Welcome to

EARLY CHICAGOU

an accommodating dank flat that fortuitously unites the North Atlantic Ocean and the Mississippi River. As the glacial meltwaters ebbed, a distinctive scoured landscape gradually embraced flora and fauna. Native families came, left, returned.

Strangers arrived and the tales begin. Accounts of an earlier time and its characters are recorded within these pages. Our compendium denotes the locale and presents a wide variety of information concerning Chicago's earliest period, long before the settlement developed into a midwest metropolis. Many people came, mattered and moved along; some settled. We have included a lot to tell the whole story: meet native Americans, the French, some Canadians, traders, soldiers, settlers, women and children.

We entreat those who love Chicago to glance backward, then join us until the exodus of the area's native inhabitants in the summer of 1835. Share our fascination in the rendezvous.

Foreword to *Early Chicago* by Mayor Richard M. Daley

For well over a century, the City of Chicago has fascinated people from all over the world. Carl Sandburg famously coined it the "city of the Big Shoulders." Chicago was the setting for some of the 20th century's important works of literature, the backdrop for stories by such literary giants as Theodore Dreiser, Richard Wright, Willa Cather, Nelson Algren, Saul Bellow, and James T. Farrell.

Why such interest in Chicago? First, it is the archetypal Great American City; an economic powerhouse that has been one of the strongest forces behind the unparalleled prosperity Americans enjoyed during this century. Uncommon foresight and vision matched with practical business sense created a city that lies on the shores of Lake Michigan geographically, but impacts every corner of the earth economically.

Chicago also fascinates because of its remarkable diversity. People from all over the country and the world have come to Chicago to turn their dreams into reality. Today, 2.8 million people reside in the city. One hundred languages are spoken in the metropolitan area, which is home to one million foreign-born residents. Partly because of its diversity, Chicago is regarded as one of the world's great cultural capitals.

Rising up just behind the natural beauty of the lakefront and Grant Park is Chicago's world famous skyline, one of the most picturesque anywhere. The juxtaposition of steel, concrete, and glass with sand, parkland and water is dazzling and stands as a testament to our ability to live harmoniously with nature while simultaneously putting a distinctive stamp on it.

Still, I sometimes look at the shoreline and wonder how it must have looked to the earliest Native Americans who discovered the area they called Chicagoua. Or to Jean Baptiste Point de Sable, who, by the mid 1780s, had settled at the mouth of the Chicago River.

For anyone interested in Chicago's early history, this book – the first to treat the history in an encyclopedic manner – is an essential reference. All of us who love Chicago owe a great debt of gratitude to Dr. Ulrich Danckers and Jane Meredith for bringing the beginning of the city's remarkable story to life in these pages.

CHICAGOUA, OR *ALLIUM TRICOCCUM*, IN BLOOM

Painting by Jane Meredith

A

Compendium

of the

Early History
of Chicago

to the Year
1835
when the Indians left

by

ULRICH DANCKERS & JANE MEREDITH

JOHN F. SWENSON, Contributing Editor

with a contribution from

Helen H. Tanner

Be it remembered that in the 225th year of the independence of the United States of America,
and in conformity to the Act of Congress of the United States
"An Act for the Encouragement of Learning, by securing the copies of maps, charts and books,
to the Authors and Proprietors of such copies, during the time herein mentioned,"
Ulrich Danckers, Jane Meredith, and John F. Swenson, of the said country,
have deposited with the Library of Congress, the title of a book,
the right whereof they claim as Co-Authors and Co-Proprietors, in the words following,
to-wit:
"A Compendium of the **Early History of Chicago** to the Year 1835 when the Indians left."

Published by Early Chicago, Incorporated, River Forest, Illinois, in the year 2000.
Copies may be ordered by calling (708) 366-7002, or by fax to (708) 366-3485.
Printed by Inland Press, Menomonee Falls, Wisconsin.
Library of Congress Card Catalog Number: 99-96900
© 1999 by Ulrich Danckers & Jane Meredith
ISBN: 0-9675823-0-X
977.3

Library of Congress Cataloging-in-Publication Data:

Ulrich Danckers & Jane Meredith
A Compendium of the Early History
of Chicago to the Year 1835 when the Indians left

1. Chicago—History—to 1835.   2. Chicago—History—Encyclopedia.
3. Chicago—Genealogy.   4. Indians of North America—Northwest.
5. Point de Sable, Jean Baptiste—Biography.   6. Kinzie, John—Biography.
7. Peoria—History.   8. Fur Trade—Northwest.   9. Chicago—Bibliography.

This volume was printed in AGaramond fonts and was formated by the authors to harmonize with the style prevalent at the time when printing presses made their Chicago debut.

PREFACE

With this book we invite you to explore the past, in order to more fully experience the present. These pages deal with a time before Chicago grew its big shoulders and before its grand buildings arose; a time when one could stand on the lake dunes and gaze west across a prairie stretching to the horizon. With luck or by chance, clouds of passenger pigeons might pass overhead, darkening the sky.

As the authors, we believe that this book offers something new to anyone who wants to learn about the origins and early history of Chicago. For the first time an encyclopedic arrangement of thousands of items of historical significance, scattered in hundreds of earlier books, journals and source documents, has been systematically brought together to form a cohesive whole. We have tried hard to avoid making this a mere compilation of dry facts. Many early residents and visitors are quoted verbatim and breathe life into these times; illustrations in the style of the era have been used to facilitate the reader's involvement.

Our main focus has been the period prior to 1835, a pivotal year, during which the native Americans were forcefully escorted west beyond the Mississippi, and the local language and customs had just swung decisively from French/Indian to English. Few Chicagoans may consider that, prior to the multi-ethnic city we all recognize, a small community of mixed Indian and French culture had already existed for more than a century, Chicago's oldest and deepest root, and well worth exploring.

For those who favor a chronologic approach, the book begins with a timeline. Many maps illustrate the progression of geographic knowledge as Europeans advanced toward Chicagoland throughout the 15th to 18th century. Those who would like to further explore Chicago's past on their own are referred to the extensive bibliography, or may make use of the section "A Guide to Local Historical Monuments."

Results of recent historical research have been incorporated whenever possible. In this we have appreciated the help of Chicago scholar John F. Swenson, who has contributed three essays and much guidance.

ACKNOWLEDGMENTS

Gathering and organizing the large amount of information needed to prepare this volume was only possible with the help of many knowledgeable people who readily came to our assistance. Everyone contributed and all have our gratitude.

Michael Kaplan of the Newberry Library was the first, who introduced us to John Aubrey. David Buisserat, then of the library's Hermon Dunlop Smith Center for the History of Cartography, enhanced our love of maps and gave direction. Through David Karrow we learned of Yolanda Dembowski's valuable identification of early North American maps at the Service historique de la Marine, Vincennes, France; Paul Braffort and Ananda Abeydeera of Paris enabled us to acquire photographs. Evelyn Swanson introduced us to the promise of desktop publishing in lieu of small note cards. Appreciating the worth of our endeavor, Father Joseph Downey of Loyola University Press greatly encouraged us.

At the Chicago Academy of Sciences, then north on Clark Street, Louise Zumac generously shared library books and collection items relative to the flora and fauna of our locale. Later on a walk in Ottawa Trail Woods to Laughtons' Ford with Ed Lace, a historian with the Forest Preserve District of Cook County, we experienced his expertise and love of the environment; we traced and traipsed a bit of Chicago's early history. Any unknown birds we may have seen or heard were identified by David Willard of the Field Museum. Phil Parillo, also at the museum, told us about that greenheaded fly we missed. We encountered James Van Stone's work at the museum through Cora Sallee of the Forest Park Historical Society and curator at the Forest Park Library; she introduced us to the native American silver artifacts found along the Des Plaines River, on display with other relics. At a Chicago Map Society meeting, we heard James A. Marshall present his research concerning the importance of the Hopewellian earthworks in and near Chicago. Through the Chicago Maritime Society we met Ralph Freese and Jack Kelly, true historian-artisans devoted to enlivening the past with hands-on demonstrations of blacksmithery and canoeing. Leon Toussaint, another historian-raconteur, outlined county histories through the lives of the Beaubiens. David Wendell of Rosehill Cemetery submitted family particulars we could not find elsewhere. Laura Linard, curator of special collections at the Chicago Public Library, granted access to early documents. In Evanston Janice Klein and Penelope Berlet allowed us to visit the fine collections of the Mitchell Museum of the American Indian during renovation.

Many of the suburban and county historical societies and museums hold keys to understanding what happened in Chicago in this early time, and we found staff members always ready to help, specifically: Frank Lipo and June Atkinson, Oak Park Historical Society; Sue Faul, Riverside Museum; Kathy Hussey-Arntson, Wilmette Historical Museum; E. Keating and Arden Newey, Lisle Station Park and Lisle Historical Society; Helen Sauvageau, Plainfield Historical Society; Nancy Desmond, Isle a la Cache Museum; Margaret Bedard, Kankakee County Historical Society. We needed more assistance from farther away: Janice Hildebrand of Sheboygan County (Michigan) Historical Research Center, and Rita L. Maroney, the historian at the Office of the U.S. Postmaster General, Washington, D.C.

We collaborated several years with Paul Petraitis who provided the rich history of the Calumet region and helped us determine an encyclopedic format for the center section of the book. As our effort slowed we encountered the work of Donald Schlickan, an architect, artist, and Chicago historian, who had combined his multiple skills to create the renderings and paintings which we happily include; his two color plates of Fort Dearborn exhibit unmatched accuracy. When the Harold Washington Library opened in October 1991, Ron Mounce became our invaluable resource adjunct by browsing, ever alert in noting how much we had missed. Mary Feely has been our indispensable proofreader. Dr. Helen H. Tanner of the Newberry Library, well-known as a native American historian, has contributed an important history of the local Indian tribes. John F. Swenson, an allium specialist, historian, contributing editor, continues to extend and enrich us with new understanding of our Chicagou and Jean Baptiste Point de Sable. Thank you very much, everyone.

CONTENTS

A

CHICAGO CHRONOLOGY

Beginning with

PREHISTORIC EVENTS

and
Ending with the Year

MDCCCXXXV

CHICAGO AREA CHRONOLOGY

A series of early published maps of the Americas forms an integral part of this chronology. They were selected to show the advance of recorded geographic knowledge, beginning with the first fragmentary recognition by Abraham Ortelius in 1570 of the continental outlines, documenting the penetration of the interior by the early explorers through the gateway of the St. Lawrence River, showing for the first time all five Great Lakes on the map of Nicolas Sanson in 1650, and eventually recording a place called *Chicagou* in its now familiar position on the map of Guillaume Delisle in 1718.

The universe is thought to have begun **30 billion years ago**, according to the big bang theory.

4.6 billion years ago   The planet Earth forms.

3.5 billion-570 million   Precambrian period. At its beginning, the earliest traces of life on Earth, blue-green algae, develop in the oceans; during its later stages, the Earth experiences its first glacial age (800-600 million years ago).

570-500 million   Cambrian period, during which a profusion of plants, sea shells, and trilobites thrives on the ocean floors.

500-440 million   Ordovician period, marked by the development of vertebrate fish. Toward the end of this period, marine or fresh water arthropods begin to colonize the land, the first multicellular animals to do so.

440-410 million   Silurian period. Plants appear on the dry lands. A warm, shallow sea covers what is now Chicagoland and beyond, the deposits of which harden into Niagara limestone, the bedrock that underlies Chicago. Though located at an average depth of 50 to 100 feet, the limestone does

outcrop in multiple locations.

410-360 million   Devonian period, during which vertebrate animals (*Amphibia*) first develop legs and begin to colonize the land. The first insects appear, initially wingless.

360-320 million   Mississippian period, marked by an abundance of marine animals called crinoids.

320-290 million   Pennsylvanian period, which includes the second glacial age. Reptiles develop from amphibians.

290-245 million   Permian period. Reptiles dominate the lands.

245-210 million   Triassic period, marked by the development of both dinosaurs and mammals.

210-140 million   Jurassic period, when dinosaurs dominate and give rise to the first birds (*Archaeopterix*).

140-65 million   Cretaceous period, ending with a mass extinction of dinosaurs.

65 million   The Cenozoic era begins, during which time mammals diversify and establish dominance.

55 million   Gradual cooling begins (Cenozoic decline), associated with continental drift and the dissolution of Pangaea, the early single continent, first into Gondwanaland, and then into the continents known today.

10 million   Mountain glaciers appear in the Northern Hemisphere, marking the beginning of the third glacial age, which technically continues to the present time, although the Earth currently experiences a warm interglacial period.

4 million   The earliest hominids develop in Africa, south of the Sahara, and will remain restricted to this continent for the next three million years.

2.5 million   The genus *Homo* emerges with its initial species *Homo habilis* ('handy man').

1.7 million   *Homo erectus* ('upright man') appears in eastern Africa, the first hominid to devise complex tools and use fire.

1 million   *Homo erectus* begins its migration from Africa to Europe and Asia.

120,000   *Homo sapiens* ('wise man') develops and gradually replaces all other ancestral species of man.

40,000-15,000   latest period of ice age of the Northern Hemisphere (glacial maximum at 18,000 years ago), causing the sea to drop by 500 feet—compared to the current level—with formation of a broad land bridge (paleocontinent of Beringia) between northeast Asia and Alaska. **During this period, various groups of people appear in North and South America.** In addition to traditionally recognized Siberians, ancestors of most Indians, the latest anthropological and genetic studies of human remains find strong affinities with Europe, southeast Asia, Australia, and Japan. They seem to have come in small groups, perhaps by sea as well as land; no evidence yet suggests migration away from the Americas. While archeology confirms habitation as early as 12,500 years ago [Monte Verde site, Chile], more recent finds at the same site strongly suggest 33,000 years ago. At approximately 4,000 B.C., the Inuit are the last to arrive.

15,000   Start of a warming period for the Northern Hemisphere and Chicagoland that still continues. With temperatures rising, the Wisconsin glacier, which had covered Chicagoland completely, begins to retreat.

12,000   In full retreat, the Wisconsin glacier leaves behind early geographic features: the terminal (Valparaiso) moraine, trapping meltwater that forms Lake Chicago, and gravel and sand; a layer of impermeable clay that causes a high water table and swampland. Indian tribes, now well established in North and South America, are widely dispersed, resulting in a great diversity of languages and cultures; milder temperatures bring migrating Indians, who follow the large game from the central plains east across the Mississippi River and into the Chicago locale.

10,500   Lake Chicago, larger and deeper than present-day Lake Michigan, overflows through the Des Plaines and Calumet Sag low areas. As the residual northern portion of the glacier gradually melts over the next 6,000 years, the waters find access to the St. Lawrence River in the north, causing successively lower lake levels (the Glenwood, Calumet, and Tolleston phases), defining shore ridges that will be recognizable well into the 20th century by the course of the Indian trails they first determined.

9,000   Lake Chicago overlays the area eventually covered by the City of Chicago. A near arctic climate prevails and coniferous forests slowly overrun the tundra. Musk ox, caribou, and moose are likely local inhabitants.

8,000   Indian presence is established in southwestern Illinois at the Madoc Rock Shelter and elsewhere.

6,000   Blue Island, Stony Island, and Mount Forest [Argonne Forest] remain true islands in Lake Chicago; Indian occupation of the Illinois River valley begins.

4,000   Lake Chicago's level temporarily drops to 480 feet. (The current level

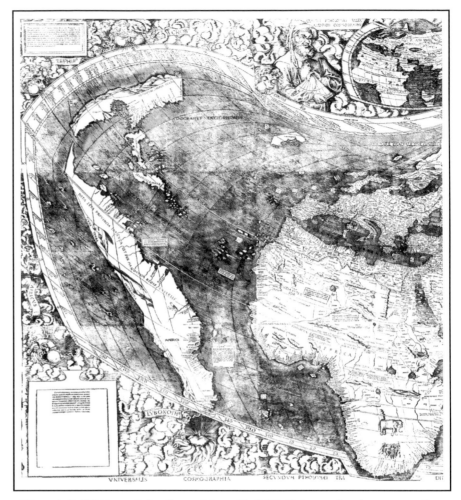

Western half of Waldseemüller's wall map of the world of 1507. Little more than the eastern coastlines of North and South America, and some Caribbean islands, were known at that time. Waldseemüller believed that [see] Amerigo Vespuci had discovered the new continent, and named it after him. The word *America* can be found in the lower third of the southern continent. [94]

of Lake Michigan is 580 feet.) Lake Calumet forms from Calumet Bay, dries, then reforms as waters rise again. Local forests change from balsam fir and spruce to oak and hickory.

2,000 to 1,000 A.D.   Artifacts and inscriptions found throughout North America have been convincingly compared to similar evidence in Scandinavia, North Africa, Western Europe, the Iberian peninsula, and the Mediterranean; many suggest ocean voyages, with references to and images of ships.

------------------------------------ Anno Domini ------------------------------------

1000   The Indian Mississippi culture begins in the fertile flood plains of the Mississippi River valley, particularly near Cahokia, Illinois, where large mounds are constructed and where a community of 20,000 will florish until 1300.

The Norse again reach North America at *Vinland*, probably Newfoundland, from their colonies on Iceland and Greenland where they lived until the 15th century or later.

1295   Marco Polo returns from his 25-year journey into China and writes his travel account, widely circulated in manuscript, a narrative which plays a major role in making this fabled exotic land of the Orient a place to dream of and reach.

1492   On April 17, Spain's King Ferdinand agrees to finance Christopher Columbus' voyage to find the westward route to China.

Columbus' first transatlantic expedition leaves the harbor of Palos, Spain, in three small caravels, weighing anchor on August 3. On October 12, Columbus sights one of the islands within the eastern Bahamas, an island he names San Salvador and where he lands, there claiming the territory for Castile (Spain) by raising the flag on October 12.

1493   On November 3, Columbus lands on Dominica in the Lesser Antilles on his second expedition to the new world. After extensive exploration of many islands, large and small, he returns to Spain June 11, 1496.

1494   On June 7, the Treaty of Tordesillas is signed by Castile (Spain) and Portugal, sanctioned by Pope Alexander VI, roughly establishing a meridian of longitude between Portugal and Castilian "Asia," meaning the Americas. That these were new continents only gradually dawned on Europeans; the Magellan-Del Cano circumnavigation of 1519-22 finally confirmed speculation begun after Columbus' first voyage.

1497   Giovanni Caboto (John Cabot), a naturalized Venetian in English service, reaches the North American mainland, probably northern Maine or Nova Scotia, on June 24, and claims the land for King Henry VII, conflicting with that of Spain [see 1494]. After this single landing he coasts north-easterly for a month and returns to Bristol. On a second voyage, in 1498, Cabot and his ship are lost at sea, but evidence points to a southeasterly passage as far as the Carribean and Cuba.

1499   Amerigo Vespucci accompanies the Spanish conquistador Alonzo de Ojeda on an expedition to the New World. Vespucci's recognition and description of South America as a continent will lead the German cartographer

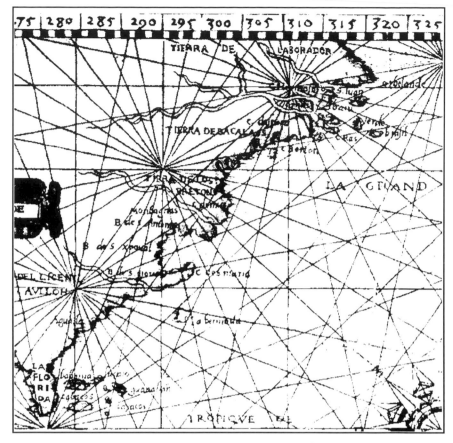

A portion of Nicolas de Nicolai's 1553 navigational chart, incorporating many details of Cartier's 1534-35 exploration of the St. Lawrence River and Gulf [upper third of image]. The land to the north he calls *Labrador*. [94]

Martin Waldseemüller to name the New World after him.

1507   Martin Waldseemüller publishes the first map that uses the word *America*.

1513   On September 29, Vasco Núñez de Balboa, Spanish conquistador, reaches the Pacific Ocean upon crossing the land bridge of Panama, and thus confirms the presence of another ocean between America and Asia.

1519   Alonzo de Pineda, Spanish conquistador, explores the Gulf of Mexico and arrives at the mouth of the Mississippi River, but does not pursue the inlet. This large gateway to the North American continent remains unused by Europeans for nearly two more centuries.

1522 On September 7, navigator Juan de Elcano returns to Spain, completing the first circumnavigaton of the globe with an expedition that began under Ferdinand Magellan on September 20, 1520.

1534 Jacques Cartier, commissioned by King François I, explores the Gulf of St. Lawrence in search of the northwest passage to Cathay and its riches, beginning the process of French discovery that will in time reach Chicagou and beyond. On July 24, he claims for the king this undefined area, over the protest of the local Iroquois leader, Donnacona. By a ruse he kidnaps two of the latter's sons and takes them back to France for training as interpreters. This treachery sows the first seeds of the growing Iroquois distrust of the French which will become burning hatred and destruction by the late 17th century.

1535-36 Cartier, on his second voyage, explores the St. Lawrence from Quebec [*kebec*, narrows] to Hochelaga (Montreal) with guidance from Donnacona's sons and others; he learns of the Great Lakes to the West. Both great river entrances to North America, the Mississippi and the St. Lawrence, are now

Northeast portion of Abraham Ortelius' 1570 map of America. Geographic knowledge of the coastal region is growing rapidly. No hint yet of the Great Lakes of the interior. The mythical region of [see] Chilaga near the upper reaches of the St. Lawrence River is shown. [94]

known to Europeans. He and his large crew overwinter, many dying of scurvy before he learns the cure, a vitamin-rich infusion of white cedar bark. The next May Cartier leaves for France with several Iroquois, now including Donnacona, who spins fabulous tales, mostly untrue, of the riches of Canada [*kanata*, settlement].

1541 Cartier is now merely a subaltern of Jean-Francois de La Rocque de Roberval, who disastrously fails to comply with a royal commission as the king's lieutenant-general to found a colony in Canada; the resulting disillusionment and failure to find riches causes France to ignore North America until the time of Champlain, just after 1600.

1565 On August 28 Phillip II, king of Spain, proclaims himself monarch of North America.

1570 Abraham Ortelius publishes *Theatrum Orbis Terrarum*, the first modern atlas of the world that provides the most accurate depiction of settlement within the Americas. The atlas will be continually revised and expanded well into the next century.

1603 Samuel de Champlain, often regarded as the founder of Canada or *Nouvelle France*, begins his career of exploration and colonizing as a passenger on a voyage from France. First as cartographer, then as explorer, shrewd

Sebastian Münster's 1540 wood engraving map of the New World, showing the St. Lawrence river inlet behind an early version of Newfoundland [named *Corterati*]. What is to become Canada is named *Francisca* in honor of French King Francis I.

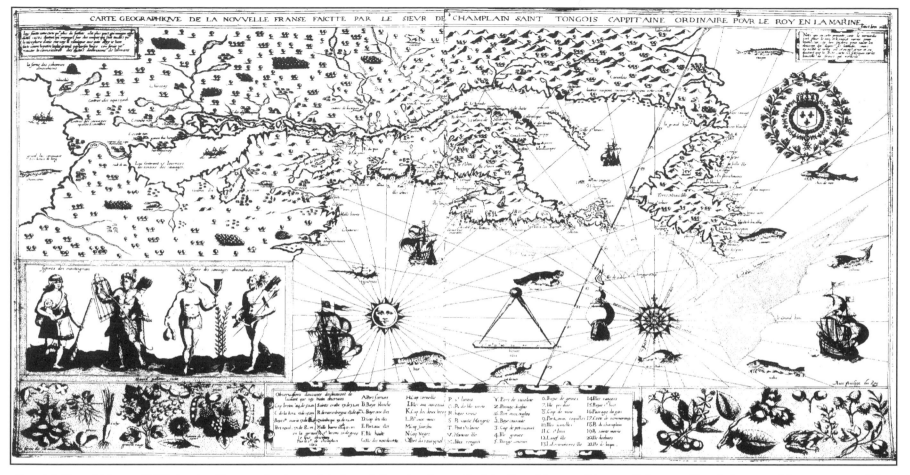

Samuel de Champlain's map of 1612, based on his own explorations, and the first to indicate the existence of a chain of great lakes west of the upper St. Lawrence River. In the years to follow, as governor of New France, his maps become more detailed and accurate. [94]

observer, visionary, and (from 1620 to 1636) *de facto* governor, his reports fill six volumes. In 1608, he founds Quebec; he discovers Lakes Ontario and Huron; of his maps, none earlier than that of 1612 has been found. His achievements secure Canada and its Indian trade for France.

1608   At a large Algonkin village called Stadacona, Samuel Champlain founds the city of Quebec.

1609   James I of England grants to the Virginia Company of London an amended charter enlarging its boundaries "from sea to sea, west and northwest," which becomes the basis for Virginia's claims to western lands includ-

ing Illinois, to 41° north, just above Peoria, which it will finally cede to the United States in 1784, as part of the settlement of debts arising out of the American Revolution.

1612   Samuel de Champlain, as governor of *Nouvelle France*, begins to prepare maps documenting the new terrain he is exploring, the first to be published in Paris the following year.

1615   The first mission among Indians in North America is established near Quebec in Huron territory by French Récollect priests.

1626   Fathers Jean de Brébeuf and Anne de Noüé establish the first Jesuit

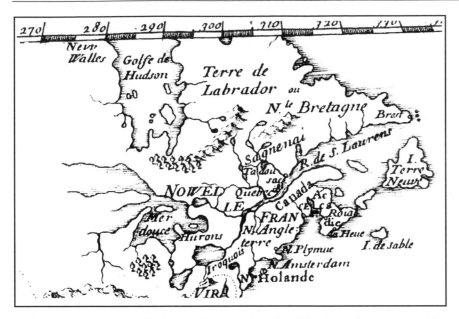

This portion of Pierre Du Val's 1655 map of America shows that all five Great Lakes are known, with the western shores of Lakes Superior and Lake Michigan not yet delineated. Du Val, son-in-law of the cartographer Nicolas Sanson, borrows much from his famous teacher, but in this instance surpasses him in clarity of arrangement. Lake Huron is called *Mer douce* [sweet sea]; the other lakes are unnamed, although Sanson's 1656 map will label Lakes Superior, Erie, and Ontario with the names used today, though Lake Michigan is still *Lac de Puans*. [94]

mission among the Huron at Green Bay, where Récollect priests had earlier labored.

1632   The *Jesuit Relations*, an annual report on the religious and political activities in Canada, is first published in Paris.

1634   Jean Nicollet, who lived and traded from 1618 to 1633 among various Indian groups in present Ontario to strengthen fur trade relationships, is sent by Champlain to visit Indians at *Baie des Puants* (Green Bay); he is the first European known to have crossed upper Lake Michigan, searching for the ocean route to China as well. Nicollet ascends the Fox River but does not reach the portage to the Wisconsin River; he learns of the *Iliniouek* (Illinois) people to the south and returns to Quebec in the autumn of 1635.

1636   Charles Huault de Montmagny is appointed governor of New France, the first to bear this title; he succeeds Champlain, the *de facto* governor since 1620. Montmagny's name meaning *great mountain* is translated by the Iroquois as *Onontio*, the title given by all Indians to subsequent governors for more

than a century.

1640   The *Mission de Sainte-Marie* is established by Jesuit priests among Huron tribes near present-day Midland, Ontario. This is the first permanent fortified European mission on the Great Lakes; many more missions follow.

1642   Montreal is founded under the name Ville-Marie at the location of Hochelaga, where for many years a settlement of some sort had been proposed. The village quickly becomes the hub of the fur trade.

1644   The Iroquois begin to war against the Huron and their allies, the French.

1647   The Iroquois, armed by and allied with the Dutch and English, are deadly rivals of the Huron, associates of the French for the fur trade; they now begin their systematic destruction of the Huron nation. This virtual genocide is completed by 1649, marked by the gruesome martyrdom of St. Jean Brebeuf, the great ethnographer of these people; the surviving Huron take refuge with various other peoples near Quebec.

1650   Nicolas Sanson d'Abbeville, French cartographer, publishes in Paris the first map of North America that shows all five Great Lakes.

1655   Médard Chouart Des Groseillers, enterprising trader and explorer, may be the first European to travel the western shore of Lake Michigan, presumably passing the site of Chicago; the exploration was probably inspired by Nicollet's 1634-35 voyage and his own experiences in the Huron country since 1646.

1661   Louis XIV appoints Jean Baptiste Colbert as minister of the French colonies in North America. Marquis de Tracy is appointed governor and Jean Talon is appointed intendant of Canada, then with a population of 3,000 European civilians and 1,300 French officers and troops.

1662   On April 23, English King Charles II grants Connecticut a charter that allows the extension of its western border to the "South Sea." This will later become the basis for Connecticut's claim to Illinois country, which it maintains until September 13, 1786.

1663   Louis XIV, ending more than a century of New France's rule by a series of privately-owned companies, quasi-private rule, declares it a royal province and establishes a government system like that of the French provinces. There is a governor in charge of military and external affairs, Marquis Alexandre de Prouville de Tracy, and an intendent for internal administration, the great Jean Talon; they are key members of the *Conseil Souverain*, an executive- and legislative-like council and supreme judicial court. New France's population is approximately 2,000.

Father Marquette's map of 1673, the first to
show the western shore of Lake Michigan. [357]

1665   Minister Colbert sends the first breeding stock horses to the St. Lawrence River colonies, introducing a new species to the continent.

Jesuit Father Allouez founds the *Mission de Saint-Espirit* and begins missionary work among the Huron and Ottawa at Chequamegon Bay, Lake Superior [near present-day Ashland, WI]; he remains three years, until relieved by Father Marquette.

1669   Father Allouez establishes the *Mission de Saint-François-Xavier* at Point Sable, Wisconsin, but within two years it is moved to De Pere on the Fox River, a few miles above Green Bay.

1670   Des Groseillers and his relative Pierre-Esprit Radisson, after suffering unfair treatment by Governor Jean de Lauson, participate in funding the English financed Hudson's Bay Company, beginning a series of events leading to the British conquest of 1763.

1671   Fathers Dablon and Marquette found the *Mission de Saint-Ignace* on the north side of the strait of Mackinac. A small fortified and garrisoned trading post is established at the same location in order to control the Indian fur trade.

Fathers Dablon and Allouez explore the entire shoreline of Lake Superior and create an invaluable map that will be published in the *Jesuit Relations* of 1672.

At Sault-Sainte-Marie, Simon François d'Aumont, sieur de St. Lusson, takes possession of the entire interior of the North American continent for France, extending *Nouvelle France*.

The name *Chicagou* is first mentioned in a report to the French court by Father Pierre Charlevoix: "Chicagou at the Lower End of Lake Michigan."

1672   In September, Intendant Talon and Governor Frontenac appoint Louis Jolliet and Father Jacques Marquette to explore westward in an effort to locate the rumored great river. On December 8, Jolliet arrives at the *Mission de Saint-Ignace* to inform Marquette of his appointment.

The *Jesuit Relations*, an annual report on the religious and political activities in *Nouvelle France* that had been published in Paris since 1632, is discontinued as a result of initial suppression of the Jesuits by French authorities.

1673   On May 17, Louis Jolliet and Father Marquette begin their quest from the *Mission de Saint-Ignace*. They travel in two canoes and in the company of five *donnés*. After first heading south on Lake Michigan, they travel up the Fox River and portage to the Wisconsin River [Fox-Wisconsin Portage].

On June 17, they discover the Mississippi River by canoeing down the Wisconsin River.

On June 25, they make contact with the Illinois along the banks of the later state of Iowa.

On July 17, after reaching the Arkansas River and now aware of the Spanish at the lower Mississippi River, they return northward.

On August 25, they enter the Illinois River and find that the Illinois population is concentrated at Kaskaskia; the Indians befriended them, and Father Marquette promises to return.

In September 1673, Chicago's recorded history begins. Louis Jolliet and Father Marquette portage to the Chicago River and discover the future site of Chicago; this is the first historically confirmed presence of Europeans at Chicago. During this portion of their journey, Jolliet conceives the idea that a canal between the Chicago River and the Des Plaines River can join the Great Lakes with the Mississippi River.

On September 30, Louis Jolliet and Father Marquette reach the *Mission de Saint-François-Xavier* at Green Bay.

Upon completion of the journey, Father Marquette prepares a map that documents their exploration.

1674   Jolliet reports the discoveries of his 1673 joint exploration with Father Marquette to Governor Frontenac, and presents him with a map of the Great Lakes and the Mississippi River basin. Unfortunately, the map was redrawn from memory because the original was lost on his return trip to Quebec, in a canoe accident that nearly cost him his life.

On October 25, Father Marquette sets out from the *Mission de Saint-François-Xavier* on the Wisconsin-Fox River for his second trip to the Kaskaskia village on the Illinois River to establish a mission.

On December 4, Father Marquette arrives at Chicago again, in the company of *donnés* Pierre Portenet and Jacques Largillier. Early severe blizzards force the group to winter in an improvised cabin near the portage.

1675   Father Marquette, ill from a gastrointestinal infection, is visited at the Chicago hut during the winter by Indians with whom he trades, and by the fur traders Pierre Moreau and The Surgeon [Jean Roussel], who advises the ailing father.

On March 30, Father Marquette and his two companions leave their winter quarters and travel to Kaskaskia. On arrival during the Easter week, April 11-14, Father Marquette establishes the *Mission de la Conception* near Starved Rock, Illinois. Marquette's illness worsening, his companions escort him during the last week of April back to Lake Michigan, then north along the lake's eastern bank, heading for Saint-Ignace.

On May 18 or 19, Father Marquette dies and is buried near what will later be Ludington, Michigan.

Governor Frontenac grants René-Robert Cavelier, sieur de La Salle, permission to explore the lands west and south of Lake Michigan and to claim them for the French Crown.

1677   In April Father Claude Allouez, Father Marquette's successor in the Illinois country, visits the Chicago area. He spends several days in a native village along the Des Plaines River, then moves on to the great village opposite Starved Rock, and carries on mission work with the Kaskaskia intermittently until 1687.

1680   In February, La Salle and Tonti build the short-lived Fort Crevecoeur at the lower end of Lake Peoria, the first such structure built by Europeans in the Illinois River valley.

1681   Melchisédech Thèvenot, Paris-based French scholar and chronicler of explorations in the New World, publishes the first map to mark the Jolliet-Marquette discoveries of 1673, and also the earliest to attach the name *Michigan* (*Michigami*) to one of the Great Lakes.

1682   In January La Salle, with Tonti, Father Membré, the physician Jean Michel, and others, begins a Mississippi expedition from Chicago by way of the portage and the Illinois River. On February 5, the expedition enters the Mississippi, and on April 9, the men reach the Gulf of Mexico where La Salle stakes France's claim to the entire Mississippi River valley, the Province of *Louisiane*.

1683   During the winter of 1682-83, La Salle's *engagé* Antoine Brassard selects the site, probably on Hickory Creek near present New Lennox, IL, where André Eno (Hunault) and Jean Filatreau were briefly in a small shelter "at the portage of Chicagou," enlarged in the spring and garrisoned by about 20 of La Salle's men. This location fits La Salle's notation in his letter of June 4, 1683, that it is 30 leagues (72 miles) from Fort St. Louis and is about 20 miles south of the main Chicagou *portage des chenes*, which La Salle disliked and avoided after his 1681-82 southward journey.

Tonti and crew build Fort St. Louis on *Le Rocher* [Starved Rock]; La Salle visits here and returns to his Chicagou fort, from which a portage route leads to the Calumet River system and Lake Michigan. La Salle writes three letters from this fort to the governor of New France. Meanwhile, unknown to La Salle, the new Governor de La Barre, replacing his sponsor Frontenac, joins with Montreal merchants jealous of La Salle's Illinois monopoly and sends troops and traders to take over Fort St. Louis under joint command with the experienced Tonti. La Salle learns of this treachery en route to his Chicagou fort, for which he has requisitioned munitions and falconets (small cannons), but his pleas are ignored by de La Barre, who has trade plans of his own. La Salle abandons the Hickory Creek fort in September and, taking with him his Indian friends Ouiouilamet and Nanangouci, leaves for France to ask the king to oust de La Barre's people from Illinois and back his expedition to colonize and secure the mouth of the Mississippi. De La Barre is silent partner of trading ventures with the Iroquois and even encouraged them to attack other French traders; this duplicity is the final detail which prompts his removal from office; Denonville replaces him.

1684   La Salle gets royal authority and financing for a three-ship, 300-person expedition to establish a French colony on the mouth of the Mississippi. He is also granted a royal order returning his Louisiana interest. The flotilla finally sets sail on August 1 and, after a series of hardships largely caused by La Salle's intransigence, sails past her destination, the mouth of the Mississippi.

Oliver Morel de la Durantaye, French commandant at Michilimackinac, comes south to Illinois with 60 of his men to assist Tonti, who commands at Fort St. Joseph (Starved Rock), against Iroquois attacks. Durantaye builds a post or fort at Chicago, and is there visited by Tonti the following year. Within less than a year, Durantaye returns to Michilimackinac, and the post likely becomes a depot.

1685   La Salle's colonizing expedition arrives at Matagorda Bay in Spanish Texas, which in no way resembles the mouth of the Mississippi. Through his blunders and the incompetence of others, his ships and most of the colony's supplies and equipment are lost. He founds a short-lived colony, in which most of the inhabitants eventually die of sickness and attacks by Indians who are constanly lurking nearby. [La Salle's lost ships have recently been found, raised, and preserved by marine archaeologists.]

1686   La Salle desparately, but unsuccessfully, tries to find the Mississippi by overland excursions and loses several of his best men during the effort. This produces lasting enmity toward him which leads to his assasination the next year by mutinous members of the expedition. Meanwhile Tonti, hearing at Fort St. Louis vague news of La Salle's Texas troubles, goes to the Gulf with 25 Frenchmen and 18 Indians, in an unsuccessful search east and west of the Mississippi, leaving a letter for La Salle with the Mongoulascha (La Salle's Quinipissa) Indians near present Venice, LA, which in 1699 will help convince d'Iberville that he has found the mouth of the Mississippi by ship (which he knows only under its local name, Malbanchya). On his return, Tonti passes through Chicagou just before the Iroquois raid it. [Tonti's rescue mission, though unsuccessful, acquainted many of the French with the Mississippi and the Gulf coast and must have stimulated informal private travel in advance of official settlement beginning in 1699.]

About July 1, Iroquois destroy the French-Miami settlement and post at Chicagou, scattering its people.

1687   Jean-Baptiste Louis Franquelin, royal hydrographer, revises his 1684 map of North America, marking the Chicagou settlement on the south branch of the river, unaware of its recent destruction.

After La Salle's murder on March 19, six survivors of his expedition, including their leader Joutel, set off by land route from Texas for Canada to send rescuers to the dying colony, but it is destroyed, and most people, including Father Membré, will be killed by the local Indians. Joutel's memoirs, published in French but not fully in English, are an essential record of this harrowing trip.

Joutel and his five companions [Père Anastase Douay, Abbé Jean Cavelier {La Salle's brother}, Jean Baptiste Cavelier {no relation}, a pilot named Tessier, and a young Parisian named Barthelemy] reach Fort St. Louis on September 14, where they meet Father Allouez and Tonti, from whom, at Father Cavelier's insistence, they conceal the death of La Salle. Joutel sketches the geography of the Chicagou area and the history of Allouez's short-lived Chicagou settlement at the time Durantaye maintained a fort here, but not its destruction by Iroquois about July 1, 1686. He arranges for interpreter-guides to lead them to Chicagou, which they reach on Sept. 25. Joutel learns that Chicagou is named for the local woodland wild garlic, *Allium tricoccum*, which he tastes and describes the following spring. After spending a week in the area, which Joutel describes minutely (including the site for the canal proposed by Jolliet), they set off up Lake Michigan's western shore but Cavelier, with his hidden agenda, frightens them into returning to the reluctant hospitality of the now-crowded Fort St. Louis.

Governor Denonville organizes a massive French-Indian raid on the Seneca, in part as retaliation for Iroquois attacks on French traders and settlements, including the destruction of the Chicagou settlement, which presumably scattered Durantaye's garrison as well as its French and Miami settlers. Denonville's raid destroyed Iroquois crops and heightened their hostility toward the French. Tonti returns to Fort St. Louis from the Denonville raid and becomes well acquainted with Joutel, a retired fellow soldier. Joutel had unwisely invested, and ultimately loses, his life savings in La Salle's chimerical scheme. Father Cavelier promises to reimburse Joutel but ignores him once they return to France. But Cavelier also loses his investment; his ploy to conceal his brother's death and be paid from his bankrupt estate will be defeated when creditors finally learn the truth.

1688   On March 29, Joutel and his party once again reach Chicago and remain until April 5. Joutel finalizes his research of the name *Chicagou*, en route to Canada and France, where they arrive too late to arrange rescue of La Salle's Texas colony.

Franquelin prepares a new map of North America, prominently showing "Fort Checagou" and "Ft. Crevecoeur," both of which were already destroyed at the time of publication, but evidence to the world of France's occupation in support of her claim to Louisiana.

Vincenzo Maria Coronelli, the Venetian cartographer to Louis XIV, prepares a map and globes incorporating reports of Jolliet, Marquette, La Salle, Tonti, and others.

1689   Baron Lahontan, a French officer and unreliable historian, travels in the Great Lakes region and later publishes a report in which he claims to have passed through the Chicago *portage des chênes* on April 24.

A Spanish party investigates reports of La Salle's illegal Texas colony given by two survivors. The party finds the place in ruins, many unburied bodies, and the remains of Joutel's vegetable garden.

1690   Miami settle at Chicago, locating their village on the main part of the river; a second settlement soon forms on the south branch. French traders, soldiers, and missionaries will follow shortly.

1691   Constantly lurking Iroquois raiders seen around Fort St. Louis prompt Tonti, with the advice of Indian leaders, to set up a new fort among eight Indian villages at the wide south end of Peoria Lake, on the Illinois River's east bank. Tonti calls it *Fort St. Louis de Pimiteoui* (or *Pimitesi*), meaning *place of fat game*, from the multitude of animals drawn to the pastures and shallow waters along the beach in front of the fort. De Liette, Tonti's cousin, describes in his writings the game of lacrosse played by the Indians on the extensive meadow behind these villages. The elevated location of the fort commands river traffic through the outlet of the lake, and is used for successive forts until 1763, when the last French garrison was withdrawn; its charred ruins were well known 10 and more years after that. The United States built Fort Clark opposite this site, on the west bank, in 1813, in the middle of a French village begun by Jean Baptiste Maillet about 1790.

1693   Lt. Nicolas d'Aillebout, sieur de Mantet is dispatched by Governor Frontenac [whom the King had reappointed for a second term, following Denonville] to the Chicagoland area to set up a fort and deal with Indian troubles. He builds and commands the fort which is shown on the map he and Louvigny, former commandant at Michilimackinac, draw in 1697, on

which it is called *fort des françois et 8iatanons* [8iatanon, or Ouiatanon, an early name for Wea, a subtribe of the Miami].

In April, Pierre You de la Découverte, one of La Salle's men on the 1682 trip to the mouth of the Mississippi, is married at Chicagou to an Indian woman, Chicago's first recorded marriage.

Also that month, La Forêt sells half of his share in the Illinois colony's exclusive trading rights to Michel Accault at "Checagou," payment to be made there in August, making it Chicago's first recorded business transaction and the potentially largest of all time—one-quarter of Illinois' trade.

1696   The Jesuit *Mission de l'Ange Gardien* is established at Chicagou by Father Pierre François Pinet, probably on the present site of the Merchandise Mart. Two Miami villages exist nearby.

A glut of furs prompts Louis XIV to suspend the fur trade and withdraw the garrisons of the Great Lakes posts, including Mantet's at Chicagou; Tonti is exempted from this order.

1697   Tonti, Michel Accault, and François de La Forêt receive permission from Governor Frontenac to establish a fortified trading post at Chicagou that is managed by Pierre de Liette, Tonti's cousin, and lasts until c.1705.

Probably in this year Antoine Laumet, who had acquired the title of nobility "Antoine de la Mothe, sieur de Cadillac" under questionable circumstances, then commandant at Michilimackinac, visited the Great Lakes posts, including Chicagou, "on the Garlic River" with the Miami village, and writes a report of his findings.

The *Mission de l'Ange Gardien* is closed for one year by order of anti-Jesuit Governor Frontenac.

Pierre Le Moyne, seigneur d'Iberville, an explorer, fierce soldier, and Indian diplomat, is selected by Pontchartrain, minister of marine, to find the mouth of the Mississipi and secure the river and Louisiana against Spanish and English incursions.

1698   D'Iberville's expedition to the Gulf of Mexico is outfitted at Brest, France. In aid of his search, he had interviewed experienced travelers, including Joutel, who declined to join him; he also has many Spanish navigational charts and aids, and he reads or takes along the mostly inaccurate reports of Hennepin and others as well as knowledge gathered by La Salle and Tonti. The Spanish, apprehensive of d'Iberville's mission, hasten to strengthen Pensacola Bay and prevent him from landing there. Ironically, when d'Iberville arrives in 1699, the ill-supplied Spaniards, many of them convicts, must beg food from the better provisioned French.

The *Mission de l'Ange Gardien* at Chicagou is reopened. Governor Frontenac, protector of La Salle and Tonti, and silent partner of many trade enterprises, dies.

1699   On New Year's Eve 1698, Pierre Le Moyne, seigneur d'Iberville, on orders of King Louis XIV, sets sail from St. Dominque (Haiti) determined to find the mouth of the Mississippi [which La Salle had discovered traveling doswnstream in 1682, but could not find by sea in 1684] and establish French control of the water route between New France (Canada) and Louisiana by building a fort on or near the Gulf of Mexico; he begins his methodical search at Choctawhalchee bay in late January and on March 2 finds the three mouths of the locally named Malbanchya river, which La Salle had described under its upriver name, Mississippi, when claiming Louisiana for France in 1682. For three more weeks he explores the river to Baton Rouge and beyond, and interviews Indians, some of whom remembered La Salle and Tonti. A 1686 letter, written by Tonti to La Salle, is retrieved from the local Mongoulascha (La Salle's Quinipissa) Indians, which clinches d'Iberville's identification of the Malbanchya (its Choctaw name) as the Mississippi. Now convinced that he has found his objective, he returns to his anchorage at Ship Island opposite present Biloxi, MS, and establishes *Fort Maurepas* (commonly called Fort Biloxi) at present Ocean Springs, MS. This first French habitation in Louisiana is a military base, not a settlement, and its garrison of 80 soldiers under sub-Lieutenant M. de Sauvole, plus a few civilian officials with their families, is in place by May 2 when d'Iberville leaves for France. It is in effect the capital of Louisiana until abandoned for *Fort Louis* on Mobile Bay in April 1702, where a civilian village is soon established.

In March, the *Mission de Sainte Famille de Caoquias* (later also called *Mission de Saint-Sulpice*) is established by Father Pinet at Cahokia.

On October 21, Father St. Cosme, en route from Quebec to the Illinois River for the purpose of planning further missionary work among the Indians, visits the Chicago *Mission de l'Ange Gardien* under Fathers Pinet and Bineteau. With him are Fathers Montigny and Davion, with Tonti as their guide. The party stays until October 24 and visits again on its return trip to Canada during the Easter week of 1700. In his report, Father St. Cosme mentions two large Miami villages near the mission house.

1700   In February, alarmed by English exploration and trade on the Mississippi, d'Iberville builds and garrisons Fort Mississippi [also called *Fort La Boulaye*], near present Phoenix, LA, below New Orleans. M. de Sauvolle, commandant at Fort Maurepas, has written to Illinois to invite workers to

the coast, and in February several come from Fort St. Louis de Pimiteoui and Cahokia bearing furs they sell to d'Iberville, who sells them at New York on his way back to France. Thus is begun the major trade route downriver from Illinois to lower Louisiana and New Orleans, first for furs and ultimately for food. New France and Louisiana are now linked, as Jolliet and La Salle had envisioned, forming a major element of French strategy and potential containment of English expansion.

In early September, Father Jacques Gravier visits the *Mission de l'Ange Gardien* while on a trip to the Mississippi River by way of the Chicago portage.

By this time an estimated 16,000 French people live in the huge portion of North America then claimed by France. The territory extends from the arctic tundra south to New Orleans and the Appalachian Mountains, from the Rockies east to the Atlantic Coast, past New England. Quebec, the capital of *Nouvelle France*, had been founded in 1608. Reports by early visitors, such as Father St. Cosme, suggest that a few Frenchmen with Indian wives already live at Chicago in 1700; their names, however, are unrecorded.

1701   Antoine Laumet, the self-styled Cadillac, persuades the king to let him establish Detroit and Fort Pontchartrain and abandon Michilimackinac, where he had commanded. He also forces the Jesuits, whom he dislikes, to abandon their mission there; the autocratic Laumet is essentially a dictator and rules with an iron hand. Many French settlers are induced to come; Laumet forces many Indians to leave their homes and move to Detroit, which intensifies a long period of inter-tribal conflict, especially the Fox wars, and assured that the Fox would be permanent enemies of the French. Henri Tonti's brother Alphonse commands the garrison.

At this time Chicagou is merely a trading post with a few French habitants; as the Fox wars begin, the Illinois River route becomes hazardous even for the French traders, who increasingly favor the Maumee-Wabash-Ohio river route to the Illinois country, ultimately to be secured by posts at *Les Miamis* (Fort Wayne), Ouiatanon (Lafayette), and Vincennes, all in present Indiana; Chicagou village becomes intermittently deserted. These wars last until 1740, and control of the portage will remain in the hands of often hostile Indians until the Treaty of Greenville in 1795.

1703   Guillaume Delisle, royal cartographer to Louis XIV, completes his map of North and Central America and the Caribbean, incorporating all documented reports of travelers to date.

1710   Joseph Kellogg of Deerfield, MA, captured there at age 13 by Indians in a 1704 raid and abducted to Caughnouaga, Quebec, has learned Indian ways and joins six French *voyageurs* on a trading trip to the Mississippi. They

Excerpt from Delisle's 1718 map, showing Chicagou and both branches of the Chicago River, a settlement or an Indian village on each branch. The Des Plaines River is called Chicagou R. [605]

spend the winter at Michilimackinac. In the spring of 1711, they pass through "Chigaguea," finding no settlers, then down the Illinois River to Cahokia and Kaskaskia, French villages which he later describes, and to the confluence of the Ohio and Mississippi, whence they return to Canada. Kellogg is the first Englishman known to have visited Chicago.

1715 French soldiers establish a fortified post and trade center at Michilimackinac [later Mackinaw City] on the southern coast of the strait of Mackinac. This French outpost will florish until 1760; in 1761 British troops will take over the fort.

In November the acting governor of *Nouvelle France*, Claude de Ramezay, and Intendant Begon recommend that a fort be built in Chicago to facilitate access to the Illinois country. The recommendation is not acted upon.

1717 On September 27, most of Illinois country becomes a district of the French province of Louisiana. Illinois country is now ruled by the governor at New Orleans, who appoints all officials of the military-style Illinois government at *Fort de Chartres*. The boundaries of Louisiana are never clearly defined, but the northern line runs north of Peoria and Ouiatanon; Chicagou remains part of *Nouvelle France*.

1718 In January, John Law's *Compagnie des Indes* receives from the French Crown exclusive rights to organize, import slaves into, and commercially exploit Louisiana, of which southern Illinois is then the northernmost portion.

In June, Guillaume Delisle's map of Louisiana and the Mississippi River basin notes the location of Chicagou and accurately traces its river's course.

James Logan, British agent from Pennsylvania who surveys French routes in the West, reports coming through Chicago where he finds only ruins of a

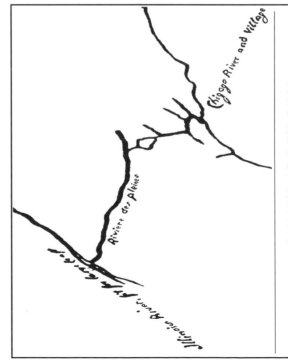

In 1761 the British military officer Lt. Dietrich Brehm visits Chicago while surveying and mapping the territory newly acquired from the French near the end of the French and Indian War. An excerpt of his map shows the "Chigago River and village," and portrays with fair accuracy the portage, Mud Lake, and the Des Pleines and Illinois rivers. His official report indicates that the village is inhabited at that time.

[in the editor's collection]

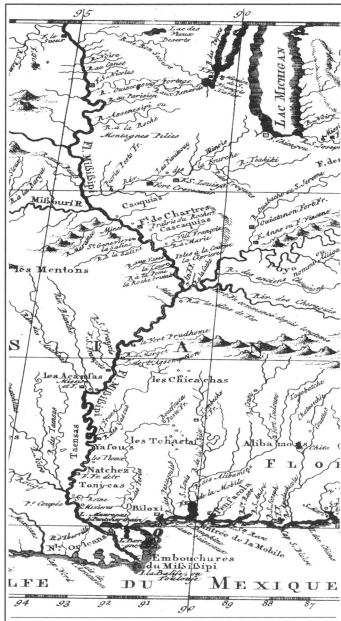

Excerpt of Bellin's *Carte de Louisiane*, 1757. By that year, the waterways between Lake Michigan and the Gulf of Mexico have been well explored and mapped. [in the author's collection]

"fort" [possibly de Liette's trading post, abandoned by 1705].

1738 In November, the Virginia legislature creates the county of Augusta, which technically includes the Illinois country.

1745 In early October, Louis Amiot is born along the Des Plaines River near Chicago and is baptized at Mackinac the following June.

1754 Beginning of the French and Indian War.

1755 Englishman John Mitchell produces a map of the British and French Dominions in North America that provides the most up-to-date information of its time, becoming the standard for the last half of the 18th century.

1759 In July, Fort Niagara falls to the British, marking the end of French dominance on the Great Lakes.

On September 18, the French surrender Quebec to the British and on November 29, Detroit. The French era in Chicago officially ends, but most French settlers remain and French influence lingers.

1761 In November an expedition under Capt. Henry Balfour, 80th Regiment, comes through the Chicago region, mapping Lake Michigan's coastline as part of the effort to incorporate the previously French territory into the British empire.

Also in this year, British Lt. Dietrich Brehm maps the "Chigago" locale.

The British reestablish Fort St. Joseph, abandoned by the French in the previous year, and establish a naval shipyard on the Niagara River.

1763 On February 10, the Treaty of Paris is signed. Great Britain has won the French and Indian War, and France renounces all North American mainland east of the Mississippi River, excluding the New Orleans area. Canada comes under the British crown and with it, Chicagoland. However, the French will continue to govern the district north of the Ohio River until 1765, when the British take over.

Spain acquires the Territory of Louisiana from the French and holds the land until 1802, when Napoleon regains the province in a secret treaty.

1764 On November 26, the Roman Catholic Jesuit order is officially suppressed in France, although its missionary activity in North America will continue until the end of the century.

1765 The English take possession of Illinois and the Great Lakes region; Chicago comes under English rule although its people are still French.

1766 On March 5, Spain takes possession of New Orleans from the French.

1769 Pontiac is murdered by a Peoria Indian in front of the Brynton, Wharton & Morgan store at Cahokia. Contrary to legend, there is no record that this provoked massive retaliation

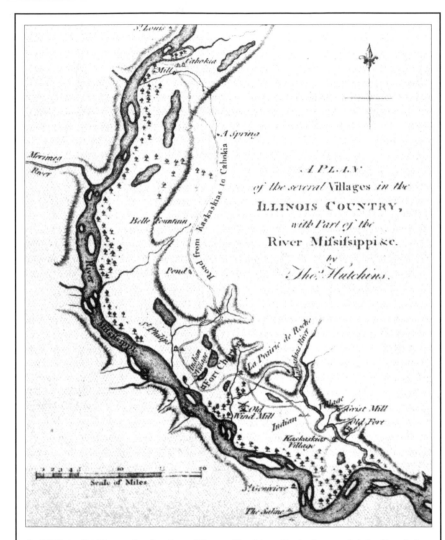

A PLAN of the several Villages in the ILLINOIS COUNTRY, with Part of the River Mississippi &c. by Thos. Hutchins.

In 1775 the British captain of engineers Thomas Hutchins, after having traveled the Great Lakes, the Ohio, and the Mississippi in 1762, prepares this map of the formerly French territory, then British. It incorporated the thriving towns Kaskaskia and Cahokia, with Fort de Chartres for protection. The soil of these bottom lands is alluvial and of astonishing fertility, and will become known as the American Bottom. [in the author's collection]

them to effectively dominate the upper lakes for years to come, even after they lose the Revolutionary War.

Thomas Hutchins, British captain of engineers who personally traversed the extensive terrain of the Great Lakes region following the transfer from French to British rule, completes a map that contains the Chikago region, noting an Indian village and fort at the entrance of the unnamed river.

1773   William Murray, of Kaskaskia, forms the Illinois Land Company, which acquires from the Indians two very large tracts of land in exchange for trade goods; one of the tracts includes the present site of the city of Chicago. The deed will later be reversed by Congress, making land purchases from the Indians by private individuals illegal.

Patrick Kennedy, a Kaskaskian trader, ascends the Illinois River and observes the ruins of the French fort at Peoria; he finds no French people in the village. His description is important, because it refutes the legend, later fabricated by land speculators around 1801, that Jean Baptiste Maillet, militia commander at Peoria, granted land there to Jean Baptiste Point de Sable in 1773.

1775   On April 19, the American Revolutionary War against the British begins at Lexington and Concord, Massachusetts.

1776   On June 7 Richard Henry Lee, of Virginia, proposes to the Continental Congress a resolution calling for a declaration of independence from Britain.

On July 4, the Continental Congress adopts the Declaration of Independence. Chicago becomes American.

There are still a few French at Chicagou as evidenced by a French-language pass issued on July 4 by George Morgan, colonial Indian agent at Pittsburgh, promising safe conduct to its inhabitants and those of Illinois (Kaskaskia and Cahokia) who wish to apply.

1778   On December 9, Virginia claims a corridor of western lands to the Mississippi River, including Illinois country, which becomes its "County of Illinois."

In this year or earlier, a French trader named Guillery from Mackinac establishes a trading post on the west bank of the north branch of the Chicago River, at the Forks. American occupation of Montreal severely reduces trade via the Great Lakes, and in 1778 and 1779, the Potawatomi and Guillery may be the sole inhabitants of Chicagou.

The armed British sloop, *Archangel*, is the first modern ship of record to enter

against the Illinois Indians; the 1723 seige which gave Starved Rock its name was an episode in the Fox wars.

1771   The British establish a shipyard and headquarters at Detroit, enabling

Lake Michigan since the loss of *Le Griffon* in 1679.

1779   On October 3, the British sloop, *Felicity*, sails past Chicago in an effort to keep supplies from rebellious American colonists along the shoreline of Lake Michigan.

1781   In January, the remnants of Fort St. Joseph are captured by a band of 65 men and some 200 Indians under the leadership of Don Eugenio Pourre and briefly occupied in the name of the King of Spain.

On October 19, the British Gen. Lord Cornwallis surrenders to Gen. George Washington after the Battle of Yorktown.

This year, and again in 1783, British licenses are issued at Montreal for traders going to the Grand Calumet River at the south end of Lake Michigan. These are the only such licenses for any place near Chicago since about 1700. In fact, there is no record of any licensed trade to Chicago except a 1770 scouting mission by a French trader named Quillet which carried no trade goods.

1782   Jean Baptiste Gaffé of Cahokia sends boats with trade goods to Chicagou to establish a trading post where none had been since about 1778. De Peyster, British commander at Detroit, sends a party to evict Gaffé but results are not recorded. As recently as 1779, French traders occasionally visited Chicagou but did not live there.

1783   On September 3, America and Britain sign the definitive peace articles in Paris, ending the Revolutionary War. Britain's claim to the Illinois country is thus terminated, and the land becames part of the United States.

1784   Virginia cedes her claimed western territory, including Illinois [see 1609], to the United States as part of the settlement for her debts incurred during the Revolution; the deed of cession reserves the right of French and other settlers to their "titles and possessions," which were never clearly defined.

Notwithstanding the 1783 Treaty of Paris, British officials in Canada develop clandestine strategies to keep the United States out of what will soon become the Northwest Territory, Illinois included. Designed to control the Indians and the fur trade, the principal element of the Canadian economy, these plans include placement of secret Indian agents at important locations and the [unrealized] creation of an Indian "buffer state."

1785   The Illinois and Chicagou rivers have become safe for trade and travel; Peoria settlers and traders, who had fled to Cahokia or Vincennes during the Revolution, have returned, and perhaps in this year [possibly as early as 1784, but certainly no later than 1788] Jean Baptiste Point de Sable, the founder of

modern Chicago, moves there from near Detroit. Illinois country is not yet sufficiently organized by United States authorities to block or expel a known agent of the British Indian Department.

1786   On September 3, Connecticut surrenders to the United States its claim to western lands, including Illinois country and Chicago [see 1662].

1787   On July 13, under President Washington, the U.S. Congress unanimously passes an ordinance creating the "North West Territory" out of all United States territorial possessions northwest of the Ohio River, including Illinois country. The same ordinance provides for a governor of said territory, for a system of representation in Congress "as soon as there shall be five thousand free male inhabitants, of full age," and further provides for the elimination of slavery within the territory, a provision that will not be enforced for decades to come. These territories are to be admitted in due time to the Union "on an equal footing with the original states." The North West Territory eventually becomes Ohio, Indiana, Illinois, Michigan, Wisconsin, and part of Minnesota.

Point de Sable and Catherine, his Indian wife of many years, travel from Chicagou to Cahokia to have their marriage solemnized by Father St. Pierre at the *Mission de Sainte Famille de Caoquias*.

On July 17 Gen. Arthur St. Clair, newly appointed governor of the Northwest Territory, inaugurates the territorial government.

1789   On August 7, Congress establishes the Department of War and Indian Administration, and Henry Knox becomes the first secretary. Congressional policy is set forward in Article 3 of the act, part of which reads as follows: "The utmost good faith shall always be observed toward the Indians; their land and their property shall never be taken from them without their consent, and their property, rights and liberty shall never be invaded or disturbed, unless in just and lawful wars authorized by Congress, but laws founded in justice and humanity shall from time to time be made, for preventing wrongs being done to them, and for preserving peace and friendship with them."

1790   In May Gen. Arthur St. Clair, appointed governor of the Northwest Territory by President Washington in 1788, finally reaches the area and starts to organize its government. He organizes St. Clair County, in present southern Illinois. First at Kaskaskia, he appoints officials and militia officers, and adopts laws without authorization to do so. He then removes to Cahokia and does likewise. In July, Governor St. Clair organizes Knox County to include Peoria and Chicago.

St. Clair and Winthrop Sargut, secretary of the Nortwest Territory, compile lists of French and American settlers in Illinois and at Vincennes, under a controversial 1788 law of the Continental Congress which was enacted to carry out the 1784 promises, in Virginia's cession of western lands to the United States, to protect these settlers in their "titles and possessions." These lists, and further lists compiled 1795-1797, open the floodgates for hundreds of fraudulent land claims, particularly at Peoria, by unscrupulous land speculators, including the future governor of Illinois, John Reynolds, and attorney Isaac Durneille, who created documents that, if authentic, would make him the sole owner of Peoria.

On May 10 Hugh Heward, Detroit trader on his latest trip to Cahokia, visits Point de Sable at Chicagou for two days, trading cloth for food and leaving his birchbark canoe in exchange for the use of a pirogue for the balance of his voyage. In mid May Heward visits Peoria and lists 10 men "settled among the Indians" there, including Maillet, commander of the St. Clair county militia.

Lt. John Armstrong, U.S. Army, makes his second trip to Illinois, a top secret mission in trader's guise to evaluate the feasibility of U.S. travel and trade up the Mississippi River from its junction with the Illinois River. Prominent people at Cahokia discourage him, and Governor St. Clair confirms. Armstrong's report of June 2 to Secretary of War Henry Knox, includes a copy of a French map of western North America and a narration of his 1789 trip to Chicago and down the Illinois River, accompanied by a copy of a map of the river basin from Chicago to the Mississippi, the most accurate of its kind for another 30 years or more.

On June 20, Chicago becomes part of newly formed Knox County, Northwest Territory.

On July 16, the District of Columbia is established as the seat of the United States government.

Antoine Ouilmette locates in Chicago on the north side of the river, near Point de Sable's homestead.

1792   On April 2, Congress authorizes establishment of the U.S. Mint.

In total disregard of the Treaty of Paris, the British create Kent County, of the Province of Upper Canada, in which they include Chicago. Although this move is in conflict with the Northwest Ordinance adopted by the U.S. congress in 1787, England will remain in *de facto* control of Illinois county until the year 1796.

Jean La Lime and his Potawatomi wife, Nokenoqua, settle in Chicago north of the river near the Ouilmette family.

1794   On August 20, Gen. Anthony Wayne defeats the Indians at Fallen

Timbers in northwestern Ohio, reducing Indian pressure that had made settlement precarious. This makes the Treaty of Greenville possible.

On November 19, Jay's Treaty is signed in London, resolving multiple serious Anglo-American diplomatic issues. Most difficulties have been the result of Great Britain's resistance in meeting all agreements of the definitive Treaty of Paris of 1783, and its clandestine agitation against the United States with the Indian tribes now in American territory.

1795   On August 3 the Treaty of Greenville is signed; by this treaty the federal government acquires, among other large tracts of land ceded by the Indians, "one piece of land six miles square at the mouth of the Chicago River."

On October 27, the Treaty of San Lorenzo between the United States and Spain settles Florida's northern boundary and gives navigation rights on the Mississippi River to the United States.

1796   On July 6, the Catholic priest Michel Levadoux travels from Cahokia to Detroit by way of the Illinois River and Chicago.

On August 15, Chicago becomes, until 1800, part of Wayne County, Northwest Territory.

On October 2, British troops leave Michilimackinac, the last frontier post to be evacuated under the terms of Jay's Treaty; this opens the upper lakes to American commerce.

On October 8, Eulalia Pelletier, granddaughter of Jean Baptiste Point de Sable and daughter of Jean Baptiste Pelletier and his wife Suzanne, is born at

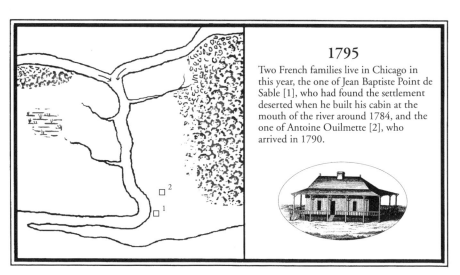

1795

Two French families live in Chicago in this year, the one of Jean Baptiste Point de Sable [1], who had found the settlement deserted when he built his cabin at the mouth of the river around 1784, and the one of Antoine Ouilmette [2], who arrived in 1790.

Chicagou; she will be baptized at St. Louis in 1799.

1800   On May 7, President Adams approves an ordinance dividing the Northwest Territory; the western portion, including Illinois, becomes the Indiana Territory. The ordinance goes into effect on July 4, 1801, and provides "that St. Vincennes, on the Wabash river shall be the seat of the government for The Indiana Territory."

In May, Point de Sable sells his estate for 600 French *livres* to Jean La Lime, with the St. Joseph trader William Burnett financing the deal. De Sable moves to St. Charles [MO] in the Spanish Territory of Louisiana.

1801   On May 3, Chicago becomes part of St. Clair County, Territory of Indiana, when St. Clair County (formerly a county of the Northwest Territory) is enlarged by proclamation.

1802   France regains the Territory of Louisiana from Spain in a secret treaty.

1803   On January 24, Chicago becomes part of Wayne County, Indiana Territory.

On March 9, Secretary of War Gen. Henry Dearborn sends orders to Col. John Hamtramck, commandant at Detroit, to have the region surrounding the mouth of the Chicago River surveyed for the feasibility of establishing a post.

In April, Capt. John Whistler and six soldiers of the First U.S. Infantry travel overland from Detroit to Chicago. After considering several locations, Whistler surveys a site at the mouth of the Chicago River with plans to construct a fort, specifically "Stockade Works Aided by Block Houses."

On April 30, Thomas Jefferson concludes successful negotiations to purchase the Louisiana Territory from France for $15 million, about four cents an acre. This more than doubles the size of the nation and enhances the strategic importance of Chicagoland for future commerce.

On June 7, the Treaty of Fort Wayne is signed between the United States and the Delaware, Shawnee, Miami, Potawatomi, Kaskaskia, Eel River, Wea, and Kickapoo, ceding 2,038,400 acres along the Wabash River near Vincennes for $4,000.

On July 14, two parties leave Detroit for Chicago: Lt. James S. Swearingen, with a company of soldiers, takes the old Sauk Trail across Michigan; the second party, led by Capt. John Whistler, sails on the schooner *Tracy* first to the mouth of the St. Joseph River, and from there on smaller boats to Chicago. The party includes Mrs. Ann Whistler, their children Sarah; John, Jr.; an older son, William; and his wife, Mary Julia.

On August 7 the Treaty of Vincennes is signed with the Kaskaskia, Cahokia, and Mitchigami, ceding for $12,000 a large area (8,911,850 acres) in central and southeastern Illinois, comprising approximately half of the present state. [Other tribes will cede their claims to the same area in the Treaties of Edwardsville in 1817 and 1818.]

On August 17, the two military parties meet at the mouth of the Chicago River to construct a fort, which Captain Whistler calls Fort Dearborn. Construction is completed by early December. The official return, dated December 31, lists 69 military personnel at the fort, among them William C. Smith, the first military physician.

On August 30 William Wells, Indian agent at Fort Wayne, issues a government license to J.B. La Geuness authorizing trade with the Indians at "Chicagou."

On December 20, the flag of France is replaced by the U.S. flag in New Orleans, marking the official transfer of the Louisiana Territory.

Louis Pettell with his Indian wife moves to Chicago late in the year.

By the end of this year, there are four civilian houses at Chicago, located on the north side of the river. From E to W, they belong to Burnett/La Lime, Ouilmette, Le Mai, and Pettell.

1804   In early May John Kinzie arrives from St. Joseph on horseback. With him are his wife, Eleanor, their son, John Harris, aged 6 months, and Eleanor's daughter, Margaret. Kinzie purchases the Point de Sable estate from La Lime and Burnett.

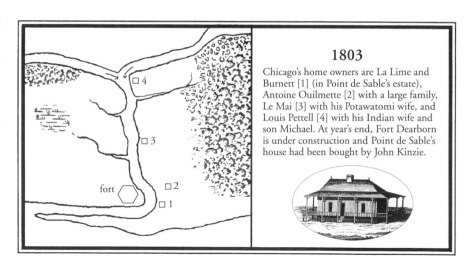

1803

Chicago's home owners are La Lime and Burnett [1] (in Point de Sable's estate), Antoine Ouilmette [2] with a large family, Le Mai [3] with his Potawatomi wife, and Louis Pettell [4] with his Indian wife and son Michael. At year's end, Fort Dearborn is under construction and Point de Sable's house had been bought by John Kinzie.

In the autumn the United States Indian Agency opens its first office at Fort Dearborn, with Indian agent Charles Jouett in charge. An attorney by training, Jouett becomes Chicago's first lawyer. He brings his wife, Eliza, and they will live in the agency house soon to be built by the soldiers.

On November 3, the Treaty of St. Louis is concluded between the United States and various leaders of the Sauk and Fox tribes, resulting in cession to the government of 14,803,500 acres of land in Missouri, Illinois, and southern Wisconsin. The Indians receive in return $22,234 and the right to live on the land as long as it is owned by the government. Later this treaty will be bitterly denounced as unfair by the Sauk leader Black Hawk, and his defiance will lead to the Black Hawk War in 1832, involving Fort Dearborn and Chicago.

In early November John Kinzie, recently appointed justice of the peace, performs the first marriage ceremony at Chicago for James Abbott and Sarah, Captain Whistler's daughter, in the rude and unfinished fort. Abbott, a young Detroit merchant, journeys to the fort to marry; afterward the couple immediately ride back to Detroit.

On December 27 Ellen Marion Kinzie, the first known child of European descent, is born at Chicago, the daughter of John and Eleanor Kinzie.

1805 The first U.S. factor, Ebenezer Belknap, arrives early in the year and remains until December.

The first U.S. Indian Agency house is built by the Fort Dearborn soldiers on the south bank of the river, immediately west of the fort.

In the autumn Meriwether Lewis Whistler, son of Lt. William and Mrs. Mary Julia Whistler, becomes the first known boy child of European descent born at Chicago.

1807 Captain Whistler struggles to keep the garrison adequately supplied in the spare wilderness; see his following letter to Secretary of War Gen. Henry Dearborn:

Fort Dearborn 6th Jany 1807

Sir   On the 11th of November last I left this fort, having leave of absence from Col Burbach for a few weeks to visit Detroit & I took Fort Wayne in my rout, for the purpose of seeing the Contractor Agent ther as he is impowered to furnish this post, with the article of meet,—At the time I left here there was not more than was sufficient for two months Issues of that article on hand, this was the occasoin of my making Fort Wayne in my rout, on my arrival ther which was on the twenty first of novemr I informed the agent, of the situation of this post as wanting the articl

of meat in particular, he replyed it was not in his power to remedy the evil accept with a few poor Beeves, nineteen in number these were sent in Dec. and arrived here in the latter part of that month I made Fort Wayne in my rout on my return purposely to gain infermation looking for better success the said agent informed me that it was not in his power to make a purchase as the bills in favour of the Contractor were protested, and the people would not sell there property without some other means than his bills, he also informed me, he was not able to Furnish Fort Wayne or this post, Capt Whipple also informed me he was under the necessity himself of procuring some Hogs (that happened thereabout) for the use of his Garrison as the agent could not supply it—These circumstances were alarming to me as being in so remoat a part of world where little could be purchased I informed the agent, I should be under the necessity of purchasing that article of my arrival at Fort Dearborn if to be had there—on my arrival I found by making a survey of what meat was in store including the nineteen head already mentioned ther was not a suffient quantity for three months Issues finding no hoaps of a further suply, I nade inquiry and found a small quanty of hoch for sail I made a purchase of it on as reasonable terms as posiable, for which I inclose the acct with my Certificate annexed therto hoaping you will acknowledge it as suffient for discharging the acct in favor of the persin of whom I made the purchase, I am Ignorant of the manner in shich I aught to draw for the payments of such purchase, but finding mysilf under the necessity of acting under the 3d and [?], article of your agreement with Olivre Phelps Esqr of the 6th June 1806 I mad the purchase and that being not suffient I have entered into an agreement with a man that happined here from Staunton for Beer, a Copy of which I have taken the liberty also to inclose this last I hoap will be a suffient quanty with what ws already on hand for six months commencing the first instant,—I am happy to find that the Contractor is gainer for what he looses on the first purchase, he gains much more on the latter—Sir   I have the Honor to be your most Obt & Humb J Whistler Capt

The Honorable Henry Dearborn Secrettary of War

N.B. I have given a draught to the person whom I mad the purchase from—but whether it is in form or not I am not a judge—

In September Maria Indiana Kinzie is born to John and Eleanor Kinzie at Chicago.

1808 Dr. John Cooper arrives on the *Adams* to succeed Dr. William Smith, becoming the second physician at Fort Dearborn.

1809 On February 9 Chicago, formerly in the Indiana Territory, becomes part of the new Territory of Illinois, with Kaskaskia as the capital.

On March 3 part of Indiana Territory, including St. Clair County with Chi-

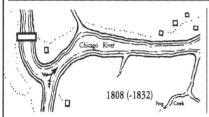

CHICAGO'S EARLIEST PUBLIC FERRY WAS AT WOLF POINT ACROSS THE NORTH BRANCH, RUN BY A NATIVE MAN • 1808

Captain John Whistler's draft of 1808 notes that at the Forks, where the "Cheykago" River branched north and south, is an Indian ferry (hollow bar), attended by a man who lives nearby. In 1829 this will be known as a privately owned ferry service, largely for the convenience of patrons of the Wolf Point Tavern, Chicago's first pub built in 1828. Locally referred to as the "grapeline" ferry, its west bank landing is located close to the tavern door.

cago, becomes the new Territory of Illinois, with Kaskaskia as its capital.

On April 28, Chicago becomes part of the new St. Clair County of the Territory of Illinois.

In late June, William Johnson journeys from Fort Wayne to Fort Dearborn and records his observations of the land he traverses, portaging, the fort and its officers.

On October 29, Charles La Lime Jouett is born to Indian agent Charles Jouett and his second wife, Susan.

1810   A bitter feud develops between the trader John Kinzie and many officers of the fort. At issue is Captain Whistler's attempt to stop Kinzie's distribution of liquor to the Indians. Politics allow Kinzie to prevail, resulting in the removal of Captain Whistler and the principal officers from the garrison in April.

In June, Capt. Nathan Heald succeeds Captain Whistler as commandant of Fort Dearborn until its disastrous evacuation on August 15, 1812.

In the summer Matthew Irving succeeds Joseph Varnum as U.S. factor.

Violent actions by Indians begin to be reported from many locations on the western front.

1811   On April 1, Dr. John Cooper resigns his commission, and Dr. Isaac Van Voorhis fills the vacancy to become the third surgeon at Fort Dearborn.

Aggressive actions by local Indians begin. On May 26 Jean La Lime, interpreter at Fort Dearborn, sends a letter of complaint to General Clark at St. Louis, regarding horse stealing by Indians.

In June Lt. Linai Helm arrives at the fort, transferring from Detroit, filling the vacancy created by the death of Lt. Seth Thompson on March 4. With him is his wife Margaret, stepdaughter of John Kinzie.

On July 7, Jean La Lime sends a letter to Fort Dearborn, complaining of Indian depredation near Fort Dearborn.

On October 1, the U.S. Indian agent Charles Jouett removes to Kentucky and does not return until 1816.

On November 7, Gen. William Henry Harrison, governor of the Indiana Territory, defeats the Shawnee at Prophetstown on Tippecanoe Creek in northern Indiana. But the victory is indecisive and most of the Indians will join the British in the War of 1812.

Within his account book on December 16, John Kinzie notes an earthquake occurring at Chicago.

In this year, Jean Baptiste Beaubien moves permanently to Chicago and builds his first house on the east side of the south branch of the river.

1812   On April 6, marauding Winnebago kill Liberty White and Jean Baptiste Cardin on Leigh's farm at Hardscrabble.

In early June, John Kinzie kills Jean La Lime during a quarrel just outside the fort. He goes north into hiding, but returns to his residence once an investigation by Fort Dearborn authority "exonerates" him during his absence.

On June 18, the U.S. Congress approves war with England. The struggle does not initially go well for the United States.

On July 12, U.S. forces invade Canada; Mackinac is lost on July 17.

In late July, Captain Heald receives instructions to encourage "the Chiefs of the different nations in the vicinity of Chicago to go" to a council at Piqua;

1812

At the beginning of the year, the following men have cabins in Chicago: John Kinzie [1], Antoine Ouilmette [2], Michel Coursoll [3], Jean B. La Lime [3a], Thomas Burns [4], François Le Mai [5], Louis Pettell [6], J.B. Chandonnai [7], Louis Buisson [8], James Leigh [9], William Russell [10], J.B. Mirandeau, Sr. [11], Samuel Clark [12], François LaFramboise [13], Alexander Robinson [14], and J.B. Beaubien [15]. Leigh and Russell also own a farm at Hardscrabble on the south branch of the river, and François Des Pins has a cabin half a mile farther upstream.

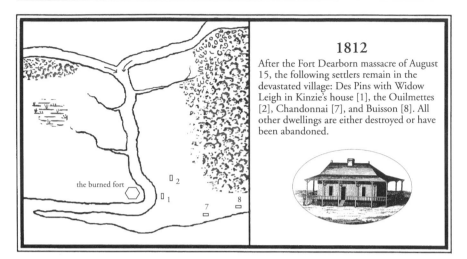

1812

After the Fort Dearborn massacre of August 15, the following settlers remain in the devastated village: Des Pins with Widow Leigh in Kinzie's house [1], the Ouilmettes [2], Chandonnai [7], and Buisson [8]. All other dwellings are either destroyed or have been abandoned.

the burned fort

John Kinzie assists and "... 17 Chiefs &c of the Potawatimies, Ottowas, Chippewas & Winebagoes set out, well satisfied, from chicago ...." [Thomas Forsyth, Sept. 7, 1812]

On August 9 the Potawatomi messenger, Winamac, brings orders from Gen. William Hull at Detroit to Captain Heald that Fort Dearborn is to be evacuated because of a possible large scale attack by Indian tribes.

On August 13, at "... a place called Terre Coupee, distant from Chicago about 90 miles ...," the Indian chiefs meet the Indian agent William Wells from Fort Wayne, with Cpl. Walter Jordan and "Winemege or Catfish a Potawatimy Chief," escorted by 20 or 25 friendly Miami, en route to Fort Dearborn with orders to assist the beleaguered inhabitants. The chiefs are directed to join them and "[a]ll returned back to Chicago, where they found a very great number of Indians."

August 15, the day of the Fort Dearborn massacre: Soon after the fort's evacuation, as the retreating party progresses south along the beach for Fort Wayne, an Indian attack kills a large number of soldiers, dependents, and civilians. Survivors are taken prisoner. Aided by friendly Indians, the Kinzie family escapes to Detroit.

On August 16, Fort Dearborn is burned by Indians and General Hull surrenders Fort Detroit.

On September 14 Chicago, formerly in St. Clair County of the Illinois Territory, becomes part of Madison County.

Ten or more private homes have existed at Chicago during this year, among them those belonging to Kinzie, Ouilmette, Buisson, and Burns, who lived on the north side of the river. Leigh lived south of the fort, with a farm four miles southwest of the fort on the south branch of the Chicago River. Clark lived near the Forks. LaFramboise and Robinson lived on the west side of the south branch and Beaubien on the east side.

1813   Antoine Ouilmette and Louis Buisson farm around the ruins of the fort.

1814   On November 28, Chicago becomes part of Edwards County, Illinois Territory.

On December 24, the War of 1812 formally ends with Britain's defeat when the United States and Britain sign the Treaty of Ghent. The United States now begins rebuilding relations with the tribes of the western Great Lakes and the Mississippi River valley.

1815   John Dean, army contractor, arrives and builds a house at the mouth of the Chicago River, south of the fort's ruins.

1816   On July 4, Capt. Hezekiah Bradley arrives on the schooner, *General Wayne*, with two companies of the Third Infantry and begins reconstruction of Fort Dearborn on the same site. With him is the fourth Fort Dearborn military surgeon, Dr. William Gale.

Charles Jouett, who had previously been the fort's Indian agent, is reappointed and arrives with his family. Lt. Taliaferro will later recall: "[s]o hostile were the Winnebagos and others that the Quartermaster had to move daily with an armed party for the security of the men engaged in felling and hewing lumber for the post."

At the Treaty of St. Louis, on August 24, the Fox and the Sauk cede to the United States, among other lands, a 20-by-70-mile strip of land, running southwest from the shore of Lake Michigan to the Fox River, its midline coinciding with the outlet of the Chicago River. This strip includes the historic portage route, and its acquisition facilitates the later construction of the Illinois & Michigan Canal. Outside this corridor, its borders known as the Indian Boundary Lines, the land is still owned by Indians.

In September Maj. Stephen H. Long, of the Corps of U.S. Topographical Engineers, explores a proposed route for the canal and visits Fort Dearborn. He submits a map of the "Illenois River" with his survey report to the acting secretary of war, George Graham, and writes: "... a canal uniting the waters of the Illinois with those of Lake Michigan, may be considered of the first importance of any in this quarter of the country."

In the autumn the Kinzie family returns from Detroit, and John Kinzie becomes the first Chicago agent of the American Fur Co. William Cox teaches school to the children of John Kinzie and others from the fort in an old bakery building on the Kinzie property.

Also in this year, the Detroit firm Conant & Mack sends John Crafts to establish a trading house at Hardscrabble on the south branch.

On October 13 the new U.S. factor, Jacob Varnum, arrives with his bride, Mary Ann.

On December 31, Chicago becomes part of Crawford County, Illinois Territory.

The U.S. Army establishes several new garrisons in the upper Northwest, in addition to rebuilding Fort Dearborn: Fort Howard at Green Bay; Fort Crawford at the mouth of the Wisconsin River; and Fort Edwards and Fort Armstrong on the Mississippi River.

1817 In May Maj. David Baker, Third Infantry, replaces Capt. Hezekiah Bradley as commandant at Fort Dearborn.

In this year, the schooner *Heartless* attempts to navigate the passage from the lake into the Chicago River, but is grounded on the sand bar and cannot be freed, becoming Chicago's first shipwreck.

From October 2 to 4, Federal Judge Advocate Samuel H. Storrow visits Fort Dearborn and recounts the following:

On the 2d of October, after walking for three or four hours, I reached the River Chicago, and after crossing it, entered Fort Dearborn, where I was kindly entertained by Major Baker and the officers of lhe garrison, who received me as one arrival from the moon. At Chicago I perceived I was in a better country. At some remotely future period, when a dense population enables the husbandman to apply artificial warmth to his grounds, means of life may be extracted from this soil which are latent at present. It requires industry, and is capable of repaying it. ✧ The river Chicago (or, in English, Wild Onion river) is deep, and about fifty yards in width, before it enters the Lake, its two branches unite—the one proceeding from the north, the other from the west, where it takes its rise in the fountain of the De Plein, or Illinois, which flows in an opposite direction. The source of these two rivers illustrates the geographical phenomenon of a reservoir [Mud Lake] on the very summit of a dividing ridge. In the autumn they are both without any apparent fountain, but are formed within a mile and a half of each other by some imperceptible undulations of the Prairie, which drain it and lead to different directions. But in the spring, the space between the two is a single sheet of water, the common reservoir of both, in the centre of which there is no current towards either of the opposite streams. The ground between the two is without rocks, and, with little labor, would admit of a permanent connection between the waters of the Illinois and Michigan. ✧ The site and relations of Fort Dearborn I have already explained. It has no advantage of harbor, the river itself being always choked, and frequently barred, from the same causes that I have imputed to the other streams of this country. In the rear of the fort is a prairie of the most complete flatness, no sign of elevation being within the range of the eye. The soil and climate are both excellent. Traces yet remain of the devastation and massacre committed by the savages in 1812. I saw one of the principal perpetrators, Nes-cot-no-meg. ✧ On the 4th of Oct. I left Chicago for Fort Wayne .... Our course was to lay, for about 60 miles, on the beach of Lake Michigan, from thence inclining eastwardly to the St. Joseph's of the Lake, and thence due south to the Miami of Lake Erie. On the night of the 4th I slept on the beach, after having forded the the little Kennomick. I call it after the Indian pronounciation—Calumet is probably the name. On our right lay an expanse of flat prairie, extending, as I supposed, to the Illinois.

1818 In April Nathaniel Pope, delegate from the Illinois Territory to the U.S. House of Representatives, convinces the assembly that the state-to-be must have its northern border extended northward by an additional 41 miles, deviating from the stipulation of the original ordinance, thereby providing access to Lake Michigan. Chicago is thus included in the state of Illinois.

On April 18, Pres. Jidentmes Monroe signs the bill that converts the former Illinois Territory into the 21st state of the Union. Chicago is now in Crawford County, Illinois. Also on this day, the U.S. Senate confirms Dr. Alexander Wolcott's appointment as Indian agent; he immediately leaves for Chicago to succeed Charles Jouett.

On August 26, the first constitutional convention for the state of Illinois, attended by 33 delegates, completes its task at Kaskaskia.

On October 4, the schooner *Hercules* is wrecked between the two Calumet River mouths after leaving Chicago; all aboard perish, including Lt. William Evileth, who had assisted in the construction of the second Fort Dearborn.

On October 6 Shadrach Bond, from St. Clair County, becomes the first governor of the state of Illinois.

On November 1, 16-year-old Gurdon Hubbard makes his first visit to Chicago in his new job as apprentice clerk for the American Fur Co.

On December 3 Illinois, previously part of the Illinois Territory since March 1, 1810, becomes the 21st state of the Union.

In this year, Dr. John Gale, Fort Dearborn surgeon, is succeeded by J. Ponte Coulant Mc Mahon, M.D., the fifth physician at the fort.

1819 On March 22, Chicago becomes part of Clark County, Illinois.

CHICAGO in 1820
Old Fort Dearborn

[306]

John C. Sullivan, a U.S. government surveyor, prepares a detailed map of the Chicago portage area and the 20-by-70-mile corridor acquired from the Indians through the Treaty of St. Louis, for which canal construction is proposed.

1820   In June Capt. Hezekiah Bradley, Third Infantry, reassumes command at Fort Dearborn.

On August 29, Henry Schoolcraft arrives at Fort Dearborn as a member of a government expedition under Lewis Cass that has explored the Northwest. Before leaving, he sketches the much-copied "View of Chicago," showing the lakefront with Fort Dearborn at the center, Kinzie's house on the right, and Indians with canoes at the sand bar in the foreground. Excerpts of Schoolcraft's account of the visit follow:

The next day's journey, 28th, carried us forty miles, in which distance, the most noticeable fact in the topography of the coast was the entrance of the Racine or Root River; its eligible shores being occupied by some Pottawattomie lodges. Having reached within ten or twelve miles of Chicago, and being anxious to make that point, we were in motion at a very early hour on that morning of the 29th, and reached the village at 5 o'clock a.m. We found four or five families living there, the principal of which were those of Mr. John Kinzie, Dr. A. Wolcott, J.B. Beaubien, and Mr. J. Crafts, the latter living a short distance up the River. The

Pottawattomies, to whom this site is the capital of their trade, appeared to be lords of the soil, and truly are entitled to the epithet if laziness, and an utter inappreciation of the value of time, be a test of lordliness. Dr. Wolcott, being the U.S. Agent for this tribe, found himself at home here, and constitutes no further a member of the expedition. Gov. Cass determined to return to Detroit from this point, on horseback, across the peninsula of Michigan, accompanied by Lt. Mackey, U.S.A., Maj. [Robert Allen] Forsyth, his private secretary, and the necessary number of men and pack horses to prepare their night encampment. This left Capt. Douglas and myself to continue the survey of the Lakes, and after reaching Michilimackinac, and rejoining the party of Mr. Trowbridge, to return to Detroit from that point. The preparations for these ends occupied a couple of days, which gave us an opportunity to scan the vicinity. We found the post (Fort Dearborn) under the command of Capt. Bradley, with a force of one hundred and sixty men. The River is ample and deep for a few miles, but is utterly choked up by the lake sands, through which, behind a masked margin, it oozes its way for a mile or two til it percolates through the sands into the lakes. Its banks consist of a black, areneceous, fertile soil, which is stated to produce abundantly, in its season, the wild species of cepa or leek. This circumstance has led the natives to name it the place of the wild leek. Such is the origin of the term Chicago. ... ✧ The country around Chicago is the most fertile and beautiful that can be imagined. It consists of an intermixture of woods and prairies, diversified with gentle slopes, sometimes attaining the elevation of hills, and it is irrigated with a number of clear streams and rivers, which throw their waters partly into Lake Michigan and partly into the Mississippi River. As a farming country, it presents the greatest facilities for raising stock and grains, and it is one of the most favored parts of the Mississippi Valley. The climate has a delightful serenity, and it must, as soon as the Indian title is extinguished, become one of the most attractive fields for the emigrant. To the ordinary advantages of an agricultural market town, it must add that of being a depot for the commerce between the northern and southern sections of the Union, and a great thoroughfare for strangers, merchants, and travellers.

On November 6, having returned with Schoolcraft in late August from the four-month Cass expedition that had included himself as physician, Indian Agent Wolcott writes to his brother-in-law in Middleton, Connecticut:

... You wanted me to write some account of my domestic affairs. The principal part of my stock consists in two horses, ten milch cows (two yoke of oxen belonging to Uncle Sam) and about ten head of young cattle. Mr. Kinzie planted for me during my absence six acres of corn from which I gathered three hundred and seventy measured bushels, more than sixty bushels to the acre, a pretty good crop that, considering the season. I intend next spring to enclose a pasture of about a hundred acres to keep my cows and twenty sheep. ... [Am now] digging a space for an ice house as I find my old one will not answer my purpose. During the winter

& spring I propose to build an additional kitchen, a store-house, a blacksmith's shop, a council house, and office, an old fashioned connecticut corn-barn, a poultry house, a smoke-house, a milk-house, and a root-house, besides putting up enclosure of palings around my yard &c. &c. Do you see I do not propose to be idle between this & the next planting season. If Uncle Sam lets me stay on this farm of his for five or six years I intend to make it one of the most convenient and inviting little posts in the country.

In this year, Dr. William S. Madison succeeds Dr. McMahon to become the sixth Fort Dearborn military surgeon.

1821 In January Maj. Alexander Cummings, Third Infantry, assumes command at Fort Dearborn.

On January 31, Chicago becomes part of Pike County, and the capital of Illinois reverts back to Kaskaskia from Vandalia.

On August 29, a treaty is concluded in Chicago between the United States and various Indian tribes which, among other large land cessions [approximately five million acres], gives the United States the right-of-way to construct the Chicago Road between Detroit and Chicago. About 3,000 Indians are in Chicago for the occasion to receive in return an immediate distribution of merchandise, grants of small parcels of land to certain individuals, government-provided instructions for the Indians in blacksmithing, agriculture, &c., and the assurance of certain annuities in perpetuity. The treaty clears the way for the Illinois & Michigan Canal project.

In September, Dr. M.H.T. Hall replaces Dr. Madison at Fort Dearborn, to become the seventh military surgeon. He remains two months and is followed by Dr. Thomas P. Hall, the eighth military surgeon, who will serve until 1823, when the garrison will be withdrawn.

In October Lt. Col. J. McNeil, Third Infantry, assumes command of Fort Dearborn and serves until July 1823.

During this year, Ebenezer Childs of Green Bay passes through Chicago and reports the following later:

In 1821, I made a trip to St. Louis in a bark canoe. ... [There] I remained two weeks, did my business, when I was advised to return by way of the Illinois River. ... We continued up the Illinois to the junction of the Kankakee and the Eau Plaine, and thence up the Eau Plaine to where I supposed we had to make a portage to Chicago River; but I could not see any signs of the portage. There had been heavy rains for several days, which had so raised the streams that they overflowed their banks. I concluded that I had gone far enough for the portage, so I left the Eau Plaine and took a northeast direction. After travelling a few miles, I found the current of the Chicago River. The whole country was inundated; I found not less than two feet of water all across the portage. That night I arrived at Chicago, pitched my tent on the bank of the Lake, and went to the Fort for provisions. ... There were, at this time, but two families residing outside of the Fort at Chicago, those of Mr. Kinzie and Col. Beaubien. ...

1822 In March, the U.S. Congress makes available property for the Illinois & Michigan Canal and appropriates $10,000 for a canal survey.

In this year, Rev. Isaac McCoy establishes an Indian Baptist mission and school where Niles will develop in the Michigan Territory. Several Chicago children attend the school as boarders, among them Josette Ouilmette and Madore Beaubien.

A military burial of the 1812 massacre victims' remnants is held sometime this year; until then the bones have remained scattered among the sand dunes south of Fort Dearborn.

On the first Monday of August, the second election for govervor and lieutenant-governor of Illinois takes place; Edward Coles, from Madison County, is elected governor.

U.S. government agent Charles C. Trowbridge travels to Fort Dearborn to fulfill provisions of the Chicago Treaty of 1821, e.g. the extension of certain services to the local Indians.

1823 On January 28, Chicago becomes part of Fulton County, Illinois.

On February 14, Governor Coles and the Illinois legislature create an Illinois and Michigan Canal Commission, charged with having the canal lands surveyed and with estimating the cost of canal construction.

On June 5, Maj. Stephen H. Long revisits Fort Dearborn (then under the command of Lt. Col. John McNeil), this time as leader of an expedition to explore the valleys of the Red and Minnesota rivers and the border country between the former river and Lake Superior, later described by the expedition's historian-geologist-mineralogist William H. Keating. Arriving with Major Long is the blacksmith and gunsmith David McKee, who settles in Chicago, initially as an employee of the Indian Agency.

On July 20 John Hamlin of Peoria, returning from Green Bay on business, obliges Dr. Wolcott and Ellen Kinzie and performs a marriage ceremony between them.

In July Capt. John Green, Third Infantry, assumes command at Fort Dearborn to serve until its evacuation in October 1823.

On August 5, Archibald Clybourn arrives as a permanent Chicago resident;

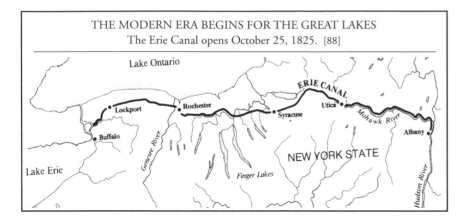

THE MODERN ERA BEGINS FOR THE GREAT LAKES
The Erie Canal opens October 25, 1825. [88]

other members of his family follow.

On September 1, a Fulton County election is held at the Kinzie house to choose a major and company officers for the 17th Regiment of the Illinois militia.

In October, Fort Dearborn is evacuated and left in the charge of Indian Agent Dr. Wolcott until its reoccupation.

The first personal property tax is levied on Fulton County residents, Chicago included. The tax rate is "5 mils to the dollar," exempting only household furniture. Amhurst C. Ransom, justice of the peace, serves as collector; he collects $11.42 in Chicago. Assuming collection of all tax due, the total valuation of the settlement was $2,284.

During this year, David Hall and James Kinzie build the Wolf Point Tavern at the Forks, on the west bank of the river. Chicago's first pub and inn will soon have its own ferry service, the "grapeline ferry" for the convenience of patrons.

1824 The U.S. Congress passes the General Survey Act, which gives the president the power to plan improvements on the Great Lakes, such as harbor or canal construction, although Congress must approve the cost. As a consequence of this act—but not until 1831—$5,000 will be appropriated for a Chicago lighthouse, and, in 1833, $25,000 for harbor improvement.

Col. René Paul and Col. Justus Post, both engineers from St. Louis, begin a survey and cost estimate of a proposed canal connecting the Chicago River with the Illinois River at Lasalle, completing their work the following year. Their estimate is $639,946 to $716,110. [When eventually built from 1836 to 1848, the cost ran over $700,000,000; *eds.*]

In June Joseph Bailly, believing he is in Michigan Territory, builds a home and trading post on the bank of the Calumet River [near Chesterton, IN], becoming the first settler in the Calumet region.

On August 22 W.T. Barry, postmaster general, requests proposals "for carrying the mail of the United States from Chicago, Ill. to Green Bay, M.T. and back once a week, on horseback, for three years, from 1st January, 1825." [The advertisement appeared in the *Chicago Democrat* between Sept. 17 and Dec. 24, 1834, possibly to highlight the community's growth in 10 years; *eds.*]

On December 1, John Quincy Adams is declared president of the United States by the House of Representatives, following a four-way electoral deadlock among Adams, Andrew Jackson, William Crawford, and Henry Clay.

1825 On January 13, Chicago becomes part of Putnam County, Illinois, but is administered by Peoria County.

On May 15, John Crafts dies; Jean Baptiste Beaubien assumes responsibility as the American Fur Co. agent.

On July 28, John Kinzie is commissioned justice of the peace of Peoria County, the first Chicagoan to hold this office.

On September 8, the Peoria Court appoints Archibald Clybourne constable for the Chicago district of Peoria County.

On October 9, the visiting Rev. Isaac McCoy gives the first Protestant sermon in Chicago.

On October 25, the Erie Canal opens as America's first man-made waterway,

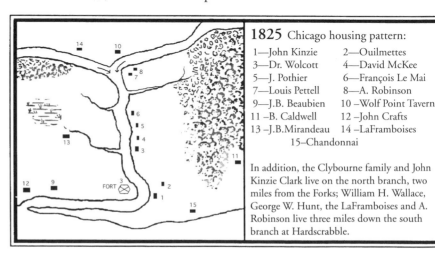

1825 Chicago housing pattern:
1—John Kinzie   2—Ouilmettes
3—Dr. Wolcott   4—David McKee
5—J. Pothier   6—François Le Mai
7—Louis Pettell   8—A. Robinson
9—J.B. Beaubien   10—Wolf Point Tavern
11—B. Caldwell   12—John Crafts
13—J.B. Mirandeau   14—LaFramboises
                 15—Chandonnai

In addition, the Clybourne family and John Kinzie Clark live on the north branch, two miles from the Forks; William H. Wallace, George W. Hunt, the LaFramboises and A. Robinson live three miles down the south branch at Hardscrabble.

and establishes a new route for trade with and emigration from the settled East.

In December, William H. Wallace opens a trading post at Hardscrabble on the south branch.

Also in this year, Heinrich Rothenfeld, first German settler, comes to Chicago, but settles further west at what will soon become Dunklee's Grove. A 1 percent Putnam County property tax assessed on 14 Chicago residents yields $90.47. Alexander Robinson opens his tavern on the west bank of the river, near the Forks.

John H. Fonda, trader and mail carrier of Prairie du Chien, passes through Chicago and will later record his experience:

> [Lake Peoria] ... *At length the councils were concluded, and our* [Indian] *guide signified his willingness to procede. Under his direction we paddled along until we came to the Des Plaines river, from which we passed into a large slough or lake* [Mud Lake] *that must have led us into a branche of the Chicago river, for we followed a stream that brought us opposite Fort Dearborn. At this period, Chicago was merely an Indian Agency; it contained about 14 homes, and not more than 75 to 100 inhabitants at the most. An Agent of the American Fur Company, named Gurdon S. Hubbard, then occupied the Fort. The staple business seemed to be carried on by Indians and run-away soldiers, who hunted ducks and muscrats in the marshes. There was a great deal of low land, and mostly destitute of timber. The principal inhabitants were the agent, Mr. Hubbard, a Frenchman by the name of Ouilmette, and John B. Beaubien. It never occurred to me that a large city would be built up there. ... But to go on with my story, we departed from Fort Dearborn in a fishing boat and proceded north along the Lake shore toward Green Bay.*

1826   On July 29 Elizabeth, John Kinzie's daughter from his first marriage, marries Samuel Miller, with her father officiating as justice of the peace.

On August 7, a state election is held by the Chicago precinct of Peoria County at Indian agent Wolcott's house and 35 ballots are cast to chose a governor [Ninian Edwards], lieutenant-governor, and a member of Congress [Daniel Cook].

In this year, Mark Beaubien arrives with his wife, Monique, and children, purchasing a small log cabin on the south bank near the Forks from James Kinzie.

Stephen J. Scott settles at Grosse Pointe with his family. David and Bernardus Laughton open a trading post on the south branch at Hardscrabble, but within a year move to the Des Plaines River to build and maintain a trading post and

tavern.

1827   On March 2, by an act of Congress, the federal government grants to the State of Illinois alternate sections, six miles wide, of public land along both sides of the proposed route of the Illinois & Michigan Canal. The money realized in land sales will be used to meet canal construction costs.

On May 18, Deborah Watkins files Chicago's first divorce procedings in a Peoria court against her spouse, Morrison Watkins, for being "an habitual and excessive drunkard who sought the companionship of women contrary to his marriage vows &c. &c."

During the summer [June to August], the Winnebago uprising in Wisconsin causes much concern in the Chicago settlement, where Fort Dearborn has been ungarrisoned since 1823. A company of militia is organized in July under the command of Jean B. Beaubien. Gurdon Hubbard goes to Danville and returns with 100 men for reinforcement, the "Vermillion Rangers," but no action occurs.

In early July, the unoccupied Fort Dearborn is struck by lightning; the barracks on the east side, the storehouse at the south gate, and part of the adjoining guard house are destroyed.

In this year, the brothers John and Samuel Miller build their tavern on the projection of land between the north branch and the main channel of the Chicago River, opposite Wolf Point. Archibald Clybourne builds the first slaughterhouse for cattle to supply the garrison.

1827-28   John H. Fonda returns again during the winter and later shares:

> ... *I was mail-carrier in the North-West before there was a white settlement between Prairie du Chien and Fort Snelling. ... It was the winter of 27, that the U.S. Quartermaster, having heard of me through some of the men with whome I was a favorite, came to me one day and asked me if I could find the way to Chicago. I told him it wasn't long since I made the trip by the Lake. He said he wanted a person who was not afraid to carry dispatches to the military post at Fort Dearborn. I said I had heard that the Indians were still unfriendly, but I was ready to make the attempt. ... [willing to] carry the mail between Fort Howard, at Green Bay, and Fort Dearborn, commanded by Capt. Morgan, that stood on a point now forming a part of the City of Chicago. ... I chose a companion to go on the tramp with me. He was a Canadian, named Boiseley, a comrade with me for many years. It was in the company of this Boiseley that I presented myself before the Quarter-Master, and reported ourselves ready for the start.* ✧ *He intrusted me with the—not mail-bag, but a tin canister or box of a flat shape, covered with untanned deer-hide, that contained the dispatches and letters of the inhabitants.*

... One noon we arrived at the southern terminus of our journey at Fort Dearborn —after being on the way for more than a month. It was in January, ... and with the exception that the Fort was strengthened and garrisoned, there was no sign of improvement having gone on since my former visit [1825]. This time I was on business, and I advanced up to the sally-port with a sense of my importance, was challenged by the sentry, and an orderly conducted me to the Adjutant's office, where I reported myself as the bearer of dispatches for the commanding officer. Captain Morgan was in the office, and, advancing, intimated that he was that person and took the case of letters, directing me to await his further orders. Getting a pass, I went outside the pallisades to a house built on the half-breed system —partly of logs and partly of boards. This house was kept by a Mr. Miller, who lived in it with his family. Here Boisely and I put up during the time we were in the settlement. I received my orders from Morgan about the 23d of January, and prepared to return with other letters. We started up one branch of the Chicago river, and after leaving this we followed the Des Plaines, taking pretty much the same way we had come.

1828   On January 6, John Kinzie dies hours after suffering a cerebral stroke.

On May 11, a Peoria County election for constable is held at the agency house; nine votes are cast; elected are David Hunter and Henley Clybourne.

On August 4, the Chicago precinct casts 33 votes in a congressional election.

On August 28, Alexander Doyle is elected justice of the peace. David Hunter and Henley Clybourne are reelected as constables.

On October 3, Fort Dearborn is reoccupied with a military garrison. The commanding officer is Capt. and Bvt. Maj. John Fowle, Fifth Infantry. With him is Dr. Clement Alexander Finley, who becomes the ninth Fort Dearborn physician.

On October 20, 69 men—among them 61 from Chicago—petition the Illinois General Assembly to set off a new county from Peoria County to be named Michigan County; proposed boundaries embrace all territory in Illinois north of the Kankakee River and east of the Fox River. The legislature does not act on the petition.

On November 3, U.S. presidential elections are held at J.B. Beaubien's house; 40 votes are cast. Andrew Jackson captures the presidency on a platform demanding massive, systematic removal to the West of all eastern Indians.

The Department of Indian Affairs builds the first frame house in Chicago as an award to Billy Caldwell (Sauganash) for his services on behalf of the U.S. government; the house is constructed near the corner of the later Chicago and Wabash avenues.

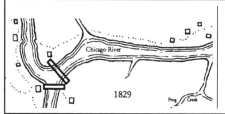

FERRY ACROSS THE SOUTH BRANCH • 1829

This ferry is authorized and licensed by the commissioners of Peoria County in June 1829. Archibald Clybourn and Samuel Miller construct it at the future Lake Street level and make crossings until 1831; Mark Beaubien continues service thereafter. Passage is free for county residents, others pay fixed rates. The main landing is on the east side, allowing for crossing to both the west and the north banks. In 1832 it will be replaced by a log bridge.

1829   On January 22, the Illinois legislature creates the Canal Commission, with powers to undertake the task of construction; the first three canal commissioners are Dr. Gershom Jayne, a druggist and physician of Springfield, Edmund Roberts of Kaskaskia, and Charles Dunn of Chicago.

In June, the first ferry across the Chicago River is licensed by the commissioners of Peoria County. It is built and initially run by Archibald Clybourne and Samuel Miller, later by Mark Beaubien. The main landing is on the east bank of the south branch [where Lake Street would later reach the river], allowing for crossing both to the west and to the north bank of the main river; the ferry will be replaced by a log bridge in 1832.

In the summer, the first wagonload of lead, from the recently discovered lead mines at Galena, arrives in Chicago, the trip taking 11 days.

On July 29, a treaty is concluded at Prairie du Chien between the U.S. government and the Chippewa, Ottawa, and Potawatomi; ceded are five million acres of additional Illinois territory. Several Chicago area residents are awarded compensation at this treaty.

On September 18, Justice of the Peace Alexander Doyle marries David Hunter and Maria Indiana Kinzie.

On October 2, Lt. Jefferson Davis of the First Infantry (later president of the Confederacy) visits Fort Dearborn from Fort Winnebago, where he is stationed, in search of some deserters.

On November 27, the Welland Canal is completed, linking Lakes Erie and Ontario, bypassing Niagara Falls.

On December 8, the Peoria County Commissioners Court grants Archibald Caldwell Chicago's first tavern license for Wolf Point Tavern.

In this year, Mark Beaubien, who has lived on the south bank near the Forks since 1826, begins to take in guests and calls his house the Eagle Exchange Tavern. His daughter, Emily, later recalls: "... and then came along a man that considered himself a sign painter and he painted a blue eagle for the Eagle Exchange ... the 'Old Blue Eagle,' we called it."

1830 On February 24, William Howard and Frederick Harrison, Jr., complete a map of proposed piers for construction of the harbor at the mouth of the Chicago River.

On March 26, Lt. J.G. Furman writes one of several letters from Fort Dearborn to the editor of a Maryland periodical, sharing details of an earlier hunt, beginning: ... *The day was lovely—'the scy so cloudless, clear, and purely beautiful, that God alone was to be seen in heaven,'—the broad blue face of the lake, unruffled by a breath of air, shone in the morning sun like one vast mirrow of polished silver. And the woods were so silent, that the cheering cry of the huntsmen and the wild melody of the hounds were echoed from a thousand points. Everything thus being propitious, we crossed the Chicago, and persued our route through the thick woods on its north side.*

On April 19, the first canal lot sells to Henry Rotley in Chicago, consisting of 80 acres at $1.25 per acre, totaling $100, "being the highest bid therefore."

Certificates of purchase are being exchanged for land patents from the governor.

In May, Dr. Elija Harmon comes to Chicago, and in December begins to serve as the 10th medical officer of the Fort Dearborn garrison, continuing to attend private patients in the village.

On June 9, Reverend See is issued a license by the Commissioners Court of Peoria County to maintain a ferry across the mouth of the Calumet River, which Johann Mann operates for him.

In June, Stephen Forbes and his wife, Elvira, begin teaching school to some 25 students in a log building belonging to J.B. Beaubien, engaged for this purpose by Beaubien and Lt. David Hunter. The children are partly from the garrison and partly from the settlement.

During the summer William Guyon, Henry Belin, and Frederick Harrison conduct surveys in northern Illinois in preparation for construction of the Chicago harbor and the Illinois & Michigan Canal.

On July 24, a special election for justice of the peace and for constable is held at James Kinzie's house; 56 votes are cast. John S.C. Hogan becomes justice of the peace and Horacio Smith is elected constable.

On August 2, 32 people vote in the general election of Peoria County. John Kinzie's house serves as the polling place for the Chicago precinct; John Reynolds from St. Clair County is elected governor. The poll list of voters

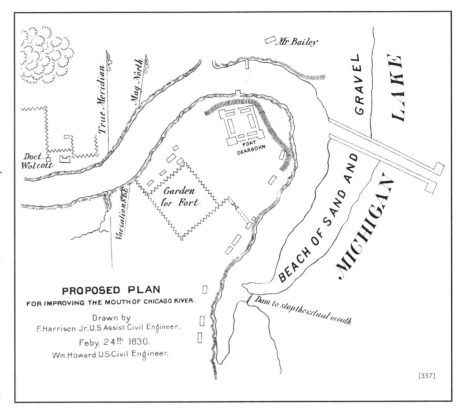

PROPOSED PLAN
FOR IMPROVING THE MOUTH OF CHICAGO RIVER.
Drawn by
F. Harrison Jr. U.S. Assist. Civil Engineer.
Feby. 24th 1830.
Wm. Howard. U.S. Civil Engineer.

[357]

includes Jonathan Bailey, J.B. Beaubien, Madore Beaubien, Leon Bourassa, James Brown, Billy Caldwell, Jean B. Chevallier, John L. Davis, Russel E. Heacock, John S.C. Hogan, James Kinzie, B.H. Lawton, Joseph LaFramboise, Stephen Mack, John Mann, Daniel McKee, Alexander McDale, Rev. William See, Stephen J. Scott, Joseph Tibeaut, Daniel Van Eaton, Rev. J. Walker, Peter Frique, Mark Beaubien, Laurant Martin, Jean B. Secor, Joseph Bausky, Michael Welch, Francis Ladusier, Lewis Ganday, John Van Horn, and Peresh Le Clerc [likely Pierre Le Clerc; *eds.*].

On August 4 James Thompson, canal surveyor for the commissioners of the Illinois and Michigan Canal Company, completes the first survey and plat of Chicago. The plat covers canal section 9, bordered by Madison, State, DesPlaines, and Kinzie streets, embracing approximately three-eighths of a square mile, the "original town." What was once referred to as the "Fort Dearborn settlement," now rapidly becomes Chicago in everyone's mind. Ottawa, at the other end of the planned Illinois & Michigan Canal, is also platted this year.

With Thompson's new street pattern, Mark Beaubien realizes that his Eagle Exchange Tavern now stands in the middle of a street; he moves the building to the southeast corner of Market and Lake streets.

On September 4, the first auction sale of canal section lots, as laid out on Thompson's map, is held. Each lot sale averages $35, though the highest price is $100 for an 80-by-180-foot riverfront lot. Thus settlers, who until then had the status of squatters on government land, for the first time acquire legal title to their property, marking the beginning of Chicago as an organized community. The sale receipts will provide funds for the planned conctruction of the Illinois & Michigan Canal.

On October 26, Dr. Alexander Wolcott dies.

On November 25, a Peoria County election is held for justice of the peace. Twenty-six votes are cast and Stephen Forbes defeats William See.

Chicago in 1831

[537A]

On December 14, First Lt. David Hunter, Fifth Infantry, assumes command of Fort Dearborn.

In this year, Walter Newberry visits Chicago and buys, as a speculative investment, 40 acres of land just north of the river. John Dixon, an Indian trader and the only permanent settler in a vast area held by the Sauk and Fox, assumes control of the ferry where the Chicago-Galena road crosses the Rock River. John Mann and his wife, Arkash, establish a tavern on the east bank of the mouth of the Calumet River, where he runs a ferry. Elijah Wentworth, Sr., opens an inn on Sand Ridge, eight miles north, and Russell Heacock opens "Heacock's Point," a tavern on the south branch. That the fur trade east of the Mississippi is rapidly declining is now evident to all concerned.

1830-31   The winter snow covers the Chicago area for several weeks at a four-foot depth, and the temperature remains at minus 15 degrees Fahrenheit for three weeks; the season is remembered as the "winter of the deep snow" by the earliest settlers.

1831   On January 15, Cook County is created by an act of the Illinois General Assembly, with Chicago as the permanent county seat. This new county also includes all or portions of Lake, McHenry, DuPage, and Will counties.

On March 3, the U.S. Congress approves an appropriation of $5,000 to build the first lighthouse on Lake Michigan, to be built within the year at Chicago.

On March 7, the first county commissioners are elected: Samuel Miller, Gholson Kercheval, and James Walker; Richard J. Hamilton is elected first judge of the Probate Court. They are sworn in by Justice of the Peace John S.C. Hogan when they meet the following day, and the commissioners then grant licenses to sell merchandise, keep tavern, run an auction house, and operate a ferry. In addition, William See is appointed city clerk and Archibald Clybourne is appointed county treasurer.

On March 31, Jonathan Bailey is appointed Chicago's first postmaster by William T. Barry, postmaster general under President Jackson. Bailey then lives in the old Kinzie house, out of which he conducts the first postal activities; soon after, he opens a post office at the Forks.

In April, the Cook County commisssioners order the first two county roads to be mapped out, one by way of Madison Street and Ogden Avenue to the Des Plaines River [Riverside], the other along State Street and Archer Avenue "to the house of widow Brown on Hickory Creek."

On May 20, the troops are withdrawn from Fort Dearborn under Lt. David Hunter's command, until the Black Hawk scare prompts reoccupation. During the hiatus, Indian Agent Thomas J.V. Owen becomes caretaker.

In June, the state grants Cook County permission to sell 24 canal lots separately, the proceeds of which will be used for the erection of public buildings.

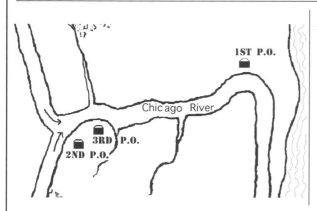

CHICAGO'S FIRST THREE POST OFFICES • 1831-1834

John S.C. Hogan, Chicago's third postmaster, in the summer of 1834, moves the post office from its 2nd location on Lake and South Water streets to its 3rd location on Franklin and South Water. Under Chicago's first postmaster, Jonathan N. Bailey, postal service had begun in April, 1831, out of the old Kinzie House where Bailey then lived.

On July 15, the Napier brothers, Joseph and John, arrive on the schooner *Telegraph* with their families and friends, and soon move west to form the Napier settlement.

In late September, c.4,000 Indians come to Chicago for their annual annuity, which is distributed by Colonel Owen, John Kinzie and Gholson Kercheval assisting. Potawatomi chief Big Foot attempts to use the occasion to agitate for war against the settlers, but finds few supporters.

In October, Richard J. Hamilton is appointed commissioner of Cook County's school lands.

On October 30, Chicago's lighthouse collapses. Construction had been completed by a Samuel Jackson only days earlier. A replacement will be built the following year, immediately west of Fort Dearborn on the military reservation, to remain a prominent landmark until 1857.

Also in this year, George Bickerdyke and Mark Noble, Jr., begin building a sawmill just north of Lake Street on the east bank of the Des Plaines River. The mill, reportedly the only one within 20 miles of Chicago, will become vital to the settlement and growth of the Oak Park and River Forest communities. A tannery building is constructed, owned, and operated by John Miller and Benjamin Hall at the Forks, just north of Millers' Tavern. Dexter Graves builds the Mansion House hotel on the north side of Lake Street, near Dearborn Street. Mark Beaubien adds a two-story frame house adjacent to his cabin and calls the new structure "Sauganash Hotel" in honor of his friend Billy Caldwell. Thomas Jefferson Vincent Owen succeeds the late Dr. Wolcott as Indian agent. Chicago's first ferry service is licensed to transport passen-

gers across the river. Mark Beaubien is appointed ferryman; he pays a $50 license fee, with James Kinzie posting a $200 surety bond. The first Cook County property tax assessment in Chicago for the year 1831, one-half percent "[o]n town lots, on pleasure carriages, on distilleries, on all horses, mules and neat cattle above the age of three years, on watches with their appurtenances, and on all clocks," yields $148.29. Three sailing ships visit Chicago during the year, the *Napoleon*, the *Telegraph*, and the *Marengo*.

1831-32 A debating society is organized during the winter and meets regularly at the fort, Jean Baptiste Beaubien presiding.

1832 In March the first "public building" is erected with county funds ($12), a roofless construction built by Samuel Miller [who asks for $20 but settles for $12]; it is the so-called estray-pen, used for temporary holding of runaway farm animals, and located on the southwest corner of the public square.

On April 4, Cook County's first financial statement shows that for the preceding year, the tax collected on real estate and personal property amounted to $148.29.

On April 5, the aging Sauk Chief Black Hawk leads approximately 1,000 Sauk warriors and their families eastward across the Mississippi into Illinois and Wisconsin, forbidden territory previously ceded to the United States by the Indians; hostilities begin in mid-May. By August, an overwhelming force of 7,000 U.S. soldiers under Generals Atkinson and Scott will have dispersed and destroyed the Indian band, with all hostilities ending by September 30 in the complete rout of the Indians.

On April 25, the county surveyor Jedediah Woolsey is instructed to lay out a street connecting the settlement with the lakeshore and does so by extending South Water Street westward.

On May 20, in preparation for the construction of the harbor and the Illinois & Michigan Canal, "Map No. 1 of the Survey of the Michigan & Illinois Canal," completed by Henry Belin in 1831, is filed with the Topographical

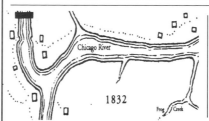

FIRST LOG BRIDGE ACROSS NORTH BRANCH • 1832

Built by Sam Miller, this floating log bridge initially accommodated only foot passage, but by late 1833, it will have been strengthened to also accept teams. A short distance north of where the *grapeline ferry* was, replacing same, its eastern end is located where the southeast corner of Kinzie and Canal streets will be.

Bureau of the Engineer Department in the U.S. Army.

In late May, Rev. Adam Payne, an itinerant preacher who has shared a well appreciated sermon at the fort just two days earlier, is killed by Indians on his westward journey, becoming one of the first victims of the Black Hawk War.

On June 17, Fort Dearborn is formally regarrisoned for the Black Hawk War with two companies of regulars from the Second Infantry, arriving from Niagara under Commandant Maj. William Whistler. With them is Dr. Samuel G.J. DeCamp, the 11th Fort Dearborn surgeon, who relieves Dr. Harmon.

On July 10, to fight Black Hawk and his warriors, troops arrive in Chicago from Detroit on board the two first steamboats under the command of Gen. Winfield Scott. With them arrives the cholera and Fort Dearborn becomes a hospital. The sick are treated by Drs. De Camp and Harmon, but with no adequate treatment for cholera available, one in four patients dies—58 soldiers die, and are buried at a site that will later become the northwest corner of Lake Street and Wabash Avenue, although at least 20 are committed to a sea burial. General Scott makes "Rat Castle" (nickname for the Wolf Point tavern) his headquarters. Most civilians flee the settlement.

On August 6, Philo Carpenter opens the first drugstore, likely in Mark Beaubien's small log cabin on the southeast corner of Lake and Market streets, adjacent to the Sauganash Tavern.

On August 19, the first meeting of a Sunday school class is held under Philo Carpenter's direction in an unfinished log building on the Fort Dearborn reservation; 13 children and five adults attend.

In August, a Cook County election is held and 114 votes cast: Joseph Duncan of Jacksonville is elected to Congress, James M. Strode of Galena as state senator, Benjamin Mills of Galena as state representative, Stephen Forbes as sheriff, and Elijah Wentworth, Jr., as coroner.

On September 15, the so-called "Black Hawk Purchase" is signed at Fort

CHICAGO in 1832 [12]

Armstrong with the defeated Sauk and Fox, but also with the Winnebago, ceding their remaining homeland in southeastern Wisconsin and northwestern Illinois, as well as a 50-mile-wide strip of land in Iowa, along the west bank of the Mississippi. By eliminating the Indian threat to homesteaders on the Illinois prairies, this treaty contributes much to the steady stream of newly arriving Easterners in Chicago.

In the autumn, the number of new arrivals in Chicago reveals a rapid increase, fanned by (1) the relative safety from Indian attacks, resulting from the victory over Black Hawk and the subsequent Treaty of Fort Armstrong; (2) glowing reports of the fertile lands of Illinois, spread by soldiers returning east from the Black Hawk War; and (3) the developing Illinois & Michigan Canal fever. Most immigrants continue west from Chicago following refreshment, inquiry, and supply acquisition, but a significant number recognize the settlement's potential and remain.

On October 20, another treaty is concluded with the Potawatomi; a large area of land south of Chicago, between Lake Michigan and the Illinois River, is ceded to the United States. Annual annuities are promised and monetary claims are paid to many Chicagoans.

On November 2, John S.C. Hogan, co-owner and manager of a variety store at the northeast corner of South Water and Lake streets, becomes the second postmaster, following Bailey. Hogan subdivides the store with separate doors

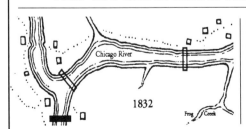

FIRST LOG BRIDGE ACROSS THE SOUTH BRANCH • 1832

Anson H. and Charles Taylor had help from the soldiers of Fort Dearborn when they built this floating bridge just north of Randolph Street. Naked Indians were frequently seen amusing themselves by diving from it. Solid enough for wagons, the bridge was maintained until 1840, supplemented by ferries at Lake, Clark, State and Rush streets [shown by hollow bars for Lake and Clark].

and uses the eastern half as a post office.

Also during this year, the first two bridges across the Chicago River are built, both made of floating heavy logs strung together, and capable of being detached to let river traffic pass. Samuel Miller builds the first one across the north branch at the present Kinzie Street level, replacing the 1829 ferry. The brothers Anson and Charles Taylor build the second bridge across the south branch just north of Randolph Street. Heavier than Miller's bridge, it supports wagons, and will be in service until 1840. The first major surgical procedure is performed in Chicago by Dr. Harmon, who removes the frozen foot of a *métis* mail carrier. The German born John Planck comes to Chicago with the Ebinger brothers; by the year1834 they will have all removed to Dutchman's Point [Niles], where Planck will open his tavern in 1835.

1833   On February 3 Dr. Philip Maxwell arrives as the 12th of the Fort Dearborn surgeons, replacing Dr. DeCamp and serving at the fort together with Dr. George F. Turner, who is the 13th and last physician appointed to the fort. Dr. Maxwell will later become a private medical practitioner in town.

In February, Kinzie's Addition to Chicago is platted by George W. Snow, acting under Captain Hunter's direction and in the presence of John H. Kinzie; bounded on the south by the river (with the sand bar at the river's mouth understood by some to be included), west by State Street, east by the lakeshore, and north by Chicago Avenue.

In March, the U.S. Congress votes and President Andrew Jackson signs an appropriation of $25,000 for construction of a Chicago harbor.

Also in March, a state road connecting Chicago with the left bank of the Wabash River, opposite Vincennes, is completed.

On April 17, the first shipment of western produce (287 bbls. beef, 14 bbls. tallow, 152 hides [4,659 lbs.], and 2 bbls. beeswax) leaves the port of Chicago for the East on Oliver Newberry's schooner *Napoleon*.

On May 1 Father St. Cyr arrives, the first Catholic priest permanently assigned to Chicago; on May 5 he conducts his first Mass, then proceeds to organize St. Mary's parish.

On May 14, Capt. and Bvt. Maj. John Fowle, Fifth Infantry, reassumes command at Fort Dearborn to serve until June 19.

On May 19, Presbyterian minister Rev. Jeremiah Porter, recently accompanying a troop transfer from Fort Brady to Fort Dearborn, preaches his first sermon in the fort's carpentry shop; on June 26 he organizes the First Presbyterian Church with nine settlers and 17 others from Fort Dearborn.

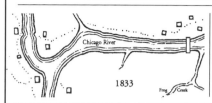

THE DEARBORN FERRY AT OLD POINT • 1833

Chicago River

1833

Frog Creek

On August 10, 1833, the locals elected five village trustees. One of their first official actions was the establishment of the Dearborn Street ferry. There was no charge for using it. In service nearly one year, the ferry was replaced in 1834 by Chicago's first drawbridge.

Spring weather revives Chicago's marked acceleration of population growth that had begun in the preceding fall, slowing during the winter; the population will increase exponentially for the next three years.

Also in the spring, the lake schooner *Austerlitz*, owned by Oliver Newberry, carries east the first shipment of pork from Chicago.

The brick manufacturer Tyler Blodgett arrives and builds a kiln on the north bank between Clark and Dearborn streets, employs the German immigrant brickmaker Heinrich Lampmann, and together they operate the first brickyard.

On June 19, Maj. George Bender, Fifth Infantry, assumes command at Fort Dearborn to serve until October 31. On the same day, John Dean Caton arrives and soon opens his law office in Dr. Temple's building on Lake Street; within six months, Caton will be appointed town attorney.

On July 1, construction of the Chicago harbor begins under the supervision of Maj. Bender, with the building of a set of piers through the sand bar that blocks the harbor mouth. The military has little experience or expertise in such matters, and six years of on-and-off work will be necessary to complete the project, at a cost overrun of more than $100,000.

In late July, at a meeting of the "Qualified Electors" of the Chicago precinct of Cook County in the Peter Pruyne & County drugstore, a 12-to-1 vote is cast for the incorporation of the "Town of Chicago" [pursuant to the Act of Incorporation of February 12, 1831], Thomas J.V. Owen, presiding; Dr. Edmund S. Kimberly, secretary; voting for incorporation: Owen, Kimberly, John S.C. Hogan, C.A. Ballard, George W. Snow, Richard J. Hamilton, Dr. J.T. Temple, John W. Wright, George W. Dole, Hiram Pearsons, Alanson Sweet and Mark Beaubien; against: Russell Heacock.

On August 5, a notice is posted of an election to be held on August 10, for the purpose of choosing five trustees for a village board.

On August 10, the first village board, consisting of five trustees, is elected and meets in the Sauganash Hotel to organize the town government. The trustees are: Indian Agent Thomas J.V. Owen, George W. Dole, Madore B. Beaubien, John Miller, and Dr. Edmund S. Kimberly. The board defines the town limits as follows: "Beginning at the intersection of Jackson and Jefferson streets; thence north to Cook street, and through that street to its eastern extremity in Wah-bon-seh; thence on a direct line to Ohio street in Kinzie's addition; thence eastwardly to the lake shore; thence south with the line of beach to the northern United States pier; thence northwardly along said pier to its termination; thence to the channel of the Chicago River; thence along said channel until it intersects the eastern boundary line of the town of Chicago, as laid out by the canal commissioners; thence southwardly with said line until it meets Jackson street; thence westwardly along Jackson street until it reaches the place of beginning." [Ordinance 1, extended on November 6]

On August 12, the new village board of trustees elects Col. Thomas J.V. Owen as its president and appoints Isaac Harmon as village clerk.

Also during August, Colbee C. Benton, a traveler from New Hampshire, visits Chicago and later prepares a detailed journal of this trip:

(Tuesday Aug 20) — I have had a good opportunity to view the town and country about, and I find Chicago a very pleasant place, as I have before thought. It is situated on the southwestern shore of Lake Michigan at the mouth of the Chicago River, and already it has the appearance of considerable business. It is laid out into lots on each side of the river, and between the two branches, which come together about one mile from the lake. ... The lots are mostly owned by the United States government and the state of Illinois. ... and can not be sold until the legislatures meet again, which will not take place until sometime in 1834. The lots being owned as they are is of great disadvantage to the place and to the appearance of it. It prevents the erection of good buildings, for no one would be willing to risk a large amount of property on public land which must be brought into market and sold under the hammer. ✧ At present the town presents a singular and very peculiar appearance. The lots, many of them, are improved with temporary buildings, some not more than ten feet square, and they are scattered about like cattle on the prairie. They are mostly new. I believe there has been one hundred built this year, all without any regard to beauty, and they are set on blocks so that they can move them at the shortest notice. It will depend some on the length of the purse of the occupant whether the building shall be moved at the time the lots come into the market. ✧ The north side of the river is partly owned by individuals, but it is not much settled yet; some few buildings near the lake. The settlements are in the forks of the river (which consists of one new tavern house two stories high, one other old-looking tavern, one large store building, and a number of log dwellings), and on the south side is the most, which consists of two large, two-story taverns, three or four large storehouses, and a great number of small dwellings and shops. This street [originally Water Street, now Upper Wacker

Drive] extends to the land occupied for the Fort, and is the principal place of business. ✧ The Fort and public buildings are situated on the shore of the river and lake, and it is much the most pleasant part of the town, rendered more pleasant on account of its being elevated a little higher than the rest of the land about. Fort Dearborn, as it is called, is an old fort and it has that appearance, except that the buildings have lately been whitewashed, which makes it appear a little more respectable. It is surrounded by a post fence which would not be much protection against a few pieces of heavy cannon. It answers, and has answered very well, however, as a good and safe refuge from the revenge and cruelty of the savages. It is occupied at present by two companies of forty-eight men each, but in all probability they will soon be unnecessary residents. If emigration continues at the same rate it has done the past season, the country will very soon be able to defend themselves; when that time comes the soldiers will be removed to some other station and the land will be sold and laid out and made to constitute a part of the town. ✧ ... The inhabitants are a singular collection of beings. "All nations and kindred and people and tongues." Black and white and red and grey, and they live in all manner of ways. Some men do their own cooking. I saw one little hovel which contained a family, and near it was two stakes and a pole across it where they hung on the pot and done all their cooking, & all of it in the principal street. ✧ I was surprised to observe the masculine appearance of the women. They were in the street as much as the men, and seemed to prefer a seat outside of their dwelling places rather than to sit down under their own roof. And finally I have seen a good deal to surprise, interest, and amuse me for the few days that I have remained here.

In August Chicago's population stands at between 150 and 200. Among these are four physicians: Assistant Surgeon Philip Maxwell (at Fort Dearborn), Dr. Elijah D. Harmon, Dr. Edward S. Kimberly, and Dr. John T. Temple. There are also nine lawyers: Russell E. Heacock, Richard J. Hamilton, Lewis C. Kercheval, Robert Nelson Murray, Giles Spring, John Dean Caton, Alexander N. Fullerton, Edward W. Casey, and Peter D. Hugunin.

Also in August, the New York land speculators Arthur Bronson and Charles Butler visit Chicago and in time proceed to buy 19 town blocks and 80 acres of adjoining land, later selling most of it at enormous profits before the collapse of land prices in 1837.

On September 4, George W. Dole is named treasurer of the town of Chicago by the town board of trustees.

On September 26, a treaty is signed in Chicago between the United States and an assembled c.6,000 members of the so-called United Bands of Chippewa, Ottawa, and Potawatomi, who surrender their remaining claims to Illinois land [c.5,000,000 acres] and agree to be relocated to reservations west of the Mississippi River by the end of 1835, in exchange for half a million dollars in cash, with an equal amount allocated for annuities to be paid later.

Also in September, two visitors from the East, Charles J. Latrobe and Patrick Shirreff, arrive and witness the town and the ongoing land cession treaty with the Indians; Latrobe left an account of what he observed in his book, *The Rambler in North America*, and Shirreff in his book, *A Tour Through North America; Together with a Comprehensive View of the Canadas and the United States, as Adapted for Agricultural Emigration*. Excerpts of Latrobe's experience follow:

Meanwhile, the village and its occupants presented a most motley scene. The fort contained within its palisades by far the most enlightened residents in the little knot of officers attached to the slender garrison. ... Next in rank to the Officers and Commissioners may be noticed certain store-keepers and merchants resident here, looking either to the influx of new settlers establishing themselves in the neighborhood, of those passing yet farther to the westward, for custom and profit, not to forget the chance of extraordinary occasions like the present. Add to these a doctor or two, two or three lawyers, a [government] land agent, and five or six hotel keepers. These may be considered as stationary, and proprietors of the half a hundred clapboard houses around you. Then for the birds of passage, exclusive of the Pottawatamies, of whom more anon, and emigrants and land speculators, as numerous as the sand. ✧ You will find horse-dealers and horse stealers—rogues of every description—white, black, brown, and red; half-breeds, quarter-breeds, and men of no breed at all; dealers in pigs, poultry, and potatoes; men pursuing Indian claims, some for tracts of land, others, like our friend 'Snipe,' for pigs which the wolves had eaten; creditors of the tribes, or of particular Indians, who know that they have no chance of getting their money if they do not get it from the Government Agents; sharpers of every degree; peddlars, grog-sellers; Indian Agents and Indian traders, of every description, and contractors to supply the Pottawatamies with food. The little village was in an uproar from morning to night, and from night to morning; for during the hours of darkness, when the housed portion of the population of Chicago strove to obtain repose in the crowded plank edifices of the village, the Indians howled, sang, wept, yelled, and whooped in their various encampments. With all this, the whites seemed to me to be more pagan than the red men. You will have understood, that the large body of Indians collected in the vicinity consisted not merely of chiefs and warriors, but in fact the greater part of the whole tribe were present; for where the warrior was invited to feast, at the expense of the Government, the squaw took care to accompany him; and where the squaw went, the children or papooses, the ponies, and the innumerable dogs followed, and here they all were living merrily at the cost of the Government. ... ✧ The interior of the village was one chaos of mud, rubbish, and confusion. Frame and clapboard houses were springing up daily under the active axes and hammers of the speculators, and piles of lumber announced the

preparation for yet other edifices of an equally light character. Races occurred frequently on a piece of level sward without the village, on which temporary booths afforded the motley multitude the means of 'stimulating,' and betting and gambling were the order of the day. Within the vile two-storied barrack, which, dignified as usual by the title of hotel, afforded us quarters, all was in a state of most appalling confusion, filth, and racket. The public table was such a scene of confusion that we avoided it from necessity. The French landlord was a sporting character, and everything was left to chance, who, in the shape of a fat house-keeper, fumed and toiled round the premises from morning to night. Within there was neither peace nor comfort, and we spent much of our time in the open air. A visit to the gentlemen at the fort, a morning's grouse-shooting, or a gallop on the broad surface of the prairie, filled up the intervals in our perturbed attempts at reading or writing indoors, while awaiting the progress of the treaty. ....

In September, Eliza Chappel opens a school in the log cabin that had been the initial store of Stephen Wright, at the southeast corner of Lake and Market streets.

In the autumn, the first jail is built on the northwest corner of the public square, existing until 1853.

On October 8, Asahel Pierce arrives and soon opens a blacksmith shop on the west bank (Lake and Canal streets) to manufacture his "bull plow."

On October 16, John Calhoun arrives with his two apprentices and printing equipment, and moves into an unfinished building at the southwest corner of South Water and Clark, from which he will soon begin to publish the *Chicago Democrat*.

On October 19, Rev. Allen B. Freeman, who had come two months earlier with his wife, organizes the first Baptist church of Chicago.

Between October 20 and 24, by order of the County School Commissioner Colonel Hamilton, all but four of the 144 blocks in the school section [Section 16; immediately south of the town, between Madison Street and Roosevelt Road] go on public sale at an average price of $6.72 per acre, and bring $38,865—a larger than anticipated yield. John Bates is the auctioneer.

On October 23, Charles Cleaver arrives and later will build a soap factory on the south side. Also that day, George David arrives from the East and records:

Oct. 23. Completed today the remaining 13 miles of our journey and entered the long looked for town of Chicago at night fall, and after much trouble in seeking for an asylum; put up by the recommendation of Mr. Winson at Brown's boarding house, thus terminating our wanderings and here we found a resting place, here we "lit on the spot we could call 'home.' " The day had been fine & mild, hardly a zephyr breathed to ripple the glass surface of the lake, but when we reached the open prairie the wind arose and before morning it blew so hard that I fancied the roof of the boarding house in which we were would have fallen about my ears but the roof being stronger than my faith it was in the same elevated condition when I awoke as when I went to sleep.

On October 31, Capt. D. Wilcox, Fifth Infantry, assumes command at Fort Dearborn and serves until December 18.

Also in October, St. Mary's Church opens its door as the first Catholic church.

On November 6, the town board of trustees extends the town's boundaries by adding to the existing official town area the tract bounded by State Street on the west, Ohio Street on the north, the lakeshore on the east, and Jackson Street on the south.

On November 7, the town board of trustees adopts the first code of local laws; the document bears no seal but is attested by "Isaac Harmon, Secretary." The ordinances will be published in the *Chicago Democrat*, beginning on December 10.

On November 8, Gov. John Reynolds of Illinois acknowledges Town President Owen's request for a special session of the legislature to consider construction of a railroad from Chicago to the Illinois River.

On November 16, the carpenter and shipwright Nelson R. Norton moves to Chicago; in the spring of 1834 he will build the Dearborn Street drawbridge.

On November 26, the first issue of the *Chicago Democrat* appears.

On December 4, John Dean Caton is appointed town attorney by the board of trustees; George W. Snow is appointed town assessor and surveyor; and a committee for bridges and ferries is selected, consisting of G.W. Dole, Medore Beaubien, Dr. Kimberly, and John Miller.

On December 10, the *Chicago Democrat* prints the first village ordinances.

On December 18, Maj. John Green, Fifth Infantry, assumes command at Fort Dearborn and serves until September 16, 1835.

On the same day, Granville T. Sproat opens the private English and Classical School for Boys in a small building on South Water Street, corner of Franklin.

On December 31, the *Chicago Democrat* prints additional new ordinances.

Also in this year, Gurdon S. Hubbard formally moves from Danville, Illinois, but in preceding years he has spent so much time in Chicago that the villagers already consider him as one of their own.

The stonemason Alanson Sweet and the plasterer William Worthingham build Chicago's first brick house under contract for John Noble on the north side of the river [Kinzie Street], on a lot adjacent to the later Lake House Hotel.

The first Tremont House is built and then run by Alanson Sweet at the northwest corner of Lake and Dearborn. Dexter Graves and Rufus Brown open their boarding houses, and Wentworth's Buckhorn Tavern opens on Flag Creek.

Silas B. Cobb builds the two-story Green Tree Tavern for James Kinzie, later to be called Chicago Hotel, and later yet, Lake Street House.

George W. Dole, as agent for Oliver Newberry, opens the first slaughterhouse; in the following year, the first beef will be exported to the East.

Jerry Church revisits Chicago from Cleveland; an excerpt from his journal of impressions and commentaries follow:

We there took the beach of the Michigan lake and followed it to Chicago, and there we found a large town built up in three years; for it was only three years since we were there with the black oxen and wagon, and at that time there were but half a dozen houses in the place. It was very surprising what improvements had been made in the western country in that short time. Look at an Indian wigwam town changed into an American city in the course of three or four years! I know of a number of places in the west that would have been improved in the same way, if the government had let the currency alone, and had not taken what I call the one thing needful from us. The consequence now is, the land lies uncultivated, and nothing but a wild Indian sitting wrapped up in a red blanket on a log, where we might have had a good native American, or at least some imported voters from "the land of steady habits," to have been the cultivators at this time.

John Bates remembers that "... [i]n 1833 the settlement of the new town, so far as buildings showed, was mostly on what is now Water Street. ... Up and down Water Street, between what is now State and Wells streets, now Fifth Avenue, all the business houses and stores were built. Also nearly all the cabins for dwellings. You could from every store and dwelling, look north across the river, as there were no buildings on what is now the north side of that [S Water] street. At that time a slough [Frog Creek] emptied into the river, at what is now the foot of State Street, and was a sort of bayeau of dead water through which scows could be run up as far as Randolph Street, near the corner of Dearborn, and there was a dry creek up as far as where the Sherman House now stands. There was a foot-bridge of four logs run lengthwise across the creek near the mouth of the creek."

1833-34 "A mild autumn is followed by a severe winter, with the temperature dropping to minus 29 degrees."

1834 On January 1 Charles Fenno Hoffmann, author and visitor from New York, arrives in Chicago. Of his visit he left an account in *A Winter in the Far West, by a New Yorker*; he writes in the *New York American*, No. XVIII, 1834:

Chicago, Jan. 10, 1834—I have been here more than ten days, without fulfilling the promise given in my last. It has been so cold, indeed, as almost to render writing impracticable in a place so comfortless. The houses were built with such rapidity during the summer as to be mere shells; and the thermometer having ranged as low as 29 below zero during several days, it has been almost impossible, notwithstanding the large fires kept up by the attentive landlord, to prevent the ink from freezing while using it, and one's fingers become so numb in very few moments when thus exercised, that, after vainly trying to write in gloves, I have thrown by my pen, and joined the group composed of all the household around the bar-room fire. This room, which is in an old log cabin aside of the main house, is one of the most comfortable places in town, and is, of course, much frequented, business being, so far as one can judge from the concourse that throng it, nearly at a stand still. Several persons have been severely frostbitten in passing from door to door; and, not to mention the quantity of poulty and pigs that have been frozen, an ox, I was just told, has perished from cold in the streets at noonday. An occasional Indian, wrapped in his blanket, and dodging about from store to store after a dram of whiskey, or a muffled Frenchman, driving furiously in his cariole on the river, are almost the only passengers abroad; while the wolves, driven in by the deep snows which preceded this severe weather, troop through the town after nightfall, and may be heard howling continually in the midst of it. ✧ The situation of Chicago, on the edge of the Grand Prairie, with the whole expanse of Lake Michigan before it, gives the freezing winds from the Rocky Mountains prodigious effect, and renders a degree of temperature which, in sheltered situations, is but little felt, almost painfull here.

—The bleak winds

Do sorely ruffle; for many a mile about,

There's scarce a bush.   H

On January 7, the publication date of the seventh issue of the *Chicago Democrat*, Nelson P. Perry, a "man of color," announces that he is in town for the next three weeks and "at all times ready to furnish music."

On January 28, the 10th issue of the *Chicago Democrat* announces meetings of the Chicago Temperance Society at the Presbyterian meeting house and of the Polemic Society of Chicago, to debate the issues of Congress and of internal improvements. From the editorial in that issue, reflecting the sudden momentum acquired by the town's growth rate during the past year, John Calhoun writes:

In some of the first numbers of our paper we made some very general remarks, respecting Chicago and vicinity, but we find from the many letters of inquiry, &c. that arrive in every mail from all parts of the United States, that our observations were far too limited; and having become more acquainted with the surrounding country, from longer residence in it, we shall again resume the subject in a more particular manner. ✧ Chicago is situate on the river of the same name, which is divided into the north and south branches, about three-quarters of a mile from its mouth. These branches come from nearly opposite directions, from whose junction the river runs in nearly a due east course, till it empties into the Lake. The River from the junction to the Lake, is over two-hundred feet in width, and from twenty to thirty feet in depth, and both branches are navigable for several miles for vessels of any size. The town is situate on both sides of the river and branches, extending from the Lake some considerable distance west of the junction. ✧ The Spring of 1833, may be marked as a new era in the history of Chicago, and in fact all the Northern parts of the State of Illinois: or indeed that may be referred to as the commencement of their improvement. At that time Chicago did not contain more than five or six regular stores, and now may be counted from twenty to twenty-five; then it did not contain over one hundred and fifty inhabitants, whereas now there are from eight to ten hundred; then it did not contain more than thirty buildings, now may be seen over one hundred and eighty. ✧ During the past summer, eighty vessels have arrived, bringing goods and property to a vast amount: yet notwithstanding the immense importation of merchandize during the past season, hardly three good assortments could now be made out in this place. After the fall stock of Goods had arrived, every store was crowded to excess—now they look quite empty. But the mercantile business has not alone flourished; indeed that in the business of Chicago, has been of but small moment. Building and real improvements have been the great order of the day. To describe the want that has been for building materials and mechanics, would be only to incite incredulity.

Also in January, Ashbel Steele keeps the Eagle Hotel in town.

On February 2, the 11th issue of the *Chicago Democrat* announces the appointment of Lt. James Allen as superintendent of harbor.

On February 11, the 12th issue of the *Chicago Democrat* announces the schedule of mail arrival and departure from all directions, and informs the public that the village board has again revised the town boundaries to include all land east of State Street, from Chicago Avenue on the north to 12th Street on the south, excepting the military reservation of Fort Dearborn.

On Saturday, February 15, the Chicago River rises three feet and swells to an unusual volume and force, due to heavy rains on the two preceding days. The occurrence is fortuitous—in conjunction with the southern pier that had been constructed in 1833, under Major Bender, the freshet facilitates ongoing harbor construction, under Lt. James Allen, by cutting a 30-foot-wide and 10-to-12-foot-deep channel through the large sand bar that had accumulated in front of the river outlet.

On February 18, the 13th issue of the *Chicago Democrat* announces: a new post office opening at Walker's Grove [Plainfield]; a citizens' "voice of people" meeting to discuss the communication between Lake Michigan and the Illinois River by canal or railroad, led by P.F.W. Peck and Richard J. Hamilton; and evening entertainment, arranged by Mr. Bowers, "*Professeur de tours Amusant*," at Dexter Graves' boarding house, on Monday, February 24.

On March 4, in the 15th edition of the *Chicago Democrat* appear the following notices: a new post office opens at the Napier settlement; and James Allen, agent, solicits offers of timber for harbor construction.

On March 28, the 17th edition of the *Chicago Democrat* carries the following notices: Rev. John M. Peck advertises his *Guide for Emigrants*, and announces the upcoming publication of his *Gazettier of Illinois*; Lt. E. Kirby Smith, post adjutant at Fort Dearborn under Major Green, announces a $30 reward to anyone who can provide information leading to the capture of William W. Morin, a soldier who has deserted.

On April 8, the 19th edition of the *Chicago Democrat* notifies its readers that an eclipse of the sun will take place on November 13, and that post office clerk Bates is looking for a man with some knowledge of gardening.

On May 4, the *Michigan* becomes the first steamboat to enter the Chicago River and pass through the recently completed Dearborn Street drawbridge.

On May 14, the 24th edition of the *Chicago Democrat* announces that all free, white, male citizens over 18, under 45, are to meet "on the first Saturday in June" [June 2], at noon, at the house of the sheriff of Cook County, S. Forbes, on the west bank of the Des Plaines River, for the purpose of electing a colonel to organize the militia of Cook County. [Jean Baptiste Beaubien was elected, and the losing candidate was John Mann; *eds.*]

On May 21, the 25th edition of the *Chicago Democrat* informs readers that 250 to 600 people have arrived at Chicago during the past week, and that Edmund S. Kimberly will be a candidate for representative of the Illinois house.

In May regular sessions of the Circuit Court of Cook County begin in Chicago, under the Hon. Richard M. Young. Also this month the first divorce under local Chicago jurisdiction takes place, namely between Daniel and Angelina Vaughan (née Herbert), with Angelina suing.

On June 11, the second recorded public commercial entertainment performance takes place, that given by Mr. Kenworthy, ventriloquist.

The *Chicago Democrat* of June 18 publishes the first advertisement for Joshua Hathaway's map: "Lithographic Maps of Chicago. – Mr. Jno. H. Kinzie procured while in New York a few copies of Lithographic maps of this Town. They are beautifully executed, and contain the Town Plat, together with the School Section, Wabansia, and Kinzie's Addition."

On June 19, Chicago's first public concert is given by Mr. C. Blisse.

On June 21, Cyrus Hall McCormick is granted a patent for his reaping machine. [He did not remove from Cincinnati to Chicago until 1847; *eds.*]

There had been intermitent Methodist sermons since 1826, but this summer the congregation is formally organized, and on June 30 a contract is signed for building the First Methodist Church at the corner of North Water and Clark streets, to be built by John Stewart and Rev. Henry Whitehead at a cost of $580. On the same day Miss Catherine Bayne, from Scotland, opens a boarding and day school for young ladies on Randolph Street, between Clark and Dearborn.

On July 12, the *Illinois* becomes the first major sailing vessel to enter the river under full sail, "her top-masts covered with flags and streamers," passing the Dearborn Street drawbridge and docking at Newberry & Dole's wharf.

On July 14, John D. Caton is elected justice of the peace with a vote count of 172 to 47. Judge Caton would later remember that it was not until the spring of 1834, that Chicago streets became a reality, though platted four years earlier: "... There was not even a wagon track upon any street in Chicago. Every one drove where he pleased across the Prairie from one building to another. ◇ It was early in that spring of 1834 that I found myself at the crossing of Dearborn and Lake streets looking west; and for the first time I could see where the street was by the line of buildings on either side of it. This was the first time I ever noticed a street in Chicago made perceptible by the buildings on both sides of it. Then for the first time could I fully realize that our little settlement was assuming the appearance of a town."

In the summer, Postmaster Hogan moves the post office from Lake and South Water streets to a blacksmith shop, which he rents from Mathias Mason, on the southwest corner of Franklin and South Water streets, where Thomas Watkins becomes postal assistant.

On August 11, John H. Kinzie is elected president of the town board of trustees, replacing Thomas J.V. Owen; elected with him as board members are G.S. Hubbard, E. Goodrich, J.K. Boyer, and John S.C. Hogan.

On August 26, Aaron Russell and Benjamin H. Clift open Chicago's first book and stationery store on South Water Street, between Wells and LaSalle.

On September 1, the town trustees pass the first Sunday liquor law, providing for a $5 fine for the offence of keeping a tippling house or grocery store open on Sundays, with half of the amount going to the complainant.

On September 25, the town is divided into four wards, and a firewarden is appointed for each: first ward—W. Worthington; second ward—E.E. Hunter; third ward—Samuel Resique; and fourth ward—James Kinzie.

On October 2, the town trustees authorize the borrowing of $60, Chicago's first loan on the faith of the community; the funds are intended to drain and improve State Street.

On October 6, John Sweeney shoots the last bear [400 pounds] in Chicago, in the woods near Randolph Street, between LaSalle and the river; occasional sightings continue to be reported near the town as late as 1837.

The first murder trial occurs in early October. The laborer John Fitzpatrick had beaten his wife, Elizabeth, and she died from the injuries; attorney James Collins' excellent defense causes the jury to acquit the defendant.

On October 12 Rev. Palmer Dyer, who had arrived two days earlier, gives Chicago's first Episcopal service to the newly organized St. James Episcopal congregation at the Presbyterian Church, by the gracious invitation of Rev. J. Porter. Soon thereafter, John Kinzie furnished a building on the southeast corner of State [then Wolcott] and Kinzie streets as a place of worship; in 1840, this building will become known as "Tippecanoe Hall."

On October 21 the following notice appeared in the *Chicago Democrat*:

On Saturday last [October 16], about 10 o'clock a.m., a building on the corner of Lake and LaSalle streets, and the one attached, were discovered to be in flames. Our citizens repaired to the scene of conflagration with a promptitude worthy of commendation and succeeded in arresting its progress, after distroying [sic] two other buildings adjoining. The wind being high at the time, threatened the destruction of a number of the surrounding houses, but, by the exscertion [sic] of our citizens, were saved from the devastation. The loss of the sufferers will be severely felt, as some of them lost their all. A building on the corner, occupied as a dwelling, loss $300. There was in the house $220 in money, $125, being in Jackson money, was found in the ruins. The remainder, the rag currency, was destroyed. A building owned and occupied as a cabinet shop, and another building as a groceriy by H. Rhines, together with dwelling, furniture and tools, loss $1,200. A building owned and occupied as a dwelling by James Spence, loss $500. The fire commenced by a coal from a shovel in carrying from one building to another. The want of suitable officers to take charge and oversee in cases of fire is much felt, and we understand the Trustees have suitable regulations in respect to it.

On October 18, a Chicago Cemetery Association is organized for the purpose of finding sufficient burial space, other than the then common practice of burying deceased relatives on private family property.

On the evening of October 24, a spontaneous meeting of prominent citizens is held at the Presbyterian Church to adopt measures to suppress gambling. Col. R.J. Hamilton opens the meeting, Col. John H. Kinzie presides, and Hans Crocker is appointed secretary. A committee of nine is appointed to ascertain the extent of gambling in the town and to identify those engaged,

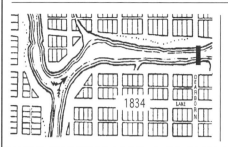

DEARBORN STREET DRAWBRIDGE • 1834

The street pattern adopted in 1830 is now evident. Dearborn Street bridge is built by shipwright Nelson R. Norton in the spring of 1834. The 300 foot long wooden structure, with a 60-foot mobile section for passage of river traffic, turned out to be quite unreliable. It is frequently in need of repair and is particularly unpopular with southside residents who see business, formerly transacted on their side of the river, now being conducted at northside warehouses. The bridge will be removed in July 1839.

while another committee of five is appointed to draft resolutions. On October 25 all meet again and adopt seven prepared resolutions, acting under authority of existing anti-gambling laws of the state of Illinois. The resolutions are published in the next *Chicago Democrat* [October 29].

On October 28 a large number of Indians gather in Chicago to receive their annual annuity in trade goods, in accordance with the provisions of the Chicago Treaty of the previous year. Poorly organized, the distribution of goods becomes tumultuous. A brief description appears in the *Chicago Democrat* of November 5: "On Monday of last week, the Indian annuities were paid. Considerable drunkenness among the Indians was observed, but we are informed that the evil was greatly diminished from last year. A number died while there, and two Indians were killed by being stabbed by others."

John Calhoun's 1854 eyewitness account of the 1834 distribution of the promised annuity of trade goods follows.

About $30,000 worth of goods were to be distributed. They assembled to the number of about 4000. The distribution took place by piling the whole quantity in a heap upon the prairie on the west side of the river near the corner of Randolph and Canal streets. The Indians were made to sit down upon the grass in a circle around the pile of goods—their squaws sitting behind them. The half-breeds and traders were appointed to distribute the goods, and they leizurely walked to the pile and taking an armful proceeded to throw to one and another of those sitting upon the grass, and to whom they were appointed to distribute, such articles as they saw fit, and then returned to the pile to replenish. Shortly the Indians began to show an anxiety not to be overlooked in the distribution and at first got on their knees, vociferating all the time in right lusty Indian gibberish. Then they rose on one foot, and soon all were standing, and they began to contract the circle until they finally made a rush for the pile. I saw then a manner of dispersing a mob that I never saw exemplified before or since. The crowd was so great around the pile of goods that those who were back from them could not get to them and the outsiders at once commenced hurling whatever missiles they could get hold of,

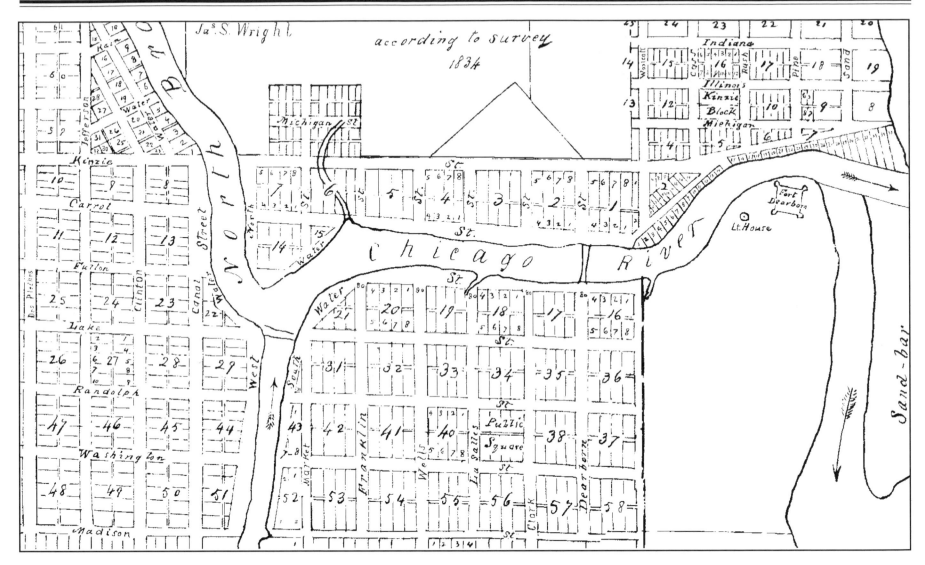

Shown above is part of a **manuscript map of Chicago** that resulted from surveys **James S. Wright** adapted in **1834**. It formed the basis of the first printed map of the town. The large rectangular portion borderd by Kinzie, Wolcott (now State), Madison and DesPlaines streets represents the original town as surveyed four years earlier by James Thompson. It is flanked on its east by the Fort Dearborn reservation. North of Kinzie Street are shown part of the Kinzie Addition (east, with the unnumbered "Kinzie Block" between blocks 10 and 12) and the triangular Wabansia Addition, bordered by Kinzie and Jefferson streets and the north branch of the river. Blocks and lots of real estate are systematically numbered. When trying to identify a numbered lot, one first needs to find the block. If the lots within a given block are not numbered, one can refer for guidance to the numbering system used in a nearby block within the same section.

literally filling the air and causing them to fall in the center where the croud was most dense. These, to save a broken head, rushed away, leaving a space for those who had hurled the missiles to rush in for a share of the spoils.

In the autumn, a cholera vigilance committee is appointed by the town trustees. No cholera materializes, but the committee becomes the forerunner of the first Chicago Board of Health, to be established in 1835.

On November 10, the digging of a public well is authorized in the Kinzie Addition on the north side of the river (corner of Cass [Wabash] and Michigan [Hubbard] streets) at a cost of $95.50; this is the first community effort to provide villagers with pure water. Horse carts (backed into the lake and filled with water by means of a bucket) deliver the water, with prices varying from one shilling or five to 10 cents per barrel. [Not until January 18, 1836, will the Illinois State Legislature pass a law incorporating the Chicago Hydraulic Company, of which George W. Dole will be the president; the real estate panic of 1837 delayed organization and action of the company until 1840.]

On December 2, the Chicago Lyceum for Social and Intellectual Pursuits is formed by a group of book-oriented intellectuals. They hold weekly meetings in the courthouse for debating cultural subjects and for the purpose of accumulating a library.

Also this year, Mark Beaubien opens his second hotel, the Exchange Coffee House, later called the Illinois Exchange, and sometimes the New York Exchange, on the northwest corner of Lake and Wells; the establishment is initially run by Mr. and Mrs. John Murphy.

Lathrop Johnson and George Stevens begin building the New York House on the north side of Lake Street; they will open for business in 1835.

Charles Butler of New York organizes the American Land Co., through which he channels large funds to Chicago, fueling the land boom that began in 1833.

1834-35 "A mild winter with little snow—front doors are open throughout the season, and cows graze on the river banks."

1835 On January 31, the state of Illinois authorizes Chicago to establish its own police force; prior to this time, law enforcement was a function of military authorities, the U.S. Indian agent, and later the county sheriff. Yet not until August 15 does the town board appoint the first police constable.

On February 6, the General Assembly of Illinois approves the Chicago School System.

On February 11, the Illinois General Assembly endorses the Articles of Incorporation of the Town of Chicago which the town trustees had voted on Au-

gust 10, 1833.

On February 12, the Illinois legislature grants a charter to the State Bank of Illinois, a branch of which will open in Chicago mid-December; this will be the first banking facility in town, with John H. Kinzie as president.

On May 16, the following article appears in the *Niles' Register*:

The public mind being at this time directed with considerable interest toward the town of Chicago in Illinois, as a place destined to take rank very soon among the first commercial cities of the west, a few remarks relating to the prospects of this place may not be uninteresting to the public: Chicago contains at present between three and four thousand inhabitants. Three years since it was only a military station. The state is rapidly settling with emigrants of industry and character as well as of means, and will soon out-run Ohio. Chicago is one of the finest harbors on Lake Michigan, and there can not be a finer one anywhere: twenty to twenty-five feet of water in front of the town, and completely embayed from any lake winds; and at the same time the town is not half a mile from the lake. Nature has done every thing to render Chicago the finest city of the west. It will command the trade of the Illinois River and Mississippi by means of the canal; and the west and east by the navigation of the lakes, and, as Hoffman says in his winter in the west, it is destined to be the New Orleans of the west. ✧ It is stated, that New York has extended her long-armed speculation to Chicago—and that about 150 building lots, 40 feet front and of suitable depth, have been sold in that city, for $300 or $400 each.

Capt. Jack Wagstaff anchors the *Illinois* offshore near the north bank of the Chicago River on May 25 to unload cargo and a few families. The following day the Gale family arises and Edwin remembers: "We were ready for an early breakfast of fried perch and bass just out of the river, and venison steak, and griddle cakes with wild honey and maple syrup. We made haste with our meal, eager to get out for a stroll in order to view our surroundings, and become acquainted with the place that we felt was to be our future home. ✧ What strikes us especially on going out is the entire absence of streets, of which, properly so called, there is not one, no, not even a ditch to mark the roads. Moreover, there is nothing to indicate where they ultimately will be, save the surveyor's stakes. And, as there are no streets, so there are no sidewalks. Occasionally, near the houses, we come across stepping-blocks, short pieces of cord wood thrown down to keep pedestrians out of the mud, but by their use in the spring, they had, in most cases, been pressed down to near the level of the adjoining path."

On May 28, the U.S. Land Office opens for the sale of land obtained through the 1833 Indian Treaty; the office is located above Thomas Church's grocery store on the east side of Lake Street, between Clark and Dearborn. Receipts for land sales during the first two weeks exceed $500,000. Also this month, J.B. Beaubien purchases 75 acres of the Fort Dearborn reservation at the U.S.

Land Office for $94, but the purchase will later be declared invalid by the Supreme Court ("Beaubien land case").

On June 6 the following article appears in the *Niles' Register*:

Three years ago the number of inhabitants in Chicago was fifty-four,—now it is four thousand, including about forty merchants. Five churches have been erected, of various sizes, and for various denominations. A steamboat communication, twice a week, is established with Buffalo, and by sloops and schooners, flour is transported from one place to the other at a freight of 25 cents per barrel. Water lots, 45 feet deep by 200, have been sold at from two to seven thousand dollars. So much for the enterprise of freemen.

Also on June 6, Capt. William Gordon of the U.S. Army, in charge of an exploring party of Potawatomi and several white men, acquires supplies from Capt. J.B.F. Russell, disbursing agent in Chicago; soon after the party travels westward as far as Fort Leavenworth to scout suitable locations for Indian resettlement, an agreement of the 1833 Treaty at Chicago.

On June 8, the first issue of the second Chicago weekly, the *Chicago American*, appears; the date on the issue mistakenly reads May 8, a result of a printer's error. The paper is published by editor and owner T.O. Davis, located on South Water Street, near the drawbridge.

On June 19, the first board of health forms, replacing the Cholera Vigilante Committee; the board receives inadequate funding and is minimally active.

Also this month, the third town board election takes place. Hiram Hugunin becomes president, and elected as board members are W. Kimball, B. King, S. Jackson, E.B. Williams, F.C. Sherman, E. Loyd, and George Dole.

On June 29, the *Michigan* docks with the Hon. Lewis Cass, secretary of war, on board; leading townsmen, T.J.V. Owen and R.J. Hamilton, immediately invite him to a public dinner, though circumstance renders departure within hours; graciously he responds: "… But I beg leave to return my sincere thanks for the honor you have conferred on me, and for the favorable sentiments you have been pleased to express."

On July 4, Postmaster Hogan announces new post office hours in the *Chicago American*: 6 a.m. to 7:30 p.m., adding "N.B. [note well] Postage of Letters must be paid when taken: hereafter no credit will be given."

On July 6, the Illinois Secretary of State A.P. Field certifies the Articles of Incorporation of the Town of Chicago, originally passed by the town trustees on August 10, 1833.

In the July 18, *Chicago American* editor Thomas Davis reports that "[t]he amount of money received at the Land Office in this town for lands sold from the 28th May till the close of the land sale is a little over 386,500 dol-

lars, of which about 353,500 were for lands sold at auction, and the balance under the pre-emption law. The exact amount cannot as yet be ascertained."

During the summer, the first building erected for specific school purposes is financed by John S. Wright and built by Joseph Meeker on the Presbyterian church's property; Ruth Leavenworth is the teacher.

On August 5, a new town ordinance outlaws as a fire hazard the stacking of feed hay in the town's central area.

On August 7, John Calhoun bills the town of Chicago $5, "To printing 100 bills [handbills] 'Laws and Ordinances.'"

On August 15 the third village board appoints Oremus Morrison as the first police constable, and the town surveyor is directed to lay out the first two cemeteries: 10 acres of land on the north side of the river (for Protestants; east of Clark Street, near Chicago Avenue), and 16 acres on the south side (for Catholics; at the foot of 23rd Street); each will be fenced in September, and thereafter burial will be forbidden elsewhere.

Also on that day, the *Chicago American* lists the first brewery among as many as 95 business enterprises in town—little doubt the Chicago Brewery, begun in June by the Crawfords.

On August 18, the Chicago Bible Society is organized and chooses Rev. Isaac T. Hinton as its first president; the society's mission is to make Bibles available to all who can read.

Also that day, the last war dance of the Potawatomi takes place. The Indians had come to Chicago to receive their last annuity in preparation for their westward relocation. John D. Caton's eyewitness description follows: ... *I shall close this paper with an account of the great war dance which was performed by all the braves which could be mustered among the five thousand Indians here assembled. The number who joined in the dance was probably about eight hundred. Although I can not give the precise day, it must have occurred about the last day of August, 1835. It was the last war dance ever performed by the natives on the ground where now stands this great city, though how many thousands have preceded it no one can tell. They appreciated that it was the last on their native soil—that it was a sort of funeral ceremony of old associations and memories, and nothing was omitted to lend to it all the grandeur and solemnity possible. Truly, I thought it an impressive scene, of which it is quite impossible to give an adequate idea by words alone. ✧ They assembled at the council-house, where the Lake House now stands, on the north side of the river. All were entirely naked, except a strip of cloth around the loins. Their bodies were covered all over with a great variety of brilliant paints. ✧ On their faces, particularly, they seemed to have exhausted their art of hideous decoration. Foreheads, cheeks, and noses were covered with curved stripes of red or vermillion, which were edged with black points,* and gave the appearance of a horrid grin over the entire countenance. The long, course, black hair, was gathered into scalp locks on the top of their heads, and decorated with a profusion of hawk's and eagle's feathers, some strung together as to extend down the back nearly to the ground. They were principally armed with tomahawks and war clubs. They were led by what answered for a band of music, which created what may be termed a discordant din of hideous noises, produced by beating on hollow vessels and striking sticks and clubs together. They advanced, not with a regular march, but a continued dance. Their actual progress was quite slow. They proceeded up and along the bank of the river, on the north side, stopping in front of every house they passed, where they performed some extra exploits. They crossed the North Branch on the old bridge, which stood near where the railroad bridge now stands, and thence proceeded south along the west side to the bridge across the South Branch, which stood south of where Lake Street bridge is now located, which was nearly in front, and in full view from the parlor windows, of the Sauganash Hotel. At that time this was the rival hotel to the Tremont, and stood upon the ground lately occupied by the great Republican wigwam where Mr. Lincoln was nominated for the presidency—on the corner of Lake and Market streets. It was then a fashionable boarding-house, and quite a number of young married people had rooms there. The parlor was in the second story fronting west, from the windows of which the best view of the dance was to be obtained, and these were filled with ladies as soon as the dance commenced. From this point of view my own observations were principally made. Although the din and clatter had been heard for a considerable time, the Indians did not come into view from this point of observation till they had proceeded so far west as to come on line with the house, which was before they had reached the North Branch bridge. From that time on they were in full view all the way to the South Branch bridge, which was nearly before us, the wild band, which was in front as they came upon the bridge, redoubling their blows to increase the noise, closely followed by the warriors, who had now wrought themselves into a perfect frenzy. ✧ The morning was very warm, and the perspiration was pouring from them almost in streams. Their eyes were wild and blood-shot. Their countenances had assumed an expression of all the worst passions which can find a place in the breast of a savage; fierce anger, terrible hate, dire revenge, remorseless cruelty, all were expressed in their terrible features. Their muscles stood out in great hard knots, as of wrought to a tension which must burst them. Their tomahawks were thrown and brandished about in every direction, with the most terrible ferocity, and with a force and energy which could only result from the highest excitement, and with every step and every gesture they uttered the most frightful yells, in every imaginable key and note, though generally the highest and shrillest possible. The dance, which was ever continued, consisted of leaps and spasmodic steps, now forward and now back and sideways, with the whole body distorted into every imaginable unnatural position, most generally stooping forward, with the head and face thrown up, the back arched down, first one foot thrown far forward and then withdrawn, and the other similarly thrust out, frequently squatting quite to the ground, and all with a movement almost as quick as lightning. Their weapons were brandished as if they would slay a thousand enemies at every blow, while the yells and screams they uttered were broken up and multiplied and rendered all the more hideous by a rapid clapping of the mouth with the palm of the hand. ✧ To see such an exhibition by a single individual would have been sufficient to excite a sense of fear in a person not over nervous. Eight hundred such, all under the influence of the strongest and wildest excitement, constituting a raging sea of dusky, painted, naked fiends, presented a spectacle absolutely appalling. ✧ When the head of the column had reached the front of the hotel, leaping, dancing, gesticulating, and screaming, while they looked up, with hell itself depicted in their faces, at the "chemokoman squaws" in the windows, and brandished their weapons as if they were about to make a real attack in deadly earnest, the rear was still on the other side of the river, two hundred yards off; and all the intervening space, including the bridge and its approaches, was covered with this raging savagery glistening in the sun, reeking with steamy sweat, fairly frothing at their mouths as with unaffected rage, it seemed as if we had a picture of hell itself before us, and a carnival of the damned spirits there confined, whose pastimes we may suppose should present some such scenes as this. ✧ At this stage of the spectacle, I was interested to observe the effect it had on the different ladies who occupied the windows almost within reach of the war clubs in the hands of the excited savages just below them. Most of them had become accustomed to the sight of naked savages during the several weeks they had occupied the town, and had even seen them in the dance before, for several minor dances had been previously performed, but this far excelled in the horrid anything which they had previously witnessed. Others, however, had just arrived in town, and had never seen an Indian before the last few days, and knew nothing of our wild western Indians but what they had learned of their savage butcheries and tortures in legends and in histories. To those most familiar with them, the scene seemed actually appalling, and but few stood it through and met the fierce glare of the savage eyes below them without shrinking. It was a place to try the human nerves of even the stoutest, and all felt that one such sight was enough for a lifetime. The question forced itself on even those who had seen them most, what if they should, in their maddened frenzy, turn this sham warfare into a real attack? How easy it would be for them to massacre us all, and leave not a living soul to tell the story. Some such remark as this was often heard, and it was not strange if the cheeks of all paled at the thought of such a possibility. However, most of them stood it bravely, and saw the sight to the very end; but I think all felt relieved when the last had disappeared around the corner as they passed down Lake Street, and only those horrid sounds which reached them told that the war dance was still progressing. They paused in their progress, for extra exploits, in front of Dr. Temple's house, on the corner of Lake and Franklin streets; then in front of the Exchange Coffee House, a little further east on Lake Street; and then again in front of the Tremont, at that day situate on the northwest corner of Lake and Dearborn streets, where the appearance of the ladies in the windows again inspired them with new life and energy. From thence they passed down to Fort

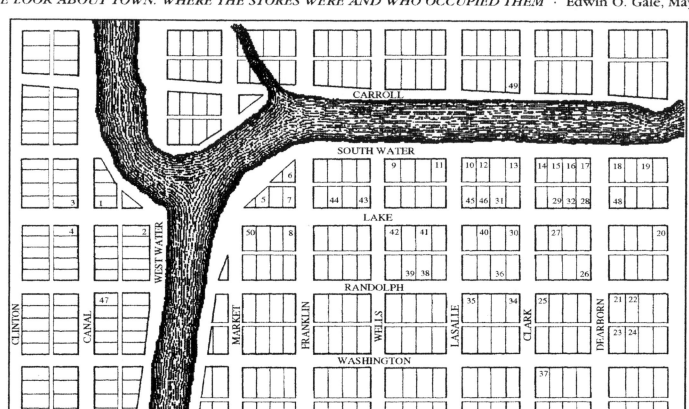

WE LOOK ABOUT TOWN. WHERE THE STORES WERE AND WHO OCCUPIED THEM · Edwin O. Gale, May 26

1. Green Tree Tavern
2. Alexander Robinson
3. Goss & Cobb
4. Asahel Pierce
5. John S.C. Hogan
6. John T. Temple
7. Clemens Stose
8. George Snow
9. Mosely & McCord
10. P.F.W. Peck
11. Philo Carpenter
12. Stephen F. Gale
13. Issac D. Harmon
14. Harmon & Loomis
15. Pruyne & Kimberly
16. King, Jones & Co.
17. Medore Beaubien
18. Newberry & Dole
19. James A. Marshall
20. St. Mary's Church
21. Willis Jones
22. Alvin Calhoun
23. James Collins
24. Ashbel Steele
25. Seth Warner
26. J.K. Botsford
27. Thomas Church
28. Tremont House
29. Joseph Meeker
30. Presbyterian Church
31. Frink & Bingham
32. N.Y. Clothing Store
33. Hogan's Auction
34. Court House
35. Jail & John Beach
36. John Calhoun
37. Robinson Tripp
38. Francis C. Sherman
39. Bernard Blasy
40. Joseph Peacock
41. Thomas Cook
42. Oliver Hanson
43. Illinois Exchange
44. New York House
45. Solomon Lincoln
46. H.H. Magie
47. W.H. Stowe
48. Mansion House
49. First Methodist
50. Sauganash

This 1835 map was assembled by Ron Mounce from information provided by Edwin O. Gale in his book, *Reminiscences of Early Chicago and Vicinity*. Chicago, 1902.

Dearborn, concluding their performanse in the presence of the officers and soldiers of the garrison, where we will take a final leave of my old friends, with more good wishes for their future welfare than I dare hope will be realized.

In the September 5 *Chicago American*, editor Davis notes that "Carpenters, Masons and Laborers are still very scarce in this town, and command high wages. Many buildings intended to be erected this season will have to lie over for want of mechanics to put them up."

On September 9, a post office is opened in the community of Calumet.

In the September 12 *Chicago Democrat* Capt. J.B.F. Russell requests "for the removal of the Indians. FROM 10 to 40 OX TEAMS. The waggons to be strong and well made, with good canvass or cotton covers, to keep every thing within dry—to carry with it a bucket for tar or grease—to be supplied with an axe, or hatchet, hammer and nails. Each wagon to have two yoke of Oxen, to carry 1500 lbs, if required, and to travel daily twenty miles, if necessary. …"

On September 16, Capt. D. Wilcox, Fifth Infantry, reassumes command at Fort Dearborn, serving until August 1, 1836.

On September 19, the first fire department commences with the town board's resolution to acquire two engines and 1,000 feet of hose.

On September 21, Christian B. Dobson's wagon train of ox teams leaves Chicago to rendezvous with the Potawatomi encamped on the Des Plaines River, 12 miles away. The Indians number less than 1,000, well under the several thousand people anticipated. Four groups form—led by Alexander Robinson, Billy Caldwell, Waubonsee, and William Holiday, assisted by Robert Kinzie and Gholson Kercheval. All leave on September 28, "emigrating to the land allotted them west of Mississippi." In western Missouri, the Indains will refuse to go farther and settle, until removed by force in the summer of 1837.

On September 29, the town is organized into four school districts at a meeting held at the First Presbytarian Church by leading citizens, among them John H. Kinzie, R.J. Hamilton, John Wright, and John Watkins.

Throughout the autumn, a Grecian style one story brick courthouse with basement, that includes Corinthian columns and broad steps, is erected on the northeast corner of the public square, corresponding to the southwest corner of Clark and Randolph streets; the structure houses the courtroom, with county offices below.

In the October 7 *Chicago Democrat*, editor John Calhoun acknowledges: "We would be wanting in our duty to the officers engaged in the work, were we not to notice the great improvements which have been made in the streets of our town the past season. They are alike credible to this new place and the officers engaged in superintending them.—We have not, as yet, paved streets;

but one year since we had nothing in the shape of a street in the place beyond the sticking up of stakes, and here and there a building on the line, showing where a street was intended to be. Now the principal streets are well turnpiked, and so graduated and ditched as to drain them thoroughly."

On October 31, many townspeople gather in the Presbyterian church "for the purpose of expressing views and sentiments in relation to propriety and necessity of our Legislature adopting some more effective and energetic measures for the immediate construction of the Illinois and Michigan Canal, than what has heretofore been done." A committee forms to draft resolutions that express the citizens' sense of urgency.

In the November 4 *Chicaco Democrat*, John Calhoun reaffirms that "[o]ur merchants are, without an exception, prosperous, and extending their imports. The bustle of our docks, & the number of waggons thronging the streets for merchandise, are indications of prosperity which cannot be mistaken. Give us the canal, and we shall, as if by magic, assume an attitude of importence, both in numbers and wealth, which will not only make Chicago the pride of the state, but the wonder of the west." He says that 20 tons of coal were within the week received from Albany, shipped by way of the lakes, another "fact to demonstrate to our southern citizens, that they have great need of the canal." On the same day the village board, compounding its commitment to a fire department, creates a detailed ordinance with 52 sections concerning fire codes. In December the newly organized volunteer department will purchase its first fire engine at a cost of $894.38 from Hubbard & Co., and construction of a frame engine house (24 by 12 feet) will begin on the LaSalle Street side of the public square.

On November 18, the *Chicago Democrat* publishes "PUBLIC NOTICE. Leases of the Wharfing Privileges on Lots in the Town of Chicago, for the term of 999 Years," and the ordinance adopted in regard to such privileges. In response, townspeople meet the following Saturday morning at Trowbridge's Coffee House, the "largest group of citizens ever witnessed," and organize under S.B. Morris; Giles Spring presents a set of resolutions that condemns the town council's measures and advocates substitution. Citizens' claims, applications and petitions for wharfing privileges flood the clerk's office for many weeks.

The results of a census recently taken are reported in the November 28 *Chicago American*, listing Cook County's as 9,773, up 300 percent in two years.

Sometime this autumn, Dr. Daniel Brainard has come to town on horseback, dismounting and opening an office; in two years he will obtain a charter for Rush Medical College [now Chicago's Rush-Presbyterian-St. Lukes Medical Center].

On December 5, the officers of Chicago's first banking facility are announced in the *Chicago American*, with John H. Kinzie as president; called "Chicago Branch of the State Bank of Illinois," it opens for brisk business sometime in mid-December at the corner of LaSalle and South Water streets. The concern will fail in 1837. The *Marine Journal* listing this day notes that there have been no arrivals or clearances, "[t]he river is filled with ice."

The Chicago Lyceum sponsors a debate on December 8 at 7 o'clock at the Presbyterian church: "Is the removal of the Indians west of the Mississippi by the United States Government, consistent with faith, humanity and sound Policy?" The disputants are Dr. J.T. Temple (affirmative) and T.A. Harding (negative).

In the December 9 *Chicago Democrat*, the editor reports that "[t]he population of Chicago, according to the last census is 3279. There are 44 stores (dry goods, hardware and groceries,) 2 book stores, 4 druggists, 2 silversmiths and jewelers, 2 tin and copper manufactories, 2 printing offices, 2 breweries, 1 steam saw mill, 1 iron foundary, four storage and forwarding houses, 3 taverns, 1 lottery office, 1 bank, 5 churches, 7 schools, 22 lawyers, 14 physicians, a lyceum and a reading room. Nine brick buildings have been erected the past season, among which, are a tavern, three stories high, and a county clerk's office. The foundations of two churches (episcopal and baptist) were laid, but could not be completed owing to the want of materials." Continuing, he writes that the many buildings made of brick are the result of the lack of materials of proper quality, but because "there has been discovered on the North Branch, two miles from Chicago, a superior quality of clay, free from lime stone, which has been the great defect in the clay heretofore used," the brickmaking business may become more extensive.

The Chicago Harmonic Society gives the first public concert on December 11 at the Presbyterian church; tickets cost 50 cents. Among the selections for several performers are "Wreath" and "Oh! Lady fair," glee for three voices, and a violin solo: "Spring of Shillalah, with variations," by Samuel Lewis.

On December 12 the "Fire Kings," the first engine firefighting company, is organized; Hiram Hugunin, then president of the town board of trustees, is soon after elected chief of the fire department.

George P. Delaplaine, later U.S. general, visits the town this month and will write the account of his experience that follows:

Left Cincinnati in December, 1835, then a lad, in the company of Capt. Garret Vliet, a well known surveyor, who was coming to Wisconsin on service for the government. We went to Milwaukee overland via Terre Haute and Chicago. There were only two taverns in Chicago, at the time, and everything was in a decidedly crude condition. I remember one incident, trivial in itself, but illustrative of our experience during our brief stay. The guest who had preceded me in the occupancy of my room in the hotel, had caught a muscrat in the adjoining marsh and taken it with him to his quarters, as a pet. He went off and forgot the animal, which fed upon one of my boots during the night, for want of better provender.

The *Chicago American* on December 19 reports that "Capt. Russel, who left here some weeks since in charge of the emigrating Indians, has returned." William Montgomery advertises "CHRISTMAS PRESENTS.--- 12 setts splendid Ear Drops, 21 setts splendid Breast Pins, 12 Finger Rings, Necklaces, Lockets, Safety Chains, &c."

"The Prairies around Chicago are still burning." [*Chicago Democrat*, December 30]

Throughout this year, many new hotels and inns have opened: in town—the New York House, the Steam Boat Hotel, Flusky's Boarding House, Fay's Boarding House, Ike Cook's Saloon, Hollis Newton's Tavern and Hotel, Kelsey's Boarding House, Lincoln's Coffee House, and the Western Hotel; on access roads to Chicago—Ellis Inn (S), Kettlestrings' Tavern [Oak Park], Planck's Tavern at Dutchman's Point, Half-Way-House [Plainfield, Ottawa Road], Castle Inn [Brush Hill Trail], and Patterson's Tavern [Winnetka].

A speculative mania for land within and beyond Chicago has begun, prompted by the plans of the federal government to build the Illinois & Michigan Canal. Large amounts of money flow in from the East through investors who include Arthur Bronson, Charles Butler, and Edward Russell. The auctioneer Augustus Garrett reports sales of $1,800,000 worth of real estate in 10 months.

Observations within a *New York Times* article, reprinted in the *Chicago Democrat* [December 9], reads "… Lands in that place and its vicinity, are constantly rising in price, and business is uncommonly action. Success to the new city of the West. Her flourishing condition may, in a great degree, be attributed to New York enterprise; and we should take an interest in every thing that concerns her prosperity." The crash will come in 1837.

1835-36 "Regular weather, pleasant winters—a few cold days in 1836—fields covered with plenty, no failures of crops known; fruit abundant; peaches fine."

MAPS THAT LEAD TO CHICAGO

1507 Waldseemüller, Martin
  "Universalis cosmographia secundum Ptolomaei traditionem et Americi Verpucii aliorumque lustrationes," Saint-Dié [Castle of Wolfegg, Württemberg]

1540 Münster, Sebastian
  "Novae Insvlae, XVII Nova Tabvla" [reedition: Ptolemy's *Geographia*], Basel [Service historique de la Marine, Vincennes]

1553 Nicolai, Nicolas de
  "Novveau Monde," navigational chart [Bibliothèque Nationale, Paris]

1570 Ortelius, Abraham
  "Americae sive Novi Orbis, Nova Descriptio," *Theatrum Orbis Terrarum*, Antwerp [Newberry Library, Chicago]

1612 Champlain, Samuel de
  "Carte Geographiqve de la Nouvelle Franse," *Les Voyages du Sieur de Champlain*, Paris, 1613 [Newberry Library, Chicago]

1655 Du Val, Pierre
  "Amerique/Autrement/Nouveau Monde/et Indes Occidentales/Par P. Du Val d'Abbeuille/Geographe Ordinai du Roy ...," [Bibliothèque Nationale, Paris]

1656 Sanson d'Abbeville, Nicolas
  "Le Canada, ou Nouvelle France, &c.," Paris [Newberry Library, Chicago]

1671 Allouez, Jean and Dablon, Claude
  "Lac Superievr et avtres lievx ou sont les Missions des Peres de la Compagnie de Iesvs Comprises sovs le nom D'ovtaovacs," *Jesuit Relations*; Paris, 1672 [Newberry Library, Chicago]

1673 Marquette, Pére Jacques
  holograph [Archives de la Compagnie de Jésus, St. Jérôme, Quebec]

1674 Jolliet, Louis
  "Carte de la descouverte/du Sʳ Jolliet ou l'on voit la communication/du Fleuve Sᵗ Laurens avec les Lacs Frontenac/Erié, Lac des Hurons, et Ilinois ..." [Service historique de la Marine, Vincennes]

c.1674 *Manitoumie* II [Bibliothèque Nationale, Paris]

1681 Thèvenot, Melchisédech
  "Carte de la decouverte faite l'an 1673 dans l'Amerique Septentrionale," *Recueil de Voyages*; Paris [Newberry Library, Chicago]

1686 Franquelin, Jean-Baptiste Louis
  "Amerique Septentrion" [Service historique de la Marine, Vincennes]

1688 Coronelli, Marco Vincenzo
  "Partie Occidentale/du Canada ou de la Nouvelle/France/ou sont les Nations des Ilinois, de Tracy, les/Iroquois, et plusieurs autres Peuples;/Avec la Louisiane Nouvellement decouverte etc. ..." [Service historique de la Marine, Vincennes]

1697 Louvigny, Louis de la Porte de
  "Carte du Fleuve Missisipi auec les Noms des peuples qui L'habitent et des Etablissements des Espagnols et Anglois qui en sont proches par de la porte de louuign[y]" [Service historique de la Marine, Vincennes]

1718 Delisle, Guillaume
  "Carte de la Louisiane et du Cours du Mississippi," Paris [Newberry Library, Chicago]

1733 Popple, Henry
  "A Map of the British Empire in America with the French and Spanish settlements adjacent thereto," London [Newberry Library, Chicago]

1744 Bellin, Jacques Nicolas
  "Carte des Lacs du Canada," *Journal d'un Voyage Fait par Ordre du Roi dans l'Amerique Septentrionale*, Pierre F.X. de Charlevoix; Paris [Newberry Library, Chicago]

1755 Mitchell, John
  "A Map of the/British and French Dominions/in North America, ...," London [Newberry Library, Chicago]

1757 Bellin, Jacques Nicolas
  "Carte de la Louisiane et Pays Voisins," Tom. XXI [Collection of Ulrich F. Danckers, M.D.]

1761 Brehm, Lt. Dietrich
  "Chigago River and village" Public Records Office, London

1771 Hutchins, Thomas
  "A Plan/of the several Villages in the/Illinois Country,/with Part of the/River Mississippi &c." and "A/New Map/of the Western Parts of/Virginia, Pennsylvania,/Maryland, and North Carolina; ..., the Whole of the Illinois River...," *A Topographical Description of Virginia, Pennsylvania, Maryland, and North Carolina, Comprehending the Rivers Ohio, Kenhawa, Sioto, Cherokee, Wabash, Illinois, Mississippi, &c.*; London, 1778 [Newberry Library, Chicago]

1778 Carver, Capt. Jonathan
   "A/New Map/of/North/America, From the/Latest Discoveries/1778," *Travels through the Interior Parts of North America in the Years 1766, 1767, and 1768*; London [Newberry Library, Chicago]

1808 Whistler, Capt. John
   draught of Fort Dearborn [National Archives, Washington, D.C.]

1816 John Melish
   "Map of the United States with the Contiguous British & Spanish Possessions," Philadelphia [National Archives, Washington, D.C.]

1816 Long, Maj. Stephen H.
   "A Map/of the/Illenois River/from the Mouth to Gomo's Village 200 miles/St. Louis September 20" [National Archives, Washington, D.C.]

1818 Smith, Captain
   "Map of Chicago River" [The War Department, Washington, D.C.]

1819 Sullivan, Capt. John C.
   "Northern Boundary Illinois Bounty Lands" [National Archives, Washington, D.C.]

1819 Smith, Daniel D.
   "A Map of all the Lands belonging to the Kickapoo Tribe of Indians in the State of Illinois Ceded to the United States by Treaty signed at Edwardsville in the State of Illinois July 30th …" [National Archives, Washington, D.C.]

1821 Walls, John
   Survey of the Chicago River, Mud Lake and part of the DesPlaines; 18 June [U.S. General Land Office, Washington, D.C.]

1823 Lucas, Fielding, Jr.
   "Illinois," *General Atlas Containing Distinct Maps of All the Known Countries in the World* [Collection of Ulrich F. Danckers, M.D.]

1823 Tanner, Henry Schenk
   A New American Atlas, Containing Maps of the Several States of the North American Union [National Archives, Washington, D.C.]

1824 Post, Col. Justus and Paul, Col. René
   "Map of the proposed Illinois & Michigan Canal," Illinois Canal Commission [National Archives, Washington, D.C.; Illinois State Archives, Record Group 491, Springfield]

1830 Howard, William and Harrison, Frederick, Jr.
   "Map of the mouth of Chicago River Illinois with the plan of the proposed piers for improving the Harbor" [National Archives, Washington, D.C.]

1830 Harrison, Frederick, Jr. and Guyon, William B.

"Map No. 1 of the Survey of the Michigan & Illinois Canal," proposed route; survey completed by Henry Belin, Topographical Bureau, Engineer Department, U.S. Army; 20 May 1832 [National Archives, Washington, D.C.]

1830 Thompson, James
   Plat of the Original Town, Chicago [authenticated MS copy, 1837; Chicago Historical Society Library]

1830 Lyon, Lucius
   "Map/of the/Boundary Line/between/Ceded and Unceded/Lands/surveyed … comformably to the stipulations of the Treaty of/Prairie du Chien of/1829" [National Archives, Washington, D.C.]

1831 plat of the Fractional Township at the mouth of the Chicago River [Illinois State Archives, Springfield]

1833 Carver, David
   "Plat of Town of Chicago" [copy of the 1830 James Thompson plat; Illinois State Archives, Record Group 491, Springfield]

1833 map of Chicago, with notation: "sent to Washington to secure an appropriation to improve the harbor, March 2, 1833" [MS copy, Chicago Historical Society Library]

1834 Hathaway, Joshua, Jr.
   "Chicago with the School section, Wabansia and Kinzie Addition"; Peter A. Mesier, Lithographer; New York [Chicago Historical Society Library]

1834 Wright, James Stephen
   town survey; Peter A. Mesier, Lithographer, New York [National Archives, Washington, D.C.; Newberry Library, Chicago]

1835 Miller & Co., Lithographers; New York
   "Map of Lots at Chicago for Sale by Franklin & Jenkins on Friday, 8th of May, 1835, at 12 O'clock at the Merchants Exchange" [Chicago Historical Society Library]

1835 Mesier, Peter A., Lithographer; New York
   73 Building Lots in Chicago to be sold at Auction by Jas. Bleeker & Sons on Thursday, 2nd of October" [Chicago Historical Society Library]

1836 Talcott, Edward B.
   "Chicago with the Several Additions compiled from the recorded plats in the Clerk's Office, Cook County, Illinois," "The lots in the original town … will be offered for sale … on the 20th of June 1836"; Peter A. Mesier, Lithographer; New York [Newberry Library, Chicago; Chicago Historical Society Library]

1837 Bradley, Asa F.
"Map of the city of Chicago"; Nathaniel Currier, Lithographer; New York [exact copy of map drafted in 1836-1837, as sworn by Asa F. Bradley; Chicago Historical Society Library]

1837 Mitchell, Samuel Augustus
"The Tourist's Pocket Map of the State of Illinois" [Newberry Library, Chicago]

1837 "A map of the town of Chicago;" filed May 29, 1837; record in Book H, pp. 111-12; "W.F. Thornton, W.B. Archer and G.S. Hubbard, late Commissioners of the Illinois and Michigan Canal, certify that this map of the town of Chicago is the identical map by which they were governed in selling lots belonging to the said town on the 20th and following days of June last past. Chicago, May 22, 1837" [Chicago Historical Society Library]

1837 Allen, Capt. James
"Improvement of the Harbour of Chicago" October 15; Capt. Thomas J. Cram's annual report, Engineer Department, U.S. Army [National Archives, Washington, D.C.]

1884 Andreas, Alfred Theodore
"Map of Chicago in 1830," *History of Chicago. From the Earliest Period to the Present Time*, vol. 1:112-13

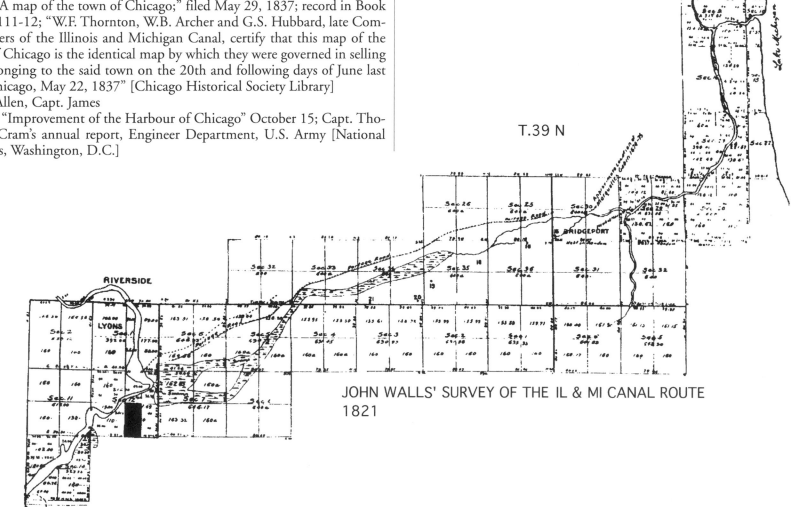

T.39 N

JOHN WALLS' SURVEY OF THE IL & MI CANAL ROUTE
1821

ENCYCLOPÆDIA CHICAGOUA

or

A LEXICON

of

PERSONS, PLACES and THINGS ARCHAIC

Relating to the

HISTORY

of

CHICAGO

to the
Year

MDCCCXXXV

Explanation of symbols and abriviations used in the following text:

✦ Person still listed in the 1839 *City Directory* with address and/or occupation as indicated.

➡ Chicago street named after person or group.

✳ Important map; see also map list on page 51.

★★★ Chicago's 1st   First-of-its-kind event for Chicago.

▲ A historical monument existent in the Chicago area; see Monument Section, beginning on page 402.

❀ A portrait of this person shown elsewhere in this book as indicated.

⚜ *Fleur-de-lit*, here used to highlight official representation of the French crown.

N   north
S   south
E   east
W   west

In conjunction with settlements and counties, the names of states are given as abbreviated by the United States Postal Service.

[ ]   Small numbers in brackets refer the reader to numbered bibliographic entries as the source.

Abbott, Constant   on 1833 list of early setlers; listed in the *Chicago Democrat* on Jan. 1 and April 1, 1834, as having unclaimed letters at the post office. [319]

Abbott, James   (1774-1858) Detroit fur trader and member of prominent Detroit family; married Sarah Whistler at Fort Dearborn in early November 1804. John Kinzie performed the ceremony of Chicago's second recorded marriage; served as postmaster for the Michigan Territory until May 1833; later that year was awarded $2,300 as an American Fur Co. agent in the treaty negotiated at Chicago; the couple lived in Detroit and raised three chil-

dren: Sarah, Madison, and William.

Abbott, Lucius, M.D.   later husband of [see] McKillip, Margaret. [12]

Abbott, Titus H.   partner of [see] Asahel Pierce in the firm Pierce & Abbott, a smithy "nearly opposite Chicago Hotel" in 1833; notice of dissolution appeared May 7, 1834; an unclaimed letter notice in the *Chicago Democrat* on Sept. 2, 1835, may imply that Abbott moved on.

Abell, Sidney   also Abel; attorney from Pensylvania; third postmaster of Chicago, appointed by President Van Buren on March 3, 1837, to succeed John S.C. Hogan; came to Chicago in 1834 and advertised on Feb. 17 and May 25, 1835, a law office on Lake St., one door E of the New York House, and on June 24, an office with "Esq. Harmon on Dearborn St., two doors S of Eagle Coffee House" [Isaac Dewey Harmon was not a trained lawyer, but sometimes advised others on legal matters]; ✦ postmaster, 37 Clark St.; in 1840 married Martha Jane Lowry of Springfield, IL. [12, 733]

Academy   see English and Classical School for Boys.

Acay, Gabriel   voted in a general election on July 24, 1830, held at the Kinzie house.

Accault, Michel   also Aco, Ako, Accau; French fur trader and associate of La Salle during the years 1669-1680; traveled in the Northwest with Father Hennepin in 1680; in 1694 he married a young Illinois woman, Marie [Aramipinchicoue] Rouensa, at the Peoria mission; he partnered Tonti and La Forest in a Chicago trading post, managed for them by Pierre de Liette, Tonti's cousin, from 1697 to c.1702. [46, 241, 259, 647, 649]

Aco   see Accault, Michel.

Adams   a 150-ton United States government brig on the Great Lakes, built in 1799 in the Rouge River shipyard, named after the president, outfitted in 1803 and used, among other missions, to supply Fort Dearborn from Detroit beginning in 1804. Dr. Cooper came to the fort on the *Adams* in 1808. During the 1812 war General Hull sur-

NEW BLACKSMITH SHOP.

PIERCE & ABBOTT,

WOULD respectfully inform the inhabitants of Chicago and the neighboring settlements, that they have commenced the above business in said town, nearly opposite the Chicago Hotel, where they are ready to wait upon all those who may have any kind of work to do in their line of business, on the most liberal terms. They will manufacture *Prarie Ploughs*, to order, and on the shortest notice. By strict attention to business, they hope to receive a share of patronage.

Dec. 10, 1833.   3

rendered the ship to the British, who renamed it *Detroit*; the Americans recaptured the vessel later that year; stranded and burned at Black Rock. [48]

Adams, Charles   born in 1813 at Norwalk, CT; arrived in September 1835; later returned to Norwalk, where he was still alive in 1885. [12]

Adams, George   U.S. Army private at Fort Dearborn, enlisted in Aug. 21, 1806, and reenlisted in 1811; killed in the initial battle of the massacre of Aug. 15, 1812.

Adams, James   received one vote at Chicago in his 1834 bid for governor of Illinois; lost to Joseph Duncan of Jacksonville, who had 199 votes.

Adams, John   (1735-1826) Massachsetts native; second president of the United States, serving from 1797 to 1801; under Adams the Northwest Territory was divided and Chicago became part of the new Territory of Indiana in 1801; ➡ Adams Street (200 S).

Adams, John Quincy   (1767-1848) Massachsetts native; sixth president of the United States, serving from 1825 to 1829; during his term the Erie Canal was opened in 1825, establishing a major route for immigration to the West and thereby initiating a new era for Chicago; ➡ Quincy Street (220 S).

Adams, Joseph S.   (1794-1885) born in Staffordshire, England; sergeant of the Fifth U.S. Infantry regiment; transferred from Fort Brady to Fort Dearborn in May 1833, arriving on the same vessel with [see] Reverend J. Porter. When the troops moved on to Fort Howard late in December 1836, only Adams, Lt. L.T. Jamison and Maj. J. Plympton remained behind. As ordnance-sergeant of the post, Adams moved his family from the village into the fort and stayed until the end of May 1837, considering himself the last soldier [as opposed to officer; Jamison was the last officer] of Fort Dearborn and, retiring from the military to a claim in [Northfield Township], began to farm; with his wife Hannah had several children, among them a son Ralph, who married a daughter of Alderman [see] Bernard Ward, and a daughter who became the wife of Dr. Allen W. Gray; after his death on June 9, 1885, his widow lived in Evanston. Adams detailed his reminiscences of this period in a 1881 letter to John Wentworth. [12, 13, 708]

Adams, William   baker; arrived June 1833 and remained until 1836; in partnership awhile with Johann Wellmacher, the dissolution of which was listed in the *Chicago Democrat* on March 25, 1834 [a "Willie Adams and his sisters" attended school under Miss Eliza Chappel in 1833, possibly William Adams' children]. [12]

Adams, William Henry   (c.1813-1882) arrived in 1832 from New York; served under Capt. G. Kercheval in the Chicago militia during the Black Hawk War; voted at the first town election on Aug. 10, 1833; ◆ surveying, mapping, &c., Lake Street; married Elizabeth Bradley on June 23, 1839; became alderman in 1849; died on June 6, 1882. [12, 714, 733]

Additions to Chicago   during the early part of the speculative land boom, several additions to the original town plat were made in quick succession to accommodate the demand for real estate; these were the Breese & Beaubien Addition, the Canal Addition, the Carpenter (or Carpenter & Curtiss) Addition, the Duncan Addition, the Fort Dearborn Addition, the Kinzie Addition, the Newberry Addition, the Russell & Mather Addition (or North Branch Addition), the J.B.F. Russell Addition, the Wabansia Addition, the Wight Addition, and the Wolcott Addition. For details, see individual entries. Also to be counted as additions are the fractional Sections 15 and 22 along the lakeshore, immediately S of the Breese & Beaubien Addition, both formally incorporated as shown on the 1836 ✳ map by E.B. Talcott [see map list on page 51].

Agency   see United States Indian Agency.

agency houses   for the first Fort Dearborn, the two-story structure in which the U.S Indian agent would conduct his business, was built by the soldiers in 1805, a short distance W of the fort, outside the stockade, near the south bank of the river, with the U.S. factor's house between the agency and the fort; "an old-fashioned log-building [covered with split oak siding], with a hall running through the centre, and one large room on each side. Piazzas extended the whole length of the building, front and rear." A letter of Oct. 9, 1807, from Captain Whistler to Secretary Dearborn, indicated that a house for the "agent and Factor Interpreter" was being built at that time on the N side of the river, where, according to Whistler, the Indians would find it easier to camp, but as it turned out, only the interpreter's building was constructed on the N side. On Aug. 16, 1812, the Indians burned the fort, the agency and the factory. [Where the agency house had stood, the soldiers of the next fort would later erect a large hexagonal barn.] For the second fort, the agency house was on the N side of the river, close to the bank, W of the Kinzie house. It may have begun as the [see] Burns house, built c.1809 by [see] Ezekiel Cooper, and later enlarged, remodeled, and occupied in succession by the Indian agents Jouett and Wolcott for themselves and their families. By the time Dr. Wolcott married, the building had become known as [see] "Cobweb Castle." A third agency house was later built immediately S of the fort on the lakeshore, apparently to have separated the conduct of business from the Wolcott family's living space; this structure was purchased in 1822/23 by Crafts and J.B. Beaubien and enlarged to serve as a trading post for the American Fur Co. of which they were the Chicago agents. [12]

Agnes Barton   schooner from Buffalo, NY, under Captain Ludlow; called at Chicago on Sept. 14, 1834.

ague   see malaria.

Aix sponsa   Wood Duck; see ducks.

Ako   see Accault, Michel.

Albee, Cyrus P.   arrived from Vermont in 1834, and did various work, settling on meat marketing; an unclaimed letter was noted in the *Chicago Democrat* on Jan. 2, 1835; ◆ Funk's Market, corner of Lake and Dearborn streets; married Harriet Wilson of Ohio in 1843. [13]

Alexandre   also Alexander; a brother within the *Séminaire des Missions Étrangeres*; among those who came from Quebec to visit the *Mission de l'Ange Gardien des Miamis à Chicagoua* on Oct. 21, 1698. When the group left for the Illinois River on the 24th, he remained behind at the mission until Easter of 1699, when members of the party picked him up on the return trip to Quebec; likely a lay brother who assisted the abbés, his full name is not known but his distinction is that of being one of the earliest visitors to Chicago.

Alexander, Isaac H.   owner-assignee of 80 acres of Chicago land in Section 28, Township 39, prior to 1836 (Andreas, *History of Chicago*, pp. 112-113). [12]

Alexander, Samuel   member of the initial canal commission created by Illinois Governor Cole in 1823 to have the canal lands surveyed and a cost estimate prepared. [12]

Algonkin   also Algonquin; the term for a group of related North American Indian tribes, sharing a similar language and living between the eastern seaboard and the Great Lakes at the time the first Europeans appeared; so identified by Champlain and others in the early 1600s; allied with the French in conflict against the Iroquois. Both the Miami and the Potawatomi, the two tribes dominant in succession in Chicagoland from the time the Europeans arrived to that of the forced relocation of all Indians beyond the Mississippi, were among the Algonkins; other peoples who spoke Algonkian languages were the Ojibwa [Chippewa], Ottawa, Sauk, Fox, Illinois, Maskouten and Shawnee; ➡ Algonquin Avenue (5600 W).

Algonkian   also Algonquian; a group of related North American Indian languages spoken by the Algonkins.

Allen, Lt. James   (c.1806-1846) native of Ohio; Fifth Infantry; as cartographer, accompanied an 1832 expedition led by Henry B. Schoolcraft into Minnesota to establish the true headwaters of the Misssissippi River, and in 1834, published a ✳ map thereof; stationed at Fort Dearborn as brevet second lieutenant from May 14, 1833, to January 1834; present during the Indian Treaty of Chicago in September 1833, and among the witnesses who signed the document; superintended early harbor construction as a temporary assignment from the U.S. Army Engineer Department and replaced Major Bender in January 1834, as harbor superintendent, serving until September 1838; with C. Petit and Henry Moore began the Chicago Reading Room Association in July 1835; advanced to captain on June 30, 1837; later that year on October 15, he submitted a ✳ map, *Improvement of the Harbour of Chicago*, with Capt. Thomas Cram's annual report to the U.S. Army Engineer Department; ✦ steamboat builder and captain, boarding at the Lake House. [12]

Allen, John [P.?]   a John Allen is listed as private on the Fort Dearborn muster roll, Dec. 31, 1810; arrived from New York in 1833; ✦ John P., boot- and shoemaker, *North Water* Street.

Allen, Nathan   arrived from New York in 1834 and became county commissioner in 1836; married Diana Madison on July 17, 1836. [12]

Allen, Thomas   born c.1808 in Brome County,

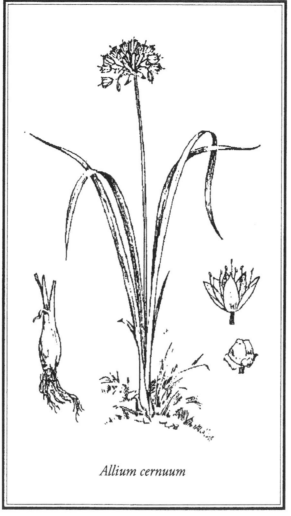

Allium cernuum

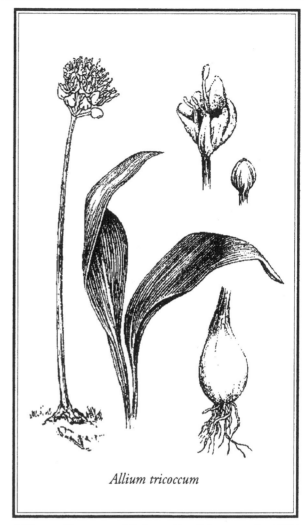

Allium tricoccum

NY; arrived in October 1835; still lived in Chicago in 1878; later moved to [Glencoe]. [12, 351]

Allen, Thomas   from Pittsfield, MA; died in Chicago on Sept. 20, 1835, at age 25, per notice in the September 26 *Chicago American*.

Allin, John   U.S. Army private at Fort Dearborn under Captain Heald, enlisted in November 1810; seriously wounded during the initial battle of the massacre of Aug. 15, 1812; executed by the Indians later that evening. [12]

Allison, George and John   English; came in 1832 with their parents and brothers; would become farmers, remaining on the family's property near [Wheeling]. [13]

Allison, Thomas   English; came in 1832 with his wife Mary and four young sons (Thomas, John, George and William); shortly thereafter purchased a farm near Clybourn Place, three miles N of the settlement; in 1834 moved farther N [Northfield Township] and continued to farm; built the first bridge across the Des Plaines River in 1834/35, at his own expense. [13]

Allium   Latin for garlic, a word of Celtic or Gaelic origin; a genus of the plant family *Alliaceae*, containing *Allium canadense* (wild onion, used for food by the Indians; found in sunny and lightly wooded areas); *A. stellatum* (prairie wild onion, on rocky banks in the interior); *A. cernuum* (wild nodding onion, prairie habitat); and *A. tricoccum* (wild garlic; French, *ail sauvage*; on wooded river banks; broad-leaved and blooming white). With extensive research John F. Swenson convincingly demonstrates [see page 377] that the Indian name *chicagoua* for *Allium tricoccum* is the word that was adapted for the settlement's name. The plant once grew abundantly along wooded river banks in the Chicago region and can still be found in some of Chicagoland's forest preserves, private gardens, and at Morton Arboretum. See illustrations on pages 57 and frontispiece. [647]

Allouez, Père Claude Jean   (1622-1689) French Jesuit; born in St. Didier, France; arrived at Quebec in 1658 and served at Trois Rivères and other St. Lawrence settlements for seven years; founded the *Mission de Saint-Esprit* among the Ottawa and other tribes at Chequamegon Bay on western Lake Superior in 1665, and the *Mission de Saint-François-Xavier* in 1671 on the Wisconsin Fox River, a few miles above Green Bay [near De Pere]. In the *Jesuit Relations* of 1666-1667, Father Allouez referred to Lake Michigan as "Lac Illiniones, as yet unexplored," and recorded that the Fox called the lake "Match-i-hi-gan-ing"; submitted a valuable ✴ map, *Lac Svperievr et avtres lievx ou sont les Missions des Peres de la Compagnie de Iesvs Comprises sovs le nom D'ovtaovacs*, with Father Dablon that was printed in the *Jesuit Relations* of 1672. Father Allouez was Father Marquette's immediate superior in 1673 when the father and Jolliet discovered the Chicago site, and first visited Chicago on April 10, 1677 to find 80 Illinois warriors encamped along the Des Plaines River [the chief greeted him with a 100-word welcome address, ★★★ Chicago's 1st oration] and willing to escort him to a larger village at Kaskaskia, opposite Starved Rock, carrying on Marquette's mission work with the Kaskaskia intermittently until 1687. There exists some evidence of a short-lived Jesuit mission and village in Chicago under Father Allouez at the time Durantaye maintained a fort here (1684-85). This infant settlement was destroyed and its inhabitants scattered by an Iroquois raid in about July 1886. Danonvilles's 1887 attack on the Senecas was in part retaliation for this raid. Father Allouez's name is engraved on the Marquette monument of 1926 at Chicago. After his death he was buried at the *Mission de Saint-Joseph* [Niles, MI], founded under his direction in the 1680s; Father Aveneau succeeded him there in 1690. [12, 605, 611, 649, 681, 682]

Alscum, Madaline   or Olscum; French *métis* servant girl indentured to Susan Randolph, wife of Indian agent Charles Jouett; lived with the family at Chicago from 1816 to 1818; in 1818 married Joseph Ozier, a soldier from Fort Dearborn.

Amberg, Adam   resident by 1833; German Catholic immigrant and member of St. Mary's Church. [12, 342]

Ament, Anson   (1816-1850) from Kentucky; during the Black Hawk War, enrolled in Capt. James Walker's company as private on June 19, 1832, with brothers Edward and Hiram; requested a furlough and on July 19 joined Captain Naper's company as private with brother Calvin, mustered out on Aug. 15; his wife's name was Sarah. [12, 714]

Ament, Calvin   (1814-1850) from Kentucky; with brother Anson, enrolled as private in Captain Naper's company on July 19, 1832, during the Black Hawk War; mustered out on Aug. 15. [342]

Ament, Edward Glenn   (1806-1888) eldest son of John Viele and Eunice Ament; in 1821 homesteaded within Bureau County; worked for Joseph Ogee, an Indian interpreter, in 1824 at Peoria, where he met Mark Beaubien and John Kinzie; during 1825-1826, worked for the Clybourne brothers in Chicago, voting on Aug. 7, 1826; joined his brothers working inthe lead mines at Galena, then returned again to homestead in 1828; met Peter Specie in 1831 and was persuaded to resettle near Chicago, involving all brothers; joined Captain Walker's company as private on June 25, 1832 with Hiram and Anson, mustered out August 12; married Emily Ann Harris in 1832 (died in 1836), married Mary Luce in 1839; in 1885, was living at 160 LaSalle St. [351, 458, 714]

Ament, Hiram   born 1810 in Kentucky; enrolled as private in Captain Walker's company with Edward and Anson during the Black Hawk War, June 25, 1832, mustered out August 12; married Nancy C. Harris (Emily Ann's sister) in 1832, who died in 1833. [458, 714]

Ament, John Lawson   (1809-1850) born in Kentucky; son of John Viele and Eunice Ament; married Sarah Ann Hodges in 1829.

America   a 60-ton schooner from Buffalo, NY, under Captain Foster; called at Chicago in September 1835; wrecked on Lake Michigan in 1841. [48]

America, naming of   see Vespucci, Amerigo.

American Bottom   an expression frequently found in 18th- and 19th-century literature, meaning a stretch of fertile bottom land of the Mississippi River valley in southern Illinois; the land had encouraged the development of flourishing French settlements by 1750, when Chicago was merely an isolated grouping of cabins within a vast wilderness. H.S. Tanner [see entry] in 1832 explained the term as follows: "[t]he American Bottom, as it is called, reaches along the Mississippi from the mouth of the Kaskaskia to Alton, or a little above the entrance of the Missouri; a distance of nearly 90 miles. The soil of these bottoms is alluvial, of astonishing fertility, often embedding trees and other vegetable matter." [44, 529]

American Fur Co.   (1811-1842) chartered in New York State in 1808 by John Jacob Astor and launched in 1811; the company's headquarters were in Michilimackinac, with agents in Chicago and elsewhere in the Midwest. The company had a profound influence on the economic and social life of early Chicago from 1816 to 1832, supplying the Indians with manufactured goods from the East in exchange for the natural resources harvested by them. In addition to fur, the Indians furnished [see] fish from the rivers and lakes, which the company salted or dried for shipment. John Kinzie (1816-1823/1825-1827), John Crafts (1823-1825), and Jean Baptiste Beaubien (1827-1835) were the Chicago/Fox River area agents; Antoine Deschamps (1817-1824) and Gurdon S. Hubbard (1824-1835) were agents for the Illinois River trade. Depletion of wildlife caused trade to diminish as early as 1827 and because the trapping was done by Indians, the fur trade ended in 1835 with the removal of the Indians. Also see Traders' Brigades; Crooks, Ramsey; Stuart, Robert; Matthews, William. [12, 296]

American Hotel   also called American Inn; on North Water Street near Kinzie Street, operated by William McCorristen from 1836-1839; was the former Steamboat Hotel, which in 1835 was managed by John Davis, and later that year by J. Dorsey. [Nye, visiting in 1837, said of it: "dirty and poor food."]

American Land Corporation   eastern firm organized in 1834 by Charles Butler, specializing in western land investments and capitalized at one million dollars. Butler became its first president and through the business channeled large funds to Chicago, fueling the 1833-37 land boom; for more details, see Butler, Charles; Bronson, Arthur.

Amiot, Louis   also Amyot, Lammiot; born near Chicago late in 1745 (★★★ **Chicago's first** recorded birth of a child of European ancestry), the son of Jean Baptiste Amiot, a French Canadian blacksmith who with his Ottawa wife Marianne had their son baptized at Michilimackinac on June 14, 1746; translated from the French, the church record reads: "the said child having been born at

the Rivière aux plains [Des Plaines River] near chikago at the beginning of the month of October last." The Amiots were a large French family; Louis' paternal grandfather may have been Sieur Charles Joseph Amiot of Michilimackinac, located within the fort as shown on a contemporary map (1749) by Michel Chartier de Lotbiniére. [Family records may be found in the *Collections of the State Historical Society of Wisconsin* 19:17, *eds.*] Louis' birth is of particular interest, supporting the belief that there was a nearly continuous settlement of French families in the Chicago region throughout the 18th century. [649]

anarchy   with regard to the Illinois country, a breakdown of jurisdictional authority that began in 1781 in what had been Illinois County of Virginia, when the Virginia Act of 1778 that had created the county expired; anarchy lasted until the spring of 1790. A breakdown of the local criminal justice system developed. Murders and other crimes went unpunished, and certain persons established themselves as overlords. In 1790, civil jurisdictions were reorganized as part of the new Northwest Territory of the United States.

Anas discors   see teal, blue winged.

Anas platyrhynchus   mallard; see ducks.

Anastasius, Père   see Douay, Père Anastase.

Anderson, Alex   in late November 1835 filed a petition and an affidavit in support of his claim for wharfing privileges along the Chicago River.

Anderson, John   (c.1815-1847) unclaimed letter existed per notice in the July 2, 1834, *Chicago Democrat*; married Marie C. Tremblay in Chicago in 1835; died in Chicago.

Anderson, Joseph   laborer; arrived in 1826 and voted on August 7 of that year, a state election held at Indian agent Wolcott's house; also voted in 1830. [498]

Anderson, Susan   listed as owner of 80 acres of Chicago land in the SE quarter of Section 6, Township 39, prior to 1836, as per Andreas, *History of Chicago*, pp. 112-113.

Anderson, Capt. Thomas Gummersall   (1779-1875) British trader at Milwaukee from 1803 to 1806, competing there with two French traders, LaFramboise [François] and Le Claire [Pierre]; rode south in 1804 to Chicago to greet "new neighbors," the first garrison of the unfinished Fort Dearborn. As an elderly man he wrote a narrative of this visit and of the dinner with Captain Whistler and family, still quartered in one of the log cabins belonging to the local traders. In the War of 1812 Anderson fought for the British. [Quaife considers Anderson's narrative unreliable, but he was no doubt at Fort Dearborn, therefore the account is within the bibliography; *eds.*] [11]

Andreas, Alfred T.   (1839-1900) co-author, editor, and publisher of *History of Chicago, From the Earliest Period to the Present Time*, three volumes, published 1884 to 1888; also publisher of *History of Cook County, Illinois* in 1884 and *History of Milwaukee* in 1881; his manuscript notes are within the collections of the Chicago Historical Society. [12-14]

Andrew steam sawmill   built in 1830 on the Detroit-Chicago road just E of La Porte, IN.

Andrews, David   New Jersey surveyor and civil engineer, arrived in 1834 (unclaimed letters noted on Oct. 8, 1834; July 1, 1835; and Jan. 2, 1836); did surveys throughout Cook County and for early government land sales; became the first settler on Wolf Ridge by 1838, operating a sand farm near 126th Street and Wentworth Avenue; in 1840 married Sophia Caroline Ward of Will County Following Andrews' death in 1885, the family donated land for the construction of W Pullman Park, the highest elevation in Chicago, with many old trees that include black oak. [13]

Andrews, David   tailor; in partnership with Thomas Eels; advertised in the *Chicago Democrat* on Oct. 22, 1834, a shop located one door N of the Tremont House; ◆ tailor, North Side.

Andrews, Prestly   U.S. Army private at Fort Dearborn, enlisted in July 11, 1806; badly wounded during the initial action at the massacre of Aug. 15, 1812, and killed later that night. [12]

Angelica   armed British sloop patrolling Lakes Michigan, Huron, and Erie during the period of British control; built at Detroit in 1771. [48]

Anker Site   in the summer of 1958, archaeological excavations were made at the former Howard Anker farm on the N side of the Little Calumet River where an early Indian village once existed, c.1400-1500; an unusual number and variety of found artifacts among many burial sites exhibited widespread contact and trade with tribes within the Mississippi River valley. These artifacts included marine shell beads, disc and face pipes, effigy bowls and copper beads, finger rings, earplugs, and necklaces, bracelets. [*Chicago Area Archaeology*, Illinois Archaeology Survey no. 3 (1961): 89–138]

Ann   schooner on Lake Michigan under Captain Ransom in 1821, delivered American Fur Co. trade goods from Michilimackinac to James Kinzie at Chicago; wrecked that year, with loss of life, off Long Point, Lake Erie.

annuities   see Indian annuities.

Antelope   a 75-ton schooner built at Perrysburg, OH in 1828; called at Chicago with passengers and merchandise from Buffalo, NY on July 11, 1835, under Captain Edwards, and returning later in July from Michigan City. [48]

Archangel   armed British sloop patrolling Lakes Michigan, Huron and Erie during the period of British control; built at Detroit in 1774. [48]

Archer Trail   see Old Chicago Trail.

Ariadne   a yawl for six to eight passengers and freight on regular passage between St. Joseph and Chicago, c.1833.

Armour, George   (c.1812-1881) arrived from England in 1835.

Armstrong, Lt. John   (1755-1816) from New Jersey; in spring 1789, explored the Illinois River and its connection with Lake Michigan. In the process he visited Chicago and traversed the portage, observing later "[a]t the carrying place of Chicago,

the water happened to be very high, in consequence of the rains that had lately fallen, for it is the over flowing of the water of the branches that makes the carrying place so easy at high water. A Battoe [*sic*; see *bateau*] may pass at such time without carrying anything. ... But at low water, or in a dry Season, all must be carried 9 miles ...." In 1790 he was sent on a top-secret United States government mission to assess the feasibility of exploring the Missouri River. Visiting St. Louis and Cahokia disguised as a trader, he reported that such a mission was dangerous and impossible. His report of June 2, 1790 contains a detailed ✳ map of the Illinois River system, including the portage; the map was not drawn by Armstrong, but acquired by him from an unknown source, probably in St. Louis. Also see entry on Mount Joliet for Armstrong's description. He was later appointed a judge in Cincinnati and treasurer of the Northwest Territory. [640,649]

Armstrong, William H.   arrived from the West Indies in 1835 and worked for Gurdon Hubbard; an unclaimed letter existed per notice in the Sept. 2, 1835 *Chicago Democrat*; ◆ clerk, G.S. Hubbard & Co. [351]

Army Engineers   see Corps of Engineers [Topographical Engineers]. [423]

Arnold, Isaac Newton   (1813-1884) lawyer from Harwick, NY; came in the autumn of 1836 (1835, according to others); initially employed by Augustus Garrett to draft real estate and general contracts during the land boom; became the first elected city clerk in March 1837; ◆ attorney and counsellor at law, Clark Street, listed as Arnold & Ogden by his partner [see] Mahlon D. Ogden; married Harriet Augusta Dorrance in 1841; later served in Congress; eventually honorary president of the Chicago Historical Society. [12. 597]

Arnwaiskie, Theotis   married Daniel Bourassa on May 20, 1823, John Kinzie J.P. officiating.

arpent   an old Parisian unit of land measure, both of distance (30 *toises* = one *arpent* = c.192 feet) and area (one square *arpent* = 0.84 acres). This and other

ISAAC NEWTON ARNOLD

Parisian measures were the official standards in all of New France; see also league. [649]

artificer   one of several civilians at frontier military posts, such as Fort Dearborn, hired under the authority of the commanding officer to perform such specialized work as carpentry, brickmaking, ironworking, gunsmithing, &c.; many treaties with the Indians obligated the government to provide such workers to serve the Indians in keeping their firearms, knives, and tools in condition; subject to military discipline while employed.

Ashbrook, Thomas   U.S. Army private; enlisted in Dec. 29, 1805, and served at Fort Dearborn until his enlistment expired in Dec. 29, 1810; did not reenlist, thereby escaping the massacre of Aug. 15, 1812. [12]

Assenisipia   see Western Territory.

Assgood, Dexter   misspelling in Andreas' *History of Chicago* for [see] Hapgood, Dexter J.

Astor, John Jacob   (1763-1848) born in Waldorf, Germany, arrived in New York in 1783; first sold bakery goods, then toys, then furs in 1786 at Montreal, buying and shipping to London; by

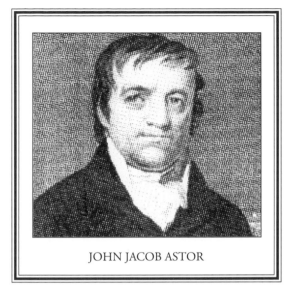

JOHN JACOB ASTOR

1808, with the surrender of the northern posts to the United States, he began the Southwest Co. and soon acquired other fur trading concerns; was granted a charter in 1809 by New York State for the [see] American Fur Co., for which many Chicago traders eventually worked; launched the company in 1811; agents were first sent to Chicago in 1817 and the company controlled much of the settlement's economic and social life through 1833. Astor lived in New York, while his company's main business was in Michilimackinac, with agents throughout and beyond the Northwest; in 1834 he sold his interests in the American Fur Co., apparently never having visited Chicago; died in New York; ➡ Astor Street (50 E). [12]

Atalanta   schooner from Buffalo, NY, under Capt. Joseph Caskey; called at Chicago on July 1, 1834; Caskey, age c.35, died in Buffalo shortly thereafter, as per notice in the *Chicago Democrat* of Sept.10, 1834; on Nov. 6, 1835, the vessel returned to Chicago from Buffalo under Captain Shepherd.

Athena   female Negro slave of John Kinzie in 1812, serving as cook and housemaid; wife of Henry, also one of Kinzie's slaves; survived the massacre of 1812

in the boat with the Kinzies, but lost her husband in the trade [see Black Jim] for Captain Heald's release. [12]

Atkins, Eliphalet   on 1833 list of early settlers; unclaimed letter notice in the *Chicago Democrat* on Jan. 1, 1834.

Atkinson, Joseph   replaced William Hissey as partner to [see] Thomas Jenkins, as noted in the Aug. 15, 1835, *Chicago American*; Jenkins & Atkinson, a general store on South Water Street between Dearborn and Clark, existed until January 1836.

Atlanta   100-ton schooner that brought merchandise for Hubbard & Co. in the summer of 1834; built at Fairport [Harbor], OH, in 1832. [48]

attorneys   see lawyers.

auctioneers   John Bates (1832); David Carver (1833); James A. Marshall, M.D., W. Montgomery (1835); Augustus Garrett (1835); and Mr. Greenleaf [first name unknown](1835).

Auguel, Antoine   also Aguel, Auguelle; nicknamed Picard; traveled with Father Hennepin in 1680; member of La Salle's 1682-83 expedition to the mouth of the Mississippi, passing through Chicagoland in January 1682 on the way south; was later honored by the French Crown for his service. [46]

Aurora Borealis   32-ton lake schooner, built in Huron, OH in 1816; called at Chicago on Aug. 8, 1835, coming from Oswego, NY, under Captain

Allen. [48]

Austerlitz   134-ton schooner owned by Oliver Newberry; carried the first shipment of pork east from Chicago in the spring of 1833; on July 9 arrived from Buffalo with skilled workmen and many supplies for the Chicago harbor project, and as late as November 18, under Captain Smith, brought a "full cargo of Merchandize, &c. for citizens of this village"; piloted by Captain McKinstry, brought lumber and 15 passengers from Detroit on April 27, 1834, and returned with merchandise from Buffalo four times through November; called at Chicago twice under Captain Robertson in 1835 until, with full cargo for St. Joseph and Chicago, as per notice in the Nov. 28, 1835 *Chicago American*, was driven ashore by storm below Grand River.

Austin, Dr. William G.   a druggist and physician; unclaimed letter notice for him in the *Chicago Democrat* on Jan. 1, 1834; on May 25, 1835, a notice in the *Chicago Democrat*, placed by attorney A.G. Leary, indicates that Leary and Austin shared an office on Lake Street, "two doors below Cook's Coffee House"; later on August 7 advertised in the *Chicago American* his drugstore for botanics and his practice of "botanic healing art which is not connected by ties of consanguinity to the Thompsonian system," with his office yet on Lake Street, near the post office, "three doors E. of Cooke's coffee-house" [the Mansion House]; was one of three directors for the Young Men's Temperance Society, organized on December 19 that year; ✦ Dodge & Austin, Drs., Lake Street, W of Dearborn. [12, 221]

Autray, Jean François Bourdon, sieur de   also Autry; born in Quebec in 1647; member of La Salle's 1682-83 expedition to the mouth of the Mississippi, passing through Chicagoland in January 1682 on the way south; was later honored by the French Crown for his service. [46]

Aveneau, Père Claude   Jesuit missionary who succeeded Father Allouez at St. Joseph in 1690 and there served the Miami for more than 20 years.

Awbenabi   Potawatomi warrior, also known as He-Looks-Black, who took part in the Fort Dearborn massacre; is believed to have survived. [12]

Axtel, Almond   on 1833 list of early settlers.

Axtel & Steele   unclaimed letter listed in the *Chicago Democrat* on Jan. 1, 1834.

Ayers, Thomas   also Ayres; arrived in 1830; voted on July 24, 1830 [see Chronology].

Aythya valisineria   canvasback; see ducks.

Babcock, Ralph and Morgan   arrived in 1833, and moved on to [now] Lombard where they claimed land along the Du Page River; it was first named Babcock's Grove after them. [314a]

Babcock, Charles   on 1833 list of early settlers. [319]

Bachelor's Grove   large wooded area in the SW Chicagoland area where an early settlement began following the acquisition of land tracts in 1832 by four bachelors [see Rexford brothers]; it is now mostly part of the Tinley Creek division of the Cook County Forest Preserve District. Tinley Creek's early name was Bachelor's Grove Creek.

Badin, Father Steven D.   also Stephen Theodore Baden; from Ahoille, France; first Catholic priest ordained in the United States (Baltimore, 1793); missionary among the Potawatomi on the St. Joseph River near Niles [MI] when he came to Chicago in October 1830 to baptize many young children within the Catholic community, among whom were Helene and Susanne, daughters of Billy and Nanette Caldwell; in the 1830s he built a small log chapel on St. Mary's Lake, N of South Bend, IN (its replica would later be erected on the University of Notre Dame campus). The territory assigned to him as missionary extended from St. Mary's Lake S to Bardstown, KY, encompassing Cincinnati and obligating him to frequent lengthy travel; substituted occasionally for Father Cyr in Chicago, when the latter had to be absent. [12, 268, 544]

Bailey, Amos   arrived in 1834 from Vermont; a carpenter by trade, became county surveyor in 1836; in the winter of 1836-37 he commissioned [see] Asa Bradley to create a ✳ real estate map of Chicago that included all new subdivisions; ✦ carpenter and surveyor; in 1885 lived in Pacheco, Contra Costa County, CA. [12, 164, 351, 733]

Bailey, Bennett   (1811-1881) arrived from Hartford County, MD in August 1834; ✦ carpenter and builder; active in Chicago until his death on Nov. 11, 1881. [12, 351]

Bailey, C.F.W.   on 1833 list of early settlers. [319]

Bailey, Maj. David   of Tazewell County; with 12 privates voluntarily escorted Chicago horsemen returning from Ottawa with news of Indian unrest; remained to command "Bailey's Odd Battalion" of four companies of voluntary Cook County militia (led by Capt. H. Boardman, Capt. J.S.C. Hogan, Capt. Holden Seissons, andCapt. James Walker) from May 24 until mid June 1832, stationed at Fort Dearborn during the Black Hawk War; the battalion disbanded June 11 when Maj. Gen. John R. Williams of Michigan Territory arrived with nearly 100 territorial militiamen. [714]

Bailey, Jonathan Nash   from Vermont; probate judge and postmaster at Mackinac between 1825 and 1829, and village president in 1826; arrived at Chicago not later than February 1830 and moved into the old Kinzie house (as shown on the Harrison & Howard ✳ map of Feb. 24 of that year); voted in the August 2 election; bought real estate on the north bank of the river in block 2, which he soon sold to James W. Lee [see map on page 44]; became sutler to Fort Dearborn in 1830 (according to James Bucklin, who visited Chicago in that year); was appointed ★★★ **Chicago's 1st** postmaster by William T. Barry, postmaster general, under President Jackson, on March 31, 1831; still lived in the old Kinzie house at the time of his appointment, for which he paid rent of $50 on Jan. 20, 1831, to the estate of John Kinzie; initially, postal business was conducted by Bailey at this residence, making the Kinzie house ★★★ **Chicago's 1st** post office. In the spring another office was established in a new log cabin at the Forks (NE corner of Franklin and South Water streets; often referred to as "Chicago's first post office"), built by J.S.C. Hogan. Bailey also maintained a garden at [see] *Grosse Pointe*, and at times brought vegetables to Chicago for sale or distribution; not present enough to regularly tend to the postal business, he hired Hogan as his postal clerk and deputy, who served in this capacity until the appointment of postmaster was officially transferred from Bailey to Hogan on Nov. 2, 1832. Bailey and his family left Chicago for St. Louis in May or June of 1832. Anna Maria, Bailey's eldest daughter, subsequently married Hogan on April 27, 1834, near Lewistown and returned to Chicago. [12, 704, 733]

Bailly, Joseph   (1774-1835) Anglicized from Baillé de Messein, also Joe Baies, Bayeux; born in Quebec; a fur trader at Mackinac in the late 1790s [a son Alexis, born in 1798 to his first wife, became an American Fur Co. trader in Minnesota]; in 1800 was with the American Fur Co. on the Grand River [Michigan]; licensed in 1802 by Governor Harrison of the Indiana Territory to trade with the Indians on the Grand River; met and married Marie De la Vigne (née Le Fevre, a French-Ottawa woman with three children) at Mackinac in 1810; later worked out of St. Joseph, Michigan, then moved to the Calumet River in June 1824, and built a log home on the Sauk Trail branch [near Chesterton, IN], becoming the first white settler in the Calumet region and "the only Catholic household between Detroit and Chicago;" several log structures eventually accommodated the family, and the homestead became known to occasional travelers as Baillytown. Jerry Church visited the Baillys in 1830, Roland Tinkham in 1831 and early in 1833, and Valentine Boyer's family spent an overnight with the Baillys in 1833 [their recollections of Bailly hospitality follow below]. The Baillys had a son, Robert, who died of typhoid fever while attending

Joseph Bailly's cabin, along the Calumet River [CHS]

the Cary Mission School, and three beautiful daughters who were sent to Detroit or Montreal to be educated: Ester Mary, born 1812, later married John Harrison Whistler in Chicago on Jan. 23, 1834, the Hon. R.J. Hamilton officiating; as noted in a 1842 *Chicago Daily American* obituary, she died in childbed, leaving her husband with five young children; Rozanne (also Rosene) married Francis Howe, a clerk at the Chicago branch of the Illinois State Bank; and Eleanor. Joseph Bailly died at Baillytown, aged 61. The landmark log house and other buildings still stand [see accompanying photograph]. Marie, known as Monee, later lived in Chicago briefly, but returned to the homestead; she died in 1866. [12, 141, 349, 642, 697]

Jerry Church's visit with the Baillys in 1830:

... We then prepared to leave [Ottawa], and hired a man with a yoke of black oxen and a wagon, to take us to Chicago, distant eighty miles, which we traveled in two days and a-half – two nights camped out. At last we arrived in front of a hotel, in the city of Chicago, (which at that time contained about half a dozen houses, and the balance Indian wig-wams) with our ox stage. We stayed there a week or two with the French

and Indians, and enjoyed ourselves very well. We then took passage in a wagon that was going to Michigan, through the Indian country, without any road. We followed round the beach of the Lake; camped out the first night and slept on a bed of sand. The next morning we came to an old Frenchman's house [Joseph Bailly], who had a squaw for a wife. They had three daughters, and beautiful girls they were, and entertained us very well. My brother almost fell in love with one of the old fellow's girls, and I had hard work to persuade him along any farther. He told me that he thought he felt a good deal like 'an Ingen,' and if he had an 'Ingen gal' for his wife, he thought he could be one. However, I persuaded him to travel on. ✧ We went on through the Pottawatamie nation, until we came to a place called the door-prairie. There we stopped and tried to buy a piece of land, for the purpose of laying out a town at that place. We could not get any title but an Indian one, and we concluded that would not do, so we traveled on, ...*

Roland Tinkham's visit with the Baillys in the summer of 1831:

... and just at sunset arrived at Bailey's or Bayee's, trading post. I never was weary nor hungry or had my feet sore before. We had walked 27 miles. The old trader was not home, but his daughters were. Fine girls, indeed, for this or any other country, tho' their father is an ugly, illiterate man, and their mother a full blooded Ottawa, yet he is rich and has given three of his daughters a good English education. They speak English, French and Indian with correctness and fluency; dress in the English fashion, and are quite accomplished and genteel in their manner. Henry said they are the first girls that ever made an impression on him, and as each of them has a section of prime land reserved in the treaties with U.S. by virtue of their Indian mother, he thinks he shall take at least two of them. We fared sumptuously; some mosquitoes, too.

Dr. Valentine A. Boyer's visit with the Baillys in 1833:

Departing from Laport the only place of note before

we reached the Lake shore was a French Trader's location on the Grand Calumet, consisting of six or more log shanties, for storage purposes, together with the house in which his family resided, and a stable for his cattle and horses. When we arrived there Old Mr. Baillie, for that was his name, received us very kindly and offered us one of his storage shanties, in which we found a chimney, for our accommodation. ✧ When applied to for entertainment, Mr. B. informed us he had none to provide us with, consoling us by saying, he kept no house of entertainment, but extended to us the privelage of occupying one of his 'Block houses.' Taking possession of the one pointed out, we found therein, several bunks in which was spread a bear skin or two and several deer skins. Being provided with a skillet, pans and a coffee pot, Mother and Sister [Maria] soon prepared one of the most palatable meals we had had for some time. Venison we bought from Mr. Baillie, coffee and a few – Knicks – we had provided at Pigeon [White Pigeon], so upon the whole, the meal was made that was palatable and fully appeased the appetite of the inner man. ✧ Feeling somewhat recuperated after the hearty meal we enjoyed, we began to look for our comfort, for our sleep, we found sleeping accommodations slim, Mr. Dean [Day Dean] and myself betook us to the bunk with the bear skins without divesting ourselves of any of our clothing but our coats – one of the luxuries of the expedition was an old fashioned Pennsylvania feather bed with which Mother would not part under any consideration, that was brought out of the wagon and a buffalo robe was spread on the floor, which was the bare ground, the feather bed was laid thereon and Mother and Sister were snugly and comfortably ensconsed therein. Father [John K. Boyer] and Jim [James A.] being supposed to be equally well taken care of, we all retired in anticipation of enjoying a good nights rest, as the journey from Mottville to Bailleytown had been made mostly on foot because the road led thro – a wet low swampy country a great part of the way. But alas, our anticipated enjoyment was soon blasted – and to our serious disappointment, *the famished fleas and bugs who had been the only occupants of the place for some time set about feasting on us so voraciously that fatigued as I was, having fallen asleep nearly as soon as I touched the bear-skin, I was after a few hours sleep aroused from my slumber, springing out of the bunk I hurried out of doors with all dispatch possible where I found Mr. Dean, who had preceded me, fast asleep on the wagon tongue of his wagon with the end board of the wagon for a pillow apparently thankful that he had escaped alive from the tormenting pests.*

Bailleytown   see Bailly, Joseph.

Baines, M.   arrived in 1835 and became firewarden in 1836.

Baird, Elizabeth Thérèse Fisher   see Fisher, Elizabeth Thérèse.

Baker, Bvt. Maj. David   Third Infantry; commandant of Fort Dearborn from May 1817 to June 1820; received his commission in 1799 and, before the war of 1812, served at Mackinac and Detroit; in 1823 he lost his wife and children in an epidemic at a post on the Saginaw River; became lieutenant colonel in 1829, and died at Detroit in 1836.

bakers   Johann Wellmacher (1830), Mathias Meyer (1831), William Adams (1833), Samuel C. George (1834), Josiah P. Cook (1834), Dexter Graves (1834), and Nicholas Boilvin (1835).

Balboa, Vasco Núñez de   (c.1475-1519) Spanish conquistador, who on Sept. 29, 1513, became the first European to reach the Pacific Ocean by crossing the land bridge of Panama. He confirmed what Columbus was only able to suspect, that America was not an extension of China.

Baldwin, Russel   on 1833 list of early settlers. [319]

Balestier, Joseph Neree   came late in 1835 from Brattleboro, VT; successful land speculator and lawyer who formed a partnership with [see] Thomas R. Hubbard, Hubbard & Balestier [Harriet Martineau wrote that in 1836, he realized $500 per day by merely making out titles to land]; ✦ attorney and counsellor at law, 24 Clark St.; on

Jan. 21, 1840, gave a lecture before the Chicago Lyceum on early Chicago, which in 1876 was printed as the first of the *Fergus Historical Series* pamphlets [see Bibliography]. On Sept. 21, 1841, he advertised on Wall Street in New York City; by then he had met in Chicago and married Dr. Wolcott's niece, Caroline Wolcott. [12, 31, 351]

Balfour, Capt. Henry   commandant of Fort Michilimackinac from Sept. 28 to Oct. 1, 1761; commander of a British expedition that came through the Chicago locale in November 1761 to survey former French territory and to map the coastline of Lake Michigan for the British Army under Gen. Jeffrey Amherst; the Balfour Expedition maps are within the Public Record Office, London.

Ballard, Charles A.   arrived in 1833 and purchased land from Mark Beaubien in block 31 [see map on page 44]; early in August voted "yes" for [see] incorporation, then voted in the first town election of August 10; remained in town until 1836. [12]

Ballard, Thomas   from Ireland, came in 1833 with his English wife, Ann (née Bennett); shoemakers who relocated in Long Grove.

Ballingall, Patrick   from Scotland, arrived in 1834; student at the law office of Spring & Goodrich in 1836; ✦ attorney at law, Lake St; married Philura M. Orcutt of Orleans County, NY in 1844. [12]

balloon frame   method of wooden house construction invented in the early 1830s by either G.W. Snow or A.D. Taylor, depending on the source consulted. [Duis identifies St. Mary's Catholic Church, built by Taylor, as the first balloon frame structure.] The method soon spread across the prairie and became typical for most light timber buildings, later with clapboard siding. Balloon frame houses are less wasteful of timber, increasingly precious during the construction boom of those years; the balloon frame depends on good nailing technique for its stability, rather than on an abundance of wood mortised, tenoned, and pinned together with oaken dowels, as in earlier construction; a clap-

board coat completes the job. Also see frame house. [245, 505]

Baltimore   schooner belonging to the American Fur Co. in 1817; regularly delivered supplies to Fort Dearborn.

bank   see State Bank of Illinois.

Banskey, Joseph   on 1833 list of early settlers; see Bauskey, Joseph. [319]

Baptist congregation   Mrs. Rebecca Heald, who arrived with her husband at the fort in 1810, and Reverend Isaac McCoy, who visited in 1826 from the Carey Mission [Niles, MI] and gave a sermon, were the first Baptists in Chicago. When Dr. Temple arrived in 1833, he initially attended Presbyterian services at Fort Dearborn, but then arranged through correspondence with the American Home Baptist Society to have a pastor assigned to Chicago; later in the year [see] Rev. Allen B. Freeman arrived from Vermont and by October 19 organized the first Baptist church with fourteen members: Reverend Allen and Hannah Freeman, S.T. Jackson, Martin D. Harmon, Samantha Harmon, Peter Moore, Nathaniel Carpenter, John K. Sargents, Peter Warden, Willard Jones, Ebenezer and Betsy Crane, Susannah Rice, and Lucinda Jackson. Reverend Freeman died of typhoid fever in Chicago on Dec. 15, 1834, and was succeeded by Rev. Isaac T. Hinton. Dr. Temple also promoted construction of the first Baptist meeting house, starting a subscription fund with $100; construction was completed in 1834 for about $900 at the SE corner of Franklin and South Water streets; known as the Temple Building, services were held on the lower floor and a school existed on the upper floor; Methodists and Presbyterians initially borrowed the space for their services. Not until 1844 did the congregation have a distinct brick church building, then at the SE corner of Washington and LaSalle; see Monuments for a commemorative ▲ bronze plaque once present at Wacker and Michigan. [632]

Barada, Eulalie   born in St. Louis about 1788;

neighbor of Jean Baptiste Point de Sable in St. Charles, MO; important because she has been carelessly confused with Point's granddaughter Eulalie Pelletier (born in Chicago, 1796)—confusion arises from a 1813 document, recorded in the St. Charles Co. archives, by which Point gave Eulalie (then married to her third husband, Michel Roi) all of his property in return for her promise to care for him for the rest of his life, feed his hogs and chickens, repair his house, and arrange for his burial in the parish cemetery. Contrary to the conclusions of most historians, who say that Eulalie "inherited" his wealth, the document clearly shows that he was destitute, to the point of having to borrow household utensils from Eulalie. Whether Eulalie kept her promises is not known; she was not recorded as a witness to Point's burial, although she outlived him; she does not appear in records of the title of Point's house or farm; also see Point de Sable, Jean Baptiste. [649]

Barbier, Gabriel   member of La Salle's 1682-83 expedition to the mouth of the Mississippi, passing through Chicagoland in January 1682 on the way south; was later honored by the French Crown for his service. [46]

barge   also patroon; the largest boat used on the Mississippi prior to the steamboat, powered by a crew of 40 to50 men, including the captain; carried 50 to 100 tons, too large to pass through the Chicago portage, even under the best weather conditions.

Barkenbile, C.G.   a notice in the Aug. 15, 1835, *Chicago American* offers a $5 reward for the small gold breast-pin on a gold chain that he had lost between F. Myer's grocery and the public works on August 5.

Barker, Benjamin F.   by Sept. 6, 1832, was renting a cabin for $3 a month at Chicago and by letter to his brother in the East, reported that money was plentiful and requested salt and flour; by January 1833 he chopped wood to feed his family, the only work available and observed that the situa-

tion of the Indians was desperate, thousands were starving; in March he rented a farm 8 miles N and asked for a strong wagon and barrels of salt; listed as a subscriber to the *Chicago Democrat* in November; in February 1834 he hauled wood to town with a small wagon and oxen and requested a stock of groceries; by March had a shop in town and had built a house for his family, reporting in May that competition was great and liquor was in great demand; by the end of July he wrote from Juliet—money was scare in Chicago where a grocery existed on every corner, and the country was delightful; letters to Jacob A. Barker are preserved at the Chicago Historical Society.

Barlett, Charles Herbert   came with his wife in 1834 from New Hampshire; moved to Libertyville Township in 1836 and became one of the first Lake County commissioners. [13, 304]

Barnard, Chauncey, Jr.   assisted Henry Belin in the summer of 1831 to take soundings and measurements of the Chicago River in preparation for the construction of the Chicago harbor and the Illinois & Michigan Canal.

Barnard, J.H., M.D.   arrived 1835; physician who advertised his practice in the *Chicago American* on June 3, with an office in the New York House on Lake Street; in September he entered a partnership with Dr. J.C. Goodhue, with an office on Lake Street, three doors W of the Tremont House, advertising the practice of "Physic and Surgery" in the *Chicago Democrat* throughout the autumn. [12]

Barnes, Hamilton   arrived from New York in 1832; married to Anna M. Fitch; listed as a subscriber to the *Chicago Democrat* in November 1833; ✦ carpenter, W Madison Street; became alderman in 1842; in 1885 his widow lived at 152 S Sangamon St. [12, 351]

Barnes, Joseph A.   (1805-1881) came with the Eli B. Williams family from Wartsfield, VT, arriving April 14,1833; his wife E.W. (née Miner, married in 1829) followed overland in September with her brother, Dr. Frederick Miner, and his family; ac-

quired a lot for $50 on Kinzie Street near Canal and built a house; listed as a subscriber to the *Chicago Democrat* in November 1833; removed to Elk Grove Township in the spring of 1834 and farmed; of three daughters, Adaline and Amelia survived to adulthood, while Mary died at age six; died on March 19, 1881. [12, 13, 278]

Barney, J.R.   listed as a subscriber to the *Chicago Democrat* in November 1833.

Barnum, Truman   became street commissioner on Nov. 4, 1835; ✦ teamster, corner of N Dearborn and Indiana [Grand] streets. [28]

barrens   a form of landscape found in early Illinois. H.S. Tanner [see separate entry] in 1832 described them as follows: "[t]hese are a species of country of a mixed character, uniting forest and prairie. They are covered with sparse, stinted oaks &c. and grass. The fire sweeps over them in the fall, but is not powerful enough, from want of abundant fuel, to destroy the timber. They soon become covered with thick forests, when the fire is excluded. They are not poor land, as their title, given ignorantly by the early settlers, would seem to indicate. They are generally second-rate land, productive, healthy, more rolling than the prairies, and abounding in good springs."

Barrows, Mary   on 1833 list of early settlers; assistant teacher at Eliza Chappel's normal school, with Elizabeth Beach, late in 1834; later became a missionary in Japan. [319]

Bathelemy   a young man from Paris, and a member of the ill-fated 1684 La Salle expedition to the mouth of the Mississippi River which, due to La Salle's error, ended in Spanish Texas. After La Salle's death, Bathelemy was one of the group of six who, led by Joutel, reached Chicago by overland route on Sept. 25, 1687, en route to Canada. [519, 611]

Barton, Pagan   prior to 1836, owner of 80 acres of land in Section 30, Township 39, as shown in Andreas's *History of Chicago*, pp. 112-113.

Bascom, Rev. Flavel   (1804-1891) also Bascome; Presbyterian minister from Lebanon, CT, who

REV. FLAVEL BASCOMB

came with his bride Ellen P. [née Cleaveland] in July 1833, while on his honeymoon; accepted an invitation to give a sermon at the Presbyterian *church* in the absence of Reverend Porter. Not until 1839 did he return to Chicago to become the church's pastor, succeeding Reverend J. Blatchford to serve for the next nine years. Following Ellen's death in 1837, he would marry Elizabeth B. Sparhawk of Connecticut; still lived at Hinsdale in 1885. [12, 351, 707]

bateau   also *batteau*, Mackinaw boat; relatively heavy, long, tapering boat with flat bottom and shallow draft, decked over at the stern, used by the French Canadians and dominated the Mississippi and Illinois river traffic during the French period;

able to traverse the Chicago portage during high water conditions; 25 to 50 feet in length, 8 to 12 feet wide, and 3 to 4 feet deep; could withstand heavy seas and was usually propelled by oars (four oarsmen and one steersman), but a mast and sail could be easily rigged. Trader Gurdon S. Hubbard characterized them as: "French boats—Mackinaw boats, carrying six to eight to ten tons—some larger, some smaller. They were the boats we brought our lake goods with, and returned in the summer with our furs and peltries—the same boats which formerly navigated the St. Lawrence." As soon as the Chicago harbor opened, they disappeared. Also see Traders' Brigade.

Bates, Aurilla   from Ohio; mother of Elvira, who married Stephen R. Forbes in 1830, and Sophia, who married Bernardus Laughton in 1830. When Aurilla visited Chicago in 1834, staying with the Laughtons, she suffered a cerebral hemorrhage and died; the *Chicago Democrat* of July 4 reported: "... was attacked with a severe paraletick [sic] shock, which terminated her existence."

Bates, George C.   (1812-1886) from Canadaigua, NY; prominent Detroit attorney, politician and later judge; married Ellen Marion Kinzie in 1836, six years after the death of her first husband, Dr. Alexander Wolcott. The couple lived at Detroit and had one son, Kenzie, a major, who died c.1884 in Lansing, MI; after Ellen's death, Bates practiced law in Chicago between 1861 and 1871; died in Denver, CO. [12]

Bates, John, Jr.   (1803-c.1885) born in Fishkill, NY; arrived in May 1832; early in 1833 he was hired as postal clerk by Postmaster Hogan; together they introduced, and continued for over a year, the custom of firing a gun from the door on the N side of the post office log cabin every night at sunset, responding to the nightly gun salute from the flag-lowering ceremony at Fort Dearborn; both Bates and Hogan slept in the loft of the log cabin at Lake and South Water streets that was then the post office until Bates married. Harriet Gould Brown of

JOHN BATES, JR.

Springfield, MA, married him on Nov. 13, 1833, Hon. R.J. Hamilton officiating; a daughter, Harriet Ellen, died in August 1835 at 18 months. Bates became a licensed auctioneer—★★★ Chicago's 1st —and in July 1834 built an auction store "on the street leading from the draw-bridge to the oak woods, and blue island," on the W side of Dearborn, between Lake and South Water streets, a wooden structure that in 1838 became the "Rialto,"

Chicago's second theater house; ✦ auctioneer, Lake Street Bates's skill as an auctioneer is well expressed by Edwin O. Gale: "Johnny Bates could sell anything from a canal lot to a lot of cracked pitchers, and sell his customers, too, if he really set about it, which he would sometimes do merely for the fun of the thing. He was a short man, but had the happy gift of being able to look over the head of a six-footer and catch the eye of a five foot chap behind him, in order to raise the giant's bid." In 1885 lived at 275 State St.; died in a freak railroad accident when 80 years old. [12, 13, 351]

Bates, Sophia   from Virginia, sister of Stephen Forbes' wife; married Bernard H. Laughton on Nov. 7, 1830, Reverend William See officiating.

Battles, Joe   Negro slave of Charles Jouett, U.S. Indian Agent and his wife Susan; called "Black Meat" by the Indians; arrived with them in January 1809 from Kentucky, Susan's home state.

Baumgarten, Moritz   later called himself Morris Baumgarden; arrived from Germany in 1832; additional family members included Charles [died on Oct. 16, 1882], Peter (may have arrived in 1836) and Catharine; Moritz (ward 5) and Peter (ward 6) voted in the first mayoral election of 1837; Catharine married Jacob Müller at St. Mary's Church on April 4, 1836, Father St. Cyr officiating; ✦ Morris, Morris, Jr., and Charles, carpenters, Illinois Street near North State. [12, 342]

Bauskey, Joseph   also Banskey; from France; made a purchase at the estate sale of W.H. Wallace on April 27, 1827; voted on May 11, 1828, and Aug. 2, 1830 [see Chronology]; married Deborah Scott Watkins on Nov. 25, 1828, J.B. Beaubien, J.P. officiating; died of cholera in 1832. [12]

Baxley, Capt. J.M.   from Maryland; Fifth Infantry; member of the Fort Dearborn garrison from June 20, 1833, until April 1836, with wife Mary Robbins Baxley (from Baltimore, married Nov. 13, 1822) and five children, of whom two or three attended school under Miss Eliza Chappel; present during the Indian Treaty of Chicago in September

1833, and signed as witness on the document. The eldest son, 10-year-old John Charles Merryman, died of bilious fever at Fort Dearborn on Sept. 16, 1834. Mary, 32, died at the fort on the following November 16, leaving the bereaved husband and four children; after leaving the Army, remained in Chicago four only a few years. [12, 708]

Baye de Puants, La   see Green Bay.

Bayer & Spence   Chicago area company which, under contract with Major Bender, furnished 2000 cubic yards of stone for the harbor project in the summer of 1833, at $1.90 per yard.

Bayne, Catherine   from Scotland; opened a boarding and day school for young ladies on June 30, 1834, on Randolph, between Clark and Dearborn streets, "nearly in the rear of the Presbyterian Church," where she taught "Lessons in English Reading, Grammar, Geography with use of Globes, Writing, Needle work, Embroidery and Fancy Work, Oriental Drawing, Enamel Painting, Transfer Drawing and Velvet Painting." On Sept. 15, 1835, she married William McCorristen; as late as 1840 the school was yet known in her name, but a new listing under her married name would appear in the *Chicago American* on March 2, 1841.

Beach, Elizabeth L.   assistant teacher at Eliza Chappel's normal school in late 1834, together with Mary Barrows; in 1836 married Alford B. Hale.

Beach, John   the jailer in 1835, responsible for the small log jail within a high plank palisade on the NW corner, at Randolph and LaSalle streets, according to E.O. Gale; ✦ canal contractor, Randolph Street, E of Dearborn. [266]

Beach, O.S.   member of the fire engine company No.1 in 1835 [see entry on firefighting with petition to the village board of Dec. 16, 1835].

bear   *Ursus americanus*, black bear; common in Illinois at the time of exploration by Europeans; Father Bineteau stated that for early explorers the ox [bison], bear, and deer were the main meats; Father Gravier in 1700 reported seeing more than 50 bears in one day along the Mississippi River be-

tween the present sites of St. Louis and Cairo; late in 1833 a bear was killed in the timber along the E side of the south branch of the Chicago River; it is reported that Sam George spotted and John Sweeney shot the last bear (400 pounds) in Chicago in the woods near Adams Street, between LaSalle Street and the river on Oct. 6, 1834; occasional sightings were reported near Chicago as late as 1837. All bears had disappeared from Illinois by 1860. [266]

Beaubien, Alexander   (1822-1907) born in Chicago on Jan. 28, 1822, to Jean Baptiste Beaubien and his wife Josette (LaFramboise); he was likely born on the premises of the military fort proper, prompting the local Indians to enthusiastically celebrate the event [see John Kelley's following description from *Tales*, see Bibliography]. Alexander married Susan Miles of Canadaigua, NY, in 1850; worked for the Chicago Police Department in later life, and as a private detective; his ▲ grave is in Graceland Cemetery.

... Five or six times had the stork visited Fort Dearborn before it brought little Alexander Beaubien, but on all previous visits it had left behind a full-blooded white child. The Indians manifested no interest in these children. But the Beaubien case was different. Word of the big event was passed from one tepee to another along the banks of the river, and the braves and sqaws came trooping over to the Fort wrapped in blankets and wearing their prettiest feathers. They brought presents fashioned from leather and beads for the mother and child. ✧ *That night bonfires were kindled on both banks of the river and the Pottawatomies danced as they never danced before, in honer of the first white-and-red papoose in Chicago.* [12, 42]

Beaubien Cemetery   small cemetery on land set aside by Mark Beaubien on Ogden Avenue in Lisle; Mark spent his last years living with a daughter in Kankakee where he died and was buried. See Monuments for details and occupants of the cemetery. [429]

Beaubien, Charles Henry (1803-1858) son of Jean Baptiste Beaubien and his second Ottawa wife; brother of Madore Beaubien; he, with his family, came to Chicago in 1811, but removed to Milwaukee shortly before the 1812 massacre, returning in 1818; he had a daughter, Marie (born at Mackinac on March 22, 1822), with Marie, a Chippewa consort. In 1829 Charles taught a small family school near the fort, and had become known for his skill as violinist; ◆ violinist; died at [see] *Grosse Pointe*; see schools. [12, 42]

Beaubien, Emily (1825-1920) born at Monroe, MI on July 28, 1825, to Mark and Monique Beaubien and came from Detroit with her family in 1826; married Robert Le Beau, a saddler from Newark, in 1846; in 1875 left to live in Corpus Christi, TX, returning to Aurora in 1912 where she died on Nov. 4, 1920. Acquainted with her late in life, Quaife observed: "She was a refined and charming woman, and possessed a remarkable store of memories of the scenes of her early years"; some of these memories have been preserved through interviews she granted. She had learned the Potawatomi language before the age of 10 and retained the ability to speak it all her life. She was the last member of the family to be buried in the Beaubien Cemetery in Lisle [see Monuments]. [41, 42]

Beaubien House located on the former lakeshore, a short distance N of the old river mouth, between the Dean House (S) and the Lee House (N). Jean Baptiste Beaubien built it for his family in 1817 and lived there until 1836; a bronze ▲ plaque on the east wall of the Cultural Center, at the SW corner of Randolph Street and Michigan Avenue indicates the location [see Monuments]. Beaubien successively owned and occupied many other houses in Chicago during his life.

Beaubien, Jean Baptiste (1787-1864) known as John Beaubien or Colonel Beaubien later in his life; born at Detroit to Jean Baptiste and Josette [née Bondy] Beaubien, who married in 1777; one

JEAN BAPTISTE BEAUBIEN

among 10 children born within a large (15 other children from the father's earlier marriage) well established French Canadian family (originally Cuillerier *dit* Beaubien [see *dit* entry] assumed in 1712, in honor of Sieur Michel De Beaubien, an ancestral family member); prior to 1800, Jean Baptiste served as an apprentice to Joseph Bailly at the St. Joseph River; in 1804, by which year he had traded in Milwaukee and Mackinac, he made his first visit to Chicago and moved there permanently in 1811, building his first house on the E side of the south branch, about a quarter mile S of the Forks; later he may have owned, at one time or another, every house at the lakeshore S of the Chicago River. In 1812, after the massacre, he bought the Leigh House (closest to the fort) from Leigh's widow, although he had moved with his family to Milwaukee shortly before the massacre; he returned in 1818 to reside permanently in Chicago. In 1817, Beaubien bought for $1,000 the larger Dean house at the mouth of the river and began to build an even larger house between the two that became

known as the Beaubien House. In the autumn of 1818, he was appointed American Fur Co. agent, but in 1822 John Crafts took over the agency and Beaubien worked under him as subagent; in July 1827, during the Winnebago scare, he organized a local company of militia; from 1827 to 1835 he held the Chicago area trade concession of the American Fur Co. In 1830, he purchased from the government lots 1 and 2 in block 17, and additional land in blocks 18 and 36 [see map on page 44], but later sold part of the land to Madore Beaubien and William Jones (block 17), to Seth Johnson and Robert Stewart [Stuart?] (block 36) and to Solomon Juneau (block 18); in May 1835 he bought the Fort Dearborn reservation [75.69 acres] through the local government land agent for $94.61, but the purchase was later declared invalid by the U. S. Supreme Court ("Beaubien land case"), and the land became the Breese & Beaubien Addition to Chicago, Sidney Breese having been one of Beaubien's attorneys and a party in the dispute with the federal government; late that year, filed a claim for wharfing privileges for lot 5, block 36. Between 1840 and 1858, he lived on his farm near Hardscrabble. His first Ottawa wife, name unknown, bore him a daughter, Marie; with his second Ottawa wife, Maw-naw-bun-no-quah (Mahnobunoqua), sister of Shabbona, he had Charles Henry and Madore; she died in 1811; in 1812, he married Josette, housemaid of the Kinzies and daughter of François LaFramboise; together they had George (died early), Susan, Monique, Julie, Alexander, Ellen [Helene Maria?], Philippe and Henry (twins), Marie Louise, Marguerite, Caroline, and William; Josette died in 1845; with his fourth wife, Catherine Louise Pinney (married in 1855), he had Isadore, Maurice, Pauline, and Claudia; his children totaled 19. Jean brought the first carriage to Chicago and, in 1834, shipped from Detroit Chicago's second piano, for the benefit of his daughters who had been sent to Detroit to be educated [see Ashbel Steele for the first]. He served as public administrator for Cook County; was elected a colonel of the Sixtieth Regiment of the Illinois Militia on June 7, 1834, at the house of Stephen Forbes on the Des Plaines River; in 1850 he was commissioned to or adopted the title of "Brigadier General"; died at Lisle where he had lived since 1858, and there buried in the Beaubien Cemetery [see Monuments]. ➡ Beaubien Court (120E, from 150 N to 186 N) [12, 28, 42, 159, 226, 357, 429]

Beaubien, Josette LaFramboise see LaFramboise, Josette. [12]

Beaubien land case see Beaubien, Jean Baptiste.

Beaubien, Madore Benjamin (1809-1883) first name variously spelled Medare, Medard, Medart; son of Jean Baptiste and his second Ottawa wife, Mahnobunoqua, and best known of his father's 19 children; born on the Grand River [Michigan]; came to Chicago in 1811, but his family removed to Milwaukee shortly before the 1812 massacre, returning in 1818 for permanent residency; though from a Catholic family, he attended the Baptist

MADORE BENJAMIN BEAUBIEN [CHS]

Carey Mission [Niles, MI] in 1823 and 1824, and between 1825 and 1828 attended Hamilton College in New York. Madore was regarded as "the handsomest man in Chicago" and a great charmer; was on the Aug. 2, 1830, voting list and on Aug. 10, 1833, was elected to the first Chicago Town Board of Trustees. On Dec. 14, 1834, he married Maria, daughter of his business partner, John K. Boyer, Reverend J. Porter officiating; in December 1835, he was a member of the fire engine company No.1 [see entry on firefighting for petition to the village board of Dec. 16, 1835]. His wife abandoned him in 1838 with their two children, George and Susan, and would file for divorce in 1843; his business enterprise, a store he had built in 1831 at the SW corner of Dearborn and South Water streets [✦ merchant, South Water Street] in shambles, he left Chicago for good in 1840, joining the Potawatomi at Council Bluffs, IA and later removed with them to their reserve in Kansas. He was married to an Indian woman, Keez-ko-quah, and in 1854, married his cousin, Therese LaFramboise; altogether, Madore fathered 10 children; died on Dec. 26, 1883. [12, 42, 43, 226, 429 535]

Beaubien, Mark (1800-1881) born in Detroit, younger brother of [see] Jean Baptiste; married Monique Nadeau (1800-1847), with whom he had 16 children, 14 of whom survived their mother; then married Elizabeth Mathieu, with whom he had seven. Mark came to Chicago in 1826 with Monique and children, among them [see] Emily, and purchased a small log cabin on the south bank near the Forks from James Kinzie; in 1829 he began to take in guests, calling his cabin the "Eagle Exchange Tavern." A fun-loving fiddle player, he loved to entertain his guests at night, tempting one to believe stories about his knack for boyish mischief [see following excerpts from Hurlbut]; was licensed to keep a tavern on June 9, 1830; when the town plat was published that year, he found that his business was in the middle of a street and moved the structure to the SE corner of Market

MARK BEAUBIEN [12]

and Lake streets He purchased from the government in 1830 lots 3 and 4 in block 31 on which his building stood, as well as the small block 30, later selling part of the land to Charles A. Ballard [see map on page 44]. In 1831 he built on a two-story frame house and called the structure the "Sauganash Hotel" in honor of his friend Billy Caldwell, whose Indian name was Sauganash; on June 6 that year, at the new county seat (Chicago), was granted a license to sell goods in Cook County In the late summer of 1832, he rented his original log cabin, adjacent to his tavern, to newly ar-

rived Philo Carpenter for use as ★★★ **Chicago's 1st** drugstore; an ardent enemy of alcohol, Carpenter soon moved out. Mark next let the space to John S. Wright, and in 1833, the cabin became a school under Eliza Chappel's direction. Early in August 1833, Mark was one of the "Qualified Electors" who voted to incorporate the town [for a copy of that meeting's original report, see incorporation] and on August 10 voted in the first town election; also became the first licensed ferry owner and in 1834, built his second hotel, the "Exchange Coffee House," at the NW corner of Lake and Wells streets; placed an ad in the Dec. 21, 1835, *Chicago Democrat* that read: "I Mark Beaubien, do agree to pay 25 bushels of Oats if any man will agree to pay me the same number of bushels if I win against any man's horse or mare in the town of Chicago, against Maj. R.A. Forsyth's bay mare, Now in Town for three miles on the ice"; ◆ hotel-keeper, Lake Street In 1840, Mark removed to Lisle with his family where he acquired farmland from William Sweet S of Sweet's Grove and also a cabin located immediately W of the [see] Beaubien cemetery; the cabin soon became a tavern, while yet home to the residing family. From 1851 to 1857 he used the building as a toll station for the Southwest Plank Road, with his son collecting the toll; the ▲ structure, built in the 1830s, still exists though moved; see Monuments. Later, during 1859 and 1860, he was the lighthouse keeper in Chicago. His address in 1878 was Newark, Kendall County. During the last 10 years of his life, he was troubled by failing memory, much to his chagrin because he loved to tell stories of the past; he was happiest in the company of old friends. Mark died on April 11, 1881, in the home of his daughter Mary [born Sept. 30, 1848] and son-in-law, Georges Mathieu, at Kankakee and was buried with his second wife in St. Rose Cemetery, the oldest portion of Mound Grove. His fiddle is preserved at the Chicago Historical Society. One of his sons, Napoleon, known as "Monkey," was a close childhood friend of Edwin

O. Gale; another son Mark, Jr., lived in Chicago well into the 20th century; ➡ Beaubien Court (120 E from 150 N to 186 N), a short street in present downtown Chicago, named after Mark and Jean Baptiste Beaubien who together fathered 42 children with their Indian, French and English wives, vitally contributing to the population explosion of early Chicago. [12, 42, 160, 357, 266, 429]

[*Chicago Antiquities*, p.332] ... *We have read a statement in Smith's* History of Wisconsin *to the purport that Col. Wm. J. Hamilton passed through Chicago in June, 1825 [if true, it must have been 1826; eds.], with a drove of some 700 head of cattle, procured in southern Illinois, which he had contracted to the government, for the use of the post at Green Bay. A brother of Colonel Beaubien, it is stated, assisted in getting the cattle across the Chicago River, but in rendering that service, managed to drown one of them purposely; so Beaubien told Hamilton some years afterward. He did it, he said, in order to buy the animal, knowing that he could not purchase it any other way, and he very greatly needed the beef. This "brother of Colonel Beaubien," we must believe, was none other than our famed Mark.*

[p. 333] ... *In the early days, while Mr. B. kept a tavern, possibly the old Sauganash, when emigration from the east began to pour forth the stream which has not yet subsided, Mark's loft, capable of storing half a hundred men, for a night, if closely packed, was often filled to repletion. The furniture equipment, however, for a caravansary so well patronized, it is said, was exceedingly scant; that circumstance, however, only served to exhibit more clearly the eminent skill of the landlord. With the early shades of an autumn eve, the first to men arriving were given a bed on the floor of the staging or loft, and, covering them with two blankets, Mark bade them a hearty goodnight. Fatigued with the day's travel, they would soon be sound asleep, when two more would be placed by their side, and the aforesaid "two blankets" be drawn over these new comers. The first two were journeying too intently in the land of dreams to notice this sleight*

of hand feat of the jolly Mark, and as travelers, in those days, usually slept in their clothes, they generally passed the night without great discomfort. As others arrived, the last going to bed always had the blankets; and so it was, that forty dusty, hopeful, tired, and generally uncomplaining emigrants or adventurous explorers, who went up a ladder, two by two, to Mark Beaubien's sleeping loft, were all covered with one pair of blankets. It is true, it was sometimes said, that in a frosty morning there were frequently charges of blanket-stealing, and grumbling was heard, coupled with rough words similar to those formerly used by the army in Flanders; but the great heart of Mark was sufficient for the occasion, for, at such times, he would only charge half price for lodging to those who were disposed to complain.

Frank G. Beaubien [1919] provides a valuable late episode:

Near the time of my father's death—just before he died he asked for his violin. He played an old Indian tune, the words are, "Let me go to my home on the far distant shore white man, let me go." He played it partly through but he was too weak to finish. He requested me to bring the violin and a picture of Hon. John Wentworth, taken when he was a young man and to hand them to John Wentworth. After his death I brought them to Hon. John Wentworth who was stopping at the Sherman House. I handed them to him and said that it was father's request. He took my hand, the tears came to his eyes and he could not speak and he left me and I went out deeply impressed. Mr. Wentworth gave the violin to the Calumet Club, where the old pioneers used to meet once a year until they all passed away.

Beauharnais also Beauharnois; two members of this large and influential French family played major roles in New France and are often confused. The earlier official was François de Beauharnais, seigneur de la Chaussay-Beaumont; a royal councilor, he was appointed intendant of New France in April 1705 and served until 1707. His brother was Charles de la Boische, marquis de Beauharnais (c.1670-1749), who was appointed governor of Canada in 1726 and served until 1747. [665]

beaver   *Castor canadensis*; common in Illinois at the time European settlement began; relentlessly hunted by trappers and Indians alike, initially beaver pelts were the most highly prized and used as monetary units, the value of other goods being designated as so many pelts. In 1831, beaver pelts brought $2 per pound in Chicago; later in the 1830s muskrat pelts gradually replaced beaver pelts in the fur trade; the beaver became almost extinct in this state, though a comeback has been noted in recent years.

Beben, Joseph   listed as a early settler in 1833. [319]

Beck, Lewis Caleb   author of *Gazetteer of the States of Illinois and Missouri*, published in Albany, NY in 1823; in it, Beck borrows from Schoolcraft when describing the Chicago locale:

The country around is the most fertile and beautiful that can be imagined. It consists of an intermixture of woods and prairies, diversified with gentle slopes, sometimes attaining the elevation of hills, irrigated with a number of clear streams and rivers, which throw their waters partly into Lake Michigan and partly into the Mississippi River. It is already the seat of several flourishing plantations.

Beckford, —   printer working for Calhoun's *Chicago Democrat* in 1833, together with Oscar Pratt.

Beebeau, —   see Bibeau, Louis.

Beers, Anthony   on 1833 list of early settlers. [319]

Beers, Cyrenus   hardware merchant; arrived from Connecticut in 1835, signing up in September with the "Fire Kings," an early volunteer fire brigade; married Mary Curtis of Connecticut on Nov. 21, 1838; an only infant son died in 1842; ◆ [Jabez K.] Botsford & Beers (copper, tin and sheet iron at the corner of Lake and Dearborn streets); alderman in 1843; died in 1848. [12, 351]

Beggs, Reverend Stephen Ruddel   (1801-1895) Methodist preacher from Rockingham County, VA;

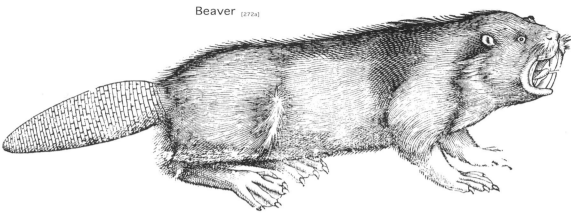

Beaver [272a]

on June 15, 1831, made a one-day visit to Chicago, where he conducted a religious service in the quarters of Dr. Harmon; married Elizabeth L. Heath on September 1, 1831, moving later that autumn to Chicago where his wife joined him the following May; they preceded Reverend Walker in their residence just N of Wolf Point, the reverand and his family arriving soon after, living together with the Beggs couple for a short while; Reverend Beggs's description [*Early History of the West and Northwest*] follows; after Elizabeth's death in 1866, he married Mrs. Sarah Frost; died at Plainfield. A notebook of sermons that belonged to the minister is preserved at the Chicago Historical Society. [12, 50, 351, 707]

... Jesse Walker was my successor in 1832. He moved his family up to Chicago as soon as possible and set to work. I attended his first quarterly meeting; it was held in an old log school-house, which served for a parsonage, parlor, kitchen, and audience-room. The furniture consisted of an old box stove, with one griddle, upon which we cooked. We boiled our tee-kettle, cooked what vegetable we could get, and fried our meat, each in its turn. Our table was an old wooden chest; and when dinner was served up, we surrounded the board and ate with a good appetite, asking no questions for conscience sake.

Belcher, William   active in the fur trade of the Northwest; served as storekeeper employed by the

sutlers of Fort Dearborn sometime between 1821 and 1830; on Sept. 4, 1830, he purchased lots 5 and 6 in block 29 from the government [see map on page 44]; in 1833 B.B. Kercheval was listed as owner of this land, but other early records show Robert A. Kinzie as proprietor.

Belin, Henry   U.S. assistent engineer under Dr. William Howard; came in the summer of 1831 to take soundings and measurements of the Chicago River in preparation for the construction of the Chicago harbor and the Illinois & Michigan Canal, assisted by Chauncey Barnard, Jr. ✳ Map No. 1 of his May 20, 1832, report, reprinted in the Dec. 10, 1834, *Chicago Democrat*, provides a graphic description of the river, which he identifies as a creek:

The survey of the creek commences at its mouth, which is obstructed by a bar. At the time it was sounded, during the summer of 1831, there was two feet water, but it is constantly altering, and sometimes completely closed. From the bar the water of the lake gradually deepens, and, 445 yards from its mouth, there is 18 feet water. ◇ *This creek, from its mouth to Fort Dearborn, a distance of 467 yards, runs parallel to the lake, (course nearly north,) from which it is separated by a narrow sand bank, its average width 100 yards; the depth varies from 5 to 6 feet. From the fort of the village of Chicago, the course is west, distance 1,150 years [sic], average width 70 yards, and from 15 to*

16 deep: at this point the stream forks. From the village, the main branch has a course east of south for 3,200 yards, average width 60 yards, depth 17 feet; thence, to the point where the line of levels commence, the course is south of west distance 5,230 yards, average width 44 yards, depth varying from 26 to 10 feet. The creek heads about 2,500 yards from the above mentioned point, in low, wet ground, which extends in a westerly direction for about four miles to Mud lake, which communicates with the river Des Plaines. [432, 681, 682]

Belknap, Ebenezer from Connecticut; first factor at Fort Dearborn; served from early 1805 to Dec. 31, 1805; was succeeded by Thomas Hayward. [544, 559]

Bell, Wilson A. purchased on Sept. 4, 1830, lots 4 and 5 in block 34 [see map on page 44] and within two years sold the land to Sullivan Blood; also purchased lot 5 in block 23 from William See [Lee?] and within two years sold it to George Stoner; enlisted as a private at Fort Dearborn on Oct. 10, 1833 and was discharged exactly three years later.

Bellair, Louis from France; present at the estate sale of W.H. Wallace on May 10, 1827, acquiring an old tent for five dollars; Mrs. Kinzie, in *Wau-Ban*, mentions him as one who beats his wife. [220]

Belle Fountain the French name by which [see] Bourbon Spring was originally known; where David Laughton died on April 12, 1834.

Belleau, Michel later corrupted to Bureau and Beuro; Quebec trader active in Illinois between 1771 and 1780; partner of Pierre Durand and Jean Baptiste Point de Sable; his 1777 trade license was bonded by Jean Orillat; took oath of loyalty to Virginia in 1778 or 1779 after Clark's conquest of Illinois, an act which served as his death warrant; met Durand at the Chicago Portage in 1779 with a large shipment of furs and 15 *engagés* from his post at the mouth of the *Rivière au Bureau*; killed by Indians, spring 1780; his estate was administered at Cahokia that year. [649]

Bellin, Jacques Nicolas (1702-1772) French cartographer who, with access to official documents of earlier explorers, prepared a ✳ map, *Carte des Lacs du Canada*, that accompanied Charlevoix's *Journal d'un Voyage Fait par Ordre du Roi dans l'Amerique Septentrionale* of 1744; the map shows the *Portage aux chênes* [Chicago Portage] starting ambiguously from the north branch of the Chicago River instead of the south branch; introduced on the map are five imaginary islands in Lake Superior, named after and apparently meant to please members of the French nobility; these islands were repeated on his ✳ map, *Partie Occidentale de la Nouvelle France ou Canada* in 1755 and copied by later mapmakers, resulting in misinformation as late as 1805 [John Cary, *A New Map of Part of the United Stated of North America*]. [605, 681, 682]

Belz John resident by 1833, German Catholic immigrant; in 1837 was married to Veronica Periolat by Father St. Cyr. [342]

Bemis, Aaron mail carrier between Fort Dearborn and Fort Wayne in 1823, whom Major Long met on his expedition to the source of the St. Peter's River and detained as a guide. [12, 394]

Bender, Maj. George from Massachsetts; Fifth Infantry, commandant at Fort Dearborn from June 19 to Oct. 31, 1833, when he resigned; followed Major Fowle both as commandant and as construction superintendent for the harbor project; under him the construction work actually began [see Shapley, Capt. Morgan L.], with Henry Handy as his assistant and Abraham V. Knickerbocker as his clerk; signed as a witness on the 1833 Treaty of Chicago; died in Washington City on Aug. 21, 1865. [12]

Benedict, — settler in 1829 on the Sauk trail (Detroit-Chicago Road); in November 1827, acted as letter carrier for Dr. A. Wolcott.

Benedict, Sheldon partnered A.W. Chambers as Messrs. Chambers & Benedict late November 1835, buying J.M. Faulkner's entire stock of goods and continuing at the old stand two doors W of

the Land Office on Lake Street; an ad in the November 25 *Chicago Democrat* assured a "stock of Groceries probably as extensive as any west of the city of New York."

Benjamin [?] child of Captain and Mrs. Heald's Negro slave, Cicely, born early in 1811 just prior to the Healds's residence at Fort Dearborn; killed and beheaded at the massacre of Aug. 15, 1812. [12, 226]

Benjamin Barton lake schooner under Captain Ludlow; came from Buffalo, NY, calling at Chicago on Aug. 30 and Oct. 23, 1835.

Benjamin Franklin lake schooner that came from Buffalo, NY, calling at Chicago on Oct. 1, 1835.

Bennett, Henry S. real estate speculator in 1834; ✦ speculator, boarded at the Illinois Exchange [Exchange Coffee House].

Bennett, Hiram on 1833 list of early settlers. [319]

Bennett, Samuel C. arrived from New York in 1835; ✦ school teacher, corner of State and Madison streets; also ✦ Mary Bennett, assistant S.C. Bennett. [12]

Bennett, Thomas on 1833 list of early settlers. [319]

Bennett, William early owner of land, prior to 1836, who with John Ludby acquired the SE quarter (160 acres) of Section 32, Township 40 N; and for his own account, 80 acres in the NE quarter, according to Andreas, *History of Chicago*, pp. 112-113, of Section 20, Township 39; ✦ soap boiler.

Benton, Addison P. on 1833 list of early settlers. [12, 319]

Benton, Col. Colbee Chaimberlain (1805-1880) successful business man and frequent traveler of Lebanon, NH, who in 1833 visited Chicago and left a detailed journal of this trip; additional excerpts from his journal [see Bibliography] can be found in conjunction with the following entries: Chicago harbor; Mann, John; Ouilmette, Louis; prairie; and in Chronology, August 1833. [53]

... (Sunday Aug 18) Left Calemic River for Chicago which is about fourteen miles distant. By the way, I

would speak of the Calemic River. It is a fine deep river and navigable fifteen miles from its mouth. With a little expense a fine harbour could be made, even better than one could be made at Chicago. The river is wider and deeper than the Chicago River and can be navigated much farther into the country. The land is cold and marshy about the outlet of the river. There is a very good place to build a town on the lake and there will be one laid out before a great while, and it must be something of a place in time. Mr. Mann claims the best part of the land by a preëmption right. There is some doubt about his claim, and if he does not substantiate it, it will be sold when government bring their lands into market, which will probably be in a year or two. ❖ For some time before we arrived at Chicago we could only see the lighthouse, but as we approached nearer we could see the Fort and one or two other buildings, and we could not see anything more until we left the beach of the lake and rose onto the prairie. There we had a grand view of an extensive prairie, and a very fine view of the town. The prairie was alive with cattle and horses and it looked very pleasant, and the principal street, which we passed through, looked lively and businesslike, altho' we afterwards found out that it was the Sabbath. There did not seem to be much attention paid to the Sabbath. I believe, however, that there was a meeting in a log dwelling or school house. I saw men about the streets as the New England people would be on a week day, and I saw some Indians drunk. They had been fighting and were covered with blood. ❖ We arrived at Chicago about noon and took up our quarters at Mr. Kinzie's new tavern, kept by Mr. Clark. ❖ I shall remain here tomorrow and perhaps longer.

Benton, Lewis   settled in the Calumet region in 1833, and may have been the first permanent resident, with a store on the W bank of the river 60 yards from its mouth; active in land speculation, advertising "Calumet Lots" for sale in the July 29, 1835 *Chicago Democrat* with Chicago agents George Dole and E.K. Hubbard; appointed postmaster of the first Calumet post office in Septem-

ber; built the first hotel in Calumet, known as "Calumet House" and constructed a bridge across the Grand Calumet River in 1836; ♦ speculator.

Berg brothers   five brothers, German Catholic family that immigrated in 1834; members of St. Mary's Church; in the first mayoral election Anton voted in the second ward and G. Berg in the fourth; Joseph later owned an inn on LaSalle Street; ♦ Anton, teamster; Joseph, saddle and harness maker, Charles E. Peck. [12, 342]

Bernard, Epolite J.   on 1833 list of early settlers. [319]

Berry, Benjamin A.   arrived from Ohio in 1835; hardware merchant; he and his wife Lydia M. lost infant children in 1837 and 1840; ♦ Berry, B.A. & Co., dry goods and grocery, South Water Street

Berry Point Trail   one of the major Indian trails of early Chicago, still traceable in the modern street pattern: northward from present Roosevelt Road and Cicero Avenue to the Lake Trail, where Lake Street and Western Avenue intersect.

Berry, Redmond   U.S. Army private at Fort Dearborn; enlisted in July 1806, and was killed at the massacre of Aug. 15, 1812. [12]

Berry, Thomas   arrived from Germany in 1835.

Bersier, John Baptist   *engagé* from Detroit; worked for William H. Wallace at Hardscrabble in 1826 and until his death in April 1827.

Bertrand, B.H.   on 1833 list of early settlers. [319]

Bertrand, Joseph   trader at St. Joseph in the 1820s and 1830s, near Potawatomi chief Topenebe's village; interacted with Chicago traders and advertised in the *Chicago Democrat*; with his Potawatomi wife Madelaine [née Bourassa] had five children (Joseph, Jr.; Benjamin; Laurent; Theresa; and Amable); the children received land grants along the St. Joseph-Kankakee River portage; his family name became the name for a town [Bertrand, MI] on the Michigan/Illinois border, a few miles S of Niles, MI [were the earlier St. Joseph settlement was]. [220]

Besson, Louis   see Bisson, Louis.

Besson, Mary   also: Bisson; see Leigh, Charles.

Best, Henry   German; came in 1831; ➡ Best Avenue (between 1436 Wrightwood Avenue and Diversey Avenue). [12, 728]

Best, William   U.S. Army private at Fort Dearborn; enlisted in April 1806, and was discharged in 1810 as unfit for duty; left the Chicago area. [12]

Bibeau, Louis   also Beebeau, Bibo; at Peoria, 1790; later an Illinois River trader in the employ of the American Fur Co.; like all other Illinois traders, he made annual passages through the Chicago portage. In John Kinzie's account book Bibeau was noted on June 20, 1808; April 28 and June 2, 1809; June 19, 1811; and July 21, 1812. On July 27, 1818, he was employed as an interpreter for one year on the Illinois River, where newly employed Gurdon Hubbard was assigned to him. [354, 404]

Bickerdyke, George B.   (1806-1880) also Bickerdike; from Yorkshire, England; carpenter who arrived on horseback from Cincinnati in 1831; acquired 10 acres that included the SE corner of Lake and Dearborn streets on which he built a shop, selling the land soon after when its value increased; bought 80 acres along the Des Plaines River [near Oak Park] and erected a steam sawmill, partnered with Mark Noble, Jr.; listed as a subscriber to the *Chicago Democrat* in November 1833; married Noble's second daughter, Mary, also from Yorkshire, on Nov. 29, 1833, the Hon. R.J. Hamilton officiating at a double ceremony (with Mark Noble, Jr.; and Charlotte Wesencraft); built a log cabin on the north branch near Elston Avenue; of five children three survived, including their first, George N., born on Oct. 2, 1834; ♦ farmer, West Indiana [Grand] Street

Bickerdyke, Joseph   (c.1819-1903) came in 1831 from Yorkshire, England, likely related to George; married Elizabeth A. Welden in 1849; later bred trotting horses; assessor and road commissioner in the 1850s; died Nov. 6, 1903.

Bickerdyke, Richard, Jr.   owned 80 acres of land

in Section 30, Township 39, prior to 1836, as shown in Andreas, *History of Chicago*, pp. 112-113.

Bickerdyke, Richard, Sr. owned 80 acres of land in Section 30, Township 39, prior to 1836, as shown in Andreas, *History of Chicago*, pp. 112-113.

Bickerdyke & Noble Chicago firm, built a steam sawmill on the E bank of the Des Plaines River in 1831, the only such mill for 20 miles; mill laborers who settled nearby began the communities of Oak Park and River Forest; also see Bickerdyke, George; Noble, Mark, Jr.

Bienville, Jean-Baptiste Le Moyne, seigneur de (1680-1767) see Le Moyne family.

Bigelow, Ellen a young woman in her late teens who arrived at Chicago with her sister, Sarah, on the brig *Illinois* on May 24, 1835, fourteen days out of Buffalo; daughters of Lewis Bigelow, a lawyer from Petersham, MA, who had moved to Peoria several months earlier with other family members; the girls left the following day by stage, arriving two days later in Peoria. Within a month, Ellen detailed their arduous journey in a letter to an aunt, and that relevant to Chicago follows below. Ellen married the lawyer William Frisby at Peoria and their daughter, Louise, was born in 1839. For additional quotations from Ellen's letter, see entries on Frink & Walker, Erie Canal, and prairie. [55a]

... Chicago I don't like at all. The town is low and dirty, though situated advantageously for commercial purposes. I saw only one place in which I would live if they would give me all they possess, and that was Fort Dearborn. I liked that. It is beautifully situated and the grounds and buildings are neat and handsome. A great land fever was raging when we were there, and I am told it has not yet abated. Property changes hands there daily, and it is thought no speculation at all if it doesn't double in value by being retained one night. ❖ I think they are all raving distracted, and if I mistake not, a few years, if not months, will reduce things to their proper level and restore them to their senses. ❖ We left Chicago in the stage for Ottawa, a route of 80 miles across the prairies, and such

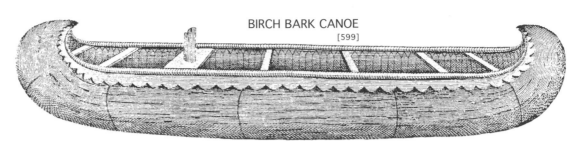

BIRCH BARK CANOE
[599]

traveling never did we behold before. The low prairie about Chicago was entirely flooded with water, and the creeks were swollen to rivers. Nothing in the shape of a bridge greeted our eyes. Streams, large and small, were all to be forded even at the risk of sticking fast in the middle of them. On the banks of the Des Plaines, about ten miles from Chicago, are found a multitude of Indians, gathering for the great council they have been holding....

Bigelow's Building located on the E side of Clark Street, between Lake and South Water, to which the post office was moved in June 1837.

Big Foot Winnebago chief whose village existed at Lake Geneva, formerly Big Foot Lake; his tribe's attacks on white settlers near Prairie du Chien in June 1827, in retaliation for disregard of earlier treaty agreements, precipitated the Winnebago War; there was no bloodshed in Chicago but considerable military and militia activities at Fort Dearborn that led to the regarrison of the fort.

Big Man see Peesotum.

Big Woods timberland along the Fox River, partially within Cook County prior to the creation of Du Page County in 1839. In the spring and summer of 1832, settlers feared that the Potawatomi who camped there would join Black Hawk and fled to Fort Dearborn.

bilious fever see malaria.

Bineteau, Père Julien also Binneteau; Jesuit priest and missionary in Maine in 1693; afterward worked with Fathers Gravier, Pinet and Marest at the *Mission de la Conception* in southern Illinois, and with Father Pinet at the *Mission de l'Ange*

Gardien at Chicago, 1698; wrote an account of the Illinois country in 1699 and died soon after of a febrile illness. [12]

Bingham, Charles K. arrived in 1835; employee of a stage line, likely Frink & Walker; ❖ Frink, Bingham & Co., 123 Lake St.

Birchard, Matthew see Fort Dearborn reservation.

birch bark canoe an Indian invention, light and strong, excellent for portaging; hot pine pitch was used to waterproof; not made in Illinois because the birch tree did not grow there.

Bird, Frederick arrived from New York early in 1833 with members of the Daniel Warren family, and soon married Louisa Warren in Chicago on May 10; moved to Geneva and later to Rock River; they had seven children, all surviving; died c.1851.

birds a number of game bird species were welcome food supplements as well as targets for sport hunting in the early days of the settlement, but many of these are no longer found today. They left their mark in the reports of pioneers and settlers and even in street names and monuments; among them were ducks, eagles, geese, grouse, passenger pigeons, prairie chickens, swans, teals, and wild turkey. For an impression of the abundance of waterfowl in Chicago in April 1829, see the report by Lt. J.G. Furman of Fort Dearborn, reprinted in Hurlbut's *Chicago Antiquities* and excerpted below. For additional information on individual species and the records left about them by early pioneers, see individual entries. [64, 357]

... We passed up the left branch [south branch] *of the Chicago to its source, and thence, in a heavy snowstorm during a night 'as black as Erebus,' through 'Lac Marais'* [Mud Lake] *into the riviere Aux Pleins. ✧ The prairie between those streams is at all times swampy; but during the spring floods, a considerable lake is formed, the waters of which flow simultaneously through the Chicago, the Aux Pleins, and Illinois Rivers, into the great northern lakes, and into the Mississippi. Here, after the waters have subsided, vast quantities of aquatic fowl congregate to feed upon the wild-rice, insects, &c. that abound in it. Swan, geese and brant, passing to and fro in clouds, keep an incessant cackling; ducks of every kind, from the mallard and canvas-back, down to the tiny water-witch and blue-winged teal, add their mite to the 'discord dire,' while hundreds of gulls hover gracefully over, ever and anon plunging their snowy bosoms into the circling waters. In April, myriads of plover and snipe take the place of the aforementioned; still later, great quantities of woodcock grouse, and ortolans, make their appearance in its neighbourhood. ...*

Birkbeck, Morris   the most prominent settler in southern Illinois who arrived in 1817 from England with his family in Edwards County, founding the town of Wanborough on what was soon known as the "English Prairie." Nearby Albion was founded by his neighbor, George Flowers; Albion is existent but Birkbeck's town faded after his death in 1825. *Urbs in Horto*, the inscription on the Chicago seal meaning "city in a garden," may be traced to a description in Birkbeck's book, *Notes on a Journey in America, from the Coast of Virginia to the Territory of Illinois* [1818], in which he expresses his delight after traveling through the large dark forests of southern Indiana: "... prairies, so beautiful with their surrounding woods, as to seem like the creation of fancy; gardens of delight in a dreary wilderness ...." [56, 250]

Bishop, Thomas   arrived from New York in 1835; ◆ bookkeeper, Philo Carpenter. [351]

bison   *Bison bison*; in early reports also called buf-

1808, Anonymous
[418]

falo, oxen, pisikious, or Illinois cattle. Father Marquette's party killed buffalo and deer for meat on their travels, finding both plentiful and he reports them grazing on the banks of the Mississippi in herds that numbered 400 animals. The animal is referred to in the concession La Salle received from the French Crown in 1678. Traveling down the Kankakee River in December 1679, Father Hennepin observed:

It seems this [the prairie] *is the element and the country of the buffalo, herds of two or even of four hundred. The paths by which they have passed are beaten like our great roads. Very fine wool instead of hair, horns almost all black, thicker than cattle's, head of monstrous size, neck short and very thick, sometimes six hands broad. Very fat in autumn, and very succulent. The Indians have this forecast not to drive these animals entirely from their countries, to pursue only those who are wounded, and the others that escape, they suffer to go at liberty without pursuing them further, in order not to alarm them too much. When the Indians have killed any cows, the little calves follow the hunters, and go and lick their hands or fingers; these Indians sometimes take them to their children and after they have played with them, they knock them on the head to eat them. The hoofs of all these little animals are dried and fastened to rods. In their dances they shake and rattle them. ✧ The ordinary skins of these wild cattle weigh from one hundred to a hundred and twenty pounds. The Indians cut off the back and the neck part which is the thickest part of the skin, and they take only the thinnest part of the belly which they dress very neatly, with the brains of all kinds of animals, by means of which they render it as supple as our chamois skins dressed with oil. They paint it with different colors, trim it with white and red*

porcupine quills, and make robes of it to parade in their feasts. In winter they use them to cover themselves especially at night. Their robes which are full of curly wool have a very pleasing appearance.
Uncontrolled hunting rapidly diminished the herds; severe winters with excessive snowfall, especially 1779/1780 and 1806/1808, in which bison are said to have perished by the tens of thousands, contributed to the decline; by 1830 all wild native bison had likely been exterminated in Illinois. Two bronze ▲ sculptures of the American buffalo exist at the E entrance of Humboldt Park; ➡ Buffalo Avenue (3300E). [341]

Bisson, Louis also: Besson, Bieson; early French trader who passed yearly through the Chicago Portage from approximately 1778 on; known from 1818 writings left by Gurdon S. Hubbard and others; frequently traded with John Kinzie at Chicago. [354]

Bisson, Mary also: Beeson, Besson; see Leigh, James.

Bisson, Pierre Sr. see Buisson, Louis.

Black Bird also known as Siggenauk, Letourneau, Mukudapenais, or Mucketepennese; Potawatomi chief from the Milwaukee area, but originally from St. Joseph; pro-American in 1777, but led the attack that became the Fort Dearborn massacre in 1812, following the strategy set by Nescotnemeg; after the attack, negotiated with Captain Heald for surrender; for his services he received the British loyalty medal. [226]

black code see slavery.

black gown term used by the Indians when addressing or referring to any Jesuit missionary.

Black Hawk (1767-1838) Ma-ka-tai-me-she-kia-kiak; anti-American leader of the Sauk Indians, and leader in the Black Hawk War of 1832; did not recognize the Treaty of St. Louis of 1804 under which his tribe was to move to the W bank of the Mississippi River; the desperate decision of this intelligent leader to defy the United States authorities and precipitate a war that would lead to de-

struction of most of his tribe can be understood only in the context of the emotional climate then prevalent among his people; as an illustration of this climate, see the following letter by a Fox chief [Apanose] to William Clark describing one of many rumors then circulating among the Indians; ➡ Black Hawk Street (1500 N). [211, 365, 520, 635]
[July 22, 1832] *Father, – We will relate one of these fables: – We were told that the Americans were determined shortly to lay hands on all our males, both young and old, and deprive them of those parts which are said to be essential to courage; then, a horde of Negro men were to be brought from the South, to whom our wifes, sisters, and daughters were to be given, for the purpose of raising a stock of Slaves to supply the demand in this country, where Negroes are scarce. ✧ We assure you, Father, that this, and many other similar stories have had a great influence on the minds of all, or at least of most, of that unfortunate band, which seems now abandoned from heaven and humanity. For the evidence of this fact, I will refer you to the enthusiastic madness with which our women urged their husbands to this desparate resort; & secondly, influenced by a belief of the above fables, they have uniformly treated the dead bodies of the unfortunate white men who have fallen into their hands, with the same indignities which they themselves so much dreaded.* [365]

Black Hawk War on April 5, 1832, Chief Black Hawk led approximately 1,000 Sauk and Mesquakie warriors and their families eastward across the Mississippi into Illinois and Wisconsin between Fort Madison and Fort Armstrong to reclaim land he maintained was illegally signed over to the United States in 1804, territory thereafter forbidden to Indian habitation. Hostilities began in mid May [see Indian Creek] and ended September 30 with the complete rout of the Indians; of 1,000 warriors only 150 survived. The United States military, 850 strong, were led by Gen. Winfield Scott; officers included Jefferson Davis, Albert Sidney Johnston, William Hamilton (son

BLACK HAWK

of Alexander Hamilton), Robert Anderson (of Fort Sumter fame), and Nathan Boone (son of Daniel Boone). Abraham Lincoln served in the Illinois militia company. For those too far S of Chicago, small fortifications were devised from Joliet to La Porte, all in anticipation of hostilities. Fear brought numerous frightened farming families to Fort Dearborn in search of protection and by May 10 about 700 people had crowded into the fort; 15 children were born in Chicago during this time. Seven militia companies were organized in Cook County and served under the company commanders, Capt. Gholson Kercheval (Chicago, May 3), Capt. Harry Boardman (May 24), Capt. J.S.C. Hogan (May 24), Capt. James Walker (Walker's Grove, June 19), Capt. Joseph Napier (Napierville, July 19), Capt. Holden Seission (July 23), and Capt. Jesse B. Brown (no written record preserved). Colonel

Owen, the Indian agent, initially commanded the fort and the local militia, assisted by Gholson Kercheval and Colonel Hamilton; Maj. William Whistler came with two companies of regulars from Niagara and reoccupied the fort, expelling settlers into the settlement. The soldiers under General Scott arrived July 8 from the east on the steamers *Sheldon Thompson* and *William Penn*, and brought cholera [for the ravages of the ensuing epidemic, see cholera]; with the arrival of the cholera, families hastened home; for an eyewitness account see Penrose, Mary A. The fort became a hospital and 200 cholera cases were admitted, 58 resulting in death. Warfare ended with the Treaty of Fort Armstrong that September, and its eviction of the Indians from Illinois and eastern Iowa. [12, 50, 211, 635, 714]

Statement that Black Hawk gave after he was captured at the end of the war:

My warriors fell around me. It began to look dismal. I saw my evil-day at hand. The sun rose clear on us in the morning; at night it sunk in a dark cloud, and looked like a ball of fire. This was the last sun that shone on Black Hawk. He is now a prisoner to the white man, but he can stand the torture. He is not afraid of death. He is no coward—Black Hawk is an Indian. He has done nothing of which an Indian need to be ashamed. He has fought the battles of his country against the white man, who came year after year to cheat his people and take away their lands. You know the cause of our making war. It is known to all white men. They ought to be ashamed of it. The white men despise the Indians, and drive them from their homes. But the Indians are not deceitful. Indians do not steal. Black Hawk is satisfied. He will go to the world of spirits contented. He has done his duty. His Father will meet and reward him. The white men do not scalp the heads, but they do worse—they poison the heart. It is no pure with them. His countrymen will not be scalped, but they will in a few years become like the white man, so that you can not hurt them; and there must be, as in the white settlements, as many officers as men, to take care of them and keep them in order. Farewell to my nation! Farewell to Black Hawk!

Black Horn Tavern see Wentworth, Elijah, Jr.

Black Jim also Black James; one of Kinzie's Negro slaves, brought by him to Chicago in 1804; first listed as Black James in Kinzie's account book on Aug. 20, 1805; at the time of the massacre of 1812, he was in the boat as a rower; was subsequently traded by Kinzie —together with slave Henry—to obtain Captain Heald from the Indians; died about 1832 or 1833. [12, 404]

Black Meat see Battles, Joe.

Black Partridge also known as Mkedepoke or Muck-otey-pokee; elder brother of Waubansee; chief of the Illinois River Potawatomi whose village was on the S side of the Illinois River, opposite the head of Lake Peoria; neutral in 1776, but friendly to the Americans during the 1812 war; warned Captain Heald of danger prior to the Fort Dearborn massacre, but could not avert the tragedy, able only to rescue Margaret Helm and arrange for the release from Indian captivity of Mrs. Leigh and her infant after the massacre; worked as clerk and interpreter in Toronto, Canada, between 1846 and his death in 1863.

black residents and visitors prior to 1836 several individuals of African descent had come to Chicago; Jean Baptiste Point de Sable (1784); Jeffrey Nash (1803); Black Jim and Athena (1804); Joe Battles (1809); Cicely (1810); Pepper (1812); Henry (1812); George White (1833); Oliver C. Hanson (1834); and Nelson P. Perry (1834). See individual entries for details.

blacksmiths an entry on Sept. 3, 1804, within John Kinzie's account book lists a man named Roberts as Fort Dearborn's blacksmith; also see Jean Baptiste Mirandeau (1811), James Kinzie (1821), Joseph Pothier (1822 or earlier), David McKee (1823), Archibald Caldwell (1827), William See (1830), Israel P. Blodgett (1832), Asahel Pierce (1833), Clemens Stose (1833), Lemuel Brown (1833), Mathias Mason (1833), James C. Hatch (Lisle 1833), Leander French (1834), and William Harman (1835).

Blackstone, John announced in the Nov. 26, 1834 *Chicago Democrat* a public sale of the personal effects of Samuel Holland, deceased, on December 24, that included a horse and traveling trunk.

Blair, George arrived from New York in August 1835 with his partner Edward Manierre; in the September 5 *Chicago American* they placed an advertisement for their tailoring establishment, Manierre & Blair, located in a store on Clark Street near Lake; ✦ tailor, (Manierre & Blair, 23 Clark St.) 260 State St.

Blake, Levi on Dec. 30, 1835, submitted a proposal to the town board to build a fire engine house for $225, underbidding Dickinson & Sheppard; awarded the contract on January 23 and completed the job by the following autumn. [12, 28]

Blake, S. Sanford arrived from Burlington, VT on June 15, 1834, later moved to Racine, WI, where he was living in 1885. [12, 351]

Blanchard, Francis G. from England, arrived in 1834; owner of 80 acres of land in Section 34, Township 39, prior to 1836, as shown in Andreas, *History of Chicago*, pp. 112-113; advertised as house and land agent in the *Chicago Democrat* on May 14, 1834, with an office on Lake Street opposite Dr. Temple's; ✦ real estate dealer, Lake Street

Blasy, Bernard [Bernhard Blasey?] from Germany, arriving in 1835; ✦ baker, Randolph Street; died in Chicago in 1883. [12]

Bleeker, James auctioneer; his ✱ map of "73 Building Lots in Chicago to be sold at Auction by James Bleeker & Sons on Thursday, 22nd of October [1835]" was published by Peter Mesier in New York [map at the Newberry Library, Chicago; eds.]. [164]

Blisse, C. a performer who entertained Chicagoans with a performance on June 19, 1834, postponed until then "owing to the badness of weather"; see entry for concert. [482]

blocks (city blocks, numerical system) in 1830, when surveyor James Thompson plotted the intersecting streets of the original town, he numbered the resulting blocks 1 though 58 [see map on page 44]; all are located in the southern half of Section 9, Township 39; later additions to the town have individual systems of block numbering, each beginning with number one.

Blodgett, Asiel Z. also Avice; son of Israel, born at Fort Dearborn on Sept. 10, 1832, during the Black Hawk scare; raised at Downer's Grove; later a railroad worker and captain in the Civil War. [218a, 319]

Blodgett, Caleb from Monroe, OH; father of Tyler K.; placed a notice in the *Chicago American*, Oct. 17, 1835, requesting information concerning the disappearance of his son Selvy E., enroute to Buffalo in 1833; ✦ brick maker, *North Water Street* near Wells.

Blodgett, Henry William (1821-1905) from Amherst, MA; arrived by wagon team in 1830 with his parents, Avis and Israel Blodgett; in the following spring the family settled at Dupage town; ✦ clerk, Philip F.W. Peck; later became a lawyer, served in both houses of the Illinois legislature, strongly opposed slavery, and was made a federal judge by President Grant in 1870. [60, 61, 218a]

Blodgett, Israel P. (1797-1864) also Bladget; blacksmith from Amherst, MA with his wife Avis (née Dodge) and son, Henry W.; farmer in 1831 near the Du Page forks, three miles S of the Naper settlement and forging the first cast-iron plow suitable for prairie use; during the 1832 Black Hawk War served as corporal in the militia company under Captain Napier; in 1835 bought land and moved to Downer's Grove; known as an ardent abolitionist. His memories were collected by his daughter Corac, and are preserved at the Downers Grove Historical Society. [13, 60, 61, 218a, 314a, 657a]

Blodgett, Tyler K. brickmaker; son of Caleb; arrived from Amherst, MA in the spring of 1833 and built a kiln; employed the German immigrant brickmaker Heinrich Lampmann, and operated ★★★ **Chicago's 1st** brickyard on the north bank, between Clark and Dearborn streets; built his brick residence—★★★ **Chicago's 1st**—on South Water Street, across the river from his brickyard, a structure 20 feet square, one and a half stories tall; late in 1835 filed a claim for wharfing privileges for lots 1 and 2, block 6; ✦ tavern-keeper, Michigan Avenue [12, 28]

Blood, Sullivan purchased lot 4 in block 34 from William A. Bell, about 1832 [see map on page 44].

Bloomingdale see Duncklee's Grove.

Blow, Lewis voted on July 24, 1830 [see Chronology].

Blue Earth local Indian who always painted his face a "ghostly blue" and kept to himself during the years 1816-1818, witnessed and described by Mrs. Susan Callis. [74]

Blue Island a wooded outcropping of pre-Glenwood moraine, nearly 12 miles S of Chicago center (between 87th and 130th streets, and E of the Calumet/Saganashkee portage), originally stretched 2 miles N to S and about 2 miles E to W, rising suddenly some 30 to 40 feet high, surrounded by swampy prairie; at the southern end were several fine springs. In an early *Chicago Democrat* editorial [1834], John Calhoun observed: "... when viewed from a distance, [it] appears shrouded in an azure mist or vapor, hence, we suppose, the appellation Blue Island." Earlier, it was an island in glacial Lake Chicago that preceded Lake Michigan. Favored by Indians who hunted there until 1837, the locale remained unsettled by whites until 1833-34. The community of Blue Island that developed (at the southern edge of the ridge where the Vincennes Road crossed Stony Creek) was for years the largest town in southern Cook County; later a regional center for the wool, brewing, and brick industries; ➡ Blue Island Avenue.

Blue Jacket legendary Ohio Shawnee war chief; born Marmaduke Van Swearingen to a white frontier family, he grew up with a burning hatred of Americans; made plans in 1794 to move to "Chicagou on the Illinois River" in British-controlled territory after Gen. Anthony Wayne's defeat of British-backed Indian forces at Fallen Timbers, near present-day Toledo, but abandoned them because the defeated Indians were forced to cede a 6-mile-square tract at the mouth of the Chicago River to the United States.

Board of Health formed on June 19, 1835, primarily in response to the 1832 cholera epidemic; its members were James Curtis, B.S. Morris, E. Peck, B. King, A.N. Fullerton, Dr. John T. Temple, J. Jackson, and H. Hugunin; preceded by the [see] Cholera Vigilante Committee of 1834. When the cholera failed to return (the next epidemic would not be until 1849), the board became inactive; in 1837 the new town charter provided for a permanent board of health, resulting in its revival. For the next two decades the board concerned itself primarily with creating a record of vital health statistics; not until 1867 did the board become an active force in public health. An Illinois State Board of Health was not created until May 25, 1877.

boarding houses see taverns, hotels, and boarding houses.

Boardman, C. a member of the "Washington Volunteers," a Chicago fire brigade existing prior to the incorporation of the town in 1833. [12]

Boardman, Harry farmer from Vermont; with Bailey Hobson, built the first grist mill two miles S of [now] Naperville, along the Joliet Road and the Du Page River in 1831; resident of the Naper settlement; during the Black Hawk War commanded, as captain, the third company of Cook County voluntary militia under Maj. David Bailey; stationed at Fort Dearborn, the unit began on May 24 and disbanded June 11, 1832; farmed in Du Page Township [Will County]. [319, 314a, 714, 734]

boats for the various types of boats used on rivers and lakes near Chicago prior to 1836, see keelboat, barge, *bateau*, *piroque*, northern canoe, birch bark canoe, Mackinaw boat; for the larger vessels on Lake

Michigan, see entries under sloop, schooner, brig, sailing vessels and steamships.

bobcat *Felix rufus*; early Illinois settlers referred to them as wildcats or lynxes, rarely bobcats; frequent in counties with heavy timber stands, but by 1900 they had disappeared. *Felix lynx*, the Canada lynx, probably never existed in Illinois; its mention by early Illinois settlers must be attributed to naive terminology. [341]

Boeske, Heinrich German immigrant, first attested to as having lived in Chicago in 1834. [342]

Bogardus, John L. Peoria county assessor in 1825, whose list of assessments provides valuable evidence about Chicago residents of that year; see taxation. Bogardus lived in Peoria where he ran a ferry and owned a fish oil production enterprise utilizing Lake Peoria fish; became justice of the peace in 1826. [12]

Boilvin & Le Beau "quite a large confectionary establishment" as described by Andrew J. Vieau; see Boilvin, Nicholas.

Boilvin, Nicholas American Indian agent at Prairie du Chien c.1800-1812, a difficult position in a British-leaning town. [7]

Boilvin, Nicholas baker, arrived from New York in 1835 with wife Betsey; partner in a confectionary store, Boilvin & Le Beau on Clark and South Water streets; on Sept. 16, 1836, the Boilvins' 19-month-old only daughter, Helen Maria, died. [733]

Boisbriant, Pierre Dugué, sieur de appointed the first governor of the "Illinois Country" in 1718 by the *Compagnie d'Orient*; built Fort de Chartres in 1720 and continued as commandant until 1725, when he became acting governor of Louisiana. [12, 665]

Boiseley Canadian friend and travel companion of John H. Fonda, who accompanied Fonda on a mail delivery errand from Fort Howard to Fort Dearborn in the winter of 1827-28. [251]

Boisrondel, François de La Salle's trusted storekeeper at Fort St. Louis (Starved Rock); member of La Salle's 1681-82 expedition to the mouth of the Mississippi, passing through Chicagoland in January 1682, on the way south; among the group with Henri Joutel that reached Chicago on Sept. 25, 1687, on the way from Texas to Canada.

Bols, William attended the estate sale of W.H. Wallace on May 10, 1827 and acquired a castor hat for $2.94. [220]

Boliveu, Nicholas was granted a license to sell goods in Cook County on June 6, 1831, at the county seat (Chicago).

Bolles, Nathan Howard arrived from New York in 1835, likely Peter's brother; one of the delegates who prepared the city charter in 1837; ✦ county commissioner, overseer of the poor, Lake Street; in 1885 his widow (Sarah K.) lived in Cleveland, OH. [12, 351]

Bolles, Peter (1790-1839) from New York; resident by November 1835, when he was elected trustee of the first Presbyterian *church* and applied for wharfing privileges; married to Harriet Elizabeth (née Rogers); chosen alderman in the newly chartered city in 1837; ✦ school inspector, Wells Street near Randolph; died in New York City during August 1839; Harriet died in childbirth early in 1840, infant Elizabeth survived. [12, 28, 351]

Bonasa umbellus ruffed grouse; see grouse.

Bond, Ezra arrived in 1832; member of the Chicago company during the 1832 Black Hawk War; died before 1852.

Bond, Heman arrived from New Hampshire in 1833; lived in a log and sod cabin at the end of Monroe Street where mid-July he accommodated [see] Charles M. Gray and others overnight; ✦ horse dealer, Adams Street near State; died in 1855. [12, 351, 733, 734]

Bond, Shadrach (1773-1832) farmer who lived near Kaskaskia before he became the first governor of the state of Illinois on Oct. 6, 1818, serving until 1822; earlier, had served as the first delegate from the Illinois Territory to Congress; ➡ Bond Avenue (3134 E). [12]

Bond, William arrived in 1832; member of the Chicago company during the 1832 Black Hawk War; ✦ laborer; later moved to Somanauk, DeKalb County where he was still living in 1885. [12]

Bonin, Augustus also Bonna; married Josette Franche before Judge Caton on Sept. 20, 1834; a subsequent notice in the *Chicago Democrat*, Sept. 22, 1935, announced: "Whereas my wife Josette, has left my house without any reasonable cause, this is to caution all persons from crediting her on my account, as I will pay no debts of her contracting."

Bonnell, J. D. visited Chicago, arriving on foot Aug. 25, 1835; later lived in Lake City, MN; in a 1879 letter [written to the *Chicago Times*, reprinted in Andreas], he described his experience:

... On arriving at Chicago I stopped overnight at the Mansion House. In the morning I commenced looking over the town and prospecting for a boarding-place, and to learn what I could find to do. The hotels were all pretty full, and their prices ranging too high for my finances, I walked across the street, where the first thing that attracted my attention was the sound of a violin. On entering a small wooden structure, there stood behind a rudely constructed counter Mr. Dalton, a recent arrival from Columbus, Ohio, a former tailor there, but who had now opened a liquor shop, and played the fiddle to attract customers. ❖ Passing east, toward the mouth of the river, was the Lake House in course of construction, east of which was the residence of Dr. Kimball [actually Dr. Kimberly; eds.], who was a partner of Mr. Pruyne in a drug store on South Water Street. Mr. Pruyne was State Senator. Opposite Dr. Kimball's was Hunter & Hinsdale's warehouse. Adjoining on the west was Newberry & Dole's warehouse, and on one part of the latter building was the hat store of McCormick & Moon, of Detroit, Mr. Moon being the partner of the Chicago store. In the back part of the store was Jesse Butler's tailor shop. In turning the corner of Dr. Kimball's residence, away to the northeast, among the sand-hills, close by the lake shore, stood a small yellow house, occupied by Parnick [Patrick] Kelsey as a boarding

LEVI DAY BOONE, M.D.

house, ostensibly run by Eve, Parnick's wife, for Mr. Kelsey was a sub-contractor in removing stumps and grubs, preparatory to the grading of the street on the North Side, through the swamps and bogs, which at that time rendered traveling almost impossible. But as Mrs. Kelsey had all the borders she could accommodate, I was obliged to seek other quarters. ✧ Dearborn Street at the time I write was the "lively" street, for Garrett's auction-room was located there, on the west side of the street, close to Cox & Duncan's clothing store, just opposite to which were Mr. Greenleaf's auction-rooms. To the latter place I was want to go of evenings and bid off town and city lots, having the next day in which to secure a purchaser, and in case I failed to sell for an advance of my purchase I returned at night and paid Mr. Greenleaf a dollar and the property was offered again for sale. ✧ The winter of 1835-1836 was a gay one for Chicago. Mr. Jackeax had a dancing-school at the New York House once a week, which called out the elite of the city. Lincoln's coffee-house was the popular drinking place, situated, I think, on the corners of St. Clair and Wells streets. Mr. Lincoln had a favorite horse, an iron grey, and quite fleet on foot, particularly so when in pursuit of a prairie wolf. Many times in the winter of 1835-1836 I have seen Mr. Lincoln mount his horse when a wolf was in sight on the prairie toward Bridgeport, and within an hour's time come in with the wolf, having run him down with his horse and taken his life with a hatchet or other weapon. ... [12]

Bonnet, Augustin   also Austin or Augtin Banny; bought a Scottish cap for 25 cents at the estate sale of W.H. Wallace on April 27, 1827; voted on July 24, 1830 [see Chronology].

bookbinders   see Ariel Bowman, Hugh Ross.

Boone, Levi Day, M.D.   (1808-1882) great-nephew of Daniel Boone; born in Kentucky, graduated from the medical department of the Transylvania University of Louisville, KY; arrived in 1835 [according to Chicago Medical Society publications, or in 1836, according to A.N. Waterman], and in the following year helped organize the Cook County Medical Society and was elected secretary at its first meeting on Oct. 3, 1836. In March 1833, Boone married Louisa M. Smith, daughter of Judge Theophilus Smith of the Supreme Court of Illinois and on Sept. 13, 1839, they lost their only daughter, Clarissa Ann, at the age of nine months; ✦ physician, [49] State Street, corner of Washington Street; in partnership with Dr. Charles V. Dyer, although they held strongly differing views on slavery, Dyer being an ardent abolitionist, and Boone giving a series of lectures in support of the scriptural warrant for human slavery [see Bibliography, A.N. Waterman]. On April 15, 1850, Boone was elected the first president of the newly formed Medical Society of Chicago; in 1855 became mayor of Chicago and served one year; trustee of the University of Chicago and an incorporator of Rosehill Cemetery; died in Chicago on Jan. 24, 1882; in 1885 his widow lived at 3029 Michigan Ave. [12, 351]

Bordenois, Augustin   *engagé* from Detroit; worked for William H. Wallace at Hardscrabble in 1826 and until his death in April 1827.

Boston   armed British schooner patrolling lakes Michigan, Huron, and Erie during the period of British control; built at Navy Island in 1764. [48]

Bosworth, Increase   with Alfred Edwards as Edwards & Bosworth, first advertised through agent [see] J.H. Phelps in the Oct. 28, 1835, Chicago Democrat; ✦ general store, South Water Street

Botsford, Jabez Kent   also John Kent; born c.1812, arrived in 1833 from Connecticut; advertised in the *Chicago Democrat* on Feb. 18, 1834 that he had opened a store "next door to Graves' tavern", and had for sale "dried peaches, butter, lard and loaf sugar" and tin ware from Detroit – "Double Patent reflecting Bakers, a first rate article" and coffee pots, milk pans, dish kettles, dippers, graters, &c. on February 25 at his variety store on the corner of Dearborn and Lake streets; on April 22 he commenced a Tin, Sheet Iron and Stove Manufactory, but also sold pork at the same location,

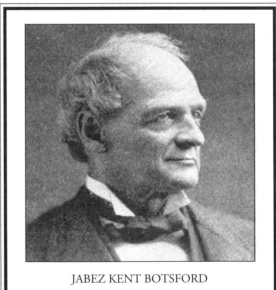

JABEZ KENT BOTSFORD

advertising as [Alexander] Fullerton & Botsford; was successful as a land speculator; yet maintaining the manufactory alone, announced in the September 30 *Chicago Democrat* that he had just returned fromNew York "with heavy stock of Tin Plate, Sheet Iron, Copper" and that he had "now on hand a large assortment of STOVES (of all descriptions) … &c. &c.;" on October 7 was among the first members of the "Pioneer" hook and ladder company, a voluntary fire brigade; married Minerva Kimball at the Naper settlement on Nov. 4, 1835; ✦ Botsford & [Cyrenus] Beers, copper, tin and sheet iron; in 1850, served on a committee that established Northwestern University; in 1885 lived at 1704 Michigan Ave. [12, 351]

Boucha, Henry   also Bouche; served during the 1832 Black Hawk War in the Chicago company under Capt. G. Kercheval. [714]

bounty lands   see Military Tract.

Bourassa, Daniel   born 1780 into a prominent family at Mackinac; son of Daniel Bourassa and Marguerite Bertrand [The wife of the St. Joseph trader Joseph Bertrand was Madelaine Borasseau, possibly a different spelling of the same name; *eds.*], brother of Leon; trader and resident at Chicago in 1817; justice of the peace; married to an Indian, then later married Theotis Arnwaiskie (May 20, 1826), John Kinzie officiating; resided was on the E side of the south branch of the river, not far from the Forks; his name appears on a poll list in 1826 and as voter on August 7; in April the following year, attended the estate sale after W.H. Wallace's death; in 1833 his many children received government stipends: Joseph Napoleon, Mark, Jude, Theresa, Stefan, Gabriel, Alexander, James, Eli, Jerome, and M.D. Bourassa. [12]

Bourassa, Joseph Napoleon   son of Daniel; present at the Treaty of Chicago of 1833.

Bourassa, Leon   also Bourissa; born in 1799, son of Daniel Bourassa, Sr. and Marguerite Bertrand, brother of Daniel; between 1818 and 1819 worked for the American Fur Co. as a boatman on Lake Huron; early resident who assisted with the inventory of the W.H. Wallace estate on April 4-5, 1827; lived immediately S of the Sauganash Hotel in 1830; in 1830, purchased canal lots 1 and 2 in block 44, and yet owner in 1833 [see map on page 44]; listed as voter on July 24 and Aug. 2, 1830, and in April 1833; also that month, representing a family of three, his name was included on the petition by Catholic citizens to Bishop Rosati in St. Louis, asking that a priest be assigned to them; married to a Potawatomi woman named Marguerite, with whom he had a son named Joel; Father St. Cyr performed an ecclesiastical burial for an infant son, Jean Baptiste, in July 1835; the family lived in a cabin on land owned at [Forest Park], where a ▲ monument [see Monuments] in the Forest Home Cemetery commemorates Bourassa and his Indian relations. [12]

Bourassa Mark   son of Daniel; married by Father St. Cyr to Josette Chevalier in March 1835, as listed in Catholic church records.

Bourbonais, Antoine   an elder independent Illinois River trader in 1818 competing against Gurdon Hubbard of the American Fur Co., but in 1821 the company employed him to consolidate its monopoly; traded at Peoria and also on the Kankakee River; lived at the Portage des Sioux, MO in 1838. [259]

Bourbonnais, François, Sr.   also Bourbonne; a French-Potawatomi believed to have settled in 1812, his house was built in 1811 or 1812, close to and SW of the fort; his wife's first name was Cattice [also Catishe]; bought "by indenture" from John Kinzie one "Negro wench"; both he and his son, François, Jr., were licensed to keep a tavern at Peoria in 1825-26 and later were beneficiaries under the Chicago Treaty of 1833, receiving one section at Soldiers' Village. [226, 567, 697]

Bourbon Springs   originally *Belle Fountain*, a term frequently used by early French settlers for several natural springs in Illinois; in the Des Plaines River valley, the name was given to a spring on Stephen Forbes' homestead at [Riverside]; when J.B. Beaubien was elected colonel of the state militia of Cook County on June 7, 1834, at Forbes's home, a celebration thereafter was improvised by emptying kegs of bourbon into the well spring, and from then on it was known as Bourbon Springs.

Bourdon, Jean   see Autray, Jean François Bourdon, sieur de.

Bowen, Erastus S.   arrived in 1833 from New York; on December 22, he and his wife Emeline lost a daughter, Safera Amelia, to scarlet fever at the Naper settlement [*Chicago Democrat*]; in 1835 his name was on a school-related petition signed on September 19; ✦ city collector, corner of South Water Street and Michigan Avenue; still living in Chicago in 1878. [12, 351]

Bowen, James   U.S. Army private at Fort Dearborn, enlisted in January 1808, killed at the 1812 massacre. [226]

Bowen, Joseph   corporal at Fort Dearborn under Captain Heald; had initially enlisted in April 1806; survived the massacre of Aug. 15, 1812, with a wound in his left upper arm; captured by the Indians and later ransomed. Thomas Forsyth and Antoine Le Clair, Sr., encountered him at Sandy Creek in April 1813, yet held captive among some Potawatomi and the only literate person able to read a recent British letter summoning the tribe's warriors to Detroit. [109, 226]

Bowers, Mr.   entertainer—*Professeur de Tours Amusant*—who came through town and advertised in the *Chicago Democrat* a performance [for 50 cents] on Monday, Feb. 24, 1834, at Dexter Graves' boarding house; note a sampling of his innumerable feats within the accompanying advertisement. [482]

Bowles, James   from Peoria; came to the estate sale of François Le Mai in Chicago on May 10, 1828 and bought a silver watch for $6.50. [220]

Bowman, Ariel   (1786-1844) Montreal bookbinder, publisher and bookseller; had moved to Duncklee's Grove by 1837, and to Chicago in 1840

EXHIBITION.

*Joy hath its limits, we but borrow
One hour of mirth, from months of sorrow.*

THE Ladies' and Gentlemen of Chicago, are most respectfully informed that Mr. Bowers, *Professeur de tours Amusant*, has arrived in town, and will give an Exhibition at the house of Mr. D. Graves, on Monday evening next.

PART FIRST.

Mr. Bowers will fully personate Monsieur *Chaubert*, the celebrated *Fire King*, who so much astonished the people of Europa, and go thro' his wonderful Chemical Performance. He will draw a red hot iron across his tongue, hands, &c. and will partake of a comfortable warm supper, by eating fire balls, burning sealing wax, live coals of fire, melted lead. He will dip his fingers in molted lead, and make use of a red hot spoon to convey the same to his mouth.

PART SECOND.

Mr. Bowers will introduce many very amusing feats of *Ventriloquism* and *Legerdemain*, many of which are original, and too numerous to mention. Admittance 50 cents, children half price.

Performance to commence at early candle light. Seats will be preserved for Ladies, and every attention paid to the comfort and convenience of the spectators. Tickets to be had at the bar.

—★★★ Chicago's 1st bookbinder.

Boyer, Cecilia   adopted daughter of John K. Boyer; married Joseph Matteson June 10, 1840, at Chicago.

Boyer, Charles E.   merchant, arrived June 1833; ✦ clerk on the canal; married Elizabeth Runyon on April 21, 1840; removed to Lockport.

Boyer, James Aurant   son of [see] Boyer, John K.

Boyer, John K.   arrived from Pensylvania on May 26, 1833, with his wife Elizabeth (née Aurant), and three children: Valentine Aurant, James A., and Maria; became street commissioner later that year and supervisor of roads and bridges in 1834; provided the first rock to begin construction of the harbor piers; became a business partner of Madore

Beaubien, who married Maria Dec. 4, 1834 [divorce proceedings were listed in Cook County, 1843]; a notice in the Sept. 3, 1834, *Chicago Democrat* announced his July 7 circuit court suit in which he sought payment for "12 pieces of cotton sheeting and about 30 lbs. of coffee" from five fellow townsmen; was one of three commissioners appointed by the ninth General Assembly of the state of Illinois on Jan. 20, 1835, "to view, survey, mark and locate a [state] road from Bloomington in M'Lean county, to the town of Chicago on lake Michigan" for two dollars per day throughout the time required; had a log cabin on South Water Street, near Newberry & Dole, where he filed a claim for wharfing privileges for the W half of lot 3, block 4 late in 1835; ✦ coroner, South Water Street, near Clark; died in 1843. [12, 28, 728]

Boyer, Maria   see Boyer, John K.; Beaubien, Madore.

Boyer, Valentine Aurant, M.D.   (1814-1890) son of John K. Boyer, arrived with his parents and siblings from Pensylvania on May 26, 1833; at that time a medical student, after his first course, which he had attended at the University of Pensylvania, from which he eventually graduated in 1836; ✦ South Water Street near Clark; became asst. surgeon of the City Guards, 16th Regiment of the Illinois Volunteers in 1840; served on the first board of trustees of the First German Lutheran Church. To facilitate his practice Boyer maintained a drugstore until its destruction by fire in 1871; served as justice of the peace from 1844 to 1852, and as surveyor of the Chicago port under President Pierce; married Mary Catherine Specht on Oct. 30, 1847; retired in 1880; in 1885 his address was 490 Fullerton Ave. A detailed letter, written in 1882 to a cousin, describes his family's experiences on the road to and in the early village [see part of the account following entries on Bailly, Joseph and Mann, Arkash Sambli]. [12, 351, 728]

Brackett, E.C.   advertised a "New wholesale wine and liquor store" on Dearborn Street in the June

VALENTINE AURANT BOYER, M.D.

27, 1835, *Chicago American*; signed up with the "Pioneer" hook and ladder company, a voluntary fire brigade, the following autumn.

Bradain, John B.   voted on Nov. 25, 1830 [see Chronology].

Bradford, Harriet   wife of William H. who served as a second lieutenant in Capt. H. Seission's company July 23 to Aug. 15, 1832; unclaimed letter notices appeared on Jan. 1 and on April 2, 1834 in the *Chicago Democrat*; also in the January 1 *Chicago Democrat*, a notice identified Harriet as administrator for her husband's estate; a final notice appeared Sept. 17, 1834.

Bradley, Asa F.   mechanic; in the winter of 1836-37 was commissioned by county surveyor Amos Bailey to create a ✱ real estate map of Chicago that included all new subdivisions; the map was printed by N. Currier in New York in 1837 [within the Chicago Historical Society's collections, comparable to E.B. Talcott's ✱ map of 1836]; ✦ city surveyor, Morrison's Row, Clark Street [164]

Bradley, Cyrus P.   came in 1833; ✦ check clerk,

H. Norton & Co.'s warehouse; went north to Racine; returned in 1848 and became city collector.

Bradley, David   born c.1809; engineer from Syracuse, NY; arrived in October 1835, and immediately built, together with William H. Stow, an iron foundry for the firm Jones, King & Co. on the south branch bank at Polk Street; ✦ plowmaker, Asahel Pierce; later made the first Chicago steam engines; in 1885 lived at 63 N Desplaines St. [12, 351]

Bradley, Maj. Hezekiah   Third Infantry; Virginia native; led two companies in the construction of the second Fort Dearborn in 1816; gathered then the bleached bones of the 1812 massacre victims, still scattered among the sand dunes, and buried them; served as commander of the fort from June 1816 until May 1817, and again from June 1820 to January 1821; died in 1826 at the age of 40; ➡ Bradley Place (3732 N).

Bradley, J.C., M.D.   surgeon-dentist who advertised services in the *Chicago American* on June 20, 1835, and later partnered Dr. Kennicott.

Bradwell, Thomas   from Loughborough, England; arrived from New York via Jacksonville with his wife Elizabeth and son in June 1834; settled at [Wheeling].

Bradwell, James Bolesworth   (1828-1907) arrived with his parents from England in June 1834; would become a lawyer and eventually a probate judge and Illinois state legislator; founded and edited *Chicago Legal News*; married Myra Colby in 1852; still lived in the city in 1878. [12]

Brady, Samuel P.   son of Gen. H. Brady; settled and built a house on the Fort Dearborn reservation in 1832; listed as one of the settlers who received cash awards as a result of the Treaty of Chicago, 1833; listed as a subscriber to the *Chicago Democrat* in November 1833; on Nov. 21, 1835, petitioned for suspension of the sale of wharfing privileges; in the December 23 *Chicago Democrat* placed a request for "50 live Grouse," for which he

would pay a liberal price, to be delivered at his store. [28]

Brady, Madame   see Sainte Ange, Pilette de.

Brainard, Daniel, M.D.   (1812-1866) born in Whitesboro, NY; received his medical degree from Jefferson Medical College, Philadelphia, where he had studied under Dr. Benjamin Rush; came on horseback in the autumn of either 1836 [Kinney and Ingals] or 1835 [Caton and Chicago Medical Society], and rented office space from the lawyer J.D. Caton; in 1837 he obtained a charter for Rush Medical College [now Rush-Presbyterian-St. Lukes Medical Center] that did not open until 1843, after his selection of qualified faculty members; also in 1837, was appointed ★★★ **Chicago's 1st** health officer of the city; in 1838 performed the second major surgical procedure in Chicago when amputating the crushed leg of a laborer injured at the construction of the Illinois & Michigan Canal [for the first major operation, see Harmon, Elijah D., M.D.]; for several years he served as editor of the *Chicago Democrat*; ✦ 17 Dearborn St.; in 1839 he also traveled to Paris for postgraduate studies (returning in 1852 to lecture and perform laboratory experiments on wound healing; received honorary memberships in French and Swiss medical societies); married Evelyn Height on Feb. 6, 1845. In 1847 Brainard was instrumental in organizing Chicago's first general hospital in Tippecanoe Hall; served as vice president of the American Medical Association in 1850, and as president of the Illinois State Medical Society in 1854; died of the cholera at the Sherman House and was buried at Graceland Cemetery; ➡ Brainard Avenue, a diagonal street, 2700 E to 3400 E. [12, 363, 364, 403]

Brandwell, Johann   German immigrant, first attested to as having lived in Chicago in 1834. [342]

Branta canadensis   see Canada goose.

Brassard, Antoine   *engagé* of La Salle; during the winter of 1682/83 he selected the site for La Salle's post in the Chicagou are, probably on Hickory Creek. [649]

DANIEL BRAINARD, M.D.

Bray, Dominick   one of Gurdon Hubbard's reliable employees who traveled to Chicago in late May 1827 to report that the Iroquois River post had been pillaged by drunken Potawatomi. [354]

Breed, Art   listed as a subscriber to the *Chicago Democrat* in November 1833.

Breese & Beaubien Addition   to Chicago; see Breese, Sidney.

Breese, Josiah S.   see next entry.

Breese & Sheppard   advertised "New Goods and New Store" in the Sept. 30, 1835, *Chicago Democrat*, located in a four story brick building opposite the Tremont House; some of the New York dry goods itemized, all of a superior quality, included: "Black, blue and fancy Cassimeres; Sattinetts; Beaverteens, moleskins, and Buffalo cloths; Vestings, Goat Hair Camblets; Calicoes and Ginghams, of every description; Black Italian Silks; Plain, figuered [*sic*], and plaid Pou de Soir; Irish Linens and Lawns, Lamb's woolshirts, woollen stockings, socks; Black and Colored Italian cravats." Josiah S. Breese was likely one of the partners, who in 1839 partnered Col. Edmund D. Taylor in Taylor, Breese & Co., a dry goods store on Lake Street, near Clark. The other partner was possibly [see] Robert Sheppard.

Breese, Sidney member of the surveying party for the Illinois & Michigan Canal that visited Chicago in 1830 under James M. Bucklin, chief engineer; served as judge during the May 1835 term of the Circuit Court of Cook County, held at the Presbyterian *church* in Chicago. As a respected lawyer, Mr. Breese became a party in the legal proceedings that followed the purchase of the evacuated Fort Dearborn Reservation by Jean Baptiste Beaubien on May 28, 1835, in the case of *The United States of America v John B. Beaubien, James Whitlock, Edmund D. Taylor, Sidney Breese, and James M. Strode.* The case was lost by Beaubien et al., and the land became the Breese & Beaubien Addition to Chicago as shown on E.B. Talcott's ✱ map [see map list on page 51]. [13, 357, 704]

Brehm, Lt. Dietrich British military officer who in 1761 visited and ✱ mapped the "Chigago" village during his survey of the territory newly won from the French near the end of the French and Indian War; he found several settlers there; his work contributed to the completion of [see] Thomas Hutchins' maps. [649]

Brevoort, Maj. Henry B. (c.1775-1858) of Detroit; skipper of the *Adams* from 1802 to 1812; noted in Kinzie's account books as visiting Chicago trading post on Aug. 29, 1809, and May 26, 1810; distinguished himself in combat against the British during the War of 1812; was appointed Indian agent at Green Bay in December 1822, removing to there in 1823 and moving his family from Detroit to Green Bay the following year; in 1829 the family returned to Detroit, where the major remained until his death; his daughter, Mrs. Mary Ann Brevoort Bristol, later wrote of her reminiscences in the Northwest [published in the *Wisconsin State Historical Collections* 8:293 {1879}], giving a lively account of her family's ancestry and activity, as well as of early pioneer life. [404]

CHICAGO BREWERY.
THE SUBSCRIBERS wish to make contracts for 4000 bushels of good sound Barley to be delivered at the Chicago Brewery, for which the highest market price will be given. Inquire at Mr. Fay's.
J. & W. CRAWFORD.
Chicago, June 13th, 1835.   tf2

breweries on June 13, 1835, an advertisement in the *Chicago American* seeks to buy a large amount of barley for what is called the Chicago Brewery; the ad is signed by J. & W. Crawford [see Crawford, James and William], presumably ★★★ Chicago's 1st brewers, who at that time lived at Fay's boarding house on Lake Street; on Aug. 15, 1835, an article in the *Chicago American* lists one brewery among nearly 95 business enterprises in town, most likely the Crawford venture; the location of this first brewery remains undetermined; by December 9 John Calhoun listed 2 breweries as existent among the businesses in Chicago. For subsequent Chicago brewmasters, see entries on William Haas, William Lill, and Konrad Sulzer.

Brewster, Franklin Detroit merchant; working with, and probable brother of William Brewster. During 1825-27, the Brewsters furnished trade goods and personnel to W.H. Wallace in Chicago, and when Wallace unexpectedly died early in March 1827, William sent Franklin on horseback from Detroit before the month's end for the purpose of "attending to the concerns of Wallace after his death."

Brewster, Hogan & Co. was granted a license to sell goods in Cook County at the county seat (Chicago) on June 6, 1831; was dissolved Feb. 20, 1834; see Brewster, William; see Hogan, J.S.C.

Brewster, William Detroit merchant; visited Chicago in 1818 for three or four weeks; returned for permanent residence in September 1833; he and his brother were assignees for Joseph Bertrand, Sr. at the Chicago treaty on September 26; by December the firm Brewster, Hogan & Co. was advertising its forwarding and commission/dry goods business in the *Chicago Democrat*, in a store at the NE corner of Lake and South Water streets; on Feb. 20, 1834, the firm was dissolved and Hogan operated the store alone; also see Hogan, John Stephen Coats.

Bridges, Mr. said to have lived on the N side of the river in 1816; according to Mrs. Susan M. Callis, a visitor that year, his house was located between the Burns house and the Kinzie house. [74]

bridges and ferries [Also see maps in the Chronology section illustrating the locations of early ferries and bridges.] Prior to 1830, there was little need for bridges over the river and its branches, although it is known from Capt. John Whistler's ✱ draft of Fort Dearborn and adjacent lands that there lived in 1808 at the Forks a man who provided Indian ferry service—★★★ Chicago's 1st documented ferry; locals and Fort Dearborn soldiers kept boats at various small piers, and most visitors and transients arrived in their own canoes, the predominant mode of travel. Antoine Ouilmette provided occasional ferry service near his cabin—built in 1790—on the N side of the river. Early in 1829, Archibald Caldwell, who then ran the Wolf Point Tavern, stretched a rope across the north branch near the entrance to the tavern and left a canoe at both ends, as a welcome gesture to potential guests; it became known as the "grapeline ferry." A second 1829 ferry was constructed in June at Lake Street by Archibald Clybourne and Samuel Miller under a license issued by the county commissioners. Additional ferries were established at Clark, State and Rush streets. [For the text of the license issued to Clybourne and Miller, see taverns, hotels and boarding houses.]

In 1832, Sam Miller built ★★★ Chicago's 1st floating log bridge of "stringers" across the north branch, N of his tavern, located opposite Rev. Jesse

DEARBORN STREET DRAWBRIDGE, BUILT IN 1834. [12]

Walker's cabin, near Kinzie Street. Meant for foot traffic only, it replaced the grapeline ferry; by late 1833, the bridge had been strengthened to accept teams.

A second bridge was built in 1832, crossing the south branch, just N of Randolph Street. Also floating, but of logs more substantial than those of its north branch counterpart, it was able to support heavy wagons, though always with difficulty. Floating log bridges could accommodate river traffic by being temporarily disconnected from shore on one or the other side. Built by Anson and Charles Taylor, the Randolph Street bridge was maintained until 1840.

In August 1833, the Dearborn Free Ferry was begun as a public service without charge, located at Dearborn Street or "Old Point," as the location

was called. The ferry preceded ★★★ Chicago's 1st drawbridge, constructed at the same site in the spring of 1834 by the shipwright Nelson R. Norton, in anticipation of the intended straightening of the eastern end of the river by a cut through the sand bar, to admit larger vessels. The bridge was 300 feet long, 16 feet wide, with a gallowlike frame at each end and a double cable draw creating an opening of 60 feet. On July 12, 1834, the day the cut through the sand bar was complete, the schooner *Illinois* entered the new harbor and was the first to pass the bridge. See Castelnau to note his drawing in 1838; the bridge lasted until 1839.

On Dec. 4, 1833, the town trustees created a committee responsible for ferries and bridges, all of which by then were in the public domain. The

committee consisted of George Dole, Madore Beaubien, Edmund Kimberly, and John Miller, who were responsible for keeping everything in working order; another bridge would not be built until 1840, at Clark Street. The only other bridge to be found in the Chicago area before 1836 was built across an arm of the Saganashkee Swamp, to facilitate the Calumet-Sag south portage route, W of the mouth of Bachelor's Grove Creek [Tinley Creek]; who built this log bridge or when, is uncertain; the bridge can be found only on a copy of the original survey drawings of 1832 [in the Chicago Historical Society Collections]. The official record of the meeting of the Peoria County commissioners of June 2, 1829, relative to the license to keep a ferry across the Chicago River, reads as follows:

Ordered: That Archibald Clybourn and Samuel Miller be authorized to keep a ferry across the Chicago River, at the lower forks, near Wolf's Point, crossing the river below the Northeast Branch, and to land on either side of both branches, to suit the convenience of persons wishing to cross. And that said Clybourn and Miller pay a tax of two dollars, and execute a bond with security for one hundred dollars. The rate for ferriage to be one-half of the sum that John L. Bogardus gets at his ferry at Peoria. Ordered: That the following rates be, and they are hereby, allowed to be charged and received by the different ferries, by their respective owners, in this county, to wit:

For each foot passenger, 6 1/4 cts.
  man and horse, 12 1/2 cts.
Dearborn sulkey chair with spring, 50 cts.
  one-horse wagon, 25 cts.
four-wheeled carriage, drawn by two
  oxen or horses, 37 1/2 cts.
cart with two oxen, 37 1/2 cts.
head of neat cattle of mules, 10 cts.
hog, sheep, or goat, 3 cts.
hundred-weight of goods, wares, and
  merchandize, each bushel of grain, 6 1/4 cts.
And all other articles in equal and just pro-

portions.

One early teamster describes crossing a log bridge as follows: *The horses' front feet would settle the planks about 6 inches, the hind ones about a foot or 6 inches more, the forward wheel about a foot and a half, the hind ones about two feet in the water. It did not seem possible to cross safely on the concern. Every time a team crossed, every plank had to be replaced before the next one could cross.*

Charles Cleaver, 1882: "There were no railes on the sides, and, as it shook and trembled under every team that crossed over, it was not surprising that, once in a while, a span of horses should jump into the river. I saw one myself that winter [1833-34]— a splendid team, just driven in from Detroit, and the best in the city—plunge into the river and drown before we could help."

Public notice of Feb. 13, 1836: *The Trustees of the Town of Chicago will not hold themselves accountable for any damage which may arise to any person by reason of crossing the bridges over the Chicago River, or over the North or South Branches thereof, the said bridges being considered dangerous, and the said Trustees not having funds out of which to repair the said bridges.*

Bridget   schooner under Captain Ludlow; came from various lake ports (Buffalo, St. Joseph, Green Bay), carrying passengers as well as merchandise; called at Chicago twice in 1834, three times in 1835; lost on Lake Michigan late in 1835.

brig   two-masted ship with square sails; the *Adams* began to call at Fort Dearborn in 1804 with supplies, continuing through 1808; the John Kinzie frequented Chicago in 1834 and 1835; those that called in 1835 were the *Illinois, Indiana, Queen Charlotte,* and *Neptune.*

Briggs, Benjamin   listed as a subscriber to the *Chicago Democrat* in November 1833; advertised in the paper on May 27, 1834 (with James O. Humphrey), as a carriage- and sleighmaker on South Water Street, Briggs & Humphrey; ✦ wagon maker, Randolph Street; listed as a member of the

Tabernacle Baptist Church in 1843. [12]

Briggs & Humphrey   yet existent in 1839, see Briggs, Benjamin.

Bristol, Charles L.   partner of [see] Wm. Hogue & Co. with Hogue and John Hale; dissolution.

Brock, General Isaac   British general in the War of 1812; counterpart to General Hull in the northwest theater; after the Fort Dearborn massacre he contended that he had no knowledge of any such attack by the Indians, which was disingenuous in view of the fact that British authorities had asked the Indians to kill every American settler W of Detroit.

Brock, Thomas   arrived in 1835, lawyer; candidate for alderman in 1837; ✦ ex-justice of the peace, corner of Madison and Clark streets; Nancy, his first wife, died in 1839; afterward, married Mrs. Ester D. Miner, whose young children (Caroline and Gideon Minor) would die of smallpox early in January 1840.

Brodeur, Jean Baptiste   also Broudeaur; in April 1833, his name was among Catholic citizens on a petition to Bishop Rosati in St. Louis, asking that a priest be assigned to them.

Bronson, Arthur   (1800-1844) New York lawyer, real estate speculator, and financier who never lived in Chicago but became the most active of Eastern promoters during the land boom between 1833 and 1837; in August 1833, visited Chicago with his friend Charles Butler, exploring and socializing, contributing a charitable donation of $50 to a Sunday school library. He could have seen only a few unsightly shacks scattered between the swampy prairie and the undeveloped shoreline, but Bronson expressed his faith in Chicago's promise: "If I were a young man and unmarried I would settle down at Chicago: it presents one of the finest fields in America for industry and enterprise, and though at present a journey to this point is attended with great privations, fatigue, exposure, and difficulty, in a few years we will think no more of going to Chicago than we now think of going to Buffalo.

There will be lines of steamships, stages, and railroads the entire distance from Albany to the Fort at St. Louis on the Mississippi, Chicago being an important and commanding point on this great thoroughfare." In 1834, Bronson purchased 19 town blocks and 80 acres of adjoining land to which Capt. David Hunter held title (half of Kinzie's and the whole of Wolcott's additions), all on the N side, paying the then-astounding sum of $20,000; after his return to the East, he continued to buy Chicago land working through at least 10 different agents, among them John H. Kinzie and Dr. Temple; Chicago lawyer James Grant handled the legal problems of the land titles; in May 1836, before the collapse of land prices in 1837, Bronson sold most of his holdings, with enormous profits, to the American Land Co. controlled by Butler. During a subsequent visit to Chicago in 1844, he became ill and died soon after of consumption in New York. [12]

Bronson, Myron K.   listed as a subscriber to the *Chicago Democrat* in November 1833.

Brooks, Captain   master of the lake schooner [see] *Jesse Smith* which, coming from [see] Shipwagen, visited Chicago on Oct. 17, 1835; ✦ Captain, schooner *Jessie Smith.*

Brookes, Henry   (c.1818-1882) also Brooks; from England, probable brother of Samuel; arrived July 27, 1833, with his wife Elizabeth Ester and a son John Howard (died in 1844 at age 12) [Andreas contributes that "the Brooks children" – Elizabeth, Margaret, and Henry – attended school under Miss Eliza Chappel in 1833, daily paddling their own canoe across the river to and from school. Henry and Elizabeth may have come with several children; *eds.*]; Mrs. Charles A. Taylor reports that Mr. Brooks brought a piano from England, and that Mrs. Brooks, assisted by George Davis, gave several concerts during the winter of 1834-35; ✦ clerk, boards Samuel Brookes; lived in Hyde Park in 1878;

died on March 3, 1882. [12, 653]

Brookes, Samuel L. arrived on July 27, 1833, from England, likely brother of Henry; applied for wharfing privileges on Nov. 20, 1835; ✦ florist, Adams Street near Dearborn. [12, 28, 351]

Brookes, Samuel Marsden born c.1818 in England, arrived in October 1833; ✦ portrait painter, Adams Street—★★★ Chicago's 1st; later studied in Milwaukee (there marrying Julia B. Jones in 1842) and Europe; moved to California in 1862. Together with Thomas Stevenson in 1856, he painted the Fox River series; still living in 1885 at San Francisco. [12]

Brookfield, William married to Emma Lolliet; their son Walter was baptized Oct. 28, 1830, by Father Badin.

Brooks, Lt. Edward E. from Kentucky; stationed at Fort Dearborn until 1819, when he advanced to the rank of captain and was transferred to Detroit; resigned from the military in 1827; served as inspector general of the Territorial Militia of Michigan at the time of the Black Hawk War and was in Chicago with the rank of colonel under Maj. Gen. John R. Williams, June 11-22, 1832; died in Detroit. [12]

Brown, Charles B. and Samuel Charles is known to have arrived in 1835; probably brothers, were enrolled as grade school students in the class taught by [see] John Watkins in December 1835. Names of corresponding parents were not recorded. [351, 728]

Brown, Daniel B. came in 1835; partnered his brother [see] Nathaniel J. and [see] Augustus Garrett in the firm Garrett, Brown & Brother until late November, then purchasing and selling real estate for Garrett, Thompson, Brown & Co.

Brown, E. advertised "Painting" first in the June 8, 1835, *Chicago American* and continued the ad into the autumn: "Carriage, Sign, Ornamental and Fancy Painting, Guilding, &c. executed in the first style," on Randolph Street, over Briggs & Humphrey's Carriage Shop.

Brown, Erastus S. arrived on June 22, 1833, in a yawl, *Ariadne,* with a load of lumber, landing where Mrs. Wright formerly lived [lakeshore, E end of Madison Street]; had been a member of the initial canal commission created by Governor Cole in 1823. [12]

Brown, James voted on July 24 and Aug. 2, 1830; his wife's name was Vienna.

Brown, Jesse B. on April 3, 1832, purchased "downtown" lot 3 in block 20 for $60 [see map on page 44], but soon after sold it to Richard J. Hamilton; as captain, took charge of one of the five volunteer militia companies raised in Cook County during the Black Hawk War. [12]

Brown, Joseph W. Brigadier General of the third Michigan Territorial Brigade, who came with his troops to Chicago during the Black Hawk War. [714]

Brown, Lemuel (1784-1883) originally from Cumberland, RI; arrived from Springfield, MA in February 1833, with his wife [Cynthia?] and an adopted daughter, Harriet, who later married John Bates on November 13; worked on the harbor project and purchased lots 5 and 6 in block 28 from Elijah Wentworth [see map on page 44]; ✦ blacksmith, Randolph Street near Dearborn; lived in Kenwood in 1878 and at Lemont in 1885. [12, 351]

Brown, Nathaniel J. born in Windsor County, VT in 1812; in the late 1820s was an agent for an older brother's first stage line between Detroit and St. Joseph; acquired woodland acreage along the Grand

PAINTING.

E. BROWN respectfully informs the inhabitants of Chicago, that he has established himself in the above business on Randolph street, over Briggs & Humphrey's Carriage Shop, where he will transact all business in his line with taste and dispatch.

Carriage, Sign, Ornamental and Fancy Painting, Gilding, &c. executed in the first style. 1tf

River in Kent County [Michigan], built a sawmill and rafted six schooner loads of pine from Granville to the coast, where the *White Pigeon* carried the lumber to Chicago for sale, arriving on April 4, 1835; remained to form a partnership with another brother, Daniel B., and [see] Augustus Garrett, opening a commission office [see Garrett, Brown & Brother] for the purchase and sale of Chicago real estate; in the December 2 *Chicago Democrat* the three men announced a new copartnership with Oliver H. Thompson—Garrett, Thompson, Brown & Co.—for the purpose of buying and selling real estate, conducting a general land agency and also an auction, commission, and mercantile business; in 1837 contracted for rock work on the Illinois & Michigan Canal, excavating a mile at [Lemont]; ✦ canal contractor; continued successfully in stone quarrying and real estate. [13]

Brown, Rufus from New York; served in the Chicago militia during the 1832 Black Hawk War; with his wife Elizabeth was a charter member of the first Presbyterian church, organized by Reverend Porter on June 26, 1833; early Sunday school meetings were held in Brown's well-reputed boarding log house, which was adjacent to that of P.F.W. Peck. Reverend Porter lived in Peck's house and had his meals at Brown's house; George David [see entry] stayed at Brown's in October 1833 with his 13 fellow travelers; ✦ warehouseman, Bristol & Porter; married Sarah Dunn Howe in 1843; in 1885 his widow lived at 45 S Ann St. [12, 714]

Brown, Samuel married Clarissa Horr on Feb. 3, 1834, per announcement in the *Chicago Democrat.*

Brown's boarding house see Brown, Rufus.

Brown, S. Lockwood arrived in 1835; later secretary of the Sunday School Union of Chicago and would write about the history of Sunday school in Chicago.

Brown, Thomas C. shipmaster, arrived from New York in 1833; married Harriet Ellston on Jan. 6, 1834.

Brown, William Hubbard (1796-1867) from

Connecticut, married Harriet C. Seward in 1822; came to Chicago from Fayette County, IL, in October 1833; listed as a subscriber when the *Chicago Democrat* first published in November; on May 28, 1834, he and J.B. Tuttle opened a grocery store on Dearborn Street, one door S of Messrs. Newberry & Dole, a partnership they dissolved on June 21; another notice in the May 20, 1835, *Chicago Democrat* announced "connexion in business … closed" with P.P. Russell, of Russell & Brown; joined the Presbyterian church on Nov. 3, 1835 and in June 1836, was chosen as an elder, a position held until 1842, when he withdrew to help form the Second Presbyterian Church; in late November 1835 he became a vice president of the Chicago Bible Society, and on the 24th filed a statement in support of David Carver's claim for wharfing privileges; ◆ cashier, State Bank of Illinois, corner of Lake and South Water streets; was appointed school agent of the city in 1840, becoming an influential friend of the Chicago school system and a philanthropist in later life; in 1856 became the first president of the Chicago Histori-

cal Society; Brown School [54 N Hermitage Ave.] would be named after him; died in Amsterdam while touring Europe. [12, 28, 97]

Browne, Bvt. 2d Lt. Gustavus buried in Chicago, one of 75 cholera victims during the 1832 Black Hawk War.

Brownell, Jeremiah on 1830 census of Peoria County; owner of 80 acres of Chicago land in the NE quarter of Section 18, Township 39, prior to 1836, as seen in Andreas' *History of Chicago*, pp. 112-113.

Brush, Henry L. in 1833 owned lot 3 in block 44 and lot 1 in block 33 [see map on page 44]; both lots had formerly belonged to John Evans.

Brush Hill Trail also Brush Hill Road, Fullersburg Road; Indian trail between Chicago and the Naper settlement; crossed the Des Plaines River at the Laughton ford, near the Barry Point Road bridge; later became the county Southwest Plank Road, then Ogden Avenue; the land that surrounded the rise known as Brush Hill later became Fullersburg, then Hinsdale.

Bruté de Remur, Most Reverend Simon William Gabriel first Catholic bishop of Vincennes, in the territory of which the diocese Chicago was included during the period 1834-1843.

Bryant, Lemuel a visitor to Fort Dearborn in 1832 during the Black Hawk scare who described the cholera-ridden soldiers in his diary, which is preserved at the Chicago Historical Society.

Buchholz, Friedrich German immigrant who came to Dunklee's Grove [Bloomingdale] with his family in 1835 from Stolzenau (near Hanover); educated and articulate, he led the local Lutheran community in worship for three years before a professional minister became available; died in a construction accident on Feb. 15, 1838, when helping a newcomer build his home. [342]

Buckeyes nickname for Ohio natives or residents, common in early Illinois. Ohio is referred to as the Buckeye State. [55a]

Buckhorn Tavern see Wentworth, Elijah, Jr.

Bucklin, James M. (1802-1890) from Providence, RI; appointed chief engineer for the Illinois & Michigan Canal construction project by the Illinois canal commissioners in the summer of 1830; he and Captain Pope, surveyor, came immediately to Chicago, moving into the Wolf Point Tavern; with help from the soldiers at Fort Dearborn under Major Fowle, they completed the job of surveying and mapping the canal route by December 31; in 1830, purchased 2 lots of block 6 from the government [see map on page 44]; in 1835 he married Mary Ann Beckwith in Alabama. Curiously, in his writings both before and after 1830, Bucklin favored a rail connection rather than a canal, and in later life worked for several emerging railroad lines; in 1830, he notes:

The journey to Chicago was alike long and memorable. North of Springfield the country was very thinly settled—no houses or improvements except at the points of the timber bordering on the streams across the prairies at intervals of thirty or forty miles. ✧ *The streams which we crossed had not yet broken through the thick*

WILLIAM HUBBARD BROWN [410]

JAMES M. BUCKLIN [Ill. St. Hist. Lib.]

matted sod upon which they flowed but were of wide expanse, the water slowly percolating underneath and through the grass. The prairies were infested with myriads of green-headed flies [see "greenheaded fly"; eds.] *whose bites were so severe on the horses we were compelled frequently to travel by night.* ❖ *In due time we reached the Des Plaines river where, for the first time, I caught a view of Lake Michigan. Away in the distance I espied a little dot on the horizon, which proved to be the flag that floated over Fort Dearborn. On the banks of the lake with naked eye we could see but little else, but with the aid of field glasses, we could discern the palisades of the fort surrounded by what looked like a few huts and some scattering Indian lodges which then comprised all there was of the settlement known as Chicago. Between us and the lake the country seemed to be an arid, concave plain, without a vestige of vegetation of any sort, recent prairie fires having entirely consumed the grass, the smoke of which was still visible.*

The Chicago River that Bucklin observed:

The water was deep, clear, and apparently pure. The banks were fringed with wild rice, and it looked like a canal, meandering through a level, green meadow. There were no trees, but we noticed a few scattering log-houses on the banks, some Indian lodges, and Fort Dearborn on the bank of the lake in the distance, which was somewhat elevated above the surface in the rear. [12, 704]

budget   for the village budget, see corporate finances.

buffalo   see bison.

Buffalo   161-ton schooner built at Huron, OH, in 1832; first called at Chicago from Calumet on Oct. 25, 1835, under Captain Beraun; sank on the Niagara River in 1839 [48]

Buffalo, NY   located at the point where the W end of the Erie Canal reaches Lake Erie, the settlement suddenly became a busy transit point for westward migration when the canal opened in 1825. Canal line boats and larger lake vessels, always crowded in the early days when westbound, exchanged pas-

sengers here. In May 1835, [see] Ellen Bigelow was among the passengers. As in Chicago, real estate speculation was rampant at that time. She gives her impression of Buffalo and vividly describes her journey to Chicago on the brig *Illinois* in a letter to a relative back home. [55a]

Buisson, Louis   (c.1758-c.1830) also Bisson; called Pierre Buison, Sr., by Eckert; Canadian trader, resident of Peoria; listed in John Kinzie's account book on May 15, 1804; May 24, 1806; June 4, 1808; lived in [owned?] a cabin in Chicago at the time of the 1812 massacre, and during its duration remained indoors with his family, N of the river near the lakeshore, half a mile N of the Kinzie house—all survived; ransomed several survivors held captive by the Indians after the massacre and spent the winter of 1812-13 at Chicago in a trading partnership with [see] Des Pins (LeMoine). When Peoria was destroyed in 1812 by Craig's militia, four houses were burned but Buisson's and Des Pins's escaped the flames; Thomas Forsyth, Indian agent there, implied that this was because they were British traders. Buisson was in Peoria in 1818 as an American Fur Co. agent for the St. Louis branch and, across the river from Fort Clark, established Trading House at Wesley City [Creve Coeur]; married to Potawatomi Sheshi Chevalier (daughter of François Chevalier), sister of Archange Ouilmette; their children included Pierre, Jean Baptiste, Michael, Nicholas, and Mary. [226, 259, 404, 649]

bull plow   crude "breaking" plow with a wooden mold-board, for turning up the sod; forerunner of the lighter "self-scouring" plow with steel mold-board that [see] Asahel Pierce would later adapt at Chicago.

Bumgarden, Morris   arrived in 1832, and still resident [Andreas] in the autumn of 1833; see Baumgarten, Moritz. [12]

Burdick, Paul   listed as a subscriber to the *Chicago Democrat* in November 1833. Dr. Boyer noted that a Mr. Burdick had his house 3 1/2 miles N of the main Chicago River, between the prairie and

the sand ridge that paralleled the lakeshore. [728]

Burke, Michael   among the Catholics who signed a petition submitted to the bishop at St. Louis in April 1833, requesting that a priest be assigned to them; married Marguerite May Kurbey in 1836; ✦ tender, south branch bridge.

Burke, Patrick   U.S. Army private at Fort Dearborn, enlisted in May 1806; was killed after the surrender at the 1812 massacre. [226]

Burley, Arthur Gilmore   (1812-1897) arrived from Exeter, NH on May 11, 1835; half brother of Stephen F. Gale; ✦ crockery, stone, earthenware; 161 Lake St.; in 1885 lived at 1620 Indiana Ave. [12, 351]

Burly Shoulders   see Shabbona.

Burman, —   U.S. Army private at Fort Dearborn, enlisted in August 1811, was killed at the 1812 massacre. [226]

Burnet, Gen. Ward Benjamin   (c.1811-1884) born in Pensylvania; second lieutenant, when he arrived with the military in August 1832 for the Black Hawk War and later became general; in 1878 lived in New York City; died on June 24, 1884. [12, 639]

Burnett, George   U.S. Army private and fifer at Fort Dearborn; enlisted in October 1806; killed by an Indian after the surrender at the massacre of Aug. 15, 1812. [226]

Burnett, William   of Scottish origin, arrived in Michigan about 1769 and had a trading post in Detroit, where John Kinzie first began work; in 1775 became a trader at the mouth of the St. Joseph River, where he lived until his death in 1814. Father Leva- doux noted in 1782 that Burnett "had cleared large fields, erected a valuable mansion house, barn, storehouses, &c., and cultivated the earth, and traded with the Potawatomi and other nations of Indians, and that he never removed from thence. His orchards contained apple, quince, peach, and cherry trees." In 1798, Burnett also maintained a trading post at Chicago, and in August of that year he wrote to a firm in Montreal "that it was understood a garrison would be sent to Chicago," a project not realized until five years later. He married Kaw-kee-me, sister of Topenebe, principal chief of the St. Joseph's band of Potawatomi; their children included John, James (continued the father's business after his death until his own in 1835), Isaac, Jacob, Abraham (interpreter for Reverend McCoy of the Carey Mission), Nancy, and Rebecca—all sent to Detroit or Montreal for their education. Burnett's sympathy was with the Americans; arrested in Mackinaw by the British and taken to prison in Montreal, but later released; was a witness on the 1800 bill of sale [with John Kinzie] when Point de Sable sold his house to La Lime—he guaranteed payment, and therefore may be regarded as the legal owner of the Point de Sable estate until it was purchased by Kinzie. In 1803 his was the only farm at Chicago known to the War Dept. as a source of provisions for the new Fort Dearborn. After the Fort Dearborn massacre, Captain and Mrs. Heald, fleeing from the Indians, were temporarily housed by Burnett in St. Joseph. The children of Burnett were granted land sections by the government in the Treaty of Chicago of 1821; most stayed in Michigan when the Potawatomi left, but Abraham, the youngest, went with the tribe to eastern Kansas and was made a chief; a hill there still bears the family name, Mount Burnett. [12, 166, 526, 527, 649]

Burns House   built c.1809 by [see] Ezekiel Cooper on the north bank of the river "nearly opposite the garrison" and W of the Kinzie house [later the SW corner of State and North Water streets]; became known as the Burns House when Thomas Burns married the widow Cooper in 1811. In this house the Potawatomi chief White Elk found and killed Mrs. Sukey Corbin and her two small children during the 1812 massacre. The Indian agent Jouett and his family occupied and enlarged a house on the north bank of the river during his second term at Chicago, from 1816 to 1819, and it was then known as the Agency house; it is uncertain if this was the former Burns House, or a separate building constructed by the soldiers in 1807, as mentioned in a letter of October 9 that year by Captain Whistler [see Agency Houses]. From 1820 to his death in 1830, the successor agent, Dr. Wolcott, lived either with his family in the officers' quarters of the garrison or in the Agency House; by then the structure had been remodelled into a double log house and partly clapboarded; at times he shared the Agency house with John Kinzie, whose own house began to crumble in the late 1820s, and who died in 1828. Wolcott's widow, with her widowed mother, Mrs. John Kinzie, and her half sister Mrs. Lenai Helm, left the house in 1831. Afterwards and until 1833, Col. R.J. Hamilton and his family lived there. [12, 74, 367]

Burns, Thomas   listed in John Kinzie's account book on Aug. 27, 1809; soldier at Fort Dearborn until 1811, when his term expired; then settled as a civilian, married the widow Mary Cooper, and moved into her house on the north bank of the river [the house may have been or at least was close to where the second Agency house, "Cobweb Castle", would be built], becoming stepfather to James, Anne(?), Frances(?), and Isabella Cooper; was wounded at the 1812 massacre as the sergeant in charge of the Chicago militia, organized earlier in the summer by Captain Heald; after the surrender, was tortured and killed by an Indian squaw with a pitchfork; three of his children died with him; his wife and two girls (Isabella Cooper and Catherine Burns) survived massacre and Indian captivity and later lived in Detroit. Isabella married George Fearson of Detroit, the younger brother of Mary Julia Fearson, wife of William Whistler. [12, 226, 404]

Burtis, Richard   listed as a member of Reverend Porter's Presbyterian *church* in June 1833. [12]

Burton, Edward   began advertising a "New Fashionable Tailoring Establishment" in the *Chicago American* on June 27, 1835; recently arrived from New York City, his shop was on Lake Street, near Franklin.

butchers   an entry on May 27, 1804, within John Kinzie's account book lists [Stephen] Draper as Fort Dearborn's butcher; self-employed butchers thereafter were Archibald Clybourne (1823); Jonas Clybourne (1824); Mark Noble, Sr. (1831); George W. Dole (1831, actually a merchant who employed butchers); Mark Noble, Jr. (1831); John Noble (1831); Sylvester March (1833); Edward Simons (1834); Cyrus P. Albee (1834); and Gurdon S. Hubbard (began meatpacking in 1834). For details, see individual entries; for a good description of the beginning of Chicago's meat industry, see *Goodspeed's History of Cook County, Illinois* [1:651].

Butler, Charles   New York investor and friend of real estate speculator Arthur Bronson, brother of Andrew Jackson's attorney general. During the winter 1832/33 Butler met Robert A. Kinzie, who while visiting New York, offered him Chicago real estate; in August 1833, Butler and Bronson visited Chicago to see the settlement and determine later land purchases; were present at the treaty with the Indians; stayed at the Green Tree Tavern of James Kinzie; for Butler's diary notes on that occasion, see Green Tree Tavern entry. As president of the American Land Co., Butler spent $100,000 in May 1835 to buy 50 acres–1000 city lots–from Bronson on the N side of the river, a fraction of the same land that Bronson had purchased in the fall of 1834 from Capt. David Hunter for $20,000. Butler had married William Ogden's sister, Eliza, and through his brother-in-law Ogden came to Chicago to supervise Butler's investments, later becoming ★★★ **Chicago's 1st** mayor. In 1881 Butler shared his earliest impressions of Chicago in a letter with Ogden (below):

In the winter of 1832-33 I was spending some time with my friend Arthur Bronson in New York as his guest. Among other topics we discussed that of a visit to the Western country the following summer for information and pleasure. We decided on the plan of a journey to Chicago the ensuing summer. [Butler and

Bronsen traveled via Niagara Falls, then Buffalo, by steamer to Detroit, by rented wagon with two horses—plus two saddle horses, with Gholson Kercheval as hired guide—to South Bend and Michigan City; *eds.*] ✧ *From Michigan City to Chicago, a distance of about sixty miles, the journey was performed by me on horseback. There was but one stopping place on the way, and that was the house of a Frenchman named Bayeux [Joseph Bailly], who had married an Indian woman. At Calumit River, which was crossed on a float, there was an encampment of Pottawatomie Indians. There were some trees on the westerly bank of the river, and in some of these the Indians had hammocks. In making the journey from Michigan City to Chicago I followed the shore of the lake nearly the whole distance.* ✧ *I approached Chicago in the afternoon of a beautiful day, the 2nd of August, (1833); the sun setting in a cloudless sky. On my left lay the prairie, bounded only by the distant horizon like a vast expanse of ocean; on my right, in the summer stillness, lay Lake Michigan. I had never seen anything more beautiful or captivating in nature. There was an entire absence of animal life, nothing visible in the way of human habitation or to indicate the presence of man, and yet it was a scene full of life; for there, spread out before me in every direction, as far as the eye could reach, were the germs of life in earth, air and water. I approached Chicago in these closing hours of day, 'So calm, so clear, so bright,'—and this was the realization of the objective point of my journey.* ✧ *But what was the condition to this objective point, this Chicago of which I was in pursuit, to which I had come? A small settlement, a few hundred people all told, who had come together mostly in the last year or two. The houses, with one or two exceptions, were of the cheapest and most primitive character for human habitation, suggestive of the haste with which they had been put up. A string of these buildings had been erected without much regard to lines on the south side of the Chicago River (South Water Street). On the west side of the South Branch, near the junction, a tavern had been improvised for* the entertainment of travelers, erected by James Kinzie, but kept by a Mr. Crook [David Clock; eds.]; and there we found lodgings.* ✧ *Emigrants were coming in almost every day in wagons of various forms, and, in many instances, families were living in their covered wagons while arrangements were made for putting up shelter for them. It was no uncommon thing for a house, such as would answer the purpose for the time being, to be put up in a few days. Mr. Bronson himself made a contract for a house, to be put up and finished in a week. There were, perhaps, from two to three hundred people in Chicago at that time, mostly strangers to each other. In the tavern at which we stayed, the partitions were chiefly upright studs, with sheets attached to them. The house was crowded with people – emigrants and travelers. Many of them could only find a sleeping-place on the floor, which was covered with weary men at night.* ✧ *The east window of my bed-room looked out upon Lake Michigan in the distance, Fort Dearborn lying near the margin of the lake; and, at this time, there was nothing, or very little, to obstruct the view between the inn and the lake, the fort and the buildings connected with it being the principal objects; and those buildings were very low structures; and I could, from my window, follow the course of the river, the water of which was as pure as that of the lake, from the point of junction to its entrance into the lake.* [12, 639]

Butler, Jesse   tailor; had a shop in 1835 on South Water Street, at the rear of the McCormick & Moon hat shop, according to [see] J.D. Bonnell. [12]

Butterfield Creek   main tributary of Thorn Creek, in the SW portion of the Calumet basin.

Butterfield, Justin   (1790-1855) lawyer, from Keene, NH; came to Chicago in 1835 to reconnoiter and settled permanently; formed a law partnership with James H. Collins which lasted many years; married to Elizabeth Pierce of New York; was a member of the first board of directors of Rush Medical College when incorporated in 1837; ✦ attorney and counsellor at law, 46 Dearborn St.,

JUSTIN BUTTERFIELD [12]

residing at Michigan [Hubbard] Street at the corner of Rush, housing sons Justin, Jr. (law student, Butterfield & Collins), William (medical student), and George. [12]

Butterfield, Lyman   (1797-1845) arrived on the schooner *Telegraph* with Capt. Joseph Naper in 1831; staked a claim and settled N of the Napier settlement [Wheaton]; came with his new wife, Amanda Hooper; second corporal in the militia company under Napier during the 1832 Black Hawk War; ✦ Columbian House, corner of Wells and South Water streets; died in Chicago. [12]

Cabot, John   (1450-c.1499) also Giovanni Caboto; Venetian navigator in the service of King Henry VII of England; on June 24, 1497, reached what may have been northern Maine or Nova Scotia, and took possession of the new land for the crown, establishing England's claim to the North American continent; returned in 1498 and explored along the coast of Cape Cod, but traveling farther south Cabot and his ship were lost at sea. [205, 317, 732]

Cachand-Ervendberg, Ludwig immigrated from Germany in 1836 and settled at Dunklee's Grove; after the death of Friedrich Buchholz (1838), became the first professional minister of the local Lutheran congregation which he named the Teuto Community; left for Texas in 1840 and was killed by Indians in 1863.

Caddy, George arrived in 1834; married Emily Oalds on Sept. 13, 1834, the ceremony conducted by I.D. Harmon.

Cadillac, Antoine de la Mothe, né Laumet (c.1657-1730) born near Toulouse, France; invented a noble background to disguise a dubious and still uncertain past; served in the French army and in 1683 came to Port Royal; settled in Quebec in 1691 and received an appointment in the colonial troops, becoming commandant at Michilimackinac (Fort de Buade) from 1694 to 1697; in a 1695 report he mentioned the name "Chicagou on the garlic river" as one of a chain of posts on Lake Michigan; within a letter [see below] written the same year, he reveals his unsympathetic and irreverent regard for the Indian race and the role alcohol played in its destruction; while visiting the Great Lakes posts in 1697, he came to Chicagou; founded Detroit on July 24, 1701 by establishing Fort Pontchartrain du Detroit, that consisted of a few buildings within a high palisade; assisted by Alphonse de Tonti as the second officer in command of the fort. Laumet induced many Indians to relocate to Detroit, a policy that lead to eventual disastrous tribal enmities and created an opportunity for British incursions. In 1710 the French crown relieved him of his position as commandant but appointed him governor of Louisiana, but he did not arrive there until 1712; served three years, then returned to France, where he died. [101, 426, 649, 665]

Excerpt from a 1695 letter by Cadillac:

What reason can one assign that the savages should not drink brandy bought with their own money? This prohibition has much discouraged the Frenchmen here from trading in the future. It seemes very strange that they should pretend that the savages would ruin themselves by drinking. The savage himself asks why they do not leave him his beggary, his liberty, and his idleness; he was born in it and wishes to die in it – it is a life to which he has been accustomed since Adam. Do they wish him to build palaces and ornament them with beautiful furniture? He would not exchange his wigwam and the mat, on which he squots like a monkey, for the Louvre!

Cahokia an Indian tribe, part of the Illinois confederacy; also, first permanent white settlement in Illinois [within St. Clair County, just N of the present town of Cahokia, IL, and two miles S of East St. Louis]; began as a Jesuit mission to the adjacent village of 2000 Tamaroa and Cahokia Indians in 1699 (see *Mission de Sainte Famille de Caoquias*). Found nearby are large Indian mounds, now known as the Cahokia Indian Mounds; archeologists have dated these to a prosperous Indian community of nearly 20,000 people that existed between A.D. 1000 and 1300; they served as burial sites and platforms for temples. The largest of the mounds is named Monks' Mound; with a height of 100 feet, and a base of 1000 by 700 feet, it is the largest prehistoric monument in the United States. Deforestation is suspected to have led to the demise of the original Indian settlement. [9, 436a, 467, 470, 493, 544]

Caldwell, Archibald born in 1806 in Pearisburgh, Giles County, VA; married Emily Hall (sister of Benjamin Hall); arrived with his wife on horseback via Fort Wayne in July 1827; cousin to Archibald Clybourne who had earlier come from Virginia, together with Caldwell's sister, Louisa Caldwell; voted on May 11, 1828 (see Chronology); from 1828 to 1830 ran the Wolf Point Tavern for James Kinzie, for which he was granted ★★★ **Chicago's 1st** tavern license on Dec. 8, 1829,

ARCHIBALD CALDWELL

by the commissioners of Peoria County; occasionally did blacksmith work; in the spring of 1829 he abandoned his wife for an Indian woman, Josette; in June 1830, sued by Emily for a divorce that was uncontested [For Mrs. Caldwell's complaint in the records of the circuit court at Peoria, see the following text as read by her attorney on June 8, 1830; Emily later married the discharged soldier Cole Weeks]; in 1830, moved with Josette to the vicinity of Green Bay where they had five boys and a girl, and "all lived in Indian style"; in 1834 piloted the schooner *Jefferson* from Green Bay to Chicago, remaining until the next year; was still alive in 1880, living at Black Creek, WI. [12]

Your oratrix lived with the said Archibald as a dutiful and obedient wife and discharging all the duties of her station with cheerfulness and obedience until some time in the spring of 1829, the said Archibald, disregarding the solem obligations of the husband and lost to every principle of justice toward our oratrix, his wife, voluntarily abandoned your oratrix, and took to himself an Indian woman by the name of Josette, with whom he has since continued to live in adultery. And your oratrix avers that the said Archibald has repeatedly cohabitated with the same Josette, an Indian woman, and has continued to live with said Josette in adultery for more than one year next before the filing of this Bill. Now your orator expresses charges that the said Archibald is and has been guilty of Adultery with said Josette in the manner aforesaid.

Caldwell, Billy (1780-1841) the illegitimate son of a Mohawk mother and an Irish father, William Caldwell, Sr., a senior captain in Walter Butler's British ranger brigade, stationed near Niagara; documents show that Billy was originally given the name Thomas, but that name was later used for a subsequently born legitimate half-brother, and he became Billy; his Indian name, acquired in adult life, was Sauganash, also Sakonosh, meaning in the Potawatomi language *English-speaking Canadian*; at age two, Billy and his mother were abandoned by his father who moved to Amherstburg, where he married Suzanne Baby of Detroit. About 1789 the senior Caldwell took Billy from his mother and included him within the growing family he had formed with Suzanne. As bastard son, he was permanently relegated to second place; here he formed strong British loyalties, received a formal education, and was eventually fluent in English, French and several Indian dialects; he entered the Indian trade as apprentice of Thomas Forsyth in 1797 at the St. Joseph and Wabash rivers; moved to Chicago in 1803 as chief clerk of the Kinzie-Forsyth fur trading partnership, an association that lasted intermittently until 1833; formed an enduring friendship with Alexander Robinson in 1804. Two of Caldwell's claims can not be documented, and are probably fictional: that he served as secretary to Tecumseh in 1807, and that he intervened to rescue some of the survivors at the Fort Dearborn massacre. In 1813 Caldwell secured for himself a commission as captain, and subsequently often referred to himself as a captain in the British Indian

Department [served until Sept. 1816], of which John Kinzie also was a member until his 1813 arrest for treason. During the war, and until 1820, Caldwell lived at Amherstburg in Canada, then returning to Chicago to work with Kinzie, Forsyth and Wolcott in the Indian trade; lived on the N side of the river; in 1826, served as election judge for Peoria County; was rewarded in 1828 for his services by the U.S. Department of Indian Affairs with ★★★ **Chicago's 1st** frame house [near what is now the SE corner of Chicago Ave. and State St.] and a 1,600 acre land grant (Caldwell Reservation) along both sides of the north branch of the Chicago River [now the North Branch Division of the Cook County Forest Preserve District, adjacent to the communities of Edgebrook and Sauganash—part of the division has been designated Caldwell Woods as a permanent ▲ memorial]. In preparation for the 1829 Treaty of Prairie du Chien, American authorities sponsored him to serve as a Potawatomi chief, and the Indians concurred; in 1830, he assisted James M. Bucklin, chief engineer, in plotting the Illinois & Michigan Canal route; voted at elections on July 24, Aug. 2, and Nov. 25, 1830; was a friend of Mark Beaubien who, in 1831, named his [see] Sauganash Tavern after him; served as interpreter under Indian agent Owen at Fort Dearborn from 1831 to 1833; helped survey the Vincennes Road in 1832; on the list of subscribers to the *Chicago Democrat* in November 1833; actively promoted the establishment of a Catholic church in Chicago; helped negotiate the Chicago Treaty of 1833 as one of the principal spokesmen for the Prairie and Lake Indians, then sold his house and reservation land to farmers and accompanied the Indians to Council Bluffs, IA. Contemporaries describe Billy as a tall, good looking man. He was married four times: first to de Nanette, the daughter of Potawatomi chief Nee-scot-nee-mag, a Catholic convert from the village on the St. Joseph River, MI. De Nanette died soon after the birth of their son [twin daughters born

earlier, Helene and Susanne, were baptized by Father Badin on Oct. 17 and 18, 1830]; his second wife, who was the daughter of his employer Robert Forsyth and an Ojibwa woman, died in childbirth the year after they married; his third wife was a *métis* woman whose name is not recorded; his fourth and last wife was a French woman named Sauqua LeGrand whom he married on Nov. 18, 1834, with whom he settled in Council Bluffs, IA, and who survived him; together, his wifes gave him eight to ten children. ✦ north branch Chicago River, fifth ward. For Caldwell's efforts to help educate Indian children of school age, see comments by John Watkins under that entry; ➡ Caldwell Avenue; also Sauganash Avenue. See Shabbona. [12, 102, 109, 149, 149a, 226, 357, 642]

Caldwell, Louisa B. from Virginia; sister of Archibald Caldwell and cousin to Archibald Clybourne, in whose company she came to Chicago in 1827; in 1830, testified at Chicago before Jean B. Beaubien, J.P. in the divorce case of Archibald and Emily Caldwell; married Willis Scott on Nov. 1, 1830, Reverend William See officiating. [12]

Caldwell reservation see Caldwell, Billy.

Calhoun, Alvin brother of John Calhoun; arrived from New York June 12, 1834, on the schooner *Hiram* with Hibbard Porter; in September 1835, signed on as a fire brigade volunteer with the "Fire Kings"; he and his wife Miranda had an only son, William Frederick, who died in September 1836, aged 17 months; was a candidate for constable in 1837; ✦ carpenter and builder, 58 Randolph St.; became mayor in 1849. [12]

Calhoun, John (1808-1859) born in Watertown, NY; owned printing equipment and published the *Watertown Eagle*, an unsuccessful venture; married Pamelia C. Hathaway in 1832; arrived Oct. 16, 1833, with his equipment and two apprentices and, after assisting with lathing and plastering, moved into an unfinished building at the SW corner of South Water and Clark streets; became ★★★

JOHN CALHOUN [12]

Chicago's 1st printer and the publisher of the *Chicago Democrat*, ★★★ **Chicago's 1st** newspaper; in November 1834 he moved to the loft above the hardware store of Jones & King on South Water Street, between Clark and Dearborn. Pamela came to Chicago in the spring of 1834, "after the measurable comforts of a home in a new village had been provided" and then regularly helped with proofreading and printing. The publisher's wide-ranging editorials reflected the views and concerns of his pioneer neighbors, such as problems with the mails [see the following text that appeared April 16, 1834]. The first issue of the newspaper appeared on Nov. 26, 1833, and the names of 144 subscribers [preserved at the Chicago Historical Society; reprinted in Andreas, 1:365] provide valuable information about inhabitants, as well as others who

lived as far as Milwaukee. In September 1835, Calhoun joined the voluntary fire brigade, "Fire Kings"; in November 1836, he decided, for personal reasons, to sell the business and found a willing buyer in Horacio Hill of Concord, NH, who signed the contract but failed to activate the deal with a down payment; John Wentworth then took over the management, and published until the paper's absorption by the *Chicago Tribune* in 1861. The *Chicago American* listed on April 22, 1837, the death of Lewis, the Calhouns' 11 month old only child; ✦ county collector, Eddy's store, 105 Lake St. Calhoun continued to live in Chicago, holding an aldermanic chair and other local political appointments, operating a hardware store and acting as land purchaser for the Illinois Central Railroad; died in Chicago. His *Chicago Democrat* accounts and subscription books (1833-41) are preserved at the Chicago Historical Society; ➡ Calhoun Avenue (2526 E), Calhoun Place (24 N). [12, 204, 351, 479, 480]

The Mails. – It is with regret that we are again compelled to find fault with the mode and manner in which the affairs of the Post Office in this section of the country are managed. – Last week we had not a single word of intelligence from the East. Owing to careless and inexcusable neglect, (a neglect which might be the means of removing the guilty offender from his office) the mail that had been sent from Chicago eastward the week previous, was returned with the self-same contents it had at its departure. This is a matter of great importance to us, especially at this season. The opening business of the Spring suffers, and we are kept in ignorance of the times at Washington, and the commercial transactions of the atlantic cities. Let some certain personages look to it. ✧ Seven or eight buildings have been raised in this town within the past week. ✧ Owing to the failure of the arrival of the last eastern mail, is our excuse for not giving cur [sic] usual variety of news this week.

Among the first items Calhoun printed on a Washington hand press were: (1) Nov. 13, 1833, "one

pack of cards" for C. Ingersoll's Traveler's Home, $2; (2) *Chicago Democrat*; (3) Dec. 6, 1833, "21/2 quire vouchers" for Col. F.J.V. Owen, $5.

Calhoun, John Caldwell (1782-1850) United States statesman and controversial political philosopher of Scottish-Irish stock from South Carolina who became secretary of war under President Monroe in 1817 and soon began to promote construction of postal and military roads between the eastern cities and the new states in the Midwest. In 1819, he urged the U.S. Congress to authorize construction of the Illinois & Michigan Canal; authorized an expedition under Michigan Territory's first governor, Lewis Cass, and chose members able to explore the territory's western reaches; this expedition reached Chicago on Aug. 26, 1820. In 1824, he was elected the nation's seventh vice president under John Quincy Adams and reelected in 1828 under Andrew Jackson; on Dec. 28, 1832, he resigned due to disagreements with President Jackson, and claimed a Senate seat he had won in South Carolina; Martin Van Buren replaced him. [12, 119, 721]

Callimink River corruption of the Indian name for the Calumet River, so called by early settlers.

Callis, Susan daughter of first Indian agent in Chicago, Charles Jouett and Susan Randolph Allen; Charles Lalime Jouett was Susan Callis' brother; she lived in Chicago from 1816 to 1818; her recollections in a letter to John Wentworth are reprinted in Andreas; for memoirs published with comments by Franz L. Brown, see Bibliography; in 1885 lived in Hopkinsville, KY. [12, 74]

calumet many alternate spellings of the word, generally starting with a *K* if used for a river, are found in early documentation and originally denote an Indian appellation meaning *deep river*: Callimink, Calumak, Kinnickinck, Kinnikinnick, Kalamick, Kennemick (Hutchins, 1778), Konnomick (Andrews, 1782), Kilomick, Killomick (Hull, 1812); meanings: (1) French word for hollow reed (shepherd's pipe). (2) Indian tobacco pipe, symbol of peace and friendship, or war, used in ceremonies; highly decorated. Encountering the Illinois, Father Marquette detailed:

There is a Calumet for peace, and one for war, which are distinguished soley by the color of the feathers which with they are adorned; red is a sign of war. They also use it to put an end to their disputes, to strengthen their alliances, and to speak to strangers. It is fashioned from a red stone, polished like marble, and bored in such a manner that one end serves as a receptacle for the tobacco, while the other fits into the stem: this is a stick two feet long, as thick as an ordinary cane, and bored through the middle. It is ornamented with the heads and necks of various birds, whose plumage is very beautiful. To these they also add large feathers, – red, green, and other colors, – wherewith the whole is adorned. [Jesuit Relations LIX].

(3) small settlement at the mouth of the Little Calumet River that grew round the ferry crossing; the ferry was first begun by Reverend See in 1830; active land speculation by agents Lewis Benton, George Dole, and E.K. Hubbard began with an advertisement for "Calumet Lots" in the July 29, 1835, *Chicago Democrat*, and a post office named Calumet was opened later that year on September 9, with Lewis Benton as postmaster; the settlement was abandoned by the 1850s. (4) also referring to the [see] Calumet region; ➡ Calumet Avenue (334 E), Calumet Expressway, Calumet Skyway.

Calumet beach   a geological term, designating the second in a series of three major concentric dune ridges left behind by the shore of glacial Lake Michigan when its level was higher than today; still visible in the landscape today. During the Calumet phase, 10,000 years ago, the lake was 35 to 40 feet higher than it is today. Each of the ridges today, where undisturbed by human activity, reflects its age by having its own characteristic set of animals and plants (the Calumet beach trees are jack pine and white pine); highways U.S. 12 and U.S. 20 now follow part of its course. For the other two ridges, see Tolleston beach and Glenwood beach.

Calumet Club   a private social club, formed in 1878 by a group of well-established citizens; the Indian word calumet was chosen because it implied goodwill and kindly greeting; many of the club's programs cultivated the knowledge of Chicago history. In 1885, the club prepared an Old Settlers' List, which gave the names and then-current addresses of all residents who had arrived in Chicago prior to 1840 and were still alive. Another list gave the names and dates of death of early settlers who died between 1879 and 1885. Both lists were later published in the third volume of Andreas' *History of Chicago*. [12, 58, 121, 684, 707]

Calumet lakes   listed from E to W, the lakes of the Calumet region are: Little Lake, Long Lake, Berry (or Bear) Lake, Lake George, Wolf Lake, Hyde Lake, Lake Calumet and, Hog Lake. Created over the last 4,000 years, these shallow "pan" lakes appear to have formed between spits and offshore ridges of Lake Chicago, crossing older NE flowing river beds.

Calumet phase   see Calumet beach.

Calumet Place   late 1830s name for a small community emerging at "Horseshoe Bend" on the Calumet River [N of Riverdale].

Calumet portage   also Calumet-Sag portage, portage des perches; a portage via the Little Calumet River and Stony Creek/Stony Brook [in part the Calumet Sag Channel] and the Saganashkee Slough to the Des Plaines River; required portaging twice, once between the Little and the Grand Calumet Rivers—separate at that time—and again through the Sag valley between Stony Brook and the Des Plaines River. Both portages connected the Great Lakes and the Mississippi River basin across a continental divide of approximately 10.5 feet above the mean lake level; usage varied with the seasons, yet, due to the size of the Calumet River system, the Calumet portage [near Palos Hills] was shorter and useable longer into each season than its northern counterpart; first mentioned by the English explorer Patrick Kennedy in 1779; destroyed during

construction of the Sanitary and Ship Canal in 1900; lesser local portages were existent around Lake Calumet and Wolf Lake. [298]

Calumet region   term applied to the land around the southern end of Lake Michigan; its name derives from the two rivers draining the mainly low and swampy region (also see Calumet). Since the retreat of the glaciers, the area has been the crossroads for passage through much of northern America's heartland; major Indian trails here intersected. To the N is the Chicago River basin; to the W the Saganashkee Slough/Sag Channel and Hickory Creek drain into the Des Plaines, and to the S is the massive Kankakee basin; Trail Creek [Michigan City] and La Porte form its eastern border. The Calumet was a paradise for hunters in the early days of Chicago and Fort Dearborn, with an abundance of deer and wild fowl. [486, 496]

Calumet River   originally Kinoumiki, according to Father Gravier's c.1696 dictionary, meaning *a boat of deep draft*—clearly not a canoe, and suggesting Europaen navigation on it by 1696; also Kennomekon, Kenomokouk, Calamick River, Calamink, Callimink River; located at the southern edge of metropolitan Chicago, draining the Calumet region into Lake Michigan; formed by the confluence of the Grand Calumet River and the Little Calumet River, some three to four miles from its mouth. When Europeans first arrived the two rivers were completely separate, with different mouths; once the rivers became joined, the mouth of the Grand Calumet River was closed by lake action. [12]

Calumet Sag   low geographic feature in the Calumet region, formerly the ancient Chicago outlet river [the Calumet-Sag Channel]; also see Saganashkee Swamp.

Camp, Samuel   purchased lot 3 in block 35 from Robert A. Kinzie in c.1832 [see map on page 44].

Campbell, Asa   U.S. Army private at Fort Dearborn; enlisted January 1805; incapacitated by illness during the evacuation, killed at the massacre of Aug. 15, 1812. [226]

Campbell, Maj. James B. of Ottawa, IL; treasurer of the board of canal commissioners in 1830, visiting Chicago in this capacity; purchased lot 4 in block 6, and lot 7 in block 8 from Clark Hollenbeck in c.1832; also purchased waterfront real estate from Mark Noble, Sr., on the E side of the north branch in August 1833, jointly with George E. Walker. In 1835, he lived with his first wife at Flusky's boarding house, was a member of the Lake House Association and, late that year, filed a claim for wharfing privileges for lot 1, block 19; ◆ real estate agent, North Clark Street; his first wife's name is not recorded, but he married again in 1840, Sarah P. Elliot; lived at 2634 Calumet Ave. in 1885. [12, 28]

Canada native word *kanata* for settlement–along the St. Lawrence River; adapted by Cartier for the land beyond; under Louis XIV in 1683, Canada was made a royal province, Nouvelle France. The appellation Canada is often used synonymously with [see] New France. [129, 217, 704]

Canada goose *Branta canadensis*; formerly among the waterfowl hunted widely for food by Indians and pioneers; still a common migrant from Canada, abundant in Illinois in the winter, but also a frequent summer resident. [64]

Canis lupus see wolf.

Canal Addition one of the early [see] additions to Chicago by which the original town, as laid out in the [see] Thompson plat of 1830, grew beyond its first borders. The 1836 Chicago ✳ map by E.B. Talcott [see map list on page 51] shows that the Canal Addition represents the portion of the NE quarter of Section 21 that lies W of the south branch of the Chicago River.

Canal Bill in 1829 the Illinois state legislature created a three-member canal commission, which began to plan for the construction of the Illinois & Michigan Canal; for details see Illinois & Michigan Canal.

Canal Commission see Illinois & Michigan Canal.

Canal Commission Addition one of the early [see] additions to Chicago by which the original town, as laid out in the [see] Thompson plat of 1830, grew beyond its first borders. The 1836 Chicago ✳ map by E.B. Talcott [see map list on page 51] shows that the Canal Commission Addition represents the western half of the NE quarter of Section 17. The entire Section 17 was formerly designated [see] canal land.

Canal Land on March 2, 1827, by an act of Congress, signed by President Andrew Jackson on May 21, 1830, the federal government granted to the state of Illinois alternative sections, six-miles wide, of public land along both sides of a proposed route for the Illinois & Michigan Canal, to be sold and the proceeds to be used to meet the canal construction costs.

Canis latrans see wolf.

cannibalism early European explorers first encountered cannibalism among Caribbean Indians. Their reports on the subject were often marked by sensationalism and exaggeration, although it was indeed widely practiced. Also in the interior of North America, where living conditions were often marginal, the hunting of members of other tribes for the purpose of devouring them was an ever-present possibility. In other situations, the consumption of particular portions or organs of an enemy killed in battle was believed to convey certain desired qualities from the victim to the conqueror. An example of such practice occurred at the [see] Fort Dearborn massacre, when the victorious Indians ate Captain Wells's heart.

Cannon, Ephraim and John children by this name, probably siblings, were enrolled as grade school students in the class taught by [see] John Watkins in December 1835. Names of corresponding parents were not recorded. [728]

capote French, diminutive of *cape*; a long cloak, often made from a blanket, usually hooded and belted at the waist, often worn by French Indian

cannibalism in the New World
wood engraving in 1509 [790a]

traders in the wilderness.

Captain White lake steamer that arrived in July 1832, with four companies of soldiers under General Scott; lacking a harbor, they were taken ashore on Mackinaw boats; among the troops was [see] Capt. J.B.T. Russell.

caravel a small sailing ship used by the Spaniards and Portugese in the 16th century. The adjacent wood engraving is from the first illustrated edition of the *Columbus Letter*. [156]

Cardin, Jean Baptiste French Canadian who came to Chicago early in 1812 and worked on Leigh's farm, where he was killed by marauding Winnebago on April 6, together with co-worker Liberty White. [226]

Carew, David on June 4, 1834, filed a petition with the town council to have a nuisance removed.

ⅅceanica Ⅽlaſſis

caravel

[28]

Carey Mission a Baptist Indian school and mission established in 1822 by Rev. Isaac McCoy, attracting emigration and a settlement [near Niles, MI] and existing until c.1830; a branch opened in 1829 on the Detroit-Chicago Road NE of La Porte, IN; also see McCoy, Reverend Isaac. [12]

cariole French, *carriole*; (1) a Canadian dog sled; (2) a light, covered cart; (3) a small carriage drawn by one horse.

Carleton, Sir Guy also Lord Dorchester; English governor of Canada, 1774-1778, succeeded by Governor Haldimand.

Carli, Paul J. (1804-1845) of German origin; in April 1834, began management of the Eagle Hotel on Lake Street and by June advertised "elegant fancy Chairs and Rocking Chairs" in the *Chicago Demo-crat*; on September 22 he announced that John Shrigley would replace him as hotel manager; married Lydia Ann Brown of Springfield, OH, on September 28, Isaac Harmon officiating; John Bates advertised an auction of Paul's "fancy store," its stock, and the building on the north point of J.S.C. Hogan's lot, on October 30; resided six miles up the north branch in 1835; ✦ candies and notions, South Water Street, near Wells.

Carpenter, Abel E. (1813-1882) born in Savoy, MA; brother of Philo Carpenter, who came in June 1833, and taught at the Yankee Settlement [Lockport]; in 1834 assisted Granville Sproat and worked in Philo's drugstore as clerk; a farmer near Warrenville in 1835, later opening a dry goods store; married Sally L. Warren on June 26, 1836, at Aurora; later lived in Aurora, where he died on Dec. 8, 1882; his widow still lived there in 1885. [12, 351]

Carpenter, Gilbert married Mrs. Minerva Hodge on Nov. 17, 1833, Reverend Jesse Walker officiating; on the list of subscribers to the *Chicago Democrat* in November 1833.

Carpenter, Philo (1805-1886) of Savoy, MA; druggist; in May 1830 he married Sarah F. Bridges, who died within the month; arrived on July 18, 1832, from Troy, NY, with a stock of drugs and medicines and opened ★★★ Chicago's 1st drugstore on August 6 in what was most likely Mark Beaubien's small log cabin on the SE corner of Lake and Market streets, immediately against which the Sauganash tavern and hotel had been built earlier in the year; on August 19 organized and conducted the first Sunday school class in an unfinished building owned by Mark Beaubien, with 13 children attending; that year he became active in the temperance movement and, no longer able to endure the proximity of the busy tavern, moved his store to the log cabin of George W. Dole in the winter of 1832-33, on the SE corner of South Water and Clark streets, and remained until the fall of 1833. By this time he had purchased from John Noble

PHILO CARPENTER

two adjacent lots in block 19 on South Water between Wells and LaSalle streets, for which he paid $75 and which gave him a 40-foot frontage on which he built a large two-story frame building with Indiana lumber; moved his store into half the structure and rented the western half to the firm of Russell & Clift; did business until 1840. An ardent enemy of alcohol and member of the Temperance Society, he advertised in the Dec. 17, 1833, *Chicago Democrat* a "Temperance Almanac for sale." Carpenter invested wisely in real estate, acquiring among other holdings, lot 8 in block 40 of the original town from James Kinzie, and a 160-acre plot W of Halsted Street between Kinzie and Madison [SE quarter of Section 8, Township 39], which later became known as Carpenter's Addition, and variously as Carpenter & Curtiss Addition. Likely the attorney [see] James Curtis (also Curtiss) was affiliated with Carpenter in these real estate proceedings. Carpenter was on the voting list for the first town board, Aug. 10, 1833; charter member of the first Presbyterian church, later becoming a deacon. [A split developed within the congregation over the issue of slavery, of which Carpenter was an ardent enemy, and many members seceded with him in 1850 to form the new First Congregational Church.] In April 1833, he married Ann Thompson of New York State; their first daughter, 9 month old Grace Ann, died Oct. 17, 1835, but eventually they became the parents of seven children. In 1834, he imported from the East ★★★ **Chicago's 1st** one-horse shay, and is also credited with having brought to town the first platform scale and the first iron scale. In August 1835, the Chicago Bible Society was founded, and Carpenter became one of its officers; on November 21, submitted a claim for wharfing privileges; ✦ druggist and apothecary, South Water Street; ➡ Carpenter Street (1032 W); living at 436 Washington Blvd. in 1885; died a well respected, successful business man and philanthropist. An account book of his store's early business transactions is preserved at the Chicago Historical Society. [12, 28, 221, 351]

Carpenter's Addition   also Carpenter & Curtiss Addition; see Carpenter, Philo; see Curtiss, James.

Carpenter, Sgt. Nathaniel   (1764-1842) native of Massachsetts; became a charter member of the Baptist congregation on Oct. 19, 1833; on the list of subscribers to the *Chicago Democrat* in November 1833; married Mrs. Eunice Hunter of Chicago at Fort Dearborn on Jan. 9, 1834, Reverend Free-

man officiating; they had eleven children; later moved to Winnebago County, where he died on Oct. 28, 1842, of an inflammatory disease.

Carrig, Thomas   arrived in 1834 from Ireland; died in 1838.

Carrington, Henry, Jr.   from Connecticut; came with his father in 1835; entered a claim near Holderman's Grove.

Carrington, Henry, Sr.   (1781-1871) from Connecticut; came with his oldest son Henry in 1835; a widower, he returned the following year with a younger son (Nathan Starr) and in 1837, acquired the Morse claim [1834, Lyons Township] and farmed the acreage; died in Connecticut. [13, 278]

Carroll, Charles   (1737-1832) American Revolutionary War hero and member of the Continental Congress, and the last surviving signer of the Declaration of Independence; ➡ Carroll Avenue (328 N, from 44 W to 4758 W) was named after him by James Thompson in 1830; its eastern portion, between Lake Street and Wells Street, still deviates from its otherwise exact EW direction by several degrees, reflecting the original course of the Chicago River's north bank [note Wright's map, page 44], though the bank itself has long since been brought into perfect EW alignment. ➡ There is also a Carroll Drive in Garfield Park.

Carroll, Patrick   married Mary Hogan on April 24, 1835, Father St. Cyr officiating.

Cartier, Jacques   (1491-1557) French navigator who explored the St. Lawrence River; commissioned by François I to look for the NW passage to Cathay, he discovered the Gulf of St. Lawrence (1534) and on a second trip in 1535, explored the St. Lawrence River as far W as [Montreal]. On May 3, 1536, in a ceremony near [Quebec], Cartier claimed the entire drainage basin of the St. Lawrence River for the French crown. He neither found a passage to China, nor did he return with the precious stones or metals as had been anticipated; consequently, French authorities lost interest in further exploration until the effort to colo-

nize North America and find the western approach to China was revived by Henry IV at the end of the 16th century. [205, 730]

Carver, David   bachelor seaman from New York; arrived late summer 1833 with the first cargo of pine on a schooner he owned; voted in the first election on August 10; a licensed auctioneer, but as merchant in 1834, shipped whitewood, pine lumber, produce, and provisions regularly between St. Joseph and Chicago, using also the *Post Boy*, *Commodore*, *Dart*, *Oregon*, *White Pigeon*, and *Llewellyn*; opened ★★★ **Chicago's 1st** lumber yard on South Water Street, between LaSalle and Wells, adding in May an auction and commission store to his storehouse, and held auctions every Saturday; in the Jan. 21, 1835, *Chicago Democrat* he announced the dissolution of his partnership with Isaac K. Palmer; continued to advertise as lumber dealer & commission merchant; in January he had communicated with the town board in relation to wharfing privileges and on November 24, submitted an affidavit in support of his claim for privileges, bolstered by a statement filed by W.H. Brown; ✦ Captain, *David Carver*. [28]

Carver, Capt. Jonathan   (1710-1780) a Massachsetts native who, from 1766 to 1768, traveled extensively throughout the northern parts of the Great Lakes and, in 1779 and again in 1781, published an account of his experiences that became a popular book, *Travels through the Interior Parts of North America in the Years 1766, 1767, and 1768* (demonstrating that in 1778 it was still possible to print a detailed ✱ map of the Great Lakes, include a number of large imaginary islands in Lake Superior, and completely ignore the Chicago site or river). [605, 682]

Casas, Don Bartolomé de las   see Las Casas, Don Bartolomé de.

Casey, Edward W.   New Hampshire lawyer who arrived in 1833 and immediately established practice in town, advertising in the May 7 *Chicago Democrat*, with an office "adjoining that of Clerk of Circuit Court"; later in August, and still in August 1835, he advertised his office with B.S. Morris as located on the second floor of Garrett's Auction Room on Dearborn Street (near the corner of South Water Street); known as a heavy drinker; served as clerk of the town board under President John H. Kinzie in 1834; returned to Concord, NH, by 1841; died on Oct. 3, 1875, at Newburyport, MA. [12]

Casey; John, Peter, Patrick, and Edward arrived in 1835 from Ireland, probably related; ✦ John [c.1794-1881] –bricklayer, corner of Market and Washington; Patrick–waiter, Mansion House; Edward and Peter–clerks, Stanton & Black; by 1879, Edward was living in California; John died in Chicago. [12, 351]

Cass, Lewis (1782-1866) born at Exeter, NH; served under Gen. William Hull in the War of 1812, and was highly critical of Hull's surrender of Detroit to the British; governor of the territory of Michigan and regional superintendent of Indian affairs from 1813 to 1831. In 1820, Governor Cass led a four-month expedition, covering 4,000 miles, in an attempt to reach the source of the Mississippi River; accompanied by Henry Schoolcraft as mineralogist, Dr. A. Wolcott as physician, and Capt. David B. Douglas as topographer; James D. Doty joined as official journalist and Charles C. Trowbridge as assistant topographer, but both took a partly separate course that bypassed Chicago. The expedition reached Fort Dearborn on Aug. 26, 1820 (see G. Hubbard's following account for a lively description of Cass' second visit in 1827). In 1821, Cass negotiated the Indian treaty in Chicago, was in charge of containing the Winnebago scare of 1827, and directed the Black Hawk War of 1832; in late June 1835, while Secretary of War, he returned to Chicago, but the steamer *Michigan* only docked and circumstance rendered departure within hours; was a member of the U.S. Senate from 1845-1857; ran unsuccessfully in 1845 as Democratic candidate for president against Zachary Taylor; later served as Sec. of State under President Buchanan; [➡ prior to 1930, Wabash Avenue, N of the river, was called Cass Avenue]. [12, 737]

[1827] *While at breakfast at Mr. Kinzie's house, we heard singing, faintly at first, but gradually growing louder as the singers approached. Mr. Kinzie recognized the leading voice as that of Bob Forsyth, and left the table for the piazza of the house, where we all followed. About where Wells Street crosses, in plain sight from where we stood, was a light birchbark canoe, manned with thirteen men, rapidly approaching, the men keeping time with their paddles to one of the Canadian boat songs; it proved to be Governor Cass and his secretary, Robert Forsyth, and they landed and soon joined us.*

Cassidy, George W. co-owner-assignee, together with William Fithian, of 240 acres of land in Section 20, Township 39, prior to 1836, as per Andreas, *History of Chicago*, pp. 112-113.

Castelnau, Francis, compte de (1812-1880) French traveler to Chicago in 1838; made a drawing of the harbor entrance, looking E to include a portion of Fort Dearborn, that was published in 1848 in Paris. It is one of the few surviving sketches of early Chicago created *in situ* as opposed to the many that were drawn later from memory. [115]

Castle Inn a hotel and tavern along Brush Hill Trail in [Hinsdale] built by [see] Orente and David Grant in 1835. [29a, 217a]

Castor canadensis see beaver.

Catfish see Winnemac.

Cathay early name for China introduced to Europe by Marco Polo; derived from the name of a pre-Mongol tribe that had conquered parts of northern China in the 10th century A.D. and held them for 200 years; early European explorers were searching for a shorter route to Cathay when they sailed westward across the Atlantic Ocean.

Catholic congregation St. Mary Catholic parish, the first organized congregation, was established in May 1833 by Father [see] St. Cyr under the authority of Bishop Joseph Rosati of St. Louis; the

ST. MARY'S CHURCH [410]

first Mass was celebrated in Mark Beaubien's log cabin on May 5, and ★★★ **Chicago's 1st** Catholic baptism took place on May 22 [George Beaubien, son of the Mark]; a modest unpainted wooden balloon frame church building, St. Mary's Catholic Church, measuring 25 by 35 feet, initially without steeple or bell, was completed in October 1833 on a canal lot at the SW corner of Lake and State streets, built by Augustine D. Taylor for $400. The price for the lot was more than anticipated, and the church was later moved twice, first to the SW corner of Michigan and Madison streets, then to the SW corner of Wabash and Madison. In 1834, Chicago became part of the newly established diocese of Vincennes under Bishop Simon Bruté, but Father St. Cyr continued to report to Bishop Rosati while remaining in Chicago. In October 1836, Father St. Cyr left, and was replaced by Father Leander Schaeffer, who served until 1840. Not until

September 1843 was the first Roman Catholic diocese created at Chicago; Reverend William J. Quarter was appointed the first bishop. See Saint Cyr, John Mary Irenaeus, for a list of petitioners; ➡ St. Mary Street (2170 N). [12, 267, 268, 578, 658]

Catie, Joseph voted at the election of Aug. 7, 1826 (see Chronology).

Catlin, Seth (1812-1863) arrived in 1834 from Massachsetts; went into commerce and banking.

Caton, John Dean (1812-1894/5) from Monroe, NY; at his arrival on June 19, 1833, with his 18-year-old brother William, Chicago had fewer than 200 inhabitants; six weeks later, there were more than 250. This made incorporation possible under the laws of the state and Caton participated in the effort. As lawyer, prosecuted ★★★ **Chicago's 1st** case of larceny in July; his office was in Dr. Temple's building on Lake Street; later, on December 4, was appointed town attorney. In 1834, he formed a law partnership with James H. Collins, opening an office on South Water Street, one door E of the corner with Lake Street, removing in June to an upstairs office two doors E of the Baptist church on South Water Street, and was also elected justice of the peace; in 1835 the partnership was dissolved and Caton traveled to New Hartford, NY to marry Laura A. Sherrill on July 28, returning with his bride; ✦ attorney at law, Clark Street; in 1842 joined the Supreme Court of Illinois, becoming chief justice in 1855; lived at 1900 Calumet Ave. in 1885; ➡ Caton Street (1652 N). See the following excerpt of Caton's reminiscences to the members of the Calumet Club and assembled old settlers on May 27, 1879. [12, 242, 351, 707]

... Let me ask John Bates over there if he remembers when we scated together up to Hard Scrabble, - where Bridgeport is now, - and he explained to me, by pantomime alone, how the Indians cought musk-rats under the ice. And let me ask Silas B. Cobbs if he remembers the trick Mark Beaubien played on Robert A. Kinzie to win the race on the ice that winter? See, now, how Mark's eye flashes fire and he trembles in

JOHN DEAN CATON [120]

every fibre at the bare remembrance of that wild excitement. This was the way he did it. He and Kinzie had each a very fast pony, one a pacer and the other one a trotter. Mark had trained his not to brake when he uttered the most unearthly screams and yells which he could pour forth, and that is saying much, for he could beat any Pottawatomie I ever heard, except Gurdon S. Hubbard and John S.C. Hogan. The day was bright and cold. The glittering ice was smooth as glass, the atmosphere pure and bracing. The start was about a mile up the South Branch. Down came the trotter and the pacer like a whirlwind, neck and neck, till they approached Wolf Point, or the junction, when Kinzie's pony began to pull ahead of the little pacer,

J. D. CATON,
ATTORNEY & COUNSELLOR AT LAW,
And Solicitor in Chancery,
ONE door east of Brewster, Hogan & Co,
South Water-street, Chicago, Illinois.
Dec. 10, 1833 3

and bets were two to one on the trotting-nag as he settled a little nearer to the ice and stretched his hear and neck further out, as if determined to win it but by a throat-latch. It was at this supreme moment that Mark's tactics won the day. He sprang to his feet in his plank-built pung, his tall form towering above all surroundings, threw high in the air his wolf-skin cap, frantically swung round his head his buffalo robe, and screamed forth such unearthly yells as no human voice ever excelled, broken up into a thousand accents by a rapid clapping of the mouth with the hand. To this the pony was well trained, and it but served to bring out the last inch of speed that was in him, while the trotter was frightened out of his wits, no doubt thinking a whole tribe of Indians were after him, and he broke into a furious run, which carried him far beyond the goal before he could be brought down. Hard words were uttered then, which it would not do to repeat in a well-conducted Sunday-school, but the winner laughed and pocketed the stakes with a heartiness and zest which Mark alone could manifest. ...

For an account of Caton representing Chicago Negroes in court to help them secure their "free paper," see the item following the entry on slavery.

Caton, William P. born 1815, arrived on June 19, 1833, with his older brother, John Dean Caton; lived at Joliet in 1885. [12, 351]

Cauchois, Jacques member of La Salle's 1682-83 expedition to the mouth of the Mississippi, passing S through Chicagoland in January 1682.

Cavarly, Alfred W. member of the surveying party for the Illinois & Michigan Canal that visited Chicago in 1830 under James M. Bucklin, chief engineer. [704]

Cavelier de La Salle, Abbé Jean brother of La Salle, born at Rouen; Sulpitian priest; survivor of the ill-fated Texas expedition; after his brother's death, was member of the group with Henri Joutel that reached Chicago on Sept. 25, 1687, on their way from *Fort St. Louis* (Starved Rock) to Canada, and then to France; died in Rouen after 1717. [519]

Cavelier, Jean Baptiste no relation to La Salle; sur-

survivor of the ill-fated Texas expedition; after La Salle's death, was a member of the group of six with Henri Joutel that reached Chicago on Sept. 25, 1687, on their way from *Fort St. Louis* (Starved Rock) to Canada, and then to France. [519]

Cavelier, René-Robert, sieur de La Salle   see La Salle, René-Robert Cavelier, sieur de.

cecropia moth   *Hyalophora cecropia*; the largest North American moth with a wingspan of up to 150 mm (5 7/8 inches); common in and around settlements in pioneer days, but rarely encountered today in Chicagoland.

cemeteries   prior to 1835, when the first cemetery was laid out, the bodies were usually buried on or near the homestead, or near that of a friend who would look after the grave. Captain Whistler's 1808 ✳ draft of the fort shows an "Indian grave yard" SE of the stockade as part of "a soldiers's garden," near the old mouth of the river. Another "old burying ground," referred to by John Calhoun, was on the lakeshore between the Hardy house and the Wright house; Judge Caton places it between Washington and some distance N of Randolph Street, and describes graves washing away in July 1832: "... half a dozen coffins sticking out of the bank and the bones hauled out and scattered on the beach." The dead from the fort were usually buried on the N side of the main river, E of Kinzie's house, near the lakeshore; John Kinzie was also buried there in 1828, but his body was later moved twice. The soldiers who died of cholera during the Black Hawk War in 1832 were buried near the Forks at a site that later became the NW corner of Lake Street and Wabash Avenue; at least 20 of those who died on board ship while anchored at Chi-

cago were committed to a sea burial (see cholera for Capt. A. Walker's letter). The people living near the Forks had a common acre on the W side of the north branch in which to bury their dead. On Oct. 18, 1834, a Chicago Cemetery Association was organized; on Aug. 15, 1835, the town surveyor was directed to lay out two tracts of land suitable for burials: 10 acres of land on the N side (for Protestants; E of Clark Street near Chicago Avenue) and 16 acres on the S side (for Catholics; at the foot of 23rd Street); these, Chicago's first official cemeteries, were fenced in September 1835, and burial was forbidden elsewhere thereafter. Henry Gherkin, a German immigrant, was the first recorded gravedigger in 1836. In 1842, the city fathers established a new municipal burial ground on a tract of land now roughly bounded by North Avenue, LaSalle, Wisconsin, and State streets; when the Civil War ended, this cemetery became the southern portion of Lake Park, later renamed Lincoln Park. Oakwoods Cemetery, on the S side, was chartered in 1853; Rosehill Cemetery was chartered in 1859, and Graceland Cemetery's charter was approved on Feb. 22, 1861—both are on the N side.

Cervus elaphus   see elk.

Chacksfield, George   (c.1808-1885) born in England; arrived in November 1835; ✦ grocery and provision store, South Water Street near Clark; still living in Chicago in 1878. [12, 351]

Chachagwessiou   Illiniois chief with whom Marquette had contact en route to Chicago during the winter of 1674-75.

Chamberlin, Horace   participant in an outing on horseback from Chicago to the Calumet River, with Rose Hathaway as partner, in the spring of 1835, as described by John D. Caton; not long after Chamberlin lost his life in the Texas revolution. [121]

Chambers, Asa W.   acquired 120 acres of land at [Western Springs] in June 1835; partnered Sheldon Benedict as Messrs. Chambers & Benedict late November that year, buying J.M. Faulkner's entire

stock of goods and continuing at the old stand two doors W of the land office on Lake Street; an ad in the November 25 *Chicago Democrat* assured a "stock of Groceries probably as extensive as any west of the city of New York." [711a]

Champlain, Samuel de   (1567-1635) French explorer whose achievements helped secure Canada and its Indian trade for France, opening the way for later discoverers to reach Chicago; first came to the banks of the St. Lawrence River in 1603 and, during his next visit in 1608, founded Quebec and discovered Lake Champlain. From 1608 to 1635, he served as the first governor of New France; Nicollet was his protégé; at the time of his death it was clear that the settlement of Quebec would endure. In his travels, Champlain had gone around Lake Ontario and as far W as Georgian Bay of Lake Huron (1613-15); in 1612 he prepared a ✳ map, *Carte Geographique de la Nouvelle Franse*, and another in c.1616, which was eventually published in 1653 by Pierre Du Val; visualized are the Great Lakes W of Georgian Bay, presumably copied by Champlain from Indian sketch maps; ➡ Champlain Avenue (634 E). [12, 94, 127, 205, 281, 322, 605]

Chance   lake schooner under Captain Wade; coming originally from Buffalo, NY, and then sailing between St. Joseph and Chicago, the vessel called at Chicago seven times in 1835, on November 11 from [see] Shipwagen; was run ashore by storm later that month on Lake Michigan, as per notice in the November 28 *Chicago American*.

Chandler, Joseph   arrived from New York on June 27, 1833; beginning in July, held an executive position in harbor construction under Maj. George Bender, together with Morgan Shapley; ✦ harbor government works. [12]

Chandonnai, Jean Baptiste   *métis* son of Chippewaqua, adopted by Charlotte Chandonnet of Mackinac; fraternal nephew of Potawatomi Chief Topenebe of St. Joseph; employed from 1792 to 1799 by William Burnett at St. Joseph; at Milwaukee after 1800; employed as chief clerk in Kinzie's store, and lived in a house N of the river near the lakeshore, between the houses of Buisson and Kinzie; was in the boat with the Kinzies at the time of the massacre of 1812 and several days later, conveyed them, Margaret Helm, and Sergeant Griffith by boat to St. Joseph; assisted in the release of Captain and Mrs. Heald from captivity after the massacre by offering a mule and a bottle of whiskey. In 1813, living at Detroit, he was charged with treason against George III and, with Kinzie, was jailed in irons in Fort Malden for trying, though a long covert agent of the British Indian Department, to win the Indians over to the U.S. side; was also wanted for the murder of his stepfather, a British army offficer who had gone to Burnett's to arrest him; "escaped to the Indians" and by July 22, 1814, was an official U.S. interpreter at an Indian treaty at Greenville, Ohio, convened by Governor Harrison and Governor Cass of Michigan Territory, by which various Indian groups, including the Potawatomi of his uncle Topenebe, allied themselves to the United States and agreed to supply warriors to fight the British; on Sept. 8, 1815, acted as an interpreter with Kinzie at the Treaty of Spring Wells near Detroit, at which the various tribes officially "repented" their pro-British activities—Chandonnai was then a valuable asset of U.S. Indian policy, a friend of the Americans; married to Marie Chapoton of Detroit, who, with their newborn child, joined him at Chicago in 1817. Within two years, Chandonnai acted as an independent fur trader in Chicago, but was then hired by the American Fur Co. to remove him from competition; at the Chicago Treaty of 1821 he was granted two sections of land on the St. Joseph River; present as interpreter at the 1833 Treaty of Chicago, dying soon after somewhere in Michigan. [12, 29, 109, 226, 235]

Chapeau, Jacques   purchased a hat at the estate sale of W.H. Wallace on Dec. 14, 1827; possibly

[see] Jacques Chaput.

Chapin, John P.   (1810-1864) born in Bradford, VT; arrived in 1832 from New Hampshire and became a member of the firm Wadsworth, Dyer & Chapin, general wholesale and retail merchants; ♦ commission merchant, South Water Street; in 1846 became the tenth mayor of Chicago and served for one year. [728]

Chapman, Charles H.   arrived in 1833 from New York with his wife Emily and appointed second ferryman for the Dearborn Free Ferry on September 3; on the list of subscribers to the *Chicago Democrat* in November 1833; owned a house on the SW corner of Randolph and Wells streets; [in his book, E.O. Gale accuses Chapman of financial double-dealings] in February 1834, Chapman settled his accounts and returned to New York, though in the *Chicago Democrat* on July 30 he advertised the rental of three buildings and on August 14 William Payne announced in the *Chicago Democrat* a lawsuit against him; in the June 8, 1835, *Chicago American* he advertised several structures for sale or rent; ♦ real estate dealer, Randolph Street [12, 266]

Chapman, George   arrived in 1833 from New York and voted in the first town election on August 10; in 1839, a George H. Chapman is listed as real estate dealer. [12]

Chapman, James   U.S. Army private at Fort Dearborn; enlisted in December 1805; left Chicago when his enlistment expired in December 1810. [226]

Chappel, Eliza Emily   (1807-1888) New York born of mixed Huguenot and Pilgrim descent; had organized a school at Mackinac; arrived in June 1833 in the company of Capt. Seth Johnson and his wife; initially lived with the family of Major Wilcox at Fort Dearborn; in September she opened a one room school, the Infant School, in a log cabin that had been the initial store of John S. Wright at the SE corner of Lake and Market streets [see Monuments, schools]; here she accommodated 25

students, her living quarters being separated from the classroom by a curtain; in January 1834, moved her class to the first Presbyterian *church* building. Eliza married Reverend Jeremiah Porter on June 15, 1835, and moved with him to Green Bay, WI; they had nine children, three of whom died in infancy; s her grave is located at Rosehill Cemetery; ➡ Chappel Avenue (2032 E). ✦ For a portrait of Eliza Chappel Porter, see page 369. [12]

Chaproffne, François   also Chapron, Francis; with wife, Rosalia, an immigrant from France to New York in 1833; arrived by lake boat in Chicago in 1835 and within a week moved to [see] *Grosse Pointe* intending to farm, becoming friends of the Ouilmette family; returned to Chicago in 1836, living at Van Buren and Canal streets; their children were Eugenié, Celestine, Zoé, and Vincent; F gardener, West Water Street, N end; in 1841 bought land and moved to Elston Avenue and Division Street, where François died several years later. Rosalia continued their horticulture enterprise. [293]

Chaput, Jacques   early member of the Catholic congregation; signed for a family of five on the 1833 petition to Bishop Rosati, asking that a priest be assigned to Chicago. [12]

Charbonneau   a *voyageur* and member of the de Montigny-St. Cosme party that came through Chicago in 1699.

Chardon, Father Jean-Baptiste   (c.1651-1743) joined Father Aveneau as missionary at the St. Joseph Mission in 1705 and remained until 1712, when the Fox War forced his withdrawal; was fluent in several Indian languages, and continued his labor among the Indians elsewhere on various assignments; his last years were spent in Quebec, where he died at the age of 92.

Chardonnais, Jean Baptiste   misnomer for [see] Chandonnais, Jean Baptiste.

Charlevoix, Père Pierre François-Xavier de   (1682-1761) born in St. Quentin, France; Jesuit scholar and traveler in America in the 1720s; traced some of Father Marquette's travels and recorded his own experiences in detail; in 1721 visited the *Mission de la Conception* in Kaskaskia; in September was at Fort St. Joseph, heading for Chicago, but stormy weather deterred him and he eventually took the St. Joseph-Kankakee River route, bypassing Chicago; in 1744 published his *Journal d'un Voyage Fait par Ordre du Roi dans l'Amerique Septentrionale*, which included a ✳ map of the Great Lakes by cartographer [see] Jacques Bellin that shows Checagou and the Portage des Chenes. Charlevoix believed that Nicholas Perrot was at the Chicago site several years (1671) before Jolliet and Marquette, but few historians agree. [12, 226, 235]

Charlotte armed British sloop patrolling Lakes Michigan, Huron, and Erie during the period of British control; built at Navy Island in 1764. [48]

Chase, Dr. Enoch Vermont born, brother of Horace; of Milwaukee, but early resident of Chicago in the early 1830s; in an 1883 letter [reprinted in Andreas] describes a visit to Chicago in 1834, when he traveled from Michigan City around the lower end of Lake Michigan; in addition to sighting Chicago, his description of road travel and enumeration of isolated houses and taverns on the roads between Michigan City and Milwaukee are of historic interest. [13]

Chase, Horace Vermont born, brother of Enoch; arrived in Chicago in 1834 and became a clerk in P.F.W. Peck's store, then worked for Chester Ingersoll at the Wolf Tavern, then as clerk in the firm of Kinzie & Hall; in the winter of 1834-35 moved to Milwaukee and remained there permanently.

Chassut, Jacques early member of the Catholic congregation; signed for a family of five on the 1833 petition to Bishop Rosati, requesting that a priest be assigned to Chicago.

Chaubenee see Shabbona.

Chavelie, Peter see Chevalier, Peter.

Cheagoumeman word for the mouth of the Chicago river as used by Franquelin ✳ on his map of New France, 1684; probably a corruption of Chicagoumeman.

Checagou misspelling of *Chicagou*.

Chechepinqua transliteration of the Potawatomi name of [see] Alexander Robinson; also Chi-Chi-Bingway, Chee-Chee-Bing-Way that mean *squinting eyes, blinking eyes.* [226]

Chequamegon Bay also Chegoimegon; near the western extent of Lake Superior; close to present Ashland, WI; site of the Jesuit [see] *Mission de Saint-Esprit*, founded by Father Allouez in 1665.

Chevalier also Chevallier; prominent family at St. Joseph and Mackinac, originally from Montreal; family name of a line of Potawatomi chiefs at St. Joseph around 1760, at Deep River in 1780 and afterwards at Lake Calumet; many names of family members are recorded, but the exact relationship of each is not always known.

Chevalier, Angelique received $200 at the Chicago treaty on Sept. 26, 1833; an obituary in the *Chicago Democrat* on Feb. 4, 1834, "Miss Angelique Chevalier, 33, died on Jan 27 at Chicago, of pulmonary disease."

Chevalier, Archange see Ouilmette, Archange Chevalier.

Chevalier, Catherine also de Catiche; daughter of François and Marianne Chevalier, sister of Archange Ouilmette and Sheshi Buisson; married [see] Alexander Robinson on Sept. 28, 1826, before John Kinzie, J.P. Robinson's first wife [Indian name unknown] nevertheless retained a position within the household.

Chevalier, François French-Potawatomi chief of a village on the NW shore of Lake Calumet, whose daughters married [see] Antoine Ouilmette, Alexander Robinson, and Louis Buisson.

Chevalier Jean Baptiste (1803-1834) son of Louis Pascale Chevalier and his Ojibwa consort; métis Potawatomi chieftain who attended the estate sale of W.H. Wallace on April 27, 1827, and bought a "bai horse paid by John Kinzie, Senr."; was on the voter list of Aug. 2, 1830; an announcement of his death on Jan. 21, 1834, in the *Chicago Democrat*, as per Louis P. Chevalier, estate administrator. [12]

Chevalier, Josette also Josephte; born 1807 at Mackinac; daughter of Louis Pascale Chevalier and his Ojibwa consort, godchild of Leon and Archange Bourassa; her marriage to Mark Bourassa by Father St. Cyr is listed in Catholic church records, March 1835.

Chevalier, Louis Pascale [Louison] born in 1720; influential French-Potawatomi chief at St. Joseph during the Revolutionary War; engaged in trade and agriculture at St. Joseph.

Chevalier, Louis early member of the Catholic congregation; signed for a family of three on the 1833 petition to Bishop Rosati of St. Louis, asking that a priest be assigned to Chicago; likely the Louis P. listed as administrator for [see] Jean Baptiste Chevalier's estate in January 1834.

Chevalier, Peter [Pierre] also Chavalié, Chevilire; voted at the election of Aug. 7, 1826 [see Chronology].

Chicago (1) also Chicagou or Checagou; Michigamea chief who lived in MO during the first half of the 18th century and visited Paris, where he became an instant sensation at the royal court; nothing points to a connection between this chief and the name of the Illinois settlement Chicago, contrary to statements by Mrs. Juliette Kinzie and Joseph J. Thompson. (2) local Miami name for the wild garlic plant *Allium tricoccum* that gave the settlement of Chicago its name; see essay by John Swenson on page 377. [406, 659]

Chicago a side-wheel steamer owned by John Griffith & Co. and Capt. John F. Wight, built on the St. Joseph River near the mouth of Hickory Creek in 1834-35; routed between St. Joseph and Chicago in 1835. [235]

Chicago, IL located in the state of Illinois at a latitude of 41 degrees, 53 minutes, and 06.2 seconds N; longitude W of the meridian of Greenwich, 87 degrees, 38 minutes, 01.2 seconds, as determined by Lt. Col. J.D. Graham, U.S.A., in

1858 at the dome of Chicago's courthouse. Chicago was incorporated as a town on Aug. 10, 1833, but incorporation was not approved by the Illinois General Assembly until Feb. 11, 1835, and not certified by the secretary of state until July 6, 1835. The municipality received a city charter on March 4, 1837. Also see Additions to Chicago; Chicago boundaries; Chicago Directory; Chicago land boom; Chicago, name, origin; Chicago, name, variants; Chicago population growth; Chicago precincts; Chicago schools; Chicago streets; Chicago Town Ordinances; Chicago Town Trustees. [58, 72, 73, 99, 215, 258, 266, 269, 273, 294, 303, 325, 375, 463, 465, 491, 498, 544, 553]

Chicago Academy   see English and Classical School for Boys.

Chicago additions   see Additions to Chicago.

Chicago American   second Chicago weekly newspaper, representing Whig views; the first issue appeared June 8, [reading May 8, due to a printer's error] 1835, under editor and owner T.O. Davis; the office was on Water Street [later called South Water Street], near the drawbridge. On April 9, 1836, the *Chicago American* became a daily paper and was sold to [see] William Stuart in 1837; Alexander Stuart acquired the paper in July 1842, and published until Oct. 18, 1842. One week later, under new ownership, the paper was reintroduced as the *Chicago Express*; in 1844 the paper became the *Chicago Daily Journal*. [12]

Chicago and New York Land Company   real estate firm prominent during the 1835-36 land boom; its agent was K. Richards, with an office above the drugstore of W.H. & A.F. Clarke, at the corner Lake and Clark streets

Chicago Bible Society   organized as a branch of the American Bible Society on Aug. 18, 1835, at a meeting of interested members of various denominations at the Methodist chapel; their mission was to make Bibles available to all who could read; Reverend Isaac T. Hinton was the first president; on November 25, the society held its first annual

meeting at which Reverend J.T. Mitchell was elected president; W.H. Brown and Lt. Jamieson became vice presidents, Thomas Wright and Reverend Hinton, recording and correspondence secretaries, Dr. J.T. Temple became treasurer, and F. Thomas, G. Goodrich and James Rockwell comprised the executive committee. [12]

Chicago Board of Health   see Board of Health.

Chicago Board of Town Trustees   first board elected on Aug. 10, 1833, with five trustees: T.J.V. Owen (president), George W. Dole, Madore B. Beaubien, John Miller, and E.S. Kimberly; the second election took place on Aug. 11, 1834; elected were J.H. Kinzie (president), G.S. Hubbard, E. Goodrich, J.K. Boyer, and John S.C. Hogan. At the third election in June 1835, eight trustees were elected: H. Hugunin (president), W. Kimball, B. King, S. Jackson, E.B. Williams, F.C. Sherman, E. Loyd, and George Dole. Also see: Chicago, Town, incorporation. [12]

Chicago Book and Stationary Store   ★★★ Chicago's 1st opened in August 1834 by Aaron Russell and Benjamin H. Clift on South Water Street between Wells and LaSalle; other merchandise, such as patent medicines, were also sold; though the partnership dissolved in October 1835, Clift carried on.

Chicago, boundaries   the area of the Chicago settlement (0.417 square miles) was initially defined by the plat published on Aug. 4, 1830, by James Thompson, surveyor for the canal commissioners; it was enclosed by Madison, DesPlaines, Kinzie, and State streets, of which only Kinzie Street was named. On Aug. 10, 1833, the same day the first village board was elected, the town limits were defined as follows: "Beginning at the intersection of Jackson and Jefferson streets; thence north to [see] Cook street, and through that street to its eastern extremity in Wah-bon-seh; thence on a direct line to Ohio street in Kinzie's addition; thence eastwardly to the lake shore; thence south with the line of beach to the northern United States pier; thence

northwardly along said pier to its termination; thence to the channel of the Chicago River; thence along said channel until it intersects the eastern boundary line of the town of Chicago, as laid out by the canal commissioners; thence southwardly with said line until it meets Jackson Street; thence westwardly along Jackson street until it reaches the place of beginning." The first increase in size of the settlement was declared by the village board on Nov. 6, 1833, adding to the existing official town area the tract bounded by State Street on the W, Ohio Street on the N, the lakeshore on the E, and Jackson Street on the S. On Feb. 11, 1834, the village board again revised the boundaries, including all land E of State Street, from Chicago Avenue on the N to 12th Street [Roosevelt] on the S, excepting the military reservation of Fort Dearborn.

Chicago Brewery   J. and W. Crawford first advertised to make contracts for 4,000 bushels "of good sound Barley to be delivered at the Chicago Brewery" in the June 13, 1835, *Chicago American*; for a reproduction of the ad, see entry on breweries.

Chicago Cemetery Association   organized on Oct. 18, 1834.

Chicago Commercial Advertiser   a weekly "liberty" [anti-slavery] paper first issued on Oct. 11, 1836, by Hooper Warren, with Edward H. Rudd as printer; the office was on Dearborn Street near South Water; it survived approximately one year.

Chicago Democrat   ★★★ Chicago's 1st newspaper, published by John Calhoun, a Jacksonian Democrat; used the eagle here reproduced as decoration on every issue beginning Nov. 26, 1833, with

"–'Where Liberty dwells, there is
my Country'–Franklin"

below its headline. Initially, the newspaper was published every Tuesday, but in 1834 there were interruptions from late December to May because printing paper did not arrive. Calhoun states in the March 25, 1835, issue: "... the publisher deems it proper to state the causes which have led to its

temporary suspension. ... Early in the fall we have made arrangements for our [paper] supply but winter set in before it was received. We have since endeavored to obtain paper from various places, but have been unsuccessful. A supply of paper will be received by the first vessels from Cleveland, and also from Buffalo, ..." Offices were located at the SW corner of South Water and Clark until late October 1833, when moved to the loft above the hardware store of Jones & King on South Water Street between Clark and Dearborn. The paper was printed on an imperial sheet; a Washington press was used, operated by manual power; the second owner and publisher, John Wentworth, took over in November 1836. Publication ceased in 1861 when the paper was absorbed by the *Chicago Tribune*. In 1834, subscription per year was $2.50, payable in advance; advertisements were $1 for 17 lines or less, and 25 cents for every extra line. [12]

Chicago-Detroit Road   see Chicago Road.

Chicago Directory   Hurlbut, in his *Chicago Antiquities*, writes of a metallic box placed into the NE cornerstone of the court building at its construction in the fall of 1835, containing several unique documents, among them a list of "every dweller in Chicago outside of Fort Dearborn"; the box has never been found. A *Chicago Business Directory*—★★★ **Chicago's 1st**, containing 277 entries, almost half of them on Lake Street, was

printed as part of a 1839 publication by Edward H. Rudd under the title *The Laws and Ordinances of the City of Chicago*, passed in Common Council; in 1843, attorney James Wellington Norris canvassed for a general directory, and Robert Fergus and William Ellis printed the listing in 1844; many subsequent directories appeared. Before 1843, there have survived only lists of voters, such as those who cast votes for the first mayoral election on Tuesday, May 2, 1837. This particular list is reprinted in the second issue of the *Fergus Historical Series*, published in 1876. The same issue also contains a 1839 Directory of the City, which Robert Fergus retrospectively assembled with the assistance of several elderly residents. Most of the citizens listed for 1839 (males only) had been living in town in preceding years, and population growth was minimal in Chicago between 1836 and 1839. [Every settler included in the encyclopedia, who was still living and working in the city in 1839 and listed in the directory is noted with ✦ and followed by the original listing; *eds.*] Another retrospective attempt, this one to assemble a comprehensive list of residents for 1833, may be found in J.R. Hayden's book. [99, 132, 243, 319, 506]

Chicago elections   see elections.

Chicago Fire Department   see firefighting.

Chicago harbor   the mouth of the Chicago River did not naturally allow fot a harbor; a sand bar diverted the river's final course southward, and just where the waters met–from Wacker Dr. to as far S as 12th Street–was dependent on the wind, lake levels, and storm activity. G.S. Hubbard considered Madison Street the "permanent mouth," but saw it move 1 1/2 miles S from the fort. [For further testimony by Hubbard, see entry on fox.] The sand bar stretched from N to S and was at times quite substantial, with juniper bushes and small willows growing on its northern portion that connected to the shore; it narrowed toward its free southern end, where the river met the lake; the mouth was usually too shallow to admit ships draw-

ing 18 inches or more. According to Alexander Robinson, who witnessed the effort, soldiers of the second Fort Dearborn first cut a channel through the sand bar in 1816, wide enough for a yawl that carried supplies to the fort; the channel clogged with sand, so the soldiers were observed to have repeated the digging in 1818, 1823, and 1829, with no lasting success. Not until March 1833 did Congress appropriate an initial sum of $25,000 for a harbor; work began in July under the direction of Maj. George Bender, commandant at Fort Dearborn, and Asst. Superintendent Henry S. Handy. Harbor construction, a precondition for the construction of the Illinois & Michigan Canal which would follow, were federal projects under authority of the U.S. Department of Engineers [but from 1838, under the authority of the Topographical Bureau], which closely monitored and guided Major Bender's efforts, as well as those of Second Lt. James Allen, who succeeded Bender as superintendent early in 1834. Prior to its completion, Charles F. Hoffman observed the effort and published the account that follows in the *New York American* [no. 18]. By July 12, the sand bar that had previously blocked the entrance to the Chicago River was breached by a man-made channel large enough to admit merchant vessels, and flanked by a 700-foot-long pier on the N and one of 200 feet on the S of the river mouth (both to be extended thereafter), creating a protective harbor 200 feet wide and from 3 to 7 feet deep, and on that day the sailing ship *Illinois* entered; soon after, the sand bar, on which unfortunate speculators had built houses, was totally washed away. In 1835, a $6,000 dredging machine [drawing existent in the National Archives, Washington, D.C.] was purchased to deepen the channel; in August Allen advertised in the *Chicago Democrat* for 20 carpenters and 40 common laborers, promising immediate employment and good wages upon application. In 1833, only two brigs and two schooners had arrived from the lower lakes; in 1834, 176 vessels

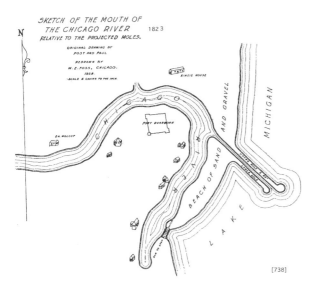

SKETCH OF THE MOUTH OF THE CHICAGO RIVER 1823 RELATIVE TO THE PROJECTED MOLES.

ORIGINAL DRAWING BY POST AND PAUL REDRAWN BY W.Z. FOSS, CHICAGO. 1923. SCALE 8 CHAINS TO THE INCH.

[738]

came; in 1835, about 250; and in 1836, by December 1, 456 ships had come, 39 of which were steamboats. Also see Chicago River; Forks; Illinois & Michigan Canal.

The town lies upon a dead level, along the banks of a narrow forked river, and is spread over a wide extent of surface to the shores of the lake, while vessels of considerable draught of water can, by means of the river, unload in the center of the place. ✧ *The Government have appropriated thirty thousand dollars for the purpose of making a safe and convenient harbour. The work is going on briskly & will probably be finished the next season. At present the vessels are obliged to anchor outside of the bar and unload by means of small boats or lighters, so called, and these have to be rowed more than a mile around the bar. When the river comes onto the beach of the lake it turn almost directly south and follows the beach, making a channel of about fifty yards between the beach and the sand bar, and it cannot be crossed even by small boats until proceeding about half a mile from the turn and then with difficulty sometimes. When the harbour is finished all this expense, time, and trouble will be saved. The work has been commenced*

on the south side of the river at the turn, and they are extending a wharf directly into the lake, cutting through the sand bar, and when finished the river will have a straight and direct channel into the lake, so that any vessel can come into the river and unload anywhere in town, saving all this distance round the bar with their freight's expense & the danger of anchoring in the lake. It will be a safe harbour and the only one in this part of the lake, and the only one that can be except the mouth of the Calemic River. Vessels will be able to run up the south branch a mile or two, and up the north branch some farther.

Chicago Harmonic Society   an ephemeral amateur group that gave the first public concert in Chicago on Dec. 11, 1835 at the Presbyterian church. [12]

Chicago Hotel   see Green Tree Tavern.

Chicago Hydraulic Company   see water works.

Chicago, incorporation   see Chicago, Town, incorporation.

Chicago land boom   see land boom.

Chicago Lyceum   the Chicago Lyceum for Social and Intellectual Pursuits, spearheaded by Dr. Egan, Dr. Temple, and Thomas Hoyne, with Royal Stewart as secretary; met first at the Presbyterian meeting house on Dec. 9, 1834; its members were a group of book-oriented intellectuals who advertised for donations to a library in the *Chicago Democrat* on December 17 and soon accumulated about 300 volumes; they held weekly meetings in Cook's Coffee House or at the courthouse for discussion of cultural subjects and to practice debating; sessions were suspended throughout the summer and early autumn of 1835, but were revived late November and held at the Presbyterian church; on December 12, Lt. L.T. Jamieson was elected president, and Dr. Temple became vice-president; its reading room was located above John Johnson's barber shop in September 1836, and later moved to the second floor of the Saloon Building; by 1841, interest in the Lyceum had faded [its library made available that year to the newly formed Young Men's

Association], but the endeavor may be noted as a forerunner of the Chicago Library System. [12, 544]

Chicago massacre   see Fort Dearborn massacre.

Chicago massacre tree   a large cottonwood tree on 18th Street, between Prairie Avenue and the lakeshore, said by eyewitnesses to have marked the site of the Fort Dearborn massacre of Aug. 15, 1812, and in particular, the location of the baggage wagon containing the twelve children of garrison personnel who were all tomahawked by one of the Indians; the tree was still standing in 1893, when an adjoining bronze memorial group ▲ (sculpted by Carl Rohl-Smith) was dedicated to mark the site's importance. The tree was cut down the next year and the sculpture now is within the Prairie Avenue Historic District park.

Chicago militia   see Fort Dearborn militia.

Chicago, name, origin   the Illinois and Miami word *chicagoua* for the locally growing wild garlic plant *Allium tricoccum* became the name for the town of Chicago. The Indians also applied the same name to two local rivers, along the wooded banks of which the plant grew in abundance; these were the present Chicago River and the Des Plaines River. For additional etymologic information, and discussion of earlier speculative theories about Chicago's name, see the essay by John F. Swenson on page 377.

Chicago, name variants   the French spelling of *Checagou* was due to an erroneous transcription of the ambiguous handwriting of La Salle, whose letter to the governor of New France began "Du Portage de Checagou 5 juin 1683." In a 1697 letter to Laval, Father Gravier mentions "[o]ur mission of Chikagoua." The United States government in the 1795 Treaty of Greenville wrote Chikago. Early variations (and misspellings) have been, in alphabetical order: Cheagoumeman (Franquelin 1686); Checago (Minet 1685), Checagou (La Salle 1683; Senex, De L'Isle 1703; Tonti, Nicolas de Fer 1718; Bellin 1744), Chegakou (Lahontan 1703), Chekagou (Tillman 1688), Chekakou (Moll), Chicago

(William Burnett 1798), Chicagou (St. Cosme 1699, De L'Isle 1703, Charlevoix 1744, Joutel), Chicagoue (Armstrong), Chicagoux (de Ligney 1726), Chigagou (Popple 1733), Chicag8 (St. Cosme 1699), Chicagoua or Chicagoüa or Chicag8a (Gravier 1696), Chicagou (DeL'Isle 1718; Mitchell 1755), Chicagoux (early French manuscript, according to Hurlbut), Chicagu (St. Cosme 1699), Chicagvv (St. Cosme 1699), Chicajo (Gen. A. Wayne 1795), Chicaqua (Sanson 1696), Chicauga (W. Jordan, Armstrong 1790), Chigagou (St. Cosme 1699), Chikago (Hutchins 1771), Chikagoe (G. La Mothe), Chikagou (St. Cosme 1699), Chikagoüa (Gravier 1700), Chikagu (St. Cosme 1699), Chiquagoux (Jean Orillat), Eschecagou and Eschickagou (De Peyster 1813).

Chicago outlet   geographic term for twin channels through the Valparaiso moraine that drained the waters of glacial Lake Chicago; through it flowed the large Chicago outlet river during the terminal period of the last ice age; the old river bed is now occupied by the Sanitary and Ship Canal, the remnants of the Illinois and Michigan Canal, the Calumet-Sag Channel and the lower Des Plaines River.

Chicago Plain   also Chicago Lake Plain; the virtually flat expanse of land uncovered by the retreat of Lake Chicago to the level of Lake Michigan that extended from the present lakefront W to Oak Park and LaGrange and S to Blue Island.

Chicago population growth   see population figures.

Chicago Portage   originally named by the French *La Portage des Chênes* [oaks], the name most commonly refers to the 1 1/2 mile stretch of wet prairie straddling the continental divide and separating the E end of Mud Lake (now Kedzie Avenue and 31st Street) from the W arm of the south branch of the Chicago River (at Western Avenue and 27th Street), and thereby separating the Mississippi River system from the Great Lakes. The distance to be portaged varied with the season: at high water, during approximately 48 days of the year, boats of two to three tons could pass without unloading, but during dry times portaging of up to 100 miles by way of the Long Portage Road became necessary, because the Des Plaines River became a bed of rocks. The portage was known and had been used by the Indians for centuries; the first confirmed use of the portage by Europeans was in 1673 by Jolliet and Father Marquette. Necessary to note is that there was at least one other portage in what is now the city of Chicago, which used the north branch of the river, and that the term *Portage de Chicagou* may have referred to more than one location. For additional detail, see entries for portage and for Mud Lake. [12, 692]

Chicago Precinct   when Chicago was part of Putnam County but administered by Peoria County from Jan. 13, 1825, to Jan. 15, 1831, a precinct was designated for voting purposes that included land E of the mouth of the Du Page River (emptying into the Des Plaines River) to Lake Michigan and N to the Michigan Territory [Wisconsin State] line. Following the organization of Cook County, in March 1831, three county voting precincts were established: one for Chicago, one at Hickory Creek, and one at the Du Page settlement.

Chicago Reading Room Association   directors Lt. J. Allen, C. Petit, and secretary Henry Moore met at the Tremont House on July 6, 1835, with the intention of obtaining a building with a room for reading and a hall for public lectures; on Aug. 22 a second notice appeared in the *Chicago American* indicating that papers for the present were deposited at Cook's Coffee House, "where they can be seen at all convenient times."

Chicago River   called *Portage Rivière* by Father Marquette, and later *Rivière de Chicagou* by other Frenchmen, although early travelers used the native name Chicago and its variants for the Des Plaines River; still later the term Chicago Creek was common. The name refers to the main stem and the north and south branches, joining at Wolf Point; early names for the north branch were Guillory (Post & Paul 1824 map), Gary River (Keating), Guarie River (Hubbard), and Guilleroi (Lieutenant Furman); headwaters for the south branch were at Mud Lake (31st Street and Kedzie Avenue), and for the north branch, near Skokie. The river once drained the Chicago plain into Lake Michigan and successively formed several mouths, the location depending on lake level, rainfall, and storm activity. In 1830, the river averaged 40 feet in width and had multiple small tributaries (sloughs) in the [downtown] region; sloughs at LaSalle Street and State Street were crossed atop logs by pedestrians on South Water Street; the sloughs were built over and eventually disappeared. At that time, the river reached the lake at a point that is now covered by the Chicago Art Institute on Michigan Avenue. The completion of the Illinois & Michigan Canal in 1848 began the process of flow reversal of the river, though not realized until completion of the Drainage and Shipping Canal in January 1900. Both canals connect the south branch of the Chicago River with the Des Plaines River, as did the Chicago portage, using the Des Plaines valley, which marks the former prehistoric outflow of the lake. For information on the river mouth with its variable location in earlier years, see next entry; on the associated sand bank and an account of early efforts to straighten the final stretch of the river and to create a harbor, see also Chicago harbor, Chicago Portage, Mud Lake, Chicago outlet. [310]

Chicago River mouth   for a description of its location and displacement over time, see Gurdon S. Hubbard.

Chicago Road   (1) local term used for the trail that connected Bailly's trading post on the Calumet Beach Trail with the Sauk Trail at Westville, IN; (2) also meaning the Chicago-Detroit Road (or Turnpike), construction of which began in 1825 along the old Sauk Trail (or Mohawk Trail), after the Treaty of Chicago of 1821 secured the right of way from the Potawatomi. Starting at Detroit, the road crossed the St. Joseph River in three places, passed through [Michigan City, IN] and skirted the shore of Lake Michigan until just S of Chicago where the road [later Cottage Grove Avenue] united with the Vincennes Road near 18th and Michigan. Inland variations became alternate stage routes during the mid 1830s and passed through either Hammond, Riverdale, Thornton, and Blue Island.

Chicago, seal the familiar corporate seal was created in 1838, its impetus being the incorporation of the city of Chicago on March 4, 1837; the seal was designed by Dr. James C. Goodhue and was often affectionately referred to as "Dr. Goodhue's Little Baby." Earlier, the first village president, Thomas J.V. Owen, used the obverse of a U.S. half dollar to create a seal. On the inscription *Urbs in Horto*, see Birkbeck, Morris. The original design by Dr. Goodhue, as shown here, has undergone several modifications in subsequent years. [56, 435]

Chicago Temperance Society an organized temperance society existed as early as 1832; a notice placed in the *Chicago Democrat*, Dec. 24, 1833, by the secretary of the society, J. Watkins, alerts members and inhabitants to meet at the Baptist Meeting House; a Jan. 28, 1834, notice redirects them to the Presbyterian Meeting House; also see Philo Carpenter, one of the most active members.

Chicago, Town, boundaries see Chicago, boundaries.

Chicago, Town, incorporation in the summer of 1833, the population level had reached 350 and Chicago's citizens prepared to incorporate the settlement as a town under the Illinois legislative act that had been passed on Feb. 12, 1831; a population of 150 was the minimum requirement. Late in June [the exact date is unknown], at a meeting of the "Qualified Electors" of the Chicago Precinct of Peoria/Putnam County, in the drugstore of Peter Pruyne & Co., a 12-to-1 vote was cast for incorporation. Thomas J.V. Owen, presiding; Dr. Edmund S. Kimberly, secretary; voting for incorporation: Owen, Kimberley, John S.C. Hogan, C.A. Ballard, George W. Snow, Richard J. Hamilton, Dr. J.T. Temple, John W. Wright, George W. Dole, Hiram Pearsons, Alanson Sweet, and Mark Beaubien; against, Russell Heacock. On Aug. 5, a notice was posted for an election to be held on Aug. 10 for the purpose of choosing five trustees. Meeting in the Sauganash Hotel, 28 voters elected the trustees who proceeded to organize the town government; they were: Indian Agent Thomas J.V. Owen, George W. Dole, Madore B. Beaubien, John Miller, and Dr. Edmund S. Kimberley. On Aug. 12, the town board met for the first time, was sworn in by Col. R.J. Hamilton, and elected Mr. Owen president and Mr. Harmon clerk. Chicago's Articles of Incorporation as a town were not approved by the Illinois General Assembly until Feb. 11, 1835, and were not certified by the secretary of state until July 6, 1835. The 28 names on the voting list of Aug. 10, 1833, are: Dr. E.S. Kimberly, Hiram Pearson, Philo Carpenter, Dr. J.T. Temple, David Carver, James Kinzie, Charles Taylor, John S.C. Hogan, George W. Snow, Madore Beaubien, G. Kercheval, G.W. Dole, G.V. Owen, R.J. Hamilton, Enoch Darling, W.H. Adams, C.A. Ballard, John Watkins, James Gilbert, Mathias Smith, Dexter J. Hapgood, Stephen F. Gale, J.B. Beaubien, Mark Beaubien, William Ninson, George Chap-

man, John W. Wright, and Eli A. Rider. [28]

Chicago, town limits see Chicago, boundaries.

Chicago, Town, Ordinances see Chronology for Nov. 7 and Dec. 4, 1833, to note the first 16 ordinances written and adopted by the first town board; also see Ordinances of the Town of Chicago.

Chicago, Town Trustees see Chicago Board of Town Trustees.

Chicago Treaties with the Indians see Treaties.

Chicago Turnpike see Chicago Road.

Chicago & Vincennes Railroad a notice in the July 18, 1835, *Chicago American* announced a meeting in Danville of commissioners G.S. Hubbard, J.H. Kinzie, G.W. Dole, P. Pryne, and William B. Archer of Vincennes; by late September its board consisted of eight men from the three towns, and subscriptions for capital stock became available for sale on Dec. 14 at the Chicago branch of the State Bank of Illinois.

Chicago, European visitors, earliest Marquette and Jolliet 1673; Marquette 1674-75; Allouez 1677; La Salle 1679; La Salle and Tonti 1681; Joutel and Cavelier 1687-88; Lahontan 1689; Tonti 1691-92; Pinet and Bineteau 1696; Montigny, St. Cosme, Davion, Tonti, and Thaumur de la Source 1699. These travelers left written records of passage through the Chicago area prior to 1700 when portaging between Lake Michigan and the Mississippi River system; while near the portage, some were detained either by bad weather conditions or by choice (mission work). Numerous others would have come through the portage during the same time period, but were illiterate or chose to leave no record. For details, see individual entries.

Chicago wards on Sept. 25, 1834, the town was divided into four wards and a firewarden was appointed for each: first ward—W. Worthington; second ward—E.E. Hunter; third ward—Samuel Resique; fourth ward—James Kinzie.

chicagoua also chicag8a; Illinois word for the locally growing wild garlic plant *Allium tricoccum*, which gave the town of Chicago its name. The first spelling of the word chicagoua or chicag8a was by Father Gravier in the 1690s, a Jesuit missionary and talented linguist, who, following the linguistic convention begun by the Jesuit St. Jean de Brebeuf in the 1630s, used the symbol "8" to signify an Illinois sound similar to the French *ou* or the English *u*; the *a* at the end of chicagoua was almost silent. For additional etymologic information see John F. Swenson's essay on page 377.

Chi-Chi-Bingway   see Chechepinqua.

Chilaga   a corruption of the native name *Hochelaga* for Montreal; according to Helen H. Tanner, "… a legendary, mythical place that kept cropping up on early maps." The name is found on maps as early as 1570, before the Great Lakes were known to western explorers, and is usually placed into what is now Canada, past the headwaters of the St. Lawrence River, far N of present-day Chicago, but on later maps is farther S; the similarity to the word *Chicago* has prompted some historians to speculate that Chilaga may be an early spelling of Chicago, but there yet is no convincing evidence, and such speculation ignores the ancient name Hochelaga. [324; personal communication from John F. Swenson]

Childs, Col. Ebenezer C.   born in Massachusetts, 1797; living at Green Bay in 1821 and within that year, visited Chicago; published his experiences [see Bibliography] in 1858. He approached by way of the Chicago portage after several days of heavy rain and "found not less than two feet of water all the way across the portage"; returning in 1827: "The place had not improved any since 1821. Only two families still resided there, those of Kinzie and Col. Beaubien." [For the complete comment by Childs on his Chicago visit, see 1821 in the Chronology.] Childs married one of the *métis* daughters of [see] Augustin Grignon of Wisconsin. [12]

Childs, Luther   involved in the first organization of a Sunday school on Aug. 19, 1832; later moved to Milwaukee; in 1840 married Susan Curtis of Chicago.

children   for a listing of the first children known to have been born to settlers at Chicago up to the year 1812, see page 110.

Chipman, Ansel   owner of Chicago land, the eastern half of the NE quarter of Section 4 of Township 39 N, prior to 1836, as seen in Andreas, *History of Chicago*, pp. 112-113.

Chippewa   armed British sloop patrolling Lakes Michigan, Huron, and Erie during the period of British control; built at Pine River in 1769. [48]

Chippewa   also Ojibwa; an Indian tribe of Algonkian linguistic stock, to which the Ottawa and Potawatomi initially belonged, but later split off; they were first encountered by the French near Sault Sainte Marie, who therefore called them *Salteurs* after 1640; the name *Chippewa* is a corruption of *Ojibwa*. The tribe has been ▲ memorialized in the granting of its name to Chippewa Woods, located in the northernmost portion of the Indian Boundary Division of the Cook County Forest Preserve District; ➡ Chippewa Avenue (2000 E).

Chipwagen   see Sheboygan.

Chittenden Road   stagecoach road of the mid-1830s [paralleling Torrence Avenue], passing the Chittenden cabin, crossing the Little Calumet River by Chittenden bridge near 130th Street, and the Grand Calumet near the state line.

cholera   having been introduced from Europe to Canada in April 1832, the Asiatic cholera reached Fort Dearborn on July 10, 1832, with soldiers on board the steamer *Sheldon Thompson* for the Black Hawk War arriving from various eastern military posts, and with soldiers on the *William Penn* arriving eight days later; the disease had manifested itself onboard ship only the day before arrival. The permanent garrison of two companies under Maj. William Whistler was evacuated and camped two miles from the fort. The fort was converted into a hospital for the 1,000 soldiers present, and the sick were treated by Dr. De Camp and Dr. Harmon; 200 became ill and 58 died. The civilian population largely withdrew into the countryside. A sec-

ond cholera epidemic occurred in 1849, and a third one in 1866. The following letter written in 1860 by Capt. A. Walker of the *Sheldon Thompson* describes some of the events.

Four steamers, the Henry Clay, Superior, Sheldon Thompson, *and* William Penn, *were chartered by the United States Government for the purpose of transporting troops, equipment and provisions to Chicago, during the Black Hawk War, but, owing to the fearful ravages, made by the breaking out of the Asiatic cholera among the troops and crew on board, two of those boats were compelled to abandon their voyage, proceeding no further than Fort Gratiot. The disease became to violent on board of the* Henry Clay *that nothing like discipline could be observed, everything in the way of subordination ceased. As soon as the steamer came to the dock, each man sprang on shore, hoping to escape from a scene so terrific and appalling. Some fled to the fields, some to the woods, while others lay down on the streets, and under the cover of the river bank, where most of them died unwept and alone. ❖ We arrived at Chicago on the evening of the 10th of July, 1832. I sent the yawl-boat on shore soon after with General Scott and a number of the volunteer officers. ❖ Before landing the troops next morning, we were under the painfull necessity of committing three more to the deep, who died during the night, making, in all, sixteen who were thus consigned to a watery grave. These three were anchored to the bottom in two and a-half fathoms, the water being so cleat that their forms could be plainly seen from our decks. This unwelcome sight created such excitement, working upon the superstitious fears of some of the crew, that prudence dictated that we weigh anchor and move a distance, sufficient to shut from sight a scene which seemed to haunt the imagination, and influence the mind with thought of some portentious evil. ❖ In the course of the day and night following, eighteen others died and were interred not far from the spot where the American Temperance House has since been erected* [NW corner of Lake Street and Wabash Avenue; eds.]. *The earth that was removed*

Indian women have given birth in the Chicago area for thousands of years, and many *métis* children, sired by early French trappers and traders, have crowded the dwellings they shared with their Indian mothers since the second half of the 18th century. Few vital statistics regarding these children were then noted. The first known Chicago-born *métis* child was Louis Amiot, his birth documented within the Catholic church records.

RECORDED BIRTHS AT CHICAGO · ARRIVALS BETWEEN
1745 & 1812

1745 October   **Louis Amiot**, son of Jean Baptiste Amiot, French Canadian blacksmith and his Ottawa wife Marianne, who baptized their son at Michilimackinac on June 14, 1746; the church record reads: "the said child having been born at the Rivière aux plains [Des Plaines River] near chikago at the beginning of the month of October last"; died in 1757.

1796 Oct. 8   **Eulalia Pelletier**, first child of trader Jean Baptiste Pelletier and Suzanne Point de Sable, granddaughter of Jean Baptiste Point de Sable; lived to adulthood.

1804 Dec. 27   **Ellen Marion Kinzie**, second child of trader John and Eleanor Lytle McKillip Kinzie; lived to adulthood.

1805 autumn   **Meriwether Lewis Whistler**, son of Lt. William and Mrs. Mary Julia Fearson Whistler at Fort Dearborn; drowned at age of seven.

1807 September   **Maria Indiana Kinzie**, fourth child of John and Eleanor Lytle McKillip Kinzie; lived to adulthood.

1807 Oct. 7   **John Harrison Whistler**, son of Lt. William and Mrs. Mary Julia Fearson Whistler at Fort Dearborn; died in 1873.

1809 Oct. 26   **Charles La Lime Jouett**, son of Charles Jouett and Susan Randolph Allen Jouett; died on Sept. 8, 1810.

1810 Feb. 8   **Robert Allen Kinzie**, fifth child of John and Eleanor Lytle McKillip Kinzie; died in 1873.

1811   **Benjamin** (?), son of Cicely, Negro slave of Capt. Nathan and Mrs. Rebekah Wells Heald at Fort Dearborn; killed and beheaded as an infant at the massacre of Aug. 15, 1812.

1811   **Sally Leigh**, daughter of James and Martha Leigh; survived the massacre of 1812.

1812 Feb. 12   **Susan Simmons**, second child of Pvt. John and Mrs. Susan Millhouse Simmons at Fort Dearborn; died in 1900, becoming the oldest survivor of the massacre.

1812 April   **Catherine Burns**, only child of Thomas and Mary Burns; survived the massacre and lived to old age.

1812 May   **Heald**, —, unnamed stillborn child of Capt. Nathan and Mrs. Rebekah Wells Heald, "born dead for want of a skillful midwife." The Healds had adamantly rejected the professional services of Dr. Van Voorhis (age 21), feeling that he was too young.

1812 Aug. 15   **Corbin**, —, unnamed 8 month old fetus of Pvt. Phelim and Mrs. Victoria Corbin; after the mother had been killed at the massacre, the fetus was cut from her abdomen, and both were scalped and beheaded.

[Editors' note: James and Martha Leigh had two young sons killed at the Fort Dearborn massacre who must have been born in Chicago during the years between 1804 and 1811, but neither their names nor their birth dates are recorded.]

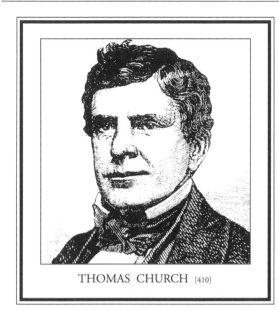

THOMAS CHURCH [410]

to cover one made a grave to receive the next that died. All were buried without coffins or shrouds, except their blankets, which served for a winding sheet, there left, as it were, without remembrance or a stone to mark their resting-place. During the four days we remained at Chicago, fifty-four more died, making an aggregate of eighty-eight who paid the debt of nature.

Cholera Vigilance Committee   appointed by the town trustees in 1834, consisting of Dr. W.B. Egan, Dr. J.C. Goodhue, A. Steele, Mark Beaubien, and J.K. Palmer—all from the S district; G. Kercheval, J. Miller, N.R. Norton, John Davis, and Hiram Hugunin from the N district; J. Kinzie, C. Taylor, and J. Bates, from the W district. The committee saw little activity because the cholera did not return until 1849, but became the forerunner of the first [see] Chicago Board of Health of 1835. [12]

Church, Henry   listed in 1833 as owner of lot 10 in block 28 of the original town, a lot that in 1830 had belonged to A. Clybourne [see map on page 44].

Church, Jeremiah (Jerry)   early visitor from Cleve-land who kept a journal and left accounts of three separate visits to Chicago during the years 1830 to 1833; traveled around the lake, stopping at Joseph Bailly's and John Mann's inns; for excerpts from his journal, see Bailly, Joseph; Mann, John; malaria. [141]

Church, Thomas   (1801-1871) arrived by schooner with his wife, Rachel (née Warriner), and two small daughters from Buffalo, NY on June 2, 1834; purchased two Lake Street lots on the S side of the street in block 28 from Archibald Clybourne for $250 each and erected ★★★ Chicago's 1st building on Lake Street, between Clark and Dearborn, a two-story 20-by-40 foot frame structure where they lived and kept a grocery store (with M.L. Satterlee, clerk); upstairs in this building, the U.S. Land Office opened on June 1, 1835; in the Sept. 2 Chicago Democrat, as agent for Buffalo [NY] Nursery, advertised "Fruit and Ornamental trees, Grape vines, Rose bushes, &c. ... Trees and Plants ordered from this Nursery will be securely packed in boxes or mats, and delivered on board of any steam boat or vessel in Buffalo, and will arrive in Chicago in perfect order," catalogues gratis; Church therefore qualifies as ★★★ Chicago's 1st nurseryman; ✦ grocery and provision store, 111 Lake St. In April 1839 Rachel died; she had borne five children, two of whom survived; on Nov. 5, 1839, Thomas married Rebecca Pruyne (widow of Peter Pruyne, daughter of Silas Sherman) who brought her own child to the marriage; became a successful real estate investor, then later the first president of the Chicago Fireman's Insurance Company; Church died in Chicago; his widow still lived at 331 Michigan Ave. in 1885; ➡ Church Street, a diagonal street on the SW side. [12, 97, 351, 653]

Church, W.E.   a person by this name claimed wharfing privileges from the Chicago

DEACON WINSLOW CHURCHILL [314a]

town board in November 1835.

churches and congregations   see entries under: Methodist church (1831), Catholic church (1833), Presbyterian church (1833), and Episcopal church (1834).

Churchill, Deacon Winslow   born in Vermont; farmed 30 years in New York; arrived in June 1834 on the schooner *LaGrange* with his wife Mercy Dodge and 11 children (three sons brought families); moved to a 160 acre claim along the Du Page River to settle at [Lombard]. ✿ For a portrait of Mercy Dodge Churchill, see page 370. [657a]

Cicely   a Negro slave girl with infant child, belonging to Captain and Mrs. Heald, came with them to Fort Dearborn in 1810; John Kinzie offered $600 for both, but was refused; perished with her child in the Fort Dearborn massacre. In 1855, long after her husband's death in 1832, Mrs. Heald petitioned the U.S. government for monetary compensation for loss of personal property suffered at

GEN. GEORGE ROGERS CLARK

the massacre of 1812; the major item in the inventory she submitted was "One negro woman, Cicely, and her child, valued at $1,000.00"; the claim was denied. [226]

Circuit Court of Cook County   regular sessions of this court began in May 1834, under the Hon. Richard M. Young at Chicago; Judges Sidney Breese and Stephen T. Logan held the first and second sessions in the 1835-1836 term.

City charter   granted to Chicago by the state legislature on March 1, 1837.

City Hotel   built in 1836-37 by Francis C. Sherman on the NW corner of Clark and Randolph streets, remodeled in 1844 and renamed Sherman House.

City West   lumber boom town on Silver Creek (Indiana dunes) founded by 1834, but abandoned following a fire several years later; the remaining buildings were moved to Michigan City and Tremont.

claim to land   early settlers were able to stake a claim by building a cabin on unsurveyed land; "...

timber claims were made by marking trees [carved initials on 'witness trees' at the four corners], and the prairie claims by plowing a furrow entirely around each." Homesteaders were able to purchase at a minimum price, $1.25 per acre, the portion of land settled and improved. "The usual quantity claimed was 160 acres; some, however, claimed more, and some less than that amount. There were some conflicting claims; but these difficulties were generally settled when the land was sold, by the one having the largest portion of the disputed claim buying the whole, and then re-deeding to each holder his proportion."

Clairmore, Jerry   see Clermont, Jeremy (Jerry).

Clamorgan, Jacques   the assumed name of a mysterious swindler of unknown origins; Clamorgan is not a genuine surname found anywhere in the world. In legend, Jean Baptiste Point de Sable's friend and benefactor; a wealthy landowner and crooked land speculator who conspired with corrupt officials of Spanish Louisiana to obtain fraudulent land "grants" for himself and others. Point de Sable, the free Negro, is unlikely to have lived within Clamorgan's space, as the "friend" was an abusive slave owner. [649]

Clarissa   ★★★ Chicago's 1st ship, built in the town for lake trade; construction began in 1835; was launched on May 12, 1836; the builder was Nelson R. Norton, a ship carpenter, and the carpenter brothers, Polemus D. and Thomas E. Hamilton.

Clark County   from 1819 to 1820 Chicago was part of Clark County in Illinois, then became part of Pike County. For detail, see Chicago jurisdictional chronology on pages 209 and 210. [544]

Clark, David   also Clock; early resident who in 1833 leased and managed James Kinzie's Green Tree Tavern once built; was followed by Edward Parsons; a David K. Clark had enlisted in Captain Walker's militia late June 1832, during the Black Hawk scare. [12]

Clark, Elijah   charter member of the first Presbyterian congregation in June 1833; on the list of subscribers to the *Chicago Democrat* in November 1833.

Clark, Gen. George Rogers   (1752-1818) Revolutionary War hero from Virginia. As a colonel of the Virginia militia, drove the British from Illinois (occupation of Kaskaskia in July 1778) and Vincennes (in February 1779). His personal credit was destroyed by the insolvent Virginia government, and he died in abject poverty, having been given hollow honors but inadequate compensation for his financial sacrifices; older brother of [see] Lt. William Clark; ➡ Clark Street [nearly paralleling the lakeshore N of the river, following the Green Bay Trail, defying the later grid pattern]. [142, 524, 649]

Clark, Henry A.   attorney and novelist; arrived in 1835 from New York; died in 1862. [12]

Clark, Henry B., M.D.   little is known about this physician who arrived in 1833 and subscribed to the *Chicago Democrat* in November; advertised in 1837 in the *Chicago American* with an office on Dearborn Street; ◆ 159 Lake St.; died at Walworth, WI before 1854. [12]

Clark, James   U.S. Army private at Fort Dearborn; enlisted on Dec. 4, 1805; left Chicago immediately when his enlistment expired on Dec. 4, 1810. [226]

Clark, James   arrived from New York in 1835.

Clark, John   Scottish friend and early Detroit business partner of John Kinzie who married his sister-in-law Elizabeth McKenzie c.1786. John Kinzie Clark was their son, born 1792 [for siblings, see Clark, John Kinzie]. Clark sold out his share of the business to Kinzie in 1797 when Kinzie established himself at St. Joseph; moved to Chicago with his son in the 1820s; for family relationships, see Kinzie family tree on page 222.

Clark, John A.   secretary of the Polemic Society of Chicago in January 1834; ◆ John Clark, Hobbie (Albert G.) & Clark, dry goods, &c., 142 Lake St.

Clark, John Kinzie   (1792-1877) also Indian

JOHN KINZIE CLARK [12]

Clark; born near Fort Wayne, son of the Scottish trader John Clark and Elizabeth McKenzie (sister of Margaret McKenzie, John Kinzie's first wife); had twin siblings Andrew and Mary (born in 1776), and an older sister Elizabeth (born in 1791); became half brother to Archibald Clybourne when his mother separated from Clark and married Archibald's father, Jonas Clybourne (see Kinzie family tree on page 222); raised among the Indians who called him Nonimoa [Prairie Wolf], while others referred to him as Indian Wolf; first came to Chicago in 1817; helped move the Jonas Clybourne family to Chicago in 1824 and initially lived with them at their north branch home; engaged at times to carry mail by horseback between Chicago and Milwaukee while living in Wisconsin with an Indian mate; married Madelaine Mirandeau (sister of Victoire) in 1825, and had at least one child with her; voted at the election of Aug. 7, 1826 [see Chronology]; appointed constable for the June term, 1827; in 1829, built a log cabin NW

[Northfield/Deerfield] near Elijah Wentworth, Sr.'s inn; after Madelaine's death, married Permelia Scott of [see] *Grosse Pointe* on July 21, 1829, Rev. Isaac Scarritt officiating in a double ceremony that also wedded Willard Scott to Caroline Hawley; had three daughters: Hadassah (1830), Elizabeth (1831) and Lucinda (died at age two); owner of 80 acres of land in the SE quarter of Section 6, Township 39, prior to 1836, as seen in Andreas, *History of Chicago*, pp. 112-113; voted at the elections of July 24 and Nov. 25, 1830 [see Chronology]; lived with Archibald in 1830 on the north branch, eight miles N of Wolf Point, remaining until 1836, then returning to [Northfield Township]; in January 1834, was secretary for the [see] Polemic Society of Chicago; died at Northfield in 1865, Permelia in 1877. [12, 544]

Clark, Mrs.   in 1857 testimony in the *Sand Bar* case, Gurdon Hubbard refers to "Mrs. Clark's house near the mouth of the river," actually the house of Caroline Clarke, Henry B. Clarke's widow; see Clarke House.

Clark, Norman   see Clarke, Norman.

Clark, Samuel   early settler and cattle dealer, married to Emmaline, built his house in 1812 near the Forks on the land between the main river and the south branch; joined the Chicago militia and was killed in the Fort Dearborn massacre; wounded in the attack, Emmaline was taken captive and soon died in captivity. [226]

Clark, Silas   U.S. Army private at Fort Dearborn, enlisted in August 1806; was reassigned to Fort Wayne in December 1810. [226]

Clark Street   ➡ formerly called Old Sand Road, running N atop an ancient sand ridge [beach of Lake Chicago]; part of the [see] Green Bay Indian Trail; also see Clark, Gen. George Rogers. The leading street in the settlement at the time of Chicago's incorporation as a town on Aug. 10, 1833, the first board of trustees quickly responded to public improvement demands and borrowed $60 for the digging of ditches on either side of Clark Street, mak-

ing the thoroughfare passable. [249]

Clark, William H.   arrived from Massachusetts in 1835; died in 1878. [12]

Clark, Lt. William   (1770-1838) younger brother of the Revolutionary War hero Gen. George Rogers Clark; together with Capt. Meriwether Lewis, led the renowned [see] Lewis and Clark expedition through the unknown NW of the continent in 1804-1806; earlier had participated in the victorious battle of Fallen Timbers under Gen. "Mad Anthony" Wayne in 1794; later became governor of Upper Louisiana, later Missouri. [12]

Clark, W., M.D.   see Clarke, William, M.D.

Clarke, Abram Fuller   (1814-1886) druggist, partner and brother of [see] Clarke, William Hull; together advertised "Paints, Oils &c." in the Nov. 18, 1835, *Chicago Democrat*, at the corner of Lake and Clark; another ad appeared on Dec. 9, the first of its kind: *Perfumery A SPLENDID assortment of Paris Perfumery, comprising French and Geneva cologne water, lavender water, milk of roses, cold cream, Antique oil for the hair, essences, pommades, pearl powder, and soaps of all kinds for washing, shaving and the toilet*; ♦ druggist, W.H. & A.F. Clarke; lived at Marietta, GA in 1885. [12, 221, 351]

Clarke, Henry Brown   (1802-1849) arrived in 1835 from Utica, NY with his wife, Caroline, (née Walker) and spent several weeks at the Tremont House until their household goods arrived; soon prospered as a merchant and land speculator, acquiring 20 acres along the shore; was member of fire engine company No.1 in December 1835; served on the first board of directors of the branch of the State Bank of Illinois that opened in December 1835; died of cholera in the 1849 epidemic; his widow's house (see Clarke House) survived the great fire of 1871. A brother-in-law, Charles Walker, also came in 1835. [12, 97, 171]

Clarke House   the ▲ Henry Brown Clarke House, also called the Widow Clarke House; built facing the lake in 1836 in the Greek revival style on acreage acquired the previous year (16th Street and Michigan Avenue), was moved in 1872 to 45th Street and Wabash Avenue, and later was moved back close to its original location, standing now on the E side of Indiana Avenue, between 18th Street and Cullerton Street; the oldest surviving house in the city. When built, the structure was at the eastern edge of a seemingly limitless prairie, nearly 11/2 miles S of the settlement; the nearest house S was the Hollis Newton tavern and hotel, another 11/2 miles distant.

Clarke, Norman (1805-1885) also Clark; from Vermont, arrived in 1835; ✦ dealer in land claims, &c.; later removed to Racine, WI, where he was living in 1878; died Feb. 28, 1885. [12, 351]

Clarke Point sand hill formed around bedrock outcroppings at 79th Street and the lakeshore; reached by a stone reinforcement on the W side; possibly used by Indians for ceremonial purposes.

Clarke, Samuel C. brother and silent partner of [see] Abram F. and William H.; opened a large drugstore in 1835 and stocked the first ice cream; ✦ druggist. [221, 544]

Clarke, Timothy B. carpenter and builder from Trumbull County, OH; a soldier in the War of 1812, he came to Illinois in 1820 to claim land in the [see] Military Tract; at Walker's Grove in 1830, moved to Chicago in 1831 and was appointed county road viewer; said to have built one of Chicago's first [see] frame houses; in 1832, his oxen team supplied provisions for Reverend Beggs' first quarterly prayer meeting; on July 23, volunteered with his son Barrett (B.B.) as privates in Captain Seission's Company during the Black Hawk War; mustered out Aug. 15. [12, 428, 714]

Clarke, William Hull (1812-1878) druggist, arrived in 1835 and, together with his brother Abram F., opened Chicago's third drugstore in May 1835, on South Water Street near Franklin; in November 1835 announced that the firm had moved to the SE corner of South Water and Clark and ad-

CHARLES CLEAVER [410]

vertised paints and oils; in September 1835 joined the Fire Kings, an early volunteer fire brigade; ✦ Clarke, Wm. H. & Abram F., wholesale druggists and apothecaries, 128 Lake St. [George P. Clarke is also listed as druggist]; became assistant engineer of the Chicago Board of Public Works in 1855; died in Chicago. His listing of Cook County residents between 1833 and 1838 is preserved at the Chicago Historical Society. [221]

Clarke, William, M.D. physician; arrived in 1833, as indicated by Hibbard Porter's account books, in which Clarke is debited for purchases made between June and December; a Dr. W. Clark is on the list of subscribers for the *Chicago Democrat*, first appearing Nov. 26, 1833; an uncollected letter addressed to him is listed in *Chicago Democrat*, January 1834. In 1834, he participated with Dr. Kimberly in an effort to establish a hospital for cholera patients outside the town limits.

Claude French-Canadian in the employ of John

Kinzie in 1812, unknown surname; lived in a shed on the N side of the river, near to and NW of the Kinzie house; at the time of the massacre he was in the boat with the Kinzies and survived.

Clay, William advertised as a hat manufacturer and dealer in the *Chicago Democrat* on May 28, 1834, at the "corner of Lake and Franklin streets, opposite Dr. Temple's."

Clear Day see Wasacheck.

Cleaveland, Henry W. and Horatio J. owners of the NE quarter of Section 32 in Township 40 N before 1836; in addition, Horatio was listed as sole owner of 80 acres of Chicago land in Section 28, Township 39, as per Andreas, *History of Chicago*, pp. 112-113. An H.I. Cleveland is listed as a subscriber to the *Chicago Democrat* in November 1833; two sisters, perhaps daughters, Miriam and Fidelia, attended school under Eliza Chappel in 1834.

Cleaver, Charles (1814-1871) English, arrived on Oct. 23, 1833; on Nov. 4, 1835, the *Chicago Democrat* advertised the Chicago Soap and Candle Manufactory of Messrs. Elston & Chaver [Chever in the Nov. 14 *Chicago American*], "on the Point between North Branch and Main River"; in late November both John T. Temple and Bernard Ward submitted depositions in support of his and [see] Daniel Elston's claim for wharfing privileges; on Nov. 27 Elston & Cleaver applied and later claimed privileges at the junction of the north branch and main stream [lots 3, 4, block 7]; he would later build a successful soap factory on the S side [38th Street]; in 1838 married Mary, daughter of Samuel Brookes, the town florist; a company town, Cleaverville, gradually developed S of the factory [later becoming the Oakland community]; ✦ candle and soap factory on south branch. Cleaver's reminiscences of early Chicago, published in 1882, provide valuable historical information; ➡ Cleaver Street (1432 W); in 1885 lived at the corner of Ellis Avenue and 43rd Street [12, 13, 351]

clergy see preachers and missionaries.

Clermont, Alexis French-Canadian, born on

ARCHIBALD CLYBOURNE [12]

Mackinac Island in 1808, lived later at Green Bay; before the Black Hawk War, served as crew member on a Durham boat for local traders, and from 1832 to 1836, served as mail carrier between Green Bay and Chicago; for excerpts from his 1888 narrative, see entries under Durham boat and Mail carriers. [147]

Clermont, Jeremy (Jerry)   also Clairmore; in 1821, employed by the American Fur Co. for the Iroquois River trade; Indian trader and resident in Chicago in 1825; was then assessed for tax purposes: owned $100 of personal property and paid $1.; voted at the election of Aug. 7, 1826 (see elections). [12]

Cleveland, H.I.   see Cleaveland, Henry W. and Horatio J.

Cleveland, OH   founded 1797 and named after Gen. Moses Cleaveland, but the spelling later changed; small settlement on Lake Erie's southern shore, similar to pre-1830 Chicago, until the opening of the Erie Canal in 1825; thereafter the mu-

nicipality grew rapidly as multitudes of immigrants from the eastern seaboard paused or pushed westward through Cleveland.

Clift, Benjamin H.   from Philadelphia; opened the [see] Chicago Book and Stationary Store next to Philo Carpenter's drugstore on Water Street on August 26, 1834, jointly with Aaron Russell; on Oct. 22, 1835, the partnership was dissolved and Clift carried on alone; was one of three directors for the Young Men's Temperance Society, organized on Dec. 19 of that year; in 1836, married Mary H. Bishop of New York. [12]

Clifton, Josiah   owner of 80 acres of land in the NW quarter of Section 8, Township 39, prior to 1836, as per Andreas, *History of Chicago*, pp. 112-113.

Clinton, DeWitt   (1769-1828) mayor of New York City; governor of New York State and sponsor of the Erie Canal; James Thompson, surveyor in 1830, named one of the first Chicago streets after him; ➡ Clinton Street (540 W).

Clock, David   see Clark, David.

Clybourne, Archibald   (1802-1872) also Clybourn; born in Giles County, VA; butcher; arrived on August 5, 1823; his parents (Jonas and Elizabeth) and other family members followed him in 1824; was appointed ★★★ Chicago's 1st constable for the Chicago district of Peoria County on Sept. 6, 1825, by the Peoria court; became a successful stockyard owner by buying cattle in central Illinois and building ★★★ Chicago's 1st slaughterhouse in 1827; business skyrocketed the following year with his acquisition of the government contract to supply fresh meat to Fort Dearborn, Fort Mackinac, Fort Howard, and Fort Winnebago [thus credited with launching Chicago as a major cattle trade center and meat market]; married Mary Galloway [see Clybourne, Mary] on June 9, 1829, Rev. Isaac Scarritt officiating (the couple would live in Jonas Clybourne's house until 1835); in the same month, was authorized to keep a ferry in conjunction with Samuel Miller; for the text of the license

see page 85; on Dec. 8, 1829, appointed trustee of the School Section; served as justice of the peace (1831); early owner of Chicago real estate, the SW quarter of Section 32 in Township 40 N, including his slaughterhouse, and became active as real estate dealer during the speculative fever that gripped the town in the early 1830s; in 1830, was listed as owning lot 10 in block 28 and lots 4 and 5 in block 5 of the original town, but by 1833 the lot in block 28 belonged to Henry Church, and lot 5 in block 5 belonged to Dr. Kimberly; member of the Universalist church; in 1831 served as a justice of the peace and as the first treasurer of Cook County; occasionally advised people on legal matters but was not a trained lawyer; advertised two butcher shops, one on the north branch, the other on market square in the *Chicago Democrat* of Dec. 3, 1833; in December 1834, he and [see] Bowman C. Dobson advertised a new store in "Clybournsville" one mile S of [Batavia] at their mill, where Mill Creek enters the Fox River. Late in November 1835, he submitted a claim for wharfing privileges along the Chicago River; sometime earlier that year the Clybournes had moved to a small frame house on Elston Road [Elston Avenue] and in 1836, moved into a 20-room brick residence on the same lot; ✦ farmer and cattle-dealer, 512 Elston Ave.; died in this house in 1872, was survived by his widow and 10 living children, four of them born before 1836: Sara Ann in 1830, Margaret E. in 1831, Martha Ann in 1833, and James A. in 1835, who took over his father's business; ▲ buried at Rosehill Cemetery; Mary died in Chicago in 1904. Clybourne was a cousin of Archibald Caldwell and also related to John Kinzie [see Kinzie family tree on page 222]; ➡ Clybourn Avenue, a diagonal NW street. [12, 28, 249]

Clybourne, Henley   (1805-1876) second son of Jonas Clybourne; arrived with his parents from Virginia in 1824; present at the estate sale following the death of William Wallace; married Sarah Benedict on May 23, 1827, the Rev. Jesse Walker officiating; elected constable on May 11, 1828, and again on Aug. 20, 1828; died in Westville, IN. For family relation with the Kinzies, see Kinzie family tree on page 222. [12]

Clybourne, Jonas butcher, father of Archibald and Henley; married (c.1786) Elizabeth Clark, née Elizabeth McKenzie, sister of Margaret McKenzie, John Kinzie's first wife; came from Virginia on April 3, 1824, with his adopted son, John K. Clark, and Elizabeth Kinzie following Archibald Clybourne; assessed in Chicago on $625 in personal property in 1825; voted on July 24 and Nov. 25, 1830. The Clybournes established themselves at "Clybourn Place," also called "New Virginia," on the W side of the north branch of the Chicago River, just short of two miles from the Forks; died in 1842 in Westville, IN. For family relation with the Kinzies, see Kinzie family tree on page 222. [12]

Clybourne, Mary (1812-1904) née Galloway; arrived in 1826 with her parents, James and Jane Galloway, and younger siblings Jane, Susan, and John from Sandusky, OH. The experience of the Galloway family's move to Chicago and temporary residence, written later by Mary and published by Andreas, gives a rare glimpse of the early settlement in the 1820s; in the spring of 1827 the Galloways moved to the Illinois River valley, where James had staked a claim [near Marseilles]; here met and married Archibald Clybourne on June 9, 1829, Rev. Isaac Scarritt officiating [Tazewell County marriage register]; until 1835, the young couple lived with Archibald's parents at "Clybourn Place" on the north branch; their large brick home of 20 rooms on Elston Road [now Elston Avenue] was not built until 1836; died in Chicago at age 92; survived by five children, among whom were James, William, and Henry. ❀ For a portrait of Mary Galloway Clybourne see page 367. [12, 728]

Clybourne, Thomas from Virginia; married a daughter of William Kinzie; arrived in 1832 with Benjamin Hall, but left when the Black Hawk War began. [706]

Clybournsville a small community that settled near the Clybourn & Dobson Mill, where Mill Creek enters the Fox River one mile S of [Batavia]; in the Dec. 17, 1834, *Chicago Democrat* Archibald Clybourne and Bowman C. Dobson advertised a new store.

Coal Burner see Shabbona

Cobb, Silas Bowman (1812-1900) born in Montpelier, VT; harness maker, arrived penniless on the schooner *Atlanta* on May 29, 1833; initially worked for James Kinzie as a carpenter in the construction of the Green Tree Tavern; soon formed a partnership with Oliver Goss (the latter living in Plainfield and silent partner), Goss & Cobb; built a two-story house and harness shop at Canal and Lake, opposite the Green Tree Tavern; they dissolved the partnership on Feb. 18, 1835, and Cobb soon moved to larger quarters at 171 Lake St., where he remained many years; his shingle read: Saddle & Harness Manufactory – Cash Paid for Hides – S.B. Cobb; among items crafted were leathern buckets [see Stose, Clemens], two required in every building, according to an 1835 fire ordinance; in October joined the "Pioneer" hook and ladder company, a voluntary fire brigade; ✦ saddle, harness, & trunk maker (same address). In 1840, he married Maria Warren in [Warrenville], who had befriended him in the company of her parents and twin sister Mary in 1833, and who then headed for the Illinois prairies [Warrenville]; see the following recollection. A skilled real estate investor, Cobb became independently wealthy during the boom period, and managed to remain so when the boom ended; considered the richest man in Chicago in 1867; his widow's address in 1885 was 3334 Michigan Ave; she died in 1888. [12, 351]

I arrived in Chicago in the spring of 1833. In October of the same year I was occupying my new shop opposite the hotel, in the building of which my first dollar was earned in Chicago. Standing at my shop one afternoon talking with a neighbor, our attention was attracted by the arrival at the hotel of a settler's

SILAS BOWMAN COBB [410]

wagon from the east. With my apron on and my sleeves rolled up, I went with my neighbor to greet the weary travelers and to wellcom them to the hospitality of Fort Dearborn, in accordance with the free and easy customs of "high society" in those days. We learned that the travelers were the Warren family, from Westfield, New York, bound for the settlement of Warrenville, Illinois, where a relative had preceded them about six months previously. There were several young women in the party, two of them twin sisters whom I thought particularly attractive, so much so that I remarked to my friend, after they had departed, that when I was prosperous enough so that my pantaloons and brogans could be made to meet I was goin to look up those twin sisters and marry one of them or die in trying.

Edwin Gale remembers: *As soon as he was able to support a wife he married one of the twin daughters of Colonel Daniel Warren.* ✧ *Jerome Beecher married the other sister. Cobb thought that he married Maria and Beecher always believed that he himself married Mary, but they only knew what the girls told*

JEAN BAPTISTE COLBERT [410]

them, for the sisters so closely resembled each other and dressed so exactly alike that it required intimate acquaintance to distinguish them. They purchased their millinery of [my] *mother, and she never could tell whether she was waiting on Mrs. Cobb or Mrs. Beecher.*

Cobweb Castle   also Cobweb Hall; nickname for the second government agency house on the north bank of the river, vacated when Dr. Wolcott died in the fall of 1830. The house had acquired its name during the time Wolcott lived there as bachelor, before his marriage to Ellen Marion Kinzie in 1823. [12]

Cochron, William   bought 168 gallons of "high wines" for $67.20 at the estate sale of W.H. Wallace on April 27, 1827.

Coffee Creek   tributary of the Calumet River in Porter County, IN, known by its French name, *Rivière du bois Franc*, as late as 1837.

Cohen, Peter   Alsatian immigrant, came in 1830;

established a variety store (clothing and dry goods) on South Water Street, two doors E of Dearborn, next to Newberry & Dole; advertised in the first issue of the *Chicago Democrat*, Nov. 26, 1833; on April 29, 1834, the store was taken over by H. Doty & Co.; after June 11, 1835, again advertised in the *Chicago Democrat*, announcing "New and Cheap Goods"—dry goods and groceries at his old stand, and on Nov. 23 submitted a claim [lot 2 block 16] for wharfing privileges; voted in the first mayoral election; ✦ merchant, South Water Street. [28]

Colbert, Jean Baptiste   (1619-1683) the "Great Colbert, powerful Minister of the Marine and Colonies" to Louis XIV, king of France, after whom Father Hennepin, La Salle, and Frontenac honorarily named the Mississippi, *Rivière de Colbert* in the 1690s; was succeeded in the office by his son (1651-1690) of the same name; French policy in New France was determined to a large degree by the Colberts.

Colbert Rivière   see Colbert, Jean Baptiste.

Cole, Parker M.   on the list of subscribers to the *Chicago Democrat* in November 1833; ✦ dry goods and groceries, Lake Street.

Cole, Sgt. W.C.   listed with his wife, Julia, as members of the Presbyterian church on June 26, 1833; most likely part of the Fort Dearborn garrison. [12]

Coles, Edward   born in Virginia; came to Chicago in 1819 from Edwardsville, IL; following Governor Bond, was elected Illinois governor on an antislavery platform in 1822 and inaugurated on Dec. 5, 1822; served until 1826; created the initial canal commission; in 1831, moved to Philadelphia; died in 1868. ➡ Coles Avenue. [12]

Colhoun, J. Edward   topographer and astronomer, came to Fort Dearborn on June 5, 1823, as a member of Maj. Stephen Long's expedition to explore the Red River; a report of this visit and the entire expedition was written by William Keating [see Bibliography].

Collett, J.A.   placed advertisements in the June 1834 *Chicago Democrat* to sell and remove a small building; on July 9, John Bates announced an auction sale involving the unexpired lease of Collett's Restoratory, two small adjoining buildings, and all furniture, cooking apparatus, and groceries.

Collins, James H.   lawyer from New York who arrived in 1834; initially formed a law partnership with John D. Caton (Collins & Caton) and opened an office on South Water Street, one door E of the corner with Lake Street, removing in June to an upstairs office two doors E of the Baptist church on South Water Street; the partnership dissolved the following year and Collins joined Justin Butterfield in July; defended successfully ★★★ Chicago's 1st murder case in the fall of 1834 [for details, see murder]; became a prominent member of the legal community and a confirmed abolitionist; his contemporary Isaac Arnold observed: "He was a good lawyer, a man of perseverance, pluck and resolution, and as combative as an English bulldog"; represented the government in the celebrated case of the Beaubien land claim; ✦ attorney & counselor at law, 46 Dearborn St.; died at Chicago of the cholera in 1854. [12]

Collinsworth, Lt. John T.   Fifth Infantry; from Tennessee, stationed at Fort Dearborn as brevet second lieutenant from May 14 to June 20, 1833; resigned in 1836, went to Texas, became inspector general and died in 1837.

Collot, Gen. Victor   French general who, in the summer of 1796, came to Chicago on a journey through the "western countries" and left a journal of his travel impressions. Collot had been Governor of Guadaloupe in the West Indies; after the British took possession of that territory, he came to North America and visited the Ohio settlements and the Illinois country before returning to his native France. [152]

Colombo, Cristoforo   (1451-1506) Christopher Columbus, acknowledged by nearly everyone as the discoverer of America though he explored only the

CRISTOFORO COLOMBO [410]

Caribbean Islands, believing himself to be off the eastern coast of Cathay (China); the first landfall may have been Samana Cay, a small island among the eastern Bahamas; the date was Oct. 12, 1492. Columbus believed himself near Cathay because he had calculated the circumference of the earth to be 25% smaller than its actual size. He never set foot on the New World continent, though once, seeing the distant land, supposed it another island. Four voyages were made during the years 1492 to 1504. A native of Genoa, he was in the service of King Ferdinand and Queen Isabella of Spain; his discoveries established Spain's claim to the North American continent. [156, 157, 176, 209, 314, 386, 447, 504, 554, 620]

Colson, Erastus college professor at the Illinois College, visited Chicago with [see] Jonathan Baldwin Turner in the summer of 1833.

Colton & M'Whorter an advertisement in the Dec. 16, 1835, *Chicago Democrat* announced a new wholesale & retail grocery on Lake Street a few doors E of Cook's Coffee House; neither the business or the grocers are listed in 1839.

Columbus 391-ton steamer built in 1835 at Huron, OH; visited Chicago later that year.

Commerce lake schooner, built in 1825; from Buffalo, NY, called at Chicago three times in 1834, twice in 1835, transporting merchandise and passengers under Captain Smith; during the summer of 1834, [see] Seth Paine arrived aboard the vessel, which also brought merchandise for Harmon, Loomis & Co.; involved in the lumber trade by 1837, when she was rebuilt and her name changed to *Hiram Pearson*.

Commissioners' Court see Cook County Court of Commissioners.

Commodore schooner; from Buffalo, NY, called at Chicago three times in 1834, twice in 1835, transporting merchandise under Captain Culver; was wrecked at Cleveland Harbor in 1845. [48]

Compagnie d'Orient see Louisiana Province.

Conant & Mack Detroit firm which established a trading house on the south branch of the Chicago River in 1816, headed by John Crafts; the American Fur Co. pitted against Crafts their agent John Kinzie, and in 1819, J.B. Beaubien; competition became too great and the firm sold its branch in 1822. The firm also built roads, and under Sec. of War John C. Calhoun was awarded a government contract to cut a road [northward extension of Woodward Avenue] through the forest at Detroit and lay it with corduroy; the firm was paid $1,000 per mile. Also see Mack, Steven, Jr. [12, 119]

Conant, Shubael partner of Steven Mack, Sr., in the Detroit firm of [see] Conant & Mack. [119]

concert ★★★ Chicago's 1st public concert was given by Mr. C. Blisse on June 19, 1834; another followed on Dec. 11, 1835, given by the Chicago Harmonic Society, which T.O. Davis described in his Dec. 19 *Chicago American* as "... a fine treat to a crowded audience of intelligence, beauty and fashion ... an agreeable entertainment." [482]

Conner, James interpreter for the Indian treaty negotiations in 1833 at Chicago, together with

Luther Rice. [559]

Connestoga wagon in Connestoga, Lancaster County, PA, broad-wheeled covered wagons were built for use by pioneers in crossing the prairie; many of the [see] "prairie schooners" roundabout the early town were Connestogas.

Constitutional Convention the first convention for the state of Illinois assembled with 33 delegates at Kaskaskia and completed its task on Aug. 26, 1818. The constitution was adopted in convention without being submitted to a vote of the people; approved by Congress on Dec. 3, 1818.

Contractor a sloop visiting Chicago under Captain Lee late in 1808 that delivered four or five barrels of whiskey to the firm of Kinzie & Forsyth, probably as supply for the Fort Dearborn garrison.

Contraman, Maj. Frederick H. also Countraman, Countryman; in June 1829 employed Pierre Lamset to haul three barrels of whiskey from the settlement to his home in the Fox River Precinct; on Sept. 3, 1834 [50 years old] elected major of the Cook County militia, chosen to command one of two battalions; announced as candidate for town mayor on Sept. 10; noted two months later per *Chicago Democrat*, married "Miss Susanna, the beautiful accomplished daughter of Captain William Lawrence, late a private of the U.S. Army, aged 12 years" in Chicago on Nov. 19; later in the *Chicago American*, in November 1835, Frederick was cited for assault and battery, with intent to kill a "Mr. Robinson of this place"; ◆ farmer, West Randolph Street.

Cook, Charles W. tanner; arrived with wife Amy in 1835 and engaged in small merchandising; became proprietor of the Mansion House and the American Temperance Hotel [no bar]; later entered the lumber business; in 1885, his widow lived at 3241 Indiana Ave. [12]

Cook County the County of Cook, named after Daniel H.P. Cook and created by an act of the general assembly of the state of Illinois on Jan. 15, 1831, which states: "The county seat thereof is

DANIEL H. POPE COOK [12]

hereby declared to be permanently established at the Town of Chicago, as the same has been laid out and defined by the Land Commissioners." The original boundaries included what is now Cook, McHenry, DuPage, Lake, and Will counties; for Chicago's earlier jurisdictional chronology, see page 209. In late October 1835, the offices of the Clerk and Recorder of Cook County were removed to the office newly erected by the county on Chicago's public square, as per notice in the *Chicago American*. The results of a census recently taken were reported in the Nov. 28 *Chicago American* and listed the county's population as 9,773, up 300 percent in two years – with 18 sawmills, 5 gristmills, 2 breweries, 1 iron foundry, and 1 glove manufactury. [13, 278, 377, 544]

Cook County Court of Commissioners   the County of Cook was created by an act of the General Assembly of the State of Illinois on Jan. 15, 1831, and the Commissioners' Court of the county

was opened on March 8, 1831. Samuel Miller, Gholson Kercheval [of Chicago], and James Walker [on the Du Page River] were sworn into office by J.S.C. Hogan, J.P. William See was appointed clerk of the court. The Circuit Court of the vast Fifth Judicial District under [see] Judge Richard M. Young now included Cook County and began to convene regularly on April 23, 1832. [12]

Cook County Medical Society   the first meeting was held on Oct. 3, 1836, at the office of the Chicago Insurance Co.; the secretary was Dr. Levi D. Boone. [On April 19, 1850, the Chicago Medical Society was formed and Dr. Boone became its first president. Today's conjoined "Chicago Medical Society–The Medical Society of Cook County" therefore seems to have had its beginning in 1836, although records are lacking to show that the society met regularly between 1836 and 1850; *eds.*]. [12]

Cook County roads   see Chicago roads.

Cook, Daniel H. Pope   (1795-1827) native of KY; newspaper man, politician, first Illinois attorney general, and later member of the U.S. House of Representatives from Illinois, winning five successive elections and serving from 1819 to 1827; credited with securing passage of the Illinois & Michigan Canal bill and land grant of 1827; in 1821 married Julia C. Edwards, daughter of Gov. Ninian Edwards; Cook County was named after him; died in Kentucky. [12]

Cook, Isaac   born c.1812; arrived from New Jersey in February 1834; in October 1835 joined the "Pioneer" hook and ladder company, a voluntary fire brigade that organized in a meeting reportedly held at Cook's saloon on South Water Street; at the same time, may also have managed the Mansion House on Lake Street under the name Cook's Coffee House; married Caroline Gibson on July 4, 1836, per notice in the *Chicago Democrat*; ✦ Eagle Saloon, 10 Dearborn St.; became sheriff in 1846 and postmaster in 1854; lived at St. Louis, MO in 1885. [12]

Cook, Josiah P.   initially ran a bakery on the corner of Lake and LaSalle streets with Samuel C. George; on Oct. 29, 1834, they reported partnership dissolution in the *Chicago Democrat*, as Bates announced an auction of "the Bakeshop with all Baking utensils" on Nov. 3; ✦ [John] baker, LaSalle Street.

Cook's Coffee House   see Cook, Isaac.

Cook's Saloon   see Cook, Isaac.

Cook Street   ➡ a short-lived diagonal street in the Wabansia Section of early Chicago; used in the official description of the boundaries of Chicago by the newly elected town board on Aug. 10, 1833. The street is evident on Joshua Hathaway's ✳ map of Chicago printed in 1834; that same year John S. Wright drew the town from surveys, identifying the street as Naler Street. See Chicago, boundaries.

Cook, Thomas   (1800-1885) from Yorkshire, England; came in June 1832; in 1833, he purchased a cart from Newberry & Dole and with cart and horse, began a lumber business on South Water Street between Randolph and Washington, buying his supplies from George Smith; by 1836, his business in teaming extended to Galena, Springfield, Detroit, and Mineral Point, WI; married by Reverend Freeman in Chicago to Alsey Scott of [Western Springs] on June 28, 1834, per notice in the *Chicago Democrat*; ✦ teamster, Desplaines Street, near Monroe; after Alsey's death married Mary Queen in 1848. [12, 13, 711a]

Cooley & Holsman   see next entry.

Cooley, R.S.   partnered [see] George Halsman in a tailoring business, Cooley & Holsman [*sic*], opposite the Eagle Coffee House on Dearborn Street; advertised "Fashions received in their season, from New York" in the July 22, 1835, *Chicago Democrat*; dissolution occurred Aug. 1; Halsman continued at the same location.

Cooley, William   settled N in Cook [Lake] County; on the list of subscribers to the *Chicago Democrat* in November 1833; married Rebecca Warner of Newton, CT on Dec. 25, 1833 "at the

JOHN COOPER, M.D. [137]

Du Page," as noted in the *Chicago Democrat* of Feb. 4, 1834.

Cooper, Ezekiel   settler who built a house on the N side of the river close to the Forks in 1809 [later known as the Burns House, near Merchandise Mart]; with wife, Mary, had four children: James (1797), Isabella (1800), Anne (1806?), and Frances (1809?); died early in 1811, of (probably) malaria; later that year, Mary remarried discharged Fort Dearborn soldier Thomas Burns, and gave birth to Catherine on April 5, 1812, the day before the Winnebago attack at Leigh's farm; only Mary, Isabella, and Catherine would survive the 1812 massacre and remain captive among the Indians for two years. [226]

Cooper, Isabella   born in 1800; daughter of Ezekiel and Mary Cooper, stepdaughter to Thomas Burns, sister of James; survivor of the Fort Dearborn massacre, although she was scalped (the scar remaining throughout her life, the size of a silver

dollar); later married George Fearson of Detroit, younger brother of Mary Julia Fearson, wife of William Whistler; for additional details, see Burns, Thomas; Cooper, Ezekiel. [226]

Cooper, James   born in 1797; son of Ezekiel and Mary Cooper, stepson of Thomas Burns, brother of Isabella; joined the Chicago militia and was killed at the Fort Dearborn massacre of 1812. [226]

Cooper, John   U.S. Army private at Fort Dearborn, enlisted in May 1808; killed defending the wagons in the massacre of 1812. [226]

Cooper, John, M.D.   (1786-1863) born at Fishkill, NY; graduate of the College of Physicians and Surgeons, New York City; enlisted as surgeon's mate on June 13, 1808, and was assigned to Fort Dearborn; arrived from Buffalo on the brig *Adams* to succeed Dr. William C. Smith; became close friend of the commandant, Capt. John Whistler, who allowed him to act as sutler for the fort (in partnership with Whistler's son, John Whistler, Jr.), a lucrative job, but a move that put both Whistler and Cooper in conflict with government regulations, and on a personal basis, with the U.S. Factor, Matthew Irwin, and with John Kinzie; Cooper resigned his commission on April 1, 1811, in resentment over Whistler's reassignment, instigated by Irwin and Kinzie. As a parting gift, Whistler gave him his copy of William Shenstone's *Poems* [this volume was later returned to the Chicago Historical Society and can be seen among the few surviving items from the first Fort Dearborn; see Shenstone, William, for a sample of his poetry]. Replaced by a former classmate, Dr. Van Voorhis, Dr. Cooper, who had maintained two saddle horses and a hunting dog at the fort, tendered his resignation and left the army, riding back to New York by way of Detroit, Fort Wayne, and Pittsburgh. [13, 109, 564]

copper   a metal known to, and used and traded by, the Indians of the Great Lakes region since prehistoric times. Rich deposits of native copper (nearly pure metal) occurred along the southern margin of Lake Superior, on Isle Royal, and else-

Indian copper effigy bird

where in the upper peninsula of Michigan. Some of the more superficial deposits were displaced southward by glacial activity ("float" copper). In 1666, Father Allouez reported: "One often finds at the bottom of the water [of Lake Superior] pieces of pure copper, of ten or twenty livres' weight. I have several times seen such pieces in the Savages' hands; ...." The local Indians did not smelt copper, as was done by tribes in the Southwest and in Central America, but used cold hammering techniques to create tools and ornaments. Tens of thousands of copper artifacts found in burial mounds and former campsites and villages in many North American locations testify to the Indians' great appreciation and resourceful adaptation of copper. See entry for Anker Site.

Corbin, Fielding   unrelated to James and Phelim Corbin; U.S. Army private at Fort Dearborn; enlisted on Oct. 25, 1811; believed killed in the initial battle at the massacre of Aug. 15, 1812. [226]

Corbin, James   U.S. Army private at Fort Dearborn; brother of Phelim Corbin; husband of Susannah (nicknamed Sukey) and father of a young son and daughter; enlisted Oct. 2, 1810; survived the massacre of Aug. 15, 1812; wounded in the heel, hip, thigh, and shoulder; later ransomed from the Indians by the trader Buisson and conveyed to Mackinac by canoe; was imprisoned by the British there but released to New York in the spring of 1814. Susan and the children were killed by an Indian when discovered hiding in the Burns house. Corbin is one of the few survivors of the massacre who left a recorded eyewitness account. [226, 561]

Corbin, Phelim   U.S. Army private at Fort Dearborn; brother of James; husband of Victoria; enlisted on Dec. 7, 1805, and reenlisted on Dec. 7, 1810; survived the massacre of 1812 and was later ransomed from captivity; both his eight months pregnant wife and the fetus were scalped and then beheaded during the attack. [Captain Heald, commandant at the fort, lists in his post-massacre report only two privates by the name Corbin, namely Fielding and James; Eckert lists Phelim in addition, and insists he is distinct from and unrelated to Fielding; Phelim and James were listed in *Niles Weekly Register* as survivors; James and Fielding were on the muster list of Nov. 30, 1810, and May 31, 1812; *eds.*] [226, 708]

Corncrackers   nickname for residents from Kentucky, common in early Illinois. [55a]

Cornelius   young lad brought from the East in 1834 by Philo Carpenter to work in his drugstore; his full name is not recorded. [221]

Coronelli, Vincenzo Maria   (1650-1718) Venetian Franciscan priest, globe- and mapmaker for Louis XIV, 1680; cosmographer to the Republic of Venice, 1685; among his important work are early maps of the North American Great Lakes region. His 1688 ✷ map of the western part of New France, *Partie Occidentale du Canada ou de la Nouvelle France ou sont les Nations des Ilinois, de Tracy, les Iroquois, et plusieurs autres Peuples …* [Service historique de la Marine, Vincennes], published in Paris by J.B. Nolin, incorporated the reports of Marquette, Jolliet, and La Salle. [605, 681, 682]

corporate seal   see Chicago, Town, seal of.

corporate finances   in 1823, when Chicago was in Fulton County, the first tax was collected, a total of $11.24 property tax based on 0.1% of assessed value. Public funds available to the town trustees in the initial years after the 1833 incorporation were frugally spent; the budget was small and even the repair of streets and bridges was not authorized unless the treasurer had sufficient funds on hand. On Oct. 2, 1834, the board voted to authorize a loan of $60, ★★★ **Chicago's 1st** loan on

IRA COUCH [410]

the faith of the community.

Corps of Engineers   of the U.S. Army; early name: Topographical Engineers; established on March 16, 1802; beginning with [see] Major Steven H. Long's 1816 first scientific survey of the Chicago portage, the officers of the corps played important roles in building the second Fort Dearborn, in mapping the proposed Illinois & Michigan Canal in the 1820s, and subsequently in directing the development of the Chicago harbor. In this context, also see separate entries on Army Engineers Dr. W. H. Howard, Frederick Harrison, William B. Guyon, Henry Belin, and William Sanford Evileth. [423]

Corron, Joseph P.   married Hannah Ann Tuckerman on Oct. 27, 1835, per notice in the *Chicago Democrat*, Oct. 28, 1835, E.W. Casey officiating, "all of Cook County."

Cottage Grove Trail   early name for branch of the Chicago-Detroit Road [originally an ancient Indian trail] that left the Vincennes Road and passed through a wooded area near 31st Street. Cottage

Grove was described by Dr. Boyer in 1833 as "a timber point running toward Chicago and about three miles distant therefrom," although the name was coined later by Charles Cleaver, who had his cottage there; survives as a two-block street; ➡ Cottage Grove Avenue (200 E), between 22nd and 24th streets.

Couch, Ira   (1806-1857) from New York State, arrived in late 1835 or 1836 with his wife Caroline E. (née Gregory) and his brother James; the brothers opened a tailor shop and haberdashery on Lake Street between Dearborn and Clark in 1836; within a year, purchased the first Tremont House and created the first grand hotel; rebuilt twice after disastrous fires in 1839 and 1849, remaining in the family until 1853; the brothers are believed to have become ★★★ **Chicago's 1st** millionaires. James married Elizabeth C. Wells in 1847 [Ira's bones are thought by some to rest in a ▲ mausoleum near the Chicago Historical Society in Lincoln Park, a former city cemetery; more likely the remains are those of his nephew with the same name Ira, son of James; the elder Ira died in Havana, Cuba, in 1857; his grave is at Rosehill Cemetery, clearly marked; the mausoleum lost its inscribed plaques long ago.]; in 1885, James' address was the Tremont House, and Ira's widow lived at 3156 Indiana Ave.; ➡ Couch Place (170 N). [12, 351]

Couch, James   (1800-1892) see Couch, Ira.

Council Bluffs, IA   location to which 5,000 Indians were moved from Chicago in 1835, in accordance with the Treaty of Chicago of 1833.

Countraman, Maj. Frederick H.   see Contraman, Maj. Frederick H.

county roads   see streets and roads.

coureurs de bois   unlicensed independent traders operating in New France and Louisiana since 1660 or earlier; required by law to be licensed by the authorities, but they were largely disregarded, and it was openly charged that governors and other officials were in collusion with the traders. Toward

Chicago's first court house 1835

the end of the 17th century, an estimated one third of the able-bodied men of the colony played an active historical part exploring the wilderness while evading the law and living among the Indians; with a thorough knowledge of waterways, they were experts on local transportation, portages, and trails; also see *voyageur, engagé.*

Coursoll, Michel   also Coursolle, Courselle; likely the Mr. Cursall whose cabin is indicated N of the river on Captain Whistler's 1808 draft of the first Fort Dearborn; a French trader from Montreal who worked among the Indians along the lower Wabash River, occasionally acquiring supplies from John Kinzie, beginning in May 1804. The account book entries identify four members of the Coursoll family who came together on June 16, 1804: Mr. Michel, Mechial, John Marie, and Fran. Marie. One or another purchased supplies through the summer of 1806; Drolett, "Coursoll's man," is noted on Sept. 14, 1805, likely a French *engagé.* According to the *Wisconsin Historical Collections,* Michel Coursolle traded on the Michigan peninsula prior to 1812, and as a British trader in 1816, was granted a lot on Drummond Island. [404]

courthouse   ★★★ **Chicago's 1st** courthouse, a brick structure with basement and first story, was built in the fall of 1835 on the NE corner of the public square framed by Randolph, Washington, Clark and LaSalle streets, where City Hall and the Cook County building now stand; ➡ Court Place, at 125 N, is a reminder. [12]

Courtney, Thomas   arrived with wife and child in 1834; built a one room cabin at Blue Island [now the corner of Grove and Ann streets], becoming the first settler.

Coutra, Louis   resident in 1825; assessed for tax purposes on $50 worth of personal property. [12]

Cox, A. Jackson   tailor from New York, arrived 1835; partner of the clothing store of Cox & Duncan [Thomas Duncan?] on the W side of Dearborn Street, near South Water Street, mentioned in [see] J.D. Bonnel's letter; ◆ tailor, 9 Clark St.

Cox, David   arrived from New York in 1835; lawyer, elected judge in 1837; ◆ hotel-keeper, corner of West Lake and North Canal streets. [12]

Cox, William L.   discharged soldier, settled at the south branch of the Chicago River around 1810; on June 2, 1811, Indians murdered his son and abducted his daughter; a posse overtook the Indians near Springfield and freed the girl; in the fall of 1816, taught school to the children of John Kinzie and others from the fort in an old bakery building on the Kinzie property. [12]

Crafts, John   (1789-1825) born in Walpole, New Hampshire; in 1816, the firm Conant & Mack of Detroit sent Crafts to establish a trading post at Hardscrabble on the south branch near the Leigh farm, selling the establishment to the American Fur Co. in 1822. [Some have maintained that Abram Edwards, of Detroit, was the proprietor of the agency at Hardscrabble, rather than Conant and Mack, and that Crafts worked for Edwards; *eds.*] Crafts is first listed in John Kinzie's account book in November 1818; in September 1820, Beaubien & Crafts is listed. A highly successful American Fur Co. agent, he moved the post to the old Dean house at the mouth of the river, then owned by Jean B. Beaubien, who had already become his partner (subagent) in the flourishing enterprise; together they built a warehouse just E of the Dean house by the edge of the river; from 1823-1825, continued to hold the area trade concession of the American Fur Co., in which Beaubien would suc-

ceed him (John Kinzie became subagent). Crafts was a frequent visitor to the Kinzie house throughout 1824 as he courted Maria Indiana Kinzie; in 1825, was assessed on $5,000 of personal property, though likely company stock; died that year on May 15 at the Kinzie house of bilious fever [malaria]. Crafts was well liked, known for dressing well, with a large wardrobe; Dr. Wolcott was administrator of Crafts' estate; the auction (June 1, 1826) of his large estate attracted many purchasers from the locale and beyond, whose names, acquisitions, and payments have been recorded and preserved in Peoria court records. [12, 170, 220, 404]

Crafts House   see Dean House.

Crandall, David   from Franklin County, NY; in 1831 came with wife Harriet (née Thurston) and son John to [Calumet Township], residing on the E side of the river; with hundreds of other families sought refuge in Fort Dearborn during the 1832 Black Hawk scare and joined [with Alva Crandall] Captain Seission's militia company late July; a daughter Sarah was born in September 1835; later moved to Will County, then to Missouri. [278, 714]

crane   see whooping crane (*Grus americana*); sandhill crane (*Grus canadensis*).

Crane, Ebenezer   listed with Betsy Crane, as charter members of the Baptist church on Oct. 19, 1833. [12]

Cratee, Madore   French trader with the American Fur Co. on the Illinois and Fox rivers; mediator with the Potawatomi; later a mail walker between Ottawa and Chicago, and Chicago and Portage [IN]; by Indian trot he could cover 90 miles a day, earning $18.

Crawford County, Illinois Territory   created by act of legislature Dec. 31, 1816; included Chicago until 1819, when the settlement became part of Clark County; for details, see Chicago jurisdictional chronology on page 209. [544]

Crawford, James and William   on April 1, 1834, there were unclaimed letters for a James Crawford at the post office; presumably brothers and ★★★

Chicago's 1st brewmasters, who in the summer of 1835, advertised in the June 13 *Chicago American* for 4,000 bushels of barley that were to be delivered to the Chicago Brewery; inquiries were taken at Mr. Fay's Boarding House on Lake Street. A later article in the *Chicago American* on Aug. 15 listed one brewery among nearly 95 business enterprises in town, suggesting that the venture was succeeding. The location of this first brewery remains undetermined. William Crawford married Elizabeth Ann Hubbard on April 17, 1836; in 1839, he was listed as a drayman, in the alley between North Clark and LaSalle. Also see breweries.

Crevecoeur   see *Fort Crevecoeur*.

Crittenden, John J.   first U.S. district attorney of the territory of Illinois, took office in 1809 under Governor Edwards.

Crocker, Hans   (1816-1889) arrived from New York in 1834; was secretary of the town's anti-gambling committee constituted on Oct. 25, 1834; was secretary for the Chicago Lyceum in 1835 and on Nov. 10 he debated the query "Would it be expedient for the United States to extend her Territory by the acquisition of Texas?" with Thomas R. Hubbard at the Presbyterian church for the Lyceum—his position was negative, as per notice in the *Chicago American*; was also vice president of the Young Men's Temperance Society, organized on Dec. 19 that year; a lawyer, removed to Milwaukee in the autumn of 1836 though still listed at Chicago in 1839 without an address; was still living there in 1885. [12, 351]

Crocker, Oliver A.   cousin of Oliver C. Crocker; member of a team that went from Chicago to Sheboygan in 1834 to build a sawmill on the Sheboygan River.

Crocker, Oliver C.   (1811-1879) also known as Colonel Crocker; born in Union, NY, on May 2, 1811; arrived in Chicago in June 1834, where he became acquainted with [see] William Payne, whom he joined in financing and undertaking an expedition to [see] Sheboygan where the party con-

JAMES CURTIS [410]

structed and operated a sawmill until 1836. The enterprise having failed, he returned to the East. In 1878, he lived in Binghampton, NY, but died on Aug. 1, 1879, during a visit to Chicago, hours after registering as an old settler at the Calumet Club. His reminiscences were printed in the *Sheboygan Times* on March 9, 1878. [12]

Croghan, George   British Indian agent; left many reports of his exploits during the 1760s, in which he also mentioned Chicago and wrote it *Chicag8*. [173, 649]

Crooks, Ramsey   (1786-1859) Scottish fur trader, manager and later part owner (with John Jacob Astor) of the [see] American Fur Co.'s entire Northwest operations; maintained close contact by correspondence with the Chicago fur traders, including John Kinzie; in 1809 visited Fort Dearborn, traveling on the sailing vessel *Salina*. [12]

Cross, Jefferson T.   owner of 80 acres of land along both sides of the south branch of the river in Section 32, Township 39, prior to 1836, as seen in Andreas, *History of Chicago*, pp. 112-113.

Cross, Solomon, Jr.   owner of 80 acres of land in Section 32, Township 39, prior to 1836, as seen in Andreas, *History of Chicago*, pp. 112-113.

Crozat, Antoine   (1655-1738) see Louisiana Province.

Crozier, John   U.S. Army sergeant at Fort Dearborn; enlisted July 1803, promoted to sergeant in December 1810; survived the massacre of Aug. 15, 1812, and escaped the Indians, reaching Fort Wayne; reported to have deserted before the massacre, but not known to have been charged officially. [226]

Cummings, Maj. Alexander   Third Infantry; born in Ireland; commandant at Fort Dearborn from January to October 1821; died in 1842. [12]

Cunningham, Hezekiah   member of the [see] Vermillion Rangers who came to Chicago for its protection during the Winnebago war of 1827; left an account of the event that may be found in Andreas.

Cursall, Mr.   see Coursoll, Michel.

Curtis, James   also Curtiss; solicitor, arrived from New York in 1835; opened an office on South Water Street between Clark and Dearborn, one door W of Jones, King & Co. (upstairs), as per *Chicago Democrat* ad on May 20; his wife's name was Mary; in 1835 or early 1836, an addition to the original town was executed by the town trustees, variously referred to as the [see] Carpenter (or Carpenter & Curtiss) Addition, implying that James Curtis was either a partner of or did the necessary legal work for Philo Carpenter in the proceedings; ◆ attorney & counselor at law, 175 Lake St.; became mayor in 1847 and again in 1850; in 1885 his widow lived in Champaign, IL. For a picture of Curtis, see this page. [12, 278, 351]

Curtis, Joseph   English; came in the spring of 1831 and erected a log cabin along the north branch

[Niles Township]; returned to England in 1850. [13]

Curtiss, L.G.   as deputy surveyor of Cook County, placed a notice in the July 15, 1835, *Chicago Democrat* stating that "Orders left at the Mansion House will be punctually attended to."

Cutwright, Peter   owner of 80 acres of land in Section 30, Township 39, prior to 1836, as per Andreas, *History of Chicago*, pp. 112-113.

Cutwright, Samuel   prior to 1836 owner of 80 acres of land in Section 28, Township 39, as per Andreas, *History of Chicago*, pp. 112-113.

Cygnus buccinator   see swan.

Dablon, Father Claude   (1618-1697) born in Dieppe, France; came to Canada as a Jesuit missionary in 1655; spent his first years at isolated missions in the wilderness, frequently ministering with Father Allouez; in 1668, founded the mission at Sault St. Marie with Father Marquette; in 1671, became superior of the *Mission de Saint-Esprit* at Chequamegon Bay [Ashland, WI]; submitted a valuable ✴ map, *Lac Svperievr et avtres lievx ou sont les Missions des Peres de la Compagnie de Iesvs Comprises sovs le nom D'ovtaovacs*, with Father Allouez that was printed in the *Jesuit Relations* of 1672; appointed superior of all Canadian missions, a position held until at least 1693 at Quebec; granted Father Marquette permission to accompany Jolliet on the 1673 expedition that led them to Chicago, and edited Father Marquette's travel reports; died in Quebec. [12, 605, 681, 682]

Dally, Joseph   a remaining letter listed in the *Chicago Democrat* on Jan. 21, 1835, may identify the blacksmith of Dally & Youngs.

Dally & Youngs   the new smithy in town, opposite the jail, with an initial advertisement in the *Chicago Democrat* on June 18, 1834.

Dalton, George   see Dolton, George.

Dalton, —   see Dolton, Charles H.

dancing schools   see Marshall, James A.; Davis,

William H.

Daniel Webster   steamer, built at Black Rock, NY in 1833; frequented Chicago in subsequent years. [48]

Danville, Illinois   on the Big Vermillion River, a 125-mile distance from Chicago; Gurdon S. Hubbard established a trading post here in 1823. The trail between Chicago and Danville later became known as Hubbard's Trace, and in 1834 was made a state road, the northernmost part of which became State Street. From Danville Hubbard led 100 militia volunteers—the "Vermillion Rangers"—on horseback to Chicago in July 1827, during the Winnebago war, to help safeguard the small settlement, unprotected because Fort Dearborn had not been garrisoned since 1823.

Darling, Enoch   arrived from Rhode Island in June 1832 and on July 23, enrolled as a private in Capt. H. Seissions' company of mounted volunteers, mustered out Aug. 15; voted in the election of the first town board on Aug. 10, 1833; remained in Chicago until 1836. [12, 733]

Darling, Lucius R.   of [what is now] Silver Lake, Kansas; arrived in 1832; later married Elizabeth, daughter of Antoine Ouilmette, following her divorce from Michael Welch; general agent of the Chicago, Alton & St. Louis Railroad in 1857. [12]

Dart   a 15-ton sloop built by Dr. L.A. Barnard at La Grange Prairie, and hauled by oxen to Niles [MI] where it was launched on the St. Joseph River. During 1834, it called at Chicago seven times (six times under Captain Barnard, on June 6 under Captain Putnam), sailing regularly between St. Joseph, Chicago, and Milwaukee with merchandise.

Daugherty, Daniel   U.S. Army private at Fort Dearborn; enlisted August 1807; killed at the 1812 massacre immediately after surrender. [226]

Davenport, Joseph and William   each purchaser of 80 acres of land in 1830 in Section 4 of Township 39 N [now the near N side].

David Carver   schooner, in 1833 owned and operated between Chicago and St. Joseph by the ear-

liest Chicago lumber merchant, [see] Capt. David Carver; unnoted on Marine Listings in both newspapers through December 1835. [12]

David, George   English visitor in 1833, travelling overland through the Midwest; little is known about him, and little is noted in his diary about Chicago, his possible destination, but his vivid description of daily travel conditions provide extraordinary insight; the editors have therefore included a generous excerpt from his unedited manuscript, transcribed from the original by R.P. Mason [Escanaba, MI]; see David's definition of "turnpiking" as a separate entry. [187]

Sept. 17th. Started at 7. Turned out very wet, the road bad. very mirey the horses worn and jaded. the waggons heavy loaded. these circumstanced combined to render the roads disagreeable in the extreme & fatiguing both to men and horses. By 3 o'clo. our poor steeds dragged us through "mud & mire" 3 miles but their efforts failed. They fairly knocked up. There was no tavern, or indeed any shelter except a half finished shanty we found in the woods a little distance from the road. Its roof was watertight & and that was very lucky, the rain continuing without interruption for the greatest part of the night, a little cessation in the evening enabled us to get our blankets in some order & and kindle some fire, but for want of a chimney we endured a great annoyance in the smoke tho' we stood it as bravely as a set of Laplanders, before it was dark we had eaten our morsel and lain down to rest. Sleep I can't say much about. Mrs. B. suffered considerable alarm from the idea that wolves would come in the dead of the night and disturb us, but her fears were groundless.

Sept. 18th. ... Autumn tints begin to variegate the foliage of the forest trees from the brightest yellow to the deepest & most brilliant shades of vermillion. The leaves of the tulip tree turn to a bright yellow and those of the Arbor Vitae to a deep vermillion. We saw between this spot and Perrysburgh several log houses in progress. One individual had raised his house a month since, and informed us that himself & 4 neigh-

bors only were engaged 4 days in putting it up and rendering it habitable. It was nearly watertight but still *deficient in comfort, and in this state he seemed much disposed to let it remain. This is a fault too prevalent among American settlers. They run up just enough for present shelter & work very hard in clearing the land for two years or so, but after that period they are the laziest people, next to the Indian. Their houses receive but little improvement, if any, and seldom or ever completely finish it. I have slept in log taverns where the landlord has laid by money and can afford to waste half his time "behind a pipe." "Glick" the Dutchman was eternally sauntering to & fro with a pipe instead of busying himself to put his house or stable in order, for the latter was miserable, & when I remarked to him on the unfinished state of his premises, replied, "I am going to fix it." A great & redeeming trait in the character of an American laborer & in which he differs widely from the English operative, is, you may accost him, ask him 20 questions, handle his tools, he will answer you readily, but never "asks you for a drink." ❖ Stump farms present a most unseemly aspect after the corn or grain has been reaped & housed. The farm has the appearance of being covered with beans stacked, or rather in shocks, from one end to another. Many people call them "niggers" by reason of these stumps always being blackened by having been burnt to destroy them as near the ground as possible. ...*

Sept. 20. ... *stopped at a Dutchman's 12 miles from Perrysburgh who housed us for the night although he kept no tavern. His name was Roop, and he was very anxious to persuade us he was a high Dutchman & not one of those low Dutchman that pour over the Atlantic in such numbers. He was a civil, accommodating chap, the only great inconvenience was the host of noisy children he had, our own being sufficient to preclude the necessity of any addition on that score. Shot the first prairie hen, a bird similar to fowl, with head like a partridge, very good eating. Entered today in the Territory of Michigan, 7 miles.*

Sept. 21 ... *We were unfortunately compelled to biv-*

ouack in a spot were we could get no water; the consequence was we could get no tea and went to sleep on roast potatoe. Before lighting our fire we were obliged to cut down all the fern & prairie grass to prevent the whole prairie catching fire, for it was not a close wood we were passing thro', but "Oak Openings" which is a light sandy soil, poor, on which nothing but burr oak will grow. This wood extends 18 miles from the settlement at 10 mile creek to Sommerfield.*

Sept. 22. Sunday. *We were upon the march at dawn "breakfastless" with 9 miles to travel, before we find water which we did not accomplish till 2 o'clo. by reason of bad horses & and bad roads, having 4 or 5 swamps to drag thro' deep enough to take the waggon wheels in up to the stocks. I at one time despaired of ever getting the horse I drove to move again till the wolves should carry him; judge of the roads when I say we were 8 hours going 9 miles. Put up at "Russell's" tavern at Somerfield and made as speedy an attack upon victuals as all circumstances would permit. Slept on the bar room floor with the landlord, his wife and three children, one of which entertained us with incessant crying and the wife found out she had chickens to cook when it was time for all to be asleep. This was a log house and one of the most comfortless; plenty of chinks to let the air in. The wind swept over the floor like a hurricane, the power of attraction of my body to the floor being very strong or I should have been carried away – "nolens, volens."*

Sept. 24. *Still remaining at Russell's tavern, the horses not sufficiently recovered or the new harness completed. The ague [malaria] is very prevalent at this place. We work at the smith's shop ourselves because the smith has the "shakings," the landlord, his brother, his wife & 3 children, the stage driver, in fact 5 people out of 6 are suffering under it. ...*

Oct. 3rd. *Bungled over 14 miles today, to Coldwater, Morse's tavern. ... Reached the tavern at 6 o'clo. A sharp frosty air. The landlord went out at night to a merrymaking. We went to bed at our accustomed time 9 o'clo. and about 2 in the morning my slumbers were broken by him, in a state of inebriation, tumbling*

over me; to get to his bedroom was his intention, but poor man he had—"Put an enemy in his mouth that Stole away his brains."—and he was fumbling in an opposite direction. There perhaps he might have fumbled till morning beams illumined the horizon had I not put him in the road and facilitated "his anchorage in blanket hay." ❖ The inmates of his hotel were beastly dirty in their actions and cooking.*

Oct. 5. ... *Reached "Sturges Prairie," 9 miles; by sunset, glorious travelling! ! 2 of our horses now are in such a condition that a London knacker would hardly give them room in his copper. ❖ Sturges Prairie is a fine open plain of 5,000 acres, nearly all under tillage; about 2 miles south of this runs the state line between the territory of Michigan & the state of Indiana. We put up at Douglass's tavern, more respectable than usual. The people of the house were greatly amused at the sight of our large bed, and well they might, for when the size of the room would permit as it did in the present instance, we made up all the mattresses into one bed which would hold 11 individuals without annoyance. ❖ Two waggons, well horsed and attended, drove up to the Inn soon after us laden with trinkets and specie for the Indians, with 6,000 of whom a treaty for land was being held at Chicago.*

Oct. 10. *A clear fine frosty morning. Passed the St. Joseph by ferry at a place called Bertrand. Passed thro' an Indian village of the tribe Potawatamies 1 mile from the river westward. These poor savages were greatly surprised at the ass's foal which accompanied us, running after us hallo-ing and clapping their hands. Crossed the Portage prairie to Ben Hardman's house, a German who, tho' he kept no house of entertainment, took us in and afforded us fire & shelter, which was truly needful. We were tired, our cattle were the same, and there was no vestige of a house else before us, tho' we could see further than our strength, at the present time, could carry us. This man's house could boast of but one room, & he had a family of 10 children, which add to himself & wife and son in law, his oldest daughter being married, and 14 of us, forming a formidable host of 27 and all, all to sleep in one room. We remarked to our host that we feared we should be troublesome but he replied "he could put two droves of quiet sheep in one stable." He was one of the early German settlers and had quite a patriarchal appearance. He wore a long and dignified beard that descended almost to his waist. We entered the State of Indiana today by taking a southerly direction after passing the Indian village, hoping to fall in with some farmer that could sell us a supply of oats. 13 miles*

Oct. 11. Got onto the Michigan road at 11, and followed it thro' mud hole, swamp & bog for 10 miles. Passed over the "wet Swamp" Terracopera prairie & rolling prairie to Well's log house, a tavern. A wet day, & cold winds; rather uncomfortable housed for Mr. Well's splendid one room mansion could not boast of a door to keep either wind or wolf out. Wolves are so numerous on this prairie that they dare let nothing loose for fear of destruction by these ravenous beasts. He told us that had it not been for his timely intervention a day or two since in the woods he should have lost a yearling calf and that too, in broad day. 12 miles

Oct. 14. "Thro' the woods & thro' the woods" 7 miles to Michigan City, a puny place with half a dozen houses on the edge of the lake with a creek running thro' the town. ❖ *We met a man on horseback before arriving at the town of whom we asked some questions relative to Chicago, and he favored us with the following luminous reply. He said "It was a rising place, but the land about it pretty much poor, wet and unhealthy and powerful frosty; they were going ahead lively with the buildings." ...*

Oct. 15. Rested all day at Hughes's Tavern [Michigan City]. It rained heavily; washed our clothes and laid in a little "grub" to last us over the beach 40 miles to the next tavern. ...

Oct. 18. ... At 2 o'clo' a yoke of oxen met us and conveyed us to "Mann's tavern" on the mouth of the Calamic at 8 o'clo' in a queerish kind of condition. Here we ate, drank, & slept with Frenchmen & squaws.

Mann was a French trader [German] who married a squaw, consequently he had plenty of Indian relations.

Oct. 22. The Calimic proved a calamitous stream and finished the career of the ass which was unfortunately drowned in attempting to swim over to follow the waggon of another party, mistaking them for us.

Oct. 23. Completed today the remaining 13 miles of our journey and entered the long looked for town of Chicago at nightfall, and after much trouble in seeking for an asylum; put up by the recommendation of Mr. Winson at Brown's boarding house, thus terminating our wanderings and here we found a resting place, here we "lit on the spot we could call 'home' ". The day had been fine & mild, hardly a zephyr breathed to ripple the glassy surface of the lake, but when we reached the open prairie the wind arose and before morning it blew so hard that I fancied the roof of the boarding house in which we were would have fallen about my ears but the roof being stronger than my faith it was in the same elevated condition when I awoke as when I went to sleep.

Davion, Rev. Antoine (-1726) native of Normandy, arrived at Quebec in 1690; priest within the *Séminaire des Missions Étrangères*; with Abbés St. Cosme and De Montigny, was directed by Father Gravier to the *L'Ange Gardien* mission at Chicago in October 1698, then continued S for work among the Akansea; remained a missionary among the Tonicas along the southern Mississippi River until 1708 when hostility mounted; removed to La Mobile or New Orleans about 1722; returned to France in 1725.

Davis, George (1809-1858) born in London; arrived in 1833; one of the earliest teachers, though initially worked as surveyor for the state government; was listed as a subscriber to the *Chicago Democrat* in November 1833; [his drawing of Wolf Point in 1834 later appeared in the *Chicago Magazine*, 1857]; opened a school during the winter of 1834-35 over a store on Lake Street, between Dearborn and Clark, and in 1835 taught school at the Presbyterian church on the corner of Lake and Clark streets; known as "a great singer" and gifted musician; married Myra Delia Willcox of Detroit in 1836; ◆ county clerk, 109 Lake St.; became alderman in 1844; from 1851 to 1856, lived with his family at Detroit, then returned to live in Chicago until his death. [12, 97, 351]

Davis, George M. arrived in 1831 from New York. [351]

Davis, Jefferson (1808-1889) U.S. statesman and only president of the Confederate States of America; born in Christian County, KY; graduated from West Point in 1828 near the bottom of his class. Throughout the following five years, he was stationed in the Northwest, mostly at Fort Crawford and Fort Winnebago; was at the latter in 1829 as lieutenant under Major Twiggs and in October was sent to Fort Dearborn in search of deserters; participated in the Black Hawk War of 1832 and was placed in charge by Colonel Taylor of conveying the captured Black Hawk from Fort Crawford to Jefferson Barracks (Missouri). Early historians, without documentation, place Davis on the Chicago and Calumet rivers in 1833 as a lieutenant in the Corps of Engineers, conducting a government survey; most likely he has been confused with Lt. James Allen, or with Allen's successor, Capt. Thomas Jefferson Cram. His poor academic record would have precluded any service in the elite Topographical Engineers, as the U.S. Army Corps of Engineers was then called [personal communication from editor of *Jefferson Davis Papers* to John F. Swenson]. Davis was inaugurated president of the Confederate States of America in 1861 at Richmond, VA. A later visit to Chicago by Davis was recorded by John Wentworth for May 21, 1881. Davis' 1829 visit is well authenticated by Lt. David Hunter, stationed at Fort Dearborn garrison; see the following excerpt by Quaife. [*Transactions*, Illinois State Historical Society, v. 30; 1923]

A member of the Fort Dearborn garrison at this time was Lieutenant David Hunter. Looking out from the fort one morning in 1829, where now swirls the greatest tide of humanity born by any bridge in the world, Hunter perceived on the north side of the river a white man. Wondering who the stranger would be, he entered a small canoe, intended but for a single person, and paddled across to interview him. It proved to be [Jefferson] Davis, and inviting him to lie down in the bottom of the canoe Hunter ferried him across to the post. The passage of time was to work a strange transformation in the relations of the occupants of that little boat in this voyage across the placid Chicago. In May, 1862, Hunter, now Major-General in the command of the Department of the South, issued an order emancipating the slaves in the states of Florida, Georgia and South Carolina. Davis, a president of the Confederacy, responded with a proclamation of outlawry against Hunter, threatening in the event of his capture by the Confederate forces to put him to death as a felon.

Davis, John   arrived from New York in 1833; was listed as a subscriber to the *Chicago Democrat* in November 1833; served on the cholera committee in 1834; in the Sept. 3 *Chicago Democrat* he gave notice that he would be leaving for Europe and requested settlement of accounts. [12, 733]

Davis, John L.   from Wales; voted on July 24 and Aug. 2, 1830 (see elections); managed the Steam Boat Hotel on North Water Street, as per ad in the *Chicago Democrat* of June 10, 1835; ✦ tailor, North Water Street near Kinzie; later moved to Milwaukee. [12]

Davis, Thomas O.   arrived from Pennsylvania in 1834; owner and editor of the *Chicago American*, the second newspaper, which began publication on June 8, 1835, located on South Water Street, near the drawbridge. A six-month subscription cost $2.50 if paid in advance, else $3. Davis additionally printed broadsides for Augustus Garrett's "Great Sale of Chicago Lots" in the Kinzie and Wolcott Additions held on June 15, and later the minutes of the Northern Baptist Association's convention at Du Page on Sept. 15, the first and third

of the four earliest remaining imprints printed at Chicago; was member of the fire engine company No.1 late in 1835 [see petition to the village board of Dec. 16, 1835, under entry for firefighting]. Late in 1837, printing was suspended because of the unavailability of paper; the newspaper continued publication under the auspices of [see] William Stuart & Co. [12, 351, 479, 480, 733]

Davy, Jacob   arrived in 1835.

Day, Lt. Hanibal   (c.1805-1891) from Vermont; Second Infantry, served as second lieutenant at Fort Dearborn from June 17, 1832, to May 15, 1833, under Capt. William Whistler. [12, 58]

Day-Kau-Ray   Decorah chief, quoted in Mrs. Kinzie's *Wau-Bun*; his words, reprinted as follows, make clear the resistance of Indians to becoming part of the white culture and society and to sending their children to such schools. During his term as Indian Agent, John H. Kinzie, referred to by the Indians as "their Father," called upon a council of Indian chiefs to invite their people to participate in broad-based government-sponsored teaching programs, designed to instruct Indians how to master modern agricultural and technical methods. When their Father's address was ended, Day-Kau-Ray, the most venerable of the assembled chiefs, arose to reply and spoke as follows:

Father, — The Great Spirit made the white man and the Indian. He did not make them alike. He gave the white man a heart to love peace, and the arts of a quiet life. He taught him to live in towns, to build houses, to make books, to learn all things that would make him happy and prosperous in the way of life appointed to him. To the red man, the Great Spirit gave a different character. He gave him a love of the woods, of a free life, of hunting and fishing, of making war with his enemies and taking scalps. The white man does not live like the Indian—it is not his nature. Neither does the Indian love to live like the white man—the Great Spirit did not make him so. ✧ Father, — We do not wish to do anything contrary to the will of the Great Spirit. If he had made us with

white skins and characters like the white man, then we would send our children to his schools to be taught like the white children. ✧ Father, — We think that if the Great Spirit had wished us to be like the Whites, he would have made us so. As he has not seen fit to do so, we believe he would be displeased with us to try and make ourselves different from what he thought good. ✧ Father, — I have nothing more to say. This is what we think. If we change our minds, we will let you know.

Dean, John   from Connecticut; army contractor; built a house at the mouth of the Chicago River in 1815 [Randolph Street]; later became a judge and civic leader; ➡ Dean Street (1700 W). [733]

Dean, Day   farmer near Detroit and teamster who, for $300, conveyed the John Boyer family to Chicago in 1833, remaining only a few days. [728]

Dean House   John Dean's house, a five room structure at the mouth of the Chicago River that was sold to Jean Baptiste Beaubien in 1817; soon after, John Crafts, agent for the American Fur Co., established the business therein, with Beaubien as subagent. Crafts and Beaubien then built a warehouse just E of the house at the edge of the river. The strategic location for lake and river traffic was an important factor in Beaubien's and Crafts' success as traders. Crafts died on May 15, 1825, and in c.1833 Henry S. Handy purchased the old Dean house. [12]

Dearborn, Gen. Henry   (1751-1829) born in New Hampshire; a Massachusetts congressman and secretary of war under President Thomas Jefferson, 1801-1809. On March 9, 1803, he wrote a letter that involved Colonel Hamtramck, commandant at Detroit, ordering the construction of a fort at the mouth of the Chicago River (see following excerpt); the fort was begun that summer and named after him; ➡ Dearborn Parkway and Dearborn Street (both 36 W). [79]

Colonel Hamtramck should be directed to send a suitable officer with six men and one or two guides to the mouth of the St. Josephs at the south end of Lake

SAMUEL GRANDIN J. DECAMP, M.D. [137]

Michigan and from thence to Chikago on the opposite side with a view to the establishment of a Post – and send by water two field pieces, a suitable quantity of ammunition and other stores for a Post at Chicago.

Dearborn Street bridge   the first of several drawbridges; see bridges and ferries.

Dearborn wagon   a light four-wheeled wagon for passengers, with top and side curtains, used in country districts, named after its inventor.

Debait, Samuel   also Debaif; arrived from Pennsylvania in 1831; member of the company under Capt. G. Kercheval during the Black Hawk War (muster role of May 2, 1832). [714, 733]

Debating Society   an organization with this name was formed during the winter of 1831-32; its membership included many of the males of the settlement and the fort, who elected Jean Baptiste Beaubien as president; in 1834, a like Polemic So-

ciety of Chicago was formed.

Debigie, Simon   spelling of name questionable, but as taken from the voting record; voted on July 24, 1830, in the Peoria County election held in Chicago.

DeCamp, Samuel Grandin Johnston, M.D. (1788-1871) born in New Jersey; graduated in 1808 from the College of Physicians and Surgeons of New York City, a classmate of Drs. Cooper and Van Voorhis; married Nancy Wood of New Jersey in 1809; became the tenth Fort Dearborn physician upon arrival as Assistant Surgeon on June 17, 1832, succeeding Dr. Harmon, and remained until Nov. 23 that year. On the night of July 10, cholera-infected troops arrived by ship under General Scott; within one week, 200 cholera cases were admitted, and the fort became a hospital under the doctor's charge; 58 soldiers died despite blood-letting [then acceptable] and calumel treatment; in April 1833, was succeeded by Dr. Phillip Maxwell. Dr. DeCamp, who had first enlisted for the War of 1812 and reenlisted in 1823, remained with the army until 1862. [12]

Deep River   the major tributary of the Calumet River system, located in Lake and Porter Counties, IN; became home for the "trader Indians" who in 1780 relocated there, chased from their original locale along the St. Joseph River by British troops.

deer   *Odocoileus virginianus*, white-tailed deer; the only native species of deer in Illinois; called ruebuck, dwarf deer, and *chevreuil* by explorers and settlers; in the early 1800s they were abundant, providing meat and hide; in August 1820 when the Lewis Cass expedition approached Fort Dearborn by canoe, Captain Douglas, the party's biologist, saw three deer sporting on the lake bank. Until 1848, venison taken locally was selling on the markets for 3 cents a pound or less, but by the late 1870s the species was nearly exterminated. [Intensive restocking of the deer throughout the state in the 1930s has resulted in numbers so plentiful that they have become a nuisance in many communi-

ties, although large numbers are taken in an annual controlled hunt; *eds.*] [241]

De Gannes   see Liette, Pierre, sieur de.

De la Vigne, Marie   (1783-1866) born in Michigan, daughter of a French-Canadian father and French Ottawa mother; mother of two children; divorced; traveled to Mackinac, where she became Joseph Bailly's wife in 1810; for more details see Bailly, Joseph.

Delaware   Lake Michigan steamship that was wrecked during a trip between Niles [MI] and Chicago in 1836, with no loss of life.

De Liette   see Liette, Pierre, sieur de.

Delisle, Guillaume   (1675-1726) also De Lisle, De L'Isle; maker of maps of the finest quality during the early 18th century, receiving the title of *premier géographe du roi* in 1718. Under his father Claude Delisle's tutelage, he began publishing maps of North America in 1700. On his 1718 ✳ map, *Carte de la Louisiane et du Cours du Mississipi*, he shows the location of Chicagou correctly and denotes the Chicago River quite accurately; the name Chicagou R. is applied to the Des Plaines River. [605, 681, 682, 718]

Dement, William   as per announcement in the *Chicago American*, married Lucinda Faucett on Dec. 12, 1835, Isaac Harmon officiating as justice of the peace.

de Montigny, Rev. François Jolliet   (-1725) came to Canada from Paris and was ordained as a priest within the *Séminaire des Missions Étrangères* at Quebec in 1693; in 1698, with Father Antoine Damien, established missions among the Natchez Indians; in the fall of 1699 he was appointed the leader of the group of seminary priests—Abbé St. Cosme among them and with Tonti as guide—who traveled to the Illinois River valley and arrived at the established *Mission de l'Ange Gardien* on Oct. 21, 1699, where Fathers Pinet and Bineteau were in charge; on Oct. 24 the party proceded S through the portage to the Tamarois Indians in the Mississippi Valley.

Denison, Micajah   U.S. Army private at Fort Dearborn; enlisted April 1806; badly wounded at the massacre on Aug. 15, 1812, taken captive, then tortured to death by the Indians that night. [226]

Denny, Capt. St. Clair   native of Pennsylvania; with the Fifth Infantry, stationed at Fort Dearborn under Major Plympton from August 1836 to December 1836; died in 1858.

dentists   see Kennicott, William H.; Bradley, J.C.; Temple, Peter.

Denonville, Jacques René de Brisay, marquis de   succeeded La Barre in October 1685 as governor of Nouvelle France during the time Illinois was part of Canada.

Densmore, Eleazer W.   born c.1820; arrived from Paris, NY in 1835; ◆ clerk, R.P. & J.H. Woodworth; in 1885, living at 2328 Indiana Ave. [12]

Depain, –   see Des Pins, François

De Peyster, Maj. Arent Schuyler   (1736-1822) New York-born British commandant at the old Fort Michilimackinac (on the Michigan shore) from 1774 to 1779, succeeded by Capt. Patrick Sinclair. De Peyster's men under Lt. William Bennet arrested Jean Baptiste Point de Sable around Aug. 1, 1779, at his trading post on *Rivière du Chemin* (Michigan City, IN), taking him to Michilimackinac. In his mostly fictitious book *Miscellanies* [1813], the aging De Peyster reports some of his experiences, much distorted by the passage of time, in the Northwest. He erroneously refers to Point de Sable as "well educated, and settled at Eschecagou, but much in the French interest." De Peyster introduced Point de Sable to Sinclair, who in turn employed him as manager of his large estate, the Pinery near Detroit. Some of De Peyster's recollections, contradicted by contemporary documents, have led most historians to the unwarranted conclusion that there was a fort which was imaginatively transformed into a trading post (run by Point de Sable) in Chicago in 1779. As De Peyster knew in 1779, this post was actually at the mouth of the *Rivière du Chemin* (present Michigan City, IN) in 1778-

79. The name De Peyster gives to Chicago in his later writings (Eschecagou or Eschickagou) is unprecedented and remains unexplained except as a result of failing memory; in earlier documents he used the French spelling *Chicagou*. From 1779-1784, De Peyster was in command at Detroit, succeeding Lt. Gov. Henry Hamilton. For additional information on De Peyster see John Swenson's essay about Point de Sable on page 388. [201, 564, 649]

De Pin   see Des Pins, François.

Deplat, Bazille   see Displantes, Basile.

de Sable, Jean Baptiste Point   see Point de Sable, Jean Baptiste.

Deschamps, Antoine   also des Champs; educated at Quebec to become a priest but at 19, engaged himself to a St. Louis fur trader; frequent user of the Chicago portage from 1778 on; aged veteran of the Illinois and Ohio River trade, living at Peoria until at least 1811; from 1817-1824 held the Illinois River trade concession of the American Fur Co., working out of St. Louis; a ranking superior to and early business partner of young Gurdon Hubbard when, en route to the portage in 1818, he pointed out the site of Guillory's former cabin near the west bank of the north branch, at the foot of [Fulton St.]; in 1821 traded at Masquigon [Muskegon, MI]; was a justice of the peace. He died at Michillimackinac, according to his death notice found in G.S. Hubbard's papers. His wife, a Cree, was sketched with a Snake woman and later painted by Karl Bodmer, the Swiss who journeyed up the Missouri River in 1833-34 with Prince Maximilian of Wied, Germany; they gathered and recorded invaluable information about the Northern Plains Indians. ✿ For the portrait of Mrs. Deschamps, see page 367. [12, 62, 354, 649]

Des Pins, François   also Du Pin, Du Pain, De Pin, Depins, Depain, DuBou; actually Lemoine *dit* Despins according to a note to Kinzie's account book; from Montreal, French settler and Illinois River valley trader [acquired supplies from

Mackinac; listed only in John Kinzie's account book on May 12, 1804, and Oct. 8, 1805, though on June 14, 1806, Antoine Ouilmette hired a wagon and a pair of oxen from Kinzie for $50 to transport Lemoine's goods over the portage to the fork of the Illinois River] who had a cabin on the south branch half a mile upstream from Leigh's farm in 1812 but lived in Kinzie's house during the autumn and winter following the Fort Dearborn massacre in a trading partnership with Louis Buisson. They were "British traders" according to Thomas Forsyth; together they ransomed several Indian captives, survivors of the massacre, probably commissioned by Robert Dickson, the British agent who visited Chicago in March 1813; married one of them, the widow of James Leigh, who had died defending the wagons. Although a layman, Des Pins had some knowledge of medicine and practiced on Mrs. Leigh's ailing infant successfully during the post-massacre period when no physicians were available. In a Jan. 27, 1814, letter written to John Lawe at La Baye [Green Bay], Colonel Dickson mentions an old Indian who demanded payment for the 20 bags of corn he had given Du Pin at Chicago. [109, 226, 404, 649]

Des Plaines River   French, *river of the plains*; also Chicagoua [native, used by the Indians, French, and early Americans, meaning *garlic river* and applied to the portion downstream from the Chicago area]; Desplaines [Hurlbut]; des Pleines [Mitchell]; O'Plaine [Chapman]; Plein [Schoolcraft]; Au Plaine [Hoffman]; Aux Plaines [Kinzie, J.]; Kikabou [Armstrong]; Kickapoo [Carey]; *Chicagou* [De Lisle]; Illinois [Thomas Jefferson]; Divine [Jolliet]; Saint Louis [Dablon]; and Laplaine; the river owed its importance and early denotation on maps and in reports to its access to either the Calumet or the Chicago portages, connecting the Mississippi River with the Great Lakes via the Illinois River (low water levels made navigation on the Des Plaines River difficult, even impossible for usage of the Chicago portage most of the year). For an extensive discussion of the river's name and history, see Bibliography: Smith, Herman Dunlop, *The Des Plaines River, 1673 to 1940*; ➡ DesPlaines Street (630 W), Des Plaines River Road (9400 W). [329, 626]

Des Plaines valley   notch in the Valparaiso moraine through which Lake Chicago once drained S, and so named the Chicago outlet.

Desplat, Bazille   see Displantes, Basile.

Detroit   began as Fort Pontchartrain du Détroit, a post established on July 24, 1701, by the French military officer Antoine de la Mothe Cadillac [true name: Laumet], with the permission of Governor Frontenac of New France; became British at the end of the French and Indian War. On July 11, 1796, the British surrendered Detroit to the Americans. Before the construction of Fort Dearborn in 1804, Detroit and Michilimackinac were the extreme western outposts of the U. S. government; in 1824, Detroit received a city charter; many immigrants traveling to early Chicago arrived via the Detroit Road around the lower end of Lake Michigan, a trip that took five days by stagecoach in 1835. [572]

Detroit   a 50-ton sloop purchased by the U.S. government in 1796 and used for troop movements throughout the Great Lakes; there is no record that it ever visited Chicago.

Detroit   schooner from Oswego, NY; called at Chicago on Aug. 24, 1834, and again on Aug. 18, 1835; was wrecked on Lake Ontario in 1842. [48]

Detroit   the U.S. brig [see] *Adams* was captured and renamed *Detroit* by the British during the War of 1812.

Deweese, David and Thomas   from Washington County, IN; staked claims with their brother [see] George Hammer in Hanover Township and returned with their families in 1835 to build log houses and farm. [13]

Dewey, Dennis S.   beginning in July 1835, placed ads in the *Chicago Democrat* for "4 first rate Journeymen Cabinet Makers to whom steady employ-ment will be given and good prices—Cash up and no Grumbling"; ✦ chair and furniture maker, 139 Lake St.

Dicken, Lewis   a child by this name was enrolled as grade school student in the class taught by [see] John Watkins in December 1835. Names of corresponding parents were not recorded. [728]

Dickson, Robert   principal British trader and shrewd agent to the Indians of the western nations, based at Green Bay; married to a Sioux woman; between 1811 and 1814, was active throughout the northwest in uniting and inciting the various tribes west of Lake Michigan against the Americans; leading Indians and Canadians, overtook Mackinac in July 1812; following the Fort Dearborn massacre, visited Chicago on March 22, 1813, possibly in an attempt to locate members of the garrison and their relatives still lingering in Indian captivity, but also to deliver pro-British chiefs' belts of wampum accompanied by British letters to the tribes inviting warriors to Detroit; the captives whom he was able to find were gathered at Chicago and taken to Mackinac, then turned over to the local British commandant, as if they were prisoners of war. [109; *Journal of the Illinois State Historical Society* 7, no. 1 (April 1917): 351-52]

Dickinson & Sheppard   on Dec. 23, 1835, submitted a proposal to the town board to build a fire engine house for $375; [see] Robert Sheppard's partner was likely his brother-in-law, who may have been Augustus, a porter at City Hotel in 1839. [28]

Dilg, Charles Augustus [Karl]   (1844-1904) valuable historian and amateur archeologist, active in Chicago between 1890 and 1910, a contemporary of Alfred Scharf; came to Chicago from Milwaukee in 1869; wrote a history column and articles for local newspapers, as well as the manuscript, *Chicago's Archaic History*, now within the Chicago Historical Society, containing sketches of historical scenes, Indian mounds, maps of the location of former Indian campsites, pioneer roads and portage routes. [206]

Dill, John S.   legal notices involving him appeared in the *Chicago Democrat* on Sept. 3, 1834, bringing suit against John C. Wickham in circuit court on Aug. 11, 1834, for repayment of $186.50.

Dimmick, Edward   on the 1833 list of early settlers; an unclaimed letter was listed by the post office on Jan. 1, 1834; married to Mary Ann Stow; ✦ painter, (Wayman & Dimmick).

dirk   a pointed straight dagger, 4 or 5 inches long, with a small handle; usually worn within the vest.

Displantes, Basile   also Basil Displat, Desplat, Deplat; listed in John Kinzie's account book at St. Joseph on Oct. 13, 1803; voted on Aug. 7, 1826, in Chicago; signed the [see] Michigan County petition on Oct. 20, 1828; signed the 1833 petition of Catholics in Chicago to Bishop Rosati requesting a priest. [404]

Ditlsaver, —   see Saver, Dill.

dit **name**   [from French *dire*, to say] an assumed name, replacing or added to the family name. The historian Milo Quaife related: "It is a matter of common knowledge that in New France men frequently acquired, in addition to their ancestral name, a second one by which they were commonly known, and that succeeding generations might lose the original name altogether, and be known only by the acquired one."

divorces   ★★★ Chicago's 1st divorce was filed on May 18, 1827, in a Peoria court by Deborah (née Scott) Watkins of Chicago against Morrison Watkins for his being "an habitual and excessive drunkard who sought the companionship of women contrary to his marriage vows &c. &c." In 1830, Archibald and Emily (née Hall) Caldwell were divorced after Archibald abandoned her for an Indian woman named Josette. In the first case under local Chicago jurisdiction, Angelina (née Hebert) sued Daniel Vaughan for divorce in May 1834; trial was held in an unfinished loft of the Mansion House on the N side of Lake Street near Dearborn; records no longer exist that document whether or not Angelina was granted the divorce.

GEORGE WASHINGTON DOLE [12]

Dixon's ferry　located where the Chicago-Galena road crosses the Rock River; earlier called "Rock River Ferry" when unreliably run in the 1820s by the alcoholic *métis* Joseph Ogee; run from 1830 on by John Dixon, Indian trader, then the only permanent settler in an area held by Sauk and Fox; in 1828, Dixon had secured a contract to carry the mail from Peoria to Galena and depended on the ferry; the land route from Fort Winnebago to Fort Dearborn included Dixon's ferry, used by Mr. and Mrs. John H. Kinzie in the early spring of 1831.

Doan, George W.　co-owner with Captain Russell of the [see] Saloon Building, built in 1837.

Dodson, Christian Bowman　(1809-1891) born in Berwick, PA; came in August 1833 as a government harbor contractor and became a friend of Archibald Clybourn; on the list of subscribers to the *Chicago Democrat* in November 1833; in December 1834, they advertised a new store in Clybournsville one mile S of [Batavia], at the Clybourn & Dobson Mill, where Mill Creek enters the Fox River; in the spring of 1835, he took part in an outing on horseback in partnership with Rebecca Sherman [later, once widowed, Mrs. Rebecca Sherman Pruyne Church] as described by John D. Caton; in 1835 and again in 1837, he contracted with the government to transport Indians from the greater Chicago region to the West, working with Capt. J.B.F. Russell in the effort of [see] Indian removal; married Harriet Newell Warren [whose early recollection is preserved at the Chicago Historical Society] of New York State in 1837 at the Naper Settlement; ✦ contractor, West Lake Street near Canal; living at Geneva in 1885. [12, 121, 207, 351, 655]

Dodson, William S.　from Pennsylvania, arrived in 1833 [with brother Christian?]; ✦ contractor, West Lake Street near Canal. [351]

Dole, George Washington　(1800-1860) arrived from New York on May 4, 1831, and served in the militia during the Black Hawk War as first lieutenant under Capt. Gholson Kercheval; initially resided on the Fort Dearborn reservation in the sutler's house/store until June 1832 and was placed in charge of building maintenance for the garrison; c.1832 purchased from James Kinzie lot 8 in block 2 [see map on page 44]; built a log house on the SE corner of South Water and Clark streets; became a clerk for Oliver Newberry and later a co-owner of the principal store in town [the settlement's third frame house, after A. Robinson's and R.A. Kinzie's] in partnership with Newberry, located at the SE corner of South Water and Dearborn streets, opposite from Beaubien's store; behind Dole's warehouse, and on his account, 550 cattle and hogs were butchered by John and Mark Noble, Jr., packed and sold in the fall of 1832, initiating Chicago's meat packing tradition; in August 1833 was one of the qualified electors who voted to incorporate the town [for copy of that meeting's original report, see incorporation]; member of the first board of trustees and was named town treasurer by the board on Sept. 4, 1833; married Louisa Towner on Jan. 28, 1837; ✦ city treasurer, Michigan [Hubbard] Street; became postmaster in 1851. Dole was an uncle of Julian S. Rumsey, who became mayor in 1861.

Dolesey, John and Peter　German immigrant brothers who voted in the first mayoral election in ward 1; ✦ Peter Dolesey, saloon, Lake Street.

Dolton, Charles H.　born in Columbus, OH, in 1825; arrived with his parents in October 1835; married S. Ellen Stronach of Maryland in 1836; removed to [Dolton] in 1838 and became a farmer and dealer in coal. [13]

Dolton, George　from Columbus, OH; came on Oct. 6, 1835, with his wife, Catharine, and children [see Charles H. Dolton] in a wagon drawn by two yoke of oxen; according to [see] J.D. Bonnell; formerly a tailor, opened a liquor store on the S side of Lake Street near Dearborn and played the violin to attract customers; removed to Sand Ridge along the Little Calumet River [Dolton] in March 1838; first ran a ferry service and later built the first bridge (and an adjoining tavern/hotel) across the river; ✦ tailor, North Water Street. [13]

donné　a male unpaid volunteer lay assistant to missionaries; Pierre Porteret and Jacques Largillier were *donnés* with Father Marquette on his 1674-75 expedition to the Illinois.

Doolittle, Elizah　storekeeper who advertised "Behold! Behold! Wanted—Five hundred cash customers" in the *Chicago Democrat* on Dec. 2, 1835, selling assorted dry goods, harnesses, carriages, and renting rooms; located in the former building occupied by M.B. Beaubien, "pleasantly situated for offices and easily accessible" on the SW corner of South Water Street and Dearborn, opposite the drawbridge; that month filed a claim for wharfing privileges for lot 1, block 17; ✦ commission merchant, corner of Dearborn and South Water; died in Joliet.

Door Prairie　located S and W of La Porte [French, meaning *the door*], IN, this arm of the Grand Prairie was the first large prairie seen by travelers coming to Chicago in the early 1800s on the Detroit-Chicago road. In explanation of the name, see the following report by Dr. Boyer (early June 1833); also see eastern woodlands; see Grand Prairie. [728] *Two tracts of heavy timber approached each other from both sides of the road to within fifty or a hundred yards of the road, through which opening a tongue of green prairie extended, uniting the expanding prairie on both sides of the timber, the road passing over this tongue of land through the points of timber on each side of it, leaving the impression on the mind of the traveller that he was passing though a door. The resemblance to a door giving rise to its name, 'Door Prairie.'*

Dorsey, L. [J.] with J. Force, assumed management of the Steam Boat Hotel [later called the American Hotel] on North Water Street on Nov. 9, 1835, following John Davis.

Doty, H. on April 29, 1834, the clothing and dry goods store of Peter Cohen on South Water Street, two doors E of Dearborn Street, was taken over by H. Doty & Co.; within a month, in the May 28 *Chicago Democrat*, he also began advertising 50 plows.

Doty, James D. 20-year-old official journalist who accompanied the 1820 Cass expedition, but was not among the detail that reached Chicago; later became governor of Wisconsin.

Douay, Père Anastase Latin, Anastasius; Récollet missionary priest and member of the ill-fated 1684 La Salle expedition to the mouth of the Mississippi River which, due to La Salle's error, ended in Spanish Texas. After La Salle's death, Father Anastasius was among the six members who, under Joutel's leadership, reached Chicago on Sept. 25, 1687, en route to Canada. [519, 611]

Dougherty, Daniel see Daugherty, Daniel.

Douglas, Capt. David Bates from New Jersey; 1813 Yale graduate and U.S. Army Corps of Engineers officer who, in August 1820, came through Chicago as the topographer and biologist of an exploring party under General Cass [see Chronol-

ogy, August 1820, for excerpts of Schoolcraft's report on the expedition's experience at Chicago]; while in Chicago, he interviewed John Kinzie and recorded near-verbatim Kinzie's eyewitness report of the 1812 Fort Dearborn massacre; died in 1848, according to some reports. The Calumet Club records a "Captain B. Douglas" who died in December 1882. [714]

Douglas Grove early neighborhood that grew round Stephen A. Douglas' property near 35th Street and Lake Shore Drive. Geographically, the grove represented the watershed between the Chicago River and the Calumet River basins. Here was the only place in Chicago where the great Midwest prairie met the lake and was visible from the shore. Gurdon Hubbard later referred to Douglas Grove when vividly describing the scenery seen as he first stepped ashore in 1818 [see entry for prairie]. A Stephen A. Douglas ▲ monument is still located there, now only known as part of Hyde Park. [354]

Douglas, Stephen Arnold (1813-1861) elected to the Illinois House of Representatives in August 1836; member of the Committee of Internal Improvements with Capt. Joseph Napier; wrote the bill that passed Feb. 27, 1837, expediting the completion of the Illinois & Michigan Canal.

Downer, J. purchased in c.1832 a parcel of land from Mark Beaubien in block 31 (see map on page 44).

Downer, Pierce (1782-1863) from Jefferson County, NY; married Lucy Ann (née Ellis) in 1808; traveled to Chicago in 1832 to join his son [see Downer, Stephen E.], then established a claim for 160 acres on the N side of [Downers Grove]. [218a, 314a]

Downer, Stephen E. native of New York, born 1809; arrived 1832 or earlier; his father, Pierce, joined him in Chicago in 1832; listed as a subscriber to the *Chicago Democrat* in November 1833; worked as a mason to construct Chicago's first [see] lighthouse under a Samuel Johnson; staked a claim

on the E side of [Downers Grove] in 1833; married Amanda Tasker on July 9, 1835, at Naper's Settlement, as per announcement in the *Chicago Democrat*. [218a, 314a]

Doyle, Alexander living at Peoria; elected justice of the peace on Aug. 28, 1828, during the period when Chicago was part of Putnam County but administered by Peoria County (Jan. 13, 1825, to Jan. 15, 1831). Doyle, a stickler for law enforcement, had jurisdiction over Chicago and once cited James Kinzie for selling a pint of whiskey without a license; for the ensuing controversy, see the following excerpt from Doyle's letter within court records of July 14, 1829, to John Dixon; on Sept. 18, 1829, officiated at the marriage of Lt. David Hunter and Maria Indiana Kinzie.

I have enclosed to you the proceedings I had before me in the case of the People vs. James Kinzie for retailing liquor without a license. The wiseacres of this place have decided that I had no jurisdiction in the case. The fact has been proven to my satisfaction there is no doubt in my mind of the correctnes of the charges. You will see that I have given a judgement in the case. If I have jurisdiction, please return the papers; if I have not, dispose of them as you think proper.

Accompanying Doyle's letter was the affidavit of Francis Laducia, who stated that he called on Kinzie to pay a bill of seven shillings; he tendered a dollar in payment and received 12 1/2 cents in change; this he gave back to Kinzie for one pint of whiskey. The sale was contrary to the criminal code then in effect, providing a fine of $10 for selling less than one quart of liquor without a license.

Doyle, John a settler at [now] Winnetka or Kenilworth in 1820, in whose cabin Elizabeth Ouilmette and Michael Welch were married on March 11, 1830, J.B. Beaubien officiating as justice of the peace of Peoria County. [96a]

Doyle, Capt. William last British commandant at Mackinac, following Capt. Edward Charleton in 1792, and serving until August 1796, when the post was surrendered to the United States persuent to Jay's Treaty of 1794.

Draper, H.M. signed a school-related petition on Sept. 19, 1835 as part of the community effort to organize the town into school districts; was a member of the fire engine company No. 1 in 1835 [see petition to the village board of Dec. 16, 1835, entry on firefighting].

Draper, Lyman Copeland (1815-1891) secretary of the Wisconsin Historical Society from 1854-1886; outstanding specialist in frontier history, compiler of the enormous Draper manuscript collection, pertaining to Western history, which is in the State Historical Society of Wisconsin at Madison; ➡ Draper Street (2540 N). [214, 315]

Draper, Stephen U.S. Army private at Fort Dearborn; listed in John Kinzie's account book on May 27, 1804 as Fort Dearborn's butcher; a private, re-enlisted July 19, 1806; severely wounded in action at the massacre of Aug. 15, 1812, captured, then killed later that night. [226, 404]

Driggs, Alfred L. sawmill owner at White Pigeon, MI, who visited Chicago in 1833 with a load of 20,000 feet of whitewood lumber, having contracted with the captain [likely David Carver] of a vessel to deliver across the lake and return, for $200; stayed for two days, finding the market disappointing, but sold his wood to "a man by the name of Williams" [probably Eli B. Williams, who had arrived on April 14, 1833]; in later years, recorded his memories and published them. [216]

Drolett "Coursoll's man," likely a French *engagé* noted in John Kinzie's account book on Sept. 14, 1805; see Coursoll, Michel. [404]

drugstores see Philo Carpenter (1832), Peter Pruyne & Dr. E.S. Kimberly (1833), William G. Austin (1835), Samuel C. Clarke (1835), William H. Clarke & Abram F. Clarke (1835), Frederick Thomas (1835), F. Thomas & Thomas Jenkins (1836). The earliest drugstores in Chicago could not survive unless other merchandise was also sold, nor was it possible to prevent other stores from offering drugs as a sideline; "book and stationery

THOMAS DRUMMOND [410]

stores" did an especially large business in patent medicines. Not until 1838 did a drugstore open that sold drugs only; owned by Leroy M. Boyce, the store's policy was maintained until his death in 1849. [221]

drug trade western-style drug supplies first reached Chicago in 1803 with the arrival of the initial Fort Dearborn physician, Dr. William C. Smith. While meant for the garrison, drugs (as well as treatment) were made available in emergencies to the civilians of the small village by Dr. Smith and his military successors. Systematic trade in drugs began when [see] P.F.W. Peck opened his general store in 1831. His stock included aloes, alum [used as astringent or as emetic], borax, copperah [copra, dried coconut meat], Epsom salt, Glauber salt, and sulfur. All subsequent general stores also sold drugs in an ever increasing variety, such as castor oil, British oil, Bateman's drops, Turlington's balsam, Godfrey's cordial, quinine, calomel, opium, snake oil, and ginseng root. Bookstores often held the exclusive

franchise for patent medicines: [see] Stephen F. Gale's bookstore advertised Brandreth's Pills, and [see] Russell & Clift sold Morrison's Vegetable Pills. Other such popular drugs were Bristol's Sarsaparilla, Dr. Egan's Sarsaparilla, Sawyer's Extract of Bark, Morrison's Hygeian Pills, Lee's English Vegetable Pills, and Dewey's Cholera Elixir. The drugstore of [see] Dr. William G. Austin (1835) advertised "botanical healing art" and specialized in botanical preparation. [12, 221]

Drummond, Thomas born c.1809; arrived in May 1835 from Bristol, ME, but soon moved on to Galena; married Delia A. Sheldon in 1839; did not settle in Chicago until 1850; attorney who later became a U.S. judge; living at Winfield in 1885. [12, 351]

Dryer, G.R. born c.1811 in Clarendon, NY; arrived in November 1835; lived at Joliet in 1878. [12]

Dubou, — probably a misspelling for [see] Des Pins, Francois. [226]

Duck, Charles H., M.D. early Chicago physician; as per Andreas: "... registered in Fergus's Directory for 1829, and was for sometime a practitioner there." [13]

ducks wild ducks have long been a favored target for hunters in the Chicagoland area, beginning with the earliest visitors; in 1699, Father Binneteau referred to the Illinois country: "Game is plentiful such as ducks [and] Turkeys." Mallards (*Anas platyrhynchus*) are the most common ducks in Illinois; some remain year around, but most migrate, breeding in the southern Canadian provinces; as a hunted species, the handsome wood duck (*Aix sponsa*) is second only to the mallard (currently 12 percent of the hunters' take); in the fall most migrate S; canvasbacks (*Aythya valisineria*), a chunky diving duck, is highly prized for its excellent taste. For an 1830 account by Lt. J.G. Furman on the abundance of waterfowl in Chicago, see birds. [64]

dug-out canoe see pirogue.

Dulignon, Jean member of La Salle's 1682-83 expedition to the mouth of the Mississippi, passing through Chicagoland in January 1682 on the way south; later honored by the French king for his service. [46]

Duncan Addition   one of the early [see] additions to Chicago by which the original town, as laid out in the [see] Thompson plat of 1830, grew beyond its first borders. The 1836 Chicago ✳ map by E.B. Talcott [see map list on page 51] shows that the Duncan Addition represents the eastern half of the NE quarter of Section 17. The entire Section 17 was formerly designated [see] Canal Land. It is likely that the addition was named after Joseph Duncan, one of the original (1825) directors of the Illinois & Michigan Canal project, who later served as governor of Illinois from 1834-1838.

Duncan, Joseph   of Jacksonville, served on the original board of directors of the then planned Illinois & Michigan Canal, constituted in 1825; elected to the U.S. House of Representatives in 1826, 1828, 1831, and 1832; served as governor of Illinois from 1834-1838. [12]

Duncan, Thomas   tailor, most likely the partner of A. Jackson Cox in the clothing store of "Cox & Duncan" on the W side of Dearborn Street in 1835, near South Water Street; ◆ tailor, Clark Street.

Duncklee, Hezekiah and Ebenezer   traveled with Mason Smith across Michigan and northern Indiana and arrived in Chicago on Sept. 3, 1833, from Hillsborough, NH; later that autumn, made a claim and built a cabin on the E side of Salt Creek [Bloomingdale, formerly Duncklee's Grove]; Ebenezer's family followed in 1834. [314a]

Duncklee's Grove   also Dunckley's Grove, named after Hezekiah and Ebenezer Duncklee; a community of German immigrants had began to form on Salt Creek as early as 1825, 25 miles from Chicago; in 1836, this was the starting point for construction of the state road to Galena; eventually renamed Bloomingdale.

Dunmore   armed British schooner patrolling Lakes Michigan, Huron, and Erie during the period of

British control; built in Detroit in 1773. [48]

Dunn, Col. Charles   of Golconda, IL; in 1830, purchased from the government lot 3 in block 2, lot 1 in block 16, and lots 6 and 7 in lot 34 [see map on page 44]; was one of the three first commissioners for the Illinois & Michigan Canal development, and visited Chicago in that capacity in the summer of 1830. [12, 704]

Dunn, James Anson, M.D.   arrived from Buffalo, NY and opened an office "in Sherman's brick block, nearly opposite the Tremont House," near the corner of Lake and Dearborn streets, advertising in the Nov. 25, 1835, *Chicago Democrat*; was corresponding secretary of the Young Men's Temperance Society, organized on Dec. 19 that year. [12]

Du Page River   known to Indians as Tukoquenone; a forked tributary of the Des Plaines River, named after an early French trader, or two brothers, the exact identity of whom is not yet certain. There were many individuals in New France by the name Pagé (sometimes Paget), from which the spelling Du Page is thought to have been naively derived. In the most comprehensive study of the subject to date, John Swenson argues that the likely choice for the owner of an early trading post at the Du Page River is a member of a prominent French family of Kaskaskia in the middle of the 18th century, by name Pierre Pagé (1715-1752), and less likely his brother Joseph Prisque Pagé (1717-1764), who owned a mill at Kaskaskia; both were murdered by Indians. At the Du Page River forks, in Du Page Township [Will County]. Stephen J. Scott, who had lived the preceding four years at [see] *Grosse Pointe* [Evanston], resettled his family in 1829, joined the following autumn by the Pierce Hawley, Harry Boardman, Robert Strong, and Israel Blodgett families. The settlement became known as Dupage town, and a post office named Dupage was established in 1830, renamed Channahon in 1849. Following the organization of Cook County in March 1831, three voting precincts were established: one for Chicago, one for Hickory Creek,

and one for the Du Page settlement. Du Page County was created out of Cook County on Feb. 9, 1839. [374, 586, 648, 649, 660, 734]

Dupage town   see previous entry.

Du Pin, Francois   see Des Pins, François.

Durand, Pierre   a Detroit trader with several years' experience in Illinois, particularly 1775-79; contemporary and fellow trader of Point de Sable. Point de Sable was working for Durand at the *Rivère du Chemin* trading post [Michigan City] in 1778 and in 1779, when he was taken into British custody and conveyed to Michilimackinac. Durand's canoe and other valuable property in Point's custody were confiscated by British forces, and he did not get reimbursed until 1784. His surviving manuscript places Point de Sable at the *Rivère du Chemin* in 1778 and 1779; for text of his narrative, see essay on page 388. [649]

Durantaye, Olivier Morel de la   commander at Michilimackinac between 1683 and 1685; in 1684, came to Illinois with 60 men to assist Tonti, then commander at Fort St. Joseph (Starved Rock), against Iroquois attacks; built a fort at Chicago in 1684 and was there visited by Tonti in 1685; within less than a year returned to Michilimackinac, and subsequently the fort may have served as a depot, its exact location uncertain but probably on the south branch of the Chicago River; died in 1727. [12, 46, 611, 675]

Durham boat   invented by Robert Durham of Bucks County, PA, c.1750; used by early traders to traverse the Chicago Portage, as well as other portages and rapids in the Midwest; was 60 ft. long, 8 feet wide, and 4 feet deep, and capable of carrying 15 tons and a crew of 7. Alexis Clermont of Green Bay supplies a crew member's account of working conditions on a Durham boat:

In the fall of 1828, Joseph Paquette, who had a place below Dutchman's Creek, took a contract for furnishing hay to Fort Winnebago, at the Fox-Wisconsin portage. I went to the portage with Paquette and his other men, to make the hay, my wages being, if I re-

member aright, seventy-five cents a day, and board. We returned home in a boat, down the Fox River. ❖ *After this I became one of a crew of a Durham boat—my first employer being Daniel Whitney; the next, Findlay Fisher Hamilton. There were generally seven men of us,—six poles and a steersman; sometimes there was a cook, but the usual custom was to have a cook for a fleet of three boats. Traders were in the habit of running such a fleet; for when we came to rapids, the three crews together made up a crew big enough to take the boats and their lading through with ease. Each boat had a captain who was steersman. Durham boats were from sixty to seventy feet long, and carried from 12 to sixteen tons.* ❖ *The round trip, from Green Bay to Portage and return, would take from sixteen to twenty days; if Lake Winnebago was rough, it might last a month. During storms on the lake, we always tried to run to Garlic Island, where there was a good harbor, also good water; but frequently we were obliged to camp on the mainland. Wages were, sometimes, for the trip; usually, however, they were $1.25 a day and board—although, in the fall, because of the cold water through which we had to work at the rapids, we got from $1.50 to $1.75. The captain got from $2.00 to $2.25—after a few seasons I became a captain. Upon reaching a rapid, going down, four of the crew would jump out. two on a side, and bear up the boat, while two men remained at the bow to pole, and the steersman kept his place at the steering oar. When the weather was cold,—for we ran during the entire season of navigation,—one man would run ahead on the bank, and light a fire to warm us, for we were completely drenched, and in a shivering condition.* [147]

Durocher, Jean Baptiste   early member of the Catholic congregation, in April 1833 his name was on the petition by citizens to Bishop Rosati in St. Louis, asking that a priest be assigned to them; probably the John Derosche who married one of the Ouilmette girls [Sophia?] and after 1835 settled with her and the tribe on the banks of the Kansas River.

CHARLES VOLNEY DYER [58]

Dury, David   in a July 7, 1834, circuit court suit John K. Boyer sought payment for "12 pieces of cotton sheeting and about 30 lbs. of coffee" from him and four others; legal notices involving him appeared in the Sept. 3, 1834, *Chicago Democrat*.
Du Sable, Jean Baptiste   see Point de Sable, Jean Baptiste.
Dutchman's Grove   also Dutchman's Point, named after the "Dutchmen" [Germans] John Schladinger, John Planck, and the three Ebinger brothers who settled there in 1833 and 1834; 12 miles N of the main river on the Milwaukee Road [Niles Township] where Planck had his tavern in 1835. [13]
Du Val, Pierre   (1619-1683) student and son-in-law of Nicolas Sanson, working in Paris as cartographer from 1658; published general atlases and military maps; an atlas of his own maps was published (1688-89) by his daughter following his

death. [26]
Du Verger   see Forget Du Verger, Father.
Dye, John   arrived in 1835; was a member of the fire engine company No. 1 in 1835 [see petition to the village board of Dec. 16, 1835, with entry of firefighting]; ❖ clerk, Lake Street.
Dyer, Charles Volney, M.D.   (1808-1878) born in Clarendon, VT; graduate of the Middlebury (VT) Medical College in 1830; moved his medical practice from Newark, NJ, to Chicago, arriving on Aug. 23, 1835; became a member of the Chicago Lyceum; served as town clerk (1836) and judge of the probate court (1837); married Louisa M. Gifford of Elgin in 1837; three of their six children survived: Stelle Louise, Charles, and Louis; ❖ with Dr. Levi D. Boone, office, 49 State St.; served as city health officer and as surgeon of the company militia and the City Guards (1838-40), earning high praise for fearless service during the cholera epidemic of 1854; was active in the "underground railroad" to send fugitive slaves to Canada, and in 1863, was appointed by President Lincoln as judge on the Mixed Court for the Suppression of the African Slave Trade; died in Lake View. [12]
Dyer, Dyson   U.S. Army private at Fort Dearborn; enlisted October 1810; survived the massacre of Aug. 15, 1812, and was ransomed from the Indians after a captivity of nearly two years. [226]
Dyer, Rev. Palmer   Episcopalian minister who preached the first service to the budding congregation on Oct. 12, 1834, but did not remain; moved to Peoria and later to Fort Snelling as army chaplain. [12]

Eagle   *Haliaeetus leucocephalus*; the American bald eagle, fairly common today along the Mississippi and Illinois rivers, and common in the early days of Chicago; patrols the banks of large water courses in search of food, and likely scouted along the coast of Lake Michigan prior to an enlarged human settlement. [64]
Eagle Exchange Tavern   opened in 1829 on the

east bank of the south branch, in the middle of [Lake Street]; Mark Beaubien had bought the log cabin in 1826 or 1827 from James Kinzie, but in 1830 when the streets were laid out, he had to move the building slightly south onto the SE corner of Market Street [North Wacker] and Lake, onto lots 3 and 4 of block 31 which he then bought; in 1831, a two-story large frame house was added and the establishment became the Sauganash Tavern. Emily Beaubien recalled that her father Mark originally sold Indian goods in a little log store, bought the cabin, and later "... made that part of the Eagle Exchange and there he kept a billiard place and in those days everything had a bar." [12, 357]

Eagle Hotel   managed early in January 1834 by Ashbel Steele and was probably located on Lake Street; kept by P.I. Carli later that year; on Oct. 7, 1835, the town board of trustees met at "Trowbridge's Eagle Hotel" [Andreas], implying that S.G. Trowbridge was then the owner.

Eals   nickname for residents from New York, common in early Illinois. [55a]

earthworks   of the [see] Hopewell. [12, 357]

eastern woodlands   a vast, almost uninterrupted mixed broadleaf and conifer forest that extended from the Atlantic seaboard to the tip of Lake Michigan prior to the arrival of Europeans on this continent. A ✳ map prepared by the historian Alfred Mayer in the 1950s dramatically reveals that the Chicago/Calumet area was the structured interface between the Grand Prairie to the west and the eastern woodlands; near La Porte, IN the prairies were still partly delineated by forest and had names: Door, Twenty Mile, Morgan, and Robinson; but upon entering Illinois, within a span of 40 miles, the prairies were the dominant landscape feature and the groves (small forests surrounded by prairie) were named. Tree types in the woodlands included oak, elm, linden, beech, maple, birch, aspen, poplar, pine, and juniper. Swamp lands within the woods, as found along the Sag, near Stony Island, and around the mouth of the Grand Calu-

met at Miller, IN, included tamarack, alder, pine, black ash, aspen, maple, willow, and buttonwood. Also see prairie.

Eastman, Lt. Jonathan   from Vermont; first lieutenant and district paymaster; in June 1812 came to Fort Dearborn with the last payment for the company's service, nine months' pay through June, prior to the massacre.

Eastman, Seth   see Schoolcraft, Henry R.

Eberhardt, A.   German immigrant, first attested to as having lived in Chicago in 1833. [342]

Ebert, Lizard   with his wife Evangeline (née Reed), witnessed the baptism of their son Henri by Father Badin in Chicago on Oct. 18, 1830.

Ebinger, Christian   (1812-1879) born in Würtemberg, Germany; gardener, immigrated in 1831 with his brothers John (married Elizabeth Planck) and Frederick, sister Elizabeth, and brother-in-law [see] John Planck; spent one year in Detroit where he married Barbara Rehly, then came with his bride to Chicago in 1832; had seven children: Christian, Henry, Margaret, Sarah, Eliza, Caroline, and William; in 1834, moved to Dutchman's Point to farm; became a preacher with the German Evangelical Association. [13, 278, 342]

Ebinger, Heinrich   German immigrant, first attested to as having lived in Chicago in 1834. [342]

Edson, Nathan   U.S. Army private at Fort Dearborn; enlisted in April 1810; waiter to Factor Matthew Irwin until late June 1812; survived the massacre of Aug. 15, 1812, and was ransomed from the Indians after nearly two years of captivity. [226]

Edward Sacket   schooner; called at Chicago from New York State ports with passengers, merchandise and lumber three times during 1834, twice under Captain Forsyth, and on Oct. 12 under Captain Dibble.

Edwards & Bosworth   see Edwards, Alfred; also see Bosworth, Increase.

Edwards, Abraham H., M.D.   (1781-1860) native of Springfield, NY; became a physician in 1803 and practiced in Indiana and Ohio; joined the army

medical corps at Detroit in 1812; was in Chicago as lieutenant colonel of the Michigan territorial militia under Maj. Gen. John R. Williams during the Black Hawk War from June 11 to June 22, 1832.

Edwards, Abram   merchant at Detroit in 1818 with branches at Mackinac, Green Bay, Fort Gratiot, and Chicago; in May 1818, visited his Chicago branch and Fort Dearborn, then under the command of Major Baker [Edwards' 1855 letter, *Wisconsin Historical Society Collections* 5]. The nature and location of Edwards' branch agency remain obscure as his report contains no description of the settlement; some historians believe that John Crafts worked for Edwards at his Hardscrabble outlet, rather than for Conant & Mack. The five day trip led from Green Bay by way of Sturgeon Bay, portaging to the shore of Lake Michigan, then south along the shore in a birch bark canoe; at night the party camped onshore, never saw any white men, but many Indians, many of which were out in canoes spearfishing for whitefish.

Edwards, Lt. Alexander H.   in Chicago during the Black Hawk War with a company of cavalry from Michigan; brother of Col. Thomas A.H. Edwards; earlier in 1816, had been a schoolmate of the Kinzie children at Detroit. [714]

Edwards, Alfred   with Increase Bosworth as Edwards & Bosworth, first advertised through agent [see] J.H. Phelps in the Oct. 28, 1835, *Chicago Democrat*; ✦ grocery and provision store, North Water Street; in 1839, Bosworth is still listed as proprietor of their store on South Water Street

Edwards County, Illinois Territory   Chicago was part of Edwards County from 1814 to 1816, then became part of Crawford County, Illinois Territory. For details, see Chicago jurisdictional chronology on page 209.

Edwards, Ninian   (1775-1833) lawyer; first governor of the Illinois Territory, commissioned by President Madison; took office on April 24, 1809; was reappointed every two years and served throughout the entire period of its existence until

WILLIAM BRADSHAW EGAN, M.D. [12]

Dec. 6, 1818; was president of the convention which drafted the state's first constitution and served as governor of Illinois from Dec. 6, 1826, to Dec. 9, 1830. The following item appeared in the *Illinois Herald* on Oct. 1, 1815. [12, 230, 231]
Notice.—I Have for sale 22 slaves. Among them are several of both sexes, between the years of 10 and 17 years. If not shortly sold, I shall wish to hire them in Missouri Territory. I have also for sale a full-blooded stud-horse, a very large English bull, and several young ones. Ninian Edwards.

Edwards, Col. Thomas Aaron Hunt in Chicago during the Black Hawk War and in command of a Cass County regiment of militia from Michigan; was temporarily in command of Fort Dearborn prior to the cholera outbreak and until Maj. William Whistler arrived; brother of Lt. Alexander H. Edwards.

Eels, Thomas S. advertising "Fashionable Tailoring" in the *Chicago Democrat* on July 22, 1834; by Oct. 22, he was in partnership with another tailor

named Andrew and located one door N of the Tremont House, advertising that they "flattered themselves to be inferior to none"; signed list for firefighting materials at a meeting at Trowbridge's Eagle Hotel on Oct. 7, 1835, and was named to the Hook and Ladder Co. on Nov. 11; living in Jacksonville, FL, in 1885. [12]

Egan, William Bradshaw, M.D. (1808-1860) also Eagan; born in Killarney, County Kerry, Ireland; graduated from Dublin Medical School; licensed to practice in New Jersey in 1830 and opened an office in Newark; married Emeline Mabbatt of New York City on Jan. 21, 1832, and in the fall of 1833, moved with his wife to Chicago. Following the completion of St. Mary's Church in October, its successful balloon frame structure prompted Dr. Egan to organize the construction of like adjoining buildings for habitation, nicknamed "Egan's Row." In the July 2, 1834, *Chicago Democrat* he offered "services in Medicine and Surgery in residence near the Maison-house"; also that year, helped organize St. James Episcopal Church, was a member of the Chicago Lyceum, became a member of the town's health committee, representing the S division and also announced in the Sept. 10 *Chicago Democrat* that he was a candidate for mayor; was a successful real estate investor during the land boom and a talented platform speaker, effectively presiding at public meetings; at the celebrated inauguration of construction of the Illinois & Michigan Canal in 1837, was selected by common consent to give the public oration, which was a resounding success; also assisted Dr. Brainard in establishing Rush Medical School in 1837; ✦ real estate dealer, boarded at City Hotel; later served as city recorder and as a state senator; was active in organizing the local Republican party; in 1853, he purchased the land holdings of Stephen Forbes on the Des Plaines River. Egan died in Chicago; in 1885, his widow lived at 624 Dearborn Ave. [12, 40, 218, 351]

Eldredge, John Woodworth, M.D. (1808-1884)

also Eldridge; native of New York State, graduated in 1834 at Fairfield Medical College, NY; arrived in 1834; became the chairman when the city's board of health was organized in 1837; ✦ Clark Street corner of South Water, Loomis' Building; in 1840 married Sophia E. Houghton of Vermont, and they had one daughter; practiced for 34 years, remaining in Chicago until he died on Jan. 1, 1884; ➥ formerly Eldredge Court, now 9th Street. [12, 351]

elections local election for county and town offices prior to Chicago's incorporation as a city were held on the following dates:
1823 Sept. 1 (Fulton County election for sheriff; Abner Eads won);
1826 Aug. 7 (Peoria County election; Ninian Edwards for governor, Daniel Cook for congressman; 35 votes were cast);
1827 (Peoria County election; no further record found);
1828 May 11 (Peoria County election for constable at Agency house; nine votes cast; David Hunter and Henley Clybourne elected);
1828 Aug. 4 (Peoria County election for member of Congress at Agency House, member of general assembly and county officers; 33 votes cast);
1828 Aug. 20 (Peoria County election at Agency House; 33 votes cast; Alexander Doyle defeated Archibald Clybourn for justice of the peace; David Hunter and Henley Clybourn reelected as constables);
1828 Nov. 3 (presidential election at J.B. Beaubien's house; 40 votes cast; Andrew Jackson won);
1830 July 24 (Peoria County, Chicago precinct election for justice of the peace and for constable, at James Kinzie's house; 56 votes cast; John S.C. Hogan defeated Archibald Clybourn for justice of the peace, Horacio Smith defeated Russell Rose for constable);
1830 Aug. 2 (for governor, held at James Kinzie's house; 32 votes cast; elected: John Reynolds; for complete poll list, see below);
1830 Nov. 25 (Peoria County election for justice of

the peace; 26 votes cast; Stephen Forbes defeated William See);

1831 March 8 (Cook County election for county commissioners; elected: Samuel Miller, Gholson Kercheval, and James Walker);

1832 August (Cook County election; 114 votes cast; Joseph Duncan of Jacksonville elected to Congress, James M. Strode of Galena for state senator, Benjamin Mill of Galena for state representative, Stephen Forbes for sheriff, Elijah Wentworth, Jr., for coroner)

1833 Aug. 10 (for village trustees; elected were: George W. Dole, Madore Beaubien, John Miller, E.S. Kimberly, and T.J.V. Owen—president);

1833 Dec. 9 (for constable); [Silas W. Sherman ran but apparently lost; made Cook County sheriff in 1834];

1834 June 7 (for colonel of the Illinois militia; elected: John B. Beaubien);

1834 June 12 (for justice of the peace; elected: John Dean Caton);

1834 Aug. 4 (Cook County election; 528 votes cast; Gen. Joseph Duncan elected for governor, William M. May for congressman, James W. Stephenson of Jo Davies County for state senator, John Hamlin for state representative, and Silas W. Sherman for sheriff);

1834 Aug. 11 (for trustees; elected were: J. H. Kinzie—president; G.S. Hubbard, E. Goodrich, J.K. Boyer, J.S.C. Hogan);

1835 July (for trustees: elected were: H. Hugunin—president, W. Kimball, B. King, S. Jackson, E.B. Williams, F.C. Sherman, A. Loyd, and George W. Dole);

1835 Aug. 5 (elected for county recorder: R.J. Hamilton; elected for county surveyor: Addison Collins; elected for justice of the peace: Sidney Abell, Edward W. Casey, Isaac Harmon, and Edward H. Hunter; elected for constable: Oremus Morrison, Luther Nichols, and John Shrigley);

1836 June 6 (for trustees; elected were: E.B. Williams—president, S.G. Trowbridge, Peter Bolles,

L.P. Updike, A.D. Taylor, William B. Ogden, A. Pierce, T.G. Wright, and J. Jackson). [12, 220] For details, where held, and outcome of elections, see Chronology.

Eliza   23-ton schooner from Cleveland, OH; called at Chicago with passengers, lumber, and merchandise four times during 1834, twice under Captain Dibble, then under Captain Burton. [48]

Elizabeth Ward   65-ton schooner from Oswego, NY, Lake St. Clair, and Detroit; called at Chicago with lumber and merchandise once in 1834 under Captain Ward, twice in 1835 under Captain Austin and twice under Captain Fearson; capsized on Lake Erie in 1845. [48]

elk   *Cervus elaphus, Cervus canadensis*; known to early settlers as serf or stag. In 1673, Father Marquette's party observed that elks were common along the Illinois River; in 1712, Father Marest reports that "the plains and prairies [on either side of the Illinois River] are all covered with buffaloes, roebucks, hinds [mature female deer or elk], stags ...." In the 1820s, elks had become uncommon in northern Illinois and by 1850 they had disappeared. [341]

El-Lewellyn   see *Llewellyn*.

Elkswatawa   Shawnee name of the Prophet; see Prophet, the.

Elliot, William   listed in 1830 as the owner of lot 5 in block 2, previously owned by James Kinzie [see map on page 44].

Ellis Inn   see Ellis, Samuel.

Ellis, Joel   arrived in 1832; ♦ butcher, Funk's Fulton market, 95 Lake St.; in 1885, lived at 62 West Jackson St. [12, 351]

Ellis, Samuel   arrived in 1832 from Massachusetts; known to have used his ox wagon to transport Philo Carpenter and George P. Snow on July 16, 1832, for the last stretch of their journey to the settlement; was a member of the Chicago company during the Black Hawk War; on the list of subscribers to the *Chicago Democrat* in November 1833; in 1835, owned more than 136 acres of beachfront

property on the S side adjacent to the lakeshore between 31st and 39th streets [in Sections 34 and 35, Township 39]; on 35th Street near Vincennes Avenue, ran a tavern called Ellis Inn; ♦ milkman, south of 22nd Street, red barn on prairie; ➡ Ellis Avenue and Ellis Park (600 E). [12, 456]

Ells, Thomas S.   signed up with the "Pioneer" hook and ladder company in October 1835, a voluntary fire brigade.

Ellsworth, Lewis   a settler from New Hampshire whose house and grove were near the Napier trading post that was fortified as Fort Payne during the Black Hawk War.

Elston, Daniel   from England; lived NW of the Forks on a diagonal wagon trail to Niles, which earlier had been an Indian trail from the Forks to Wisconsin; in 1830, he purchased a 160-acre section of land along the trail [see Woodstock Trail] that eventually became Elston Avenue [NE quarter of Section 6, Township 39 (Andreas, *History of Chicago*, pp. 112-113); advertising can be found in the first issue of the *Chicago Democrat*, Nov. 26, 1833, for the "Soap and Candle Manufactory of Messrs. Daniel Elston & Co. ... keeping constantly on hand an assortment of all descriptions of Hard and Soft SOAP, Wax and other Candles, to ensure public support. N.B. Cash paid for Tallow, ... also for good House Ashe," and in the Feb. 18, 1834, issue an ad appeared announcing "Smoke! Smoke!! Smoke House" offering a "Quantity of highly flavoured Hams, Fletches of Bacon, Mess and Prime Pork"; in the Nov. 4, 1835, *Chicago Democrat* advertised the Chicago Soap and Candle Manufactory of Messrs. Elston & Chaver [*sic*] "on the Point between North Branch and Main River"; late November both John T. Temple and Bernard Ward submitted depositions in support of his claim for wharfing privileges; on the 27th, Elston & Cleaver [see Charles Cleaver] applied and later claimed privileges at the junction of the north branch and main stream [lots 3, 4, block 7]; Daniel supported his earlier claim [lot 4, block 7] with an affidavit filed on Dec. 24; his wife was Blanche Maria; became alderman in 1837; ✦ brickmaker, Elston Road; ➡ Elston Avenue, a diagonal street on the NW side; in 1885, his widow lived in Lake View. [12, 28, 351]

Emerson, Benjamin   born in 1810 near Utica, NY; arrived in 1835 and began to sell milk; ✦ milkman, Chicago Avenue near Lill's brewery; married a Miss Kiley of Ireland in 1839 and later that year removed to a claim in Niles Township.

engagé   French term for an employee under a written contract [*engagement*] with an official license holder of the Indian fur trade on their difficult travel through the wilderness. They were characterized by exceptional hardiness and love of the outdoor life; many eventually married Indian women; some initiated trade illegally and without a license, becoming [see] *coureurs de bois*. Also see *voyageur*, a term often used synonymously with *engagé*.

engagement   see *engagé*.

Engineers   see Corps of Engineers.

Engle, Lt. James   from New Jersey; Fifth Infantry; stationed as second lieutenant with his wife at Fort Dearborn from Oct. 3, 1828, to May 20, 1831, under Major Fowle; voted on July 24, 1830 (see Chronology); resigned his commission in 1834, dying soon after. [704]

English and Classical School for Boys   also English and Classical Academy; opened in December

LIVERY STABLE.

THE citizens of Chicago are hereby informed, that a LIVERY STABLE is opened at the Point, and that preparations are being made to accommodate the public. Saddle horses, single horse Carriages will be kept on hand. All of which can be had day or night (for Cash only, at reasonable charges. All property to be returned sound as when taken from the stable, or the person hiring will be held responsible.— Horses kept by the day or week.

THOS. EPERSON & CO.

Chicago, Feb. 11, 1834.   13

1833 as a private school in the small building of the First Baptist Church on South Water Street, at Franklin. The teacher ("preceptor") and proprietor was Granville T. Sproat of Boston, who advertised the school in the December 1833 issues of the *Chicago Democrat*; in March 1834, he was joined by an assistant, Miss Sally L. Warren. In 1834, the school accepted community funds and thereby became public; the trustees included George W. Snow, Eli W. Williams, and Dexter Graves. Also see Sproat, Granville T.

Eno, André Henault [or Hunault]   a member of La Salle's party who, together with Jean Filatreau, built and occupied a "fort" at "Chicago" for several months during the winter of 1682-83, as indicated in a letter that La Salle wrote from the Chicago portage on June 4, 1683; such a structure would be the second semipermanent dwelling built by a European, the first being Father Marquette's winter hut of 1674-75; however, the heading of La Salle's letter said it was 30 leagues [72 miles] from Fort St. Louis, a distance far short of present Chicago.

Eperson, Thomas   advertised in the Feb. 18, 1834, *Chicago Democrat* the establishment of a livery stable at the Point [Wolf Point].

Episcopal congregation   the Episcopal church community was first organized in 1834 through the efforts of Dr. Maxwell, Dr. Egan, Giles Spring, Gurdon Hubbard, Margaret Helm, and John H. Kinzie and his wife Juliette; in October 1834, Rev. Palmer Dyer arrived and preached the first sermon on the 12th at the Presbyterian church, by the invitation of Rev. J. Porter. Reverend Dyer left within the week and on the following Sunday (Oct. 19), Rev. Isaac W. Hallam conducted the service and took charge of the parish; Mr. Kinzie soon furnished a building on the SE corner of State (then Wolcott) and Kinzie streets as a place of worship [in 1840, this building became known as "Tippecanoe Hall"]. The Female Sewing Society of St. James Parish held its first annual fair on June 18,

1835, and on the 20th the ladies included "A Card" in the *Chicago American* acknowledging gratitude to "Messrs. Bates & Montgomery for use of their auction room and their services." The St. James Church, a handsome edifice of brick, was constructed in 1836 on two lots at the corner of Cass [Wabash] and Illinois streets and opened on Easter Sunday, 1837; the building surpassed in comfort and appearance the frame structures that other denominations (Catholic, Presbyterian, Baptist) had erected earlier, and was the only church in town with a tower and organ. The community drew its membership chiefly from the well-to-do residential section of the N division; because John H. Kinzie was a member and a generous contributor, it was often referred to as the "Kinzie Church."

Ericson, Leif   see Leif Ericson.

Erie Canal   between the Hudson River and Lake Erie; America's first major man-made waterway; begun by New York State in 1817 and opened on Oct. 25, 1825, establishing a new route for trade with and immigration from the settled East, beginning the modern era for the Great Lakes. The canal was 363 miles long and had 83 locks, extending from the Hudson River N of Albany across the Mohawk Valley to Buffalo, NY, on Lake Erie; signaled the beginning of the "canal era" in northern Indiana, and the canal fever that fanned Chicago's real estate boom of the mid-1830s. Traveling in a boat of one of the various canal lines was no comfortable matter for westbound emigrants, as described below by [see] Ellen Bigelow, in a letter to a relative back home in Massachusetts: [On the] *"Genesee," Clinton Line, Capt. D. W. Botts. ... What they called the ladies' cabin we found to be a little, mean, dirty place, in size about six feet by ten, and into that ten and sometimes twelve persons were regularly wedged. The berths were straw mattresses thrown upon rails of which our poor bones complained most bitterly. The noise of passing through the locks with the jar occasioned by meeting other boats would have prevented us from sleeping had the straw and* *rails permitted it. We arose in the morning unrefreshed and heartily sick of canal boats. … A rainstorm came on which added much to the horror of our situation, as it drove all the gentlemen into the cabin and covered the floor with mud and water and gave us no room to turn around.* [55a]

Ernst, Anna   German immigrant, first attested to as having lived in Chicago in 1832. [342]

Escher, Jacob and Martin   also Esher; German-Protestant immigrant brothers who arrived in 1836 with their families and soon joined the German Evangelical Association. Jacob's son, John J. (1823-1901), later became bishop of the Evangelical church, author of the *Evangelical Church Catechism*, and, in 1861, founder of North Central College in Naperville. [12]

Essex   schooner from Oswego, NY; first called at Chicago with passengers and merchandise on Nov. 14, 1835, under Captain Bassett; wrecked off Bass Island in 1848. [48]

estray book   kept by Richard J. Hamilton in 1833 and 1834 in his capacity as clerk of the common Cook County court, in which he listed data on all stray domestic animals accumulating within the estray pen; the book formed the basis for periodic public sales of unclaimed animals before an appointed appraiser and a justice of the peace; animals thus sold—or "taken up"—were listed, with the amount they brought, in the *Chicago Democrat.*

estray pen   also hog pound; a corral erected with county funds in March 1832 on the SW corner of the public square, meant to hold lost hogs and cattle until their owners could claim them; was built by Samuel Miller, who asked $20 for his effort but settled for $12; the estray pen was ★★★ **Chicago's 1st** public structure.

Eustis, Lt. Col. Abram   in charge of artillery at Fort Dearborn throughout the 1832 cholera epidemic, then led the Black Hawk War troops to the field of action near Galena, where General Scott and staff had preceded them to join other forces.

Eustis, William, M.D.   from Massachusetts; Continental army surgeon between December 1775 and December 1776; hospital physician and surgeon from October 1780 to the close of the Revolutionary War; named secretary of war on March 7, 1809, serving until Jan. 13, 1813 in Washington City; beginning Dec. 30, 1809, Matthew Irwin, government factor at Fort Dearborn, reported to Eustis regularly on the irregularities he observed concerning actions of the officers and others. This, in 1811, led to the replacement of Capt. John Whistler as commandant of the fort. Dr. Eustis died on Feb. 6, 1825. [109, 326]

Evans, John   on Sept. 4, 1830, purchased from the canal commissioners lot 3 of block 44 and lot 5 of block 33; by 1833, both lots were owned by Henry Brush. [12]

Everts, Hiram   also Evarts; from Granville, NY; placed two notices in the *Chicago Democrat* on Aug. 5 and 12, 1835, for "EDUCATION," informing "the inhabitants of Chicago, that he will open a HIGH SCHOOL for Young Gentlemen on the 10th … should sufficient encouragement be offered." Terms of eleven weeks were to be available for ordinary [$5] and higher [$6] English branches and for Latin and Greek [$8] languages; testimonials were accessible at Dr. Temple's house; died in Chicago on Sept. 24 at age 23, per notice in the Sept. 26 *Chicago American.*

Evileth, Lt. William Sanford   also Eveleth, Evelith; native of Virginia; graduated from West Point in 1813; a U.S. Department of Engineers officer; employed in the rebuilding of Fort Dearborn in the summer of 1818; in October embarked on the schooner *Hercules* to return East, but lost his life on the 4th when the ship was wrecked between the mouths of the two Calumet Rivers; his body was identified by the military buttons on his clothes. [12]

Ewing, William Lee Davidson   (1795-1846) present at the 1833 Indian Treaty of Chicago, serving as the government commission's secretary; was allowed a grant of $5,000 at that occasion; served as an interim governor of Illinois in 1834 for only 15 days, succeeding Governor Reynolds and followed by Governor Duncan; was president of the Illinois Senate at the time; ➡ Ewing Avenue. [13, 559]

"Exchange, the"   colloquial term for either the Eagle Exchange Tavern or the Exchange Coffee House.

Exchange Coffee House   later called the Illinois Exchange, and sometimes the New York Exchange; second hotel built by Mark Beaubien, erected in 1834 at the NW corner of Lake and Wells streets and initially run by Mr. and Mrs. John Murphy; subsequent managers or owners were A.A. Markle in 1836, Jason Guley in 1838, Charles W. Cook in 1839 [then 182 Lake St.], and F.A. Munson in 1844. [41]

*F**aith**   armed British schooner patrolling Lakes Michigan, Huron, and Erie during the period of British control; built in Detroit in 1774. [48]

factory   see U.S. Factory System.

Fairplay   a U.S. Revenue cutter, armed single-masted U.S. revenue sailing ship that visited Fort Dearborn in 1819.

Fallen Timbers, Battle of   on Aug. 20, 1794, Gen. Anthony Wayne succeeded at Fallen Timbers, OH, in breaking Indian resistance to the continued colonization of the Midwest; his victory led to the Treaty of Greenville in the following year, the terms of which were of particular significance for the future development of Chicago. [152, 570, 625]

Farnsworth, William   (c.1795-1860) American born; entered the fur trade at Montreal, then signed up with the American Fur Co. and in 1818 was assigned as clerk in the district of Fond du Lac; in 1820, he left the company to become an independent trader on the shore of Green Bay and with success, in 1822 or 1823 married *métis* Marinette Chevalier, also a trader and popular with the Indians; there in 1832-33 he built the first sawmill on the Menominee River where Marinette, WI now exists, and in 1835 took over another sawmill at Sheboygan, which had been built during the previous year by [see] William Payne and Oliver C. Crocker, and traveled to Chicago to acquire a manager, Jonathan S. Follet. Farnsworth spent the remainder of his life in Sheboygan, until his death in the *Lady Elgin* steamship disaster.

fathom   unit of measure equal to six feet; a descriptive term expressed commonly in pioneer days, i.e.: "The fur traders' birch bark canoe was usually five fathoms and a half in length, and four feet and a half in their extreme breadth."

Faux, William   a visitor to the Birkbeck colony who left accurate but often uncomplimentary accounts of pioneer life in early Illinois in his 1823 book, *Memorable Days in America: Being an Journal of a Tour to the United States, Principally Undertaken to Ascertain, by Positive Evidence, the Condition and Probable Prospects of British Emigrants.* [240]

Faulkner, J.M.   advertised dry goods "And Ready Made Clothing, Crockery, Nails, Groceries, Hardware and Cutlery, Glass and Sash, Paints, Oils, &c. N.B. Cash paid for 5,000 bushels of Oats" in the *Chicago Democrat* on Aug. 15, 1835, "two doors west of the Land Office on Lake St." in a two story brick store just completed by A. Steele; his daughter Catherine Elizabeth was born in September that year, but died five months later; in the Nov. 25 *Chicago Democrat* he announced the sale of his entire stock to Messrs. Chambers & Benedict and solicited the continued patronage of the people of Chicago and surrounding county at his old stand.

Fay, H.K.   listed as having an unclaimed letter in the Jan. 1, 1834, *Chicago Democrat*; advertised property for sale in the June 20, 1835, *Chicago American*; then owned a boarding house on Lake Street, located opposite Dr. J.T. Temple's house.

Federal Land Ordinance of 1785   provided for land to be divided into rectangular portions, bounded by parallels and meridians. Both the east-west oriented parallels, or township lines, and the north-south oriented meridians were located six miles apart, enclosing areas of 36 square miles each, which constituted survey townships [not to be confused with civic townships]. Within each township, parallel section lines, one mile apart, would create sections of one square mile each. This system, which was specifically applied to the Midwest trans-Appalachian region by the Northwest Ordinance of 1787, resulted in the checkerboard street pattern characteristic of Chicago. The ordinance also created the office of the geographer of the United States; Thomas Hutchins became the first individual to hold the office. Also see Fielding's map on page 142. [87, 521]

Felicity   armed 55-ton British sloop, built at Detroit in 1773-74, patrolling Lakes Michigan, Huron and Erie during the period of British control to "awe the Indians and prevent the rebels building boats" [Major De Peyster, 1779]; while patrolling the western shore of Lake Michigan, piloted by Samuel Robertson, the ship passed the Chicago site on Oct. 3, 1779.

Felis concolor   see mountain lion.

Felis rufus   see bobcat.

Felis lynx   see bobcat.

Fer, Nicolas de   cartographer in Paris who, in 1718, published the ✳ map, *Le Cours de Missisipi, ou de St. Louis, fameuse riviere de l'Amerique Septentrionale* for the *Compagnie d'Occident*, compounding the "Mississippi Bubble"; Chicago is noted as *Les Checagou.*

Fergus Historical Series   see Bibliography.

ferries   see bridges and ferries.

ferry Indian   Capt. John Whistler's 1808 draft of Fort Dearborn shows a cabin at the Forks between the north branch and the main river, and notes "Indian Ferry [service across the north branch] attended by the man of this house." See map on page 25.

Field, Thomas J.   co-owner of a grocery on Dear-

born Street with George W. Reeble; the shop was raided on Oct. 25, 1834, by the sheriff in accordance with Illinois' antigambling laws, the owners arrested, and a roulette table confiscated; each unable to post bond of $1,000, they went to jail.

Filatreau, Jean   member of La Salle's party who, together with [see] André Eno, built and occupied for several months a "fort" in the Chicago area during the winter of 1682-83, as indicated in a letter La Salle wrote from Chicago on June 4, 1683. This would be the second semipermanent dwelling built by Europeans, the first being Father Marquette's winter hut of 1674-75.

Filer, Alanson   born 1812, carpenter from New York, arrived July 6, 1833; on March 4, 1834, the firm A. Filer & Co. advertised in the *Chicago Democrat* its "Cabinet and Chair Manufactory, three doors north of the Baptist meeting house," and by May 21, a second ad read "CHAIRS !!!, Clark, Filer & Co."; "N.B. Sign painting and ornamental painting neatly executed" was was added as postscript on June 10; on Nov. 16, he married Mrs. Hannah Pilkington Green; a later marriage was with Elizabeth Crews; moved to the Root River settlement late in 1835; later returned to Evanston; in 1885, lived at Racine, WI. [12]

finances   see corporate finances.

Finley, Clement Alexander, M.D.   (1797-1879) in some texts mistakenly identified as Dr. J.B. Finley; born in Newville, PA; graduated from the Medical School of the University of Pennsylvania in 1818; became the ninth Fort Dearborn physician, serving as assistant surgeon at the fort from Oct. 3, 1828, to Dec. 14, 1830, when he was followed by Dr. Harmon. Though the years were relatively uneventful, Lieutenant Furman's letters in Hurlbut's *Chicago Antiquities* describe the doctor as an active participant in regular wolf hunts near the fort; on Sept. 4, 1830, he purchased from the canal commissioners lots 5 and 6 in block 31, still in his possession in 1833 [see map on page 44]; during the Black Hawk War served under General

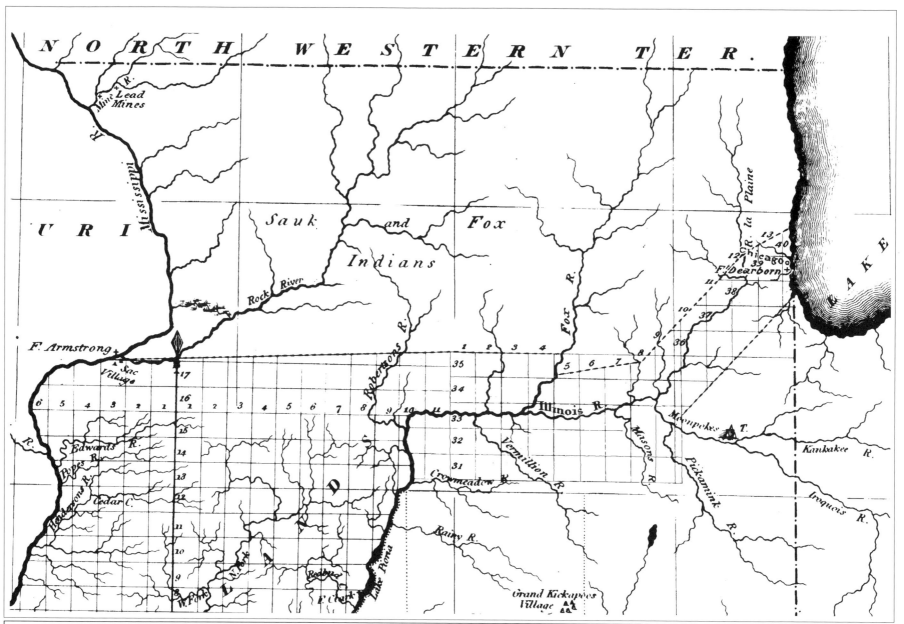

Excerpt of Fielding Lucas' map of 1823, showing that the subdivision into survey townships of 36 square miles each, mandated by the [see] Federal Land Ordinance of 1785, had been completed in the [see] Military Tract and the territory intended for IL & MI Canal construction and yielded by the Indians in the Treaty of St. Louis of 1816.

CLEMENT ALEXANDER FINLEY, M.D. [137]

Scott at Fort Armstrong; in 1846 served as medical director under General Taylor in Mexico; in 1861, became surgeon general of the army, retiring the following year. [12, 704]

Finney, Bernard   placed an ad, the first to appear, in the Aug. 12, 1835, *Chicago Democrat* that read: "$100 Reward. Ran away from the subscriber, living in St. Louis, on the 5th day of August, a mulatto man named George, about 26 or 30 years of age, about 5 feet 9 or 10 inches high, round face, rather full, and marked with the small pox, has a pleasing countenance when spoken to, and is obliging in his manners; a blacksmith by trade; had on when he left a white hat considerably worn, linen round about and summer pantaloons. It is supposed he has procured forged free papers, and will aim for some of the free states. The above reward will be paid for his apprehension and delivery to me in St. Louis, or fifty dollars for such information as may lead to his detection."

firefighting   in 1831, the Illinois legislature passed an ordinance authorizing any incorporated settlement to organize a volunteer fire company; in Chicago, however, there had existed a volunteer fire brigade prior to the town's incorporation, calling itself the "Washington Volunteers"; known members were A.V. Knickerbocker, J.J. Gilluffy, H. Williams, and C. Boardman. In November 1833, three months after Chicago's incorporation as a town, its village trustees adopted the first fire-related ordinance, requiring that rooftop stovepipes be insulated from wooden building material; Benjamin Jones served as ★★★ **Chicago's 1st** firewarden, responsible for inspecting all town buildings each month. On Sept. 25, 1834, the town was divided into four wards for firefighting purposes, and a warden was appointed for each ward to enforce the November 1833 ordinance; they were, in numerical order of the wards: William Worthington, Edward E. Hunter, Samuel Resique, and James Kinzie. The first fire in the incorporated town occurred on Oct. 16, 1834 [see the report from the *Chicago Democrat* of Oct. 21 in Chronology]. Lessons learned from this fire prompted the trustees to empower the wardens to summon bystanders to assist in suppressing fires, and on Nov. 3 they passed another ordinance making it unlawful for any person to "convey fire brands or coals of fire from one house or building to another—, unless the same be carried or conveyed in a covered earthen or fireproof vessel." On Sept. 19, 1835, in preparation for a fire department, the town board authorized the purchase of two fire engines and 1,000 feet of hose. On Nov. 4, the trustees passed an ordinance that established the Volunteer Fire Department of the Town of Chicago, headed by seven officers: the chief engineer, two assistant engineers and the four wardens; the ordinance of 52 sections, printed in the Nov. 11, *Chicago Democrat*, also mandated the possession of leather buckets: "Sec. 35. Every dwelling or other building, containing one fire place or stove, shall have one good

painted leather bucket, with the initials of the owner's name painted thereon. Every building with two or more fire places or stoves, shall have two buckets. Every owner of such building or lessee of the same for a term of years, not provided with buckets as aforesaid, shall forfeit two dollars for each deficient bucket, and the further sum of one dollar for each month he shall neglect to provide himself with such bucket or buckets, after he shall have been notified by a firewarden so to do. Sec. 36. That every able bodied male inhabitant shall, upon an alarm of fire, repair to the place of the fire, with his bucket or buckets, if he shall have any, and hence to the direction of the several officers, as is provided by the thirty-first section of this ordinance, and in default thereof each person shall pay a penalty of five dollars. Sec. 37. That every occupant, of any building shall keep the same fire buckets, in the front hall of such building, or in some other convenient and accessible place, under penalty of one dollar."

In anticipation of the official action to create a fire department, a large number of volunteer fire fighters had already in September organized themselves into the "Fire Kings," and on Oct. 7 the "Pioneer" hook and ladder company formed. The names of most of the volunteers are recorded in historical documents and in this volume, and are evidence of the cooperative spirit prevailing in an early pioneer settlement. On Oct. 23, Lewis Sely submitted a bill to the town council for a fire engine, and on Dec. 8 Hubbard & Co. communicated with the council in regard to ★★★ **Chicago's 1st fire engine** [made by John Roger & Son, Baltimore] that was ordered by the corporation [*Chicago American*, Dec. 12]. Gurdon S. Hubbard may actually have acquired the engine—for $894.38—that did not arrive until the following year. On Dec. 12, the county commission gave its permission to erect an engine house on the public square for five years, and on Dec. 15 members of Fire Engine Company No. 1 petitioned the village board for an engine house; a letter was also submitted, its unedited text follows. [12, 28, 96]

To the board of Trustees of the town of Chicago. Gentlemen,

We the undersigned members of the fire Engine Company No. 1. would respectfully represent, that the building now proposed for the Engine House, being only 12 by 18 feet, is unquestionably to [sic] small to meet the wants and necessities of the Engine company in this, to wit, The House should be sufficiently large not only for the Engine and utensils, but also room for the necessary operations of the company themselves in drying by a Stove &c the Hose—Thawing the ice &c—and room enough to hold such necessary meetings of the members as are required of them.

Your petitioners would further request, that a Cistern which would hold 3 or 4 Hogsheads of water ought to be constructed and attached to the Engine; as it will be remembered, we have only 150 feet of Hose and Suction Engine.

All which is respectfully submitted to the consideration of the board.

16th Dec. 1835

S.G. Trowbridge, T.O. Davis, H.G. Loomis, O.S. Beach, H.B. Clarke, Joel Wicks, N.F.L. Monroe, H.M. Draper, John Dye, Ira Kimberly, William McCoristen, Amos C. Hamilton, S.W. Paine, James H. Mulford, M.B. Beaubien, Edmund Peek.

Proposals to build the engine house were submitted to the town council on Dec. 23 by Dickinson & Sheppard [$375] and on the 30th by Levi Blake [$225]; Blake was awarded the contract on Jan. 23. An engine house, 12 by 24 feet, was thereafter built on LaSalle Street, between Washington and Randolph; its pine cistern held two hogsheads of water.

Fire Kings   one of the early volunteer fire brigades, this one formed in September 1834. The appellation may have been chosen by those who witnessed a traveling entertainer, who earlier in February had dazzled Chicagoans with feats of the "Fire King"; see entry for Bowers, Mr. But another source identifies Hubbard's fire engine as Fire King No. 1 and notes that the Fire Kings organized on Dec. 12 to work the engine, its members reimbursing Hubbard for its cost. [12, 96]

fires, Fort Dearborn   see Fort Dearborn fires.

First Presbyterian Church and Society of Chicago, The   see Presbyterian congregation; the epithet "First" was not used until two years after the church's founding.

Fischer, Heinrich Dietrich   (1815-1868); also, Henry Dietrich Fischer; German saddler and harnessmaker, born in Esdorf (Kingdom of Hannover); immigrated to the U.S. in 1834, and arrived in Chicago in 1834/35, where he found insufficient work in his trade and was employed in various construction jobs, including the building of the Lake House Hotel and later the Illinois & Michigan Canal; in 1836, his parents and four siblings joined him in Chicago, and the entire family moved to Duncklee's Grove [now Bloomingdale] to farm. [13, 342, 657a]

fish   early European visitors testified in their reports to an abundance of fish in the Great Lakes and their tributary rivers. [See] whitefish, lake herring, lake trout, chub, pike, walleye and yellow perch; all were harvested by the Indians with dipnets, gill nets, spears, and baited bone or copper hooks, respectively. Indians established the first commercial fisheries, trading their catch to explorers, settlers, and to the [see] American Fur Co., which dried or salted the fish and shipped the product east with the collected furs.

Fish, Elisha   served as private in Capt. James Walker's Cook County militia company under Major Bailey from May 24 until mid-June 1832, then became a corporal in Walker's second company, reorganized June 19 and active through Aug. 12, until the Black Hawk threat abated; settled within York Township in 1834; a remaining letter for him was listed in the Jan. 21, 1835, *Chicago Democrat*. [217a]

Fisher, Elizabeth Thérèse   born 1810 at Prairie du Chien; daughter of Henry Monroe Fisher and Marie Anne Le Sellier; with her mother visited Chicago by sailing ship in 1817, and described her experience in later life as Elizabeth Thérèse Baird under the title *Reminiscenses of Early Days on Mackinac Island*; for her impression, see entry for Kinzie House. Elizabeth Thérèse was the granddaughter of [see] Pierre Le Sellier, a long-term acquaintance or friend of John Kinzie, and a fellow British agent during the War of 1812. [29, 635a]

Fisher, Pitman   resident of Cook County; in the Aug. 13, 1834, *Chicago Democrat* J.B. Beaubien announced, as administrator, the public sale of his personal estate.

Fithian, William   listed prior to 1836 as co-owner-assignee, together with George W. Cassidy, of 240 acres of land in Section 20, Township 39, as per Andreas, *History of Chicago*, pp. 112-113.

Fitzpatrick, John   notice in *Chicago Democrat* on Sept. 17, 1834, reads: "An inquest was held on the body of a woman by the name of Elizabeth Fitzpatrick, residing over the North Branch of the Chicago river in this town, who was found dead in her bed on Monday morning last, with evident marks upon her person of having been murdered. The verdict of the Jury was, 'that she came to her death by violence upon her body by John Fitzpatrick, who it is said was her husband.' Fitzpatrick has been apprehended, and is now in jail awaiting his trial, at the Circuit Court to be held in this town on the first Monday of October next. We understand that both were adicted [*sic*] to habits of intemperance." Attorney James Collins' excellent defence caused the jury to acquit the defendant; ✦ laborer, corner of Chicago Avenue and Rush Street.

flag as initially decreed by Congress on June 14, 1777, the American flag had 13 stripes and 13 stars. As of May 1, 1795, a revised design stipulated 15 stripes and 15 stars in order to accommodate Vermont and Kentucky, which had since joined the Union of originally 13 states; this revised flag was the one that flew over the first Fort Dearborn and initially also over the second Fort Dearborn. On April 4, 1818, Congress ordered the flag to return to the original 13 stripes and set the number of stars at 20, stipulating that on admission of every new state one star would be added. [137]

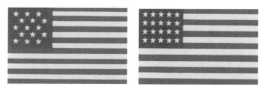

1795   1818

Flag Creek tributary to the Des Plaines River; Elijah Wentworth, Jr., built a tavern at Flag Creek in 1833, soon after followed by [see] Joseph and Robert Vial, who built a hostelry in the spring of 1834 and farmed.

Flag Creek Convention Cook County's first Democratic convention; a notice in the *Chicago Democrat* on June 24, 1835, announced a meeting at the Eagle Coffee House the following Monday to elect delegates for the convention that was later held at Joseph Vial's hostelry on July 4; Peter Pruyne was nominated for state senator.

Flagg, Reuben from Vermont; arrived in July 1830, to homestead at Walker's Grove with his wife, Betsey (née Kendall), where a daughter, Samantha, was born; became a private in the Bailey volunteer militia on May 24, 1832, within James Walker's company, then continued as a corporal

with the company that reformed on June 6. He afterward occasionally hauled lumber by oxen team to Chicago for Walker's sawmill. [734]

flogging punishment of soldiers for disobedience and other offences was not uncommon at Fort Dearborn and other army installations until 1812, when it became prohibited; a maximum of 100 strokes was delivered across the bare back in the presence of their comrades.

Flood, Capt. Peter F. (1812-1888) arrived from Ireland in June 1835; ✦ schooner *Huron*; married Mary A. Clark in 1842; in 1885, lived at 93 S Sangamon St. [12]

Florida schooner, built at Black River, OH in 1834; called at Chicago with merchandise and passengers from Buffalo/Sacket's Harbor, NY, twice in 1835 under Captain Wilson.

Flusky, — together with his wife, kept a boarding house on Franklin Street in 1835; in residence together then were Gurdon S. Hubbard, Mr. and Mrs. John D. Caton, Mr. and Mrs. Augustus Garrett, James B. Campbell and family, Mr. and Mrs. William Stewart, and Rev. and Mrs. John T. Mitchell. In an 1888 letter to Mrs. Hubbard, Caton reminisced about that time, how the Fluskys wanted to sell the house and so the boarders resolved to jointly buy to continue living there, the wives taking turns at housekeeping.

Follansbee, Charles married Sally Merriam Coburn in Chicago on Feb. 5, 1835; ✦ grocery and provision store, 24 Dearborn St.; listed in the Cook County census for 1840.

Follett, Jonathan S. in Chicago in 1835, when he was hired by the early Sheboygan trader William Farnsworth to run for him a sawmill on the Sheboygan River that Farnsworth had recently purchased from William Payne and Oliver C. Crocket. Follet and his wife Eliza thus became the first permanent settlers at Sheboygan.

Fonda, John H. early trader and mail carrier between Fort Howard and Fort Dearborn, living in Prairie du Chien; visited Chicago in 1825 and again

during the winter of 1827-28, and recorded his experiences; see excerpts concerning these times in the Chronology (1825 and 1827-28) and his description of the clothes worn under the entry for mail carriers. [12]

foolscap large sheets of sturdy writing paper; greased with bear or raccoon fat to make them more translucent, then used for want of glass in the window openings of early pioneer cabins.

Foot, — Andreas makes reference to a Mr. Foot who in 1831 succeeded [see] Stephen and Mrs. Forbes as teacher at the schoolhouse on the lakeshore, near the end of [Randolph Street]. [12]

Foot, Benjamin J. placed a notice in the Dec. 17, 1834, *Chicago Democrat* that read: "I hereby forbid any person harboring or trusting my wife, Lucy Ann, on my account, as I shall pay no charges for her after this date."

Foot, John B. from Connecticut, brother of Starr Foot; arrived in 1833; married Elizabeth Sherman on Nov. 12, 1834, Col. R.J. Hamilton officiating; ✦ blacksmith, Randolph Street, near State; moved to Leyden Township in 1840. [13, 351]

Foot, Starr also Foote; arrived in 1833 from Connecticut [had worked under William Jones on the Buffalo harbor and, following his visits to Chicago in 1831 and 1832, had been advised of the opportunities]; advertised "groceries" in the first issue of the *Chicago Democrat*, Nov. 26, 1833; became the second proprietor, after Alanson Sweet, of the first Tremont House hotel on the NW corner of Lake and Dearborn streets, followed by the Couch brothers; in the Aug. 15, 1835, *Chicago American* he noted the selling of a "valuable new two horse wagon, spring seats, &c. Also a set of double harness"; ✦ teamster, Clark Street, corner of Monroe; later superintendent of the Cook County poor for several years. [13, 351, 357]

Forbes, Elvira teacher; wife of [see] Stephen R. Forbes (née Bates), born in Vermont in 1806; sister of Sophia, wife of Bernardus Laughton, trader and innkeeper [Riverside].

STEPHEN VAN RENSSELAER FORBES

Forbes, Isaac Sawyer   older brother of [see] Stephen Van Rensselaer Forbes who also came to Fort Dearborn in the spring of 1829 with a surveying party and continued south to Louisiana; familiar with the [Riverside] locale where Stephen would homestead, he returned there with his wife and two children in 1836, bringing also his parents and other siblings.

Forbes, John, Jr.   from Preble, NY; brother of Stephen Van Renssellaer Forbes who also came to Chicago in 1830 with his wife, Mary Trowbridge, and their small son Daniel Webster; removed to [Riverside] in 1833 to homestead along the Des Plaines River, where the next year another son, Henry Clay, was born; moved farther W to the Mississippi River in 1838.

Forbes, Stephen Van Renssellaer   (1797-1879) of Scottish ancestry; born in Wilmington, VT, on July 26, son of John and Ann Sawyer Forbes; came to Fort Dearborn in the spring of 1829 with a surveying party that included his brother Isaac Saw-

yer Forbes and continued S to Louisiana; leaving Newburgh [south Cleveland], OH, in June 1830, he and his wife Elvira (née Bates) returned to Chicago, on horseback from Detroit, to both live and begin teaching school to some 25 students in a log structure belonging to J.B. Beaubien [near Randolph Street and Michigan Avenue], acquired for this purpose by Beaubien and Lt. David Hunter; the children were both from the garrison of the fort and the settlement; served as appraiser of the estate of François LaFramboise on Dec. 17, 1830; had been elected justice of the peace earlier on Nov. 25, 1830, and was later elected sheriff of Cook County in August 1832. In 1831, he squatted on a 160-acre homestead (SW quarter of Section 36, Township 39 R., 12 E.) on the Des Plaines River at [Riverside] adjoining the eastern border of David Laughton's land and including the Belle Fountain springs, where a daughter, Aurilla Anne, was born on June 3, 1834; for this property he paid $200 in 1835 and received title on Oct. 1, 1839; he built a large log house the following year; by 1836 he owned entirely, and sold, Section 36. The site of his house is now indicated by a ▲ monument [see Monuments]; here the election of Jean Baptiste Beaubien to the position of colonel of the Sixtieth Regiment of Illinois Militia took place on June 7, 1834. His sawmill later became known as Dr. Fox's mill and survived Forbes until the end of the century, when it was destroyed by fire. In 1836, his parents John and Ann Forbes, with children and grandchildren, moved from Preble, NY and settled on the Des Plaines River. In 1885, Forbes' widow lived in Cleveland, OH. [12, 51, 249, 262, 351]

Forbes, T.   on the list of subscribers to the *Chicago Democrat* in November 1833.

Force, J.   with L. Dorsey, assumed management of the Steam Boat Hotel [later called the American Hotel] on North Water Street on Nov. 9, 1835, following John Davis.

Ford, David M.   arrived from New York in 1834.

Ford, Martin M.   arrived from New York in 1834;

♦ tanner, Clark Street, NE corner of Madison; died in 1854.

fords of Chicagoland   before bridges were built in the Chicago area beginning in the early 1830s [see entry on bridges and ferries], travelers had to cross the rivers at fords. The Chicago River was fordable only over a shallow sand bar at its mouth; the main branch of the Green Bay Trail crossed here. The Des Plaines River had several fords [see map on page 147]: the South Portage Road led to Summit Ford, located a few feet N of the [Lawndale Avenue] bridge; the Old [north] Portage Road led to Laughton's Ford (formerly "Ford of the Des Plaines"; at 45th Street); a branch of the Green Bay Trail led to the Stony Ford, now just S of [U.S. Rte. 66; formerly State Highway No. 4]; the Brush Hill Trail between Chicago and Napierville crossed the Des Plaines River at the Riverside Ford, near the Berry Point Road bridge. The Calumet was fordable only at its two mouths (one S of Chicago, the other at Miller, IN), and near [135th Street and Ashland Avenue]. Stony Creek was fordable at what is now Ann Street, where the original Vincennes Road crossed. The Sag was forded near its mouth on the Des Plaines, and further E near Paddock's Creek.

Ford, Thomas   attorney; appointed judge of the sixth circuit (formed Jan. 17, 1835; inclusive of Cook and eight other counties); presided at two sessions in Chicago during 1836; was named municipal court judge by the city legislature in 1837. [12]

Forêt, Francois Daupin, sieur de la   see La Forêt, François Daupin de.

Forget Du Verger, Père Jacques François   Sulpitian missionary priest in charge of the *Mission de Sainte Famille de Caoquias* [Cahokia] up to the year 1763 when he, prior to closing the mission and selling the mission property, freed three slaves owned by the mission. An assumption by some earlier historians, that one of the slaves may have been [see] Jean Baptiste Point de Sable, has been shown to be

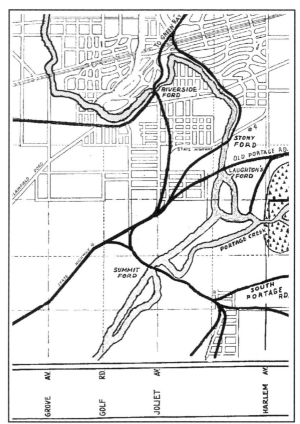

THE FORDS OF THE DES PLAINES RIVER
and their relation to the old Chicago portage trail network;
based on a map by Knight & Zeuch [413], with the 1928
street pattern superimposed; trails in solid black.

false. [399]

Forks, the name used by early settlers for the area surrounding the confluence of the branches of the Chicago River, where the growing village was first centered, although additional houses were strung along the main branch of the river toward Fort Dearborn by 1830. Not until 1892 did the original shape of the "forks," with Wolf Point forming a more acute angle than today, give rise to an unofficial emblem for Chicago in the shape of the letter *Y*, designed in March of that year by A.J. Roewad in response to a contest; first promoted by private

initiative, it was eventually adopted by the city council in 1917. The French equivalent for fork, *La Fourche*, was applied to another fork, formed by the confluence of the Des Plaines and Kankakee Rivers, where a major Indian village existed and was so named in the 1700s.

Forsyth, Robert born 1763; one of John Kinzie's five half brothers (see Kinzie family tree on page 222); both Robert and Thomas were initially in partnership with John Kinzie at Chicago in 1803; was in the service of the American government during the War of 1812; his children were Robert Allen [see next entry], Marcia, Alice, and Jane; all received $3,000 each at the 1833 Chicago treaty with the Indians, although none had Indian blood. [12]

Forsyth, Robert Allen (1798-1849) born in Detroit, son of Thomas Forsyth and his Ojibwa wife; early citizen of Chicago; served in the War of 1812; was a cadet in 1814 and later served as secretary to Governor Cass (in that capacity, accompanied him on the exploratory expedition that passed through Chicago in August 1820); was present at the Treaty of Chicago of 1833, serving on the claims committee and signing the treaty as a witness; died in Detroit. He is sometimes cited as Chicago's very first schoolteacher: at the age of 13, during a winter visit in 1810, he taught the alphabet to six-year-old John H. Kinzie, tutoring with a speller brought from Detroit. [12, 214]

Forsyth, Maj. Thomas (1771-1833) born in Detroit on Dec. 5; youngest of John Kinzie's five half brothers (see Kinzie family tree on page 222); married a Ojibwa woman with whom he fathered Robert Allen, and later in 1804, married Keziah Malott; beginning in 1802, opened trading posts at Saginaw Bay, on an island in the Mississippi near Quincy, at Chicago in partnership with John Kinzie, and at Peoria, the latter being his headquarters from 1802 to 1812, and where he lived until 1818. With Kinzie, Thomas was co-owner of a Negro slave, Jeffrey Nash, who served Forsyth in Peoria, then

ran away; the owners initiated a suit to recover him, but lost. At the outbreak of war in 1812, Forsyth was acting U.S. Indian subagent for the Illinois Territory, and among his letters to Gen. William Clark in Washington City, is included a hand-drawn ✳ map of the southwestern part of the Great Lakes region, identifying rivers, settlements, and Indian villages [preserved in the Draper Collection]; during the war, partly spent ransoming Chicago massacre captives and partly as a British prisoner, he obtained the rank of U.S. major; was replaced in 1816 by Capt. Richard Graham as Indian agent for the Illinois Territory; in 1818, he was appointed Indian agent in Missouri Territory; from 1819 to 1830, was U.S. Indian agent for the Sauk and Fox at Rock Island; after removal from office by President Jackson, lived at St. Louis until his death on Oct. 29, 1833. His manuscripts are at the Wisconsin Historical Society. [12, 109, 214, 255, 256, 635a, 681, 682]

Forsyth, William, Sr. Scottish fur trader at Niagara and innkeeper in Detroit, immigrated to New York c.1750; fought under General Wolfe at the capture of Quebec in 1759; first wife Isabel (née Martin) died in 1764; the sons he had with Isabel became half brothers to John Kinzie when he married Kinzie's widowed mother Emily in 1765 (see Kinzie family tree on page 222); died in Detroit, c.1790. His sons were George (1761; died in 1775), William, Jr. (1762), Philip and Robert (twins, 1763), and [after he married Emily Tyne Haliburton MacKinzie] Thomas (1771). William, Jr., married Margaret Lytle, the sister of Kinzie's first wife Eleanor. [12]

Forsythe, William   arrived in 1831; firewarden in December 1835; by 1837 was active in municipal politics and held official positions; ◆ merchant, West Water Street. [12, 351]

forts   basic information on the individual forts and their relevance to the Chicago area follows in alphabetical order. For a sense of the early forts of the Northwest frontier, the following short essay was contributed by Paul Petraitis:

Large and small, financed by purses both local and international, the region's many forts played significant, though fleeting roles in the history of the Midwest and the Great Lakes. The word fort *means different things to different people. Some envision a stonewalled bastion of European design, but what was more common in the Midwest during the 18th century was a fort made of logs and mud. The dictionary definitions of* a fortified place *and* an army post *also apply at different times and places. From Fort Prudhomme in the south to Fort La Pointe on the banks of Lake Superior, the French and British, and later the Americans, built a variety of structures all referred to as forts. Locally, the Fox and Potawatomi built forts as well.*

Some forts barely exist in the historical record, leaving behind no administrative archives or archeological remains. At times maps and travelers' accounts are our only clues as to their approximate location. Some local fort traditions have little or no basis in fact but nonetheless spark civic imaginations.

Others, like Fort de Chartres or Fort Dearborn, have left a detailed historical imprint. In between these large official government-built forts and the forts of the imagination lie a tantalizing spectrum of semiper-

First Fort Dearborn in 1805, with U.S. Indian Agency house on the right   [12]

manent structures, all loosely grouped under the same heading. Most Midwest forts were usually ungarrisoned and seem to have owed their existence more to the fur trade than to the fallout of international conflict.

The early Chicago area forts (1683-1696) were several, the first being built by La Salle, followed by the Jesuits and then Tonti. The last of the French forts was probably Petit Fort in the Indiana dunes, built about 1752. [Paul Petraitis]

Fort Armstrong   established on the southern end of Rock Island in May 1819 as part of the defenses in the Northwest following the war of 1812; the Treaty of Fort Armstrong of 1832 was signed under General Scott with the Winnebago, Sauk and Fox at the end of the Black Hawk War; the fort was abandoned in May 1836.

Fort Bellefontaine   established in 1805 opposite the mouth of the Illinois River above St. Louis; garrison and supplies for the fort were routed by way of Fort Dearborn, the initial shipment arriving on the *Adams*'s first voyage of the season in that year. [565]

Fort Brady   originally a French fortification E of Sault Ste. Marie on the south bank of St. Mary's River, established late in the summer of 1751 to protect fur trade interests; rebuilt as an American military post in June 1822; many troops and a commandant were transferred to Chicago in May 1833 to strengthen Fort Dearborn in the aftermath of the Black Hawk War; Fort Brady was occupied until late spring 1866. [12]

Fort Caroline   built by the French in Florida in 1562 [near Jacksonville] and destroyed in 1565 by the Spaniard Pedro Menendez de Aviléz, founder of St. Augustine.

Fort Cavendish   see *Fort de Chartres.*

Fort Chartres   see *Fort de Chartres.*

Fort Chicago name favored by some historians for the first Fort Dearborn, built in 1803, reserving the name *Fort Dearborn* for the second fort, built at the same location in 1816; yet a military return dated Dec. 31, 1803, [reprinted in the *American State Papers*, 12:175] conclusively proves that the first fort was called Fort Dearborn.

Fort Chicagou also *Fort de Checagou* [Checagou, a frequent misspelling of the French *Chicagou*, probably derived from LaSalle's ambiguous handwriting]; a permanent French military fortification in the Chicago area, the existence of which has never been proven. However, small fortified French trading posts existed without doubt in various locations of Chicagoland during the 17th century, and may be referred to as *forts* by some. Although the year of construction remains uncertain, around 1685 the French built a fort or stockade in Chicago and kept it intermittently garrisoned during the tenure of La Barre, governor of New France; in a June 4, 1683, letter written by La Salle from the Chicago portage, he speaks of a "fort" built there during the preceding winter by two of his men, André Eno and Jean Filatreau, first built during the winter of 1682-83. [This could only have been a small structure, about 50'x70', possibly at the New Lenox site, perhaps surrounded by a stockade, but not a fort in the military sense. For other such establishments, see John Swenson's essay "Chicago: Meaning of the Name and Location of Pre-1800 European Settlements" on page 377, *eds.*] Others credit Durantaye, the commandant at Michilimackinack, as the originator of a post in 1685 in Chicago, citing Franquelin's 1688 ✳ map, in which Fort Checagou is similarly positioned; sometime between 1693 and 1696 [1701-1705 according to documents cited by Faye] Nicolas d'Ailleboust de Mantet was a commander at Fort Chicagou. Both La Salle and Tonti were at Fort Chicagou, referring to it in correspondence [see the following excerpt from [*Memoir of the Sieur de Tonty*]; some scholars credit Tonti with constructing a fort or military post in the southern Chicago area [now Hegewish] in 1691-92. James Logan, British agent in Pennsylvania who surveyed French routes in the West in 1718, reported only ruins of a fort at Chicago; the fort was last officially mentioned in the text of the Treaty of Greenville, 1796. For additional evidence of a French fort at Chicago, see entry for Mantet, Nicolas d'Ailleboust, sieur de.

Excerpt from Tonty's *Memoir*:

I embarked, therefore, for the Illinois [coming from Michilimackinac in search of La Salle], on St. Andrews Day (30th of October, 1685); but being stopped by the ice, I was obliged to leave my canoe, and to proceed on by land. After going one hundred and twenty leagues, I arrived at the fort of Chicagou, where M. de la Durantaye commanded; and from thence I came to Fort St. Louis, where I arrived in the middle of January [1686]. [559]

Fort Clark built by U.S. troops in 1813 on the west bank of the outlet of Peoria Lake, opposite the east bank site of the earlier French *Fort St. Louis de Pimiteoui* that Tonti had built in 1691; burned in 1818 and 1819, only rebuilt in 1832 during the Black Hawk War but never occupied. Prior to the establishment of regular government mail service, mail was occasionally brought from Fort Clark to Chicago, but more often from Fort Wayne. [649]

Fort Conti see *Fort Niagara*.

Fort Crawford established in June 1816 at Prairie du Chien, Michigan Territory, at the confluence of the Mississippi and Wisconsin rivers, in conjunction with the construction of Fort Howard at Green Bay and the rebuilding of Fort Dearborn, to achieve military control over the region W of Lake Michigan; unoccupied from 1826 to 1827, and in 1830 was moved to new barracks on higher ground S of the first site; played a major role during the 1832 Black Hawk War, when [see] Jefferson Davis was stationed there; twice more was evacuated and regarrisoned before closure in 1856.

Fort Crevecoeur "fort of the broken heart"; built in January 1680 by La Salle and Tonti at the lower end of Lake Peoria, but shortlived. The exact location is in dispute. The name was meant to flatter Louis XIV, whose armies had won a victory nine years earlier at *Creve-coeur* in the Netherlands. When La Salle returned to Fort Frontenac for necessary supplies and Tonti left *Crevecoeur* to survey *Le Rocher* (Starved Rock) on the Illinois River in 1681, remaining discontented members mutinied, destroying the fort and the partially constructed vessel meant for exploration of the Mississippi. A ▲ mural in the Oak Park Post Office is entitled "The Foundation of Fort Crevecoeur" [see Monument Section], and also a second ▲ mural, "La Salle's Search for Tonti 1680" [see Monument Section, under La Salle]. [12, 615]

Fort Dearborn I established by the U.S. government to protect the strategic site from foreign interests; commissioned by President Jefferson and built by Capt. John Whistler and his soldiers in 1803 [arrival date, Aug. 17], although not completed until the next year; made with rough logs locally hewn, not like the whitewashed ones of the second fort. Located at a latitude of 41 minutes, 51 seconds N and a longitude of 87 minutes, 15 seconds W, the fort stood on a sandy 8-foot-high hill, on the convex side of the Chicago River as it curved from an eastern to a southern flow direction, less than 100 yards from the lakeshore. The fort had two-story barracks with pillared porches, two blockhouses—at the NW and SE corners—a double palisade, and a sally port, the soldiers' term for the tunnel dug from the smaller gate in the stockade near the NW blockhouse to the river bank; the fort flew the American flag, which at that time had 15 stripes and 15 stars, the latter being arranged in a circle. Maintaining the lonely fort in the vast wilderness and meeting the needs of its garrison was a difficult task for Captain Whistler; his unedited letter [see Chronology, page 24] to the Secretary of War Gen. Henry Dearborn reveals some of the problems that were confronted; the

FORT DEARBORN I IN 1810
by Brigitte Kozma

1808 pay scale for military personnel at the fort follows. In June 1810 Captain Whistler was transferred to Fort Detroit, and Capt. Nathan Heald took over as commandant. The fort was evacuated and many of its inhabitants were massacred on Aug. 15, 1812; for details, see Fort Dearborn massacre. The fort and the nearby Indian agency building were burned by Indians the following day and only the powder magazine, built of stone, remained; a cannon, thrown into the river by the soldiers before the evacuation, was retrieved by later residents and regularly fired at ceremonial occasions, until in 1847 it misfired and severely mutilated [see] Richard L. Wilson; it was then scrapped. For the location of the fort in the city today, one may note ▲ markers in the pavement at the corner of Wacker Drive and Michigan Avenue [see Monuments]. For a worthy description of what William Johnson found when he visited the fort in 1809, see Johnson, William. [11, 12, 103, 104, 105, 179, 215, 257, 260, 275, 326, 464 559, 708, 723]

Pay scale for military personnel in 1808:

Rank	Pay/Month	Forage Allowance	Rations/Day
COLONEL	$75	$12	$6
LT. COLONEL	$60	$11	$5
MAJOR	$50	$10	$4
SURGEON	$45	$10	$3
SURGEON'S MATE	$30	$6	$2
ADJUTANT	$10	$6	–
CAPTAIN	$40	–	$3
1ST LIEUTENANT	$30	–	$2
2ND LIEUTENANT	$25	–	$2
ENSIGN	$20	–	$2
MUSIC TEACHER	$9	–	$1
SERGEANT	$10	–	$1
CORPORAL	$8	–	$1
MUSICIAN	$8	–	$1
PRIVATE	$7	–	$1

Fort Dearborn II   established in conjunction with Fort Howard at Green Bay and Fort Crawford at Prairie du Chien in 1816 to achieve military control over the region W of Lake Michigan. The first

garrison, 112 in number, came from the Third U.S Infantry in Detroit and arrived under the command of Capt. Hezekiah Bradley on board the schooner *General Wayne* on July 4, 1816, and immediately began to build a new fort over the former one. For a description of the building site, see an excerpt from Milo Quaife's *Checagou* below. Moses Morgan was among the carpenters and other skilled laborers brought along to facilitate the effort; Alexander Robinson and Antoine Ouilmette, the locals, furnished ponies; pine timber was obtained from the wooded shore [near Lincoln Park] and rafted S along the shore. Built on the same site as the first fort, the second fort was similarly aligned to the north-south axis, but had just one blockhouse and a single palisade, all made of native oak. Early July 1827, while unoccupied by troops, the fort was struck by lightning and the barracks on the E side, the storehouse, and part of the guardhouse at the south gate were destroyed; the structure continued to be used intermittently by the military until 1834. In May 1835, the fort was sold to Jean B. Beaubien by the local government agent for $94; however, Beaubien never took possession of the fort and eventually the U.S. Supreme Court voided the contract and returned his money. In 1856, Stephen S. Wright bought the blockhouse and all that remained of the stockade, disassembling the portions the following year; in his factory, he reworked the logs as souvenir furniture for himself and his friends. The last remnant of the fort was destroyed in the 1871 Chicago fire, though according to Hurlbut, a building remained on South State Street, near the NE corner with 33rd Street in 1881, that contained reused fort timbers. For a listing of the fort's successive commandants, which also reflects the times of its occupancy, see page 152. [12, 103-5, 215, 257, 260, 326, 559, 564, 708, 723]

... on June 30, 1816, the garrison, 112 in number, arrived at Chicago on board the schooner General Wayne. *Save for the magazine, which had been built*

of brick, the fort and other public buildings were found to have been entirely destroyed, while the bones of those who had perished in the battle four years before still covered the scene of action. The houses on the north side of the river still stood, however, and certain French traders had occupied them more or less regularly during the years of the war. ❖ *... the troops disembarked and established a temporary camp in a pasture near the fort site. Some garden seeds had been brought along, and one of the first tasks was to prepare a garden, probably on the site devoted to this purpose in the years before the war. The two Chicago half-breeds, Alexander Robinson and Antoine Ouilmette, with their squaws and ponies, were engaged to prepare the ground and with the aid given by the soldiers the task was soon accomplished. For some reason, however, the garden proved a failure. An enterprising Detroit trader, foreseeing a demand for vegetables at Chicago, had sent some Canadian half-breeds in advance of the garrison, and these men had planted a truck garden in May up the south branch, in the vicinity of the Lee farm [see Leigh farm]. Its produce was now brought down to the post and in the absence of other competition was sold to the garrison at a high price.*

Fort Dearborn Addition to Chicago   see Fort Dearborn reservation.

Fort Dearborn commandants   see Fort Dearborn garrison; also see listing on page 152.

Fort Dearborn-Detroit Road   also known as the Chicago Road; retracing almost entirely the old Sauk Trail.

Fort Dearborn evacuations   (1) for the fateful evacuation of the garrison of the first fort on Aug. 15, 1812, see Fort Dearborn massacre; (2) the second fort was first evacuated in the summer of 1823 under the premature premise that it was no longer needed, but the Winnebago War prompted reoccupation on Oct. 3, 1828; (3) the fort was again evacuated in the spring of 1831, when the garrison removed to Green Bay on the schooner *Napoleon*. Reoccupation took place on June 17, 1832, by two companies of regulars from Niagara under

BRIEF HISTORY OF FORT DEARBORN & CHRONOLOGICAL LIST OF ITS COMMANDANTS

1803 April	**Captain John Whistler**, First Infantry, arrives at the mouth of the Chicago River from Detroit with six soldiers to survey the site and predetermine construction of a fort on orders from General Henry Dearborn, Secretary of War.
1803 August 17 to 1810	**Captain Whistler** returns in the company of his wife, three children and with 68 military personnel. He designs and builds Fort Dearborn, becoming the first commandant; when cold weather arrives late in 1803, the troops are modestly sheltered.
1810 to **1812** August 15	**Captain Nathan Heald** is named commandant.
1810 November to **1811** June	**Lieutenant Philip Ostrander** serves as acting commandant during Captain Heald's 9-month furlough.
1812 August 9	**Captain Heald** receives orders from General Hull to evacuate the post and to remove its occupants to Detroit.
1812 August 15	The **Fort Dearborn Massacre** occurs 1 1/2 miles south of the fort as the garrison moves out. Four to five hundred Potawatomi attack, killing 52 soldiers and civilians. Fifteen Indians are slain in the action. Captain Heald survives.
1812 August 16	Indians burn the fort.
1816 July 4 to 1817 May	**Captain Hezekiah Bradley**, Third Infantry, arrives from Detroit with a garrison of 112 men; he designs and builds the second Fort Dearborn and becomes its first commandant.
	Brevet Major Daniel Baker, Third Infantry, Commandant
1817 May to 1820 June	**Captain Hezekiah Bradley**, Third Infantry, Commandant
1820 June to 1821 January	**Major Alexander Cummings**, Third Infantry, Commandant
1821 January to 1821 October	**Lieutenant Colonel John McNeil**, Third Infantry, Commandant
1821 October to 1823 July	**Captain John Greene**, Third Infantry, Commandant
1823 July to 1823 October	Fort Dearborn remains unoccupied and is left in the care of Indian agent Dr. Alexander Wolcott.
1823 October to 1828 October 3	**Brevet Major John Fowle**, Fifth Infantry, Commandant
	1st Lieutenant David Hunter, Fifth Infantry, Commandant
1828 October 3 to 1830 December 14	Fort Dearborn remains unoccupied and is left in the care of Indian agent Thomas J.V. Owen. A portion of the structure serves as a general hospital after July 11, 1831.
1830 December 14 to 1831 May 20	
1831 May 20 to 1832 June 17	The U.S. Congress appropriates $5000 for the construction of a lighthouse which is built within the year near the NW corner of the stockade. The lighthouse collapses soon after completion and a new sturdier one is erected in 1832.
1831	

1832 June 17 to **1833** May 14	**Major William Whistler**, Second Infantry, Commandant [son of Captain John Whistler]
1833 May 14 to **1833** June 19	**Captain and Brevet Major John Fowle,** Fifth Infantry, Commandant
1833 June 19 to **1833** October 31	**Major George Bender,** Fifth Infantry, Commandant
1833 October 31 to **1833** December 18	**Captain DeLafayette Wilcox**, Fifth Infantry, Commandant
1833 December 18 to **1835** September 16	**Major John Greene**, Fifth Infantry, Commandant
1835 September 16 to **1836** August 1	**Captain DeLafayette Wilcox**, Fifth Infantry, Commandant
1836 May 28	Jean Baptiste Beaubien, colonel in the Militia of Cook County, purchases land that contains the Fort Dearborn Reservation, including the fort, for $94.61 from the U.S. Land Office in Chicago and receives a certificate. The U.S. Government later contests the sale.
1836 July	Colonel Beaubien's attorney, Murray McConnell, brings legal action of ejection from the fort against the commandant, **Captain DeLafayette Wilcox.**
1836 August 1	**Captain and Brevet Major Joseph Plympton**, Fifth Infantry, replaces Captain Wilcox as Commandant.
1836 December 29	Troops are permanently withdrawn from Fort Dearborn. Only Ordinance-Sergeant Joseph Adams and **Captain Plympton** remain, responsible for Government property.
1837 May	**Captain Plympton**, last commandant, leaves the fort; Captain Louis T. Jamison remains until late autumn, detailed on recruiting-service.
1839 March	U.S. Supreme Court vacates Colonel Beaubien's purchase of Fort Dearborn.
1839 June 20	Fort Dearborn Reservation, divided into blocks and lots by order of the Secretary of War, is sold to multiple private parties fot the highest bids; receipts total $106,042.00.
1840 December 18	Colonel Beaubien surrenders his certificate of purchase for Fort Dearborn and the purchase price of $94.61 is returned to him.
1856	Alexander Hesler photographs the abandoned fort that has become a historical landmark.
1857	A.J. Cross, city employee, tears down the lighthouse and fort, excluding the officers' quarters.
1871 October 8	The last portion of Fort Dearborn is destroyed in the great fire of Chicago.

FORT DEARBORN II IN 1832
by Donald Schlickan

Maj. William Whistler, in preparation for the Black Hawk War. (4) final evacuation on Dec. 29,1836.

Fort Dearborn fires   see (1) Fort Dearborn I, for the destruction of the fort by the Indians in 1812; (2) Fort Dearborn II, for the fire caused by lightning in 1827.

Fort Dearborn garrison   troops of the first garrison arrived on foot from Detroit on Aug. 17, 1803, and were greeted by many friendly Indians; Captain Whistler and his family arrived by ship (the *Tracy*), which the astonished Indians described as a "big canoe on wings." The first return as stated in the *American State Papers*, v. 1, pp175-176, lists the following: one captain and commandant, one second lieutenant, one ensign, four sergeants, one surgeon, 54 privates. For a listing of all subsequent commandants and their terms of office, see page 152.

Fort Dearborn massacre   on Aug. 9, 1812, an Indian runner, Winnemac, brought General Hull's order to Captain Heald to evacuate the fort and move all its inhabitants to Fort Wayne; on Aug. 13, Captain Wells and Cpl. Walter Jordan arrived from the garrison of Fort Wayne in the company of 27 [other accounts state higher numbers, up to 100; *eds.*] friendly Miami warriors to assist in the move; the evacuation began at 9 a.m. on Aug. 15, a warm and sunny day; with them was a small company of 12 militia men, local civilians organized and armed by Heald in recent months; there were two wagons for the children of soldiers and militia; most adults were either on horseback or on foot. One and a half miles south of the fort, the garrison was ambushed by c.500 Indians from behind the sand dunes, near the intersection of Prairie Avenue and 18th Street and marked by a ▲ monument [see Monuments]. The Miami escort immediately fled. Captain Heald's force at the moment of confrontation consisted of 69 U.S. military personnel and the 12 militia members; there were 20 women and 20 children in the transport; 14 women and 8 children survived; seriously

Fort Dearborn II, as sketched by Count Francis Castelnau when he visited Chicago in 1838. [115]

wounded survivors of the initial action and some others, were killed or tortured to death, or were taken prisoner and distributed among Indian tribes; those who did not die in captivity either escaped or were later ransomed, returning to civilization during the next two years. Eckert [in *Gateway to Empire*] determined that of the total of 148 men, women, and children involved, 88 lost their lives; exact losses suffered by the Indians were never ascertained.

Recorded eyewitness reports by survivors are few; the one that follows by John Kinzie was recorded near-verbatim by [see] Capt. David Bates Douglas in 1820.

On the [9] *Aug. 1812 an express a Potawatomie Indian* [Winnemac] *came there with orders to Capt. Hill* [Heald] *comdg., to evacuate the Fort if possible—the messenger expressed his doubts of the practicability of doing so unless the troups moved off immediately say the next morning & that by a rout as the Wabash Potawatamies were disaffected particulary those of Magoquous Villages and would undoubtedly stop them—✧ Capt. Hill however somewhat distrustful of the Indian & expecting Capt Wells with some Miamies did not adopt the advice—the Indian then pressed him through me & I also joined in it to go the following day—which he also declined & he was then told he might stay as long as he pleased & with this his adviser left him—by this time the Potawatomies began to come in. The idea of evacuation was known generally & talked of; they professed friendship & gave assurances that they would conduct the troups safely thro but it was always observed that they all came in hostile array. In the course of the Councils which were* held about this time Capt. Hill showed the Indians the Arms, Ammunition goods &c. which were to be given to them for their safe conduct. Things were in this state when Capt. Wells arrived with 27 Miamies about the time that Capt. Hill had determined upon evacuating—Capt. W & self advised against it as we had in the fort a sufficiency of Arms Ammunition &c to have sustained the attacks of the Indians even tho' assisted by the British. It was however determined [that the fort be abandoned]—I then advised & Capt W. agreed with me that the ammunition & liquor ought to be destroyed as the latter would only inflame them & the former would undoubtedly be used in acts of hostility against our people if not against ourselves—to this there was no other objection than Capt. H. having already shown it to them—but he acknowledged the propriety of the step & freely agreed to adopt any measure I might suggest for justifying him in sight of the Indians for taking it. Strategem was accordingly resorted to & the business of destruction was immediately commenced. It was intended to throw the powder in the river but that was prevented by an accident. As I passed out of the Fort at Dusk to wash at the River two Indians seized hold of me but perceiving who I was they desisted from using violence—their curiosity had been excited by the hammering and bustle in the fort & they desired to know what was going on. I told them we had been opening barrels of pork & flour & were preparing to march next day—this satisfied them for the present but I perceived they were on the alert & it would be unsafe to attempt throwing the powder in the River, so it was thrown in the well. On the morrow we marched by the rout of the beach. When we reached the Sand Hillocks beyond those pines (about two miles) along shore, [From this and similar evidence it is clear that Kinzie told his story by daylight and was pointing out distinctive landmarks.] Capt. Wells who was behind came round in front & spoke to me observing that we were surrounded. This I had also perceived having seen the Indian Rifles passing round our right as if forming a line to hem us in. He asked what was

best to be done. I said we must make the best defence we were able & this was agreed to—the men were faced towards the land and advanced in line up the bank. As they rose the Indians fired their first volley several fell but the soldiers still preserved their order & and pressed upon the Indians into the prairie—in the course of the battle several desperate encounters took place. Ensign Rowman [Ronan] fought until struck down the 3d time rising each time until he received the fatal blow of a tomahawk which felled him to rise no more. ✧ A sergeant [Otho Hays] pressed upon a strong Indian [Naunongee] with his bayonet & wounded him in the breast—he endeavoring to parry & to strike with his tomahawk, the Sergt did not kill him but recovered & passed his bayonet thro his body & in this situation he still cut down his antagonist with his Tomahawk. Capt. Wells and Dr. Van Voorhees [Voorhis] were killed as also 28 out of the 56 men & Capt. Hill badly wounded when the remainder cut their way into the prairie—mean time others [Indians] had passed round the beach & got among the baggage where the women & children were & here was perpetuated one of the most shocking scenes of Butchery perhaps ever witnessed—their shrieks of distress, their piteous appeals to father mother Brothers & Husbands for help & and their prayers for mercy were there unheard & disavailing—the Tomahawk & knife performed their work without distinctions of age or condition. This scene of Havoc lasted for near ten minutes. In the early part of the affray I had charge of Mrs. K who was in my boat—Mrs. Hill [Heald] & my daughter [Mrs. Helm] who were near me. Mrs. H. however in her terror soon left me & fled to her Uncle Capt. Wells by whose side she received several shot wounds. When the Indians got round to the Baggage some scuffling took place among some of them which I afterwards learned was about killing me. An order however was given out among the Indians that they should neither hurt me or my family. Capt Wells hearing this requested his neice to return to me but she still clung to him. ✧ A Potawatamie [Black Partridge] now came forward & after taking my gun

offered to take us to a place of safety but my daughter thinking his intentions hostile ran at first into the Lake but soon returned. I motioned to him to bring Mrs. Hill to us which he did & then conducted us up to that turn of the river above the Fort ✧ The Potawatamies by this time sent a messenger [Pierre Le Claire] to Capt. Hill demanding his surrender—upon what terms asked Capt. Hill. the messenger did not know but being a man whom I had brought up & friendly to the Amerns. he advised the Captain not to surrender until they should propose some terms—the Captain accordingly refused to surrender unless they would give pledge for the lives of the prisoners—this they agreed to with the exception of those who were mortally wounded & the remaining 28 men some of them badly wounded were surrendered accordingly—one man [Thomas Burns] whose wounds appeared mortal was Tomahawked by a squaw. Three were killed by a volley fired among a group in consequence of one of them having drawn a knife as if to defend himself mistaking their intentions when the Indians fired their pieces after the fight in honor of the dead. Several others were dispatched under various pretenses during the afternoon & evening so that probably not more than ten or 12 ultimately escaped the Massacre. After all was over the Indians counciled among themselves about the disposal of the prisoners. I was allowed with my family & Mrs. H. to return to my house. The remaining soldiers were distributed among the different chiefs & there only remained Capt. H. to be disposed of—a subject which caused them some discussion. They were inclined to take his life & indeed were emulous among themselves of dispatching him as being the Chief on our side. They complained moreover in a council of his having deceived them by destroying the Arms &c which he [had] shown to be delivered out to them—& they had heard that he had poisoned the flour. I answered them in his behalf by showing an order for this destruction & explained to them the obligations of our officers to obey the order of a superior—which they conceived of. I denied the adulteration of the flour & offered to eat it—indeed

156

it wanted but little to convince them that the bearer of this was a great liar. They acknowledged having deceived us & asked Capt. H. if he thought the prest. of the U.S. would forgive them. It was difficult to say—they knew from past events the pacific disposition of the prest. but if they wished to ask forgiveness I would exchange hostages, take some of their principal men & go with them for that purpose—they asked Capt. H. his opinion of the probable continuance & result of our war to which he gave a suitable reply. In this state things remained with much anxiety for him on our part when a well disposed Indian advised me to get him away or he would be killed. I then got a faithful fellow [Chandonnai] to take Mrs & Capt Hill to St. Joseph in his canoe which he did though pursued 15 miles by some of them—& [Alexander] Robinson the present interpreter took them thence to Mackinaw. ❖ Some days after 10 or 12 indians painted black & armed came across the river to my house & anticipating their demand I warned Mrs. K against the event & enjoined her to meet it with courage. They came & declared their intentions of taking satisfaction of me for Hills escape. 5 Potawatie. quieted finally with presents. I was allowed to remove to the little Colic. and went. The treatment of the dead was characteristic—Capt. W. & Dr. V.V. Name of the chief who comanded Black B[ird]. Reason of his kindness to me—his son [uncertain meaning]. Capt. Wells rec'd information the night before we marched that we should be attacked but we had then given everything away and could not retract. The Chiefs after we determined to evacuate used to eat with us every day as we had a superabundance of provision to make away with. Nuscotnoning [Nescotnemeg] was the author of the massacre. The Black Bird comanded—the Miamies knowing of the attack stayed behind & took no part—they rode past in the beginning of the foray & one a half Potawatomie made a short speech—to this effect—Potawatomie I am much astonished at your conduct—You have been treacherous with these people. You promised to conduct them safely thro. You have deceived them and are about to murder them in cold blood—let me advise you to beware—you know not what evil the dead shall bring upon you—you may by and by hear your wives & children cry & you will not be able to assist them. Potawatomie beware—so saying he rode on.

Other eyewitness reports include those by Captain Heald, Lieutenant Helm, Sgt. W. Griffith, Cpl. W.K. Jordan, and Pvt. James Corbin. An excellent report was given in a Sept. 7, 1812, letter by Indian Agent Thomas Forsyth (who arrived at Fort Dearborn the day after the massacre), written to Governor Benjamin Howard of Louisiana [Missouri] Territory and preserved in the Illinois Territorial Papers. Also see Chicago massacre tree. [36, 109, 280, 327, 407, 411, 465, 558, 561, 564, 619]

Fort Dearborn militia   a group of 15 male civilian residents who were organized into a company by Captain Heald during the crisis period between the Indian murders on Leigh's farm on April 6, 1812, and the Fort Dearborn massacre. Thomas Burns, former member of the fort's garrison, was made sergeant and given command. Three brothers (Alexis, Claude, and LaFortune LaFramboise) soon deserted, taking with them 12 of the fort's horses. The other 12 were killed in the massacre on Aug. 15, 1812. According to Eckert, their names were Thomas Burns; Charles Lee, Sr.; Charles Lee, Jr.; James Cooper; William Russell; Samuel Clark; Louis Pettell; Michael Pettell; —Henry, a "seventy year old former revolutionary soldier" and two unidentified French settlers. Unfortunately, many of the names in Eckert's writing are erroneous, especially those of the Leigh family: Charles Lee was actually [see] James Leigh. [226]

Fort Dearborn physicians   of the first fort: William Smith, 1803 until 1808; John Cooper, 1808 until 1811; and Isaac VanVoorhis, 1811 to 1812 (killed at the massacre). Of the second fort: John Gale, 1816; J. Ponte Coulant McMahon, 1818; William S. Madison, 1820; Thomas P. Hall, 1821; Clement A. Finley, 1828; Elijah D. Harmon, 1830; Samuel Grandin Johnston Decamp, 1832; Abraham H. Edwards, 1832; Erastus Winslow, 1832; Phillip Maxwell, 1833; and George F. Turner, 1833.

Fort Dearborn reservation   in 1824, at a time when the fort was not garrisoned, Alexander Wolcott, Indian agent at Fort Dearborn, suggested to J.C. Calhoun, secretary of war, that the land on which the fort stood—bordered by the lakeshore, Madison Street, State Street, and the main river—be declared a military reservation; the secretary agreed and made the necessary arrangements. For details, see the two following letters—later published in the *Chicago Tribune* of Feb. 2, 1884—one by Dr. Wolcott, the other by George Graham of the U.S. General Land Office. In April 1839, the major portion of the reservation was released by the secretary of war, J.R. Poinsett, and became the Fort Dearborn Addition to Chicago; a war office agent, Matthew Birchard, surveyed the addition, laying in lots and streets and filing the map with Cook County; all lots were sold except the portion where the lighthouse stood. [12, 13]

Fort Dearborn, Sept. 2, 1824. – The Hon. J.C. Calhoun, Secretary of War – SIR: I have the honor to suggest to your consideration the propriety of making a reservation of this post and the fraction on which it is situated for use of this agency. It is very conveniente for that purpose, as the quarters afford sufficient accomodations for all the persons in the employ of the agency, and the storehouses are safe and commodious places for the provisions and other property that may be in charge of the agent. The buildings and other property, by being in possession of a public officer, will be preserved for public use, should it ever again be necessary to occupy them again with a military force. ❖ As to the size of the fraction I am not certain, but I think it contains about sixty acres. A considerably greater tract than that is under fence, but that would be abundantly sufficient for the use of the agency, and contains all the buildings attached to the fort – such as a mill, barn, stable, &c. – which it would be desirable to preserve. I have the honor to be

Alexander Wolcott, Indian Agent.

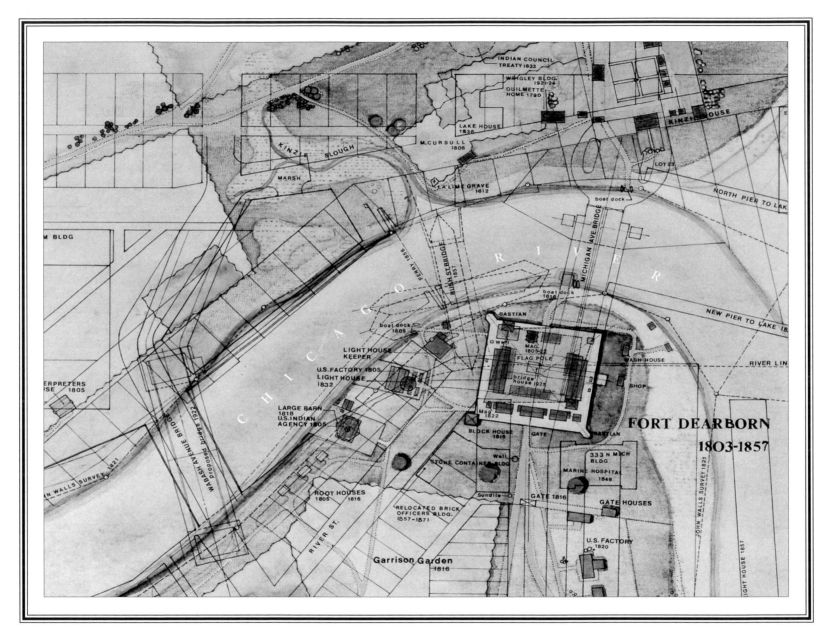

EXCERPT OF AN ARCHITECTURAL AERIAL STUDY OF CHICAGO 1812-1816 WITH FORTS DEARBORN I AND II OVERLAPPED
by Donald Schlickan

158

General Land-Office, Oct. 21, 1824. – The Hon. J.C. Calhoun, Secretary of War – Sir: In compliance with your request, I have directed that the Fractional Section 10, Township 39 North, Range 14 East, containing 57.50 acres, and within which Fort Dearborn is situated, should be reserved from sale for military purposes.

I am, &c., George Graham.

Fort de Buade   see Fort Michilimackinac.

Fort de Chartres   wooden stockade built on the banks of the Mississippi River N of Kaskaskia in 1720 by Pierre Dugué, sieur de Boisbriant, French commandant of Illinois country; planned for the protection of Kaskaskia and Cahokia; was the seat of civil and military law; Boisbriant commanded the fort until 1725, when he became acting governor of Louisiana, and de Liette replaced him; rebuilt in 1727 and 1732; reconstructed with stone in 1753; conceded to England in 1763 with the Treaty of Paris but maintained by the French until Oct. 10, 1675, when the British took possession, renaming it Fort Cavendish (though the original name is remembered); was damaged by a Mississippi flood in 1772 and thereafter abandoned. [12, 665]

Fort Defiance   built in 1793 by General Wayne at the junction of the Maumee and Auglaize Rivers (Ohio) during his successful campaign against the midwestern Indian tribes, which ended in the victory at Fallen Timbers.

Fort des Miamis   see *Fort Miami*.

Fort Edwards   built in September 1816 on the east bank of the Mississippi River opposite the mouth of the Des Moines River as security against the Potawatomi; irregularly garrisoned, abandoned in July 1824.

Fort Edward Augustus   see Fort Howard.

Fort Frontenac   built at the mouth of the Great Cataruqui River on Lake Ontario at [now] Kingston, Ontario, by Frontenac and La Salle in 1673 to safeguard settlement and provide a base for westward exploration. [12]

Fort Harrison   construction by U.S. troops began on Oct. 5, 1811, on the east bank of the Wabash River [two miles from the center of Terre Haute, IN]; was completed on Oct. 28, 1811.

Fort at Hickory Creek   early in 1683, La Salle built a fort on Hickory Creek, three miles above its mouth [New Lenox, IL], c.30 leagues from Starved Rock. [649]

Fort Howard   established at Green Bay at the mouth of the Fox River, in the summer of 1816, in conjunction with Fort Crawford at Prairie du Chien and the rebuilding of Fort Dearborn, to achieve military control over the area W of Lake Michigan. When the members of the Lewis Cass expedition visited the fort in August 1820, they observed a four-sided picketed enclosure with four towers, housing a garrison of 600-700 men, and a settlement of French-Indian inhabitants, including about 60 households scattered for three or four miles along the river; the garrison was withdrawn in 1841, regarrisoned after the Mexican War, and abandoned in 1852. Green Bay had been the site of a French post in 1684, which was rebuilt in 1717, and again occupied from 1745 to 1761 (La Baye); a British garrison was maintained here from 1761 to 1815 (Fort Edward Augustus).

Fort Holmes   fortification at the highest elevation of Michilimackinac Island, built by the British while they held the island from 1812 to 1814, but named by the Americans following reoccupation; Maj. Andrew H. Holmes of Virginia was slain in the battle of Mackinac Island, Aug. 4, 1814.

Fort Illinois   see *Fort St. Joseph de Pimiteoui*.

Fort Johnson   see Fort Ottawa.

Fort Mackinac   see Fort Michilimackinac.

Fort Malden   established by the British in 1796 (following transfer of Detroit to American rule) on the east bank of the Detroit River mouth on Lake Erie, at Amherstburg; John Kinzie of Chicago was imprisoned there for treason during part of the 1812 war. For several decades, the fort was an important British power center in the Northwest; between 1796 and 1814 Indian chiefs throughout the Northwest would annually assemble at Fort Malden, under Gen. Henry A. Proctor, to receive gifts and annuities, an attempt by the British to perpetuate their influence, though the United States had taken possession of the land. Juliette A. Kinzie contributes some understanding in *Wau-Bun* [1856]:

The Independence achieved by the United States [1783] did not alter the policy of the natives, nor did our Government succeed in winning or purchasing their friendship. Great Britain, it is true, bid high to retain them. Every year the leading men of the Chippewas, Ottawas, Pottawattomies, Menomonees Winnebagoes, Sauks and Foxes, and even still more remote tribes, journeyed from their distant homes to Fort Malden in Upper Canada, to receive their annual amounts of presents from the Great Father across the water.

The following letter from Joseph Chew to Thomas Aston Coffin exemplifies the efforts made by the British to cultivate the friendship of the Indians in U.S. territory after 1783:

Montreal 16th May 1796.

Dear Sir – A few days ago I received a Message from Thomas a famous War Chief of the Follesavoine Nation of Indians at La Ba on the Mississippi & requesting to have a Medal with his Majesty's Arms sent to him, and being well informt of His Friendship for the English & the Influence he has with his nation, and not having time to make the requisition, I send the Medal by a Gentleman who left this place today for La Ba, and now enclose a requisition and a copy of the Message to be delivered with the Medal which I hope His Lordship may not disapprove of.

Am Dr Sir Your most obedt. humble Servant
Joseph Chew.

American authorities were anxious to neutralize such British solicitations with tokens of their own, often seeking to replace British medals that had already been gratefully accepted by the Indians.

U.S. Indian Agent John Boyer reports on the effort to Governor Cass at Detroit:

Green Bay Agency [Oct. 1, 1816]

Sir – I have seen most of the principal chiefs residing in this quarter. They all appear to be friendly disposed, and have generally expressed themselves well pleased with the establishments at this place. The Winnebagoes were opposed to the building of a Fort, when they first visited me, but after I held two or three talks with their Chiefs, they left me apparently well satisfied. I have had some trouble, from the want of Medals, Armbands, and small flags, believing these necessary items would be here in a short time, I demanded from the Chiefs the medals &c. they had received from the British, promising to replace them with those of the United States, most of the Chiefs who have visited me since I made the demand, have delivered up their Medals &c. they had received, not having any to give in return, I considered myself bound to pay them well for what they gave up, and promised to replace them as soon as possible. ✧ The whole of the goods intended for this Agency has gone to Chicago, and I have only received a few articles marked for that Agency, without invoice or letter accompanying the packages. I have made this statement to the Secretary of War, and have requested him to forward on Medals &c. in the Spring.

Jno. Boyer, Ind. Agent.   [109, 406]

Fort Miami (1679)   also *Fort Miamis, Fort des Miamis*; built in November 1679 by La Salle and his men at the mouth of the *Rivière de Miamis* [in Michigan, called St. Joseph's River after c.1703]; in 1680, the fort was destroyed by mutinous expedition members. *Fort Miami* is not to be confused with a second and later fort on the St. Joseph's River, called Fort St. Joseph, and located 60 miles upstream. Another source of confusion resulted from a map error which placed a nonexistent *Fort Miamis* at Chicago [see ✱ Henry Popple's *A Map of the British Empire in North America*, 1733; eds.]. Father Hennepin helped in the construction of *Fort Miamis* and his later report leaves no doubt as to the exact location: "Just at the mouth of the river Miamis there was an eminence with a kind of platform naturally fortified. It was pretty high and steep, of a triangular form ... we felled the trees that were on top of the hill, and ... we began to build a redoubt of eighty feet long and forty feet broad."

Fort Miami (c.1712)   see Fort Wayne, Indiana.

Fort Miami (c.1750)   see Fort Wayne, Indiana.

Fort Miami (1794)   constructed in the spring of 1794 by the British on the Maumee River, a few miles above [Toledo]; the fort was meant to counter General Wayne's campaign against the midwestern Indians but failed to do so; occupied by American troops in July 1796; abandoned in 1797.

Fort Michilimackinac   there were three forts at different times, as detailed below; the third fort was called Fort Mackinac. As military outposts, they controlled the traffic on three lakes and as trade centers, the rich fur harvests of Lake Superior and the upper Mississippi valley. The traders usually lived within the walls of the forts: (1) built in 1672 by French soldiers under the command of Louis de Buade, count de Frontenac, and named *Fort De Buade* to protect a small settlement of fur traders called Michilimackinac, and the *Mission de Saint-Ignace* of Fathers Dablon and Marquette [St. Ignace, WI]; in 1694 Cadillac became commandant at *Fort de Buade*; in 1701 the fort was abandoned, as was the mission four years later; (2) built by French soldiers in 1715 on the southern shore of the strait of Mackinac at the western edge [Mackinaw City]; again, the associated settlement was called Michilimackinac; the fort remained under French rule until 1760, under the British until 1780, when moved to Mackinac Island; (3) under the last commandant of the second fort, Maj. Patrick Sinclair, a new fort was constructed on the high, strategic stone bluff on the SE end of Mackinac Island in 1780 for increased protection against attack by Col. George Rogers Clark; French and British traders and Indians accompanied Sinclair's troops, and the old fort was abandoned; under the protection of the new fort, Mackinac Island evolved as the great fur trading center of the upper lake's region, on which all Chicago traders depended. The island and the fort remained British until 1796, American until 1812 (July 19), British again until 1815, and American again until it was abandoned in September 1894; in 1959 the fort was reconstructed and is now a historical monument. [12, 530, 531]

Fort Niagara   first built as *Fort Conti* by La Salle with Tonti and Hennepin in 1679 at the mouth of the Niagara River on Lake Ontario; the ship *Le Griffon* was constructed here for western reconnaissance and fur transport; was destroyed by Indians c.1682, replaced in 1687 by the short-lived *Fort Denonville* under orders of Governor Jacques René de Brisay, marquis de Denonville, of New France, and destroyed again in 1688. The first fort at this location with the name *Fort Niagara* was built from 1725 to 1727, often called the House of Peace [now known as the French Castle, the oldest masonry structure W of the Hudson River and E of the Mississippi]; was occupied by the British in July 1759, marking the end of French dominance on the lakes; surrendered to the Americans in August 1796.

Fort Ottawa   erected in the spring of 1832 during the Black Hawk War on the south bank of the Illinois River, at its junction with the Fox River; later known as Fort Johnson.

Fort Ouiatenon   originally a small, prosperous French trading post on the west bank of the Wabash River [near LaFayette, IN] in 1717, an important settlement between Quebec and New Orleans and the center of French relations with the Wea Indians, a group related to the Miami; in 1763 taken over by the British; destroyed in 1791 by Gen. Charles Scott to protect NW territorial communities from British-allied Indians.

Fort Payne   also Paine; a trading post in Naperville, built of hewn logs by the Napier brothers in

Fort Michillimackinac as sketched by Count Francis Castelnau when he visited in 1838. [115]

1831; fortified with a stockade to protect settlers at the onset of the Black Hawk War by a company of men from Joliet under Capt. Morgan L. Payne; never saw battle. [314a]

Fort Peoria see *Fort St. Louis de Pimiteoui.*

Fort Petite misnomer for [see] *Petit Fort.*

Fort Pimiteoui see *Fort St. Louis de Pimiteoui.*

Fort Pontchartrain du Détroit French post completed by Antoine de la Mothe Cadillac on July 24, 1701; later became Detroit.

Fort Recovery built by General Wayne in 1793 on the Ohio side of the Indiana-Ohio border, Mercer Co., near the headwaters of the Wabash River, and near the Indiana Territory site of General St. Clair's 1791 defeat by the Indians.

Fort St. Clair also Fort Sinclair; built as a fortified settlement in 1764 by the British Lt. Gov. [see] Patrick Sinclair within the pine woods at the mouth of the Pine River, a tributary to the St. Clair River, about 30 miles N of Detroit; adjacent land eventually became St. Clair's private estate, the Pinery, where the later Chicago settler Jean Baptiste Point de Sable was taken to manage the estate for Sinclair from 1880-1884, prior to settling at Chicago. The Pinery [Chinguagon in Ojibwa] provided timbers and lumber for the Fort at Detroit.

Fort St. Francis see Fort Howard.

Fort St. Joseph located 60 miles upstream from the earlier short-lived *Fort Miamis*; built by La Salle in 1679 at the mouth of the St. Joseph's River; Fort St. Joseph was preceded by a mission probably established by Father Allouez in 1689, the exact date still disputed among historians. In 1691, Count Frontenac sent Sieur de Courtemanche to establish a fort, and he remained as commandant for several years. In 1696, the fort was abandoned by order of the king, but was reoccupied some time prior to 1720 and continuously occupied until 1763, when its occupants were killed during the Pontiac rebellion. Charlevoix described the approach to the fort in a letter dated 1721; it was located in what is now Portage Township on the E side of the river, a short distance downriver from the present town of South Bend, IN, near the border with Michigan. The fort guarded the much-used portage between the St. Joseph's River and the headwaters of the Kankakee. The portage began on the west bank, opposite the fort and adjacent to a large Potawatomi village; nearby was one of the three intersections between the river and the Detroit-Chicago Road. The fort was of great strategic value, and together with the community of traders that developed nearby, served also as a central depot for the fur trade. In January 1781, the remnants of the fort were captured by a band of 65 men and some 200 Indians under the leadership of Don Eugenio Pourre and briefly occupied in the name of the king of Spain. The fort was destroyed during the Revolutionary War. Also see entry for St. Joseph, the settlement that developed near the fort.

Fort St. Louis de Pimiteoui also *Fort St. Louis II, Fort Pimitoui*, Fort Peoria, Fort Illinois; built on the east bank of the Illinois River near the narrows at the outlet of lower Lake Peoria during the winter of 1691-92 by Tonti and François Dauphin de La Forêt, who had jointly acquired La Salle's fur trade concession; due to an oversupply of beaver pelts in Europe, the post did not last long. [649]

Fort St. Louis de Rocher also *Fort St. Louis des Illinois*, Rock Fort; built by La Salle and Tonti on the 125-foot-high summit of a cliff on the north bank of the Illinois River [now Starved Rock, La-Salle County], during the winter of 1682-83; the fort attracted French colonists and Indians, a settlement that eventually numbered 20,000 inhabitants; the French populace depended on New France for supplies, increasing usage of the Chicago portage; abandoned as a military post in 1702, but was a trading post until 1718, when burned by Indians.

Fort Shelby   see Fort Crawford.

Fort Snelling   on the Mississippi River [near St. Paul], seven miles below the Falls of St. Anthony; built in 1820 by the Fifth Regiment of the U.S. Infantry under Lt. Col. Henry Leavenworth.

Fort Vincennes   also *Poste du Ouabache*, *Poste Vincennes*, *Post St. Vincent Au Post*; see Vincennes, IN.

Fort Washington   built in 1790 at [Cincinnati]; served as U.S. military headquarters for the failed 1790 campaign against the Indians under General Harmar, and the likewise unsuccessful 1791 campaign under General St. Clair; not until General Wayne broke the Indians' resistance at Fallen Timbers in 1794 was the future of Chicago secured.

Fort Wayne   built 1794 by Gen. Anthony Wayne at the junction of the St. Joseph's and St. Mary's Rivers (Miamitown), a 150-mile distance from Chicago, during the weeks following the Battle of Fallen Timbers; would be the frequent site for annuity payments to Indians. On Aug. 10, 1812, Captain Wells, Indian agent at Fort Wayne, traveled to Fort Dearborn to assist the garrison in its fateful evacuation; two weeks after massacre, on Aug. 28, Fort Wayne came under Indian attack, but the siege was broken when General Harrison brought relief on Sept. 16. For a historic sketch of the community that preceded Fort Wayne, see the next entry.

Fort Wayne, IN   another historic town that, like Chicago, derives its existence from the proximity of an important portage [the Maumee-Wabash portage] between the Great Lakes and Mississippi systems; much used by the Indians and referred to by them as *Kekionga*; Father Allouez mentioned the portage in 1680. A French fort was built there in c.1712, alternately referred to as *Poste Miami*, *Poste des Miamis*, *Fort Miamis*, *Fort Saint Philippe*, or *Les Trois Rivières* [from the junction of the rivers Maumee, St. Mary, and St. Joseph]; the community that grew around the fort was known to the French as *Larabiche*. The fort was partially destroyed by Indians in 1747, but rebuilt nearby before 1750 with the same name, *Fort Miamis*; during "Pontiac's War" it fell to the Indians in 1763, and at the end of the French and Indian War the fort was seized by the British. In 1794 [see] Fort Wayne was built, giving the town its name. Prior to the establishment of regular government mail service, the mail to Chicago often arrived by way of Fort Wayne, where existed a U.S. post office at the time the first Fort Dearborn was built in 1803. [71, 288]

Fort Winnebago   prompted by the Winnebago War of 1827 as a necessary protection for the Fox-Wisconsin River portage valuable to American traders, and built in 1828-29 on the Fox River [now Portage, WI] under Major Twiggs; Lt. Jefferson Davis helped with the interior design and the procurement of logs, and traveled overland to Fort Dearborn in 1829, in search of deserters. John H. Kinzie was stationed there as Indian agent, and his wife Juliette later described life at the fort in her 1856 book *Wau-Bun*. [406]

Forth, Thomas   U.S. Army corporal; enlisted July 6, 1807; enlistment extended due to emergency; was killed during the initial battle of the Fort Dearborn massacre. [226]

Foster, Lt. Amos Bancroft   (c.1802-1832) from New Hampshire; Fifth Infantry; stationed at Fort Dearborn as brevet second lieutenant under Major Fowle from June 20, 1829, to May 20, 1831; voted on July 24, 1830 (see elections); was transferred to Fort Howard in May 1831 where, on Feb. 7, 1832, he was shot and killed by a private soldier named Doyle, whom he had punished for drunkenness; Doyle was convicted and executed. While stationed at Chicago in 1830, Amos purchased from the government six lots in block 3 [see map on page 44] and additional lots in blocks 4, 5, 6, 8, 13, 15, 18, 23, 28, and 32; at his death, the real estate became the property of the Foster family, and subsequently the title went to Dr. John Foster, the brother of Amos. [704]

Foster, Caleb   served as private in Captain Boardman's voluntary county militia and Captain Napier's company during the Black Hawk War of 1832; a uncollected letter is listed in the Jan. 1, 1834, *Chicago Democrat*; resided in the Naper settlement. [12]

Foster, John Herbert, M.D.   (1796-1874) a surgeon from Hillsborough, NH in the Black Hawk War, arrived in 1835 to take over his brother's [see Foster, Amos B.] extensive real estate holdings, becoming one of the largest owners; on Nov. 21 that year, submitted a petition for wharfing privileges, and remained to practice medicine; ✦ Lake Street; on Sept. 21, 1840, married Nancy Smith of Peterborough, NH; in later years, sold part of his late brother's land for the construction of Northwestern University; served on both the Chicago and the Illinois state boards of education; his ▲ grave site is located at Rosehill Cemetery; ➡ Foster Avenue, Foster Drive, and Foster Place, all at 5200 N.

foundry   ★★★ Chicago's 1st was built in the autumn of 1835 on Polk Street, W of the south branch; associated with this enterprise were [see] William Jones, Byram King, William H. Stow, David Bradley, and the firm Jones, King & Company.

Fowle, Capt. & Bvt. Maj. John, Jr.   native of Massachusetts; Fifth Infantry; commandant at Fort Dearborn from Oct. 3, 1828, to Dec. 14, 1830, and again from May 14, 1833, to June 19, 1833; in 1828 he ordered a ditch to be dug parallel to the N side of the fort and through the sand bar that diverted the river to the south; this first attempt to straighten the river and create a harbor was ill-conceived and the ditch rapidly filled with sand; in March 1832, the U.S. Department of Engineers placed him officially in charge of the construction project for the Chicago harbor, but he was transferred before the work began; was a charter member of the First Presbyterian Church; was killed in the explosion of the steamboat *Gazelle* at Cincinnati on April 25, 1838. [12, 704]

Fowler, Albert   born in 1802 at Monterey, MA; arrived in 1832 from New York; in November 1833 moved to Milwaukee, where he became one of the first Anglo-Saxon settlers; moved to Rockford, IL, about 20 years later, where he served as mayor.

Fowler, Elmira   milliner and dressmaker, advertised in the *Chicago Democrat*, Nov. 5, 1834, offering New York fashions and instruction for young ladies; located on Dearborn Street, "opposite new bridge."

Fowler, Hiram   listed in the July 30, 1834, *Chicago Democrat* as a candidate for county commissioner, then living at Naper's Settlement.

fox   two different species still occur in the locale, abundant when European settlement began; both range throughout the state: the red fox, *Vulpes vulpes*, inhabits the open grassland and the shrubby edge of woods, and the grey fox, *Urocyon cinereoargenteus*, prefers the woods and climbs trees; also see *waukesha*, the Potawatomi word for fox. Fox hunts were held by the garrison of Fort Dearborn along the sand bar that blocked the Chicago River entrance in the 1820s; as part of testimony given in 1856, and regarding the sand bar, G.S. Hubbard recalled the following: [341]

From the piazza of the Kinzie house we could look directly down the river about half way to the mouth, where the view was obstructed by a bank. The mouth was about where Madison street now is. The mouth

was a shifty one; it gradually went farther south. At one time it went down as far as where the Illinois Central roadhouse now is, about a mile and a half from the fort. [Independent testimony by Jacob Miller: "... river was about 200 feet below Madison street. I know I lived right there in 1834"; *eds.*] *It was then so small that we could hardly get our boats through. I should say that the mouth at Madison was the permanent mouth. We used to hunt foxes on the bar. The foxes were caught in the woods and fed and got in condition at the fort. On festival days they were taken to the upper end of the sand bar and loosed, when the dogs were put on them and they were chased in the sand. There was land enough to make the sport entertaining. The bar was about 200 feet wide, but ran off to a mere spit at the end.*

Fox Indians   also Mesquakie; an Algonkin tribe, originally living near the headwaters of the St. Croix River in Wisconsin; initially friendly trading partners (referred to as *Renards*) of the French, they allied with the Iroquois against the French, closing the Wisconsin-Fox River portage and, around 1700, the Chicago portage to nearly all traffic. This hampered French trade and settlement growth in the Illinois River valley and along the Mississippi for the next 75 years; Jesuit missions, including the *Mission de l'Ange Gardien de Chicagou*, were closed by royal order. Although with a concerted effort the French trapped and destroyed the greater part of the Fox nation in 1730 at Marameck Hill [about two miles S of the present village of Plano, IL], they never succeeded in permanently reestablishing control of the Chicago portage or of the fur trade in the Northwest, which was to be dominated by the English instead. In 1804, by the Treaty of St. Louis, the surviving Fox conveyed to the United States all their land in Illinois. [631, 699]

Fox River of Illinois   Indian names: Pishtaka, Pistikoui; its headwaters are in southeastern Wisconsin and the water flows generally in a southern direction to its junction with the Illinois River at Ottawa; those traveling from Fort Winnebago to

Chicago crossed the river, as did John H. Kinzie and his wife in 1831.

Fox River of Wisconsin   about 175 miles long, flowing generally in a northeasterly direction through Lake Winnebago and several smaller lakes, reaching the southern end of Green Bay; within 1 1/2 miles of the Wisconsin River near its origin (Swan Lake), enabling the historically important portage across the continental divide; see Fox-Wisconsin portage; another portage existed between the upper Root (Racine) and the Fox Rivers, used by the St. Cosme party in 1699.

Fox-Wisconsin portage   also see portages; this major Great Lakes/Mississippi portage was used extensively by traders before and after the discovery of the Chicago, Calumet, and St. Joseph portage routes; it is 1 1/2 miles in length. Here Jolliet and Father Marquette crossed in June 1673 to reach the Mississippi River; the portage remained in use longer than its southern counterparts; a remaining 1835 structure in Portage, WI has been adapted as a portage museum.

frame house   all structures built in Chicago prior to 1828 were log cabins; thereafter, frame houses were favored, built with many heavy squared timbers and diagonal supports, mortised, tenoned, and pinned together with oaken dowels; nails were not yet available. The method was costly in terms of both time and material; ★★★ **Chicago's 1st** frame house was owned by [see] Billy Caldwell, the second and third were built for Robert A. Kinzie and Newberry & Dole, respectively; in the early 1830s the frame house was replaced by the [see] balloon frame.

Franchere, Louis   also Francheres; early member of the Catholic congregation; in April 1833, his name was on the petition by Chicago citizens to Bishop Rosati of St. Louis, asking that a priest be assigned to them.

Francis   sloop; called at Chicago on July 23, 1835, under Captain Duchane, coming from Detroit.

François —   surname unknown; French-Potawatomi part-time employee of John Kinzie and freelance interpreter; was present at the Fort Dearborn massacre and survived. [226]

Franklin & Jenkins an auction house in Broad Street, New York City; a ✸ "Map of Lots at Chicago for Sale by Franklin & Jenkins on Friday, 8th May, 1835, at 12 O'clock at the Merchants Exchange," actually a plot of the Russell & Mather Addition which Gurdon Hubbard, then in New York, drew from memory and parcelled into lots, was printed by Miller and Co. [within the Chicago Historical Society Library]; all available lots were sold that day for $80,000 and partners Russell, Mather, and Hubbard made a profit of $77,500 on those 40 acres. [164, 705]

Franklin, Benjamin (1706-1790) scientist, author, publisher, diplomat, and a leading personality during the American Revolution; James Thompson, canal surveyor in 1830, named one of the earliest streets after him; ➡ Franklin Street (300 W).

Franquelin, Jean-Baptiste Louis (1653-c.1725) engineer, hydrographer, and cartographer in the services of Louis XIV, residing in Quebec c.1670; on his 1684 ✸ map of the Great Lakes region [*Carte de la Louisiane ou de Voyages du Sr. de la Salle &c.* ...], the Chicago River is well depicted with its two branches, and its mouth is named Cheagoumeman; a small stream originating near the lakeshore S of the Chicago site and entering the Des Plaines River from the east is named R. Checagou. On his 1686 ✸ map, *Amerique Septentrion,* a settlement on the south branch of the present Chicago River is named Chicagou. [192, 681, 682]

Franzen, Hermann B.H. German immigrant arrived in November 1835 with three adult sons (his wife, Adelheid, had died in transit); in 1837 the family moved to Duncklee's Grove. [342]

Franzen, Johann Heinrich eldest son of Hermann B.H. Franzen; the family had come in 1835, from Schale, near Osnabruc; later owned a linseed oil mill at [Bensonville], a remaining wall of which was publicly dedicated to him as an historical ▲

monument in 1934. [342]

Freeman, Rev. Allen B. (1807-1834) arrived with his wife Hannah (née Clarke) from Vermont on Aug. 16, 1833; sent at the request of Dr. J.T. Temple by the American Baptist Home Mission Society as "missionary for Northern Illinois," and organized the First Baptist Church on Oct. 19; early in December 1834, while returning from Long Grove, his horse became ill, and he stayed with the animal two days until its death, then walked the remaining 18 miles to town, became ill from exposure, and died of typhoid fever on Dec. 15; funeral services were held in the First Presbyterian Church, Rev. J. Porter delivering the sermon; Hannah gave birth to a son, called Allen after his father, a short time after her husband's death, but the infant soon died; Freeman was succeeded in office by Rev. Isaac T. Hinton; Hannah remarried Rev. Alvin Bailey on Nov. 17, 1836. [12]

Freeman, Ford on the list of subscribers to the *Chicago Democrat* in November 1833.

Freeman, Mrs. Harriet her death at age 28 is noted in the June 11, 1834, *Chicago Democrat.*

Freeman, Robert born c.1808; arrived in 1833 from Pennsylvania and later moved to Naperville; married to Adaline, daughter of Capt. H. Boardman; ✦ carpenter, Clark Street, corner of Monroe; still living at Naperville in 1885. [12, 351]

French and Indian War 1754-1763; this war represented the American phase of a worldwide nine-year struggle between France and England for supremacy in North America, won decisively by England (the war overlapped, but was not identical to the European Seven Years' War; both wars ended with different peace treaties); began over the specific issue of conflicting trading territories in the upper Ohio River valley; most Indians fought on the side of the French, but were reconciled with the British after the French defeat; the peace treaty signed in Paris on Feb. 10, 1763, ended French dominance in North America, but the land around the southern end of Lake Michigan, especially near

Chicago and the St. Joseph River, remained a French stronghold until 1780; Spain, a secondary player in this war, relinquished Florida but received Louisiana, including New Orleans. Spain recovered Florida with the Treaty of Paris in 1783 and held it until 1818. [152, 526]

French, Leander a remaining letter listed in the *Chicago Democrat* on Jan. 21, 1835, may identify [see] Asahel Pierce's partner in the smithy Pierce & French.

French train colloquial expression for a boxy wooden sleigh, 6 by 3 feet, and drawn by a two-horse tandem, used by early settlers in the Midwest.

freshet a common word in the early settlement for a sudden overflowing of a stream because of melting snow or heavy rains upstream; spring freshets in particular facilitated river traffic, predominate at the time, by making portaging easier and shorter, for example by often completely eliminating the need to portage from the Chicago River to the Des Plaines.

Friend, Aaron, Charles, and John militia volunteers in the Black Hawk War at Chicago; all enrolled in Captain Seission's company on July 23, 1832; by 1857, both Aaron and Charles were dead, John was in California. [714]

Frink & Walker stagecoach transportation company that late in 1834 bought out the stagecoach line between Chicago and Ottawa from Winter, Mills & Co., which in turn had bought out Dr. John T. Temple in February 1834; Temple had pioneered the line earlier. In 1834, Frink & Walker's Chicago terminal was at the intersection of Dearborn and Lake streets, one of the town's busiest places. The owners soon added a line to St. Charles, Elgin, and Galena, which left Chicago via Lake Street—earlier called Old Chicago Road or Elgin Road. The stage was heavy, of wood, and held 10 passengers, nine inside and one with the driver; the middle seats inside were least desirable, offering no backrest. In the September 1835 *Chicago*

FRINK & WALKER'S STAGE OFFICE.   [12]

Democrat the company announced that "[t]he coaches from Chicago to St. Louis in future will run through in five days by day light without any detention on the road. From Chicago to Peoria in two days, and from Peoria to St. Louis in three days." In 1839, the business was still run by Martin O. Walker, though then concerned with mail delivery, at the same address as Frink, Bingham & Co. Ellen Bigelow, [see separate entry] a newly arrived immigrant from Massachusetts, took the stage coach from Chicago to Ottawa in late May 1835, a 25-hour ride, and in a letter described the experience as follow:

We left Chicago in the stage for Ottawa, a route of 80 miles across the prairies, and such travelling never did we behold before. The low prairie about Chicago was entirely flooded with water, and the creeks were swollen to rivers. Nothing in the shape of a bridge greeted our eyes. Streams, large and small, were all to be forded even at the risk of sticking fast in the middle of them. In the course of [our trip] we were completely mired six times. ... In the middle of a deep slough, or swole, as they call them, you must fancy the coach buried in mud and water above the wheels. The gentlemen all out with coats off, pantaloons and shirt sleeves rolled up and standing in water about three feet deep, ready to carry the ladies across upon their backs, or in any other way most agreeable to the parties. That being done, they set their shoulders to the wheels of the carriage, the horses kicking and plunging to extricate themselves from the mire, and the driver lashing them right and left, screaming, yelling, and swearing in true stagedriver style. You can imagine what delightful business it must have been to pack

ourselves back again, covered as we all were with mud, and nine crowded into a carriage designed only for six, and containing but two seats, as an instance of the inefficiency which characterizes the people of Illinois." [55a]

Frink, John born in Ashford, CT in 1797; stage and steamboat line operator and entrepreneur; late in 1834, with Martin O. Walker took over from Winters, Mills & Co. the Chicago-Ottawa stagecoach line that had been pioneered by Dr. Temple; also operated the steamboat line from Ottawa to St. Louis; did not move to Chicago until 1836; ✦ Frink & [C.K.] Bingham, stage office, 123 Lake St.; his son John, Jr., was then a clerk with [also see] Frink & Walker in 1839, at the same address [Harvey Frink, possibly another son, is listed in 1839 as a clerk at the post office]; John's wife, Martha, died in 1843. [12]

Frique, Peter voted on July 24, Aug. 2, and Nov. 25, 1830 (see elections). [12]

Frog Creek a small spring-fed tributary to the main branch of the Chicago River before 1835 [originated in center of the Loop area]; described in 1856 from memory by Juliette A. Kinzie:

... as low wet prairie, scarcely affording good walking in the driest of summer weather, while at other seasons it was absolutely impassable. ... a muddy streamlet, or as it is called in the west, a slew, or slough, after winding around from the present site of the Tremont House, entered the river at the foot of what is now State Street. At the mouth of Frog Creek Russell Heacock had a log cabin in 1827 before moving to the Chicago River south branch. At least 2 similar small creeks emptied into the main stem from the north side. An 1831 traveler remarked: "I passed over the ground from the Fort to the Point [Wolf Point], on horseback, and was up to my stirrups in water the whole distance; I would not have given sixpence an acre for the whole of it." The locals knew better, and generally canoed that distance on the river; in 1883 John Bates recalled: "At that time [1833] a slough emptied into the river, at what is

now the foot of State Street, and was a sort of ba-yeau of dead water through which scows could be run up as far as Randolph Street, near the corner of Dearborn." [13]

Frontenac, Louis de Buade, comte de   (1620-1698) governor of New France from 1672 to 1682 and again from 1689 to 1698; an architect of French expansion in North America under Louis XIV; led French forces against the Iroquois and the English colonies. As one of his first acts, in 1672 he occupied Mackinac where he established *Fort de Buade*; in 1673 founded *Fort Frontenac*, a fur trading post on Lake Ontario; arranged for Jolliet's and Father Marquette's and for La Salle's explorations of the Mississippi; ▲ ➡ Frontenac Avenue (550 W). [193, 730]

Fuller, Benjamin   came from New York to Chicago by horse in 1834, and determined to return with his wife Olive to Brush Hill; returned also with his parents, Jacob and Candace Fuller and eleven siblings to York Township where Jacob bought land in 1835, the area later known as Fullersburg; in the autumn of 1835 Benjamin was among the blacksmiths whom Col. Russell secured to shoe the Indians' horses at their last encampment near Vial's farm before continuing westward to a reservation across the Mississippi. [29a, 217a]

Fuller, Elam   listed as owner of 80 acres of Chicago land in Section 18, Township 39, prior to 1836, as seen in Andreas, pp. 112-113. [12]

Fullerton, Alexander N.   (1804-1880) lawyer and business man, native of Chester, VT; married Julia Ann Hubbell (1808-1844) in November 1830 at Troy, NY; later there were two children; arrived by November 1833; on April 22, 1834, advertised in the *Chicago Democrat* with [see] John Botsford as Fullerton & Botsford at the corner of Dearborn and Lake streets; in 1835, started law practice with Grant Goodrich, but the firm Fullerton & Goodrich was dissolved the following year; was among the most successful of the real estate lawyers dur-

ing the land boom but afterwards favored commercial interests; owned a lumber mill in Michigan; ✦ lumber merchant, North Water Street; was active in town, Whig and later Republican politics; ➡ Fullerton Avenue, Fullerton Drive, and Fullerton Parkway (all at 2400 N). [12]

Fulton County, IL   named after Robert Fulton; was formed on Jan. 28, 1823, and included Chicago; for county business, such as ferry or tavern license applications and court appearances, early settlers had to travel to Lewistown, the county seat [see the following paragraph from an early chronicle]; in 1823 the county authorities levied a property tax, ★★★ **Chicago's 1st**, which resulted in the collection of a total of $11.42 from residents; in 1825 Chicago became part of Putnam County; for details, see Chicago jurisdictional chronology on page 209. [12, 544, 590]

When a couple wanted to get married they would generally postpone the matter until they found another couple of the same mind, or found some one who wanted a tavern license, and then they would send a man down to Lewistown to do both jobs and thus save expense, as it took a man at least two weeks, horseback, to make the trip, and he would have to camp out in the woods most of the nights because there were but few settlers along the route. [590]

Fulton Market   existent in the summer of 1835, see Ormsby, M.P.

Fulton, Robert   (1765-1815) American inventor and canal engineer; developed the first commercially successful steamboat, the *Clermont*; its maiden run on the Hudson River took place on Aug. 17, 1807, covering the 150-mile distance in 32 hours; ➡ Fulton Boulevard, Fulton Drive, Fulton Market, and Fulton Street (all at 300 N).

Funk, Absalom   born in Virginia, came from Funks' Grove [McLean County] late in 1834 to manage the butchering of the family's many hog and cattle herds that were driven between October to January to the Chicago market [until 1841]; advertised in the *Chicago Democrat* on Nov. 22, 1834,

offering $20 reward for information about a stolen horse; ✦ Funk & Doyle, butchers [James H. Doyle and also John Funk], Fulton and Illinois markets, 95 Lake St. and North Water Street, corner of North State.

Furkee, George   mentioned by East as having lived in Chicago in 1828. [208]

Furman, Lt. John Gano   (c.1801-1830) from Charleston, SC; officer stationed at Fort Dearborn from Oct. 3, 1828, to Aug. 29, 1830, the day of his death; in a letter written on Aug. 24, Ellen Kinzie Wolcott described "dangerously ill" Lieutenant Furman as "a very highly gifted and interesting young gentleman"; an enthusiastic hunter, he wrote several letters in 1830 to the editor of a Maryland periodical; these were published and later reprinted in Hurlbut's *Chicago Antiquities* of 1881; they vividly describe how local settlers and officers from the fort would meet regularly and together ride out to hunt wolf and deer—one written on March 30 follows; for Lieutenant Furman's comments on the abundance of waterfowl in Chicago, see birds. [357]

Mr. Editor: One fine morning in December last, while the dew drops were yet lingering on the faded foliage, we marshalled our forces, and sallied forth to the chase, in pretty respectable numbers for this wild, western region. We were in all nine huntsmen. A leash of greyhounds, owned by Capt. S. [Capt. Martin Scott], of the U.S.A., his excellent fox-hounds, and those of Dr. F. [Dr. Clement A. Finley] and Mr. C. [Archibald Clybourne?] formed a very efficient pack of five couples. ✧ The day was lovely—'the scy so cloudless, clear, and purely beautiful, that God alone was to be seen in heaven,'—the broad blue face of the lake, unruffled by a breath of air, shone in the morning sun like one vast mirrow of polished silver. And the woods were so silent, that the cheering cry of the huntsmen and the wild melody of the hounds were echoed from a thousand points. Everything thus being propitious, we crossed the Chicago, and persued our route through the thick woods on its north side. We had not proceeded quite a half mile, when the whole pack, de a simultaneous burst, and went off eagerly on the track. ✧ 'A wolf,' said one; 'no—a deer'—clapped rewels into his horse's sides and dashed off for the prairie to head the animal. The hounds at first ran off toward the river [north branch], in a westerly direction, and went nearly out of hearing, but soon turned and took up a northeast course, the whole pack in full concert. Having ridden about two miles from the starting point, and hearing the quick savage bark of the ground-hound slut (Cora) close by, I stopped. Mr. B. [one of the Beaubien brothers] was about thirty yards in advance of me, and glancing my eye around, I cought glimps of Capt. S., some little distance behind, urging his horse to the utmost. These observations were the work of an instant only, however, for scarcely had I alighted when a spike buck dashed through the thicket in full sight, and within shooting distance,— Cora within five or six rods of him. Mr. B and myself both levelled. The first shot was his, by the courteous rules prevalent among hunters on like occasions. He fired, but the buck did not fall; and I instantly followed his example. The shots struck on opposite sides, and were both mortal; but so rapid was the speed of the animal after we had fired, that a gentleman coming up the instant exclaimed, 'By heavens, he is not touched!' He darted for the thicket, but the black greyhound (Nero) got site of him before he reached it, and the most beautiful chase I ever recollect to have witnessed took place. The trial of speed was nobly contested for about thee or four hundred yards, the dear having about thirty yards start. The distance between them lessened by insensible degrees until the greyhound seized his prey, and sunk his fangs into his ham. After a severe struggle, the buck broke loose before Capt. S. and myself, who had dismounted, could get up to Nero's assistance. An other chase, not less beautiful than the first, took place; but Nero again seized the buck and held him till we got up. We knocked him on the head with a tomahawk, and drew the knife across his throat. As soon as the pack came up we started, and the hounds gave tongue again. Most of us went off to the prairie, to station ourselves along the points of the wood. The hounds went off to the west, and after running about a mide divided—some of them drove a deer toward the point almost at which they had taken up the trail. Mr. C. shot at it, but as no blood was found we presume it was not injured. The rest of the pack (with the exeption of Dr. F.'s beautiful black tan pup Ringwood—and well he deserves the name—who drove three deer across the prairie to the lake,) followed a track leading along the Guilleroi [north branch], and did not return until late at night. On my return from the head of the prairie, I heard the report of a gun, and on inquiry, found that Mr. S had killed a fine doe. ✧ Our sport for the day was now over; we called in squirmishers and took our way home rejoicing. At the garrison, our spoil was divided. We then retired to spend the evening with that flow of generous feelings which a fine day's sport never fails to inspire. J.G.F.

fur trade the period of the North American fur trade extended from approximately 1600 to 1850, and was originally a process by which two radically different races communicated, exchanging material and cultural goods for mutual benefit. The beaver was the major fur for most of the period, sent to Europe to be made into felt for hats. Furs shipped from Michilimackinac between June 23 and Sept. 24, 1767: 1,142 bear; 514 muskrat; 1,267 cat [cougar]; 25,008 raccoon; 853 elk; 84 buffalo; 5,798 otter; 9,556 marten; 1,457 fisher; 507 mink; 1,070 fox; 139 wolf; 310 gray fox; 1,707 red fox; 50,928 beaver; 27,037 dressed leather; and 251 castoreum [from gland of beaver]; value of trade goods shipped to upper country in 1767: 39,585 *livres*. The interlude ended when the natural resources were depleted and progressive settlement by Europeans and Americans overran the Indians and the *métis* traders; in Chicago and Illinois, the end of the fur trade came when the Indians were relocated westward beyond the Mississippi. The [see] Indian removal effort began in 1835 and took approximately three years. On July 14, 1837, the American Fur Co. informed their agents that there would be no more opportunities for trade in the vicinity of Lake Michigan and terminated their activities there. The official inventory prepared prior to public sale of the business estate of the Chicago trader William H. Wallace, who died after a short illness in March 1827, near the end of the fur trade period, lists furs acquired in Illinois: 4,014 muskrat, 692 raccoon, 431 deerskin, 252 mink, 46 marten, 115 fisher, 18 wolves, 13 wildcats, 15 otter, 8 bears, 5 fox, and 1 lynx. Other animals hunted for their skins were coyote and elk. It is significant that no beaver were listed; they had been virtually extirpated by 1827. Major firms involved in the trade were the *Compagnie du Canada* (French), Hudson Bay Company, the North West Company, the XY Company (all British), and the American Fur Co. For the type of merchandise offered to the Indians in return for pelts, see trade goods. The fur trade moved north and east after leaving Illinois. See also *coureurs de bois*. [274, 541, 649, 687, and Archives of Canada, *Dartmouth Papers* MG 23, A1 v. 5: 5630]

Fury, John U.S. Army private at Fort Dearborn; enlisted March 1808; badly wounded at the massacre of Aug. 15, 1812; found on board the British fleet on Lake Erie when it was taken by Commodore Perry, according to Captain Heald's report; Eckert writes that he was tortured to death after the battle. [226]

Gaffé, **Jean Baptiste** Cahokia and Mackinac trader in the 1780s who in 1782 sent boatloads of trade goods to Chicago. Over what period of time this post was maintained, by whom, and exactly where it was located, is not known. Late in 1783 [see] Rocheblave wrote that his wife and family were still at Chicago, implying a post or settlement. [9]

Gage armed British schooner patrolling Lakes Michigan, Huron, and Erie during the period of British control; built at Detroit in 1773. [48]

Gage, Jared arrived from NY in 1835; brother of John, married to Sarah Merrill; opened a flour and feed store on South Water Street, between Clark and Dearborn; ✦ flour dealer, South Water Streetbetween Clark and Dearborn; died on March 31, 1880; in 1885 his widow lived at Winnetka. [12, 351, 733]

Gage, John arrived from NY in 1835; brother of Jared; in 1837 built a flour mill on the W bank of the south branch, on the N side of Van Buren Street and became known as "the Honest Miller"; ✦ flour store, South Water Street, mill S Branch; school inspector from 1837 to 1841; alderman, 1840; his wife's name is unknown, but a daughter [Maria] died in 1840, according to a notice in the *Chicago American* on Dec. 28; in 1885 lived in Vineland, NJ. [12, 351, 544, 733]

Gage, Stephen T. arrived from New Hampshire in 1832 and served in the Black Hawk War as a member of the Chicago company; on the list of subscribers to the *Chicago Democrat* in November 1833. [12, 733]

Gale, Abram (1796-1889) born in Warwick, MA; married Sarah [née Silloway] at Boston in 1824; arrived on May 25, 1835, with their daughter Georgiana and sons [see] Edwin O. and William H.; purchased a house at the corner of Wells and Randolph streets, where Sarah opened ★★★ Chicago's 1st millinery store; the attic was rented to Tuthill King and his bride; ✦ [Abraham] also Mrs., New York millinery store, 99 Lake St.; the family later moved to Galewood and acquired 320 acres of public land W of town, one of the few farms within the city limits; still lived there in 1885. [12, 13, 266, 351]

Gale, Edwin O. son of Abram, arrived as a child with his parents on the brig Illinois from Massachusetts; see Chronology for the description of his first walk through town on May 26, 1835; initially stayed with his family at the [see] Green Tree Tavern, also vividly recalled in *Reminiscences of Early Chicago and Vicinity*; later lived in Oak Park. [266, 351]

Gale, John, M.D. from Rockingham County,

NH; fourth Fort Dearborn military medical officer, arrived with the rank of surgeon's mate at his post in July of 1816, under the command of Capt. H. Bradley, and assisted in the reconstruction of the fort; had enlisted in 1812 and had served with distinction during the War of 1812; remained at Fort Dearborn until succeeded by Dr. McMahon in 1818; in the early 1820s married an Iowa woman named Ne-co-mi at Fort Calhoun, NE; remained with the military and died at Fort Armstrong in 1830 with a rank of surgeon major. [12]

Gale, Stephen Francis (1812-1905) born in Exeter, NH; arrived in May 1833; half brother of [see] Arthur G. Burley; voted in the election of the first town board on Aug. 10, 1833; opened the second book and stationery store in 1835 on South Water Street, near Clark Street; ✦ bookseller and stationer, 159 Lake St. Gale also sold patent medicines, advertising Brandreth's Pills as sole authorized agent; married Medora Augusta Smith on Dec. 7, 1841; in later years headed the Chicago Fire Department; in 1885 lived at 55 S Peoria St.; ➡ Gale Street, in the NW section of the city. [12, 266, 351]

Gale, William H. son of [see] Abram, arrived with his family from Massachusetts; later moved with them to Galewood. [266]

Galena, IL this frontier settlement near the Mississippi began in 1823 when large lead deposits nearby, worked earlier by Indians, French, and English miners, began to be worked by Americans, thus precipitating the first important American mining rush [see comment by J.M. Peck in his *A Gazetteer of Illinois*, excerpt below]. The production was 5.2 million pounds in 1827, 11.1 million in 1828, 13.3 million in 1829, and 8.3 million in 1830 [see H.S. Tanner]. Lead was sold at Galena for two to three cents a pound. In the summer of 1829, the first wagonload of lead from Galena arrived in Chicago, the trip taking 11 days. The town rapidly developed after the Black Hawk War had secured western Illinois for settlers as well as miners, and became the most important commercial

center in the western country N of St. Louis. Chicago served as a way station for would-be lead miners heading to Galena from the East; in 1834, the trail from Chicago to Galena by way of Naperville and Aurora, used by General Scott's army two years earlier during the Black Hawk War, became a state road on which a stagecoach would travel between the two towns once a week. As late as 1842, Galena's wholesale trade would surpass that of Chicago. [527] J.M. Peck's 1831 comment about Galena:

Such was the crowd of adventurers in 1829, to this hitherto almost unknown and desolate region, that the lead business was greatly overdone, and the market for a while almost destroyed. ... The business is now reviving, and probably will be prosecuted in future more in proportion to the demand of lead.

Galloway, James first visited Chicago in 1824 alone and on horseback; in 1826 returned with his wife Jane and four children: Mary (14), Jane (8 or 9), Susan (2), and James (10) from Sandusky, OH; moved into a small, single room log cabin at Hardscrabble that belonged to Chief Robinson [Robinson's trading post until 1825] and endured a very harsh winter, much in fear of the Indians as mother Jane and Mary purchased wool from Ouilmette, spun yarn, and knit gloves and stockings for sale to the soldiers at Fort Dearborn; in the spring of 1827 moved to the "Grand Rapids of the Illinois River" [Marseilles] where Mary met Archibald Clybourne, who frequently came to the Illinois River valley to buy livestock for his father's butcher business; the couple married June 9, 1829, Reverend Isaac Scarritt officiating, and settled in Chicago [see also Clybourne, Mary]; James died at Chicago in 1837, as noted in the *Chicago American* on Nov. 4, seven years after his wife. [12, 728]

Galloway, Mary (1812-1904) see Clybourne, Mary; Galloway, James; Clybourne, Archibald. [12, 728]

gambling during the summer of 1834, gambling was tolerated or encouraged in a number of Chicago's taverns and shops, notwithstanding the existence of Illinois laws making gambling a criminal offence. On Oct. 24 [also see Chronology] rising anti- gambling sentiments among the townspeople resulted in a "spontaneous" meeting of leading citizens, presided over by Col. John H. Kinzie, with Hans Crocker appointed secretary. On the following day the assembly reconvened and adopted seven prepared resolutions, designed to safeguard Chicago's reputation and to insure prompt punishment of offenders. The meeting reports and text of the resolutions were published in the *Chicago Democrat* on Oct. 29, 1834. Four of the resolutions are reprinted as follows:

Resolved, That we consider those persons who for their base and selfish purposes are willing to plunder the unexperienced and thoughtless of their property, and to sacrifice the morals of this community and the reputation of this town, unworthy [of] our friendship of respect and that we will evince, by our treatment of all such persons, whenever and wherever known, our abhorrence of their occupation and contempt of themselves.

Resolved, That witnessed the introduction of persons believed to be sharpers and blacklegs, into this town, with the most indignant feelings, and that we will use all honorable means to bring these wretches and their abettors to that punishment which their base and abominable practices so richly deserve.

Resolved, That cost what it may, we are determined to root out this vice, and to hunt down those who gain by it an infamous subsistence.

Resolved, That the moral sense of this community is opposed to gambling in all its forms and that this shall be felt at home and known abroad.

Ganday, Lewis   also Ganaby or Gunday; voted in the Chicago election of Aug. 2, 1830.

"Garden City"   a nickname for Chicago that probably recalls Morris Birkbeck's description of the Illinois prairie as a beautiful garden; he published his popular *Notes on a Journey in America, from the Coast of Virginia to the Territory of Illinois*, in 1818. The Latin phrase *Urbs in Hortu*, meaning City in

a Garden, was used by Dr. Goodhue in designing Chicago's official seal. [56]

Gardiner, Alvah Noyes   also Alvin Gardner; arrived in 1830 and on May 18 married Julia Staly [Staley?], Justice J.B. Beaubien officiating; later moved to Blue Island. [708]

Garie's River   see Guillory.

Notice to Coopers.

A FEW Journeymen Coopers can have constant employment, and fair wages, by applying to the subscriber, at Chicago, Illinois.

J. J. GARLAND.

May 19, 1834.   25

Garland, J.J.   a subscriber to the *Chicago Democrat* who advertised on May 19, 1834, and thereafter for journeymen coopers, whom he would employ for fair wages; volunteered with the "Pioneer" hook and ladder company in October 1835.

garlic   for the wild garlic plant that gave Chicago its name, see *Allium*.

Garner, Richard   U.S. Army corporal at Fort Dearborn; enlisted in October 1805; wounded and taken prisoner by Indians at the massacre of Aug. 15, 1812, then tortured to death later that night.

Garow, James   voted on July 24, 1830. [226]

Garrett, Augustus   (1802-1848) from New York state, married Eliza Clark in 1825; arrived late in 1834, advertising an auction in December at his store on South Water Street N of the drawbridge; by late spring 1835, he formed a partnership with the Brown brothers and became, with little financial means, a leading land speculator and auctioneer during the canal-inspired land boom, with a business office in the auction room on the W side of Dearborn Street near Water Street, and by the end of October his sales alone were $1,8 million; among the first items printed in Chicago by T.O. Davis, other than the *Chicago American*, were broadsides to advertise Garrett's auctions; in Nov. 11, 1835 *Chicago Democrat* he advertised as A. Garrett, Auction & Commission House, No. 1,

Dearborn St.; an ad in the same issue listed "lots in the Towns of Chicago, Kankakee, Vienna, Juliett, Romeo, Dresden, Enterprize, Peru, and Bailytown"; a second ad offered " Liquors, Teas, &c." items such as 5 [see] pipes Signett Brandy, 5 pipes Swan Gin, 24 baskets champaigne Wine, & 7 qr. [quarter] casks Sherry, 10 chests hyson and young hyson tea, 4 hhds. [see hogshead] St. Croix Rum, 28 eight day brass clocks, 100 wood clocks; also see Garrett, Brown and Brother; ◆ auctioneer, real estate, boarded at Sauganash Hotel; served as mayor in 1843, 1844 and 1845; following his death on Nov. 30, 1848, his widow established the Garrett Bible Institute in Evanston. [12, 480]

Garrett, Brown & Brother   a successful partnership with [see] Nathaniel J. and Daniel B. Brown for which Garrett had printed broadsides advertising an auction on May 21, 1835, shortly after his arrival in Chicago; in December 1835 the Chicago branch of the State Bank of Illinois opened in a four-story brick building owned by Garrett, Brown & Brother at the corner of LaSalle and South Water streets, and the three men announced in the *Chicago Democrat* a new copartnership with Oliver H. Thompson—Garrett, Thompson, Brown & Co., for the purpose of buying and selling real estate, conducting a general land agency and also an auction, commission and mercantile business, at either the store in Lake Street or at the Auction & Commission Room on Dearborn.

Garrett, Thompson, Brown & Co.   see the preceding entry.

Gary, Erastus   native of Putnam, CT; brother of Jude Perin Gary and Orlinda; traveled to St. Joseph [Michigan] in 1831 to teach school; in 1832, with three others, paddled to Chicago in a dugout canoe, stayed overnight, then continued to the Napier settlement and staked a claim adjoining the NE border of the Wilson/Butterfield claim [Winfield]; built a sawmill on the Du Page River and supplied cut lumber throughout the county; married Susan Valette and had a son, Elbert, prior to

1840. [314a]

Gary, Jude Perin   arrived with his sister Orlinda in 1832, following the Black Hawk War; passed through the settlement to join his brother Erastus; married Margaret L. Kimball; became a circuit riding Methodist preacher. [314a]

Gary, William   from Pomfret, Ct; came in 1832 to [Warrenville] with his wife Lucy (née Perin) following their children [see] Erastus Gary, Jude Perin, and Orlinda. Orlinda married Jesse C. Wheaton on March 26, 1839.

General Harrison   schooner, brought a load of Michigan whitewood lumber in the summer of 1833, to be used for harbor pier construction; it returned the following year and entered the newly opened harbor.

General Hunter   a sloop on the Great Lakes; in May 1805 it brought trade goods from Mackinac to Chicago for the account of Kinzie & Forsyth, and returned to Mackinac with furs, after first visiting St. Joseph.

General Wayne   lake schooner, built at Amherstburg in 1807 as *Caledonia*; used to transport the British force from St. Joseph for the capture of Mackinac in July 1812; after the war Americans renamed the vessel *General Wayne*; during June and July of 1816, brought 112 soldiers of the Third U.S. Infantry, under Capt. Hezekiah Bradley, from Detroit to build the second Fort Dearborn.

George III   (1738-1820) king of England from 1760 to 1820, a 60-year span that included 20 years of British jurisdictional authority over Chicagoland, namely from the end of the French and Indian War (1763) to the end of the Revolutionary War (1783), and *de facto* to 1796.

George, Samuel C.   baker, arrived in 1834 from New York; spotted the last black [see] bear in downtown Chicago that year on Oct. 6; initially ran a bakery on the corner of Lake and LaSalle streets with Josiah P. Cook; on Oct. 29, 1834, they reported partnership dissolution in the *Chicago Democrat*, and John Bates announced an auction

of "the Bakeshop with all Baking utensils" on Nov. 3; in the paper on Dec. 24, George cautioned all persons from cutting timber or drawing away wood on his land in Townships 38 and 40; ➡ George Street (2900 N).

Gerber, B.   German immigrant, first attested to as having lived in Chicago in 1834. [342]

German Evangelical Association   sect founded in 1790 in Pensylvania by preacher Jacob Albrecht; became established at Chicago in 1835; among those who belonged to this exclusively German church were George C. Gross, Daniel and Christoph Stanger, Jacob Schaebele, Jacob and Martin Escher, Adam Knopp, Jacob Ott, Johan Rehm and Georg Strubler.

Ghent   lake schooner that took U.S. factor Charles Jouett to his assignment at Fort Dearborn in 1816.

Gibson, Daniel   filed an affidavit on Nov. 24, 1835, in support of the Palmer & George [see Palmer, George] claim for wharfing privileges. [28]

Gibson, Hugh G.   listed as co-owner of 160 acres of land, together with James Woodworth, in the SW quarter of Section 8, Township 39, prior to 1836, as per Andreas, *History of Chicago*, pp. 112-113.

Gilbert, Ashley   became a member of fire engine company No.1 ("Fire Kings") in December 1835, and remained active several years; ♦ bookkeeper, Horace Norton & Co.

Gilbert, James   arrived in 1833 and voted in the election of the first town board on Aug. 10. [12]

gill   liquid measure, equal to a 1/4 pint; when Fort Dearborn was dismantled in 1856, a paper dated Nov. 12, 1811, was found – "Permission is thereby granted for one gill of whiskey each: Denison, Dyer, Andrews, [Keamble?], [Burnam], J. Corbin, Burnett, Smith, McPherson, Hamilton, Fury, Grummow, Moffitt, Lynch, Locker, Peterson, P. Corbin, Van Horn, Mills"; the names were partially overmarked, implying satisfaction.

Gilluffy, J.J.   a member of the early volunteer fire brigade " Washington Volunteers."

glacial age   see ice age.

Glacial Lake Chicago   see Lake Chicago.

Gladwin   armed British schooner patrolling Lakes Michigan, Huron, and Erie during the period of British control; built at Navy Island in 1764. [48]

Glas, Joseph   U.S. Army sergeant at Fort Dearborn; date of enlistment not known, but was transferred to Fort Washington at Cincinnati late in 1811. [226]

Gleacon, Eli   prior to 1836 listed as owner of 80 acres of land in the SW corner of Section 6, Township 39, as seen in Andreas, *History of Chicago*, pp. 112-113.

Glecen, Luther   trader, attended the estate sale of W.H. Wallace on May 10, 1827, buying 5 Indian awls and 100 needles for 21 cents; Mrs. Kinzie, in *Wau-Bun*, located him later at Lake Puckaway.

Glenwood beach   a geological term, designating the highest of a series of three major concentric dune ridges left behind by the shore of glacial Lake Michigan when its level was higher than today, still visible in the landscape today. During the Glenwood phase, 12,000 years ago, the lake was 55 to 60 feet higher. Each of the ridges today, where undisturbed by human activity, reflects its age with its own characteristic set of animals and plants (the dominant Glenwood beach trees are oaks); this ridge was once part of the Sauk Trail used by Indians and early settlers and now the Glenwood-Dyer Road in southern Cook County and U.S. Highway 30 follows part of its course. For the other two ridges, see Tolleston beach and Calumet beach; also see Sand Ridge.

Glenwood phase   see Glenwood beach.

Globe   schooner from Buffalo, NY; visited Chicago with merchandise under Captain Perkins on June 24, 1834, and twice in 1835.

Godfrey, Col. Gabriel   attended the Indian Treaty of Chicago in 1821 as Indian agent. [13]

Goodhue, Josiah Cosmore, M.D.   (1794-1847) Vermont physician, graduated from the medical department of Yale University in 1829; first prac-

JOSIAH COSMORE GOODHUE, M.D. [410]

ticed in Canada, then came to Chicago in the fall of 1832 [according to publications of the Chicago Medical Society; in contrast thereto, A.H. Waterman writes of his arrival in 1835, and A.S. Hubbard remembers 1834; *eds.*]; as an agent, advertised in the Aug. and September 1835 *Chicago Democrat* the leasing of town lots; also advertised throughout the autumn an office on Lake Street, three doors W of Tremont House, with Dr. J.H. Barnard, a partnership in the practice of "Physic and Surgery"; in 1837 drafted jointly with Dr. Brainard the bill for incorporation of Rush Medical School; was active in early city government, designing the city's first seal, serving as alderman in 1837, and instrumental in founding the public school system; ✦ Dearborn Street N of Lake Street; after 1839 moved to Rockford, IL; in 1846 became a founding member of the Rock River Medical Association [predecessor of the Rockford Medical Association, 1871-1880, becoming Winnebago County Medical Society on Sept. 18, 1881; *eds.*];

in 1847 the doctor fell into an uncovered well and drowned. [12, 184]

Gooding, Joseph A. arrived in 1833; unclaimed letter(s) listed at the post office for Jan 1, 1834; married Eunice Cutting on March 14, 1837. [319]

Gooding, William E. (1803-1878) native of Bristol, NY; civil engineer on the Welland Canal; arrived May 1, 1833; squatted and later purchased land in what subsequently became known as Gooding's Grove, 30 miles SW of the settlement; in 1834 was employed by the commissioners of public works of Indiana to work on the Wabash & Erie Canal; in 1836 was selected chief engineer of the Illinois & Michigan Canal, a position held until the project was completed in 1848; died in Lockport at the age of 75. [319]

Goodrich, Ebenezer P. arrived in 1833; served as town trustee in 1834. [12]

Goodrich, Grant (1812-1889) born in New York; arrived in May 1834; one of the founders of the First Methodist church and member of the first fire company in 1835, and in November was appointed to the executive committee of the Chicago Bible Society; formed a law firm that year with A.N. Fullerton that ended in 1836; went into law practice with Giles Spring and was among the most successful of the real estate lawyers during the land boom; married Juliette Atwater of Westfield, NY, on July 24, 1836, and had four sons and one daughter; ✦ attorney and counselor at law, 107 Lake St.; eventually became a respected judge and one of the founders of Northwestern University in 1850; in 1859 was elected to the Illinois Supreme Court; in 1883 the judge recalled the following early episode; lived at 40 Rush St. in 1885; his ▲ grave site is located at Rosehill Cemetery. [12, 351, 707] From Judge Grant Goodrich's 1883 recollection: *In the winter of 1834-35, Gurdon S. Hubbard, John H. Kinzie, and others visited the Legislature at Vandalia, to urge the passage of a bill to commence the work on the* [Illinois & Michigan] *canal. They succeeded well in getting it through the House of Repre-*

sentatives, and securing the pledges of votes enough to carry it in the Senate; but two Senators who had agreed to support it changed their minds, and secured its defeat. ✧ *The indignation at Chicago was hot and fierce, and she must give some signal expression of it. A cannon was procured, effigies of the offending Senators made, and placed on the bank of a cellar, where the Tremont House now stands, and John and Robert Kinzie, and others, performed around them the ceremonies which the Indians practiced around prisoners, devoted to mockery, torture, and an ignominious death, after which one was shot into fragments from the mouth of the cannon.* ✧ *The other one was laid upon a rude bier, and carried upon the ice in the river, escorted by Geo. White, as master of ceremonies, the town bell-ringer and the only negro here. The effigy was then placed over a can of powder, which was exploded, up-heaving the ice, and blowing the senator high in the air, and tearing him into fragments, amidth the shouts and jeers of the multitude.* ✧ *We were compelled [said the Judge] to furnish our own amusements, and this is a specimen of the way in which it was done.*

Goodrich, Timothy Watson born c.1820 in Benson, NY; arrived in 1832; ✦ clerk, T.B. Carter & Co.; later moved to Milwaukee; had returned and was living at 544 Astor St. in 1885. [12, 351]

goose see Canada goose.

Goose Island an artificial island in the north branch of the Chicago River, created by the digging of an alternate channel; divided into approximately two equal halves by Division Street; ★★★ Chicago's 1st shipyard was set up on Goose Island in 1835 and thrived for several decades; in 1873 ten large schooners were built in the yard. [727]

Gordon, Eleanor Lytle Kinzie granddaughter of Juliette Augusta Magill Kinzie and daughter of Nellie Kinzie Gordon, who wrote the book *John Kinzie, the "Father of Chicago," a Sketch*, published in 1912.

Gordon, Capt. William U.S. Army; headed an exploratory party to Fort Leavenworth in 1835 that

left Chicago in June and returned on Sept. 9. The expedition fulfilled terms of the 1833 Chicago Treaty with the Indians and explored territory for Indian resettlement. The party consisted of Gordon, several other white men [including William Holiday], and 50 Potawatomi, of whom only the name Ma-chu-etah has been recorded. They drew their supplies from [see] Capt. J.B.F. Russell, disbursing agent for Indian removal in Chicago. Also see: Indian removal. [655]

Goss, Oliver   native of Vermont; resident of Plainfield in 1832, but purchased in September lot 2 of block 56 in Chicago for $70, still owner in 1833 when he formed a partnership with his longtime friend's son, [see] Silas B. Cobb, building a two-story house at Lake and Canal streets, where Cobb opened a harness shop at street level [see Goss & Cobb], renting out the upper floor; continued to live at [Plainfield] as silent partner; the partnership ended amicably in 1834; died in 1842.

Goss & Cobb   "Saddle & Harness Making" advertisement can be found in the first issue of the *Chicago Democrat*, Nov. 26, 1833; by the following June the ad featured trunkmaking; located at the corner of Lake and Canal streets

governors of British Canada   (1760-1805) their function was to represent their king who appointed them. Individual entries may be found for those governors [*] deemed to have been of special importance in the context of Chicago's early history. [665]

Sir Jeffrey Amherst
1760-1763
*General Thomas Gage
1763-1764
James Murray (first governor-general)
1764-1766
Lieutenant-Colonel Æmilius Paulus Irving
1766
*Sir Guy Carleton
1766-1778
Hector T. Cramahé (acting governor)
1770-1774
*Frederick Haldimand
1778-1784
*Henry Hamilton
1784-1785
General Henry Hope
1785-1786
Sir Guy Carleton, Lord Dorchester
1786-1796
Sir Alured Clarke (acting governor)
1791-1793
Sir Robert Prescott
1796-1799
Sir Robert Shore Milnes (lieutenant-governor)
1799-1805

governors of Illinois   (1818-1835) see individual entries for further detail.

Shadrach Bond
1818-1822
Edward Coles
1822-1826
Ninian Edwards
1826-1830
John Reynolds
1830-1834
Joseph Duncan
1834-1838

governors of French Louisiana   (1706-1763) their function was to represent their king who appointed them. Individual entries may be found for those governors [*] deemed to have been of special importance in the context of Chicago's early history. [665]

*Jean-Baptiste Le Moyne, seigneur de Bienville
1706-1707
Nicolas Daneaux, sieur de Muy
1707-1708
*Antoine de la Mothe Cadillac
1712-1715
Jean Michiele, seigneur de Lépinay et de La Longueville (acting governor, then governor)
1715-1717
*Jean-Baptiste Le Moyne, seigneur de Bienville (commander in chief)
1717-1726
Pierre Dugué, sieur de Boisbriant (acting governor)
1725-1726
— Perier
1726-1732
*Jean-Baptiste Le Moyne, seigneur de Bienville
1732-1741
Pierre François Rigaud, marquis de Vaudreuil
1743-1753
Louis Biollouart de Kerlérec
1755-1763

governors of *Nouvelle France* or French Canada   their function was to represent their king who appointed them; in New France administrative decisions were usually made by the [see] intendant, also appointed by the king. Individual entries may be found for those governors [*] deemed to have been of special importance in the context of Chicago's early history. [665]

*Samuel de Champlain
1608-1635
Marc Antoine de Brasdefer de Chasteaufort
1635-1636
Charles Huault de Montmagny
1636-1648
Louis d'Ailleboust de Coulonge
1648-1651
Jean de Lauson, Sr.
1651-1656
Charles de Lauson de Charny
1656-1657
Pierre de Voyer d'Argenson
1658-1661
Pierre du Bois, baron d'Avaugour
1661-1663
Augustin de Saffray, chevalier de Mézy
1663-1665
Jacques de Meuf de la Poterie
1665
Daniel de Rémy de Courcelles
1665-1672
*Louis de Buade, comte de Frontenac
1672-1682
*Antoine Joseph Le Fèvre de La Barre
1682-1685
*Jacques René de Brisay, marquis de Denonville
1685-1689
*Louis de Buade, comte de Frontenac
1689-1698
Louis Hector de Callières
1698-1703
Philippe de Rigault, marquis de Vaudreuil
1703-1725
Claude de Ramezay (acting governor)
1714-1716
*Charles Le Moyne, first baron de Longueuil
1725-1726
Charles, marquis de Beauharnais

1726-1747
Michel Rolland Barrin, comte de la Galissonière
1747-1749
Jacques Pierre de Taffanel, marquis de la Jonquière
1749-1752
*Charles Le Moyne, second baron de Longueuil
1752-1755
Pierre François Rigaud, marquis de Vaudreuil
1755-1760

governors of United States Territories that included Chicago (1788-1818) see individual entries for further detail.

Arthur St. Clair - Northwest Territory
appointed 1788
William Henry Harrison - Indiana Territory
appointed 1800
Ninian Edwards - Illinois Territory
appointed 1809

Graham, Richard acting secretary of war in 1817, to whom [see] Major Long reported; together with Commissioner Philips, was author of the *Report on the Region Included Within the Boundary Lines of the Indian Treaty of St. Louis, August, 1816* that accompanies Captain Sullivan's ✳ map; his brother Richard was Indian agent at Peoria in 1816. [437]

Grand Avenue ➡ former Indian trail called Whiskey Point Road in the 1860s, it obliquely cuts through the usual checkerboard street pattern of later origin.

Grand Equestrian Arena an enterprise that, according to Winslow, gave the first circus performance in a tent on Sept. 14, 1836.

Grand Prairie see prairie.

Grannis, Henry F. arrived from New York in 1834; died in 1864. [351]

Grant, James (1812-1891) born in Enfield, NC; arrived on April 23, 1834, to become the sixth lawyer; established an office at the corner of Michigan Avenue and Kinzie Street, next to the Cook County recorder's office; on April 30, 1834, married Eliza Hubbard, daughter of Ahira Hubbard; on Jan. 1, 1835, was appointed state's attorney, removing his

office to G.S. Hubbard's warehouse, SW corner of Water and LaSalle streets; was among the most successful of the real estate lawyers during the land boom; in 1836 represented large real estate interests for the New York speculator Arthur Bronson; from March 1836 to 1838 operated under a partnership arrangement, constituting the firm Grant & Peyton; ✦ attorney, North Water Street near Rush, boarded at Lake House; in 1839 moved to Davenport, IA, where his wife died in 1842; later became a judge, but returned to Chicago for receptions and camaraderie with other "old settlers"; living at Davenport in 1885. [12, 351, 707]

Grant, Orente (c.1790-) came in late autumn 1834, and made a claim along the Brush Hill Trail; built a hostelry known as Castle Inn with his brother David; became Brush Hill postmaster in March 1835. [29a, 217a]

Grant, Zachariah father of Orente and David; prior to 1836 owned 80 acres of land in Section 32, Township 39, as per Andreas, *History of Chicago*, pp. 112-113.

"grapeline ferry" local name for a privately maintained ferry service across the north branch of the Chicago River prior to 1832, when the first bridge was built; the ferry primarily served patrons of the Wolf Point Tavern.

Gratiot, Charles influential trader at Cahokia and St. Louis; his papers, mostly account books, are at the Missouri Historical Society and are a unique source for the period 1777-87.

Gratiot, Gen. Charles Brig. General of the U.S. Army in charge of the Department of Engineers, assigned by Congress as responsible for harbor improvement at Chicago on March 2, 1833; initial construction was supervised by Maj. George Bender, Fort Dearborn commandant, who received his orders related to the harbor project directly from Gratiot in Washington City [now Washington, D.C.], as did Lt. James Allen, who succeeded Major Bender as superintendent of the project.

Graue, Friedrich German immigrant from

Stolzenau, who came with his family in June 1834, together with the family of Bernhardt Koehler; both families settled at Duncklee's Grove and became members of the German Lutheran community; in 1852 built a grist mill [▲ Graue Mill; see Monuments] on Salt Creek [Hinsdale] that was restored in 1950. [342]

Graue Mill   see Graue, Friedrich

Graves, Dexter   from Norwich, NY; came in 1831 and built the Mansion House on Lake Street near Dearborn; his wife was Olive and their known children were Henry, Louisa, and Lucy (died of scarlet fever in 1844 at age 19); in c.1832 bought a lot on block 18 from P.F.W. Peck [see map on page 44]; John D. Caton reports to have stayed at Graves's hotel in July 1833 "at five dollars per week"; on March 25, 1834, an ad appeared in the *Chicago Democrat* announcing that D. Graves had commenced the Chicago Bakery on South Water Street, a few doors N of Messrs. Newberry & Dole and that he "will always keep on-hand, fresh Bread, Crackers, Cakes, &c. &c."; also that year sold the hotel to his son-in-law Edward H. Hadduck and was trustee of the English and Classical Academy; later did well in real estate; ✦ livery stable, 44 State St. [Couch Place] and ✦ Graves, (D.) & Stevens, (M.W.), Rialto Saloon, 8 Dearborn St.; in 1909 his son Henry commissioned Loredo Taft to create a ▲ monument for his father's grave in Graceland Cemetery, a haunting bronze figure entitled "Eternal Silence"; see Monuments. [12, 544]

Graves, Henry   second son of [see] Dexter Graves and his wife Olive; arrived as a 10-year old from New York with his parents in 1831; married Clementine Johnson; ✦ State Street, near Lake Street [with cousin Lorin?]; lived at 88 33rd St. in 1885. [12]

Graves, Joseph   assistant land surveyor working with William S. Trowbridge in the Chicago area in 1835.

Graves, Loren   also Lorin; arrived from New York in 1834; married Mary Jane Sevier on May 5, 1841;

✦ State Street, near Lake Street. [351]

Gravier, Père Jacques   born at Moulins, France; came to Canada in 1685 as an experienced instructor and sent to Michilimackinac the following year, succeeded Father Allouez at Kaskaskia during 1688. Though superior at Mackinac between 1695 and 1698, he returned to the *Mission de la Conception*; early in September 1700 Father Gravier visited the Gardien Angel Mission. Severely wounded by a Peoria Indian late in 1705, he sought medical attention in Mobile and France; early in 1708 returned to mission work but died soon afterward. A skilled linguist, Father Gravier prepared during the 1690s the first Illinois grammar [lost] and compiled an Illinois-French dictionary [extant], a work of 586 pages and nearly 25,000 entries. [613]

Gray, Charles McNeill   (1807-1885) arrived from Sherburne, NY, on July 17, 1834, by sailing vessel with his mother and stepfather [see] Jireh Rowley; likely George M.'s older brother; initially worked as clerk for G.S. Hubbard, later Peter Cohen; ✦ grain cradle factory, 78 Dearborn St.; married Maria Louisa Johnson of Brownsville, ME in 1839; became a successful manufacturer, contractor, and railroad man; was elected the 12th mayor in 1853; died on Oct. 17, 1885, and is buried at Graceland Cemetery. [12, 544, 734]

Gray, George M.   born c.1818 in Sherburne, NY, likely younger brother of Charles M.; arrived in June 1834; ✦ agent, C.M. Gray's factory; in 1885 lived at the Grand Pacific Hotel in Chicago. [12, 351]

Green Bay   also *Le Grand Baie, Baye des Puans, La Baye*; at the mouth of the Fox River, on the W coast of upper Lake Michigan. As to the name *Baye des Puans* (French for *Bay of Stinkers* or *Bay of Stinkards*), where the Winnebago lived, a mistranslation by early French Jesuits is believed responsible: *Quinipeg* in Algonkian means *bad smelling waters*, as salt water was so designated by them; Winnebago or Quinipeguo would therefore mean *men of the sea*, and Green Bay would have been *bay*

of the men of the sea. [Also see *puants*, for for early comment by Father Ragueneau at the *Mission de Sainte Marie* explaining why the Winnebago were so called.] In 1671, the *Mission de Saint-François-Xavier* was moved to the head of Green Bay (from Point Sable to De Pere, WI); from here Father Marquette and Jolliet started their historic expedition, in the course of which they came to what is now Chicago. Thomas Forsyth reports that in c.1812 nearly 40 French settlers lived at Green Bay, where a Jacob Franks operated a fine grist mill. Like Chicago, the settlement was the starting point for westward travel via an important portage route, in this case the Fox-Wisconsin River portage to the Mississippi, as used by Father Marquette and Jolliet in 1673.

Green Bay Indian Trail   also U.S. Military Road and later Green Bay Road; northwestern portion of the Lake Shore Trail, from Fort Dearborn to Green Bay (Fort Howard), a distance of c.225 miles; one of the major trails designated by an act of Congress as an important national route on June 15, 1832, and therefore to be improved as a national road; near Chicago the trail follows a former beach ridge of ancient Lake Chicago, now marked by the course of Clark Street, earlier referred to as Old Sand Road; at Foster Avenue NW to Howard Street at Robey Avenue, then northward along the present Green Bay Road through the northern suburbs. A branch of the Green Bay Trail leads from [see] *Grosse Pointe* [Evanston/Wilmette] SW (present Gross Point Road following the old trail), across the Des Plaines River at Stony Ford and into the Starved Rock area; an alternative branch trail followed what is now Carpenter Road See Memorials for the detail on a bronze ▲ plaque at the SW corner of Hubbard St and Michigan Avenue; also see entry for Ridge Road Trail.

Green, Jane Ann   listed prior to 1836 as owner-assignee of 160 acres of land in the NW quarter of Section 20, Township 39, as seen in Andreas, *History of Chicago*, pp. 112-113.

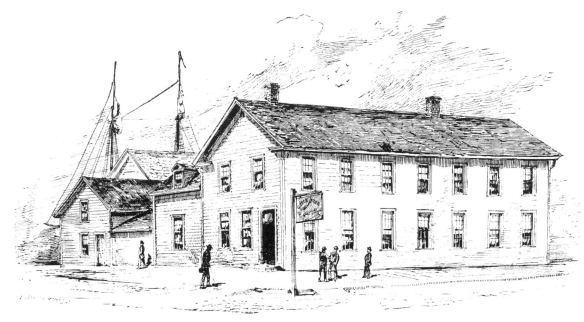

THE GREEN TREE HOTEL.   [12]

greenheaded flies also prairie flies, deer flies, horse flies; appearing greenheaded to the casual observer, they are actually green-eyed, the large eyes covering most of the head; several species were found in the prairie, belonging to the genus *Chrysops* (deer fly) and *Tabanus*, members of the latter genus being larger; they may still be found in rural Illinois. In 1833 Jerry Church noted:

We then concluded to go to the far west. We bought us a cream-coloured horse and a small red square box wagon to carry our trunks, made a spring seat in it, and got aboard and took the national road for Michigan lake, the mud about two feet deep, and as black as tar. But we waded through it, and at last arrived at a beautiful country on the St. Joseph river. Nothing troubled us then except musquitoes and prairie flies; they were very hard on us and our noble dun horse, and would almost take a suck at our red box wagon, thinking it was blood.

Green Tree Tavern acquired its name from a solitary oak tree nearby; built by Silas B. Cobb for James Kinzie as a two-story frame building in 1833; stood at the NE corner of what is now Lake and Canal Sts; had low ceilings and doors, and the windows were set with tiny panes of glass; managed by a succession of landlords, initially by David Clock, then Edward Parsons; was later called Chicago Hotel [as early as December 1833] and Lake Street House [in 1849]; in 1880 the building was moved to Milwaukee Avenue For a description of the tavern and the activities inside, see the following reports, first by Charles Butler on Aug. 2, 1833 and then by Edwin O. Gale in 1835:

Charles Butler's report:

... Our Tavern presents a fair sample of the state of things at Chicago. It is new and unfinished. The partition walls not lathed and plastered and of course, free communication between all the rooms. ... The south west window of my room looks off on the prairie, which is boundless to the sight and the sun setting in it is very beautiful. The land around Chicago is not in [the] market. It is uncultivated. Hard clay and limestone bottom. ...

Edwin O. Gale's report:

... The Greentree having no book for that purpose, we were spared the ceremony of registering. Nor was it certain that we could find accomodation until our host had returned from the kitchen, wither he had gone to consult with his efficient wife. ... The momentous council was at length ended, and we were assigned a room adjoining the one we had first entered, which was the bar, reading, smoking, and reception room, ladies' parlor and general utility place in one. ... On the east and west side of the room were the inevitable puncheon benches. The walls, ceilings, and board partitions had evidently received a coat of whitewash when the house was built, but it would require more than ocular evidence to establish the fact. Scattered around was an assortment of wooden chairs. Near the north end was a bar counter, useful not only for the receiving of drinks, but also umbrellas, overcoats, whips and parcels. The west end of the bar was adorned with a large inkstand placed in a cigar box filled with No. 8 shot, in which were sticking two quill pens—steel being unknown here, although invented in 1830. ... At the other end of the counter were a dozen or more short pieces of tallow candles, each placed in a hole bored in a 2x4 block and fortified by sixpenny nailes, standing like mourners around the circular graves in which they had seen so many flickering lights pass away into utter darkness. ✧
Hanging in a row against the wall were large cloth and leather slippers, which the guests were expected to put on at night, that mud might not be tracked into every part of the house. Under the counter was a large wooden bootjack.... Resting on a broad shelf, fastened at each end, were large pails of rain or river water, in which floated long-handled dippers, with rags crowded into spaces the rust had eaten through. Next to each pail was a looking glass, its frame veneered with mahogany. Hanging on wooden pegs were three or four towels of that shade so easily produced by dipping dirty

hands in water and rubbing briskly in the process of drying. Tied to each mirrow was a horn comb.... In the middle of the room, standing in a low box filled with lake sand, was a large stove used in winter to good advantage not only for the warms imparted to the room, but for furnishing hot water for toddies, shaving and washing as well. ... [W]e were called to supper by a large bell, which was rung by our host in a manner which required no explanation as to its meaning. In the dining room were two tables, the length of the room, covered with green-checked oil cloth, loaded with roasted wild duck, fricassee of prairie chicken, wild pigeon pot pie, tea and coffee, creamless, but sweetened with granulated maple sugar procured from our red brethren. These furnished a banquet that rendered us oblivious to chipped dishes, flies buzzing or tangled in the butter, creeping beetles and the music of the Mosquito Band.

Greene, Maj. John   native of Ireland; Third Infantry; at the rank of captain, commandant at Fort Dearborn from July to October 1823, at which time the fort was evacuated, remaining so until Oct. 3, 1828; as Major and now with the Fifth Infantry, commandant at Fort Dearborn from Dec. 18, 1833, to Sept. 16, 1835; died in 1840.

Greeenleaf, —   according to the report by J.D. Bonnell, Mr. Greenleaf was a real estate auctioneer in 1835 with his auction rooms on Dearborn Street, opposite those of his competitor Garrett; for a description of his mode of operation, see entry on Bonnell, J.D.

Greenville, Treaty of   see Treaty of Greenville, 1795.

grey gowns   Indian name for the Récollets priests, such as Father Hennepin and other clerics who traveled with La Salle in Illinois country.

Gridley, John   arrived from Onondage, NY, in 1835 with wife, Nancy (née Seely), and sons Elisha, George, and John, daughters Elizabeth, Mary, and Louisa; moved on to Lake County, near [now] Gilmer, IL, where they acquired several hundred acres of land and built a log cabin. [Information found

LE GRIFFON

on an old family cemetery marker which is, or was, located on Route 85 near Gilmer.]

Griffith, William   U.S. Army quartermaster sergeant at Fort Dearborn; enlisted May 1812; survived the massacre of Aug. 15, 1812, with the help of Topenebe before the battle began; escaped the Indians, traveling and reaching Detroit with the Healds on Sept. 22; one of the few survivors who later recorded their experience, his account of the massacre is in Robert B. McAfee's *History of the Late War in the Western Country* [see Bibliography]. [12, 226, 463]

Griffon   French, *Le Griffon*; also *The Griffin*; received its name in compliment to Count Frontenac, on whose escutcheon two winged griffins were emblazoned as supporters; first ship on the Great Lakes, weighing 45 tons and built in 1678 by Dutch shipwrights for La Salle's 1679-81 expedition to Illinois; blessed by Father Hennepin for its maiden (and final) voyage, and placed into the Niagara River above the falls; sailed to the Green Bay peninsula where La Salle, Tonti, and 32 crew members disembarked and continued their voyage with canoes; laden with furs, *Le Griffon* was lost on the return trip to Niagara in 1679, presumably foundering in the Rock Island Passage. La Salle's orders

had been for the ship to deliver its cargo and then return to meet him at the mouth of the St. Joseph River.

Grignon, Pierre and Augustin   also Perish [a diminutive of Pierre]; was a visitor to Chicago in c.1794. Through his brother Augustin a brief narrative of Pierre's visit [in the *Wisconsin State Historical Society Collections* 3] has reached posterity; see the following excerpt:

Chicago means the place of the skunk. I understood these animals were very plenty there. At a very early period, there was a negro lived there named Baptist Point de Saible; my brother, Perish Grignen, visited Chicago about 1794, and told me that Point De-Saible was a large man; that he had a commission for some office, but for what particular object, or from what government, I cannot now recollect. He was a trader, pretty wealthy, and drank freely. I know not what became of him. Augustin Grignon, Butte des Morts, WI, 1857.

In 1825 the trader Augustin Grignon lived on the Fox River between Fort Howard (Green Bay, WI) and Fort Winnebago (Portage, WI) with an Indian wife. They had many children, some of them blond and blue-eyed; one of their daughters married [see] Ebenezer C. Childs. For Pierre Grignon, also see essay on Jean Baptiste Point de Sable on page 288. [13]

Griswold, S.P.   worked for M.B. Beaubien, advertising Buffalo Ale in the Aug. 29, 1835, *Chicago American* – "Just received, a few bbls. superior Ale, and for sale low"; in October, as an auctioneer at the corner of South Water and Dearborn streets, he advertised six lots "situated in the Towns of Juliett and Kankakee."

Grisworld, Harmon   mail carrier of Niles, MI who once a week carried the mail on horseback to and from Chicago in 1831.

Gross, George C.   German immigrant in 1835, from Pensylvania; became a member of the German Evangelical Association. [342]

Grosse Pointe   also Gros Point; a name French

voyageurs gave to an area 13 miles N of the Chicago River mouth where the steeper coastline forms an obtuse angle projecting into the lake; was originally densely wooded; here, according to Thomas Forsyth, the Indians netted large numbers of whitefish every June; in 1826 [see] Stephen J. Scott and his family from Maryland homesteaded here; in 1829 the Prairie du Chien Treaty awarded the French-Indian [see] Ouilmette family of Chicago two sections of land at [see] *Grosse Pointe*, forcing Scott to abandon his homestead on the property and move to the Des Plaines River valley; settlement of this N shore region did not begin in earnest until 1835; from 1874 to 1924 a Village of Gross Point existed, later to be incorporated in the communities of Wilmette and Evanston.

grouse   the two Illinois species, the ruffed grouse (*Bonasa umbellus*) and the sharp-tailed grouse (*Tympanuchus phasianellus*) have become extirpated in the state as a result of hunting and habitat destruction, but were plentiful in pioneer days according to early reports; for an excerpt of such a report, one by Lt. J.G. Furman in 1830, see birds. [64]

Grummo, Paul   also Grummow; U.S. Army private at Fort Dearborn; enlisted in October 1810; survived the massacre of Aug. 15, 1812, and was later ransomed from the Indians. [226]

Grus americana   see whooping crane.

Grus canadensis   see sandhill crane.

Gryon   the Gryon children: Rolland, Orville, Abibail, and Charles, probably siblings, were enrolled as grade school students in the class taught by [see] John Watkins in December 1835. Names of corresponding parents were not recorded. [728]

Guardian Angel Mission   see missions.

Guerin, Byram   resident in 1835; his name was on a school-related petition signed on Sept. 19, 1835. [12]

Guild, Albert H.   arrived from New York in 1834; ✦ Guild & Durant [James T.], dry goods, &c., 149 Lake St.; died in St. Louis. [351]

Guillory, —   often misspelled Guillary, Guilleroi,

Gary, Garie, Guary, Guyari, Gauri, and Guarie; French trader whose Mackinac-based company owned a post on the W bank of the north branch of the Chicago River near the Forks, located where Fulton Street now intersects with the river. Quaife thought the trader's correct name was probably Jean Baptiste Guillory, son of Joseph Guillory and Louise Bolon, but his opinion seems based on a misinterpretation of the name on a trading license issued in 1779 to a Jean Baptiste Guillon. According to John F. Swenson, and based on the Michilimackinac baptismal registry, he was a son of Simon Guillory who died at Mackinac c.1744. Gurdon Hubbard describes a remnant of the gardens and adjacent cornfields surrounding Guillory's post, noted in 1818; Hubbard learned from Antoine des Champs, Louis Bisson, and other older *voyageurs* that the property existed prior to 1778, which would make Guillory an earlier resident of Chicago than Point de Sable, who settled there sometime between 1784 and 1788. Guillory's name, in its multiple variations as listed above, was also used in the early years, and as late as 1830, for the north branch of the Chicago River—as Guarie's River, &c. [12, 357, 564, 649]

Gulpin, Samuel G.   mentioned by East as having lived in Chicago in 1828. [208]

Gunday, Lewis   also Ganday or Louis Gouday; voted on July 24 and Aug. 2, 1830.

Gurin, Byron   listed as a subscriber to the *Chicago Democrat* in November 1833.

Gustin, William   in a July 7, 1834, circuit court suit John K. Boyer sought payment for "12 pieces of cotton sheeting and about 30 lbs. of coffee" from William and four others; legal notices involving him appeared in the Sept. 3 *Chicago Democrat*.

Gutmann, Frederick   arrived in 1833 from Bavaria with his wife, Mary; both died in Chicago, Mary in 1857, Frederick in 1869; left six children: Catherine, Barbara, George, Leonard, Adam, and Mary.

Guy, John   listed as a member of the Presbyterian Church in June 26, 1833. [12]

Guyon, William B.   also Guion; U.S. assistent civil engineer within the topographical corps under Dr. William Howard, together with Henry Belin and Frederick Harrison, Jr.; in 1830 conducted surveys at Chicago in preparation for the construction of the Chicago harbor and the Illinois & Michigan Canal; both Harrison and Guyon became ill in the summer of 1830, and Belin completed the work in 1831, with the assistance of Chauncey Barnard, Jr. [423, 681, 682]

Haas, Wilhelm   (1800-1861) also William; German immigrant beer brewer who together with Konrad Sulzer, arrived from Watertown, NY, with 150 barrels of ale and brewing equipment in 1836 [according to Hofmeister; Angle gives an unlikely 1833 as the year of their arrival]. Together they founded a brewery that initially produced 600 barrels of beer per year. The brewery was probably Chicago's second, possibly that listed in the Dec. 9, 1835 *Chicago Democrat*, the first one having been opened late summer by J. and W. Crawford [see breweries]; ✦ brewer, corner of Chicago Avenue and Pine [Michigan] Street, then in partnership with William Ogden; the brewery was sold to Michael Diversey and William Lill in 1843. [17, 342]

Hackley, Lt. James, Jr.   from Kentucky; stationed at Fort Dearborn until the end of 1818 when promoted to captain, then resigned from the military; according to Mrs. Susan Callis, he "married Rebecca [Rebekah] Wells, of Fort Wayne, daughter [niece] of Capt. William Wells," who was killed in the Fort Dearborn massacre; resigned in 1818 and died in 1831. [12, 74]

Hadduck, Edward H.   (c.1810-1881) also Haddock; born in Salisbury, NH; came in May 1833, staying initially at Dexter Graves's boarding house (Mansion House) at $5 a week, then married Louisa, Graves's daughter on Dec. 11, 1834, R.J. Hamilton officiating, and later that year purchased the hotel from his father-in-law; on Nov. 24, 1835, filed an affidavit in support of E.B. William's claim for wharfing privileges; remained in Chicago permanently, serving as alderman in 1838; ✦ commission merchant, South Water Street; died on May 30, 1881; in 1885 his widow lived at 2976 Michigan Ave. [12, 571]

Haight, Isaac   arrived from New York in 1834 and served as wood inspector in 1835; was active in local Democratic politics as a delegate to the Flag Creek convention in July 1836; ✦ North Canal Street near West Lake Street. [12, 351, 544]

Haines, Elijah Middlebrook   (1822-1889) born in Oneida, NY; arrived in May 1835; worked as a tailor and was active in politics; ✦ tailor, South Water Street between Clark and LaSalle; married Melinda Griswold on Aug. 8, 1845; later moved to Lake County and founded Hainesville; in 1885 lived in Waukegan. [12, 351]

Haines, John Charles   born in 1818 in New York State; arrived on May 26, 1835; ✦ clerk, George W. Merrill; in partnership with Jared Gage, acquired Chicago flour mills in 1846; helped organize the Chicago waterworks system in 1854; active in the Old Settlers' Society beginning in 1855; served as mayor in 1858 and 1859; president of the Illinois Savings Institution in 1859; in 1885 lived in Waukegan. [12, 351]

Haldimand, Sir Frederick   (-1791) British governor of Canada from 1778 to 1784, succeeding

HALF WAY HOUSE [738]

Governor Carleton. The *Haldimand Papers* have survived, are in the British Library, and in the *Haldimand Collection* of the Canadian Archives, and are a rich source of historical information on military actions, trade, and politics in the Great Lakes and Illinois during the American Revolution. [12]

Hale, James   a child by this name was enrolled as grade school student in the class taught by [see] John Watkins in December 1835. Names of corresponding parents were not recorded. [728]]

Hale, John P.   on March 5, 1834, submitted an application to lease wharfing privileges along the river, likely as a partner of [see] Wm. Hogue & Co.; featured in a lawsuit notice in the April 16 *Chicago Democrat* that year; by 1848 had become known as an active abolitionist. [28, 544]

Hale, Timothy R.   petitioned the state general assembly with John Mann, Nelson R. Norton, and James Kinzie, and on Feb. 11, 1835, was authorized to erect a toll bridge for "persons, wagons, and droves of cattle" across the Little Calimic [Calumet] near where the State road between Chicago and La Porte, IN, crossed; father or brother of Virginia, second wife of James Kinzie.

Half Day   also Aptakisic; chief of a Potawatomi band that planted fields near Half Day [Lake County] and hunted along the Du Page River near Naper's Settlement in the early 1830s; during the Black Hawk scare, he warned settlers on farms along the river and escorted many to Fort Dearborn; an orator for his tribe in many treaty negotiations between 1827 and 1846. [61, 697]

Half Way House   residence and tavern of [see] Dr. E.G. Wight; built in 1835 on the Ottawa Road near Walker's Grove [Plainfield, IL]. [738]

Haliburton, Jane [Alice?]   born in New York in 1759, half sister of John Kinzie from an earlier marriage of their mother, Emily Tyne, to the British Army chaplain William Haliburton (see Kinzie family tree on page 222); in June 1768 she married Sampson Flemming, a deputy commis-

DAVID HALL [12]

sioner of stores at Detroit, and when widowed, married Nicholas Low of New York; not known to have visited Chicago. [564]

Hall, Basil   English visitor to the United States whose popular travel account, *Travels in North America in the Years 1827 and 1828*, was published in Edinburgh in 1830; his work contains good descriptions of the Grand Prairie.

Hall, Benjamin   tanner, came in 1832 from Giles County, VA, with his wife Margaret [former wife of John Kinzie, née McKenzie], whom he had married in 1796; operated a tannery at the Forks with John and Samuel Miller, just N of Miller House; there were two children, David and Sarah; had purchased from Samuel Miller a lot on block 14, where the tannery stood [see map on page 44]; on the list of subscribers to the *Chicago Democrat* in November 1833; a sister (see Hall, Emily) married Archibald Callwell; built a tavern with [see] John Marshall at Dutchman's Point in 1840 and was proprietor; in 1885 lived at Wheaton. [12, 13, 351]

Hall, David   from Virginia; son of Benjamin Hall,

and half brother of James Kinzie (see Kinzie family tree on page 222); arrived in 1823 or earlier, but in that year built Wolf Tavern with James Kinzie, owning and operating the associated store as late as 1834; was clerk of the Wallace estate sale on April 27, 1827, purchasing then 6 1/4 dozen scalping knives and other goods; was clerk for the American Fur Co. under J.B. Beaubien for some time; Kinzie & Hall advertised in the June 25, 1834 *Chicago Democrat*, one door E from the corner of Lake and Canal streets, near the Point, selling dry goods, hardware, and groceries; in the Dec. 2, 1835 *Chicago Democrat* the partners announced the sale of the entire stock of goods and offered thanks to their customers. [12, 708]

Hall, E.B.   shoemaker; arrived in 1832. [351]

Hall, Emily   sister of Benjamin Hall; from western Virginia; married Archibald Caldwell early in 1827 in Virginia and traveled on horseback with her husband via Fort Wayne, arriving in July; in the spring of 1829 Caldwell abandoned her to find contentment in the nearby wigwam of an Indian woman, Josette; Emily sued for divorce in June 1830; Archibald did not contest and Emily later married the discharged soldier Cole Weeks.

Hall, George   arrived in 1832. [351]

Hall, M.H.T., M.D.   served as the seventh Fort Dearborn medical officer for a period of only two months between the terms of duty of Dr. William S. Madison and Dr. Thomas P. Hall; he arrived in September 1821. [738]

Hall & Miller   a large tannery in 1833 at the Forks, owned and operated by Benjamin Hall and John and Samuel Miller. [13]

Hall, Thomas P., M.D.   born in Maryland; completed medical training in or before 1813; succeeded Dr. W.S. Madison, becoming the eighth military physician at Fort Dearborn in 1821; was present when Captain Long's expeditionary party visited the fort from June 5-11, 1823; remained at the fort until the garrison was withdrawn in 1823; was the author of a valuable manuscript concern-

ing the Potawatomi and their medical practices, variously quoting Keating's expedition narrative [see Bibliography]; died 1825 in Georgia. [12]

Hall, William   listed as owner of 80 acres of land in the NE quarter of Section 6, Township 39, prior to 1836, as per Andreas, *History of Chicago*, pp. 112-113. A William Hall, member of the Calumet Club, died in August 1881. [12]

Hallam, Rev. Isaac William   born in Connecticut in 1809; arrived from New York in 1834 with his wife Nancy [née William of Richmond, VA, married on Feb. 19, 1833], who bore him 10 children (one boy was named John Kinzie; a daughter, Lucy William, died in 1839); took charge as the first permanent pastor of the budding Episcopalian congregation on Oct. 19, 1834, though the initial sermon (on the preceding Sunday) had been given by Rev. Palmer Dyer; in 1835 conducted the wedding ceremony of Peter Pruyne and Rebecca Sherman, and in 1836 that of Thomas Watkins and Therese LaFramboise; ✦ St. James' Church, Cass [Wabash] Street near Illinois; in 1843 returned with his family to Stonington, CT, where he was living in 1885. [12, 351]

Halsman, George   see Holsman, George.

Hamilton, Amos C.   arrived in 1835; advertised in the Nov. 25, *Chicago Democrat* a lottery and exchange office at No. 8 on the W side of Dearborn, four doors from the corner with Water Street, selling tickets to various weekly lotteries and trading in uncurrent banknotes, gold and silver; member of the fire engine company No.1 in December [see petition to the village board of Dec. 16, 1835, with entry on firefighting]; in 1837 was Whig candidate for assessor, but lost; ✦ clerk, B.F. Knapp. [12, 351, 544]

Hamilton, Henry   British colonel, served as lieutenant governor and superintendent of Indian affairs of Detroit and its dependencies from 1775 to 1779 [was succeeded in that position by Major De Peyster]; on Feb. 25, 1779, was captured by George Rogers Clark at Vincennes and became an Ameri-

REV. ISAAC WILLIAM HALLAM [12]

can prisoner at Williamsburg; after release, served as governor of Canada in 1785, and later became governor of Dominica.

Hamilton, Henry Raymond   Chicago author of *The Epic of Chicago*, a historical review of the city's early years, published in 1932; son of Henry E. Hamilton, who edited *Incidents and Events in the Life of Gurdon S. Hubbard*; grandson of Col. Richard J. Hamilton, and first cousin twice removed of Gurdon S. Hubbard.

Hamilton, John   U.S. Army private and drummer at Fort Dearborn; enlisted in July 1808; killed in action at the massacre of 1812. [226]

Hamilton, Polemus D.   born 1813; arrived in 1834 from Wales, NY, with his brother Thomas E.; erected many of the first frame buildings in the town, the first being a store for James Woodruff at the corner of South Water and Wells streets; purchased acreage at the Yankee Settlement [Lockport] in 1835; helped Nelson R. Norton build the *Clarissa* in 1835, acquiring half ownership of the

RICHARD JONES HAMILTON [12]

vessel upon completion in 1836; married Cynthia Holmes of New York in 1836 (three children: David G., Mary J., and Maria E.); ◆ carpenter, Clark Street; lived at 126 Clark St. in 1885. [12, 351]

Hamilton, Richard Jones (1799-1860) often noted as R.I. Hamilton; also referred to as Colonel Hamilton, a title of deference to his activities in the Chicago militia during the Black Hawk War; born in Danville, KY, came to Illinois in 1820; married Diana W. Buckner in 1822, daughter of an historic Kentucky family; admitted to the bar in 1827 while justice of the peace for Jackson County; circuit-riding lawyer in 1829; was elected first judge of the probate court in March 8, 1831; second lawyer to settle in Chicago [Russell Heacock had come in 1827], arriving on April 9, 1831, from Vandalia with a notary commission and with the governor's appointment as Cook County recorder, replacing Reverend See in this office; with him came his wife and two children, Richard N. and Sarah, who later attended school under Miss Eliza Chappel

in 1833; all lived in the Agency house on the N side of the river from 1831 to 1833; became the first clerk of the Cook County Circuit Court and served from 1831 to 1837; in October 1831, was appointed commissioner of the county's school lands and held this office until 1840, and in this capacity arranged the sale of the Chicago school section; subsequently held numerous other official county positions; in c.1832, Hamilton purchased lots in blocks 20 and 21 from Jesse B. Brown and J.S.C. Hogan, respectively [see map on page 44]; served under Captain Kercheval in the Chicago militia during the Black Hawk War, listed on the muster roll of May 3, 1832. Diana attended Reverend J. Walker's first sermon in 1832 and was active in the Methodist Church; a second daughter Eleanor (or Ellen) was born in 1832, and a third, Diana B. in 1834, shortly before her mother's death. In August 1833, Hamilton was one of the "Qualified Electors" who voted to incorporate the town [for a copy of that meeting's report, see entry on incorporation], and in September was present at the Indian Treaty of Chicago and signed the document as a witness; late in 1835 he and W.E. Owen filed a claim for wharfing privileges for lot 4, block 19; that year he married Harriet L. Hubbard, sister of Henry G. Hubbard, of Chicago, the latter two being children of Ahira Hubbard and cousins of Gurdon S. Hubbard; as per notice in the *Chicago American*, their daughter Pauline died at 16 months on Aug. 16, 1839; ◆ clerk circuit court, corner of Clark and Randolph; Harriet died at age 27 in 1842; married Mrs. Priscilla P. Tuly in 1843; his ▲ grave site is located at Rosehill Cemetery; ➡ Hamilton Avenue (2100 W). [12, 28]

Hamilton, Thomas E. from Erie County, NY; arrived in 1834 with his brother Polemus D. and went into business erecting frame houses; in 1835 helped build the *Clarissa*, purchasing quarter interest the following year; ◆ carpenter, Madison Street, corner of LaSalle.

Hamilton, Lt. Thomas see Whistler, Catherine.

Hamilton, William Stephen born in New York City; son of famous statesman Alexander Hamilton; came to Fort Dearborn in 1823 while returning from a cattle drive from southern Illinois to Green Bay; in his employ was John Hamlin, a justice of the peace, enabling then the marriage of Dr. Wolcott and Ellen Marion Kinzie; see Hamlin, John. [12]

Hamlin, John as justice of the peace of Fulton County and while returning from a business trip to Green Bay, performed the marriage ceremony at Fort Dearborn between Dr. Alexander Wolcott and Ellen Marion Kinzie on July 20, 1823; stocked provisions for the American Fur Co. as its Peoria representative; at times covered the Chicago trade of the company, as in 1824, when Crafts left for Mackinac; in 1825 sent the first shipment of produce to Chicago in keelboats on the Illinois River to the mouth of the Kankakee, changing to Durham boats for delivery up the Aux Plaines River; as a member of the Whig party, became state senator in 1834; ➡ Hamlin Avenue and Hamlin Boulevard (3800 W). [12, 544]

Hammer, George from Washington County, IN; staked a claim in Hanover Township with those of his brothers, [see] David and Thomas Deweese; returned with his wife Elizabeth (née Coulter) and children [see John Hammer] to build a log house and farm in 1835; died in 1882. [13, 278]

Hammer, John farmer; born in 1820 in Washington County, IN; came with his brother's family in 1835 to Hanover Township; married E. Browning in 1842. [13, 278]

Hamtramck, Col. John Francis born in Canada; in 1794 commanded the left wing of General Wayne's army at Fallen Timbers; in March 1803, as commandant of the First Infantry at Detroit, and as ordered by General Dearborn, directed Capt. John Whistler to erect barracks and a strong stockade at Chicago (the first Fort Dearborn); died later in April and was succeeded at Detroit by Maj. Zebulon Pike. [544]

Hanchett, John L.   born c.1805; arrived from New York in June 1835; married L.J. Moore from Massachusetts on April 27, 1837; ✦ surveyor and engineer on the Illinois & Michigan Canal; held an office at the public works; lived at 371 Wabash Ave. in 1885. [12, 351]

Handy, Henry S.   (c.1804-1846) later called Major Handy; arrived from Washington City in 1832 as a bricklayer and mason; by 1833 had purchased from J.B. Beaubien the old Dean House, located on the lakeshore S of the fort and lived there with his family; married to Laura W. Bellows, who later divorced him (per notice in the *Chicago American*, 1843); an Emily Handy attended school under Miss Eliza Chappel in 1833, presumably their daughter; on March 10, 1833, General Gratiot appointed him assistent superintendent [under Maj. George Bender] of the harbor project; when Major Bender left Oct. 31, 1833, he carried on as acting superintendent until Second Lt. James Allen was given the superintendent position by Gratiot in January 1834. While supervising construction, Handy showed prudence and foresight, demonstrated in an excerpt of a letter written to General Gratiot in Washington City, in the autumn of 1833 [see below]; a partnership with [see] Charles Taylor was dissolved March 4, 1834; later active in community affairs, such as the Infant School organization; ✦ Major Handy, bricklayer and plasterer [listed with Joy Handy, same profession]; died at Bayfield, MI; in 1885 divorced wife Laura was listed as widow and lived at 11 Page St. [12]

I would suggest propriety of purchasing the pork and beef that may be required next season as soon as possible for the reason that the emigration to this place and the neighboring country will be such next season that provisions will be extremely high. The treaty continued so long this fall and the number of Indians and whites were such that provisions are now as high as in Washington City. Hogs and beef can be bought at a very low rate within one hundred and twenty miles from this place and driven on foot and slaugh-
tered at or near Chicago. By so doing, nearly half of the expense could be saved for provisions.

Handy House   see Dean House.

Hannah   48-ton schooner, built at Black River, OH in 1816; coming from St. Joseph, it called at Chicago under Captain Sprague on July 10 and 16, 1835.

Hanson, Joseph L.   from England, arrived in 1835; opened a grocery store and signed up with the "Pioneer" hook and ladder company, a voluntary brigade; as per announcement in the *Chicago American* of Nov. 5, 1836, married the schoolteacher Ruth Leavenworth "last Thursday evening"; ✦ grocery and provision store, 146 Lake St. [12, 351]

Hanson, Oliver C.   Negro from S. Domingo; arrived in 1834 and opened a barbershop; still living in Chicago in 1880. [351, 544]

Hapgood, Dexter J.   arrived in 1832; early member of the Catholic congregation, who among other citizens in April 1833, added his name [misinterpreted as Assgood] to the petition presented to Bishop Rosati of St. Louis, asking that a priest be assigned to them; lived eight miles S of [Wheeling]. [12, 351]

harbor   see Chicago harbor.

Harding, J.A.   also T.A. and F.A.; debated Dr. J.T. Temple within the Chicago Lyceum forum that met at the Presbyterian church on Dec. 8, 1835; the question was whether or not the removal of the Indians west of the Mississippi by the U.S. government was "consistent with faith, humanity, and sound Policy"; was elected secretary of the Lyceum on Dec. 12; was one of three directors for the Young Men's Temperance Society, organized on Dec. 19.

Hardscrabble   early name for the area that, beginning c.1809, included the [see] Leigh farm on the south branch of the Chicago River at [now] 24th Street; later residents of the locale included Chief Robinson, the Laughtons, the Laframboises, the Galloways, Crafts, Wallace, and the Heacocks.

Harlem   name of an early community in the area that was originally Noyesville [Oak Park and River
Forest].

Harman, William   blacksmith; arrived in 1835; ✦ North Water Street, near N State; lived at 210 South Water St. in 1885. [12, 351]

Harmar, Gen. Josiah   Pennsylvania native; led an unsuccessful campaign against the midwestern Indian tribes in 1790; resigned in 1792; died 1813. Not until General Wayne succeeded in defeating the Indians at Fallen Timbers in 1794, was western settlement a viable choice. Harmar's papers are in the Clements Library, University of Michigan.

Harmon, Charles Loomis   arrived from Vermont in 1832; son of Dr. Elijah D. Harmon, older brother of Isaac; the brothers ran a dry goods store on the SW corner of South Water and Clark streets in 1833 and 1834; on March 1, 1834, the firm's name became Harmon, Loomis & Co. when their cousin [see] Horatio G. Loomis joined them; unsuccessful candidate for alderman in 1837; ✦ Harmon, (Horatio G.) Loomis & Co., wholesale grocers, same location; married Abba Ann Curtis on Dec. 14, 1840.

Harmon, Edwin R.   born c.1816 in Fredonia, NY; arrived in August 1833, likely a relative of Dr. E.D. Harmon; ✦ clerk, Harmon & Loomis; lived in Chicago in 1879, but by 1885 lived at Aurora. [12, 351]

Harmon, Elijah Dewey, M.D.   (1782-1869) early Chicago physician, born in Bennington, VT; studied medicine in Manchester, VT; married Welthyan Loomis on Oct. 30, 1808; see sons Charles and Isaac; entered the army as a surgeon in 1812, resuming private practice at the end of the war; came in May 1830 and served as (the 10th) medical officer of the garrison following Assistent Surgeon Finley, also practicing privately; for a short while he lived and practiced in the old Kinzie House, where his shingle is said to have been displayed; acquired ownership of 138.24 acres of beachfront land in Section 22, Township 39, as per Andreas, *History of Chicago*, pp. 112-113; his family followed one year later; was the second civilian physician to

ISAAC DEWEY HARMON [412]

Captain Kercheval in the militia during the Black Hawk War, listed on the muster roll of May 3, 1832; the brothers jointly owned a store in 1833 and 1834 on the SW corner of South Water and Clark, advertising in the first issue of the *Chicago Democrat*, Nov. 26, 1833, as C. & I. Harmon, dry goods and crockery; on March 1, 1834, the firm's name became Harmon, Loomis & Co. when their cousin [see] Horatio G. Loomis joined them; appointed town clerk by the first board of trustees, elected on Aug. 10, 1833; also served as justice of the peace for Cook County in the early 1830s; his residence in 1833 was on the N side of the river, near the Forks; in the Aug. 6, 1834, *Chicago Democrat* his company offered for sale the first "2 cases Artificial Flowers" available in town, and in the June 27, 1835, *Chicago American* advertised "STUART'S Celebrated Confectionary And a choice lot of Perfumery"; his name was on a school-related petition signed on Sept. 19 and in December he was appointed judge of probate for Cook County; ✦

ISAAC N. HARMON [412]

establish practice in Chicago (Dr. Wolcott was the first); performed ★★★ **Chicago's 1st** major surgical procedure in the winter of 1832-33 by amputating the frozen foot of a Canadian *métis* mail carrier who had come from Green Bay on horseback; served under Captain Kercheval in the militia during the Black Hawk War, listed on the muster roll of May 3, 1832, and during the cholera epidemic of 1832, cared for the soldiers of the garrison, earning high praise from Maj. William Whistler, commanding officer. Harmon's house was on the N side of the river, between the Forks and Colonel Hamilton's house, where he kept his unusually extensive medical library; elected justice of the peace as per *Chicago American*, Aug. 8, 1835; from 1834 on he lived mostly in Texas [though listed in Fergus' 1839 *Directory*], but often visited Chicago; is buried at Graceland Cemetery. [12]

Harmon, Isaac Dewey (1814-1886) son of Dr. Elijah D. Harmon, and brother of Charles L.; clerk for the Detroit merchant Oliver Newberry prior to his coming to Chicago in 1831; served under

ELIJAH DEWEY HARMON, M.D. [137]

dry goods merchant, 8 Clark St.; on Oct. 26, 1842 married Anna M. Huntoon of St. Charles; occasionally advised people on legal matters, but was not a trained lawyer; for a letter by Isaac to his brother Charles, describing the collapse of the first lighthouse, see entry on lighthouse; lived at 4333 Ellis Ave. in 1885. [12, 351]

Harmon, Issac N. born c.1826 in Fredonia, NY; arrived as a child on Aug. 3, 1833, presumably in the company of Edwin R. Harmon, but the relationship is unknown, likely in-laws of Dr. E.D. Harmon; still lived in Chicago in 1879. [12, 351]

Harmon, Isaac and Martin children by this name, possibly siblings, were enrolled as grade school students in the class taught by [see] John Watkins in December 1835. Names of corresponding parents were not recorded. Isaac is probably identical with Isaac N. of the previous entry. [728]

Harmon, Loomis & Co. see Harmon, Charles Loomis; see Loomis, Horatio G. On Nov. 21, 1835 both men submitted a claim for wharfing privi-

```
100 BARRELS SALT, 30 Barrels Whis-
       key, and 1 Cask of old Whiskey, of
superior quality, just received by
             HARMON, LOOMIS & CO.
Chicago, June 9th, 1835.                    tf 2
```

leges on lot 1, block 18, and in the Dec. 5 *Chicago American* advertised "New Store of Napersville." The account books of early transactions of the dry goods, grocery and hardware business in Chicago and those of the branch store at Naperville are preserved in the Chicago Historical Society. [28]

Harmon, Martin D. arrived from Vermont in 1833; became a charter member of the First Baptist Church congregation on Oct. 19, and plastered John Calhoun's printing office in November of that year, together with Willard Jones; an enthusiast early in 1834 to promote temperance societies within the county. [12, 544]

Harmon, Samuel on the list of subscribers to the *Chicago Democrat* in November 1833.

Harper, — according to J.J. Flinn, a white man named Harper was accused in 1833 under the vagrant law and sold at auction; for detail, see White, George. [249]

Harrington, H. arrived from Vermont in 1835. [351, 733]

Harrington, James see Herrington, James, Sr.

Harris, Benjamin born 1802 in Pensylvania; served as member of the Chicago Company in the Black Hawk War of 1832; married to Sarah Cortright (1824); purchased real estate in block 8 [see map on page 44] and soon after sold the land to Lt. Enoch Thompson; died in Iowa. [12, 733]

Harris, William (1785-1865) settler in the Fox River valley by 1831 with his wife, Rebecca (née Coombs, married 1814), and children Hiram, Nancy, Emily Ann; was among the refugees seeking temporary shelter at Fort Dearborn during the early months of the Black Hawk War. [239]

Harrison, Frederick, Jr. U.S. assistant civil engineer under Dr. William Howard, together with

Henry Belin and William B. Guyon; conducted surveys at Chicago in 1830 in preparation for the construction of the harbor and the Illinois & Michigan Canal; both Harrison and Guyon became ill in the summer of 1830, and Belin completed the work in 1831, and ✷ "Map No. 1 of the Survey of the Michigan & Illinois Canal" was filed on May 20, 1832 within the Topographical Bureau, Engineer Department, U.S. Army; under Howard, Harrison also prepared the manuscript ✷ map [National Archives, Washington, D.C.] of the mouth of the Chicago River, dated Feb. 24, 1830, incorporating the proposed piers for improving the harbor. [423, 681, 682]

Harrison, William Henry (1773-1841) from Virginia; served as lieutenant and favorite aide throughout General Wayne's campaign against the Indians in the Northwest; appointed governor of the Indiana Territory in 1800 by President John Adams when Illinois and Chicago were still part of that territory; in 1804, as governor of Indiana Territory, he negotiated with leaders of the Sauk and Fox tribes the Treaty of St. Louis, resulting in cession to the government of 14,803,500 acres of land in Missouri, Illinois, and southern Wisconsin. The Indians received in return $22,234 and the right to live on the land as long as it was owned by the government. At a later time, this treaty was bitterly denounced as unfair by the Sauk leader Black Hawk, and his defiance led to the Black Hawk War in 1832, in which Fort Dearborn and the surrounding settlement became involved. In 1809, Governor Harrison concluded the Treaty of Fort Wayne with the Potawatomi, Delaware, Miami, and Eel River tribes. This ceded to the United States three tracts of land containing more than 2.5 million acres on the upper Wabash River. The treaty was bitterly denounced by Tecumseh and his followers, and helped precipitate the War of 1812; later as general, Harrison further weakened Indian resistance at the Battle of Tippecanoe in 1811; became the ninth president of the United States in

1840 (campaign slogan: "Tippecanoe and Tyler, too"), serving only 32 days before he died; ➡ Harrison Street (600 S). [12, 427]

Harry a Negro boy brought from Kentucky by Gholson Kercheval; lived as an indentured servant with the John H. Kinzie family at the Agency house during part of 1831 [Note: indenture was for a definite term, slavery was permanent].

Hartzell, Thomas trader on the Illinois and Kankakee Rivers; first settler [Hennepin] in Putnam County in 1816, running a ferry there until 1831; attended the estate sale of W.H. Wallace on May 10, 1827, buying chintz shawls; on Sept. 4, 1830, the first day of land sales by the canal commissioners, bought three choice downtown lots in blocks 20 (lot 1) and 29 (lots 7 and 8) [see map on page 44]; in 1835 acquired the store of P.F.W. Peck at the SE corner of South Water and LaSalle streets.

Hatch, Luther and James C. brothers and farmers, arrived in 1832 and moved W to become the first settlers of [Lisle]; Luther was on the list of subscribers to the *Chicago Democrat* in November 1833; James built his home in 1833, establishing a wagon and blacksmith shop on his farm, and married Cornelia Whitlock. According to John J. Flinn, a man named Hatch, likely either Luther or James C., initiated ★★★ Chicago's 1st criminal trial in the spring of 1833 by complaining to Russell E. Heacock, then justice of the peace, that a fellow boarder at Old Geese's Tavern had robbed him of $34 in Bellow's Falls money [issued by a private bank, a practice common during the land boom from 1833-1838; see money]. The ensuing dramatic proceedings involved James W. Reed as constable, John D. Caton as prosecuting attorney, and Giles Spring as defense attorney, and are detailed in Flinn's book. [249, 314a]

Hathaway, Joshua P., Jr. took a census of the settlement in the summer of 1833 and reported that there were 43 houses and less than 100 men, women, and children; made the earliest published real estate ✷ map, "Chicago with the School Section, Wabansia and Kinzie Addition" in 1834 [followed shortly by the Wright map], compiled from the four original surveys as filed in the Cook County clerk's office; the map is referred to in a notice in the *Chicago Democrat* of June18, 1834, as follows: "Lithographic Maps of Chicago. – Mr. Jno. H. Kinzie procured while in New York a few copies of Lithographic maps of this Town. They are beautifully executed, and contain the Town Plat, together with the School Section, Wabansia, and Kinzie's Addition." Arthur Bronson partnered Kinzie in New York and there had 600 maps printed by Peter A. Mesier for $120.15; the men's correspondence on the matter is preserved within the Chicago Historical Society Collections. [164]

Hathaway, Rose   sister of Pamelia Calhoun (the printer's wife); visited Chicago in the spring of 1835 as described by John D. Caton. [121]

Hatheway, Abraham   squatter at [see] *Grosse Pointe* in 1834, ran a tavern, and said to have counterfeited negotiable Mexican dollar pieces. [580]

Hawley, Caroline   daughter of Pierce Hawley, who had come from Vermont and settled in the Fox River precinct of Peoria Co; married [see] Willard Scott on July 22, 1829, Rev. Isaac Scarritt officiating in a double ceremony that also wedded the groom's sister Parmelia to John Kinzie Clark at Holderman's Grove. Some later remembered that a short while before the marriage, a young Indian chief offered Mr. Hawley 10 ponies and a large quantity of furs for his daughter; to this proposal the young woman demurred, and her father informed the suitor that such was not the custom, that their religion did not permit the sale of daughters for wives.

Hawley, Pierce H.   originally from Vermont; moved with his family (and the family of his brother Aaron) to Vincennes in 1814, to the junction of the Fox and Illinois rivers in 1822, to Holderman's Grove in 1825 where he was taxed as resident of the second precinct of Peoria County, and in June 1830, placed a claim along the E fork of the Du Page River, buying additional land from Israel Blodgett, and there built a homestead; served as private both under Captain Kercheval in the Chicago company and in Captain Napier's volunteer militia during the Black Hawk War; also see Hawley, Caroline.

Hayes, Otho   U.S. Army sergeant at Fort Dearborn; listed as sawyer in John Kinzie's account book in June and July 1804; promoted to sergeant on April 23, 1811; killed in hand-to-hand combat at the massacre in 1812, after mortally wounding the Potawatomi chief Naunongee. [226, 404]

Hayward, Thomas   second factor at Fort Dearborn; succeeded Ebenezer Bellknap early in 1805; resigned in the spring of 1807 and was succeeded by Joseph B. Varnum. [544, 559]

Heacock, Russell E.   (1779-1849) also signed his name Hickok; born in Litchfield, CT; carpenter and ★★★ **Chicago's 1st** practicing lawyer; was admitted to the bar in 1816 and also that year married Rebecca Osborn in Jefferson County, IL; both arrived by sailing ship on July 4, 1827; initially lived in the old officers' quarters of Fort Dearborn, unoccupied at that time, then moved to a log cabin on the S side of the river, at the mouth of Frog Creek; by March 1828 they were at "Heacock's Point" [Bridgeport], one mile S of Leigh's farm, on the other side of the river; Serena, a daughter, was born in 1828, and later a son named Reuben B. On Dec. 7, 1830, Heacock received a license to keep a tavern "five miles from Chicago"; helped organize Cook County and brought the first suit in its circuit court; on Sept. 10, 1831, was appointed justice of the peace; in August 1833 he was one of the "Qualified Electors" who voted to incorporate the town [for a copy of that meeting's original report, see entry on incorporation], and was the only one to vote against incorporation; his reasons are unknown; prior to 1836, owned 160 acres of land along both sides of the south branch of the river in Section 32, Township 39 (Andreas, *History of Chicago*, pp. 112-113); in May 1835 opened a second story law and land agency office at the corner of Lake Street and Franklin, opposite the Exchange Coffee House; ◆ attorney, justice of peace, corner of Adams and Clark; was nicknamed "Shallow Cut" during the canal debate, because he favored a shallow rather than deep excavation [state bankruptcy later made a shallow cut necessary]; died of cholera in Chicago, after suffering a debilitating stroke six years earlier, leaving numerous descendents. [12, 249]

Heacock's Point   Russell E. Heacock's property on the E side of the south branch, one mile S of Hardscrabble, where he settled in 1828 and for which location he received a liquor license in 1830 and ran a tavern.

Heald, Capt. Nathan   (1775-1832) born in Ipswich, NH; promoted to U.S. Army captain of the First Infantry regiment on Jan.31, 1807; was commandant at Fort Wayne when, in June of 1810, he was ordered to Fort Dearborn to take over the command of the transferred Captain Whistler; remained until the fort's disastrous evacuation on Aug. 15, 1812. While on furlough in 1811, he traveled to Louisville, KY, and on May 23 married Rebekah Wells (1790-1857), daughter of Capt. Samuel Wells, a noted Indian fighter of Kentucky, and niece of Capt. William Wells, Indian agent at Fort Wayne at that time; in the spring of 1811 Rebekah joined her husband at Fort Dearborn, accompanied by a slave, Cicely, and Cicely's infant. Rebekah bore him five children, of whom two died early; in May 1812, at Fort Dearborn, Rebekah gave birth to a son "born dead for want of a skillful midwife," as recorded in the captain's journal [she had refused Dr. Van Voorhis' services, because he was "too young"]. Captain and Mrs. Heald were among the wounded survivors of the Fort Dearborn massacre, while Cicely and her child were killed. Topenebe and Pokagon took the Healds to St. Joseph, found shelter for them in the house of trader William Burnett, and from there Alexander Robinson conducted them by boat to Mackinac for a fee of $100; in September 1812 they reached Detroit. Heald received an honorable discharge in 1814. [12, 226, 410, 544, 559]

Heald, Mrs. Rebekah Wells born in Jefferson County, KY, in 1790; see Heald, Capt. Nathan. ❀ For a portrait of Rebekah Wells Heald, see page 368. [12, 410]

Healy's Slough see Ogden's Slough.

Heartless a schooner on Lake Michigan that arrived at Fort Dearborn in 1817 and attempted to navigate passage into the Chicago River, but was grounded and could not be freed; became ★★★ **Chicago's 1st shipwreck.**

Helm, Mrs. Margaret see McKillip, Margaret. [12, 226]

Helm, Lt. Linai Taliafero born in Virginia, of German extraction; came to Fort Dearborn as U.S. Army second lieutenant in June 1811, filling the vacancy created by the death of Lieutenant Thompson earlier in the year; had married Margaret McKillip on June 10, 1810, stepdaughter of John Kinzie: the union ended in divorce in 1829, with Margaret charging infidelity and drunkenness [records still preserved at the circuit court of Peoria]. Both were among the survivors of the Fort Dearborn massacre of Aug. 15, 1812; they became separated during the action, and he was taken prisoner by the Indians and removed to the Illinois River by the Ottawa chief Mittatasse, from whom he was ransomed on Aug. 30, with Black Partridge as intermediary, by the trader and U.S. Indian agent Thomas Forsyth in return for two horses and a keg of liquor. For the only son of their union, see Helm, William Edwin. Helm was promoted to first lieutenant on Jan. 20, 1813, and to captain on April 15, 1814; he resigned from the U.S Army later that year on Sept. 27; was again at Chicago with his wife in April 1818, noted in Kinzie's account book as Capt. L.T. Helm; died Oct. 5, 1838. [12, 226, 326, 327, 404]

Helm, William Edwin born Oct. 18, 1821, in Chicago; only son of Lt. Linai T. Helm and Mar-

garet McKillip; when his parents were divorced in 1829, his mother was awarded custody; lived in Detroit with his mother and stepfather, Dr. Lucius Abbott, later in Chicago and, after serving in the Civil War, in St. Louis.

He-Looks-Black see Awbenabi.

Hennepin, IL town on the Illinois River, named after the French missionary.

Hennepin, Père Louis (1640-c.1705) born in Ath, Belgium; studied under [see] Father Ribourde at the monastery in Béthune, France; Récollect missionary associated with Robert Cavelier de La Salle during La Salle's 1679-81 expedition; wrote about this and other western trips made in 1683, supplementing the text with an early ✳ map (1698) of the middle west. To his apparent discredit is his unlikely claim [see his 1697 publication] that he traveled prior to La Salle on the Mississippi from Illinois to the river's mouth and back, all in 43 days. In 1679 Hennepin mentions "Michican Lake," and notes that the French refer to it as "Illinois," most Indians as "Illinouk," and the Miami as "Misch-i-gon-ong," meaning *great-lake-place-of*. An observation of the landscape is detailed below, c.1683. [12, 265, 330-4, 611]

Boundless prairies interspersed with tall trees; you could find the finest pieces in the world; fruit trees and wild grape vines producing clusters a foot and a half long which ripen perfectly, herbs and grain in greater abundance than in the best lands in Europe. The air, very temperate and healthy, a country watered by countless lakes, rivers, and streams, mostly navigable. [265, 605]

Henry a Negro slave owned by John Kinzie in c.1812. [226]

Henry, — Chicago militia private; settler, killed at the Fort Dearborn massacre. [226]

Henry Clay lake steamer; called at Fort Dearborn in the fall of 1828 with territorial Governor Cass on board; Cass had come from Green Bay where he had met and negotiated a treaty with the Winnebago.

Henry, Patrick the eloquent orator of the American Revolution, who subsequently became governor of Virginia; when in 1778 the state extended its territorial claim to include the Illinois region, his authority as governor included Virginia's "Illinois County." In 1784 Virginia ceded Illinois to the United States; see jurisdictional chronology on page 209.

Henry Roop schooner under Captain Gould; coming from Buffalo, NY, the vessel called at Chicago on Sept. 29, 1835; was lost near Sandusky in 1843. [48]

Hercules schooner on Lake Michigan in 1818, under contract for the American Fur Co. at Mackinac; wrecked on Oct. 4 that year between the two Calumet Rivers after leaving Fort Dearborn; all aboard perished, among them [see] Lt. William Evileth.

Herndon, John F. served as a member of the Chicago militia company in the Black Hawk War of 1832. [12]

heron *Ardea herodias*; the great blue heron, largest of the herons in Illinois and one of the most numerous; still common where the upper Chicago River flows through quiet forest preserves within the busy metropolis. [64]

Heron, James E. native of Pensylvania; had been sutler at Mackinac in 1821, came to Fort Dearborn in 1822 to work as sutler with [see] Henry Whiting, but the association ended the following year when he became sutler at Fort Howard; died in 1845. [12]

Herrick, R.E. on the list of subscribers to the *Chicago Democrat* in November 1833.

Herrington, Crawford younger brother of James Clayton, Jr.; came in 1835 with his wife Rachel, and opened a drayage concern at his brother's store [Geneva], hauling furs procured to Chicago and returning with town goods – $3 a day for the seven-day round trip; erratic compensation from James resulted in his family's return to Pensylvania in 1837. [233]

Herrington, James Clayton, Jr. (1798-1839) in May 1833 brought his family from Crawford County, PA, to claim his father's land and cabin, but his wife (Mary Charity Patterson, married 1819) was later said to be "not satisfied with the moral tone of Chicago as a place to rear her sons" [they would have 10 children in all]; a notice in the *Chicago Democrat* of Oct. 22, 1834, reports that Herrington's horse was stolen by a deserter; in April 1835 he sought to enhance his investment ["a good grove of timber & water" in his father's words] and began to homestead in the Fox River valley; opened a store that initiated a leading role in the founding of the community of Geneva. [233]

Herrington, James Clayton, Sr. Harrington on J.S.C. Hogan's register and in Andreas' index; engineer and surveyor, applied to work as surveyor of the Huron Territory and traveled from his native Pensylvania to Fort Dearborn in 1830; awaiting confirmation, he made a claim for 106.95 acres of land along the lakeshore, S of 12th Street, in Section 22, Township 39, as per Andreas, *History of Chicago*, pp. 112-113; letters to his sons express faith in the fertile soil and the value of ownership; contracted ague as private in Capt. J.S.C. Hogan's company during the Black Hawk War [July 1832] and returned home. [12, 155, 233, 714]

Hessey, William advertised the rental of a house near the Point in the Oct. 8, 1834 *Chicago Democrat*; ◆ ready-made clothing, Randolph Street near bridge.

Hesslington, George also Heslington; from Yorkshire, England; came in 1833 with his wife Ann and daughter Annie [married James Blann in 1850] and acquired land to farm in Northfield Township; on the list of subscribers to the *Chicago Democrat* in November 1833. [13]

Heward, Hugh trader from Detroit to the Illinois River who visited Point de Sable on May 10, 1790, at Chicago, stayed two nights, and bought provisions; stopped at Peoria, where he visited and named in his journal 10 Frenchmen who were

REV. ISAAC TAYLOR HINTON, D.D. [12]

"settled among the Indians"; left a manuscript journal, a transcript of which is in the Chicago Historical Society. This is in effect the only 18th-century census of Peoria. His journal proves that Point de Sable lived at Chicago in 1790, although he may have settled as early as 1784. [337]

H. Hubbard schooner from Buffalo, NY; called at Chicago under Captain Brown on Aug. 15, 1834, and Nov. 14, 1835.

Hickling, William (1814-1881) English by birth, arrived in March 1835, together with his later business associate and brother-in-law George E. Walker; together built a sawmill on land secured from Mark Noble, Sr., along the north branch of the Chicago River, sold it, then built another on the Des Plaines; the venture was unsuccessful, and both removed to Ottawa, where they engaged in merchandising; there Hickling became Ottawa's first mayor; married twice: first Mrs. Clark, youngest sister of G.E. Walker, and later to a Miss Caswell; the last 12 years of his life was spent in Chicago, active in the

Chicago Historical Society; died on Aug. 25, 1881. [12]

Hickory Creek early settlement on the Hickory Creek, a tributary of the Des Plaines River [New Lenox Township, NW Will County]; begun in 1829 by Aaron Friend and Joseph Brown; following the organization of Cook County, in March 1831, three county voting precincts were established: one for Chicago, one for Hickory Creek, and one for the Du Page [now Dupage] settlement. For La Salle's 1683 activities in the greater Chicago area, probably on Hickory Creek, see John F. Swenson's essay on page 377. Also see Chronology section, year 1683.

Higgins, Montgomery & Company real estate firm prominent during the 1835-36 land boom.

Hill, Irad on the list of subscribers to the *Chicago Democrat* in November 1833.

Hinton, Rev. Isaac Taylor, D.D. (1799-1847) successor to Reverend Allen B. Freeman at the First Baptist Church, arrived from Richmond, VA, on July 26, 1835 with wife Sarah [née Mursell, married 1822], six children, and a nurse; all initially lived in Dr. Temple's house (comment by Mrs. Temple, as related by daughter Lenora Maria: "father kept a Baptist hotel"); had been educated at Oxford and recently arrived from England; in August helped establish the Chicago Bible Society and was elected president, then became corresponding secretary at its first annual meeting in November; also directed services at the First Presbyterian Church from 1835-1837, still without a permanent pastor; ◆ First Baptist Church, LaSalle Street; remained with the church until 1842. Reverend Hinton wrote a book entitled *A History of Baptism Both from Inspired and Uninspired Writings*, making him ★★★ **Chicago's 1st** author; died in New Orleans of yellow fever. [12]

Hiram 60-ton schooner; visitor to Chicago from multiple lake ports, carrying lumber, furniture, merchandise, and occasionally passengers in 1834, calling three times under Captain Bassett; between

BAILEY HOBSON [314]

June 15 and Oct. 22, 1835, the vessel transported lumber nine times from [see] Shipwagen under Captain Rathbourn; on Nov. 8 and 28, 1835, the vessel arrived from Kalamazoo; ran ashore and was wrecked in 1838. [48]

Hissey, William of Hissey & Jenkins; see Jenkins, Thomas.

Hitchcock, Lambert Connecticut chairmaker who traveled to Chicago and St. Louis in 1835 to take orders for kits of chair parts that local chair makers could acquire and assemble; in a letter written to his partner, he stated that three chairmakers were to be found in Chicago, "the London of the West" with 4,000 to 5,000 inhabitants. [171]

Hitchcock, S.S. dissolved his copartnership with Samuel M. Phelps on Aug. 8, 1835, as noted in the Aug. 15 *Chicago American*; Phelps continued alone, but the business was not identified.

Hix, Jonathan on the list of subscribers to the *Chicago Democrat* in November 1833.

H. Norton schooner from Buffalo, NY; called at Chicago under Captain Oliver on Aug. 21, 1834; ran ashore on Lake Michigan in 1842. [48]

Hobson, Bailey (1798-1850) from North Carolina, arrived in 1830 alone on horseback; returned with his wife, three children, and brother-in-law in March 1831; married to Clarissa Stewart in 1821; Quakers, the first settlers of now [Lisle Township] along the Du Page River; built a gristmill with Harry Boardman two miles S of [now] Naperville and ran a tavern to serve the mill customers who came in large numbers and often had to wait; served as private under Captain Boardman, then under Captain Napier in the Cook County voluntary militia during the Black Hawk War after the family had fled to Fort Dearborn; the Hobson children were all educated in eastern colleges and convents, some in Europe. ❀ For a portrait of Clarissa Stewart Hobson, see page 372. [12, 314a]

Hobson Tavern built c.1834 by [see] Bailey Hobson on the Joliet Road, two miles S of Napier's Settlement [now Naperville], near his and Harry's Boardman's gristmill on the Du Page River; see photograph. [314a]

Hoffman, Charles Fenno (1806-1884) author; visitor to Chicago from New York early in 1834, when the modest settlement had just begun to rapidly grow; reported his findings to newspapers during his travels, such as the article of Jan. 10, 1834, in the *New York American*, dealing with the cold spell he encountered while in Chicago [see Chronology, January 1834]; later gave an interesting account of his visit in book form, *A Winter in the Far West*; for his impressions on how Chicagoans entertained themselves, see entry under Wabano; died on June 7, 1884, a member of the Calumet Club. [12, 338, 339]

Hoffman, George W. within a Michigan volunteer militia that formed at Niles in May 1832, responding to a request for aid by Major Owen, Indian agent in Chicago.

Hog Lake also known as Winnemac Swamp; like many of the lakes and swamps of the Calumet region, Hog Lake's size varied according to the season; at its largest, the lake stretched nearly to Vin-

JOHN STEVEN COATS HOGAN [12]

cennes Avenue on the W, 67th Street on the N, and Stony Island on the S; during dry spells a small pond was existent amid the large wet prairie; like Lake Calumet the depression was formed by a combination of wave action and gradually lowering lake levels about 3,000 years ago; also see Calumet Lakes.

hog pound see estray pen.

Hogan, Charles L.P. arrived in 1834; ✦ dry goods and grocery store, Lake Street near Franklin; became county commissioner in 1845. [351]

Hogan, John Stephen Coats (1805 -1868) born in New York City; arrived in 1829, sent from Detroit by Oliver Newberry to build and operate a store; was elected justice of the peace on July 24, 1830, with 33 votes over A. Clybourne's 22; voted in the following Aug. 2 election; served as postal clerk and deputy for Postmaster Bailey; was appointed postmaster by William T. Barry, postmaster general under President Jackson on Nov. 2, 1832, following Bailey; partner of the firm

Brewster, Hogan & Co., purchased on Sept. 4, 1830, from the canal commissioners lots 1, 2, 5, 6 in block 21 and later additional land in block 40 [see map on page 44], and in 1831 built a 20-by-35-foot log cabin on the NE corner of South Water and Lake streets, which was subdivided, with separate doors, and was to be both store for his firm and sleeping arrangements (western part) with the post office (eastern part); served as lieutenant under Captain Kercheval in the militia during the Black Hawk War, listed on the muster roll of May 3, 1832, then as captain of a Cook County volunteer company within Maj. David Bailey's battalion stationed at the fort between May 24 and June 11. In August 1833. Hogan was one of the "Qualified Electors" who voted to incorporate the town [for a copy of that meeting's original report, see entry for incorporation]; earlier in 1833 employed John Bates, Jr., as clerk to run the postal business, and in the summer of 1834 employed a second clerk John L. Wilson; probably in July, Hogan moved the post office to a building on the SW corner of Franklin and South Water streets, where Thomas Watkins became postal assistant.; in the July 30, 1834, *Chicago Democrat* he advertised "Dry goods and Groceries, S. Water st., one door below Post Office"; applied for wharfing privileges on Nov. 21, 1835. During the land boom Hogan was an active and successful promoter and speculator, but lost his fortune in the crash of 1837; Sidney Abell succeeded him as postmaster on March 3, 1837, and he left Chicago afterward though listed in Fergus' *Directory*: ◆ dry goods and groceries, 236 Lake Street Later Hogan tried his luck in California during the gold rush, with unknown success; on his way stopped at the Potawatomi reservation where he was hailed as a long lost brother; was married twice: first on April 27, 1834, to Anna Maria Bailey, eldest daughter of the previous postmaster, who died in 1837, then to the widow Mary S. Ainslie in Boonville, MO, on March 20, 1848; died in Boonville. An example of Hogan's easygo-

Hollenback's cabin, 1831   [239]

ing jovial style follows. [12, 28, 172]

A humorous episode occurred at the log cabin store of J.S.C. Hogan on Lake and South Water streets that was the Chicago post office in the fall of 1832, when a customer complained to the then merchant and part-time postmaster John Hogan about the way the letters, to be picked up by addressees [there was no carry-out in those days], *were stacked up unsorted in a corner of the grocery shelf. Explained the postal patron: the country where he came from usually provided in its post offices little orderly boxes, called "pigeon holes," alphabetically arranged &c. On his next visit the customer found to his surprise that Mr. Hogan had nailed a series of old boots, soles first, to one of the exposed logs inside the store, with the gaping holes perfectly ready to accommodate letters and to serve the public in – as we would say today – an efficient and effective manner.* [184, 249]

hogshead   a liquid measure of 63 gallons, or a barrel large enough to contain at least 63 gallons, abbreviated hhd.; a term used by those involved in [see] firefighting.

Hogue, William   Wm. Hogue & Co. advertised "50 bbls. [early abbreviation for barrels] of whiskey" and "50 boxes Glass, and for sale low for cash" in the Sept. 10, 1834 *Chicago Democrat*; notice of the company's dissolution by mutual consent of Charles L. Bristol, John Hale, and Hogue appeared in the *Chicago American* on July 22, 1835.

Hoit, Thomas and Sarah   known from a notice in the *Chicago Democrat*, Sept. 24, 1834, announcing that Sarah, formerly of Stafford County, NH, had died on Sept. 16 at age 43; a Thomas Hoyt is on the list of subscribers to the *Chicago Democrat* in November 1833.

Holbrook, John C.   native of Boston, arrived in 1835 and on June 10, advertised in the *Chicago Democrat* his store for "Hats, Clothing, Boots &

Shoes, Wholesale and Retail … receiving additions to assortment every 15 or 20 days, through the season" on South Water Street, one door from Dearborn Street; late September the advertisement read "the Boston Clothing Store, Agent for the Manufacturers"; in October signed up with the "Pioneer" hook and ladder company, a voluntary fire brigade; married to Betsey N. Huntoon; ✦ boots and shoes, South Water Street [12]

Holderman's Grove   [Newark, Kendall County] originally Weed's Grove; the only settlement between Peoria and Chicago in the late 1820s; location of the John K. Clark-Permelia Scott and Willard Scott-Caroline Hawley double wedding on July 21, 1829, Reverend Isaac Scarritt officiating.

Holiday, William   member of an exploratory party under [see] Capt. William Gordon that left Chicago in June and returned in September in conjunction with the Indian removal effort; one of four men—with Alexander Robinson, Billy Caldwell, and Waubonsee—who organized the Potawatomi encamped along the Des Plaines River in late September and led the Indians westward for the new reservation beyond the Mississippi. [655]

Hollenback, John, Clark, David S., and George brothers [?], born in Muskingum County, OH; came with their families in 1829 (John in 1828); on Sept. 4, 1830, Clark purchased lot 7 in block 8 and lots 7 and 10 in block 44 [see map on page 44]; sold his lot in block 8 to James B. Campbell soon after and he and his relatives moved to the Fox River valley to stake out claims [Kendall County]; a son of Clark (Clark Jr.) was nine years old when they arrived; a son of George (George M.) was born in 1831, the first male white child born in Kendall County. The Hollenback families were among the refugees who sought protection at Fort Dearborn during the Black Hawk scare. George's house, built in 1831, was the first in Kendall County, its appearance typical of log dwellings [see painting on page 188]. [239]

Holmes, John   arrived from England in April

1835.

Holsman, George   also Halsman; tailor, advertised in the July 22, 1835, *Chicago Democrat* as Cooley [R.S.] & Holsman; they dissolved the partnership on Aug. 1, and with an ad on the 10th he continued "tailoring in the most Fashionable style"; located on Dearborn Street, "nearly" opposite the Eagle Coffee House; in the Nov. 25 *Chicago Democrat* he announced that he had removed to a building "nearly" opposite the New York House on Lake Street; ✦ saloon, Lake Street near LaSalle.

Holt, Isaac   U.S. Army sergeant at Fort Dearborn; promotion to sergeant was in April 1811; killed in action at the massacre of Aug. 15, 1812; his wife was captured but survived and afterward lived in Ohio. [226, 249]

Holy Spirit Mission   see *Mission de Saint-Esprit.*

Hondorf, John   early resident of German extraction, and member of the Catholic congregation; his signature is on a petition in April 1833 to Bishop Rosati of St. Louis, requesting a priest for Chicago. [17, 342]

honey   widely collected from wild bee colonies by the Indians, *voyageurs,* and traders as a favorite staple and trade object.

Hooker, James L.   born c.1819 in Sackett's Harbor, NY; arrived in June 1834; ✦ clerk, Joseph H. Gray; in 1879 lived at Watertown, NY. [12]

Hoosier   nickname for Indiana natives or residents, common in Chicago as early as 1833 [see Wellmacher, Johann for the advertising he devised]; name for the wagons, drawn by three yokes of oxen, that came throughout the 1830s with produce from the Wabash River country. [55a]

Hope   armed British schooner patrolling Lakes Michigan, Huron, and Erie during the period of British control; built in Detroit in 1771. [48]

Hopewell   name given to an extraordinary cultural development that blossomed among prehistoric Indian tribes in northeastern North America between 500 B.C. and A.D. 500, characterized by the construction of large, elaborate, geometric, and

other earthworks. They served as burial mounds, often containing offerings of high artistic accomplishment, but were likely also used for other ceremonial purposes. The earthworks were first noted in southern Ohio, but Hopewellian structures can be found from western New York to Kansas, including the Chicago region. As James A. Marshall has observed, their design and execution indicates a knowledge of geometry apparently lost to succeeding tribes, as well as the employment of a unit of measure. A possible Hopewellian earthwork in what is now downtown Chicago, the serpent mound [called lizard mound by Albert F. Scharf], was formerly a prominent feature in the landscape, but is now covered by the Belmont el-station near the intersection of Sheffield and Oakdale Avenues; another possible work was the Chicago Pyramid Mound at Cheltenham Beach (7800 S). Marshall has located approximately 45 such sites within 60 miles of Chicago's Loop and writes that "about a dozen of those works would, if restored, be regarded as spectacular." Burial mound building was not restricted to the Hopewell culture, but was already practiced during the Adena culture, which preceded it, and continued into the Temple Mound Period, which endured until the arrival of the Europeans in North America. Also see Indian prehistory. [206, 370, 450, 451, 452, 596]

Hopkins, Henry   on the list of subscribers to the *Chicago Democrat* in November 1833.

Horn, John van   see van Horne, John.

Horner, William   German immigrant, first attested to as having lived in Chicago in 1833. [342]

hotels   see taverns, hotels, and boarding houses.

horses, wild   as reported by [see] H.S. Tanner in 1832, wild horses of a small size could be found on the Illinois prairie at that time. "They are of the same species as the Indian ponies, and are the offsprings of the horses which were brought here by the early French settlers, and suffered to run at large."

house numbering   systematic numbering of houses

began only in 1839, starting on State Street; prior to this time, the relationship of a structure to the nearest street corner or well-known landmark was used to guide a customer or stranger; examples from early newspaper ads read: "three doors west of Tremont House on Lake Street," or "South Water Street near draw bridge," or "two-story house opposite Exchange Coffee House, corner of Lake and Franklin."

Howard, Dr. William   civil engineer, appointed in September 1829 by the topographical bureau of the U.S. Army's engineer department to supervise the surveying effort for construction of the harbor and the Illinois & Michigan Canal; working under him were Asst. Engineers Henry Belin, Frederick Harrison, Jr. and William B. Guyon; both Howard's and Harrison's names are on the ✷ map of the E end of the Chicago River's course, prepared by [see] Harrison in 1830. [12, 423, 681, 682]

Howe, Captain   master of the commercial sailing vessel *El-Lewellyn* [*Llewellyn*] that operated between Chicago and Green Bay in 1834; in June that year contracted with [see] William Payne to transport partner [see] Oliver C. Crocker, several men, and mill equipment to Sheboygan.

Howe, Frederick A., Sr. and Frederick A., Jr.   junior was born c.1828 in Buffalo, NY, and was a child when both arrived in June 1834; ✦ [Sr.] justice of the peace, 97 Lake Street; Fred Jr. was a member of the Chicago militia in 1844, and still lived in Chicago in 1879. [12, 351]

Howe, Sarah D.   dress-, cloak-, and habitmaker, advertised in the *Chicago Democrat* on Aug. 18, 1835; located on Lake Street in the house of Dr. Austin, three doors E of the Mansion House; by Sept. 9 she requested "4 active young ladies as apprentices"; ✦ Miss Howe, milliner and mantuamaker, corner of Lake and Wells streets; in 1843 married Rufus B. Brown.

Hoyne, Lenora Maria Temple   daughter of Dr. John T. Temple, a 12-year-old when the family came in 1832; witnessed the Indian war dance in

1835 [see her following report of the event and an earlier memory of baptism by Reverend Freeman in 1834]; on Sept. 17, 1840, married the lawyer Thomas Hoyne, who had arrived from New York City in 1837 and would die on July 27, 1883; in 1885 lived at 267 Michigan Ave. [12]

While we were living in the cottage the great Indian War Dance took place. Poor mother was almost crazed with fear. She laid down on the bed and covered her head with a pillow to shut out the fiendish yells of the red devils who were dancing before our door, brandishing their tomahawks and knives, firing pistols and making the air ring with their horrid noises. There were nearly a thousand warriors, naked excepting the breech-cloth about their loins and in all their war paint which made them still more hideous. I stood on a chair at the window and peeped through the shutters to see the fiends. And I can assure you that they were more like an army of devils than anything one can imagine. The picture was indelibly fixed in my mind and as I write is vividly before me. I think if I were an artist I could put it on canvas as it appeared to me on that day.

[For another account of the same war dance, one by J.D. Caton, see Chronology, Aug. 18, 1835.]

I was baptised in the month of February. The day was cold. The ice in the lake was cut far enough for the candidates to walk out into the water and we were immersed. When we reached the shore our clothing was frozen so hard we could not bend it. We were wrapped in blankets and driven home. None of the candidates of whom there were five took cold or felt any bad effects from the exposure. We all felt that we had followed our dear Savior down into the water and he would care for us.

Hoyt, Thomas   on the list of subscribers to the *Chicago Democrat* in November 1833. See Hoit, Thomas.

Hubbard, Augustus   from Chamion, KY; a notice in the Oct. 21, 1835 *Chicago Democrat* announced his death of bilious fever at age 24, at the residence of J. Curtiss.

Hubbard, Ahira   came from Middleborough, MA in 1830, an uncle of Gurdon S. Hubbard and the father of Henry G., Harriet L. and Mary Ann, whom Gurdon married in 1842 as his third wife; on the list of subscribers to the *Chicago Democrat* in November 1833; brought his wife Serena (née Tucker) and daughter from Massachusetts in 1836; died of the cholera at 70 on Aug. 15, 1849, and was ▲ reburied at Graceland Cemetery on Oct. 23, 1868.

Hubbard & Co.   business partnership that involved Gurdon, Elijah, and Henry as "Commission & Forwarding Merchants," first advertising insurance in the July 2, 1834 *Chicago Democrat*, representing Howard Fire Insurance Co. of New York; advertisements in the *Chicago American* beginning early June 1835 included "POT-8-OES, Cider, Dried Apples" and "20 BBLS. SPERM OIL, for sale by Hubbard & Co."; with extensive new stock, [see] Henry King took over the dry goods store late October

Hubbard, Eber   arrived in 1835 from New York; remembered as having cut down the N wing of the Dearborn Street bridge in 1839.

Hubbard, Elijah Kent   (1813-1839) arrived from Connecticut in 1834; member of one of the town's antigambling committees constituted on Oct. 25; real estate speculator and member of the board of directors of the first Chicago branch of the Illinois State Bank in 1835; advertised as an agent for Howard Fire Insurance Co. of New York in the summer of 1835; active in railroad promotion in the late 1830s; ✦ banker, 47-51 Dearborn St. [12]

Hubbard, Gurdon Saltonstall   (1802-1886) born

GURDON SALTONSTALL HUBBARD
AT AGE 30   [705]

GURDON SALTONSTALL HUBBARD
IN HIS LATER YEARS

in Windsor, VT; in 1815 his father, a lawyer impoverished by speculation, moved the family to Montreal, where young Gurdon found employment in a hardware store; on April 28, 1818, he became an employee of the American Fur Company under agent William W. Mathews, the agreement stipulating service for five years at $120 a year [thereafter he received $1,300 yearly]; came from Montreal through Chicago for the first time on Oct. 1, 1818, at age 16 when assigned to the Illinois River Brigade under Antoine des Champs, where he worked with [see] Louis Bibeau; when des Champs retired, Hubbard succeeded to the position of superintendent of the Illinois River trading posts. A fellow employee, Noel Le Vasseur, worked with him in the Iroquois and Kankakee River regions and became a close friend; during his early years in the Northwest, Hubbard married 15-year-old Watseka, niece of Tamin, chief of the Kankakee Potawatomi; the union lasted two years and resulted in two children, both of whom died in infancy; Watseka later married Le Vasseur, who succeeded Hubbard in charge of the Iroquois River post at Bunkum, now called Iroquois, IL. When in 1827 Hubbard resigned his position, he purchased from John Jacob Astor the Illinois trading interests of the American Fur Co. (held until 1835), and went into business for himself at Danville, establishing subsidiary posts from Chicago to the Wabash and Ohio Rivers; his frequent travel between Danville and Chicago gave the name "Hubbard Trace" to the connecting trail. As a young man, the Indians called him Che-mo-comon-ess, meaning "the little American"; later he became Papa-ma-ta-be, meaning "swift walker." From Danville Hubbard led 100 militia volunteers—the Vermillion Rangers—on horseback to Chicago in July 1827 to help safeguard the small settlement during the Winnebago scare [For a description of Hubbard's appearance at that time, see entry for Vermillion Rangers]. In the spring of 1831, he married Eleanora Berry; they had one child, Gurdon S. Hubbard, Jr., born in 1838. During 1832-33 he served as a member of the Illinois legislature; in 1833, formally moved from Danville to Chicago, but in preceding years he had spent so much time supplying the villagers with pigs raised in the Danville region that they had long before considered him as one of their own; had already [1830] purchased from the government four lots (1, 2, 7, 8) constituting the eastern half of block 19 [see map on page 44], a choice parcel. Large debts to the American Fur Co. initially kept him from participating in the land boom, but he successfully handled the real estate investments for a distant Connecticut relative, Edward E. Russel, and by 1835 had accumulated sufficient capital to invest on his own account; concentrating on "water lots" and those along major traffic routes [on Nov. 6 that year submitted a petition for wharfing privileges in front of block 19, lots 1 and 2], he also purchased land in Milwaukee, Green Bay, and Racine, and eventually opened a land agency that served eastern customers. Within several years he became the town's largest meat packer and owner of the largest warehouse, a lake shipper, a director of the Chicago branch of the Illinois State Bank, an insurance man, a member of the Illinois & Michigan Canal Board in 1836 and one of the incorporators of the first waterworks; ♦ Hubbard & Co., forwarding and commission merchants. In 1842, a widower since 1840, he married his cousin, Mary Ann Ellis Mills Hubbard; in 1879 his address was 243 White St., but in 1885 he lived at 143 Locust St.; Hubbard's papers are at the Chicago Historical Society; ➡ Hubbard Street (430 N). Also see Hubbard, Henry George; for family relations with Col. Richard J. Hamilton, see the Hamilton entry; for Hubbard's description of the prairie scenery, see prairie. For Hubbard's first impression of Chicago in 1818, and for Roland

Tinkham's impression of Hubbard, see below. [12, 28, 352-4, 705]

Hubbard's report:

We started at dawn. The morning was calm and bright, and we, in our holiday attire, with flags flying, completed the last twelve miles of our lake voyage. Arriving at Douglas Grove, where the prairie could be seen through the oak woods, I landed, and climbing a tree, I gazed in admiration on the first prairie I had ever seen. The waving grass, intermingled with a rich profusion of wild flowers, was the most beautiful sight I had ever gazed upon. In the distance the grove of Blue Island loomed up, beyond it the timber on the Desplaines River, while to give animation to the scene, a herd of wild deer appeared, and a pair of red foxes emerged from the grass within gunshot of me. ✦ *Looking north, I saw the whitewashed buildings of Fort Dearborn sparkling in the sunshine, our boats with flags flying, and oars keeping time to the cheering boat song. I was spellbound and amazed at the beautiful scene before me. I took the trail leading to the fort, and, on my arrival, found our party camped on the north side of the river, near what is now State street. A soldier ferried me across the river in a canoe, and thus I made my first entry into Chicago, October 1, 1818.*

From Roland Tinkham's letter, describing Hubbard in 1831:

G.S. Hubbard is quite a gentleman, speaks good English and French, and knows every Indian tongue, and almost every Indian person in this 200 miles, and in some directions much further. He has been in the Indian trade since he was 16 years old; he is now about 30. His Influence among them is great; they all know him and appear to love and fear him. He is quite rich.

Hubbard, Henry George   arrived from Massachusetts in 1829; signed up with the "Pioneer" hook and ladder company in October 1835, a voluntary fire brigade; son of Ahira Hubbard, brother of Harriet L. and Mary Ann, and cousin of Gurdon S.; married to Julia Elvira Smith; ✦ G.S. Hubbard

& Co.'s warehouse; died in 1849; in 1885 his widow lived at the Hotel Bristol, Chicago. [Andreas writes that Hubbard Street, originally Michigan Street, was "named after Henry George Hubbard, the brother of Gurdon S. Hubbard"; he was not a brother but his cousin, and the first part of Andreas' statement is given little credence by the editors.] [12, 351]

Hubbard's Folly   early critics referred thus to the first brick warehouse building that Hubbard built in 1834 at the SW corner of Water and LaSalle streets; earlier brick structures were the powder magazine of the first Fort Dearborn (1803) and a brick house built by Alanson Sweet and William Worthingham under contract for John Noble (1833) N of the river on a lot adjacent to the later Lake House Hotel.

Hubbard's Trace   also Hubbard's Trail or Vincennes Trail; established by Gurdon S. Hubbard between 1822 and 1824, leading from Fort Dearborn S to Danville and beyond to Vincennes; along this route he established trading posts 40 to 50 miles apart. Hubbard's Trace was made a state road in 1834, its southern part referred to as Dixie Highway, and its northernmost part later State Street in Chicago.

Hubbard, Thomas R.   in partnership with [see] Joseph N. Balestier, Hubbard & Balestier; first advertised "Money To Loan" in the Nov. 14, 1835 *Chicago American*; applications were accepted (post paid) for the "loan of monies for a term of years on bond and mortgage, on good lands, unencumbered and under improvement, in any part of the State of Illinois, at 12 per cent, interest, payable semi-annually"; ✦ attorney at law, corner of Clark Street and Lake.

Hudson Bay Company   (c.1770-1823) one of three large English fur trading companies in the Northwest after 1780, picking up where and what the French traders had left; its rivals were the XY Company and the North West Company; was later fused with the latter.

Hugunin; Hiram, Peter Daniel, Robert and Leonard C.   brothers from New York; arrived in 1833 on their yacht *Westward Ho* after a three-month journey from Oswego; when their ship could not cross the sandbar in front of the Chicago River mouth, they paid to have oxen to pull the vessel across into the harbor. Hiram (c.1798-1866) was the captain; became a member of the first sanitary vigilante committee in 1834, chief engineer of the voluntary fire brigade in 1835, and president of the village board in June of the same year; in the August *Chicago Democrat* he advertised as agent for the Northwestern Fire and Marine Insurance Co. of Oswego; the following month his home was destroyed in a prairie fire; then served as delegate to the state Democratic convention at Vandalia; prior to 1836, owned 80 acres of land in Section 32, Township 39 as per Andreas, *History of Chicago*, pp. 112-113; ✦ merchant on W Water Street, near Lake; in 1840 served on the board of school inspectors; his wife, name unknown, died in 1842; Hiram died at Waukegan. Peter Daniel (c.1783-1865) applied for wharfing privileges on Nov. 21, 1835; listed as Daniel, ship chandler, in 1839; moved on and became a Wisconsin county judge. Leonard C. is known to have lived at 232 S. Halsted [old numbering system], was well liked by the Indians and associated freely with them when hunting and fishing; ✦ speculator; lost one arm in a duck hunting accident, but continued to be an inveterate hunter; died on Nov. 6, 1882. [12, 28, 351]

Hugunin, Edgar   arrived from New York in 1835; later moved to Wisconsin. [351]

Hugunin, Edward   arrived from New York in 1835; later moved to California, where he died in 1878, age 64. [351]

Hugunin, John Clark   (c.1811-1865) arrived from New York in 1835; in January 1837 he advertised a reward for the return of one of his runaway slaves; ran for alderman in the same year; ✦ dry goods and grocery, South Water Street; died at Milwaukee. [12, 351]

Hugunin, Robert arrived from New York in 1833; known to have been in the naval service during the 1812 war; commanded the lake schooners [see] *Lucinda* and *Jefferson* in 1834; ✦ Captain Robert Hugunin. [351]

Hulbert, Eri Baker (1807-1852) from Otsego County, NY; in 1831 married Mary Louisa Walker, sister of [see] Almond and Charles Walker; joined his brothers-in-law as partner of [see] Walker & Co. in 1836; his wife and son, William Ambrose, joined him the following year, and thereafter George and Eri Baker, Jr., were born; ✦ (Chas. Walker & Co.); left the business in 1841, continuing as a successful merchant through 1851; left for California in 1852, dying in transit. [736]

Hull, Gen. William native of Massachusetts; U.S. Army general; died in 1825; see War of 1812; see Fort Dearborn massacre. [12]

Humphrey, James Oscar arrived in 1834 from New York; carriagemaker who partnered [see] Benjamin Briggs under the name Briggs & Humphrey; ✦ wagonmaker; moved to Ohio and still living at Willoughby in 1885. [12, 351]

hundredweight a unit of weight, equal to 100 pounds in the United States, 112 pounds in England.

Hunt, Charles H. in July and throughout the month of August 1835, his notices in the *Chicago Democrat* advertised a "High School for Young Ladies"—its first term of 11 weeks commencing Aug. 8, delayed until the 17th, offering ordinary [$6] and higher [$7] "branches of English" as well as the Latin, Greek and French languages [$8]; satisfactory credentials could be seen at office of Henry Moore, Esq.; the outcome of this venture has not been recorded. [12]

Hunt, George W. independent trader, working with William Wallace, who spent the winter of 1825-26 in Chicago in successful competition with the American Fur Co.; in April 1827, again or still in Chicago, prepared an inventory of the Wallace estate. [12]

Hunt, William Nelson U.S. Army private at Fort Dearborn; enlisted in October 1810; survived the massacre of Aug. 15, 1812, but froze to death as an Indian prisoner. [226]

Hunter & Hinsdale according to the report by [see] J.D. Bonnell, a warehouse on South Water Street in 1835, immediately E of Newberry & Dole. [Identity of the owners could not be established; eds.]

Hunter, First Lt. David (1802-1886) born and died in Washington City [now Washington, D.C.]; 1822 graduate from West Point; was elected constable in Chicago on May 11 [with Henley Clybourne, nine votes cast] and again on Aug. 20, 1828; assigned to the Fifth Infantry, company A at Fort Dearborn beginning Oct. 3, 1828; known to have carried mail between Chicago and Fort Wayne in 1828, on horseback, with two foot soldiers carrying muskets; voted on July 24, 1830; served as acting commandant of the fort from Dec. 14, 1830, when Major Fowle began a six-month leave of absence, until May 20, 1831; married Maria Indiana Kinzie on Sept. 18, 1829, Peoria Judge Alexander Doyle officiating; taught school to children of the settlers near the fort; was at the fort during the 1829 visit by Lt. Jefferson Davis and helped him cross the river [for his description, see entry on Davis, Jefferson]; succeeded Dr. Wolcott as appointed administrator of John Kinzie's estate after Wolcott died in 1830, and took over his real estate claim of 80 acres in the NE corner of Section 9, Township 39, immediately W of the Kinzie property; in 1833 supervised the platting of the Kinzie Addition, and joined in partnership with John H. Kinzie to establish a forwarding and commissioning business; ✦ Illinois Street, near Rush. Hunter advanced to the rank of Bvt. Major General in 1865 as commander of the Department of the South during the Civil War, and was part of the military commission which sat in judgement on the Lincoln conspirators. [12, 351, 707]

The following is an excerpt from a 1879 letter of his Chicago reminiscences:

More than half a century since, I first came to Chicago on horseback, from St. Louis, stopping on the way at the log-cabins of the early settlers, and passing the last house at the mouth of Fox River. I was married in Chicago, having to send a soldier one hundred and sixty miles, on foot, to Peoria, for a license. The northern counties in the State had not then been organized, and were all attached to Peoria County. My dear wife is still alive, and in good health; and I can certify, a hundred times over, that Chicago is a first-rate place from which to get a good wife.

Hunter, Edward E. arrived from Kentucky in 1833 and in November, on the list of subscribers to the *Chicago Democrat*; became firewarden for the second ward in September 1834, and supervisor of roads and bridges in November; his name was on a school-related petition signed on Sept. 19, 1835; served as county treasurer in 1837; died in California. [12, 351, 707]

Huntington, Alonzo (c.1808-1881) lawyer from Shaftsbury, VT; arrived with his wife (1833) Patience Lorraine Dyer, sister of Dr. Charles V. Dyer, in the fall of 1835; became state's attorney for the seventh Illinois district in 1837 and held that office until 1841; ✦ attorney and counselor at law, Lake Street; his first two children (Stella Aurelia, age 2, and Susanna Maria, age 4) died on Dec. 21 and 22, 1839, respectively, of malignant scarlet fever; there were six children altogether, of whom only two survived to adulthood; Huntington is still listed in Chicago in 1879, and died on Nov. 17, 1881. For a portrait of Huntington, see page 194. [12]

Huntoon, Capt. Bemsley also Bengsley; arrived from Massachusetts in 1835 and soon became owner of a steam sawmill on the north branch of the Chicago River, a little S of Division Street, at the mouth of a contributory stream; in 1837 served as school inspector; ✦ steam sawmill, north branch. [12, 145, 733]

ALONZO HUNTINGTON [12]

Huntoon, George M.   came from Massachusetts in 1832; ◆ constable, N State Street near Kinzie; married Maria Reed on Nov. 28, 1839; lived in [Evanston]. [13, 733]

Hurd, Niram F.   on the list of subscribers to the *Chicago Democrat* in November 1833; in the June 25, 1834, issue he placed a notice that a trunk with brass letters *WKD*, containing clothing, had been found and could be claimed from the subscriber on Lake Street

Hurlbut, Henry H.   early member of the Chicago Historical Society and corresponding member of the Wisconsin State Historical Society; in 1882 published his book, *Chicago Antiquities*, a critically researched lifelong collection of early historical data; ➡ Hurlbut Street (5800 N). [351]

Huron   schooner from Huron, OH; carried lumber and passengers between several lake ports and called at Chicago under Captain Hunt—and later under Captain Eno—four times in 1834 (deliver-

ing merchandise "direct from New York" for John Wright) and again on Sept. 30, 1835.

Huron   a French epithet meaning *bristly head*; archaic French word identifying four advanced Iroquoian tribes whose collective name for themselves was *wendat*; united with the French against the Iroquois in the fur trade; lived within Huronia, located around Lake Simcoe, S and E of Georgian Bay, in palisaded and semi-permanent villages; first met the French under Champlain, welcoming many early French missionaries. Enemies of the Iroquois since prehistoric times, they suffered greatly when in the mid 17th century the Iroquois first acquired and used firearms; most were driven W into Michigan, Wisconsin, and Illinois [in the Calumet region from about 1700 to 1720]; once a great nation, few remain today, mostly in Oklahoma; ➡ Huron Street. (700 N).

Hurtt, Nathan A.   U.S. Army private at Fort Dearborn; enlisted on Dec. 29, 1811; deserted before the massacre of Aug. 15, 1812, was captured by the Indians, escaped and reached Fort Wayne. [226]

Hutchins, Thomas   (1730-1789) born in Monmouth County, NJ; served in the French and Indian War; British captain of engineers and cartographer who personally traversed the Ohio and Mississippi Rivers in 1762, enabling him to prepare accurate maps of the Great Lakes region following the transfer from French to British rule in 1765; his reconnoitering tours through 1775, providing observations and surveys, resulted in a 1778 publication in London, *A Topographical Description of Virginia, Pennsylvania, Maryland, and North Carolina, Comprehending the Rivers Ohio, Kenhawa, Sioto, Cherokee, Wabash, Illinois, Mississippi, &c.,* that included important ✱ maps of the "Chikago" region, noting an "Indian Village and Fort at the Entrance" of the unnamed river [shown in detail but not entirely correct—see Brehm, Lt. Dietrich]; resigned his British commission in 1780 and within a year was named "geographer to the United States."

[*Michigan History Magazine* 10 (July 1926): 358-73; 681, 682]

Hyde, Norman   probate judge of Peoria, who personally appraised the estate of François Le Mai at Chicago on May 10, 1828. [220]

Hyde, Thomas S.   from Massachusetts; signed on with the "Pioneer" hook and ladder company in October 1835, a voluntary fire brigade; likely the Thomas Hyde of Davis, [Robert A.] Kinzie & Hyde, a hardware on Kinzie Street near Cass [Wabash] listed in 1839. [12, 733]

Hyde, William   listed as owner of 80 acres of land in the NW quarter of Section 6, Township 39, prior to 1836, as per Andreas, *History of Chicago*, pp. 112-113.

Iberville, Pierre Le Moyne, seigneur d'Ardillières et d'   (1661-1706) see Le Moyne family.

ice age   in this summary of the history of glaciation of the earth the editors distinguish between *glacial ages*, each measured in many millions of years and separated from each other by very long warm periods, and *ice ages*, which are measured in thousands of years, fall within the glacial ages, and are separated from each other by warming periods of comparable length. During the last billion years, there have occurred three glacial ages: the first lasting from 800 to 600 million years ago, the second from 480 to 350 million years ago, and the third one, which began 10 million years ago and is considered still in progress. The last three distinct ice ages of this third glacial age began 280 thousand, 180 thousand, and 40 thousand years ago, respectively. A warming trend, possibly of short duration in geologic terms, began 15,000 years ago and has

THE THREE GLACIAL AGES OF THE EARTH

MILLONS OF YEARS AGO

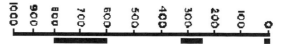

lasted until now; repeated glaciation of northern Illinois during this last ice age has had such a profound impact on Chicagoland's geography that the history of its organic life can only be fully understood in relation to these early events; references to the ice ages and their effects, as well as to other important geological events, will therefore be found throughout this volume; also see Lake Chicago. [261, 312, 361, 720]

Idie, Christopher   purchased lot 1 in block 43 from Joseph LaFramboise in c.1832 [see map on page 44].

Ile de la Cache   see *Isle a la Cache.*

Illini   native term for an Algonkin confederacy of five tribes, consisting of the Peoria, Cahokia, Kaskaskia, Tammarai [Tamoroa, Tamarois], and Mitchagamie [Michigamea]. The plural form of the word used by the Indians was Irenouaki; at Green Bay in 1634, Nicollet learned of the Iliniouek people to the south; the French transliterated the word as *Illinois*. In 1673 Father Marquette still found the Illini living SW of Lake Michigan and along the banks of the Illinois River, but from 1722 on they came under attack by Fox Indians and were soon brought close to extinction by invading tribes during the next several decades. An Illini Indian of the Peoria tribe murdered the Ottawa chief Pontiac in 1769, but contrary to legend, there is no record that this provoked massive retaliation against the few remaining Illinois; the 1722 seige which gave Starved Rock its name was an episode in the Fox wars. Though many Illini, having retreated to the Rock of St. Joseph of La Salle fame, were starved into submission and then massacred by the Ottawa and Potawatomi in 1769, a legendary event which gave the locale its name, Starved Rock; in 1837 the remaining survivors sold their title to the land and removed to a Kansas reservation. Also see the entry for Starved Rock. James Gray in *The Illinois* gives a good description of the appearance and customs of the Illini, gleaned from early eyewitness accounts. [45, 284, 649]

Illinois   (1) originally a French word for the Illini tribe; (2) state of the U.S. since 1818, named after the Illini tribe; ➡ Illinois Street (500 N). See Illinois State.

Illinois   a 100-ton schooner, built and operated by Capt. Augustus Pickering at Sacket's Harbor, NY, in the winter of 1833-34; called at Chicago six times in 1834 [first visit on June 10], four times in 1835; the first large sailing ship to enter the mouth of the Chicago River under Captain Pickering through the newly completed breach of the sandbar that until then (July 12, 1834) had always blocked access to the river; after stopping at the wharf of Newberry & Dole, the *Illinois* passed through the open Dearborn Street drawbridge to Ingersoll's wharf in front of the Western Stage House. The sailing was a much celebrated event, the *Chicago Democrat* reporting that "the banks of the river were crowded with a delighted crowd" that "hailed with loud and repeated cheers," and once the Illinois docked, "[h]er decks were immediately crowded by the citizens." [118]

Illinois   a 21-ton brig under Captain Wagstaff, calling at Chicago from Buffalo, NY, on Sept. 9, 1834 with 100 passengers; in 1835 it returned three times, bringing merchandise in addition to passengers. In May 1835, [see] Ellen Bigelow took passage on the *Illinois* and described the overloaded ship and the journey to Chicago in a letter to a relative back home. [55a]

Illinois   lake steamer built in 1837 for Oliver Newberry, designed for the Chicago trade; on its for-ward deck was mounted a brass cannon from the first Fort Dearborn, accidentally recovered from the river by dredging in 1833, and acquired by Newberry to be used for several years to announce the ship's arrival in port.

Illinois & Michigan Canal   envisioned as early as 1673 by Jolliet, and in the 1680s by Joutel, as a means to connect navigation on the Great Lakes with that on the Mississippi River system, and again proposed by Galatin in 1808; recommended for construction by President James Madison in 1814; in 1816, Maj. Stephen Long of the Corps of Topographical Engineers was sent to explore the practicability of the project and made a highly favorable report to the acting secretary of war, George Graham: "... a canal uniting the waters of the Illinois with those of Lake Michigan, may be considered of the first importance of any in this quarter of the country"; in January 1819, Secretary of War John C. Calhoun submitted a report to Congress urging the construction of the canal as a national effort; the Indian Treaty of Chicago in August 1821 secured the necessary Illinois land, and federal authorization for the project was given by Congress with the ordinance of March 30, 1822; this led to the creation by Governor Cole and the Illinois legislature of an initial commission on Feb. 14, 1823, charged to survey the canal lands and estimate the cost of canal construction; the commissioners were: Thomas Sloo, Jr., of Hamilton County; Theophilus W. Smith, later of Chicago; Emanuel J. West; Erastus Brown; and Samuel Alexander. The commissioners visited Chicago in 1823 and later employed two civil engineers, Col. Justus Post, of Missouri, and Col. René Paul, of St. Louis, to perform the task in 1824 and 1825; on March 2, 1827, by an act of Congress, signed by President Andrew Jackson on May 21, 1830, the federal government granted to the State of Illinois alternate sections, six miles wide, of public land along both sides of a proposed route for the Illinois & Michigan Canal, to be sold and the proceeds to be used to meet the canal construction cost; on Jan 22, 1829, the Illinois legislature created the canal commission, with powers to undertake the task; the first three canal commissioners were Dr. Gershom Jayne, a druggist and physician of Springfield, Edmund Roberts of Kaskaskia, and Charles Dunn; the commission had the towns of Ottawa and Chicago—at either end of the proposed route—platted, and in September 1830 the lots were offered to the public at auction; in September 1829 Dr. William Howard of Baltimore, MD, a civil engineer in the employ of the U.S. Corps of Engineers, had been given the charge to again survey the proposed canal route; assistant engineers F. Harrison, Jr., William B. Guyon, and Henry Belin were assigned to him, and all became involved in the survey effort of 1830 and 1831. Construction of the Chicago harbor with elimination of the obstructing sandbar at the river mouth, a precondition for the future canal, began in July 1833 and by July 12, 1834, the first merchant vessel entered the river mouth [see Chicago harbor]. Construction of the canal was delayed until enough bonds could be sold to finance the project, estimated at $4,043,000; the editorial of the Jan. 16, 1836 *Chicago American* begins: "Illinois and Michigan Canal Bill Has Passed ! ! !"; a new board of canal commissioners was then appointed, consisting of Gurdon S. Hubbard, William F. Thornton, and William B. Archer, and subsequently J.B. Fry, and construction began on July 4, 1836, under Chief Engineer [see] William Gooding with the festive groundbreaking

ceremony, amid a frenzy of real estate speculation. Work was interrupted by the 1837 economic downturn and 12 years would pass before the canal opened to barge traffic on April 26, 1848. The canal contributed vitally to the city's early growth, but its importance was soon overshadowed by that of the railroads; within Chicago proper virtually all traces of the canal have disappeared, but much of the canal SW of Chicago remains and is now being carefully preserved by governmental effort and is made accessible to the public; ➡ Canal Street (500W); Lock Street (1500 W), adjacent to where the Bridgeport lock of the canal once was. ▲ See Illinois and Michigan Canal National Heritage Corridor in the section "A Guide to Early Chicago Historical Monuments." [76, 348, 557, 575, 704, 661]

Illinois country   an appellation used in early verbal and written communication, before political subdivision had established sharply defined borders, designating the land where the [see] Illini or Illinois lived and largely, but not entirely, coinciding with the valley of the Illinois River. Its strategic importance as an essential link between Canada in the north and Louisiana in the south was recognized as early as 1673 by its first visitor, Louis Jolliet, and became increasingly apparent to later travelers, such as the French Jesuit Father Vivier who, in an excerpt from a 1750 letter, expressed his sentiments as follows:

Among the Illinois, Nov. 17, 1750.

... For the rest, this country is of far greater importance than is imagined. Through its position alone, it deserves that France should spare nothing to retain it. It is true, that it has not still enriched the King's coffers, and that convoys to and fro are costly; but it is nonetheless true that the tranquillity of Canada and the safety of the entire lower part of the Colony depend on it. Assuredly, without this post there can be no communication by land between Louisiana and Canada. There is another consideration: several regions of the same Canada and all those on the lower part of the river would be deprived of the provisions

they obtain from the Illinois, which are often a great resource to them. By founding a solid establishment here, prepared to meet all these troubles, the King would secure the possession of the most extensive and the finest country in north America. To be convinced of this one has but to glance at the well-known map of Louisiana, and to consider the situation of the Illinois country and the multitude of Nations against whom the post usually serves as a barrier. ...

Illinois, County of   created on Dec. 9, 1778 by Virginia, embracing the entire Northwest; the state never exercised any control over Chicago, and ceded the land to the United States in 1784; for details, see Chicago jurisdictional chronology on page 209. [8]

Illinois Exchange   see Exchange Coffee House.

Illinois Land Company   see Murray, William.

Illinois River   the first white men to discover and travel on the river (Aug. 25, 1673) were Jolliet and Father Marquette, who noted on his hand-drawn map only the name of the one Indian village along the river, Kachkaska [Kaskaskia, now Utica, IL]; though Jolliet lost his map before reaching Montreal, he named the river Rivére de St. Louis (quoted later by Father Dablon); early names used by others include: Seignlai (La Salle), Seignelay (Frs. Hennepin and Membre), and R. de St. Louis (Father Dablon, quoting Jolliet). Together with one of its tributaries, the Des Plaines River, the river forms part of the Chicago Portage route between the the Great Lakes and the Mississippi. [163, 284]

Illinois State   statehood was granted on Aug. 24, 1818; the area covered by the new state was comprised of the Illinois Territory but the northern border of the territory was extended 41 miles to include Chicago and the contemplated canal; the capital was located in Kaskaskia from 1818 until moved to Vandalia in 1820, and again relocated to Springfield in 1840. For additional details see Chicago jurisdictional chronology on page 209. [44, 59, 63, 78, 81, 85, 89, 144, 230, 233, 252, 271, 340, 347, 360, 366, 379, 456, 492, 511, 523, 548, 584, 644]

Illinois state roads   see entry on streets and roads.

Illinois Territory   created by separation from the Indiana Territory by the ordinance of Feb. 9, 1809; "that from and after the first day of March next, all that part of the Indiana Territory which lies west of the Wabash River and a direct line drawn from the Post Vincennes due north to the territorial line between the U.S. and Canada, shall for the purpose of temporary government, constitute a separate territory and be called 'Illinois'; effective March 1, 1809 and lasting until statehood was gained on Aug. 24, 1818; capital: Kaskaskia; governor: Ninian Edwards. For additional detail, see Chicago jurisdictional chronology on page 209. [80, 109, 253]

incorporation   of the town of Chicago, on or close to Aug. 3, 1833; the approximate date on which the leading citizens ["Qualified Electors"] of the village chose a president and a clerk, and decided by majority vote to incorporate the village as a town in accordance with the law of the state. The exact date is not known with certainty because it was omitted on the official handwritten report filed by the clerk on Sept. 5, 1833; for an unedited typed copy of the report see below. Legislative approval, making incorporation official, followed in due course; also see Chronology entry of Aug. 10, 1833; the vote for incorporation of the city took place on March 4, 1837.

At a Meeting of the Citizens of Chicago convened pursuant to publick notice given according to the Stature for Incorporating Towns, Th. J.V. Owen was chosen President & E. S. Kimberly was chosen clerk. The Oaths were then administered by Russel E. Hickok a Justice of the Peace for Cook County. When the following vote was taken on the propriety of incorporating the Town of Chicago, County of Cook, State of Illinois

For Incorporation: C.A. Ballard, John S.C. Hogan, G.W. Snow, R.J. Hamilton, J.T. Temple, John Wright, G.W. Dole, Hiram Pearsons, Alanson Sweet, E.S. Kimberly, T.J.V. Owen, Mark Beaubien
Against Incorporation: Russel E. Heacock

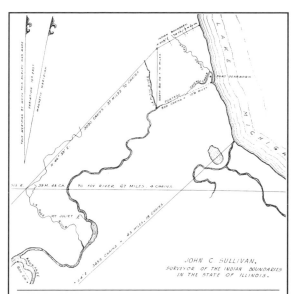

The Indian boundary lines near Chicago as seen on an excerpt of the surveyor's map, used in the treaty at St. Louis in 1816. [413]

For Incorporation 12   against Incorporation 1
We certify the above poll to be correct
Th.J.V. Owen, President   Ed.S. Kimberly, Clerk

Indian agent   see United States Office of Indian Affairs.

Indian annuities   periodic payments of money (annuities) to Indian tribes or individuals were made in accordance with various treaty agreements over the years; other distributions were made in the form of merchandise useful to Indians; payments were part of the compensation Indians would receive for ceding ancestral homelands to the U.S. government, which in turn would make most of the land available to white settlers. The payments were made by the Agent of Indian Affairs, and began at Fort Dearborn as early as 1808 under Agent Charles Jouett, for annuities due from Treaties of Detroit and Greenville, and as late as 1834. See Chronology, November 1834, for an eyewitness account of an annuity distribution. [12]

Indian Army Trail   Indian trail that led from the Indian village at Chicago to the Winnebago village [now Beloit] in Wisconsin; followed by General Scott and his men in the Black Hawk War; a portion is now Addison Road in Lombard.

Indian boundary line   northern and southern borderlines of the 20 mile wide corridor ceded by the Fox and Sauk to the United States on Aug. 24, 1816, at the Treaty of St. Louis; running SW from the shore of Lake Michigan to the Fox River and its midline coinciding with the outlet of the Chicago River, this strip included the portage route, and its acquisition prepared the way for the later construction of the Illinois & Michigan Canal; outside the corridor, the land was still owned by Potawatomi, Ottawa, and Chippewa tribes until the Chicago Treaty of 1833. The lines bounding the purchase were surveyed in the winter of 1818-19 by John C. Sullivan and his assistant, James M. Duncan; the land between them was surveyed in 1821 and immediately thrown open to preemption and homestead claims. ➡ The northern boundary line is still recognizable in the Chicago street pattern, marked by diagonal streets that defy the checkerboard pattern: nearest the lakeshore, by the four sections of the interrupted Rodgers Avenue; further SW, by Forest Preserve Avenue between Plainfield Avenue and Narragansett Avenue; by additional scattered remnants in the suburbs, such as the Indian Boundary Road in River Grove, and the Indian Boundary Drive in Melrose Park; by diagonal portions of the border between Melrose Park and Stone Park; and, lastly, by the NW border of the triangular Randolph Park in Hillside. The southern line is marked within Chicago only by the short section of Harbor Avenue between Green Bay Avenue and Avenue O, while in the SW suburbs it follows I-55 in its diagonal course.

Indian corn   *Zea mays L.*; also Indian wheat; staple food of the Indians; extensively grown by the Potawatomi in the valleys of the Des Plaines and Fox Rivers for their own use and for trade; brought to the early western trading posts in bark-woven

A collection of Indian signatures

sacks on the backs of ponies. In 1809, Alexander Robinson came by boat to Chicago and purchased from the Indians 100 bushels of corn to transport back to St. Joseph, an occurrence that provides some sense of a trade and its volume rarely noted.

Indian Creek   in LaSalle County, IL; site of the massacre of May 20, 1832, where Sauk Indians killed 14 members of three settler families (Hall, Davis, Pettigrew), abducted two of the Hall daughters, and burned down several houses during the early part of the Black Hawk War; the girls were ransomed by the U.S. government after six months and had been well treated; the massacre immediately caused a large number of settlers elsewhere to seek temporary shelter at Fort Dearborn.

Indian Department   see U.S. Office of Indian Affairs.

Indian prehistory   Indians first entered Illinois as small mobile bands during the late phase of the last ice age approximately 12,000 years ago, hunting large Pleistocene animals. Indian prehistory (prior to the arrival of Europeans) is divided into four periods: (1) The Paleoindian Period [to 8000 BC], when the climate was colder than now, a mixed tundra and open spruce forests occupied the land, and large game was still plentiful. (2) The Archaic Period [8000–500 B.C.], when the climate had come to resemble that of today; large game had disappeared but smaller animals were plentiful and wild plant food was gathered; campsites from this period have been found in many Illinois locations, including Starved Rock; in addition to distinctive stone tools, the Indians left knives and points hammered out of [see] copper nuggets. (3) The Woodland Period [500 B.C.–A.D. 1000],

marked by the introduction of primitive pottery and the development and use of domesticated plants; villages grew larger and became more permanent, and the dead were buried beneath mounds; trading networks were established; within this period is the existence of the [see] Hopewell Culture [300 B.C.–A.D. 400]. (4) The Mississippian Period [A.D. 100–1673], a development marked by large permanent villages with substantial partly sunken earth lodges and nearby cemeteries in the upper Illinois River valley. Maize (Indian corn) and the common bean were introduced from Mexico and were extensively cultivated, together with native squash. The period found its highest expression along Cahokia Creek in southern Illinois, where in the 12th century a settlement of approximately 30,000 inhabitants surrounded a series of man-made truncated pyramids, used for ceremonial purposes. The largest form covered 16 acres and is still visible in the landscape, and is now known as Monks' Mound because Trappist monks lived there in the early 1800s and tilled its surface, long after the original people had disappeared.

Indian removal   U.S. policy first conceived by Thomas Jefferson in 1803 for the systematic removal of Indians en masse to reservations W of the Mississippi; became law under President Jackson with passage of the Indian Removal Act of 1830. Fulfilling the terms of the 1833 treaty at Chicago, Congress approved an appropriation of $9,453 on March 3, 1835, to cover the expenses of an exploring party of 50 Potawatomi from the Chicago agency for the purpose of Indian resettlement. The party of Indians and several white men, led by Capt. William Gordon of the U.S. Army, left after June 6, traveling as far as Fort Leavenworth before returning to Chicago in early August. From the Chicago area most Indians were moved later in September 1835, first to a reservation in Clay County, MO, near Fort Leavenworth, but two years later, because of hostile Missouri settlers, were transported to Council Bluffs, IA. Later, a third removal

took them to a reservation in Kansas. Following the initial removal in 1835, additional efforts became necessary, because some of the Indians had stayed behind, and others had returned, having been dissatisfied with their newly assigned lands. In 1839, there were still some Potawatomi residing near Chicago. For additional details, see entries on Christian B. Dobson, who received the contract to furnish transportation in 1835 and 1837, and Capt. John B.F. Russell, who was the disbursing agent in 1835. [655]

Indian sugar   see maple sugar.

Indian trails   the major ancient Indian trails in and around Chicago, as well as additional trails that developed before 1830, are still visible on modern road maps, often as diagonal streets: Lincoln Avenue, Clark Street, Ogden Avenue, Archer Avenue, and Vincennes Avenue. With the coming of Europeans, the trails first became bridle paths, then roads for wagons, then stage and mail routes. For information on individual major trails in the area, see entries under Sauk (Sac) Trail, Vincennes Trail, Hubbard Trace, Calumet-Tolleston Beach Trail,

Trail Creek Trail, Lake Shore Trail, Green Bay Trail, Portage Trail, Lake Trail, Cottage Grove Trail, Archer Trail (Old Chicago Trail), Berry Point Trail, and the Fort Dearborn-Detroit Road. [610]

Indian treaties   see treaties with the Indians.

Indian tribes   attempts to divide the North American Indian population into clearly defined tribes has been most difficult. To quote the historian Reuben Gold Thwaites: "The migration of some of the Indian tribes were frequent, and they occupied overlapping territories, so that it is impossible to fix the tribal boundaries with any degree of exactness. ... The tribes were so merged by intermarriage, by affiliation, by consolidation, by the fact that there were numerous polyglot villages of renegades, by similarities in manner, habits, and appearance, that it is difficult even to separate the savages into families. It is only on philological grounds that these divisions can be made at all." However, if one were to list in sequence the various tribes encountered by the early French explorers and missionaries on their gradual advance from the Gulf of St. Lawrence to the Chicago River, the following can be distinguished with relative assurance: (1) member tribes of the Algonkian language family were the first Indians encountered by the explorers, specifically the Montagnai of the St. Lawrence River region; progressing farther S and W, they met like tribes of the upper Great Lakes, Ottawa, Chippewa, Kickapoo, Mascouten, Sauk, Fox, Potawatomi, Miami and Illinois; (2) a second language family was the Iroquois with five tribes—the Mohawk, Oneida, Onondaga, Cayuga and Seneca, usually secured within palisaded villages S and E of Lakes Erie and Ontario, but their ferocious raids as far W as the Mississippi terrorized all other native groups and eventually the French; related to, but often at war with the Iroquois, were the Huron of Canada, among whom the Jesuits established their earliest missions; (3) members of the Southern Indians, another language family, among them the Seminole and Cherokee, would

[116]

not have been encountered by the New France missionaries and explorers, except on journeys down the Mississippi to visit French Louisiana; (4) the fourth family, the Dakotah or Sioux, occupied the most western country beyond the Mississippi and were a nomadic and war-prone people; at the time of the French arrival, one of their peripheral tribes, the Winnebago, lived near Green Bay, in peace with the Algonkin groups who surrounded them. For those tribes relevant to the Chicago locale, see individual entries for additional detail. The basic reference work is Volume 15 of the Smithsonian's *Handbook of North American Indians.* [57, 62, 68, 114, 116, 117, 120, 200, 254, 300, 402]

Indiana   schooner from Buffalo, NY, piloted by Capt. W. Whitaker; arrived at Chicago on Sept. 26, 1834; on Oct. 1, 20 passengers collectively thanked him in the *Chicago Democrat*, recommending to the public "a superior vessel both for safe speed and safety"; returned five more times in 1835 under Captain McQueen.

Indiana   brig from Buffalo, NY; arrived in Chicago under Captain McKinstry on Oct. 22, 1834; returned four times in 1835.

Indiana Territory   created in 1800, with its capital at Vincennes; formerly part of the Northwest Territory; included Illinois from 1800 to 1809, as well as Wisconsin; William Henry Harrison, later the U.S. president, was appointed the first governor. For additional detail, see Chicago jurisdictional chronology on page 209. [513]

Indians   specifically American Indians, now often referred to as Native Americans. Those members of the human race who were the exclusive inhabitants of the Americas before the arrival of the Europeans in 1492. The first people encountered were called Indians in the mistaken belief by early westbound explorers that they had reached Asia, when in reality they had reached America. Native Americans are believed to be the descendents of nomadic Siberian hunters who crossed from Asia to North America in successive waves, beginning c.50,000 years ago, over dry land bridges that existed during the last ice age. They advanced to the Chicago area c.10,000 years ago. Before the arrival of the Europeans, the Indian population was thought to number several million. Through interaction, hostile and not, with the newcomers their numbers have been greatly reduced, and much of their culture has vanished. See Monuments. [57, 62, 68, 114, 116, 117, 120, 200, 254, 300, 402, 408, 459, 475, 552, 591, 601-3, 610, 642, 643, 651, 655, 681, 682, 697, 703, 728]

Infant School   in September 1833 Miss Eliza Chappel, later the wife of Reverend J. Porter, opened a school by this name in a log house that had been the first store of Stephen Wright at the SE corner of Lake and Market streets; the community response was favorable, involving active participation by Dr. Temple and Henry Handy; in the summer of 1834, better accomodations were found at the first Presbyterian church [SW corner of Lake

[117]

and Clark streets]; the first school that received an appropriation from the school fund of the town in 1834, and thereby became ★★★ **Chicago's 1st public school**; later accepted older students, and eventually became a boarding school. Miss Chappel resigned in the winter of 1834-35, and Miss Leavenworth took charge, followed later by Mrs. Joseph Harmon.

Ingals, Henry and Charles Francis   from Connecticut; in late spring, 1834, traveled to Michigan City with siblings and $1,000 in silver within a trunk; the brothers walked but shipped the trunk as freight to Chicago, then took a stage to Ottawa, eventually settling near Beardstown. Charles remembered the Chicago prairie as "a continual scene of sloughs and mud holes." The account may be found in the *Journal of the Illinois State Historical Society* 26.

Ingalls, Augustus   (1805-1889) arrived in 1834 from Belchertown, MA, and settled in Addison Township. [314a]

Ingersoll, Chester   from Vermont; served as sergeant during the Black Hawk War in Capt. James Walker's company in the summer of 1832; moved to Chicago and became landlord of Wolf Tavern, replacing William Wattles in late fall, 1833, renaming the tavern Traveler's Home and later, the Western Stage House; on Dec. 12 that year married Phoebe Weaver [age 21] from New York, the Hon. R.J. Hamilton officiating; in the Aug. 27, 1834, *Chicago Democrat* he advertised the sale of town lots at the newly platted town [Plainfield] NE of Walker's Grove to where he had removed, 40 miles from Chicago; farmed until 1849, then left for California. Mrs. Ingersoll is listed as an actress and teacher of dancing in 1839, boarding at the Lake House. [12, 351]

intendant   in New France during the period from 1665 to 1760, the highest-ranking administrator in charge of the affairs of the colony. While the governor represented the French king, the intendant made and supervised all major administrative decisions; both officials were appointed by the king and were answerable to him personally. Prior to 1665, only governors were appointed and were expected to fulfill both functions. Listed below in chronological order of their service are all intendants of New France; those marked [*] have a separate entry for additional information. [665]

*Jean Talon...1665-1668
Claude de Bouteroue......................... 1668-1669
Jean Talon..1669-1675
Jacques Duchesneau.............................1675-1682
Jacques de Meulles................................1682-1686
Jean Bochart deChampigny....................1686-1702
*François de Beauharnais.......................1702-1705
Jacques (père) and Antoine Denis (fils) Raudot.....
....1705-1710
Jacques Raudot, alone............................1710-1711
Claude Michel Bégon............................1712-1726
Claude Thomas Dupuy.........................1726-1728
Gilles Hocquart.....................................1728-1748
François Bigot...1748-1760

Iroquois   a confederated group of five Indian tribes or nations (Mohawk, Oneida, Onondaga, Cayuga and Seneca) of the Huron-Iroquois linguistic stock that existed S of the St. Lawrence River and Lake Ontario and struggled against the Huron for control of the fur trade between 1630 and 1665. In general, the Iroquoi were allied with the British against the French; together with the Fox, they limited French access to the Illinois River valley and the upper Mississippi around 1700 by controlling the portages, including Chicago's; the blockade lasted for approximately 75 years; they severely decimated both the Huron and the Illinois tribes, which were friendly toward the French.

Irving Park Road ➡ the course of an early Indian portage trail from the north branch of the Chicago River to the Des Plaines River; located at 4000 N and passes Portage Park at Central Avenue; Irving Park, originally called Irvington, was an early settlement along this road, named after Washington Irving (1783-1859).

Irwin, Matthew of Philadelphia; government factor at Fort Dearborn, succeeding Joseph B. Varnum; appointed in 1808 but began his duties at the fort in the summer of 1809. [The factory was the U.S. government store selling to Indians. Beginning Dec. 30, 1809, Irwin's letters to William Eustis, the secretary of war, exposed the corruption, illegal trading, smuggling, threats, and British orientation of several officers at Fort Dearborn, John Kinzie, Billy Caldwell, and others; he expressed fear for his own life as a result of his exposé; the killing of La Lime suggests his fears were not groundless.] Serving until July 5, 1812, Irwin did a total of $4,712.57 of agency business; leaving for Mackinac on a mission to find a replacement for the Indian interpreter, Jean B. La Lime, who had recently been killed by John Kinzie, and requesting that Dr. Van Voorhis cover the factory store, he thus escaped the Fort Dearborn massacre of Aug. 15; arrived at Mackinac on Aug. 16 and was captured by the British and Indians at the surrender of Fort Mackinac, but survived; in 1815 served as factor at Green Bay; married Nancy Walker in 1816 and a son (William) was born in 1817; died c.1845. [12, 109, 226, 649]

Isham, Giles S. resident in 1835, when his name was on a school-related petition signed on Sept. 19. [12]

Isle a la Cache an island in the Des Plaines River near what is now Romeoville, IL; was an important camping and hiding place for Indians and pioneers. Known to the French fur traders as long ago as Father Marquette's second trip to Illinois; his report strongly suggests that [see] "the Surgeon" and Pierre Moreau stashed their goods on the island in 1674. The site was a convenient one day canoeing distance from Chicago on the way to the Indian villages along the Illinois River. On the island is now located a fine museum, the ▲ Isle a la Cache Museum, also listed in the section "A Guide to Early Chicago Historical Monuments."

Jackeax, Mr. organized a dancing school once a week at the New York House during the winter of 1835-36, "which called out the elite of the city," according to [see] J.D. Bonnell.

Jackson a schooner that called at Chicago on Oct. 29, 1819; John Kinzie requested to send goods to Mackinac.

Jackson, Andrew (1767-1845) native of SC; seventh U.S. president, serving from 1829-1837; during his two terms, although he was vehemently opposed to internal improvements such as the Chicago harbor and the Illinois & Michigan Canal, Chicago rapidly developed from a sleepy settlement into a vibrant city. Jackson's Tennessee home was The Hermitage, E of Nashville; he was buried on the grounds of this estate; ➡ Jackson Boulevard, Jackson Drive (both at 300 S); Hermitage Avenue (1732 W).

Jackson, Carding arrived from New York in 1835; in later years, served as deputy grand master of the Masons; ◆ farmer, Vincennes Avenue

Jackson, Charles in the summer of 1833 furnished 500 logs, at $3.75 a log, for the Chicago harbor project under contract with Major Bender; each log was 30 feet long, 14 inches in diameter, and hewn on two sides.

Jackson, Daniel leading New York merchant in the early 1830s, supplied trade goods to Chicago with the help of Robert A. Kinzie; introduced Bronson to Kinzie; visited Chicago at the time of the 1833 Treaty with the Indians and signed the document as a witness.

Jackson, Ezra a child by this name was enrolled as grade school student in the class taught by [see] John Watkins in December 1835. Names of corresponding parents were not recorded. [728]

Jackson, Oren arrived from New York in 1835.

Jackson, Samuel T. (1800-1849) born in Connecticut; employed on the public works of the Buffalo harbor [had worked under William Jones there]; recommended to and appointed by the federal government to build the public works of Chicago; said to have arrived from Buffalo by schooner in May 1833 with his wife Lucinda [née Davis, married Nov. 21, 1822], but others report him to have been the building contractor who erected the first Chicago lighthouse in 1832 that collapsed before the end of the year (for details, see entry for lighthouse); in 1833 was construction foreman in charge of the pile driver at the harbor site under Maj. Geo. Bender; in 1837 served as alderman of the fifth ward while also working as a foreman of harbor improvements; ◆ Government works, near Garrison; responsible for all government property in Chicago until his death by cholera. [12, 13]

jail ★★★ Chicago's 1st jail was built in the fall of 1833 on the NW corner of the public square; existent until 1853.

Jamboe, Paul voted on Aug. 7, 1828 [see Chronology].

Jamieson, Lt. Louis Thornton Fifth Infantry; from Virginia, came from Fort Brady to serve at Fort Dearborn when regarrisoned, from May 14, 1833, to December 1936; ★★★ Chicago's 1st librarian, in charge of the library at the fort to "encourage reading among its inmates"; on the list of subscribers to the *Chicago Democrat* in November 1833; was a charter member of the first Presbyterian church; signed as witness on the September 1833 Indian Treaty of Chicago; successful real estate dealer during the speculative fever that gripped the town in the early 1830s; during 1835 he su-

LT. LOUIS THORNTON JAMISON

pervised harbor construction and in November became a vice president of the Chicago Bible Society and president of the Lyceum the following month; wife Nancy died in February 1837, and in May, he became the last military occupant of Fort Dearborn after Captain Plympton and Sgt. Joseph Adams left; later married Mary E. McClure; ◆ Capt. Louis T. Jamieson, Garrison; died in 1858 in TX. [12]

Jay's Treaty   see treaties, 1794.

Jayne, Gershom   physician and druggist of Springfield; one of the first three commissioners for the development of the Illinois & Michigan Canal who visited Chicago in the summer of 1830, and may have acquired five lots in block 4. [704]

J.C. Spencer   86-ton schooner from Buffalo, NY, under Captain Walker, built at Black River, OH in 1834; called at Chicago with passengers and merchandise on June 20, 1835, and again on Aug. 7 and Nov. 13; lost on Lake Michigan in 1843. [48]

Jefferson   lake schooner, called at Chicago on Nov.19, 1834, from French Creek, NY, with Capt.

Robert Hugunin; piloted by Archibald Caldwell from Green Bay to Chicago; called again on Sept. 14, 1835, under Captain Briggs; lost on Lake Michigan in 1844. [48]

Jefferson Barracks   near St. Louis; western headquarters of the U.S. Army during the Fort Dearborn era.

Jefferson, Joseph   born in 1828 at Philadelphia; youngest of a family of comedians, father and grandfather with identical names; the family gave several guest performances in Chicago in the summer of 1838 at the [see] Rialto, where Joseph's uncle Alexander McKenzie was manager and promoter; they moved on to Galena, Dubuque, Springfield, and farther south. While beyond the time frame set for this book, the editors include Joseph's unique impression left by the journey and the fledgling town on the mind of a bright child visitor. [12, 367, 482]

In the year 1838 the new town of Chicago had just turned from an Indian village into a thriving little place, and my uncle [Alexander McKenzie] had written to my father urging him to join in the management of the new theatre which was then being built there. ... He had scarcely finished the letter when he declared that our fortunes were made, so we turned our faces toward the setting sun. ... As I remember it, our journey was long, but not tedious. We traveled part of the way in a fast-sailing packet-boat on the Erie Canal, the only smoke issuing from the caboose stove-pipe. I can remember our party admiring this craft with the same enthusiasm that we now express in looking at a fine ocean steamer. She was painted white and green and enlivened with blue window blinds, and a broad red stripe running from bow to stern. Her name was the Pioneer, *which was to us most suggestive, as our little band was among the early dramatic emigrants to the far West. The boat resembled Noah's ark with a flat roof, and my father, like the patriarch of old, took his entire family on board, with this difference, however—he was required to pay his passage, it being understood between him and the*

captain that he should stop a night in Utica and one in Syracuse, give a theatrical entertainment in each place, and hand over the receipts in payment of our fare. ... ✧ In a few days we steamed up the beautiful lakes of Huron, Erie, and Michigan. The boat would stop some times for hours at one of the stations to take in wood, or a stray passenger, and then the Indians would paddle out to us in their canoes offering their beadwork and moccasins for sale. Sometimes we would go ashore and walk on the beach gathering pebbles, carnelians, and agates. I thought them of immense value, and kept my treasures for years afterwards. ... ✧ So day by day passed, till one night a light is espied in the distance, then another, and then many more dance and reflect themselves in the water. It is too late to go ashore, so we drop anchor. At sunrise we are all on deck, looking at the haven of our destination, and there in the morning light, on the shores of Lake Michigan, stands the little town of Chicago, containing two thousand inhabitants. ... ✧ The captain said he had enjoyed a splendid trip, such fun, such musik and singing and dancing. "Well, good-bye all," "Good luck"; and off we go ashore and walk through the busy little town, busy even then, people hurrying to and fro, frame buildings going up, board sidewalks going down, new hotels, new churches, new theatres, everything new. Saw and hammer,—saw, saw, bang, bang,—look out for the drays !—bright and muddy streets,—gaudy-colored calicos,—blue and red flannel and striped ticking hanging outside the dry-goods stores,—barrooms,—real-estate offices,—attorneys-at-law— oceans of them. ✧ And now for the new theatre [Rialto], newly painted canvas, tack-hammer at work on stuffed seats in the dress-circle, planing boards in the pit, new drop-curtain let down for inspection, "beautiful!" ... ✧ With what delight the actors looked forward to the opening of a new theatre in a new town, where dramatic entertainments were still unknown—repairing their wardrobes, studying their new parts, and speculating on the laurels that were to be won! ✧ After a short season in Chicago, with the varying success which in those days always attended the drama, the company went to Galena for a short season, traveling in open wagons over the prairie. Our seats were the trunks that contained the wardrobe ... these smooth hair trunks ... so one may imagine the difficulty we had in holding on while jolting over a rough prairie.

Jefferson, Joseph father of the boy in the previous entry; following their 1838 performance, partnered his brother-in-law, Alexander McKenzie, in the management of the Chicago Theatre on Dearborn Street; ◆ Jefferson & McKenzie.

Jefferson, Thomas (1743-1826) native of Virginia; third U.S. president, serving from 1801-1809; principal author of the Declaration of Independence; had a life-long interest in ethnology in general and in United States relations with the Indians in particular; in 1803 he nearly doubled the seize of the United States and assured its dominance in North America by spearheading the acquisition of Louisiana from France. Under Henry Dearborn, Jefferson's secretary of war, the first Fort Dearborn was built on the bank of the Chicago River; ➡ Jefferson Street (600 W). On Aug. 10, 1833, the town board defined Jefferson Street as the town's western limit.

Jeneaux, Pierre worked for W.H. Wallace from July 1826 to May 1827; voted on Aug. 7, 1826 [see Chronology].

Jenkins, Thomas operated a general store on South Water Street in 1835 between Dearborn and Clark, first in a partnership with William Hissey (dissolution July 19), then with Joseph Atkinson, advertising as Jenkins & Atkinson in the Aug. 15 *Chicago American* (dissolution on Nov. 27); in October signed up with the "Pioneer" hook and ladder company, a voluntary fire brigade; in January 1836 he formed a partnership with the druggist next door, Frederick Thomas, and within months succeeded as sole owner of the entire business, continuing as a combination drug and variety store under the name Chicago New Drug and Medicine Store; ◆ dry goods, &c., Lake Street near

Clark.

Jesse Smith schooner, built at Clayton, Lake Ontario, in 1832; came from Oswego, NY, when it first called at Chicago on June 13, 1834 under Captain Boothe with passengers and merchandise, then specialized in lumber transport from Green Bay; there were six more calls in 1834, and eight in 1835, first under Captain Drurian, then Captain Brooks—returning from [see] Sheboygen on Oct. 17, as per notice in the the *Chicago Democrat*. [48]

"Jesuit Drops" a patent medicine compounded of brandy and laudanum; addictive; appearently enjoyed by members of the British Indian Department during the war of 1812, among them Billy Caldwell. [149a]

Jesuit Relations documents published annually by Sébastien Cramoisy in Paris from 1632 to 1673, consisting of the regular relations (reports) sent by North American missionaries to their Jesuit superiors; they have become an important source of historic, geographic, and ethnographic information on 17th-century New France, including the Chicago area. In 1858, the Canadian government reissued the Cramoisy series in Quebec; from 1896 to 1901, under the editorial guidance of the historian Reuben Gold Thwaites, then secretary of the State Historical Society of Wisconsin, not only the *Jesuit Relations* but numerous additional related documents–spanning a period from 1610 to 1791– were translated into English from the original French, Latin, and Italian and were published together by the Burrows Brothers Co. in Cleveland, OH, under the title *Jesuit Relations and Allied Documents* [73 volumes]; see Bibliography under *Jesuit Relations and Allied Documents*. In 1925, Edna Kenton published in a single volume a selection of the most important *Relations*, thereby making this essential historical material available to a broad readership. [208, 399, 665]

Jesuits members of the Society of Jesus which, from 1611 to 1763, played a major role in establishing New France; as missionaries the Jesuits

sought to convert Indians to Catholicism, an effort that led them deep into the North American continent, including the future site of Chicago [see Marquette, Père Jacques]. Through their [see] *Jesuit Relations,* allied documents, and map-making efforts they described and interpreted the New World to a seventeenth century Europe watching

Title page of an issue of the *Jesuit Relations* for the years 1641/1643

with fascination. Historians of subsequent centuries have much to thank them for; Edna Kenton [see Bibliography] wrote as follows: "... the records of the Jesuits speak for themselves as authentic documents and for their writers as scholars, most of them; as statesmen, some of them; but for all of them, above all else, as brave men. To them we owe, and we will owe always the best we have of our early history, written on the spot and in the hour of its making." The first Jesuit missionaries to arrive in New France were Father Pierre Biard and Father Ennemond Massé (1611). Missionary work among the Indians demanded great sacrifices; for a 1697 report from Father François De Crepieul, S.J., detailing some of the daily problems confronting him during his 26 years of service in the wilderness, see below.

Father Framçois' report, taken unedited from *The Jesuit Relations and Allied Documents*, lxv, Doc. clxx: *THE LIFE OF A MONTAGNAIX MISSIONARY, PRESENTED TO HIS SUCCESSORS IN THE MONTAGNAIX MISSION FOR THEIR INSTRUCTION AND GREATER CONSOLATION.*

By Father François De crepieul, Jesuit, and an unprofitable servant of the Missions on canada from 1671 to 1697,—which completes the 26th wintering of The Service of The Tadoussak Mission, and the 4th at The Mission of st. Xavier,—at chegoutimy, April 21, 1697.

The life of a Montagnaix Missionary is a Long and slow Martyrdom:

Is an almost continual practice of patience and of Mortification:

Is a truly penitential and Humiliating life, especially in the cabins, and on journies with the Savages.

1 The cabin is made of poles and Birch-bark; and Fir-Branches are placed around it to cover the Snow and The frozen Ground.

2 During nearly all the day, The Missionary remains in a sitting or kneeling position, exposed to an almost continual smoke during The Winter.

3 Sometimes he perspires in the day-time and most frequently is cold during The Night. He sleeps in his clothes upon The frozen Ground, and sometimes on the Snow covered with Fir-Branches, which are very hard.

4 He eats from an ouragan (dish) that is very seldom clean or washed, and in most cases is wiped with a greasy piece of skin, or is Licked by The dogs. He eats when there is anything to eat, and when some is offered to him. Sometimes the meat is only half-cooked; Sometimes it is very tough, especially when Smoked (dried in the smoke). As a rule, they have a good meal only once—or, when provisions are abundant twice; but it does not last long.

5 The savage Shoes, or the dogs' hairy skins, serve him as napkins, as the hair of the Savage men and women serves them.

6 His usual Beverage is water from the Streams or from some pond—sometimes melted snow, in an ouragan that is usually quite greasy.

7 He often scorches his clothes, or his blanket, or his stockings during the Night—especially when the cabin is small or narrow. He cannot stretch himself, but he corles himself up, and his head rests upon the snow covered with fir-branches; this chilles his brain, and gives him toothache, &c.

8 He always sleeps with his clothes on, and takes off his cassock and his Stockings only to protect himself against vermin, which always swarm on the Savages, especially the Children.

9 Usually when he wakes he finds himself surrounded by dogs. I have sometimes had 6, 8, or 10 around me.

10 The smoke is sometimes so strong that it makes his eyes weep; and when he sleeps he feels as if some one had thrown salt into his eyes; when he Awakes, he has much difficulty in opening them.

11 When the Snow Thaws, while he is walking upon Lakes or long Rivers, he is so dazzled for 4 or 5 days by the water that drops continually from his eyes that he cannot read his Breviary. Sometimes he has to be led by the hand. This has happened to father Silvy, to father Dalmas, and to myself; while on the march I could not see further than the edge of my Snowshoes.

12 He is often annoyed by little Children, by their cries, their weeping, &c.; and sometimes he is made ill by the stench of those who have Scrofula, with whom he even Drinks out of the same kettle. I have spent more than 8 days in the cabin of Kawitaskawat, the chief man among the Mystassins, and have slept near his son, who was troubled with that disease; and the stench from him often caused me nausea, both by day and night. I have also eaten and drank from his ouragan.

13 He is sometimes reduced to drinking only water obtained from melted snow, which smells of smoke and is very dirty. For 3 Weeks I have drank nothing else, while I was with Strangers in the Region of Peokwagamy. I have never seen Savages dirtier than these, as regards eating, drinking and sleeping. Among them the meat was often covered with moose-hairs or Sand. An old women, with her long nails, gathered up handfuls of grease in the Kettle into which Snow had been thrown, and then offered it to us to eat, in a very dirty ouragan: and all drank broth out of the same Kettle.

14 In the summer-time, while Traveling, especially on the Saguenay and on the great River, he often drinks the very dirty water obtained from Ponds. During 3 days, while detained by contrary winds, we drank no other water. Sometimes the Wind compels him to take refuge in Places where there is none at all. This has happened to me more than once—indeed, more than 3 times. I have even been obliged to drink from Ponds in which I Saw toads, &c.

15 In most cases during the winter, while on long and difficult journeys, he does not find a drop of water wherewith to quench his thirst, although exhausted with toils and fatigues.

16 He suffers greatly from cold and from smoke, before the Cabin is finished, for 2 or 3 hours when the Weather is very severe in winter. His shirt, which is whet with perspiration, and his soaked stockings, render him Benumbed with cold; he suffers also from Hunger, because in most cases he has had nothing but a piece of dried meat, eaten before the camp was struck.

17 Suffering and hardship are the appanages of these holy but arduous Missions. Facit Deus ut iis diu immoretur et immoriatur Servus Inutilis Missionum Franciscus, S.J. (God grant that in them may long remain and die the Useless Servant of the Missions, François, S.J.) [12, 205 208, 399, 518]

Jewett, William P.   voted on July 24 and Nov. 25, 1830 (see elections); on the first day of government land sales in 1830, he purchased lots 5 and 6 in block 28 [see map on page 44], but by 1832 these lots were listed in the name of Lemuel Brown.

jikag   also *jigak*; Chippewa word for *skunk*; this has given rise to a theory that the original name "Chicago" means *skunk* rather than *wild garlic*; for more details see entry under Chicago name.

John Grant   93-ton schooner from Buffalo, NY; arrived under Captain Nelson at Chicago with passengers and merchandise on June 15, 1835, and later on Sept. 30 and Nov. 18; capsized on Lake Erie in 1845. [48]

John Grant Jr.   schooner under Captain Rogers; called from Buffalo, NY, with merchandise on July 9, 1834.

John Kinzie   brig, built in 1833; piloted by Captain Bristol in 1834, under Captain Grove in 1835; first called at Chicago from Detroit on May 25, 1834, calling five more times that year, twice in 1835; carried merchandise, lumber, and passengers. [48]

Johnson, David   name in the customer account book of the printer John Calhoun under the date of Aug. 22, 1834. [12]

Johnson, Lathrop   (1802-1881) from Cazenovia, NY; came in September 1834 [1832 according to Gale]; builder and co-owner of New York House with George Stevens; the hotel was built on the N side of Lake Street in 1834 and opened in 1835; a notice in the *Chicago American* on June 15, 1835, announced the dissolution of a livery partnership with J.N. Stuart; the partnership with Stevens was dissolved on Sept. 1 though they worked together through December, when he alone announced the

hotel would be "kept as heretofore"; late that year filed a claim for wharfing privileges for lot 4, block 19; in the spring of 1836 organized the first stage to Milwaukee on the Green Bay Road; ✦ [Johnston] boarded at New York House; left for Lake Superior in 1846. [544]

Johnson, Peter   arrived from Maryland in 1833 and was, with his wife Maglen E., in the group of first communicants of St. James Episcopal Church, together with Dr. Maxwell and members of the John H. Kinzie family. [12, 733]

Johnson, Sanford   a builder from Virginia, arrived in 1833; served in the voluntary fire brigade in 1835; ✦ [Johnston] carpenter, boarded at Chicago Hotel. [12]

Johnson, Capt. Seth   Second Infantry; served at Fort Dearborn from June 17, 1832, to May 15, 1833, under Maj. William Whistler; his wife (née Spence, sister of [see] Agnes and James Spence), active in organizing the library of the Presbyterian church, lived with him at the fort; conducted religious services at the fort during the winter of 1832-33, with villagers invited and attending; in c.1832 he purchased from J.B. Beaubien, together with Robert Stewart [Robert Stuart?], lot 3 in block 36 [see map on page 44]; in 1834 returned to Chicago as a civilian; ✦ north branch, W side; Seth, Jr., is also listed as a student with Dr. J. Jay Stuart; in 1843, became collector of revenue for the Chicago port. Also see McClure, Josiah E., for a possible daughter of Captain and Mrs. Johnson. [12, 432]

Johnson, William   member of the Fort Dearborn garrison that had arrived from Fort Brady in the spring of 1833, together with Reverend Porter; became a charter member of the first Presbyterian church when it organized on June 26, 1833; purchased in c.1833 from Robert A. Kinzie lots 5 and 8 on W Water Road in block 44 [see map on page 44]. In 1839 a William Johnson is listed with a haircutting and shaving saloon [*sic*] on Clark Street [12]

Johnson, William   traveled to Chicago from Fort Wayne in 1809, wrote a detailed account of his experience, and observed that Fort Dearborn was "the neatest and the best wooden garrison in the United States"; more of his notes follow. [378]

... The road still keeps the shore of the lake. Twelve miles further is the mouth of the Great Calumet. Here the sand mountain ends. Twenty miles further is the mouth of the Little Calumet. These two rivers are of the greatest consequence to the traders on the lake. They are both about twenty yards wide at their mouth, but very deep. One of them is considerably longer than the other; and there is a communication between them, which in case of storm on the lake the trader can go up one several miles, then across into the other and down it into the lake. It is twelve miles from the mouth of the little Calumet to the mouth of Chicago river. Here the United States have erected a garrison (Fort Dearborn) for the protection of the trader in this quarter of the country. This garrison does great honor to Capt. John Whistler who planned and built it. It is the neatest and best wooden garrison in the United States. This place guards the entrance of Chicago river. ✧ Between the Chicago and the Illinois rivers, there is a direct water communication. The river Plein, which is one of the main forks of the Illinois, has its source near the bank of the lake, and nine miles from Fort Dearborn it turns West. At this bend there is a long pond communicates with it, which runs eastwardly toward the lake and terminates in a small creek which runs into the Chicago river. This creek is about two miles long; and in the Spring of the year any kind of craft may sail out of the lake to the Mississippi without being unladen. The U.S. factor at Fort Dearborn measured the elevation of land between the lake and the river Plein, and found it to be four feet on the side of the lake and five on the side of Illinois. Thus by digging a canal of nine** feet deep, a passage could be got at any season in the year from the Falls of Niagara to the mouth of the Mississippi without a single foot of land carriage. The Canal would be about six miles long, through a beautiful prairie, and there is a quarry

of limestone near this place which would make excellent casing for the Canal. (**I do not understand this—why an elevation of 4 feet on one side and 5 on the other should be added together.) ❖ *While at Fort Dearborn I was informed that there were some boats at the Portage which would cross the next day. I accordingly went, in company with W. Varnum and Captain Whistler's son, to the portage. The water was low, it being about the 28th of June. The boats could not pass below; but I saw them sail out of the river Plein into the pond, and through it into the creek before mentioned, and down it into the Chicago river. The loads were brought over the portage in wagons; and they were re-loaded (into the boats) at the head of the Chicago.* ❖ *There is a custom house kept at Fort Dearborn, where all traders are obliged to make an entry of their goods.* ❖ *The public officers are Major Charles Jewet [Jouett], agent for Indian affairs; W. George [Joseph] B. Varnum, factor and commissary; Capt. John Whistler commandant; Lieut. Hamilton and Thompson. There are about sixty soldiers in garrison at Fort Dearborn; and so healthy has the place been that Captain Whistler, commandant, informed me he had lost but six men in nearly eight years, and he has the same men now that he had when he built the garrison; and although their term of enlistment expired still they all enlisted again—a sure sign that he is a good officer.* ❖ *Fort Dearborn is beautifully situated on the bank of the lake. It is bounded on the land side by an extensive prairie, interspersed with groves of trees, which gives it a beautiful appearance.* ❖ *Lake Michigan abounds with fish of an excellent quality. The white fish is caught here in great plenty. This is probably the best fresh water fish in the waters of the United States. The surge of the lake beating always against the shore, frequently throws out large fish on the land. I took up several perch and pickerel, that would weigh ten pounds, some of them alive. The shore is frequented by flocks of crows, buzzards, gulls, &c. which soon destroy the fish that is thrown out on the shore.*

Johnston, Samuel   voted on Aug. 7, 1826 and May

11, 1828 [see Chronology]; was present at the sale of the W.H. Wallace estate on April 27, 1827.

Jolliet, Adrian   older brother of Louis Jolliet; became the first Canadian to have traveled the Great Lakes westward [September 1669] seeking copper mines, under the directive of Jean Baptiste Talon, intendant of New France; never returned from this trip into the wilderness.

Jolliet, Louis   (1645-1700) Canadian explorer, born in Trois Rivères; educated at the Jesuit College of Quebec; headquartered as trader and explorer at Sault Ste. Marie from 1669; after 1673 became the official Canadian cartographer. With Father Marquette, Jolliet was one of the first Europeans recorded to have passed through the Chicago River; passage took place in September 1673, when they were eastbound and returning from a 2,500 mile trip, commissioned by Governor Frontenac, that took them from the *Mission of St. François Xavier* by way of Prairie du Chien to the Mississippi, S to the Arkansas River, and back through the Illinois River, Des Plaines River, Chicago Portage, Chicago River, and Lake Michigan. In his report Jolliet commented on the advantage for trade were the Chicago Portage replaced with a canal [as recorded by Father Dablon in his letter of Aug. 1, 1674]: "We could go with facility to Florida in a bark, and by very easy navigation. It would only be necessary to make a canal by cutting through but half a league of prairie, to pass from the foot of the Lake of the Illinois to the St. Louis [Illinois] River, which empties into the Mississippi." A ✱ map, *Carte de la descouverte du Sr Jolliet ou l'on voit la communication du Fleuve St Laurens avec les Lacs Frontenac, Erié, Lac des Hurons, et Illinois ...* [Service historique de la Marine, Vincennes], was recreated in 1674 to replace the original map that Jolliet lost in a canoe accident at Lachine while returning to Montreal to report the details of his and Father Marquette's journey. During 1674, Jolliet returned to the Chicago area and became more familiar with the terrain; married Claire F.

Bissot Oct. 7, 1675; was appointed *maître d'hydrographie* of Canada in 1697. A portion of Jolliet's report in 1673 follows. [12, 195, 198, 199, 263, 282, 286, 633, 681, 682, 718]

The river we named for St. Louis rises near the lower end of the lake—most beautiful, most suitable for settlement. Where we entered the lake is a harbor, sheltered from the wind, abounding in catfish and sturgeon. Abundant game there—oxen, cows, stags, does, and turkey. Sometimes we saw the grass there very short, and at other times, five or six feet high; hemp, which grows naturally there, reaches as high as eight feet. Nothing would be wanting there, no better soil can be found either for corn, for vines, or for any other fruit whatever.

[Also see Jolliet's description of the prairie under that entry.]

Jombo, Jock   mail carrier between Chicago and Green Bay (once a week) during the years 1834-35, as reported by Oliver C. Crocker.

Jones, Benjamin   arrived in 1833; "grocery, provision store, storage, forwarding and commission" advertisement can be found in the first issue of the *Chicago Democrat*, Nov. 26, 1833; in the third issue, Jones announces more specifically that he can arrange for shipping to and from New York on the Erie canal; selected ★★★ **Chicago's 1st** firewarden, responsible monthly for the inspection of each building; on Dec. 7, 1833, was appointed ★★★ **Chicago's 1st** street commissioner by the village council, but resigned shortly thereafter and was succeeded by Silas Sherman and Oremus Morrison; ✦ grocer on South Water Street; died in 1881. [12]

Jones, Clark & Co.   a firm identified by Andreas as competitive in the lumber trade in 1835. [13]

Jones, Fernando   (1820-1911) son of [see] William and Anna Jones, joining his father in Chicago in 1835 at age 15; began work at the U.S. Land Office as an office boy under James M. Strode, as well as at his father's hardware store; ✦ clerk, Thomas Church; on July 7, 1853, married Jane

FERNANDO JONES [410]

Grahame of Northern Ireland, who died in 1905; lived all his life in Chicago, and at 83 recalled one of the first accidental deaths occurring in the community; his story follows. [12]

It was about daylight one morning in the fall of 1835 that I was awakened by some one pounding on the door of the store in South Water street where I was sleeping. It was my father's hardware store, and it stood ... between Clark and Dearborn. I got up and found Alex Beaubien there, all exited, telling me there was a man lying in a mudhole over in the prairie, and that the fellow would die there if he were not picked up. ✧ *I dressed and hurried over toward the place, picking up a Frenchman as I followed the boy to the spot. When we got there we found a man sunk to his waist in the mud and water, and in this position he had fallen over on his face. Evidently he had been drinking or he would have avoided the hole, which was well marked and known by every teamster.* ✧ *The man was a Frenchman and had been dead several hours. We got his body out of the mire and called a wagon, taking him over to the house of the sheriff*

[Orsemus Morrison, Chicago's first constable and coroner; *eds.*]. *An inquest was held, finding his death to have been accidental. ... Today* [1903] *the point of chief interest in the story is in the fact that the hole in which the man was drowned in water and mud was just ... at Clark street and Jackson boulevard. ...*

Jones & King   hardware store on South Water Street between Clark and Dearborn; see Jones, William and King, Byram. Beginning in November 1834, John Calhoun printed the *Chicago Democrat* in the loft above the store; ✦ [Jones, King & Co.] wholesale hardware merchants, South Water Street

Jones, King & Co.   the "company" in the firm's name was Henry B. Clark; advertisements—"Rotary engines, Arery's patent" (manufactured in Buffalo), dry hides, Timothy seed, winter apples, and souse—appeared under this name throughout the summer and fall of 1835 in the *Chicago Democrat*, as an iron foundry was erected near the south branch bank at Polk Street; on November 20 Jones and King submitted an application for wharfing privileges; by December the first lot of castings had been produced; the foundry was built by William H. Stow and David Bradley of Syracuse, NY; within a few years Chicago's first steam engines were made.

Jones, Rhodias   U.S. Army private at Fort Dearborn; enlisted as private in December 1807; killed in action at the massacre of Aug. 15, 1812. [226]

Jones, Willard   from Massachusetts; arrived in 1833 and was a founding member of the first Baptist church at its first meeting on Oct. 19; in November he plastered John Calhoun's printing office, together with Martin Harmon; on Oct. 1, 1835 married Mrs. Marcia Delia Farnsworth of Blue Island and moved to Lake County [12, 733]

Jones, William   (1789-1868) native of Massachusetts; a chief of police and a superintendent of workers on the Buffalo harbor; in the summer of 1831, traveled by steamer from Buffalo, NY, and arrived at Chicago on horseback from Elhart; observed the settlement's "promise and potency" and returned

in February 1832, to buy lots 2 and 7 in block 17 from J.B. Beaubien, one on Lake Street and one on South Water Street, for $100 each [see map on page 44]; in 1833, at the school sale, he bought block 133 in the school section (on Clark and Twelfth streets) for $152; in the spring of 1834 he established a stove and hardware store [in partnership with his future son-in-law Byram King, "Jones & King"; jointly they applied for wharf privileges] at the South Water Street location; Jones and King were co-owners of the first [see] foundry in Chicago; in November 1834 the loft above the store was rented to John Calhoun for his print shop; his wife Anna (née Gregory, married 1824) and their children Louis, [see] Fernando, Kyler K., James, Mariah, Emily (married King in 1836), Albert (died in 1836), and possibly more, would join him in May, 1835; became a member of the fire engine company No.1 ("Fire Kings") in December 1835; ✦ justice of the peace, Dearborn Street, corner of Randolph; in 1840 began serving as chairman of the new board of school inspectors; buried at Oakwood Cemetery. [12]

Jordan, Walter K.   U.S. Army corporal from Pensylvania; stationed in 1812 at the Fort Wayne garrison; his family (wife Elizabeth "Betcy" Wort) remained in Pensylvania; accompanied Captain Wells and a contingent of Miami to Fort Dearborn where they arrived on Aug. 13, 1812, in order to lend protection for the planned evacuation of the fort on Aug. 15; he survived the massacre, escaped his Indian captors, and arrived back at Fort Wayne on Aug. 27; on the next day, the Indians attacked the fort and did not abandon their siege until General Harrison brought relief on Sept. 16. Jordan is one of few survivors of the massacre who later gave an eyewitness account of the event in writing; below are quoted excerpts from one of Jordan's letters. [36, 226]

[Oct. 12,1812] *Betcy I now lift my pen to inform you that I am In a good State of health after a long and* [word missing] *Journy threw the Indian Cunty*

CHARLES JOUETT [410]

I Started [word missing] *fort wayn on the 1 of august With Cao Wells and* [word missing] *to goe to fort dearborn on lake michigan wich is 200 miles from fort wain....* [Referring to the massacre] *tha first Shot the fether out of my Cap the nex shot the appolet of my Shoulder and the 3 Broke the handle of my Sword I had to Surrender My Self to 4 Dame yallow indians tha Marche up to whar Wells lay and one of them Spok English and Said Jordan I now you you gave me some toBacco at fort wain you Shant be kild but See What I will doe with your Captain He then Cut of his head and Stuck it on a pol while another tuck out his hart and divided it among the Chieffs and tha Eate it up raw....*

Josette   Indian woman for whom Archibald Caldwell, then of Chicago, abandoned his wife Emily in 1830; Emily divorced him in the same year; Josette and Archibald moved to the Wisconsin wilderness in 1830, had several children, and lived Indian style.

Joste, Bernard   a notice in the June 17, 1835, *Chi-cago Democrat* identifies a "packet of papers, bills, notes, &c." found in the woods N of town, belonging to the "German pedlar."

Jouett, Charles   (1772-1834) also Jowett; born in Charlottesville, VA, as the youngest of nine children of a prominent family; friends and neighbors of Thomas Jefferson; studied law and initially practiced in Charlottesville; served as U.S. Indian agent at Detroit from 1802 to 1805; married Eliza Dodemead on Jan. 22, 1803; became ★★★ Chicago's 1st lawyer in residence when assigned as Indian agent at Fort Dearborn in the fall of 1804 and given the charge of maintaining relations with the Potawatomi, Sauk, Fox, Chippewa, Ottawa and Miami by periodically distributing presents and holding councils with the chiefs; initially Jouett and his wife lived in the Agency house that the soldiers had built immediately W of the fort; Elizabeth died within a year, leaving him one daughter; around 1808 he built a house on the N side of the river, near the Kinzies, and brought a bride from Kentucky (Susan Randolph Allen, married 1809), a Negro slave (Joe Battles, whom the Indians called "Black Meat"), and an indentured *métis* servant girl (Madaline Alscum or Olscum); a son named Charles La Lime was born in 1809 but died the next year; serving until 1811, Jouett then resigned and settled in Kentucky, thereby escaping the destructive events at the fort in 1812; served a second term at Fort Dearborn, from 1816 to 1818, bringing his wife Susan and, by then, three daughters to Chicago and, according to Andreas, lived in the old Burns House; he was known among the Indians as the "White Otter" and was highly esteemed by them; in 1818 Dr. Alexander Wolcott assumed the office of agent. Jouett died in Kentucky. [12, 74]

Jouett, Charles La Lime   (1809-1810) son of Charles Jouett, Indian agent, and his second wife Susan; was born Oct. 26, 1809, and died on Aug. 9, 1810, at the age of 11 months; named after Jean B. La Lime, a good friend of Jouett, who was killed

A
JOURNAL
Of the LAST
VOYAGE
Perform'd by
Monſr. de la Sale,
TO THE
GULPH of MEXICO,
To find out the
Mouth of the *Miſſiſipi* River;
CONTAINING,
An Account of the Settlements he endeavour'd to make on the Coaſt of the aforeſaid *Bay*, his unfortunate Death, and the Travels of his Companions for the Space of Eight Hundred Leagues acroſs that Inland Country of *America*. now call'd *Louiſiana*, (and given by the King of *France* to M. *Crozat*,)till they came into *Canada*.
Written in French by *Monſieur* J O U T E L, *A Commander in that Expedition*; *And Tranſlated from the Edition juſt publiſh'd at* Paris.
With an exaɕ Map of that vaſt Country, and a Copy of the *Letters Patents* granted by the K. of France to M. *Crozat*.
LONDON, Printed for *A. Bell* at the *Croſs-Keys* and Bible in *Cornhill*, *B. Lintott* at the *Croſs Keys* in *Fleet-ſtreet*, and *J. Baker* in *Pater-Noſter-Row*, 1714.

by Kinzie in 1812; he is among the first children of white settlers born in Chicago.

Journal des Jésuites   see Laval de Montmorency, Mgr. François.

Joutel, Henri   La Salle's confidential deputy; naturalist, survivor, and historian of La Salle's ill-fated 1684-87 sailing expedition from France to Texas. Traveling north and overland with five companions (Père Anastase Douay, Abbé Jean Cavelier (La Salle's brother), Jean Baptiste Cavelier (no relation),

1494	June 7	Spain			seat of gov:	Spanish royal court
1497	June 24	England			capital:	London
1536	May 3	France			capital:	Versailles
1565	Aug. 28	Spain	Florida		capital:	St. Augustine
1609		England	Virginia Company of London		capital:	London
1662	April 23	England	Connecticut		capital:	London
1671	June 14	France			capital:	Versailles
1672		France	Province of *Nouvelle France*		prov. gov.:	Quebec
1682	April 9	France	[*Louisiane*; see note on next page]		prov. gov.:	[New Orleans]
1763	Feb. 10	England			capital:	London
1774	June 22	England	Province of Quebec		prov. gov.:	Quebec
1778	Dec. 9	Virginia		Illinois County	state gov.:	Williamsburg
1783	Sept. 23	U.S.			seat of gov.:	Philadelphia [provisional]
1787	July 13	U.S.	Northwest Territory		seat of gov.:	Philadelphia [provisional]
1790	June 20	U.S.	Northwest Territory	Knox County	county seat:	Vincennes
1796	Aug. 15	U.S.	Northwest Territory	Wayne County	county seat:	Detroit
1800	July 4	U.S.	Territory of Indiana	St. Clair County	seat of gov.:	Washington City
1801	Feb. 3	U.S.	Territoty of Indiana	St. Clair County	county seat:	Cahokia
1803	March 1	U.S.	Territory of Indiana	Wayne County	county seat:	Detroit
1805	June 30	U.S.	Territory of Indiana	St. Clair County	county seat:	Cahokia
1809	March 1	U.S.	Territory of Illinois	St. Clair County	county seat:	Kaskaskia
1812	Sept. 14	U.S.	Territory of Illinois	Madison County	county seat:	house of Thomas Kirkpatrick
1814	Nov. 28	U.S.	Territory of Illinois	Edwards County	county seat:	Palmyra
1816	Dec. 31	U.S.	Territory of Illinois	Crawford County	county seat:	house of Edward N. Cullom
1818	April 8	U.S.	State of Illinois	Crawford County	county seat:	Palestine
1819	March 22	U.S.	State of Illinois	Clark County	county seat:	Aurora
1820	Dec.	U.S.	State of Illinois	Clark County	county seat:	Vandalia
1821	Jan. 31	U.S.	State of Illinois	Pike County	county seat:	Cole's Grove
1823	Jan. 28	U.S.	State of Illinois	Fulton County	county seat:	house of Ossian M. Ross
1825	Jan. 13	U.S.	State of Illinois	Putnam/Peoria Co.	county seat:	Peoria
1831	Jan. 15	U.S.	State of Illinois	Cook County	state capital:	Kaskaskia
1837	March 4	U.S.	State of Illinois	Cook County	state capital:	Springfield

Notes to
A CIVIL JURISDICTIONAL CHRONOLOGY
From 1497 to 1795, the territorial claims that included Chicago were overlapping and contested.

1494	June 7	With the Treaty of Tordesillas, Pope Alexander IV sanctions Spain's claim to terrirory that subsequently will include the entire North American continent.
1497	June 24	Giovanni Caboto reaches northen Maine or Nova Scotia, and takes possession of the new land for Henry VI and England.
1536	May 3	In the name of the French crown, Jacques Cartier, from a point near Quebec, annexes the entire drainage basin of the St. Lawrence River.
1565		Phillip II, king of Spain, proclaims himself monarch of North America. On Aug. 28, St. Augustine is founded by Pedro Menéndes de Aviles. No attempt is then made by the Spanish crown to control the country that extends northward.
1606		King James I of England grants a charter to the Virginia Company of London allowing the extension of its western border west and northwest [at a 45 degree angle] "from Sea to Sea," which claim is maintained by the state of Virginia until 1784.
1662	April 23	England's crown grants a charter to Connecticut allowing the extension of its western border "to the South Sea on the west," which claim is maintained by Connecticut until Sept. 13, 1796.
1671	June 14	Simon St. Lusson, at Sault Ste. Marie, formally takes possession of all the interior of North America for France, as an extension of New France.
1672		The French crown declares *Nouvelle France* a royal province of France.
1682	April 9	LaSalle takes possession of the valley of the Mississippi and its tributaries for King Louis XIV. Chicagoland thus straddles the watershed between this new French claim (*Louisiane*) and the earlier one of 1536 (Canada). The exact administrative border between the two French provinces is disputed to this day. *De facto*, Chicago was always ruled from Canada as long as it was under the French crown, while southern Illinois was ruled from Louisiana.
1763	Feb. 10	The Treaty of Paris ends the French and Indian War. France relinquishes to England all claims to continental North America, except for Louisiana.
1774	June 22	The Quebec Act provides civil government to the English province of Quebec, including Chicago.
1778	Dec. 9	Under Patrick Henry, as governor and by action of both houses of the Virginia legislature, civil jurisdiction is extended westward into what was designated the County of Illinois. The claim is based on the charter granted by James I and the conquest by Virginian forces under George Rogers Clarke in 1778-79. On March 31, 1783, Virginia cedes this claim to the United States.
1783	Sept. 23	On this date the deed of cession is signed by the United States and Britain, transferring the power of government to the United States.
1825	Jan. 13	Both Peoria County and Putnam County are created by an act of the Illinois legislature. Chicago is located in Putnam County, but is administered by Peoria County officials.

a pilot named Tessier, and a young Parisian named Barthelemy), he reached *Fort St. Louis* on Sept. 14, 1687, then spent time in Chicagou from Sept. 25 to Oct. 3, 1687, while waiting in vain for bad weather to clear for the trip to Canada; was forced to return to *Fort St. Louis* for the winter, and was again at Chicagou from March 29 to April 5, 1688, after which he continued to Quebec. In his 1688 journal, Joutel gave sufficient information about the wild garlic plant he found in the area woods to allow the historian-botanist John F. Swenson to trace the name Chicago to the plant *Allium tricoccum* nearly 200 years later [see Swenson's essay on page 377]. An excerpt of Joutel's journal, as it pertains to his Chicagou experience, follows. [12, 384, 385, 519]

At length we set out, the 21st of March, from Fort St. Louis. The Sieur Boisrondet [Francois de Boisrondel, La Salle's trusted storekeeper at Fort St. Louis], *who was desirous to return to France, joined us. We embarked on the river, which had then become navigable, and before we had advanced five leagues, met with a rapid stream, which obliged us to go ashore, and then again into the water, to draw along our canoe. I had the misfortune to hurt one of my feet against a rock which lay under the water, which troubled me very much for a long time. We arrived in Chicagou on the 29th of March, and our first care was to seek what we had concealed at our former voyage, having—buried our luggage and provisions. We found it had been opened, and some furs and linnen taken away, almost all of which belonged to me. This had been done by a Frenchman, whom M. Tonty had sent from the fort during the winter season to know whether there were any conoes at Chicagou, and whom he had directed to see whether anybody had meddled with what he had concealed; and he made use of that advise to rob us. The bad weather obliged us to stay at that place until April. This time of rest was advantagous for the healing of my foot; and there being but very little game in that place, we had nothing but our meal, or Indian wheat, to feed on; still we*

discovered a kind of manna, which was a great help to us. It was a sort of tree, resembling our maple, in which we made incisions, whence flowed a sweet liquor, and in it we boiled our Indian wheat, which made it delicious, sweet, and of a very agreeable relish. There being no sugar canes in that country, those trees supplied that liquor, which being boiled up and evaporated, turned into a kind of sugar, somewhat brownish but very good. In the woods we found a sort of garlic, not so strong as ours, and small onions very like ours in taste, and some charvel of the same relish as that we have, but different in leaf. The weather being somewhat mended, we embarked again, and entered upon the lake on the 5th of April, keeping to the north side, to shun the Iroquois.

Juliett　schooner under Captain Shooks, built at Black River, OH, in 1834; carried merchandise and passengers between Buffalo, Detroit, and Chicago; first called at Chicago on July 1, 1834, returning three times that year, four in 1835; sank on Lake Erie in 1871. [48]

Juneau, Laurent Solomon　(1793-1856) French Canadian; early trader at Green Bay and Milwaukee, where he settled in 1818 at the age of 21 years and took an Indian wife; first worked for Jaques Vieau (Milwaukee's first permanent white settler, whose daughter Josette he married later), then became the local agent of the American Fur Company; founded Milwaukee, served as its first postmaster, first village president, and was elected first mayor in 1846. In 1833, he purchased from J.B. Beaubien lot 1 in block 18 on South Water Street [see map on page 44]. Father St. Cyr reports that on June 5, 1833, he baptized Juneau's daughter Marguerite and on June 28, 1833, gave communion to Mme. Juneau Solomon [*sic*] in St. Mary's Church in Chicago; visited Chicago many times, one of the better documented visits occurring in June 1832 during the Black Hawk crisis; Juneau was on the list of subscribers to the *Chicago Democrat* in November 1833; in the July 2, 1834, *Chicago Democrat* he offered land to lease along South

Water Street; moved to Dodge County, WI in 1852. [714]

jurisdiction　for an overview of the chronology of the civil jurisdictional relationships of Chicago, see page 209.

justice of the peace　the first Chicagoan to hold this office was John Kinzie, who was commissioned on July 28, 1825, when Chicago was in Peoria County [Kinzie had twice before been recommended for the office, namely in 1821 under Pike County jurisdiction, and in 1823 under Fulton County jurisdiction, but there is no record that he was commissioned on these occasions.] Alexander Wolcott and J.B. Beaubien were commissioned on Sept. 10, 1825; John L. Bogardus of Peoria was appointed on Jan. 15, 1826; Billy Caldwell and James Walker of Plainfield on April 18, 1826; John S.C. Hogan was elected justice on July 24 and commissioned on Oct. 9, 1830; Steven Forbes was elected on Nov. 25, 1830. The remainder fall into the Cook County period: Russel Heacock on Sept. 10, 1831; Archibald Clybourne and William See, commissioned on May 2, 1832; Isaac Harmon, elected June 4, 1832; John Dean Caton elected July 12, 1834; E.W. Casey, Sidney Abell, and Edward H. Hunter elected Aug. 9, 1835. [12]

Kankakee River　in Miami: Theakiki, Theakike; corrupted by the French to *Quin-qui-que, Kiakiki*, then to *Kankakee*; among the many portages in the Chicago region were those between the Calumet and various tributaries of the Kankakee River.

Karamone　Winnebago chief, present at the Fort Dearborn massacre; survived the encounter. [226]

Kaskaskia　native meaning: cicada [Father Gravier]; (1) Illinois village with 74 cabins encountered by Father Marquette in 1673 [near Utica, IL]; (2) Indian tribe, part of the Illini confederacy; Jolliet and Father Marquette stopped at the friendly tribal village in 1673 on their way up the Illinois River, and in April 1675 Marquette founded among them the *Mission de la Conception*; about the year 1700, mission and tribe were relocated to Kaskaskia; the tribe was moved to northeastern OK in 1832; (3) town in southern Illinois settled in 1703; became the commercial and cultural center of Illinois for the next 100 years; was made the capital of the Territory of Illinois in 1809, and remained capital during the early statehood period until 1837, when Springfield became the capital; was county seat of St. Clair County from 1809-1812. For details, see Chicago jurisdictional chronology on page 209. Kaskaskia was destroyed in 1881 when the Mississippi River suddenly changed its course. [455, 493, 544]

Kawbenaw also known as The "Carrier"; young Potawatomi chief who took part in the Fort Dearborn massacre and is credited with saving the life of Rebekah Heald; survived the encounter; his wife attempted to steal Rebekah' saddle blanket. [226]

Keah Keakah Miami subchief; leader of the Miami Indian escort of 27 warriors at the [see] Fort Dearborn massacre in 1812; survived the encounter. [226]

Keamble, — U.S. Army private at Fort Dearborn in 1812; first name not known; believed to have been killed in action at the massacre of 1812. [226]

Keating, William Hypolitus (1799-1840) geologist, mineralogist, and historian for Maj. Stephen Long's expedition which visited Fort Dearborn in June 1823; was not favorably impressed by Chicago's appearance nor by its prospects, describing them in unflattering terms, but nevertheless spoke in favor of an Illinois & Michigan canal; for some of Keating's astute comments, see the following excerpt; for his complete report, see Bibliography. [294]

In the afternoon of the fifth of June, we reached Fort Dearborn (Chicago), having been engaged eight days in traveling a distance of two hundred and sixteen miles, making an average of twenty-seven miles per day. ✧ *At Fort Dearborn we stopped for a few days, with a view to examine the country and make fur-*

ther preparations for the journey to the Mississippi. ✧ *We were much disappointed in the appearance of Chicago and its vicinity. We found in it nothing to justify the great eulogium lavished upon this place by a late traveler, who observes that 'it is the most fertile and beautiful that can be imagined'* [Schoolcraft, in 1820]. *'As a farming country,' says he, 'it unites the fertile soil of the finest lowland prairies with an elevation which exempts it from the influence of stagnant waters, and a summer climate of delightful serenity.' The best comment upon this description of the climate and soil is the fact that, with the most active vigilance on the part of the officers, it was impossible for the garrison* [of Fort Dearborn], *consisting of from seventy to ninety men, to subsist themselves upon the grain raised in the country, although much of their time was devoted to agricultural pursuits. The difficulties which the agriculturist meets with here are numerous; they arise from the shallowness of the soil, from its humidity, and from its exposure to the cold and damp winds which blow from the lake with great force during most part of the year; the grain is frequently destroyed by swarms of insects; there are also a number of destructive birds of which it was impossible for the garrison to avoid the baneful influence, except by keeping, as was practised at Fort Dearborn, a party of soldiers constantly engaged at shooting at the crows and blackbirds that depredated upon the corn planted by them. But, even with all these exertions, the maize seldom has time to ripen, owing to the shortness and coldness of the season. The provisions for the garrison were for the most part conveyed from Mackinaw in a schooner, and sometimes they were brought from St. Louis, a distance of three hundred and eighty-six miles up the Illinois and Des Plaines rivers ....* ✧ *The appearance of the country near Chicago offers but few features upon which the eye of the traveler can dwell with pleasure. There is too much uniformity in scenery; the extensive water prospect is a waste uncheckered by islands, unenlivened by the spreading canvas, and the fatiguing monotony of which is increased by the equally undiversi-*

fied prospect of the land scenery, which affords no relief to the sight, as it consists merely of a plain in which but few patches of thin and scrubby woods are observed scattered here and there. ✧ *The village presents no cheering prospect, as, notwithstanding its antiquity, it consists of but few huts, inhabited by a miserable race of men, scarcely equal to the Indians from whom they are descended. Their log or bark houses are low, filthy and disgusting, displaying not the least trace of comfort. Chicago is perhaps one of the oldest settlements in the Indian country; its name, derived from the Potawatomi language, signifies either a skunk, or a wild onion; and either of these significations has been occasionally given for it. A fort is said to have formerly existed there. Mention is made of the place as having been visited in 1671 by Perrot, who found 'Chicagou' to be the residence of a powerful chief of the Miamis. The number of trails centring all at this spot, and their apparent antiquity, indicate that this was probably for a long while the site a large Indian village. As a place of business, it offers no inducement to the settler; for the whole annual amount of the trade on the lake did not exceed the cargo of five or six schooners even at the time when the garrison received its supplies from Mackinaw. It is not impossible that at some distant day, when the banks of the Illinois shall have been covered with a dense population, and when the low prairies which extend between that river and Fort Wayne, shall have acquired a population proportionate to the produce which they can yield, that Chicago may become one of the points in the direct line of communication between the northern lakes and the Mississippi; but even the intercourse which will be carried on through this communication, will we think at all times be a limited one; the dangers attending the navigation of the lake, and the scarcity of harbours along the shore, must ever prove a serious obstacle to the increase of the commercial importance of Chicago.*

keelboat a large flat boat used early on the rivers, carrying from 20 to 30 tons; usually manned by 10 hands, including a steersman and a captain or

master or "patroon" [Canadian jargon]; could ma-
neuver the Chicago portage during favorable water conditions; upstream travel was tedious and
time-consuming, the trip from New Orleans to
Louisville, KY—a distance by river of 1,500 miles,
took from three to six months, rowing and staking
most of the way, sometimes supported by a sail, if
conditions were right.

Keeney, G.W. advertised his "wholesale and retail establishment, a few doors below Newberry &
Dole" in May 1834 issues of the *Chicago Democrat*. He sold an extensive assortment of cooking
stoves and tin, sheet iron and copperware, hollow
ware, plows and plow castings.

Keepoteh Potawatomi warrior present at the 1812
Fort Dearborn massacre; at the direction of his chief
Topenebe (Burnett connection) he boarded the
Kinzie boat and helped save the Kinzie family. [226]

Kelley, Henry also Kelly; worked for Samuel
Miller; voted on Aug. 7, 1826, and July 24, 1830.

Kellogg, Joseph (1691-1756) in February 1704,
Joseph and his two sisters were captured by Indians during their raids on Deerfield, MA, and taken
to the Montreal area; by 1710 he had learned Mohawk and perhaps other Indian languages; became
a naturalized French subject. In 1710, he joined a
Canadian trading party bound for Illinois; after
overwintering at Michillimackinac, the six *voyageurs*
coasted down the western shore of Lake Michigan
to Chicago, where they portaged into the Illinois
River, traveling down it to the Mississippi, then
returning up the Illinois, Kankakee, St. Joseph, and
Lake Michigan en route back to Mackinac and
Montreal. Some years later, back in Massachusetts,
he dictated his observations to the future Governor of Massachusetts Paul Dudley, who forwarded
the text to London. Kellogg described various villages where he had visited, but he said nothing
about a European settlement at "Chigaguea," although he described the land, vegetation, and game,
evidence that there were no French people at Chicago in 1711; the place had been abandoned in

favor of Detroit and also Cahokia and Kaskaskia,
which he did describe. Kellogg is ★★★ **Chicago's
1st** English visitor. [*Mississippi Valley Historical Review* 23,
1936: pp. 345-54; 205, 649]

Kelsey, Patrick a subcontractor in 1835, clearing
the land on the N side to prepare for street grading; also ran a small yellow boarding house among
the sand hills N of the river with his wife Eve, as
noted by [see] J.D. Bonnell; voted in the 1837 city
election; ✦ laborer, Chicago Avenue near North
Dearborn Street; still listed in the 1844 directory.
[12, 13]

Kelso, John U.S. Army private at Fort Dearborn,
enlisted in December 1805; accepted discharge on
Dec. 17, 1810, when his term expired; stayed to
be a tutor to the Kinzie children and then a field
hand on Leigh's farm; on April 6, 1812, marauding Winnebago attacked and he escaped with
Charles Leigh, Jr., and alarmed the garrison at the
fort; rejoined the army May 3 as a private and was
killed in action at the massacre of Aug. 15. [226]

Kennicott, Hiram lawyer; member of the large
Kennicott family of lawyers and physicians from
New York; arrived in 1834 and soon after built a
cabin in Vernon Township [Lake County]; created
saw- and gristmills on the Des Plaines River and
opened a general store; became justice of the peace
on Oct. 17, 1835; later moved to CO. [351]

Kennicott, Jonathan Asa, M.D. (1824-1862)
from Albion, NY; younger brother of [see] Dr.
William H. Kennicott; arrived with his family from
New York in 1832 as a child; obtained his degree
from Rush Medical College in 1843, but practiced
dentistry the next three years with his brother;
married Marie Antoinette Fisk in 1854. [12, 13]

Kennicott, William Henry, D.D.S. ★★★
Chicago's 1st dentist, who opened his office in May
1834 at the Eagle Tavern, as advertized in the *Chicago Democrat*, and practiced in town for many
years, for some time joined in his office by his
brother, [see] Jonathan Asa; was one of 14 siblings,
mostly boys, and between 1832 and 1835 the en-

tire family came to Chicago from New York State,
although not at the same time, and most of them
settled in the N and NW periphery of the original
town, where they acquired much land; married
Caroline P. Chapman from New York in 1838; ✦
dentist, Lake St.; in 1849 was an unsuccessful
candidate for mayor; a successful physician and hor-
ticulturist; died in 1853. See the story below about
an essential helpmate to Dr. Kennicott, related by
A. T. Andreas. Col. Adolphus S. Hubbard, in about
1880, listed the following additional male members of the Kennicott family as: Dr. John A.; James
H. (attorney, died in Mexico in 1840); Dr. Levi
(moved to Black Hawk, IA); Hiram (moved to Silver Cliff, CO); Dr. Jonathan Asa; Alonzo (farmer
in Barrington); and Joseph (farmer in Arlington
Heights). According to Lloyd Lewis, Hiram, in
1834, built a store, gristmill, and sawmill at Vernon
on the Des Plaines River. [12, 351, 432]

A.T. Andreas, in 1884, reported the following
about Dr. Kennicott's horse: *After a long career of
usefulness the equine* [of Dr. Kennicott], *becoming
unfit for service, was turned loose to shift for himself,
and, finding some choice picking in the court-house
square, he made that a resort. The citizens recognized
the old animal and, compassionating his condition of
marasmus, assembled and determined upon giving the
veteran a donation party. At the appointed time they
flocked to the square with provender and building
material. A shed was constructed by the embryonic
humane society, and the food stored therein. Then a
procession was formed, with the equine beneficiary at
its head, and after parading the streets to the martial
music of fife and drum, the steed was installed in his
stable, where he existed until spring, when Death
mounted the pale white horse, and rode him to the
happy hunting grounds. Peace to his mane(s).*

Kennison, David (1736-1852) also Kinison; born
in Kingston, NH; U.S. Army private at Fort Dearborn, enlisted on March 14, 1808; listed in John
Kinzie's account book in the spring and summer
of 1812; survived the massacre [in a conflicting

KEOKUK [705]

report, Kinison died at the massacre, which suggests this Kennison may be an imposter]; captured; later returned to live in Chicago. By his own information and count, Kennison was the last survivor of the Boston Tea Party and died at the age of 115 years. A curiosity of sorts, he was made "manager" of Rice's Theater in 1848, which prompted him to advertise as noted below; was buried in the city cemetery that would later become Lincoln Park, where a large granite ▲ boulder with bronze (now aluminum) plaque commemorates him [see Monuments]; ➡ Kennison Avenue (4500 W). [12, 226, 404, 559]

David Kennison's published notice:

I have taken the Museum in this city, which I was obliged to do in order to get a comfortable living, as my pension is so small it scarcely affords the comforts of life. If I live until the 17th of November, 1848, I shall be 112 years old, and I intend making a donation party on that day at the Museum. I have fought in several battles for my country. All I ask of the generous public is to call at the Museum on the 17th of

November, which is my birthday, and donate to me what they think I deserve.

Kent County, Canada   Chicago was defined as part of Kent County of the Province of Upper Canada of England when the county was created in 1792; although the action was in conflict with U.S. claims as expressed in the Northwest Ordinance of 1787, England remained in *de facto* control of the county until 1796. [544]

Kenworthy, Mr.   a traveling ventriloquist who delighted his audience in Chicago on June 10 and 11, 1834. At "Bromback Hall" [Traveller's Home] he promised to "offer for the amusement of his visitors, his Whims, Stories, Adventures &c. of a Ventriloquist, as embodied in his entertaining monologue of the Bromback Family" (seven distinct characters) as well as "performing many other very interesting feats." [482]

Keokuk   (1790-1848) blue-eyed Sauk *métis* leader born in Illinois; his name meant *Watchful Fox*; respected for his forceful personality, wisdom, and remarkable oratory; during the War of 1812, when the Sauk and Fox tribes divided their loyalties, his fellow Sauk leader Black Hawk fought the Americans, while Keokuk remained uninvolved; in 1832 he refused to join the Black Hawk War. A bronze bust of Keokuk is kept in the U.S. Senate; ➡ Keokuk Avenue (4144 W). [12, 211]

Kercheval, Col. Benjamin B.   Indian agent at Detroit in 1821, where he hired blacksmith David McKee as a federal employee and sent him to Chicago in 1823, to be retained at Fort Dearborn and teach the Indians, as stipulated in the Chicago Treaty of 1821; on Sept. 27, 1830, he is listed among the first buyers of two choice downtown lots [in block 29, lot 5 and 6; see map on page 44], which he conveyed to Robert Kinzie, assignee; other early records show William Belcher as the initial owner; trustee for William Burnett at the Chicago treaty on Sept. 26, 1833.

Kercheval, Gholson   also Kerchival or Kircheval, Goldson; from Kentucky; younger brother of Lewis

C. Kercheval; arrived in 1830 and worked as a clerk for Robert Kinzie; had his own small trading establishment by 1831 in one of the log cabins at Wolf Point [according to Mrs. Kinzie in *Wau-Bun*]; purchased real estate in block 16, selling it soon after to Anson H. Taylor [see map on page 44]; served as Indian agent at Fort Dearborn between agent Dr. Wolcott's death [Oct. 26, 1830] and agent Thomas J.V. Owen's arrival in the spring of 1831, then as subagent with James Stuart; was one of the first three Cook County commissioners elected on March 7, 1831; became captain of the Chicago militia during the Black Hawk War, listed on the muster roll of May 3, 1832 [for the complete list of militia members who served under Kercheval, see Andreas, 1:269]; on Nov. 25, 1833 married Felicite Hotchkiss of Kaskaskia, the Hon. R.I. Hamilton officiating, making him brother-in-law to Owen, who was married to Felicite's sister, Emeline; in 1834 was a member of the Cholera Vigilance Committee; in 1836 served as a director of the newly organized Chicago Hydraulic Company; ✦ real estate, River Street; in 1885 his widow lived at 204-1/2 Clark St. [12, 351]

Kercheval, Lewis C.   (c.1800-1852) attorney from Kentucky, arrived in 1831 and joined his younger brother Gholson in the Indian trade at the latter's trading post; in 1832 served as county commissioner; married Nancy Stephens of Joliet, as per notice in the *Chicago Democrat*, Nov. 4, 1835; ✦ inspector, port of Chicago, boarded at City Hotel; see Edwin O. Gale's vivid description of Lewis that follows; later he moved to San Francisco and died in 1852; his widow lived at 204-1/2 Clark St. in 1885; ➡ Kercheval Avenue (4600 W). [12, 97, 351] Gale's description of Lewis C. Kercheval:

As I recall that smooth stern-faced man with short, straight, gray hair and tall commanding figure advantageously set off in a well-fitting Websterian blue coat with large brass buttons, moving among us with erect carriage (especially after he became President of the Washingtonian Society), with slow step and precise dignity, conscious that he was Colonel by courtesy, Justice of the Peace by the votes of his fellow citizens and Inspector of the Port by the friendship of Old Hickory, it is hard to realize that this was the same person who was so much interested years before at that insignificant trading cabin, in the patronage of beaded squaws and painted bucks.

Kettlestrings Grove   early community, now Oak Ridge.

Kettlestrings, Joseph   (1808-1883) immigrated from Yorkshire, England, in 1832 with wife Betty Willis (born 1802, married 1828) and small children William and Ann. The Methodist family spent the first winter in Cincinnati, OH, where the third child, Hanna, was born; came to Chicago in 1833; placed a claim (173 acres) on "the first dry land W of Chicago," later called Kettlestrings' Grove [then Oak Ridge and, from 1871 on, Oak Park] where eight more children were born: Ellen, Mary, Joseph, Jr., Dora, Elizabeth, Thomas, Mary Ann, and Walter. Joseph, Sr., initially hauled lumber for the Chicago firm Bickerdyke & Noble [having known Bickerdyke in England and then been invited to work for him] which maintained a steam lumbermill on the E bank of the Des Plaines River [just N of the present Lake Street bridge]. The family lived in a log cabin near the mill until he built the first house in 1835 [at 1135 Lake St., now recognized by a ▲ bronze plaque]. That year he acquired an ownership interest in the mill and also sufficiently enlarged his house to serve as what was first known as Kettlestrings' Tavern, later Oak Ridge

House; while he worked at the mill, Betty boarded mill hands and managed the inn. From 1843 to 1855, the family lived predominantly in Chicago for the benefit of the children's schooling. It is not clear whether Kettlestrings' reported habit of selling parcels of his land only with a binder never to sell liquor on the property stemmed from sound business principles or from an ardent disdain of alcoholic beverages on ethical grounds. He died on Oct. 17, 1883, and Betty on Jan. 21, 1885; their ▲ graves are at Forest Home Cemetery. [12]

Kettlestrings' Tavern   see Kettlestrings, Joseph.

Kewanee   Ojibwa word for prairie hen; ➡ Kewanee Avenue (4200 W).

Keyes, Edward   purchased on Sept. 4, 1830, lots 5 and 6 in block 8, and lot 9 in block 28 [see map on page 44]; by 1833, the latter belonged to John Noble, the former to Enoch Thompson; according to a notice in the *Chicago Democrat* on July 29, 1835, an Edward Keyes died that month in LaSalle County, IL.

Kickapoo   an Indian tribe of the central Algonkin group that included the closely related Sauk and Fox; first noted as "Kicapous" between the Fox and Wisconsin Rivers by Father Allouez, 1667-70.

Kile Tavern   also Kyle Tavern, A Farmers Hotel and Stage Coach Stop, and Ten Mile House; historic stagecoach stopover; on Vincennes Trace near what is now 83rd Street; built c.1836.

Kilpatrick, Samuel   U.S. Army private at Fort Dearborn, enlisted in December 1805; was ill at the time of the massacre of Aug. 15, 1812, and was killed in the sickwagon. [226]

Kimball, Harlow   born in New York; visited in 1833; his enthusiastic testimony aroused John Calhoun's interest and led to his own return in 1834; ✦ merchant, Clark Street; died on Aug. 25, 1881. [12, 243]

Kimball, Henry N.   arrived from New York in 1835 and served as county treasurer that same year; ✦ vessel owner. [243]

Kimball & Porter   see next entry.

Kimball, Walter   (c.1809-1882) born in Rome, NY; arrived in September and subscribed to the *Chicago Democrat* in November 1833, present in Calhoun's office while the first issue of the *Chicago Democrat* was printed; with Porter [Hibbard Porter?] opened a dry goods, crockery, and hardware store on the SE corner of South Water and Clark streets in November 1833, the building having been previously occupied by P. Carpenter's drugstore, and subsequently by the Clarke drugstore; by Dec. 1, 1835, Kimball & Porter had moved to the NW corner of Clark and Lake streets, remaining until 1840. Kimball served on the village board of trustees and also on the board of directors of the first bank in Chicago in 1835 (State Bank of Illinois); ✦ probate judge, corner of Clark and South Water streets; in 1849 became clerk of the superior court; died on Aug. 17, 1882. [12, 351]

Kimberly, Edmund Stoughton, M.D.   (1803-1874) also Kimberlee, often mistakenly referred as to "Dr. Kimball" by Andreas; born at Troy, NY; received his medical degree from the College of Physicians and Surgeons in New York City; married Marie Theresa Ellis in 1829; arrived at Chicago in the fall of 1832 with his family and a young business man, Peter Pruyne; bought land from the Clybourne family on Franklin Street [lots 5 and 6 in block 5; see map on page 44]; began private practice and opened a drug and variety store under the name of Peter Pruyne & Company on South Water Street, between Dearborn and Clark (the second such store, P. Carpenter's was the first); soon became regarded as the leading druggist in town, although he continued to practice medicine. The town meeting in early August 1833 that decided Chicago's incorporation took place in the Prune & Kimberly drugstore, and Dr. Kimberly acted as secretary and voted "yes" [for a copy of that meeting's report, see entry on incorporation]; his signature is on the election notice of Aug. 5, and he was elected trustee on Aug. 10. Prior to 1836, he owned 80 acres of land in Section 32, Town-

EDMUND STOUGHTON KIMBERLY, M.D. [137]

ship 39, as per Andreas, *History of Chicago*, pp. 112-113; in 1837 he became a trustee of Rush Medical School. When Pruyne died in 1838, Kimberly moved the drugstore into Tremont House, destroyed by fire in 1839; ✦ residence, North Water Street next to the Lake House Hotel; served as city health officer from 1837 to 1841; in 1854 retired to his country home in Lake County, where he remained until his death; in 1885 his widow lived at Barrington Station, IL. For Edwin O. Gale's description of him, see below; ➡ Kimberly Avenue (4700). [12, 39, 221, 351]

Gale's description of Dr. Kimberly:

He was a tall, slender, dignified gentleman, one of the old school of courtly, kindhearted practitioners, ever responding as readily to the call of the poor and obscure as to the wealthiest and most prominent. Glasses were not so commonly worn then as at present, and his gold-rimmed spectacles always seemed to add

to the confidence his patients reposed in him. He was our family physician as long as he practiced here.

Kimberly, George A. [E.?]   arrived [or born? son of Edmund?] in Chicago in 1834; mentioned by Andreas as managing a singing group with the name "Minstrels" in 1850.

Kimberly, Ira   arrived from New York in 1834 and served as a member of the voluntary fire department in 1835 [see petition to the village board of Dec. 16, 1835, with entry on firefighting].

Kimberly, John and Lewis   children by this name, probably siblings, were enrolled as grade school students in the class taught by [see] John Watkins in December 1835. Names of corresponding parents were not recorded. [728]

Kinder, David   private at Fort Dearborn under Captain Heald; killed in action at the massacre of Aug. 15, 1812 [approximate spelling given the poor imprint on Captain Heald's list; not on Eckert's list].

King, Byram   also Byron or Byran; arrived in 1834 from New York; partner in the hardware firm of Jones, King & Co. on South Water Street between Clark and Dearborn, established in 1834, and which subsidized ★★★ Chicago's 1st foundry built on Polk Street in 1835; was among the members of the first board of health appointed June 19, 1835, and elected to the town board of trustees in July 1835; served as clerk for School District No. 4 later in September; on July 7, 1836, married Emily Jones , his partner's eldest daughter; ✦ Jones, King & Co.; died in 1841. [12]

King, Henry   arrived in 1834 from New York; with an ad in the Oct. 28, 1835, *Chicago Democrat*, announced that he had taken over Hubbard & Co. with an extensive "assortment of Fall and Winter Goods": Dry Goods, Ready made Clothing, Bonnets ["Ladies Florence gipsey bonnets; leghorn Tuscan corded edge and fancy do.; Misses do.;—straw bands"], Groceries, Hardware, Heavy Goods, Wooden and other Ware, Jewelry and Fancy Articles, House Keeping Articles, Guns and Rifles,

Fur Goods, Boots and Shoes; ✦ dry goods &c., N Dearborn Street near Kinzie Street; in 1843 the *Chicago Democrat* notes Henry and Ann G. King as involved in a forced house sale by default of payment, the mortgage transferring to William Ogden for Arthur Bronson; possibly identical with Henry W. King mentioned by Andreas as a prominent member of the Westminster Presbyterian Church in the 1850s. [12]

King, Nathaniel   also Nat, likely younger brother of Tuthill; salesman in [see] Tuthill King's clothing store in 1835, listed as clerk in 1839.

King, Nehemiah   practical surveyor and engineer, member of the Ohio legislature, judge; received $125 at the treaty in Chicago on Sept. 27, 1833; recommended for county commissioner for the Chicago precinct in the April 16, 1834; *Chicago Democrat*; chosen as nominee for the state house of representatives at the Ottawa convention in June that year.

King, Maj. Sherman   a corporal in Captain Boardman's voluntary county militia late May into June, 1832, and second lieutenant in Captain Napier's militia company between July 19 and Aug. 18, 1832, during the Black Hawk War; held the rank of major in 1833, and that year married Mrs. Amanda Morrison on Dec. 1, Stephen M. Salisbury officiating; resided at Brush Hill. [217a]

King, Thomas J.   in October 1835 he signed up with the "Pioneer" hook and ladder company, an early volunteer fire brigade.

King, Tuthill   born 1803 in New York; arrived with his bride in April 1835; the two initially lived in the attic of William Jones's house on the corner of Wells and Randolph streets; was observed by E.O. Gale as proprietor of the New York Clothing Store, assisted by Nat King, and by June he advertised "3 doors north of the Tremont House, in Dearborn" in the *Chicago American*; member of the voluntary fire department; ✦ New York clothing store, 115 Lake St.; active in public education as a member of the board of the Dearborn Seminary in the 1850s; lived at 85 Washington St. in 1885. [12, 266, 351]

Kingsbury, Col. Jacob (-1837) from Connecticut; in command at Detroit, Mackinac and other northwestern military posts from 1804 on; for a while was the superior authority of several posts that included Fort Wayne and Fort Dearborn. The *Kingsbury Papers*, including his correspondence and other documents, are of primary importance as a source for northwestern history; the papers exist in the archives of the Chicago Historical Society. Colonel Kingsbury left the military service in 1815 and died in 1837. [400]

Kingsbury, Maj. Julius Jesse Backus (c.1797-1856) Second Infantry; served at Fort Dearborn from June 17, 1832, to May 31, 1833, under Col. William Whistler, during which time he purchased from Robert A. Kinzie lot 5 of block 35 of the original town [see map on page 44]; married to Jane Creed Stebbins, who as a widow lived at Old Syme, CT, in 1885. [12]

Kingston, John Tabor early Wisconsin pioneer who visited Chicago in the spring of 1835, before the opening of navigation on the Illinois & Michigan Canal; his accounts are published as *Early Western Days*; lived at Necedah, WI, in 1885. [12]

Kingston, Paul a Scottish Presbyterian, from Lewistown, IL, where he was a storekeeper and active in church affairs; arrived with his family in 1830 and helped organize the Presbyterian church; had a son named John, and at least two daughters; on Sept. 4, 1830, bought real estate in blocks 20 (lot 7), 29 (lots 9 and 10), and 32 (lot 4) [see map on page 44]; in the Sept. 23, 1834, *Chicago Democrat* he advertised land for sale on the Du Page River at the Walker's Grove settlement [Plainfield]; on Dec. 5, 1835, applied for wharfing privileges; on May 18, 1841, married Mrs. Mary Yard of Little Fort [Waukegan]. [28, 319]

Kinison, David see Kennison, David.

Kinnikinnick a form of pipe tobacco used by the Indians; usually dried leaves mixed from a variety

THE OLD KINZIE MANSION AS IT APPEARED IN 1832.   [12]

of plants, varying from tribe to tribe and usually not containing what we now know as the tobacco plant, still always irritating to the mucous membranes; the word also meant [see] Calumet.

Kinzie Addition the NW quarter of Section 10, embracing the old Kinzie homestead, but consisting of only 102 acres (because the lake occupies its eastern extent), instead of the 160 acres the Kinzies were entitled to claim in September 1830; in *Wau-Bun*, Mrs. Juliette A. Kinzie relates an exchange of opinions [see below] between her mother-in-law Eleanor and Robert A. Kinzie concerning the land that the Kinzies were entitled to but failed to claim. The addition was surveyed in February 1833 by George W. Snow, at the request of Captain Hunter and in the presence of John Harris Kinzie; bounded on the S by the river (with the sand bar at the river's mouth, understood by some to be included), W by State Street, E by the lakeshore, and N by Chicago Avenue. [12] Juliette Kinzie quoting Eleanor and Robert:

Now, my son, said his mother, to Robert, *lay your claim on the cornfield at Wolf Point. It is fine land, and will always be valuable for cultivation—besides, as it faces down the main river, the situation will always be a convenient one.* The answer was a hearty laugh. *Hear mother*, said Robert. *We have just got a hundred and two acres—more than we shall ever want, or know what to do with, and now she would have me go and claim fifty-eight acres more! Take my advise, my boy*, repeated his mother, *or you will live one day to regret it.*

Kinzie Block all blocks (and the lots within each) of the original Kinzie Addition were available for

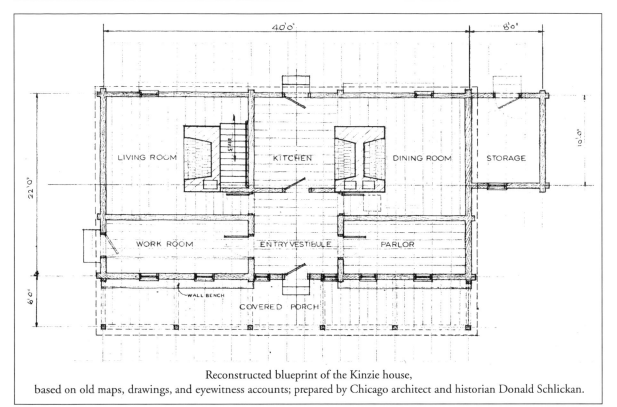

Reconstructed blueprint of the Kinzie house,
based on old maps, drawings, and eyewitness accounts; prepared by Chicago architect and historian Donald Schlickan.

sale by 1834, except block 11—the "Kinzie Block" (shown on John S. Wright's ✱ manuscript map), bounded by Rush, Illinois, Cass [Wabash], and Michigan [Hubbard] streets; John H. Kinzie had begun to build his brick residence there in 1834, on the NE corner of Cass and Michigan streets, and "Kinzie Church" or the St. James Church, was constructed in 1836, on two lots at the SE corner of Cass and Illinois streets.

Kinzie, Eleanor Lytle McKillip (1769-1834) first child of John and Sarah Lytle (also Little) of Philadelphia; sister of Margaret, who married William Forsyth, Jr.; widow of Daniel McKillip; second wife of John Kinzie [see Kinzie family tree on page 222]; like Kinzie's first wife, Eleanor spent part of her childhood (four years) as a prisoner of the Indians, in her case under the relatively benevolent super-

vision of the famous Seneca chief Cornplanter; into the marriage with Kinzie she brought a daughter, Margaret, who later married Lieutenant Helm. With John Kinzie she initially had a child who died in infancy, then John Harris in 1803, Ellen Marion in 1804, Maria Indiana in 1807, and Robert Allen in 1810, the last three born in Chicago; died in New York of cancer of the face. [226]

Kinzie, Elizabeth (1791-1832) daughter of John Kinzie and his first wife Margaret McKenzie; sister of William and James (see Kinzie family tree on page 222); lived with her mother in Virginia, but after 1816 joined her father in Chicago where, on July 29, 1826, she married Samuel Miller, with her father, as county justice of the peace, performing the ceremony. During the Black Hawk War

she moved with her husband into Fort Dearborn for protection; while living in the fort she became very ill, and died in July 1832. [12]

Kinzie, Ellen Marion (1804-1860) daughter of John Kinzie and Eleanor McKillip, known as Nell; family documents show her first name as Eleanor, like that of her mother, but she usually signed "Ellen M." (see Kinzie family tree on page 222); ★★★ **Chicago's 1st** child born of European parents within the eventual city limits of Chicago; the date was Dec. 27, 1804 [see Eckert; also see testimony by Mrs. Ann Whistler in Hurlbut, *Chicago Antiquities*; her published obituary erroneously gives 1805 as her birthyear]. Ellen Marion married Dr. Alexander Wolcott on July 20, 1823; the ceremony is often said to have been **Chicago's 1st** recorded marriage, but is actually the third [for the first, see You de la Découverte, Pierre], and became possible when John Hamlin of Peoria, who had recently received a commission as justice of the peace from Fulton County, happened to stop at Fort Dearborn while herding cattle from southern Illinois to Green Bay; it was Hamlin's first such official act, performed awkwardly because he was unfamiliar with the procedure, but much appreciated: followed by a feast on duck and venison, with everybody invited, John Kinzie playing the wedding march on his violin, and dancing until dawn. The couple had two children by April 24, 1829, when the proud father wrote his sister, Frances Magill in New York, and shared that "Master Natty Bumppo and Miss Mary Chatham [Mary Ann] who, besides readings & spellings, help their uncle Robert to set his nets & bring in the ducks & pigeons that he shoots, drive the sheep to the fold, feed the chickens, and chase the old cock turkey all over the premises...." In a letter written Aug. 24, 1830, to her sister-in-law, Ellen disclosed that they had lost their son on July 7; her husband died later on Oct. 26. Dr. Wolcott had purchased from the government in 1830 the entire block 1 of the original town [see map on page 44] and ownership transferred to his widow. She remained at Cobweb Castle with her half sister Margaret Helm until 1831 when, following an auction of household goods, both moved to Fort Howard, together with their sister Maria Indiana Hunter, whose husband's transfer from Fort Dearborn came due. In 1836 she married the Hon. George C. Bates of Detroit and they had one son, Kenzie Bates; Ellen died at Detroit; ➡ Ellen Street (1282 N); Marion Court (1838 W). [12, 226]

Kinzie, Emily née Tyne; mother of John Kinzie; daughter of a London carriagemaker; was the widow of British army chaplain William Haliburton when she married John Kinzie's father, the captain and army surgeon John Mackenzie in December 1761, bringing a daughter, Jane Haliburton, into the marriage [see Kinzie family tree on page 222]; widowed again in 1763, she married William Forsyth, Sr., in 1765.

Kinzie & Hall the partnership of James Kinzie and David Hall that had created Wolf Tavern in 1823, advertised a new store in the June 25, 1834, *Chicago Democrat*, one door E from the corner of Lake and Canal streets, near the Point, selling dry goods, hardware, and groceries; in the Dec. 2, 1835, *Chicago Democrat* they announced the sale of the entire stock of goods and offered thanks to their customers.

Kinzie House built by its first owner, Point de Sable, sometime between 1784 and 1790 on the north bank of the main portion of the Chicago River, where the river turned S until it reached the lake. When Jean B. La Lime and William Burnett bought the property from Point de Sable in 1800, the main building measured 22 by 40 feet, with at least eight outbuildings, including barn and ice house. Kinzie purchased the property in 1803. Elizabeth Thérèse Fisher Baird visited Chicago in 1817 with her mother Marienne LaSallier Fisher, and recollected a brief description of its interior in later life. George W. Dole remembers: "[it] stood on where Pine [State] Street would later be, and S of North Water Street; from the front of the house's

piazza, E. of its center, you could look down the river as it ran up the lake, and have a fair view of a boat coming up or going down ...." The inventory and sale bill after Kinzie's death imply that the house was heated with four metal stoves. The land on which the house stood belonged to the U.S. government since the Treaty of Greenville of 1795 which, however, the Chicago area Potawatomi did not recognize. They gave the land to Kinzie as a gift on Nov. 4, 1806. Title to the land from the United States was not acquired until 1830. Under both Point de Sable and Kinzie, and before regular hotels existed in town, the house would at times serve as an inn, "upon the express or implied understanding that payment was expected" (Hurlbut). Near the end of its existence, it was used as a medical practice and residence by Dr. Harmon and as a post office by J. Bailey. For a roster of successive owners and occupants see entry on Kinzie House chronology. For additional information on the house see John H. Kinzie's and E.T.F. Baird's reports below, the picture on page 217, the blueprint by Donald Schlickan on page 218, as well as the 1857 issue of *Chicago Magazine*. [29, 162]

Elizabeth Thérèse Fisher Baird's description of the old Kinzie House:

... a large, one-story building, with an exceptionally high attic. The front door opened into a wide hall, that hospitably led into the kitchen, which was spacious and bright, made so by the large fire-place. Four rooms opened into the hall, two on each side, and the upper story contained four rooms.

John H. Kinzie's 1857 description of the house:

Every feature of the old home is distinct in [my] recollection. The Lombardy poplars, which perished long ago, and the cottonwoods which once were but saplings planted by [my] own hands, and which have stood until the more recent days as mementoes of the past; the rough-hewn logs which formed the wall of [my] home, the garden and the shrubbery, the fence paling that surrounded it, and the green lawn at the front of the house, gently descending to the water of

the river; the tiny boat floating idly at the foot of the walk; and, as the crowning mark of the picture, standing upon the opposite shore, upon the highest part of the elevation, the old fort, the whitewashed walls of the block-houses, the barracks and the palisades, glistening in the bright sun, while a gentle slope of green grass extended from the enclosure to the very water's edge. It was a beautiful sight. Over all this rose the few pulsations of human progress, as seen in an occasional Indian, with his canoe or pony or pack of furs; a French Canadian loitering here and there; a soldier pacing his rounds about the fort, or idly strolling over the prairies, or hunting in the woods.

Kinzie House chronology in the spring of 1778, possibly earlier, Jean Baptiste Point de Sable settled at Chicago to farm and trade with the Indians, building a rude log cabin on the north bank of the river where it turned S to meet the lake. By the time he sold the cabin in 1800 for 6,000 livres ($1,200), he had developed the property into a commodious, well-furnished French-style house with numerous outbuildings.* Successive owners and occupants include:

Point de Sable   c.1784-1800, owner
Jean La Lime/Wm. Burnett   1800-1803, owner**
Dr. William C. Smith   1803 (with La Lime)
John Kinzie family   1803-1829 (expt. 1812-1816)
Widow Leigh & Mr. Des Pins   1812-1816
Anson Taylor   1829-1831 (residence and store)
Dr. E.D. Harmon   1831 (res .& medical practice)
Jonathan N. Bailey   1831 (residence/post office)
Mark Noble, Sr.   1831-1832
Judge Richard Young   1832 (circuit court sessions)
unoccupied and decaying   1833 and thereafter, nonexistent by 1835

* see listing of assets: Quaife, Milo M. *Documents: Property of Jean Baptiste Point Sable; 1928.*

** a careful reading of the Point de Sable-La Lime sales contract indicates that William Burnett was not just signing as a witness, but also financing the transaction, therefore controlling ownership. [649]

Kinzie, Hunter & Co. by 1835, David Hunter

and John H. Kinzie were active in the necessary and profitable lumber trade; ◆ forwarding, commission merchants, North Water Street near Rush. [13]

Kinzie, James (1793-1866) son of John Kinzie and his first wife Margaret McKenzie; brother of William and Elizabeth [see Kinzie family tree on page 222], born in Detroit on April 2. It is believed that James and his siblings accompanied their mother to Virginia on her separation from John Kinzie. James returned to the Midwest in 1816 and on Aug. 3, 1818, became an employee of the American Fur Co., maintaining posts at Milwaukee and Racine; his illegal sales of whisky to the Indians caused the Indian agent [Wolcott] at Chicago to direct him to close his business in Milwaukee, and he moved to Chicago that same year (1821); built and occupied a cabin at the forks on the E side of the south branch, and used it as a store. In 1823 he built the Wolf Tavern with his half brother David Hall, who then sold out to James; in 1826 sold his cabin to Mark Beaubien, who converted it into the Eagle Exchange Tavern; in 1828 claimed $22.18 against the estate of François Le Mai, including an item of March 19, 1828, "Amt. of expense incurred by hunting the corps [of Le Mai]." Canal engineer James Bucklin, who visited Chicago in 1830, reports that James was a trained blacksmith. About 1830, James bought lots in blocks 2, 11, 12, 21, 22, 23, 40, and 41 [see map on page 44], selling much of it again within a few years; served as private under Captain Kercheval in the Chicago militia during the Black Hawk War, as listed on the muster roll of May 3, 1832; in 1833 built the Green Tree Tavern at the NE corner of Lake and Canal streets; partnering David Hall again, Kinzie & Hall advertised a new store in the June 25, 1834, *Chicago Democrat*, one door E from the corner of Lake and Canal streets, near the Point; was appointed Cook County's first sheriff by the governor, was listed in July 1834 as a candidate for county commissioner, and became firewarden of the fourth

ward later on Sept. 25, also was ★★★ Chicago's 1st appointed auctioneer [see a sample of his activity below; also see Wabansia Addition for James's involvement in real estate ownership and transfer] and served as trustee of the school section; on Nov. 21 he applied for wharfing privileges, filing a claim two days later, a petition on Nov. 25 and another on Dec. 5; in the Dec. 2 *Chicago Democrat* that year, Kinzie & Hall announced the sale of the entire stock of goods and offered thanks to their customers; first married Leah See, daughter of Reverend William See (born in 1815) and they had three children; she died in 1837, survived by two small children; with a second wife, Virginia Hale, he had nine children; ◆ real estate agent, North Canal Street; later moved to Racine, WI, where he lived until his death. [12, 28, 220]

In the Dec. 10, 1833, issue of the *Chicago Democrat* appeared an announcement that James Kinzie, auctioneer, would sell on Dec. 13 the following real estate:

Lot 7, Block 8, and house, formerly occupied as a meeting-house, opposite the bridge on the north branch of the Chicago River. [The meetinghouse is the log cabin formerly occupied by Reverend See, and later by Reverend Walker, and the bridge was Chicago's first bridge, begun in 1832 as a floating log bridge for foot traffic only. The exact location of both structures would have been difficult to determine, were it not for Kinzie's exacting announcement, which places lot 7 at the SW corner of Kinzie and Canal streets; *eds.*] [12, 704]

Kinzie, John (1763-1828) principal trader at Chicago from 1804 to 1812; born a British subject in Quebec, Dec. 27, 1763, an allegiance he maintained until about the time of the Fort Dearborn

massacre, Aug. 15, 1812; then became a secret U. S. Indian agent while also serving in the Detroit area in the British Indian Department; was imprisoned in Canada by British authorities upon information given by Tecumseh, but escaped and eventually reestablished business at Chicago in late 1816.

He was born Kenzie but changed spelling to Kinzie. His father, John Kenzie or MacKenzie, was a Scottish surgeon in the British army and died about 1763. His mother, Emily or Anne Tyne, had been first married to British army chaplain William Halliburton and then, in 1761, to Kenzie; was widowed twice; about 1764 she married William Forsyth, member of a prominent trading family. Forsyth became Kinzie's stepfather, and his five sons, from this and a previous marriage, became John's stepbrothers.

The Forsyth family, and John Kinzie, moved to Detroit by 1779, and were enumerated in that year's census. The tradition that the five Forsyth sons were born in Detroit is inconsistent with the censuses of 1762, 1765, and 1768, in which no Forsyths are recorded.

Kinzie was described as a domineering man, with quick temper and a sharp tongue; owned and played a violin; outspoken in his anti-American sentiments and actions until his business was destroyed, most of his customers having been killed in the Fort Dearborn massacre. With his first wife Margaret, née McKenzie but not related, he lived in Detroit and had three children: William, James, and Elizabeth; the marriage ended in divorce [the children stayed with their mother, but would all live in Chicago later in life]. He was a member of John Askin's Detroit military company under British rule; the United States did not govern Detroit until 1796.

Kinzie started in the Indian fur trade about 1780 under William Burnett and was long associated with this wealthy merchant, who had been financing his operations as late as 1801. As a trader and silversmith, Kinzie did business at the Miamis Town (Fort Wayne, IN) in 1789, but being a British subject, he lost his business and had to flee before the advancing army of General Harmar in 1790. He settled further down the Maumee and again had his establishment destroyed at the time of General Wayne's victory at Fallen Timbers in 1794. From 1796 to early 1804 he had an establishment on the St. Joseph River, near present South Bend, IN, and then moved to Chicago. In 1800 he and Burnett inventoried and appraised the Chicago farm operated by [see] Jean Baptiste Point de Sable as part of a nominal "purchase" by Burnett's employé Jean La Lime; this farm was then generally known as Burnett's and as the sole local source of farm products; Kinzie bought it in 1803.

An extract from Kinzie's account book (originals destroyed in the 1871 Chicago fire) at the Chicago Historical Society has its first entry at Chicago (he used the French spelling Chicagou for several years) in May 1804. He was appointed justice of the peace at Chicago, Indiana Territory, by Governor Harrison in that year, but no records survive of this office. He bought the former Point de Sable farm from La Lime, who was really a nominee for Burnett, in 1803 and moved there with his family in 1804. His family included his second wife Eleanor (née Little or Lytle, widow of McKillip), their infant son John Harris, and Margaret McKillip, Eleanor's daughter from her first marriage. In Chicago they had three more children: Ellen Marion in 1804, Maria Indiana in 1807, and Robert Allen in 1810. Kinzie was a farmer, merchant, and Indian trader in Chicago from 1904 to 1812, as proprietor or partner with his stepbrothers Thomas and Robert Forsyth, sometimes supplying the garrison of Fort Dearborn when the official sutler failed to provide goods. In 1807 he entered into a partnership with Lt. William Whistler, son of the commanding officer, as sutlers to the fort (starting Nov. 26, per accounts) until its dissolution on Aug. 21, 1809. The sutler's contract was then awarded by the commandant Captain Whistler to his son William and the new surgeon's mate Dr. Cooper; they charged the soldiers higher prices than Kinzie did. Whistler, Sr. was removed from his command for various acts of incompetence and misconduct and was replaced by Capt. Nathan Heald in the summer of 1810. Cooper left Chicago and the army in 1811. By suspicious means Kinzie in January 1812 formally got the sutler's contract from Heald who, like his predecessor, prevented the soldiers from dealing with any other merchant who might offer lower prices. Since the soldiers spent about two-thirds of their pay with the sutler, this contract was a valuable one. The United States factor (Indian trader) Matthew Irwin called Kinzie's arrangement a "monopoly" and wrote that Heald and other officers paid lower prices than the enlisted men, in addition to which Kinzie had increased prices substantially since getting his exclusive deal. Kinzie's business grew and prospered; he had agents on the Rock River, at Milwaukee (probably Pierre Le Sellier), at Peoria (Thomas Forsyth) and "generally throughout the Indian Country." He employed the *métis* children of the Milwaukee traders Mirandeau and La Framboise as household servants; employed in his business Billy Caldwell (chief clerk), Jean Baptiste Chandonnai and Alexander Robinson; bought, held, and sold slaves [see Nash, Jeffrey; Black Jim; Henry].

Sometime in June 1812, Kinzie killed his neighbor and frequent customer Jean La Lime, the U. S. interpreter at Fort Dearborn. He hid in the woods near his home for a few days and then fled Chicago after dispatching Caldwell, and in July his Peoria partner Forsyth, to Vincennes to plead his case with Governor Harrison, in 1811 the victor at Tippecanoe as General Harrison. Forsyth was a secret U. S. Indian agent, now reporting to Gov. Ninian Edwards of the Illinois Territory, while Caldwell, whom Governor Harrison's staff tried in vain to recruit to the United States' side, was shortly thereafter commissioned captain in the British Indian Department. Kinzie may have been another target for Harrison's recruiting efforts, as he was an important Indian trader and clandestine agent of the British with many secrets of value to the United States.

Meanwhile Kinzie went to Milwaukee, arriving June 21. He was now a fugitive from U. S. justice as a result of what he called the "unfortunate affair" of La Lime's killing. For eight days in late June and early July Kinzie attended a secret war council of pro-British Indians at Milwaukee convened by British orders to plan a series of attacks on American posts and settlements, including Chicago. He was initially denied admission to their council by some Indians who suspected, not without reason, that he was an American spy, but his British credentials, recently enhanced by his killing of the informant La Lime [see below], soon won him a seat at this meeting; also, Pierre Le Sellier, the British interpreter at Milwaukee, a frequent Kinzie customer and probably his agent as well, may have vouched for him. The story of this council is told in Kinzie's letter to Forsyth of July 7, 1812, written at the site of present Ottawa, IL, while en route to Peoria.

Meanwhile an inquest into the killing of La Lime took place at Fort Dearborn, presided over by Captain Heald. Surprisingly, it was held in Kinzie's absence, and he was acquitted on grounds of self-defense. Suppression of a homicide charge would have given the U. S. authorities some leverage to enlist him as a covert American agent, a role he soon played at considerable personal risk. His

John Kinzie's Relatives

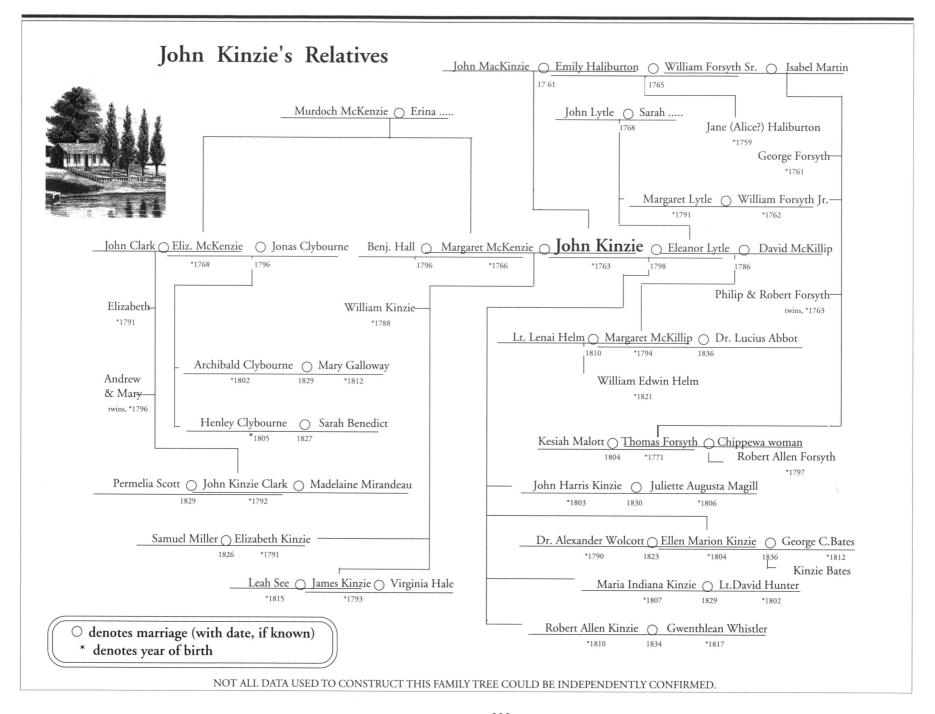

John MacKinzie ○ Emily Haliburton ○ William Forsyth Sr. ○ Isabel Martin
1761   1765

Murdoch McKenzie ○ Erina .....

John Lytle ○ Sarah .....
1768

Jane (Alice?) Haliburton
*1759

George Forsyth
*1761

Margaret Lytle ○ William Forsyth Jr.
*1791   *1762

John Clark ○ Eliz. McKenzie ○ Jonas Clybourne   Benj. Hall ○ Margaret McKenzie ○ **John Kinzie** ○ Eleanor Lytle ○ David McKillip
*1768   1796   1796   *1766   *1763   1798   1786

Elizabeth
*1791

William Kinzie
*1788

Philip & Robert Forsyth
twins, *1763

Lt. Lenai Helm ○ Margaret McKillip ○ Dr. Lucius Abbot
1810   *1794   1836

Archibald Clybourne ○ Mary Galloway
*1802   1829   *1812

Andrew & Mary
twins, *1796

William Edwin Helm
*1821

Henley Clybourne ○ Sarah Benedict
*1805   1827

Kesiah Malott ○ Thomas Forsyth ○ Chippewa woman
1804   *1771

Robert Allen Forsyth
*1797

Permelia Scott ○ John Kinzie Clark ○ Madelaine Mirandeau
1829   *1792

John Harris Kinzie ○ Juliette Augusta Magill
*1803   1830   *1806

Samuel Miller ○ Elizabeth Kinzie
1826   *1791

Dr. Alexander Wolcott ○ Ellen Marion Kinzie ○ George C. Bates
*1790   1823   *1804   1836   *1812

Kinzie Bates

Leah See ○ James Kinzie ○ Virginia Hale
*1815   *1793

Maria Indiana Kinzie ○ Lt. David Hunter
*1807   1829   *1802

○ denotes marriage (with date, if known)
* denotes year of birth

Robert Allen Kinzie ○ Gwenthlean Whistler
*1810   1834   *1817

NOT ALL DATA USED TO CONSTRUCT THIS FAMILY TREE COULD BE INDEPENDENTLY CONFIRMED.

222

absence from Heald's cursory inquiry foreclosed any breach of security by a potential disclosure of his shifting loyalties. The 1809-1812 letters of Irwin to William Eustis, secretary of war, and other documents in the U. S. National Archives (published in 1948, in Vol. 16 of the Territorial Papers of the United States) report these activities and suggest these and other elements of a complex scenario. Kinzie may have killed La Lime to silence him as Irwin's informant inside the fort on treasonable activities by Heald, other officers of the fort, and Kinzie himself. Irwin expressed his fear that his life and La Lime's were in danger; threats had been made. Irwin had been exposing to authorities in Washington Kinzie's profiteering and corruption, his bribery to get the Fort Dearborn sutler's contract, his bringing smuggled liquor and Indian trade goods from British Amherstburg to Chicago, and a twenty-year history of anti-American and pro-British activities, latterly joined in by Heald, Lt. Linai Helm (Mrs. Kinzie's son-in-law), and Ensign Ronan. All of these officers paid lower prices than the enlisted men, whom over their protests Heald had forbidden by a written order to deal with any other trader. All of this despite Kinzie's oath of loyalty to the United States taken when he was appointed justice of the peace by Governor Harrison of Indiana Territory in 1804, and sutler in 1812 by Captain Heald. Irwin left Chicago ostensibly to recruit his own successor and La Lime's replacement, before he, too, could be assaulted. In the aftermath of the Indians' murderous attack at Leigh and Russell's farm on April 6, 1812, Kinzie and Helm had threatened to kill, and then expelled from the Chicago area, the local pro-American French, Ottawa, and Chippewa. In May other members of the garrison, perhaps not coincidentally, almost succeeded in killing Jean François Réaume, a British interpreter and sometime Kinzie customer, after he had given Heald valuable intelligence on dangerous Indian activities and the plans of Robert Dickson, a top British agent. Attacks on Chicago by Indians had been anticipated as early as

1809; they would be initiated on orders of the British Indian Department at Fort Malden in Amherstberg, opposite Detroit.

The apparently unauthorized and premature Winnebago attack on Sargent Leigh's farm in April warned Chicago of imminent danger, and the June war council at Milwaukee was concerned that this attack would have placed Fort Dearborn on high alert. But despite this, the Fort Dearborn attack, first of a series, was ordered, and occurred on Aug. 15, 1812, quickly escalating from an assault on a military objective into the atrocities of a massacre of military and civilian personnel. The Kinzies, Healds, and Helms escaped being killed. Kinzie gave an account of the massacre to Forsyth upon the latter's arrival at a suddenly peaceful Chicago the next day, after his visit to Harrison's office at Vincennes to mitigate Kinzie's crime of killing La Lime. The timing of Forsyth's movements and his missing the massacre by the slender margin of a single day bespeak forewarning more than coincidence. Billy Caldwell was also elsewhere on August 15, perhaps for the same reason. For several years, starting in 1813, he was an officer and ultimately commander of the British Indian Department at Fort Malden, not returning to Chicago until after 1820.

Exactly when Kinzie's loyalty changed to the United States can only be guessed. The Indians' destruction of his business at Chicago by the massacre in August, 1812, was perhaps the unintended consequence of a British order to the Indians to attack Fort Dearborn. This shocking carnage might well have caused him, at least privately, to switch sides, but instead he moved into British-held territory and assumed a new active role in the British Indian department, about the time his most important employe, Billy Caldwell, got his captains commission. Perhaps before the massacre, but after Kinzie killed La Lime, Harrison's staff, having failed to win Caldwell to the United States' cause, had succeeded in recruiting Kinzie as a U. S. agent with the

help of Forsyth. The latter, already a secret agent, had met Kinzie at Peoria about July 2 before going to Harrison's headquarters at Vincennes. Kinzie, who must have known of Forsyth's clandestine service, wrote him on July 7, giving details of the just concluded Milwaukee war council, the sort of disclosure no loyal British agent would make.

These conjectures would help to explain Kinzie's bizarre acquittal. This remarkable resolution of a homicide charge would have been a *quid pro quo* forcing Kinzie into the secrete service of a government he had long disdained. The days he spent in hiding in Chicago after the killing might have seen the start of a clandestine process to recruit Kinzie in exchange for his acquittal. The roles of Heald, Helm, and the other officers who voted acquittal might also have been the price of the government's overlooking their nefarious activities as reported to the Secretary of War by Irwin, as well as the price of their silence on the subject of Kinzie.

After the massacre, the Kinzies and Mrs. Helm were escorted to safety at Burnett's post at the mouth of the St. Joseph River by Jean Baptiste Chandonnai, Kinzie's métis clerk, who was also a British interpreter. Chandonnai was involved as well in ransoming the Healds from Indian captivity and getting them to Burnett's. The role of the Indians and others in these rescues has been variously interpreted but may be related to the fact that Kinzie had only six weeks earlier participated in the war council at Milwaukee, and that he and Chandonnai were covert agents of the British Indian Department, which had ordered the attack. Kinzie resumed trade at his old post on the St. Joseph River by Sept. 9, 1812, with Caldwell, Chandonnai and Helm among his customers. By January 1813, Kinzie and his family were in British-held Detroit, Caldwell was a newly-commissioned captain in the British Indian Department at Amherstburg, and Chandonnai and Helm again appeared in Kinzie's account book. The Kinzies lived in a large house on the northeast corner of Jefferson Avenue and Wayne Street, although

Kinzie himself appears to have spent part of his time at the St. Joseph post, where the last entry in his accounts is dated March 22, 1813.

Later in 1813, probably in August or September, Kinzie and Chandonnai were charged with treason against George III and jailed in irons in Fort Malden. While acting (so far as the British knew) as a British agent, he and Chandonnai, on leave from their trading post, were taking gunpowder to Tecumseh's forces, which were fighting alongside British troops in the present Toledo-Sandusky area against Harrison's advancing army. They were also trying, "in a correspondence with the enemy" (that is, as secret U. S. agents), to win the Indians over to the American side. Tecumseh complained to Maj. Gen. Henry Procter, the British commander, and Kinzie and Chandonnai were arrested. In the days of August and September, about the time of this arrest, American forces had repulsed the British-Indian sieges of Fort Meigs (present day Fremont, OH), which Tecumseh had demanded, emboldened by massive Indian reinforcements dispatched by Dickson from many places in the upper Midwest. Commodore Perry had beaten a British fleet near Put-In Bay, thus giving the United States control of Lake Erie and imperilling British supply lines. With American chances of victory improving, Kinzie was now on the winning side, but exposure removed him and Chandonnai from the field.

Chandonnai "escaped to the Indians," probably with covert assistance, but Kinzie was sent in irons to Quebec and from there on a ship to England, perhaps to prevent him from also mysteriously escaping and giving British secrets to U. S. authorities, such as he had probably given U. S. secrets to his British contacts for many years. Ironically, at the end of September, Procter's British troops withdrew from the Detroit area and, after dismantling Fort Malden, retreated eastward with the remainder of Tecumsehs forces. Upbraided by Tecumseh for cowardice, Proter took a stand at

Moraviantown on the Thames River, fighting a loosing battle in which Tecumseh was killed. Billy Caldwell was wounded during this campaign. Kinzie was already outside the war zone and in the hands of stern British justice. But the ship carrying him was forced into port in Nova Scotia by a storm, and he escaped in the confusion. Remarkably, he eluded capture by the British authorities and by Indians, suggesting that he returned to Detroit via U. S. territory, a remarkable feat for a presumably impecunious prisoner. He was able to resume his business by August, 1814, in Detroit, now for nearly a year held by the United States.

Tecumseh had told Procter in 1813 they would kill Kinzie if the British didn't, and the Indians had been offered a large reward in early December, 1814, by Lt. Joseph Cadotte of the Indian Department to bring Kinzie in alive as a prisoner to Mackinac, or failing that, to kill him, along with Chandonnai. The latter, a nephew of Topenebe, the local Potawatomi leader, was also wanted for the murder of his stepfather, a British army officer who had gone to Burnett's to arrest him. On July 22, 1814, while a fugitive from British justice, Chandonnai was an official U. S. interpreter at an Indian treaty at Greenville, Ohio, convened by Governor Harrison and Governor Cass of Michigan Territory. The various Indian groups, including the Potawatomi of his uncle Topenebe, allied themselves to the United States and agreed to supply warriors to fight the British. Kinzie, who returned from exile about this time, now was a new and patriotic U. S. citizen looking for a non-secret government job as Indian agent or interpreter, and also seeking to reestablish his business at Chicago. In the spring of 1815, after the Treaty of Ghent ended the War of 1812, he complained about Cadotte's reward offer to Governor Cass. This complaint was referred to James Monroe, then U. S. secretary of state as well as secretary of war, and at Monroe's urging Governor Robinson of Canada ordered a military court of inquiry to hear the Kin-

zie and Chandonnai cases. United States intervention for these men at the highest official level suggested that they had acted in furtherance of United States interests and under clandestine directions, at great personal risk. The record of this hearing was published in 1890, in Vol. XVI of the Michigan Pioneer and Historical Collections. It contains extensive sworn testimony about the activities of Kinzie and Chandonnai, both unequivocally established to have been British subjects and agents up until the time of their treason.

Cadotte was acquitted with the court's commendation for his actions in the matter, and a copy of the record was sent to Washington. Even before this court of inquiry, Kinzie and Chandonnai were received as useful U. S. citizens, and on Sept. 8, 1815, acted as interpreters at the Treaty of Spring Wells near Detroit, at which the various tribes officially "repented" their pro-British activities; Kinzie and Chandonnai had apparently repented privately and were now valuable public assets of U. S. Indian policy. Kinzie had always been on good terms with the Indians, who saved him and his family from harm at the time of the Fort Dearborn massacre, possibly on orders of the British Indian Department. His eyewitness account of the massacre [see Fort Dearborn massacre], another version of what he had told Forsyth the next day, describes the events. During the war of 1812 his home was occupied by the "British traders" from Peoria, Louis Buisson and François Lemoine dit Des Pins, suggesting that the British had an interest in preserving the property as a supply base to build a new fort at Chicago, plans which never materialized.

In the autumn of 1816, Kinzie and his family returned to their Chicago homestead, but he never regained the prosperity he had enjoyed before the war [see his letter to his son at entry Kinzie, John Harris]. In 1818 he became subagent under the U. S. Indian agent in Chicago. Plans were made but not carried out to have him live at

JOHN HARRIS KINZIE [12]

present Ottawa, IL. He may have gotten this position with the help of Governor Cass and his relative Robert A. Forsyth, Jr., secretary of the Indian Department, both of whom he accompanied at six Indian treaties at St. Mary's, Ohio, in the fall of 1818. He was also the Chicago representative of John Jacob Astor's American Fur Company as John Kenzie, Jr., "clerk." On Dec. 2, 1823, he was elected justice of the peace of Fulton County, in which Chicago was then included, and on July 28, 1825, he was sworn in to the same office for Peoria County. He died a few hours after suffering a cerebral stroke on Jan. 6, 1828. His initial burial place was near the fort, south of the river; then his body was moved across the river to the cemetery northeast of his home, where the dead from Fort Dearborn were usually buried; in 1835 his remains were moved to the north side cemetery, now Lincoln Park, and finally to Graceland Cemetery; · Kinzie

Street (400 N). For John Kinzie's family tree and family relationships with other Chicagoans, see page 222. Also see *John Kinzie* (a brig on Lake Michigan, built in 1833). [12, 109, 220, 226, 279, 559, 404-7, 649]

Kinzie, John Harris (1803-1865) also Colonel Kinzie; Shaw-nee-aw-kee (Potawatomi name of his father, bestowed on John Harris after his father's death); eldest son of trader John and Eleanor Kinzie [see Kinzie family tree on page 222)]; born on July 7 in Sandwich, Ontario; came to Chicago in October 1804 with his parents, where he lived until 1812, when the family escaped to Detroit for the next four years; returned with his family to Chicago in 1816 and worked for the American Fur Co. under Robert Stuart from 1818 to 1823, liv-

ing on Mackinac Island, during which time he became an accomplished violin player; [for a 1821 letter he received on Mackinac from his father at Chicago, see below]; transferred to Prairie du Chien in 1823 to learn the Winnebago language; served as private secretary to Governor Cass of Michigan Territory in 1826, and during this year accompanied a delegation of Winnebago to Washington; in 1827 was at the Treaty of Butte des Morts, and in 1830 became Indian subagent at Fort Winnebago, compiling vocabularies of both the Winnebago and the Wyandotte languages while serving until 1833, when he resigned and returned to Chicago again, opening a variety store [May 14, 1834 ad in the *Chicago Democrat*: "Salt, Nails, Window-Glass, Iron &c. &c."]; about 1830 he had bought lots in blocks 2, 5, 20, and 32 (see map on page 44) and also that year on Aug. 9, had married Juliette Augusta Magill of Middleton, CT, the niece of his brother-in-law Dr. Alexander Wolcott; they had two sons and three daughters; Juliette later became the author of *Wau-Bun*. John Harris became the second town president when elected on Aug. 11, 1834, serving for one year; advertised in the *Chicago American* late summer and autumn of 1835, as merchant with a forwarding and commissioning business opposite Fort Dearborn, which, as well as a lumber concern, was soon partnered by his brother-in-law Maj. David Hunter; was also involved in efforts to secure a charter for the Chicago and Vincennes Railroad that fall; in late November submitted a claim [lots 1 and 2 of block 2] for wharfing privileges; served as president on the first board of directors of the branch of the State Bank of Illinois that opened in December 1835; ◆ Kinzie & Hunter, forwarding, commission merchants, North Water Street near Rush. Later in life he served as registrar of public lands (appointed by President Harrison in 1841), canal collector (1848), and paymaster in the army, appointed by President Lincoln in 1861, with the rank of major; with an increasingly heavy workload, he died suddenly on a railroad train on June 21, 1865. His brick residence stood at the NE corner of Cass [Wabash Avenue N of the river] and Michigan streets. [12, 226]

Letter from John Kinzie to son John H.:

Dear Son: I received your letter by the schooner. Nothing gives me more satisfaction than to hear from you. It does give both myself and your mother a pleasure to hear how your conduct is talked of by everyone that hopes you every advantage. Rather let this stimulate you to continue the worthy man, for a good name is better than wealth, and we can not be too circumspect in our line of conduct. Mr. Crooks speaks highly of you, and try to continue the favorite of such worthy men as Mr. Crooks, Mr. Stewart [Ramsey Crooks and Robert Stuart together were managing the American Fur Co. on Mackinac Island] *and the other gentlemen of the concern. Your mother and all of the family are well, and send their love to you. James is here, and I am pleased that his returns are such as to satisfy the firm.* ✧ *I have been reduced in wages, owing to the economy of the Government. My interpreter's salary is no more, and I have but $100 to subsist on. It does work me hard sometimes to provide for your sisters and brothers on this, and to provide for my family in a decent manner. I will have to take new measures. I hate to change houses, but I have been requested to wait Conant's arrival* [Mr. Conant of Conant & Mack, Detroit, competitors of the American Fur Co., which bought C & M out in 1822]. *We are all mighty busy, as the treaty commences to-morrow, and we have hordes of Indians around us already. My best respect to Mr. Crooks and Stewart, and all the gentlemen of your house.* ✧ *Adieu. I am your loving Father. John Kenzie.* [Aug. 19, 1821]

Announcement in a September 1830 issue of the *North-Western Journal*, published weekly in Detroit:

Married

on the 9th inst. at New Hartford, Oneida County, N. Y. by the Reverend Mr. Adams,
Mr. John H. Kinzie,
Agent of Indian Affairs at Fort Winnebago,

to
Miss Juliette Auguste Magill.

Kinzie, Juliette Augusta   (1806-1870) née Magill, born Sept. 11 in Connecticut [see Kinzie family tree on page 222]; sister of William Magill who, as a boy in 1823, spent some time at Fort Dearborn with their uncle Dr. Alexander Wolcott; married her uncle's brother-in-law John Harris Kinzie on Aug. 9, 1830, and moved with him to Chicago in 1834; in later years she wrote the book *Wau-Bun, the "Early Days" in the North-west* (published 1856), which recorded much information about early life in Chicago and what we now call the Midwest, although her text is not always historically accurate. [Mrs. Kinzie was not, as is often said, Chicago's first author; that honor goes to Rev. Isaac T. Hinton, D.D.; eds.] ❀ For a portrait of Juliette Magill Kinzie, see page 371. [12, 405-8, 558]

Kinzie, Margaret McKenzie   born 1766; daughter of Murdoch and Erina McKenzie of Virginia; first wife or consort of John Kinzie, prior to his Chicago period; sister of Elizabeth McKenzie, who became a like consort to John Kinzie's early trading partner Alexander Clark [see Kinzie family tree on page 222]. In the early 1770s, they had been captured by the Shawnee and raised among them; years later they were given to or ransomed by Kinzie and Clark. Kinzie and Margaret had three children: William, James, and Elizabeth, who returned with their mother to Virginia after the parents separated. Clark and Elizabeth had four children: Elizabeth, John Kinzie, and twins Andrew and Mary; all of whom also returned to Virginia. There both sisters found new husbands. Elizabeth married Jonas Clybourne, and Margaret married Benjamin Hall, and both families would eventually settle at Chicago, forming the Virginia branch of the Kinzie family and settling along the north branch. [12]

Kinzie, Maria Indiana   born in Chicago in September 1807 of John and Eleanor Kinzie; in 1824-25 she was courted by the trader John Crafts, whose untimely death at the Kinzie House in May 1825

ended the budding relationship; married [see] Lt. David Hunter, later general, on Sept. 18, 1829 [see Kinzie family tree on page 222]; for the marriage license the lieutenant sent a soldier on foot 160 miles to Peoria; moved with her husband to Fort Howard when he was transferred in 1831; both enjoyed a long life together. [12, 226]

Kinzie, Robert Allen   (1810-1873) also Major Kinzie; fourth surviving child of John and Eleanor Kinzie, born (Feb. 8) and died (Dec. 13) in Chicago [see Kinzie family tree on page 222]; with his family, survived the 1812 massacre and escaped to Detroit, returning to Chicago in 1816; during his teens attended school in Detroit for several years; from 1825 to 1827 worked for his brother John Harris at Prairie du Chien, later at Fort Winnebago, and from 1829 to 1840 he remained in Chicago, mostly in trade. In 1830 he entered at the government land office, on behalf of his mother's family,

ROBERT ALLEN KINZIE [12]

a claim for the 102 acre tract lying N of the river between State Street and the lake, and ★★★ **Chicago's 1st** deed on record from Governor Reynolds conveys lots 5 and 6, block 29, original town, to Robert Kinzie for $109 [conveyed to Kinzie as assignee of Benjamin B. Kercheval on Sept. 27, 1830, and recorded on Dec. 2, 1831; Kinzie at that time was entitled to claim additional land, but failed to do so. [For the record on an exchange on that subject between Robert and his mother, see Kinzie Addition]. With James Kinzie he built and operated a store (Chicago's second frame building, after Billy Caldwell's residence) on the W side of Wolf Point in 1832 near Wentworth's Tavern; advertised whitefish for sale in the March 4, 1834, issue of the *Chicago Democrat*, which later in November, identifying him as with the firm Kinzie & Forsyth, announced that on Nov. 8 he married Gwenthlean (1817-1894), daughter of Col. William Whistler, Rev. Isaac Hallam officiating; in 1835 became a partner in the hardware firm of Davis, Kinzie & Hyde, and resided on the N side of Michigan Avenue, SE of the old Kinzie mansion; late November that year he filed a claim for wharfing privileges; ✦ Davis, Kinzie & [Thomas] Hyde, hardware, Kinzie Street near Cass [Wabash]. After 1839, he lived successively in Walnut Grove, IL; Des Moines, and Kansas. In 1861 he was appointed paymaster in the army with the rank of major, and remained in this service until his death; buried at Graceland Cemetery in the family grave; in 1885 his widow lived at 3308 Wabash Ave. [12, 226, 351]

Kinzie slough   a swamp on the N side of the Chicago River, drained by a small creek entering the river about 200 feet W of the Kinzie House.

Kinzie, William   born 1788; eldest son of John Kinzie and Margaret McKenzie, John's first wife; brother of James and Elizabeth [see Kinzie family tree on page 222]; married in Virginia, then moved to Elkhart, IN, where he died; never resided in Chicago. [12]

Kitchimokman   Potawatomi name for Americans,

meaning *Big Knives*, a term used by all Algonkian language speakers.

Klingmann, William   German immigrant, first attested to as having lived in Chicago in 1835. [342]

Knaggs, Whitmore   Indian agent, attended the Chicago Treaty of Aug. 29, 1821; at the W.H. Wallace estate sale on May 10, 1827. [220]

Knickerbocker, Abraham V.   arrived in 1833 from New York and worked as clerk for harbor improvements under Supt. Maj. George Bender, receiving $30 per month; was a member of the "Washington Volunteers," a Chicago fire brigade existing prior to incorporation; made a claim for wharfing privileges with Edmund Kimberly in 1835; in 1836 was among the first officers of the Chicago Marine and Fire Insurance Company; in 1837 he served temporarily as acting superintendent of the harbor when Lieutenant Allen, superintendent since 1834, was reassigned; ✦ clerk, government works. [12]

Knickerbocker, H.W.   born c.1812 in New York; came in October 1833; by 1879 he lived at Naperville, and was still living in 1885. [12]

Knight, James   a child by this name was enrolled as grade school student in the class taught by [see] John Watkins in December 1835. Names of corresponding parents were not recorded. [728]

Knowles, Joseph   see Noles, Joseph.

Knox County, Northwest Territory   Chicago became part of Knox County in 1790, but was simultaneously claimed by England as part of Kent County of the Province of Upper Canada from 1792 on. British authorities were in *de facto* control in Chicago and the Northwest until 1796, when Chicago became part of Wayne County, Northwest Territory; for details, see Chicago jurisdictional chronology on page 209. [436a, 544]

Koerner, Gustave Philip   originally Körner; born at Frankfort, Germany, in 1809; a liberal university student familiar with American constitutional law, he fled the chaos of Europe in 1833 and settled in St. Clair County, Illinois; became professionally active as a lawyer in the Illinois court system and

politically involved in the state and national campaigns of 1856 and 1858, and President Lincoln's election. Koerner visited Chicago in 1836, leaving with a sense—learned and objective—of the immensity of "life in this new Eldorado." [416]

Kohler, Bernhard   German immigrant in June 1834, who came with his family from Stolzenau and later moved to Duncklee's Grove [now Bloomingdale]. [342]

K. Utica   schooner from Kalamazoo, called at Chicago on Aug. 4, 1835.

Labaque, Francis   arrived in 1832 and served in the Black Hawk War under Capt. Gholson Kercheval. [12]

La Barre, Antoine Joseph Le Fèvre   governor of New France when Illinois was part of Canada; succeeded Governor Frontenac in 1682 and was succeeded by Governor Denonville in 1684; in- imical to La Salle; died 1688; also see Chronology for the year 1683.

Lacker, Frederick   see Locker, Frederick.

Lac de Puans   see Lake Michigan.

La Clair, Peter   see Le Claire, Pierre.

Lac Marais   see Mud Lake.

"La Compt, Madam"   real name Marie Joseph La Marche, wife of Louis Le Comte; both residents of Cahokia c.1772 to after 1808.

"Madam La Compt" was a real person whose life story has been fictionalized and conflated with those of her mother and daughter by the master of unreliable Illinois history, [see] John Reynolds, who "remembered" a legend that she had lived in Chicagou in 1765 as Mme Pilette de St. Ange." He had known two of these three women but wrote as if they had been one person, "Madame La Compt," long after they were all dead. Reynolds boasted that he wrote his book, published 1859, entirely from memory "which may be relied upon," but many fragments of history, dimly remembered by him or his informants, reassembled to produce an abundance of legends, including this one. In

Reynolds' defense it may be noted that these three women bore similar given names: Marie Joseph, Marie Josephte, and Marie Josette. The published vital records of St. Joseph, Michillimackinac, and Cahokia (there are none for Chicago before 1833) permit a sketch of these three remarkable women, and of the two women from whom they were descended. All five are given here in reverse chronological order.

(1) Marie Josette Languedoc born c.1773 in Cahokia; married there on May 1, 1791, to Michel Pilet *dit* St. Ange, Cahokia. Reynolds, who moved to Illinois about 1800, knew her until she died at Cahokia in 1843; there is no evidence that she and her husband ever lived in Chicagou, as Reynolds claimed, especially not in 1765. After 1800 Michel's brother, Louis Pilet did live in Chicagou as well as Peoria, but his name has been unfortunately garbled to Pettle and Petelle in Kinzie's account book, and this decidedly non-French name has concealed his true identity. The 1787 census of Cahokia, written in French, spells their surname, and that of their brother Charles, as *Pilet*. Louis "Pettle" or "Pelette" was a frequent customer of John Kinzie from December 24, 1803, to July 21, 1812. In the U.S Peoria land claims hearing of 1820 he is Louis Pilette; Reynolds, who was heavily involved in the various land claim proceedings, would have known of him.

(2) Marie Joseph La Marche the real "Mme Le Comte," born at St. Joseph after July 28, 1853, baptized July 4, 1756; married [1] Joseph Languedoc at Cahokia on Jan. 16, 1772; married [2] Louis Le Comte, native of *Ange Gardien* parish, Quebec, at Cahokia Jan. 27, 1775. Confusion as to their having lived at Chicagou may have arisen because Chicagou was the site of the *Ange Gardien* mission 1696-1702. Louis was still alive on Jan. 21, 1808. Reynolds knew both him and his wife; she probably died before her daughter, Marie Josette, the year of whose death, 1843, he falsely attributed to her mother, Marie Josephte Esther L'Arche, baptized Jan. 1, 1734 at age about one

year, thus creating a woman who supposedly lived a remarkable 109 years.

(3) Marie Josephte (Josette) Esther L'Arche (L'Archeveque) born at St. Joseph c.1733, baptised there Jan. 1, 1734. She married [1] Jacques Bariso de la Marche on Aug. 2, 1784; they had children including three sons still living at Cahokia in 1890, but he died after July 1756, and she then married [2] Charled le Boeuf *dit* La Flamme; they had children who were minors at his death, date unknown; two of them were living at Cahokia in 1790. As the wife of La Flamme she might have lived at Chicagou in 1763, when there were "a few French families" present, but they were at Cahokia by 1772 when her daughter married Joseph Languedoc there. She married [3] Thomas Brady of Cahokia, marriage contract June 8, 1779; her son Philippe La Flamme came of age about 1783, and Esther (as she often appeared in St. Joseph church records) seems to have been alive then. But she was certainly dead by Oct. 1, 1794, the date on which Brady's second (?) wife, Josephine Charlier, was buried at Cahokia. Reynolds could not have known Esther, who died when he was but a child.

(4) Marie Magdeleine Réaume born c.1714, date of death not known; married [1] Augustine L'Archeveque (L'Arche) before 1729; he died before July 1748, and she married [2] Louis-Therese Chevalier, leader of the St. Joseph community; they were both alive in 1780 when the paranoid Governor Sinclair ordered the elderly couple relocated to Michillimackinac. She and her husband were the celebrated personalities and great Indian diplomats; Reynold may have heard their stories from her granddaughter and great-granddaughter and attributed them to "Madame La Compt."

(5) Symphorosa Ouaouaboukoue, probably a Menominee of Green Bay (*La Baye*); married there before 1714, [1] Jean Baptiste Réaume, official interpreter at the post. Symphorosa died before 1752, when Réaume married [2] Marie Matchi-

ouagakouat informally at *La Baye* in 1752, solemnized at Michillimackinac Aug. 15, 1754, thus rendering legitimate their 11-month old son, Jean Baptiste *fils*. Later male members of the Réaume family were well-known traders, interpreters, and Indian diplomats; the legends of these men may still have echoed in Cahokia in the 19th century, and found their way into Reynolds' malleable memory. [559, 584, 595, 649]

Lacrosse name given by French pioneers to a ball game they saw the North American Indians play, who in turn called it *baggataway*; oldest organized sport in America; De Liette, Tonti's cousin, described in his writings how he saw the game being played by the Indians on the extensive meadows behind the native villages at Lake Peoria; it was not taked up by white men until c. 1840. [649]

Laducier, Francis also Laducia, Ladusier; voted on Aug. 7, 1826, and on Aug. 2, 1830; testified against James Kinzie before Justice Alexander Doyle on July 7, 1829, in the proceedings concerning the unlicensed sale of whiskey by Kinzie [Laducia owed seven shillings, paid with a dollar, receiving 12 1/2 cents in change with which he bought a pint of whiskey, unlawful as Kinzie had no license to sell less than a quart]; according to Wentworth, Laducier had no family and died at Archibald Clybourne's house. [12]

Laducier, Jean Baptiste voted on July 24, 1830 [see elections].

La Forêt, François Daupin de also Delaforêt, Delaforest; La Salle's lieutenant who commanded *Fort Frontenac* until 1685; administered Fort St. Louis with his cousin Tonti in the Illinois country between 1685-1689; in 1689, following La Salle's death, was granted the exclusive Illinois trade rights with Tonti and together built *Fort St. Louis* II at Lake Peoria in 1691; in April 1693, La Forêt sold half of his share in the Illinois colony's trading rights to Michel Accault at "Checagou," payment to be made there in August, making it ★★★ **Chicago's 1st** recorded business transaction and the largest of all time—one-quarter of Illinois' entire trading rights; companion of Tonti, de Liette, and Accault, with whom he worked intermittently at Chicagou from 1696 to c.1702 in a fur trading venture, with a trading post [near Tribune Tower]; by 1710 had replaced Cadillac as commandant at Detroit, where he died in 1714. [46, 259, 649]

La Fortune, Jean Baptiste actually named Tellier *dit* La Fortune or Lafortune; Mackinac *métis* engaged as interpreter at St. Joseph, 1818 to 1819; worked for William H. Wallace as interpreter at Hardscrabble in 1826; voted on Aug. 7 that year [see Chronology]. [220]

LaFramboise, Alexis (1763-1800) also Alexander; second son of Jean Baptiste Fafard *dit* LaFramboise and Geneviève le Bissoniere of Trois Rivières, Canada; brother of [see] François, Claude, and Joseph; successful Mackinac fur trader who opened up a second post at Milwaukee by the mid 1780s; married Josette Blondeau Adhemar in 1792 at Mackinac; had turned his Milwaukee trading post over to François by 1795.

LaFramboise, Alexis born 1794, son of François and his Potawatomi wife Shaw-we-no-qua; one of three Chicago militia members who survived the Fort Dearborn massacre of 1812 by deserting, traveling to Milwaukee with his parents; in 1817 returned to live in Chicago; early in 1833, by which time he was married and had two children, his name (for a family of four) appeared on the petition by Catholic citizens to Bishop Rosati of St. Louis asking that a priest be assigned to them. [12, 226]

Laframboise & Bourassa a partnership between one of François' sons (Claude, Alexis or Joseph) and Leon Bourassa; awarded $1,300 at the Treaty of Chicago, Sept. 26, 1833, in settlement for a claim accepted against one or more Indians (Treaty Schedule B).

LaFramboise, Claude also Glaude or Glode; son of Jean Baptiste Fafard *dit* LaFramboise and Geneviève le Bissoniere of Trois Rivières, Canada; brother

of François, Alexis, and Joseph; successful fur trader at Green Bay; boatman at St. Joseph in 1819.

LaFramboise, Claude (1795-1872) son of François and his Potawatomi wife Shaw-we-no-qua; one of three Chicago militia members who survived the Fort Dearborn massacre of 1812 by deserting, traveling to Milwaukee with his parents; in 1817 returned to live in Chicago; assessed on $100 personal property in 1825; voted on Aug. 7, 1826; worked for W.H. Wallace as an interpreter in 1826 and 1827; was granted a reservation on both sides of the Des Plaines River at the Prairie du Chien Treaty of 1829; his wife's name was de Nacouche and one son, Joseph, was baptized by Father Badin on Oct. 18, 1830; served as private with his brother Joseph under Captain Kercheval in the Chicago militia during the Black Hawk War, listed on the muster roll of May 3, 1832; early in 1833 was a member of the Catholic community, his name (for a family of four) appearing on the petition by Catholic citizens to Bishop Rosati of St. Louis asking that a priest be assigned to them; ✦ Claude Laframboise; died in KS. [12, 220, 226]

LaFramboise, François possibly Alexis' son, born c.1793 and baptized at Mackinac in 1797; voted on Aug. 7, 1826; ran a trading house with his uncle on the W bank near the forks between Madison and Washington streets; is not listed among the heirs to the estate when François died in 1830. [12]

LaFramboise, François also François Dauphin de la Forest Laframboise; son of Jean Baptiste Fafard *dit* LaFramboise and Geneviève le Bissoniere of Trois Rivières, Canada; brother of Joseph, Alexis, and Claude; member of the large LaFramboise family of French traders at Mackinac and Milwaukee; sent from Mackinac to Milwaukee to run Alexis' trading post by 1795, but incurred the enmity of local Indians and the business failed; known to be at Milwaukee as trader for several years after 1800 as noted by [see] Thomas G. Anderson in 1803; he and his Potawatomi wife Shaw-we-no-qua [Madaline, according to Eckert] were the parents

of Claude, Joseph, Alexis, LaFortune, and Josette; the family moved to Chicago in 1810 or 1811 and lived along the E side of the south branch, about a mile S of the forks, but left for Milwaukee shortly before the 1812 massacre; they returned in 1817 and purchased the Leigh farm from John Crafts, and, with nephew François, ran a trading house on the W bank near the Forks between Madison and Washington streets; voted on July 24, 1830; died in Chicago on April 26, 1830, and Stephen Forbes was appointed appraiser of his estate, which was divided equally between Claude, Joseph, Alexis, and Josette (Mrs. J.B. Beaubien), each receiving a fourth: $253.04. [12, 226 565]

LaFramboise, Joseph (the Indian Chief) son of François and his Potawatomi wife Shaw-we-no-qua; became a Potawatomi chief by marriage to Therese Peltier; assessed on $50 of personal property in 1825; voted on Aug. 7, 1826; his wife worked for W.H. Wallace in 1826 and 1827, making shirts and performing various services; Joseph voted on Aug. 2, 1830; purchased from the government in 1830 a lot constituting the northern part of block 43 (see map on page 44) but sold the land soon after to Christopher Idie; sons Jean Baptiste and Ambroise were baptized on Oct. 12, 1830, by Father Badin; served as private under Captain Kercheval in the Chicago militia during the Black Hawk War, so listed on the muster roll of May 3, 1832; early member of the Catholic congregation, signing for a family of seven on the April 1833 petition to Bishop Rosati of St. Louis, asking that a priest be assigned to Chicago; son François was baptized on Aug. 8, 1833; acted as one of the principal spokesmen for the Prairie and Lake Potawatomi at the Chicago Treaty of 1833; was granted an annuity of $200 per year for life, as well as one section of land on the Des Plaines River immediately S of the northern Indian boundary line, for himself and his six children in the treaty [a part of his reservation is now within the Indian Boundary Division of the Forest Preserve District of Cook

County, and is described on Forest Preserve maps]; his daughter Therese married the postal clerk Thomas Watkins, and years later, after their divorce, married Madore Beaubien. In 1835, Joseph went W with the Potawatomi, but was still listed in Chicago's 1839 *City Directory*: ✦ Joseph LaFromboise, Indian chief. [12]

LaFramboise, Joseph (the trader) (1775-1809) son of Jean Baptiste Fafard *dit* LaFramboise and Geneviève le Bissoniere of Trois Rivières, Canada; brother of François, Alexis, and Claude; respected Mackinac fur trader; moved to Milwaukee in 1802, after having acquired François' financially stressed property in that town two years earlier; established a trading post at Grand River, MI, where he was murdered by an Indian in the autumn of 1806; his wife [see] Madeline Marcot LaFramboise carried on the business with skill and great success, with her headquarters at Milwaukee. [565]

LaFramboise, Josette (1797-1845) baptized at Mackinac in 1797; daughter of François and his Potawatomi wife Shaw-we-no-qua; employed as nursemaid by the Kinzie family, where she witnessed the killing of La Lime by John Kinzie; in 1812 she married the widowed Jean Baptiste Beaubien as his third wife, but remained with the Kinzies when, shortly before the 1812 massacre, her husband with the children from earlier marriages removed to Milwaukee; at the time of the massacre, she was with the Kinzies in a boat and survived; later she joined her husband in Milwaukee until 1818, when the entire family returned to Chicago; Jean B. and Josette had George (died early), Susan, Monique, Julie, Alexander, Ellen, Philip and Henry (twins), Marie, Margaret, Caroline, and William. [12, 226]

LaFramboise, LaFortune born 1797, son of François and Potawatomi wife Shaw-we-no-qua; Chicago militia member in 1812 who escaped death in the Fort Dearborn massacre by deserting, fleeing to Milwaukee; in 1817 he returned to live in Chicago; was not listed among the heirs to the

estate when his father died in 1830. [226]

LaFramboise, Madelaine Marcot (c.1780-1846) daughter of French trader J.B. Marcot and his Ottawa wife Misigan (Marie); sister of Thérèse Schindler; devoted widow of Joseph, who was murdered by an Indian in 1807 on the upper Grand River [near Grand Haven, MI]; acquired a license to trade the following year and continued the business to great acclaim at Michilimackinac, becoming an employee of the American Fur Co.; in 1818 listed as trader on Grand River; described by contemporaries as "a woman of a vast deal of energy and enterprise—of a tall and commanding figure, and most dignified deportment"—"[a] woman of extraordinary ability, spoke French remarkably well, and, in deportment and conversation, a lady highly esteemed; [after her husbands death …] she took control of the business, and continued as a trader in the [American Fur] Company's employ." Madame LaFramboise appears to have never been in Chicago, but was well known by Indians and traders alike throughout the Northwest. Her oldest daughter, Josette, in 1817 married Capt. Benjamin K. Pierce, elder brother of a future president of the United States. [565]

LaFramboise, Therese daughter of Joseph LaFramboise; married post office clerk Thomas Watkins in 1836, but the marriage did not last; in 1854, as widow Hardin, she married her cousin Madore Beaubien in KS.

LaGrange lake schooner, built in Buffalo, NY; called in July 1833 to deliver supplies for harbor construction; in 1834 made four visits under Captain Cushwa, one which brought the [see] Deacon W. Churchill family to Chicago, and in July delivered "a lot of original still and landscape Paintings, in elegant guilt frames" which were sold "very cheap for cash" by J.H. Mulford; in 1835 the vessel returned twice under Captain Gauchvois, on July 14 and Sept. 10; sank at Pt. Pelee in 1847. [48]

Lahontan, Louis Armand de Lom D'Arce, baron de also La Hontan; spent several years (1683-

1693) in French military service in the Northwest and published in 1703, his volume *New Voyagesto North America*, describing travels that took him as far W as the longitude of Santa Fe, and including a ✱ map, *Carte de la Rivière Longue*, the western parts of which are conjectural and rely on information and sketches he collected from the Indians; on it he shows the Chicago portage extending from the lake directly to the Illinois River, omitting the Chicago River and Mud Lake; his spelling is *Chegakou*. Lahontan claims to have passed through Chicago on April 24, 1689; historians often found him unreliable. [420, 421]

Laird, George W., James, and William received treaty money at Chicago on Sept. 27, 1833; in 1834 George built a tavern at [now] Naperville which he named [see] Pre-Emption House; a copartnership between George and William was dissolved in November 1833, according to an announcement by George in the *Chicago Democrat* in July 1834; the same announcement reported that he conducted business "in the old stand at Pau Pau" [Lee County, IL], and had "just received a splendid assortment of New-Goods from New York" and would "sell as cheap as the cheapest." By Oct. 22, George had become postmaster of the Paw Paw post office, providing lists of remaining letters to the *Chicago Democrat* until at least April 1836. In the May 27, 1835, *Chicago Democrat* Philinda Laird placed a notice as administratrix of William's estate at Ottawa. [217a, 314a]

La Jeunesse, Jean B. also La Geuness; French Canadian fur trader who was granted a U.S. government license to trade with the Indians at "Chicagou" on Aug. 30, 1803. The license was granted by William Wells, then Indian agent at Fort Wayne, and states that "No Liquors [are] to be carried to the Indian Country on any account whatever." The document is within the Chicago Historical Society Collection.

Lake Chicago also Glacial Lake Chicago; term used by geologists for a lake that preceded Lake

Michigan; was formed when the Wisconsinan glacier retreated from the Chicago area, beginning about 14,000 years ago. Lake Chicago's level, at its highest, was almost 60 feet higher than the level of present Lake Michigan and the lake completely covered the area now occupied by Chicago. Its northern outlet into the St. Lawrence River was still blocked by remnants of the glacier and it drained through the so-called Chicago outlet, a notch in the Valparaiso moraine, into the Mississippi system. Its western shores reached to where Oak Park and LaGrange now exist. As the glacier shrank in stages, the major three of which are often referred to as the Glenwood phase (50 feet above the level of Lake Michigan; c.12,000 years ago), the Calumet phase (35 feet; c.10,000 years ago), and the Tolleston phase (20 feet; less than 8,000 years ago); each left behind many sandy beach ridges. The lake's southern shores were dammed by the hills of the Tinley-Valparaiso terminal moraine systems; as the glacier retreated farther and cleared the northern outlet, the lake level fell further and Lake Chicago became Lake Michigan. [309, 346]

Lake County   what is now Lake County was originally within the boundaries of Cook County and determined the Lake Precinct by commissioners in September 1835; became a portion of McHenry County in 1837 until March 1, 1839, then acquired its own status as a county. [299, 304]

Lake House   hotel on the N side of the river, near the bank opposite the fort, at Rush, Kinzie, and Michigan streets, facing the latter; ground was broken in 1835, completed in the fall of 1836; three stories high and built of brick, the hotel was elegantly furnished and construction cost was $100,000; was owned by the Lake House Association, whose members were G.S. Hubbard, Gen. D.S. Hunter, John H. Kinzie, Dr. W.B. Egan, and Maj. James B. Campbell; was managed by Jacob Russel from 1836 to 1839.

Lake Illinois   earlier name for Lake Michigan. Jolliet used Lake of the Illinois, but also Lac Missihiganin. [Early attempts by Europeans at transliteration of an Indian names usually resulted in a variety of spellings; *eds.*]

Lake Michigan   created by glacial action during the ice ages, its size varied much during its early development; these various stages have been given different names by geologists [see Lake Chicago]; during the last several millennia the level of Lake Michigan has averaged at 580 feet above sea level, with deviations of up to eight feet occurring in 500 to 600 year cycles, upon which there are superimposed 20 to 30 year cycles with lesser deviations. When the Europeans first visited Lake Michigan, the larger cycle was at its peak and the water level was probably eight feet higher. According to Father Allouez, the Fox word was Match-i-hi-gan-ing, and according to Father Hennepin in 1679, the Indian name was Misch-I gon-gon, meaning *great lake-place-of.* Earlier names used for Lake Michigan were Lake of the Illinois or Lac Illinois (Frs. Marquette and Dablon, Jolliet, La Salle), Lac St. Joseph (Father Allouez), Lac Dauphin (La Salle and Father Membre), Miesitgan and Missigan (Father St. Cosme), Missihiganin (Jolliet), and Lac de Puans (Sanson); according to Shea, Father Marest was first to use the name Lake Michigan, explaining that it was wrong to call it Lake Illinois, because the Illinois did not live nearby. [94, 346, 565]

Lake Peoria   see Peoria, IL.

Lake Shore Trail   much used by Indians and pioneers, this trail extended from Michilimacinac to

The Lake House in 1857,
viewed from across the river, with the lighthouse and the blockhouse of Fort Dearborn in the foreground to the left.

Green Bay, S along the shoreline and around the lower end of the lake, with an extension to Detroit (Fort Dearborn-Detroit Road).

Lake Trail the major E-W trail of the early settlement, still traceable in the modern street pattern, closely following the course of Lake St. from the lakeshore westward through the suburbs of Elmhurst, Addison, and Elgin, then N along the E shoreline of the Fox River.

La Lime, Jean B. also Lalime; Canadian; an early agent of William Burnett, the St. Joseph trader, and later a free-lance trader who lived in Chicago as early as 1792 [according to an Aug. 17, 1792, entry in Burnett's account book]; from 1804 on, he was Indian interpreter at Fort Dearborn—a well educated man and on friendly terms with the officers of the fort; bought [for William Burnett] the Point de Sable property in 1800 for 6,000 French *livres* and sold it to John Kinzie in 1803, but stayed in Chicago, living after the sale in the interpreter's house on the N side of the river, nearly opposite the mouth of Frog Creek; was a friend of the Fort Dearborn physician Dr. William Smith, who called him "a very decent man and a good companion," and with whom he had lived in the "borrowed" Kinzie house during the winter of 1803-04; was killed by John Kinzie during a quarrel in the spring of 1812 [the exact date of his death is not to be found in readily accessible records, and invites further research. Eckert gives March 23; Quaife gives April as the month; however, it could not have been earlier than May 15, since on this date the U.S. Factor Irwin wrote a letter from Fort Dearborn to the Secretary of War W. Eustis in Washington, reporting a death threat against "the Interpreter." La Lime was married to a Potawatomi woman Nokenoqua (Noquee-noqua), and had a son John La Lime [who received land grants on the St. Joseph River at the Chicago Indian Treaty of 1821]. La Lime was initially buried about 200 yards from Kinzie's house on the N side of the river [the southern end of Rush Street], within plain view of the front door and piazza, a gravesite that Kinzie afterward would tend well. According to Winslow, his bones are said to be now in the possession of the Chicago Historical Society. [12, 109, 564]

Lampmann, Heinrich S. later Henry S. Lampman; German immigrant brickmaker, ★★★ **Chicago's 1st,** who arrived in 1833 from Ann Arbor and was employed by Tyler K. Blodgett at Blodgett's new brickyard; in 1885 lived at Litchfield, MI. [12, 342]

Lampmann, J. German immigrant, first attested to as having lived in Chicago in 1833. [342]

Lamset, Pierre also known as Peter or Basil Lamsett, Peter Lampsett, Peter Specie, Peter Pecie; *métis*, Indian trader and resident of Chicago in 1825, when he was assessed for tax purposes, owning $100 of personal property and paying $1 in tax; made two purchases at the estate sale of W.H. Wallace of May 12, 1828, including a martingale; had a claim one mile S of Hardscrabble on which Russell Heacock settled in 1828; in 1830 Lamset settled in the Fox River valley at what later was called Specie Grove; is known to have hired himself out to new settlers, using a breaking plow he owned to prepare the prairie for cultivation; was among the refugees seeking shelter at Fort Dearborn during the early phase of the Black Hawk War; owned land in Kendall County until 1835, when he sold out and moved to Vermillian County [12]

land boom in 1835-36 a speculative mania for land within and beyond Chicago developed, prompted by the plans of the federal government to build the Illinois & Michigan Canal. Large amounts of money flowed in from the East through investors such as Arthur Bronson, Charles Butler, and Edward Russell. Dr. William B. Egan of Chicago is said to have bought a tract of land in 1834 for $300 and sold it again in 1836 for $60,000; Augustus Garrett, one of the major entrepreneurs, is said to have sold $1.8 million worth of property in 10 months. The deals were often shady, as highlighted by this note in *Chicago American*, July 2, 1836: "The rapidity with which towns are thrown into the market is astonishing. Houses are born in a night, cities in a day, and the small towns in proportion." The boom ended in 1837 with a financial crash, precipitated by action of Congress, which had passed a law on June 23, 1836, regulating the deposits of public money and discrediting the issues of any bank unable to redeem its issues in species. Most speculators lost their fast-won fortunes. Even the military officers stationed at Fort Dearborn had been unable to resist the lure of real estate speculation, as the fragment of a feverish letter written by Commandant Major Wilcox [see below] may demonstrate. The dizzying pace of land value appreciation in the early 1830s is demonstrated by one particular lot with 20-foot frontage in the 100 block of Lake Street, W and immediately adjoining the property of Thomas Church: it sold for $7 in 1830, for $250 in 1834, and for $800 in 1836. [12]

Excerpt of Major Wilcox letter:

Fort Dearborn, 6. June 1835

... every house in town is filled to overflowing, from Ten to Fifty arriving daily. Captain Hunter sold his Land here for 25000 and the Bronsons have been offered 100,000. I suppose it will bring 150,000. so you see what speculations are going on here, I am sorry that I have made out so badly for you, but if you are disposed to trade on the 500. I have no doubt I can mak in 1000 in a year, or if you will make anyone else here your agent they will be able to do the same; Lieutenant Jameson received a commission from Maj Whiting last night to purchase to the amount of 1000 for him, the Lots are very high but going higher every day. I have purchased one for 1000. and one for 200. since I sold the house my water Lot is worth about 4000 now, you may think that I talk too much about lots; but there is an opportunity here of making something such as few officers have, and I should feel that it would be wrong to neglect it. had I done so at first coming here I should have made more money. now, I think it a positive duty lay up something for my Fam-

ily.   *Monday 8. since Saturday one ship one Brig and Ten Schooners have come into Port; yesterday passengers were landing all day, say 200 landed, and about the same number on board the morning. on Saturday evening. Mr. Walter Newberry one of the Bronson Firm, sold one Block of 8 lots (which Dr. Wolcot bought of the Canal Commissioners) for $35.000. after the great land sale here I intend to enter a Quarter Section and I will if you think proper enter one for you at the same time, say a half section in a body, I should like to get it near Juliet, it is a flourishing Village and I have three of four find Building Lots there; I wish you could be here this spring for a few days. ...*

Sample sales receipt from 1831 by M.F. Walker:

Received, Chicago, August 15, 1831, from P.F.W. Peck, Eighty Dollars, in full for Lot No. 4, block 18, in the plan of the "Town of Chicago," and in full of all claims to this date. (signed) *M.F. Walker.* [This lot is located at the SE corner of South Water and LaSalle streets, and in 1854 was valued at $42,000, in 1864 at $60,000; *eds.*]

land claims   see preemption laws

land office   see United States Land Office.

Landon, Jacob   U.S. Army private at Fort Dearborn; enlisted November 1807; wounded in action at the massacre of Aug. 15, 1812, and killed by the Indians after surrender. [226]

Lane, James   from Ireland, born 1803; arrived May 20, 1835; worked at the meat market at Old Dearborn street bridge; married Mary Higgins on Sept. 21, 1838; ◆ boarding house, corner of North Water and Dearborn streets; was an alderman in 1847; Mary died in 1877 and in 1885 James still lived at 12 Lane Place. [12, 351]

Langlade, Charles de   French military officer during the French and Indian War, active mostly in Wisconsin; his father was the earliest [c.1745] permanent settler in Green Bay, WI; his mother was an Indian; was married to an Indian early in life but in 1754 married a French woman; swore allegiance to the British government at the end of the

French and Indian War and was of great service through his knowledge of and influence over the local Indian tribes. In 1779, military orders from Major De Peyster brought the then British Captain Langlade to St. Joseph and his men apprehended Jean Baptiste Point de Sable at his trading post at *Rivière du Chemin* on suspicion of sympathizing with the Americans. [69]

Larabiche   see Fort Wayne, IN.

Larant, Alexander   voted on Aug. 7, 1826 [see Chronology].

Largillier, Jacques   (c.1644-1714) born in France; well-connected and prosperous trader and associate of Jolliet who accompanied Father Marquette as *voyageur* on his 1673 exploration of the Mississippi with Jolliet, and again on his last expedition in 1674, without Jolliet; later retired from business and entered the services of the Society of Jesus; died at Kaskaskia.

Larrabee, William M.   arrived from Canada in 1834 with his wife Elizabeth Caroline Bellamy; Elizabeth died at age 29 on May 19, 1837; married Mary Margaret Haight thereafter; served in the voluntary fire department; ◆ bookkeeper, William B. Ogden; alderman in 1846; in the 1850s was associated in leading positions with the Galena and Chicago Union Rail Road; died on Sept. 28, 1879; in 1885 his widow lived in Geneva. [12, 351]

La Salière, Pierre   also Le Sallier, but properly: [see] Le Sellier, Pierre.

LaSalle   168-ton schooner from Buffalo, NY; called at Chicago under Captain Stewart on Sep.13, 1835; capsized near Racine in 1849. [48]

LaSalle, IL   town on the Illinois River, named after the French explorer.

La Salle, Père Jean Cavelier de   elder brother of René Robert Cavelier de La Salle, the explorer; born at Rouen, France; Sulpitian priest; survivor of the ill-fated Texas expedition; after his brother's death in Texas was a member of the group with Henri Joutel that reached Chicago on Sept. 25, 1687, via

Fort St. Louis (Starved Rock), continuing to Canada, and then to France. [191]

La Salle, Nicolas de   member of René-Robert Cavelier de La Salle's 1682-83 expedition to the mouth of the Mississippi, which took the party through Chicagoland in January 1682 on its way S; the two La Salles were not related. [46]

La Salle, René-Robert Cavelier, sieur de (1643-1687) born at Rouen, France; La Salle immigrated in 1667 to Montreal, where his brother Jean served as a priest of the Sulpician order; from a local landowner, René-Robert soon developed into one of the great explorers of the New World. As a protege of Governor Frontenac, he began his voyages in 1668; his movements in 1670 cannot be clearly traced, but by some historians, Magry among them, he is credited with a visit to the Chicago portage, and from there S to the Ohio River, in 1670; most authorities believe however that Marquette and Jolliet, in 1673, were the first Europeans to visit the site of Chicago, while La Salle reached Chicago for the first time in 1679, on his way to St. Joseph and the Illinois River; in 1674 La Salle visited France and in 1675 the king rewarded him for his explorations with a patent of nobility and with ownership of *Fort Frontenac*, which La Salle had built in 1673 and named after the governor. In 1678, the king granted him a monopoly in the trade of buffalo skins [see text of the letters patent below], Tonti came from France to join him as his lieutenant, and that year La Salle had the first Great Lakes sailing vessel built, *Le Griffon*; La Salle built *Fort Niagara* and *Fort Miamis* in 1679, *Fort Crevecoeur* in 1680, and *Fort St. Louis de Rocher* and *Fort Chicagou* in the winter of 1682-83, with *Fort St. Louis de Rocher* becoming the first permanent European fortress in the Midwest. His design was to establish a colony in the Illinois country to serve as a bridgehead from which to penetrate the Mississippi valley. During their famous 1681-82 voyage to the Gulf of Mexico La Salle and Tonti passed

René-Robert CAVELIER, sieur de LA SALLE [46]

through Chicago in January 1682; in their company were Father Membré, the surgeon Jean Michel, and approximately 20 other Frenchmen. On April 9, 1682, at the mouth of the Mississippi River La Salle solemnly took possession of the entire Mississippi Valley for France, calling the territory *Louisiane*, after the French king; the official account of this expedition is known as the *Proces Verbal*. In his reports, La Salle began in approximately 1681 to use the word *Chicagou* to indicate specifically the site of the present city; two of La Salle's letters, written at *Chicagou* and dated June 4 and Sept. 1, 1683, indicate that he spent considerable time there during this year; it is believed that La Salle built a fort or post in the southern Chicago area, possibly near Blue Island or Hegewisch, in 1683. Leaving Tonti in charge at Fort St. Louis, La Salle left Illinois for the last time in the fall of 1683 and traveled to France, from there to prepare his intended colonizing ocean voyage to the mouth of the Mississippi; his ships overshot their goal,

stranding La Salle and his men on the Texas coast, and La Salle was murdered on March 19, 1687, in Texas by discontented members of his expedition. ➡ LaSalle Drive and LaSalle Street (both at 140 W). [12, 46, 54, 131, 169, 192, 194, 384, 424, 519, 613, 672, 673, 675]

Letters Patent, granted by the king of France to the Sieur de La Salle in 1678:

LOUIS, by the grace of God, King of France and of Navarre. To our dear and well-loved Robert Cavelier, Sieur de la Salle, greetings:

We have received with favor the very humble petition, which has been presented to us in your name, to permit you to endeavor to discover the western part if New France; and we have consented to this proposal the more willingly, because there is nothing we have more at heart than the discovery of this country, through which it is possible a road may be found to penetrate to Mexico; and because your diligence in clearing the lands which we granted to you by the decree of our council of the 13th of May, 1675, and, by Letters Patent of the same date, to form habitations upon the said lands, and to put Fort Frontenac in good state of defence, the seigniory and government whereof we likewise granted to you, affords us every reason to hope that you will succeed to our satisfaction, and to the advantage of our subjects of the said country. ✧ For these reasons, and others thereunto moving us, we have permitted, and do hereby permit you, by these presents, signed by our hand, to endeavor to discover the western part of New France, and, for the execution of this enterprise, to construct forts whereever you shall deem it necessary; which it is our will that you shall hold on the same terms and conditions as Fort Frontenac, agreeably and conformably to our said Letters Patent of the 13th of March, 1675, which we have confirmed, as far as is needful, and hereby confirm by these presents. And it is our pleasure that they be executed according to their form and tenor. ✧ To accomplish this, and everything above mentioned, we give you full powers; on condition, however, that you shall finish this enterprise within

five years, in default of which these presents shall be void and of none effect; that you carry on no trade whatever with the savages called Outaouacs, and others who bring their beaver skins and other peltries to Montreal; and that the whole shall be done at your expense, and that of your company, to which we have granted the privilege of the trade in buffalo skins. And we command the Sieur de Frontenac, our Governor and Lieutenant-General, and the Sieur Duchense, Intendant, and the other officers who compose the supreme council of the said country, to affix their signatures to these presents; for such is our pleasure. Given at St. Germain en Laye, this 12th day of May, 1678, and of our reign the thirty-fifth.   Louis.

Las Casas, Don Bartolomé de   (1474-1566) Spanish Dominican friar, missionary, and bishop of Chiapas who championed native rights; first Catholic priest ordained in America; published *Brevissima Relacion* in 1552, in which he described the gruesome cruelties inflicted on the Indians and chronicled the fate of the doomed races of the Antilles; active in the West Indies, Peru, and Central America, he became the first known advocate of the abolition of American slavery; ➡ Las Casas Avenue (4924 W). [112, 113]

La Tendre, Jean Baptiste   also Letendre; a French Canadian voyageur married to a Potawatomi woman called Keecheeaqua (Big Woman); later worked as a hired hand, first in the Milwaukee business of Jacques Vieau and then that of Solomon Juneau; for the latter, he made numerous trips to Fort Dearborn as a runner, carrying heavy loads of specie [largely silver coins] used for annuity payments or in trade with the Indians, who would not accept paper money; on Nov. 7, 1830, was baptized in Chicago by Father Badin; when the Potawatomi were removed from Milwaukee in 1837, he went with them to KS.

La Toupine   see Moreau, Pierre.

Lathrop, Samuel S.   born c.1810 in RI; arrived in September 1834; in October 1835 he signed up with the "Pioneer" hook and ladder company, an early volunteer fire brigade; remembered in Andreas as having built a picket fence in 1835 around the isolated grave of Baptist minister Reverend A.B. Freeman; lived at Bristol, IL, in 1885. [12, 351]

Latrobe, Charles Joseph (1801-1875) English traveler and author who, in September 1833, visited Chicago, coming from Detroit via Niles, MI; witnessed the land session treaty then being negotiated with the Potawatomi; the detailed and perceptive description of his Chicago experience is recorded in his 1835 book, *The Rambler in North America, 1832-1833;* ➡ Latrobe Avenue (5232 W). [See excerpts from Latrobe's report in Treaty 1833, Chicago, and in the Chronology, September 1833.] [12, 425]

Latta, James U.S. Army private at Fort Dearborn; enlisted April 1810; taken prisoner by Indians at the massacre of Aug. 15, 1812, then tortured to death the following day. [226]

Latzky, John on Oct. 1, 1835, married Potily Morris, Father St. Cyr officiating.

Lauer, Kaspar German immigrant who arrived with his wife Eva in 1835. On Sep, 18, 1854, he became the first Chicago police officer to die in the line of duty, 1854. [342]

Laughton & Taylor in 1828 a firm by this name existed at "Farm House, Chicago," selling groceries and whiskey; presumably one or both of the Taylor brothers, Anson and David, were involved as partners together with the Laughton brothers, David and Bernardus. Anson Taylor soon after rented the old Kinzie house and kept a like stock of goods.

Laughton, David and Bernardus H. also Lawton; Bernardus was also called Bernard or Barney; brothers originally from New England; their father John had owned a trading post on an island in Lake St. Clair, MI; David is listed in John Kinzie's account book between February and May of 1822; in 1823 they received from Dr. Wolcott a license to trade with the Indians at the Vermillion River; both were employed as traders by the American Fur Co.; in

1825 Bernardus had a trading post at Grand Detour on the Rocky River, MI; together owned a trading post at Hardscrabble in 1826, half a mile S of Chief Robinson's cabin, but in 1827 moved to the Des Plaines River, where they built both a trading post [Lyons] and a tavern, the oldest such establishment W of Chicago. In 1830 David homesteaded, and on Sept. 29 purchased from the State of Illinois 160 acres consisting of the SE quarter of the Canal Section 35, Township 39 R, 12 E [now a part of Riverside]; he also owned land to the S [Lyons]; there is no record of land ownership by Bernardus, who must have built on David's land, probably in partnership. Bernardus voted that year in the Aug. 2 election and later on Nov. 7 married Sophia Bates from Vermont (sister of Mrs. Elvira Forbes), with whom he had a son named David Henry. [In 1834, Stephen and Elvira Forbes homesteaded immediately to the E of the land owned by David and described above.] David is said to have had three Indian wives in succession, who all died before him. His last wife, a Potawatomi woman named Waish-kee-shaw, and their son Joseph received a small land grant in the Chicago Treaty of 1833. Bernardus died on April 4, 1834, and David, age 43, died shortly after on April 12 at Belle Fountain; both brothers were buried by Steven Forbes, who was living with them at that time. Isaac Harmon was the administrator of David's will. David left a nuncupative will in favor of his nephew David Henry, but the probate court recognized instead an earlier will written in favor of a Jacob Harsen; with a letter of administration dated Dec. 1, 1834, G.W. Snow announced an auction of the David's estate's "Stock, Furniture, &c." [with that of Daniel Outhet] at Bates' Auction Room on Dec. 31. [12, 262, 404]

Laughtons' ford also earlier, Ford of the Des Plaines; where the N portage trail crossed the Des Plaines River, once 200 feet wide, with a shallow bottom of rock and gravel, as the Niagara limestone underground here extends to the surface.

Counting from upstream, it is the third of four fords between Riverside and Summit, following Riverside ford and Stony ford (the last is Summit ford); named after the [see] Laughton brothers who built their trading house on the east bank of the river in 1827, along the old N portage road 12 miles from Chicago. The site is between Lyons and Riverside, within the Ottawa Trail Woods Forest Preserve on Harlem Avenue, at the level of 46th Street

Laughtons' trading house and tavern also see previous entry. In addition to the trading post which the Laughton brothers appear to have owned jointly, Bernardus also built and maintained a tavern, taking in overnight visitors. An inscribed granite boulder [▲ see Monuments] marks the exact location of the former trading house, confirmed by archeological excavations [according to Forest Preserve historian Ed Lace]. It is unlikely that the tavern was under the same roof; most historians maintain that the tavern was probably further upstream at the Riverside ford, approximately one mile NE from the trading house, on land that is now part of the town of Riverside, where the Laughtons also owned land. In her book *Wau-Bun*, Mrs. Kinzie describes a visit to Laughtons' tavern in March 1831 while traveling with her husband from Fort Winnebago to Fort Dearborn. An excerpt follows, preceding a less well known 1835 account by Chandler Gilman. [12]

Mrs. Kinzie's account:

It was almost dark when we reached Laughton's. The Aux Plaines was frozen, and the house was on the other side. By loud shouting, we brought out a man from the building, and he succeeded in cutting the ice and bringing a canoe over to us, but not until it had become difficult to distinguish objects in the darkness. ✧ A very comfortable house was Laughton's, after we reached it—carpeted, with a warm stove—in fact, quite a civilized style. Mr. Weeks, the man who brought us across, was the major-domo during the temporary absence of Mr. [Bernardus] Laughton. Mrs.

[Sophia] *Laughton was a young woman, and not ill-looking. She had complained of the loneliness of her condition and having been brought out there into the woods; which was a thing she had not expected when she came from the east.*

Mr. Gilman's account:

At half-past eight we stopped at a small log hut to breakfast. The public part of the establishment (for it was a sort of inn) consisted of two little rooms; in one was a table, which, when we entered, the combined exertions of a black wench, a tall strapping country girl, and the landlady (the very ugliest woman I ever saw by the by) were covering with materials for a substantial breakfast. In one corner of the other room was a straw bed, on which a poor pallid wretch was extended; his shrunk features, wasted form, and the general appearance of debility, plainly indicating a victim to the fever of the country. Opposite the sick man's bed, another corner of the room was occupied by a bar, at which several persons were taking in poison—in other climates the seed of disease, in this of death—in the shape of antifogmatics, fever killers, &c. The other end of the room was crowded with the persons and the luggage of an emigrant family.... From the contemplation of these miserable emigrants we were summoned to our breakfast.

Laumet   see Cadillac, Antoine de la Mothe, né Laumet.

Laval de Montmorency, Mgr. François   first bishop of Quebec who, in 1658, founded the Seminary of Quebec (*Séminaire des Missions Étrangères*), an institution that sent many missionary priests into the Illinois country during the 17th century, and later became Quebec's Laval University. Some came to Chicago, among them [see] Abbés Montigny François Jolliet de Montigny and Anthony Davion. Among the extraordinary treasures still kept at Laval University is the *Journal des Jésuites*, an informal day-to-day journal kept by the Jesuit fathers at their house in Quebec from 1645 to 1686, unedited and not meant for publication, unlike the *Jesuit Relations*, and therefore more re-

vealing to historians in many ways. [399]

Lavaye, Francis   lived at Chicago in 1828. [220]

Law, John   (1671-1729) see Louisiana Province.

Lawton   see Laughton.

lawyers   attorneys were abundant even in the settlement's earliest years; as Joseph Jefferson expressed in his autobiography, referring to Chicago in the year 1838: "... attorneys-at-law, oceans of them." Those who visited or settled before 1836 are listed below, with the time of their arrival: Charles Jouett (1805; U.S. Indian agent, did not practice in the community); Russell E. Heacock (1827); Richard J. Hamilton (April 1831); Lewis C. Kercheval (1831); Robert Nelson Murray (1831); Giles Spring (1833; arriving a few days before Caton); John Dean Caton (June 1833); Alexander N. Fullerton (1833); Edward W. Casey (1833); Peter D. Hugunin (1833); James Grant (April 1834); James H. Collins (1834); Hans Crocker (1834); Patrick Ballingall (1834); Justin Butterfield (1834); Henry Moore (1834); James B. Bradwell (1834); Albert G. Leary (1834); Buckner S. Morris (1834); Ebenezer Peck (1834); Sidney Abell (1834); Hiram Kennicott (1834); J. Young Scammon (September 1835); Henry A. Clark (1835); David Cox (1835); Thomas Drummond (1835); Alonzo Huntington (1835); Francis Peyton (1835); Lucien Peyton (1835); Edward G. Ryan (1835); Theophilus W. Smith (1835); James M. Strode (1835; earlier as circuit rider); James Curtis (1835); William Stuart (1835); Thomas Brock (1835); William B. Ogden (1835); Thomas Ford (1835); and Royal Stewart (1835). In addition to those named who resided in Chicago, there were from 1831 on "circuit riding" lawyers (such as [see] James M. Strode, Benjamin Mills) from southern Illinois towns, who would come and go, often traveling with judges (such as [see] Richard Montgomery Young). Circuit riding to other towns was practiced equally by the Chicago lawyers; memories of a circuit riding lawyer, excerpted from Isaac N. Arnold's *Recollections of the Early Il-*

linois and Chicago Bar.

I have known the trip to Springfield to take five days and nights, dragging drearily through the mud and sleet, and there was an amount of discomfort, vexation and annoyance about it sufficient to exhaust the patients of the most amiable. But the June journey was as agreeable as the December trip was repulsive. A four-in-hand, with splendid horses, the best of Troy coaches, good company, the exhilaration of great speed over an elastic road, much of it a turf of grass, often crushing under our wheels the most beautiful wild flowers, every grove fragrant with blossoms, framed in the richest green; our roads not fenced in by narrow lanes, but with freedom to choose our route; here and there a picturesque log cabin, covered with vine; boys and girls on their way to their log school-houses, and the lusty farmer digging his fortune out of the rich earth. Everything fresh and new, full of young life and enthusiasm, these June trips to Springfield would, I think, compare favorably even with those we make today in a luxurious Pulman car. But there were exceptions to these enjoyments. Sometimes torrents of rain would, in the course of a few hours, so swell the streams that the log bridges and banks would be entirely submerged, and a stream which a few hours before was nearly dry, became a foaming torrent. Traveling at such times was never agreeable, and was sometimes a little dangerous.

lead   see Galena, IL.

league   measure of distance used in Paris and New France, including early Illinois; one league is 2 *toises* (paces). A *toise* equals 1.949 meters, from which one may calculate that one league (Father: *lieue*) equals 2.411 statute miles. Most writers, ignorant of this legally mandated use of the Parisian *lieue* as a land and surveyor's measure, refer to the nautical league, which, as a subdivion of a degree of latitude, would have been useless on land, particularly in any travel not in a straight line. The nautical league was about three English miles, which leads to misleading equivalents. [649]

Leary, Albert Greene   arrived from Maryland in

1834; attorney, who later became a member of the state legislature; on May 25, 1835, advertised his office in the *Chicago Democrat* as located on Lake Street, "two doors below Cook's Coffee House [the Mansion House], with Dr. W.G. Austin;" his wife was Virginia (née Leary), a niece of President Taylor; ✦ attorney and counselor at law, Dearborn Street; died in 1853 in New Orleans.

Leavenworth, Ruth   teacher in 1835 at the Infant School at the first Presbyterian church, succeeding Miss Eliza Chappel, and being later succeeded by Mrs. Joseph Harmon; during her tenure in 1835, John S. Wright financed the building of a schoolhouse for the Infant School, creating its own quarters on the W side of Clark Street, just S of Lake Street. As per announcement in the *Chicago American*, on the Nov. 3, 1836, Miss Leavenworth married grocer Joseph L. Hanson, Reverend Hinton officiating; ✦ [the couple's home and grocery/provision store] 146 Lake St. [12, 243]

Le Clair, Antoine, Sr.   native of Montreal; first became an Indian trader at *Parc aux Vache*, marrying a Potawatomi woman in 1792; moved his family to Milwaukee in 1800 and continued trading, traveling to Detroit yearly in the spring to select goods that were later brought by a vessel that also stopped at St. Joseph and Chicago, returning with furs. Le Clair was observed by [see] Thomas G. Anderson in 1803, and his visits to Chicago were indicated in Kinzie's account books on Nov. 8, 1804; Sept. 3, 1806; and July 9, 1807; an adventure to Kankakee was noted on Nov. 28, 1808. The family removed to Peoria in 1809, and lived there until October 1812, when Peoria was destroyed. On May 1, 1810, Le Clair again outfitted with Kinzie for a Kickapoo adventure. From June 15 to July 11, 1812, Le Clair made a circular tour from Peoria to Chicago, Milwaukee, Coshquainong, down the Fox River to its mouth, and home again; in a July 14 report to Thomas Forsyth, then U.S. Indian agent in Peoria, he detailed the impressions he gained of Indian attitudes at this critical time, the beginning

of the war with England: "... I understood by Indians whom I was formerly acquainted with that all their talk is war with the Americans, and were only waiting (and that with impatience) for word from the British, and the first place they meant to attack was the Garrison at Chicago ...." His son, Antoine, Jr., was a United States interpreter for the Fox and Sauk Indian agency at Rock Island in 1832 and, upon Black Hawk's capture in August, translated biographical testimony. [109, 404, 691; *Wisconsin Historical Collections* 11 {1888}: 238-242]

Le Claire, Pierre   also Peter or Pieriche (diminutive) LaClair, LaClerc; *métis* Potawatomi who lived near Fort Dearborn in 1812 and worked for John Kinzie; G.S. Hubbard recalls that starting before daylight, La Claire "... carried the news of the war of 1812 ... sent by Major Robert Forsythe to his uncle, Mr. John Kinzie, ... [walking] from the mouth of St. Joseph River around Lake Michigan, a distance of ninety miles, in one continuous walk," then dining with the Kinzies' before reporting to the officers at Fort Dearborn by 9 p.m.; during the massacre of Aug. 15, he played a role in the surrender negotiations of the survivors. Early in 1817, Kinzie's account book indicates that Pierre had returned to Chicago. Under the Chicago Treaty of Aug. 29, 1821, as a son of Moi-qua [name of his Indian parent, as listed in the treaty document], he received a section of land on Elkhart River, and at the Treaty of Prairie du Chien of 1829, was awarded a section of land at the Pawpaw Grove; married Margaret Pachequetachai (also Pechequetaroai) on Jan. 1, 1827, John Kinzie, J.P., officiating; voted on July 24 and Aug. 2, 1830 (see elections); in 1832 served as official interpreter with the Indian Agency, and during the Black Hawk War served as private in Captain Boardman's Cook County company, then in the company of Potawatomi. In early 1833, by which time he and his wife had one child, was an early member of the Catholic congregation and his name, for a family of three, was on the petition by Catholic citizens

to Bishop Rosati of St. Louis asking that a priest be assigned to them; noted in 1857 as residing in Indian country. [226, 404, 714]

LeClerc, Peresh   also Peresh [correctly, Pieriche, a diminutive for Pierre], Peres La Clerc, the Stutterer, or Pierre Moran; a Potawatomi-Kickapoo who was employed by John Kinzie in 1812 and worked for him again in 1816; not identical with Pierre Le Clerc [La Claire]. Peresh was rumored by some to have used his influence to bring about a merciless attack on the evacuating garrison. [12, 74, 226]

Le Comte, Madam   also La Compt; see Saint Ange, Michel Pilet *dit*.

Lee, Charles   see Leigh, James.

Lee farm   see Leigh farm.

Lee House   see Leigh House.

Lee, James W.   in 1833 listed as owner of lot 7 in block 2, land that first belonged to Jonathan Bailey and then to James Kinzie; see map on page 44; on March 13, 1836, a notice appeared in the *Chicago Democrat* indicating that James W. Lee had died in Cleaveland, OH, and that his Cook County property was for sale, its value considered sufficient to cover his debts.

Lee, William   see See, William.

Leflenboys, Joseph   at the county seat (Chicago) was granted on June 6, 1831, a license to sell goods in Cook County [12]

Legg, Benjamin   a child by this name was enrolled as grade school student in the class taught by [see] John Watkins in December 1835. Names of corresponding parents were not recorded. [728]

Legg, Isaac   arrived with his family from Tennessee in 1833; ✦ real estate dealer, sixth ward, near Lill's brewery.

Legre, Felix   also LeGree; blacksmith, murder victim in 1835 on the road from Chicago to Ottawa, between Laughtons' ford and the house of Elijah Wentworth, not far from Buckhorn Tavern; notices of the murder appeared in the *Chicago Democrat* on July 8, and in the *Chicago American* on July

11; the convicted murderer was [see] Joseph E. Norris.

Le Griffon   see *Griffon*.

Leif Ericson   Viking discoverer of North America c.A.D. 1000; member of a prominent family of Norwegian origin; his father, Eric Thorvaldsson (Eric the Red) founded the earliest Scandinavian settlement in Greenland. In Leif's time, there already existed a dim awareness of lands in the North Atlantic ocean W of Greenland; on a journey in the year 999, Leif sailed from Norway to Greenland, missed its southern tip, and landed at "Vinland" [probably Newfoundland]; realizing his mistake, he promptly returned to Greenland, reaching it before the autumn of 1000; colonies that he and other Norse explorers subsequently founded in North America did not survive long; ▲ see Monuments.

Leigh farm   usually referred to as "Lee farm," "Lee's place" and later as "Hardscrabble;" the buildings were located on the W side of the south branch of the Chicago River [at 24th Street, Bridgeport], with cultivated land on both sides of the river, occupying about 20 acres; the farm belonged to James Leigh and his partner William Russell; Leigh had his main house on the lakeshore just S of Fort Dearborn. On the evening of April 6, 1812, when both Leigh anf Russell were not on the premises, a party of Winnebago killed two of Leigh's men (Liberty White and Jean B. Cardin) at the farm, while John Kelso and Leigh's son escaped. A later owner of Leigh's farm was John Craft, who outfitted it as a trading post for the Detroit merchant house, Conant & Mack; François LaFramboise, Sr., later purchased the property from Craft.

Leigh House   also Lee House; James Leigh's main residence, built in 1804 on the lakeshore, just S of the fort. Leigh's widow sold the house to J.B. Beaubien in 1812; when Beaubien bought the Dean House for his residence in 1817, he used the Leigh House for a barn; by 1832 it was roofless, and Capt. A. Walker, commander of the *Sheldon*

SCALE 1/8 INCH TO 1 FOOT.

THE "LEE FARM", OR "HARDSCRABBLE", 1839, AFTER DATA GIVEN BY ALEX. BEAUBIAN, SON OF COL. J.B. BEAUBIAN.   CHAS. A. DILG

[206]

Thompson, purchased the remnants as firewood for his steamship when he delivered soldiers for the Black Hawk War. See the following excerpt of a letter from the captain, published in the *Chicago Tribune* in 1861. [12]

The number of buildings at that time (1832), where your populous city now stands, were but five [Captain Walker appears to refer only to the part of town E of the forks; eds.], three of which were log tenements—one of them, without a roof, used as a stable. We remained four days after landing the troops, procuring fuel for the homeward voyage, &c. The only means of obtaining anything for fuel was to purchase the roofless log-building used as a stable. That, together with the rail fence enclosing a field of some three acres nearby, was sufficient to enable us to reach Mackinaw. Being drawn to the beach and prepared

for use, it was boated aboard by the crew, which operation occupied most of four days to accomplish.

Leigh, James   also, but erroneously, Mr. Lee, or Charles Lee, Sr.; Leigh pronounced his name as in "Lee," but the correct spelling and his correct first name are evident from an autograph letter [see below] he wrote on March 30, 1811, to Col. Jacob Kingsbury, preserved in the *Kingsbury Collection* of the Chicago Historical Society. Apparently John Kinzie, who was a flexible speller, initiated the mistake in his account books, listing him interchangeably as "Sargent Leigh" or "Sargent Lee," but once (1805) listed him with his full name "Sargent Jas. Leigh." For the wrong first name [Charles instead of James], N. Matson, in his 1882 book, *Pioneers of Illinois*, quotes as authority Leigh's surviving daughter Mary, but one must allow that she lost her father when she was 12 years old, became permanently separated from her mother at the same time, was nearly 86 when interviewed by Matson, and is not quoted verbatim; Captain Heald, in an official report on the killing of two white men at the Leigh farm on April 6, 1812, spells Leigh's name correctly. Leigh and his family came to Fort Dearborn with the first contingent of soldiers in 1803, his position was that of recruiting sergent; when his term expired about 1809, he remained and acquired a house on the lakeshore immediately SE of the fort near the mouth of the river; in addition, and together with William Russell, he owned a farm on the south branch [see Leigh Farm]. Leigh and his oldest son John [age 16] joined the Chicago militia in the summer of 1812; James and John, daughter Lilly [age 10], and two younger sons were killed in the Fort Dearborn massacre, while his wife Martha, daughter Mary, and infant Sally, born 1811, survived. The Indian chief Black Partridge fell in love with Leigh's widow during her captivity but she married the French trader Du Pin [see Des Pins], afterward living with him and Sally for four years in the abandoned Kinzie House. Mary was ransomed from Indian captivity in the spring of 1813 and later married a Frenchman named Besson [Bisson, Beeson?]; ➡ Lee Place (740 N). [12, 226, 404, 459, 649]

Letter from James Leigh to Col. Jacob Kingsbury:
Chicago, March 30th 1811
Sir. It is with a degree of deference I presume to address myself to you not being personally known when I was in the Army—to solicit you for an indulgence which you have it in your power to grant—On my retiring from the Army I got liberty from Captain Whistler to reside on the reserve and which I have made considerable improvements not far distant from the Garrison—I have got a large stock of cattle and find them to be troublesome in the fall of the year to the fences and to evade having any difficulty I got liberty from Lieutenant Ostrander to make a small improvement on the out lines of the reserve near the

Portage distant from the Garrison about 3 miles and which I find will be of great benefit to me to reside there in the fall and winter months. ❖ *I request from you—your liberty to improve about 20 acres. The timber which lies on this land is overgrown sugar tree [maple] and basswood which can not be of any benefit for repairing the garrison. I have cleared this winter about 10 acres and have built a small house thereon—If you will grant me the favour of my settlement I shall esteem it a great favour—it is not Sir with any idea to be independent of any garrison order which may be issued from time to time that I selicit—only to hold it comfortable thereto—I beg to refer you to Captain Whistler whom I expect will give you any further information relative thereto, he being acquainted with the situation of it. I rem. Sir your most ob. and very humble S't. James Leigh*

Le Mai, François also Le May, Lemay, May, L'May; best known as the French Canadian trader who, according to Mrs. J.H. Kinzie, sold John Kinzie his Chicago house, misinformation [see below] perpetuated by most historians until Quaife found and published the original sales contract in 1928; by some writers the first name is given as Pierre, which seems to be in error, since Father Garraghan found Francis Le May to be among "habitans a Chicagou" who took their children to St. Louis to be baptized in 1799; earlier, on Aug. 1, 1790, the name of a François L'May was on the roll of a company of the first Regiment of the County of St. Clair, and it is likely that this was the same person. Le Mai was a *métis* trader, with a Potawatomi wife, who owned one of the four houses already located on the N side of the river at the time the first Fort Dearborn was built in 1803. In historical accounts, Le Mai is frequently confused with Jean La Lime; Juliette Kinzie popularized the mistake in her book *Wau-Bun*, reporting that her father-in-law bought his house from Le Mai; but La Lime purchased the house from Point de Sable for William Burnett in 1800 and sold it to John Kinzie in 1803. Le Mai died in March 1828, apparently out-of-doors and

in the vicinity of the village; in 1828 James Kinzie claimed $22.18 against the estate of Francis May, including an item of March 19, 1828, "Amt. of expense incurred by hunting the corps [of Le May];" the estate sale took place on May 10; ➡ LeMai Avenue (5232 W). [12, 220]

Lemoine, François also Lamoyne, Lamoine, Lemoine *dit* Despins; see Des Pins, François.

Le Moyne family this family of an immigrant to New France became of extraordinary importance for the cause of France in North America. The father, Charles Le Moyne (1626-1685), born in Dieppe, Normandy, France, as the son of the inkeeper Pierre Le Moyne and Judith Duchesne, arrived in Canada in 1641, age 15; he settled in Montreal after first traveling extensively with the Jesuit fathers to their Great Lakes missions; played a vital role in the defence of the colony against the Iroquois; was made a chevalier in 1668; and by the time of his death had become the richest man in Canada. With his wife Catherine Thierry he had 12 sons and two daughters. Their eldest son, Charles Le Moyne, first baron de Longueuil (1656-1729), was sent by his father to France for education and military training. While there, he married Claude-Élisabeth Souart. In 1683, the young couple moved to New France, where Charles had a distinguished military career defending French settlements against Iroquois and English attacks; in 1700 he became the first Canadian-born baron; served as interim governor of New France from 1725-1726. His son, Charles Le Moyne, second baron de Longueuil (1687-1755), was also trained as a military man and served as interim governor in 1752. Pierre Le Moyne, seigneur d'Iberville et d'Ardillières (1661-1707) was Charles's and Catherine's third and most illustrious son; he established his reputation as a heroic soldier and sea captain in the defence of French trade interests in James Bay and Hudson Bay against English encroachment. In 1698, the French king determined to repeat La Salle's effort, unsuc-

Pierre LE MOYNE, seigneur d'IBERVILLE [483]

the New England coast and on Newfoundland and at Hudson Bay, demonstrating his courage and leadership. In 1698, he joined d'Iberville on his successful expedition to the mouth of the Mississippi River, where they established the Biloxi post. D'Iberville returned to France, leaving de Bienville in charge; his efforts flourished, and by 1706 de Bienville became the first governor of Louisiana, a position he held twice more in later years [see governors]. In 1718, he established a trading post between Lake Pontchartrain and the Mississippi River, which he called Nouvelle-Orléans [New Orleans]; returned to France in 1741, retiring from public life; died in Paris. [430a, 483, 665]

Leonard, Michael   U.S. Army private at Fort Dearborn; enlisted in April 1810; killed in action at the 1812 massacre. [226]

Leroi, Joseph   made small purchases at the W.H. Wallace estate sale of April 27, 1827.

Le Sellier, Pierre   also, but improperly, as Le Sallier, Lasalière, La Sallier, and La Salière; French trader at Milwaukee, the St. Joseph River, Muskegon, and Michillimackinac between 1804 and 1818, and a frequent customer at John Kinzie's trading post in Chicago during those years; later he lived in what is now Lee County on the Rock River, becoming its first white settler [memorialized in 1937 by the placement of a marker near the remnants of his cabin in Kingdom, c.7 miles NE of Dixon, IL]; during the War of 1812 he worked for the British cause, and was much in demand; in 1815, as officer of the British Indian Department for eastern Wisconsin, he gave the Indians news of the end of the war; in 1818, he worked as an employee of the American Fur Co. for about one year, and became acquainted with Gurdon Hubbard; acted as local guide for the expedition under Maj. Stephen Long, by whom he was engaged at Chicago in 1823; Keating, a member of the expedition, describes him as a "man, who had lived for upward of thirty years with the Indians, had taken a [second] wife among the Winnebagoes, and settled on the headwaters

cessful in 1685, to colonize at the mouth of the Mississippi, and he entrusted Pierre Le Moyne with the task. With his youngest brother Jean-Baptiste, Pierre sailed along the coast W of Florida and on March 2, 1699, their ship entered a channel of the Mississippi delta. A fortified trading post was built at Biloxi Bay [Ocean Springs], the beginning of the colony of Louisiana. Subsequent exploits brought him to various Caribbean islands, where cruel pillaging by his men left some of the local native settlements in ruins and damaged his reputation; died of a tropical fever early in 1707 in Havana, Cuba. Jean-Baptiste Le Moyne, seigneur de Bienville (1680-1767), was the last of the sons, and was raised under the influence of his older brothers after his father's death; he learned seamanship at an early age, and his brother d'Iberville included him among his crews; took part in the campaigns against the English in 1696 and 1697 along

of Rock river ...." Le Sellier's first wife was Thérèse Marcot, born in c.1776 as daughter of Jean Baptiste Marcot and an Ottawa woman, variably named Thimotée or Marie Nesketh. Le Sellier and Thérèse had a daughter, Marie Anne, who became the wife of Henry Monroe Fisher of Prairie du Chien, and the mother of [see] Elizabeth Thérèse Fisher. In 1817 Elizabeth and her mother visited the Kinzie family, and Elizabeth later wrote about the experience, describing the interior of the Kinzie house. Le Sellier's 1823 service as guide for Major Long is the last record of him. He was over 80 years of age at the time. His remains are likely to be found in one of the many graves near his Lee County cabin. [29, 109, 394, 404, 635a, 635b]

Letendre, Jean Baptiste   see La Tendre, Jean Baptiste.

Levadoux, Father Michel   Sulpician priest who in 1796 was appointed vicar-general of the Northwest Territory by Archbishop Carroll of Baltimore; took charge of the Detroit church and from there made multiple trips to Mackinac, sanctioning marriages and conducting baptisms; in the summer of 1796 he visited Cahokia and returned to Detroit via the Illinois River and Chicago; in a later report he wrote: "Then, continuing my journey [from Peoria, then a small village on the Illinois River where he had performed several marriages and baptisms], I reached the border of Lake Michigan, that is to say, a village called Chicago. I remained here only a day and a half. I was visited by a great Indian chieftain and a large number of his braves. I embarked on the Lake the 8th of July." Father Levadoux does not mention any of the French settlers living in Chicago at that time. He was recalled in 1801, afterward returning to France. [268]

Le Vasseur, Noel   (1799-1879) also Levasseur; born in St. Michel d'Yamaska, Canada, on Dec. 25 to poor parents; illiterate all his life; a contemporary and friend of [see] Gurdon S. Hubbard. At age 18 he became a *voyageur* working for Astor out of Michilimackinac, then interrupted employment

NOEL LE VASSEUR [345]

for one year to live with an Indian tribe near Prairie du Chien, learning the language. Early in 1820, he traveled to the Illinois River valley by way of the Chicago portage and established a trading post for the American Fur Co. on the Iroquois River at a place earlier called Bunkum, now Iroquois, IL. Hubbard soon followed and operated the post with Le Vasseur's assistance until 1827, when Hubbard left and Le Vasseur succeeded him. He married Watseka (Potawatomi), Hubbard's first wife, and with her had three children; he remained at the post until c.1835. In 1837, he married Ruth Bull of Danville (eight children), and in 1861, he married Elenor Franchere of Chicago; he is buried in Bourbonais, IL.

Lewis and Clark expedition   provided with detailed orders from President Thomas Jefferson and medical instructions from the preeminent physician Dr. Benjamin Rush, Capt. Meriwether Lewis and Lt. William Clark sailed with a party of 34 from St. Louis up the Missouri River in May of 1804 on their historic mission to explore the unknown West and its native people; they followed the muddy river to its source, crossed the conti-

nental divide, and traveled down the Columbia River to its mouth on the Pacific Ocean; when they returned to St. Louis in September 1806 with good maps and a wealth of carefully recorded information, they had done much to dispell ignorance and open the West to settlement; during the following decades, many enthusiastic pioneers and settlers would pass through Chicago. [719]

Lewis, John   a child by this name was enrolled as grade school student in the class taught by [see] John Watkins in December 1835. Names of corresponding parents were not recorded. [728]

Lewis, Capt. Meriwether   (1774-1809) Virginia born; together with Lt. William Clark, led the famous [see] Lewis and Clark expedition through the unknown Northwest of the continent in 1804-1806; in 1808 Lewis was appointed governor of Louisiana by President Jefferson but died the following year. [719]

Lewis, P.J.   subscribed to the *Chicago Democrat* in November 1833.

Lewis, Samuel   first announced in the *Chicago Democrat* on June 22, 1835, and repeated a month later in the *Chicago American*: "… that when a sufficient number of scholars offer themselves, he intends commencing a VOCAL and instrumental music school; at his room on S. Water will attend to repairs and tuning of Piano Fortes and other instruments"; an ad on Aug. 19 announced he has "begun teaching the science of Music" in A. Garrett's Auction Room; by Nov. 9 had removed to the third story of the four-story building on Lake Street, over the store of Messrs. Breese & Shepard; in 1836 married Eleanor Watts, Reverend Hallam officiating. [544]

libraries   for Chicago's earliest public libraries and book collections, see Jamison, Lt. Louis T.; Meeker, Joseph; Chicago Lyceum. Of private libraries there were few before 1836, but Dr. Elijah Harmon was known for his unusually large collection of medical texts.

license, Indian trade   see La Salle, for letters patent

from the king to trade in buffalo skins; see *engagé*, *coureurs de bois*.

Liette, Pierre, sieur de   (c.1665-1729) wrote his name Delliette; the name De Gannes, sometimes attributed to him as his pen name, is actually the name of an as yet unidentified copyist; was a younger first cousin of Tonti (son of Tonti's mother's brother) and joined him at Fort St. Louis in 1687; divided his time from 1691 to 1705 between the Miami at Chicago and the Illinois at Fort St. Louis II, Peoria, which he had helped build. In Chicago he ran a trading post in partnership with François Daupin de La Forêt, Michel Accault, and Henri de Tonti [located probably near today's Tribune Tower] which he had to close, leaving in 1705 after the king revoked his trading license; continued as French commander and trader in the Illinois country until 1720. From de Liette's memoirs: "Most beautiful, you begin to see its fertility at Chicago, unwooded prairies, requiring only to be turned up by the plow, most temperate climate." [12, 101, 190, 241, 259, 649]

lighthouse   on March 3, 1831, the U.S. Congress approved an appropriation of $5,000 to build the first lighthouse on Lake Michigan; the lighthouse was built that year on the south bank of the Chicago River, at the location where the first U.S. factory building had stood from 1805 to 1812, just W of where Rush Street bridge later met the river bank; it was built by Samuel Jackson [or Samuel Johnson, according to {see} Stephen Downer]; it was 50-feet-tall with walls 3-feet-thick, but collapsed on Oct. 30; a sturdier one was erected in 1832 at the same location. It was 40 feet tall, with a stationary light from four oil lamps and with a 14-inch reflector, no lenses, visible from five to seven miles. There was a bell fog signal. A prominent landmark, the structure remained until 1857; Samuel C. Lasby was the first keeper of the light, at a salary of $350 per year, and Jean Baptiste Beaubien was the last lighthouse keeper. The following letter of Oct. 31, 1831, from Isaac D. Harmon describes the collapse of the first lighthouse: [12, 289]

Dear Brother: We have had a flattener pass over the face of our prospects in Chicago. The light-house, that the day before yesterday stood in all its glory, the pride of this wondrous village, is now "doused." For about a week past, cracks have been observed in it, and yesterday they began to look "squally." Mr. Jackson (the man who contracted to erect the building), ordered some of the stones, which looked likely to fall, to be taken out. Yet he and his men assured people there was no danger of its falling. Jackson said, "You can't get it down," but there were others who were not so sure. My father [Dr. Elijah D. Harmon], in the afternoon, told them it leaned to one side. They laughed at him, and so confident were some of its standing, that, but a few hours before it fell, they went upon the top of it; and amongst the rest, some women. Stones kept dropping from the hole in it; and, about nine o'clock in the evening, down tumbled the whole work with a terrible crash and a noise like the rattling of fifty claps of thunder. The walls were three feet thick, and it had been raised fifty feet in hight; so you must know it made some stir when it fell. The first thing father said to the workmen when he went out was: "Does it lean any now." They were 'horn of their locks,' and had nothing to say. Various reasons were assigned as the cause of its falling. Jackson wants to make it appear that it was owing to the quicksand under the building, which made it settle, and said that a lighthouse can not be made to stand here. It would be greatly for his interest to have this story believed; as, by this means he would probably get pay for what he has done; otherwise, he will not. People here, and those that are well qualified to judge, say there is no such thing as quicksand about it, and that it was all owing to the wretched manner in which it was built. I am inclined to believe them. Judging from the piece of wall now standing, the mortar looks like dry sand, and the wall is two-thirds filled up between with stones not bigger than a man's head. Finis. Yours affectionate, Isaac D. Harmon.

Lill, William (1808-1875) an English brewer; arrived on foot in 1835 from Louisville, Kentucky; initially worked for William B. Ogden grading streets; worked with and for the brewery begun by Wilhelm Haas and Konrad Sulzer, soon after partnered by Haas and William B. Ogden; ✦ corner of Chicago Avenue and Pine [Michigan] Street; in 1843 he teamed with Michael Diversey to purchase the brewery; ➡ Lill Avenue (2534 N). [12, 17, 342]

Lincoln Avenue ➡ known earlier as [see] Little Fort Road, leading toward Waukegan, where an early but fictitious French trading fort was believed to have been. It was actually at Milwaukee.

Lincoln, O.S. roller boy for John Wentworth at the *Chicago Democrat* in 1836, and ★★★ **Chicago's 1st** newspaper carrier. [12]

Lincoln's Coffee-House as reported by [see] J.D. Bonnell, a popular drinking establishment near a corner of Wells Street, N of the river, in the winter of 1835-36. [The editors could not establish the identity of the owner, who frequently ran down wolves when sighted on the prairie, on his fast gray horse.]

Lincoln & Reader see next entry.

Lincoln, Solomon arrived from New York in 1833; subscribed to the *Chicago Democrat* in November 1833, and in December advertised the opening of a tailor shop on the S side of Lake Street, near LaSalle; referred to as the "prairie tailor" as the location at that time was considered out on the prairie; on Sept. 28, 1834, his wife Ester (née Cobb), also from New York, died at age 27 from bilious fever; in the Oct. 7, 1835, *Chicago Democrat*, Lincoln advertised with a partner—Lincoln & Reader: "Four or five Journeymen Tailors will find steady employment, by applying to the subscribers immediately"; became a fire warden in December; ✦ tailor and clothier, 156 Lake St. [Reader's identity is not known; *eds.*] [12]

Linctot, Daniel Maurice Godfroy de born c.1730, probably at Detroit; his father had been a respected officer in the French army in Canada, his mother

also French; Cahokia trader who became an Indian agent for the Americans and a major under George Rogers Clark during the Revolutionary War, when military maneuvers brought him to Chicago, probably more than once; contemporary of Jean Baptiste Point de Sable, and acquainted with him; prepared a manuscript ✱ map of the Great Lakes. [69, 559]

Lindsley, A.B. also Lindsay; government agent sent to Fort Dearborn in 1822 to close out the factory under Jacob Varnum and sell its holdings; for the goods in stock, valued at nearly $16,000, Lindsley realized only $1,250; also see United States Factory System. [559]

Lisle, IL village SW of Chicago along what is now Ogden Avenue. Settlement began in 1832 with the brothers James C. and Luther Hatch; by 1834 the settlement had its own post office under Postmaster John Thompson, who conducted business from his home. In 1840, Mark Beaubien bought farmland from William Sweet and a cabin, living there and also opening a tavern within; the building still exists and the Beaubien family cemetery is nearby.

Little Fort historically unsubstantiated French fort at [Waukegan]; was actually at Milwaukee as noted in a 1779 ship's log and other 18th century documents; the name was changed to Waukegan in 1847, "wakiegan" allegedly meaning house or fort in Algonkian, particularly a white man's dwelling. In Father Gravier's c.1696 dictionary, "wakagamiwi" means a bay, which is present at Waukegan. The Algonkian word "waku" means bent or crooked. Lincoln Avenue leading toward Waukegan, was formerly called Little Fort Road. Also see *Petit Fort*. [John F. Swenson]

Littleton, Samuel voted on July 24, 1830 [see Chronology].

Little Turtle (c.1747-1812) Michikiniqua, also Mechecunnaqua; Miami Indian chief and renowned orator, born near Fort Wayne, IN; in 1782 abducted and raised 12 year old William Wells, who later became his son-in-law; devised the strat-

LITTLE TURTLE [357]

egy that led to the defeat of General Harmar in 1790, when Indians resisted the infiltration of the Northwest by settlers; the Indian victory was short-lived and, within five years, Gen. Anthony Wayne defeated the Indians and forced the signing of the 1795 Treaty of Greenville. During the negotiations Little Turtle denied the existence of a former "fort" at Chicago, as recited in the treaty; he said, "we have never heard of it," the authoritative refutation of a persistent myth. Little Turtle always abided by this treaty, and did not join forces with Tecumseh in the War of 1812; died on July 14. [12]

Little Woods   local term for the forested area on the E side of south branch of the Chicago River.

Livingston, John R.   arrived from New York in 1835; in October signed up with the "Pioneer" hook and ladder company, an early volunteer fire brigade; ✦ real estate agent, boarded at Lake House.

livre   former French monetary unit and a silver coin, later replaced by the franc. Point de Sable sold his Chicago house and associated property in 1800 for 6,000 livres, then the equivalent of $1,200.

lizard mound   of Chicago; see Hopewell Indians.

Llewellyn   also *El-Llewellyn*; a schooner mastered by Captain Howe in June 1834 when [see] William Payne contracted to transport men and sawmill equipment to [see] Shipwagen; newly introduced in late May 1835 as *Llewellyn* and plied as a packet boat between David Carver's pier at Chicago and Calvin Britain's pier at St. Joseph throughout the season until October, carrying passengers and merchandise; piloted by Captain Clark beginning June 23, then Captain Howe beginning July 25, the vessel called 17 times that year.

Lobbeke, Friedrich   German immigrant, first attested to as having lived in Chicago in 1832. [342]

Locker, Frederick   U.S. Army private at Fort Dearborn; enlisted April 1810; killed in action at the massacre of 1812. [226]

Lockwood, Samuel Drake   (1789-1874) served as Illinois Supreme Court justice from 1825-1848; ➡ Lockwood Avenue (5300 W). [12]

Logan, Hugh   U.S. Army private of Irish extraction at Fort Dearborn under Captain Heald; enlisted in May 1806; taken prisoner by Indians at the massacre of Aug. 15, 1812, and killed later in the day. [226]

Logan, James   a British agent, sent into the Illinois country in 1718 by Sir William Keith, royal governor of Pennsylvania, to survey French routes in the West, knowledge of which might later prove useful to the British; he reported only ruins of a fort at Chicago. [12, 441]

Logan, Stephen T.   judge of the October 1835 term of the Circuit Court of Cook County, held at the Presbyterian church; presided over about 100 civil cases that were divided among 25 or 30 members of the bar.

log houses   prior to 1828, all cabins or houses constructed by early Chicago settlers were made out of locally cut and roughly hewn logs; this is true also for the first and the second Fort Dearborn, built in 1803 and 1816, respectively. Initially, the French method of construction predominated; it called for planting the logs used for the walls of the cabin vertically into the ground. These structures had a short life span, due to the easy access of soil moisture to the wood, with early onset of rot. Later houses were built with logs set on a stone foundation and arranged horizontally. The floors of log cabins and much of the furniture were made of [see] puncheons, as was the stockade of Fort Dearborn. Beginning in 1828, the construction of frame houses was introduced and soon became the dominant method of building construction. Also see entry on "balloon frame" construction, first used in Chicago in the early 1830s.

London, England   seat of jurisdictional control over Chicago and the Midwest from 1763 until 1796. For details, see Chicago jurisdictional chronology on page 209. [544]

Long, Lt. Edwin Ramsay   from North Carolina; Second Infantry; served as brevet second lieutenant at Fort Dearborn from June 17, 1832, to May 15, 1833, under Capt. William Whistler; died in 1846.

Long Knives   in Shawnee, Shemanese; in Potawatomi, Chemokemon; by these terms the Indians referred to the United States soldiers, especially the officers (referring to their swords) and the Virginians.

Long Portage Road   see Portage Trail.

Long, Maj. Stephen Harriman   (1784-1864) from

[157A]

TYPICAL EARLY FRENCH ILLINOIS LOG HOUSE

MAJ. STEPHEN HARRIMAN LONG

New Hampshire; graduate of Dartmouth College and professor of mathematics at West Point from 1815 to 1818; as major within the U.S. Corps of Topographical Engineers and acting engineer of fortifications, he was sent by Secretary of War William H. Crawford to explore the route of the proposed Illinois & Michigan Canal in September 1816; in the process, and traveling by way of Michigan City around the lower end of the lake, he visited the recently rebuilt Fort Dearborn, where Capt. H. Bradley was in command, and then made a manuscript ✳ map of the "Illenois River" [National Archives, Washington, D.C.] that in March 1817 accompanied a report submitted to George Graham, then acting secretary of war: "... a canal uniting the waters of the Illinois, with those of Lake Michigan, may be considered the first in importance of any in this quarter of the country, and, at the same time, the construction of it would be at-

tended with very little expense, compared with the magnificence of the object." On June 5, 1823, he revisited Fort Dearborn (then under the command of Lt. Col. John McNeil), this time with an expedition to explore the valleys of the Red and Minnesota Rivers and the border country between the former river and Lake Superior, described by the expedition's historian-geologist-mineralogist William H. Keating [see Bibliography]; also with him were Thomas Say as entomologist, Samuel Seymour as artist, and J. Edward Colhoun as topographer and astronomer; they stayed at the fort until June 11; ➡ Long Avenue (5400 W). [12, 394, 437, 681, 682]

Loomis, Horacio G.   born c.1814 in Burlington, VT; came on May 3, 1834; joined his cousins Charles and Issac Harmon in their store to form the "mercantile business Harmon, Loomis & Co.;" was a member of the fire engine company No.1 ("Fire Kings") in December 1835 [see petition to the village board of Dec. 16, 1835, with entry on firefighting]; ✦ (Harmon & Loomis), SW corner of Clark and South Water streets; in 1848 became a charter director of the Chicago Board of Trade, and in 1851 served on the board of the Chicago City Hydraulic Company; lived in Naperville in 1879, but by 1885 lived in New York; ➡ Loomis Street (1400 W). [12 351]

Loraine   sloop built at Black River, OH, in 1834; called at Chicago first under Captain Kimball on Aug. 25, 1834, then under Captain Johnson on Aug. 10, 1835.

Losier, Oliver   subscribed to the *Chicago Democrat* in November 1833; likely [see] Lozier, Oliver.

Louis XIV of France   (1638-1715) the Sun King; his long reign lasted from 1643 to 1715; from 1682 on he formally ruled Chicagoland from Versailles, as part of the French colony of New France, with Quebec as its capital. See picture on page 244.

Louisiana Province   the territory was claimed for France by [see] La Salle on April 9, 1682, when his

LOUIS XIV

expedition reached the mouth of the Mississippi River; in accordance with international custom of the time, the claim included the entire Mississippi basin and the draining systems of its tributary rivers and therefore included parts of what is now metropolitan Chicago. Louisiana became a colony in 1699 when [see] d'Iberville, sailing from France, arrived at the mouth of the Mississippi and built the first settlement called Fort Maurepas (Fort Biloxi) at present Ocean Springs, MS; in 1702, the small community was moved to Fort Louis on

Mobile Bay, and in 1706 d'Iberville's brother de Bienville became the first governor of the colony [see governors]. In 1713, the French government granted a 15-year lease for development and exploitation of the entire colony to a rich merchant, Antoine Crozat, whose expectations of large gold and copper mines and of lucrative trade with Mexico were, however, soon disappointed; in August 1717 he surrendered his lease to the Duc d'Orleans, French regent since the death of Louis XIV (1715). The following month an association called *La Companie d'Orient* (also *Banque Général*, *Companie des Indes*, Louisiana Company, Company of the West, and Company of the Colonies) was formed in Paris. John Law, a shrewd and unscrupulous adventurer from Scotland who had become a Paris banker and friend of the regent, controlled the company that obtained a charter to last for 25 years. Granted extensive privileges that included the printing of paper money (produced in huge amounts) and a monopoly of the tobacco trade, Law also imported the first black slaves to Louisiana and attracted European settlers, among them many Germans. For a short time, France was carried away by a wave of speculation in Mississippi stocks, but in 1720 the "Mississippi bubble" burst and Law, losing his hold on the company, fled to France; living in obscurity, he died at Venice (1729). In 1722, the regent placed control of the company in the hands of three commissioners, who continued to encourage agricultural development, and the seat of government was moved from Mobile to New Orleans the next year. In 1731, the company surrendered its charter and Louisiana became a royal province of France; in 1732, de Bienville again became governor with full powers. All along, the Chicago portage was the essential travel link between Louisiana and the older French colony of [see] New France, and the resident traders of the small Chicago village benefited from its strategic location. When France lost the French and Indian War in 1763, it was forced to cede all its posses-

sions in North America to England, except that the portion of Louisiana west of the Mississippi became Spanish. In 1800 Spain, by a treaty which was never published, ceded its holdings back to France, from which it was acquired by the United States through the Louisiana Purchase in 1803. For additional details, see Chicago jurisdictional chronology on page 209 and the Chronology section for the year 1699. [431, 438, 665]

Louvigny, Louis de la Porte de   (1662-1725) French officer under the command of Frontenac who first arrived in New France in 1683. He was sent to Mackinac with a relieving contingent of soldiers in 1690, and served there as commander of the fort, when Great Lakes Indians threatened to rebel against the French; in the following years Louvigny, together with his fellow officer Sieur d'Aillebout de Mantet, carried on the work begun by La Salle; their joint memoir was published by Margry [see Bibliography] and includes a 1697 ✳ map [Service historique de la Marine, Vincennes] of the Mississippi showing all forts for which La Salle had been responsible, as well as the fort at Chicagou built in 1693 by Mantet. [448, 559, 681, 682, 718]

Lovett, Joseph   (1789-1855) born in New London, CT; came in 1833 and filed a claim in Jefferson Township near John K. Clark; returned to Chicago with his wife Lydia (née Crouch) and family in 1835. [278]

Lowe, James M.   arrived from Massachusetts in 1834; ✦ clerk, circuit court clerk's office; served as city clerk in 1843; charter member of the Reformed Presbyterian Church in 1845. [12, 733]

Lowe, Samuel J.   arrived from England in 1834 with his wife and at least one child, Samuel J. Lowe, Jr.; ✦ high constable, deputy-sheriff [until 1842], 125 Clark St.; his first wife Roxana L. died in 1839, and on Dec. 30, 1841, he married Eliza J. Beattie; member of the board of the Mechanics' Institute in 1848; died in 1850. [12, 97]

Loy, Andrew   U.S. Army private at Fort Dearborn;

enlisted in July 1807; was killed in action at the Fort Dearborn massacre. [226]

Loyd, Alexander   (1805-1871) arrived from Ireland in 1833; subscribed to the *Chicago Democrat* in November 1833; originally a storekeeper, but by 1837 was counted among the principal contractors and builders of Chicago; ✦ Wells Street; served as mayor (Democrat) in 1840. [12]

Lozier, Oliver   arrived in 1833 from New York; as per notice in the *Chicago American* of Aug. 15, 1835, he filed for divorce from his first wife Olive, who did not appear in court on Oct. 12; on March 18, 1836, advertised a rifleshop "nearly opposite New York House;" on June 1, 1837, married Mary Ann Topley; ✦ painter and glazier, corner of Canal and Jackson streets

Lozon, Clemon and Morice   *engagés* from Detroit; worked for William H. Wallace at Hardscrabble beginning in the summer of 1826 and continuing until his death in April 1827; Morice's contract included "trade and traffic with the Indians." [220]

Lucanus elaphus Fabr.   giant stag beetle, the largest of the North American staghorn beetles, the males growing up to 6 cm (2 3/8 inches) in length; once common in northern Illinois; needs decaying oak trunks for the larvae to mature; lacking such, it disappeared from the Chicago region during the first half of the 20th century.

Lucas, Fielding, Jr.   son of a publisher; bookseller in Baltimore who published in 1823 the *General Atlas Containing District Maps of all the Known Countries in the World* which included, five years after statehood, an Illinois county ✳ map. Chicago then existed at the eastern end of the long panhandle of Pike County; N of the settlement the land, undivided, still belonged to the Indians.

Lucier, Charles   made small purchases at the estate sale of W.H. Wallace on April 27, 1827; his wife was Isabelle (née Plante); on Oct. 28, 1830, his daughter Marie Isabelle was baptized in Chicago.

Lucinda   schooner transporting lumber, merchandise, and passengers between Chicago and St. Joseph in 1834 under Capt. Robert Hugunin; its first Chicago call, from Oswego, NY, was on June 18; eight more calls followed that year, and after the last one on Aug. 17 the ship departed for French Creek, NY. [Captain Hugunin returned to Chicago with the *Jefferson* on Nov. 19, 1834.]

Ludby, John   arrived from England in 1834 and, together with William Bennet, acquired the SE quarter of Section 32 in Township 40 N, prior to 1836, as per Andreas, *History of Chicago*, pp. 112-113; in addition, on his own acquired 80 acres in Section 32 of Township 39. In the Sept. 30, 1835, *Chicago Democrat* advertised a Soap & Candle Manufactory on Lake Street, "a few doors above the New York House"; on hand he kept "Sperm and Dip'd. Candles of the first quality. Also, Hard and Soft Soap, Neats Foot Oil, which he will sell for cash, or exchange for Ashes, Grease or Fat, on the most reasonable terms"; in late November 1835, he submitted a deposition in support of his claim for wharfing privileges, while William Ludby, J.H. Collins, William Saltonstile and Thomas Stannig all filed affidavits in favor of his claim. [12, 28]

Ludby, William   see previous entry.

Lumbard, Hiram   subscribed to the *Chicago Democrat* in November 1833.

lumber mills   probably first in the area was the Andrew steam sawmill, built in 1830 on the Detroit-Chicago Road E of La Porte, IN; sometime in 1831 James Walker opened a sawmill at Walker's Grove and throughout 1832, lumber was occasionally hauled to Chicago by oxen team; also in 1831 the steammill built by the Chicago firm Bickerdyke & Noble on the east bank of the Des Plaines River [just N of Lake Street bridge, becoming the nucleus for the development of Oak Park and River Forest communities] met the growing demand for building materials and would furnish the lumber for the Chicago River piers when harbor construction began in 1833, with Indians among the workers; in 1832 the Vail mill opened on Trail Creek

near Michigan City. Charles Cleaver reports that there was in 1833-34 a small sawmill, run by water power, "about five or six miles up the North Branch, where they had built a dam across the stream, getting a three or four foot head of water; there was also a small steam sawmill, run by Captain Bemsley Huntoon, situated a little S of Division Street, at the mouth of a slough that emptied itself into the river at that point, in both of which they sawed such timber as grew in the woods adjoining, consisting of oak, elm, poplar, white ash, &c." All local mills combined could not satisfy the need for lumber during the Chicago boom period, and increasingly lumber had to be hauled on wagons from Indiana or by ship from Michigan. The first lumber merchant [see] David Carver plied his schooner in the summer of 1833 between St. Joseph and his lumberyard, located between LaSalle and Wells streets; by 1835 competition included Kinzie, Hunter & Co., and Jones, Clark & Co. [13]

Lupton, Benjamin   born in England in 1817; came to America in 1831 and to Chicago late in 1833, where he apprenticed himself to the blacksmith Mathias Mason; remained with him three years, returning to England to marry Mary Arrowsmith; returned with his bride and settled at Dutchman's Point [Niles], opened the first blacksmith shop in 1840 and worked there for over 20 years.

Lutra canadensis   see river otter.

Lyceum   see Chicago Lyceum.

Lynch, Michael   U.S. Army private at Fort Dearborn; enlisted in December 1805; wounded badly and taken prisoner by Indians at the massacre of Aug. 15, 1812; killed for inability to keep up the following day en route to the Illinois River. [12]

Lyon, Lucius   United States Surveyor from Detroit; surveyed the boundary line between unceded land and land ceded by the Potawatomi, Chippewa, and Ottawa tribes at the Treaty of Prairie du Chien, July 26, 1829; the survey ✳ map was made soon after ratification in 1830 under the direction of

Hon. J.H. Eaton, secretary of war. [681, 682]

Lyon, William P.   placed several ads in the *Chicago Democrat* and the *Chicago American* in July and August of 1835 to advertise his intended wholesale grocery that opened Sept. 1 on South Water Street near the drawbridge; his stock included a "large and well selected assortment of GROCERIES; comprising a general variety of Wines, Teas, Sugars, Coffee, &c."; on Sept. 12 he advertised "Boots & Shoes. A few pair of gentlemen's superior waterproof boots lined with India Rubber."

Lyons, IL   an early community on the Des Plaines River SW of Chicago, although not incorporated until 1888; already well known in 1834, when it was described in a gazetteer (according to Benedetti) as follows: "Lyons is a town site on the Des Plaines at Laughton's old trading house, twelve miles west of Chicago. It has a saw mill, three houses and a tavern." The Laughton brothers were the first to homestead here in 1827; they also built the tavern. They were attracted to the ford that accommodated the crossing of the Old Portage Trail; it soon became known as Laughton's ford. The saw mill was built by Stephen Forbes in the early 1830s and stood on the E side of Riverside Ford; it changed hands several times and burned down near the end of the century, when it was known as Dr. Fox's Mill. [12, 51]

Lytle, John and Sarah   also Little; John Kinzie's second set of parents-in-law, the parents of Margaret Lytle Forsyth and Eleanor Lytle Kinzie [see Kinzie family tree on page 222].

Mabury, James   U.S. Army private at Fort Dearborn; enlisted in April 1806; killed at the massacre of 1812. [226]

Ma-chu-etah   also Mah-che-o-tah-way; member of an 1835 exploring party under [see] Capt. William Gordon that left Chicago in June and returned in September in conjunction with the Indian removal effort.

Mack, Stephen, Jr. (1799-1850) born in Poultney, VT; early white settler in the Rock River valley c.1822, with a strong Chicago connection; son of Col. Stephen Mack, Sr., of Detroit, partner of the trading firm [see] Conant & Mack; lived at Bird's Grove and later at Rockton, worked as Indian trader for the American Fur Company and for his own account, shipping his merchandise through Chicago; married to Ho-no-ne-gah, a Winnebago who bore him 11 children; in 1823, 1824, and 1826, received from Dr. Wolcott licenses to trade with the Indians at the Rock River; voted in Chicago on May 11, 1828, and again on July 24 and Aug. 2, 1830 (see elections); on April 3, 1832, he purchased lots 7 and 8 in block 43 on E Water Road, next to and S of Joseph LaFramboise's lot [see map on page 44]; enlisted in the Black Hawk War, serving in Captain Brown's company, then was garrisoned and served in Capt. J.S.C. Hogan's company; at the 1833 Chicago Treaty his *métis* children Rosa and Mary were awarded monetary compensation. [12, 13]

Mackay, Lt. Aeneas arrived in Chicago by canoe on Aug. 28, 1820, as a member of Governor Cass' expedition to explore the upper Mississippi; stayed at John Kinzie's house, then continued to Detroit.

Mackinac see Michilimackinac.

Mackinac Island see Michilimackinac Island.

mackinaw Ojibwa word for turtle.

Mackinaw of or from Mackinac Island; common spelling for Mackinac [see Michilimackinac] from about 1812 on; if the spelling is Mackinac, pronunciation today is as though *Mackinaw*, rhyming with *paw*; ➡ Mackinaw Avenue (3332 E).

Mackinaw boat see *bateau*.

MacKinzie, John also Mackenzie, McKensie [Quaife]; father of John Kinzie; a surgeon of Scottish descent who served in the British army per appointment of Feb. 2, 1756, then lived in Quebec, and later in Detroit, where he had married in 1761, then died in 1763; his wife and mother of John Kinzie, was the widow Emily Haliburton (née

Tyne); their son John was born in Quebec in 1763 [see Kinzie family tree on page 222].

Mackraragah according to Eckert, a Winnebago chief who took part in the Fort Dearborn massacre and survived the action. [226]

Madison County, Illinois territory. Chicago was part of Madison County from 1812 to 1814, then became part of Edwards County; for details, see Chicago jurisdictional chronology on page 209. [436a, 544]

Madison, James (1751-1836) Virginia native; fourth United States president who served from 1809-1817; in 1814 asked Congress to authorize construction of a canal at the Chicago portage; Congress did not act on this recommendation until 1822. Under his administration, the second Fort Dearborn was built at Chicago in 1816; ➡ Madison Street (N-S baseline for Chicago's street numbering system since 1909).

Madison, William S., M.D. born in Kentucky; sixth Fort Dearborn military surgeon who had enlisted as a surgeon's mate at the beginning of the War of 1812, and resigned in 1815; rejoined the army in 1820 and came to Fort Dearborn with the rank of surgeon major, succeeding Dr. McMahon and being succeeded by Dr. M.H.T. Hall in 1821; was killed in action against hostile Chippewa in 1821 after leaving Fort Dearborn.

Mad Sturgeon see Nescotnemeg.

magazines see periodicals.

Magellan, Ferdinand (1480-1521) Portuguese explorer who initiated and led the first circumnavigation of the earth for the Spanish crown; the Strait of Magellan at the southern end of South America, which he discovered and through which he sailed, was named after him. He died on April 27, 1521, before the voyage was completed, and only one of his five ships, navigated by Juan Del Cano and with 18 of his men, returned to Spain. The voyage lasted from Sept. 20, 1520, until Sept. 7, 1522.

Magie, Haines H. dry goods merchant and co-owner of Magie & Wilkinson; was a member of

the fire engine company No.1 ("Fire Kings") in December 1835; ✦ H.H. Magie & Co., 130 Lake St. [12]

Magie & Wilkinson grocers, advertising a new store in the *Chicago Democrat* on June 11, 1835, on LaSalle Street, "a few doors south of Hubbard's brick store;" the partner was likely [see] Elias R. Wilkinson; among the dry goods itemized were "Blue and figured twill'd Jeans, Grodeswa Silks, plain and striped Sattinetts, Bobbinett Laces, Rowen Cassimeres and French Bombazines."

Magill, Arthur W. and Frances brother-in-law and sister of [see] Dr. Alexander Wolcott, Jr., and parents of William and Juliette Augusta (who married John H. Kinzie); each corresponded with him at Chicago before his death in 1830, with letters that are preserved at the Chicago Historical Society; ✦ Arthur W. Magill is listed with two others, likely sons—Alexander W., a clerk, and Julian, a clerk with Kinzie & Hunter.

Magill, William nephew of Dr. Alexander Wolcott, brother of [see] Juliette Augusta Magill Kinzie; as a boy in his teens, he spent some time at Fort Dearborn in the early 1820s as guest of his uncle. In a letter to William's mother, dated "Chicago Jany 10, 1823" Dr. Wolcott speaks of tutoring William in French and mathematics, and remarks that he is able to shoot to kill grouse on the wing; the exact duration of William's stay is not known.

mail carriers private contractors appointed by the United States government to transport mail between the widely-separated post offices; often unreliable. Their modest pay was frequently docked for poor performance. Postage stamps, invented in England in 1837, were not used in the United States until 1847. Among known mail carriers of this early period are Bemis (1823), John Kinzie Clark (1825), John H. Fonda (1825-1828), David McKee (1826), Elijah Wentworth, Jr., (1830), Jock Jombo (1834-35), Alexis Clermont (1832-1836); a *métis* mail carrier, whose name is not recorded, arrived on horseback from Green Bay in the winter of 1832-33 with his feet frozen, one of which required amputation by Dr. Harmon—★★★ **Chicago's 1st** major surgery. See entries of individual names for details; see entry on postal service for the mail system after March 1831; for a firsthand account on the work of a mail carrier see below for an excerpt from the 1888 narrative of Alexis Clermont. [147, John F. Swenson]

During the Black Hawk War (1832), I served on the home-defence company of volunteers, under Colonel Tyler, to protect Fort Howard. That disturbance over, I ran the mail on foot, from Green Bay to Chicago, the contractor being Pierre B. Grignon. I would start out from the post-office in Shantytown, taking the Indian trail to Manitowoc. Only twice would I see the lake between Green Bay and Milwaukee—at Sauk River, twenty-five miles north of Milwaukee, and at Two Rivers. From Milwaukee I went to Skunk Grove, then to Gros Point, where I struck the lake again, and then I would see no more of the lake until I reached Chicago. ✧ At Gros Point, Michael Quelmit [Michael Ouilmette, son of Antoine and Archange Ouilmette; eds.] had a little trading post. As for Indians, there were large villages of them at Manitowoc and Sheboygan, not many at Milwaukee, and I do not recollect that there were any villages between Milwaukee and Chicago. If I remember aright, there were at this time but ten houses in Chicago. John, James, and Robert Kinzie, I remember well; also the postmaster, John Logan. ✧ In making my trips I was not alone. An Oneida Indian always accompanied me. The load was limited to sixty pounds, and we usually had that weight. As a rule it took us a full month to make the round, From Greenbay to Chicago and return. We carried two shot-bags filled with parched corn; one of them hulled, the other ground. For the greater part of our diet we relied upon the Indians, or on what game we could kill; the bags of corn were merely to fall back upon, In case the Indians had moved away, as they were apt to, on hunting and fishing expeditions. At night, we camped out in the woods, wherever dark-ness overtook us, and slept in the blankets which we carried on our backs. In Chicago we merely stopped overnight, and promptly returned the way we came; we were delayed by a tardy mail from Detroit, which reached Chicago by steamer in summer, by foot, overland, in winter. ... Our pay was usually from $60 to $65 for a round trip such as I have described, although in the fall it sometimes reached $70. I made my last overland trip to Chicago in the summer of 1836.

According to John H. Fonda, the attire of a mail carrier in 1827 included the following:

A smoke-tanned buckskin hunting shirt, trimmed leggins of the same material, a wolf skin chapeau with the animal's tail still attached, and moccasins of elk hide. A heavy mountaineer's rifle with shortened barrel and with a shoulder strap. A powder horn hung from the shoulder. The waist belt held a sheath knife, a pair of pistols, a pouch of mink skin with rifle bullets and a short-handled ax.

Main Poc also Main Poche; Potawatomi chief who lived near the junction of the Kankakee and the Des Plaines Rivers early in the 19th century; inveterate enemy of the Americans; outspoken in his complaints about unequal justice, as applied by the white authorities; organized threatening demonstrations against Fort Dearborn in 1808 and was an active marauder during the years leading up to the Fort Dearborn massacre; fought with Tecumseh's forces near Malden in 1812. [12, 559]

malaria a common disease in Chicagoland and southern Illinois in pioneer days, wherever swamps, ponds, and wet bottom lands allowed mosquitoes to thrive; the illness was called ague, or bilious fever when liver function became impaired; medical historians believe that the disease came from Europe with early explorers around 1500; early travel accounts and letters from the Midwest abound with reports of the ague, such as those of Jerry Church and Roland Tinkham, the details of which are extracted below; also see entry for Sherman, Phinneus.

From the Journal of Jerry Church, when he had "A Touch of the Ague" in 1830:

... and the next place we came to of any importance, was the River Raisin, in the state of Michigan. There we met with a number of gentlemen from different parts of the world, speculators in land and town lots and cities, all made out on paper, and prices set at one and two hundred dollars per lot, right in the woods, and musquitoes and gallinippers thick enough to darken the sun. I recollect the first time I slept at the hotel, I told the landlord the next morning I could not stay in that room again, unless he could furnish a boy to fight the flies, for I was tired out myself; and not only that, but I had lost at least half a pint of blood. The landlord said that he would remove the musquitoes the next night with smoke. He did so, and after that I was not troubled so much with them. We stayed there a few days, but they held the property so high that we did not purchase any. The River Raisin is a small stream of water, something similar to what the Yankees would call a brook. I was very much disappointed in the appearance of the country when I arrived there, for I anticipated finding something great, and did not know but that I might on the River Raisin find the article growing on trees! But it was all a mistake, for it was rather a poor section of country. ✧ We then passed on to Chicago, and there I left my fair lady-traveler and her brother, and steered my course for Ottawa, in the county of Lasalle, Illinois. Arrived there, I put up at the widow Pembrook's, near the town, and intended to make her house my home for some time. I kept trading round in the neighborhood for some time, and at last was taken with a violent chill and fever, and had to take my bed at the widow's, send for a doctor, and commence taking medicine; but it all did not do me much good. I kept getting weaker every day, and after I had eat up all the doctor-stuff the old doctor had, pretty much, he told me that it was a very stubborn case, and he did not know as he could remove it, and thought it best to have counsel. So I sent for another doctor, and they both attended me for some time. I still kept getting

worse, and became so delirious as not to know anything for fifteen hours. I at last came to and felt relieved. After that I began to feel better, and concluded that I would not take any more medicine of any kind, and I told my landlady what I had resolved. She said that I would surely die if I did not follow the directions of the doctor. I told her that I could not help it; that all they would have to do was to bury me, for my mind was made up. In a few days I began to gain strength, and in a short time I got so that I could walk about. I then concluded that the quicker I could get out of those "diggins" the better it would be for me. So I told my landlady that my intention was to take my horse and wagon and try to get to St. Louis; for I did not think that I could live long in that country, and concluded I must go further south. I accordingly had my trunk re-packed, and made a move. I did not travel far in a day, but at last arrived at St. Louis, very feeble and weak, and did not care much how the world went at that time. However, I thought I had better try and live as long as there was any chance.

From a letter by Roland Tinkham, relative of Gurdon. S. Hubbard, describing his observations of malaria during a trip to Chicago in the summer of 1831:

... the fact cannot be controverted that on the streams and wet places the water and air are unwholesome, and the people are sickly. In the villages and thickly settled places, it is not so bad, but it is a fact that in the country which we traveled the last 200 miles, more than one half the people are sick; this I know for I have seen it. We called at almost every house, as they are not very near together, but still there is no doubt that this is an uncommonly sickly season. The sickness is not often fatal; ague and fever, chill and fever, as they term it, and in some cases bilious fever are the prevailing diseases.

Also see David, George, as he described the prevalence of ague in settlements on the road to Chicago in 1833 (diary entry of Sept. 24).

Malast, John Baptiste   voted on Aug. 7, 1826 [see Chronology].

Malford, James H.   was a member of the fire engine company No.1 in December 1835 [see petition to the village board of Dec. 16, 1835, with entry on firefighting]; likely [see] Mulford, James H.

Malzacher, Louis   German immigrant who arrived in 1833; on May 2, 1837, he voted in the second ward for the mayor; ✦ grocery and provision store, 181 Lake St. [12, 342]

Malzacher, M   German immigrant, attested to as having arrived and lived in Chicago in 1833; probably a brother of Louis Malzacher. [342]

Mammut americanum   see mastodon, American.

Manierre, Edward   born c.1812 in New London, CT; arrived Aug. 4, 1835; with his partner George Blair placed an advertisement in the Sept. 5 *Chicago American* for their tailoring establishment, Manierre & Blair, located in a store on Clark Street near Lake; half-brother of George; married Margaret Ann Spangler in 1839; ✦ Manierre & Blair (George), merchant tailors, 43 Clark St.; served as alderman in 1848; lived at 2352 Prairie Ave. in 1885. [12, 351]

Manierre, George   (1817-1863) halfbrother of Edward; arrived from CT in 1835; in 1836 became a deputy clerk of the circuit court and a law student; ✦ attorney and counselor at law, 105 Lake St.; married Ann Hamilton Reid of Scotland on Sept. 17, 1842; served as alderman in 1846; later circuit court judge; buried at Graceland Cemetery; his widow lived at 1928 Calumet Ave. in 1885. [12, 351]

Mann, Archange Sambly   (corrupted to Arkash Sambli); adopted *métis* daughter of Antoine Ouilmette; during the Fort Dearborn massacre she remained at home with her family, and all survived the encounter; in 1813 married a Tousaint Tremble in Cahokia but the alliance ended in divorce in 1830; she then married John Mann in Chicago on Aug. 3, 1830, Reverend See officiating, and lived with her husband at the mouth of the Calumet

GEORGE MANIERRE [12]

River until 1838, managing Reverend See's ferry; was a beneficiary under the Treaty of 1833 in Chicago; the comments of Mrs. Charles A. Taylor and Dr. Valentine A. Boyer, who visited the Manns in 1832 and 1833, follow respectively; for additional information, see Mann, John. [12, 226, 654]

Mrs Charles A. Taylor's comments:

We found our new host ... with a half-breed wife. Numerous children of all ages nearly filled this cabin. They were pushed aside for our comfort, as we were obliged to spend the night under their roof, which covered two rooms. One was used for a sleeping room, devided by a blanket. The woman shared my bed, with her infant. In spite of discomforts, we slept well. ◇ *As customary among the Indian traders, we found Mr. Mann living with an Indian Squaw, a female appearently of the higher order of her class, a nat and tidy matronly woman of sympathizing tendency who manifested the disposition to administer to the wel-*

fare of the female portion of our party.

Dr. Boyer's comment:

... As customary among the Indian Traders, we found Mr. Mann living with an Indian Squaw, a female apparently of the higher order of her class, a neat tidy matronly woman of a sympathizing tendency who manifested the disposition to administer to the welfare of the female portion of our party.

Mann, John   also Mann, Johann; of German origin; voted on July 24, Aug. 2, and Nov. 25, 1830; on Aug. 3, 1830, married Archange Sambli Ouilmette Tramblay; they became early members of the Catholic congregation—he signed for a family of five [Andreas erroneously notes four] on the 1833 petition to Bishop Rosati, asking that a priest be assigned to Chicago; in 1832 or 1833 tried to get into the Chicago lumber business and poled a raft of square building timber from the Calumet to the Chicago River, but found no takers, until Joseph Adams bought it, in friendship, and passed it on to Nelson Norton, who used it for the Dearborn Street bridge; in the Dec. 10, 1833, issue of the *Chicago Democrat* John gave notice that he had found a pocketbook; declared candidate for colonel of the Cook County militia but lost to J.B. Beaubien in the election of June 7, 1834. John and Arkash lived from 1830 to 1838 at the mouth (E side) of the Calumet River, where they kept a tavern and ran a ferry that was owned by Reverend See. John became a serious alcoholic and his wife would leave him in 1838 to return to her Potawatomi tribe; he then moved to Wisconsin. For a description of overnight stays at Mann's inn by three separate visitors in 1830 and 1833, see excerpt from Harriet Warren Dodson's journal under Warren, Daniel, and from those of Jerry Church and Colby C. Benton below. [12, 53, 141, 342, 654, 728]

Jerry Church's overnight in 1830:

It was fifty miles from the old Frenchman's [Joseph Bailly] house to the Calamink river, where the first white man lived in the road. He had a half-breed Indian wife, and kept the ferry across the Callamink

river at its mouth [John Mann and his wife Arkash]. We thought we could reach his house the first day, but our horse got weary of traveling in the sand, on the beach of the Michigan lake, and we were forced to stop. We unhitched our horse and turned him out to graze on the sand rushes and juniper berry bushes, and my friend and myself had to lay down to sleep in part of an old canoe that had floated ashore, and fight the musquitoes all night, without any thing for supper, or any thing else for comfort. Next morning we traveled on until ten o'clock before we came to the crossing place, both tired and hungry. I was as near gone as any man could well be and live. I went to the hut and asked the man if he could give us some breakfast. He said he could not, for he had nothing in the house for his own family. He said that he had sent to Chicago for provisions by a wagon, and it had not returned, and he could not give us anything for breakfast. I told him I must have something to eat before I went farther, if I had to kill a young papoose and roast him. I saw a gun standing in the corner of the hut and I loaded it and went out on the beach and shot a black bird, took it down to the water and picked off the feathers and dressed it in good order, and went back to the house and asked the woman if she would roast it for me. She said she would. She also said she had a little coffee, and would make me a cup of coffee. I told her that was very kind indeed, and requested her to make it as soon as possible, which she did, and gave us a few Indian Cranberrys, and we fared sumptuously. I asked the man what the bill was. He said not anything; and I gave the woman a dollar, and told her that I should always remember her while I lived for saving my life. We then crossed the river and had twelve miles to go to Chicago.

Another trip by Church later in the same year:

We had to camp out three nights, and in the course of our journey, stopped at the house where the Indian woman saved my life by roasting the blackbird, at the mouth of the Callamink river. The man said he knew me, and that he was better prepared now than he was at that time. He said he could now give me something

to eat, and not only that, but some good old whiskey to drink beside. I told him such news as that was always pleasant to me, and I hoped he would always be blessed with plenty of those good things. ...

En route from Michigan City to Chicago, Colbee C. Benton stopped for the night of Aug. 17, 1833, and reports as follows:

It has been a beautiful day—a cool, refreshing breeze from the lake has favored us, which we found quite comfortable; and it was well for us, for we could not find anything else to refresh ourselves or horses until we arrived to the mouth of the Calemic River [Calumet River], a distance of fifty miles. We found great quantities of sand cherries, but we never saw any before and did not dare to eat many. They resemble our black cherries, only a little larger, and grow on low bushes on the dry sand, and are very sweet indeed. ✧ About noon we saw an Indian but he run [sic] and hid from us, and after traveling about half way across the beach we passed an Indian camp. We stopped and borrowed a dipper to dip up some water. I proposed stopping to dine with them as they had just got their dinner ready, but my companion said I could if I would eat out of the same dish, a dish filled with corn and fish without even being scaled, all thrown in whole and jumbled up together into a real chowder. I finally concluded not to dine and we proceeded. We seemed to be traveling all the time in the same spot; we seemed to be following a point of land but did not seem to gain any. It was like going round a bay, there was all the time a point extending out. And finally it was no more nor less than a bay consisting of the south end of Lake Michigan. ✧ The lake was gently rolling and it looked powerful and magnificent. Its waters were clear and pure and cool and good to drink. The shore of the lake is sandy all the way round the south end of it, and in some places the sand hills and sandy plains extend back into the country for miles; and in some places there are extensive marshes bordering on the lake, seemed to be parted only by a little winnow of sand. It is more marshy near the mouth of the Calemic River, and we traveled along the shore of some small lakes, only had to cross a little sand bar. The whole country on the south shore of Lake Michigan is cold, marshy land or barren, sandy land for some miles from the lake. We found some coal on the shore, which was an evidence that there is a bed of it somewhere in the vicinity. ❖ *We arrived at Mann's log house at the mouth of the Calemic about five o'clock p.m., very hungry and very much fatigued after having rode fifty miles without any to eat; and our horses, too, were weary and hungry, but we could not get anything but marsh hay. Yet we were determined to remain till next day. Mr. Mann, the proprietor of this splendid establishment, married a squaw and we had a squaw supper. Quite a decent cup of coffee, tho'. After supper I borrowed a gun and went up the river after game. I saw a great many ducks but they were flying at a distance. I saw some in the river but the marsh about the river was so wide and the grass so high that I could not get a shot at them.* ❖ *In the evening Mr. Mann returned from Chicago with some oats and we succeeded in getting a few for our horses—but a few, however, for there were some more travelers arrived in the evening and we were obliged to divide. Some of the travelers had been to Chicago and some had been down into the state of Illinois. After each one told his most marvelous stories we retired to a log hut recently erected for a lodging room. There were three things called beds, which were occupied by six of us, and two were obliged to sleep on the floor.*

Manning, Joel arrived from Massachusetts in 1835; served as election judge in 1837; ❖ secretary to canal commissioners. [733]

Manning, John served as corporal in Captain Boardman's voluntary county militia late May 1832 into June and as second sergeant under Captain Napier in July 1832 during the Black Hawk War. [12, 714]

Mansion House hotel built in 1831 by Dexter Graves on the N side of Lake Street near Dearborn, almost opposite the Tremont House. Graves sold out to Edward Haddock [his later son-in-law] in 1834, who sold the hotel to Abram A. Markle

in 1835; in an ad in the *Chicago American*, Aug. 7, 1835 [see Austin, William G., M.D.], it is referred to as [see] Cook's Coffee House; the hotel was later moved at least twice, and was destroyed by the fire of 1871. [12]

Mantet, Nicolas d'Aillebout, sieur de French officer under the command of Frontenac who was sent to and stationed near Chicago with a relieving party during the period from 1693 to 1696 [or 1701-1705, according to documents cited by Faye] when Great Lakes Indians in the St. Joseph region threatened to rebel against the French; a fort was constructed, probably at the mouth of the Chicago River; in the following years Mantet, with his fellow officer Louis de la Porte de Louvigny, proposed to carry on the work begun by La Salle; their joint memoir was published by Margry [see Bibliography]. Mantet assisted Louvigny in the preparation of the 1697 Louvigny ✳ map, which calls the Calumet River, *R. de Chicagou*. [718]

maple sugar produced in large quantities by midwestern Indians, especially within the forests along the eastern shore of Lake Michigan. E.O. Gale, in his *Reminiscenses of Early Chicago*, writes: "For I remember how as a boy [1835] I prized the granulated maple sugar we were want to purchase from the squaws. It was put up in small birch bark boxes ornamented with colored grasses, and in large baskets made of the same material holding some 25 pounds. After the departure of the larger tribes, we were occasionally enabled to purchase it from straggling bands coming from the north or Michigan." Also see: Henri Joutel, for an excerpt from his journal with a description of maple sugar encountered in 1688 at Chicago.

Marco Polo traveled to China in 1270 via the traditional overland route, going east from Europe; when he returned 25 years later, he wrote a bestseller about his experiences, a book that played a major role in making this fabled land of the Orient that he called Cathay, a place to dream of and reach; the dream had remained alive for 200 years when

Columbus, in 1492, set out to find a more direct way to China; he found America instead.

Marengo 104-ton schooner, built in 1831; arrived from Detroit in October 1831 with goods for Newberry & Dole and with many immigrants; in 1834 the vessel made five calls at Chicago, two more in 1835, all under Captain Dingley, covering the route to Buffalo; sank on Lake Erie in 1856. [48]

Marest, Père Gabriel (1662-1714) born at Laval, France; Jesuit missionary serving at the *Mission de la Conception* in southern Illinois in 1693 and later, working with Frs. Gravier, Bineteau and Pinet; in his letter of Nov. 9, 1712, to his superiors, he was the first to use the expression "Lake Michigan," explaining that Lake Illinois was inappropriate because the Illinois did not live nearby; his brother Father Joseph J. Marest also served as a missionary in the Midwest at approximately the same time and was stationed at Michilimackinac in 1711.

Mariah Antonette schooner afloat on Lake Erie in 1827; under Captain Scoville, made three calls at Chicago from Buffalo, NY in the summer of 1834, beginning June 30; brought merchandise to Hubbard & Co.

Markle, Abram A. arrived in 1835; served in the first engine company of the voluntary fire department the same year; managed the Mansion House hotel on the N side of Lake Street, near Dearborn, in 1835, and in 1836, managed or owned the Exchange Coffee House at the NW corner of Lake and Wells streets; ❖ late Illinois Exchange, 192 Lake St. [12]

Markoe, Hartman a vice president of the Young Men's Temperance Society, organized on Dec. 19, 1835; ❖ dry goods merchant, Lake Street

Marquette, Père Jacques, S.J. (1637-1675) born in Laon, France; became a Jesuit priest and was assigned, at his request, to New France to do missionary work, arriving at Quebec on Sept. 20, 1666; learned six Indian languages, including Illinois; in 1668 founded the *Mission de Sault Ste. Marie*; in 1669 took over *Mission du Saint-Esprit* that Father

PÉRE JACQUES MARQUETTE, S.J. [577]

Allouez had founded at Chequamegon Bay in 1665; from there in 1669 he wrote a letter to his superiors at Quebec in which he first expressed a deep interest in exploring the lands that lay further W [see an excerpt from his letter below]; in 1671 he founded the *Mission de St. Ignace*; appointed by his superior Father Claude Dablon to accompany Louis Jolliet, the two began their voyage at St. Ignace on May 17, 1673, and traveled the Mississippi River; with them were five *voyageurs* (the names of four are believed to be Jacques Largilliers, Pierre Moreau, Jean Plattier, and Jean Thiberge); on their return trip, the party passed through the Chicago portage and thus became the first Europeans documented to have visited the site that was later to become Chicago. On Oct. 25, 1674, Marquette headed S again, this time only in the company of Pierre Portenet and Jacques Largilier; surprised by early cold weather, they spent the 1674/75 winter in a makeshift structure, probably a lean-to on high ground on the south branch of the Chicago River; after a brief Easter visit to the Kaskaskia village, they returned by way of

Hickory Creek to the Calumet River and Lake Michigan. Marquette is credited with founding the *Mission de la Conception* at Kaskaskia [Utica, IL] on the Illinois River in April 1675; on his way back to St. Ignace, Marquette died on May 16 of amebiasis near [now] Ludington, MI, on the E coast of Lake Michigan; ➡ Marquette Avenue (2700 E); Marquette Drive, (6600 S); Marquette Road (6700 S and 6600 S); Marquette Park, at Marquette Road and Kedzie Avenue; ▲ see section Guide to Monuments for details.   [12, 49, 161, 195, 197, 208, 282, 298, 307, 581, 585, 611, 629, 633, 634, 663, 681, 682, 718]

Excerpt from a 1669 letter by Father Marquette, as edited and reprinted in the *Jesuit Relations*: "When the Illinois come to trade at the Point they pass a great river which is almost a league in width. It flows from north to south and to so great a distance that the Illinois, who know nothing of the use of the canoe, have never as yet heard of its mouth, &c. It is hardly probable that this great river discharges itself into the Atlantic in Virginia; we are more inclined to believe that it has its mouth in the gulf of California, &c...." Marquette then expressed the hope for an opportunity to "visit the nations who dwell along its shores, in order to open the way to many of our Fathers, who for a long time have awaited this happiness. This discovery will give us a perfect knowledge of the sea either to the south or to the west."

Marquette's map   the "holograph" [handwritten or hand-drawn] ✶ map and report prepared by Father Marquette during the 1673 voyage with Jolliet, both unknown until rediscovered in 1844 by a local Quebec public official [see Viger, Jacques], are kept in the Archives de la Compagnie de Jésus, St. Jérôme, Quebec.

Marquette's prayer book   a small manuscript book of praying and catechism, prepared for him by Father Claude Allouez, entitled *Praeces Ilinicae* [Illinois Prayers], which he carried on his journeys to Illinois; preserved at Quebec, facsimile published there in 1908. [649]

MARQUETTE / LAON MARKER
For description, see Monument Section, page 410

marriage   ★★★ Chicago's 1st; in 1804 Sarah Whistler, eldest daughter of Capt. John Whistler, married James Abbott, a Detroit merchant; the marriage took place at Fort Dearborn and was officiated by John Kinzie, who then was a justice of the peace of the Indiana Territory.

Marsh, Sylvester   (1803-1884) born in New Hampshire; arrived in 1833; initially worked for Gurdon Hubbard as a meat packer; in 1834, temporarily in partnership with Edward Simmons (dissolved as per notice in the *Chicago Democrat* of Aug. 6, 1834), he built his own packing house on Kinzie Street, near Rush, and opened a butcher shop on Dearborn between Lake and South Water streets; ◆ Marsh & Dole (George W.), butchers, Dearborn Street; served in the Chicago militia as second lieutenant during 1840-41; in 1855 moved to Concord, NH; died on Dec. 30, 1884. [12, 13]

Marshal Ney lake schooner owned by Oliver New-berry, called on Chicago in August 1830 and October 1832.

Marshall, Humphrey from Kentucky; second lieutenant under General Scott, assisted with the deposition of the remains of soldiers during the cholera epidemic of 1832 [see cemeteries]; died in 1872, having attained the rank of brigadier general.

Marshall, James Augustus, M.D. born in England in 1809; physician and lecturer from New York who visited Chicago on April 20, 1832, remaining only a few hours to explore the potential of opening a practice; in his words, "This might be a place of some importance, but the ground is too low"; he was irritated by the croaking of innumerable bull frogs, later writing: "I found the place too small for me to hope to make anything of my profession, the garrison being supplied with one of the best in the country, in the person of Dr. Phillip Maxwell, so we shipped at once for Navarino, Green Bay, Wis." However, on Aug. 5, 1834, Dr. Marshall returned to Chicago, arriving on the

---

DANCING.

JAS. A. MARSHALL has the honor of announcing to the Ladies and Gentlemen of Chicago and vicinity, that his First Quarters Tuition in the above polite accomplishment, will commence on Friday the 21st inst. at Messrs. Johnson & Stevens' Assembly Room, (New-York House) one door north of the Exchange Coffee House. Those wishing to become pupils will please leave their address at the Exchange Coffee House, where they will be duly honored.

Hours of Tuition for Misses and young Masters. from 2 until 5 o'clock, P. M.; and from 6 until 9 for the elder class of Gentlemen.

Nov. 19, 1834.—3w51.

J. A. M. respectfully requests the company of his patrons, and those who wish to patronize his School to attend on Friday evening, where they can enjoy themselves in a few sets of Quadrilles. Tickets may be had of J. A. Marshall for one dollar each.

---

schooner *Nancy Dousman*; on Nov. 19, 1834, he announced in the *Chicago Democrat* the opening of a dancing school at the New York House; E.O. Gale, in *Reminiscences of Early Chicago*, refers to him as "Little Jimmy Marshall," confirming that he was a physician by training, but worked here as a dancing master and as an auctioneer of canal lots with John Bates; on Sept. 3, 1836, married Andalusia Shattucks, who died in 1837; in 1838 married Rosanna M. Shattucks; ◆ auctioneer, commission, &c., South Water Street; lived at 2906 Indiana Ave. in 1885. [12, 265, 351, 544] **AD**

Marshall, John subscribed to the *Chicago Democrat* in November 1833; built a tavern with [see] Benjamin Hall at Dutchman's Point in 1840. [13]

Martin, George arrived in1833 and moved on to [now] Naperville, where he built the first frame house. [314a]

Martin, Laurent voted in Chicago on Aug. 2, 1830 (see elections).

Martineau, Harriet (c.1799-1876) English author and traveler to Chicago in 1836, who left a vivid account of her visit, contributing a valuable perspective; her description of the prairie between the town and the Des Plaines River follows; see Bibliography. [12, 453, 454]

[comparing the prairie with the Salisbury Plain of her native England] *A single house in the middle of the Salisbury Plain would be desolate. A single house on a prairie has clumps of trees near it, rich fields about it; and flowers, strawberries, and running water at hand. But when I saw a settler's child tripping out of home-bounds, I had a feeling that it would never get back again. It looked like putting out into Lake Michigan in a canoe. The soil round the dwellings is very rich. It makes no dust, it is so entirely vegetable. It requires merely to be once turned over to produce largely; and, at present, it appears to be inexhaustible. As we proceeded, the scenery became more and more like what all travelers compare it to,—a boundless English park. The grass was wilder, the occasional footpath not so trim, and the single trees less*

majestic; but no park ever displayed anything equal to the grouping of the trees within the windings of the blue, brimming river Aux Plaines.

Mas, Jean member of La Salle's 1682-83 expedition to the mouth of the Mississippi, which passed through Chicagoland in January 1682 on its way S; was later honored by the king for his services. [46]

Mascoutens Algonkian, "people of the little prairie"; Indian tribe related to the Potawatomi; Father Allouez found them at Green Bay in 1670, and Father Marquette reported seeing them near Chicago in 1674; driven S and westward by neighboring tribes to eventual settlement along the Fox River, WI.

Mason, Matthias (1801-1876) blacksmith; arrived in 1833 and subscribed to the *Chicago Democrat* in November; married to Maria Rice (1800-1873); first had his shop on Franklin Street, between Lake and South Water, then moved in July 1834 to Lake Street, near Dearborn, renting his former smithy to John S.C. Hogan for use as a post office; his apprentice was [see] Benjamin Lupton; advertising for "Matthias Mason & Co.—blacksmith, on Main-street nearly opposite Graves' Tavern" can be found in the first issue of the *Chicago Democrat*, Nov. 26,1833. [Graves' Tavern in 1833 was on Lake Street]; removed to Indian Creek [Lake County] in 1835; died at Sutherland, IA on Dec. 20, 1882. [12]

massacre see Fort Dearborn massacre.

massacre tree see Chicago massacre tree.

mastodon, American *Mammut americanus*; prehistoric elephant-sized large mammals with well developed upper tusks that flourished mostly during the interglacial periods. Fossil remains are common throughout Illinois, occurring within the Chicagoland area—one was discovered in the summer of 1883 on the S side of Wicker Park near Milwaukee Avenue, 1 1/4 miles E of Humboldt Park. The Perry mastodon, found at Glen Ellyn in 1963, is existent in the Edwin F. Deicke Exhibit Hall at

Wheaton College. [341]

Mather, George   see Russell & Mather Addition.

Matthews, William W.   first personnel manager at Montreal of the American Fur Co. for the entire Northwest; required pre-employment physicals before hiring *voyageurs*; organized the traders' brigades that would fan out into the wilderness to service the remote outpost; responsible for starting young Gurdon S. Hubbard in the fur trade, hiring him for five years at $120 per year in 1818. [12]

Maur's Hotel   on the Chicago Road, at Calumet, in 1834. [12]

Maxwell, Philip, M.D.   (1799-1859) born at Guilford, VT; studied and originally practiced medicine in New York State; 12th of the Fort Dearborn surgeons, serving at the fort with Dr. George F. Turner; received his appointment as surgeon's mate with the U.S. Army on July 13, 1832, and arrived at Fort Dearborn on Feb. 3, 1833 to replace Dr. S.G.J. DeCamp; witnessed the 1833 Chicago Treaty with the Indians; remained at Fort Dearborn until its abandonment on Dec. 26, 1836; ✦ Garrison. After his resignation from the Army in 1844, he became a private practitioner in Chicago, serving as city physician in 1845, and as state representative from 1849 to 1852. His spirited discussions at the billiard table of the old Tremont House with Dr. Egan, a like large man of wit and overflowing humor, have become legend. In 1855, Dr. Maxwell retired to Lake Geneva, WI; little is known of his family; a Celia Maxwell attended school under Miss Eliza Chappell in 1833—presumably his daughter. The doctor's *Prescription and Diet Book of the Sick and Wounded at Fort Dearborn, 1832-1836* is preserved at the Chicago Historical Society; ➡ Maxwell Street (1330 S). [12, 97]

May   likely a schooner, mastered by [see] Capt. James Rough; brought supplies to Fort Dearborn or John Kinzie, as noted in Kinzie's account books for the years 1804, 1806, and 1808. [404]

May, Francis   see Le Mai, François.

Mayer, Leo   German immigrant, first attested to

PHILIP MAXWELL, M.D.   [137]

as having lived in Chicago in 1833. [342]

Mayer, Nathaniel   arrived from Alsace-Lorraine in 1834; married to Blondine D. (1799-1879); a son, Leo, was born at Fort Dearborn on June 26, 1834, who grew up in Chicago and would become prominent in the city's fire department. [Apparently the same family, though various sources spell the name differently: in Andreas' second volume, it is Leo Myers; on A. Hubbard's list it is Leo Meyer; *eds.*] [12, 342, 351]

M' Cauley, —   at a coroner's inquest, reported in the June 10, 1835 *Chicago Democrat*, the body of an Irish woman was identified as that of M'Cauley [McAuley] who, inebriated for several days, had come to her death by "a fracture to the scull, caused by a violent blow or fall."

McCall, James A.   came in the fall of 1833 from Victoria, Canada, and worked as a tanner for John

Miller in the tannery immediately N of Miller's Tavern; a notice in the *Chicago Democrat* of May 1, 1839, indicates that a James McCall had died, and Elizabeth McCall was the administrator of his estate.

McCall, John H.   brother of James A.; arrived in the winter of 1834-35 from upper Canada.

McCarty, Duncan   U.S. Army private at Fort Dearborn; enlisted in December 1805; killed after surrender at the massacre of 1812. [226]

McCarty, Richard   trader in Michilimackinac during the Revolutionary War; licensed by British authorities to trade with the Illinois, his business brought him to Chicago periodically; siding with the Americans after the war, he moved to Vincennes.

McClellan, James   teacher at the English and Classical School for Boys; succeeded Dr. Henry Van Derbogart in 1835. [12]

McClintock, James   arrived in 1830 and settled in Lyons Township; lived in Gowen, IL, in 1885. [12, 278, 351]

McClintock, Wilson   arrived in 1832; he and his wife Catherine lost a two-year-old son, Franklin, of encephalitis on April 19, 1836, as per notice in the *Chicago Democrat*, April 20; served as commissioner of streets in 1836, as election judge in 1837; on Sept. 12, 1840, the *Chicago Daily American* announces the death of his (second?) wife Charlotte; died in 1838 at Bachelor's Grove.

McClure, Charles   arrived from Canada in 1835; was elected town trustee in 1835 but declined the position; ✦ carpenter. [351]

McClure, Josiah E.   arrived from Canada in 1835; a notice in the *Chicago Democrat* of Jan. 14, 1837, announced his marriage to Harriet Johnson, "daughter of a U.S. Army captain" [perhaps {see} Capt. Seth Johnson, who served at Fort Dearborn in 1832-33 and remained in Chicago after 1834 as a civilian; *eds.*]; ✦ McClure & Co., commission merchants, 89 Lake St.; lived at 2120 Michigan Ave. in 1885. [12, 351]

McConnell, Edward (1805-1878) born in Dublin; came to Montreal in 1823, and arrived in Chicago from Detroit on board the *Marshal Ney* in August 1830, staying at Miller's Tavern a short while, then moved to Springfield, where he became connected with the U.S. Land Office; served in the Black Hawk War; returned to Chicago in 1835 to become chief clerk for Edmund D. Taylor, receiver of the Chicago Land Office; invested extensively in Chicago real estate; ✦ gardener, Lumber Street near Canal Street; married Charlotte McGlashan in 1844; died on May 11, 1878, and was survived by his wife and sons John, George, and Benjamin F.; his widow lived at 101 Washington St. in 1885. In a letter, written to H.E. Drummer on July 18, 1835, McConnell notes the accelerating growth of the town. [12, 13, 351, 457]
Excerpt of McConnell's letter:
Chicago is improving very fast. They are about building an Episcopal Church. The ladies had a fair some time since for the purpose of raising money to buy an organ and obtain about fifteen hundred dollars for their "notions and fixings," they did not get any of my money for I had none about that time. There is some talk about building a Theatre to cost 20 thousand dollars. A Tavern is building which is to cost 18 thousand when complete There is a great deal of capital here there are more than a dozen who are worth upward of a thousand dolls each. Chicago is entirely Eastern in manners and people. Upward of twohundert families landed last week from down East. Twelve sail lay at harbor at one time discharging their cargoes ....

McConnell, Murray (1798-1869) New York born; a Jacksonville speculator who purchased a portion of the Fort Dearborn reservation from Jean Baptiste Beaubien in 1836, and attempted to execute an action of ejection against DeLafayette Wilcox, commandant at Fort Dearborn, but lost in court. [12]

McCord, Jason merchant; arrived in 1834 from New York; in October 1835 he signed up with the "Pioneer" hook and ladder company, an early volunteer fire brigade; late that year he and [see] Flavel Moseley filed a claim for wharfing privileges for lot 4, block 19; ✦ Mosely [Flavel] & McCord, merchants, on South Water Street; served as alderman in 1841 and 1843; died in 1871. [12]

McCord, John (1803-1873) born in Orange County, NY; came in 1833, acquired land in Palos Township and farmed; served as county assessor and tax collector; married Harriet Paddock of New York in 1839. [278]

McCormick & Moon according to [see] J.D. Bonnell's report, a hat store on South Water Street between Dearborn and Michigan in 1835 [in part of the Newberry & Dole warehouse], representing the branch of a Detroit firm and run by Mr. Moon; Jesse Butler had his tailor shop in the rear. [12, 13]

McCorrister, William time of arrival uncertain; a notice in the *Chicago Democrat* of Sept. 16, 1835, indicates that on Sept. 15 he had married the teacher [see] Catherine Bayne; member of the fire engine company No.1 in December [see petition to the village board of Dec. 16, 1835, with entry on firefighting]; from 1836 to 1839 he operated the American Hotel on North Water Street

McCoy, John soldier in the Revolutionary War who in c.1833 homesteaded on the Sauk Trail, W of [Chicago Heights], a short distance E of what is now Western Avenue The site is located in the Thorn Creek Division of the Forest Preserve district of Cook County. McCoy came to Chicago by way of Ohio, perhaps explaining the substantial grove of Ohio buckeye trees now near his cabin site. His cabin served as a "station" on the underground railroad for escaped slaves. [Information furnished by Ed Lace, July 1996]

McCoy, Rev. Isaac Baptist minister; his wife's name was Christina; in charge of the Carey Mission [Niles, MI], a Baptist mission school established by him for the benefit of Ottawa and Potawatomi children, but attended mostly by their *métis* relatives; Josette Ouilmette attended and Madore Beaubien spent 1823-1824 at this school; observed the payment of the Indian annuity at Chicago in October 1825, and at Indian agent Wolcott's suggestion, on Oct. 9 he addressed the Indians on the subject of the mission; the sermon was delivered in English and was ★★★ Chicago's 1st such event; the school existed from 1822 to 1829, and the mission was closed when the Indians and *métis* settlers were relocated; in 1840 McCoy published *History of Baptist Indian Missions*— embracing remarks on the former and present condition of the aboriginal tribes, their settlement within the Indian Territory, and their future prospects; died at Louisville, KY, in 1846 at age 62. [12, 468]

McDale, Alexander voted in the Aug. 2, 1830, election; listed as owner of 80 acres of land in the NW quarter of Section 6, Township 39, prior to 1836, as per Andreas, *History of Chicago*, pp, 112-113. [12]

McDaniel, Alexander (1815-1898) born in New York State; first listed as living in Chicago in 1833; an unclaimed letter is listed on Jan. 1, 1834; by 1836 he lived at [Wilmette]; married Emeline C. Huntoon on Nov. 27, 1842. [96a, 319]

McDonnell, Charles submitted a petition for wharfing privileges late in 1835, accompanied by a report of the committee on wharfs and public grounds; ✦ grocery and provision store, 30 Market [Franklin] St.

McDuffie, Bvt. Second Lt. George W. was buried in Chicago in 1832 as one of 75 cholera victims during the Black Hawk War.

McForreston, W. arrived in 1835 and served as a member of the first engine company of the voluntary fire department in the same year.

McGowan, Patrick U.S. Army private at Fort Dearborn; enlisted in April 1806; survived massacre of 1812 and subsequent Indian captivity. [226]

McGrath, Thomas arrived from Ireland in 1835. [351]

McGregor, A. identified in a *Chicago Democrat* ad of May 28, 1834, as the supplier of pine timber in 12-to-60-foot lengths and 6-to-14-inch squares, available through P. Prune & Co. at "as reasonable terms as can be had in Chicago" [possibly Alex McGregor, who had worked under William Jones on the Buffalo harbor, and, following his visits to Chicago in 1831 and 1832, had been advised of the opportunities].

McHarry, John arrived from New York in 1834; a notice in the *Chicago Daily American* of July 7, 1842, announced his marriage to Mary A. Scovill on June 29. [351]

McIlvaine, Caroline Margaret (1868-1945) associated with the Chicago Historical Society between 1901 and 1927, serving as invaluable librarian (many accessions), lecturer, secretary, and installation exhibit director; introduced or edited other writers' important contributions concerning Chicago's history.

McKay, James arrived from Scotland in 1835. [351]

McKee, David (1800-1881) born in Loudoun County, VA; government blacksmith and gunsmith of Scottish ancestry; came on June 5, 1823, initially as an employee of Col. Benjamin B. Kercheval, Indian agent at Detroit, arriving from Fort Wayne in the company of the expedition lead by Maj. Stephen H. Long, and remained until 1832; spoke fluently the Potawatomi language; assessed on $100 of personal property in 1825, and voted locally in 1826 and 1830; built his house and smithy on the N side of the river just W of the agency house [now corner of Franklin and Kinzie streets] in or before 1825, and employed William See and Joseph Porthier; in 1827-28 he made monthly trips on horseback between Chicago and Fort Wayne, via Niles, MI, to carry the mail "on account of the Government," the round trip taking two weeks on horseback; married Wealthy Scott (Stephen H. Scott's daughter of [see] *Grosse Pointe*) on Jan. 23, 1827, John Kinzie, J.P. officiating; a son, Stephen, was born on Sept. 18, 1830; bought in 1830 from the government lot 1 in block 5, lot

7 in block 4, and lot 7 in block 49 [see map on page 44]; during the Black Hawk War served in the Chicago militia under Captain Kercheval, being listed in the muster roll of May 3, 1832; later that year moved to a farm in [DuPage County] and later to Kane County; applied for wharfing privileges in Chicago on Nov. 21, 1835; after Wealthy's death, married a Sarah W.; died in Aurora on April 8, 1881. [12, 28, 441]

McKenzie, Elizabeth born 1768; daughter of Moredock and Erina McKenzie, sister of Margaret, John Kinzie's first wife (see Kinzie family tree on page 222); both sisters had been raised by Shawnee Indians as captives, but were later ransomed; married John Clark, an early Detroit friend of John Kinzie; their children were twins Andrew and Mary (1776), Elizabeth (1791), and [see] John Kinzie Clark (1792); after her separation from John Clark, she married Jonas Clybourne of Virginia and moved to Chicago in 1824. [12]

McKenzie, John see MacKinzie, John.

McKenzie, Margaret see Kinzie, Margaret McKenzie.

McKillip, Daniel Eleanor Kinzie's first husband (see Kinzie family tree on page 222); was killed in 1794 by General Wayne's troops at Fallen Timbers when fighting on the side of the Indians.

McKillip, Eleanor see Kinzie, Eleanor McKillip.

McKillip, Margaret (1794-1844) later Margaret Helm, Margaret Abbott; daughter from an earlier marriage of John Kinzie's second wife Eleanor (see Kinzie family tree on page 222); was born at New Settlement, Ontario, on Lake Erie in 1794, the year her father, Daniel McKillip, was slain at Fallen Timbers; was raised in Detroit by her grandparents, where she married Lt. Linai T. Helm on June 10, 1810; came to Fort Dearborn in 1811 with her husband; survived the massacre with the help of Black Partridge and Waubinema [the moving legend being embodied in a Chicago bronze ▲ statue, see Monuments] and was hidden from the Indians first in the Kinzie House, then in that of the Ouil-

mette family, were she escaped Indian searches dressed as a French woman; after several days Chandonnais conveyed her, the Kinzies, and Sergeant Griffith to St. Joseph; was reunited with Lieutenant Helm in New York. They had one son in 1821, William Edwin, but she divorced her husband in 1829 at the Peoria Circuit Court, charging infidelity and drunkenness; was awarded $800 at the Treaty of Prairie du Chien on July 29, 1829 "for losses sustained at the time of the capture of Fort Dearborn in 1812 by the Indians"; on Jan. 25, 1836, she married Dr. Lucius Abbott of Detroit, where she died in 1844. [226]

McMahon, J. Ponte Coulant, M.D. born in Washington City; became a surgeon's mate with the Third Infantry of the U.S. Army on Nov. 21, 1817; fifth Fort Dearborn surgeon, arriving in 1818 to succeed Dr. John Gale; served at the fort until 1820, when he left on account of ill health, and was followed by Dr. W. Madison; resigned from the Army in 1834 and died in 1837.

McMurray, Andrew from Tennessee; notice in the *Chicago Democrat* of June 25, 1834, reports his accidental drowning at age 22 in the north branch of the Chicago River on June 23.

McNeil, Lt. Col. John from a Scottish-Irish family that had established itself in New Hampshire in 1718; at 6 feet 6 inches, he was the rival of General Scott in size; commandant at Fort Dearborn from October 1821 to July 1823; married to Elizabeth Pierce, half sister of President Franklin Pierce; a daughter was born to them, possibly the first child born at the new fort; died in 1850.

McPherson, Hugh U.S. Army private and drummer in the military band at Fort Dearborn; enlisted in October 1807; killed in the initial action at the massacre of 1812. [226]

Meacham, Harvey, Silas, and Lyman from New York; arrived in 1833, and acquired the NW quarter of Section 4 in Township 39 N, as per Andreas, *History of Chicago*, pp. 112-113; later Harvey settled what became known as Meacham's Grove [Medinah, three miles NE of Bloomingdale]; Lyman's wife died in the autumn of 1833, and was buried in a coffin made from wagon box boards, and within the precinct's first election [then still Cook County], he was selected justice of the peace at Elk Grove. [314a]

Méachelle Potawatomi chief in the Chicago locale who alleged to have, as a child, observed the massacre of the last Illinois Indians at Starved Rock at the hands of the united Potawatomi and Ottawa, and as an old man related the event to John D. Caton. For this there exists no contemporary documentation.

Mechkigi Potawatomi chief, living temporarily at Chicago in the late 1770s when the village had been abandoned by white settlers and traders during the Revolutionary War; both Mechkigi and Nanaloibi, a fellow chief, were much courted at the time by both British and American agents.

medical society see Cook County Medical Society and Chicago Medical Society; also see physicians.

Meeker, Joseph S. (1805-1872) born in New Jersey; carpenter who came to Chicago with his wife Adeline in the summer of 1833 and joined the Presbyterian congregation in September, constructing their first meeting house later that fall at Lake and Clark streets; having brought with him from the East a small collection of books suitable for religious education [Edwin O. Gale called them "biographies of goody-goody boys"], he donated them to the church and became librarian for the congregation when its Sunday school was formally organized on March 16, 1835; also that year constructed Chicago's first schoolhouse, built for that purpose, on part of the Presbyterian church property, for which the promoter and benefactor John S. Wright paid him $505.93; his name was on a school-related petition signed on Sept. 19, as he was active in public school organization; in October signed up with the "Pioneer" hook and ladder company, an early volunteer fire brigade; ♦ carpenter and

builder, 165 Clark St.; died in Chicago. [12, 351]

Meleagris gallopavo see turkey, wild.

Melish, John (1771-1822) Philadelphia map publisher of Scottish descent who, in 1816, published the first wall ✱ map to show the entire extent of the United States, *Map of the United States with the Contiguous British & Spanish Possessions*; the map became very popular and went through 23 editions. [681, 682]

Membré, Père Zenobius (Zénobe) O.F.M. (1645-1689) born in France; Franciscan priest who spoke the Illinois language and served briefly at the *Mission de la Conception* in southern Illinois in 1679; was present in 1680, together with Frs. Hennepin and Ribourde, when La Salle built Fort Crevecoeur at Lake Peoria; later was the chaplain for La Salle's and Tonti's expeditionary party via Chicago [January 1682] to the mouth of the Mississippi, and for La Salle's final, fatal expedition that ended in Texas [1684-1687]. Here Father Membré was killed by hostile Indians as one of the last surviving members of the abandoned French Texas colony. [12, 295, 519, 611]

Menard, Pierre, Sr. (1766-1844) French fur trader and merchant from Saint Antoine, Canada, who settled at Kaskaskia in 1790; was elected to the first Illinois senate in 1812; served as senate president until 1818, when he became Illinois' first lieutenant governor; visited Chicago in 1835, ruefully sharing then with Father St. Cyr that he once owned part of the Kinzie estate, having paid $50 at the time, but later sold the land to John Kinzie for the same price [his name is on the list of purchasers of choice lots of Sept. 27, 1830, the first day of government land sales; together with E. Roberts he had owned lot 4 of block 29 {see map on page 44}, but by 1833 Roberts was listed as the sole owner]. Menard's bronze statue is on the grounds of the capitol building in Springfield; ➡ Menard Avenue, Menard Drive [both at 5800 W]. [267, 268, 451]

Ménard, Père René (1605-1661) born in Paris, came to Canada as a Jesuit instructor in 1640; pre-

ceded Father Allouez as missionary priest among the Ottawa at Keweena Bay on the S shore of Lake Superior in 1660-61, assisted by Adrien Jolliet; died soon in the northern woods. [His name is listed on the Marquette monument of 1926, but we find no evidence of Father Ménard having worked in or visited Illinois; *eds.*] [12]

Menéndez de Avilés, Pedro Spanish expedition leader who founded St. Augustine in 1565; became the earliest permanent settlement on the North American continent and claimed jurisdiction N to and beyond the Chicago region.

Mermet, Père Jean (1664-1716) born at Grenoble, France; came to Canada in 1698 as a Jesuit teacher; in 1699 he served at the *Mission de l'Ange Gardien* in Chicago, and was placed in charge when Father Pinet left for the Peoria mission; subsequently served under Father Aveneau at the St. Joseph Mission until 1702; completed his mission work in Kaskaskia with Father Marest.

Merrick's Hotel mentioned in Enoch Chase's 1834 letter as existent on the Chicago Road, half-

PIERRE MENARD, SR. [345]

way between Calumet and Chicago. [12]

Merrill, A. subscribed to the *Chicago Democrat* in November 1833.

Merrill, George (1812-1901) born in Canada; arrived in 1834 with the Joseph Lovett family and settled on Lovett's claim one mile NW of Whiskey Point in Jefferson Township; married to Julia Lovett. [13]

Merrill, George W. from New Hampshire, arrived in 1835; in October signed up with the "Pioneer" hook and ladder company, an early volunteer fire brigade; ◆ dry goods merchant, 166 Lake St.; later became prominent in the railroad business (Fox River Valley Line) and was a member of the second Presbyterian church. [12, 351]

Merrill, Isaac on the post office list of unclaimed letters for April 1, 1834.

Mesier, Peter A. New York lithography firm that published several of the first maps of Chicago in the 1830s, one being the ✳ map of "73 Building Lots in Chicago to be sold at Auction by James Bleeker & Sons on Thursday, 22nd of October" [existent in the Newberry Library; those involved were likely in New York; *eds.*].

Mesquakie Indians see Fox Indians.

messisipi Father Allouez's spelling of Mississippi; he was one of the first to have heard of the great river from prairie Indians, among them the Illinois, who occasionally visited his *Mission de Saint-Esprit*, established in 1665.

Metea Potawatomi chief, took part in the Fort Dearborn massacre.

Methodist congregation occasional visits to Chicago by clergy from the Methodist Fox River mission took place as early as 1826, among them Rev. Isaac Scarritt's visit in 1828, during which he conducted a well attended service at Fort Dearborn; in 1830 the blacksmith and Methodist Episcopalian preacher Rev. William See moved to Chicago and delivered Sunday sermons on an irregular basis; in late 1831 Rev. Stephen R. Beggs arrived, moved into Reverend See's former residence, the

"school house" on the river's W side, just N of Wolf Point, where in 1832 he was first joined and then succeeded by Rev. Jesse Walker; regular Sunday service began at the "school house," at the house of Mark Noble, Sr., and elsewhere; the congregation was not formally organized until 1834 when it acquired its own 28-by-36-foot frame building in the second half of that year, built by John Stewart and Rev. Henry Whitehead at a cost of $580, at the corner of North Water and Clark streets; religious services were held here until 1836. At the end of 1834, Reverend Walker became superannuated, and was followed by Rev. John T. Mitchell in 1835; Whitehead received a license to preach in 1834 and did so on occasion in 1835, prior to Reverend Mitchell's term. On Nov. 20, 1835, the congregation was incorporated as the Methodist Episcopal Church of Chicago, and in 1857 was renamed First Methodist Episcopal Church of Chicago. [12]

Methodist Episcopal Church of Chicago see Methodist congregation.

métis French, designating an individual of mixed parentage: Indian and French or French Canadian; Abbé Thaumur de la Source, visiting the Chicago area in 1699 with the St. Cosme party, relates in a letter: "I will mention also, that many Canadians marry among the Illinois"; *métis* were in the majority in Chicago from c.1790 to 1832, not counting the members of the Fort Dearborn garrison. [533-4, 536-7]

Mett, Oliver mentioned as having lived at Chicago in 1828. [220]

Meucret, Gilles member of La Salle's 1682-83 expedition to the mouth of the Mississippi, which took the party through Chicagoland in January 1682 on its way S; was later honored by the king for his services. [46]

Meules, M. Jacques de intendant of New France, 1682-1686.

Meyer, Leo see Mayer, Nathaniel.

Meyer, Mathias German baker who arrived in the

spring of 1831 and opened a bakery at Wolf Point; died in 1851; considered Chicago's first settler of German birth by some, but Wellmacher and van Horne are recorded earlier. [342]

Miami Indians northern branch of the Algonkian speaking tribes, inhabiting the country between the Wabash and the Illinois Rivers; related to the Illinois and speaking a similar language; the Wea (French, Ouiatanon) were a subtribe of the Miami; inhabited Chicagoland as well as the areas of Milwaukee, Racine, Kenosha, Waukegan, and Whiting, IN at the time of arrival by the first European explorers; throughout the late 1660s into the 1670s, they traveled to the Green Bay region to trade; in c.1690 a band of Miami established a village on the main portion of the Chicago River, and a second village soon developed on the south branch, attracting French soldiers, missionaries, and traders; in 1695 Cadillac mentioned a visit to Mackinac by "the Illinois of Chicagou," but they were more likely Miami. About 1700 de Liette, who ran a trading post in Chicago at that time, estimated 300 families in each village, with a total population between 3,000 and 4,000. During the middle of the 18th century, the Illinois were decimated by wars with the Potawatomi, Kickapoo, Ottawa, Chippewa, Sac, Fox, and Winnebago and were forced to relocate S into the upper Wabash and Maumee River valleys, much reduced in numbers; they left the Chicago region permanently about the year 1718, though Charlevoix made reference to them there in 1727. Little Turtle, who signed the Treaty of Greenville, was their most well-known leader, with a large village where Fort Wayne was erected in 1794. The Potawatomi then became the dominant tribe near Chicago and remained so until the forced relocation of all Indians by the U.S. government. For a firsthand description of appearance and character traits of the Miami, see under entry for St. Cosme; ➡ Miami Avenue (6124 N). [12, 124, 651]

Miami River also *River of the Miamis*; early name

for [see] St. Joseph River; sometimes confused with two other, similarly named rivers: the *Miami of the Lake*, an early name for the Maumee River of Ohio until about 1816, and the *Great Miami*, which flows into the Ohio River near Cincinnati.

Miamitown   British settlement in Indiana at the site of the later Fort Wayne; John Kinzie owned a substantial trading establishment here in 1789, which he abandoned when fleeing before the advancing army of General Harmar in 1790.

Michel, Jean.   French Canadian surgeon for La Salle's 1681-82 expedition to the mouth of the Mississippi River, passed through the Chicago portage in January 1682 on the party's way S; was later honored by the king for his services; Michel is the second European physician known to have been to Chicagoland; see Surgeon for the first one. [46]

Michigamea   also Mitchagamie, Mitchigamie; an Illinois tribe, part of the Illini confederation.

michigan   Algonkin word meaning *great water*; ➤ Michigan Avenue (100 E). [Michigan Street, now Hubbard Street, is existent on James S. Wright's survey manuscript in 1834 and Edward B. Talcott's "Chicago with the Several Additions compiled from the recorded plats in the Clerk's Office, Cook County, Illinois," published in 1836; *eds.*]

Michigan   first steamboat (472 tons) to have cabins on deck; owned by Oliver Newberry, and first to enter the Chicago River and pass through the recently completed Dearborn Street drawbridge on May 4, 1834; was built with two engines side by side of 80 horse power each, each with a propeller, at Detroit in the spring of 1833; was commanded by Captain Pickering (later by Capt. C. Blake, according to N. Norton and the June 8, 1835, *Chicago American*); one of three steamers to call at Chicago during that year. The *Michigan* made additional calls on Aug. 21, 1834 (Captain Pease), and in 1835 under Captain Blake on June 29 and July 26, each time coming from Buffalo, NY.

Michigan   130-ton schooner built at Perrysburg, OH, in 1832; first called at Chicago on July 20,

The Steamboat Michigan.

Capt. C. BLAKE, will leave Chicago for Detroit and Buffalo on the morning of the 28th of June, at 9 o'clock. For freight or passage, apply to the master on board, or to

NEWBERRY & DOLE.

Chicago, June 8, 1835.   3w1

1834, coming from Buffalo, NY; returned on July 20 and Nov. 9, 1835, under Captain Dixon. [48]

Michigan City, IN   earlier name, *Rivière du Chemin*, Trail Creek; for centuries this had been an important point of convergence of multiple Indian trails; early Lake Michigan port at the mouth of Trail Creek and on the beach route portion of the Detroit-Chicago road; the Cahokia trader Pierre Durand had a post there in 1778-79, where Jean Baptiste Point de Sable was arrested by the British Lieutenant Bennet under order from Major De Peyster on suspicion of sympathizing with the French and Americans; other settlers arrived in the 1820s; on the bank of Trail Creek the Vail sawmill opened in 1832, one of many to furnish lumber for the

Chicago boom; the road from Detroit to Chicago passed through Michigan City, IN, and in 1835 the Detroit-Michigan City portion took three days by stagecoach, the Michigan City-Chicago portion took two days. In the July 15, 1835, *Chicago Democrat*, John Calhoun reported receiving the first issue of *Michigan City Gazette*, its editor writing of "a young city … with its four story frame buildings." [69, 70]

Michigan City road   inland branch of the Chicago-Detroit Road that passed through Baillytown, [Hammond, Riverdale, and Roseland].

Michigan County, IL   proposed in 1828 by a petition to the Illinois General Assembly, originating in Chicago, which the new county was meant to include, but never created; for details, see Chronology, Oct. 20, 1828.

Michigan Lake   see Lake Michigan.

Michilimackinac   this name applies not only to the entire region of the strait formed by the confluence of Lakes Michigan, Superior, and Huron, but also, and specifically, to the following three distinct sites: (1) Point Ignace on the northern mainland, (2) Mackinac Island in the strait, and (3) Mackinaw City on the southern mainland. At Point Ignace, where the town of St. Ignace is now located, a settlement of French fur traders already existed when, in 1671, the *Mission de Saint-Ignace* was moved here from Mackinac Island. A small fort was added for the protection of the traders and the mission; from here Father Marquette and Jolliet left to explore the Mississippi and found the Chicago site in 1673. From 1683-1685, [see] Oliver Morel de la Durantaye served as commandant at the fort, the same Durantaye who in 1684 came to Chicago to construct a fort that he left garrisoned intermittently for the protection of local traders. In 1715, the French moved fort and mission to a site on the southern shore of the strait, but the name Michilimackinac remained the same; it is now Mackinaw City. From 1761 to 1796, the fort was under British control, from 1796 to 1812

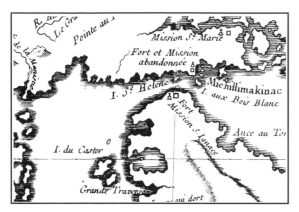

Excerpt from Jacques Nicolas Bellin's 1744 map of the Great Lakes, showing the Michillimackinac locations of the successive French missions and forts in this strategic area.

American, from 1812 to 1815 British again, and since then it has remained American. Here were the western headquarters of the American Fur Co., and to this place the Chicago traders sent their furs, and from here they received their supplies and pay. Prior to 1830, Michilimackinac had been the site of the only—and remarkably active—town within a vast wilderness, and a way station for men and supplies destined for frontier military fortifications at Green Bay, Chicago, Prairie du Chien, and St. Anthony Falls.

Michilimackinac Island   Ojibway, *mitchimakinak* or *grand turtle*; small island in the Straits of Mackinac, later called Mackinac Island; here Father Dablon began the *Mission of Saint-Ignace* in 1670, but removed to the mainland of the upper peninsula the following year [St. Ignace], after Father Marquette had joined him.

Miguly, Rudolph   also Rudolphy Migleley; arrived in 1834 from Germany; ✦ grocery, Randolph Street, near LaSalle; lived on 2430 Prairie Ave. in 1885. [12, 351]

Military Tract   also bounty lands; a popular name given to a section of the state of Illinois, set apart under an act of Congress, passed May 6, 1812, as bounties of land, 160 acres each, for soldiers in the war with Great Britain commencing the same year; the tract was located between the Mississippi and the Illinois Rivers [see map on page 142], was surveyed in 1815-16, and was comprised of 207 townships each measuring six miles square, plus additional fractional townships, altogether providing 3.5 million acres for claims. Settlement of such claims [320 acres per veteran] began to stimulate growth in 1823; both the Military Tract and Chicago were part of Pike County then and most of the pioneers came through Chicago.

militia   see Fort Dearborn militia.

Miller & Company   New York lithography firm that published a real estate ✳ map of Chicago in 1835, "Map of Lots at Chicago for Sale by Franklin & Jenkins on Friday, 8th May, 1835, at 12 O'clock at the Merchants Exchange" [within the Newberry Library; those involved are unknown, likely partners in New York; *eds.*].

Miller, Charles   first listed as living in Chicago in 1833; married Mary Curtis on Aug. 21, 1842; listed as barber and hairdresser in 1844 Chicago *Directory*. [319]

Miller, George G.   purchased real estate in blocks 18 and 36 [see map on page 44] and soon thereafter sold it to George Walker prior to 1833.

Miller House   also Miller's Tavern; originally a log cabin built in 1820 by Alexander Robinson on the projection of land between the north branch and the main channel of the Chicago River, opposite Wolf Point [see picture on page 376]; in 1827 Samuel Miller and his brother John, with Archibald Clybourne holding a partnership interest, added a two-story house to the cabin, fronting the river; John Fonda and Boiseley stayed there in January 1828; initially used as a store and as shelter for travelers, the structure soon became a regular tavern, licensed on April 13, 1831; when Sam Miller removed to Michigan after his wife's death in 1832, P.F.W. Peck moved in with goods and managed a store.

Miller, Jacob   from Virginia; cousin of John and Samuel Miller, also of Benjamin Hall; arrived in June 1832 with Thomas Clybourne just before the Black Hawk War and served as a volunteer private in Captain Hogan's company; left and returned with his family to settle on May 25, 1834; did blacksmithing, helped in harbor and pier construction; reported later that at that time the mouth of the Chicago "river was about 200 feet below Madison street. I know I lived right there in 1834"; made a government claim on Mill Creek [tributary of the Des Plaines River] in late summer of 1835 and built a saw- and gristmill soon after; served as justice of the peace; ✦ blacksmith on N State Street, corner of Indiana [Grand]; lived at 42 Clybourn Ave. in 1885. [12]

Miller, John   brother of Samuel Miller; came in 1831; ran a tannery with Benjamin Hall immediately N of Sam Miller's tavern; purchased Wellmaker's four lots on block 14, and by 1830 the Miller brothers, together with Hall, owned the entire block; elected town trustee (first board) on August 10, 1833; ✦ tanner, north branch and fire warden, fourth ward; died at Galesburg. [12]

Miller, Joseph   German immigrant, first attested to as having lived in Chicago in 1835. [342]

Miller, Peter   U.S. Army private at Fort Dearborn; enlisted in December 1805; declared unfit for service early in 1811 but reenlisted later on July 24; one of the sick soldiers killed within or near the sick wagon at the 1812 massacre. [226]

Miller, Ralph   U.S. Army private at Fort Dearborn; enlisted in December 1805; left Chicago when his term expired Dec. 19, 1810. [226]

Miller's Tavern   see Miller House.

Miller, Samuel   brother of John; arrived in 1826 or earlier; married Elizabeth Kinzie on July 29, 1826, John Kinzie J.P. officiating; according to G. Hubbard, "Samuel Miller bought a small log cabin on the opposite side of the river from Wentworth, and south of the present Kinzie Street bridge, to which he added a two-story log building [in 1827], finishing the outside with split clapboards. These two public buildings [Wolf Point Tavern and Miller's Tavern] were the first Chicago could boast"; was licensed to operate a tavern with Archibald Clybourne on May 2, 1829, and licensed to operate a ferry at the forks on June 2, 1829, again jointly with Clybourne; with his brother in 1830, purchased from the government the land in block 14 on which their buildings stood [see map on page 44]; was elected Cook County commissioner on March 7, 1831, when the board was first created; received a county license as an innkeeper on April 13, 1831; in March 1832 built a roofless estray pen on the SE corner of the public square, ★★★ **Chicago's 1st** public building, for which he billed the town $20 but received only $12, because it did not meet specifications agreed upon; also in 1832 built ★★★ **Chicago's 1st** bridge, 10 feet wide and for foot traffic only, made of floating logs, that crossed the north branch at where Kinzie Street; during the Black Hawk War served in the Chicago militia under Captain Kercheval, being listed in the muster roll of May 3, 1832. In July of that year, his wife died and Miller with several children moved to Michigan where their uncle, William Kinzie, had his home; also see entries for Miller House, estray pen and Kinzie, Elizabeth; ➡ Miller Street (1028 W). [12, 13, 351]

Mills, Benjamin   circuit riding attorney who in traveling from Galena to Chicago in early April of 1832, in the company of attorney (see) James M. Strode and Judge Richard M. Young, became aware of the early unrest of the Black Hawk War, and warned the Chicago settlement of the impending danger. [12]

Mills, Elias   U.S. Army private at Fort Dearborn; taken prisoner by Indians at the massacre of 1812, and remained in captivity at the Indian villages along the Fox River for nearly two years; was then ransomed through the help of Michael Buisson, son of the trader Louis Buisson. [226]

Milwaukee, WI   early names include Milwakee, Milwakie, Milouaki, Melloki, and Melleoki;

Chicago's rival town on the western shore of Lake Michigan, about 90 miles N of Chicago at the mouth of the river of the same name, was incorporated as a town in 1837. The town was preceded by an Indian village of the same name, meaning *fine land* in Algonkian. French traders had settled as early as 1743, the first one of (fragmentary) record being a Frenchman named St. Pierre, who lived there from 1764 to at least 1779. Prominent among the early Milwaukee trading families were those founded—usually in joint partnership with Indian spouses—by Jacques Vieau (1795), Jean Baptiste Mirandeau (1798), Alexander LaFramboise, Antoine Le Clair and Laurent Solomon Juneau. There was frequent contact and interaction between them and the Chicago traders. In August 1820, when the Lewis Cass expedition came through, they found "a trading post, two American families, and an Indian village." By 1834 Milwaukee started to grow rapidly, but eventually would not keep pace with Chicago, whose phenomenal growth was due to the construction of the Illinois & Michigan Canal. In the early 1830s, the trip by stagecoach between Chicago and Milwaukee took 1 1/2 day at a cost of $3 in the summer, $5 in the winter; ➡ Milwaukee Avenue, diagonally crossing the checkerboard street pattern and extending toward Milwaukee. An early Indian trail led from Chicago to Wisconsin and Milwaukee, later becoming the Elston Road. Milwaukee Avenue is of later origin, built in the middle of the 19th century as the Northern Plank Road. [691]

Miner, Aaron   a Revolutionary War veteran, likely a relative of Frederick; joined family within Elk Grove Township in 1834. [278]

Miner, Frederick T., M.D.   (c.1793-1861) arrived from Vermont Sept. 28, 1833 with wife Miranda and an 11-year-old son, Rush [named after Dr. Benjamin Rush], and his sister E.W. Barnes; soon moved on to Elk Grove Township, farming the next 30 years, practicing medicine simultaneously; subsequently moved to Arlington Heights, where he

died. [13, 278]

Miner, Horace   voted in election of Nov. 25, 1830 [see Chronology].

Mirandeau, Jane   also Genevieve; long worked with her sister as a domestic servant for the Kinzie family prior to the Fort Dearborn massacre; received a quarter section of land [160 acres] in the 1829 treaty, next to the land granted to her sister Victoire Mirandeau Pothier, near Billy Caldwell's reservation; some of her land is now part of the North Branch Division of the Cook County Forest Preserve District.

Mirandeau, Jean Baptiste, Jr.   also Miranda; born in 1796; worked as a servant in the households of John Kinzie and Dr. Wolcott; early member of the Catholic congregation, signing for himself and two of his sisters on the 1833 petition to Bishop Rosati, asking that a priest be assigned to Chicago. [12, 226]

Mirandeau, Jean Baptiste, Sr.   also Miranda, Maranda; educated member of a prominent Quebec French family; became an early permanent settler, blacksmith, and trader at Milwaukee (c.1789); listed in John Kinzie's account books on Oct. 1, 1805, April 30, and Aug. 7, 1807, prior to moving with his family to Chicago in 1810 and occupied a house SW of the fort on Frog Creek, doing blacksmith work at Fort Dearborn in 1811-12, but returned to Milwaukee shortly before the massacre. In 1816, the family came again to Chicago as he had become an employee of the American Fur Co. and was a close friend of John Kinzie; had married an Ottawa woman, with whom he had 10 children: two died very young; the others, in the order of their birth, were [see] Jean Baptiste, Jr., Joseph, Louis, Madelaine, Victoire [see separate entry], Rosanne, Genevieve [see Jane], and Thomas. Jean Baptiste, Sr., died in the spring of 1818 or 1820, and was said to have caused his death by heavy drinking. Madeline married [see] John K. Clark in 1825. Thomas and his three brothers received the sum of $1,200 at the Chicago Treaty of 1833, with

John H. Kinzie acting as trustee for the fund. [12, 226, 404]

Mirandeau, Victoire born in the winter of 1800-01; fifth *métis* child of Jean Baptiste Mirandeau; never attended school, learning to read or write, but spoke French, English, and several Indian languages; often visited the Ouilmettes with her sister Madeline while the father did blacksmith work at the fort, and both became eyewitnesses to the La Lime homicide in 1812; worked as servant with her sister Jane for the Kinzie and Wolcott families prior to the Fort Dearborn massacre; married Joseph Pothier at Fort Dearborn on May 24, 1828, J.B. Beaubien officiating as justice of the peace; received 320 acres of land in the 1829 treaty, between land granted to her sister Jane and Billy Caldwell's reservation; some of her land is now part of the North Branch Division of the Cook County Forest Preserve District; lived in Chicago from 1816 to 1835, after which date the Pothiers (with three children) moved to Milwaukee, her childhood home, where her husband died in 1875 and she lived to an advanced age. [12]

missions listed in chronological order are those North American missions considered relevant to the discovery and history of Chicago; many others, not mentioned here, have existed. All attempted to bring Catholicism to the Indians and in the process furthered the exploration and subjugation under the French crown of what later became New France and Louisiana. The first French cleric to arrive with the early colonizers was the secular priest Jessé Fléché in 1610, followed by the Jesuit fathers Pierre Biard and Ennemond Massé in 1611; in 1615 three Récollet priests, the abbés Denis Jamay, Jean d'Olbeau, and Joseph le Caron reached Quebec and soon began missionary work among the Hurons. [612]

Mission de Saint-Joseph founded in **1634** by the Jesuit fathers Jean de Brébeuf, Antoine Daniel, and Ambroise Davost among the Huron (where Récollet priests had earlier labored) at Georgian Bay, on the eastern shore of Lake Huron; destroyed by the Iroquois in 1649.

Mission de Saint-Esprit [Holy Spirit Mission, *La Pointe du St. Esprit*] major Jesuit mission founded in **1665** by Father Claude Allouez at Chequamegon Bay of western Lake Superior [Ashland, WI] and taken over by Father Marquette in 1669; Father Claude Dablon reported in 1670 that Indians who identified themselves as belonging to the Illinois tribe had come N to trade at this mission.

Mission de Sault-Sainte-du-Marie major Jesuit mission founded in **1668** by Fathers Marquette and Dablon at an Ojibwa village [Sault Ste. Marie; the oldest permanent European settlement in Michigan].

Mission de Saint-Françoi Xavier founded in **1669** by Father Allouez, first on Green Bay [Point Sable, WI], but moved in 1671 to [De Pere, WI] on the Fox River a few miles above Green Bay, from where Father Marquette and Louis Jolliet started their historic expedition, in the course of which they came to what is now Chicago; remained the closest mission to the north.

Mission de Saint-Ignace founded in **1671** by Father Marquette at Michilimackinac [Point St. Ignace, Michigan Peninsula] and named after the founder of the Jesuit Order, Ignazius de Loyola; in exploring, both Fathers Dablon and Marquette had considered Mackinac Island before deciding to build the mission on the shore of the peninsula. By 1700 a thriving trade and French government center had evolved round the mission, but its importance declined with the founding of Detroit in 1701.

Mission de la Conception [**Mission of the Immaculate Conception**] founded in April **1675** by Father Marquette at the Kaskaskia village near [Utica, IL], after having first made contact with the Indians in August 1673 in the company of Jolliet; the mission became the parent house for several others, among them the St. Joseph mission in Michigan and the Guardian Angel Mission at Chicago;

the original site of the mission is now known as the Zimmerman archaeological site. After Father Marquette, the mission was tended in succession by Fathers Allouez, Bineteau, Membré, Ribourde, Gravier, and Marest; mission and village were moved S in 1691 to Lake Peoria for greater safety from Iroquois attacks, and then in 1700, to the future site of St. Louis, and finally in 1703, to the Kaskaskia River, near its junction with the Illinois River. The mission existed until 1832, at which time the Indians were removed to Oklahoma.

Mission de Saint-Joseph probably founded before **1689** by Father Allouez; the first preserved written document about the mission is a letter of 1706 by Father Marest; located on the bank of the St. Joseph River in the lower Michigan Peninsula at [Niles, MI]; active as late as 1773; here is the grave of Father Allouez, who died in 1690. [565]

Mission de l'Ange Gardien des Miamis à Chicagoua [**Guardian Angel Mission**] founded in **1696** by Father Pierre François Pinet on the Chicago River, where he served with Father Julian Bineteau, and later with Father Jean Mermet. [This is generally thought to have been the first mission in Chicago; however, there exists some evidence in records left by Joutel and Perrot that Father Allouez maintained a short-lived mission during the years 1684-85 when Durantaye built and commanded a French fort in Chicago.] The fathers maintained close contact with the *Mission de la Conception*, then at Lake Peoria under Father Jacques Gravier. On Governor Frontenac's order Father Pinet closed the mission for political reasons in 1697, then reopened it the following year. In 1699, three priests from the *Séminaire des Missions Étrangères* of Quebec visited, conducted to Chicago by Tonti. One of them, Abbé St. Cosme, supplied a vivid picture of the mission in his report [see excerpts with entry on St. Cosme], also indicating that French traders lived nearby. At its peak the mission was surrounded by a Miami village of 150 cabins. From 1699 on it was intermittently occupied, permanently abandoned by

1702 because of of the increasing danger of Fox and Iroquois attacks. [12, 267, 268, 290, 649]

Mission de Sainte Famille de Caoquias [Holy Family Mission of the Cahokias; also *Notre Dame de Kahokia*; also *Mission de Sainte Famille de Tamaroa*, and (later) *Mission de St. Sulpice*] founded in **1699** by Father Pinet at the great village of Cahokia among the Tamaroa; Father Pinet died soon thereafter, and his place was taken by Father Gravier. The mission was closed in 1763 by Father Forget, who at that time freed three slaves owned by the Church. [565, 649]

missionaries see preachers and missionaries.

Mississippi a 77-ton schooner from Cleveland under Captain Freeland; called at Chicago on Oct. 24 and Nov. 9, 1835.

Mississippian Culture see Indian prehistory.

Mississippi bubble see Louisiana Province.

Mississippi River *great river* in Algonkian: *missi* meaning *great*, *sepe* meaning *water* or *river*. Earlier names given to this river were Rio del Espiritu Santu (Pineda, the first to discover one or more of its outlets in 1519), El Rio Grande del Florida (DeSoto), R. de la Conception, and Missipi (Marquette); during most of the French period, before 1700, the Mississippi River was called Rivière de Colbert (Jolliet, La Salle, Hennepin, Membré) after Louis XIV's minister. [197, 198]

Missouratenou see Mount Jolliet.

missouri Algonkian word for dugout canoe or [see] pirogue, as distinguished from the birchbark canoe [Father Gravier's *Dictionary*].

Mitchigami also Michigamea, Mitchagamie, Mitchigamie; Illinois tribe, part of the Illini confederacy.

Mitchell, John London mapmaker who came to Virginia as a botanist early in the 18th century; was able to draw upon the maps and other records in the Admiralty Office and the Board of Trade; in 1755 produced *A Map of the British and French Dominions in North America*, the most up-to-date ✳ map at its time and the standard for the last half

of the 18th century, followed by 20 additional editions until 1799; died in England in 1768.

Mitchell, Rev. John T. Methodist minister who succeeded Rev. Jesse Walker in leadership of Chicago's early Methodist congregation near the end of 1834, and who was in turn succeeded by Rev. O.T. Curtis in 1836; is said to have been a graduate of Illinois College at Jacksonville; in 1835 lived with his bride at Flusky's boarding house, and on Nov. 25 was elected president of the Chicago Bible Society. [12, 544]

Mitchell, S. Augustus Philadelphia mapmaker who, in 1836, published *The Tourist's Pocket Map of the State of Illinois*; the ✳ map showed the proposed Illinois & Michigan Canal and the division of the canal corridor into townships, a first step toward the sale of canal land to finance the project; a popular map that had many subsequent editions.

Mittatass a principal warrior of the Ottawa, involved in the Fort Dearborn massacre; held Lieutenant Helm prisoner after the massacre, releasing him to the trader Thomas Forsyth in return for two horses and a keg of liquor. [226]

Mkedepoke see Black Partridge.

Mo-ah-way also Moaway; a Potawatomi Indian whose name translates *wolf*, who once lived on the land now called [see] Wolf Point; first reported by Juliette Kinzie in her book *Wau-Ban*; received land and monies in the Indian treaties of 1829 and 1833. [697]

Moffett, William U.S. Army private at Fort Dearborn; enlisted April 23, 1806; listed in Kinzie's account books on Nov. 4, 1806, and Feb. 11, 1807, and April 10 and July 21, 1812; believed killed in action at the massacre of 1812. [226, 404]

Mohawk one of five nations of the Iroquois confederacy who inhabited upper New York State; the Indian word means *savage, ferocious*; ➡ Mohawk Street (532 W).

Mohawk Trail also see Sauk Trail; Indian trail leading W from Albany, NY, to Chicago and beyond, by way of Buffalo, Cleveland, and Sandusky; the

portion from Detroit to Chicago became known in the early 18th century as the Chicago Road or Chicago Turnpike.

Mohr, M. Swiss born c.1807; arrived in May 1835; living at Walworth, WI, in 1885. [12]

Molere, Pierre married to Angelique Vandette; Catholic church records reveal that in Chicago on Oct. 18, 1830, Father Badin baptized their children: Monique, Agatha, and Joseph.

money (1) paper money: Initially the economy of the Ancien Régime was based on barter, and whatever few French coins were available. Newly imported coins tended to rapidly disappear. The first paper money issued on the North American continent was the French card money, a brainchild of the Canadian Intendant Jacques de Meulles. In 1685, he arranged to have ordinary game cards cut into quarters, each quarter was stamped with the French crown and lilly symbol, then signed by the governor, intendant, and treasurer of Quebec. The people were ordered to accept this makeshift money as valid tender. It proved highly unstable in value, and it is not likely that any of it reached Chicagoland. On the East Coast, the Massachusetts Bay Company began to issue properly designed paper money in 1690; not until May 10, 1775, did the U.S. government issue paper money; before that time, and for decades thereafter, notes were issued by virtually thousands of small private banks, by some city governments, or by local enterprises such as railroad companies, printed for them by engraving and printing firms. Lieutenant Allen, in charge of Chicago harbor construction and obliged to pay his workers, complained that he "... must endure taking and circulating ... a motley kind of money of which I can know little or nothing"; when a bank failed, which happened often, holders of its money were out of luck. Before 1840, most bills were black and white. (2) Coins: Silver coins were safer than paper money, but all coins were in short supply. England failed to make enough coins available for the colonies. Spanish-milled silver *Reales* pieces ("8 bits"; "pieces of eight") were therefore accepted as official currency in colonial days; they came in two forms: "pillar dollars" had the Spanish coat of arms on one side, the pillars of Hercules on the other, and were coined from 1745-1770; "bust dollars," showing Carolus III and IIII [IV] instead of the pillars, were minted from 1772 to 1825; some of the "bust dollars" were counterstamped in London with the head of George III of England to validate them as legal British currency [which gave rise to the sarcastic contemporary saying "Being short of silver to make money pass, they stamped the head of a fool on the head of an ass"] but the public accepted them, stamped or not; slightly larger than the United States silver dollar, which they inspired, their higher silver content made them more acceptable even after the U.S. Mint began producing dollars; smaller Spanish *escudo* denominations were also available. The colony of Massachusetts had began to strike silver shillings in 1652, but was later forbidden by the English king to continue. In 1792, the dollar was established as the monetary unit of

the nation, and that year the government began striking coins in its first mint at Philadelphia, but the initial supply was limited. Other foreign coins used in North America include the French *livre* and *centime* pieces, some English guineas and shillings, Portuguese *rei* pieces, Virginia halfpennies, and privately minted Welsh halfpennies. For illustrations of some of the coins used in Chicago before 1836, see page 264.

During the Chicago land boom (1833-1837), the need for money overtook even the capacity of private banks to issue notes. Often one man would repay another by exchanging work for work. For a description of how various business entities began to create their own money (scrip) and how the resulting currency chaos led to the sudden collapse of the boom, see the following recollections of an eyewitness (printed in *Magazine of Western History*):

Canal scrip was money; the bank bill was money; and the private individual decided it was necessary, in order to keep the ball rolling until the future should realize the wildest dreams, that he must take his turn at making money. Nearly every man in Chicago do-

ing business was issuing his individual script, and the city abounded with litle tickets, such as "Good at our Store for 10 cents," "Good for a Loaf of Bread," "Good for a Shave," "Good for a Drink," &c. &c. When you went out to trade, the trader would look over your tickets and select such as he could use to the best advantage. The times, for a while, seemed very prosperous. We had a currency that was interchangeable; and for a time we suffered no inconvenience from it, except when we wanted some specie to pay for our postage. In those days it took twenty-five cents to send a letter. But after a while it was found out that men were over-issuing. The barber had outstanding too many shaves; the baker too many loaves of bread; the saloon-keeper too many drinks. Want of confidence became general; each man became afraid to take the tickets of another. Some declined to redeem their tickets in any way, and some absconded. ... Of a sudden the ripple had been made, and the circle of distrust had spread beyond recall. [517]

Monks' Mound   see Cahokia.

Monroe   341-ton steamboat, built in 1834 at Monroe, MI, and an occasional visitor to Chicago in

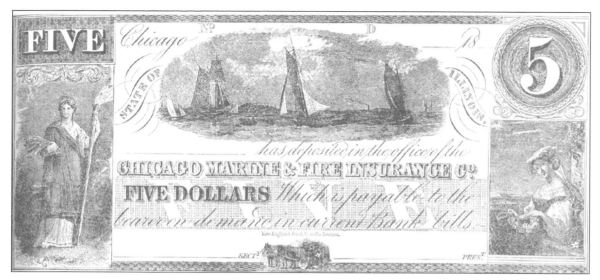

subsequent years; its first call at Chicago was on Aug. 20, 1835, under Captain Whittaker, when it came from Buffalo, NY. [48]

Monroe, James (1758-1831) Virginia native; fifth United States president, serving from 1817-1825; under Monroe Illinois became a state of the Union on Aug. 24, 1818; ➡ Monroe Street, Monroe Drive, both at 100 S.

Monroe, N.L.F. arrived from Connecticut in 1834, signing up in October with the "Pioneer" hook and ladder company, an early volunteer fire brigade [also see petition to the village board of Dec. 16, 1835, with entry on firefighting]; on Aug. 5, 1837, a legal notice involving a Nelson Monroe appeared in the *Chicago American*. [733]

Monselle, Charles early member of the Catholic congregation; in April 1833 his name was on the petition by Catholic citizens to Bishop Rosati of St. Louis, asking that a priest be assigned to them.

Montgomery, John prior to 1836 he owned 80 acres of land in Section 30, Township 39, as per Andreas, *History of Chicago*, pp. 112-113; a notice in the *Chicago Daily Journal* of Sept. 21, 1842, announced the Sept. 19 marriage of a John H. Montgomery to Miss Mary Chivel, "both of this city."

[12]

Montgomery, Loton W. married to Elizabeth Montgomery; opened his shop on South Water Street, E of the corner with Dearborn, and advertised in the Dec. 17, 1833, issue of the *Chicago Democrat*, "Boot and Shoe Making, next to Peter Cohen"; ✦ [living or working at] United States Hotel.

Montgomery, William born in Pennsylvania c.1817; arrived in 1833; on July 6, 1835, advertised in the *Chicago Democrat* "auction and commission on South Water Street, at David Carver's old stand" [between LaSalle and Wells streets], and thereafter placed ads frequently in the paper; one month later he "Wanted a Man to Ring Bell for Auctions"; also in 1835 acted as distributor of the *Saturday Evening Post, Casket*, and *Book of Nature*; married Virginia Alice Temple in 1843. [544]

Montigny, Abbé François Jolliet de (1661-1725) born and died in Paris; ordained in Quebec in 1693; became a member of the Seminary of Quebec; leader of the *Séminaire des Missions Étrangères* delegation [of which Abbés St. Cosme and Davion were members] that visited Chicago in October 1698 to consult with Fathers Pinet and Bineteau,

on the way to work among the Arkansea along the Mississippi; founded a mission at Tamarois, of which the Jesuits complained; returned through Chicago in April 1699; was vicar general to the bishop of Quebec and director of the Ursulines; in 1700, was sent from France to China, where he endured great hardship as a missionary.

Montreal canoe a heavy-duty birchbark French canoe, referred to as "the workhorse of the fur trade"; 35 to 40 feet long, capable of transporting more than three tons of freight with a 7-to-12-man crew.

Monuments a separate section of this book deals with early historical monuments, arranged in alphabetical order.

Moon, — partner in the Chicago branch of the Detroit hat store, [see] McCormick & Moon.

Moore, Henry arrived from Concord, MA, in 1834, admitted to the Illinois bar on Dec. 8, 1834; initially served as deputy to Colonel Hamilton, the circuit court clerk, but in June of 1835 began an individual legal practice, advertising in the July 4 *Chicago American* an office in John H. Kinzie's new store; with C. Petit and Lt. J. Allen began the Chicago Reading Room Association in July; his name was on a school-related petition signed on Sept. 19, 1835, and on Nov. 22 submitted a petition for wharfing privileges; in 1837 became a trustee of Rush Medical School; ✦ attorney and counseller at law, 9 Clark St.; on account of poor health, removed soon after to Havana, Cuba; died in 1841 at Concord, MA; his widow lived at Yorkville, Kendall County, in 1885. [12]

Moore, Peter member of the Baptist church and present at its initial organizational meeting of Oct. 19, 1833; on June 3, 1834 married Jane Parks "of the DesPlain" or "the DesPages," J.D. Caton officiating. [12]

Moran, Pierre see LeClerc, Peresh

Moras, Antoine of Detroit; *engagé* in the party of [see] Hugh Heward, which stopped in Chicago at Jean Baptiste Point de Sable's farm from May 9 to

11, 1790, on the way from Detroit to Cahokia.

Moreau, Pierre one of five *voyageurs* who took part in the 1673 expedition of Father Marquette and Louis Jolliet to the Mississippi and the Chicago site. During Marquette's second trip to the Illinois River in December 1674, Moreau was in Illinois territory on his own account as a trader under the name *La Toupine* [French, *the mole*], and learning from the Indians that Marquette was camped at the Chicago River and ill, he brought a man with medical knowledge to the camp; in reference to this man, Marquette only denotes "the surgeon." There has been much speculation in the past as to the true name of this doctor; some earlier historians believe that his name was Louis Moreau, unrelated to Pierre Moreau; John F. Swenson identifies him as [see] Jean Roussel or Rousselière; ▲ see Monuments.

Morgan, Achilles resident of Vermillion County in 1827, when he came to Chicago as captain of 100 militia volunteers from Danville [Vermillion Rangers] to lend protection during the [see] Winnebago War. [12]

Morgan, E. subscribed to the *Chicago Democrat* in November 1833.

Morgan, Col. George Indian agent appointed by the Continental Congress and a prominent trader in Kaskaskia; in 1776 he issued safe-conduct passes to "the French people in Chicago" to visit Pittsburgh. The names of these settlers are not recorded. It is known, however, that in 1778 and 1779 Pierre Durand, a Cahokia trader, passed through Chicago en route to Point de Sable's earlier trading post at *Rivière du Chemin* and encountered only Indians. [649]

Morgan, Moses carpenter from Detroit who came with the garrison of the second Fort Dearborn in 1816 to assist in the reconstruction of the fort; in his old age wrote a narrative of his experience.

Morin, William M. native of New York; became a private at Fort Dearborn when Lieutenant Allen enlisted him on Dec. 8, 1833; known as a carpen-

ter and cabinetmaker; in 1834 he deserted and the March 25 issue of the *Chicago Democrat* carried a notice promising $30 reward for information leading to his capture, by order of Major Green. [12]

Morris, Buckner Stith (1800-1879) born in Augusta, KY; attorney; married Evelina Barker in Kentucky in 1832; arrived in 1834 via the Wabash River to Vincennes, from there on horseback to Chicago; formed a law partnership with J. Young Scammon; in August 1835 advertised an office with Edward Casey on Dearborn Street, near South Water Street, second floor of Garrett's auction room; subsequently had an illustrious law career that included being elected mayor of Chicago in the spring of 1838; ✦ (alderman), attorney, &c., Saloon Building. Evelina died in 1847; in 1850 Buckner married Eliza A. Stephenson, who died in 1855; he died on Dec. 16, 1879, and is buried at Rosehill Cemetery. [12]

Morris, Joseph E. see Norris, Joseph E.

Morris, Potily on Oct. 1, 1835, married John Latzky, Father St. Cyr officiating.

Morrison, Charles arrived from New York in 1835; ✦ drayman, 135 Clark St. [The five Morrison brothers had worked under William Jones on the Buffalo harbor and, following his visits to Chicago in 1831 and 1832, had been advised of the opportunities]; had died by 1879. [351]

Morrison, Daniel (c.1819-1880) arrived from New York in 1835; ✦ drayman, 135 Clark St.; died on Nov. 9, 1880. [12]

Morrison, Ephraim (c.1814-1880) born in Oneida County, NY; arrived in October 1834; ✦ hat and cap factory, Dearborn Street, between Lake and South Water; died on June 15, 1880. [12, 351]

Morrison, Ephraim, Jr. arrived from New York in 1835; ✦ teamster, 111 Madison St.; died in 1880. [351]

Morrison, Ezekiel born in New York c.1810; arrived in 1833; ✦ carpenter, 123 Clark St.; by the 1850s had become a leader in the emerging railroad industry; lived at 125 Clark St. in 1885. [12, 351]

BUCKNER STITH MORRIS [12]

Morrison, James M. arrived from New York in 1833; a member of the fire engine company No.1 ("Fire Kings") in December 1835, and a firewarden in 1836; ✦ carpenter, 131 Clark St.; had died by 1879. [12, 351]

Morrison, Orsemus arrived from New York in 1833 to attend the first sale of school lands and bought a 200 foot lot at the SE corner of Clark and Madison streets for $62 in silver, where he built a frame tenement house from timber cut on the north branch; also acquired land within block 7 of the School Section Addition, fronting Harrison Street (416 feet) and Halsted Street (400 feet) for $61; married to Lucy Paul; a very large man, weighing 300 pounds; appointed street commissioner in the fall of 1833, jointly with Silas W. Sherman; collector and constable—★★★ Chicago's 1st—in July 1835; in the Dec. 9 *Chicago Democrat* he placed the notice "Pewter Up All persons who is not known by the Collector, owning property on the corporation or as agent for such, will please to call at his office in front of the (Eagle Coffee House) and pay his tax by the first of January, …"; again constable in June 1836; alderman for the second ward in 1837; ✦ street commissioner, collector, coroner, 153 Clark St.; in 1885 his widow lived at 1510 Washington Blvd.; for one of his first official acts as constable and coroner, see Fernando Jones' story under entry Jones, Fernando. [12, 351]

Morse, Reverend Jedediah sent by Secretary of War John Calhoun to visit northwestern Indian tribes and government factors in 1820 in order to gain information helpful in determining future policies of the United States factory system; at Fort Dearborn he found that factor Jacob Varnum's fur trade for all of 1818 amounted to only $25; Congress abolished the factory system in 1822. [12]

Mortt, August U.S. Army private of German extraction garrisoned at Fort Dearborn, enlisted July 9, 1806; listed in Kinzie's account books on Nov. 4, 1806; May 10, 1807; and Dec. 9, 1811; survived the massacre of 1812 but was killed by his Indian captors during the winter of 1812-13. [226, 404]

Moselle, Charles arrived in 1832 and served under Capt. Gholson Kercheval in the Chicago militia during the Black Hawk War. [714]

Mosely, Flavel also Moseley; arrived from New York in 1834; active as a volunteer fireman; served as school inspector and promotor of community schools; ✦ Mosely & McCord (Jason), merchants, South Water Street; member of the Presbyterian church; on the board of education in the 1850s; died in Chicago in 1867. [12]

Mount Joliet also *Mont Jolliet*, Mount Juliet, Monjolly; Indian name: *missouratenoui* [*pirogue mound*; *missouri* means *pirogue*]; a distinct alluvial mound that formerly stood on the western bank of the Des Plaines River, about 40 miles SW of Chicago; was described by early travelers as having had the form of a truncated cone, 60 feet high,

1,300 feet long at the base, and 225 feet wide, its top perfectly level, its regular sides sloping at 45 degrees; observed by Abbé St. Cosme in 1699, and shown on maps as early as 1674 (Louis Jolliet) and 1778 (Thomas Hutchins). An entry in the journal of [see] Hugh Heward records a French village near the mound in 1790. In 1789, while exploring the Illinois River and the portage connecting with Lake Michigan, Lieutenant Armstrong observed Mount Joliet and described it in his report to the government [see below]. The mound no longer exists; parts were leveled during the construction of the Illinois & Michigan Canal, and its clay core was mined in production of tiles and bricks for the growing city. [414, 640]

Lieutenant Armstrong describing Mt. Joliet:
Mount Juliet stands on a delightful Grassy plain and is a beautiful work of nature. The side that fronts the water is about fifty perches in length [one perch equals 5 1/2 yards; eds.] and is nearly thirty in breadth. … Its perpendicular height above the Surface of the plain is 60 or 70 feet; the top is perfectly level. It is upward of two hundred yards from the water side ….

mountain lion *Felis concolor*; panther, cougar, puma, catamount or painter; this animal was encountered and hunted in Illinois by early explorers but was never plentiful. When Charles Jouett, Indian agent, brought his bride Susan on horseback from Kentucky to Fort Dearborn mid winter in 1808, he kept the "panthers," whose frequent cries the party could hear during the night, away with the help of campfires. Mountain lions were still reported seen in the 1830s near S Chicago and in the Indiana dunes; probably all mountain lions were exterminated in Illinois before 1870. For bobcat, *Felix rufus*, see separate entry. [74, 341]

Moyan, John U.S. Army private at Fort Dearborn, enlisted on June 28, 1806; killed in action at the massacre of 1812. [226]

Mud Lake known as "le petit lac" by the French; also Lac Marais, Swamp Lake, Portage Lake; a swampy, elongated lake, its western end divided

into N and S arms, both now eliminated by construction, was 5 miles in length and located in the depression left behind when the ancestral Chicago River changed course and flow direction c.3800 years ago; instead of continuing to follow the old outlet of glacial Lake Chicago and run into the Des Plaines River, the water broke its banks near Lake Street and ran into Lake Michigan. Mud Lake straddled the divide between the Great Lakes and the Mississippi River system, representing the central portion of the Chicago Portage route, stretching from the Chicago River's south branch (Albany Avenue and 31st Street) to the beginning of Portage Creek (Harlem Avenue and 49th Street); Portage Creek flowed from Mud Lake into the Des Plaines River. For an account on the abundance of water fowl on Mud Lake in pioneer days, see birds.

Mulford, Edward H. (c.1794-1878) was a major in the War of 1812 and once an escort of General LaFayette; watchmaker; arrived in 1833 with his wife, Rebecca, to engage in the jewelry business of his son [see] James H. Mulford; a second son, Edward H. Mulford, Jr., also joined the business of his brother (not later than 1839); in 1836 Edward, Sr., acquired from the government 160 acres of land at $1.25 per acre at [see] *Grosse Pointe* and built a cabin on the W side of Ridge Road Trail to secure his preemption claim; ✦ Major E.H. Mulford, Illinois Street near State; held a commission as justice of the peace; died on March 5, 1878, in Evanston. [12, 351]

Mulford, James H. son of Edward H. Mulford; arrived late in 1832 or in 1833; subscribed to the *Chicago Democrat* in November 1833; jeweler and seller of novelties and art objects, with a store one door S of the post office, which at that time was at the NE corner of Lake and South Water streets; on Jan. 7, 1834, Mulford advertised in the *Chicago Democrat* watches and jewelry, adding that he would pay "cash for old silver"; in June and July of that year he had for sale, "at reasonable prices," American, French, and English engravings, as well as original still life and landscape paintings; in August 1835, he requested 500 ounces of tortoise shell for the "highest cash"; ✦ James H. & Edward H. Jr. Mulford, jewelers, &c., Dearborn Street. [12]

Mullarky, Thomas   a child by this name was enrolled as grade school student in the class taught by [see] John Watkins in December 1835. Names of corresponding parents were not recorded. [728]

Müller, Jacob   also Mueller; born c.1810 in Rohbach, Germany; arrived in May 1834; married Catharine Baumgarten; still lived in Chicago in 1879. [12]

Muller, Peter   a Frenchman or *métis*; lived at Wolf Point c.1826, near Alexander Robinson; voted in election of Nov. 25, 1830; Peter's wife was Robinson's half sister who, later as widow, continued to reside there until c.1842.

Münster, Sebastien   (1489-1552) scholar, cosmographer, cartographer; first to reintroduce Solinus and Ptolemy, and arrange with his collaborators in atlas form various, then modern, separate maps for each of the four continents known at the time; viz. Europe, Africa, Asia, and America; of particular interest is ✳ "Novae Insvlae, XVII Tabvla," printed in Basel in 1540. [502]

murder   ★★★ Chicago's 1st murder trial after the town had incorporated took place in the fall of 1834, Circuit Judge Young presiding in an unfinished 20-by-20 foot store on Dearborn Street, between Lake and Water streets. In a drunken fit, the Irish laborer John Fitzgerald, on returning home and finding something not to his liking, had beaten his wife, Elizabeth, and she had died from the injury. Thomas Ford was the prosecuting district attorney, and James Collins successfully defended the accused before the jury; he was acquitted. The second murder trial in Chicago did not occur until 1840, although a murder occurred and a suspect was indicted in 1835, the trial was held in Iroquois County because of a change of venue. For details of this case, see Norris, Joseph E.

Murphy, Hiram P.   arrived in 1835 and remained

in Chicago. [351]

Murphy, James K.   born c.1824 in Ireland; arrived in August 1835; ✦ clerk, John Fennerty [fancy dry goods store, South Water Street]; still lived in Chicago in 1879. [12]

Murphy, John   (1799-1881) born in Ireland, married Bridget Rogers on April 26, 1835, Father St. Cyr officiating; said to have moved to [now] Lake County.

Murphy, John   (1803-1850) born in County Cork, Ireland, and a strict Catholic, arrived with his wife, Harriet [née Austin, a strict Baptist], in June of 1834; the children of this alliance, reports John Wentworth, were all baptized in both religions; ran Mark Beaubien's Exchange Coffee House for two years and in 1836 managed the Sauganash, renaming it United States Hotel, but in 1837 he built his own United States Hotel W of the river [West Water Street, corner of Randolph]; served as alderman in 1839, and again in 1844; died of cholera on Aug. 14, 1850, while still residing at his hotel; in 1885, his widow lived at 351 West Adams St. [12, 351, 357, 706, 707]

Murphy, N.   married Mrs. M. Frauner in 1834, said to have been the first Chicago marriage in which Father St. Cyr officiated.

Murray, John   came with his wife, Amy (née Napier), and their son [see next entry], Robert Nelson, and in-laws, Joseph and John Napier, and their families on the *Telegraph* in July 1831, immediately journeying W in prairie schooners to land along the Du Page River, where Joseph Napier had previously made a claim; served as private in Harry Boardman's company, part of Major Bailey's Cook County voluntary militia, from May 24 until mid-June 1832, stationed at Fort Dearborn during the Black Hawk War.

Murray, Robert Nelson   born c.1814 in Washington, NY; arrived on the *Telegraph* in July 1831 with his parents, John and Amy Murray, all traveling westward to the Du Page River to homestead within the Naper settlement; served as corporal in the

Chicago militia company under Captain Napier during the Black Hawk War; became an attorney and later a county judge; living in Naperville in 1885. [12, 351]

Murray, William   an enterprising Englishman who lived in Kaskaskia in 1765, established in 1773 the "Illinois Land Company" and, in the presence of the civil and military officials of the town, acquired from the several assembled Indian chiefs two very large tracts of land in exchange for trade goods, weapons, horses, cattle, and other specified items. In the deeds, one of the designated boundaries was "Chicagou or Garlick creek," such that the site of the present city was included in the grant; the deeds were later declared null and void by the U.S. Supreme Court, based on the well-established rule that the Indian-owned frontier lands could be sold by them only to a government. Furthermore, these purported grants were illegal under then-prevailing British law and George III's Proclamation of 1763, as well as earlier French and later American law. [12, 608]

Musham, Harry Albert   (1886-1973) born in Chicago, grandson of a lake schooner captain, son of an 1871 fire marshal; naval architect, pioneered a system of weather forecasting based on the fluctuation of the water levels in the Great Lakes; in 1939 was chairman of the Fort Dearborn Memorial Commission, submitting a report on the location of the first Fort Dearborn that determined the city's placement of pavement markers; in 1943 published research on the location of the 1812 massacre or battle. [*Journal of the Illinois State Historical Society* 36:21–40]

muskrat   *Ondatra zibethicus*; abundant in Illinois in pioneer days and still plentiful; gradually replaced beavers as a trade item in the late phase of the fur trade (1830s) when the supply of beaver pelts dwindled in the Midwest and NW regions. Elijah Wentworth, Sr., related that, when he came to Chicago in 1827, "a great deal of the land in Chicago, along the river and lake, was low and marshy with numerous muscrat houses scattered about." [341]

Myers, Frederick A. soldier stationed at Fort Dearborn who kept a journal of events from early 1832 to February 1834, preserved at the Chicago Historical Society; after leaving the army he became a fur trader among the Ojibwa, living with an Indian woman and writing an English-Ojibwa dictionary; by August 1835 was back in Chicago, owner of considerable downtown property and selling groceries; his name was on a school-related petition signed on Sept. 19; married to Sene Hayden; said to have died of cholera and was buried at the northside cemetery that later became Lincoln Park. [12, 314a]

Myers, Leo see Mayer, Nathaniel.

Nation du Feu *nation of fire*, erroneous French term for a group of Great Lakes Indians that included the Mascoutens, also known as the Prairie Band of the Potawatomi, and the Chippewa or Ojibwa. The native word *Mascouten* means *prairie*, not *fire*.

Nanaloibi Potawatomi chief, living temporarily at Chicago in the late 1770s when the village had been abandoned by French settlers and traders during the Revolutionary War; both Nanaloibi and Mechkigi, a fellow chief, were much courted at the time by both British and American agents.

Nancy Dousman 130-ton schooner built at Black River, OH, in 1833; in 1834 called at Chicago four times under Captain Saunderson [Sanderson?] with lumber and passengers, bringing, among others, Dr. James A. Marshall on Aug. 15; returned once in 1835 under Captain Shooks on Aug. 16, coming from Detroit. [48]

Naperville, Illinois earlier also Napiersville and Napierville, and initially Napier's or Naper's Settlement and Napersville; see Napier, Joseph. This settlement was larger than Chicago in the early 1830s, yet in Cook County; now in DuPage County, initially its county seat. In the July 23, 1834, *Chicago Democrat* a notice reads:

A meeting of the settlers in Naper's Settlement, is requested to be holden at the house of Joseph Napier, on the second day of August next, at 3 o'clock, P.M. for the purpose of ascertaining the minds of the settlers about subscribing to resolutions that we will not crowd upon any settler's claim, nor countenance it in others, and we will not bid upon improvements or claims, nor countenance that, and to appoint a committee to examine claims when they are reported as being unreasonable. A Settler. Napier's Settlement, July 11, 1834.

On July 7, Morris Sleight had written to a friend that the settlers around the settlement had agreed "... they will not bid against each other; anything to the contrary they have declared Club law, and are determined to put it in force." [171, 586, 677]

Napier, John later Naper; brother of [see] Joseph Napier; arrived with wife, Betsy, and two children from Ohio on July 15, 1831; steamer sailor on Lake Erie from 1828 to 1830; captain of a steamer between Buffalo and Detroit; commanded the *Telegraph* to Chicago; settled W along the Du Page River [Naperville]; a corporal in the Cook County volunteer militia under his brother during the Black Hawk scare in 1832. [12, 586]

Napier, Joseph (1788-1862) later Naper; of Scottish descent, Napier being the original Scottish spelling; from Vermont, elder brother of John; sailor and captain of sailing vessels on Lake Erie until 1830; built the schooner *Telegraph* on the bank of the Ashtabula River, then sailed to Chicago with his wife, Almeda, their two children, his brother and sister, Amy Murray, their families and acquaintances, arriving on July 15, 1831 to deliver the vessel to its new owner; soon after the families journeyed W to a claim previously made on the west bank of the Du Page River (becoming a neighbor of Stephen J. Scott, who in late spring had sown crops in anticipation) and established a settlement [Naperville]; opened a store among the new log structures, for about a year in partnership with P.F.W. Peck who had arrived with the brothers on the *Telegraph*;

brought hardware for a grist- and sawmill, built and run by [see] Bailey Hobson; in September 1831, organized a local school district and hired a teacher, sending six of his own children to the school. From July 19 to Aug. 15, 1832, during the Black Hawk War, Joseph, in the rank of captain, organized and commanded the militia company of mounted volunteers of that part of Cook County [For the complete list of militia members who served under Napier, see Andreas, vol. 1:271.]; in 1837, he served as representative to the Illinois House of Representatives for Cook County, working on a committee with Stephen A. Douglas; later platted the town of Naperville; ➡ Naper Avenue (6600 W). [12, 586]

Napieralski, Capt. Joseph born in c.1800 at Kaliszy, Poland; said to have been the first Polish immigrant to Chicago, arriving in 1834; served as captain in the Polish army during the disastrous 1831 war with Russia, fleeing to the United States by way of Prussia and Norway; other members of his company followed him to the United States in subsequent years; remained in Chicago until his death, his story being reported by one of his descendents, Emilia Napieralska. [576, 544]

Napoleon 107-ton lake schooner, built in 1828 at Detroit for Oliver Newberry; called at Chicago frequently during the 1830s; dispatched from Detroit in May 1831 to help with the evacuation of the Fort Dearborn garrison, then under Lt. David Hunter as acting commandant in the absence of Major Fowle. On April 17, 1833, the *Napoleon* left the port of Chicago with the first shipment of western produce for eastern markets, carrying beef, tallow, hides, and beeswax belonging to merchant George W. Dole; John Stewart was then the master. In 1834, the ship called at Chicago seven times under Captain Stuart with passengers and merchandise, mostly from Buffalo, NY; in 1835 called three times under Captain Chase [Case?]. [12]

Nash, Jeffrey a Negro slave purchased at Detroit on Sept. 5, 1803, by John Kinzie and Thomas Forsyth, apparently first taken to Chicago and later to Peoria, where he worked for several years in the business his masters owned jointly, before he ran away, making his way to St. Louis and eventually to New Orleans, where he is said to have had a wife and child. Forsyth and Kinzie initiated a suit to recover him but were denied ownership by the Louisiana Supreme Court, based on the Ordinance of 1787. [556]

Naunongee also Nan-non-gee; Potawatomi chief of a large Indian village at the mouth of the Calumet River; was severely wounded at the 1812 massacre at Fort Dearborn by Sgt. Otho Hayes with a bayonet thrust, who at the same time lost his life from a tomahawk blow to his head; the only Indian chief known to have died [later at his village] because of the massacre. [226]

Navigator schooner from Buffalo, NY; called at Chicago under Captain Rice on Nov. 5, 1834.

N.C. Baldwin 145-ton schooner from Buffalo, NY; called twice at Chicago with passengers and merchandise under Captain Sweet in 1835, on June 20 and Oct 22. [48]

Neads, John from Virginia; U.S. Army private at Fort Dearborn; enlisted in July 1808; taken prisoner with his wife, Sarah, and child by the Indians after the massacre of 1812; all three died in captivity, John between Jan. 15 and 20, 1813; the four year old son had died of exposure when tied to a tree and left behind by the Indians; the mother died soon after from hunger and cold. [226]

Neff & Co. placed an ad in the Aug. 22, 1835 *Chicago American* asking for "8 or 10 first rate journeymen carpenters, who will be paid from $1.75 to $2.00 per day."

Nelson, — U.S. Army private at Fort Dearborn, originally from Maryland, enlisted in May 1809; following the massacre of 1812, he died of exposure during the following winter while in Indian captivity. [226]

Neptune brig from Buffalo, NY; called at Chicago under Captain Wilkesson twice in 1834 with po-

FIRST SHIPMENT OF GRAIN FROM CHICAGO'S FIRST DOCK.   [12]

tatoes and bacon, on July 2 and Oct 20.

Nescotnemeg also Nuscotnemeg, known as Wild Sturgeon; Potawatomi; planned the Fort Dearborn massacre of 1812 as one of the principal chiefs involved; was severely wounded in the chest then, but survived; his village was on the Kankakee River. [226]

New Connecticut schooner from Buffalo, NY; called at Chicago under Captain Baxter on Sept. 27, 1834, under Captain Kennedy on July 22, 1835.

Newberry Addition the Walter L. Newberry Addition to Chicago, comprising 40 acres; it occupied the eastern half of the western half of the NE quarter of Section 9, the land loosely enclosed by

Kinzie, Franklin, Chicago, and LaSalle streets, adjacent to the W side of the Wolcott Addition; purchased in 1833 for $1,062, estimated value in 1864 at $750,000.

Newberry & Dole Detroit merchant house, forwarding, commission, and retail, opened a Chicago branch in 1829 through J.S.C. Hogan, whom the firm sent from Detroit; a flour and provision store in one of the first three frame buildings on the corner of South Water and Dearborn streets, opposite Beaubien's store, owned jointly by Oliver Newberry and George W. Dole. On Jan. 14, 1833, they advertised "shot guns for sale" in the Chicago Democrat. During the same year the firm entered the meat packing business in grand style; see below the text of ★★★ **Chicago's 1st** bill of lading for beef; the partners applied for wharfing privileges on Nov. 21, 1835. The account books (1831-38) of this storage, forwarding, and commission business are preserved in the Chicago Historical Society. [12]

Text of Newberry & Dole's Bill of Lading:

Shipped in good order and well conditioned by Newberry & Dole on board of the schooner called Napoleon, *whereof is master for the present voyage John Stewart, now lying in the port of Chicago, and bound for Detroit, to say: O. Newberry, Detroit. –87 bbls. [barrels] beef; 14 bbls. tallow; 2 bbls. beeswax; 152 dry hides, weighing 4,695 lbs. Being marked and numbered as in the margin and to be delivered at the port of Detroit in like good order (the dangers of the lakes and rivers excepted) unto consignees, or to their assignees— he or they paying freight at — per bbl. bulk. In witness whereof the master of said vessel hath affirmed to two bills of lading, all of this tener and date, one of which to be accomplished, the other to stand void, Chicago, April 17, 1833. John Stewart.*

Newberry, Oliver   a native of East Windsor, CT, older brother of Walter L.; lived in Detroit from 1920 until 1862, the year of his death; in c.1825 he became active in lake shipping, and within a few years owned a fleet of vessels in addition to docks, stores, warehouses, and offices at various points around the Lake Erie shore; in 1829 sent J.S.C. Hogan from Detroit to Chicago to build and operate a store for him; purchased in 1830 from the government lot 4 in block 16 and subsequently from G.W. Dole lot 4 in block 17 on South Water Street [see map on page 44], where Hogan, in 1831, developed the business into the "principal store in town" under the name Newberry & Dole, "licensed to sell goods," located on the corner of South Water and Dearborn streets, with its own dock on the river. On April 3, 1832, Newberry purchased eight choice lots in Sections 16 and 17 for a total of $238, and secured the appointment as official sutler to Fort Dearborn. Of

Walter Loomis Newberry [410]

the many sailing ships he owned, the *Napoleon*, the *Savage*, the *Austerlitz*, and the *Marshall Ney* made visits to the Chicago harbor; his *Michigan* was the first steamer to pass the new Dearborn Street drawbridge in 1834, and on July 12 the *Illinois*, the first large commercial sailing vessel, landed at the wharf of N & D; ◆ forwarding commission merchant, North Water Street corner with Rush. [12, 118]

Newberry, Walter Loomis   (1804-1868) born in East Windsor, CT, younger brother of Oliver Newberry; early leading citizen of Chicago who, during an early visit in 1830, had bought a 40 acre plot just N of the river in Section 9, reaching from Kinzie Street to Chicago Avenue, and who returned in 1833 to make his fortune. He was one of the few successful land speculators able to retain his wealth during the panic of 1837 and the depression from 1839 to 1842; ◆ attorney and real estate, office Newberry & Dole. In 1841 he organized and served as first president of the Young Men's Association of Chicago, that later became

the Chicago Library Association; married Julia Butler Clapp on Nov. 22, 1842; served as alderman in 1851. In his will he left half his fortune—$2.1 million—to provide for the establishment of a Chicago library which, long after his death, developed into a world renowned research and reference institution bearing his name; ➡ Newberry Avenue (828 W). [12]

New France   see also Canada; early name for the original French possessions in northeastern North America, initially extending from the St. Lawrence River and its basin, including the Great Lakes, and S through the Mississippi River basin to the Gulf of Mexico; thanks to the faithfully drawn and kept records of the Jesuit missionaries, few periods in history have been so well illuminated as the French regime in North America; in 1717 the southern portion became the Province of Louisiane. The area now occupied by Chicago straddles what was the border between New France and Louisiana Province; the border followed the divide between the Great Lakes and the Mississippi drainage systems. Also see Louisiana Province, as well as the table on page 209 on Chicago jurisdictional chronology. [128, 129, 217, 222, 362, 368, 396, 666, 680]

New Lenox, IL   site of a 1994 archeological discovery possibly related to La Salle's 1683 activities in the greater Chicago area; this Hickory Creek site was excavated and mapped by archaeologists in 1994, and promptly reburied because it is part of a municipal golf course owned by the New Lennox Park District; for details, see John F. Swenson's essay on page 377. Also see Chronology section, year 1683.

New Orleans   location first sighted in 1699 by de Bienville and d'Iberville as an Indian portage from the lower Mississippi to Lake Pontchartrain and the Gulf of Mexico; founded as a French settlement in 1718 by de Bienville, it became the capital of Louisiana Province in 1722, and was named in honor of the Duke of Orleans, French regent at the time. From 1717 to 1763, the Chicago area was formally a part of this province and was under the jurisdiction of New Orleans. For additional details, see Chicago jurisdictional chronology on page 209.

New York   80-ton schooner, called at Chicago on Aug. 5, 1834, coming from Cleveland, and again on Nov. 5, 1834, coming from Buffalo; called once in 1835, on July 31 from Buffalo.

New York Exchange   see Exchange Coffee House.

New York House   hotel built in 1834 on the N side of Lake Street and opened in 1835; the initial owners and managers were Lathrop Johnson and George Stevens, then Johnson alone until 1839, when L.M. Osterhould took over.

newspapers   for Chicago's first newspapers, see *Chicago Democrat* (Nov. 26, 1833); *Chicago American* (June 8, 1835).

Newton, Hollis   owned a 48 acre plot where he ran a roadside hotel and tavern three miles S of Chicago in 1835; died on Aug. 25, 1835. [12]

Niagara formation   a thick layer of solid limestone underlying large parts of the Great Lakes region, derived from sediments of shallow warm seas that existed during the Silurian period 400 million years ago. In the Chicago area the rock is usually found at a depth of 50 to 75 feet, underneath the silt, sand, and gravel left by the Wisconsin glacier, but it comes to the surface in many locations, such as at Stony Island, Stony Ford, and Riverside Ford. Chicago's skyscrapers depend on the limestone foundation for a solid footing, and much of Chicago's building material, such as lannon stone, is so derived.

Nichols, E.C.   arrived from New York in 1832. [351]

Nichols, Luther   (1805-1881) born in Gilbertsville, NY; arrived for the Black Hawk War from Fort Niagara, with his wife, Ellen, and one daughter, Adeline A.; as corporal under the immediate charge of Maj. William Whistler in June 1832, he helped bury the cholera victims of General Scott's army, was discharged late in 1833; elected constable on Aug. 5, 1835; ◆ drayman, 50 Dearborn St.; in 1855, as the Chicago police captain under Mayor Levi Boone, he confronted the rebels during the "Lager Riots"; died on May 2, 1881. Adeline later married Abram Heartt; her early recollections are preserved in the Chicago Historical Society. [12, 351, 544]

Nickols, Patterson   advertised "Ohio Flour and Butter, for sale at J. Kinzie's Ware House" in the Dec. 12, 1835, *Chicago American*; ◆ livery stable keeper, Kinzie Street near North State.

Nicollet, Jean   (1598-1642) also Nicolet; born in Cherbourg, France, immigrated to Quebec in 1618; lived several years among the Algonkins along the Ottawa River and learned their language; as an agent of Champlain, the governor of New France, was sent W in 1634 to explore unknown territory, seeking the "men of the sea" [see Green Bay]; traveled with seven Huron Indians through the Straights of Mackinac to Green Bay, becoming the first European to see Lake Michigan and to set foot on the territory that later became Wisconsin; on the shores of Green Bay he met the Winnebago, for whom he dressed in embroidered colorful Chinese damask, believing he had reached Cathay; farther up the Fox River in Wisconsin he encountered the Mascouten; for a description of Nicollet's momentous encounter see the passage from Du Creux' *Historia Canadensis* below. Nicollet was married to Marguerite Couillart; was frequently consulted on Indian matters until his untimely drowning near Quebec in 1642; ➡ Nicolet Avenue (7044 W). [12, 100, 205, 383]

Excerpt from Du Creux' *History Canadenses*:

When he [Nicollet] *was two days distant* [from the Winnebago], *he sent forward one of his own company to make known to the nation to which they were going that a European embassador was approaching with gifts, who, in behalf of the Huron, desired to secure their friendship. The embassy was received with applause, and young men were immediately sent to meet him, who were to carry the baggage and the equipment of the Manitourinion (wonderful man) and escort him with honor. Nicolet was clad in a Chinese robe of silk, skillfully ornamented with birds and flowers of many colors; he carried in each hand a small pistol. When he had discharged these, the more timid persons, boys and women, betook themselves to flight, to escape as quickly as possible from a man who, they said, carried the thunder in both hands. But the rumor of his coming having spread far and wide, the chiefs, with their followers, assembled directly to the number of four or five thousand persons; and the matter having been discussed and considered in a general council, a treaty was made in due form. Afterward each of the chiefs gave a banquet after their fashion; and at one of these, strange to say, a hundert and twenty beavers were eaten.*

Niles, IL   see Dutchman's Grove.

Niles, MI   historic town 92 miles E of Chicago; site of 17th century Jesuit mission and 18th century St. Joseph post; located on the St. Joseph River, 25 miles from its mouth, and was accessible to small steamboats from the lake by 1837. By 1831, Niles had its own post office, one year after White Pigeon, 35 miles E of Niles. Early Chicago mail went first through White Pigeon, then through Niles by horseback; beginning in September 1833 there was stagecoach service between Niles and Chicago. [357, 618]

Nine Mile Prairie   term used by early settlers for the stretch of prairie between the Chicago settlement and the ferry on the Des Plaines River. For a description, see entry on Harriet Martineau.

Ninson, William   arrived in the fall of 1832 and voted in the first town election in 1833. [12]

N. Norton   schooner from Buffalo, NY; called at Chicago under Captain Oliver on Aug. 21, 1834; ran ashore on Lake Michigan in 1842. [48]

Noble, John   (c.1802-1885) son of [see] Mark Noble, Sr., and brother of Mark, Jr.; born in Yorkshire, England; butcher, arrived in June 1831; raised cattle with his brother on the S side; the cattle were slaughtered at Madison Street and Michigan Av enue, and packed at G.W. Dole's warehouse at Dearborn and South Water streets; some remember that during the Black Hawk War of 1832 the brothers made available 152 steers to the soldiers at the fort and to the refugees from the countryside, alleviating famine. The brothers bought from the government and private sellers a lot of real estate in blocks 8, 10, 18, 19, 23, 28, and 56 [see map on page 44], selling much again within a few years. Sometime in 1833, John built with Mark, Jr., and sister Mary a log cabin on the north branch [at Belmont Avenue], yet he also lived in ★★★ **Chicago's 1st** brick house, built for him by Alanson Sweet and William Worthington on Kinzie Street near Lake and Rush; on Aug. 13, 1834, the firm "Wesencraft & Noble" advertised in the *Chicago Democrat* for a "first rate sawyer" for their steam sawmill; ✦ real estate, resided at Dutchman's Point; died on Jan. 13, 1885; ➡ Noble Street (1400 W). [12, 351]

Noble, Mark, Jr.   son of [see] Mark Noble, Sr., and younger brother of [see] John Noble; arrived with his family in June 1831; partnered George Bickerdyke who erected a steam sawmill on the Des Plaines River in 1832; married Charlotte Wesencraft of Buffalo on Nov. 29, 1833, the Hon. R.J. Hamilton officiating at a joint ceremony, also the marriage of George Bickerdyke and Mary Noble; partnered his brother raising and butchering cattle, and in buying and selling land; ✦ real estate, Dutchman's Point; sometime afterward left for TX; had died by 1879. [12, 351]

Noble, Mark, Sr.   (c.1765-1839) English butcher who arrived in August 1831 with his family, among them the adult children John; Mark, Jr.; Elizabeth; and Mary (see separate entries); sometimes referred to as "Father Noble," for he was a fervent Methodist Episcopalian and often organized prayer meetings in his home and elsewhere before a pastor was regularly available; occupied the old Kinzie House on the N side of the river where he organized prayer meetings, replaced with a small cabin he built at

corner of State and South Water streets; once the northern pier construction of the river mouth in 1832 resulted in accretion of additional beach sand, he entered a claim for 29 acres of the new beach property with the U.S. Land Office; daughters Elizabeth and Mary helped organize the first Sunday school with Philo Carpenter on Aug. 19, 1832; ✦ farmer, Dutchman's Point; as per notice in the *Daily American*, died Nov. 25, 1839. The farmhouse Mark built in 1833 on a prairie ridge was sold by his widow, Margret, in 1846, and still exists as the southern wing of the Noble-Seymour-Crippen House at 5622 N. Newark Ave. in Norwood Park.

Nolan, Michael   on Aug. 29, 1835, married Mary Green, Father St. Cyr officiating.

Noles, Joseph   also Knowles; U.S. Army private at Fort Dearborn; enlisted in September 1910; taken prisoner by Indians at the massacre of 1812 and later ransomed. [226]

Norris, J.   placed an ad in the Dec. 16, 1835, *Chicago Democrat* announcing that "A FEW GENTEEL BOARDERS can be accommodated at the long House between the Methodist and Episcopal Meeting House, just across the Draw Bridge."

Norris, Joseph E.   though listed also as Morris, actually Joseph Thomasson; indicted in Cook County for the 1835 murder of a man [Felix Legree] on the road to Ottawa, between Laughtons' Tavern and the house of Elijah Wentworth, Jr. [Flag Creek]; James Grant was the prosecuting attorney, Henry Moore the public defender; during an attempt to escape, the prisoner injured an innocent bystander, the jeweler Edward Mulford. Because of a change of venue, the trial was held in Iroquois County and led to the execution of Norris by hanging on June 10, 1836. [13, 707]

North, August   private at Fort Dearborn under Captain Heald; taken prisoner by Indians at the massacre of Aug. 15, 1812, and killed later. [226]

North Branch Addition   also known as the [see] Russell & Mather Addition.

North Water Street   ➡ (400 N); running parallel to and immediately N of the main part of the Chicago River, so named by James Thompson in his original plat of Chicago, 1830.

North West Army   during the Black Hawk War, the Wolf Point Tavern [Rat Castle] in Chicago became the headquarters of the North West Army of the United States while General Scott was in the settlement.

North West Company   (1783-1821) one of three major rival British fur trading companies in the Canadian north, competing with the Hudson Bay Co. and the XY Co. during the era of fur trade; was founded in 1783, headquartered at Grand Portage Bay, its agents only occasionally penetrating as far S as Chicago; in 1803 the company removed from French to British territory and eventually fused with the Hudson Bay Co., which lasted until 1823.

Northwest Ordinance   an "Act to Provide for the Government of the Territory North West of the River Ohio," passed by the Continental Congress in 1787, and ratified by the U.S. Congress in 1789; created the mechanism by which future states, including Illinois, would be formed and governed. [571]

Northwest Territory   officially "the Territory Northwest of the River Ohio"; created by the Continental Congress, when it passed the Northwest Ordinance; Chicago was part of the Northwest Territory of the United States from July 13, 1787, to May 7, 1800; on the latter date, Chicago became part of the Indiana Territory. See jurisdictional chart on page 209. [59, 152, 512, 544, 571]

Norton, Nelson R.   born in Hampton, NY, in 1807; carpenter and shipwright who came on Nov. 16, 1833; in the spring of 1834 he built the Dearborn Street drawbridge, ★★★ **Chicago's 1st** 16 feet wide, 300 feet long, and with an opening of 60 feet; with the carpenter brothers Polemus D. and Thomas E. Hamilton in the spring of 1835, built the first commercial sailing vessel in Chicago, the sloop *Clarissa*, which was owned by the three carpenters and which was launched on May 12, 1836; late in 1835 he filed a claim for wharfing privileges for lot 3, block 2; ♦ bridge-builder, NW corner of State and Indiana [Grand] streets; removed to Aldon, MN, in 1839 and still lived there in 1885. [12, 351]

Norton, W. A.   became a fire warden in December 1835. [12, 28]

Nouvelle France   also *Nova Francia* [Latin], Canada; French term meaning *New France*, as on Du Val's map on page 12; *Nouvelle France* began with the exploration of the St. Lawrance Gulf and River in 1534 by Jacques Cartier, followed by his annexation of the entire St. Lawrence drainage system in 1536 in the name of François I, king of France; it became an official province of France in 1672, and remained French territory until 1763. Chicagou was part of *Nouvelle France.*

Noyesville   name of an early community in the area that is now Oak Park; a Noyesville Post Office was opened on Aug. 10, 1846, and remained so named until 1871, when it became the Oak Park Post Office.

Nuscotnemeg   see Nescotnemeg.

Oak Park, IL   formerly known as [see] Noyesville; western suburb, approximately 10 miles from Lake Michigan, developed on an old sand bar (geologists term it the Oak Park spit) that formed 11,000 years ago on the shore of Lake Chicago; first settler was Joseph Kettlestrings (1833) from Yorkshire, England, who worked at a steam sawmill on the east bank of the Des Plaines River, just N of Lake Street bridge, built in 1831 by the Chicago firm Bickerdyke & Noble and later owned by Ashbel Steele, River Forest's first permanent resident. The mill gave Oak Park [and River Forest] its start by attracting laborers; earlier names are Kettlestrings' Grove and Oak Ridge; the name Oak Park was not used until 1872, and incorporation did not occur until 1902;

MAHLON DICKERSON OGDEN [678]

➡ Oak Park Avenue (6800 W). [166, 701]

Oak Ridge   (1) an early name until 1871 for the community of Oak Park; (2) a wooded sand ridge that extended from near Douglas Grove (Lake Shore near 35th Street) in a SW direction towards Blue Island; this ancient shoreline of Lake Chicago had long been a popular Indian trail and was surveyed as a northern portion of the Vincennes Trail in 1833-34.

Oak Ridge Inn   see Kettlestrings, Joseph.

Oakwood Cemetery   see cemeteries.

Oak Woods   early name for what is now called Hyde Park.

Odocoileus virginianus   see white-tailed deer.

Ogden Avenue   see Ottawa Trail.

Ogden's Slough   a slow moving creek that drained part of the swampland in the triangle between the main part of the Chicago River and the south branch; emptied into the south branch below 12th Street; a similar rivulet, a short distance farther S, was called Healy's Slough. [728]

Ogden, Mahlon Dickerson   younger brother of William, a lawyer who came in 1836; ♦ attorney, [Issac N.] Arnold & Ogden, Clark Street; died on Feb. 14, 1880. [12]

Ogden, William B.   (1805-1877) born in Delaware County, NY; studied law; became a member of the New York legislature and was active in the Erie Railroad project; arrived in June 1835 to handle his brother-in-law Charles Butler's real estate investments; immediately involved himself in town governmental affairs, and in September 1835 he was vested with authority by the town board to purchase in the East and deliver two fire engines. When he returned with them in 1836, he came to stay, bringing his younger brother Mahlon, also a lawyer; a Democrat, William became the first mayor of the city of Chicago by election on May 2, 1837, defeating John H. Kinzie of the Whig Party; ♦ real estate dealer, Kinzie Street near N State, his brother handling much of the business; ➡ Ogden Avenue, a diagonal street in the SW of

WILLIAM B. OGDEN [678]

Chicago. For the origins of this street, see Brush Hill Trail. [12, 98]

Ogee, Joseph *métis*, lived earlier at Peoria and prior to 1830 on Rock River at a crossing and settlement later called Dixon's Ferry; came to Chicago to make purchases at the estate sales of W.H. Wallace on May 10, 1827, and again at the estate sale of François Le Mai on May 12, 1828; was an alcoholic, rendering his ferry service unreliable; in 1830 Dixon bought the ferry and its attached property from Ogee. [220]

Ohio 187-ton steamboat for passengers from Buffalo, NY; built at Sandusky, OH, in 1830; called three times at Chicago under Captain Cotton in the summer of 1834 (June 26, July 17, July 20); capsized at Toledo in 1842. [48]

Ojibwa Indians see Chippewa Indians.

Old Chicago Trail also Archer Trail; originally a portage trail, representing the northern part of the Old Chicago Trail from Bloomington, broadened to a wagon trail in 1834; paralleling the south branch and the Des Plaines River, crossing the latter at [Summit], where Van Austen's tavern was in the 1830s, continuing on the E side of the river to [Brighton], then entering SW of the town at Archer Trail. The first wagon loads of grain, produced by early prairie farmers for shipment to eastern ports, reached Chicago on this trail.

"Old Geese" nickname of [see] Wentworth, Elijah, Sr.

Old Point according to Alexander Beaubien, the location at the river where Dearborn Street later crossed; Dearborn Street bridge was called Old Point Bridge by some.

Old Sand Road early name for the southern portion of the Green Bay Trail; paralleling the lake and following an ancient shoreline [Clark Street]; see Green Bay Indian Trail.

Old Settlers' Society formed on Oct. 22, 1855, with J. H. Kinzie as president, Col. R.J. Hamilton as vice president, J.Y. Scammons as treasurer, George T. Pearsons as secretary; committee for an-

nual festival: G.S. Hubbard, John S. Wright, and John C. Haines; eligible for membership were those who resided in Chicago prior to January 1837, as well as male children of members, born in Chicago prior to 1837, eligible upon reaching the age of 21.

Old Settlers' List see Calumet Club.

Olin, Nelson enterprising Milwaukee resident who made a business trip to Chicago in October 1835 and whose account can be found in his *Reminiscences of Milwaukee* during 1835-36; see the following excerpt of his report, reprinted in the *Wisconsin Magazine of History* 8 (1929-1930):

After returning from the land sale [at Green Bay], *I purchased a yoke of cattle and picked up what hides I could find about Milwaukee and started for Chicago for a load of flour. I paid 2 cents for hides in Milwaukee on the way down, and sold the same in Chicago at twelve and one-half cents per pound. Purchased 12 barrels of flour at $10 per barrel and a yoke of Hoosier cattle, that could not be driven one rod without being led with a rope or behind another pair of cattle, at $60. After getting my cattle together and my flour on the wagon, I started for Milwaukee. I drove out from the store hous on the Main Street, and had not gone ten rods before the wagon was in the mud to the axles. I was stalled and had to roll out every barrel of flour before the wagon could be hauled out. After loading again, I made another move to ward Milwaukee. The bridge that spanned the Chicago River, a stream one rod in width, was made of black-oak poles lying just above the water* [floating log bridge; *eds.*]. *It was one of the poorest excuses for a bridge I ever saw. Above the forks of the Chicago River a boy of fifteen years could at that time run and jump across it without much exertion. After crossing the river the road was very muddy for one-half mile out of town, but then I found very good roads until I reached Root River* [now Racine], *where I came to heavy timber. From that point to Milwaukee there was just no road at all. When I got fastened to trees that could not be drawn over, there was no such thing as backing Hoo-*

Rat de Bois

[259]

sier cattle. I would hitch my lead oxen to the hind end of the wagon and haul it back until loose. In this way I worked my way to Milwaukee. My flour sold at $15 per barrel. It went like hot cakes.

Olscum, Madaline see Alscum, Madaline.

Ondatra zibethicus see muskrat.

O'Neil, Thomas arrived from Ireland in 1834.

O' Neil, John arrived from Ireland in 1834; tinsmith, who at some time served as town collector; ✦ farmer, corner of 22nd and Halsted streets; in 1857 he began a five year term in the penitentiary for the murder of his neighbor Michael Brady. [12, 351]

opossum *Didelphis virginiana*; common indigenous animal throughout the state of Illinois; appears to have been less frequent in pioneer days than it is today; called *rat de bois* [forest rat] in early French accounts of explorers and missionaries [ref. *Jesuit Relations*]. See picture on page 275. [259, 341]

Ordinance of 1784 a federal act for the government of the Western Territory, the provisions of which were never acted upon and which was superseded by the Federal Land Ordinance of 1785.

Ordinance of 1785 see Federal Land Ordinance of 1785.

Ordinance of 1787 see Northwest Ordinance.

Ordinances of the Town of Chicago the following ordinances are those passed by the trustees, here presented in summary language and in chronological order, based on the complete text published in the *Chicago Democrat* on the dates indicated below. Only the first 16 were numbered. [357, 592]

Passed Nov. 7, 1833 [see *Chicago Democrat*, Nov. 26, Dec. 3, 10, and 17, 1833]:

[1] Defines town limits: Jefferson St. on the W; Ohio St. [and both eastern and western projections thereof] on the N; Lake Shore and Fort Dearborn Reservation [E].

[2] Names four streets S of Washington St.: Madison, Monroe, Adams, Jackson.

[3] Makes restraining of pigs in the village streets a requirement.

[4] Makes the shooting of a firearm within the village a punishable offence.

[5] Makes the removal of timber from either Chicago bridge an offence.

[6] Regulates the fireproof passing of stovepipes through the walls or roof of any house.

[7] Regulates the running of horses through the streets.

[8] Prohibits the "indecent exhibition" of stallions within the town limits.

[9] Prohibits dumping of garbage, construction material, &c. in village streets.

[10] Prohibits dumping of dead animals into the river.

Passed Dec. 4, 1834, at the house of Dexter Graves [see *Chicago Democrat*, Nov. 10, 17, 24, 31, 1833, and Jan. 7, 1834]:

[11] Names George W. Snow as assessor & surveyor of the town.

[12] Sets the town-tax collector's compensation at 10 percent of the tax roll.

[13] Creates a bridge maintenance committee, appointing G.W. Dole, Medore B. Beaubien, Edmund S. Kimberly, and John Miller.

[14] Makes John Dean Caton town attorney.

[15, 16] Regulates the use of riverfront property and the application process for wharfing privileges.

Passed June 6, 1834, at the house of E.H. Hadock [see *Chicago Democrat*, June 18, 25, and July 2, 1834]:

• Details the duty of the assessor regarding taxable property.

• Details the duty of the supervisor of streets.

• Empowers the supervisor of streets to draft male residents between the ages of 21 and 60 for the duty of street repair, three days a year.

Passed July 11, 1834 [see *Chicago Democrat*, Aug. 6, 13, and 20, 1834]:

• Levies a tax of quarter of 1 percent on all taxable property for the year 1834.

• Instructs the surveyor to graduate South Water Street such that water will flow N into the river.

• Gives instructions to the tax collector.

Passed July 30, 1834 [see *Chicago Democrat*, Aug. 27, 1834]:

• Further details the duties of the tax collector, including the requirement to post a bond.

Passed Sept. 1, 1834, at the house of Starr Foot [see *Chicago Democrat*, Sept. 3, 10, 17, and 24, 1834]:

• Prohibits the selling or dispensing of alcoholic beverages by any "tippling house or grocery" on Sundays;

• Orders the town attorney to prosecute all offences of the previous ordinance.

Passed Sept. 25, 1834, at the Tremont House [see *Chicago Democrat*, Oct. 1 and 8, 1834]:

• An ordinance to prevent fire.

[Sec. 1] Divides the town into four wards as follows: E of LaSalle St. and between Jackson and South Water—first ward; N of Jackson and between LaSalle and East Water—second ward; N of the river—third ward; W of the north and south branches of the river—fourth ward.

[Sec. 2] Appoints firewardens, one for each ward: (1) William Worthingham, (2) Edward E. Hunter, (3) Samuel Resigue, and (4) James Kinzie.

[Sec. 3] Regulates the fireproof passing of stovepipes through the walls or roof of any building.

[Sec. 4] Describes the duty and authority of the firewardens.

[Sec. 5] Sets fines for violators.

[Sec. 6] Repeals the earlier fire ordinance of Nov. 6, 1833 (Ordinance Six).

Passed Sept. 29, 1834 at the Tremont House [see *Chicago Democrat*, Oct. 1, 1834]:

• Makes it unlawful to remove dirt or sand from any of the town streets, unless for the purpose of repairing those streets by order and permission of the supervisor of streets.

Passed Oct. 13, 1834, at the Tremont House [see *Chicago Democrat*, Oct. 22 and 29, 1834]:

• A fire ordinance.

[Sec. 1] Further details the authority and duty of firewardens.

[Sec. 2] Makes the warden, in whose ward a fire breaks out, "Warden in Chief," subjecting the other three wardens to his authority.

[Sec. 3] Assigns a numbered badge or plate to each firewarden, designating his ward, to be worn on his hat.

Passed Nov. 3, 1834 at "the Exchange" [see *Chicago Democrat*, Nov. 5, 12, 19, 26 and Dec. 3, 1834]:

• An ordinance for the further prevention of fires. Makes it unlawful to carry or convey firebrands or coals of fire between buildings within the town limits, unless transported in a covered earthen or fireproof container.

Passed Aug. 5, 1835 [see *Chicago Democrat*, Aug. 12, 19, 26, and Sept. 2, 1835; also see the Illinois Regional Archives Depository]:

• An omnibus ordinance.

[Sec. 1] Declares that anyone guilty of violating the laws and ordinances herewith can expect penalties.

[Sec. 2] Makes it unlawful to place obstacles (timber, stone, &c.) on public passages (streets, sidewalks, &c.) without permission of president or trustee, except for those related to building construction, and then may only block one half of the passage for no longer than two months.

[Sec. 3] Makes it unlawful to place casks or crates on the walkway in front of a building further than four feet, or in the street, unless with permission.

[Sec. 4] Makes it unlawful to for any animal,

wagon, or cart to cross a sidewalk, unless to enter a lot or yard.

[Sec. 5] Makes it unlawful to ride or drive over a bridge faster than at the pace of a walk.

[Sec. 6] Makes it unlawful for anyone to damage pavements, walks, sewers, drains, or to dig holes or ditches without permission, or to obstruct repair.

[Sec. 7] Makes it unlawful to dispose anything (e.g. straw shavings) into sewers, drains or ditches, obstructing its purpose.

[Sec. 8] Makes it unlawful to possess a billiard table, nine or ten pin alley for public use without a specific license.

[Sec. 9] Makes it unlawful for an owner with a billiard table, gambling equipment, or liquor for sale, to allow the gaming house to become disorderly.

[Sec. 10] Makes it unlawful to conduct oneself disorderly, to riot, to create a disturbance in the streets with in the town, or to form crowds for unlawful purpose.

[Sec. 11] Makes it unlawful to dump on streets or into the river any dead animals or putrid meat, fish entrails, decaying vegetables, or any other offensive substance.

[Sec. 12] Makes it unlawful to dump any "nuisance" into any lot.

[Sec. 13] The president or any trustee, on finding "any nuisance" in the street or in any lot, may order the perpetrator to remove it.

[Sec. 14] Makes it unlawful to any grocery or "tippling house" to sell beer on the "Sabbath, or first day of the week."

[Sec. 15] Makes it unlawful to burn hay, straw, chips, or any combustible material in any street or in any lot without permission from a trustee.

[Sec. 16] Chips or other combustible material accumulating within buildings must be removed at least once a week.

[Sec. 17] Makes it unlawful to dump chips or other combustible material on streets.

[Sec. 18] Redefines how stovepipes must be passd through the roof or wall of buildings.

[Sec. 19] Forbids the carrying of open fire through streets or lots.

[Sec. 20] Forbids fireworks or the firing of guns within town limits.

[Sec. 21] Creates firewardens for each district and defines their duties.

[Sec. 22] Forbids the stacking of hay in the area bordered by Washington, Canal, and Kinzie streets, and the lake.

[Sec. 23] Sets penalties for the offenses against the foregoing ordinances.

Passed Oct. 19, 1835 [see *Chicago Democrat*, Oct. 28 and Nov. 4, 1835]:

• An omnibus ordinance.

[Sec. 1] Sets the time when the trustees appoint three inspectors of elections, attendant to the annual election of trustees and all special town elections.

[Sec. 2] Sets the time of polling in such elections; declares poll lists to be kept in the same manner as that of the state law.

[Sec. 3] Describes inspectors' responsibilities following elections, compliant with state law.

[Sec. 4] Specifies the inspectors' filing of canvasses with the clerk of the county court circuit.

[Sec. 5] Designates special elections to fill vacancies in the offices of trustees.

[Sec.6] Authorizes trustees to appoint from time to time as many police constables as they may think proper.

[Sec. 7] Directs trustees to chose time and place of their meeting by resolution. Makes the president the presiding officer and gives him "only a casting vote."

[Sec. 8] "The trustees shall meet annually hereafter on or before the second Tuesday in June and by ballot appoint a president, clerk treasurer, attorney, street commissioner, police constable, collector of taxes, and town surgeon, two mearurers of wood, two measurers of lumber, two measurers and weighers of grain, and such other officers as the trustees may deem necessary for the good of said town: if for any cause the above officers are not appointed on the day above mentioned, the trustees may adjourn from day to day until they are appointed."

[Sec. 9] Requires that bonds be filed by the treasurer, street commissioner, and collector(s) of a height deemed appropriate by the trustees.

[Sec. 10] Describes the duties of the police constable, which includes the duty "to attend all fires within the limits of said town."

[Sec. 11] Describes the duties and the powers of the trustees, which includes the power "to arrest all dissolute and riotous persons."

[Sec. 12] Defines the duties of town assessor.

Passed Nov. 4 [see *Chicago Democrat*, Nov. 11, 18, 25 and Dec. 2, 9, 16, 1835; also see Illinois Regional Archives Depository]:

• An omnibus ordinance.

[Sec. 1] Declares that anyone guilty of breaching the laws and ordinances herewith can expect penalties.

[Sec. 2] The fire department consists of the chief engineer, two assistants, four wardens, in addition to trustees (all ex-wardens) and (as many as appointed by trustees) fire engine men, hose men, hook and ladder and axe and saw men.

[Sec. 3] Details the chief engineer's responsibilities.

[Sec. 4] Details the assistant chiefs' responsibilities.

[Sec. 5] Details the firewardens' assignment and responsibilities.

[Sec. 6] Fire companies—"The firemen shall be redivided into companies, to consist of as many members as the Board of Trustees shall from time to time direct, to attend to the fire engines, hose carts, hooks and ladders, axes, saws, and other fire apparatus, belonging to the Town of Chicago; and each of the companies shall on the first Monday of December in each year, choose from among their own numbers a Foreman, Assistant Foreman, and

Clerk, in such manner as they think proper."

[Sec. 7] Details each company's responsibilities and duties.

[Sec. 8] Details the foreman's responsibilities.

[Sec. 9] Declares that any neglect, inattendance or apparatus maintenance failure will result in penalty.

[Sec. 10] Declares that any neglect of assistance without sufficient excuse will result in penalty or expulsion.

[Sec. 11] Declares that misuse of apparatus for private purpose will result in penalty.

[Sec. 12] Defines in principle the required headgear: black leather cap with identification in white.

[Sec. 13] Details the numbers and responsibilities of the hook, ladder, axe, and saw men.

[Sec. 14] Regulates fire attendance.

[Sec. 15] Details the state of readiness of fire equipment.

[Sec. 16] Specifies fine if a fireman is absent when needed.

[Sec. 17] Defines required headgear for hook, ladder, axe, and saw men: black leather cap with identification in white.

[Sec. 18] Addresses the numbers of fire hose men selected.

[Sec. 19] Describes the fire hose men's responsibilities.

[Sec. 20] Specifies the hierarchy among fire hose men.

[Sec. 21] Defines required headgear for fire hose men: black leather cap with a coil pictured and identification in white.

[Sec. 22] Defines the badges of office at fires—the president and trustees each to carry a staff with gilded flame atop.

[Sec. 23] Defines required headgear: white leather cap with Chief Engineer in black.

[Sec. 24] Defines required headgear: white leather caps with Engineer No. 1 and Engineer No. 2 in black.

[Sec. 25] Defines required headgear: brim hat, white crown with warden in black; also to carry a white trumpet.

[Sec. 26] Defines required headgear: black leather cap with Foreman and engine company identification in white.

[Sec. 27] Defines required headgear: black leather cap with "Foreman" and hook and ladder company identification in white.

[Sec. 28] Defines required headgear: black leather cap with Assistant and identification in white.

[Sec. 29] Declares that any fireman neglectful of his responsibilities will be noted.

[Sec. 30] Describes the duties of the constable during a fire.

[Sec. 31-33] Declares town residents subject to and under the authority of the fire warden during a fire.

[Sec. 34] Details the penalty for damaging town firefighting equipment.

[Sec. 35-37] Requires residents to keep leather fire buckets in their buildings, buckets that are painted and labeled with the owner's name or initials; instructs residents when to use them.

[Sec. 38] Designates Attorney E.W. Casey, Supervisor of Roads and Bridges Edward E. Hunter, and the firewarden to handle all cases in which a resident contests a penalty.

[Sec. 39] Lowers penalty for stacking hay within the town limits from $25 to $5.

[Sec. 40] Specifies locations for the public posting of ordinances.

[Sec. 41-44] Sets election rules.

[Sec. 45] Declares that unexpected vacancies in offices must be filled by special election.

[Sec. 46] Authorizes the board of trustees to appoint police constables as needed.

[Sec. 47] Authorizes the board of trustees to determine when they will meet.

[Sec. 48] Sets the appointment date for town officials on or near the second Tuesday in June.

[Sec. 49] Requires that the treasurer, the commissioners, and the tax collectors be bonded.

[Sec. 50] Defines the duties of the town constable.

[Sec. 51] Defines the duties of town trustees.

❖ ❖ ❖ ❖ ❖ ❖

Oregon schooner on the Chicago-St. Joseph route in 1834 under Captain Brooks, making 13 calls at Chicago that year, carrying lumber, merchandise, and passengers; on Sept. 9, 1835, the vessel called under Captain Howard, coming from Buffalo, NY.

Orillat, Jean wealthy trader and merchant at Montreal in the 1760s and 1770s; in May 1770, he financed the travel of two canoes licensed to go to "Chiquagoux" under the direction of Jean Baptiste St. Cire [St. Cyr] with eight additional *engagés*, probably to scout a locale for a future trading post, but never established by him [see Gaffé]. Likely Orillat himself had visited or passed through Chicago in connection with his trading activities, because he is known to have traveled to Cahokia; financed many trading expeditions, including one *Chicago American* as representative of A. Dart & Co. of Ohio Furnace, "having on hand, at this place a lot of Stoves and Castings" at the first door W of the Fulton Market, opposite the Tremont House; "N.B. A few cast iron ploughs, first quality and cheap."

Ortelius, Abraham (1527-1598) geographer and friend of Gerhard Mercator; traveled extensively in communication with other geographers and cartographers; in 1570 published the first modern atlas of the world, *Theatrum Orbis Terrrarum*, in Antwerp. Among 70 maps, many by other mapmakers, is the ✱ map *Americae sive Novi Orbis, Nova Descriptio* that provided the most accurate depiction of settlement within the Americas in the late 16th century; the atlas was continually revised and expanded into the next century. [94, 392, 605]

O'Rourke, James arrived from Ireland in 1832; in 1836 he assisted Capt. J.B.F. Russell in the removal of the Indians from Illinois.

O'Rourke, Peter, Jr. arrived from Ireland in 1832.

O'Rourke, Peter, Sr. arrived from Ireland in 1832 [likely with his sons Peter and James], and began to farm, frequently selling the produce in town.

Osborn, Andrew L.   born c.1814 in Ridgefield, CT; arrived in July 1835; in 1836 he worked for John Calhoun as a typesetter; in the late 1840s was member of a group planning railroad construction; by 1841 had married Lucy F. Northam of Noble County, IN, and moved to La Porte, where he still resided in 1885. [12, 351]

Osborn, James T.   arrived in 1832 and served that year in the Chicago militia under Capt. G. Kercheval in the Black Hawk War. [714]

Osborne, William   (c.1811-1884) born in Ridgefield, CT; arrived on May 1, 1834; successful as a partner of Silas B. Cobb in the boot, shoe, hide and leather trade; served in the volunteer fire department in 1837; ✦ boot, shoe and leather merchant on 141 Lake St.; he and his wife were members of the Presbyterian church; died on Jan. 2, 1884. [12, 351, 733]

Oscom, Antoine   listed as an interpreter employed on Sept. 25, 1818, in Chicago by the American Fur Co.

Osterhardt, Levi M.   also Osterhoudt, Osterhaudt; in 1833 he ran the Sauganash Hotel and later George Doltons's tavern/hotel on the Calumet River at 134th Street and Indiana Avenue; ✦ [L.M. Osterhoudt] New York House, 180 Lake St.; died on Nov. 15, 1881. [12, 243, 357]

Ostrander, Lt. Philip   (1784-1813) born in New York; enlisted with the U.S. Army in 1801; served first at Mackinac, then at Fort Wayne; came to Fort Dearborn with Captain Heald in 1810 as lieutenant and served there until 1811; was acting commandant while Captain Heald was on leave from November 1810 to June 1811. Afterward, he resumed his former station at Fort Wayne; in 1813 refused court-martial "for firing upon a flock of birds passing over the fort" and died in confinement. [288]

Ottawa, IL   town at the junction of the Fox and the Illinois Rivers, where coal was first found in the United States, three miles W along the Illinois

River; originally laid out by Gurdon Hubbard and others as "Carbonia," and in 1830 was platted, as was Chicago, by order of the canal commissioners, since they represented the termini of the proposed Illinois & Michigan Canal route. Early steamboats from the Mississippi found the Illinois River navigable up to Ottawa, making a stagecoach line desirable between Chicago and Ottawa; such was organized by Dr. Temple in 1833. The canal did not open until 1848. In May 1835, [see] Ellen Bigelow took the coach trip from Chicago to Ottawa—25 hours—and described it in some detail in a letter to a relative back home in the East. [55a]

Ottawa   one of the Algonkin tribes; the first native tribe to contact the French explorers in 1633; migrated westward among the Great Lakes and became known as one of the four tribes to comprise the Chippewa, existing in the Georgian Bay area; the Algonkian word *ottawa* means *to trade.*

Ottawa Trail   Indian trail between Chicago and the Joliet area, representing the continuation of the Long Portage Road across Stony Ford, later Ogden Avenue, designated in 1831 as the first official Cook County highway, accommodating stagecoachs and wagons SW to Ottawa and beyond in the years to follow; ▲ commemorated in the name Ottawa Trail Woods of the Salt Creek Division of the Cook County Forest Preserve District, through which it passed [see Monuments].

Ouiatanon   also Ouiatenon; see Wea.

Ouilmette, Antoine   (1760-1841) also Ouilmet, Houillamette, Willamette, Wilmette, Wilmot, Wemet; a Catholic *métis* [probably part Potawatomi], born at Lahndrayh near Montreal; was initially employed by the American Fur Co.; came to Chicago in July 1790 [his statement], and built his cabin on the north bank of the Chicago River, a short distance W [N, according to Andreas] of the one owned by Point de Sable, likely sometimes working with him. From his cabin he provided ferry service across the river, if ever the need arose; in 1804 his neighbors on the north bank were Le Mai,

Pettle, and Kinzie; by the latter he was periodically employed, and like Kinzie, he transported traders and other travelers over the Chicago portage—as noted in Kinzie's account book on June 14, 1806, when he hired a wagon and a pair of oxen for $50 to transport Des Pins' [Lemoine's] goods over the portage to the fork of the Illinois River. In 1825, his name was on the first Chicago tax list [was assessed on $400 of personal property that included cows, horses, sheep, wagons, and farm implements, and paid $4 in taxes] and in 1826, on the first poll list. In 1796, Ouilmette had married Archange Chevalier [see separate entry], a French-Potawatomi woman with whom he had eight children: Joseph [removed to Marilton County, WI, to farm in the 1840s], Josette, Louis [also Lewis; see separate entry], François [Francis], Michel [known as Michael or Mitchell, under which name he served during the Black Hawk War in the Chicago militia under Captain Kercheval, being listed in the muster roll of May 3, 1832; ran a small trading post at [see] *Grosse Pointe* in the early 1830s], Elizabeth, Archange, Sophia [married I.J. Martell], and an "adopted" girl named Archange Chambly (Arkash Sambli). Elizabeth married Michael P. Welch on May 11, 1830, Justice J.B. Beaubien officiating, but divorced him in 1834 and married Lucius R. Darling; Archange Chambly married a Tousant Tramble (also Trombla) at Cahokia in 1813, divorced him in 1830, then married [see] John Mann that year, divorcing him in 1838. Like most Frenchmen, Ouilmette survived the Fort Dearborn massacre of 1812 by not joining the militia but remaining neutral and indisposed during the attack, cultivating the fort's garden during the following years. The Prairie du Chien Treaty of 1829 awarded his *métis* wife and their children a grant of two sections of land at [see] *Grosse Pointe* [forcing Stephen J. Scott to abandon his homestead on the property and move to the Des Plaines River valley], and the Chicago Treaty of 1833 awarded him monetary compensation for losses suffered in 1812; in 1829 the family removed to [see] *Grosse Pointe* and farmed, but may already have built a cabin there earlier, since the Ouilmette farm is used in the wording of the 1829 treaty as a boundary marker. The family was involved early in the Catholic community, and his name was on the petition by Chicago's citizens to Bishop Rosati of St. Louis asking that a priest be assigned to them. When the Potawatomi were relocated W of the Mississippi in 1835, Antoine and Archange followed them in 1836 or later; Archange died at Council Bluffs, IA, in 1840 and Antoine died on Dec. 18, 1841. [12, 96a, 291, 226, 292, 404]

Ouilmette, Archange Chevalier (c.1764-1841) born at Sugar Creek, MI; daughter of François and Marianne Chevalier, sister of Shesi [Pierre] Buisson and Catherine [Alexander] Robinson; wife of Antoine Ouilmette, whom she married in 1796 at [see] *Grosse Pointe*, 12 miles N of Fort Dearborn; see Ouilmette, Antoine. [96a, 226]

Ouilmette, Archange Sambly (Arkash Sambli)   see Mann, Archange Sambly.

Ouilmette, Louis   also Lewis; son of [see] Antoine and Archange Ouilmette; an escort for Colbee C. Benton, visitor in 1833 who described him in his journal, excerpted as follows:

Wednesday Aug 21; Today has been very pleasant. I called upon the Agent and was introduced to my new companion, Louis Wilmot [Ouilmette]. He is half French and half Indian; rather short but very strong and active-looking. His complexion is that of an Indian, and his hair is long, straight, and black. He wears a hat, blue calico shirt, moccasins, and pantaloons, and he also wears a red belt round his waist in which is fastened his tomahawk and scalping knife. He has lived with the Indians more or less for six years and understands their tongue very well, and can speak English and French. ... And after draining a couple of bottles of beer, we left Chicago in company with an old Indian, for Gross Point about twenty miles north on Lake Michigan, where we arrived about ten o'clock in the evening. Stayed with the old Indian whom I

liked very much. He could talk some English and seemed quite a philosopher. While passing along the sandy shore of the lake the dogs ran after a deer. It was dark, and he expressed his astonishment at the wonderful power of the dog – his seeing, running, and scenting the track. Says he: 'If a man should attempt to run in de dark wood, first he know, he have a stick right in his eye,' and says he, 'There be a great many strange things in dis world, and I spose all for de best,' &c. We turned our horses into a little field near the log mansion. Eat some crackers and went to bed in the same room with the old Indian and his squaw. Our bed was on the floor. When I was undressing says the old Indian: 'I spose you would not think it very modest to take off your clothes and go to bed before the ladies.' However, I did not feel very delicate in the presence of his old squaw.

Outhet, Daniel   arrived 1832 from Yorkshire, England, with wife Elizabeth, (née Fox), and daughter Jane (born 1823); they were among those who took shelter at Fort Dearborn during the Black Hawk War; according to estate administrators' notices in the *Chicago Democrat* on Dec. 3, 1834, and March 23, 1836, both Daniel and Elizabeth had died by 1836 [John C. Outhet, probably Daniel's brother, arrived from England in 1836, became a wagonmaker, employed William Wayman and served as alderman in 1854; he married Maria Sherman in 1842.]; Jane married William Wayman in 1844.

Owen, Thomas Jefferson Vance   (1801-1835) born in Kentucky; son of Maj. Ezra Owen, Indian fighter and companion of Daniel Boone; became U.S. Indian agent in 1830, serving in Chicago as successor of Dr. Wolcott from 1831 to 1833; purchased multiple lots of real estate from both the government and private sellers in blocks 2, 9, 10, 11, and 21 [see map on page 44]; under him as subagents served Gholson Kercheval and James Stuart, as interpreter Billy Caldwell, and as blacksmiths David McKee and Joseph Porthier; assumed responsibility as caretaker of Fort Dearborn on May

20, 1831, and served until June 17, 1832. A Catholic, he signed the petition of April 1833 to [see] Bishop Rosati, representing a group of 10; in early August that year he was one of the "Qualified Electors" who voted to incorporate the town, serving as president of this meeting [for a copy of the meeting's report, see entry on incorporation]; member of the first village board of trustees (Aug. 10, 1833), which elected him ★★★ **Chicago's 1st** village president on Aug. 12; having no town seal, he used the obverse of a United States half-eagle coin as the earliest town seal. In September he was one of three United States officials when the land session treaty was negotiated with Indians at Chicago. Owen had married Emeline Hotchkiss on July 9, 1823, daughter of Miles Hotchkiss of Kaskaskia; this made him a brother-in-law of Gholson Kercheval, who married Emeline's sister Felicite; died in his home on Oct. 15, 1835, and his funeral services were conducted by Father St. Cyr; ➡ Owen Avenue (7700 W). ✹ For a portrait of Emeline Hotchkiss Owen, see page 372. [12, 319]

Owen, W.E.   late in 1835 he and [see] R.J. Hamilton filed a claim for wharfing privileges for lot 4, block 19.

Owen, William and George   children by this name, probably siblings, were enrolled as grade school students in the class taught by [see] John Watkins in December 1835. Names of corresponding parents were not recorded. [728]

oxen   castrated bulls of a domestic breed, commonly used for pulling heavy loads by traders and early settlers; in July of 1804 Capt. John Whistler expressed to Colonel Kingsbury annoyance due to the scarcity of corn to feed public oxen, likely used in the fort's construction; in their description of the Chicago Portage [April 4, 1819], U.S. Commissioners Graham and Philips noted a "well beaten wagon road" over which "boats and their loads are hauled by oxen and vehicles kept for the purpose by the French at Chicago." Also see prairie schooners.

Ozier, Joseph   a soldier at Fort Dearborn in 1818, the year he married Madaline Alscum, *métis* servant girl indentured to Susan Randolph, wife of the Indian agent Charles Jouett. [12]

Packet boat   originally identified as the carrier of the mail, later a vessel that routinely traveled a particular route, carrying freight and passengers. In 1832, H.S. Tanner published *View of the Valley of the Mississippi, or the Emmigrant's and Traveler's Guide to the West* that noted "[a] line of packets is established between this place and Detroit and Buffalo." J.D. Caton writes that [see] David Carver owned a schooner, better known as *The Chicago Packet*, or simply the *Packet*; yet only in the July 30, 1834, *Chicago Democrat* did Captain Howe advertise the schooner [see] *Phillips* as the *Packet*, plying regularly between Chicago and St. Joseph. On May 25, 1835, Carver introduced a new schooner [see] *Llewellyn* as the "Chicago & St. Joseph Packet" that plied regularly that summer.

Page, F.M.   from New Hampshire, arrived in 1834 and soon moved to Elk Grove Township, later to [Arlington Heights]; married Selina Noyes in 1836; eight children, of whom seven survived: John, Sarah, Helen, Hannah, Hiram, Frederick, Martha, and George; F.M.'s father, John Page, served as governor of New Hampshire in 1838-39. [278]

Pagé, Joseph Prisque   (1717-1764) brother of Pierre Pagé.

Pagé, Pierre   (1717-1752) early French trader, and likely contender for the honor of having the [see] Du Page River named after him; he was primarily based in Kaskaskia, but probably had a post on the Du Page, facilitating his frequent business travels between Kaskaskia and Michilimackinac via Chicagou. [649]

Paine, Christopher   also Payne; arrived in April 1831, settling his wife and six children near the Hobsons, along the Du Page River; fled with his family to Fort Dearborn during the Black Hawk

scare in May 1832, then served as private in Captain Boardman's voluntary county militia and later Captain Napier's company; an uncollected letter is listed in the April 1, 1834, *Chicago Democrat*. [12, 351]

Paine, Seth   also Payne; arrived penniless from Vermont in the summer of 1834, the boat passage on the schooner *Commerce* having taken his last dollars; was a member of the fire engine company No.1 in December 1835; married Mrs. Francis Jones in 1836; initially had hired out with the firm Taylor, Breeze & Co., but soon teamed up with Theron Norton to run a dry goods store; ✦ Paine & Norton, 117 Lake; farmed a while in Lake County; in later years became established as a banker and editor, and developed into a fanatical socialist and abolitionist. [12]

Palmer, Dr. George W.   naval doctor; announced his Georgetown marriage to Jane R. O'Neil on June 22, 1834, in the July 2 *Chicago Democrat*; a claim for wharfing privileges was submitted under Palmer & George on Nov. 21, 1835, for which a deposition was filed on Nov. 24 with David Gibson's supporting affidavit; but the claim [lot 2 block 16] by George Palmer was certificated later that year by the town surveyor [Talcott]. [28]

Palmer, Isaac K.   arrived from New Hampshire in 1834; served on the cholera vigilance committee in 1834; in October 1835 he signed up with the "Pioneer" hook and ladder company, an early volunteer fire brigade; in the Jan. 21, 1835, *Chicago Democrat* David Carver announced the dissolution of his partnership in David Carver & Co., with Palmer; married Almira Clement on June 2, 1836; ✦ City wood inspector; listed as living in the second ward in 1840; later moved to Ohio. [12, 351]

Panama   schooner from Buffalo under Captain Chandler, called at Chicago with merchandise on July 2, 1834.

panis   an American Indian slave, as opposed to a black slave; the word was common in the 18th century, and is derived from the fact that the Illinois

had enslaved an extraordinary number of Pawnee and then made them available to the French settlers. This bondage prevailed throughout New France and Louisiana, beginning almost with the first settlements in Illinois, and was authorized by an edict of the then-intendant of New France at Quebec, Jacques Raudot, on April 13, 1709. The word is existent in early French-Canadian Catholic birth and baptism records.

panther   early Illinois settlers usually meant *Felix concolor*, the [see] mountain lion, when they talked of panthers.

Parc aux Vaches   also *Parc Vache* or Cowpens; see St. Joseph.

Pariolet, Caesar   placed the following notice in the Sept. 10, 1834, *Chicago Democrat*: "Whereas my wife Hannah, has voluntarily left my bed and board, without any just cause or provocation, this is to forbid all persons harboring or trusting her on my account, as I shall pay no debts of her contracting."

parishes   see religion.

Park, F.D.   arrived from Maine in 1831 and still lived in Chicago in 1879. [733]

Parkman, Francis   (1823-1893) American historian who contributed much information to our knowledge of the early Northwest; see Bibliography.

Parson, H.C.   arrived in 1834; served in the first engine company of the voluntary fire brigade in 1835. [351]

Parsons, Edward   second manager of the Green Tree Inn [built and owned by James Kinzie in 1833], succeeding David Clock; ✦ Parsons & Holden [Charles N.], grocery & provisions, corner of Lake and So. Water.

Parsons, T.E.   served as a corporal in the Chicago militia company under Captain Napier during the Black Hawk War in 1832. [12]

passenger pigeon   *Ectopistes migratorius*; once very abundant in Illinois, these large doves became extinct near the end of the 19th century as a result of

PASSENGER PIGEON

overhunting; the last reported sighting was from River Forest in May 1923. Bossu observed in 1768: "When one approaches the country of Illinois, one sees during the day, clouds of doves, a kind of wood or wild pigeon. A thing that may perhaps appear incredible is that the sun is obscured by them. ... sometimes as many as 80 of them are killed with one shot." John Calhoun reports that in 1832 he "stood on the tops [of dunes at the beach of the Kinzie Addition] and shot pigeons as they passed below me when they were flying." [64]

patent medicine   see drug trade.

Patterson, Erastus   arrived in 1835 from Woodstock, VT, with his wife and five children and moved N of the Ouilmette Reservation (Wilmette), where he opened a tavern on the seldom traveled road to Root River; after his death in 1837, his widow kept the tavern for some years.

Patterson, Jacob G.   subscribed to the *Chicago Democrat* in November 1833.

Patterson, John   arrived from Scotland in 1835; later moved to St. Louis, MO; possibly identical with J.W Patterson who, according to Andreas, was editor for the paper *Young America* in 1854.

Pattinson, Richard   English trader who established a trading post on the St. Joseph River in 1803 near that of William Burnett; known to have done business with Messrs. Kinzie & Forsyth in 1808.

Paul, James K.   teamster, arrived in 1831 from Lafayette, IN. [351]

Paul, Col. René   born in Santo Domingo, educated in France; St. Louis engineer in 1809; employed by the initial canal commission in 1824 to have the canal lands surveyed and a cost estimate prepared; worked with Col. Justus Post on the project, together creating ✳ "Map of the proposed Illinois and Michigan Canal." [12, 681, 682]

Paw Paw   also Paupau, Pau Pau, or Papaw; (1) a small tree, *Asimina triloba* [*asimina* being also the Algonkian name], of the custard-apple family, having an oblong edible fruit with many seeds; (2) a large grove in Lee County that attracted early settlers who included [see] George and William Laird; George announced continued business at his store in the *Chicago Democrat* in July 1834, and by October was noted as the postmaster of the Paw Paw post office, providing lists of remaining letters to the *Chicago Democrat* until at least April 1836. Paw Paw, IL, exists to this day as a small village and is located eight miles NW of Earlville, IL.

Payne, Rev. Adam   an itinerant preacher who came in May of 1832 and delivered an eloquent and well attended sermon just outside the walls of Fort Dearborn; two days later, traveling westward on horseback, he was killed by Indians, becoming one of the few white victims of the Black Hawk War.

Payne, William   (1806-1868) born in England on Dec. 22; immigrated to the United States at age 20; first lived in Buffalo, NY, until arriving in Chicago in 1834; placed an ad in the *Chicago Democrat* of Aug. 13, 1834, announcing a circuit court suit to recover "Mechanics claims, &c. against specific houses owned by Charles H. Chapman." In June that year, Payne had contracted with Captain Howe, master of the *El-Lewellyn*, to transport men and sawmill equipment to [see] Shipwagen, then partnered [see] Oliver C. Crocker in the enterprise, which failed after a year; the partnership was dissolved as per notice in the *Chicago Democrat* of Oct. 28, 1835; ✦ William Payne. He moved to Milwaukee and other parts of Wisconsin, but in 1858 he returned to Chicago and entered the wood and coal business; died in Chicago on Nov. 1, 1868. In 1885, a William H. Payne lived in Fremont Centre, IL. [12]

Peacock, Joseph   see Sobrano, Margaret; ✦ Peacock & Thatcher [David C.], gunsmiths, 153 Lake St. [12, 351]

Peailleur, James Mitchell   subscribed to the *Chicago* Democrat in November 1833.

Pearsons, George T.   arrived from Ohio in 1832; years later when the Old Settlers' Society was formed on Oct. 22, 1855, he became the secretary; later moved to Springfield, where he died. [351]

Pearsons, Gustavus C.   arrived from Ohio in 1832; later moved to Valejo, CA. [351]

Pearsons, Col. Hiram   (1811-1868) New Hampshire born, arrived in 1832 from Ohio; in early August 1833 he was one of the "Qualified Electors" who voted to incorporate the town [for a copy of that meeting's report, see entry on incorporation]; was on the voting list for the first town board on Aug. 10, 1833; initially a house painter, he became a highly successful land speculator in the early 1830s, advertising "lots for sale" in the *Chicago Democrat* in Jan. 28, 1834, and in the Feb. 18 issue advertised "Storage and Commission, Merchant – lot and Storehouse on South Water Street"; in November 1835 became trustee of the Presbyterian church and later that year filed a claim for wharfing privileges for lot 2, block 5; served as city treasurer and west-side alderman in 1837; ✦ real estate dealer, North Dearborn Street He failed to retain his wealth during the financial panic of 1837, and in 1850 continued W to San Francisco, then a boom town as Chicago had been in 1832; there he succeeded in renewing his fortune; died in California; ➡ Pearson Street (830 N). Also see *Hiram Pearson*, a lake schooner. [12, 28, 86, 320, 351]

Pecie, Peter   see Lamset, Pierre.

EBENEZER PECK [12]

Peck, Ebenezer (1805-1881) native of Portland, ME; studied law in Montreal; married Caroline I. Walker of Vermont in c.1826; arrived as a lawyer from Canada in 1835, and was briefly associated with John D. Caton; member of the volunteer fire department; worked as town board clerk in 1836 and during the year helped organize the Galena & Chicago Union Railroad; was elected state senator in 1838 to fill the unexpired seat of Peter Pruyne, serving until 1840; ✦ attorney and internal improvement, canal board; in 1844 he wrote editorials for the *Chicago Democratic Advocate* and *Commercial Advertizer*; later became judge on the U.S. Court of Claims and a close friend of Abraham Lincoln; died on March 25, 1881. His descriptive letters of the early town are preserved at the Chicago Historical Society. [12, 707]

Peck, Rev. John Mason (1789-1858) Baptist missionary who first came W in 1817 and whose job-related extensive traveling, gift of observation, and publication of guidebooks made him a recognized authority on the Midwest; in 1831 he published *A Guide for Emigrants, containing Sketches of Illinois, Missouri and the Adjacent Parts*; in 1834, *A Gazetteer of Illinois*, advertising both in the *Chicago Democrat*. He thus helped facilitate the phenomenal population growth by immigration to Illinois and Chicago in the early 1830s; in a February 1834 letter Peck describes Chicago and showed his prophetic vision: "Chicago will eventually become the greatest place for business and commerce in all the north west." [527-9]

Peck, Philip Ferdinand Wheeler (1809-1871) from Providence, RI; arrived with a small stock of goods for the western market from Buffalo, NY, in July 15, 1831, on Capt. Joseph Napier's schooner *Telegraph*; initially lived in and sold goods, including some then popular household medicinals, from a small log store that he built near the fort, NW of J.B. Beaubien's home, then moved to the Napier settlement and began a partnership with the Napier brothers in retail sales; in 1832, following the Black Hawk scare, during which he served under Captain Napier in the militia, he returned, acquiring three lots on South Water Street in block 18 [see map on page 44]; maintained a store in the old Miller's Tavern, after Miller had left the state, but in the autumn erected, with lumber from James Walker's sawmill and with the help of John S. Wright, a frame building in which he then kept a store at the SE corner of South Water and LaSalle [Caton places it on Wells Street] streets; in May of 1833 Reverend Jeremiah Porter rented the second floor as his living quarters and for initial Sunday school and religious services; on Nov. 6 filed a petition for wharfing privileges; advertised in the Dec. 3, 1833, issue of the *Chicago Democrat* the availability of dry goods and hardware. On June 20, 1835, he married Mary Kent Wythe, a teacher from Philadelphia; they would raise eight children. In the fall of 1835, Peck sold his store and became a successful real estate investor; in October signed up with the "Pioneer" hook and ladder company, an early volunteer fire brigade; on Dec. 4 filed a petition [lot 4, block 18] for wharfing privileges; built ★★★ **Chicago's 1st** brick residence in 1836 at the corner of South Water and LaSalle streets; ✦ real estate speculator, 242 Clark St.; died from an injury sustained in the Great Fire; in 1885 his widow lived at 2254 Michigan Ave. [12, 28, 221, 351]

Peek, Edmund was a member of the fire engine company No. 1 in December 1835 [see petition to the village board of Dec. 16, 1835, entry on firefighting].

Peesotum also known as Big Man; minor Potawatomi chief who, at the Fort Dearborn massacre of 1812, killed Captain Wells and ate his heart. [226]

pelican *Pelicanus erythrorynchos*, the American white pelican; still found in Illinois, usually in small numbers; according to Bohlen, six birds were sighted in the Calumet region in 1977. David McKee, who lived in Chicago from 1823 to 1832, shared his memory of the Chicago River: "Excellent fish abounded in it, and over it hovered wild geese, ducks and sandhill cranes in vast flocks, and pelicans and swans were sometimes seen." [64]

Pelletier, Eulalie Marie see Pelletier, Jean Baptiste; also see Point de Sable, Suzanne.

Pelletier, Jean Baptiste French trader; married Suzanne, Jean Baptiste Point de Sable's daughter, in 1790, for which purpose the family traveled to Cahokia; thereafter they appear to have lived with Point de Sable in Chicago. A daughter, Eulalie Marie, was born on Oct. 8, 1796, the second *métis* child born at Chicago; she was baptized on Oct. 7, 1799, again at Cahokia. In 1800 de Sable sold his property, and the Pelletier family probably moved to Peoria, where in 1807 Pelletier signed by mark a petition about his alleged land claim at Peoria.

Pemeton, David arrived in 1831 and was a member of the Chicago company during the Black

Hawk War of 1832 under Capt. Gholson Kercheval. [12, 714]

Pemwotam Kickapoo chief of village at N end of Peoria Lake in 1812; hostile to United States; name often confused with [see] Pimiteoui and Peoria.

Pennsylvania 395-ton steamboat, built along Lake Erie in 1832, making runs from Buffalo to Green Bay and Chicago in 1835; [see] J. Young Scammons arrived on the *Pennsylvania* when it called at Chicago on Sept. 20, 1835 under Captain Allen.

Penoyer, Augustus subscribed to the *Chicago Democrat* in November 1833.

Penrose, Lt. James Wilkinson born in Maryland; with the Second Infantry stationed at Sackett's Harbor in 1832, then sent W for the Black Hawk War where he served as brevet second lieutenant at Fort Dearborn from June 17, 1832, to May 31, 1833, under Capt. William Whistler; died in 1849 of disease contracted in the Mexican War; see also Mary A. Penrose, his wife. [12]

Penrose, Mary A. born in New York; daughter of Col. William Hoffman, Sixth Regiment, U.S.A.; wife of Lt. James W. Penrose with whom she came, bringing their infant son William, to Chicago during the Black Hawk War and stayed 18 months. With Fort Dearborn crowded by soldiers who had contracted cholera, was one of many dependent civilians who had to find makeshift housing in the small community; the following is an excerpt from her reminscences in 1879. [12]

In the year 1832, probably in May, my husband … was ordered ordered from Sackett's Harbor to Chicago, with several other companies of the same regiment, under Colonel Whistler. At what point we took the sailing vessel I do not remember, but it was probably at Buffalo. On arriving at Chicago, the troops were first landed in little boats. Then the officers' families were sent on shore. A storm having arisen, it was three days before Colonel Whistler's family and the wife of Major Kingsbury were able to land. ✧ There were in Chicago at that time about twelve houses. I think that all of these were made of logs. Our quar-

ters were in the fort. The troops took possession of the fort, relieving a company of militia from Michigan. About six weeks after our arrival, our little company was increased by the arrival, on a steamer [Shelden Thompson], of General Scott, with several other companies. These had been sent to Chicago to proceed to Rock Island to fight the Indians there. ✧ The boat brought not only the troops but also the cholera. At twelve o'clock A.M., Lieutenant Summer (afterwards General Summer of the War of the Rebellion) came to the fort and ordered all the families in the fort to leave before sunrise, stating that at that time the troops down with the cholera would be moved into the fortification. ✧ I had then a little babe who is now Brevet Brigadier-General William H. Penrose of the 3rd Infantry U.S.A. ✧ I remember the names of the following families: Colonel Whistler, Major Kingsbury, Captain Johnson, Lieutenant Day, Lieutenant Long, and my own. In my own family was, besides the before-mentioned babe, my husband's mother and two sisters. Four of these families, finding the house of Mark Beaubien vacant (his owner having left an hour before, without taking anything with him), with joy went into that building. Mrs. Johnson and I, with my family were, however, not so fortunate, for even the four-roomed house of Mr. Beaubien could only hold four families. Going on about one mile we came to the house of a butcher, containing but one room. Exhausted, I threw myself on my mattress, which the soldiers had carried down from the fort, and there I laid during the night. ✧ The next morning in vain did we seek for a house. A rail fence was, however, in sight. Into one corner I moved. A few boards made the floor. A carpet kept off the wind from our heads and backs. Other boards formed a far from waterproof roof. Here we remained three days and three nights, cooking on the ground. My companions in misery were Mrs. Johnson and family. ✧ After three days Captain Johnson and my husband secured a lot of green lumber. In site of our fence stood the frame of a house. To this the green boards were soon nailed and a temporary partition put in. Here our two families

moved. Mr. Penrose's mother and sister nightly crawled up a ladder to their beds. ✧ General Scott, who from the steamer had gone to the hotel at the Point [Wolf Point Tavern], after five days made his appearance. Everyday he would ride up to our house and, looking up to the open end of the frame, would talk with the ladies, invariably dwelling upon the fact that they were in more comfortable quarters than Mrs. Scott, who was then at West Point. Our cooking had to be done in the open air. Generally we got more sand than salt in our food. ✧ After remaining in these quarters, the house of the Indian Agent, Colonel Owen, having been vacated through fear of the afore-mentioned disease, we obtained permission to move into it, on the condition of permitting the Colonel to remain with us. The house stood on the North Side, and contained four or five rooms on a floor. The family of the Colonel had left even their dishes, and had gone to Springfield. ✧ I remained in the house of the Indian Agent, until Colonel Owen's family returned. I then had to seek for other quarters. My sister and myself got into a log canoe and, paddling across the Chicago River, called on the officer in charge (Colonel Whistler) and requested from him permission to again take up our abode in the fort. After a little perseverance we succeeded in obtaining two rooms. About six week afterward the troops that had been in Rock Island returned to Chicago and from thence were sent to the posts from which they had been collected. In all I remained in Chicago about eighteen months.

Peoria one of the five native tribes of the Illinois confederacy encountered along the western Mississippi River bank by Jolliet and Father Marquette in 1673; their native name was Peouaraoua (Pe8ara8a), probably meaning *dreamer*, an allusion to the traditional vision quest practiced by young Indian males; ➡ Peoria Street (900 W).

Peoria County, IL Chicago never belonged geographically to Peoria County, but when the settlement became part of Putnam County on Jan. 13, 1825, Peoria County took over its county administrative functions for Putnam County In 1825, county authorities levied a property tax and collected the following amounts from Chicago residents: $50 from the American Fur Company, $10 from J.B. Beaubien, $6.25 from Jonas Clybourne, $5.72 from D. Wolcott, $5 from John Kinzie, $4 from A. Ouilmette, and $1 from F. LaFramboise. On Jan. 15, 1831, Chicago became part of Cook County, both geographically and administratively. For details, see Chicago jurisdictional chronology on page 209. Also see entry for Peoria, IL. [436a, 469, 544]

Peoria, IL   town in central Illinois on the Illinois River, where its course widens to form Peoria Lake [early name, Lake Pimiteoui], and county seat of Peoria County; early on often called Le Ville de Maillet after the settler Jean Baptiste Maillet; here La Salle had built [see] *Fort Crevecoeur* in 1680, and United States troops later built [see] Fort Clark in 1813. Several early Chicagoans had strong connections with Peoria, and many historians have uncritically accepted the theory that one of them was Jean Baptiste Point de Sable, the "father of modern Chicago", who is said to have purchased land in Peoria in 1773 and lived there some time before resettling on the Chicago River. However, it has recently been established by John F. Swenson that the legend was started by unscrupulous land-jobbers who submitted manufactured documents to U.S. government commissions for the purpose of obtaining land grants. For detail, see the essay on Peoria's early history by Swenson on page 395. Chicago was administered from Peoria during the period when Chicago officially belonged to Putnam County (Jan. 13, 1825, to Jan. 15, 1831) and residents had to travel S for official business before the courts, or to get married. On Oct. 5, 1829, the *Galena Advertizer* reported: "He who travels by land, after leaving the little village of Peoria on the Illinois River, passing alternately forests and prairies for the distance of 170 miles, sees no trace of civilization; all is rude and wild and uncultivated, just as nature fashioned it." Alexander Doyle was

the justice of the peace at that time and keen to enforcing the liquor laws: in 1829 he cited James Kinzie for selling one pint of whiskey. Licenses to open taverns or run a ferry were issued only in Peoria; therefore the Peoria County archives are an invaluable source of information for these years. Also see entry for Peoria County, IL. [33, 210, 220, 259, 544]

Pepin, Joseph   voted on Aug. 7, 1826, and on July 24, 1830 [see Chronology]; was present at the 1827 estate sale of W.H. Wallace.

Pepper   Negro slave owned by John Kinzie in Chicago; believed to have been killed during the 1812 massacre. [226]

Peresh   see LeClerc, Peresh; [correctly, Pieriche, a diminutive for Pierre].

periodicals   while no such literature was published in Chicago until long after 1835, publications were advertised in the daily newspapers and were ordered by mail from the East and from Europe by surprisingly many; among available titles were the *New York Farmer; Mechanics' Magazine* and *Register of Inventions and Improvements; Apprentice's Companion; Quarterly Journal of Agriculture, Mechanics, and Manufactures; Register of Debates in Congress; Pennsylvania Gazette Casket; Atkinson's Casket; Novelist's Magazine; The Athenian Literary Gazette; The Youth's Companion; National Intelligencer;* also see entry for Royal Stewart.

Perkins, Maj. Isaac   public administrator for the Peoria court who came to Chicago to conduct the estate sale of W.H. Wallace on April 27, 1827; at that sale he bid on a horse for $34, and won. [220]

Perkins, T.   arrived from Massachusetts in 1834; served in the first engine company of the voluntary fire brigade in 1835. [351, 733]

perogue   see pirogue.

Perren, Julius   came to Niles Township in either 1832 or 1833 and built a cabin near Dutchman's Point on the north branch; remained until his death, 1873. [13]

Perrot, Nicolas   (c.1644-1717) French military of-

ficer, born in France; came to New France in the 1660s; explorer of the Great Lakes and the Wisconsin Fox River area during the years 1670-1690; rendered valuable services as French agent to consolidate alliances with the Indians of Wisconsin and Illinois in the struggle with the Iroquois and the English who had interrupted French trade in the west; Charlevoix writes that Perrot came by canoe and with an escort of Potawatomi to Chicago where the Miami were then encamped (1671), but the historian Shea concludes the likelihood was only by inference, and is "not borne out by the manuscript of Perrot, to which he refers." Through contact with the Miami in the early 1690s, discovered the lead mines along the Mississippi, noted on Louvigny's ✳ map in 1697. [12, 37, 718]

Perry, Albert   arrived from New York in 1835. [351]

Perry, Nelson Peter   early member of the Catholic congregation, and the only Negro; in April 1833 his name was on the petition by Catholic citizens to Bishop Rosati of St. Louis asking that a priest be assigned to them; as per notice in the *Chicago Democrat* of Jan 7, 1834: "at all times ready to furnish musik, Man of Color." For a description of this musician in action, see Wabano.

Peter Pruyne & Company   the second drugstore in Chicago, owned by Dr. Kimberly, a practicing physician, and managed by Peter Pruyne; opened in the fall of 1832 on South Water Street, between Clark and Dearborn; the firm built the first privately owned shipping dock on the river across the street from the store. [221]

Petersen, Frederick   U.S. Army private at Fort Dearborn; enlisted in June 1808; killed in action at the massacre of 1812. [226]

Petit Fort   (1) a little known French structure of modest size built c.1752 just off the Lake Shore trail, near Dune Creek [Indiana Dunes State Park]; the only local site identified with military activities between British and United States troops during the Revolutionary War, when a skirmish between St. Joseph-based British troops and a St.

Louis-based raiding party composed of Spanish and American settlers occurred [1780]; still standing in 1811, where General Hull camped enroute to Chicago; may have been a fur cache with minimal creature comforts that continued to be used by St. Joseph fur traders and others like Alexander Robinson, Billy Caldwell, and Joseph Bailly. The exact location remains uncertain; Scharf and others have assumed various sites somewhat farther inland than the location of the marker just E of the main parking lot; if any remnant of the fort survived into the 1830s it may have been destroyed by the 1838 fire that levelled the short-lived dunes community of City West [or Bailly, the town Joseph Bailly conceived and platted, but did not live to see realized]. (2) There was also a *Petit Fort de Milouaki* in 1779 at Milwaukee, not at Waukegan, as commonly supposed.

Petit Lac   see Mud Lake.

petitions   petitions listing early settlers constitute valuable historical resources, although the names are often misspelled; one such list may be found with the entry Saint Cyr; another one with firefighting.

Pettell, Louis   the real name was Louis Pilet, but also found as Pettle, Pelette, and Pilette; one of three French Canadian Pilet brothers (Michel, Charles) listed in the 1787 census of Cahokia; soon after 1800, but certainly by the time the first Fort Dearborn was built, Louis lived with his wife Angelique (her father was François Ouellet of Peoria) and son, Michael, in Chicago near the Forks in one of four log houses (among Ouilmette, Le Mai, and La Lime) along the north bank of the Chicago River, but also maintained a house in Peoria; noted in John Kinzie's Chicago account book first in 1804 soon after Kinzie's arrival, and was a regular customer through July 21, 1812; both father and son joined the Chicago militia and were killed during the massacre. For more information on the Pilet family, see entry "La Compt, Madam." [12, 226, 404]

Pettijohn, George   served as private in Captain

Seission's company during the Black Hawk War of 1832; settled in Palos Township in 1834. [278, 714]

Pettit, Charles M.   also Petit; arrived from New Jersey in 1834 and served as town treasurer in 1835, succeeding J.S.C. Hogan; with Lt. J. Allen and Henry Moore began the Chicago Reading Room Association in July that year, and later on Dec. 12 was elected treasurer of the Lyceum. [12, 351, 733]

Peyton, Francis   attorney; arrived from Virginia in 1835; partner of James Grant in 1836; lawyer for John B. Beaubien before the U.S. Supreme Court in the Fort Dearborn claim in 1839; ◆ Lake Street [12]

Peyton, Lucien   attorney; arrived from Virginia in 1835; ◆ West Lake Street, near North Canal. [351]

Phelps, J.H.   as agent for [see] Edwards & Bosworth, advertised "GOOD LIVING" in the Oct. 28, 1835, *Chicago Democrat*, "5 Tons of Cheese from Chautauge N. York said to be a better article than was ever offered (of the kind) in Chicago. 1500 lbs good Butter. Also a genteel assortment of DRY GOODS" that could "be found in the East half of the building known of late as the Mansion House."

Phelps, Samuel M.   dissolved his copartnership with S.S. Hitchcock on Aug. 8, 1835, as noted in the Aug. 15 *Chicago American*; continued alone, but the business was not identified; reported in the Nov. 11 *Chicago Democrat* that a "Camlet Cloak" had been found on Oct. 27.

Phillips   lake schooner that sailed up the river on July 14, 1834, two days after the *Illinois*, which had been the first ship to enter the new harbor and sail beyond Dearborn Street bridge; announcements of the weekly run between Chicago and St. Joseph (also Michigan City and Milwaukee) as a packet boat, always landing at the Newberry & Dole wharf, began in the *Chicago Democrat* on July 30; carried passengers and merchandise, usually under the command of Captain Howe, later Capts. Drouland, Drureau, and Andrews; made 18 calls at Chicago in 1834, 10 in 1835.

Phillips, Ezekiel   listed prior to 1836 as owner of

80 acres of Chicago land in Section 28, Township 39, as seen in Andreas, *History of Chicago*, pp. 112-113.

Phillips, H.   attended the Indian Treaty of Chicago in 1821 as paymaster of the U.S. Army.

physicians   of early Chicago and Fort Dearborn, or traveling through, in chronological order of arrival [For details, see individual entries.]   [65, 66, 137, 172, 181, 184, 188, 213, 359, 630, 738]
Father Marquette's "Surgeon" [possibly Jean Roussel]—1675; Jean Michel—1682; William C. Smith—1803 (Fort Dearborn); John Cooper—1808 (Fort Dearborn); Isaac Van Voorhies—1811 (Fort Dearborn); John Gale—1816 (Fort Dearborn); J. Ponte Coulant McMahon—1818 (Fort Dearborn); Alexander Wolcott—1818; William S. Madison—1820 (Fort Dearborn); M.H.T. Hall—1821 (Fort Dearborn); Thomas P. Hall—1821 (Fort Dearborn); Clement A. Finley—1828 (Fort Dearborn); Charles H. Duck—1829; Elijah D. Harmon—1830 (Fort Dearborn, town); E.G. Wight—1831; Samuel Grandin Johnston Decamp—1832 (Fort Dearborn); Abraham H. Edwards—1832 (Fort Dearborn, temporary); Erastus Winslow—1832 (Fort Dearborn, temporary); Edmund S. Kimberly—1832; James Augustus Marshall—1832; Phillip Maxwell—1833 (Fort Dearborn, town); George F. Turner—1833 (Fort Dearborn); John T. Temple—1833; Valentine A. Boyer—1833 (as medical student, graduated in 1836); William Bradshaw Egan—1833; Henry B. Clarke—1833; Frederick T. Minor—1833; Henry Van der Bogart—1834; William Clarke—1834; Peter Temple—1834; William G. Austin—1834; Charles V. Dyer—1835; James Anson Dunn—1835; J.H. Barnard—1835; H. Spring—1835; John Herbert Foster—1835; George W. Palmer—1835.

piasa   also piasa bird; Indian pictographs along the Mississippi River; Jolliet, Father Marquette, and later travelers on the Mississippi, told of two large paintings on high bluffs of the east bank near [Alton, IL], said to represent fabulous animals of Indian mythology, one of them often referred to as a "thunderbird." Abbé St. Cosme remarked in 1699 that they were "almost effaced"; they have since completely disappeared; the following is Father Marquette's description of the images, translated by Shea. [19, 38, 46]

As we coasted along rocks [near Alton], *frightful for their height and length, we saw two monsters painted on one of these rocks, which startled us at first, and on which the boldest Indian dare not gaze long. They are as large as a calf, with horns on the head like a deer, a fearful look, red eyes, bearded like a tiger, the face somewhat like a man's, the body covered with scales, and the tail so long that it twice makes the turn of the body, passing over the head and down between the legs, and ending at last in a fish tail. Green, red, and a kind of black, are the colors employed. On the whole, these two monsters are so well painted, that we could not believe any Indian to have been the designer, as good painters in France would find it hard to get conveniently at them to paint them. This is pretty nearly the figure of these monsters, as I drew it off.*

Piche, Peter   see Lampset, Peter.

Pickering, Augustus   captain of the schooner (see) *Illinois.*

Pierce & Abbott   see Pierce, Asahel

Pierce, Asa   arrived from New Hampshire in 1835. [351, 733]

Pierce, Asahel   born c.1812 in East Calais, VT; arrived on Oct. 8, 1833; early blacksmith and pioneer of agricultural implements who built a smithy on the west bank (Lake and Canal streets) with lumber he hauled 40 miles from Plainfield and with old blacksmith tools purchased from Reverend William See, and began to manufacture the [see] bull plow in early spring, 1834. The firm Pierce & Abbott [see Abbott, Titus H.] announced in the Dec. 10, 1833, issue of the *Chicago Democrat* their blacksmith shop as being located "nearly opposite the Chicago Hotel" (Green Tree Tavern), and announced dissolution of the firm—but continua-

tion of business at the same location—in the May 7, 1834 issue, readvertising as Pierce & French on June 25; in 1835 he brought his bride, Persis B. Abbott of Vermont to Chicago; their children were: Aurora S., Abbe A., Francis S., George H., and William S.; ✦ plow- and wagonmaker, 18 Market St.; served as village board member in 1836 and as alderman in 1837, and in 1842 on the school board; in 1885 lived at 732 Bowen Ave; ➡ Pierce Avenue (1532 N). [12, 351]

Pierce & French   Asahel Pierce readvertised his blacksmith shop on June 25, 1834, implying a new partnership.

Pierce, Samuel   listed prior to 1836 as owner of 80 acres of Chicago land in Section 28, Township 39, as per Andreas, *History of Chicago*, pp. 112-113. [12]

Pierce, Smith D.   arrived from New Hampshire in 1833; ✦ ship chandler on North Water Street; announced bankruptcy [then in Du Page County] in the *Chicago American* of April 20, 1842; later moved to Belmont, IA, where he still lived in 1885. [12, 351, 733]

Pike County, IL   from 1821 to 1823 Chicago was part of Pike County, then became part of Fulton County; for details, see Chicago jurisdictional chronology on page 209. Pike County is shown on Fielding Lucas' 1823 ✹ map on page 142 and consisted largely of the Bounty Lands between the Mississippi and the Illinois Rivers, from which a panhandle extended northeast to Chicago. This corridor comprised the land acquired by the federal government from the Indians through the 1816 Treaty of St. Louis, land through which construction of a canal between the Great Lakes and the Mississippi River system was contemplated. Pike County was named after Capt. Zebulon Montgomery Pike, former commander of Fort Massac on the Ohio River, who explored the headwaters of the Mississippi River and other western and southwestern territories during the years 1805 to 1808. Lewis Caleb Beck, in *Gazetteer of the States of Illinois and*

Missouri, 1823, describes Chicago as follows:
Chicago, a village in Pike county, situated on Lake Michigan, at the mouth of Chicago creek. It contains 12 or 15 houses, and about 60 or 70 inhabitants. From this place to Greenbay, by the way of the Lake, the distance is 275 miles, and 400 to the island of Michillimackinac. On the south side of the creek stands Fort Dearborn. [436a, 544]

Pilburn, John S.   purchased from the canal commissioners on Sept. 4, 1830, lot 4 in block 35.

Pilet, Louis   see Pettell, Louis.

Pilot   lake schooner, built in 1821 at Cleveland; visited Chicago from Detroit under Captain Keith in September 1825 with 72 barrels of trade goods for the trader William H. Wallace. [220]

Pimiteoui   native name of Indian village at [now] Peoria.

Pimiteoui, Lac de   see Peoria, IL. The native word *pimiteoui* referres to the *fat* game then found in the area of this lake.

Pineda, Alonzo de   Spanish conquistador who, in 1519, explored the Gulf of Mexico; he became the first European to reach the mouth of the Mississippi River, but did not pursue its relevance; this important entrance to the North American continent remained unused for nearly two more centuries; the Spaniards turned their attention to Central and South America, where they found greater riches.

Pinery   see Fort St. Clair; see Jean Baptiste Point de Sable.

Pinet, Père Pierre François, S.J.   (1660- 1702) born in Limoges or Périgueux, France; came to Canada in 1694 and was first sent to Michilimackinac; served two years at *Mission de Saint-Ignace;* in 1696 he and Father Binneteau opened the *Mission de l'Ange Gardien des Miami de Chicagoua* in 1696, becoming ★★★ Chicago's 1st clergymen. Father Pinet usually spent the winter months—when the Indians left to hunt—further S on the Illinois River, where he had begun a mission among the Tamaroa; the Guardian Angel Mission lasted until 1701, probably located on the N shore of the main stem of the Chicago River; in June 1702, he began work among the Kaskaskia, but died at Cahokia in August. [290]

Pioneer   230-ton steamboat built at Black Rock, OH, in 1825; on Jan. 21, 1834, a *Chicago Democrat* advertisement noted that it would "ply between St. Joe and Chicago" that year, mostly for passenger traffic, and did so, beginning June 2 under Captain Wight; all 12 subsequent calls were under Captain Spires, the last on July 9; upon departure she was wrecked "in a very severe blow, on the bar at the mouth of the St. Joseph River"; passengers bound for Chicago had just boarded and were all rescued (*Chicago Democrat*, July 16). [48]

Pioneer   an early fire brigade, formed by volunteers Oct. 7, 1835, in anticipation of the creation of the Chicago Fire Department of Nov. 4, 1835; an announcement in the Nov. 11 *Chicago Democrat* names the members of a Hook and Ladder Company (the entire Pioneer brigade and Thomas S. Eells) who have been selected by the town board of trustees; also see firefighting.

pipe   a large cask for wine, oil, &c., having a capacity of about two hogsheads, or 126 gallons.

pirogue   also pirogue; a dug-out canoe, made from a single tree trunk; were commonly used by Indians of the Americas, and are still made by them in the Amazon basin. North of Illinois, where paper birch trees grow, birch bark canoes were preferred over perogues. Perogues are durable but heavy, impractical for portaging; manned by six to seven hands, able to carry up to three tons, depending on size. In 1680, Tonti saw pirogues 50 feet long.

Plainfield, IL   see Walker's Grove.

Planck, Johann   also John Plank; born at Hesse-Darmstadt in 1808; after immigration spent a year in Detroit, then came to Chicago in 1832 with the [see] Ebinger brothers, and in 1834 moved to and built a house at Dutchman's Point [Niles], just N of the claim of Christian Ebinger; farmed there and kept a tavern with whiskey for sale to travelers and

Indians; on July 1, 1839, a legal notice (attachment) appeared in the *Chicago American* involving Plank; later he became a preacher of the Methodist Episcopalian Church, in which capacity he spent four more years in Chicago; was married to Elizabeth Ebinger, while his sister Elizabeth married John Ebinger. [342]

plank roads   an early version, usually referred to as corduroy roads and described by travelers as "soul trying," was used on swampy portions of access roads to Chicago by 1832; the "corduroy" consisted of tightly placed small-caliber logs. A systematic effort at improving street conditions in and near Chicago by using planks, flattened on top, did not begin until the year 1849. Its history is beyond the scope of this book, but did begin with Lake Street, covered 3 miles of road, cost the city $31,000, and was quickly abandoned as impractical. Ogden Avenue became a major southwestern plank road, built in 1850; a toll was due from those who used it, and [see] Mark Beaubien, who kept a tavern on this road in Lisle, collected the toll from 1851 to 1857. [12]

plants   of Chicago and Illinois, see vegetation.

Plattier, Jean   one of five *voyageurs* who accompanied Jolliet and Father Marquette in 1673 to the Mississippi and the Chicago site.

Plympton, Capt. & Bvt. Maj. Joseph   (1787-1860) Fifth Infantry; born in Sudbury, MA; married Eliza Mathilda Livingston of New York City in 1824; commandant at Fort Dearborn from Aug. 1, 1836, to May 1837; died in New York.

Poindexter, Thomas   U.S. Army private at Fort Dearborn; enlisted in September 1810; taken prisoner by Indians as one of the sick soldiers on the wagon at the massacre of 1812; tortured to death the same day. [12, 226]

Point   short for [see] Wolf Point.

Point de Sable, Catherine   see next entry.

Point de Sable, Jean Baptiste   (1745?-1818) [dates furnished by Chicago Dept. of Cultural Affairs]; also Point de Sable, Point du Sable, Pointe du Sable,

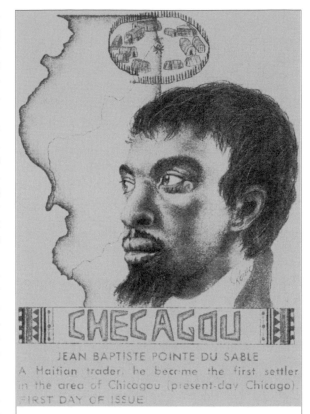

JEAN BAPTISTE POINT DE SABLE.
Design for the stamp issued in his honor by the U.S. Post Office in 1987. The likeness is fictitious, since no original portrait is known. Later research established that he did not come from Haiti, and that the incorrect spelling "du" Sable was adopted long after his death.

Point de Saible [Andreas], De Saible, De Sable, Du Sable, Point Sable [Pierce, Quaife]. Founder of modern Chicago; had a prosperous farm at the mouth of the Chicago River c.1785-1800; best known of the early Chicago settlers prior to 1800; of African descent, place of birth unknown; definitely documented by his partner [see] Pierre Durand as having a trading post in 1778-1779 at the mouth of the *Rivière du Chemin* [Michigan City]; from 1779-1784 he managed the estate of the British Lt. Governor Patrick Sinclair near Detroit, the

Pinery; about 1785 he settled in Chicago at the site of the present Tribune Tower, where he farmed and traded; was illiterate and signed by mark, later by traced initials; an excellent farmer and manager, he created a sizable estate; according to some historians, he held a commission as clandestine British Indian agent at that time; his wife was Catherine, an Indian, with whom he had two children: Jean Baptiste, Jr., and Suzanne, the latter presenting him with a grandchild on Oct. 8, 1796, in Chicago, named Eulalie Marie Pelletier; sold his estate in 1800 to Jean B. La Lime [who was really a nominee for [see] William Burnett] for 6,000 French *livres* and moved to St. Charles, now Missouri, where he bought a smaller farm and invested in real estate deals that failed by 1809, leaving him destitute for his remaining years. In 1987, the U.S. Post Office issued a stamp in his honor. For a more detailed account of his life, see an essay by John Swenson on page 388. ➡ De Saible Street (3756 S). [12, 162, 484, 564, 569, 649]

Point de Sable, Suzanne   see previous entry; married Jean Baptiste Pelletier of Detroit in 1790, for which they had to travel from Chicago to Cahokia.; the Pelletiers lived in the Chicago house of Jean Baptiste Point de Sable until it was sold in 1800. On Oct. 8, 1796, they had a daughter named Eulalie Marie Pelletier, Chicago's second recorded birth of an early settler's child [for the first, see Amiot, Louis]; they traveled to St. Louis to have the child baptized on Oct. 7, 1799.

Point of Oaks   also *Point aux Chenes*; an oak grove on the Tolleston Beach Ridge, just S of the southern arm of the western end Mud Lake, accompanying a portion of the Chicago portage. The grove defines the early French appellation of the portage, *Portage des Chenes* (Portage of the Oaks) that Jacques Bellin noted between the north branch of the "Checago" river and the Des Plaines on his 1755 ✳ map. A French settlement is believed to have existed at the Point of Oaks in the 1740s and subsequent decades, near where [see] Louis Amiot may

have been born. [526]

Pointe St. Ignace   on the northern mainland of the strait of Mackinac; the chapel at the *Mission de Saint-Ignace* became the final resting place for the bones of Father Marquette.

Pokagon, Leopold   also Pokegan, Pokagun; born a Chippewa, enslaved by the Potawatomi until proven, then adopted by tribe, marrying Topenebe's brother's daughter; with Topenebe, took the Healds safely to St. Joseph following the 1812 massacre; the second principal chief of the St. Joseph Potawatomi, and present at the Treaty of Chicago of 1833; in the fall of 1834, and in the company of Topenebe and Waubansee, he went to Washington City and protested against ratification of the treaty, claiming that Billy Caldwell, Alexander Robinson, and Joseph LaFramboise had not represented them well in the negotiations; died in 1841 at age 66. [728]

Polemic Society of Chicago   a notice in the Jan. 28, 1834 issue of *Chicago Democrat* read: "For debate: Has the Congress of the United States constitutional power to make internal improvements?"; the secretary was John Kinzie Clark; on Nov. 21 members met at the Episcopal church and the question for debate was "Is a Monarchy more favorable to Literature than a Republic?," Mitchell/Kennicott in affirmation against Spring/Wright. [544]

police   not until Jan. 31, 1835, was Chicago authorized by the State of Illinois to establish its own police force; prior to that date, limited law enforcement was provided by military authorities and by the U.S. Indian agent at Fort Dearborn. When Chicago became, successively, part of several territorial or state counties, law enforcement was the responsibility of the county sheriff; James Kinzie, for example, became the first sheriff of Cook County, and Stephen R. Forbes served as such in 1832. In 1833 the carpenter James W. Reed served as constable [although without authorization from Springfield], delivering warrants for Justice Heacock or guarding an occasional prisoner. Two years

PONTIAC [738]

following the town's incorporation of 1833, the third village board, on Aug. 15, 1835, appointed O. Morrison as ★★★ **Chicago's 1st** "Police Constable." [12, 249]

Polk, Edmund   (1776-1859) born in Pennsylvania; served in the War of 1812 under General Harrison; came from Kentucky and Indiana with his wife, Margaret (née Brown), and family in 1833 to homestead in [Lyons]; an uncollected letter for Mary is listed in the April 1, 1834, *Chicago Democrat*; the couple's children included Henry H., James, William, Wesley, Wilson, John, Samuel, Margaret, and Mary. [13, 278]

Pontiac   (1720-1769) a great Ottawa chief who, in 1763, organized a major uprising of Indian tribes (Ottawa, Potawatomi, Ojibwa) of the Northwest against the British. During "Pontiac's War" Fort St. Joseph, with a garrison of 15, was overrun on May 25, 1763. Pontiac's effort to take Detroit, however, a key element in his goal "to drive the dogs which wear red clothing into the sea" did not succeed, and by 1764 the confederacy that he had formed fell apart. In 1769 he was killed by a Peoria Indian at Cahokia; ➡ Pontiac Avenue (8332 W). [12, 37, 572]

Pool, Jasper W. (c.1803-1883) born in Philadelphia, PA; came in October 1831; resided on North Water Street and was listed as a captain; in 1879 lived at 149 W Washington St., and died Jan. 24, 1884. [12, 351]

Poor, Jonathan H. arrived in 1832 and became a charter member of Chicago's first Presbyterian church when it was organized on June 26, 1833. [12, 351]

Pope, Captain surveyor for the board of canal commissioners who, together with the chief engineer of the project, James M. Bucklin, lived in the Wolf Point Tavern during the second half of 1830 to map the canal route. [704]

Pope, Nathaniel secretary of the Territory of Illinois under Governor Edwards, a cousin of the governor, and delegate to the U.S. Congress from the territory from 1815 to 1818; judge in the federal district court established in Illinois in 1819; when in April 1818 a bill for an enabling act to provide statehood for Illinois was being considered in the U.S. House of Representatives, Pope convinced the assembly that the new state of Illinois should have its northern border moved N by an additional 61 miles, deviating from the stipulation of the ordinance, in order for the state to gain access to Lake Michigan. Thus Chicago became part of the state of Illinois, and Illinois became more closely allied to the northern states, else possibly siding with southern slave states during a civil war yet to come. Pope was first judge to hold federal court in Chicago in 1837, the session taking place over Meeker's store on Lake Street, between State and Dearborn. [12]

Popple, Henry mapmaker and secretary to England's Queen Anne; on his 1733 ✳ map, *A Map of the British Empire in America with the French and Spanish Settlements Adjacent Thereto*, he spells Chicago as "Chigagou," shows the portage and Mud Lake, places a Fort Miamis at the mouth of the Chicago River, omits the north branch, and gives the Des Plaines River a fictional shape. [682]

population figures when Father Marquette and Louis Jolliet first came through Chicago in 1673, they found no Indian settlements. In c.1696, however, two large villages of Miami existed, one on the main part of the river, the other on the south branch, and they soon attracted French traders, missionaries and soldiers. By 1700, a population of close to 4,000 was estimated by de Liette, who then ran a trading post at Chicago. There is reason to believe that a few Frenchmen formed family units with Indian women in the Chicago area, beginning with the establishment of Father Pinet's Jesuit mission in 1696 and continuing throughout the 18th century. Population figures are not existent for these early years. In the 1800 census of the Indiana Territory, to which Chicago then belonged, there were "100 souls" at Peoria, but Chicago was not mentioned.

All figures quoted for later years should be regarded with caution. For various reasons, there is no way of accurately determining the number of residents in Chicago for any given year prior to 1835. Many of the white newcomers were unregistered migrants, temporary workers, and others who would sooner or later move further west. To quote H.R. Hamilton: "To be sure it was not difficult to establish a status as resident; any person who stopped in Chicago long enough to pay a week's board was considered a resident and if he bought a lot or hung up a sign of some kind he became an old inhabitant." Most figures found in earlier literature refer only to male residents with voting privileges, or only to whites, omitting Indians or even *métis*, without specific acknowledgment. During the early boom period the population could triple within a single calender year, and therefore totals quoted for such years vary greatly, often by several hundred percent, depending on the month the count was made. The figures listed below have been proffered by various early visitors and commentators, among them de Liette, Schoolcraft, Colbert, Andreas, Beck, Hurlbut, Currey, and Lindell. For some years multiple divergent figures were obtained; in these instances the range is shown by presenting the lowest and highest figure for a given year. [12, 44, 154, 178, 350, 357, 373, 435, 565]

1700	residents:	3,000-4,000	(mostly Indians)
1800		families: 2 or 3
1803		families: 4
1812	residents:	c.40
1820	residents:	c.60	houses: 10-12
1821	residents:	60-70
1825	residents:	75-100	homes: 14; voters: 35
1829	residents:	30	families: 8
1830	residents:	40-100	houses: 12-20
1831	residents:	60	houses: 12
1832	residents:	100-600	houses: 30
1833	residents:	200-4,000	buildings: 43-180
1834	residents:	800-2,000
1835	residents:	1,500-4,000	(+1,500 transients)
1836	residents:	3,500-4,000
1837	residents:	4,179	(census year)
1838	residents:	4,000
1839	residents:	4,200
1840	residents:	4,470-4,853

porcupine *Erethizon dorsatum*; according to Hoffmeister, there are no reliable reports of porcupines occurring in Illinois during historic times, but the animal is mentioned in early French accounts as *porc-epic*, and as having been observed along the banks of the Illinois River. [341]

portage any place or route over which boats and supplies are carried or transported overland between navigable bodies of water. Of major importance to Chicago and its development was the Chicago Portage, which links the Great Lakes with the Mississippi River system; specifically, it links the south branch of the Chicago River (called *Portage Riviére*

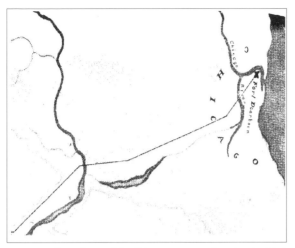

Major Long's 1816 map of the Chicago portage region, showing Mud Lake. The point where the portage road [straight line] crosses the Des Plaines River, would later be known as Laughton's ford. [413]

by Father Marquette) with Mud Lake, which drains into the Des Plaines River-Illinois River-Mississippi chain. For additional details, see entries on Mud Lake and on Chicago Portage.

Indians and early explorers used many other portages to cross the continental divide between the Great Lakes and the Mississippi River. Even in the Chicago area, there existed secondary portage routes, as between the north branch of the Chicago River and the Des Plaines River, of which present day Portage Park [bordered by Central, Berteau and Long avenues, as well as Irving Park Blvd., the latter marking the course of the old Indian portage trail] is a reminder; another lesser portage occasionally used was located further N at the level of Euclid Avenue, also between the Chicago River and the Des Plaines River; maps of the Des Plaines Division of the Cook County Forest Preserve District indicate the western end of the portage. Yet another is the [see] Calumet portage. Additional old portages of importance to the Lake Michigan trade made use of the proximity between the St. Joseph and Kankakee rivers, the Calumet

and various tributaries of the Kankakee River, the Milwaukee and Fox rivers, the Root River and the Fox River, and the Fox and Wisconsin rivers; the latter portage of two mile length having been used by Jolliet and Father Marquette when they discovered the Mississippi in 1673. The following is from de Liette's memoirs, describing his Chicago portaging experience c.1688, and the particular difficulties caused by the shallowness of much of the Des Plaines River. [12, 355, 640]

Excerpt from Litte's memoirs:

The Illinois country is undeniably the most beautiful that is known anywhere between the mouth of the St. Lawrence River and that of the Mississippi, which are a thousand leagues apart. You begin to see its fertility at Chicago which is 140 leagues from Michillimackinac, at the end of Lake Michigan. The Chicago is a little stream only two leagues long bordered by prairies of equal dimensions in width. This is a route usually taken to go to this country. At this river a portage is made, of a quarter of a league in low water and of an arpent in high water. One finds a streamlet for half a league which comes from two little lakes that extend a league and a half, at the end of which, on the rising ground at this point, is made a short portage simply of ones baggage. When the water is favorable one reëmbarks at once, but when it is low it is necessary to go a league. This is called the Portage of the Oaks; and it costs considerable effort to get the boat into this streamlet, which empties into the river [Des Plaines] which the French call the Illinois. However, this is not the Illinois, as we only come to that stream twenty leagues farther on. The passage is very difficult on account of the low waters which virtually render this river impracticable, because one ordinarily reaches this region only in summer or autumn. There are ten places where for half a league it is necessary to take out half of the baggage, and very often to remove it entirely, until the deep water is reached. It is necessary also sometimes to carry the canoe. There is a place even, called Mount Joliet, where there are four leagues of rapids, and where this must nearly always be done.

This present-day remnant of the portage creek that connected Mud Lake with the Des Plaines River was photographed by the author. It can be found in the Chicago Portage National Historic Site at 48th Street and Harlem Avenue. Beavers have returned to the now stagnant waters and have left their mark on the tree in the foreground.

For another description of the portage, this one at high water in 1789, see entry on Armstrong, Lt. John.

Portage Creek   small creek which drained Mud Lake into the Des Plaines River, located halfway between Riverside and Summit at 49th Street; was part of the Chicago Portage route.

Portage des Chenes   also *Portage aux chênes*; French, Portage of the Oaks, an alternative name for the Chicago portage; see Point of Oaks. On Bellin's 1744 ✱ map of the Great Lakes the *Portage aux chênes* is erroneously shown to arise from the north branch of the Chicago River, instead of the south branch.

Portage des Perches   French, *Portage of the Poles* or *Perch*; see Calumet portage.

Portage Lake   see Mud Lake.

Portage Park   see Portage.

Portage River   according to Gurdon Hubbard, old name of the south branch of the Chicago River, used by local traders and trappers before 1800.

Portage Trail   also known as North Portage Trail, Old Portage Trail, and Long Portage Road; one of the major trails of early Chicago, parts of which are still traceable in the modern street pattern. From the Forks, the trail roughly followed but stayed N and W of the south branch; when it reached Mud Lake, the trail followed its northern shore [there was also a lesser known South Portage Trail]; as to the modern street pattern, it ran from Cicero Avenue and 34th Street to Madison and Stewart streets, keeping fairly parallel to but S of Ogden Avenue. For a map of the eastern ends of the Chicago portage trails, their connections to other trails, and their relation to the fords across the Des Plaines River, see page 147.

Porter, George B. (1791-1834) from Pennsylvania; secretary of war in 1828, when he argued the need to regarrison Fort Dearborn because of the restlessness of Indian tribes in northern Illinois; became governor of Michigan Territory, appointed Aug. 6, 1831 by President Jackson, succeeding Governor Cass; one of three officials negotiating the land cession treaty with the local Indian tribes at Chicago in September 1833; died of cholera at Detroit on July 6, 1834. [12]

Porter, Hibbard (1806-1879) born in Jefferson County, NY; arrived in September 1833; a note in the *Chicago Democrat* of Dec. 31, 1833, indicates that his wife, Mary S. (née Shull), died in Watertown, NY, after an illness of four days; ✦ Bristol & Porter [forward/commission concern, agents for C.M. Reed], corner of State and South Water streets; died on May 30, 1879. [12, 351]

Porter, Rev. Jeremiah (1804-1893) Presbyterian minister, born in Hadley, MA, arrived on May 11, 1833, on the schooner *Mayflower* with Captain Fowle, Major Wilcox, and two companies of soldiers from Fort Brady (Sault Ste. Marie), where he had been serving as chaplain to the troops as a member of the American Home Mission Society; he came ashore on May 13; preached ★★★ **Chicago's 1st** sermon on Sunday morning, May 19, 1833, in the carpenter shop of Fort Dearborn, and on the same afternoon was invited to give another service in Father Walker's log schoolhouse at Wolf Point; found quarters above Philip Peck's store

REV. JEREMIAH PORTER [12]

on the SE corner of South Water & LaSalle streets On June 26, 1833, he organized the first Presbyterian church with nine settlers and 17 people from the fort; was an ardent moralist and enemy of alcohol, see below a quotation from a letter he wrote to a fellow preacher in 1833; often baptized believers in the river or at the beach. On June 15, 1835, he married the schoolteacher Eliza Chappel; that year the church had its own building and the congregation was self-supporting, and he removed to Peoria; lived at Detroit in 1885; his ▲ grave site is located at Rosehill Cemetery. Also see Presbyterian congregation; Presbyterian church. [12, 549, 550, 707]

Excerpt, Aug. 27, 1833 letter to Reverend Hovey, Indiana: ... *The Sabbath by multitudes is most shamefully abused; twenty stores & groceries are dealing out liquid death, while there are but two real temperance stores in the place and those kept by members of my church. In addition to these evils profaneness prevails to an extent such as I never witnessed before. The teams from the Wabash that visit us daily, seem to come loaded with cursing and bitterness. Their drivers appear almost as degraded as the miserable heathen around us. But profaneness does not stop with them. Many who call themselves gentlemen & move in the highest circle of society are embellishing, or polluting, almost every sentence they utter with some oath or curse. ...*

Porteret, Pierre one of five *voyageurs* with Father Marquette and Jolliet on their historic expedition from St. Ignace mission on May 17, 1673, and again with Father Marquette on the latter's 1674-75 trip to the Illinois region.

Porthier, Joseph see Pothier, Joseph.

Porter, William of Vandalia; secretary of the board of canal commissioners, and member of the surveying party for the Illinois & Michigan Canal that visited Chicago in 1830 under James M. Bucklin, chief engineer. [704]

Post Boy one of the first schooners, piloted by Captain Hixon from Michigan City and St. Joseph, that delivered oats and lumber to David Carver at Chicago on April 16 and 20, 1834; grounded near Michigan City later that month.

Post, Col. Justus engineer from Missouri; served as a colonel in the 1812 war. In 1823, employed by the initial canal commission, he surveyed the proposed path of the Illinois & Michigan Canal, together with René Paul creating ✳ "Map of the proposed Illinois and Michigan Canal"; ➡ Post Place (228 W). [Of interest may be the fact that Chicago's first and second post offices, under Postmaster Hogan, were located less than a block away from the short street named Post Place; could the street actually have been named for the post offices, rather than for Justus Post, as Hayner and McNamee believe? *Eds.*] [12, 320]

Post, T.M. professor at the Illinois College, visited Chicago in the company of [see] Jonathan Baldwin Turner during the summer of 1833.

postal service ★★★ Chicago's 1st postmaster was Jonathan N. Bailey, appointed by William T. Barry, postmaster general under President Jackson, on March 31, 1831; he initially worked out of the old Kinzie House, where he resided at the time of his appointment, and shortly thereafter out of a log cabin on the NE corner of Lake and South Water streets, 20-by-45 feet and built by John Steven Coats Hogan, but only half of it was used for postal services, the other half serving as a store. Bailey hired Hogan as ★★★ Chicago's 1st postal clerk; he succeeded Bailey as postmaster on Nov. 2, 1832, and hired as postal clerks John Bates (1833) and John L. Wilson (1834); also in 1834, probably in July, Hogan moved the post office to a blacksmith shop that he rented from the blacksmith, Mathias Mason, on the SW corner of Franklin and South Water streets, where Thomas Watkins became postal assistant; Sidney Abell succeeded him as postmaster on March 3, 1837. Postal business was slow prior to 1832, when mail would arrive once a week by horseback from Niles, MI; in 1833, still weekly, a one-horse wagon was needed, and later the same year one with two-horses. Dr. Temple secured a contract from the postmaster general for carrying the mail between Chicago and Ottawa, had a post-carriage shipped by boat from Detroit and on Jan. 1, 1834, made the first coach trip to Ottawa, via Walker's Grove [Plainfield]; in 1836 direct mail routes were established from Chicago to Galena and Springfield. Arriving mail was not carried out, and had to be picked up at the post office. Notices would appear periodically in the *Chicago Democrat*, listing remaining letters; if not claimed, they would be regarded as dead letters. For movement of mail prior to April 1831, see entry under mail carriers. [12]

Potawatomi dubbed *Poux* by the French, a contraction of the full name, which means *keeper of the fire*; called *canoe people* by the Illinois, because waterways were their primary avenues of travel in birch bark canoes; an Algonkian tribe that occupied the southern shore of Lake Superior and the region about the Sault Ste. Marie when missionaries first came to New France; from there they relocated to Green Bay and along the western shore of Lake Michigan. By 1750, they had spread S to the Chicago and the St. Joseph region and beyond, displacing the Miami from Chicagoland and the Illinois from the Illinois River valley. At the beginning of the 19th century their homeland was northern Illinois, and they were the major Indian tribe to interact with the European immigrants in the Chicago region. Their alliances differed from village to village: the band under Black Bird, at the mouth of the Milwaukee River, was pro-American; Black Partridge's people, at the mouth of the Chicago, and those of Windigo, at Lake Peoria, were neutral; Topenebe's people, at St. Joseph, and those of Main Poche, on the Kankakee River, were pro-British. In 1835, the Chicago Potawatomi were relocated by the federal government to lands W of the Mississippi; ➡ Potawatomie Street (8630 W). [35, 120, 148, 229, 509]

Potawatomi war dance for an eyewitness description of the great war dance in Chicago on Aug. 18, 1835, see Chronology under that date; also see Hoyne, Leonora Maria Temple. [120, 357]

Pothier, Joseph also Porthier; arrived 1821 or 1822; French Catholic blacksmith and striker for David McKee; built his house in 1825 on the N side of the Chicago River, just W of McKee's house; voted in the elections of Aug. 7, 1826, and of July 24, 1830 (see elections); on May 24 [Nov. 5?], 1828, he married [see] Victoire Mirandeau, J.B. Beaubien officiating as justice of the peace; they had three children, of whom Marie and Helene were baptized by Father Badin on Sept. 26, 1831. In the 1829 treaty at Prairie de Chien, Victoire received 1 1/2 section of land as a reservation on the Chicago River, between land granted to her sister Jane Mirandeau on the S and Billy Caldwell's reservation on the N; some of her land is now part of the North Branch Division of the Cook County Forest Preserve District. Pothier was an early member of the Catholic congregation, signing for a family of five on the 1833 petition to Bishop Rosati of St. Louis, asking that a priest be assigned to Chicago; the family moved to Milwaukee in 1835, where Joseph died in 1875. ✱ For a portrait of Victoire Mirandeau Pothier, see page 369. [12]

Poulx, Jean Babtiste see Proulx, Jean Baptiste.

Poux early French for Potawatomi.

Powell, George N. arrived in 1833; subscribed to the *Chicago Democrat* in November 1833; ◆ tavern-keeper, Milwaukee Avenue, known as "Powell's Tavern"; a notice in the *Chicago Democrat* of Sept. 25, 1839, involves him in a pending court case; died prior to 1852. [351]

Powers, William G. born c.1813 in Auburn, NY; came in May 1835; ◆ general merchant, boarded at the Lake House; in 1885 a William C. Powers was listed as living at 198 LaSalle Ave., but according to Adolphus Hubbard, William G. had died by 1879. [12, 351]

prairie according to Beecher, the French used the word to designate the grassy fields of l'Ile de France around Paris, and then the French *voyageurs* transferred the appellation to the more extensive grasslands of the New World, the dominant type of landscape in Illinois before the arrival of the American farmer. The Grand Prairie extended from near the shore of Lake Michigan to the Mississippi, from Vincennes, IN, to the Wisconsin border, interrupted only by the occasional groves of trees, described by early visitors as resembling "islands of blue in a sea of green." Botanical scholars distinguish between the eastern "tall grass prairie," on the eastern edge of which Chicagoland was located, and areas of short grass and mixed grass distributed between the tall grass prairie and the Rocky Mountains. When cultivated, the prairie soil was so rich and deep that it did not require fertilizer for 100 years; but breaking the sod required gang plowing with four to eight yoke of oxen. Prior to destruction by settlers of the woods near the lake, the prairie reached the lakeshore only along a four-mile stretch between Oak Woods [now Hyde Park] and the main Chicago River. While there were low lying areas of "wet prairie," across which travel was impossible during periods of rain, most of the prairie soil was well drained, dark, and rich, and thickly covered with Indian grass, bluejoint turkeyfoot (big bluestem), prairie beard grass (little bluestem), bluejoint, and many wildflowers, among them wild sunflowers. Also see eastern woodland, prairie fire; ➡ Prairie Avenue (300 E), originally part of an old trail linking Fort Dearborn with Fort Wayne in Indiana. See descriptions of the prairie below by Jolliet, Hubbard, Walker, Benton, and Bigelow. Also see Hall, James, as well as entries under prairie fire; under entry on Bucklin, James M., for his description of traveling though the prairie; under entry on Father Hennepin. [47, 121]

[Jolliet, 1673] *At first, when we were told of these treeless lands, I imagined that it was a country ravaged by fire, where the soil was so poor that it could produce nothing. But we have certainly observed the contrary; and no better soil can be found, either for corn, for vines, or for any other fruit whatever.* ❖ *There are prairies three, six teen, and twenty leagues in length, and three in width, surrounded by forests of the same extent; beyond these, the prairies begin again, so that there is as much of one sort of land than of the other. Sometimes we saw the grass very short, and, at other times, five or six feet high; hemp, which grows naturally there, reaches a height of eight feet.* ❖ *A settler would not spend ten years in cutting down and burning the trees; on the very day of his arrival,*

he could put his plow into the ground.

[Gurdon S. Hubbard, 1818] *Arriving in Douglas Grove, where the prairie could be seen through the oak woods, I landed, and climbing a tree, I gazed in admiration on the first prairie I had ever seen. The waving grass, intermingled with a rich profusion of wild flowers, was the most beautiful sight I had ever gazed upon. In the distance the grove of Blue Island loomed up, beyond it the timber on the Desplaines River, while to give animation to the scene, a herd of wild deer appeared, and a pair of red foxes emerged from the grass within gunshot of me.*

[Henry S. Tanner, in 1832] *The prospect of passing through these prairies in the spring season is delightful. .. Often isolated clumps of trees stand like an island in the midst of the prairie. ... The scene is forever changing, always picturesque, and beautiful.* ❖ *The prairies are generally undulating, seldom exactly level, often slightly concave, so that in some cases, they have stagnant waters over their surface in the spring. Their soil is various but fertile. From May to October they are covered with tall grass and flower-producing weeds. In June and July, these prairies seem like an ocean of flowers, of various hues, and waving to the breezes which sweep over them. The heliotrope or sunflower, and other splendid vegetables which grow luxuriantly over these plains present a striking and delightful appearance. ... The prairies are difficult to plow, on account of the firm grassy sward which covers them. But when subdued, they become fine arable lands.*

[Capt. A. Walker, from his ship, 1832] *There was no harbour accessible to any craft drawing more than two feet of water, hardly sufficient to admit the bateau in which the troops were landed. But little else was seen besides the broad expanse of prairie, with its gentle undulating surface, covered with grass and variegated flowers, stretching out far in the distance, resembling a great carpet interwoven with green, purple and gold; in one direction bounded only by the blue horizon, with no intervening woodland to obstruct the vision. The view in looking through the spy-glass from the upper deck of our steamer, while laying in*

the offing, was a most picturesque one, presenting a landscape with small groves of underwood, making the picture complete; combining the grand and beautiful in nature, far beyond anything I had before seen.

[Colbee C. Benton, 1833] *The country about Chicago, for the distance of twelve miles from the lake, is mostly a low prairie covered with grass and beautiful flowers. Southwest from the town there is not one tree to be seen; the horizon rests upon the prairie. North, on the lake, is sandy hills and barren. Between there and the north branch is a swampy, marshy place, and there is a marshy place on the south branch. The town stands on the highest part of the prairie, and in the wet part of the season the water is so deep that it is necessary to wade from the town for some miles to gain the dry prairie. Notwithstanding the water standing on the prairie and the low, marshy places, and the dead-looking river, it is considered a healthy place. It has almost a continual lake breeze, which will explain in a measure the healthiness of the place. And another reason is the cleansing of the river water by the winds driving the pure lake water into and then running out again.*

[Ellen Bigelow, 1835] *In all my life, I never saw or dreamt of so beautiful a sight as the rolling prairies. ... Nothing can equal the surpassing beauty of the rounded swells and the sunny hollows. The brilliant green of the grass, the numberless varieties and splendid hues of multitudes of flowers, I gazed in admiration too strong for words. We were at times in the midst of this vast expanse of plain, where not a tree was visible. Far as the eye could reach, nothing could be seen but "airy undulations" and smooth savannas. We occasionally found a grove, beautiful as can be imagined, entirely free from underbrush and made up of a great variety of the finest forest trees, some peculiar to this section of the country, as the cottonwood, coffeetree, hackberry and many others. Black walnut grows to an immense size and is very abundant.*

prairie chicken   *Tympanuchus cupido;* the greater prairie-chickens were an integral part of the tall grass prairie and vanished with it; today they survive in Illinois only in small remnant flocks on managed sanctuaries. They were hunted extensively by the pioneers and hated by the early farmers as pests who ferreted out and ate the newly planted grains; everyone was enlisted in the war against them, and sometimes fields had to be planted two or three times a season to replace the "varmint-snitched" seeds. Among early Chicagoans, many liked to hunt prairie chickens for pleasure and food; to quote Edwin O. Gale: *I have frequently seen him* [Capt. L.C. Hugunin] *and Richard L. Wilson, likewise an excellent shot, return from a day's sport with their buggy well loaded with prairie chickens they had shot within the present city limits.* [64]

Prairie du Chien   an early Wisconsin pioneer community on the Mississippi first settled by French traders in the 18th century; later, even though it was in the U.S. Territory, British traders stockpiled arms and ammunition there for use in recapturing the area; in c.1800 the U.S. government set up an Indian Agency there under Nicolas Boilvin to undermine British trading influence; during the 1812 war a United States expeditionary force from St. Louis took possession of Prairie du Chien and built Fort Shelby in 1814, but the fort soon surrendered to the British; in 1816 United States troops occupied Prairie du Chien and built Fort Crawford which, like Fort Dearborn, was intermittently garrisoned until regarrisoned after the Winnebago War; for treaties of Prairie du Chien of 1825 and 1829 and their significance for Chicago, see those entries.

prairie fire   periodic fires occurred on a regular basis, usually in the fall, and appear to have been a factor in spreading the prairie eastward into the woodlands and limiting the growth of trees and bushes to the vicinity of rivers and ponds. Barce described them as follows: *...giant conflagrations, feeding on the tall, dry grass of the autumn savannas,*

and fanned into a fiery hurricane by the western winds, at night time illuminated the whole heavens, and sweeping onward with the speed of the wild horse, left nothing behind them but the blackened and smoking plains. One such spectacular prairie fire about Chicago occurred in October 1834, and a recently erected building of Capt. Robert Hugunin, located two miles out into the prairie, was lost. For another description of the aftermath of a prairie fire near Chicago in 1830, see the entry for Bucklin, James M., for an excerpt of his report.

prairie fly   see green-headed fly.

prairie schooner   a name given to heavy wooden carts, a successor to the [see] Connestoga wagon, for use with five or six yoke of oxen, used for long-distance hauling across the prairie to and from Chicago, and elsewhere in the west; most Chicago-bound wagons came from the Wabash country and brought lumber, with the trip taking several days, and the crew taking provisions along and camping out at night; after selling their cargo and some of their oxen at Chicago, they would purchase salt, groceries, or dry goods, and "sail" home again; early Chicago merchants, such as J.K. Botsford and Thomas Church, and others on Market and South Water Street, benefited much from the prairie schooner trade that began with the boom period of the early 1830s.

Pratt, Oscar   printer working for J. Calhoun's *Democrat* in 1833, together with Beckford. [13]

preachers and missionaries   the first missionaries in New France, in the Illinois region, and in Chicago were French Roman Catholic, and they accompanied early French explorers. A secular priest, Messieur Jessé Fléché, was in 1610 the first active missionary in New France. Then followed members of essentially one of two orders—Jesuits, founded by Loyola, or Récollects, founded by St. Francis. The first Jesuits arrived in 1611, Frs. Pierre Biard and Ennemond Massé, and the first Récollets in 1615, Frs. Denis Jamay, Jean d'Olbeau, and Joseph le Caron. The first Illinois mission was

founded by the Jesuit Father Marquette in 1675, serving the Kaskaskia along the Illinois River, and the first Chicago mission in 1696 by Frs. Pierre François Pinet and Julian Bineteau. Best known of the Récollects in Illinois is probably Father Hennepin, who accompanied La Salle on his early travels. Beginning in 1764, the Jesuits were suppressed by the French authorities and had to abandon their missions and activities in Illinois and elsewhere. For information on individual missionaries and preachers, relevant either by their actual presence in the Chicago region or because they prepared the way for others, see the following separate entries: Claude Dablon (Catholic, 1655); Claude Allouez (Catholic, 1877); Jacques Marquette (Catholic, 1673); Louis Hennepin (Catholic; 1679); Zinobius Membré (Catholic, 1682); Claude Aveneau (Catholic, 1690); Julian Bineteau (Catholic, 1693); Pierre François Pinet (Catholic, 1696); Jean François Bisson de St. Cosme (Catholic, 1699); François Jolliet de Montigny (Catholic,1699); Thaumur de la Source (Catholic, 1699); Anthony Davion (Catholic, 1699); Brother Alexandre (Catholic, 1699); Stephen D. Badin (Catholic, 1796); Isaac McCoy (Baptist, 1826); Jesse Walker (Methodist, 1826); Isaac Scarritt (Methodist; 1828); William See (Methodist, 1830); Stephen R. Beggs (Methodist, 1831); Adam Payne (1832); Jude Perin Gary (Methodist, 1832); Joseph Rosati (Catholic, 1833); John Mary Irenaeus St. Cyr (Catholic, 1833); Jeremiah Porter (Presbyterian, 1833); Flavel Bascom (Presbyterian, 1833); Allen B. Freedman (Baptist, 1833); Henry Whitehead (Methodist; 1833); Jean T. Mitchell (Methodist, 1834); Palmer Dyer (Episcopalian, 1834); Isaac W. Hallam (Episcopalian, 1834); Isaac Taylor Hinton (Baptist, 1835); and Friedrich Buchholz (Lutheran, 1835).

Pre-Emption House   name of a tavern which [see] George W. Laird built in the Naper settlement in 1834; county elections were held here; located on the corner of Water and Main streets, it was still

PRE-EMPTION HOUSE [314a]

standing in 1928. [314a]

preemption laws   by preemption right is understood the right of a settler, who occupied a parcel of land before the area had been surveyed by the federal government, to purchase it at the minimum price of $1.25 per acre, once the government began to sell the land. The right would shield him from having to bid competitively against others, especially land speculators. To secure a claim, a structure had to be built on the land. In 1841, Congress passed the general preemption law, but in earlier years, even before 1830, it had already granted preemption rights in response to local demands. From May 28 to June 30, 1835, the Government Land Office in Chicago sold land to bona fide settlers who had made their claims earlier under the preemption laws and now came to secure their titles.

Presbyterian congregation   was first organized on June 26, 1833, by [see] Rev. Jeremiah Porter, with 25 original members, 16 of them soldiers and officers from Fort Dearborn, among them the commandant Maj. DeLafayette Wilcox; the nine civilian members were Stephen Wright, John S. Wright, Philo Carpenter, Rufus Brown, Mrs. Elizabeth Brown, J.H. Poor, Mary Taylor (Mrs. Charles H. Taylor), Elizabeth Clark, and Mrs. Cynthia Brown. In the congregation's first year, the membership increased to 66, and one of the active promoters was Stephen S. Wright. Initially services were held in the carpenter shop of the fort, sometimes at Reverend Walker's log cabin and schoolhouse at Wolf Point. The first communion was held on Sunday, July 7, 1833. Mr. Wright used to bring the "church library from Sabbath to Sabbath in a pocket handkerchief from his log store near the fort" [block 17, on Lake Street] until their own meeting house had been built by Joseph Meeker at a cost of $600 in an open field, the location later becoming the SW corner of Lake and Clark streets, and then dedicated on Jan. 4, 1834. Access was initially difficult because the its lot was "surrounded by sloughs and bogs." In the Aug. 19, 1835, *Chicago Democrat* a notice invites townspeople to attend a sale of the Presbyterian Juvenile Society's work on the next Saturday at Mrs. C. Taylor's house. On Nov. 24, 1835, the congregation formally assumed the name "The First Presbyterian Church and Society of Chicago"; afterward Reverend Porter moved to Peoria, and not until July 1837 did the congregation find another pastor (Rev. John Blatchford); during the interval the pulpit was partly graced by Rev. Isaac T. Hinton, pastor of the first Baptist church, and others. The Chicago Harmonic Society gave a public concert on Dec. 11, 1835, at the Presbyterian church, ★★★ **Chicago's 1st** public concert. Between 1835 and 1837, the structure doubled as courthouse, in which hundreds of cases were tried, including the case involving J.B. Beaubien's claim of the Fort Dearborn reservation. Under Reverend Blatchford the church had to be moved to Clark Street, S of Washington Street, because the title to the original plot had not been secured. In 1842, a Second Presbyterian Church organized itself in Chicago. See below Edwin O. Gale's comments on the first prayer house of the Presbyterian congregation. [12, 514, 550]

Considering that it was not designed for the Baptists it should have been placed nearer the future sidewalks as the long planks leading to the door could scarcely be distinguished from the water in the evening and bewildered Christians were occasionally immersed without the aid of clergy. It was not a very prepossessing structure and when one of our citizens with considerable local pride was showing it to a new arrival he feld deeply chagrined as his friend remarked: "I have often heard of God's house, but I never saw his barn before."

President   schooner from Buffalo under Captain Sweet, built at Black River, OH, in 1829; used for merchandise and passenger traffic; made three calls at Chicago in 1834 (April 20, June 12, Aug. 13) and two in 1835 (June 19 [delivering "supplies in Drugs, Perfumery, Oils, Paints, and Dye stuffs" to Frederick Thomas' apothecary], Sept. 9); capsized on Lake Erie in 1836. [48]

Price, Jeremiah   arrived from New York in 1835; purchased from John Noble and P.F.W. Peck lots 4 and 6 in block 18 and additional land in block 19 [see map on page 44]; ran for assessor in 1837; ✦ firewarden, South Water Street, near Wells Street; died in 1851. [12, 351]

Price, Robert   first advertised in the Nov. 28, 1835, *Chicago American* as R. & W. Price, "London and New York Fashionable Tailors" in a store on Lake Street within one block of the Tremont House, "prepared to execute, in the neatest manner, and at the shortest notice, all work entrusted to them"; ✦ tailor and clothier, 153 Lake St.

Prickett, William   U.S. Army private at Fort Dearborn; enlisted in June 1806; according to Eckert, he was one of the three soldiers killed in the volley fired after surrender at the massacre of Aug. 15, 1812. [226]

Prince Eugene   104-ton Canadian steamer, built in 1832; from Buffalo under Captain Patterson, called at Chicago on July 12, 1834, with merchandise; wrecked at St. Joseph in 1835. [48]

printing   see John Calhoun and Thomas O. Davis.

prison   ★★★ Chicago's 1st, a small log building, containing a single oaken cell, was erected on the LaSalle and Randolph corner of the public square in the autumn of 1833.

Procès Verbal   an official notarial French account or affidavit; for example, the report of the taking possession of Louisiana by La Salle in the name of the king of France in 1682. [46]

Procter, Maj. Gen. Henry A.   British commander during the 1812 war; disclaimed responsibility for the Fort Dearborn massacre; ordered Fort Dearborn captives ransomed from the Indians; pardoned Captain Heald. [109]

Procyon lotor   see raccoon.

Prophet, The   Temskwatawa; ordered the arrest of Chicagoan John Kinzie for treason because, as an officer of the British Indian department in 1813, he was attempting to win Tecumseh's Indians to the American side; a Shawnee chief, trusted advisor, and mystic philosopher of great influence among the tribes of the Midwest in the early 19th century. Together with his half brother Tecumseh, he started a movement for confederated Indian regeneration and resistance to the advance of the American white settlers, but their effort met with disaster in the battle of Tippecanoe in 1811, and in subsequent developments in the War of 1812, which ended British influence in the Midwest and deprived the Shawnee of British support they had formerly enjoyed. [212, 609]

prostitution   appears to have become a publicly acknowledged Chicago problem for the first time in 1835, when the town council decreed a $25 fine for anyone convicted of keeping a brothel.

Proulx, Jean Baptiste   also Proux, Poulx; present at the W.H. Wallace estate sale in 1827; early member of the Catholic community, in April 1833 his name was on the petition by Catholic citizens to Bishop Rosati of St. Louis asking that a priest be assigned to them. In 1781, a Canadian trade license was issued to a Bazile Proulx to trade at the Grand Calumet, near present Gary, IN. [649]

Pruyne, Peter   a young man with business acumen who arrived early in 1833 with the family of Dr. Kimberly; they promptly opened up a drugstore on South Water Street, W of Dearborn Street, next

THE PROPHET [410]

to the Kimball & Porter store; an ad for "P. Pruyne & Co." is in the Dec. 3, 1833, issue of the *Chicago Democrat*. On Aug. 26, 1835, he married Rebecca, only daughter of Silas W. Sherman, Reverend Hallam officiating; they had one child. On Nov. 21 of that year, he submitted a claim for wharfing privileges; in December became a director of the Chicago branch of the Illinois State Bank. Served as state senator, but his term was cut short by death in November 1838. In November 1839, Rebecca married [see] Thomas Church, who also had lost his spouse earlier that year. [12, 28, 221, 544, 653]

Puants   French for *to stink*; early French (*Puans à la Baie*) and British colonial term for member of the [see] Winnebago tribe. In the *Jesuit Relations* of 1647, writing from the *Mission de Sainte Marie*, Père Ragueneau explained why the Winnebago were so called: *On* [Lake Michigan] *dwell other nations whose language is unknown,—that is, it is neither Algonkin nor Huron. These peoples are called the Puants, not because of any bad odor that is pecu-liar to them; but, because they say that they come from the shores of a far distant sea toward the North, the water of which is salt, they are called 'the people of the stinking water.*

The *Puants* [Winnebago] inhabit the land surrounding Green Bay.

Puants, Bay of   early name for [see] Green Bay, *Stinking Waters*; actually, the original meaning of the term referred to the fact that the Winnebago, who lived there, were erroneously thought to have come from eastern coastal regions, where water carries an ocean smell.

public building   ★★★ Chicago's 1st, see estray pen; public square.

public square   first designated by James Thompson on his ✳ plat of August 1830, bounded by Clark, Washington, LaSalle, and Randolph streets. The first public building erected with public funds on the SW corner of the square was the estray pen, a roofless corral for loose cattle, followed by the first courthouse, built on the NE corner in the fall of 1835.

public well   ★★★ Chicago's 1st such well was dug and lined with stones in the Kinzie Addition (corner of Cass [Wabash] and Michigan streets) at a cost of $95.50, completed on Nov. 10, 1834, the first community effort to provide villagers with pure water.

Pugh, Jonathan H.   born in Kentucky; second lawyer to become established in Springfield (1823 or earlier); as a circuit rider, he represented Deborah Watkins in her divorce from [see] Morrison Watkins—the first recorded divorce; was canal commissioner in 1830, visiting Chicago in that capacity that summer, and on Sept. 4, purchased lot 1 in block 18 for $24 [see map on page 44; in 1835 this choice lot on South Water Street belonged to Isaac D. Harmon]; died in 1833. [37, 220]

Pugsley, Augustus   subscribed to the *Chicago Democrat* in November 1833.

Pukes   nickname for Missouri natives or residents, common in early Illinois. [55a]

puncheons the halves of a split log, with the faces smoothed by an ax or adze; the stockade of Fort Dearborn was made of puncheons, as were the floors of log cabins and much of the furniture.

punk tinder, such as dry fungus or dry rotten wood, used to ignite a fire in conjunction with sparks from steel and flint.

Putnam County Chicago became part of Putnam County on Jan. 13, 1825, but county administrative functions were handled by adjacent Peoria County In 1831, Putnam County became part of Cook County. For details, see Chicago jurisdictional chronology on page 209. [436a, 544]

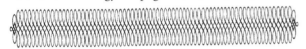

Quebec oldest city in Canada; the first European explorer to visit the site was the Frenchman Jacques Cartier in 1535, finding a large Algonkin village called Stadacona, where in 1608 Samuel Champlain founded the present city; became the capital of the French Province of New France in 1683; from 1783 to 1791 the city served as capital of Quebec Province of England, and from 1791 to 1841 as capital of the Province of Lower Canada; New France or Canada under either authority included Chicago and much of Illinois, which were therefore under Quebec jurisdiction for long periods; for further details on Chicago's jurisdictional chronology see page 209. Quebec's additional importance for Chicago's early history derives from the activities of the Jesuit missionaries who throughout the late 17th century were directed by Church authorities based there, and by the export of fur from the Northwest and the import of supply from Europe which was funneled almost exclusively through Quebec. [544]

quarter section equals 160 acres; see section.

Queen Charlotte brig from Buffalo, NY under Captain Cotton, called at Chicago on Aug. 20 and Oct. 9, 1835.

Rabbie, Jean Baptiste early member of the Catholic community; in April 1833 his name was on the petition by citizens to Bishop Rosati of St. Louis asking that a priest be assigned to them; ✦ [John] boarded at LaFramboise.

Raber, John early resident who arrived in 1834 from Germany and joined St. Mary's congregation. [342]

Raber, Philip German immigrant, first attested to as having lived in Chicago in 1833; ✦ laborer, State Street [342]

raccoon *Procyon*, an exclusively New World genus; *Procyon lotor* occurs throughout the state of Illinois; raccoons are excellent swimmers and climbers, are omnivorous, and remain near water; they have adapted well to suburban life and may be more abundant now than any time earlier. [341]

Racine River see Root River.

railroads on May 24, 1830, the first passenger railroad in the United States began service between Baltimore and Elliott's Mills, MD, a distance of 13 miles. Not until Jan., 16, 1836, was the first railroad chartered in Chicago—the Chicago and Galena Union Railroad, and not until November 1848 was the first 10-mile segment of this line, between the north branch of the Chicago River and the Des Plaines River, put into service; see also Chicago and Vincennes Railroad.

Rand, Socrates (1804-1890) born in Wendell, MA; engaged in harbor building, gradually making his way westward to Detroit; subscribed to the *Chicago Democrat* in November 1833, and arrived in February 1834; acquired 320 acres of land along the Des Plaines River in Maine Township after one year and farmed; was elected justice of the peace in 1835; in 1844 was part of a group of Chicago citizens representing their town in Peoria at a state school convention; married Fanny Wicker in 1850; lived in Des Plaines in 1879, and at 161 North Carpenter St. in Chicago in 1885. [12, 13, 278, 351]

Randolph, John (1773-1833) cousin of Thomas Jefferson and senator from Virginia from 1825 to 1827; Randolph County in Illinois is named after him; James Thompson, the surveyor who came from Randolph County and laid out the early street pattern in 1830, named ➡ Randolph Street (150 N) after him.

Ransom, Captain master of the schooner *Ann*, a vessel on Lake Michigan that delivered American Fur Co. trade goods from Michilimackinac to James Kinzie at Chicago in September 1821.

Rasle, Père Sebastian Jesuit priest who, in 1692, restored the *Mission de la Conception* in Peoria, which had been empty since Father Allouez had left in 1687.

Rat Castle nickname for the Wolf Point Tavern.

Rathbourn, Captain master of the commercial lake schooner [see] *Hiram* in 1835.

raven *Corvus corax*; once common in the Midwest; at the time of Fort Dearborn they could often be observed flying along the lakeshore and eating dead fish among the sand dunes. The population declined rapidly during the 19th century; now virtually extinct in Illinois, with the most recent sighting in Chicago on Oct. 13, 1953; ➡ Raven Street (6300 N). [64]

Rawley, Calvin purchased on Dec. 4, 1832, from the Cook County commissioners lot 4 in Section 38 [see map on page 44] for $53.

Raymond, Elisha name on the Chicago post office list of unclaimed letters of Jan. 21, 1835.

Reader, Daniel L. born c.1810 in Milton, PA; arrived in July 1833; lived in Chicago in 1879, at Aurora in 1885. [12]

real estate boom see land boom.

Réaume, Jean François also Reheaum; was arrested near Fort Dearborn in late April 1812, under suspicion of being a British agent, taken to the fort, and interviewed by Captain Heald. Being satisfied with his answers, Captain Heald released him, promising safe passage. However, when Réaume left the fort he was attacked by soldiers of the fort and was almost killed. Able to return to the fort, he remonstrated. Captain Heald then assured him that on his second departure for Fort Malden, no Americans would harm him. [109]

Récollects also Récolets; the Reformed Fathers of St. Francis, a branch of the Franciscan order of the Roman Catholic Church, known as such in France, Belgium, and Holland; zealously intent on missionary work among North American Indians, they were among the first to arrive (1615), shortly after the Jesuits (1611); many eventually came to Chicago and the Illinois country; the Indians called them "gray gowns"; for individual names, see entry for preachers and missionaries.

Red Bird Winnebago chief whose murders of two whites precipitated the Winnebago War and who surrendered himself after the war to Maj. William Whistler, then in command at Fort Howard, to be tried "under the white man's law," even though he was considered innocent under Indian law, the killings having been committed in justified retaliation to transgressions by white settlers and lead miners; a proud man, Red Bird died soon after in prison while awaiting sentence; for a description of his dramatic surrender see the following account by Milo M. Quaife, 1913:

About noon of the following day a body of Indians was described approaching Whistler's camp. As they drew nearer the voice of Red Bird singing his death song could be heard. The military was drawn out to receive the delegation and a dramatic ceremony ensued. On the right and slightly advanced was the band of musicians. In front of the center, at a distance of a few paces, stood the murderers, Red Bird and WeKau; on their right and left, forming a semicircular group, were the Winnebagos, who had accompanied them. All eyes were fixed on the magnificent figure of Red Bird: six feet in height, erect, and perfectly proportioned, his very fingers 'models of Beauty'; on his face the most noble and winning expression; his every movement embued with grace and stateliness; his dress of barbaric splender, consisting of a suit of white deer skin appropriately fringed and decorated, and over the breast and back a fold of scarlet cloth; no wonder he seemed to the spectators, even the hostile race, 'a prince born to command and to be obeyed.'

Reeble, George W. co-owner of a grocery on Dearborn Street with Thomas J. Field; the shop was raided on Oct. 25, 1834, by the sheriff in accordance with Illinois' antigambling laws, the owners arrested, and a roulette table confiscated; unable to post bail of $1,000 each, they went to jail.

Reed, Charles (1784-1863) married Chloe Roby in 1807; arrived from Virginia on March 2, 1831; soon moved to Joliet and constructed a dam and mill, but sold out and may have returned to Chicago; possibly the forwarding and commission merchant Charles M. Reed listed at the corner of South Water and State streets in 1839; married Sally Joyce in 1840 as per notice in *Chicago Daily American* of July 6. [12]

Reed, James W. arrived early in 1833 and as a constable that spring served a warrant for justice Hancock; subscribed to the *Chicago Democrat* in November 1833; cabinetmaker with a shop on South Water Street, between Franklin and Wells; in August 1834 was elected supervisor of roads and bridges, serving until November; paid John Calhoun $7 on Sept. 7, 1835, "To print blanks for census"; in 1839 lived at Blue Island. [12, 249, 351]

Reed, Thomas legal notices involving him appeared in the *Chicago Democrat* on Sept. 3, 1834, bringing suit against John C. Wickham in circuit court for repayment of $82.50, and in the *Chicago American* on Sept. 10, 1836; entered a claim [[lot 1 block 6] for wharfing privileges late November 1835; ✦ teamster, 115 Lake St.

Rees, James H. (c.1812-1880) born in Stroudsburg, PA; surveyor, arrived on Aug. 11, 1834; became city surveyor in 1836; active in the voluntary fire brigade; ✦ draftsman and surveyor, William B. Ogden; married Harriet Frances Butler on June 4, 1844, as per notice in the *Chicago Weekly Journal*; in 1849 was involved in the planning of the Galena & Chicago Union Railroad; died on Sept. 23, 1880; in 1885 his widow lived at the Southers Hotel. [12, 351]

Reheaum, Jean François see Réaume, Jean François.

Reichert, Jacob known only from the following notice that appeared in the Aug. 8, 1835, *Chicago American*: "My wife, Mary Bremley, left my house and bed on Saturday, 8th inst., without any just cause, and is supposed to have went away with some Hoosier countrymen, who probably, knew her better than I did. All persons are hereby notified, that debts contracted by said Mary after this date, will not be paid by me. The person or persons who took her away from my house will be handsomely rewarded by keeping her forever. CH. Jacob Reichert."

religion see the following major entries: missions; preachers and missionaries; Catholic congregation [1833]; Presbyterian congregation [1833]; Baptist congregation [1833]; Methodist congregation [1834]; Episcopal congregation [1834]; Chicago Bible Society.

Renards French term for the Fox Indians.

Reserve Avenue ➡ 8730 W (4444 N to 5240 N), named after the former reservation of Chief Alexander Robinson, through whose land it ran; see Robinson, Alexander; see reservation.

Resigue, Samuel arrived in 1834; served as firewarden of the third ward, appointed Sept. 25, 1834; ✦ carpenter, Illinois Street near Cass [Wabash] Street [351]

Rexford early name for Blue Island, appearing on some maps of 1835-1838.

Rexford House also Rexford Tavern; see Rexford, Stephen.

Rexford, Heber S. and Norman brothers; came in 1832 and made claims at the Yankee Settlement [Lockport] and at Bachelor's Grove [Morgan Park]; each returned with their families, but to settle at Blue Island, Norman in 1835 and Heber much later; Norman died in 1883, and Heber on March 6, 1885. [12, 13]

Rexford, Stephen   born in Charlotte, VT, in 1804; brother of Thomas; arrived in Chicago from Buffalo, NY, on July 27, 1832, and within two years made a farming claim at Bachelor's Grove [now part of the Tinley Creek Division of the Cook County Forest Preserve District] and there built a large double log house; assisted Maj. William Whistler at Fort Dearborn in 1833 with distributing provisions for the assembled Indians; served as Cook County commissioner; married Susan Wattles of Ripley, NY, on Dec. 30, 1835, Reverend S.T. Hinton officiating, and had five children with her; later relocated to Blue Island, where in 1836 he joined his brother Thomas in building and running the Rexford House on the Vincennes Trace (111th Street and Vincennes Avenue), a traders' hotel on an important trail junction, "visible for miles" on the southern end of the Blue Island ridge. Susan died in 1849; Stephen married Elvira Barber and still lived in Blue Island in 1879; Blue Island ➡ Rexford Street (short N–S street at approximately 2300 W and 133rd Street) [12, 13]

Rexford, Thomas   brother of [see] Stephen Rexford, from Charlotte, VT; built a four-room log cabin at Blue Island in 1835 near [Longwood Drive] and opened a tavern; in 1836 he and Stephen built the Rexford House.

Reynolds, John   early governor of Illinois and author of two unreliable works on the state's history: *Pioneer History of Illinois* and *My Life and Times*. He wrote these in the final years of his life, as he boasted, from memory, "which may be relied upon." As an example of his garbled recollections, see entry under Sainte Ange, Pilette de. He was a lawyer in Cahokia who, according to federal documents (*American State Papers, Public Lands*, Vol. 2, Washington, D.C., 1834) published in his lifetime, was involved (as was his lawyer-judge father Robert) in corrupt and fraudulent land-jobbing as early as 1804. Inaugurated as the fourth governor of the

state on Dec. 9, 1830; served until Nov. 17, 1834, when he resigned to assume office as representative in Congress. [583, 584, 649]
From the *Illinois Herald*, Kaskaskia, IL, Dec. 16, 1815:

To the poor people of Illinois and Missouri Territory: To the above class of mankind whose pecuniary circumstances will not admit of feeing a lawyer, I tender my professional services as a lawyer, in all courts I may practice in, without fee or reward. John Reynolds.

From the *Missouri Gazette* and *Illinois Advertizer*, Saturday, May 25, 1816:

FIFTY DOLLARS REWARD will be given to any person who will deliver to me, in Cahokia, a negro boy named Moses, who ran away from me in Cahokia about two months since. He is about 16 years old, well made, and did belong to Messrs. McNight & Brady in St. Louis, where he has been seen frequently, and is supposed to be harbored there or about there. He had on a hunting-shirt when he left me. May 14, 1816. John Reynolds.

Rhines, Henry   owned a residence, grocery, and cabinet shop on LaSalle Street, between Lake and Randolph in 1834, which was destroyed in the town's first fire in October 1834, an estimated $1,200 loss [see Chronology]; on Sept. 22, 1835, he placed an ad in the *Chicago Democrat* offering a $100 reward for information leading to the conviction of those who vandalized the frame reconstruction of his house on the same lot; ✦ deputy sheriff and constable, 44 LaSalle St. In 1844 he lost an election bid for the office of marshal, being branded by his abolitionist opponent as a "negro-catcher"; in 1885 his widow Minerva lived at 273 West Jackson St. [12, 351, 544]

Rialto   name of Chicago's second theater building [the Sauganash, in 1837 and 1838, served as the first], located at the W side of Dearborn Street, between South Water and Lake; a wooden frame structure that had been constructed in 1834 by John Bates and used as an auction house; in 1838

was refurbished for theater performances by Harry Isherwood and Alexander McKenzie, and accommodated the entertainments of the [see] Joseph Jefferson family that same year. By the following year, the Rialto had become known as the Chicago Theatre, and Joseph Jefferson partnered McKenzie as manager. [482]

Ribourde, Père Gabriel de la   (c.1615-1680) taught at the Béthune monastery in France; Récollect priest who, as Father Membré's superior, served with him at the mission de la Conception in southern Illinois in 1679; together with Frs. Membré and Hennepin, he was with La Salle when Fort Crevecoeur was built on Lake Peoria; was murdered by Kickapoo in 1680 while returning to Canada with Tonti and Father Membré. [12, 399, 665]

Rice, Luther   interpreter for the Indian treaty negotiations at Chicago in 1833, together with James Conner.

Richard, Father Gabriel   Sulpician priest of St. Ann's Church in Detroit who visited Chicago in December 1821, saying Mass, baptizing local children, and preaching to the garrison; he was also a congressman for the Michigan Territory, elected in 1824; one of his major achievements was to procure an appropriation for a government road between Detroit and Chicago. [119, 268, 544]

Richard, Robert Kerr   also Richards; in about 1832 purchased from James Kinzie lot 6 in block 2 and from William Lee lot 3 in block 23 [see map on page 44]. On Oct. 27, 1835, he debated the query "Should the General Government make further appropriations to aid this state in the construction of the Illinois and Michigan Canal?" with John D. Caton at the Presbyterian church for the Chicago Lyceum—his position was affirmative, as per notice in the *Chicago American*.

Richards, James J.   born in Salina, NY, in c.1824; arrived in July 1835; ✦ clerk, Illinois Street; later removed to [Evanston] where he still lived in 1879. [12, 351]

Rickman, Richard U.S. Army sergeant at Fort Dearborn; enlisted in May 1806; reassigned to Washington City in August 1811. [226]

Rider, Eli A. arrived in 1832 and voted on Aug. 10, 1833; subscribed to the *Chicago Democrat* in November 1833; advertised on Sept. 10, 1834, in the *Chicago Democrat* that he had a two-story house for sale on South Water Street; was a member of the second engine company of the voluntary fire brigade in 1837; ✦ clerk, for C.L.P. Hogan. [12, 351]

Ridge Avenue, Ridge Boulevard, Ridgeland Avenue, Sand Ridge ➡ Chicago area streets and forest preserves named after the ridges on top of which they extend for much of their distance; the ridges were formed by the shore of glacial Lake Chicago during its Glenwood phase (50 feet above the present level of Lake Michigan).

Ridge Road Trail former name for Ridge Avenue at [see] *Grosse Pointe* [Evanston]; follows an ancient shore ridge and was a fork of the Green Bay Trail.

Riley, James, John and Peter Ottawa *métis* brothers who lived near Fort Dearborn, serving as interpreters for Indian agent Jouett and others when needed; their father was a trader at Saginaw Bay and became later a Schenectady judge; all three may have been in Chicago at the time of the massacre, but their role and fate is uncertain. In 1839, a John Riley is listed as warehouseman for Newberry & Dole on Michigan Street [12, 226]

Riverdale settled in 1836 along the Michigan City Road S of the Calumet River; also known as Sand Ridge; ➡ Riverdale Avenue, near the far southern city limits.

River Forest, IL western suburb 12 miles from the lakeshore, bordering on the east bank of the Des Plaines River; was originally part of the larger communities of Noyesville, then Harlem; the first permanent settlers were [see] Ashbel and Harriet Steele (1836) who had first lived in Chicago; became part owner of a steam sawmill that had been built by Bickerdike & Noble in 1831 on the east bank of

the Des Plaines River, just N of Lake Street bridge, giving River Forest [and Oak Park] its start by attracting laborers. [301, 318, 701]

river otter *Lutra canadensis*, formerly common along major waterways and their tributaries in Illinois, now greatly restricted; Hoffmeister reported that in 1816, 400 otter furs were exported from Illinois. [341]

Riverside, IL community on the Des Plaines River 12 miles SW of early Chicago; in 1831 Stephen Forbes built the first ▲ log house [see Monuments], choosing the site for its strategic location near a ford, and because his brothers-in-law, the Laughtons, lived nearby in [now] Lyons. Beginning in 1869, and guided by the noted landscape architect Fred. Law Olmsted, the community began to developed into a unique residential town of curving streets that deviate from the customary checkerboard pattern of the Midwest and contribute to its special charm. [262, 490]

Riverside Ford also known as an ▲ Indian ford [see Monuments], it is the most upstream of four fords between Riverside and Summit; located immediately downstream from the Barry Point Road bridge; here a branch of the Green Bay Trail from [see] *Grosse Pointe* crossed the river and led to the Illinois River valley. [262]

Rivière du Chemin see Michigan City.

Rivière de Colbert see Colbert, Jean Baptiste.

roads see streets and roads.

Roberts,— blacksmith at Fort Dearborn in 1804; see blacksmiths.

Roberts, Edmund resident of Kaskaskia and one of the first three commissioners for the development of the Illinois & Michigan Canal, appointed in 1829; member of the surveying party for the canal that visited Chicago in 1830 under James M. Bucklin, chief engineer; when the government land sales began in Chicago on Sept. 27, 1830, he was among the first buyers, possibly as agent; the land that later became known as the [see] Russel & Mathers addition was originally entered under

the names Russel, Mathers, and Roberts; he additionally purchased lot 4 in block 2, lot 2 in block 18, and with P. Menard, Jr., lot 4 in block 29 [see map on page 44]. [12; 704]

Robinson, Alexander (1789-1872) Potawatomi, Che-che-pin-qua or Chee-Chee-Bing-Way (*Blinking Eyes*); also called Chief Robinson; brother of Mollaire Robinson; prominent Chicago trader and Potawatomi chief; born at Mackinac, son of a Scottish trader and a Green Bay Ottawa *métis* mother; early in life worked for Joseph Bailly at St. Joseph, then within the Calumet area; was a close friend of John Kinzie years before Kinzie settled at Chicago and where, by 1812, he had a house on the E side of the south branch, immediately S to that of the LaFramboises. At the Fort Dearborn massacre Robinson helped in the rescue of Captain and Mrs. Heald, conveying them by boat to St. Joseph and, for a fee of $100, guided them and Sgt. Griffith to Mackinac, again by boat. He returned to Chicago "in about 1815" [his own testimony] and until 1816, joined Ouilmette in farming around the fort, while most or all other settlers had fled in the wake of the massacre; when Kinzie returned in 1816, Robinson lived with his first wife (Indian, name unknown) on the N side of the river near [the intersection of Dearborn and Kinzie streets] and worked for Crafts in the fur trade, later for Kinzie; in 1820 he is said [R. Blanchard] to have built the cabin to which Sam Miller and Archibald Clybourne added a two-story addition in 1827, fashioning Miller's Tavern; until 1825 maintained a cabin and trading post at Hardscrabble, and was assessed on personal property of $200 that year; adapted an Indian store and tavern, with liquor license (issued on June 9, 1830), near Wolf Point; in 1830 this location became part of block 29 [see map on page 44], and he purchased the land from the government, lots 1 and 2. Robinson could not read or write, but David McKee reported that he kept accurate accounts with pencil and paper by means of characters of his own to represent quan-

ALEXANDER ROBINSON [410]

lities and was a model of uprightness; on Sept. 28, 1826, he married Catherine Chevalier [de Catiche] as a second wife, John Kinzie, J.P. officiating, whose father François Chevalier was the Potawatomi chief of a village on the NW shore of Lake Calumet; children John, David, and Maria Ann were baptized on Oct. 18, 1830, by Father Badin, and by 1833 there were five children (there would be 14); he never divorced his first wife, who retained a position within the household; was an early member of the Catholic congregation—signed for a family of eight on the 1833 petition to Bishop Rosati of St. Louis, asking that a priest be assigned to Chicago. After Chief Chevalier's death, and during the 1825 Treaty at Prairie du Chien, Robinson was appointed chief of the United Potawatomi, Ottawa and Chippewa, later representing them [the "Prairie and Lake Indians"] at the Chicago Treaty of 1833. Although his tribe went W after the treaty, he remained near Chicago; for services rendered to the government, Robinson and his wife had received at the 1829 Treaty of Prairie du Chien their own reservation grant of two land sections on the banks of the Des Plaines River [Schiller Park], where they lived until their death. The ▲ house they are believed to have lived in was still standing on their reservation (now Cook County Forest Preserve land) in 1993, but has since then been destroyed by fire. Robinson died on April 22, 1872, and was buried on the banks of the Des Plaines River near his home, as were his second wife and three children. An inscribed ▲ granite boulder marking the grave sites can be found in the forest preserve on the W side of the 4800 block of East River Road. Also commemorating his and his second wife's names are "Robinson Woods," "Catherine Chevalier Woods," and "Che-che-pin-qua Woods," all portions of the Indian Boundary Division of the Cook County Forest Preserve District [see Monuments]. Some say that Robinson died at the age of 110, but historic records make this unbelievable; he himself admitted complete ignorance of his birth date. Yet Robinson's life was exceptionally long, spanning a remarkable succession of events that transformed Chicagoland from wilderness to a modern western town; ➡ Robinson Street (1700 W). [12, 226, 357, 457, 588]

Robinson, J.H.   placed a notice in the Oct. 10, 1835 *Chicago American* in regard to "a large calf skin Pocket Book" that was stolen on the night of Oct. 5 at the New York House; the loss included "$250 in bank notes, and sundry Lend Certificates, Bonds, Notes and other accounts," necessitating a reward of $100 for detection and conviction of the thief.

Robinson, Mollaire   sister of Alexander Robinson, whom Emily Beaubien knew as a young child when Emily lived directly across the river in her father's Sauganash Hotel, recalling later that "[s]he was crazy and had several children and Father Badin came there." [41]

Robinson's Tavern   see Robinson, Alexander.

Robinson's reservation   see Robinson, Alexander.

Rocheblave, Philippe François de Rastel, chevalier de   last British governor of the Illinois country; commandant at Kaskaskia who surrendered the post to George Rogers Clark on July 4, 1778, and, as prisoner, was taken to Virginia, his wife and children remaining in Kaskaskia; by 1783, he had regained his freedom and wrote in a letter of Nov. 6, 1783 to General Haldimand that he had to travel from Quebec into the Illinois country and "find Mrs. Rocheblave and the rest of the family at Chikagou." It is not known with whom the Rocheblave family had found refuge at Chicago, perhaps [see] Jean Baptiste Gaffé, who opened a post there in 1782. [457, 649]

Rockford Trail   early area trail used by Indians and settlers, leading NW from Fort Dearborn, largely coinciding with Grand Avenue.

Rockwell, James   arrived from Massachusetts in 1834; his ad in the *Chicago American* of June 8, 1835, read "Furniture Warehouse, manufacture of cabinet furniture, on South Water Street, a location formerly occupied by Clark, Filer & Co."; became a charter member of the Chicago Bible Society in August and was appointed to its executive committee in November; served as firewarden in 1836; ◆ furniture dealer, Lake Street near Franklin Street; later moved to Batavia, where he still lived in 1885. [12, 351, 733]

rod   a measure of length equal to 16.5 feet or 5.5 yards, frequently used in early Chicago.

Rodgers, John V.   master mechanic from New York State who, in Chicago in 1834, joined William Payne and Oliver C. Crocker in an effort to construct and operate a sawmill in [see] Sheboygan.

Rogers, Edward Kendall   (c.1812-1883) also Rodgers; born in Ipswich, MA; arrived in November 1835; went into general mercantile business; married Mary B. Curtis in 1837; ◆ Horace Norton & Co. [grocers and provisions, South Water Street]; was the first merchant to receive and handle pig iron; member of the Chicago Bible Society (1840);

on the first board of trade (1848); in 1879 he lived at 359 Ontario St. where, after his death on May 2, 1883, his widow continued to reside until at least 1885. [12, 351]

Romp   schooner under Captain Chaver, called at Chicago on July 18, 1834, from Ogdensburg, NY; called again on July 30, coming from Michigan City and going to Detroit.

Ronan, George   graduated from West Point in March 1811 and immediately reported to Fort Dearborn as ensign; killed in action at the massacre of 1812. [226]

Root River   Indian: *Kipikaoui* or *Kipikawi*; also Racine River; a portage existed from the upper Root River to the Fox River; empties into Lake Michigan at Racine, WI. Schoolcraft passed near its mouth on August 1820 on his way to Chicago and described the presence of Potawatomi lodges.

Rosati, Father Joseph   bishop of St. Louis in 1833, when he received a petition by Chicago Catholics for a priest to be assigned to them; he promptly responded by sending Father St. Cyr; for the names on the petition, see St. Cyr. [12, 267]

Rose, Niles   Chicagoan who died on April 2, 1834; little more is known about him, but he gave rise to two intriguing notices in the *Chicago Democrat*; see text below.

Notice in the April 8, 1834 issue:
A man by the name of Niles Rose, residing about 8 miles up the north branch of the Chicago river, died on Wednesday of last week, in consequence of intemperance. A caution to drunkards.

Notice by the editor in the next issue, April 16:
We are requested by Mr. Russel Rose to state that no such person as Niles Rose resided up the north branch of the Chicago river. We understand, however that Niles Rose was a resident of this town [Chicago], and that the cause was intemperance.

Rose, Russel   voted on July 24, 1830, and received 21 votes for constable, but lost to Horatio Smith.

Rosette   the *métis* handmaid of the Whistler women, living with them at the fort.

Ross, Hugh   arrived 1836 from Scotland; ★★★ **Chicago's 1st** bookbinder and paper ruler; in partnership with [see] Ariel Bowman he opened up shop in the Saloon Building on Clark Street; ✦ 24 Clark St. [12, 351]

Ross, John   listed prior to 1836 as owner of 80 acres of Chicago land in Section 28, Township 39, as per Andreas, *History of Chicago*, pp. 112-113.

Rothenfeld, Heinrich   German immigrant to the Chicago area in 1825; he likely came through the settlement but moved on to what became known as Dunklee's Grove [Bloomingdale] as its first settler, soon attracting other Germans. [342, 544]

Rough, Capt. James   lake captain who resided in Buffalo, master of the *May*, which brought supplies to Fort Dearborn and/or to John Kinzie, as indicated in his account books on June 16 and Nov. 2, 1804; Jan. 15, 1806; and July 12, 1808. [404]

Roulx, Jean Baptiste   misspelled by Andreas for [see] Proulx, Jean Baptiste.

Roussel, Jean   also Rousselière; possibly the unnamed surgeon in Father Marquette's 1674-75 journal; see Surgeon, the.

Rowley, Jrieh   born in 1777, Monroe County, NY; War of 1812 captain and Erie Canal contractor; came by sailing vessel on July 17, 1833, with his wife Polly Gray (née Olmstead), four sons, stepson [see] Charles M. Gray, and in-laws; chartered a prairie schooner within two days and journeyed to Homer Township [Will County] to settle. [734]

Rue, John C.   carpenter and builder; arrived from New York in 1834; ✦ 156 Clark St.; by 1885 lived at 131 S Jefferson St. [12, 351]

Rumsey, Julian Sidney   (1821-1886) born in Batavia, NY; arrived on July 28, 1835, to work in a shipping business owned by two of his uncles, Walter L. Newberry and George W. Dole; ✦ clerk, Newberry & Dole; became mayor in 1861 and lived in Chicago until at least 1879; ➡ Rumsey Avenue, at 8500 and 8700 S. [12, 351]

Runyon, Armstead   native of Kentucky; arrived October 1830 and moved on to Lockport Township [Will County]; served as corporal in Captain Seission's company during the Black Hawk War; moved to California in 1849, died there in 1875.

Rush Medical College   first Chicago medical school, named after Dr. Benjamin Rush, one of four physicians to sign the Declaration of Independence; brainchild of Dr. Daniel Brainard, who arrived in Chicago in 1835 or 1836; received its charter on March 2, 1837, two days before Chicago received its city charter, but the school did not open for instruction until 1843. Now it is part of Rush-Presbyterian-St. Luke's Medical Center; ➡ Rush Street (65 E). [12, 364]

Russel, Benjamin   voted in the election on Aug. 7, 1826.

Russell, Aaron   from Boston; jointly with Benjamin H. Clift, he opened the "Chicago Book and Stationary Store" on Aug. 26, 1834, in the frame building belonging to Philo Carpenter on South Water Street between Wells and LaSalle, Carpenter using the western half for his drugstore; on Oct. 22, 1835, the partnership was dissolved, and Clift carried on alone. [12]

Russell & Clift   partners of ★★★ **Chicago's 1st** "Chicago Book and Stationary Store," who also held the exclusive franchise for Morrison's Vegetable Pills, a patent medicine; the initial ad listed available book titles, "[t]ogether with very superior Drawing paper, bristol board, gold leaf, very good; paper hangings, patent rulers, almanacs for 1836, drawing pencils, blank deeds, some on parchment paper; Mitchell's new pocket maps of the United States, Illinois, and Indiana; pocket compasses, &c. &c."; see Russell, Aaron. [12, 221]

Russell & Mather Addition   also referred to as the North Branch Addition; in the spring of 1835 Gurdon S. Hubbard, together with Messrs. George Mather and Edward A. Russell, purchased for $5000 an 80 acre tract of land constituting the western half of the NW corner of Sect. 9, Twp. 39, bounded by Kinzie Street on the S, Jefferson Street on the E, Chicago Avenue on the N, and on the W ending just beyond Halsted Street; it shares its southern border with the Original Town and part of its eastern border with the Wabansia Addition. [705]

Russell, Edward A. a distant relative of G.S. Hubbard from Middletown, CT; worked for the American Fur Co. in 1818, and occasionally traveled to Chicago on business; visited again in 1833, and through Hubbard was alerted to the profit potential during the 1833–37 land boom. Hubbard then managed Russell's substantial investments; the land that later became known as the [see] Russell & Mather Addition was originally entered under the names Russel, Mathers and Roberts. [705]

Russell, Capt. John B.F. (1800-1861) from Massachusetts; arrived on July 15, 1832, under the command of General Scott in conjunction with the Black Hawk War; remained in Chicago, bringing his family in 1835; on detached service for the Indian Department of the U.S. government, he became the disbursing officer [with his office in John H. Kinzie's store] for the transportation by wagon trains of 5000 Potawatomi from Chicago to Clay Co., MO in 1835, in accordance with the 1833 treaty; working with [see] Christian B. Dobson, who had received the contract to furnish transportation, he advertised in Sept. 1835, in both newspapers for 10 to 40 ox teams of two yoke each with which to remove the last of the Indians. Russell became co-owner, with George W. Doan, of the Saloon Building at the SE corner of Lake and Clark, built for them in 1836; the structure was used initially as the city hall from 1837 to 1842; ◆ Captain U.S.A., corner of Indiana [Grand] and North State streets; died on Jan. 3, 1861. [12, 733] Notice placed by Capt. Russell in the *Chicago Democrat* on Sept. 9, 1835:

Wanted, for the removal of the Indians.
FROM 10 to 40 OX TEAMS. The waggons to be strong and well made, with good canvass or cotton covers, to keep every thing within dry—to carry with it a bucket for tar or grease—to be supplied with an axe, or hatchet, hammer and nails. Each waggon to have two yoke of Oxen, to carry 1500 lbs. if required, and to travel daily twenty miles, if necessary. A per diem allowance will be paid, commencing on the day the team is accepted, which will include all allowances, except to the teamsters, a pound of bread and meat will be issued and forage to the oxen. This allowance to continue until the arrival of the party at the country allotted to the Indians west, and a day's pay for each twenty miles for their return to Chicago. The United States will not be responsible for any accident that may accrue.—The teamsters are implicitly to obey all reasonable orders and directions from the government agents. No teamster under 18 years of age will be accepted. It is reserved to the government agent in charge of the party, to discharge a team at any time by allowing him his return pay as above stipulated. Proposals to be made to the subscriber, at his office, in Col. John H. Kinzie's store, on or before the 19th of September.
J.B.F. Russell,
Capt. U.S. Army, Military Disb'g Agent.

Russell, P.P. a notice in the May 20, 1835, *Chicago Democrat* announced "connexion in business … closed" with William H. Brown, of Russell & Brown.

Russell, William early settler and part-owner of the Leigh farm on the south branch; married to Tess (?); their house [according to Eckert] was on the lake shore, just S of the Leigh House; both Russells were killed at the 1812 Fort Dearborn massacre, he as a member of the Chicago militia. A William Russell purchased land in Peoria in 1807, which supposedly had formerly belonged to Jean Baptiste Point de Sable; it is not known if this was the same William Russell. [12, 226]

Ryan, Edward George (1810-1880) born in Ireland; came in 1835; ◆ attorney and counselor at law, 8 Clark St.; in 1840 he served as editor of the newly established *Weekly Tribune*; in 1842 moved to Racine, and in 1874, became chief justice of Wisconsin; died on Oct. 20, 1880. [12, 351]

Ryan, Thomas purchased on Sept. 4, 1830, lot 2 in block 20 [see map on page 44]; a legal notice appeared in the *Chicago American* on Aug. 5, 1837, involving a Thomas Ryan.

Sabine, William A. first advertised in the June 8, 1835 *Chicago American* as a "Storage, Forwarding & Commission Merchant" on North Water Street, specifying the following week: "30 bbls. Cider – A prime article"; continued weekly to advertise new assorted goods; also worked that summer at David Carver's pier, scheduling passengers and unloading or loading freight that was shipped on the *Llewellyn* between Chicago and St. Joseph; ◆ Sabine & Co., North Water; boarding house, 161 Lake St., upstairs.

Sac Indians abbreviated corruption of *Sauk* or *Ousa-ki*; see Sauk Indians.

Sackett, Joshua S. joined Captain Hogan's Cook County volunteer company as private on May 24, 1832 during the Black Hawk scare; built the first log house and kept a tavern in Lyons Township; acquired prior to 1836 the eastern half of the NW quarter of Section 32 of Township 40 N, as per Andreas, *History of Chicago*, pp. 112-113; in 1885 lived in Garden Prairie, Boone County, IL. [12, 51, 278, 714]

sagamite Illinois word for a soup made by boiling "Indian wheat" [corn] in maple syrup.

Saganashkee Slough also Sauganash, Ausagonoshkee, Ausoganashkee; also known as Grass Lake, the Pass, and the Sag, the swamp is an arm of the Des Plaines River that occupied the southern part of the former glacial outlet of Lake Chicago; rising and falling lake levels during the last 12,000 years have rendered "the sag" alternately with an eastward current, then a westward current, and often with no current; lower lake levels about 3,500 years ago caused the separation of the sag swamps from the headwaters of Stony Creek—N of Lanes Island—and of the sloughs near Tinley Creek, also known as Bachelor's Grove Creek—S of Lanes Island. The area is thought to have been the site of possible European military encampments, both French and British, during their respective periods of dominance. For a pre-1836 bridge across an arm of the Saganashkee Swamp, see entry for bridges and ferries. Much of the ▲ Saganashkee Slough has survived as part of the Palos Division of the Cook County Forest Preserve District, where this prehistoric outlet of Lake Chicago can be visited [see Monuments].

Saginaw Algonkin, *mouth of the river*; ➡ Saginaw Avenue (2638 E).

sailing vessels the era of large sailboats on Lake Michigan began in 1679 with *Le Griffon*, built for La Salle; they alone crisscrossed the lakes until 1818 when *Walk-in-the-Water* became the first steamboat on Lake Erie. Fort Dearborn and the settlement were visited by two to three ships per year, rarely more, throughout the spring and fall, while coastal small-boat transportation was used during the other seasons. Preserved letters of the St. Joseph trader William Burnett reveal that as early as 1786 it was not unusual for sailing ships from Mackinac to stop at Chicago, although most commerce along the shores of Lake Michigan was carried out by canoe or *batteau*. Among the few ships that are known to have come to Chicago by 1835, are the *Felicity* in 1779; the *Tracy* in 1803; the *Adams* and the *May* with multiple visits from 1804 to 1810; the *General Hunter* in 1805; the *Contractor* in 1805 and 1808; the *Salina* in 1809; the *General Wayne* and the *Ghent* in 1816; the *Tiger, Heartless,* and the *Baltimore* in 1817; the *Hercules* in 1817 and 1818; the *Jackson* and the *Fairplay* in 1819; the *Pilot* in 1825; the *Young Tiger* and the *Sheldon* in 1826; the *Savage* in 1828, the *Napoleon* in 1830, 1831, and 1833; the *Marshal Ney* in 1830 and 1832; the *Telegraph* and the *Marengo* in 1831; the *Dart* in 1832; the *Austerlitz,* the *David Carver,* and the *Westward Ho* in 1833 and 1834; the *General Harrison,* the *LaGrange* in 1833 and 1834; the *El-Lewellyn,* the *Nancy Dousman,* and the *Jefferson* in 1834; the *Detroit* in 1834 and 1835; and the

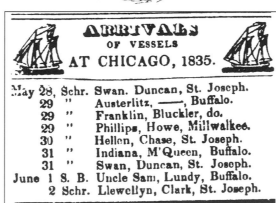

From the *Chicago Democrat* of June 3, 1835

Hiram, the *Jesse Smith,* and the *Chance* in 1835. The *Clarissa* was the first sailing ship built at Chicago and was launched in 1836.

In 1833, only two brigs and two schooners arrived from the lower lakes; in 1834, 176 vessels came (among them the *Illinois* and the *Phillip,* first and

second to sail into the new harbor beyond Dearborn Street bridge). In 1835, about 250, and in 1836, by Dec. 1, 456 ships had come, 39 of which were steamboats. See individual entries for various vessels. Also see steamships, and boats.

Saint Ange, Pilette de see "La Compt, Madam."

Saint Augustine, FL settlement in Florida, founded by Pedro Menédez de Avilés in 1565; oldest permanent European settlement in North America, and capital of Spain's territorial claim that stretched N to Newfoundland; in theory, the Chicago region was under the jurisdiction of St. Augustine for part of the 16th century. See table on Chicago Jurisdictional Chronology, page 209.

St. Charles Trail early area trail used by Indians and early settlers, leading W from Fort Dearborn at Lake Street.

St. Clair, Gen. Arthur (1734-1818) born in Scotland; came to America in 1757, to Illinois in 1790; soldier of the Revolutionary War; on Feb. 1, 1788, appointed first governor of the Northwest Territory, which included Illinois. In 1791, he fought an unsuccessful campaign against the midwestern Indian tribes, which opposed continued colonialization; in 1794 the Indians were decisively beaten at Fallen Timbers by General Wayne; ➡ St. Clair Street (200 E, from 500 to 720 N), originally Sand Street. [12, 594]

St. Clair County erected and named by Gov. Arthur St. Clair in 1790 in SW Illinois, as a subdivision of the Northwest Territory; in 1800 became part of Indiana Territory, in 1809 part of Illinois Territory [see Knox County]. For details, see Chicago jurisdictional chronology on page 209. [5, 436a, 544, 595]

St. Cosme, Abbé Jean François Buisson de (1667-1707) missionary, born in France, ordained in 1690, stationed in Quebec; on Oct. 21, 1699, Abbé St. Cosme, on the way to southern Illinois, visited the Chicago area and the flourishing *Mission de l'Ange Gardien,* as well as a large village of the Miami nearby; then in charge were Fathers Pinet and

Bineteau. The leader of the visiting group was Abbé Montigny; others with him were Abbé Davion, Brother Alexandre, and Tonti as their guide; on Oct. 24 the party proceeded S through the portage (Brother Alexandre remained temporarily) to the Tamarois in the Mississippi Valley. On his return trip to Quebec during Easter of 1700, then with Abbé Thaumur de la Source, St. Cosme again stopped at the mission; his impression of these visits to Chicago are detailed in a letter to the Bishop of Quebec; for an excerpt, see below. In 1707, Abbé St. Cosme was killed by Sitimache while descending the Mississippi. [290, 613]

From a 1700 letter written by Abbé St. Cosme:

Monsieur Montigny, Davion, and myself went by land to the house of the Reverend Jesuit Fathers, the Mission of the Guardian Angel, found there the Reverend Father Pinet and the Reverent Father Binneteau, recently arrived from the Illinois country, slightly ill. Their house is built on the bank of a small river, with the lake on one side and a vast prairie on the other. The village of savages contains over a hundred and fifty cabins, and a league up the river is still another village, almost as large. They are all Miamis. You can see no finer looking people, neither tall nor short usually, legs that seem drawn with an artists pen, they carry their load of wood gracefully with a proud gait as finely as the best dancer; faces as beautiful as white milk, the most regular and the whitest teeth imaginable, full of life, yet lazy, tattooed behind from shoulder to heels; proud, vain, they are given to begging, are cowardly, licentious, entirely given up to their senses, jealous as Italians, thievish, gourmands, vindictive, perfidious, much given to debauchery, especially the men; the reverend Jesuit fathers, who speak their language perfectly, manage (if one may say so) to impose some check on this by instructing a number of girls in Christianity. This often greatly incenses the older men and daily exposes these fathers to ill-treatment and even to being killed.

Abbé St. Cosme reports how a small boy got lost in Chicago in 1699:

The next day we began the [Chicago] portage, which is about three leagues long when the water is low, and only a quarter of a league in the spring, for you embark on a little lake [Mud Lake] that empties into a branch of the Illinois, and when the waters are low you have to make a portage to that branch. We made half our portage that day, and we should have made some progress further, when we perceived that a little boy whom we had received from Mr. de Muys [A French military officer, who became Governor of Louisiana in 1705; eds.], having started on alone, although he had been told to wait, had got lost without anyone paying attention to it, all hands being engaged. We were obliged to stop and look for him. It was a very unfortunate mishap, we were pressed by the season and the waters being very low, we saw well that being obliged to carry our effects and our canoe it would take us a great while to reach the Illinois. This made us part company, Mr. de Montigny, de Tonty, and Davion, continued the portage next day, and I with four other men returned to look for this little boy, and on my way back I met Fathers Pinet and Binneteau who were going with two Frenchmen and one Indian to the Illinois. We looked for him again all that day without being able to find him. As next day was the feast of All Saints this obliged me to go and pass the night at Chikagou with our people, who having heard mass and performed their devotions early, we spent all that day too in looking for that little boy without being able to get the least trace. It was very difficult to find him in the tall grass, for the whole country is prairies; you meet only some clumps of woods. As the grass was high we durst not set fire to it for fear of burning him. Mr. de Montigny had told me not to stay over a day, because the cold was becoming severe; this obliged me to start after giving Brother Alexander directions to look for him and to take some of the French who were at Chicag8.

[From a letter later written by Abbé Thaumur de la Source, another member of the de Montigny/ St. Cosme party, we learn with some satisfaction the following:

I will tell you that Mr. de Montigny took a boy twelve or fifteen years with him, who got lost while making the first portage in the prairies. Mr. de St. Cosme remained with five men and spent two days looking for him without being able to to find him, and during this time I and two others with Mr. de Montigny made a portage of two leagues. This boy made his way to Chicagou, where Brother Alexandre was, thirteen days after. He was utterly exhausted and was out of his head. Eds.]

Saint Cyr, Father John Mary Irenaeus (1803-1883) born in Lyon, France; arrived at St. Louis in August 1831; ordained as deacon in 1832; raised to priesthood on April 6, 1833, by Bishop Joseph Rosati of St. Louis; first Catholic priest assigned to Chicago [April 16, 1833] in response to a petition sent by local Catholics to the bishop that month [This petition is preserved and is of considerable historic interest, in that it contains the names of all petitioners and the size of each one's family, reprinted below]; Catholics then numbered 128, or c.90 percent of the population. After a journey of 12 days from St. Louis, Father St. Cyr arrived on May 1, in the company of Anson Taylor, who had been dispatched from Chicago to serve as escort; he celebrated his first Mass in Mark Beaubien's 12-by-12-foot log cabin at the SE corner of the Forks on May 5. From this modest beginning he soon formed the Parish of [see] St. Mary's and built his church near the SW corner of Lake and State streets; the building was completed [constructed with pine lumber that David Carver supplied from Michigan] in October 1833. By 1835 Father St. Cyr's flock numbered 400, Indians and Negroes [see Perry, Nelson Peter] alike; additional duties were to travel to outlying isolated settlements, as far as the Fox River valley, to perform baptisms &c. In 1837, he was recalled to the diocese of St. Louis; died on Feb. 21, 1883. Father St. Cyr's letters from Chicago to Bishop Rosati are preserved in the St. Louis Archdiocesan Archives. [12, 267, 268]

Petition letter to the Bishop of St. Louis, Joseph

FATHER JOHN MARY IRENAEUS ST. CYR [12]

Rosati, received on April 16, 1833, and answered the following day, asking that a priest be assigned to Chicago:

To the Right Reverend Bishop of the Diocese of Missouri, of St. Louis, &c., &c.

We, the Catholics of Chicago, Cook County, Ill., lay before you the necessity there exists to have a pastor in this new and flourishing city. There are here several families of French descent, born and brought up in the Roman Catholic Faith, and others quite willing to aid us in supporting a pastor, who ought to be sent here before other sects obtain the upper hand, which very likely they will try to do. We have heard several persons say were there a priest here they would join our religion in preference to any other. We count about one hundred Catholics in this town. We will not cease to pray until you have taken our important request into consideration.

Written in French and listing the following persons, giving for each the number of family members being represented, for a total of 128 individuals: *Thomas J. V. Owen – 9; J. Bt. Beaubien – 14; Joseph Laframboise – 7; Jean Pothier – 5; Alexander Robinson – 8; Pierre LeClerc – 3; Alexis Laframboise – 4; Claude Laframboise – 4; Jacques Chaput – 5; Antoine Ouilmet – 10; Leon Bourassa – 3; Charles Taylor – 2; J. Bt. Miranda and sisters – 3; Louis Chevallier and family – 3; Patrick Walsh – 2; John Mann – 5; B. Caldwell – 1; Dill Saver – 1; Mark Beaubien – 12; Dill Vaughn – 1; James Vaughn – 1; J. Bt. Rabbie – 1; J. Bt. Proulx; J. Bt. Tabeaux – 1; J.B. Durocher – 1; J. Bt. Brodeur – 1; Mathias Smith – 1; Antoine St. Ours – 1; Bazille Desplat – 1; Charles Monselle – 1; John Hondorf – 1; Dexter Hapgood – 1; Nelson Peter Perry – 1; John S.C. Hogan – 1; Anson H. Taylor – 1; Louis Franchere – 1.* Entry on the reverse side: *Major Whistler's family, about 6.*

St. Mary Catholic Church   see Catholic congregation.

St. James Church   see Episcopal congregation.

St. Joseph   this community of traders in Michigan territory, close to the current Michigan-Indiana border, was a famous frontier crossroad in the second half of the 18th century, where the Chicago Road from Detroit was joined by the trail from Fort Wayne; was preceded by the Jesuit [see] *Mission de Saint-Joseph*, built c.1685, and developed in association with nearby Fort St. Joseph, nick-named *Parc aux Vaches* or *cow pasture* by the inhabitants, where buffalo cows would earlier return to calve. Its location was on the St. Joseph River two miles S of Niles, MI, near the intersection of the Detroit-Chicago road and the St. Joseph-Kankakee portage route. During the Revolutionary War the principal trader was Louis (Louison) Chevalier, whose co-operation was sought by the warring parties because of his thorough familiarity with the land and its inhabitants. Another important trader was William Burnett, between c.1778

and 1814, with whom John Kinzie and Jean La Lime apprenticed; from 1796 to 1800 Kinzie had a trading post here, and a small stream in the area is still known as Kinzie Creek. The community is not to be confused with present day St. Joseph at the mouth of the St. Joseph's River, opposite Benton Harbor, MI. [216]

St. Joseph   schooner under Captain Burnham, built at Black River, OH, in 1835, called at Chicago on June 24, 1835, with passengers and merchandise; in the July 8 *Chicago Democrat*, a notice itemized "60 M. ft. pine lumber, 100 M. shingles, 20 bbls. flour, and 60 bbls. bulk merchandize: the largest cargo ever discharged at this port," delivered from Grand River, MI; returned five more times that year, going to St. Joseph and Buffalo, NY. [48]

St. Joseph River   early name, Miami River or *Rivère des Miamis*; the French first met the Miami among several villages along the river, replaced by the Potawatomi; La Salle's sailing vessel, *Le Griffon*, had been under orders to meet him at the mouth of the river, but perished in 1679 before completing its mission. Draining mostly Michigan territory, the river's mouth is located at [Benton Harbor]; gave access to the much-traveled St. Joseph-Kankakee portage, where a large Potawatomi village existed and where Fort St. Joseph was located from c.1712 to its destruction during the Revolutionary War; broadly meandering through Michigan, the river was crossed by the Detroit-Chicago road three times. In 1826, Congress allocated funds for the improvement of the St. Joseph harbor at the mouth of the river, the first federal harbor project on Lake Michigan, and in the following year the sloop *Savage* became the first vessel to enter the river, though actual work on the harbor did not begin until 1833. [235]

St. Lawrence River   in eastern Canada; the wide mouth of the river was first shown on the 1511 ✳ map of Ptolemy, as edited by Sylvanus; the river became the original gateway for European conquest of what was later known as New France, which eventually included the Chicago region. French-man Jacques Cartier, in 1535, was the first to leave a record of sailing into the gulf of St. Lawrence and then into the river "until land could be seen on either side." In 1610, Champlain founded Quebec along the St. Lawrence River. The first Jesuit missionaries, Fathers Biard and Massé, arrived in 1611; ➡ St. Lawrence Avenue [600 E].

St. Louis schooner from Buffalo under Captain Vorce, called at Chicago with passengers and merchandise on June 30 and Sept. 9, 1835.

St. Louis, Rivière de Jolliet's name for the Illinois River.

St. Louis, Treaty of see Treaty of St. Louis 1816.

St. Lusson, Simon François Daumant, sieur de proclaimed at Sault-Ste.-Marie in 1671 that "all the adjacent countries, rivers lakes and contiguous streams" belonged to the king of France, Louis XIV; afterward Talon reported that a cross and post with the arms of France had been erected "... in the presence of seventeen Indian nations, assembled on [that] occasion from all parts, all of whom voluntarily submitted themselves to the dominion of his majesty, whom alone they regard as their sovereign protector." The many Indian nations had been brought together by [see] Nicolas Perrot. [565]

St. Ours, Antoine in April 1833 his name was on the petition by Catholic citizens to Bishop Rosati in St. Louis asking that a priest be assigned to them. [12]

St. Pierre, — possibly the earliest permanent trader in Milwaukee, where he is said to have lived from 1764 until at least 1779. A nephew of St. Pierre, Morand, was encountered and interviewed by Captain Robertson when his boat, the *Felicity*, visited Milwaukee in 1779, but the notes in his log are ambiguous. [565, 649]

Salienne Potawatomi *métis* youth of about 14 in 1812 who lived near Fort Dearborn, possibly with the Riley brothers, and occasionally served as interpreter at the fort; was in the procession when the evacuation got underway, but survived the massacre of 1812 by joining the Indians at the beginning of hostilities. [226]

Salisbury, Stephen Milburn born in 1796 at Weymouth, MA; married Eliza Bagley on Sept. 1, 1831, and nine days later left with his wife for Chicago; noted in a journal the steady course of travel by horse and wagon until Sept, 28: "At daylight we started again and arrived at the ferry across the grand Calimine about sunrising at which place we took breakfast. Went on again and reached Chicago a little before Sun setting & put up at Mr. Grave's in the Fort which is called Fort Dearborn." The couple soon after moved to farmland at [Wheeling] where they would raise a family; enlisted as sergeant in Napier's company during the Black Hawk War; in several *Chicago Democrat* announcements he officiated in marriages, presumably as justice of the peace. [12, 714]

sally port first Fort Dearborn soldiers' term for the tunnel they dug from the storehouse in the NE corner of the stockade to an underground room at the river bank, containing a water well; meant to assure access to water in case of a prolonged siege.

Saloon Building three-story brick building erected in 1836 by Capt. J.B.F. Russell and George W. Doan at the SE corner of Clark and Lake streets, then the largest hall W of Buffalo devoted to public meetings and serving as city hall for the first five years; ▲ see Monuments. [It was named after the French *salon*, meaning *large reception hall* or *meeting hall*, and not meaning *drinking establishment*, a connotation that developed in America at a later time] [12]

Salter, John an entry on June 16, 1804, within John Kinzie's account book lists [John] Salter as Fort Dearborn's shoemaker. [404]

Saulteurs see Chippewa.

Saltonstall, William also Saltonstile; arrived from Michigan in 1835 and petitioned on Nov. 21 for wharfing privileges; ◆ fish dealer, W Madison Street; wife Mary died in 1839, according to notice in *Daily American*. He later married Sarah

Aikens. [28, 351]

Sambli, Arkash see Mann, Arkash Sambli.

sandhill crane *Grus canadensis*; in earlier days was frequently seen in the area, as reported by David McKee, a resident along the Chicago River from 1823 to 1832: "Excellent fish abounded in it, and over it hovered wild geese, ducks and sandhill cranes in vast flocks, and pelicans and swans were sometimes seen"; now an uncommon migrant and rare summer resident in northern Illinois. [64]

Sand Ridge early name for a settlement along the Michigan City Road S of the Calumet River [Riverdale]. Locations called Sand Ridge can be found both S and NW of downtown Chicago; the name refers to the long sandy beach ridge created by early Lake Chicago during the [see] Glenwood beach stage 12,000 years ago. Indian trails followed the ridge and early pioneer cabins were built atop to avoid the moisture of the surrounding swamps. ▲ In Calumet City, IL, this once prominent geological feature is memorialized by the names Sand Ridge Nature Center and Sand Ridge Prairie, both representing parts of the Thorn Creek Division of the Cook County Forest Preserve District [see Monuments]. Another known Sand Ridge was N at [Jefferson] on which Elijah Wentworth, Sr., established Wentworth Hotel in 1836. [13]

Sanford, Rathburn subscribed to the *Chicago Democrat* in November 1833.

Sanitary Drainage and Ship Canal completed in 1900, it was a successor to the Illinois & Michigan Canal (construction of which was started in 1836); it was the Sanitary Drainage and Ship Canal that, on completion, consistantly reversed the flow of the Chicago River. Each canal is a separate entity, the two partially paralleling each other, and both following the course of the prehistoric natural Chicago outflow of the southern end of glacial Lake Chicago through the Des Plaines valley, connecting the Great Lakes with the Mississippi River system by way of the Illinois River.

Sansamani Winnebago chief, participant in the

Fort Dearborn massacre; survived. [226]

Sanson d'Abbeville, Nicolas (1600-1667) influential cartographer and founder of the great French school of cartography of the 17th century; as tutor to Louis XIV and *Géographe du Roi* he had access to the records of the royal court and of the Jesuits, detailing exploration and conquest of North America. In 1650, he published the first ✳ map of *New France to show all five Great Lakes* (more maps would follow); California is shown as an island. In 1673, Jolliet and Father Marquette carried his 1656 ✳ map of Florida with them on their trip to the Mississippi River valley.

Sargents, John K. member of the first Baptist church, present at its organizational meeting on Oct. 19, 1833; a John Sargent resided at [Lisle] in 1830. [12]

Satterlee, Merrit Lawrence S. born c.1813 in Litchfield, CT; worked as clerk in Thomas Church's grocery store on Lake Street in 1835; ◆ clerk, Thomas Church; became partner in 1840; married Emily Twogood in 1844; in 1885 lived at 2704 Michigan Ave. [12, 351]

Sauganash often used as *the Sauganash*, also *Sakonosh*, meaning in Potawatomi language *English-speaking Canadian*; Indian name of (see) Billy Caldwell; ➡ Sauganash Avenue, Caldwell Avenue. For other spellings and applications of the word, see also Saganashkee Swamp.

Sauganash Tavern later United States Hotel; landmark tavern that was begun in 1829 as the Eagle Exchange Tavern, owned by Mark Beaubien; originally a log cabin, it was enlarged by the addition of a two-story blue shuttered clapboard building that opened in 1831 under the name Sauganash Tavern, at the SE corner of Lake Street and Market [Wacker Drive], and became the social center of the town. Levi Osterhardt ran the Sauganash until he moved S to run George Dolton's tavern/hotel on the Calumet River. On Aug. 10, 1833, the first town trustees were elected here. Beaubien sold the tavern to John Murphy in 1834, who renamed it

THE SAUGANASH HOTEL   [12]

United States Hotel, until his new United States Hotel on the W side of the river had been completed. From 1837 to 1839, the structure served as Chicago's first theater under the promoters Isherwood and McKenzie, then became a hotel again under the old name Sauganash, and under a succession of owners; was destroyed by fire in 1851. At the same location stood, in later years, a building called "the Wigwam," where Abraham Lincoln was first nominated for President; the Wigwam fell victim to the fire of 1871. [12, 160, 351]

Sauk Indians also Sacs, Sakis or Ou-sa-kies; Algonkin tribe that may have originally dwelt near Quebec as Black Hawk claimed; first encountered by the French near Saginaw Bay, MI; allied with the Fox when Father Allouez encountered them in 1666-67 at Green Bay; by 1718 they had gravitated S to Rock River and were pro-British; along the Wisconsin River in 1766, where their large village on Sauk Prairie was visited and described by Jonathan Carver. Black Hawk, believing that a treaty in 1802 had tricked the tribe into selling their land E of the Mississippi, began a border war in 1831 [see entry on Black Hawk War] which involved Cook County; at its close the surviving Sauk retired to Iowa, and from there to Kansas and Oklahoma. [12, 111, 151]

Sauk Trail also Sac or Mohawk Trail; central part of the principal E–W interregional Indian route that spanned most of the North American continent, crossing through the Calumet region from Rock Island to Detroit; the Santa Fe Trail and the Oregon Trail are western extensions; the trail coincides with portions of Indiana Highway 2, U.S. 330, and U.S. 30 [Lincoln Highway]. Avoiding swamp land, common throughout the Calumet region, the trail followed the top of the Valparaiso moraine and the Glenwood Beach ridge. To reach the westbound part of the Sauk Trail from Fort Dearborn, the traveler would use one of two connecting trails, the first one coinciding with modern day Archer Avenue, the other with Ogden Avenue (formerly the Brush Hill Trail), reaching the Sauk Trail at Aurora. The eastbound portion could be reached by way of the Tolleston Beach Trail to Bailly's trading post. In later years the Beach Trail from Chicago to Bailly's and the Sauk Trail as it continued to Detroit were collectively called the Chicago Road. A portion of the Thorn Creek Division of the Cook County Forest Preserve District is called the ▲ Sauk Trail Woods (containing Sauk Trail Lake), and through it runs the Sauk Trail Road of S Chicago Heights, becoming Lincoln Highway further E [see Monuments]. [699]

Sault Ste. Marie   French mission founded in 1668 by Frs. Marquette and Dablon at an Ojibwa village, later supported by a trading post; a town remains existent, the oldest permanent European settlement in Michigan.

Sauter, Charles and Jacob   early German immigrant brothers who came with their families in 1834; ◆ boot and shoemakers, 212 Lake St. Charles (1802-1882) was an alderman in 1844 from the second ward; Jacob was later a member of a band with Nicholas Berdell that played for dances at John Berg's Inn on LaSalle Street and at the "Ten Mile House" [83rd Road and Vincennes Road]. [342]

Savage   a 30-ton schooner built for Oliver Newberry in 1827 at St. Clair, under the command of Captain Hinckley, loaded with supplies for the garrison of Fort Dearborn in the fall of 1827, was driven by contrary weather to seek shelter in the mouth of the St. Joseph River, remaining there for the winter; was the first entry of a sailing vessel into that river; presumably, cargo was delivered in the spring of 1828. [118, 235]

Savage, Henry W.   resident in 1835; his name was

on a school-related petition signed on Sept. 19, 1835. [12]

Saver, Dill   his real name may have been Ditlsaver, first name unknown; early member of the Catholic community; in April 1833 his name, not completely legible, was on the petition by citizens to Bishop Rosati of St. Louis asking that a priest be assigned to them. [12]

sawmills   see lumber mills.

sawyers   some of the first sawyers, who prepared planks and boards to construct the first Fort Dearborn, were so listed in John Kinzie's account books throughout 1804 and 1805: Otho Hayes, Richard Garner, John Suttenfield, and Corporal McCabe. [404]

Saxton, Mr.   head of several clerks working in Madore Beaubien's store, whom Andrew J. Vieau replaced in 1835; left for Racine, WI.

Say, Thomas   the "father of descriptive entomology in America," Say came to Chicago and Fort Dearborn on June 5, 1823, as a member of Maj. Stephen Long's expedition to explore the Red River &c.; the report of this visit   and of the entire expedition—was written by William Keating [see Bibliography]; his major work was *American Entomology*, published in Philadelphia, 1824-1828; in 1826 he joined the Utopian colony at New Harmony, IN, where he died of a fever in 1834.

Scammon, Jonathan Young   (1812-1890) born in Whitefield, ME; lawyer, arrived in Sept. 20, 1835 on the steamboat *Pennsylvania* from Buffalo, and on Dec. 7, 1835, replaced Henry Moore [who went into legal practice of his own] as deputy to Colonel Hamilton, the circuit court clerk; subsequently he formed a law partnership with Buckner S. Morris; assisted William Ogden in preparing the plans for the Chicago & Galena Union Railway; was a practicing Swedenborgian (New Jerusalem Church), but was initially the only one in town; in 1837 married Mary Ann Haven Dearborn of Bath, ME; ◆ attorney and counsellor at law, 105 Lake St. He went on to become one of the early bankers

JONATHAN YOUNG SCAMMON [12]

of Chicago; served as alderman in 1845; following Mary Ann's death in 1858, he married Mrs. Maria Sheldon Wright in 1867; accumulated a large fortune but suffered great losses in the fire of 1871; lived in Hyde Park from at least 1879 on. Also see the March, 1857, issue of *Chicago Magazine*. [12, 97, 351, 597, 707]

Scarritt, Rev. Isaac   (1775-1861) Methodist Episcopal minister from Connecticut, succeeded Rev. Jesse Walker as superintendent of the Fox River mission in 1828, and that summer visited Chicago, residing at Miller's Tavern, where, on a Sunday evening, he conducted a religious service that was well attended by both civilians and soldiers from the fort; performed the marriage ceremony that united Archibald Clybourne and Mary Galloway on June 6, 1829, and the double ceremony for John Kinzie Clark with Permelia Scott and Willard Scott with Caroline Hawley on July 22, 1829; in 1831 built a log house at Napierville for himself and his family, and kept a horse and a cow; in the July 30, 1834, *Chicago Democrat* he (of Fountaindale) is listed as a candidate for county commissioner. In 1858, he removed to Joliet where he lived until his death. [12]

Schaefer, Leander   German Catholic priest who immigrated in October 1836; he first assisted and then succeeded Father St. Cyr at St. Mary's Church, initially the only Catholic community; he died in 1837 and Father Timothy O'Meara took his place. [12, 544]

Schanck, Lewis G.   (1801-1864) from New Jersey; said to have been the first settler in Lake County; in 1833 he accepted a contract to take soldiers and supplies from Chicago to Green Bay in sleighs; aided the Indian removal in 1837.

Scharf, Alfred Frederick   (1847-1929) valuable historian and amateur archeologist, active in Chicago between 1890 and 1910, a contemporary of Charles A. Dilg; born in Saxony, Germany, and settled with his family at Peru, IL, in 1855; came to Chicago in 1864 to support his family, working in a cigar factory and news depot; continuously collected and documented Indian artifacts, noting Chicago area trails and camps on a map in 1898; written materials are within the Chicago Historical Society.

Schlickan, Donald W.   born in Chicago in 1925; architect, historian, and artist who has lived and worked in the city throughout his life; designer of the 1982 replica of Fort Dearborn for the city. He has combined his multiple skills to accurately measure and graphically pinpoint topographical relationships between Chicago dwellings of the early 19th century and the modern metropolitan street pattern. In particular, he has determined the exact location of the outlines of both the first and the second Fort Dearborn with reference to the present Michigan Avenue bridge, improving the results of earlier studies that had been used to place historical markers into the Michigan Avenue pavement [see the Fort Dearborn listing in Monuments]. For illustrations by Schlickan, see pages 154, 158, and 218.

Schmidt, Johann   German immigrant, first attested to as having lived in Chicago in 1835. [342]

Schnaebele, Jacob   German immigrant in 1835, coming from Pennsylvania; became a member of the German Evangelical Association. [342]

Schneider, J.   German immigrant, first attested to as having lived in Chicago in 1832. [342]

Schneitmann, L.   German immigrant, first attested to as having lived in Chicago in 1835. [342]

Schoolcraft, Henry R.   (1793-1864) native of New York; mineralogist, anthropologist, author [see extensive bibliography]; lived at Sault Ste. Marie and was for 20 years the U.S. Indian agent associated with Fort Brady; was married to a Chippewa; in August 1820 he came through Chicago as a member of an exploring party sent out by the secretary of war, John C. Calhoun. For Schoolcraft's comment on the reproduction and printing of a sketch made at that time of the village, as seen from the lake, see below. For the image itself, see page 28. For his description of Chicago, its vicinity and its prospects, as he saw them, see Chronology, August 1820. Schoolcraft died in Washington City. [12, 599-604]

I took the sketch which is reproduced in the fourth volume of my Ethnological Researches, Plate xxvii [adapted by Seth Eastman], from a standpoint on the flat of sand which stretches in front of the place. The view embraces every house in the village, with the fort; and if the reproduction of the artist in volume IV. may be subjected to any criticism, it is perhaps that the stockade bears too great a proportion to the scene, while the precipice, observed in the shore line of sand, is wholly wanting in the original.

school districts   in September 1835, there existed in Chicago two public and four private [see] schools; on Sept. 19 a petition was signed by 19 residents requesting a public meeting to consider organizing the township for school purposes. The result was the division of the town into four school districts; the boundaries of each are detailed in Andreas. [12]

"school-house"   occasionally used name for Reverend Jesse Walker's cabin and meeting house on the W side of the north branch [SW corner of Canal and Kinzie Sts]; the structure stood about 30 yards from the river bank and in early 1833 was temporarily used for school purposes [see Chicago schools].

school section   the Northwest Ordinance had reserved the land value of Section 16 of each survey township for educational purposes. Chicago's school section was the square mile area SW of the original Thompson ✳ plat and was bordered by State Street, Twelfth Street [Roosevelt Road], Madison Street, and Halsted Street; on Dec. 8, 1829, J.B. Beaubien, Archibald Clybourne, and Samuel Miller were appointed as the first trustees. By order of the county School Commissioner Colonel Hamilton, all but four of the 144 blocks in this section went on public sale, which occurred Oct. 20 to 24, 1833, and brought $38,865, a larger than anticipated yield. John Bates was the auctioneer [also see Chicago schools].

schoolteachers   see teachers.

schools   in earlier times, efforts to educate children were left to each family; in the winter 1810-11, Robert A. Forsyth, age 13, was privately engaged to teach reading to six year old John H. Kinzie with the help of a speller that had been brought from Detroit. In 1816, the retired soldier William A. Cox taught school in an old bakery shack on the Kinzie estate, and his pupils were likely the Kinzie children and three or four more from the fort. An unknown sergeant taught at the fort in 1820, and Russell Heacock did so in 1826. In 1829, Charles H. Beaubien taught the Jean Baptiste and Mark Beaubien children at a small family school near the garrison. In June 1830, Stephen Forbes and his wife Elvira were employed by Mr. Beaubien and Lieutenant Hunter of the fort and began to teach a class of about 25 children, ages 4 to 20, in a house owned by J.B. Beaubien, located at the lakeshore near the foot of Randolph Street; this

arrangement lasted for about one year. Some traders could afford to send their children away for schooling; Josette Ouilmette and Madore Beaubien went to the Baptist mission school in Niles, MI, and Joseph Bailly sent his three daughters to Detroit or Montreal; most children were not so favored. In October 1831, Richard J. Hamilton, esq., was appointed commissioner of school lands for Cook County, and the school fund remained in his charge until 1840. In the autumn of 1832 John Watkins, privately employed by Richard Hamilton and Thomas Owen, began teaching school in Hamilton's old horse stable on the N side of the river, halfway between the Forks and the lake; after the first quarter, the class (12 children, "four of them white") was moved to Father Walker's house at Wolf Point; subsequently, in 1833, Hamilton and Owen had a new structure built on the north bank of the river, just E of Clark Street, for the use of Watkins and his class. The era of public schooling began with Miss Eliza Chappel who, in September 1833, opened an Infant School for about 25 children [age up to 12 years] in a log house on the SE corner of Lake and Market streets, owned by Mark Beaubien and previously used by John Wright and his son John S. as their initial store. In the summer of 1834, the school was moved, for better accommodation, to the Presbyterian church [SW corner of Lake and Clark streets]. In 1835,

when Miss Chappel married Reverend Porter and was succeeded by Ruth Leavenworth, the school received its own building, financed by John S. Wright, on Clark Street and on the grounds of the church property, constructed by Joseph Meeker; this was the first school to receive, in 1834, an appropriation from the school fund of the county, and thereby became ★★★ **Chicago's 1st** public school [In October 1833, most blocks of land of the Chicago School Section had been sold at auction, providing the first funds for public schools]. On Dec. 18, 1833, Granville T. Sproat came from Boston and opened an English and Classical School for Boys in a small building, belonging to the first Baptist church, on South Water Street, near Franklin; in March 1834 he was joined by an assistant, Miss Sarah L. Warren; other early teachers at this school were Dr. Henry Van der Bogart, Thomas Wright, and James McClellan; the school also became public in 1834. During the winter of 1834-35, George Davis opened a school above a store on Lake Street, between Dearborn and Clark; in 1835 Davis taught school at the Presbyterian church. Also see Sunday school. For an excerpt from a 1879 letter describing his experience as a teacher, see entry on Watkins, John; and from a letter by Sally Warren, on commuting to school, see entry for Warren, Sally L.

schooner   small seagoing fore and aft rigged vessel, with two or more masts.

Scott, Deborah   daughter of Stephen J. and Hadassah Scott; see Watkins, Deborah Scott. [12]

Scott, Capt. Martin B.   from Vermont; Fifth Infantry; stationed at Fort Dearborn from Nov. 4, 1829, to Aug. 20, 1830, under Major Fowle, and presented to visiting James M. Bucklin that summer as "the celebrated rifle and pistol shot"; was killed in battle, as colonel, in Mexico on Sept. 8, 1847. [704]

Scott, Permelia   daughter of Stephen J. and Hadassah Scott; married [see] John Kinzie Clark on July 21, 1829, Reverend Scarritt officiating, in a

double ceremony that also wedded her brother Willard to Caroline Hawley; lived with John K. at [Northfield]; a daughter from this marriage, Hadassah Clark, married Walter Millen of Du Page County in 1846; died in 1877, surviving her husband by 12 years. [12, 706]

Scott, Philip   subscribed to the *Chicago Democrat* in November 1833.

Scott, Seth   listed as owner of 80 acres of land, in the NW quarter of Section 18, Township 39, prior to 1836, as seen in Andreas, *History of Chicago*, pp 112-113.

Scott, Stephen J.   (1788-1852) from Connecticut, where he was owner and master of a schooner doing trade on the Atlantic; in 1825 he moved with his family from New York State to St. Joseph [Michigan], then crossed the lake to Chicago on the schooner *Sheldon* in August 1826, settling at [see] *Grosse Pointe*; his wife was Hadassah (née Trask) and their children were: Willis, Willard, Wealthy, Deborah, and Permelia; purchased numerous items at the estate sale of W.H. Wallace on April 27, 1827. In 1829 he was appointed "constable pro tem" for the Chicago region by Alexander Doyle, justice of the peace at Peoria; that year the family removed to the forks of the Du Page River when Archange Ouilmette, at the Treaty of Prairie du Chien, was granted acreage that included the Scott homestead. Scott voted in the elections of July 24, Aug. 2, and Nov. 25, 1830; later resettled his family at Naperville. When the Laughton brothers both died in April 1834, Scott took over and operated their tavern on the Des Plaines River, together with Stephen White of [Lyons]; in 1849 went to California and died there. [12, 51, 706-8, 734]

Scott, Wealthy   daughter of Stephen J. and Hadassah Scott; married [see] David McKee; a son was born on Sept. 18, 1830, and named Stephen J. Scott McKee. [12, 706]

Scott, Willard   (1808-1890) born in New York; arrived in August 1826 with his parents (see Scott,

Stephen J.). While hunting with his father, they found appealing land along the Du Page River, and when Archange Ouilmette's land grant necessitated their relocation, the family chose to resettle at the forks of that river. On July 22, 1829, he married Caroline Hawley, Rev. Isaac Scarritt officiating, in a double ceremony that also wedded his sister Permelia to John Kinzie Clark; their children were: Thaddeus Scott (Aug. 7, 1830); Williard, Jr. (Oct. 9, 1835); and Alvin (May 28, 1838); voted in the election of July 24, 1830. During the 1832 Black Hawk War he served as private under Captain Napier in the Chicago militia company; later resided at [Naperville], where he built and managed the three-story Naperville Hotel; still lived there in 1885. [12, 351, 706-8, 734]

Scott, William H.   listed prior to 1836 as owner of 80 acres of land in Section 34, Township 39, as per Andreas, *History of Chicago*, pp. 112-113.

Scott, Willis   born c.1809 in New York; arrived in August 1826 with his parents (see Scott, Stephen J.); on Nov. 1, 1830, married Mrs. Lovisa B. Caldwell, the Reverend William See officiating (a daughter, Alice Lovisa, later married Arthur Warrington); he worked for Dr. Finley at the fort and for the Clybournes; was living at the settlement until 1832; moved to Waukegan, returning to live in Chicago in c.1866; Sarah Barney was his second wife; lived at 199 W Washington St. in 1885. Henry Hurlbut (*Chicago Antiquities*) learned from Willis that the Kinzie house on occasion doubled as an inn, payment expected. [12, 351, 606, 706, 734]

Scott, Gen. Winfield   (1786-1866) fought in the Black Hawk War of 1832 as commander in chief of the U.S. Army and made "Rat Castle" his headquarters in Chicago; a very tall man, 6 feet 6 inches in height; he had taken and would take part in the Revolutionary and the Mexican-American Wars. As a member of the Whig party he ran for president in 1852; died on May 29, 1866; ➡ Scott Street (1240 N). [12, 607]

scrip   see money.

seal of Chicago   see Chicago, Town, seal of.

Sebrara, Margaret   also Sobraro; arrived in 1835 on the steamer *Niagara* from Michigan; on Oct. 13, 1842, married the gunsmith and later successful lumber dealer Joseph Peacock, who came to Chicago in 1836.

Secoes, Jean Baptiste   also Secor; voted in elections on Aug. 7, 1826, and Aug. 2, 1830; did odd jobs for James Kinzie and probably for others; according to Wentworth he died of the cholera in 1832.

section   a surveyed square area of land, one mile on each side, representing 1/36th of a [see] township in accordance with the [see] Federal Land Ordinance of 1785, and each section containing 640 acres. Further subdivision, such as sections into city blocks, is governed by local factors such as geographic features, patterns of population growth, &c. For the division of the original town of Chicago into numbered blocks, see map on page 44.

Section 9   of Survey Township 39, Range 14 of the U.S. land survey, one of the alternate sections which by the Federal Act of 1827 had fallen to the canal commission [extending from State Street W to Halsted and from Madison N to Chicago Avenue]. The original town ✳ plat, prepared in 1830 by James Thompson, surveyor for the canal commission, covered most of the southern half of Section 9.

Section 16   next section S of Section 9; a [see] school section.

Sedgwick, Charles H.   name in the customer account book of the printer John Calhoun under the date Sept. 6, 1835; possibly the same Sedgwick who prior to 1835 co-owned downtown property in Section 9 on Township 38, together with Charles Bronson and Dr. Temple. [12]

See, Rev. William   (1787-1858) born in Charleston, VA; Methodist Episcopal minister, blacksmith, and ferry owner; lived in Kentucky, Missouri, and Morgan County, IL, before coming to the Calumet River in 1830; on June 9 of that year was issued a license by the commissioners court of Peo-

ria County to keep a ferry at that stream, which the tavern owner Johann Mann operated for him; voted on Aug. 2 and Nov. 25, 1830; in September 1830 seemingly purchased lots 3, 4, 5, and 6 in block 23 [old transaction lists show a William Lee as initial purchaser, probably a misspelling; see map on page 44], which soon after he sold to Walter Selver; received eight votes for justice of the peace, but Stephen Forbes won with 22 votes. Later as blacksmith, worked for David McKee, and was also Chicago's first resident Methodist preacher. His sermons and appearance were vividly, though unflatteringly described by the author of *Wau-Bun*, Juliette Kinzie, whose sensibilities were ruffled by the less-than-spotless hands of this hard working preacher during the service; for a sample of her reaction to Reverend See, see below. Some authors doubt that See was ever ordained and refer to him as an exhorter rather than a preacher, but on two marriage certificates preserved at Peoria he describes himself as "an ordained minister of the Methodist Episcopalian Church." Edwin O. Gale describes him as follows: "—not a very scholarly man, yet conscientious and earnest, making up in lungs what he lacks in learning, and in blows any deficiency in ideas." His first wife was Minerva (née Moss) and they lived on the W shore of the north branch, in view of the Forks [SW corner of Canal and Kinzie Sts]; their daughter Leah, born 1815, became James Kinzie's first wife; See would marry again, to a woman named Mary, then to Lemira Mellan. His cabin, later called the "school-house," was subsequently occupied by Reverend Beggs, then Father Walker. He was the fourth blacksmith to come to Chicago after Mirandeau (1811), McKee (1823), and Pothier (1828 or earlier). See officiated at the following marriage ceremonies: John Mann with Archange Tramble on Aug. 3, 1830, and Willis Scott with Lovisa Caldwell on Nov. 1, 1830. On March 8, 1831, he was appointed clerk of the commissioners court of Cook County, followed in this office by Colonel Hamilton in 1832; in 1835 sold his blacksmith tools to Asahel Pierce and removed to Pulaski, WI; died there on Aug. 20, 1858. [12, 266, 406]

Excerpt from Juliette A. Kinzie's *Wau-Bun:*

There also was a Mr. See lately come into the country, living at the Point, who sometimes held fourth in the little school-house on a Sunday, less to the edification of his hearers than to the unmerciful slaughter of the 'King's English.'… Once upon a Sunday we were rowed up to 'the point' to attend a religious service, conducted by Father S–, as he was called. We saw a tall slender man, dressed in a green frock coat, from the sleeves of which dangled a pair of hands giving abundant evidence, together with the rest of his dress, that he placed small faith in the axiom—'cleanliness is a part of holiness.'

Seission, Holden (1790-1878) also Holder Sisson; native of RI; lived in New York, then farmed in Indiana; arrived in Chicago in October 1831, settling in Lockport Township [Will County]; commanded, at the rank of captain, one of seven Cook County volunteer militia companies during the Black Hawk War, defending the northern Illinois frontier; his company was organized on July 23, 1832, and disbanded on Aug. 15; served as one of the three commissioners of newly formed Will County with James Walker. [13, 714, 734]

Sely, Lewis on Oct. 23, 1835, submitted a bill to the town council for a fire engine; on Dec. 8 Hubbard & Co. communicated with the council in regard to an engine that was then ordered by the corporation; see entry for firefighting. [28]

Selvey, Walter also Selver; an early settler who by 1831 had claimed or acquired much land in Du Page Township; in Chicago purchased real estate in c.1832 from William See in block 23 [see map on page 44], and sold real estate in block 17 to John Wright; transacting business poorly, he lost his property and wealth, dying in poverty near Aurora. [734]

Seminary of Quebec also *Seminaire (Societé) des Missiones Étrangères* or Seminary (Society) of For-

eign Missions; see Laval de Montmorency, Mgr. François. [693]

Semple, Hamilton of Pekin; temporary resident in May 1832; accompanied volunteers back to Chicago from Ottawa during the Black Hawk scare.

Sergents, John L. listed as subscriber of the *Chicago Democrat* for November 1833.

serpent mound of Chicago; see Hopewell Indians.

Seymour, Samuel artist and painter of landscapes, came to Chicago and Fort Dearborn on June 5, 1823, as a member of Maj. Stephen Long's expedition to explore the Red River &c.; the report of this visit—and of the entire expedition—was written by William Keating [see Bibliography]. [12, 394]

Shabbona (1775-1859) alternate spellings: Shabnai (Clifton), Shabonee (Hurlbut), Chabonee (G.S. Hubbard), Chaubenee, Chamblee (Hurlbut), Shawbonee (A.T. Andreas), Shaub-e-nee (B.L. Pierce), Shau-bee nay (Juliette A. Kinzie), Shaubena (E.G. Mason), and Shabbona (J.A. Clifton, F. Beaubien); also called Coal-Burner, Burly Shoulders. Son of an Ottawa father and a Seneca mother, born near the Maumee River in Ohio, brother of Maw-naw-bun-no-quah [Jean Baptiste Beaubien's second wife], he married the daughter of the Potawatomi chief Spotka and became himself an important Potawatomi chief when his father-in-law died. The tribe, living near the town of Ottawa, later moved to Shabonee's Grove [DeKalb County, IL], where they remained until 1837. After the death of his wife he married a second and later a third time, and had children with all. He was friendly to early settlers in Chicago and was a friend of Billy Caldwell; fought with Tecumseh and the British against the United States in the War of 1812 but later became reconciled to the advance of the new republic; was not at Fort Dearborn on Aug. 15, 1812; opposed the Winnebago uprising of 1827 and the Black Hawk War of 1832. In 1830 he assisted James M. Bucklin, chief engineer, in plotting the Illinois & Michigan Canal route; par-

SHABBONA [410]

ticipated in the Treaty of Chicago in 1833. He migrated W with his tribe in 1836, but later returned to Shabonee's Grove; died on July 27, 1859, and was buried at Morris. A fine old photograph (ambrotype) was made in 1857 by the photographer H.B. Field and is preserved in the Chicago Historical Society. A portion of the Thorn Creek Division of the Cook County Forest Preserve District is named ▲ Shabbona Woods to commemorate his name [see Monuments]. For a small episode from Shabbona's later life, see the following excerpt from an article by Frank G. Beaubien. [12, 37, 226, 460, 697]

I remember when I was a little boy of five years of age when my father [Mark Beaubien] kept the light-house, the Indians would come and camp in our yard. That was the time the Indians used to come once a year to get their pay from the government, they always came to our house. Father used to place me on the table and play his violin and I would dance for the Indians and old Indian Chief Shabbona would give me maple sugar and a pair of moccasins for the dance. I always looked for him. The last time I saw him he came to our house on Pine street on the North side, it was the year 1858. He died in 1859. His wife and children used to come to our house after his death, when we moved to Naperville and bring her children and grandchildren with her.

Shapley, Capt. Morgan L.   arrived from New York on June 27, 1833; beginning in July held an executive position in harbor construction under Maj. George Bender, together with Joseph Chandler; he describes how the piers were begun in late summer in a letter to John Wentworth that follows; a notice in the *Chicago Democrat* of June 11, 1834, announced his wedding on June 8 to Nancy Stewart, Reverend Porter officiating; ◆ Government works, near the Garrison; later moved to Meridian, TX, where he still lived in 1885. [12, 351, 708]

An excerpt from Captain Shapley's letter to John Wentworth:

There were two or three stores on South-Water Street. Mark Beaubien, the noted fiddler, had a hotel at the head of Lake Street. There were less than a dozen dwelling shanties in the entire town. The first stone was procured about three miles up the south branch of the river. The work was commenced on the south side of the river. The ties and timber were procured upon the Calumet River, and were rafted into the Lake. The next year, 1834, the work was commenced upon the north side of the river, Lieut. James Allen, superintending.

Shawbonee   see Shabbona.

Shawnee   a term meaning *southerners*; an Algonkin tribe, originally located in Tennessee and South Carolina, but by the time of the French and Indian War they had relocated to the upper Ohio valley, SE of the Chicago region; spearheaded Indian resistance to the advancement of white settlers under their great leaders Tecumseh and The Prophet, but met defeat at the battle of Tippecanoe in 1811; what is left of the tribe lives now in Oklahoma.

Shea, John Gilmary D.   (1824-1892) productive American historian; Jesuit who later obtained dispensation to resign from the society; editor of written materials of early French explorations and mission work in New France throughout the 19th century; translator and publisher of Father Marquette's travel reports; born in New York, died in New Jersey; see Bibliography. [611-13]

Shedaker, John   voted in the Peoria County election of Nov. 25, 1830; came to Chicago in 1831, and served in the Black Hawk War of 1832 under Capt. G. Kercheval as a member of the Chicago company. [714]

Sheboygan   earlier names and spellings by the first settlers: Ship-wi-wia-gan, Chipwagen, Shipwagen, Shipwagan, Shipwagon; phonetic spelling in Indian languages: shab-wa-wa-go-ning (Potawatomi), saw-be-wa-he-son (Menominee), Jigai-gan (Ojibwa); pioneer settlement on the western shore of Lake Michigan 130 miles N of Chicago, at the mouth of the Sheboygan River, begun in the summer of 1834, when a group of men from Chicago built a cabin and sawmill by the rapids of the river, two miles from its mouth, to exploit the heavily forested region. The effort was financed and led jointly by William Payne and [see] Oliver C. Crocker. With them were several hired hands, among them the mechanic John V. Rogers, Charley Ware, H.O. Stone, an interpreter named Beaubrin [Beaubien?], and Crocker's cousin, Oliver A. Crocker. The first lumber was sawed in February 1835, and was shipped to Chicago as early as the ice had melted. But difficulties developed with the local Indians, and spring freshets washed out the mill dam. Discouraged, they sold mill and cabin in the summer of 1835 for $10,000 to William Farnsworth, a trader and entrepreneur who had been living in what is now Sheboygan County since c.1818. Farnsworth went to Chicago in 1835 to engage Jonathan S. Follett to run the sawmill for him, and he and Mrs. Eliza Follett became the first permanent settlers of the new community.

Sheldon   schooner; visited in 1826 under Captain Sherwood, bringing the Stephen J. Scott family to [see] *Grosse Pointe*. [706-8]

Sheldon Thompson   241 tons, the first three-masted steam brig on the Great Lakes, and probably the first steamer to navigate the length of Lake Michigan, built in 1825 at Huron, OH. The brig regularly serviced Chicago and, on the occasion of requiring fuel, its Capt. Augustus Walker, would purchase, dissemble and take on board an old log cabin. In 1832, together with the *William Penn*, it brought troops and General Scott—as well as the cholera—to Chicago for the Black Hawk War; the first steamboats to visit Chicago.

Shenstone, William   (1714-1763) English poet; a volume of Shenstone's poems was brought to Fort Dearborn by Capt. John Whistler in 1803. On leaving Chicago in 1810, he presented it to Dr. J. Cooper, who carefully treasured the gift; the book was later returned to Chicago and can be viewed among the collections of the Chicago Historical Society, one of very few items from the first Fort Dearborn that have survived. [617]

 SONG XII. 1744.

O' ER desert plains, and rushy meers,
    And wither'd heaths I rove;
Where tree, nor spire, nor cot appears,
    I pass to meet my love.

But though my path were damask'd o 'er
    With beauties e 'er so fine;
My busy thoughts would fly before,
    To fix alone — on thine.

No fir-crown'd hills cou'd give delight,
    No palace please mine eye:
No pyramid's aereal height,
    Where mouldering monarchs lie.

Unmov'd should Eastern kings advance,
    Could I the pageant see:
Splendour might catch one scournful glance,

Not steal one thought from thee.

Sheppard, Robert   lumber merchant from Scotland, arrived in 1834; possibly the partner of Josiah S. Breese, [see] Breese & Sheppard, who opened a dry goods store late September 1835; later on Dec. 23, as Dickinson & Sheppard, submitted a proposal to the town board to build a fire engine house for $375; ✦ carpenter and builder, Cass [Wabash] Street near Ohio; died in 1871, leaving a wife, son (Robert D. Sheppard), and two daugh-

ters; in 1885 a Mrs. Samantha Dickinson Sheppard, invited as an old settler by the Calumet Club, lived at 510 West Jackson St., Robert's widow. [12, 28]

Sherman, Francis Cornwall   (1805-1870) brother of Silas W. Sherman; came in April 1834 from Newton, CT, by way of Detroit, his family following later; married to Electra Trowbridge (1825) of Connecticut; was a manufacturer of brick but alert to any business opportunity; made the bricks for Archibald Clybourne's 20-room residence on Elston Road [Elston Avenue] in 1835; that July was elected a village trustee; started the City Hotel at the SE corner of State and Lake streets in 1837, which later became the Sherman House; ✦ contractor and builder, 85 Clark St.; in 1841, 1862, and 1863 he served as Chicago's mayor; died on Nov. 12, 1870; Electra died on Nov. 12, 1881. [12]

Sherman, Joel Sterling   born in c.1817 in Newton, CT; arrived in September 1834; son of Silas W. Sherman; married Harriet R. Botsford (niece of J.K. Botsford) of Connecticut in 1839; ✦ farmer, Northfield; lived in E Northfield in 1885. [12]

Sherman, Mrs. H.   of White Creek, NY; placed an ad in the *Chicago Democrat* on Nov. 26, 1834, offering her services of millinery and dressmaking, within "a room in the house of H. Kimball, two doors east of Mansion House."

Sherman, Phinneas   arrived in 1832 with wife and daughter, both named Elizabeth, and claimed land along the Des Plaines River [near Higgins Road, Proviso Township]; moved to Norwood Park Township in 1834 on account of the prevalence of ague near the river; on Nov. 12, 1834, the daughter married [see] John Foot. [13, 278]

Sherman, Rebecca   daughter of [see] Silas W. Sherman; participant in an outing on horseback in the spring of 1835, as described by John D. Caton; married Peter Pruyne on Aug. 26, 1835, and after Pruyne's death married Thomas Church on Nov. 5, 1839. [121]

Sherman, Silas W.   arrived from Connecticut in

1832; brother of Francis C., father of Rebecca and Joel Sterling; assistant deputy to Cook County Sheriff Stephen Forbes in 1832; was appointed street commissioner [jointly with O. Morrison] in the autumn of 1833, when Benjamin Jones resigned from the post; ran for constable at the election on Dec. 9, per announcement in the *Chicago Democrat* of Dec. 3; elected Cook County sheriff on Aug. 4, 1834; later that year Sherman became actively involved in organizing the town into school districts, his name being on a school-related petition signed on Sept. 19, 1835; ✦ ex-sheriff, 48 Clark St.; active member of the Episcopal St. James' Church. [12]

Sherror, David   U.S. Army private at Fort Dearborn; enlisted in October 1810, killed in action at the massacre of 1812. [226]

shipping   for information on early Great Lakes and river transportation pertinent to Chicago, see individual entries under boats, sailing vessels, steam ships.

Shipwagen   also Ship-wi-wia-gan, Shipwagon, Shipwagun, Chipwagen; see Sheboygan.

shipwrecks   associated with early Chicago, prior to 1836, see *Le Griffon* (1679), the *Heartless* (1817), the *Hercules* (1818), the *Ann* (1821), the *Pioneer* (1825), the *Utica*, the *Austerlitz*, the *Marengo*, and the *Chance* (1835). Frequent early shipwrecks and other near disasters led to the United States development of the Chicago harbor.

Shirreff, Patrick   also Shiereff; Scottish agriculturist who visited Chicago in September 1833 and gave a description of what he found in *A Tour Through North America; Together with a Comprehensive View of the Canadas and the United States, as Adapted for Agricultural Emigration*; see Bibliography. [544, 618]

Short, Hugh   arrived from New York in 1835; died in Milwaukee. [351]

shoemakers   an entry on June 16, 1804, within John Kinzie's account book lists [John] Salter as Fort Dearborn's shoemaker; also see E.B. Hall (1832), Loton W. Montgomery (1833), Solomon

Taylor (1833), William Henry Adams (1833), William Hartt Taylor (1834), Charles and Jacob Sauter (1834), Thomas Whitlock (1835), and George Willoughby (1835). [404]

Shrigley, John   arrived from England in 1834; a notice in the Sept. 17, 1834 *Chicago Democrat* announced the death of an only young son, Charles Rollins, from "dropsy in his head"; on Nov. 8 the paper gave notice that the Eagle Hotel had been relinquished by Paul J. Carli [to Shrigley]; elected constable on Aug. 5, 1835, as per notice in *Chicago Democrat*; in the Oct. 24 *Chicago American* E.K. Hubbard advertises Shrigley's dwelling in the Kinzie Addition available to rent on Nov. 1; elected high constable on May 3, 1837, for a two-year term; ✦ tavernkeeper [Dutchman's Point], succeeding Benjamin Hall. [13, 351, 544]

Sibley, Henry H.   began employment with the American Fur Co. at Mackinac under Robert Stuart in 1830; during that year he had occasion to accompany John H. Kinzie on a trip to Chicago, writing later about his sighting in an autobiography; for an excerpt of his experience, see below.

We embarked on a sail vessel called the "Napoleon," commanded by Captain Chesley Blake, one of the oldest and best sailors on the lakes, and after an uneventful voyage, varied only by short landings at ports on the South shore of Lake Michigan, we reached Chicago, where we remained several days. I found on the present site of the "Queen City of the Lakes," in May 1829 [The author is probably mistaken and means 1830, as is apparent from related correspondence; eds.], a small stockade constructed for defense against the Indians, but abandoned, and perhaps half a dozen dwellings, occupied by the Beaubien and other families, and a single store stocked with a small, but varied, assortment of goods and provisions. A more uninviting place could hardly be conceived of. There was sand here, there, and every where, with a little occasional shrubbery to relieve the monotony of the landscape. Little did I dream, that I would live to see, on that desolate coast, a magnificent City of more than

Fox engraved on silver plate.
From the Forest Park Library history room.

half a million of inhabitants, almost rivaling metropolitan New York in wealth, and splendor. ... Our craft returned to Mackinac without accident, ... and I entered upon my duties as office clerk on the first of June following, finding a home in the charming family of Mr. Stuart.

Sibley, Solomon   U.S. commissioner who, with Gov. Lewis Cass, negotiated the Treaty of Chicago in August 1821 with the local Ottawa, Chippewa, and Potawatomi tribes; Henry R. Schoolcraft was the secretary. [12, 544]

Siggenauk   see Black Bird.

silver   a precious metal highly valued for ornamental purposes by Indians of the Chicago area; once John Kinzie, a trained silversmith, fashioned and sold many pieces of silver jewelry to the tribes. The books of the St. Joseph trader William Burnett show that he imported from the East silver "brooches" of various kinds and sizes by the thousands, and sent his agent Jean B. La Lime thus supplied on trading trips to Indian villages. On Dec. 11, 1803, at Chicago La Lime acquired two silver thimbles from John Kinzie; Francis Ducharme bought two large crosses for $7.50 in January 1807, on the same day a brooch was exchanged for six [musk]rats, as noted in Kinzie's account books. On display at the

▲ Forest Park Library are articles [see Indian silver, in the Monuments section] that once belonged to Indians who lived along the Des Plaines River at the time of death; burial mounds were later leveled to create the Forest Park Cemetery. The artifacts found were traded sometime between 1760 and 1820 when silversmiths in Quebec and Montreal crafted laminated ware for the North West Company; items of adornment include wristbands, armbands, brooches, gorgets, and earrings. [404, 688]

Simmons, John   U.S. Army corporal at Fort Dearborn, of German extraction; enlisted on March 14, 1810; married to Susan Millhouse; two children: David (born 1809, died in the massacre) and Susan (born 1812 at the fort and survived the massacre; see Simmons, Susan); John was killed in action at the massacre. His wife and infant Susan were taken to the Green Bay area by Indians and subjected to much hardship, but eventually arrived at Susan's parents' home in Ohio after walking more than 1,000 miles; died at Springfield, IA, in 1857. [226, 564, 619, 725]

Simmons, Susan   (1812-1900) born at Fort Dearborn on Feb. 18 to Cpl. John and Susan Simmons of Ohio; her married name was Winans; she died on April 27 in Santa Anna, CA, as the last survivor of the Fort Dearborn massacre; see Simmons, John, for more details. [226, 564, 619, 725]

Simons, Edward   arrived from Ohio in 1834; owned a meat market on Lake Street, temporarily in partnership with Sylvester Marsh, dissolved as per notice in the *Chicago Democrat* of Aug. 6, 1834; he continued "to supply at the Boston Market." To Simons fell the task of butchering the last black bear killed in Chicago on Oct. 6, 1834; he reported that the animal weighed 400 lbs; ✦ butcher, Archibald Clybourn; in 1885 the widow, Laura Bronson Sprague Simons, lived at Pacific, Cook County, IL. [12, 351]

Simonton, Lt. Isaac Pierce   from Ohio; Fifth Infantry, stationed at Fort Dearborn during the time of the Treaty of Chicago in September 1833, and signed as witness on the document; died Feb. 21, 1842. [567]

Sinclair, James   (c.1801-1871) tinsmith from New York; came in 1835; married to Lydia Ann Hicks; ✦ 58 Washington St.; in 1885 his widow lived at 366 State St. [12, 351, 733]

Sinclair, John   arrived from New York in 1832. [12, 351, 733]

Sinclair, Patrick   British captain and lieutenant governor of the Province of Quebec (which included Chicago at that time), founded [see] Fort St. Clair (Fort Sinclair, the Pinery) in 1764 near Detroit, where he employed Jean Baptiste Point de Sable as manager of his estate from 1779 to 1784; suceeding Colonel De Peyster, he served as commandant of the old Fort Michilimackinac (on the Michigan shore) from 1779 to 1781. Under his command a new fort was constructed on the island in the straits, his forces were moved there on May 24, 1781, and the old fort was abandoned. [564]

Sits Quietly   see Toponebe.

Skokie   a swampy lake in the 18th century; full name: *Kitchi Wabaskoki*; forming the headwaters of the northern branch of the Chicago River; the remnants are the Skokie Lagoons, near the town of Skokie, IL.

slavery   widely practiced in North America by the Indians before and after the arrival of the Europeans, the latter also having, in general, no principal objection to slavery at the time. Father Las Casas, active in Peru, Central America, and the West Indies, was a rare exception with his active antislavery stance. The possession of both black and Indian slaves was officially sanctioned by the New France government in 1709 [for more details see entry on *panis*]. Even Father Marquette owned a slave who belonged to the Illinois tribe, presented to him in 1673 by the Ottawa, and whom he used as a guide. In 1718, the French trading concern *Compagnie d'Orient* under John Law was given permission by the French crown to import African slaves into Louisiana, of which Illinois was then the northern extension. Black slaves first came to Illinois in 1720. In 1724, the treatment of slaves became regulated by the government through the *Code Noir*, a relatively humane document for its time. The price for a male black slave was fixed at 660 *livres*, which made slaves affordable only to the very affluent. The main French distribution point for black slaves was Ste. Dominque; Jamaica served this purpose for the British. In 1732 there were 168 slaves in Illinois, in 1732 there were 317, and in 1752 the number reached 445, as opposed to 768 Frenchmen. Indian slaves, called *panis* [singular and plural], were kept as well by affluent Frenchmen, probably entering the market as sold captives of warring tribes; registers kept by notaries for the purpose of recording civic affairs—such as the *Registre des Insinuations des Donations aux Siege des Illinois*—give ample evidence of the practice. Slaves had no family names, only first names; they adopted a family name only if they were freed. On April 14, 1775, the Philadelphia Quakers under Benjamin Franklin organized the first American society dedicated to the abolition of slavery. The Ordinance of 1787 for the temporary government of the North West Territory passed unanimously by Congress on July 13, made slavery unlawful with the following passage: "There shall be neither slavery or involuntary servitude in the said Territory, otherwise than in the punishment of crime, whereof the party shall have been duly convicted." However, the law was not enforced, and slavery continued, although gradually to a lesser extent, in all parts of the Old Northwest. Governors Reynolds and Edwards of Illinois and Governor Dodge of Wisconsin all held many slaves. [See Edwards, Ninian; see Reynolds, John, for slave ownership-related newspaper ads; see also Finney, Bernard.] John Kinzie bought, held, and sold slaves: see Nash, Jeffrey; Black Jim; Athena; Pepper; and Henry. Captain and Mrs. Heald brought the slave girl [see] Cicely with them to Fort Dearborn in

$100 REWARD.

RANAWAY from the subscriber near Jackson, Missouri, on the 7th Sept. last, a Negro fellow named SQUIRE, 30 years old, 6 feet high; wore a white hat, cassinett pantaloons and check shirt. He had a scar upon his left temple. I bought him from Henry Dickson, of Jefferson city, and he has been hired at Massey's Iron Works for some time. I think he will make for one of those places or to a free state. He spoke of going to the Indians in Arkansas, to some of the other negroes. I will give one hundred dollars for him, delivered to me at this place, or twenty dollars for him delivered in some jail so that I get him again. Information directed to the subscriber at this place, or to Dr. Esselman, Nashville, Tennessee.

JAMES C. ESSELMAN,
Carnsville, Giles county, Tennessee.
January 18, 1836.—3m46.

1810; Cicely had a young child, and both she and the child were killed at the massacre of 1812; Mrs. Heald claimed $1,000 personal property loss from the U.S. government for the death of the two slaves, but her petition was denied. Military officers at army posts were encouraged to purchase slaves rather than to take servants from the ranks. U.S. Indian Agent Charles Jouett brought the slave Joe Battles from Kentucky in 1809. Jefferson Davis was accompanied by his slave, Pemberton, throughout his years of service in the Northwest. In 1819, the Illinois legislature enacted a general code of law that included "the black code" which required all free Negroes coming into the state to bring with them certificates of freedom and to have these recorded with county clerks. This code remained at least partly in effect until 1865. Those found without a certificate might be sold into peonage for a year. It was illegal to bring slaves into the state and set them free. It was legal to whip slaves for going more than 10 miles from home without permit.

Not until Dec. 18, 1865, when the 13th Amendment to the U.S. Constitution was ratified, did slavery finally end in Chicago and Illinois. [12, 82, 105, 112, 113, 308, 316]

Excerpt from the *Magazine of Western History*, relative to the Negro population of Chicago in 1833: *August of 1833, there resided in Chicago six or seven colored men, all of whom had come from free States. The law givers of Illinois, however, had not contemplated such a contingency, the earlier population having come mostly from slave States. The laws had provided that if a negro was found in the State without free papers, he should be prosecuted and fined, and if necessary, sold to pay the fine. ✧ Some enemy of the black man ... felt it to be his duty or his interest, to prosecute these early representatives here of the proscribed race. They were duly apprehended, and J.D. Caton undertook their defence, and pleaded their case before the "court" of county commissioners. ... ["Court" was then the legal designation of that body.] and the young lawyer overcame their natural modesty, or their unwillingness to assume a function hitherto unheard of. They ended by acceding to the learned jurist's expositions of the law, and as the highest accessible representatives of the judiciary of the sovereign State of Illinois, they granted to his grateful clients the required certificates of freedom, which were never questioned, and passed for excellent 'free papers.' ✧ For his services in this case, Mr. Caton received one dollar from each of the beneficiaries from the decision ....*

Sleight, Capt. Morris   New York merchant and sea captain; farmer near the Naper settlement from July 1834 to 1837, who wrote letters and kept a diary — all preserved at the Chicago Historical Society.

slew   see slough.

Sloan, Douglas   subscribed to the *Chicago Democrat* in November 1833.

Sloo, Thomas, Jr.   of Hamilton County; member of the initial canal commission created by Illinois Governor Cole in 1823, to have the canal lands surveyed and a cost estimate prepared.

sloop   single-masted sailing vessel with a mainsail and a jib, rigged fore and aft.

slough   also slew; early midwestern term for an elongated depression in the landscape, as were frequent in the low, wet parts of the prairie near Chicago, containing a slow-moving streamlet or pond at least part of the year. Frog Creek [see] ran in such a slough, emptying from the S into the main branch of the river at State Street; another slough, unnamed, emptied at LaSalle Street, coming from the SW beyond Randolph Street. Also see Ogden's Slough.

smallpox   also variola; an epidemic viral disease with potentially fatal outcome, brought to America by European immigrants at an early time; the Indians proved highly vulnerable. Abbé St. Cosme reported the devastation among the Arkansas Indians in 1699: "It is not a month since they got over the small pox which carried off the greatest part of them. There was nothing to be seen in the village but graves"; in a 1794 letter by Guillaume la Mothe, interpreter at Mackinac, to Joseh Chew, secretary for the Department of Indian Affairs at Montreal: "There is likewise at Chikagoe Fifty Indians died of the Small Pox which alarms the Indians much in this Post." The French Canadian population of Chicago suffered less, but there were annual smallpox mortalities from the beginning, with major outbreaks in 1857, 1864, 1865, 1872, and 1873. Not until 1880 was the disease brought under control by vaccination. [213]

The following is an account by Andrew J. Vieau, Sr., on the 1832 smallpox epidemic among the Potawatomi:

In the winter of 1832-33, the small-pox scourge ran through the Indian population of the state. Father [Jacques Vieau of Milwaukee] and his crew were busy throughout the winter in burying the natives, who died off like sheep with the foot-rot. With a crooked stick inserted under a dead Indian chin they would haul the infected corpse into a shallow pit dug for its reception and give it a hasty burial. In this

work, and in assisting the poor wretches who survived, my father lost much time and money; while of course none of the Indians who lived over, were capable of paying their debts to the traders. This winter ruined my father almost completely.

Smith, Barton   legal notices involving him appeared in the Sept. 3, 1834, *Chicago Democrat*; in a July 7 circuit court suit John K. Boyer sought payment for "12 pieces of cotton sheeting and about 30 lbs. of coffee" from Barton and four others.

Smith, C.   C. Smith & Co. advertised an "extensive assortment of HATS of every description" in the Nov. 4, 1835, *Chicago Democrat*; the "New Hat and Cap Establishment" was a few doors S of the Auction Store on Dearborn Street.

Smith, Charles B.   came in 1835 from Warsaw, NY; married Abigail Woodbury of New York in 1843. [351]

Smith, Chester   enlisted during the Black Hawk War as first lieutenant in Walker's company from June 19 to Aug. 12, 1832.

Smith, Daniel D.   created ✳ *A Map of all the Lands belonging to the Kickapoo Tribe of Indians in the State of Illinois Ceded to the United States by Treaty Signed at Edwardsville in the State of Illinois July 30th 1819* [National Archives, Washington, D.C.]. A Captain Smith of the U.S. Engineering Department made a ✳ *Map of the Chicago River* [The War Department, Washington, D.C.] in 1818; nothing else is known that can identify him as Daniel D. Smith. [326, 681, 682]

Smith, Eli and Elijah   likely brothers who arrived with their wives in June 1831, as part of the Hampshire Colony wagon train from Massachusetts, an organized Congregational church of 18 members; stayed overnight at "The Wolf," Elijh Wentworth's tavern; an Elijah Smith is listed as a merchant tailor at 48 Clark St. in 1839. [12, 234]

Smith, Lt. Ephraim Kirby   from Connecticut; served at Fort Howard and Mackinac during the 1820s; Mrs. Mary Ann Brevoort Bristol gives a vivid account of a canoe trip with almost disastrous outcome in the company of Lieutenant Kirby on the Fox River of Wisconsin on July 13, 1827, in her *Reminiscences of the Northwest* [see Brevoort, Maj. Henry B.]; arrived on May 29, 1833, as first lieutenant of the Fifth Infantry at Fort Dearborn and remained until July 1834, and again served at the fort from Oct. 23 to December 1836; present at the Indian Treaty of Chicago in September 1833, and signed as witness on the document; in March 1834, as post adjutant under Major Green, placed a notice in the *Chicago Democrat* promising $30 reward for information leading to the capture of a deserter; managed the first Chicago ball in 1834; died Sept. 11, 1847, in Mexico at the battle of Molino del Rey. [12, 351]

Smith, Ezra B.   from Nassau Village, NY; a young clerk employed in John Holbrook's store three months before dying of bilious fever; an obituary in the Aug. 12, 1835, *Chicago Democrat* noted his funeral on the 13th at the Exchange Coffee House.

Smith, George   (1808-1899) native of Aberdeenshire, Scotland, who came in 1834 and resided in Chicago until 1861; listed prior to 1836 as owner of 80 acres of land in the SW quarter of Section 18, Township 39, also as owner-assignee of additional 80 acres in Section 24, Township 39 (Andreas, *History of Chicago*, pp. 112-113); by 1834 Smith owned a lake vessel and imported lumber to Chicago; in October 1835 he signed up with the "Pioneer" hook and ladder company, an early volunteer fire brigade; in later years became an influential banker and a director of the Galena and Chicago Union Railroad; he formed the "Scottish Illinois Land Investment Company," a successful venture of the early boom period. Later he owned a castle in Scotland; his 1885 address was the Reform Club, London, England; died on Oct. 7, 1899. [12, 13, 351, 623]

Smith, Horacio G.   was elected constable at the special Peoria County election for constable and justice of the peace on July 24, 1830, receiving 32

GEORGE SMITH [12]

votes for constable to defeat Russell Rose, who had 21 votes [Chicago was then part of Putnam/Peoria County].

Smith, James A.   arrived from New York in 1835; in October 1835 signed up with the "Pioneer" hook and ladder company, an early volunteer fire brigade; ◆ James A. Smith & Co., hat and cap manufacturers, 127 Lake St.; a notice in the *Chicago Daily American* of April 30, 1840, announces dissolution of his partnership with a John M. Smith; died on July 23, 1875. [12, 351]

Smith, Jeremiah and Jeduthan [Judrithan?]   listed prior to 1836 as co-owners of 160 acres of land in Section 34, Township 39, as per Andreas, *History of Chicago*, pp. 112-113. Jeremiah arrived in 1831 and served in the Black Hawk War of 1832 as a member of the Chicago company; in the Dec. 17, 1834, *Chicago Democrat* he reported an "Estray Steer" and requested that its proven owner pay damages and collect the animal. [12, 351]

Smith, John, Jr.   U.S. Army private and fifer at Fort Dearborn; son of John Smith, Sr.; enlisted in

June 1806; taken prisoner at the massacre of Aug. 15, 1812, and later ransomed from the Indians. [226]

Smith, John, Sr.   U.S. Army private at Fort Dearborn; father of John Smith, Jr.; enlisted in April 1808; taken prisoner at the massacre of 1812 and killed by the Indians later in the day. [226]

Smith, John, Sr.   made a petition claim for wharfing privileges in 1835.

Smith, John T.   filed a claim for wharfing privileges for lot 3, block 16 late in 1835. [28]

Smith, Lawrence   on Oct. 27, 1835, married Mary Welsh, Father St. Cyr officiating.

Smith, Mason   born in Potsdam, NY, which he left on Aug. 13, 1833, and arrived on Sept. 3, traveling with Hezekiah and Ebenezer Duncklee across Michigan and northern Indiana; moved on to [Bloomingdale] that autumn.

Smith, Mathias   may have been a soldier at Fort Dearborn under Lieutenant Hunter until May 20, 1831, when he was discharged and remained in Chicago; voted in the elections of July 24 and Nov. 25, 1830, and Aug. 10, 1833; early member of the Catholic congregation, in April 1833 his name was on the petition by Chicago's citizens to the bishop in St. Louis asking that a priest be assigned to them; active thereafter in organizing St. Mary's Church; member of the first engine company of the voluntary fire brigade. Emily Beaubien later recalled that Smith became a friend of the Mark Beaubien family and lived with them in the 1830s; that he had been a soldier both in France under Napoleon and in America; died before 1850 and was buried in the ▲ Beaubien Cemetery at [now] Lisle. [12, 41]

Smith, Philip   U.S. Army private; enlisted on April 30, 1806, and reenlisted on April 30, 1811; believed to have been killed during the initial battle of the Fort Dearborn massacre. [226]

Smith, Theophilus Washington   (1784-1846) attorney from New York City, arrived in 1830; member of the initial canal commission created by Illinois Governor Cole in 1823 to have the canal lands surveyed and a cost estimate prepared; became a member of the Illinois Supreme Court, impeached in 1832, but acquitted; in 1833 his daughter Louise married Dr. Levi Boone [mayor in 1855], and in 1841 his daughter Lucy married F.C. Russell; served as one of the delegates to draw up Chicago's city charter late in 1836; was one of the initial trustees of Rush Medical School in 1837; ✦ judge, Illinois Supreme Court, boarded at City Hotel. [37, 351]

Smith, William   arrived in 1831 and served in the Black Hawk War of 1832 as a member of the Chicago company; ✦ teamster, Adams Street between State and Dearborn. [12]

Smith, William C., M.D.   ★★★ Chicago's 1st military physician; stationed at Fort Dearborn, arriving with Captain Whistler in 1803 and remaining until 1808; Army records show that he enlisted as surgeon's mate on July 2, 1802, and was mustered out on June 27, 1810; though most of the garrison had to pass the first winter in unfinished quarters, the doctor had the good fortune to live in the Point de Sable homestead with Jean La Lime, who held the estate for Burnett, until Kinzie arrived in 1804 and acquired the property; he then moved into the fort; in 1808 was succeeded at the fort by Dr. John Cooper. [628]

Snow, George Washington   came from Vermont or New Hampshire in 1832; married to Elizabeth (née Manierre); surveyor of the Kinzie Addition in February 1833, working under Capt. David Hunter; in August he was one of the "Qualified Electors" who voted to incorporate the town. [For a copy of that meeting's original report, see entry on incorporation.] On Dec. 4, a village ordinance appointed him assessor and surveyor for one year, allowing $3 per day for services rendered. In February 1834, he served as trustee of the English and Classical School for Boys; in October 1835, he signed up with the "Pioneer" hook and ladder company, an early volunteer fire brigade, and later played a leading role in the fire department; later

on Nov. 21 applied for wharfing privileges. Snow is considered by some the inventor of the [see] balloon frame method of the construction of wooden buildings, which was widely utilized by builders in early Chicago, while other historians credit his contemporary [see] A.D. Taylor; Snow's own house, thus constructed, was in the S division; ✦ Geo. W. Snow & Co., lumber merchants, South Water Street; in 1885 his widow lived at 321 Dearborn Ave. [12, 28, 245, 351, 505]

Soules, Rufus   acquired prior to 1836 the western half of the NW quarter of Section 32 in Township 40 N, as per Andreas, *History of Chicago*, pp. 112-113; in the March 9, 1836, *Chicago Democrat*, he advertised to circulate subscription papers; died in May 1885. [12]

Source, Abbé Thaumur de la   see Thaumur de la Source, Abbé Dominique Antoine.

South Bend, IN   a historic town that developed near the bend of the St. Joseph River because of the proximity of an important portage between the Great Lakes and the Mississippi systems [the St. Joseph–Kankakee River portage], an alternate to the Chicago portage; La Salle camped there when portaging to the Kankakee in 1679. Frenchman Alexis Coquillard, Sr., started the settlement in 1822 by establishing a trading post, known as "Big St. Joseph Station" [for "Little St. Joseph Station," see Fort Wayne]; a post office then opened at "South Hold," another early name prior to 1830, and that year [see] Father Stephen T. Badin, who came often to Chicago, built a small log chapel on nearby St. Mary's Lake; the town was platted in 1831.

South Fork   early tributary to the south branch of the Chicago River that entered the south branch just E of the point where Archer Avenue now crosses the harbor section of the river; the southern end, which originally may have been more than two miles in length, now terminates in the old stockyard district.

South Water Street   ➡ also "Water Street" as a col-

loquial term before 1834, when the other three Water Streets (N, W, and E) had not yet been built up; one of Chicago's oldest streets, and the only one recognizable as a street as late as 1833 by virtue of its row of early houses, although poorly aligned. Named on the [see] Thompson ✳ plat of 1830, it originally ran all the way between Fort Dearborn and the Forks along the south bank of the Chicago River. In 1832, few business establishments were present, and most of these were clustered at the W end; expansion proceeded from here eastward to Dearborn Street, then around onto Lake Street, on which construction proceeded on both sides back to the junction of Lake, Market, and South Water streets, the beginning. In 1920, the part of South Water Street that was W of State Street became Wacker Drive. For a description of the scene, see John Bates' following 1883 recollection [Bates lived until 1885] of early South Water Street:

In 1833 the settlement of the new town, so far as buildings showed, was mostly on what is now Water Street. There was nothing on Lake Street except perhaps the Catholic church [St. Mary's] begun on the northwest corner of Lake and State. Up and down Water Street, between what is now State and Wells streets, now Fifth Avenue all the business houses and stores were built. Also nearly all the cabins for dwellings. You could, from every store and dwelling, look north across the river, as there were no buildings on what is now the north side of that street. At that time a slough [Frog Creek] emptied into the river, at what is now the foot of State Street, and was a sort of bayou of dead water through which scows could be run up as far as Randolph Street, near the corner of Dearborn, and there was a dry creek up as far as where the Sherman House now stands. There was a footbridge of four logs run lengthwise across the creek near the mouth of the creek. At the time there was no bridge across the main river, and never had been.

Southwest Company   begun by John Jacob Astor in 1808 at Montreal when northern posts were surrendering to the United States; among several companies that became the American Fur Co. in the Northwest after the 1812 war; John Kinzie worked for this company as an independent agent (listings within his account book on Oct. 15, 1817, and May 1, 1818) during part of his residency in Chicago, and eventually the American Fur Co. [404]

Spain, Solomon D. listed prior to 1836 as owner of 80 acres of land in Section 34, Township 39, as per Andreas, *History of Chicago*, pp. 112-113.

Spaulding, S.F. arrived from New York in 1834; in October 1835 he signed up with the "Pioneer" hook and ladder company, an early volunteer fire brigade; in 1885 lived at Staunton, IL. [12, 351, 733]

Specie Grove see Lamset, Pierre.

Specie, Peter see Lamset, Pierre.

Spence, Agnes participant in an outing on horseback from Chicago to the Calumet River, with John D. Caton as partner, in the spring of 1835, as described by Caton; [see] James' and Mrs. Seth Johnson's sister; married a J.D. Wilson on May 3, 1843, in Chicago. [121]

Spence, James born in England; arrived from Pensylvania early in 1834; was a brother of [see] Mrs. Seth Johnson; had a claim at Big Woods, five miles N of the Chicago River, which he leased to John K. Boyer in anticipation of returning to England; in October he became the victim of the town's first fire, which destroyed his house at the corner of LaSalle and Lake streets, an estimated $500 loss; ◆ canal contractor, 17 Clark St.; died that year as per notice in the *Chicago Daily American* of Nov. 4, 1839. [351, 728]

Spence, John C. arrived from Pensylvania in 1834; ◆ hatter, 19 Clark St. [351]

Spohrer, K. German immigrant, first attested to as having lived in Chicago in 1833. [342]

Spriggs, William lawyer from Maryland; became one of the first three judges of the U.S. Court for the Territory of Illinois in 1809, serving with Jesse B. Thomas and Alexander Stuart.

Spring, Giles (1807-1851) Massachusetts born,

came in May 1833; advertised his office in that year's Dec. 17 issue of the *Chicago Democrat* as being located "second door W of Franklin and South Water," and soon became a highly regarded Chicago lawyer; at a large meeting of concerned citizens on Nov. 21, 1835, he introduced resolutions of condemnation in regard to the town council's [see] wharfing privileges ordinance, circulated a remonstrance, and filed a deposition in support of Anson and Taylor's claim on Nov. 24; married Levantia Budlong of New York in 1836, as per notice in the *Chicago Democrat* of July 24. In February 1836, he formed a partnership with Grant Goodrich that lasted until he was elected to the bench in 1849; ◆ 107 Lake St. According to contemporaries, he died prematurely at age 44, "a victim to the free use of intoxicating liquors." [12, 13, 28, 351]

Spring, H., M.D. advertised as physician and surgeon in the *Chicago American* of Sept. 12, 1835, in an office on Dearborn Street with Giles Spring, likely his brother; aged 32, died of a lingering illness on Nov. 11 that year as per notice in the Nov. 14 *Chicago American*.

Springfield, IL settled in 1818 by trappers and hunters; named after a nearby Spring Creek; became the permanent seat of Sangamon County in 1825 and was chosen as the Illinois state capital in 1837, the year Lincoln moved to the town; was chartered a city in 1840.

Sproat, Granville Temple (c.1808-1887) schoolteacher from Boston who arrived late spring, 1833; opened the English and Classical School for Boys in a building belonging to the First Baptist Church congregation on South Water Street, corner of Franklin, on Dec. 17, 1833; subscribed to the *Chicago Democrat* in November, and in the first issue of the *Chicago Democrat* of Nov. 26, 1833, published a letter regarding the importance of education, followed by ads in the December issues promoting his newly opened "Academy." In the fall of 1834, with the school securely underway, he chose to move on, taking a position as teacher in a school

for Chippewa Indians on Mackinaw Island; at Chicago he was succeeded as teacher by Dr. Henry Van der Bogart; died in New York; ➡ Granville Street (6200 N). For an excerpt from G. Sproat's reminiscences of Chicago in 1833, see below. [12, 631, 728]

I shall never forget the pleasant hours spent with [my pupils], *during the beautiful summer months, in that nicely furnished school room, the windows of which looked out toward the south, not a building between it and the broad expanse of, prairie, stretching far away, clothed with its beautiful vesture of flowers.* ✧ *Autumn came and brought a change in our surroundings. From the long rains the streets of the village soon became deluged with mud. It lay in many places half-leg deep, up to the hubs of the carts and wagons, in the middle of the streets, and the only sidewalk we had was a single plank stretched from one building to another. The smaller scholars I used to bring to school and take home on my back, not daring to trust them on the slippery plank. One day I made a misstep and went down into the thick mire, with a little one in my arms. With difficulty I regained my foothold, with both overshoes sucked off by the thick slimy mud. I never recovered them.*

Stacey, Moses came to Chicago from New York in a sailing vessel in 1835, and quickly moved on to settle in [now] Lombard, IL. [314a]

stag beetle see *Lucanus elaphus*.

stagecoach see Frink & Walker.

Stanger, Christoph and Daniel German immigrant brothers from Pennsylvania, arrived in 1835 and soon formed the first branch nucleus of the [see] German Evangelical Association, which was not formally organized until 1843; they settled near [now] Wheeling. [12, 304, 342]

Stannig, Thomas in 1835 submitted an affidavit in support of [see] John Ludby's claim for wharfing privileges.

Starr, James U.S. Army private at Fort Dearborn; enlisted in November 1809; killed at the massacre of 1812. [226]

Starved Rock   a tall rock or cliff in LaSalle County, on the S side of the Illinois River, upon which the French explorer La Salle erected a fort in 1682 and named it Fort St. Louis du Rocher; the fort existed until 1718. Nearby was a large village of Illinois Indians, said to have been inhabited by 7,000 to 8,000 souls in 1680. In subsequent decades the Illinois were gradually dispersed by marauding Fox and Iroquois Indians; a colorful fiction to explain its name is given by Quaife: A group of Illinois was starved into submission on the rock by Fox Indians in c.1722. A legend in Andreas claims that a remnant, having retreated to the rock, was starved and then massacred by the Ottawa and Potawatomi in retaliation for the 1769 assassination of the Ottawa chief Pontiac by an Illinois Indian. Alvord exploded this myth, stating that a thorough search had produced no reliable references to this alleged episode. Near the rock, coal was first found in this area, and was used in the forge erected within the fort. Also near the rock, in the Illinois River town Peru, was the final destination of a daily steamboat run from St. Louis beginning in 1833, with stage connection offered to Chicago in 1834 first by Dr. Temple's line, and later by the line of Frink & Walker. For Francis Parkman's 1897 description of Starved Rock as a great national monument, see below:

The cliff called 'Starved Rock' now pointed out to travelers as the chief natural curiosity of the region, rises steep on three sides as a castle wall to the height of a hundred twenty-five feet above the river. In front, it overhangs the water that washes its base; its western brow looks down on the tops of the forest trees below; and on the east is a wide gorge or ravine, choked with the mingled foliage of oaks, walnuts and elms; while in its rocky depth a little brook creeps down to mingle with the river. From the rugged trunk of the stunted cedar that leans forward from the brink, you may drop a plummet into the river below, where the catfish and the turtles may plainly be seen gliding over the wrinkled sand of the clean shallow current. The cliff is accessible only from behind, where a man may climb up, not without difficulty, by a steep and narrow passage. The top is about an acre in extent.

State Bank of Illinois   charter approved by the legislature on Feb. 12, 1835; a branch of this bank was ★★★ **Chicago's 1st** such facility, opening mid-December 1835 at the corner of LaSalle and S. Water streets in the four-story brick building owned by Garrett, Brown & Brother, with William H. Brown as cashier, Ezra L. Sherman as teller; the board of directors consisted of: president John H. Kinzie, directors G.S. Hubbard, Peter Pruyne, E.K. Hubbard, R.J. Hamilton, Walter Kimball, H.B. Clarke, G.W. Dole, and E.D. Taylor; bank checks were available Dec. 19, as per notice in the *Chicago American*; the bank failed in 1837.

State Street   ➡ Chicago's main street and its name have a history that begins among the early traders. After Gurdon S. Hubbard established his trading post in Danville in 1823, 120 miles S of Chicago, he pioneered a trail between the two settlements that, in time, became known as Hubbard's Trace. By 1834, the trace had developed into an important route of travel between the Wabash country and the new town, and that year the state of Illinois elevated it to the status of state road, in anticipation of which the surveyor James Thompson, in 1830, gave its northern portion the name State Street.

Steam Boat Hotel   opened in 1835 on North Water Street, near Kinzie Street, and was operated by John Davis; on Nov. 9 of that year, J. Dorsey and J. Force announced in the *Chicago Democrat* that they had assumed management and "that nothing shall be wanting to render their House worthy of a call from a few of the many who visit this flourishing village"; was renamed American Hotel in 1836.

steamboats   beginning in 1832, lake steamers would visit Chicago; the *Sheldon Thompson* under Capt. A. Walker came first on July 10, followed eight days later by the *William Penn*, both bringing troops for the Black Hawk War – as well as the cholera. In that year H.S. Tanner published *View of the Valley of the Mississippi, or the Emigrant's and Traveler's Guide to the West* that noted a steamboat was trading between Chicago "... and Newburyport, on the St. Joseph's, in Michigan Territory." Others followed during the years 1833-1835, including the *Daniel Webster, Monroe, Columbus, Anthony Wayne, Bunker Hill, Michigan, Ohio, Thomas Jefferson, Uncle Sam, Pioneer, United States, Pennsylvania*, and the *Chicago*; additional steamers were on the upper lakes, but never made it to Chicago, as was the ill-fated *Walk-in-the-Water*, the first steamboat built in 1818, run on the lakes, and which sank within the year. See separate entries under the boats' individual names; also see entry under sailing vessels.

Steele, Ashbel   (1794-1861) also Steel; of English descent, born in Derby, CT; bought land in Chicago in 1830 and moved with his wife Harriet (née Dawley, 1827) and children in 1833, bringing with the furniture ★★★ **Chicago's 1st** piano; in November he plastered John Calhoun's printing office; in 1834 he served on the cholera vigilante committee and managed briefly the Eagle Hotel on Lake Street; was elected Cook County coroner on Aug. 4, and was part of the hunting party that killed the last black bear in Chicago on Oct. 6; in 1836 he and his family became the first settlers at [River Forest], building a large house near Lake Street and the Des Plaines River [now forest preserve]; ✦ mason builder, third ward; purchased part ownership of a steam sawmill at the east bank of the river, just N of the Lake Street bridge, that had been built in 1831 by the Chicago firm Bickerdyke & Noble, the only such mill within 20 miles of Chicago; elected county sheriff on Aug. 10, 1840; appointed postmaster of Noyesville [early name for River Forest/Oak Park] on June 14, 1849. He died on Sept. 26, 1861; his widow lived in Maywood in 1885 and died on July 25, 1895; the ▲ family grave is at Forest Home Cemetery. [12, 301, 351]

Steele, Richard   subscribed to the *Chicago Democrat* in November 1833; became an early settler in [Lake County], where his son Albert B. was born on June 20, 1835; that year he, Thomas McClure, and Mark Noble were appointed viewers to lay out a road from Chicago to the state line, crossing the Des Plaines River. [304]

Stein, Charles   from Siefersheim, Germany; came to America in 1834 and to Chicago in 1835; conducted a small boot and shoe trade; married Magdalena Berg in 1841, Barbara Werner in 1847, and finally Maria A. Mutti, year unknown; his widow lived in Blue Island in 1885. [13]

Stephens, Capt. Robert   enrolled from July 23 to Aug. 15, 1832, as lieutenant in Seission's militia company during the Black Hawk War; on Oct. 29, 1835, married Nancy, daughter of Lewis Kercheval, in Joliet in a ceremony conducted by Cornelius C. Van Horn as per notice in the *Chicago American.* [714]

Stevens, George   co-owner, with Lathrop Johnson, of the New York House, a hotel on Lake Street built in 1834 and opened in 1835; on Sept. 1, 1835, the partnership was dissolved, though they worked together through December, when Johnson assumed responsibility; a George F. Stevens is listed as a drayman in 1839.

Stevens, Owen R.   listed as owner of 80 acres of land in the NW corner of Section 6, Township 39, prior to 1836, as per Andreas, *History of Chicago,* pp. 112-113.

Stevenson, Benjamin   second of three delegates from the Territory of Illinois to Congress during the territorial period from 1809 to 1816; the others were Shadrach Bond and Nathaniel Pope.

Stewart   two "maiden ladies" by this name, dressmakers, lived with the family of Major Handy in the old Dean House; they were presumed to be relatives. [728]

Stewart, John   listed on April 17, 1833, as master of the schooner *Napoleon* upon which George Dole's first beef shipment (287 barrels) was carried east; member of the Methodist congregation who, together with Henry Whitehead, constructed the first permanent Methodist church building at the corner of North Water and Clark streets in the second half of 1834; married to Ellen Adell Millen; ✦ Captain, steamer *Michigan.* For the text of a bill of lading, executed by Captain Stewart, see entry "Newberry & Dole." [12]

Stewart, Robert   also Stuart; listed as having in c.1832 purchased from J.B. Beaubien, and together with Seth Johnson, lot 3 in block 36 [see map on page 44]. Conceivably, this listing may have referred to [see] Robert Stuart, manager of the American Fur Co. at Mackinac, who occasionally came to Chicago on business, and whose name is spelled variously in Andreas. [12]

Stewart, Royal   attorney; assisted in Col. Hamilton's office late November 1834 and advertised subscriptions to *American Plough Boy, New-York Farmer, Rail-Road Journal and Register of Internal Improvements,* and *Mechanics Magazine and Register of Inventions*; became secretary of the Chicago Lyceum in December 1834; was admitted to the Illinois bar on Jan. 8, 1835, then advertised his services in the *Chicago American* on June 8; voted in 1837; ✦ Lake Street [12, 13]

Stewart, William   lived with his wife at Flusky's boarding house in 1835.

Stiles, David   ran a log tavern on the W bank of the south branch of the Chicago River in October 1834, mentioned in an 1883 letter by [see] Enoch Chase, who found "not a vestige of civilization except the wagon tracks and it was the dreariest road I have ever traveled" between Stile's Tavern and the one run by the Laughtons on the Des Plaines River; his name was on a school-related Chicago petition signed on Sept. 19, 1835. [13]

Stolp, Frederick   (1781-1873) served in the War of 1812; brickmaker from Columbia County, NY; at age 52 walked on foot from New York to Chicago in 1833 and on to Naperville Township, where he found suitable clay for brickmaking and chose land; in 1834 he walked back to New York to fetch his nine children and his wife Jannetje [née Janett W. Pepper, married 1813]; returned with family in September 1835 and acquired a claim E of Big Woods. [314a, 657a]

Stone, H.O.   member of the team that went from Chicago to [see] Sheboygan in 1834 to build a sawmill on the Sheboygan River. The venture failed, and the party returned to Chicago in 1835. H.O. Stone is possibly identical with Horatio O. Stone of the next entry.

Stone, Horacio O.   (1811-1877) from New York, arrived on Jan. 11, 1835; a shoemaker by training but opened a hardware store and speculated in real estate business, maintaining each business for nearly 40 years; ✦ groceries & provisions, South Water Street; a notice in the *Daily Chicago American* of Dec. 30, 1839, announced the death of two daughters within five days, one-year-old Aurora and five-year-old Semantha. His first wife's name was Jane Ann; later he married Elizabeth Yager. In 1854, he began the manufacture of pianos; in his later years owned much downtown property; died on June 20, 1877; ➡ Stone Street (80 E). [12, 37, 351]

stone quarry   the quarry nearest to the early settlement was located just S of [see] Healy's Slough. According to Valentine Boyer, from here came the stones used for initial harbor pier construction, delivered under contract in a large wooden boat by James Spence and John Boyer, who also built the boat. [728]

Stoner, George   in c.1832 purchased lot 5 in block 23 [see map on page 44] from Wilson Bell [initially the lot belonged to William Lee].

Stony Creek   branch of the Calumet River that used to flow eastward into the Calumet at Fay's Point, S of Blue Island, helping to drain the southern Chicagoland swamps. However, in times of high water, Stony Creek flowed both eastward into the Calumet and westward into the Saganashkee swamp. Tributaries were Midlothian Creek and Bachelor's Grove Creek [now in Tinley Creek]. The

Calumet-Sag Canal has replaced Stony Creek.

Stony Ford between Riverside ford and Laughton's ford; approximately 150 feet S of the Ogden Avenue bridge over the Des Plaines River; owes its shallowness and name to the fact that limestone of the Niagara formation here reaches the surface; this was the convenient crossing point for the old Indian trail from Chicago that preceded Ogden Avenue, continuing from the ford into the Illinois River valley.

Stony Island a rocky outcropping, part of the laminated limestone formation deposited 400 million years ago by a shallow tropical sea and referred to as the Niagara formation by geologists, it formed an island in Lake Chicago, Lake Michigan's precursor; what remains of this elevation is located along ➡ Stony Island Avenue (1600 E) and between 92nd and 93rd streets

Storrow, Samuel Appleton (1787-1837) U.S. judge advocate from 1815 to 1820; visited Fort Dearborn from Oct. 2 to 4, 1817, traveling overland from Detroit by way of Fort Gratiot [on the St. Clair River] and Green Bay during a three month inspection tour of the western forts. Visits to the lonely fort were rare, and visitors were well received by Commandant Major Baker and the garrison. Mr. Storrow described his Fort Dearborn experience in a letter to Major General Brown, written on Dec. 1, 1817, and in his publication *Tour of the Northwest, 1817*; for an excerpt, see Chronology, 1817. [12, 560]

Stose, Clemens, Sr. also Clement Stoce, Stokse, Stoze; German born, came from Pennsylvania; his arrival varies by account from 1833 to 1836, the earlier more likely; E.O. Gale observed Stose's smithy, where he made calumets and tomahawks for the Indians, on Franklin Street in 1835, bringing the total to three; in 1839 was elected alderman from the second ward; ✦ Stose & White [?], blacksmiths, Randolph Street near Wells; probable date of death, Oct. 18, 1881; Andreas noted the existence of an old leathern fire bucket with the name "C. Stoze" among the artifacts of the Chicago Historical Society. [12, 265, 351]

Stow, William H. (c.1806-1881) born in Utica, NY; arrived with his wife Celia in July 1834; was a member of the fire engine company No.1 ("Fire Kings") in December 1835; built and operated that year the Western Hotel on the SE corner of Canal and Randolph streets, which he held until 1852. Together with David Bradley, he also built in 1835 a foundry on Polk Street near the river, in which were later made the first Chicago steam engines; ✦ foundry, W Randolph Street; served as alderman in 1839; died on Aug. 18, 1881. Celia was active in the Presbyterian church and in 1885, lived at 2236 Michigan Ave. [12, 351]

Stowe, Henry M. also Stow; arrived from New York in 1834; ✦ iron merchant, 11 and 13 Clark St.; later moved to San Francisco; as an Old Settler listed in 1885, he was again living in Chicago. [12, 351]

Stowell, Augustine served under Captain Naper in the Chicago company during the 1832 Black Hawk War. [12, 714]

Stowell, Calvin M. served under Captain Naper in the Chicago company during the 1832 Black Hawk War. [12, 714]

Stowell, Walter arrived in 1831; served as third sergeant under Captain Napier in the Chicago company during the 1832 Black Hawk War; later moved to Newark, IL, where he became postmaster. [12, 714]

streets and roads the first streets of Chicago created by organized governmental activity were those planned and named by [see] James Thompson, surveyor for the Illinois & Michigan Canal Commission, who published his ✳ plat on Aug. 4, 1830. For several years most of these streets existed only on paper. As late as 1833, only one row of poorly aligned houses remotely resembled a street, that of South Water Street. The area mapped by Thompson is what, in the context of this book, is called the "original town," bounded by Kinzie Street on the N, State Street on the E, Madison Street on the S, and Desplaines Street on the W. At the time neither State, Madison, nor DesPlaines streets were named, and it must be realized that until much later in the 1830s the actual settlement was considerably smaller than the area covered by the plat. Thompson's checkerboard arrangement of streets reflects the mandates of the [see] Federal Land Ordinance of 1785, modified by geographic features of the landscape and preexisting village paths. The next authority to establish streets or roads, after the canal commission, was the Cook County Board of Commissioners which, during its second court session (June 6, 1831), ordered the first two county roads to be laid out, one "from the town of Chicago [by way of the later Madison Street and Ogden Avenue] to the house of B. Lawton, from thence to the house of James Walker, on the Du Page River, and so on to the west line of the county." The second was to run "from the town of Chicago, the nearest and best way [along the later State Street and Archer Avenue] to the house of Widow Brown, on Hickory Creek." Jedediah Wooley became the first county surveyor in 1831 and, on April 25, 1832, was instructed to lay out a street leading from the settlement to the lakeshore, 50 feet wide; his description reads as follows: "From the east end of [S] Water street, in the town of Chicago, to Lake Michigan. Direction of said road is south 88 1/2 degrees east from the street to the lake, 18 chains 50 links."

The third agency responsible for the creation and maintenance of streets was the Chicago Village Board, which in November 1833 named four streets S of Washington Street, namely Madison, Monroe, Adams, and Jackson, and on June 6, 1834, created the office of supervisor of streets.

A state road, constructed under authority of the government in Springfield, connecting Chicago with the left bank of the Wabash River, opposite Vincennes, was completed in March 1833; an interstate road, built with federal funds during the years from 1827 to 1836 [see entry on Richard, Father Gabriel], connected Chicago with Detroit, closely following the ancient Indian trail and connecting with Michigan Avenue in Chicago; Catlin says: "... it was nothing to boast about in the driest season and was at times impassable in wet weather." The Green Bay Indian Trail from Chicago to Green Bay had been designated by an act of Congress as an important national route on June 15, 1832, and therefore to be improved as a national road. Surveyed in 1833, in 1834 it was cut to a width of two rods as far as Milwaukee and improved with corduroy through the swamps and with log bridges over the streams.

Chicago's street pattern of today reflects both the land ordinance with its N-S orientation and the much earlier arrangement of pioneer and Indian footpaths and wagon trails, the latter yielding only to natural geographic features.

For an 1835 eyewitness account on the quality of construction of cross-country plank roads through the wilderness, see Prof. J.B. Turner's coach report below; as to another method of roadbuilding, see entry for turnpiking. [119, 320, 538]

We selected this route because it would take us over the famous government road being built from Detroit to Chicago, and we had had delightful visions of bowling along a smooth highway built by government money and government engineers. But, alas! instead of being honest corduroy, as required in the contract and advertised in glowing colors, each tree felled and laid side by side with its neighbor tree, at right angles to the right of way, and all spaces carefully filled with dirt, the whole one unbroken, smooth surface, the trees were felled helter-skelter and left just as they happened to fall, but all were covered with dirt and rounded up smooth and even before the inspector came. The first spring rains had washed away the earth. Naked trunks of trees, at all angles and of all sizes, stretched over the impassable morasses of Indiana. By September, the whole route was strewn with broken vehicles, wagon wheels, and parts of stage-coaches. The men walked behind, carrying rails on their shoulders to pry out the wheels, when skilful driving could not prevent their slipping between the tree-trunks and they were in danger of being wrenched off.

striker   assistant who does the hammering for a blacksmith.

Strode, James M.   from TN; circuit riding attorney who traveled from Galena to Chicago in early April 1832, in the company of attorney [see] Benjamin Mills and Judge Richard M. Young; they became aware of the early unrest of the Black Hawk War, and warned the Chicago settlement of the impending danger; from 1831 on Strode lived in Galena, and intermittently came to Chicago, the first time for several days in 1831. In August 1835, he was the Democratic nominee for state senator and won; moved to Chicago in August 1836; on July 7, 1836, he was commissioned as register for the U.S. Land Office [succeeding James Whitlock], with its office on Lake Street, between Clark and Dearborn; ♦ register land office, Saloon Building, Clark Street. After 1837, he was a practicing member of the Chicago bar and a prosecuting attorney until 1848. [12, 351, 544]

Strong, Robert   born in Greensboro, VT in 1806; came in July 1831 with his wife Caroline [née Trowbridge/Willey?]; served as private in Captain Boardman's voluntary county militia and under Capt. J. Brown in the Chicago militia during the Black Hawk War in 1832; bought a claim from Walter Selvey, settling near Dupage town; listed in the *Chicago Democrat* of April 8, 1834 as secretary of the Fountaindale Temperance Society. [12, 734]

Stuart, Alexander   of Virginia; became one of the first three judges of the U.S. Court for the Territory of Illinois in 1809, serving with Jesse B. Thomas and William Spriggs; in 1885 lived at Birmingham, AL. [12]

Stuart, James   subagent to Indian agent Thomas J.V. Owen, 1831-33 at Fort Dearborn, serving with Gholson Kercheval.

Stuart, J.N.   partner of [see] Lathrop Johnson in a livery stable enterprise; notice of the June 15, 1835, dissolution appeared in the *Chicago American* throughout that summer.

Stuart, Robert   (sometimes misspelled as [see] Robert Stewart, as in Andreas' *History of Chicago*) managing partner of the American Fur Co.'s entire Northwest operations at Mackinac from 1817 to 1834, part of this time with Ramsey Crooks; had migrated from Scotland to Canada in 1805 and joined John Jacob Astor's firm five years later, and remained with the firm until 1834, when he moved to Detroit. In 1831, he had as an employee [see] Miss Eliza Chappel, who taught the young children in the Stuart family and later became an early Chicago teacher. In 1833, he was in Chicago for the Indian Treaty and presented a request for $17,000 for losses allegedly suffered by the company though Indian activities since 1812; died suddenly in Chicago in 1848, where he had again come on business. [12]

Stuart, William   lawyer; arrived from New York in 1835; his wife was Eliza G.; advertised in the Nov. 14 *Chicago American* and in the Dec. 5 *Chicago Democrat* as attorney, counselor, solicitor, and general land agent at an office in Sherman's Brick Block, nearly opposite Tremont House on Lake; late in 1837 William Stuart & Co. acquired and began republication of [see] T.O. Davis' *Chicago American*; ♦ publisher and editor of *Chicago Daily American*, corner of South Water and Clark streets [his brother Alexander is listed as pressman]; followed Abell as postmaster in 1841 and sold the paper to his brother the following year. [12, 13]

Stubbs, S.A.   born c.1807 in New Jersey; arrived in 1835; still lived in Chicago in 1879. [12]

Sturtevant, George W.   placed an ad in the Oct. 28, 1835, *Chicago Democrat* in regard to a lost red pocketbook, containing sundry papers, two promissory notes, and an agreement for a lot in Juliett.

Sucker   an early good-natured nickname for residents of Illinois, loosely used [actually referred to miners from southern Illinois, who would ascend the Mississippi to Galena in the spring and descend the river home in the autumn, like sucker fish]; see entry on Wellmacher, Johann for his bakery advertisement.

sulky   a light two-wheeled horse-drawn carriage having only one seat.

Sullivan, Daniel   submitted a claim for wharfing privileges on Nov. 27, 1835. [28]

Sullivan, Capt. John C.   U.S. government surveyor for the commission established to delineate boundaries negotiated with the Chippewa, Ottawa, and Potawatomi in August 1816 at the Treaty of St. Louis; a copy of his ✱ map of 1819 is in the Newberry Library and shows the Chicago portage region and the 20 by 70 mile corridor linking it to the upper Illinois River. [682]

Sullivan, Mary Ann   a child by this name was enrolled as grade school student in the class taught by [see] John Watkins in December 1835. Names of corresponding parents were not recorded. [728]

Sulzer, Konrad [Conrad]   (1807-1873) German-Swiss immigrant druggist and brewmaster; in 1833 he met Wilhelm Haas at Watertown, NY; arrived in Chicago with 150 barrels of ale and brewing equipment in 1836 [according to Hofmeister; Angle gives an unlikely 1833 as the year of their arrival]. Together they founded a brewery that initially produced 600 barrels of beer per year; their brewery was not the first such enterprise in Chicago, but the more successful [see entry on breweries]; soon became a farmer on a 100 acre plot N of Chicago; ✦ gardener, Lake View [annexed in 1889]. An Andrew Sulzer is listed in 1839 as a brewer at the corner of Pine [Michigan] Street and Chicago Avenue, the brewery then partnered by Wilhelm Haas and William Ogden. The Sulzer Regional Public Library of Chicago at 4455 N. Lincoln Ave. has been named in honor of Conrad Sulzer. [17, 342]

Summers, William   listed prior to 1836 as owner of 80 acres of land in the SE quarter of Section 18, Township 39, as seen in Andreas, *History of Chi-*

cago, pp. 112-113.

Summit   a suburb SW of Chicago, named for the highest elevation of the watershed—the summit—through which the Illinois & Michigan Canal was constructed; ➡ Summit Avenue (800 W).

Summit Ford   the southernmost of four fords across the Des Plaines River; located at [Lawndale Avenue], where the South Portage Trail of the Chicago Portage also crossed.

Sunawewonee   chief of Prairie Potawatomi from near Peoria; one of the principal chiefs during the Fort Dearborn massacre, which he survived. [226]

Sunday school   first meeting of a Sunday school class took place under Philo Carpenter's direction on Aug. 19, 1832, in an unfinished log building on the Fort Dearborn reservation, belonging to Mark Beaubien; 13 children and five adults attended; subsequent and regular meetings were held at the fort, Rufus Brown's house, Mark Noble's house, Father Walker's cabin at the Point, and upstairs in Mr. Peck's store. Other active participants were Luther Childs, the daughters of Mark Noble, Sr. (Elizabeth and Mary), Mrs. Seth Johnson, and Mrs. Charles Taylor. In August of 1833, the New York investor Arthur Bronson visited Chicago in the company of his friend Charles Butler, exploring and socializing, and made a charitable donation of $50 for the Sunday school library. According to S. Lockwood Brown: "the children at that time were mostly half breeds and French who were not much accustomed to restraints and the only way by which they could be got together was to call for them at their homes. Ten of the teachers generally devoted the entire Sabbath to this work regularly." On March 16, 1835, the First Presbyterian Church, in existence since June 26, 1833, formally organized its Sunday school program, with Joseph Meeker as librarian.

Surgeon, The   Chicagoland's first western physician, known through the writings of Father Marquette, who must have known him but did not reveal the name of this surgeon and unlicensed

fur trader; while Marquette spent the winter of 1674-75 on the banks of Chicago River's south branch, the surgeon visited him in the company of Pierre Moreau but is not recorded as having treated him for an eventually fatal intestinal disease. Some earlier historians believed that his name was Louis Moreau, unrelated to Pierre Moreau. John F. Swenson identifies him as Jean Roussel or Rousselière. [649, 738]

Suttenfield, John   U.S. Army private at Fort Dearborn; enlisted in September 1807; badly wounded at the massacre of 1812, taken prisoner and killed by the Indians the next day. [226]

sutler   person authorized to establish himself near a military command to sell liquor, tobacco, food, services, "black ball" (boot black), brushes, thread, &c. to the soldiers—any goods not customarily furnished by the government. It was generally believed that more than three-fourths of the soldiers' pay was spent at the sutler's. The position became especially lucrative when soldiers were under order not to buy goods at other local stores, although prices there might be substantially lower. The status of sutlers was recognized by the Articles of War, which provided for the regulation of hours of business, prices, and the quality of the goods sold; sutlers were appointed by the local commander, and were subject to military order. At Fort Dearborn, the agent in charge of the [see] U.S. factory generally had the implied right to trade; however, the following exceptions were made: from 1807-1809, John Kinzie and John Whistler, Jr. (the commander's son), held the position jointly; from 1809-1811, Dr. John Cooper and John Whistler, Jr., jointly; from 1811-1812, John Kinzie; from 1820-1823, Henry Whiting (with James E. Heron in 1822); in 1830, Jonathan N. Bailey (according to James M. Bucklin); in 1832, Oliver Newberry (with George W. Dole as clerk). [105, 109, 704]

swan   *Cygnus buccinator*, trumpeter swan; the largest North American waterfowl, formerly hunted widely for food by Indians and early settlers. Father Marquette who saw them in northern Illinois in 1673, Abbé St. Cosme (in 1699), and de Liette (in 1702) all described them as abundant along the Illinois River; hunted widely for food by Indians and pioneers. David McKee, resident from 1823 to 1832, referred to the Chicago River when he recalled: "Excellent fish abounded in it, and over it hovered wild geese, ducks and sandhill cranes in vast flocks, and pelicans and swans were sometimes seen." [64]

Swan schooner under Captain Gilbert (sometimes under Captain Duncan), first called at Chicago on June 1, 1835, coming from St. Joseph; called 15 more times in that year with passengers and merchandise, serving the W coast traffic of Lake Michigan; as per notice in the Nov. 28, 1835, *Chicago American*, the vessel was unheard from following lake storms and feared lost.

Swearingen, Lt. James Strode (1782-1864) native of Virginia; as an officer familiar with the territory between Detroit and Chicago, he was asked to conduct the troops of the first Fort Dearborn along the old Sauk trail to the chosen site, and then remained to assist in the construction under Capt. John Whistler. The trip took 35 days, and all arrived on Aug. 17, 1803; he did not become a permanent member of the garrison. A journal of his experience survives, including a ✳ map redrawn by Albert Scharf. During the 1812 war he advanced to become quartermaster general of the U.S. Army, with the rank of colonel; soon after the war he received an honorable discharge; died on Feb. 3, 1864. [12, 544, 564, 646, 724]

Sweeny, John also Sweeney; came in the spring of 1834; during the following October shot the last black bear in a tree near the intersection of Adams and LaSalle [see bear]; ✦ carpenter, boarded with Henry Goodrich [a farmer on Dearborn Street near Washington]; still lived in Chicago in 1885. [12, 266, 351]

Sweet, Alanson (1804-1891) stonemason; arrived from Owasco, NY, in 1832; initially a resident of

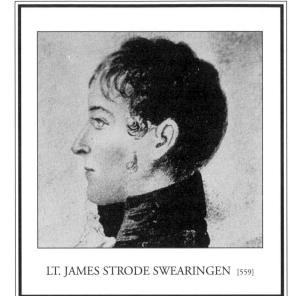

LT. JAMES STRODE SWEARINGEN [559]

the Napier settlement and served as first lieutenant in the militia under Captain Napier; under contract for John Noble and with William Worthingham, built ★★★ Chicago's 1st brick house in 1833 on the N side of the river [Kinzie Street] on a lot adjacent to the later Lake House hotel; was one of the 12 who voted for incorporation at the public meeting early in August [for a copy of that meeting's report, see entry under incorporation]; that year he also built and managed the first Tremont House hotel and married Emily Shaw at St. Joseph; in the July 16, 1834, *Chicago Democrat* he reported the loss of two saddles, items he generously loaned but were then missing; later lived in Evanston, but died in Chicago; Emily died in 1892. [12, 14, 351]

Sweet, Richard M. came in 1830 or 1831 from New York and promptly moved first to [Lisle], then the Napier settlement; in 1832 served as a private in the Chicago company under Captain Napier during the Black Hawk War; subscribed to the *Chicago Democrat* in November 1833, and placed an

ad in the Dec. 3 issue, offering 1,500 bushels of corn for sale from his barn on the E branch of the Du Page River, with 300 bushels or less also available from A. Sweet at Chicago; in 1856 became a member of the Old Settlers' Society. [12, 351]

Sweet, Stephen came in 1830, then removed to Kendall County with [see] Pierre Lamset. [239]

Sweet, William settled at [Lisle] in the 1830s and built a log structure that [see] Mark Beaubien acquired in 1840 and adapted as a tavern and later a toll house.

Tabeaux, Jean Baptiste in April 1833 his name was on the petition by Catholic citizens to the Bishop Rosati in St. Louis asking that a priest be assigned to them. [12]

tailors John L. Davis (1830), Charles A. Taylor (1832), Solomon Lincoln (1833), Francis H. and Francis Taylor (1833), Elmira Fowler (1934), Thomas S. Eels (1834), Sarah D. Howe (1835), Edward Burton (1835), Thomas Duncan (1835), A. Jackson Cox (1835), Elijah Middlebrook Haines (1835), George Halsman (1835), Edward Manierre (1835), Robert Price (1835), and Ira and James Couch (1835-36).

Talcott & Prescott as per notice in the Dec. 26, 1835, *Chicago American*, a map of the Town of Kankakee, drawn by Talcott and Prescott for $25, was missing and its return requested by investors James B. Campbell and Justice [Justin] Butterfield; E.B. Talcott's partner may have been Eli S. Prescott, listed in 1839 as receiver at the U.S. Land Office, 175 Lake.

Talcott, Edward Benton (c.1812-1886) native of Rome, NY, brother of [see] Mancel, Jr.; came in 1835 to work as an engineer on the Illinois & Michigan Canal, eventually becoming the superintendent of the entire project; in November, as town surveyor, prepared a map of the lots along the river for which [see] wharfing privileges leases were sold on the 23rd; on the 24th filed an affidavit in support E.B. William's claim for privileges, and later also a certificate for George Palmer's claim; prepared an early ✳ map, *Chicago with Several Additions compiled from the recorded plats in the Clerk's Office, Cook County, Illinois*, printed in 1836 by Peter Meiser in New York [within the Newberry Library and the Chicago Historical Society]; ✦ U.S. marshal; in 1885 lived at 1235 Wabash Ave.; died in Chicago on Feb. 8, 1886. [12, 28, 164, 351]

Talcott, Mancel, Jr. (1817-1878) also Mancil; born in Rome, NY, brother of [see] Edward B.; came in 1834 from New York, walking from Detroit, soon after was farming along the Des Plaines River in Maine Township [Park Ridge]; ✦ farmer, Milwaukee Avenue; married Mary H. Otis in 1841; after 1850 was a miner in California, returning to become a stone-dealer; established and managed banks; served as county commissioner and member of the Chicago city council and police board; died on June 5, 1878. [12, 37, 278, 351]

Talcott, Mancel, Sr. also Mancil; father of Edward B. and Mancel, Jr.; arrived in 1832 from New York; his wife Betsy subscribed to the *Chicago Democrat* in November 1833; died in 1857. [278, 351]

Taliaferro, Lt. Lawrence (1794-1771) from Virginia; arrived at Fort Dearborn on July 4, 1816, and, as asst. quartermaster and ordnance officer, superintended the reconstruction of the fort under Captain Bradley; from 1819 to 1840 served as Indian agent at Fort Snelling. [650]

Talley, Alfred Maurice arrived from SC in 1834 or 1835; married to Mary Monica Taylor; ✦ compositor, *Chicago Democrat* office. [351]

Talon, Jean Baptiste (1625-1691) first intendant of justice, police, and finance in New France from 1665 to 1668, and again between 1669 and 1675; a powerful official next to Frontenac, setting policy and issuing trade licenses. Chicago was within the region under his jurisdiction. Also see entry on intendants; see ▲ Monuments.

Tamaroa also Tamoroa, Tammaraia, Tamarois; tribe within the Illini nation; among them, at Ca-

JEAN BAPTISTE TALON [46]

hokia, Father Pinet founded the *Mission de Sainte Famille* in c.1699, while gradually closing the *Mission de l'Ange Gardien de Chicagou*.

Tanner, John trapper, trader, and Indian interpreter who in 1820 journeyed from Mackinac to St. Louis by way of the Chicago Portage and Illinois River and left a valuable account of the crossing of the portage in the dry season; had been captured by the Ottawa as a boy and was raised by them. [652]

Tanner, Henry Schenk (1786-1856) succeeded John Melish as America's preeminent map publisher in Philadelphia; in 1823 he published *A New American Atlas, Containing Maps of the Several States of the North American Union*, containing a scrupulously accurate ✳ map of Illinois; in 1832 he published *View of the Valley of the Mississippi, or the Emmigrant's and Traveler's Guide to the West* that described Chicago as "the principal port on Lake Michigan .., a growing place...." [682]

tannery ★★★ **Chicago's 1st** was built in 1831

just N of Miller's Tavern at the Forks; was owned and operated by John Miller and Benjamin Hall.

Tappen, Lt. Alexander Harper native of Ohio; brevet second lieutenant with the Fifth Infantry, stationed at Fort Dearborn from Oct. 15, 1835 to September 1836; died in 1851.

taverns, hotels, and boarding houses no clear distinction is possible between taverns, inns, hotels and boarding houses; listed below in chronological order are the early regular establishments, omitting the Kinzie house, which is known to have taken in, on occasion and for pay, travelers and others in need of temporary housing. Many of the listed taverns were located in what are now Chicago's suburbs; a general description of these was given in a letter by [see] Ellen Bigelow, who traveled by stagecoach from Chicago to Ottawa in May 1835:

Upon the prairies every house was a tavern. We usually found them about fifteen miles apart. They are all built of logs, and strongly indicate the indolence which seems the pervading spirit in Illinois. The site selected for them is generally a hollow, rather than an eminence, and the rich soil about them forms a bed of mud, which is trodden in and around the house without the slightest regard to comfort or cleanliness. Large apertures between the logs admit the dust and rain in plentiful showers, which is disposed of by being suffered to find its way through the gaping seams in the rough, hard floor, ... For details on taverns beyond their construction dates listed below, see individual entries. [12, 55a, 234, 314a, 357]

Wolf Point Tavern (1823) ★★★ **Chicago's 1st**, was also familiarly called Rat Castle or Old Geese's Tavern, its later names: Traveler's Home and Western Stage House; Robinson's Tavern and Store (1825); Miller House, also called Miller's Tavern (1827); Laughtons' Tavern, on Des Plaines River (1827); Eagle Exchange Tavern, renamed Sauganash Tavern, later United States Hotel (1829); Heacock's Point, on south branch, S of Hardscrabble (1830), Mann's Tavern, on Calumet River (1830); Wentworth's, [Jefferson] (1830);

Buckhorn Tavern, [Lyons] (1830); Mansion House (1831); Green Tree Tavern, later called Chicago Hotel, then Lake Street House (1833); Tremont House (1833); Dexter Graves' boarding house (1833); Rufus Brown's boarding house (1833); Wentworth's Black Horn Tavern, on Flag Creek (1833); Exchange Coffee House, later called Illinois Exchange and sometimes New York Exchange (1834); Eagle Hotel (1834); Stiles Tavern, on south branch (1834); Pre-Emption House in Naper's Settlement (1834); Hobson Tavern on Dupage River (c.1834); New York House (1835); Half-Way-House of Dr. E.G. Wight [Plainfield, Ottawa Road] (1835); Castle Inn [Brush Hill Trail] (1835); Ellis Inn (1835); Steamboat Hotel, later called American Hotel, also American Inn (1835); Western Hotel (1835); Flusky's Boarding House (1835); Fay's Boarding House (1835); Kettlestrings' Tavern, later Oak Ridge Inn [Oak Park] (1835); Planck's Tavern, Dutchman's Point (1835); Ike Cook's saloon (1835); Hollis Newton's Tavern & Hotel (1835); Patrick and Eve Kelsey's boarding house (1835); Lincoln's Coffee House (1835); Patterson's Tavern [Wilmette] (1835); Lake House (planned in 1835, opened in 1836); Rexford House, Blue Island (1836).

Beginning in 1829, tavern licenses were required and rates were set by the county commissioners; for the official text of ★★★ **Chicago's 1st** tavern license, issued to Archibald Clybourne and Samuel Miller on May 2, 1829, see below; the second license went to Archibald Caldwell in December 1829; the third and fourth licenses were granted on June 8, 1830, to Alexander Robinson and Mark Beaubien, each; the fifth and last license granted by the Peoria commissioner to a Chicagoan was that for Russell Heacock on Dec. 7, 1830.

On May 2, 1829, Archibald Clybourne and Samuel Miller received a tavern license from the Peoria County Commissioners' Court with the following stipulations—*Ordered: That a license be granted to Archibald Clybourne & Samuel Miller to keep a tavern at Chicago in this state, and that the rates which were allowed heretofore to J.L. Bogardus in the town of Peoria be allowed to the said Clybourne and Miller—and that the Clerk take bond and security of the parties for one Hundred dollars—License eight Dollars':*

Each half-pint of wine, rum, or brandy ...... 25 cts.
" pint " " " " .... 37 1/2 "
" half-pint gin ....18 3/4 "
" pint " .... 31 1/4 "
" gill of whisky ....6 1/4 "
" half-pint " ....12 1/2 "
" pint " ....18 3/4 "
" pint cider or beer ....6 1/4 "
" breakfast, dinner, or supper .... 24 "
night's lodging ....12 1/2 "
Keeping horse overnight on grain or hay .... 25 "
The same as above, 25 hours .... 37 1/2 "
Horse feed ....12 1/2 "

taxation　★★★ **Chicago's 1st** tax levy occurred in 1823 as a Fulton County property tax; the total collected from Chicago residents amounted to $11.42, based on a property assessment of $2,242. In 1825, when Chicago was part of Peoria/Putnam County, 14 residents were deemed to own taxable property worth a total of $9,047, and a 1 percent levy yielded $90.47. The list of County Assessor John L. Bogardus shows the following breakdown: J.B. Beaubien ($10), John Crafts ($50), Jonas Clybourne ($6.25), Dr. Wolcott ($5.72), John Kinzie ($5), A. Wilemet ($4), John K. Clark ($2.50), Alex. Robinson ($2), David McKee/Claude Laframboise/Jeremy Clermont/Peter Piche ($1 each), Joseph Laframboise/Louis Coutra ($0.50). On April 4, 1832, Cook County's first financial statement showed total taxes collected for the preceding year on real estate holdings and personal property as $148.29.

Taylor, Abner　native of ME; arrived in 1833; contractor and builder; a merchant later with the wholesale dry goods firm J.V. Farwell & Co. [351]

Taylor, Anson H.　(1805-1878) from Connecticut, brother of Charles and Augustin; married to Elizabeth Leahy; arrived in 1827; in 1828 a firm named Laughton & Taylor existed at "Farm House, Chicago" and sold groceries and whiskey—possibly a temporary partnership with one of the Laughton brothers ["sold goods here in 1829 at the Forks on the West Side," according to Frank G. Beaubien]; rented the old Kinzie residence from 1829 to 1831 and maintained a store; in 1831 he rented half of Madore Beaubien's cabin on the SW corner of South Water and Dearborn streets as a tailor shop; together the brothers built the floating log bridge across the south branch of the Chicago River at Randolph Street in 1832; some time that year he purchased lot 7 in block 16 [see map on page 44] from Gholson Kercheval, a lot that had initially belonged to J.B. Beaubien. As an early member of the Catholic community, his name was on the April 1833 petition by citizens to Bishop Rosati of St. Louis asking that a priest be assigned to them, then he was delegated by the congregation to go to St. Louis and escort Father St. Cyr to Chicago (see St. Mary's church); submitted a deposition in regard to wharfing privileges on Nov. 24, 1835; ◆ general supply store, near the Garrison. [12, 42, 351]

Taylor, Augustin Deodat　born 1796 in Hartfort, CT; brother of Charles and Anson; arrived with his wife Mary [née Gillett] in June 1833; began work on St. Mary's church, soon completing the structure with the (see) balloon frame method (regarded by some historians as the inventor, though others acknowledge G.W. Snow); later built the St. Patrick's, St. Peter's, St. Joseph's [1836], and St. James' churches [1837]; his last church was built in Naperville; filed a deposition in regard to wharfing privileges on Nov. 24, 1835; was elected to the town board in 1836; ◆ carpenter and builder, 74 Lake St. [Deodat is also listed as carpenter with A.D. Taylor]; Mary died in 1844; in 1845 he married Mary Grovan; served as alderman in 1853; in 1885 his residence was at 398 West Taylor St. [12,

245, 268, 505]

Taylor, A.W. arrived in 1831; served under Capt. G. Kercheval in the Chicago company during the Black Hawk War in 1832; subscribed to the *Chicago Democrat* in November 1833. [12, 351]

Taylor, Charles A. brother of Anson and Augustin; initially a tailor by trade; following his brother Anson, he arrived from Connecticut in June 1832 via Detroit by wagon with his wife Mary and Mary's sister Julia Willcox, then a little girl. James Kinzie's Wolf Tavern was available at that time, and they leased or ran the business for about one year, "neat and orderly"; with Anson built the floating log bridge across the south branch at Randolph Street later that summer; in April 1833 his name was on the petition by Catholic citizens to Bishop Rosati of St. Louis asking that a priest be assigned to them; later that year Charles and Mary chose to become charter members of the first Presbyterian church under Reverend Porter; voted in the election of the first town board on Aug. 10, 1833; entered into a construction partnership with Major Handy and in 1834 built a house on the corner of Canal and Madison streets, but by March the partnership was dissolved as per notice in the *Chicago Democrat* (March 18); submitted a deposition in regard to wharfing privileges on Nov. 24, 1835, and later that year filed a claim for privileges for lot 3, block 18; prior to 1836 acquired the western half of the SW quarter of Section 4 of Township 39 N, according to Andreas, *History of Chicago*, pp. 112-113; ✦ tailor, Clark Street; died in TX in 1867; in 1885 his widow lived at 199 S Peoria St., Chicago. [Mary was a sister of Orlando Willcox, later a U.S. general, who, as a child, visited Chicago repeatedly and occasionally attended Reverend Porter's Sunday school; an article in the *Chicago Tribune* of Sept. 20, 1903, is compiled from Mary's diary and vividly depicts the family's experiences on the road to Chicago and in the early village.] [12, 357, 654, 728]

Taylor, Daniel see Taylor, William Hartt.

Taylor, Elias employed as clerk by W.H. Wallace in 1826 and 1827.

Taylor, Col. Edmund Dick (1802-1891) born in Virginia; had served in the Black Hawk War at the rank of colonel; arrived in April 1835 with the appointment as receiver of public moneys for the U.S. Land Office, working out of Thomas Cook's store after June 1 on Lake Street; was on the first board of directors of the branch of the State Bank of Illinois that opened in Chicago in December 1835; in 1837 became active in promoting plans for the Galena & Chicago Union Railroad; ✦ Taylor, Col. Edmund D., Taylor, [Josiah S.] Breese & Co., dry goods, &c., Lake Street near Clark; before 1885 moved to Mendota, IL, but died in Chicago in 1891. [12, 37]

Taylor, Francis (1822-1903) son of [see] Francis H. and Louisa; came with his parents to Wolf Point in 1833; ✦ tailor, Francis H. Taylor; married Sarah Conally.

Taylor, Francis Horace (1797-1889) arrived from Connecticut in 1833; had married Louisa Plantade in 1818; was elected to the city board of trustees at the first city election in 1837; ✦ tailor, Wolf Point [until 1863]; tailors George H. and Charles H. Taylor are also listed with Francis H. Taylor in 1839; before 1885 had moved to Niles, MI, where he died. [12, 351]

Taylor, Henry arrived in 1833. [351]

Taylor, L.D. born c.1820 in Hartfort, CT; relative of the brothers Anson, Charles, and Augustin; came in June 1834; ✦ at Augustin D. Taylor's [carpenter]; still lived in Chicago in 1879. [12]

Taylor, Solomon arrived from Connecticut in 1833; ✦ boot- and shoemaker, Lake Street; his wife Lucy Ann died in 1844, aged 39. [351]

Taylor, William subscribed to the *Chicago Democrat* in November 1833; listed as owner (prior to 1836) of 80 acres land in Section 28, Township 39, as seen in Andreas, *History of Chicago*, pp. 112-113; as per notice in the *Chicago Democrat* of Jan 28, 1834, he offered hay for sale, "3 miles south";

a William Taylor is listed as compositor at the *Daily American* office in 1839. [12]

Taylor, William Hartt born in Newport, CT; arrived in June 1834; lived at the SE corner of Wabash Avenue and [Congress Street] as a shoe merchant; in the Sept. 9, 1835, *Chicago Democrat* he offered "STEADY EMPLOYMENT and Good Wages" to eight good journeymen boot- and shoemakers; in November was elected trustee of the first Presbyterian church; was active in the volunteer fire department in 1837; ✦ listed with Daniel Taylor, boot and shoemaker, 120 Lake St.; in 1857 he and his wife were still active church members; later moved to Brookline, MA. [12]

Taylor, W.W. arrived from New York in 1834; still living in Chicago by 1879. [12, 351]

teachers for Chicago's earliest schoolteachers, see entries under Robert A. Forsyth (1810); William L. Cox (1816); Elvira and Steven R. Forbes (1830); Mr. Foot (1831); John Watkins (1832); Eliza Chappel (1833); Mary Barrows (1834); Elizabeth Beach (1834); Granville T. Sprout (1833); George Davis (1833); Dr. Henry Van der Bogart (1834); Thomas Wright (1834); Sally L. Warren (1834); George Davis (1834/1835); Ruth Leavenworth (1835); Samuel C. Bennett (1835); and James McClellan (1835).

Taken Up

BY William Taylor, living in Cook county, Ill. a yellowish brindle OX, some light colour in the face and on the belly, right horn a little topped, right ear cropped, also the under ride of the left ear cropped and a slit in the same; supposed to be about six years old: appraised by Thomas Hoyt, M. D. Harmon, and Henry Walton, to eighteen dollars, before Isaac Harmon, a Justice of the Peace for said county and state.

Attest—RICH'D. I. HAMILTON, *Clerk Com. Cm Cook co. Ill.*

1

teal, blue-winged this small ducklike bird with powder-blue wing patches is a fairly common summer resident in Illinois, but was in greater abundance in earlier days, according to reports not unlike the one by Lt. J.G. Furman of June 13, 1830, reprinted in Hurlbut's *Chicago Antiquities*. [64, 357]

Tecumseh (1774-1813) Ohio born; great Shawnee chief who spent much time in his life traveling between Indian tribes of the Midwest to attain his goal of a grand Indian confederacy, formed to halt the relentless advance of white settlers into Indian lands; he denounced the Treaty of Fort Wayne; contemporary and associate of Little Turtle, Shabonna, and Billy Caldwell; was half brother of Temskwatawa, also called "The Prophet"; reported John Kinzie's attempts to win Indian allies to the American side, resulting in the arrest of Kinzie for the capital crime of treason, because in 1813 Kinzie was still a British subject and officer of the British Indian department. Tecumseh died on Oct. 5, 1813, in battle against General Harrison at the Thames River, Ontario. Also see Tippecanoe, Battle

TECUMSEH

of. [12, 212, 609]

Telegraph schooner, built in 1830 by Capt. Joseph Napier on the bank of the Ashtabula River in Ohio and used in 1831 to transport Joseph and his brother John, their families, P.F.W. Peck, Lyman Butterfield, Harry T. Wilson, and others to Chicago, arriving on July 15; the schooner was then sold and the passengers journeyed W to stake claims or settle along the Du Page River.

temperance a Chicago Temperance Society existed by 1832 and met at Reverend Walker's log cabin at the Point, but the exact date of its organization is not recorded. Carpenter in 1832 wrote and circulated the first "total abstinence pledge"; a record of a meeting on Jan. 30, 1834, exists and reveals that Dr. Temple was president, Dr. Goodhue vice president, Philo Carpenter secretary and treasurer, and the following were the additional members of the executive committee: Capt. D. Wilcox (USA), Mr. M.D. Harmon, Dr. H. Van der Bogart, and Lt. J.L. Thompson (USA). Strong feelings concerning the alcohol issue [specifically the selling of liquor to the Indians] had already appeared very early, playing a role in the conflict between John Kinzie and Capt. John Whistler that led to Whistler's transfer in 1810; illegal sales of whisky to the Indians caused the Indian agent at Chicago to direct James Kinzie to close his business at Milwaukee in 1821; Alexander Doyle, justice of the peace in Peoria with jurisdiction over Chicago, was intent on enforcing the liquor laws, and in 1829 he cited James Kinzie for selling one pint of whiskey without a license. Tavern licenses were first issued in 1829, the first one granted to Archibald Clybourne and Samuel Miller on May 2, 1829. The temperance issue would detonate with the "lager riots" in 1855 under Mayor Levi Boone. [184]

Temple Building the two-story structure, built through the efforts of Dr. John T. Temple; located at the SE corner of Franklin and South Water streets, opened in 1834; the upper floor was used mainly for religious services (Baptists), the lower

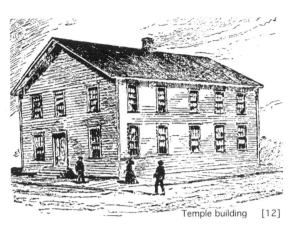

Temple building [12]

for school activities; also accommodated J.D. Caton's law office and Dr. Brainard's medical office.

Temple, John Taylor, M.D. (1804-1877) native of Virginia, medical degree from the University of Maryland in 1824, practitioner of homeopathic medicine who arrived on July 4, 1833, with his wife Elizabeth [née Staughton, 1824] and four children; became a precinct elector and voted for the incorporation of the town at a meeting late in July; in August he was one of the "Qualified Electors" who voted to incorporate the town [for a copy of that meeting's report, see entry on incorporation]; was on the voting list for the first town board on Aug. 10; built a substantial frame house on the corner of Wells and Lake streets as his residence, and an office on the SW corner of Franklin and South Water streets He had come to Chicago with a contract from the U.S. postmaster general to carry the mail between Chicago and Fort Howard at Green Bay; the route was soon discontinued by governmental order, and he was given the route between Chicago and Ottawa; imported for this purpose an elegant post-carriage from Detroit, and on Jan. 1, 1834, made the first coach trip past Laughton's Tavern on the "high prairie" Ottawa Trail over Brush Hill (elevation with heavy growth of scrub oak, highest point W of the fort) via

JOHN TAYLOR TEMPLE, M.D. [137]

Walker's Grove, taking attorney J.D. Caton along; later that spring the service was taken over by Winters, Mills & Co. On Jan. 12, 1834, Elizabeth Temple was baptized by Reverend Freeman in Lake Michigan near the foot of Randolph Street, remembered as ★★★ **Chicago's 1st** lake baptism, and the family arrived for the occasion in the above mentioned stagecoach. In 1834, the Temple children attended school under the Miss Eliza Chappel and the "Temple Building" (see previous entry) was completed; on Sept. 10 that year an ad in the *Chicago Democrat* announced a partnered medical practice between John and his younger brother, Peter; John co-owned in 1834 with Bronson and Sedgwick a major portion of real estate in Section 9, Township 39, and under his own name purchased lots in blocks 20 and 40 [see map on page 44] from the government and from John S.C. Hogan. The doctor was very active in organizing the First Baptist Church, was a member of the

school board, petitioned for wharfing privileges, became treasurer of the Chicago Bible Society and vice president of the Lyceum, was a member of the first Board of Health in 1835, and a trustee of Rush Medical School in 1837; ✦ 218 Lake St. Dr. Temple moved to Galena in 1842, then to St. Louis where he assisted in the founding of the St. Louis School of Osteopathy; died there on Feb. 24, 1877. Lenora Maria, his daughter and age 10 when the family came to Chicago, left an eyewitness account of the 1835 Indian war dance, as well as an account of her own lakeshore baptism [for her accounts see Hoyne, Lenora Maria Temple]; ➡ Temple Street (1300 W) was named after him, but renamed N Troop Street. [12, 28]

Temple Mound Period   see Hopewell culture.

Temple, Peter, M.D.   (1812-1889) from Virginia; arrived in 1834 and announced in the *Chicago Democrat* of July 7, his intention to practice dentistry on Franklin Street, near Lake Street, adjacent to Dr. John T. Temple's office; in August that year became co-partner with [his brother] Dr. Temple; married Lucy Welford Mathews on Jan. 1, 1835; ✦ real estate agent, block 17, School Section; unsuccessful in real estate, he became a practitoner of homeopathy; later moved to Lexington, MO; died on Mar. 18, 1889. [12, 351]

Temskwatawa   Shawnee name of "the Prophet"; also Elkswatawa; see Prophet, The.

Territory of Illinois   see Illinois Territory.

Territory of Indiana   see Indiana Territory.

Tessier, —   pilot and survivor of La Salle's ill-fated Texas expedition; was a member of the group with Henri Joutel that reached Chicago on Sept. 25, 1687, on their way from Fort St. Louis (Starved Rock) to Canada.

Tessier, —   a pilot and member of the ill-fated 1684 La Salle expedition to the mouth of the Mississippi River which, due to La Salle's error, ended in Spanish Texas. After La Salle's death, Tessier was one of the group of six who, led by Joutel, reached Chicago by overland route on Sept. 25, 1687, en

route to Canada. [519, 611]

Teuto   original name of the [Elmhurst-Addison] settlement, derived from the preponderance of German immigrants.

Teuto Community Church   formed in 1834 at Dunklee's Grove, near Addison, by Lutheran German immigrants; first led in worship by a lay preacher, Friedrich Buchholz, and from 1838 on by its first minister, Ludwig Cachand-Ervendberg.

Thaumur de la Source, Abeé Dominique Antoine a priest within the *Séminaire des Étrangères* who in April 1700 returned to Chicago with Monseigneur de Montigny from the Louisiana mission; left a letter describing the experience, published by Shea in 1861; had been a student of Father Charlevoix in Quebec, and was ordained there; he is known to have lived at Cahokia in 1721.

theatre   the pioneer village of Chicago had no established place of regular theatrical entertainment until Harry Isherwood and Alexander McKenzie opened a theatre in the Sauganash Hotel in October 1837, and in 1838 created the [see] Rialto theatre on the W side of Dearborn Street, between South Water and Lake streets Prior to 1837, there were only offered occasional shows by traveling entertainers in improvised quarters; one of these was a Mr. Bowers, who called himself *Professeur de Tours Amusant*, who advertised in the *Chicago Democrat* a performance for the date of Monday, Feb. 24, 1834, at Dexter Graves' boarding house; a second delightful performance followed on June 11 given by another ventriloquist, a Mr. Kenworthy. Otherwise, Charles Cleaver reports that "the store keepers played checkers while waiting for customers, and, after closing played cards. Those religiously inclined went to prayer meeting at least once a week, and Mark Beaubien played the fiddle at the Sauganash Hotel for those who wished to dance." [482]

Thèvenot, Melchisédech   (1620-1692) French scholar and author, chronicling French explorations and discoveries, among them Jolliet's and Father

Marquette's voyage; introduced the word *Michigan*; see next item and Bibliography. [12, 657]

Thèvenot's map   first printed ✳ map of the Mississippi River, entitled *Carte de la découverte faite l'an 1673*, published in 1681 in *Recueil de Voyages*. This map presents the territory between the southern end of Lake Michigan and the Mississippi and depicts in surprising and accurate detail the Chicago River with south branch, the Des Plaines River, and the portage with [Mud Lake] between them. Some historians believe that Thèvenot's map was derived from two Jesuit ✳ maps [*Manitoumie* I, II; c.1674; Bibliothèque Nationale, Paris] that coalesced Jolliet-Marquette cognizance and were taken to Paris with *Jesuit Relations* to be examined and re-presented; the composite map was engraved by Liebaux and included within *Recueil de Voyages*.

Thibeaut, Joseph   also Thibaut; voted in elections on July 24 and Aug. 2, 1830; his wife's name was de Charlotte; a son, also named Joseph, was baptized on Oct. 18, 1830, by Father Badin.

Thiberge, Jean   one of five *voyageurs* who traveled with Father Marquette and Jolliet to the Mississippi and the Chicago site in 1673.

Thomas, Frederick   English druggist from New York, opened Chicago's fourth drugstore in June 1835 on South Water Street, between Dearborn and Clark—the Chicago New Drug, Medicine, Paint, and Oil Store; among the advertised powders, pills, salts, waters, and drops was Thomas' Tincture for Augue and Fever at 50 cents per bottle, and "Physicians' Prescriptions and Family Recipes accurately dispensed"; also included was the availability of "Bleeding, Leeching and Teeth Drawing," thereby making him ★★★ **Chicago's 1st** barbersurgeon; later on Aug. 8 he entered the following ad in the *Chicago American*: "Any information respecting on Henry Thomas, an Englishman by birth (two years since following the mercantile trade as clerk, in Louisville, KY) will be thankfully received by his anxious brother." On Nov. 25, he was appointed to the executive committee of the

Chicago Bible Society; in January 1836 entered into a partnership with Thomas Jenkins, who had a general store next door, and the new firm advertised as Jenkins & Thomas; two months later the partnership was dissolved, and Jenkins succeeded to the entire business under the new name, Chicago New Drug and Medicine Store. [221]

Thomas Hart   schooner from Buffalo, called at Chicago on July 9, 1834, with merchandise under Captain McUmber; called again on Sep.14, 1835, under Captain White, coming from Oswego, NY; wrecked on Lake Ontario in 1842. [48]

Thomas Jefferson   built at Erie, PA, in 1834; with 150 horse power, the 428-ton steamboat from Buffalo called at Chicago on June 14, 1835, with merchandise and passengers under Captain Wilkins, then left for Green Bay. [48]

Thomas Jefferson   schooner under Captain Briggs, called at Chicago on Oct. 2, 1835, coming from Green Bay.

Thomas, Jesse B.   Speaker of the House of the Indiana Territory in 1808, when Illinois country was part of that territory; when elected to Congress he campaigned for and achieved a separate Territory of Illinois, effective March 3, 1809; in 1818 he presided at the convention that drafted Illinois' first state constitution. [12]

Thomas, Robert and William   children by this name, probably siblings, were enrolled as grade school students in the class taught by [see] John Watkins in December 1835. Names of corresponding parents were not recorded. [728]

Thompson & Wells   real estate firm prominent during the 1835-36 land boom.

Thompson, Lt. Enoch   stationed at Fort Dearborn in 1830 and voted in the Peoria County election for justice of the peace on Nov. 25 of that year; purchased from Benjamin Harris lot 6 in block 8, which in 1830 had belonged to Edward Keyes [see map on page 44]; on Nov. 21, 1835, submitted a petition for wharfing privileges. [351]

Thompson, James   came to Kaskaskia from SC in 1814; skillful surveyor and prominent local politician in Randolph County, IL; canal surveyor for the Illinois & Michigan Canal Commission who, on Aug. 4, 1830, completed a ✳ plat of Chicago (a 267-acre portion of Section 9, Township 39, Range 14 E of the third principal meridian, a system of surveying governed by the [see] Federal Land Ordinance of 1785). The map was lithographed in St. Louis. This was the first effort to give shape and outline to the small settlement and established the foundation for legal titles to Chicago real estate; in the process Thompson gave name to many of the downtown streets, including Randolph Street, which he named in honor of his home county. The area mapped was bound by what is now Kinzie Street on the N, State Street on the E, Madison Street on the S, and DesPlaines Street on the W, but at the time neither State, Madison, nor DesPlaines streets were named, and it should be realized that until much later in the 1830s the actual settlement was considerably smaller than the area covered by the plat; the original plat in the Recorder's Office was destroyed by the 1871 fire, but copies are within the Chicago Historical Society. The task completed, he returned home and later became a judge. [12, 164, 351, 704]

Thompson, Lt. James L.   born in TN; Fifth Infantry; member of the Fort Dearborn garrison from June 20, 1833, until April of 1836; subscribed to the *Chicago Democrat* in November 1833; died by drowning on June 21, 1851. [12]

Thompson, John   first postmaster at [Lisle]; set up the post office in a room of his house in 1834; an uncollected letter is listed in the Jan. 1, 1834, *Chicago Democrat*.

Thompson, Oliver H.   came from Vermont in 1835 and on Nov. 21 submitted a claim for wharfing privileges; a notice in the Dec. 2 *Chicago Democrat* reveals his copartnership with A. Garrett and the Brown brothers, now [see] Garrett, Thompson, Brown & Co.; in 1838 his name was on the petition of citizens opposed to granting a license for a permanent theatre at the Rialto; ✦ dry goods and groceries, 102 Lake St., and an alder-

man; married Emma Ann Heartt in 1840. [12, 351]

Thompson, Robert   arrived in 1831 and served as a member of the Chicago company in the Black Hawk War of 1832 under Capt. Gholson Kercheval. [12, 351, 714]

Thompson, Lt. Seth   from Ohio; second in command at Fort Dearborn under Captain Heald until his death from a brief febrile illness on March 4, 1811; the vacancy was filled by Lieutenant Helm in June 1811.

Thompson plat   see Thompson, James.

Thorn, Platt   subscribed to the *Chicago Democrat* in November 1833.

Thornton, William F.   (1789-1873) native of Virginia; canal commissioner, appointed to a new board in 1836 together with Gurdon S. Hubbard and William B. Archer. [12, 351]

Thrall, Edward L.   subscribed to the *Chicago Democrat* in November 1833; advertised in the paper on May 28, 1834, that he had "cloths, cassimere and readymade clothing" for sale on South Water Street, at what used to be Charles Taylor's stand.

Thurston, John Gates   (1794-1873) a mercantile business man who traveled overland from Lancaster, MA, to Chicago in 1836, with his brother-in-law George Lee, and kept a journal that was published only in 1971. [Although slightly beyond the time frame, the editors have included excerpts on subjects that were still reflecting pre-1836 conditions; see below.] [662]

Chicago. This place has become one of considerable importance. Its growth has been of little more than three years standing, and it contains three or four thousand inhabitants and is destined to become a place of great trade in the way of supplying the vast country beyond it on the northwestern lakes and frontier. It is now the grand focus for speculators from all parts of [the] union who resort here to make sale of their lands and newly manufactured towns which are made to appear like cities on paper, tho there is scarcely a house in them. This making of cities is a great trade here,

and what cannot be sold at auction or at private sale in this state are sent to the New York or other Eastern markets to gull the Yankees with. Altho there is enough lotted and now in market which when built upon will hold a population of fifty millions of people; yet the trade is still in a flourishing state and will continue so as long as there can be fools enough found to purchase. This bubble however must burst and probably soon. ✧ There is a remnant of several tribes of Indians, mostly Winnebagoes, still remaining in this place who are to remove beyond the Mississippi this fall. They are about forty in number. They inhabit a building nearly in front of the hotel where I am staying, which has enabled me to witness many of their sports, such as foot races, horse races, card playing, dances, &c. There is a large piece of vacant ground in the rear of the building in which their sports are kept up daily. Today I witnessed one such as I have never heard of before, which was that of making two horses fight. This was done by surrounding them with a crowd so dense that they could not break through the ring and then compelling them to fight by goading them with pikes, clubs, and all manner of missiles. The poor animals being beset in this manner, to which was added the horrid shouts and yells of the Indians, fought at times with desperation for near two hours till they were wholly exhausted. They were covered with blood and gashes from head to foot, and the kicks and bites which they alternately received. From the desperation with which they fought one would have thought [it] would have demolished them both long before they gave up the fight. It was judged by the spectators they would never recover from the bruises they received, but the Indians drove them out on the prairie and that was the last I saw of them. Never did I witness any sport that was so universally enjoyed as this seemed to be, not only by the men but squaws, children, and all were delighted beyond measure.

Thwaites, Reuben Gold, LL.D.   (1853-1913) born in Massachusetts; historian, journalist, author; authority on western history and editor of the *Wisconsin State Historical Journal*; was a major contributor to our knowledge of Chicago history; see Bibliography. [37, 665-9]

Tiger   the 62-ton schooner that brought [see] Factor Jacob Varnum, his bride, and factory goods from Mackinac to Fort Dearborn on Sept. 13, 1816. [48]

timothy   *Phleum pratense*; a perennial grass species introduced from Europe by early American settlers and used as a hay crop for livestock. In June 1834, John H. Kinzie advertised "Timothy and Clover Seed" for sale in several issues of the *Chicago Democrat*, and again in the Aug. 15, 1835, *Chicago American*; in the Nov. 11, 1835, *Chicago Democrat* Jones, King & Co. advertised 40 bushels of the best quality timothy seed. [information derived from Ed Lace, August 1996].

Tinkham, Roland   a relative of Gurdon S. Hubbard and Henry Raymond Hamilton who, in the summer of 1831, traveled from Massachusetts to St. Louis by way of Chicago; his letters describing the experience are quoted in Hamilton's book *The Epic of Chicago*; for excerpts, see below; also see malaria and Hubbard, Gurdon S.

Arrived at Chicago, having been nearly five days making the journey from St. Joseph. For three or for days I was near being sick in consequence of fatigue and exposure. Chicago is a very small place compared to what I expected; it was the fort and garrison that gave it importance, but since the troops have been removed to Green Bay it is rather a dull place. Here we saw two Indians to one white man. They are almost all Pottawatomies and still own a very extensive tract of country, from Michigan to the Mississippi. Peres La Clerc is here,– the brave, as he is called, who fired the first shot at the massacre of Fort Dearborn, at Chicago. His manhood is nearly departed. His proud spirit was not tamed by his foes, but by his whiskey. ❖ Chicago is on three points where the river forks, about one half mile from the lake. The country on every side is low land prairie, and while we were there it was very wet all around. There is not a frame building in the place, tho' several are covered with clapboard. Cottonwood, which is only a species of

Balm-of-Gilead, grows on the streams and wet places of Chicago. There is no road from this place except such as follow Indian trails. ... ❖ We spent 11 days in Chicago,– hunted, fished, walked about, looked at Indians and squaws and French; went to one court, a curious affair, but the story is long, and I have no time to tell it.

Tinley-Valparaiso terminal moraine   a system of gravel and clay hills left behind 15,000 years ago by the retreating Wisconsin glacier that scooped out Lake Michigan's lake bed; it now surrounds, at some distance, the southern end of Lake Michigan.

Tippecanoe, Battle of   (Nov. 7, 1811) a temporary setback for the Indian confederacy under Tecumseh and The Prophet, who had spent years trying to organize a united front against the relentless advance of white settlers into Indian territory. The battle took place on Tippecanoe Creek near the large Indian village Prophetstown, 150 miles N of Vincennes; General Harrison, commanding c.1,000 well trained soldiers, while victoriously destroying the village, fumbled his attack and suffered nearly 25 percent casualties among his men; he had to wearily retreat to Fort Harrison. Most Indians continued their aggressive stance and were soon to join the British in the War of 1812. [152]

Tippecanoe Hall   a large warehouse on the NE corner of Kinzie and Wolcott [State] streets, acquiring the name during the presidential campaign of 1840 as a place for political meetings, and in 1847 became the first general hospital in Chicago under the leadership of Dr. Brainard; however, it already existed in 1834, when the space served as the first place of worship for the budding Episcopal congregation under Reverend Hallam.

tippling house   drinking establishment; an ordinance was passed on Sept. 1, 1834, providing for a fine of $5 for keeping a tippling house or grocery open on Sunday.

Tipton, John   (1786-1839) Indiana surveyor and

legislator who in 1821 visited Chicago and Fort Dearborn and described what he saw in his journal, *Surveying line between Indiana and Illinois, 1821.* [670]

Todd, John   (1750-1782) born in Montgomery County, PA; was appointed county-lieutenant or commandant of "Illinois County" by Patrick Henry, the governor of Virginia on Dec. 12, 1778, when Illinois was part of that state; arrived at Kaskaskia in May of 1779 to assume office, but remained in Illinois only until the end of the year, asking to be relieved early of his office. With his departure, and with the Virginia Act of 1778 that had established the county soon expiring, the government situation became anomalous, and a time of civil anarchy began for Illinois that lasted until 1790, when Illinois civil jurisdictions were organized as part of the new Northwest Territory of the United States; ➡ Todd Street (500W).

Tolleston beach   a geological term, designating the lowest of a series of three major concentric dune ridges left behind by the shore of glacial Lake Michigan when its level was higher than today; they are still visible in the landscape today. During the Tolleston phase, less than 8,000 years ago, the lake was 20 feet higher than today. Each of the ridges, where undisturbed by human activity, now reflects its age by having its own characteristic set of plants (cottonwood, sand cherries, junipers) and animals. Indians and early settlers journeying between Fort Dearborn and Michigan City would follow a trail on top of this ridge to avoid the low swampy places; Joseph Bailly's property was on the Tolleston ridge. For the other, higher ridges, see Calumet beach and Glenwood beach.

Tolleston phase   see Tolleston beach.

tomahawk   hatchet-shaped traditional Indian weapon; those with iron blades were furnished to the Indians in large numbers by the fur traders.

Tombien, Jean Baptiste   also Toubien; voted in the election on July 24, 1830.

Tonti, Alphonse de   (1659-1727) younger brother

of Henri de Tonti, and part-owner of Henri's company; accompanied Cadillac to Detroit and assisted in the construction of Fort Pontchartrain du Detroit, becoming the second officer in command of the fort until his death.

Tonti, Henri de   (1650 -1704) Americanized, Henry de Tonty; a Neapolitan in exile, explorer in the service of France, faithful companion to La Salle, who spent 26 years in North America, during which time he came to Chicago on many more occasions than has been recorded by historians. Along the Niagara River in 1678, Tonti directed the construction of [see] *Le Griffon*. In the fall of 1680 Tonti, in the company of Father Membré, passed through the Chicago portage from the Illinois valley to Green Bay (having reached the Illinois River with La Salle by way of the Kankakee portage). On Jan. 7, 1681, Tonti met La Salle at Chicago and together they used the portage on their way to the Mississippi, the mouth of which they reached on April 8, 1681. Tonti had lost his right hand in earlier war action and wore an iron prothesis, greatly admired by the Indians. For the end of December 1685 Tonti recorded in his writings [see Bibliography] a visit to a French fort at Chicago then under the command of Durantaye. Tonti was also with La Salle during the fateful Texas expedition, where the latter was assassinated. Tonti, with a small remnant of the expeditionary force (among them Father Anastasius Douay, Joutel, Jean Cavelier [La Salle's brother], Moranget [La Salle's nephew and godson], and another nephew with the name Cavelier) eventually returned to Canada, passing through Chicago on Sept. 25, 1687. Tonti and François Daupin de La Forêt built Fort St. Louis on the Illinois River in 1690-91, which Tonti maintained in subsequent years. Tonti was a partner of La Forêt and Accault in a Chicago trading post, managed for them by Pierre de Liette, Tonti's cousin, from 1697 to c.1702. In 1699, Tonti guided the St. Cosme party when it passed through Chicago. In 1700, a royal

HERNRI DE TONTI [259]

decree obliged Tonti to go to Louisiana, where he rendered signal services to Captain d'Iberville. Tonti died during a yellow fever epidemic in La Mobile; named after him are the ▲ Henry DeTonty Woods, a portion of the Palos Division of the Cook County Forest Preserve District [see Monuments]; ➡ Tonty Avenue (6150W). [12, 196, 259, 430 503, 672-5]

Topenebe   also To-pay-nah-bay and Sits Quietly; Potawatomi chief at St. Joseph; brother of Kawke-mee, wife of St. Joseph trader William Burnett; fraternal uncle of J.B. Chandonnais; a friend of the Kinzies and the Healds, whom he helped survive the 1812 massacre, and yet pro-British. Topenebe went to Washington in the fall of 1834 and in the company of Pokagon and Waubansee, protested against ratification of the Treaty of Chicago of 1833, claiming that Billy Caldwell, Alexander Robinson and Joseph LaFramboise had not represented them well in the treaty negotiations. [226]

Topographical Engineers   earlier name for the U.S. Army [see] Corps of Engineers.

Tordesillas, Treaty of   see Treaties.

town crier   village employee in charge of public announcements; in 1833 the job was held by George White, a black man with a voice "the volume of a fog-horn."

township, survey   six mile square parcels of land marked off by government surveyors in accordance with the [see] Federal Land Ordinance of 1785; each township is subdivided into 36 numbered sections, each section containing 640 acres; these survey townships are not identical with the civic townships organized later. Chicago's downtown area is in Township 39. Also see Fielding's map on page 142.

Town Trustees   see Chicago Town Trustees.

Tracy   53-ton United States military schooner built in 1802 at the River Rouge shipyard, named after Connecticut's Senator Uriah Tracy; the *Tracy*, with Josiah R. Dorr as its master, carried Captain Whistler and his family to Chicago in 1803, while the soldiers took the land route from Detroit, to begin the task of building Fort Dearborn; in 1809 the ship struck a reef in Lake Erie and sank. The *Tracy* in 1803 was not the first commercial sailing vessel

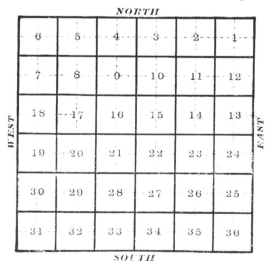

TOWNSHIP GRID
IN ACCORDANCE WITH THE U.S. LAND ORDINANCE OF 1785

to reach Chicago, as is sometimes stated; preserved letters of the St. Joseph trader William Burnett reveal that as early as 1786 it was not unusual for sailing ships from Mackinac to stop at Chicago, though most commerce along the shores of Lake Michigan was carried out by canoe or *bateau*.

trade goods many different items appealed to the Indians and were therefore imported from the East or from Europe in massive quantities and exchanged for furs, the latter being the only item of interest to the white trader; recorded inventories of Chicago traders provides an idea of the type of merchandise. The trader John Kinzie was a trained silversmith and, with specialized tools within his smithy, supplied the Indians with silver ornaments; in 1806 one of his silver brooches was accessible for "six rats" [muskrats] and "2 large silver crosses" sold for $7.50. On an American Fur Co. invoice for goods sent to James Kinzie at Chicago from Michilimackinac in September 1821, items listed included various kinds of cord, thread, flannel, cotton and ribbon, scissors, sleigh bells, iron jews'-harps, foolscap paper, double bolt padlocks, hoes, and kettles of tin, brass, and copper. When William Wallace reordered stock in September 1826, goods included playing cards, shot, powder, snuff, tobacco, whiskey, animal traps, groceries, pork, cooking utensils, and tools; after his death at Hardscrabble in March 1827 following a short illness, his official inventory contained, apart from the pelts collected, the additional items: 168 gallons of highwines, 10 ivory combs, 23 tomahawks, 800 gun flints, Indian mirrors, scalping knives, fox tail feathers, hawkbells, brass thimbles, verdigris, 32 black silk handkerchiefs, mourning shawls, chintz shawls, arm bands and wristbands in large and small sizes, headbands, five different sizes of brooches, 1,375 pair of earbobs, blankets, Indian awls, and needles. For the types of furs received from the Indians in return, see fur trade. [544]

Trader Indians term designating former residents of the St. Joseph River valley who, in 1780 and following the destruction of Fort St. Joseph in the Revolutionary War, fled to the Deep River, the major tributary of the Calumet River in Indiana; they included several Potawatomi, Ottawa, and Chippewa bands.

Traders' Brigades units of the mobile sales force of the American Fur Co., organized by personnel manager William Matthews; each brigade consisted of 5-20 *bateaux*; each *bateau* had four oarsmen, a steersman, and a capacity of six tons. From the company's headquarters at Mackinac the brigades would fan out into the wilderness to service the remote trading posts.

Trail Creek see Michigan City.

Trail Creek Trail connecting the Sauk Trail with the Lake Shore Trail between [La Porte and Michigan City], paralleling Trail Creek.

trails for early trails of the Chicago area, see Indian trails.

Traveler's Home and Western Stage House see Wolf Point Tavern.

treaties listed below in chronological order are the treaties between governments, or with Indian nations, that significantly affected the Chicago area. [152, 387]

1494 – Tordesillas treaty signed on June 7, 1494, between Spain and Portugal, and sanctioned by Pope Alexander VI; settled conflicts arising from the discoveries of Columbus' first voyage; gave Spain exclusive rights to a vast region that included all of the still unknown North American continent in return for a commitment to convert the heathens. Based on this treaty, the Chicago region may be said to to have been a Spanish domain when European colonialization of the New World began. [679]

1632 – St. Germain treaty signed on March 29; one of several successive attempts to settle conflicting interests of France and England with regard to the North American continent; in this treaty Canada is ceded to the French crown.

1763 – Paris treaty concluded between England and France on Feb. 10, 1763, ending the French and Indian War. France ceded all of Canada to Britain, except that Britain granted France limited fishing rights and the small islands of St. Pierre and Miquelon; in the south, Britain obtained Louisiana as far west as the Mississippi from France, and Florida from Spain.

1783 – Paris treaty established the independence of the United States from England on Sept. 3, 1783, as a result of the American Revolution. Secondary participants at the treaty negotiations were France and Spain; Spain demanded Illinois, based in part on the "conquest" of Fort St. Joseph in 1781, but received Florida.

1794 – London (Jay's Treaty) negotiated between the United States (represented by Chief Justice John Jay) and Great Britain, and signed on Nov. 19. The treaty adjusted a group of serious Anglo-American issues arising out of the Definitive Treaty of Peace of 1783 as well as disagreements that developed subsequently. Some of these problems directly affected the Chicago area, such as Great Britain's refusal to evacuate six controlling frontier posts in United States territory, and the active intrigue by clandestine British Indian agents against the United States with the western Indian tribes. It is believed by some historians that the Chicago trader and farmer Point de Sable may have been one of those agents. Great Britain agreed to evacuate all posts by June 1, 1796. Point de Sable moved west in 1800. [152, 649]

1795 – Greenville hopelessly defeated by Gen. Anthony Wayne at the battle of Fallen Timbers in 1794, various Indian tribes [Wyandot, Delaware, Shawnee, Ottawa, Chippewa, Potawatomi, Miami, Eel River, Wea, Kickapoo, Piankashaw, Kaskaskia], through their representatives, met with Wayne at Greenville [Ohio] and agreed to substantial territorial cessions in southern and western Ohio, some land in southeastern Indiana, small tracts around Michilimackinac in Michigan, and "one piece of land, six miles square at or near the mouth of the

Chicago River, emptying into the southwest end of Lake Michigan, where a fort formerly stood" [the area now bordered, roughly, by the lakeshore on the E, Cicero Avenue on the W, Fullerton Avenue on the N, and 31st Avenue on the S]. Treaty negotiations began on June 16, 1795, and ended on Aug. 10, becoming the first of a long series of treaties by which the Indian title to the northwestern land was transferred to the United States. [625]

1795 – San Lorenzo concluded on Oct. 27, the treaty between the United States and Spain settled Florida's northern boundary and gave navigation rights on the Mississippi River to the United States, the latter being an essential precondition for Chicago's later founding and growth.

1803 – Fort Wayne June 7, with the Delaware, Shawnee, Miami, Potawatomi, Kaskaskia, Eel River, Wea, and Kickapoo, ceding 2,038,400 acres along the Wabash River near Vincennes for $4,000.

1803 – Vincennes treaty concluded on Aug. 7, with the Kaskaskia, Cahokia, and Mitchigami, ceding for $12,000 a large area in central and southeastern Illinois (8,911,850 acres), comprising approximately half of the present state; other tribes ceded their claims to the same area in the Treaties of Edwardsville in 1817 and 1818.

1804 – St. Louis concluded on Nov. 3; negotiated by Governor Harrison with leaders of the Sauk and Fox tribes, resulting in cession to the government of 14,803,500 acres of land in Missouri, Illinois and southern Wisconsin; the Indians received in return $22,234 and the right to live on the land as long as it was owned by the government. At a later time, this treaty was bitterly denounced as unfair by the Sauk leader Black Hawk, and his defiance led to the Black Hawk War in 1832, in which Fort Dearborn and the surrounding settlement became involved. [12]

1809 – Fort Wayne treaty concluded on Sept. 30 by William Henry Harrison, then governor of Indiana Territory, with the Potawatomi, Delaware, Miami, and the Eel River tribes; it ceded to the United States three tracts of land containing more than 2.5 million acres on the upper Wabash River. The treaty was bitterly denounced by Tecumseh and his followers, and helped precipitate the War of 1812.

1809 – Vincennes concluded on Dec. 9 with the Kickapoo; resulted in government acquisition of 138,240 acres for a $2,700 payment to the Indians.

1816 – St. Louis (*Portage des Sioux*) on Aug. 24 the Chippewa, Ottawa, and Potawatomi chiefs met with a U.S. commission under Governor Edwards of Illinois and ceded to the United States a tract of land, 20 by 70 miles, that extended from Lake Michigan to the Illinois River and included Chicago, the portage, and the area for which construction of a canal between the Great Lakes and the Mississippi River system was proposed; included in the cession was some land in southwestern Wisconsin. The Indians were told that by ceding their land along the Illinois River they, too, would share in the benefits of increased trade when the canal became a reality. As it turned out, they would be ten years gone before even a portion of the project was completed in the mid 1840s. See Capt. John C. Sullivan.

1821 – Chicago treaty negotiated late summer that year and concluded on Aug. 29 near the Kinzie house on the northern bank of the river by commissioner Gov. Lewis Cass and Solomon Sibley with the Potawatomi, Ottawa, and Chippewa; attracted an assemblage of 3,000 natives and procured from the tribes a large tract of land [nearly 5 million acres] of western Michigan territory, extending from the Grand River to the Indiana line, in return for an immediate distribution of merchandise, grants of small parcels of land to certain individuals, government-provided instructions for the Indians in blacksmithing, agriculture, &c. and the assurance of certain annuities in perpetuity. The children of St. Joseph trader William Burnett, Potawatomi *métis*, were among those granted land sections by the government. The treaty cleared the way for the Illinois & Michigan Canal project, and also conveyed to the government the right of way for the construction of the Chicago Road between Detroit and Chicago, which was begun in 1825. The last Indian land in southern Michigan had now been secured, but the territory adjacent to the Chicago site in northern Illinois and southern Wisconsin was still sought. Subagent John Kinzie signed as a witness. [600]

1825 – Prairie du Chien treaty concluded on Aug. 19 with Winnebago, Sioux, Chippewa, Sauk, Fox, Potawatomi, and Iowa; no land was ceded, rather tribal lands boundaries were determined. Gen. William Clark of St. Louis and Gov. Lewis Cass of Detroit were the U.S. commissioners; during the negotiations Alexander Robinson and Billy Caldwell were appointed chiefs by the assembled Indians. Agreements reached at this treaty were soon to be breached by aggressive settlers, precipitating the Winnebago War of 1827.

1827 – Butte des Morts treaty concluded on Aug. 11, Gov. Lewis Cass presiding, formally ending the Winnebago War and settling questions resulting from the Treaty of Prairie du Chien of 1825.

1829 – Prairie du Chien treaty concluded on July 29 with the Chippewa, Ottawa, and Potawatomi, who ceded 5 million acres of territory described as follows: "Beginning on the western shore of Lake Michigan at the northeast corner of the field of Antoine Ouilmette, who lives near Gross Point, about twelve miles north of Chicago; thence running due west to Rock River; thence down said river to where a line drawn due west from the most southern bend of Lake Michigan crosses said river; thence east along said line to the Fox River of the Illinois; thence along the northwestern boundary line of 1816 to Lake Michigan; then northwardly along the western shore of said lake to the place of beginning"; multiple Chicago area residents, past and present, were awarded compensation at this treaty, among them Mrs. Helm, who received $800 "for losses sustained at the time of the capture of Fort Dearborn by the Indians," and $485 went to James Kinzie "for debts owed to him by the Indians"; 2 1/2 sections of land on the Chicago River were awarded to Billy Caldwell; two sections of land on the Des Plaines River to Alexander Robinson; other parcels of land went to Victoire Pothier, Jane Mirandeau, Claude LaFramboise, and Archange Ouilmette and her children. The United States was represented by the commissioners John McNeil, Pierre Menard, and Caleb Atwater; Indian agents Alexander Wolcott and Thomas Forsyth and the subagent John H. Kinzie were present.

1832 – Fort Armstrong (Rock Island) this was the so-called "Black Hawk Purchase," signed on Sept. 15 with the defeated Sauk and Fox, but also with the Winnebago, ceding their remaining homeland in southeastern Wisconsin and northwestern Illinois, as well as a 50-mile-wide strip of land in Iowa along the west bank of the Mississippi. By eliminating the Indian threat to homesteaders on the Illinois prairies, this treaty contributed much to the rapidly increasing stream of newly arriving Easterners at Chicago.

1832 – Camp Tippecanoe treaty concluded on Oct. 20, with the Potawatomi; a large area of land south of Chicago and between Lake Michigan and the Illinois River was ceded to the United States; an annual annuity of $600 was granted to Billy Caldwell, and monetary claims were paid to several Chicagoans who included Gurdon S. Hubbard ($5,573).

1833 – Chicago this treaty occasioned the last and greatest Indian council ever held at Chicago; negotiations between an assembled 6,000 Potawatomi (the so-called United Band of Chippewa, Ottawa, and Potawatomi, represented largely by Billy Caldwell, Alexander Robinson, and Joseph LaFramboise) and U.S. government representatives resulted in the sale of five million acres of Great Lakes land and the relocation to reservations west of the Mississippi of all Indians; in exchange the

tribes received half a million dollars in cash, with an equal amount allocated for annuities to be paid later. Numerous local *métis* received individual annuities and/or land reservations. Debts owed by Indians to white traders were satisfied by the government; thus Robert Stuart, managing director of the American Fur Co., attended to claim compensation for his company amounting to $17,000, allegedly resulting from hostile or fraudulent Indian activities. The associated festivities culminated in a dramatic Indian war dance by 800 braves, described in detail by John D. Caton [for excerpt, see under entry for Caton, John D.; for excerpts of other eyewitness accounts see also entry on Hoyne, Leonora Maria Temple, and that of English traveler Latrobe's, which follows below]. The commissioners for the government, appointed by Secretary of War Lewis Cass, were George B. Porter, governor of Michigan Territory, Thomas Owen, local Indian agent, and William Weatherford, an Illinois politician. The treaty was concluded and signed on Sept. 26 by the three commissioners and by 77 Indian chiefs. All ranking members of the commission, the village and of Fort Dearborn signed as witnesses, among them the interpreters Luther Rice and James Conner, Maj. Geo. Bender, Capt. D. Wilcox, Capt. J.M. Baxley, Lt. L.T. Jamison, Lt. E.K. Smith, Asst. Surgeon P. Maxwell, Asst. Surgeon George F. Turner, Lt. J. Allen, Lt. I.P. Simonton, Robert A. Kinzie, Robert A. Forsyth, and the visiting Daniel Jackson. Thus a major step in the Indian removal program of President Jackson was accomplished, but not everyone was happy. Topenebe and Pokagon, the principal chiefs of the St. Joseph Potawatomi, went to Washington City in the fall of 1834 in the company Waubansee and protested against ratification of the Treaty of Chicago of 1833, claiming that Billy Caldwell, Alexander Robinson, and Joseph LaFramboise had not represented them well in the treaty negotiations. The Indians were first moved in 1835 to a reservation in Clay County, MO, near Fort Leavenworth,

but two years later, because of hostile Missouri settlers, were transported to Council Bluffs, IA. Later, a third removal took them to a reservation in Kansas. In the wake of the treaty, serious charges were made in Congress of the diversion of funds meant as compensation for the Indians; the point was made that Maj. Robert A. Forsyth, a major beneficiary himself and a relative of the Kinzies, was inappropriately allowed by Governor Porter to serve as a member of the committee on claims, and that as a result of this the descendents of John Kinzie and Robert Forsyth, all without Indian ancestry, claimed and were granted large compensations [altogether $42,516; *eds.*] for losses allegedly suffered during the War of 1812 by their parents; and that, if those claims were indeed valid, the payments should not have come out of the funds designated for the Indians. Governor Porter was confronted with these charges by President Jackson, but defended himself successfully and the allocation of funds remained largely as the committee had decided, except that in the end there was not enough money and the Indians suffered further reductions. [Details of this controversy may be found in Milo Quaife's *Documents: The Chicago Treaty of 1833*, in the *Wisconsin Magazine of History* 1, no.1 (1917); *eds.*]

Charles Joseph Latrobe, observing the Treaty of Chicago in 1833:

[September] ... *we had to follow the old Indian trail for a hundred miles round the lower shores of the lake. When within five miles of Chicago, we came to the first Indian encampment. Five thousand Indians were said to be collected round this little upstart village for the prosecution of the Treaty, by which they were to cede their lands in Michigan and Illinois. ❖ I have been in many odd assemblages of my species, but in few, if any, of an equally singular character as with that in the midst of which we spent a week in Chicago. ... We found the village, on our arrival, crowded to excess; and we procured, with great difficulty, a small apartment, comfortless and noisy from its prox-*

imity to others, but quite as good as we could have hoped for. The Potawatomies were were encamped on all sides—on the wide, level prairie beyond the scattered village, beneath the shelter of the low woods which chequered them, on the side of the small river, or to the leeward of the sand hills near the beach of the lake. ... ❖ A preliminary council had been held with the chiefs some days before our arrival. The principal commissioner had opened it, as we learned, by stating that as their great Father in Washington had heard that they wanted to sell their land, he had sent Commissioners to treat with them. The Indians promptly answered, by their organ, 'that their Great Father in Washington must have seen a bad bird which had told him a lie; for, that far from wishing to sell their land, they wished to keep it'. The commissioner, nothing daunted, replied, 'that nevertheless, as they had come together for a council, they must take the matter into consideration.' He then explained to them promptly the wishes and intentions of their Great Father, and asked their opinion thereon. Thus pressed, they looked at the sky, saw a few wandering clouds, and straightway adjourned sine die, as the weather is not clear enough for so solemn a council; ... there seemed no possibility of bringing them to another Council in a hurry. ❖ But how sped the Treaty? you will ask. Day after day passed. It was in vain that the signal gun from the fort gave notice of an assemblage of chiefs at the council fire. Reasons were always found for its delay. One day an influential chief was not in the way; another, the sky looked cloudy, and the Indian never performs any important business except the sky be clear. At length, on the 21st of September, the Pottawatomies resolved to meet the Commissioners. We were politely invited to be present. The council fire was lighted under a spacious open shed on the green meadow on the opposite side of the river from that on which the Fort stood. From the difficulty of getting all together, it was late in the afternoon when they assembled. There might be twenty or thirty chiefs present, seated at the lower end of the enclosure, while the Commissioners, Interpreters, &c., were at the up-

per. The palaver was opened by the principal Commissioner. He requested to know why he and his colleagues were called to the council. An old warrior arose, and in short sentences, generally of five syllables, delivered with a monotonous intonation and rapid utterance, gave answer. His gesticulation was appropriate, but rather violent. Rice, the half-breed interpreter, explained the signification, from time to time, to the audience, and it was seen that the old chief, who had got his lesson, answered one question by proposing another, the sum and substance of his oration being that the assembled chiefs wished to know what was the object of their Great Father in Washington in calling his Red Children together in Chicago! This was amusing enough, after the full explanation given the week before at the opening session, and particularly when it was recollected that they had feasted sumptuously during the interval at the expense of their Great Father; it was not making very encouraging progress. A young chief arose, and spoke vehemently to the same purpose. Hereupon the Commissioner made them a forcible Jacksonian discourse, wherein a good deal which was akin to threat was mingled with exhortations not to play with their Great Father, but to come to an early determination whether they would or would not sell and exchange their territory; and this done, the council was dissolved. One or two tipsy old chiefs raised an occasional disturbance, else matters were concluded with due gravity. ... The glorious light of the setting sun, streaming in under the low roof of the Council-House, fell full on the countenances of the [Commissioner and the whites] as they faced the West, while the pale light of the East hardly lighted up the dark and painted lineaments of the poor Indians, whose souls evidently clave to their birth-right in that quarter. Even though convinced of the necessity of their removal, my heart bled for them in their desolation and decline. Ignorant and degraded as they may have been in their original state, their degradation is now ten-fold after years of intercourse with the whites; and their speedy disappearance from the earth appears as certain as though it were already sealed and ac-

complished. ... In fine, before we quitted Chicago on the 25th, three or four days later, the Treaty with the Pottawatomies was concluded—the Commissioners putting their hands and the assembled chiefs their paws to the same.

From the letter of an eyewitness to the 1833 Treaty, J.B. Turner, written that autumn:

The next day, after the sale [Treaty] had been completed, the place was filled with drunken Indians, in all stages of helplessness, and all wanting to fight. Under the influence of liquor, the Frenchman dances, the Italian sings, the American talks, and the Irishman and Indian want to fight. When dangerously drunk, the squaws would gather about them, throw them down, and sit upon their backs—often an unsteady and rocky seat. Three heavy squaws were sometimes sitting on one squirming, yelling Indian. I became frightened; I had heard how revengeful an Indian was, what little regard he had for his squaws. I thought, when they came to themselves and found their squaws had been sitting on their backs, there would be a terrible massacre and so I told the Indian agent my fears. 'You must be a tenderfoot,' he said. 'An Indian is always grateful to any one who restraines him when he is drunk; but let any of one try it when he is not, and he will follow them as long as he lives to take his revenge.' This proved to be true. When they awoke from their drunken sleep, all was peaceful and quiet.

Tremont House   the first Tremont House was one of the town's "fashionable" hotels, built and run in 1833 by Alanson Sweet, located at the NW corner of Lake and Dearborn; Starr Foot then acquired the establishment and by 1835 it was bought by the Couch brothers; was destroyed by fire on Oct. 27, 1839. The second Tremont House [built on the opposite, SE corner] existed from 1840 to 1849, and a third one was built of brick in 1850; ➡ Tremont Street (5636 S), its course being far from where the Tremont House was located. [12, 357]

Tripp, Robinson   [sometimes listed as Dr. Robinson Tripp, for unknown reasons; eds.] born c.1804 in Vermont; arrived in 1834; active in the Methodist community; ✦ carpenter, 119 Lake St.; in 1885 lived at 1408 Wabash Ave. [12, 351]

Trois Rivières, Canada   Three Rivers; vital early fur trading village on the St. Lawrence River in New France, where Nicollet and Father Marquette spent time and Jolliet was born.

Trois Rivières, IN   see Fort Wayne.

Trowbridge, Charles C.   U.S. Government agent from Detroit, 20 years old when he accompanied as assistant topographer the 1820 Cass expedition, but was not among the detail that reached Chicago that year; in 1822 he did visit Fort Dearborn to prepare for certain services awarded to local Indians in the Chicago Treaty of 1821, and left a description of his visit in a paper read before the Historical Society of Michigan in May 1864, part of which was reprinted in Hurlbut [see Bibliography]. A successful Detroit banker in 1833, he came to the assistance of Major Bender, then commandant of Fort Dearborn and superintendent of harbor construction, when Bender could not locally cash the treasury warrant he had received from the U.S. War Department to pay construction costs. [12, 357]

Trowbridge, Samuel G.   arrived in 1834; served as foreman of the first engine company of the volunteer fire company in 1835 [see petition to the village board of Dec. 16, 1835, entry on firefighting], and probably owner of the [see] Eagle Hotel at that time; in 1836 he became a member of the town board, county treasurer, as well as a charter member of the first Unitarian church; ✦ mail contractor, Clark Street [12, 351]

Trowbridge, William S.   arrived in 1835 as a trained land surveyor; in that year, assisted by Joseph Graves, he surveyed land around the mouth of the Sheboygan River, as recorded by [see] Oliver C. Crocker; participated in the real estate boom at that time and made a modest fortune, then settled at Milwaukee. [12]

trumpeter swan   see swan.

Tukoquenone   see Du Page River.

Tuller, Jonathan Alden   listed prior to 1836 as owner of 80 acres of land in Section 28, Township 39, as per Andreas, *History of Chicago*, pp. 112-113.

turkey vulture   *Cathartes aura*; fairly common migrant in Illinois, arriving in early spring; while rarely seen in Cook County today, these large birds were reported to have nested near Chicago as late as 1854; in 1832 John Calhoun observed them scavenging for fish along the lakefront. [64]

turkey, wild   *Meleagris gallopavo*; French, *poules d'inde*; indigenous to the Chicago locale prior to 1833; writes Father Hennepin, referring to the Illinois country: "On the 16th of October [1679] we began to find a great abundance of game, and our Indian, a very excellent hunter, killed stags and deer, and our Frenchmen very fat poule d'inde"; Father Binneteau, in 1699: " Game is plentiful such as ducks and turkeys." G.S. Hubbard reported that for the officers and men at Fort Dearborn part of their "amusement at that time, in the fall, were generally hunting deer, wolves, turkey and foxes," and David McKee recalled: "Deer were plenty, and bear, wild turkeys and otter were fond on the Desplaines"; became extirpated in Illinois but was reintroduced, and is now reestablishing itself near Chicago. [46, 64]

Turner, George F., M.D.   assistant surgeon at Fort Dearborn, with Dr. Maxwell at the fort during the time of the Treaty of Chicago in September 1833, signing as witness on the document; had become assistant surgeon on July 23 that summer, the 13th and the last of the medical officers appointed to the fort; was promoted to surgeon in January 1840; died at Corpus Christi, TX, on Oct. 17, 1854. [12, 738]

Turner, John   born c.1806 in Philadelphia, PA; arrived in April 1835; ✦ John and Leighton Turner, livery stables, corner of N State and Kinzie streets [Leighton's year of arrival could not be determined; lived in Evanston in 1885.] John married Sarah Patterson in 1843; still lived in Chicago in 1879,

his address for 1885 is Ravenswood. [12, 351]

Turner, Jonathan Baldwin   born 1805 in Massachusetts; became a faculty member of the Illinois College at Jacksonville in early 1833; that summer he traveled N on horseback from Aug. 28 to Sept. 26 in the company of two other professors (T.M. Post and Erasmus Colton), to Chicago to observe the Indian Treaty procedures, later writing about the event. [For excerpts from a letter written about a travel encounter with Potawatomi see below; about Indian activities at Chicago in the wake of the treaty, see entry for Treaty 1833, Chicago; his comments on road construction in Illinois, see entry for streets and roads. [107, 432]

At Quincy we heard that a party was going from Galesburg, and so we pushed onto that place, where we found a party of Pottawatomie Indians, who were going to attend the giving up of their land at Chicago to the government. They, through an interpreter, allowed us to go with them. We started in true Indian style, the young chief and braves first, older men next, followed by the squaws and their papooses with their ponies and camping outfit, and we last of all. In single file we rode through the tall prairie-grass, in many places higher than our heads while we were on horseback, through the theater of the last season's Indian war [Black Hawk War of 1832] to Lake Michigan. We were not altogether comfortable with our strange traveling companions, for the Indians were not well pleased with the idea of giving up their land at Chicago. But they treated us well, and the novelty of the proceedings made it interesting. Suddenly, when about fifty miles from Chicago, their young chief in front snatched up his gun, cocked it, and said something over his shoulder to the one immediately behind him, and so went the word down the whole line, the excitement growing as the guns clicked, clicked. We were alarmed, as we had seen nothing and could see nothing to cause the sudden excitement. Professor Colton was sure they intended to murder us, and wanted us to put spurs to our horses and at least make an attempt to escape; they had gotten us far out on the prairie and intended to wreak their vengeance on us, the only whites within reach. But Professor Post and I persuaded him that would be foolish; we could not possibly escape in a race, for their horses were tougher and fresher than ours. We had better watch and try some other way, if they really intended to kill us. By this time the squaws and children were equally excited, all jabbering at once. Not a thing could we understand, and not a word from us could they understand. Soon, however, we noticed they were looking not at us, but far away to the south. By rising in our stirrups and looking in the same direction, I saw a deer bounding over the high grass. The Chief left the line and started after him. ❖ When we reached Chicago I told the Indian Agent [Colonel Owen] *there of the incident, and said surely he could not get the deer. 'Yes, he will; he will follow him for days, and never leave the trail until he catches him.' And, sure enough, in two days he came in with the deer slung over the pony's back in front of him.*

turnpiking   a commonly employed method of building early roads during the first half of the 19th century; George David, a 1833 land route traveler to Chicago, gives the following definition: "The meaning of turnpiking is, ploughing up the soil from the sides of the road and throwing it, or 'hagging' to the center to drain the water off, then as it is only hardened by time the road consequently remains bad for some time"; Webster, in the second edition of the *New International Dictionary of the English Language*, reads: "to throw into a rounded form, as the path of a road." [187]

Tuttle, James B.   arrived from Massachusetts in 1831; subscribed to the *Chicago Democrat* in November 1833; on May 28, 1834, he and William H. Brown announced in the *Chicago Democrat* that they had opened a grocery store on Dearborn Street, one door S of Messrs. Newberry & Dole, a partnership they dissolved on June 21; James continued, advertising a "New Store" with the same goods, at the same location on July 2. Groceries included "Muscavado, Havana, loaf and lump Sugar; Sul-

tana Raisins; Maderia, Brazil and fiber Nuts; Snuff; Champaine, Claret and Porter"—items similar to those stocked by other grocers. On July 16 he added a variety of West India fruit preserves. [351, 733]

Tympanuchus phasianellu   sharp-tailed grouse; see grouse.

Uncle Sam   280-ton steamboat from Buffalo under Captain McKinstry, built at Grosse Isle, MI, in 1832; called at Chicago with passengers, furniture, &c on June 14, 1834, and again on July 9; a third call on July 29, coming from Detroit, was made under the command of Captain Lundy. [48]

Underwood, John Milton   arrived from Massachusetts in 1835; ✦ bookkeeper, Kinzie & Hunter; married J. Helen Sturtevant in 1842; later returned to Massachusetts where he lived at Danvers in 1885. [12, 351]

United States   37-ton steamboat from Buffalo under Capt. Asa E. Hart, built at Huron, OH, in 1835; called at Chicago with freight and passengers on July 16, 1835, and again on Oct. 8 that same year. [48]

United States   schooner from Buffalo under Captain Burke, called at Chicago on Sept. 30, 1835.

United States Army Corps of Engineers   see Corps of Engineers.

United States Factory System   suggested by President Washington, an idea to supply the wants of the aboriginal population by establishing "Indian stores," the first two factories were opened in the SW in 1795, then four more under President Jefferson in 1803, one each in Fort Wayne and Detroit; in 1805 four additional ones at Fort Dearborn, Green Bay, Prairie du Chien, and Fort Edwards were intended to break British control of the trade and cultivate friendly relations with the Indians by supplying superior goods at reasonable prices; their impact was limited. Between 1805 and 1808, three different factors administered at Fort Dearborn in short succession: Ebenezer Bellknap,

Thomas Hayward, and Joseph B. Varnum [the latter in 1807 and 1808], brother of Jacob B. Varnum (see below). Matthew Irwin successfully served from 1809 to 1812. During the time of the first fort, the factors lived in a house built for them by the soldiers in 1805 on the S side of the river, between the agency house and the fort, the same location where the lighthouse would be built in 1832. In 1812 the Indians burned the fort, the agency, and the factory. [Where the agency house had stood, the soldiers would eventually erect a large hexagonal barn.] Jacob B. Varnum served as factor from 1816 until 1822. During the time of the second fort, the factory building was located immediately S of the fort. By 1820, the factory system was critically evaluated for its continued existence [see entry under Morse, Rev. Jedediah]; opposition from powerful private companies, their influence in Congress, and unfavorable reports from territorial governors such as Cass, all foreshadowed its demise; for a sample from such a report, one by T.L. McKenney of the Office for Indian Trade and directed to the secretary of war, see below. Congress abolished the factory system in 1822; for the end of the factory at Fort Dearborn, also see Lindsley, A.B. [12, 105]

[July 5, 1821] *Sir — I have the honor respectfully to represent that for three years last past the two factories on the Lakes, one at Chicago, the other at Green Bay, have been in a measure useless to the Indians and in a pecuniary point of view to the Govt. also. This state of things is owing entirely to the unsuitable provisions which exist for the regulation of the trade. Hordes of private adventurers availing themselves of the looseness of the system have crowded into these parts on acct. of the superiority of the Furs which are taken there, and level all sorts of policy but their own, by the powerful agency which they derive from the free use of spirituous liquors as an article of their commerce, and after which the Indians, however afflicting they know the consequence to be, will go.* [T.L. McKenney of the Office for Indian Trade to the secretary of war.]

United States Hotel   see Sauganash Hotel.

United States Indian Agency   see United States Office of Indian Affairs.

United States Land Office   opened on May 28, 1835 in Thomas Church's frame house on the E side of Lake Street (between Clark and Dearborn; land office upstairs, Church's grocery store downstairs), with James Whitlock as registrar, Col. E.D. Taylor as receiver of public funds, and Fernando Jones as clerk; in the same month the office held its first sale of public land in Chicago and the entire northern Illinois district and thereby contributed strongly to the increasing flood of new arrivals, such as farmers, speculators, and adventurers. The receipts for land sales during the first two weeks exceeded half a million dollars.

United States Office of Indian Affairs   created by Congress, which gave to the President the authority to appoint Indian agents in 1793; agencies were centers through which the office administered and maintained relations with one or more tribes; until 1849 the office was under the War Department, thereafter under the Department of the Interior; the first Indian agent who granted a license to trade with the Indians at "Chicagou" was William Wells of Fort Wayne on Aug. 30, 1803; for Indian agents at Fort Dearborn, see Jouett, Charles (1804-1811 and 1816-1818); see Wolcott, Alexander (1818-1830); see Owen, T.J.V. (1831- 1833). For the work and concerns of Indian agents, as reflected within correspondence between Governor Edwards to Agent Thomas Forsyth, see the following letters. [12, 105]

[Edwards to Forsyth]
Elvirado, Illinois Terr., May 16, 1814.

The object of my wishing you to return to Peoria, is the preservation of peace between us, and the Potawatomies. As however experience has fully convinced us that there can be no neutrality with savages, in the vicinity of conflicting powers, and as we have found them faithless in all their promises, it becomes equally our interest and our duty, ...

[Forsyth to Edwards] *St. Louis, Sept. 3, 1814.*

I wrote by the mail that left this place on the 21st ult. which I hope you received safe. You will please observe, that the Indians are all now busily employed with their corn, and as soon as that is done, (which will be towards the latter end of the month) they will remove to their wintering places. I do not see how the Potawatomies of Illinois river can commence their hunt, as they receive no presents, can get no credit and having nothing to purchase ammunition to commence hunting: and as they are surrounded by Indians who receive presents from us and the British, they must and will be obliged to visit the enemy at Green Bay or Chicago, should the latter make an establishment at that place [or] at Chicago, according to the promise to the Indians formerly. It is true that should Mackinaw fall, it may have a great effect, but nevertheless presents are very tempting to the Indians, particularly to whose who are naked, for I can assure you that I never saw Indians so much in want of everything, as the Potawatamies of Illinois river are at present. ❖
At the distribution of gunpowder at Rock River which the Saukies, Foxes, Kickapoos &c received from the British at Prairie du Chien, they shewed it to the Potawatamies who were there, and asked them if their American Father gave them any gunpowder, saying you see how your British Fathers his children.

Updike, Peter Lewis   arrived from New Jersey in 1835; was a member of the fire engine company No.1 ("Fire Kings") in December 1835, a town trustee in 1836; married to Elizabeth (née Trowbridge); ◆ Updike & McClure (Andrew), carpenters and builders (Court Place) Dearborn Street; in 1849 was one of the incorporators of the Chicago Gal Light & Coke Co. [12, 351]

Updyke, P. J.   subscribed to the *Chicago Democrat* in November 1833.

Urbs in Horto   Latin, *city in a garden*; inscription on Chicago's seal; for probable origin, see Birkbeck, Morris. [56]

Urocyon cinereoargenteus   see fox.

Ursus americanus   see bear.

Utica   schooner from Buffalo under Captain Rhodes, first called at Chicago on July 24, 1835, and made five additional visits that year.

Vail sawmill   opened in 1832 on Trail creek upstream of [Michigan City]; one of several mills that supplied lumber for the Chicago boom.

Valparaiso moraine   terminal moraine at the southern end of the Wisconsin glacier that scooped out the bed of Lake Chicago, predecessor to Lake Michigan.

Van Austen's tavern   existed in the mid 1830s, where the Old Chicago Trail crossed the Des Plaines River at [Summit]. [Van Austen may possibly have suceeded the {see} Laughton brothers at their tavern and trading house, as did Stephen J. Scott temporarily, when the brothers both died in 1834; *eds.*]

Vandalia   became capital of the State of Illinois in December 1820, replacing Kaskaskia, and remained capital until 1840, yielding the title to Springfield; for details, see Chicago jurisdictional chronology on page 209.

Van Buren, Lt. Abraham   born in New York; son of President Martin Van Buren, was stationed as second lieutenant at Fort Dearborn from Oct. 3, 1828, to March 1829 under Major Fowle; died on March 15, 1873.

Van der Bogart, Henry, M.D.   (1810-1835) a graduate of the medical college in Fairfield, NY, in 1833; arrived in the spring of 1834 and soon afterward taught at the English and Classical School for Boys, replacing Granville T. Sproat as principal and by the year's end, was succeeded by Thomas Wright; became engaged to Sally Warren, a teacher who worked under him, but he died of typhoid on April 8, 1835, at the Warren home [Warrenville]; Sally married Abel E. Carpenter in 1836. Transcripts of his letters (1833-34) concerning school experiences are preserved at the Chicago Historical Society. [12]

Vanderberg, M.   subscribed to the Chicago Democrat in November 1833.

Van Eaton, David voted in the elections on Aug. 2 and Nov. 25, 1830. [12]

Van Horn, Cornelius C. also Van Horne; came from New York in 1832, settling in New Lenox Township [Will County]; became a private that year in Capt. J.S.C. Hogan's Cook County volunteer company within Maj. David Bailey's battalion stationed at the Fort Dearborn between May 24 and June 18; postmaster of the Juliet [Joliet] post office between July 1834 and April 1835, providing lists of remaining letters that were published in the *Chicago Democrat;* just prior to the land sale in May, he was in town advertising in the *Chicago Democrat* and selling "[a] number of valuable improved farms, situate along the line of the Illinois and Michigan Canal, some of the best locations in the country." [134, 714]

Van Horne, James U.S. Army private at Fort Dearborn; enlisted in May 1810; taken prisoner at the massacre of 1812 and later ransomed from the Indians. [226, 688]

Van Horne, John also van Horn; German immigrant to Chicago in 1830; according to Mayor Wentworth, van Horne was the first German settler to vote in Chicago in the Peoria County election on July 24 and Aug. 2, 1830. Van Horn, whose name suggests Dutch rather than German ancestry, competes with Johann Wellmacher for distinction of having been ★★★ **Chicago's 1st** German immigrant. [12, 342]

Vansickle, Martin worked one month for $10 for William H. Wallace at Hardscrabble early in 1826; voted in the election on Aug. 7, 1826 (see elections).

Van Voorhis, Isaac, M.D. (1790-1812) member of an old Dutch family of Fishkill, NY; graduated in 1808 from the College of Physicians and Surgeons in New York City, a classmate of Dr. John Cooper; at age 20 he became a military physician (surgeon's mate, appointed March 1, 1811) at Fort Dearborn under Captain Heald; arrived at the fort

in the summer of 1811, replacing Dr. Cooper, who had resigned his position in the spring; was killed in action at the massacre of 1812; his sensitivity and visionary quality become apparent in the following portion from a letter sent home from the lonely fort:

In my solitary walks I contemplate what a great and powerful republic will yet arise in this new world. Here, I say, will be the seat of millions yet unborn; here the asylum of oppressed millions yet to come. How composedly would I die could I be resuscitated at that bright era of American greatness—an era which I hope will announce the tidings of death to fell superstition and dread tyranny. [12, 226]

Varnum, Jacob Butler (1788-1874) from an influential Massachusetts family, appointed U.S. factor at the new Fort Dearborn in 1816 by Captain Bradley, succeeding Matthew Irwin after an interval of four years without a factor. Varnum had recently married Mary Ann (née Aiken, of Detroit) at Mackinac and brought his bride with him to the fort; arriving on the *Tiger* on Sept. 13, 1816, the couple was assigned an unused log cabin outside the stockade as both living quarters and factory store; on June 27, 1817, his wife died during childbirth; she was buried, holding the stillborn infant in her arms, a few feet from the cabin [their remains later moved to the city cemetery]; Jacob married 19-year-old Catherine Dodemead of Detroit on Aug. 8, 1819, and brought her back to the fort, where the soldiers had meanwhile built a more adequate factory; there the couple lived until 1822, together with Catherine's sister Mary and two servants; in 1821 attended the Indian Treaty of Chicago; later removed to Washington City, where he lived until his death. [12, 560, 689]

Varnum, Joseph Bradley, Jr. (1785-1867) older brother of Jacob B., who entered government service with the help of his influential father, arrived at Fort Dearborn on Aug. 20, 1807, to serve as U.S. factor until 1808 [though observed by William Johnson late June, 1809], then was transferred

to Mackinac; he escaped capture by the British in 1812, entered the fur trade until 1817, then moved to New York and became a merchant.

Vasseur, Noel see Le Vasseur, Noel.

Vaughan, Daniel W. German immigrant in 1831; married Angeline Herbert on July 9, 1831; made history as defendant in ★★★ **Chicago's 1st** local divorce proceedings [see notice in *Chicago Democrat* of May 16, 1834], involving Angeline as petitioner, Daniel as respondent; the outcome is not known; see divorces. [In 1827 a Chicago couple had divorced in Peoria, then the county seat; *eds.*] [12, 342]

Vaughn, Dill and James early members of the Catholic community, in April 1833 their names were on the petition by citizens to Bishop Rosati of St. Louis asking that a priest be assigned to them.

vegetation by the year 1832, approximately half of Illinois still consisted of [see] prairie. In the same year [see] H.S. Tanner listed the prevalent woody plants as follows: "The kinds of timber most abundant are cotton-wood, sycamore, hickory, ash, sugar-maple, beech; black, white, red, post, and jack oak; black and white walnut, blue and white ash, sweet and sour or black gum, red and water elm, black and honey locust, linden, buck- eye, pecan, hackberry, catalpa, mulberry, box elder, wild cherry, willow, dogwood, sassafras, persimmon, with smaller underwood of sumac, plum, crab apple, grape vines, pawpaw, hazel, &c. &c. The cotton-wood and sycamore grow along the streams. In the southern end, on the streams which flow into the Ohio and Mississippi toward their junction, the cypress grows." Also see barrens. [311, 313]

vermillion a red pigment applied by the Indians and made available to them by the fur traders.

Vermillion Rangers also Vermillion County Battalion; in July 1827 Gurdon S. Hubbard, then of Danville (on the Big Vermillion River), was in the Kinzie house at Chicago when Governor Cass of the Territory of Michigan made a surprise visit to warn of impending danger from the restive

Winnebago. Hubbard sped to Danville in record time and led 100 militia volunteers from the Vermillion County Battalion—the Vermillion Rangers—on horseback to Chicago to help safeguard the small settlement, unprotected because Fort Dearborn had not been garrisoned since 1823; Achilles Morgan was chosen by the volunteers as captain, and Hezekiah Cunningham, serving as a private, later gave an account of the experience; additional names of participating militia members may be found in that report. Another contemporary was Henry W. Blodgett and his description of Hubbard's appearance at that time follows. [12]

The picture of him, as he led his Vermillion County rangers up before the old fort, will ever remain in my memory. I think without exception, he was the nearest to my ideal of a frontier soldier, of anyone I have ever seen. Splendid in physique, six feet and something more in height, he rode a splendid horse, and dressed in just enough of the frontier costume to make his figure a picturesque one. He wore buckskin leggins, fringed with red and blue and a jaunty sort of hunting-cap. In a red sash about his waist was stuck, on one side, a silver-handled hunting-knife, on the other, a richly mounted tomahawk. His saddle and horse accoutrements were elegant, I might say fantastic, and altogether he made a figure ever to be remembered.

Versailles, France   France having taken formal possession of the North American Northwest, including Chicago, in 1671, Versailles became the ultimate jurisdictional capital for Chicago in that year, and remained so until 1763. For details, see Chicago jurisdictional chronology on page 209.

Vespucci, Amerigo   born March 9, 1451 in Italy, accompanied the Spanish conquistador Alonzo de Ojeda on a 1499 expedition to the New World. Vespucci's description of the coast of Brazil and his recognition of a continent in his *Quatuor Americi Navigationes* in 1504 led the German cartographer Martin Waldseemüller to suggest naming South

America after him; the name was later adapted for North America. [446]

Victory   armed British schooner patrolling Lakes Michigan, Huron, and Erie during the period of British control; built at Navy Island in 1763. [48]

Vial, Joseph   came in the fall of 1833 from Elmira, NY, and was listed as a subscriber to the *Chicago Democrat* in November; acquired 270 acres the following spring at Flag Creek [Lyons Township]; farmed with his sons Robert and Samuel; built a hostelry on Plainfield Road, where the first stages stopped near Elijah Wentworth, Jr.'s, tavern; married to Louisa Smith; their children also included Martha and Nathaniel; notified settlers [June 24, 1835, *Chicago Democrat*] and hosted Cook County's Democratic convention at Flag Creek on July 4, 1835, that nominated Peter Pruyne for state senator. Early Vial family diaries, kept between 1832 and 1848, are within the Flagg Creek Historical Society collection at the [see next entry] Robert Vial House. [13, 278, 711a]

Vial, Robert   born in Chester, NY; arrived in 1833 with his family and farmed the homestead with his father and brother Samuel; married Mary R. Ketchum. The house he built in c.1856, existent now at 7425 Wolf Road in [Burr Ridge], has been renovated under the direction of the Flagg Creek Historical Society and is an information resource center for the Illinois & Michigan Canal Commission. [13, 278, 351, 711a]

Viaux, Charles   also Vieau; son of [see] Jacques Vieau, older brother of Andrew J., Sr.; married to one of Jean Baptiste Mirandeau's daughters; subscribed to the *Chicago Democrat* in November 1833; died in KS in 1876. [691]

Vieau, Andrew J., Sr.   son of [see] Jacques Vieau, born at Green Bay in 1818; one-quarter Indian; came to Chicago in 1835 and worked as head of several clerks in Madore Beaubien's store, returning the next year to Milwaukee; served as bookkeeper for Laurent Solomon Juneau, and soon bought him out; married Rebecca R. Lawe of Green

Bay. [691]

Vieau, Jacques   born 1762; early settler (1795) and trader of Milwaukee who, until 1819, was the local agent of the American Fur Co., when Solomon Juneau took over; also had posts in Kewaunee, Sheboygan, and Manitowoc, and his trade with Indians reached as far S as Chicago; in 1836 removed to his former homestead in Green Bay; his wife was Angeline, daughter of the La Baye trader Joseph LeRoi and an Indian woman; see Vieau, Andrew J., Sr. [691]

Viger, Jacques   local Quebec historian and public official who in 1844, discovered Father Marquette's "holograph" [handwritten or hand-drawn] ✳ map and report of his 1673 expedition with Jolliet. Jolliet's map and report were lost in a 1674 catastrophe before they could be delivered to the authorities. [306, 693]

Vincennes, IN   town in southern Indiana on the Wabash River, founded under the Louisiana governor Pérrier as a military post in 1727 (most probable date) by the French explorer François Margane (Morgan) de la Valtrie, sieur de Vincennes, and named after its founder; the fort was also called Poste du Ouabache and served to counter the English influence with the Indians and to secure French control of the fur trade; later occupied first by the British, then by U.S. troops under Gen. George Rogers Clark; in 1800 became the capital for the Indiana Territory, which included Chicago. For details, see Chicago jurisdictional chronology on page 209; ➡ Vincennes Avenue; see Vincennes Trail. [122]

Vincennes Trail   also Vincennes Trace, Hubbard Trail, Hubbard Trace, Old Chicago Road, Pottawatomie Trail, Oak Ridge; Indian trail from Fort Dearborn S to Vincennes, IN; an important and much traveled regional and interregional route for Indians, traders, Indiana farmers, and military alike; was surveyed by the state of Illinois in 1833-34 and eventually became, for much of its course, Illinois Highway 1; ➡ its northern portion is still known as Vincennes Avenue.

Vincent, Aiken   also Akin; arrived in 1835; a notice in the *Chicago Democrat* of Dec. 14, 1842, announced his marriage to Sarah Ann Clark on Dec. 6; in 1885 lived at 96 Artesian Ave. [If Aiken Vincent's arrival date, as given by Adolphus Hubbard, is in error—as his spelling of Vincent's first name appears to be—he may be identical with the Englishman Mr. Vincent of the following entry; *eds.*] [351]

Vincent, Mr.   an English bachelor who in 1833 occupied a new frame house at Vincent's Prairie, five miles N of the Chicago River; the Boyer family stayed there initially and enjoyed his fine library, as Dr. Boyer later related. [728]

Virginia fence   a zigzag fence of wooden rails crossing at their ends.

voting lists   such lists of early settlers constitute valuable historical resources, although the names are often misspelled.

voyageur   in New France or Canada, a person who transported goods and men by rivers and lakes to trading posts for the fur companies, or any woodsmen or boatsmen of the early period; also see *coureurs de bois* and *engagé*. Mrs. Kinzie's description of *voyageurs*, in *Wau-Bun*, follows:

They were unlike any other class of men. Like the poet, they seemed born to their vocation. Sturdy, enduring, ingenious and light-hearted, they possessed a spirit capable of adjusting itself to any emergency. No difficulties baffled, no hardship discouraged them; while their affectionate nature led them to form attachments of the warmest character to their 'bourgeois' or master, as well as to the native inhabitants among whom their engagements carried them.

Vulpes vulpes   see fox.

Wabano   colloquial term used in early Chicago for an all night dancing opportunity held at the Lake House or Mansion House or Sauganash Hotel, preceded by dinner at 6 p.m. and followed by breakfast at 7 a.m., in which the dancers usually participated. For the text of a printed invitation by the sponsor, followed by Charles Fenno Hoffman's eyewitness report on such an event itself, see below.

Grand WA-BA-NO.
Mssrs. H. and L. Harmon
are respectfully solicited
at Mr Graves Assembly Rooms
on Wednesday, February Five, at 6 P.M.
managers.
R.A. Kinzie, J.D. Harmon, J. Spring,
E.K. Smith, M.D. Culver, M.B. Beaubien.
Chicago, Feb. 1, 1834.

We had not been here [Chicago] *an hour before an invitation to a public ball was courteously sent to us by the managers; and though my soiled and travel-worn ridingdress was not exactly the thing to present one's self in before the ladies of an evening, yet, in my earnestness to see life on the frontier, I easily allowed all objections to be overruled by my companions, and we accordingly drove to the house in which the ball was given. It was a frame building, one of the few as yet to be found in Chicago; ... we were ushered into a tolerably-sized dancing room, occupying the second story of the house, and having its unfinished walls so ingeniously covered with pine-branches and flags borrowed from the garrison, that, with the whitewashed ceiling above, it presented a very complete and quite pretty appearance. It was not so warm, however, that the fires of cheerful hickory, which roared at either end, could have been readily dispensed with.* ✧ *An orchestra* [platform] *of unplaned boards was raised against the wall in the center of the room; the band consisted of a dandy negro with his violin* [Nelson P. Perry], *a fine military-looking bass drummer from the fort, and a volunteer citizen, who alternately played an accompaniment upon the flute and triangle. Blackee, who flourished about with a great many airs and graces, was decidedly the king of the company; ... As for the company* [of guests], *it was such a complete medley of all ranks, ages, professions, trades and occupations, brought together from all parts of the world, ... that it was amazing to witness the decorum with which they comingled on this festive occasion. ...The gayest that was ever called by quadrille-playing Benoit never afforded me half the amusement that did these Chicago cotillions. Here you might see a veteran officer in full uniform balancing to a trademan's daughter still in her short frock and trousers, while there the golden aiguillette of a handsome surgeon* [Dr. Maxwell, no doubt; *eds.*] *flapped in unison with the glass beads upon a scrawney neck of fifty. ... Those raven locks, dressed a la Madonne, over eyes of jet, and touching a cheek where blood of a deeper hue mingles with the less glowing current from European veins, tell of a lineage drawn from the original owners of the soil; while these golden tresses, floating away from eyes of heaven's own color over a neck of alabaster, recall the Gothic ancestry of some of 'England's born.' How piquantly do these trim and beaded leggins peep from under that simple dress of black, as its tall nut-brown wearer moves, as if unconsciously, through the graceful mazes of the dance. ...* ✧ *'This is a scene of enchantment to me, Sir,' observed an officer to me, recently exchanged to this post, and formerly stationed here. 'There were but a few traders around the fort when I last visited Chicago; and now I can't contrive where the devil all these well-dressed people have come from!' ...* ✧ *I made several new acquaintances at this new-year's ball, and particularly with the officers of the garrison, from whose society I promised myself much pleasure during my stay.*

[Mr. Hoffman was not to be disappointed. His book tells of exciting wolfhunts &c. he enjoyed during the next few days in the company of his new-found friends; *eds.*] [339]

Wabansa stone   see Waubansee stone

Wabansia Addition   also listed as Wahponseh Addition; the plat for the Wabansia Addition to Chicago was filed for record on June 10, 1834; first shown on Hathaway's ✱ map of 1834, it is a triangular piece of land, bordered by Kinzie Street, Jefferson Street, and the north branch; named after the Potawatomi chief [see] Waubansee. James Kinzie held a dominant proprietary interest in this addition, as shown by the following action taken by the Illinois General Assembly early in 1835: "An Act to authorize James Kenzie to alter the Town Plat of the town of Wabansie. Section 1. Be it enacted by the people of the State of Illinois, represented in the General Assembly, That James Kenzie, proprietor of the town of Wabansie, be, and he is hereby authorized to so alter and amend the plat of said town as to make it conform to the survey thereof: *Provided*, said alteration shall not interfere with the wishes, rights or interests of individual claimants. Section 2. That this act shall take effect from and after its passage." [Approved, Jan. 26, 1835.]

Wabansie   see Waubansee

Wabash River   the word *Wabash* is possibly Miami: *ouabachei* or *ouabachioui*, meaning *white metal* or *silver*; trading posts, some which later became larger settlements, were established along the Wabash River many decades earlier than at Chicago; Vincennes was a French post in 1702, personally established by Sieur Juchereau, Lieutenant General of Montreal, and at least by 1721 there were traders living near the Miami village of Ke-ki-ong-a, where Fort Wayne would be. Once Chicago became a boom town in 1833, it served as an attractive outlet for the agricultural products of the Wabash River valley, and a steady stream of wagons lumbered to the market on South Water Street, up and down what is now Wabash Avenue. See the following impression by Colbee C. Benton in 1833. [697]

... The trade of Chicago seems to be with the inhabitants in the vicinity of the Wabash River, at least a considerable share of it. They come with large covered waggons drawn by three or four yoke of oxen, generally loaded with wheat which they exchange for salt. They travel very cheap indeed. Their way is across an extensive prairie nearly the whole distance, which is about one hundred and twenty miles to the Wabash River. They carry their victuals with them, and when night comes they turn their oxen onto the prairie and sleep in their waggons. At Chicago they do the same, and I saw them cooking by their fires, making coffee, kneading bread. and baking it on the coals. A large space is occupied by their teams and there is a number present all the time. They seem to live as comfortable as many of the inhabitants. There are a number of settlements in the vicinity of Chicago which do part of their trading here, but not all. ...

Wabash and Erie Canal   452 miles from Toledo, OH, to Evansville, IN; begun in 1832, completed 1856; partially closed in 1860 and abandoned in 1875; the longest United States canal, but ill-fated and short-lived because of the growing importance of the railroads.

Wabinsheway   White Elk, a Potawatomi chief of unusually tall stature, known to have killed Sukey Corbin and her two small children in the Burn's house during the Fort Dearborn massacre; suspected to have killed many children in the children's wagon. [226]

Wabonsia   see Waubansia

Wade, Captain   master of the lake schooner [see] *Chance* that visited Chicago on Nov. 11, 1835.

Wade, David   born c.1812, came in 1832; served under Capt. G. Kercheval as a member of the Chicago company in the Black Hawk War of 1832. [12]

Wadhams, Seth   born c.1818 in Goshen, CT; arrived on July 4, 1835; ✦ clerk, boarded at Illinois Exchange; living at Elmhurst in 1885. [12, 351]

Waggoner, Anthony L.   U.S. Army private at Fort Dearborn, enlisted in January 1811; badly wounded at the 1812 massacre and killed by the Indians later that night. [226]

Wahponseh Addition   see Wabansia Addition.

Waldseemüller, Martin Hylacomylus   (1470-1521) German cartographer working at St. Dié, France, whose world ✱ map, contained in *Cosmographio Introductio*, 1507, and initiating the appellation *America*; thus credit was given to Amerigo Vespucci for recognizing that the New World was of continental proportions. [247]

Walker, Almond   brother of [see] Charles Walker; visited Chicago on business from New York in 1834 and 1835; ✦ (Charles Walker & Co.).

Walker & Co.   [see Charles Walker] grocers and provision merchants located on South Water Street between Dearborn and State; the range of merchandise offered is later itemized in the *Chicago Morning Democrat*, Feb. 27, 1840: "leather, groceries, calicoes, flannels, socks, mittens, &c.&c. Fools cap and letter paper, threshing machines, fanning mills, double waggons, shiffle trees, neck yokes, &c.&c. Pork, flour and salt, 500,000 ft. pine lumber, different kinds." [736]

Walker, Augustus   captain of the *Shelden Thompson*, the first steamship on Lake Michigan, built in 1830; on July 10, 1832 arrived for the Black Hawk War with General Scott and soldiers infected with the cholera, and afterward came regularly to Chicago; for his impression of the prairie, as viewed from his ship, see entry for prairie; of the ravages of the cholera on board ship, see entry for cholera. [12, 708]

Walker, Charles   (1802-1869) native of Plainfield, NY; brother of Almond; visited in 1834, came permanently in 1835, and became a successful merchant and land speculator; on Nov. 23 he submitted a petition for a delay in deciding the question of the right to wharfing privileges; the brothers formed [see] Walker & Co. in 1836 when brother-in-law [see] Eri Baker Hulbert joined them from New York; the firm shipped the first wheat from Chicago to the East in 1838, to Walker's mills in Burlington Flats, NY; ✦ Walker & Co., South Water Street near State; from 1851-52 was president of the board of trade and within a few years was involved in railroad development; through his first wife Mary [married 1826, died 1838] he was a brother-in-law to [see] Henry Brown Clarke; married Nancy Bentley in 1841, who lived until 1881. [12, 28, 97, 351, 736]

CHARLES WALKER [410]

Walker, Charles H. son of [see] Charles Walker and Mary (née Clarke); came as a child with his parents from New York in 1835; followed his father in business, renaming the company C. Walker & Sons, and served as president of the board of trade in 1856 and 1857; later moved to LA. [12]

Walker, George E. Ottawa [IL] resident who accompanied the 1830 board of canal commissioners on their visit to Chicago that summer; purchased waterfront real estate from Mark Noble, Sr., on the E side of the north branch in August 1833, together with James B. Campbell, and in November subscribed to the *Chicago Democrat*; built a cabin on the river sand bar that was washed away in 1834; moved from Ottawa in 1835, and in that year lived with his wife at Flusky's boarding house. Also see Hickling, William. [12, 704]

Walker, George H. (c.1811-1866) arrived in 1832; served under Capt. G. Kercheval as a member of the Chicago company in the Black Hawk War; about that time purchased from George Miller lot 8 in block 18 and and lots 5 and 6 in block 36 [see map on page 44]; died at Milwaukee, aged 55. [12, 714]

Walker, Hugh purchased the downtown lot 5 in Section 31 on April 5, 1832 for $61.

Walker, James Barr (1793-1850) native of Virginia; met and married Jane G. Walker in LaSalle County; accompanied his father-in-law Reverend Jesse Walker among the Potawatomi villages along the Fox River as early as 1826; made a claim in 1828 at what became Walker's Grove [Plainfield]; purchased lot 4 in block 10 [see map on page 44] at the initial Canal Commissioners' land sale in Chicago on Sept. 4, 1830, and was still listed as owner in 1833; one of the first three Cook County commissioners elected on March 7, 1831, (with Samuel Miller and Gholson Kercheval); during the commissioners' second session on June 6, the first county road was ordered to be laid out "from the town of Chicago to the house of B. Lawton, from thence to the house of James Walker, on the Du Page River, and so on to the west line of the county." During the Black Hawk War he commanded one of five Cook County militia companies with the rank of captain; ran a gristmill and also a sawmill that provided lumber in the autumn of 1832 for Chicago's first frame structure, belonging to P.F.W. Peck; subscribed to the *Chicago Democrat* in November 1833; became postmaster at Walker's Grove in February 1834, until early July; later served as commissioner of Will County; died at Plainfield on Aug. 27, 1850. [37, 734]

Walker, Rev. Jesse (1766-1835) Virginia born Methodist preacher, usually known as "Father Walker"; his wife was Susannah; in his earlier years did missionary work in Tennessee, Kentucky, Missouri, and Arkansas; from 1824 on he was minister and superintendent of the Fox River Methodist mission; applied for and received on June 6, 1826, a license to run a ferry across the Illinois River at the mouth of the Fox River; initially came to Chicago from Peoria in the spring of 1826, at which time he delivered ★★★ **Chicago's 1st** Methodist sermon. In the fall of 1830, he was placed in charge of the Chicago Mission District, and voted in elections on Aug. 2 and Nov. 25. In 1832, he moved to the settlement to succeed Reverend Beggs, residing, as had Reverend Beggs, in the double-room log house formerly used by Reverend See, located near the Forks on the W side of the north branch; that winter of 1832-33, jointly occupied the space with John Watkins, who conducted school in one room during the week, where Walker preached on Sundays. Susannah died in 1832; he remarried in 1834 (Rebecca, who submitted a petition for wharfing privileges on Nov. 23, 1835). Late that year he, becoming superannuated, was succeeded by Rev. J.T. Mitchell and in 1835 removed to Walker's Grove, dying on Oct. 5; the remains of his first wife were disinterred and buried with him in a single large coffin. [12, 28, 37, 50, 734]

Walker, Martin O. partner of John Frink in [see] Frink & Walker; took over from Winters, Mills & Co. the Chicago-Ottawa stagecoach line late in 1834 that had been pioneered by Dr. Temple; ✦ mail contractor, 123 Lake.

Walker's Grove a notice in the Feb. 18, 1834, issue of the *Chicago Democrat* announced the opening of a new post office at Walker's Grove [Plainfield]; Rev. Jesse Walker lived and died there in retirement, but the name derives from his son-in-law and earlier resident [see] James Barr Walker.

Walkins, Samuel arrived from Virginia in 1830; possibly a misprint, [see] Watkins, Samuel. [351]

Walk-in-the-Water built at Black Rock, NY; first steamboat on the Great Lakes W of Niagara, with a maiden voyage in August 1818; a 338-ton, 135-foot schooner-rigged paddle-wheeler with wood-burning boilers, it was actually a sailing vessel with an auxiliary engine; carried the members of the 1820 Lewis Cass expedition on the first leg of their voyage from Buffalo to Detroit. The *Walk-in-the-Water* was never in Chicago, though it had navigated the northern parts of Lake Michigan. On Oct. 31, 1821, the ship was caught on Lake Erie

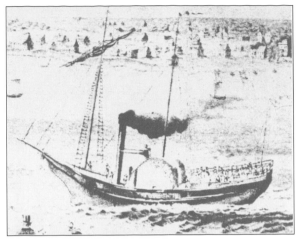
Walk-in-the-Water

by a violent gale, was stranded at Point Abino near Buffalo Creek and broke apart on Nov. 1 with no loss of life. George Washington Whistler, who spent his childhood years from age three to 10 at Fort Dearborn, made a painting of the ship in 1820, showing Detroit in the background. [565]

Wallace, William Henry (1790-1827) Montreal-born experienced fur trader of Scottish origin; in mid May 1818 was working for the American Fur Co. in Montreal, where he dispatched Gurdon S. Hubbard to the Illinois River; thereafter was a trader for the company on the lower Wabash River until 1823; in September 1825 purchased supplies and merchandise from William Brewster of Detroit, also from New York merchants, and by late December began a trading post at Chicago, renting for this purpose a cabin at Hardscrabble from Antoine Ouilmette; his enterprise was sometimes referred to as "Wallace & Davis," suggesting a partnership with John H. Davis, another former employee of the American Fur Co.; employed several *engagés* at Chicago, most of whom came from Detroit (Glode [Claude] LaFramboise and Jean Baptiste *dit* La Fortune, interpreters, and Martin Vansickle, John B. Bersier, Augustin Bordenois, and Clemon and Morice Lozon). He died a bachelor on or soon af-

ter March 2, 1827, when he was last attended by Dr. Wolcott for an infectious disease; the sale of his large estate on April 27 attracted many purchasers from the area and beyond, whose names, acquisitions, and payments have been recorded and fortuitously preserved in Peoria court archives. [12, 220]

Wallace & Davis see Wallace, William H.

Walls, John U.S deputy surveyor; made a ✳ survey of the Chicago River, Mud Lake and part of the Des Plaines River, dated June 18, 1821. [413]

Walsh, Michael see Welch, Michael P.

Walsh, Patrick arrived early in 1833 from Ireland; in April he signed for a family of two the petition by Catholic citizens to Bishop Rosati of St. Louis, asking that a priest be assigned to them. [Possibly identical with {see} Patrick Welch; the preserved list of petitioners does not show the original signatures but was written by one hand, and several of the names are clearly misspelled.] [12]

Walters, J.C. was a member of the fire engine company No.1 ("Fire Kings") in December 1835; possibly Joel C. Walter listed in 1839 as an employee of H. Norton & Co. [grocers and provisions, South Water Street].

Wapiti see elk

wampum Algonkin: wampùmpeag, a string of shell beads; also skins decorated with certain kinds of seashells, used by Indians as an exchange medium in lieu of money. During the War of 1812, Main Poc and other pro-British chiefs provided belts of wampum, "all painted with vermillion" and "about two fathoms long & nine inches wide," that accompanied British letters to the councils of various tribes in the midwest, inviting the warriors to come to Detroit for provisions and merchandise that included kegs of gunpowder. [109, 697]

war dance for eyewitness accounts of the Great Indian War Dance at Chicago in 1835, see Chronology, 1835; also see entry on Hoyne, Lenora Maria Temple.

Ware, Charley member of a team that went from

Chicago to Sheboygan in 1834 to build a sawmill on the Sheboygan River.

War, French and Indian see French and Indian War.

War of 1812 provoked by England's maritime policy and its undermining of United States relations with the Indians of the Northwest; war was also facilitated by an American desire to take Canada from the British and Florida from Britain's ally, Spain. Though poorly prepared, and with incompetent military leadership in command, Congress approved war with England on June 18, 1812, by a close vote. Initially British troops moved against Gen. William Hull in the Northwest, dislodging United States forces in quick succession from Mackinac (July 17, 1812) and Detroit (Aug. 16) and forcing the disastrous evacuation of Fort Dearborn on Aug. 15. After many months the United States employed better prepared troops and the British suffered serious setbacks, particularly in naval confrontations. On Dec. 24, 1814, the war-tired enemies signed the Treaty of Ghent, which left the various contested borders as they were before the war, but ended British interference in United States Indian affairs and left the Indians powerless to check further United States advance on its western frontier. Fort Dearborn was soon rebuilt (1816) and an organized settlement slowly evolved, by 1830 necessitating the James Thompson's ✳ platting of a potential town .

War, Revolutionary see Revolutionary War

Ward, Bernard called "Barney," came to Chicago in May 1833 with troops from Fort Brady [also see Adams, Joseph, who was his sergeant at that time, later becoming his in-law when his son Ralph married a daughter of Ward]. When his term expired, he retired from the military and became a teamster; filed a deposition in favor of D. Elston's claim for wharfing privileges on Nov. 25, 1835, and submitted his own claim [lot 5 block 7] later that year; was married to Ruth Marshall; daughter Claricy and son Henry A. were baptized on July

24, 1836; in 1837 he became the first alderman from the fifth ward; ✦ teamster, fifth ward. John Wentworth relates [1881] that Barney lived on an island in the Chicago River near the Forks, approachable from the N side by a footbridge, "since cut away," and that Henry was born on the island on March 28, 1834. [12, 28, 351, 708]

Ward, Henry A. see Ward, Bernard.

ward structure of Chicago see Chicago wards.

Warden, Peter listed as one of the founding members of the first Baptist church on Oct. 19, 1833, and a subscriber to the *Chicago Democrat* in November. [12]

Warner, Seth P. from NY; blacksmith for Ashbel Steele observed by E.O. Gale late May 1835, in the smithy on the S side of Randolph, E of Clark Street; ✦ clerk, Charles Walker & Co., South Water Street; retired to Austin, IL.

Warren 65-ton schooner from Ashtabula under Captain Heacock, first called at Chicago on July 18, 1834, and again on Aug. 16 when it came from Buffalo.

Warren, Daniel born c.1780 in Massachusetts; arrived from Westfield, NY, in April 1833 and soon acquired land 30 miles W on the W branch of the Du Page River [Warrenville]; his son-in-law Fredrick Bird followed in May, and his son Julius (nicknamed "Colonel," though only known to have been a lieutenant) arrived in July with sisters Philinda, Sally, Louisa (Mrs. Bird), and her three children. While Daniel began to build a house on his claim, Julius returned to New York and in the fall of 1833 accompanied the remainder of the family: mother Nancy [née Morton, born c.1785], sisters Harriet, Mary and Maria (twins), and Jane; they boarded at the Green Tree tavern, then continued to the homestead. During the short stay in Chicago, Maria befriended Silas B. Cobb, and they later married; for Cobb's humorous story of the initial encounter, see Cobb, Silas Bowman. Eventually, the Warrens owned a large hotel at [Warrenville]. According to [see] Emily Beaubien

"Col. Warren was a great dancer." In 1888 Harriet N. Warren Dodson of Geneva wrote the family history from which the following is an excerpt, relating the family's overnight stay at [see] John Mann's tavern on the Calumet River. [151, 207] [late October 1833, on the road from New York to Chicago]

... Only our mother was in the wagon during the day. When we were within a few miles of the Calumet it commenced raining, the walking was very heavy in the deep sand, the horses were driven as near the lake as possible on account of the depth of the sand any distance from the shore, and we began to fear we must stay another night on the dismal shore, when there came up behind us a man with a cart and a pair of oxen attached to it, who seeing us came to the wagon and asked if some of us would accept a place in his rough vehicle, at the same time saying we were but a mile or two from the Calumet, where he himself was to remain overnight. Mother hesitated a moment before accepting the kind offer. In the meantime my twin sisters had entered the cart and were quickly gone from sight. It was beginning to rain quite heavily and with our anxiety about the two sisters it seemed the next hour was the longest one we ever experienced. We at last reached the shaggy settlement at the mouth of the Calumet river. Just before we drove up in front of the only house to be seen in the dusk of the evening, a man drove past us with a pair of horses having as we afterwards learned just come from Michigan City, and seemed to be very angry because someone had disturbed his hay just on the road back of us. Said he would like to know who had pulled his hay down. The little man, driver of the cart in which the sisters had been riding, stepped up to him and told him he had taken a handful or two of hay on the roadside to make a more comfortable place for two young ladies to ride in the cart he was driving. We found out the large angry man was the owner and proprietor of the place. His name was Mann, but he seemed in his anger to be a savage. My mother hearing the loud talk went at once to the big man and said whatever there was to

pay for the hay she was the one to settle it as it was taken for her daughters' benefit. He seemed to be ashamed of himself at once, and said no more, but the little man with the cart was very indignant at his conduct and would not cross the "ferry" the next morning. Said he would risk drowning himself and oxen rather than pay such a mean man to bring him across. We watched him safely across the next morning before we went on the "ferry" ourselves, because we were told the quicksand made it dangerous crossing, and this is the last we saw of the little man with the little cart and small yoke of oxen almost as speedy as horses and well matched and well broken. We wished to have come across him again to thank him for his kindness once more, but from this simple experience we learned a rough exterior often covers a gentle heart, and that "appearances are deceitful sometimes." Mr. Mann had an Indian wife. The Mann house seemed full of people. We were marched to a small house of one room with one bed resting upon what was called a prairie bedstead, made fast to the house by two posts with cross pieces for slats. Our mother's bed was brought from the wagon, the excuse for a bed being taken from the rude bedstead, placed on the floor and three of the sisters with our traveling wraps on, camped on it and slept quite sweetly; mother and the younger sister occupying the bedstead whereon her bed had been placed. I think mother slept some toward morning, after the exitement of that wearisome day. The following day we arrived in Chicago.

Warren, Sally L. [erroneously named Sarah by Andreas]; daughter of Nancy and Daniel arrived from New York in 1833; served as assistant school teacher to Henry Van der Bogart at the English and Classical School for Boys on South Water Street; she started her job on March 21, 1834, at a salary of $300 per year; they became engaged but Henry succumbed to typhoid in 1835; in 1836 she married Abel E. Carpenter and moved to [Aurora]. See the following description of her daily commuting problems to school:

[1858] *I boarded at Eld. Freeman's; his house must*

have been situated some 4 or 5 blocks S.-E. of the meeting-house, with scarce a house between. What few buildings were there then, were mostly on Water Street. I used to go across without regard to streets. It was not uncommon, in going to and from school, to see prairie-wolves, and we could hear them howl any time in the day. We were also frequently annoy'd by Indians, but the great difficulty we had to encounter was mud. No person, now, can have a just idea of what Chicago mud used to be [in 1834]*; rubbers were of no account. I got me a pair of gent's Brogands, and fastened them tight about the ankle, but would go over them in mud and water, and was obliged to get a pair of men's boots made.*

Wasachek   also known as Clear Day; Potawatomi warrior, brother of Nescotnemeg and Waubinema; wounded at the Fort Dearborn massacre, but survived. [226]

Washington, George   (1732-1799) a native of Virginia, who became the first president of the United States, serving from 1789 to 1797. The residency at Chicago of Point de Sable, best known of the village's 18th century traders, roughly coincides with Washington's term as president; ➡ Washington Street and Washington Boulevard, (100 N).

Washington Volunteers   a fire brigade existing prior to the incorporation of the town in 1833; see firefighting.

Water Street   see South Water Street.

waterworks   prior to 1834 the water of Lake Michigan and of the Chicago River was considered drinkable without reservations; private enterprises catered to the convenience of the villagers by delivering water to the doors in barrels on two-wheeled horse carts, the price varying from 5 to 10 cents per barrel. The first public effort made by the village board to assist the inhabitants in securing clean water occurred on Nov. 10, 1834, when the board authorized the expenditure of $95.50 to have a well dug in the Kinzie Addition. Not until Jan. 18, 1836, did the Illinois State Legislature pass a law incorporating the Chicago Hydraulic Company, of which George W. Dole was the president; the real estate panic of 1837 delayed organization and action of the company until 1840. [12, 138]

Watkins, Deborah Scott   arrived from New York in 1826 with her parents [see Scott, Steven J.] and husband Morrison Watkins; married in 1821, they had two children, but were divorced in 1828; in the Peoria court records Deborah claimed "repeated and brutal cruelty and drunkenness"; her attorney was Jonathan H. Pugh, and this appears to have been ★★★ **Chicago's 1st** official divorce. On Nov. 5, 1828, Deborah Watkins married Joseph Bauskey of Chicago, who died of cholera in 1832.

Watkins, John   (1802-1897) born at Scipio, NY; came in May 1832; was secretary of the Chicago Temperance Society in 1833, and voted in the election of the first town board on Aug. 10 and in November subscribed to the *Chicago Democrat*; employed by Col. Hamilton and Col. Owen, he had begun to teach school that autumn in Hamilton's old horse stable on North Clark Street; when the school was moved to Father Walker's house at Wolf Point, Walker and Watkins cohabited, the former preaching on Sundays, the latter teaching during the week; in the July 2, 1834 *Chicago Democrat* he included a list of schoolbooks he had just received, available for sale in the "subscribers School room opposite the Printing Office." His name was on a school-related petition signed on Sept. 19, 1835; his teacher's salary then was $500 per year; left the town in 1836 to live in the vicinity of Joliet.

Winslow [428] published the following list of 24 children who were enrolled in the class taught by John Watkins in December 1835. For ten of these children [*] the editors found no corresponding family names of possible parents in Chicago at that time. Clearly, records of many early Chicago residents have not survived to this day.

Gryon, Rolland*	Gryon, Orville*
Gryon, Abigale*	Gryon, Charles*
Jackson, Ezra	Harmon, Isaac
Harmon, Martin	Owen, William
Owen, George	Kimberly, John
Kimberly, Lewis	Dicken, Lewis*
Brown, Samuel	Brown, Charles B.
Hale, James	Thomas, Robert
Cannon, Ephraim*	Cannon, John*
Lewis, John*	Knight, James*
Thomas, William	Legg, Benjamin
Sullivan, Mary Ann	Mullarky, Thomas*

For excerpts from a 1879 letter by Watkins, describing his Chicago experience, see below; also see schools. [12, 351, 728]

I arrived in Chicago in May, 1832, and have always had the reputation of being its first school teacher. I have never heard my claim disputed. I commenced teaching in the fall after the Black Hawk War, 1832. My first school was situated on the North Side, about half way between the lake and the forks of the river, then known as Wolf Point. The building belonged to Colonel Hamilton, was erected for a horse stable and had been used as such. It was 12 feet square. My benches and desks were made of old store-boxes. The school was started by private subscription. Thirty scholars were subscribed for, but many subscribed who had no children. So it was a sort of free school, there not being 30 children in town. During my first quarter I had but 12 scholars, only four of them were white; the others were quarter, half, and three-quarters Indian. After the first quarter I moved my school into a double log-house on the West Side. It was owned by Reverend Jesse Walker, a Methodist minister, and was located near the bank of the river, where the North and South branches meet. He resided in one end of the building, and I taught in the other. On Sundays, Father Walker preached in the room where I taught. In the winter of 1832-3, Billy Caldwell, a half-breed chief of the Pottawatomie Indians, better known as Sauganash, offered to pay the tuition and buy books for all Indian children who would attend school, if they would dress like the Americans, and he would also pay for their clothes. But not a single one would accept the proposition conditioned upon the change of apparel. [The reluctance of Indians to dress their children in European fashion and send them to white-run schools is readily understood if one reads the words of the Winnebago chief Day-Kau-Ray, see entry under that name; *eds.*]

Watkins, Morrison   also Munson; arrived in 1826; for details, see Watkins, Deborah Scott.

Watkins, Samuel   arrived from Virginia early in 1830, marrying Mary Ann Smith on April 15, 1830, Justice J.B. Beaubien officiating; a legal notice appeared in the *Chicago American* on March 6, 1841, referring to a case "Samuel Watkins vs. Nathaniel Blood." [351]

Watkins, Thomas   arrived in 1834; popular postal clerk under Postmaster Hogan at the post office on the SW corner of Franklin and South Water streets (1834), and later under Postmaster Abell; listed as agent for the *Philadelphia Saturday Courier* and *Catholic Herald* in the Sept. 30, 1835 *Chicago Democrat*; married Therese LaFramboise in 1836, but the marriage did not last [she later married Madore Beaubien]; ✦ clerk, post-office; for "Long" John Wentworth's description of the wedding, see below. [12, 351, 706]

I remember attending the wedding of one of the LaFramboise daughters. She was married to a clerk in the Post-office. The clerk was the one who delivered the letters, and of course was well known to all our citizens, and was remarkably popular. ✧ *He went to the printing office and had fifty cards of invitation struck off. But when people went for their letters they politely hinted that they expected a card of invitation to the wedding. So he was compelled to go to the printing office and have fifty more struck off. These did not last long, and he had one hundred more.* ✧ *Then he said that tickets were of no use, and everybody might come; and about everybody did come. The ceremony was performed by Reverend Isaac W. Hallam, pastor of the St. James' Episcopal Church.* ✧ *The house was of no particular use, as it was full and surrounded with people.* ✧ *This wedding made a strong impression on my mind, as it was the first time I ever saw*

the Indian war-dance. Some of the guests not only had their tomahawks and scalping knifes, bows and arrows, but a few of them had real scalps which they pretended they had taken in the various Indian wars. Their faces were decorated with all the favorite pictures of the Indians. And some of our young white men and ladies played the part of the Indian so well that it was difficult to distinguish them from the real ones. ✧ *It has been a wonder to me that, while our professors of musik have been inventing so many different kind of dances, none of them have reproduced the Indian war-dance, which to me is much more sensible than nine-tenth of those which are now practiced at so many of our fashionable parties. ...*

Watlon, Nelson C.   born in c.1815, Essex Co., NY; came in January 1834; in 1879 he lived in San Francisco. [12]

Watseka   Gurdon S. Hubbard's first wife, niece of Tamin, chief of the Kankakee Potawatomi; married in 1824 at age 15, two children were born but died early; after Hubbard divorced her and left the area, she married Hubbard's friend and fellow trader Noel Le Vasseur, bearing him three children; a town S of Chicago on Hubbard's Trace bears her name. ❀ For a portrait of Watseka, see page 368. [705]

Wattles, William Wallace   arrived in 1832; landlord of the Wolf Point Tavern, succeeding Charles Taylor in 1833; John D. Caton reports staying there under Mr. Wattles' care during his first night in town on June 19, 1833; in the fall of the same year Chester Ingersoll took over the lease; removed to [Plainfield]. [263, 357]

Wattles' Hotel   see Wolf Point Tavern.

Waubansee   also Wabansa, Wabansie, Wabansee, Wapunsy, Waubonsa, Wabonsia, Wahponseh—the name meaning *A Little Eastern Light*; chief of prairie Potawatomi with a summer village on the Fox River near [Aurora], wintering on the Kankakee and Illinois Rivers; younger brother of Black Partridge; British ally in the War of 1812, when he was of middle age; took part in the Fort Dearborn massacre and survived; was a friend of the Kinzie

WAUBANSEE [CHS]

family and protected its members. Participated in the Treaty of Chicago of 1833 and signed the document, but in the fall of 1834 and in the company of Pokagan and Topenebe went to Washington and protested against ratification of the treaty, claiming that Billy Caldwell, Alexander Robinson, and Joseph LaFramboise had not represented them well in the negotiations; died in 1846; ➡ Wabansia Avenue (1700 N). See also Wabansia Addition; Waubansee stone. [12, 226, 642, 697]

Waubansee stone   a glacial boulder that appears to be red granite, about eight feet in height, with a face carved into one of its upper surfaces, reported to be that of the Potawatomi chief Waubansee. The stone was hollowed out on top and is believed to have been used earlier by the Indians to mill corn; later the unordinary stone was hauled within the stockade of the second fort, and a talented soldier chiseled the face. Much later the sculpted form was purchased by the Hon. I.N. Arnold and stood for years on the lawn of his residence on Pine [Michi-

WAUBANSEE STONE [410]

gan] Street; following the great fire of 1871, the stone was placed atop a pile of collected fragments; existent within the Chicago Historical Society. [728]

Waubinema also Waubeeneemah, the name meaning *White Sturgeon*; Potawatomi chief from the Illinois River, and brother of Nescotnemeg and Wasachek; participated in the Fort Dearborn massacre and helped to save Margaret Helm; survived. [226]

Wau-Bun (1) title of the book by Juliette Kinzie, *Wau-Bun. The "Early Days" in the North-West*, published 1856; (2) Algonkian word, meaning *dawn* or *east*, also *light, white*. [406]

Waukesha Potawatomi, fox; ➡ Waukesha Avenue (5700 W).

Wayman, Samuel born in Ely, England, in c.1809; arrived from Quebec in August 1833; in November subscribed to the *Chicago Democrat*; ✦ painter, (Wayman & Dimmick); became a farmer in [Arlington Heights]; married Emma Kinder in 1846; lived at 142 Aberdeen St. in 1885. [12]

Wayman, William (1817-1892) arrived from England in 1834; became apprentice to [see] John C. Outhet; ✦ wagonmaker, Randolph Street near Franklin; married Jane, daughter of [see] Daniel Outhet, in 1844; served as alderman in 1854; lived at 251 Fulton St. in 1885; died on April 23, 1892.

[12, 351]

Wayne County Chicago became part of Wayne County of the Northwest Territory in 1797, and part of Wayne County of the Territory of Indiana in 1803; both times the county seat was Detroit. Early jurisdiction determines that some of Chicago's early court records remain at Detroit, such as those documenting Point de Sable's sale of his estate to La Lime. For details, see Chicago jurisdictional chronology on page 209. [436a, 544]

Wayne, Gen. Anthony "Mad Anthony" Wayne, who had acquired a brilliant reputation in the Revolutionary War, was given by President Washington the task of breaking Indian resistance to continued colonization of the Midwest, after Gen. Josiah Harmar and Gov. Arthur St. Clair had failed. Wayne routed the Indians on Aug. 20, 1794, at Fallen Timbers; this victory led to the Treaty of Greenville in the following year, the terms of which provided, among other conditions, a stipulation of vital significance for the future of Chicago, namely the cession by the Indian tribes to the United States government of "one piece of land, six miles square at or near the mouth of the Chicago River, emptying into the southwest end of Lake Michigan, where a fort formerly stood." Wayne died on Dec. 15, 1796; ➡ Wayne Avenue (1332 W). [12]

Wea French, *Ouiatanon*; *8iatanon* on Louvigny's ✳ map of 1697; subtribe of the larger Miami nation; encountered at Chicago by early French visitors.

Weatherford, William arrived in 1833; became assistant Indian agent and served as one of three United States officials when the Chicago land session treaty of September 1833 was negotiated with the assembled Potawatomi. [12]

Weaver, D. advertised a building for sale or to rent in the Nov. 12, 1834 *Chicago Democrat*.

Webb, Lt. James Watson (1802-1884) from Claverack, NY; Third Infantry; transferred to Fort Dearborn in June 1821, and appointed adjunct to

the post; early January 1822, John Kinzie was alerted by a Potawatomi chief of the imminent Sioux and Winnebago raid on the garrison posted at the Falls of St. Anthony, and Webb was sent to Fort Armstrong by Commandant McNeil to notify and render military aid to the outpost. Webb and an Indian guide reached the cabin of [see] Pierre Le Sellier on the Rock River, who discouraged the journey while the Winnebago were on the warpath; they continued to Fort Armstrong and the outpost was spared. Webb resigned from the army as a rear adjutant in 1827; he died June 7, 1884. [326, 635a, 635b, 704]

Weeks, Cole also Weicks; was licensed to trade on Oct. 23, 1824, for one year at Rocky River, MI; voted in the election of Aug. 7, 1826; a discharged soldier working for Kinzie [according to Wentworth], and Mrs. Kinzie writes [*Wau-Bun*] that he was employed by the Laughtons in 1831 as "major-domo" to run the tavern during temporary absences of Mr. Laughton; at the estate sale of W.H. Wallace on April 27, 1827 he bought "1 black silk vest, old" for 25 cents; married the divorced Emily Hall Caldwell. [262, 357, 406, 706]

Welch, John listed prior to 1836 as owner with his brother [see] Patrick of 160 acres of land in the SE quarter of Section 20, Township 39, as per Andreas, *History of Chicago*, pp. 112-113; ✦ farmer, S Branch, N of 22nd Street [12]

Welch, Michael P. also Walsh; arrived from Ireland in 1829; a discharged soldier and bugle player; was said to have been ★★★ Chicago's 1st native Irishman in residence; married Elizabeth Ouilmette (daughter of [see] Antoine Ouilmette) on March 11, 1830, J.B. Beaubien officiating as justice of the peace of Peoria County, in John Doyle's cabin at [now] Winnetka or Kenilworth; voted in the elections of July 24 and Aug. 2 that year; on June 16, 1834, a son Joseph was baptized and by late October Elizabeth sued for divorce, later marrying Lucius Darling of KS; left Chicago after reenlisting, joining Capt. Jesse Brown's Rangers. [12, 96a, 351]

Welch, Patrick arrived in 1833; prior to 1836 he owned with his brother John 160 acres of land in Section 30, Township 39, as per Andreas, *History of Chicago*, pp. 112-113; married Elizabeth Corcoran in 1837; a son John was baptized in 1838; ✦ farmer, S Branch, N of 22nd Street; died prior to 1880. [12, 351]

Welcome armed British sloop patrolling Lakes Michigan, Huron, and Erie during the period of British control; built in Michillimackinak in 1775. In the summer of 1780, she carried [see] Jean Baptist Point de Sable from there to Lieutenant Governor Sinclair's Pinery, near present St. Clair, MI. [48, 649]

well see public well.

Wellmacher, Johann [John Wellmaker] German immigrant baker who soon Anglicized his name; came in 1830 and probably became ★★★ Chicago's 1st settler of German origin, although the same distinction was claimed by John van Horne; born at Frankfurt/Main, came to Pennsylvania at age 17, later worked in the lead mines of Galena, where he is said to have made $2,500. Upon his arrival, he first worked at the Fort Dearborn bakery and, according to John Wentworth's reminiscences, "made a nice profit selling bread to the Indian settlers"; voted in the elections of July 24 and Nov. 25, 1830; that year purchased from the government lots 1, 2, 7, and 8 of block 14, but later sold them to John Miller [see map on page 44]; during the Black Hawk War he served in the Chicago militia under Captain Kercheval, being listed in the muster roll of May 3, 1832; later opened his own shop, Wellmaker & Co., also dubbed "Man Trap," advertising in the *Chicago Democrat* on Dec. 10, 1833 [see notice below]; an association with William H. Adams was dissolved on March 21, 1834. The *Chicago American* of July 1, 1837, carried a legal notice, "John Wellmaker vs. Antoine Ouilmet"; died at Hickory Creek, IL. [12, 351]

Hoosiers, Woolverines and Suckers, Behold !!!!!! The subscribers respectfully tender to their above named friends, and to his liberal patrons, the Pottawatamies, their sincere thanks for past favors, and informs them that they have on hand at their Man Trap, one door north of Mr. R.A. Kinzie's Store, a constant supply of fresh Bread Cakes, Pastry, &c.; also, LIQUORS, of every description, which they will sell at reduced prices, and his friends can come and get tired for nothing. John Wellmaker & Co. [See also Hoosiers, Wolverines, and Suckers.]

Wells, Absalom earliest settler on Thorn Creek in southern Cook County, where he built his cabin and trading post in c.1833 N of Rt. 30 on or near Halsted Street The site is marked on maps of the Thorn Creek Division of the Cook County Forest Preserve District. Wells came to the Chicago Heights area by way of Ohio, perhaps explaining the large grove of Ohio buckeye trees near the site of his cabin. [information obtained from Ed Lace, July 1996]

Wells, William (1770-1812) born in Pennsylvania; kidnapped at the age of 12 by Miami after the family has moved to Kentucky, and was raised by Chief Little Turtle (Michikiniqua); fought with the Indians against American troops until 1791, when he transferred his allegiance; was with General Wayne at the battle of Fallen Timbers; married to Sweet Breeze, Little Turtle's daughter, who died c.1808, then married Mary Geiger of Kentucky; was an uncle of Rebekah Wells, who married Capt. Nathan Heald; served as chief interpreter at the treaty of Greenville and later as Indian agent at Fort Wayne, issuing in August 1803 a government license to [see] J.B. La Geuness authorizing trade with the Indians at "Chicagou." In that year, he was ordered by Henry Dearborn, secretary of war, to mark out a road from Fort Wayne to Chicago and to inquire into sources of food for the new fort in addition to the farm of William Burnett, which had been operated by Point de Sable from c.1785 to 1800. On Aug. 13, 1812, he arrived at Fort Dearborn with Cpl. Walter Jordan and an es-

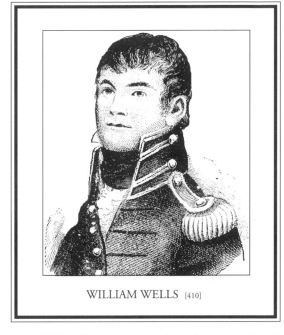

WILLIAM WELLS [410]

cort of friendly Miami, with orders to assist the beleaguered occupants; on Aug. 15, following brave resistance, he was killed by Peesotum and his heart was removed and eaten [For the gruesome details, see excerpt of letter by eyewitness Jordan.]. Wells's rank of captain, often attached to him, was not official at the time of his death; ➡ Wells Street (200 W). ✽ For a portrait of Sweet Breeze (dated 1810; Wells's daughter, according to one source), see page 370. [12, 36, 37, 226, 358, 649]

Welsh, Patrick also Welch or [see] Walsh, Patrick.

Wentworth, Elijah, Jr. (1803-1875) born in Lincolnville, ME; son of Elijah Wentworth, Sr.; came in 1827 with his parents from southern Illinois; in 1830 carried mail between Fort Wayne and Fort Dearborn; sometime that year he built and/or kept the Buckhorn Tavern on the Des Plaines River [Lyons]; married Eliza Jane Weed on Jan. 15, 1832 (she died in 1836; later he married twice more); joined Captain Hogan's Cook County volunteer company as corporal on May 24, 1832, dur-

ELIJAH WENTWORTH, JR. [12]

had four daughters: Lucy, Eliza, Zebiah, and Susan, and three sons, Elijah, Jr.; Hiram; and George (Eliza and Hiram married early and settled elsewhere); the family was very active organizing the Methodist church. Some of Elijah, Sr.'s, reminiscences of their journey to Chicago have been represented and are given in excerpt form below; a description of this industrious family by a contemporary follows. [12, 13, 351, 590]

[In 1827] the Wentworths started from Lewistown with two two- horse wagons. ... [Mr. Wentworth] said that on his trip north, after he left Canton they did not see any white people until they reached Peoria; and not one from Peoria to Ottawa; and not one from Ottawa to Chicago. They camped out at night and slept in their wagons. With their flint-lock guns they killed all the game they needed, and with the provisions they carried with them they fared well on their journey. When they arrived at Chicago they found some fifty soldiers at Fort Dearborn and some forty or fifty wigwams scattered down the Chicago river and some on the lakeshore. There were five or six stores or trading posts, and their trade was chiefly with the Indians. There were not more than ten or twelve white families in Chicago. Some of the traders had married squaws and were raising big families of half- breeds. Mr. Wentworth said a great deal of the land in Chicago, along the river and lake, was low and marshy with numerous muskrat houses scattered about. Mr. Wentworth went back about four miles from the lake and located on a fair eighty-acre tract and improved. His daughters here bought buckskin from the Indians and resumed the manufacture of gloves and mittens. Mr. Wentworth was a shoemaker, and his sons engaged in farming. The mother and her daughters carried on an extensive business in manufacturing buckskin gloves and mittens and buckeye and straw hats. The buckskins were bought of the Indians, who killed the deer and dressed the hides beautifully. The buckeye timber came from the river bottoms. The men prepared that very tough and elastic timber by working it into splits that were braided into very useful and

ELIZA WENTWORTH

handsome hats. They very much resembled the Panama hats afterwards so generally worn by gentlemen on hot weather. The straw used in making the straw hats was cut with a sickle or reap-hook about the time the grain began to form, because it would toughen better than at any other time. The straw was bound into sheafs and laid away for future use.

ing the Black Hawk scare; later served as second coroner; subscribed to the *Chicago Democrat* in November 1833, and on Dec. 17 he advertised his newly opened tavern "at Flag Creek, 18 miles south [actually SW, Lyons Township] of Chicago," called the Black Horn, on the later stage road to Joliet; died in Galesburg. [12, 13, 351, 117a]

Wentworth, Elijah, Sr. (1776-1863) born at Stoughten, MA, where he became a shoemaker and farmer; married Lucy Walker in 1799; first lived at Vandalia, IL, then in Fulton County after 1823; traveled to Chicago in 1827, and the following January rented the Wolf Tavern at the Forks from James Kinzie for $300 per year, becoming its landlord and immediately effecting a popular milieu, being visited "daily" by the officers of Fort Dearborn (he was familiarly known as "Old Geese"). In the same year he purchased from the government the entire block 28 [see map on page 44], but sold part or all of it within two years to Lemuel Brown; by the autumn he gave up his lease and established a log inn, called Wentworth's, eight miles N on Sand Ridge [Jefferson Township]. Lucy and Elijah

Wentworth, George arrived from southern Illinois in 1827 with his father Elijah Wentworth, Sr.; voted in the election of July 24, 1830. [12]

Wentworth, "Long" John (1815-1888) born at Sandwich, NH; graduated from Dartmouth College in 1836, and came on Oct. 25; in November he became editor of the *Chicago Democrat*, taking over for John Calhoun, and three years later owned the paper; ◆ editor and publisher, 107 Lake St.; married Roxanna Marie Loomis in 1844; served as Chicago's mayor from 1857 to 1858, and again from 1860 to 1861. In 1885, widowed, he lived at the Sherman House hotel; his ▲ monument at Rosehill Cemetery is a 72-foot-tall obelisk, tallest of all monuments in private cemeteries in Chicago, uninscribed and designed by himself; he was 6 feet

"LONG" JOHN WENTWORTH [12]

6 inches tall. Though Wentworth's life in Chicago falls beyond the time frame set for this book, he took an active interest in the people and events that preceded him, seeking and publishing a great deal of invaluable historical information [see Bibliography]; ➡ Wentworth Avenue (200 W). [12, 706-9]

Wentworth, Uriah   filed for divorce from his wife Betsey in the October term of the Cook Circuit Court, as noted in the Aug. 12, 1835 *Chicago Democrat*.

Wentworth, Zebiah Walker   daughter of Elijah Wentworth, Sr.; born in 1810 in ME; married Elijah Estes and moved to Bay View near Milwaukee; prior to 1836 she owned 80 acres of land in Section 30, Township 39, as per Andreas, *History of Chicago*, pp. 112-113. [12]

Wesencraft, Charles   also Wiesenkraft, Wisencraft, Wesincraft; German immigrant arriving with his wife in 1833; subscribed to the *Chicago Democrat* in November 1833; was one of the first Methodists gathering for Reverend Jesse Walker's services; their daughter Charlotte married Mark Noble on Nov. 29, 1933, the Hon. R.J. Hamilton officiating at a joint ceremony with the wedding of George Bickerdyke and Mary Noble; on Aug. 13, 1834, "Wesencraft & Noble" advertise in the *Chicago Democrat* for a "first rate sawyer" for their steam sawmill; ◆ carpenter and wagonmaker, corner of Clinton and Monroe streets [A William Wesencraft, painter, is listed at the same corner]. Charles and his wife later moved to Niles, where "Wiesenkraft's Point" is still known. [12, 342]

West, Emanuel J.   member of the initial canal commission created by Illinois Governor Cole in 1823, to have the canal lands surveyed and a cost estimate prepared. [12]

West, H.C.   subscribed to the *Chicago Democrat* in November 1833; owner of 80 feet of land on Lake Street, NW corner of Lake and Clark, for which he paid $300 earlier in 1833; sold it for $1,000 in the fall of that year [in 1856 the land was appraised at $100,000].

West Fork   small tributary to the south branch, entering from the NW, near the E end of the Chicago Portage; today there remains only a block-long canal, ending blindly at the W end of the harbor section of the south branch, near the corner of Leavitt and 27th streets

Western Hotel   a small hotel built and operated in 1835 by W.H. Stow on the SE corner of Canal and Randolph streets

Western Territory   created by ordinance of the U.S. Congress in 1784 under leadership of Thomas Jefferson, but never realized; was superseded by the Ordinance for the North West Territory of July 13, 1787. If the Ordinance of 1784 had passed, Chicago would now be located in a state named Assenisipia.

Westward Ho   sloop, arrived in 1833 with the [see] Hugunin brothers; the only vessel listed on the first marine listing in the *Chicago Democrat* on April 4, 1834, its arrival from Michigan City with cargo, corn, and oats. In May and through October the vessel actively connected the few towns along the northern and southern coast of Lake Michigan– Milwaukee, [see] Ship-wi-wia- gan, and St. Joseph, carrying merchandise and passengers, 10 in 1835; most always under the command of Captain Banks; Captains Freeman, Abel, or Harrison also piloted on occasion.

wharfing privileges   on Nov. 6, 1833, both G.S. Hubbard and P.F.W. Peck petitioned the town board for wharfing privileges; on Dec. 4 the town trustees determined such privileges as to which owners of lots bordering on river banks could build wharves up to 80 feet long for an annual fee of $15; however, the town corporation retained the right to revoke such privileges and to purchase any privately constructed wharves; in January 1834 Daniel Elston agreed to buy wharfing improvements on block 7 and David Carver communicated with the board on related matters; by Nov. 1, 1835 only a W.E. Church [Thomas?] had also filed a claim for privileges. On Nov. 15, the town board redetermined the sale of leases, then to be sold to qualifying applicants willing to construct within two years a dock, 5 feet wide, along the entire river front lot owned or occupied by them. The trustees' intention was to achieve in due time a continuous dock along the Chicago River and its branches within the original town, a dock to be "left open at all times for public uses as tow and foot path, the top of the said docks to be of an uniform height along the whole length of the river three feet above ordinary high water mark." [12, 28]

From the Nov. 18 *Chicago Democrat*:

PUBLIC NOTICE.

Leases of the Wharfing Privileges on Lots in the Town of Chicago, for the term of 999 Years.
Will be sold upon the following conditions, viz: One-fourth part of the purchase money to be paid at the time of sale, and the remaining three-fourths in three equal annual payments, bearing an interest at the rate of six per centum per annum; the owner or owners, occupant or occupants of the lots fronting the river,

will have the preference of purchase at a minimum price fixed by the Board, which can be known by applying to the Clerk of the Board, where a map or profile of the lots can be seen. Sale to take place at the store of Messrs. Jones, King & Co., on Monday the 23d Nov. inst., at 10 o'clock in the forenoon. The Board of Trustees will hold a special meeting, on Saturday afternoon, at 2 o'clock, at "Trowbridge's Coffee House," to grant preferences to such owner or owners, occupant or occupants of lots, as desire to obtain the same at the minimum price.   By order.

 E. PECK, Clerk.   Nov. 15, 1835.

But on Saturday morning at Trowbridge's Coffee House the "largest group of citizens ever witnessed" organized under S.B. Morris, with Henry Moore as secretary, and Giles Spring presented a set of resolutions that condemned the measures adopted by the Board of Trustees and advocated their substitution; after much debate citizens agreed only to remeet at 1:30, their inaction lending approval of the ordained measures. During the day S.P. Brady filed a petition for suspension of the sale of privileges while many others begin to flood the Clerk's office with claims, applications and petitions for privileges. In another meeting that evening of those opposed, the condemnation resolutions were passed and a remonstrance was circulated for signatures, which by the following Tuesday evening included over 200, more than half of legal town voters. The remonstrance cited the Board's measures as "illegal" because in the act of incorporation, there existed no clause granting the corporation the land or any other property (to lease); the measures were "unjust" because lots had only been sold to a few for one third their value, thereby depriving the town treasury in which all were equally interested; and the measures were "detrimental to the future welfare of the town" because few would have possession of the river (except where streets existed), depriving the many of free access to it unless at great delay and expense. On Nov. 23, Charles Walker petitioned for a delay in deciding the question of

the right to privileges, but claims, applications, petitions, affidavits, and depositions for privileges would continue to be submitted through the end of the year, including several for the Baptist [lot 4, block 20] and Methodist Episcopal [E half of lot 4, block 19] churches. The *Chicago American* republished the town board's ordinance of Nov. 15 on the Dec. 5, and on the 12th published the following letter from a reader:

The law of this State requires, every person or persons laying off a town or an addition thereto, before they offer any of the lots for sale, or lease the same for a longer term than five years, to have the map or plot of said town or addition, certified, acknowledged and recorded in the Recorder's Office. For a violation thereof, the forfeiture is only $25, for each and every lot so leased, &c. to be sued for and recovered in the name of the Treasurer of the county, one half thereof to the use of the county and the other to the town, &c. ✧ *The records of the Recorder's Office of Cook county, will show the fact, that "the lots or wharfing privileges" of Chicago, were leased on the 23d day of November last, by the Trustees of Chicago, and that on the 27th was the acknowledgment before Justice Harmon, Esq. and the certificate of the Surveyor the 28th, and filed in the office for record the 28th, five days after the execution of the leases for the short term of 999 years, a little way beyond the five years named in the statute. The law makes it the imperative duty of the county Treasurer to prosecute all such violations and forfeitures, and from the known vigilance of the Treasurer in the discharge of his duties, the Trustees, therefore, had as well be looking up the Shu-ne-ah.* ✧ *Then comes another and far more important question to be settled. That is, the payment of forfeiture. Is it to be done out of the corporate funds of the funds of the individual Trustees, who so pertinaciously and presumptuously persisted in a wrongful act, and against the wishes of a majority of the citizens of the town.*

 A CITIZEN.

The records of the early town board meetings are preserved at the Illinois Regional Archives Deposi-

tory, Ronald Williams Library, Northeastern Illinois University and contain the names of applicants, petitioners or claimants for wharfing privileges, usually giving the date of the application and often the location; this information is summarized as follows:

G.S. Hubbard [11/6/33, block 19, lots 1+2]

P.F.W. Peck [11/6/33]

Daniel Elston [1/1/34, block 7, O.T.]

John Hale [3/5/34]

W.E. Church [November 35]

A. Clybourne [11/20/33]

William Jones & Byron King [11/20/35]

 Palmer & George [11/21/35]

Kimberly & Knickerbacker (Knickerbocker?) [11/21/35]

William Saltonstile [11/21/35]

P. Pruyne [11/21/35]

Harmon & Loomis [11/21/35, block 18, lot 1]

Phili Carpenter [11/21/35]

Enoch Thompson [11/21/35]

John S.C. Hogan [11/21/35]

George W. Dole, Newberry & Dole [11/21/35]

 Peter Bolles [11/21/35]

Piter D. Hugunin [11/21/35]

D. McKee [11/21/35]

James Kinzie [11/21/35]

 Anson H. Taylor [11/21/35]

George W. Snow [11/21/35]

John H. Foster [11/21/35]

O.H. Thompson [11/21/35]

 Henry Moore [11/22/35]

Alex Anderson [11/23/35]

 Peter Cohen [11/23/35]

Rebecca Walker [11/23/35]

E.B. Williams [11/24/35]

John Ludby [11/24/35]

 William V. Smith [11/24/35]

Daniel Carver [11/24/35]

P. Cohen [1835, block 16, lot 2]

Methodist Episc. Church [11/24/35; block 19, lot 4, E 1/2]

D. Elston & Charles Cleaver [11/27/35, block 7, lot 3+4]

Daniel Sullivan [11/27/35]

Paul Kingston [12/5/35]

John T. Temple [12/9/35]

T.G. Wright [1835, 1/4 block 1, O.T.

P.F.W. Peck [1835, block 18, lot 4]

John T. Smith [1835, block 16, lot 3]

R.A. Kinzie [1835]

C. McDonnell [1835]

Bernhard Ward [1835, block 7, lot 5]

J.B. Campbell [1835, block 19, lot 1]

Daniel Elston [1835, block 7, lot 4]

Thomas Reed [1835, block 6, lot 1]

J.H. Kinzie [1835, block 2, lot 1+2]

Baptist Church [1835, block 20, lot 4]

George Palmer [1835, block 16, lot 2]

Moseley & McCord [1835, block 19, lot 4]

R.J. Hamilton & W.E. Owen [1835, block 19, lot 4]

N.R. Norton [1835, block 2, lot 3]

E.B. Williams [1835, block 16, lot 3]

Lathrop Johnson [1835, block 19, lot 4]

Wheeler, Russell E. arrived in 1834; ✦ Wheeler & [Burr] Peck, wholesale liquor dealers, Dearborn Street; later removed to Milwaukee where he died. [351]

Wheeler, Talman arrived from Vermont in 1831; active within Grace Church (Protestant Episcopal) in 1851. [12]

Whig 97-ton schooner from Oswego, NY, under Captain Davis, called at Chicago on June 29, 1835.

Whistler, Ann wife of Capt. John Whistler, daughter of Sir Edward Bishop. Eloped with John to the United States; lived at Fort Dearborn during his term from 1803 to 1810; died in 1878.

Whistler, Catherine daughter of Capt. John and Ann Whistler; married Lt. Thomas Hamilton, who served in his father's regiment at Detroit; they both came to Fort Dearborn in 1803, remaining until 1810, when he was transferred to Fort Bellefontaine.

Whistler, George Washington (1800-1849) born at Fort Wayne; younger son of Capt. John Whistler, three years old when he arrived with his parents and 68 officers and soldiers at the building site of Fort Dearborn on July 4, 1803; played within and near the stockade until age 10 when his father was transferred back to Detroit; became internationally successful as a military railroad builder, engineering the 400 mile railway link between Moscow and St. Petersburg. His second wife, Anna Mathilda McNeill, gave birth in 1834 to James Abbott McNeill Whistler, who became the well-known American painter. [12]

Whistler, Gwenthlean H. (1817-1894) daughter of Col. William Whistler, born at Fort Howard, where she spent her first 11 years, followed by three years at Fort Niagara; lived with her parents at Fort Dearborn in 1832 and 1833; a notice in the *Chicago Democrat* of Nov. 12, 1834, announced her marriage to Robert Allen Kinzie, youngest child of John and Eleanor Kinzie, Reverend Hallam officiating. [410]

Whistler, James Abbott McNeill (1834-1903) painter and etcher who lived and worked in London; born on July 10 at Lowell, MA, son of George Washington Whistler and grandson of Capt. John Whistler, who built the first Fort Dearborn.

Whistler, Capt. John (1758-1829) born in Ireland of English parents; came to America during the Revolution with troops under General Burgoyne; taken prisoner at Saratoga and returned to England; upon discharge, eloped with Ann Bishop to Hagerstown, MD, married her, and entered the American army in 1791; served under General St. Clair in the disastrous 1791 campaign against the Indians and was wounded; later served under General Wayne at Fallen Timbers (1794); directed by Col. Hamtramck of the First Infantry at Detroit under General Dearborn's order to travel to "Chikago" via St. Joseph with six men and guides to reconnoiter the route and site, and thereafter take command and lead a company in the transport of materials necessary to erect barracks and a strong stockade in the summer of 1803; remained commandant of the fort, which he named Fort Dearborn, until April 1810 when transferred to Fort Detroit; serving with Captain Whistler at Fort Dearborn were his son Lt. William Whistler and his son-in-law Lt. Thomas Hamilton; by appointing his younger son, John Whistler, Jr., to the position of sutler to the fort (initially in partnership with John Kinzie, who was later replaced by Surgeon's Mate Dr. Cooper, whom Captain Whistler had befriended) and by giving orders forbidding military personnel to make purchases at the competing store in the village, owned by John Kinzie, Whistler caused strong animosity to develop between two opposing factions involving the fort, the village, and the U.S. Factor Matthew Irwin (who reported regularly and in detail about conditions at the fort to the Secretary of State W. Eustis in Washington City), which may have been a factor in the killing of the fort's Indian Interpreter Jean B. La Lime by Kinzie, and which led to Captain Whistler's reassignment; in 1808 he submitted an invaluable ✱ draft of the fort and its environs [National Archives, Washington, D.C.] to the secretary of war. Whistler had 15 children, not all of whom survived, and he was chronically in debt on his $40 per month captain's salary; died at Bellefontaine. For details on several of his descendants who were born or lived at Fort Dearborn, see Whistler, William; Whistler, Catherine; Whistler, Sarah; Whistler, George Washington; Whistler, John Harrison; Whistler, John, Jr; and Whistler, Meriwether Lewis. [12, 109, 164, 681, 682]

Whistler, John, Jr. son of Capt. John Whistler; was in his late teens when living with his parents at Fort Dearborn from 1803-1810; in 1812, then an ensign in the United States military, John Jr. was severely wounded at the battle of Maguago, and in 1813 died as a first lieutenant of what may have been cholera. [12, 109, 404]

Whistler, John Harrison (Oct. 7, 1807-1873) grandson of Capt. John Whistler, born at Fort Dearborn to Lt. William and Mary Julia (née Fearson) Whistler; on Jan. 23, 1834, he married

Ester Bailly, the daughter of Joseph Bailly, trader at the Calumet River; Col. R.J. Hamilton officiated, and the notice appeared in the *Chicago Democrat* of Jan. 29, 1834.

Whistler, Mary Julia Fearson (1788-1878) born at Salem, MA; wife of William Whistler, Capt. John Whistler's oldest son, whom she married in 1802 in Detroit at age 14; both lived at Fort Dearborn during Captain Whistler's turn as commandant. In 1834, their daughter Gwenthlean married Robert Allen Kinzie. The following excerpt is from a letter written by Mary Julia F. Whistler:

The United States Schooner 'Tracy,' ... on arriving at Chicago, anchored half a mile from the shore, discharging her freight from boats. Some 2,000 Indians visited the locality while the vessel was here, being attracted by so unusual an occurrence as the appeerence in these waters of 'a big canoe with wings.' There were then here but for rude huts, or trader's cabins, occupied by white men, Canadian French with Indian wifes. ... There was not at that time, within hundreds of miles, a team of horses, or oxen; and as a consequence, the soldiers had to don the harness, and with the aid of ropes, drag home the needed timber.

Whistler, Meriwether Lewis (1805-1812) son of Lt. William and Mary Julia Whistler, born at Fort Dearborn in the autumn of 1805, the second male birth of a child of European descent; remained in Chicago until 1810, when his father was transferred; drowned at the age of seven at Newport, KY.

Whistler, Sarah eldest daughter of Capt. John Whistler, who had come with him to Chicago in 1803 to live at Fort Dearborn; in 1804 she married [see] James Abbott, a Detroit merchant—Chicago's second marriage; officiated by John Kinzie, who at that time held a commission as justice of the peace of the Indiana Territory; the couple returned to Detroit.

Whistler, Maj. William (1784-1863) born in Maryland as the oldest son of Capt. John Whistler, first commandant of Fort Dearborn. With his

MAJ. WILLIAM WHISTLER [12]

wife Mary Julia (née Fearson), he, then a lieutenant, arrived from Detroit at the mouth of the Chicago River on Aug. 17, 1803, to help build the fort. In 1807 he entered into a partnership with [see] John Kinzie as sutlers to the fort, indicated by an entry in Kinzie's account book on Nov. 26, until dissolved on Aug. 21, 1809; this dissolution was a major factor in the enmity that was to develop between Kinzie and William's father, the commandant. In 1810, he was transferred to Fort Wayne; during the Winnebago War was in command at Fort Howard; he was in command at Fort Niagara when he received orders on Feb. 23, 1832, to proceed to Fort Dearborn, which he regarrisoned during the Black Hawk War, serving as commandant of the post from June 17, 1832, to May 14, 1833. In November 1834, his daughter Gwenthlean married Robert Allen Kinzie. ❀ For a

portrait of Mary Fearson Whistler, see page 373. [12, 357]

White Dog an Indian chief living in or near Chicago during the years 1816-1818 as witnessed and described by [see] Mrs. Susan Callis. [74]

White Elk see Wabinsheway.

whitefish Lake Michigan whitefish, when in season, was spear-fished from canoes by the Indians in large numbers at [see] *Grosse Pointe* and further north. See reports under entries for Abram Edwards and for William Johnson. Also see entry under fish.

White, George a black man who served as Chicago town crier from 1833 on, and was remembered for summoning the town people to chase "the last black bear" that was sighted late in 1833 in the timber along the south branch of the Chicago River [Sightings of bears near Chicago have been recorded as late as 1837.]; sold water to the residents (charging more for lake than for river water); worked as an auctioneer. In the Fourth of July parade of 1836 he rode behind the cannon; ◆ City Crier, at Market Street, or at Stanton & Black's. [12, 249, 351, 466]

J. J. Flinn, in *History of the Chicago Police*, tells the following episode:

[In 1833 George White] *called the inhabitants together to attend the sale of a man named Harper under the vagrant law. Harper had once been a man of some respectability and education, but border life and border whiskey had so demoralized him that the community determined upon taking this extreme measure. There was a large attendance at the sale, Constable Reed acting as auctioneer. Negroes had been sold in this way, but the sentiment of the people revolted against the sale of a white man. Finally the negro town-crier bought Harper for a quarter, but some of the villagers helped the unfortunate vagrant to escape to the woods that night. He never was seen in these parts again.*

White, Liberty from New England; in the spring of 1812 he was in charge of the Leigh's farm at Hardscrabble, where he was killed and frightfully mutilated by marauding Winnebago on April 6. [12, 226]

White Pigeon   schooner built at Black River, OH, in 1832; in 1834 it connected Buffalo, NY, with Chicago, carrying passengers, lumber, and merchandise, beginning with its first call in that year on April 20 under Captain Disbrow; five more calls were made later that year, and two calls in 1835 under Captain Noel; lost on Lake Michigan in 1859. [48]

White Pigeon, MI   town 30 miles E of Niles, MI, where a post office was opened in 1830 (one year before Niles, MI), to which Major Fowle of Fort Dearborn despatched couriers once a month. [357]

White Raccoon   Potawatomi chief from the Iroquois River area, Illinois; took part in the Fort Dearborn massacre and survived. [226]

White, Stephen   (1807-) born at Hanover, NH; early resident of [Lyons] who made periodic visits from the East beginning in 1830, settling permanently in 1840; with Stephen Scott operated the Laughtons' tavern at [Riverside] following their deaths in April 1834; in 1837 married Elizabeth Gregg of Cleveland. In c.1853 White purchased from Stephen Forbes the mill on the Des Plaines River, passing it on to Dr. Fox, his son-in-law, who replaced the original structure with a two-story stone building that stood until the end of the century, known as the "Dr. Fox' Mill." [13, 51, 262, 278]

White, Thomas   born in Ireland; arrived in 1835; had died by 1878. [12]

Whitehead, Rev. Henry   (1810-1885) circuit-riding Methodist preacher and carpenter, born in 1810 at Chatham, England; arrived on Sept. 14, 1833 from the Sault Ste. Marie mission; when not assigned to any circuit, he would ply his carpentry and construction trade; together with John Stewart, he constructed the first permanent Methodist church building in the early autumn of 1834 at the corner of North Water and Clark streets, but two years later it was moved across the river to the corner of Clark and Washington. Earlier he had

advertised, as Whitehead & Co., for rental property in the July 30 *Chicago Democrat*, and on July 31 married Elizabeth Jenkins, Reverend Allen Freeman officiating (notice in *Chicago Democrat*, Aug. 6, 1834); there would be five children. Whitehead served temporarily as preacher in early 1835, between the tenures of Reverend J. Walker and Reverend J.T. Mitchell, and to make ends meet, he opened a small store on the corner of State and Madison streets, run by his wife when he was on circuit. In 1884 he made his last appearance at the Calumet Club, of which he had become a member; died on April 10, 1885, and buried at Rosehill Cemetery. [12, 140]

whitewood   much of the lumber brought to Chicago during the construction boom of the early 1830s was referred to then as whitewood; this might have come from Linden or Basswood trees, from several species of poplar, or from all of the above. John D. Caton recalled that the whitewood David Carver brought from St. Joseph in 1833 was a species of poplar.

Whiting, Capt. Henry   retired army officer of New York; purchased the merchandise of Fort Dearborn's unsuccessful factory once it closed in 1820 and became a sutler to the fort, together with [see] James E. Heron, during the years 1821-22; in 1824 he organized an independent trading post but was quickly bought out by Crafts, acting on behalf of the American Fur Co. [12]

Whitlock, Charles   arrived in 1835; had died by 1879. [351]

Whitlock, James   appointed registrar of the U.S. Land Office on March 4, 1835, his upstairs office in Thomas Cook's building after its completion June 1 on Lake Street; was still working in Chicago the following year when, as per notice in the *Chicago Democrat* of Feb. 24, he acted as administrator for the estate of David L.W. Jones, his father-in-law from Henderson, KY, who died in his home on Aug. 18, 1835. [12]

Whitlock, Thomas   (1800-1853) arrived in 1835

to explore, then settled in Chicago in 1836; married to Antoinette Haight (1826); ♦ boot and shoemaker at 104 Lake St.; two daughters: Cornelia and Antoinette; active in the founding of Trinity Church (Episcopal) in 1842. [12, 351]

whooping crane   *Grus americana*; formerly among the waterfowl hunted widely for food by Indians and pioneers, and occasionally seen flying with sandhill cranes in the Chicago area; now a very rare migrant in Illinois. [64]

whortleberries   blueberries; collected by Indians; received as a gift by Father Marquette from the visiting "surgeon"; see appropriate entries for details.

Wickham, John C.   legal notices involving him appeared in the *Chicago Democrat* on Sept. 3, 1834; two suits were brought against him in the circuit court on Aug. 11, 1834, for repayment of monies: $186.50 by John S. Dill and $82.50 by Thomas Reed.

Wicks, Joel   arrived in 1834 and served on the first engine company as a volunteer fireman [see petition to the village board of Dec. 16, 1835, with entry on firefighting].

Widow Brown   her name became well known when in April 1831 the Cook County commissioners mapped out the first two county roads, one by way of the old Brush Hill Trail (now Madison Street to Ogden Avenue) to Laughton's ford on the Des Plaines River at [Lyons-Riverside], "thence to the house of James Walker, on the Du Page River, and so on to the west line of the county"; the other along State Street to Archer Avenue "to the house of widow Brown on Hickory Creek." Hickory Creek is a tributary of the Des Plaines River (now) in NW Will County, where a settlement was begun in 1829 by Aaron Friend and Joseph Brown. The "Road to Widow Brown's House" can be found on several early Chicago maps.

Widow Clarke House   see Clarke House.

Wiesenkraft, Charles   see Wesencraft, Charles.

Wight, E.G., M.D.   came from Massachusetts to Chicago in 1831, moved to [now] Naperville, IL, in 1832, and to Plainfield, IL, in 1835, but continued to see patients as far as Chicago; built the first frame house on the road between Chicago and Ottawa, IL, in 1835 as a tavern and dwelling and called it "Half-Way-House"; when blind in later life, he continued practicing with the help of his son, Roderick B. Wight, M.D. [born in Kinderhook, NY, in 1825; graduate of Rush Medical School]. [738]

Wight's Addition   on the 1836 map of Chicago prepared by E.B. Talcott [see map list on page 51] is an 80 acre addition to the town under this name, the identity of its bearer remaining uncertain. It may refer to Reverend J. Ambrose Wight who, according to Andreas, first came to Chicago in September 1836 and spent three weeks of November with a surveying party on the Illinois & Michigan Canal led by E.D. [E.B.?] Talcott, likely the same man who prepared the map referred to above. Wight then associated himself with John Wright, the land speculator. The name given to the addition may also be a misprint for the name Wright; the [see] John Wright family was active and very successful in speculations during the land boom preceding 1837. The addition consists of the eastern half of the SE quarter of Section 5. [12]

wild rice   Indian staple food, growing in marshes around Chicago. John Calhoun recalled that after harbor construction in 1834, the terminal portion of the Chicago River that had run parallel to the lakeshore and had then become isolated and shallow, "filled up with wild rice."

Wilbourn, John S.   on Sept. 4, 1830, purchased lot 1 in block 2 and lot 4 in block 35 [see map on page 44]; by 1835 other owners were on record for these lots. [12]

Wilcox, Capt. & Bvt. Maj. De Lafayette   born in Connecticut; married to Sarah Grey Hunt in 1803; served with distinction in the War of 1812; arrived with his company (Fifth Infantry) on May 12, 1833, from Fort Brady, where he had been previously stationed; served as commandant of Fort

Dearborn from Oct 31 to Dec 18, 1833, and again from Sep.16, 1835, to Aug. 1, 1836. He was a charter member and elder of Chicago's first Presbyterian church, and signed as witness on the 1833 Indian Treaty of Chicago document. As the last commandant of the fort, Captain Wilcox became defendant in the lawsuit Murray McConnell vs. De Lafayette Wilcox, occasioned by J.B. Beaubien's purchase of the Fort Dearborn reservation in May 1835 [see Fort Dearborn II]; died in FL in 1842. [12]

Willcox, Gen. Orlando   see Taylor, Charles.

Willcox, Myra Delia   a sister of [see] Charles A. Taylor's wife Mary, and a visitor to the Taylor family's home at Wolf Point Tavern in 1832; in 1836 Myra married [see] George Davis.

Wild Sturgeon   see Nescotnemeg

Wilkinson, Elias R.   likely [see] Haines H. Magie's partner in Magie & Wilkinson, advertising a new grocery in the June 11, 1835, *Chicago Democrat*; was recording secretary of the Young Men's Temperance Society, organized on Dec. 19 that year ✦ listed with Thomas B. Carter & Co., fancy dry goods, &c., 118 Lake St.

William Penn   one of the two first steamboats to visit Chicago, arriving on July 18, 1832, with the *Sheldon Thompson* arriving on July 10. They brought Gen. Winfield Scott and his soldiers for the Black Hawk War, and introduced the cholera to Chicago. In July 1833, the vessel brought supplies for harbor construction.

Williamsburg, VA   capital of the state of Virginia during the years 1778 to 1781, when Illinois was claimed by Virginia as Illinois County, and the Chicago site was governed from Williamsburg.

Williams, Eli B.   (1798-1881) born in Tolland, CT; arrived with his family and Joseph A. Barnes on April 14, 1833, and opened a small grocery in a frame building on South Water Street; in February 1834 became trustee of the English and Classical School for Boys, and beginning May 21 in the *Chicago Democrat*, advertised 200 bushels of pota-

toes for sale; was elected to the town board in July of 1835 and again in 1836, serving as president during the latter year; his name was on a school-related petition signed on Sept. 19, 1835; applied for and claimed [lot 3 block 16] wharfing privileges in late November 1835, for which E.H. Haddock and Edward Talcott submitted supportive affidavits on the 24th; in 1837 Williams was instructed by the board to take steps to incorporate the town as a city; ✦ recorder, corner of Clark and Randolph streets, and groceries, &c., South Water Street, between Dearborn and State streets; in 1853 he became register of the U.S. Land Office in Chicago; died on March 24, 1881, and in 1885 his widow resided in the Palmer House hotel. [12, 28, 351]

Williams, H.   a member of the "Washington Volunteers," a fire brigade existing prior to the incorporation of the town in 1833. [12]

Williams, John R.   (1782-1854) born in Detroit, where he became an influential merchant and political leader; major-general of the territorial militia in 1832; his command assembled in Detroit in response to the Black Hawk threat; came to Chicago with 120 men on June 11, 1832, leaving again on June 22.

William Stuart & Co.   see Stuart, William.

Williston, Robert   subscribed to the *Chicago Democrat* in November 1833.

Willoughby, George   first advertised a "Boot Shoe & Leather Store" in the *Chicago Democrat* on June 24, 1835, located on LaSalle Street, two doors N of Lake Street; stocked a variety of leathers, including sole leather, either oak tanned from Baltimore or hemlock tanned from New York or "the best in market" calf skin, tanned in Philadelphia; tendered was "Cash paid for HIDES and SKINS."

Wilson, Charles Lush   (1818-1878) born in New York City; arrived in September 1834; brother of Richard L. and John L. Wilson; became editor of the *Chicago Daily Journal* in 1851. [12, 37]

Wilson, Harry T.   arrived from Vermont in 1831

FOR SALE.

ON CONSIGNMENT, 4000 lights Window Sash made by hand,

JNO. WILSON & CO.

Chicago, June 12, 1835.   tf2

on the *Telegraph* with Capt. Joseph Napier, then staked a claim and settled in [Wheaton]. [12]

Wilson, John L. (1812-1888) arrived from New York in 1834; brother of Charles L. and Richard L.; had a general store on Dearborn Street, which he advertised in the *Chicago Democrat* during September and October that year; became assistant to postmaster Hogan in the summer of 1834, together with John Bates; on June 4, 1835, J.L. Wilson & Co. advertised "New Goods … extensive stock of Dry Goods, Groceries, Hardware, Crockery, &c."; in October he signed up with the "Pioneer" hook and ladder company, an early volunteer fire brigade; ◆ on the canal [with brother Richard L.]; served as sheriff in 1856; lived at the Revere House in 1885 at Chicago. Among his papers (existent at the Chicago Historical Society) are several sheets that note Chicago's weather between 1830 and 1835, details that are included within the Chronology. [12, 498]

Wilson, Richard L. (1814-1856) born in Albany, NY; arrived in 1834; brother of Charles L. and John L. Wilson; ◆ canal contractor, on the canal; in 1845 became an editor for the *Chicago Daily Journal*; on April 3, 1847 he lost his left arm and right thumb when a ceremonial cannon, used on the public square, misfired; appointed postmaster on April 23, 1849, by President Taylor. [12, 37, 97]

"Windy City" this nickname for Chicago was not coined until the 1850s, when local boosters, among them John Stephen Wright and William (Deacon) Bross, plied the eastern states to promote Chicago with dazzling visions of its potential; they were often ridiculed for what many thought were wild flights of fancy but the future showed that these "windbags" had understated their case. As far as actual average wind velocity, Chicago is not in the lead among United States cities.

Winnebago for an explanation of their early name, *puants*, see that entry; a tribe of the Siouan family, calling themselves Otchungras, *people of the parent speech*. When first met by the French (Nicollet) in 1634, they occupied all of southern Wisconsin and, at times, the Chicago region; they were called *Puans a la Baie* or *Puans* by the French. Later, as allies of Tecumseh, they opposed the advent of the Americans, but in 1828, 1832, and 1840 were forced to cede all their Wisconsin lands and move to Minnesota, later to upper MO; about half the tribe later returned to Wisconsin and lives on land they have purchased; ➡ Winnebago Avenue (2200 W).

Winnebago schooner built at Green Bay in 1829; coming from Oswego, NY, under Captain Greene, the vessel called at Chicago on Aug. 16 1834.

Winnebago War also Winnebago Scare, Red Bird War; ending a decade of quiet frontier life and lasting from June to August of 1827, it was brought about by aggressive disregard by white settlers of boundaries agreed upon at the treaty of Prairie du Chien in 1825 and began with the killing of a white farmer (Gagnier) and a discharged soldier (Lipcap) three miles from Prairie du Chien by members of Big Foot's band of Winnebago. While there was little further bloodshed, the events precipitated a near panic in pioneer settlements, including Chicago, which had been without a garrison at Fort Dearborn since 1823. Quick action by Governor Cass, who visited Chicago early in July of 1827, resulted in a strong military response, a force under General Atkinson, some of which was quartered at Fort Dearborn; most members of this temporary garrison were 100 militia volunteers of the Vermillion County Battalion from Danville, the "Vermillion Rangers," hastily recruited by Gurdon S. Hubbard. Confronted with a large assembled military force, the Indians decided to settle their grievances in another treaty, conducted in August of the same year; the events prompted authorities to regarrison Fort Dearborn and Fort Crawford, and also establish the new Fort Winnebago at the Wisconsin Portage. Also see Cass, Lewis.

Winnemac also Winamac, Catfish; Potawatomi chief from the Mississinewa River, IN, who was a participant and signer of the Treaty of Greenville (1795); later lived on the St. Joseph River; on Aug. 9, 1812, he was the messenger who brought General Hull's orders to Captain Heald that Fort Dearborn was to be evacuated; sided with the British in 1812; participated in the Fort Dearborn massacre and was killed later during that war by a Shawnee chief who fought on the side of the United States; ➡ Winnemac Avenue (5032 N). [12, 226]

Winnemeg Potawatomi warrior from the Illinois River near Peoria Lake; often confused with Winnemac; participant in the Fort Dearborn massacre; survived. [226]

Winslow, Erastus, M.D. surgeon's mate for the seventh Regiment of the Michigan Territory Militia under Maj. Gen. John R. Williams, in Chicago during the Black Hawk War from June 11 to June 22, 1832.

Winston, William a former British officer who, at age 50, arrived in the company of John Bates in 1833 and stayed three years at Chicago, speculating in land during the boom period. [12]

Winters, J.D. advertised with Winters, Mills & Co. in the Feb. 18, 1834, *Chicago Democrat*: "The New Line of splendid four horse Post Coaches in Illinois – From Ottawa by way of Holderman's Grove, Walker's Grove and Laughton's to Chicago, once a week, 80 miles, through one and one half days, fare $5.00"; a postscript noted that one coach from Chicago to Dixon's ferry and Galena left every Thursday, "thus making a perfect connection with the Detroit mail. J.D. Winters & Co."

Winters, Mills & Co. took over the first stagecoach line Chicago-Ottawa from Dr. John T. Temple in February 1834 and ran it until later the same year, when it was purchased by [see] Frink & Walker; see Winters, J.D.

Wisconsin glacier   feature of the last ice age; the southern portion of the Wisconsin glacier covered what is now Lake Michigan; when the glacier began to retreat, approximately 14,000 years ago, Lake Chicago was formed. Lake Chicago decreased in size in successive phases, its current remnant being Lake Michigan.

Wode, John   German Catholic immigrant in 1833; married to Katharina (née Kannenkoth); on July 13, 1833, Father John St. Cyr baptized their twins at St. Mary's Church. [342]

Wolcott, Alexander   son of [see] Dr. Alexander Wolcott's older brother Henry; came from Connecticut in 1834; ◆ clerk, Steamer Geo. W. Dole, for St. Joseph; became Cook County surveyor; died on Aug. 11, 1884. [12]

Wolcott, Alexander, Jr., M.D.   (1790-1830) physician and Indian agent at Chicago; born in East Windsor, CT, on Feb. 14, 1790, as a member of a large and influential New England family; graduated from Yale College in 1809, but must have received his medical degree elsewhere, as the Yale medical department was not established until 1814; from 1812-1817 he was a surgeon's mate and surgeon in the U.S. Army; for the next year he practiced private medicine at Vincennes, IN, then accepted President Monroe's appointment as Indian agent in Chicago (confirmed by the Senate on April 18, 1818), immediately left for Chicago, and succeeded Agent Charles Jouett. In 1820, Dr. Wolcott accompanied Gov. Lewis Cass of the Territory of Michigan on his expedition to the source of the Mississippi River, together with Henry Schoolcraft as mineralogist. Writing on Nov. 6, 1820, to his brother-in-law, Arthur W. Magill in Connecticut, Indian Agent Wolcott listed his possessions and improvements made to "Uncle Sam's" farm on which he had harvested more than 60 bushels of corn to an acre, and expressed the hardships of his life – unprosperous, bad food, dangers, corrupt competitors. In June 1821, writing his sister Frances Magill, he described his crops anew and advised that pride

ALEXANDER WOLCOTT, JR., M.D. [137]

was the more appropriate response to life than humility; in August he and Governor Cass played leading parts at the Chicago Treaty with the Indians. Wolcott was an uncle of [see] Juliette Augusta and William Magill; William spent some time with him at Fort Dearborn's agency house as a teen-ager in 1822-23. Later on July 20, 1823, Wolcott married [see] Ellen Marion Kinzie (age 16), John Hamlin, J.P. officiating, with many local Indian chiefs attending the simple but impressive ceremony; the couple had a son [name unknown to the eds.] and a daughter, Mary Ann, who shared jointly with her mother in the father's will. Wolcott farmed extensively on Fort Dearborn land [see Chronology entry of Nov. 6, 1820], and also conducted a limited medical practice in addition to his government job, making him ★★★ **Chicago's 1st** private physician; William H. Wallace was among his patients. When the garrison was evacuated that autumn, Wolcott

moved with his wife from the agency house on the N side of the river – the former [see] Burns house (which had acquired the nickname "cobweb castle" while Wolcott was still a bachelor) that Jouett had begun to remodel and that he enlarged with "a kitchen, root-house, ice-house, store-house, dairy, and one hundred feet long of stables"– into Fort Dearborn, reversing his move in 1827, when the Winnebago War required reoccupation of the fort by military personnel. In 1825, he was assessed on $572 of personal property; became justice of the peace for Peoria County on Dec. 26, 1827. Wolcott was held in high esteem by Indians and whites alike; Schoolcraft said of him: "... as a gentleman [he was] commanding respect by his manners, judgment and intelligence." He died on Oct. 26, 1830; that year he had purchased from the government the entire block 1 of the original town [see map on page 44] that was later transferred to his widow (still listed in her name in 1833), had lost his son in July, and his niece Juliette had married his brother-in-law John H. Kinzie in August. His remains were first buried near the fort, later transferred to the City Cemetery [Lincoln Park], and still later to the Kinzie family plot at Graceland Cemetery; ➡ Wolcott Avenue (1900 W); earlier, State Street, N of the river, was called Wolcott Street. [12, 37]

Wolcott, Henry H.   a brother of Dr. Alexander Wolcott; Henry joined Alexander in 1830 or earlier; ◆ clerk, W.L. Whiting [produce and commission merchant]; remained in town until 1846; his son, named Alexander after his uncle, became a well known city surveyor.

Wolcott's Addition   consisted of the eastern half of the NE quarter of Section 9 (80 acres, immediately E of the Kinzie Addition) and the claim to it was part of Dr. Wolcott's estate when he died in 1830; David Hunter administered the estate, and sold the land to the speculator Arthur Bronson of New York in the late summer of 1834; the land became the Wolcott Addition to Chicago in 1835. In 1830 the parcel had been purchased for $130;

WOLF POINT in 1828, with Wolf Point Tavern on the left, Miller's Tavern on the right [58]

in 1864 it was estimated at $1.5 million. [12]

wolf *Canis lupus*, the grey wolf or timber wolf, abundant in Illinois until the early 19th century. Early Chicagoans complained that wolves "stole pigs and robbed hen houses and in deep winter were a threat to human life"; note also the reference to wolves in [see] George David's travel account of Oct. 11, 1833. In 1834, wolves still left the dense shrubbery along the E side of both branches of the Chicago River to search for food in the village; wrote Judge James Grant: "We hunted that winter [1834-35], twice a week when the weather was favorable, and killed many wolves in the present city limits." The wolf disappeared from Illinois sometime before 1860, in part because destruction of wolves was encouraged by law and bounties were paid. Early reports from Illinois that mention a "black" wolf, probably also referring to *Canis lupus*; there occur several variations in size and color. Distinct from this is *Canis latrans*, the coyote, also sometimes called prairie wolf or small wolf. They are larger than the coyotes of the Southwest, and have survived in Illinois until

today. The *Chicago Democrat* of Jan. 14, 1834, reported that a man had been frozen on the prairie between Chicago and Blue Island and reduced to a "few mangled remains," and there was a rumor afoot about a missing woman. [187]

Chicago Democrat, Jan. 28, 1834:

Two weeks since we mentioned it was rumored that a woman had been frozen to death, on the Prairie, near Blue Island, which has since proven to be the melancholy fact that her name was Mrs. Smith, wife of Mr. Smith residing at Blue Island, who left this place 2nd of January (which was the coldest day we have experienced this winter) for her home, and when within a mile and a half of her dwelling, she sank benumbed and exhausted to rise no more. When found, she was dreadfully mangled and torn to pieces by the wolves. She has left a husband and five children to mourn her untimely death. ✧ We are requested by Mr. Smith to return thanks to the citizens of Chicago, for their kind assistance in supplying his family with necessities, while absent from home, during the inclement season, which has deprived him of the partner of his bosom.

For a picture of the prairie wolf see page 401.

Wolf Lake largest of the Calumet chain-of-lakes, bisected by the Illinois-Indiana state line; filled with low hanging vegetation and the home of many snakes, the land presented a formidable obstacle to the first government surveyors; it is now the only one of the lakes devoted to wildlife preservation. In earlier days during rainy periods, the lake would absorb neighboring Hyde Lake [to the W] and George Lake [to the E] and would drain directly into Lake Michigan through one or two outlets; Gurdon Hubbard dubbed one of these "Pine creek" in 1822. In drier times, Wolf Lake drained westward into the Little Calumet River. Several major Indian villages were located near Wolf Lake, especially on the ridge between it and the Grand Calumet River to the S; ➡ Wolf Lake Boulevard (3500 E). Also see Calumet Lakes.

Wolf Point also the Point; an obtusely angular prominence of the W bank of the Chicago River "forks" at the point where the N and south branches meet; was the site of Wolf Point Tavern, the first public house in Chicago. Historically incorrect is the term "Wolf's Point," as well as the reference to the projection of land between the North branch and the main channel as Wolf Point, although now frequently so used. Virgil Vogel had contributed that the point existed on the NE bank where a small creek created a peninsula and, citing a passage in *Wau-Ban*, that Mo-ah- way, a Potawatomi Indian whose name translates *wolf*, once lived on the land. The larger Wolf Point area, including the land adjacent to the opposite banks of the river with its Green Tree and Miller's Taverns, became the initial social and economic core of Chicago and remained so into the early 1830s. In 1904 the shape of the forks gave rise to the Chicago emblem *Y*. See entry on Forks. [12, 697]

Wolf Point Tavern also called Wolf Tavern or, familiarly, Rat Castle, Old Geese's Tavern, and later Traveler's Home and Western Stage House; it was the first such public house in Chicago; built in 1823 by James Kinzie and David Hall on Wolf point

WOLF POINT in 1828, with Wolf Point Tavern on the left, Miller's Tavern on the right [58]

[now 338 N; corner of W Water and N Canal streets]. A sign with a painted wolf hung on a tree branch by the door, but no name was written on it; the work was believed to be that of a lieutenant from the fort—probably Lieutenant Allen painted the shingle. The tavern was later rented to Archibald Caldwell, who obtained ★★★ **Chicago's 1st** tavern license in 1829 [granted by the Peoria County Commissioners' Court on Dec. 8], when such was required. Early in 1830, and until 1832, Elijah Wentworth, Sr. [nickname: "Old Geese"] took over the management, paying Kinzie $300 per year. During those years it was often referred to as Old Geese's Tavern. Alternatively, the early settlers referred to it as *Rat Castle* even though it was the best-run tavern in town. In June of 1832, Charles Taylor and his wife Mary rented and ran the business for about one year, and it was General Scott's headquarters during the Black Hawk War of that

year; in 1833 William W. Wattles bought it; later in 1833 Chester Ingersoll bought the tavern and operated it under the name *Traveler's Home and Western Stage House*; in 1834 it ceased to be a public house. [12]

Wolfram, Henry   owned and operated a farm in the early 1830s, located between [Halsted Street, George Street, Diversey Avenue and Sheffield Avenue]; ➡ Wolfram Street (2832 N). [320]

Wolf Ridge   a wooded sand ridge near 115th Street and Racine Avenue that was home to a large number of wolves.

Wolverine   nickname for Michigan natives or residents, used in Chicago as early as 1833 [see advertising by Wellmacher, Johann]; the predatory mammal (*Gulo gulo*), from which the name is derived, vanished from Illinois as settlement began. Michigan is referred to as the Wolverine State. [341]

women of early Chicago   for an alphabetical list-

ing by maiden name, if known, of the pioneer women of Chicago, see page 367.

Wood, Alonzo Church   born in Farnham, Canada c.1809; came in August 1834; ✦ mason and builder, Cass [Wabash] Street, near Ohio Street; in 1879 he listed himself as residing in Granby, P.Q [?]., while in 1885 he resided at 69 Clinton St. [12, 351]

woodlands, eastern   see eastern woodlands; also see Little Woods.

Woodstock Trail   early area trail used by Indians and early settlers, leading NW from Fort Dearborn, partly coinciding with the later [see] Elston Avenue.

Woodruff, Alson   date of arrival uncertain; subscribed to the *Chicago Democrat* in November 1833; a notice in this newspaper on April 1834 announced the death of his wife, Mandane, at age 24.

Woodruff, James   his store, a frame structure at the corner of South Water and Wells streets, was

ALONZO CHURCH WOOD [410]

Mary Galloway Clybourne [12]

Note from the editors:

During the years covered by this book, men received most of the attention and most of the credit for whatever was accomplished. Women worked and suffered just as much, but they remained in the background. Records from the era reflect this attitude; many stories of immigrant families describe in great detail the many proud accomplishments of husband and children, but barely mention the name of the wife and mother, and sometimes not even that. Only occasionally has there been enough known about a pioneer woman to allow for an encyclopedic entry of her own.

The editors recognize this failing of the historical record, and have observed any information about women with particular interest. In this compilation all their names are listed, and for each one the name of the male partner is given, so that she can be located readily in her partner's encyclopedic entry in this book. It is hoped this listing will facilitate future genealogical studies.

ALPHABETICAL LISTING
OF
WIVES & CONSORTS
IN
EARLY CHICAGO

Arranged by maiden names, when known; otherwise by married name. All names are followed by that of the consort.

Many of the early traders and settlers were allied to Indian women; if the native women's first names are unknown, they are recorded together by tribe at the beginning of the listing.

For women or men known to have been allied more than once at different times of their lives, the number behind an individual's name indicates that this is his or her first, second, third, or fourth alliance, respectively.

Cree woman — Deschamps, Antoine
Native, tribe unknown — Clark, John Kinzie 1
Native, tribe unknown — Laughton, David 1
Native, tribe unknown — Laughton, David 2
Ojibwa woman — Caldwell, Billy 2
Ojibwa woman — Forsyth, Thomas 1
Ottawa woman — Beaubien, Jean Baptiste 1

Abbott, Persis B. — Pierce, Asahel
Adams, Hannah — Adams, Joseph S.
Aikens, Mary Ann — Varnum, Jacob B. 1
Aikens, Sarah — Saltonstall, William W. 2
Allison, Mrs. — Allison, Thomas
Ainsle, Mrs. Mary 2 — Hogan, John S.C. 2
Allen, Susan Randolph — Jouett, Charles 2
Alscum, Madaline — Ozier, Joseph
Ament, Sarah — Ament, Anson
Arnwaiskie, Theotis — Bourassa, Daniel, Jr.
Arrowsmith, Mary — Lupton, Benjamin
Atwater, Juliette — Goodrich, Grant

Mme Antoine Deschamps

Aurant, Elizabeth — Boyer, John K.
Austin, Harriet — Murphy, John
Bagley, Eliza — Salisbury, Stephen M.
Bailey, Anne Maria — Hogan, John S.C. 1
Bailly, Ester Mary — Whistler, John Harrison 1
Baley, Eliza — Salisbury, Stephen M.
Barber, Elvira — Rexford, Stephen 2
Barker, Evelina — Morris, Buckner S. 1
Barny, Sarah — Scott, Willis 2
Bates, Elvira — Forbes, Steven R.
Bates, Sophia — Laughton, Bernardus H.
Baumgarten, Catharine — Müller, Jacob
Bayne, Catherine — McCorristen, William
Beach, Elizabeth L. — Hale, Alford B.
Beattie, Eliza J. — Lowe, Samuel J. 2
Beckwith, Mary Ann — Bucklin, James M.
Bellamy, Elizabeth C. — Larrabee, William M. 1
Bellows, Laura W. — Handy, Henry S.
Benedict, Sarah — Clybourne, Henley
Bennet, Mary — Bennet, Samuel

Watseka Hubbard Le Vasseur [705]

Rebekah Wells Heald [410]

Bennett, Ann
Bentley, Nancy
Berg, Magdalena
Berry, Elenora
Berry, Lydia M.
Bertrand, Margurite
Bisbee, Laura
Bishop, Ann
Bishop, Mary H.
Bissot, Claire F.
Boardman, Adaline
Boilvin, Betsey
Bolles, Sarah K.
Botsford, Harriet R.
Bourbonnais, Cattice
Bowen, Emiline
Bowen, Nancy
Boyer, Maria
Bradford, Harriet
Bradley, Elizabeth

Ballard, Thomas
Walker, Charles 2
Stein, Charles 1
Hubbard, Gurdon S. 2
Berry, Benjamin A.
Bourassa, Daniel
Rexford, Heber S. 1
Whistler, Capt. John
Clift, Benjamin H.
Jolliet, Louis
Freeman, Robert
Boilvin, Nicholas
Bolles, Nathan H.
Sherman, Joel Sterling
Bourbonnais, François, Sr.
Bowen, Erastus S.
Prescott, Eli Sherbourne 1
Beaubien, Madore B. 1
Bradford, William H.
Adams, William Henry

Bridges, Sarah
Brock, Nancy
Brookes, Elizabeth Ester
Brookes, Mary
Brown, Harriet Gould
Brown, Caroline
Brown, Cynthia?
Brown, Lydia Ann
Brown, Margaret
Brown, Vienna
Browning, E.
Buckner, Diana W.
Budlong, Levantia
Butler, Harriet F.
Caldwell, Emily Hall 2
Caldwell, Louisa B.
Calhoun, Miranda
Caswell, Miss
Chapman, Caroline
Chapman, Emily
Chapoton, Marie
Chappel, Eliza Emily
Chapronne, Rosalia
Chevalier, Archange
Chevalier, Catherine
Chevalier, Josette
Chevalier, Sheshi
Chival, Mary
Clapp, Julia Butler
Clark, Eliza
Clark, Emmaline
Clark, Mary A.
Clark, Mrs.
Clark, Eliz. McKenzie 2
Clark, Sarah Ann
Clarke, Hannah
Clarke, Mary
Cleaveland, Ellen P.
Clement, Almira
Cobb, Ester
Coburn, Sally Merriam

Carpenter, Philo 1
Brock, Thomas
Brookes, Henry
Cleaver, Charles
Bates, John, Jr.
Clarke, Henry B.
Brown, Lemuel
Carli, Paul J.
Polk, Edmund
Brown, James
Hammer, John
Hamilton, Richard J. 1
Spring, Giles
Rees, James H.
Weeks, Cole
Scott, Willis 1
Calhoun, Alvin
Hickling, William 2
Kennicott, Dr. William
Chapman, Charles H.
Chandonnai, Jean B.
Porter, Rev. Jeremiah
Chapronne, François
Ouilmette, Antoine
Robinson, Alexander 2
Bourassa, Mark
Buisson, Louis
Montgomery, John H.
Newberry, Walter L.
Garrett, Augustus
Clark, Samuel
Flood, Capt. Peter F.
Hickling, William 1
Clybourne, Jonas
Vincent, Aiken
Freeman, Rev. Allen B.
Walker, Charles 1
Bascom, Rev. Flavel 1
Palmer, Isaac K.
Lincoln, Solomon
Follansbee, Charles

Colby, Myra
Collins, Mrs?
Conally, Sarah
Cook, Amy
Coombs, Rebecca
Cooper, Mary 1
Cooper, Mrs. Mary 2
Corbin, Susan (Sukey)
Corbin, Victoria
Corcoran, Elizabeth
Cortright, Sarah
Couillart, Marg
Coulter, Elizabeth
Crane, Betsy
Crandall, Amanda
Crews, Elizabeth
Crouch, Lydia
Curtis, Abba Ann
Curtis, Mary
Curtis, Mary

Bradwell, James B.
Collins, James H.
Taylor, Francis
Cook, Charles W.
Harris, William
Cooper, Ezekiel
Burns, Thomas
Corbin, James
Corbin, Phelim
Welch, Patrick
Harris, Benjamin
Nicolet, Jean
Hammer, George
Crane, Ebenezer
Prescott, Eli Sherbourne 2
Filer, Alanson 2
Lovett, Joseph
Harmon, Charles L.
Beers, Cyrenus
Curtis, James

Victoire Mirandeau Pothier [12]

Curtis, Mary — Miller, Charles
Curtis, Mary B. — Rogers, Edward K.
Curtis, Susan — Childs, Luther
Cutting, Eunice — Gooding, Joseph A.
Davis, Lucinda — Jackson, Samuel T.
Dawley, Harriet — Steele, Ashbel
de Charlotte — Thibeaut, Joseph
De la Vigne, Marie — Bailly, Joseph
de Nacouche [Native] — LaFramboise, Claude
de Nanette [Potawatomi] — Caldwell, Billy 1
Dearborn, Mary Ann H. — Scammon, J. Young 1
Dewey, Huldah — Wright, John
Dickinson, Samantha — Sheppard, Robert
Dodemead, Catherine — Varnum, Jacob B. 2
Dodemead, Eliza — Jouett, Charles 1
Dodge, Avis — Blodgett, Israel P.
Dodge, Mercy — Churchill, Deacon Winslow
Dolton, Catharine — Dolton, George
Dorrance, Harriet — Arnold, Isaac Newton
Dyer, Patience Lorain — Huntington, Alonzo

Ebinger, Elizabeth — Planck, John
Edwards, Julia C. — Cook, Daniel H.P.
Elliott, Sarah P. — Campbell, Maj. James B.
Ellis, Lucy Ann — Downer, Pierce
Ellis, Maria Theresa — Kimberly, Dr. Edmund S.
Ellston, Harriet — Brown, Thomas C.
Elston, Blanche Maria — Elston, Daniel
Ester, Elizabeth — Brookes, Henry
Farnsworth, Mrs. Marcia — Jones, Willard
Farrar, Caroline F. — Wilson, Charles Lush
Faucett, Lucinda — Dement, William
Fearson, Mary Julia — Whistler, Maj. William
Fisk, Marie Antoinette — Kennicott, Dr. John A.
Fitch, Anna M. — Barnes, Hamilton
Follett, Eliza — Follett, Jonathan S.
Forsyth, — — Caldwell, Billy 2
Fox, Elizabeth — Outhet, Daniel
Franche, Josette — Bonin, Augustus
Franzen, Adelheid — Franzen, Herman B.H.
Frauner, Mrs. M. — Murphy, N.
Freeman, Hannah Clarke — Bailey, Rev. Alvin.
Frink, Martha — Frink, John
Frost, Mrs. Sarah — Beggs, Rev. Stephen R. 2
Fuller, Candace — Jacob Fuller
Fuller, Olive — Benjamin Fuller
Gage, Mrs. — Gage, John
Galloway, Jane — Galloway, James
Galloway, Mary — Clybourne, Archibald
Gary, Orlinda — Wheaton, Jesse Childs
Geiger, Mary — Wells, William 2
Gibson, Caroline — Cook, Isaac
Gifford, Louisa M. — Dyer, Dr. Charles V.
Gillett, Mary — Taylor, Augustin D. 1
Grahame, Jane — Jones, Fernando
Graves, Louisa — Hadduck, Edward H.
Graves, Olive — Graves, Dexter
Gray, Polly Olmstead — Rowley, Jrieh
Green, Mrs. Hannah P. — Filer, Alanson 1
Green, Mary — Nolan, Michael
Gregg, Elizabeth — White, Stephen
Gregory, Anna — Jones, William

Eliza Chappel Porter [12]

Gregory, Caroline E. — Couch, Ira
Griswold, Melinda — Haines, Elijah M.
Grovan, Mary — Taylor, Augustin D. 2
Gutmann, Mary — Gutmann, Frederick
Haight, Antoinette — Whitlock, Thomas
Haight, Mary Margaret — Larrabee, William M. 2
Hale, Virginia — Kinzie, James 2
Haliburton, Emily Tyne 2 — MacKinzie, John
Haliburton, Jane (Alice?) — Flemming, Sampson
Hall, Emily 1 — Caldwell, Archibald 1
Harris, Emily Ann — Ament, Edward Glenn 1
Harris, Nancy C. — Ament, Hiram
Hathaway, Pamelia C. — Calhoun, John
Hawley, Caroline — Scott, Willard
Hayden, Sene — Myers, Frederick A. 2
Heald, Rebekah Wells 2 — Hackley, Lt. James, Jr.
Heartt, Emma Ann — Thompson, Oliver H.
Heath, Elizabeth L. — Beggs, Rev. Stephen R. 1
Height, Evelyn — Brainard, Dr. Daniel
Helm, Margaret McKillip 2 — Abbott, Dr. Lucius

Sweet Breeze Wells [CHS]

Herbert, Angeline
Heslington, Annie
Hicks, Lydia Ann
Higgins, Mary
Ho-no-ne-gah [Winnebago]
Hodges, Sarah Ann
Hodge, Mrs. Minerva
Hoffman, Mary A.
Hogn, Mary
Holmes, Cynthia
Holt, Jane?
Holton, Sophia
Hooper, Amanda
Horr, Clarissa
Hotchkiss, Emeline
Hotchkiss, Felicite
Houghton, Sophia E.
Howe, Sarah Dunn
Hubbard, Eliza
Hubbard, Elizabeth Ann

Vaughan, Daniel W.
Blann, James
Sinclair, James
Lane, James
Mack, Stephen, Jr.
Ament, John Lawson
Carpenter, Gilbert
Penrose, Lt. James W.
Carroll, Patrick
Hamilton, Polemus D.
Holt, Isaac
Eldredge, Dr. John W.
Butterfield, Lyman
Brown, Samuel
Owen, Thomas J.V.
Kercheval, Gholson
Eldredge, Dr. John W.
Brown, Rufus
Grant, James
Crawford, William

Hubbard, Harriet L.
Hubbard, Mary A.E.
Hubbell, Julia Ann
Hugunin, Mrs.
Hunt, Sarah Grey
Hunter, Mrs. Eunice
Huntoon, Anna M.
Huntoon, Betsey
Huntoon, Emaline C.
Ingersol, Sarah
Jamison, Nancy
Jenkins, Elizabeth
Johnson, Clementine
Johnson, Harriet
Johnson, Maria Louisa
Johnson, Mrs.
Jones, —
Jones, Emily
Jones, Mrs. Francis
Jones, Julia B.
Josette [Native]
Joyce, Sally
Kannenkoth, Katharina
Kawkeeme [Potawatomi]
Keecheeaqua [Potawatomi]
Keez-ko-quah [Native]
Kelsey, Eve
Kendall, Betsey
Kercheval, Nancy
Ketchum, Mary R.
Kiley, Miss
Kimball, Margaret L.
Kimball, Minerva
Kinder, Emma
King, Ann G.
King, Mrs.
Kingston, Mrs.
Kinzie, Elizabeth
Kinzie, Ellen Marion 1
Kinzie, Margaret McK. 2
Kinzie, Maria Indiana

Hamilton, Richard J. 2
Hubbard, Gurdon S. 3
Fullerton, Alexander N.
Hugunin, Hiram
Wilcox, De Lafayette
Carpenter, Sgt. Nathaniel
Harmon, Isaac D.
Holbrook, John C.
McDaniel, Alexander
Smith, William V.
Jamison, Lt. Louis T.
Whitehead, Rev. Henry
Graves, Henry
McClure, Josiah E.
Gray, Charles M.
Johnson, Peter
Whitlock, James
King, Byram
Paine, Seth
Brookes, Samuel M.
Caldwell, Archibald 2
Reed, Charles
Wode, John
Burnett, William
La Tendre, Jean Baptiste
Beaubien, Madore B. 2
Kelsey, Patrick
Flagg, Reuben
Stephens, Robert
Vial, Robert
Emerson, Benjamin
Gary, Jude Perin
Botsford, John Kent
Wayman, Samuel
King, Henry
King, Tuthill
Kingston, Paul 1
Miller, Samuel
Wolcott, Alexander
Hall, Benjamin
Hunter, Lt. David

Mercy Dodge Churchill [314a]

Kurbey, Marguerite May
LaFramboise, Josette
LaFramboise, Therese 1
Lauer, Eva
Lawe, Rebecca R.
Lawrence, Susanna
Leahy, Elizabeth
Leary, Virginia
Leavenworth, Ruth
LeGrand, Sauqua
Leigh, Martha 2
Leigh, Martha 1
LeRoi, Angeline
Livingston, Eliza
Lolliet, Emma
Loomis, Roxanna Marie
Loomis, Welthyan
Love, Eunice
Lovett, Julia
Lowe, Roxana L.

Burke, Michael
Beaubien, Jean Baptiste 3
Watkins, Thomas
Lauer, Kasper
Vieau, Andrew J., Sr.
Contraman, Frederick H.
Taylor Anson H.
Leary, Albert Greene
Hanson, Joseph L.
Caldwell, Billy 3
Des Pins, François
Leigh, James
Vieau, Jacques
Plympton, Capt. Joseph
Brookfield, William
Wentworth, John
Harmon, Dr. Elijah D.
Ament, John Viele
Merrill, George
Lowe, Samuel J. 1

Juliette Magill Kinzie [12]

Indian Woman with Child
sketch by Catlin

Lowry, Martha Jane	Abell, Sidney
Lozier, Olive	Lozier, Oliver 1
Luce, Mary	Ament, Edward Glenn 2
Lytle, Eleanor 1	McKillip, Daniel
Lytle, Margaret	Forsyth, William, Jr.
Mabbatt, Emeline	Egan, Dr. William Bradshaw
MacKinzie,	
Emily Tyne Haliburton 3	Forsyth, William, Sr. 2
Madison, Diana	Allen, Nathan
Madelaine [Potawatomi]	Bertrand, Joseph
Magill, Juliette Augusta	Kinzie, John Harris
Maglen, E.	Johnson, Peter
Mahaffy, Mary	Young, George
Manierre, Elizabeth	Snow, George W.
Malott, Kesiah	Forsyth, Thomas 2
Marguerite [Potawatomi]	Bourassa, Leon
Marshall, Ruth	Ward, Bernard
Martin, Isabel	Forsyth, William, Sr. 1
Mathews, Lucy Welford	Temple, Peter
Mathieu, Elizabeth	Beaubien, Mark 2

Maw-naw-bun-no-quah [Ottawa]	Beaubien, Jean Baptiste 2
Mayer, Blondine D.	Mayer, Nathaniel
McClintock, Catherine	McClintock, Wilson 1
McClintock, Charlotte	McClintock, Wilson 2
McClure, Mary E.	Jamison, Lt. Louis T. 2
McGlashan, Charlotte	McConnell, Edward
McKenzie, Elizabeth 1	Clark, John
McKenzie, Margaret 1	Kinzie, John 1
McKillip, Eleanor Lytle 2	Kinzie, John 2
McKillip, Margaret 1	Helm, Lt. Linai T.
Medora Augusta	Gale, Stephen Francis
Meeker, Adeline	Meeker, Joseph S.
Mellan, Lemira	See, Rev. William 3
Merrill, Sarah	Gage, Jared
Miles, Susan	Beaubien, Alexander
Millen, Ellen Adell	Stewart, John
Millhouse, Susan	Simmons, John
Miner, Mrs. Ester D.	Brock, Thomas 2
Miner, E.W.	Barnes, Joseph A.
Miner, Miranda	Miner, Frederick T.
Mirandeau, Madeline	Clark, John Kinzie 2
Mirandeau, Victoire	Pothier, Jean
Montgomery, Elizabeth	Montgomery, Loton W.
Moore, L.J.	Hanchett, John L.
Morris, Potily	Latzky, John
Morrison, Mrs. Amanda	King, Sherman
Morton, Nancy	Warren, Daniel
Moss, Minerva	See, Rev. William 1
Mulford, Rebecca	Mulford, Maj. Edward H.
Mursell, Sarah	Hinton, Rev. Isaac T.
Mutti, Maria A.	Stein, Charles 3
Nadeau, Monique	Beaubien, Mark 1
Napier, Amy	Murray, John
Napier, Betsy	Napier, John
Neads, Sarah	Neads, John
Nichols, Ellen	Nichols, Luther
Noble, Margaret	Noble, Mark, Sr.
Noble, Mary	Bickerdyke, George
Nokenoqua [Potawatomi]	La Lime, Jean B.
Northam, Lucy F.	Osborn, Andrew L.

Noyes, Selina	Page, F.M.
O'Neil, Jane R.	Palmer, Dr. George W.
Oalds, Emily	Caddy, George
Ogden, Eliza	Butler, Charles
Orcutt, Philura M.	Ballingall, Patrick
Olmstead, Polly Gray	Rowley, Jrieh
Osborn, Mrs.	Osborn, William
Osborn, Rebecca	Heacock, Russell E.
Otis, Mary H.	Talcott, Mancel, Jr.
Ouellet, Angelica	Pettell [Pilet], Louis
Ouilmette, Archange S. 1	Tramblay Tousaint
Ouilmette, Elizabeth 1	Welch, Michael P.
Ouilmette, Marie Louise	Welch, John
Outhet, Jane	Wayman, William
Pachequetachai, Margaret	LeClaire, Pierre
Parks, Jane	Moore, Peter
Patterson, Mary Charity	Herrington, James C., Jr.
Patterson, Mrs.	Patterson, Erastus
Patterson, Sarah	Turner, John
Paul, Lucy	Morrison, Orsemus

371

Clarissa Stewart Hobson

Emeline Hotchkiss Owen [319]

Peltier, Therese	LaFramboise, Joseph
Perin, Lucy	Gary, William
Periolat, Veronica	Belz, John
Pierce, Elizabeth	Butterfield, Justin
Pierce, Elizabeth	McNeil, Lt. John
Pinney, Catherine Louise	Beaubien, Jean Baptiste 4
Planck, Elizabeth	Ebinger, John
Plantade, Louisa	Taylor, Francis H.
Plante, Isabelle	Lucier, Charles
Point de Sable, Catherine [Native]	Point de Sable, Jean Baptiste
Point de Sable, Suzanne	Pelletier, Jean Baptiste
Polk, Mary	Polk, Edmund
Pomeroy, Ruth S.	Bascom, Rev. Flavel 3
Pruyne, Rebecca S. 2	Church, Thomas 2
Queen, Mary	Cook, Thomas 2
Reed, Evangeline	Ebert, Lizard
Reed, Maria	Huntoon, George M.
Rehly, Barbara	Ebinger, Christian
Reid, Ann Hamilton	Manierre, George

Rexford, Julia R.	Rexford, Norman
Rhines, Minerva	Rhines, Henry
Rice, Maria	Mason, Mathias
Robbins, Mary	Baxley, Capt. Joseph M.
Robinson, Catherine?	Chevalier, Louis Pasquale
Rogers, Bridget	Murphy, John
Rogers, Harriet Elizabeth	Bolles, Peter
Russel, Tess?	Russell, William
Russell, Mrs.	Russell, Capt. John B.F.
Saltonstall, Mary	Saltonstall, William 1
Sambli, Arkash 1	Tramble, Tousant
Sauter, Mrs.	Sauter, Charles
Sauter, Mrs.	Sauter, Jacob
Scovill, Mary A.	McHarry, John
Scolville, Almeda	Napier, Capt. Joseph
Scott, Alice Lovisa	Warrington, Arthur
Scott, Alsey	Cook, Thomas 1
Scott, Deborah 1	Watkins, Morrison
Scott, Permelia	Clark, John Kinzie 3
Scott, Wealthy	McKee, David
Sebrara, Margaret	Peacock, Joseph
See, Leah	Kinzie, James 1
See, Mary	See, Rev. William 2
Sevier, Mary Jane	Graves, Lorin
Seward, Harriet C.	Brown, William Hubbard
Shattucks, Andalucia	Marshall, Dr. James 1
Shattucks, Rosanna M.	Marshall, Dr. James 2
Shaw, Emily	Sweet, Alanson
Shaw, Jessy	Worthingham, William
Shawenoqua [Potawatomi]	LaFramboise, François, Sr.
Sheldon, Delia A.	Drummond, Thomas
Sherrill, Laura A.	Caton, John Dean
Sherman, Elizabeth	Foot, John
Sherman, Elizabeth	Sherman, Phinneas
Sherman, Maria	Outhet, John C.
Sherman, Mrs.	Sherman, Silas W.
Sherman, Rebecca 1	Pruyne, Peter
Shull, Mary S.	Porter, Hibbard
Silloway, Sarah	Gale, Abram
Smith, Elizabeth	Rexford, Heber S. 2
Smith, Jane Elvira	Hubbard, Henry G.

Smith, Louisa	Vial, Joseph
Smith, Louisa M.	Boone, Dr. Levi D.
Smith, Lucy	Russell, F.C.
Smith, Mary Ann	Watkins, Samuel
Smith, Medora Augusta	Gale, Stephen F.
Smith, Nancy	Foster, John Herbert
Sobrano, Margaret	Peacock, Joseph
Spangler, Margaret Ann	Manierre, Edward
Sparhawk, Elizabeth B.	Bascom, Rev. Flavel 2
Specht, Mary Catherine	Boyer, Dr. Valentine A.
Spence, —	Johnson, Seth, Capt.
Spence, Agnes	Wilson, J.D.
Sprague, Laura Bronson	Simons, Edward
Staly, Julia	Gardiner, Alvah N.
Staughton, Elizabeth	Temple, John Taylor
Stebbins, Jane Creed	Kingsbury, Julius J.B.
Stephens, Nancy	Kercheval, Lewis C.
Stephenson, Eliza A.	Morris, Buckner S. 2
Steward, Harriet C.	Brown, William H.
Stewart, Clarissa	Hobson, Bailey

Mary Fearson Whistler [357]

Stewart, Nancy	Shapley, Morgan L.
Stolp, Jannetje	Stolp, Frederick
Stone, Jane Ann	Stone, Horatio O. 1
Stow, Mary Ann	Dimmick, Edward
Stowe, Celia	Stowe, William H.
Stronach, S. Ellen	Dolton, Charles H.
Stuart, Eliza G.	Stuart, William
Sturtevant, J. Helen	Underwood, John M.
Sweet Breeze [Miami]	Wells, William 1
Talcott, Angelina	Wright, Daniel
Talcott, Betsy	Talcott, Mancel, Sr.
Tasker, Amanda	Downer, Stephen F.
Taylor, Lucy Ann	Taylor, Solomon
Taylor, Mary Monica	Talley, Alfred Maurice
Taylor, Mrs.	Taylor, William Hartt
Temple, Lenora Maria	Hoyne, Thomas
Temple, Virginia Alice	Montgomery, William
Thibeaut, Charlotte	Thibeaut, Joseph
Thompson, Ann	Carpenter, Philo 2
Thurston, Harriet	Crandall, David

Topley, Mary Ann	Lozier, Oliver 2
Towner, Louisa	Dole, George W.
Trask, Hadassah	Scott, Stephen J.
Tremblay, Marie C.	Anderson, John
Tramble, Arkash Sambli 2	Mann, John
Trowbridge, Caroline	Strong, Robert
Trowbridge, Electra	Sherman Francis C.
Trowbridge, Elizabeth	Updike, Peter Lewis
Trowbridge, Mary	Forbes, John, Jr.
Tucker, Serena	Hubbard, Ahira
Tuckerman, Hannah Ann	Corron, Joseph P.
Tuly, Mrs. Priscilla P.	Hamilton, Richard J. 3
Turner, Catherine B.	Wright, John Stephen
Twogood, Emily	Satterlee, Merrit L.
Tyne, Emily 1	Haliburton, William
Valette, Susan	Gary, Erastus
Vandette, Angelique	Molere, Pierre
Vieau, Angelicia	Juneau, Peter
Vieau, Josette	Juneau, Laurent S.
Waish-ke-shaw [Potawatomi]	Laughton, David 3
Walker, Caroline	Clarke, William Brown
Walker, Caroline I.	Peck, Ebenezer
Walker, Lucy	Wenthworth, Elijah, Sr.
Walker, Jane G.	Walker, James Barr
Walker, Mary Louisa	Hulbert, Eri Baker
Walker, Nancy	Irwin, Maj. Mathew
Walker, Rebecca?	Walker, Rev. Jesse 2
Walker, Susannah	Walker, Rev. Jesse 1
Wallace, Lydia	Whistler, John Harrison 2
Ward, Sophia Caroline	Andrews, David
Warner, Rebecca	Cooley, William
Warner, Rebecca	Scarrit, Isaac
Warren, Harriet Newell	Dodson, Christian B.
Warren, Louisa	Bird, Frederick
Warren, Maria	Cobb, Silas Bowman
Warren, Sally L.	Carpenter, Abel E.
Warriner, Rachel	Church, Thomas 1
Watkins, Betsey	Wooley, Jedediah
Watkins, Deborah Scott 2	Bauskey, Joseph
Watkins, Therese LaF. 2	Beaubien, Madore 3

Watseka [Potawatomi] 1	Hubbard, Gurdon S. 1
Watseka [Potawatomi] 2	Le Vasseur, Noel
Wattles, Susan	Rexford, Stephen 1
Watts, Eleanor	Lewis, Samuel
Weaver, Phoebe	Ingersoll, Chester
Weed, Eliza Jane 1	Wenthworth, Elijah, Jr.
Weldon, Elizabeth A.	Bickerdyke, Joseph
Wells, Elizabeth C.	Couch, James
Wells, Rebekah 1	Heald, Capt. Nathan
Welch, Elizabeth O. 2	Darling, Lucius R.
Welsh, Mary	Smith, Lawrence
Wentworth, Betsey	Wentworth, Uriah
Wentworth, Zebiah W.	Estes, Elijah
Werner, Barbara	Stein, Charles 2
Wesencraft, Charlotte	Noble, Mark, Jr.
Wesencraft, Mrs.	Wesencraft, Charles
Whipple, Maria E.	Wilson, John Lush
Whistler, Catherine	Hamilton, Lt. Thomas
Whistler, Gwenthlean	Kinzie, Robert Allen
Whistler, Sarah	Abbott, James
Whitlock, Cornelia	Hatch, James C.
Wicker, Fanny	Rand, Socrates
Willcox, Myra Delia	Davis, George
Willcox, Mary	Taylor, Charles A.
Willey, Caroline	Strong, Robert
William, Nancy	Hallam Rev. Isaac W.
Williams, Mrs.	Williams, Eli B.
Willis, Betty	Kettlestrings, Joseph
Wilson, Harriet	Albee, Cyrus P.
Wolcott, Caroline	Balestier, Joseph Neree
Wolcott, Ellen Kinzie 2	Bates, George C.
Wolcott, Frances	Magill, Arthur W.
Wood, Nancy	DeCamp, Samuel G.J.
Woodbury, Abigail	Smith, Charles B.
Woodruff, Mandane	Woodruff, Alson
Wort, Elizabeth (Betcy)	Jordan, Walter
Wright, Mrs.	Wright, Daniel
Wright, Mrs. Maria S.	Scammon, J. Young 2

the first building that Polemus and Thomas Hamilton completed following their arrival in 1834.

Woodworth, James H.　born at Greenwich, NY, in 1804; arrived in 1833; listed as co-owner of 160 acres of land, together with Hugh G. Gibson, in Section 18, Township 39, prior to 1836, as per Andreas, *History of Chicago*, pp. 112-113; late in 1835 filed a claim for wharfing privileges for the W half of lot 4, block 19; ◆ wholesale dry goods merchant, 103 Lake St. [with Robert P. Woodworth]; in 1848 and 1849 he served as Chicago's mayor. [12]

Wooley, Jedediah　also Woolsey, Woolley, Jedidah, Jediah; born in New York; came in 1830; in the same year he purchased from the canal commissioners lot 9, block 44, for $50 [see map on page 44], and still owned it in 1833; he also acquired the western half of the NE quarter of Section 4 in Township 39 N, as per Andreas, *History of Chicago*, pp. 112-113; became the first county surveyor in 1831 and, on April 25, 1832, laid out a street leading from the settlement to the lakeshore, 50 feet wide; his description read as follows: "From the east end of Water street, in the town of Chicago, to Lake Michigan. Direction of said road is south 88 1/2 degrees east from the street to the lake, 18 chains 50 links." He married Betsey Watkins in January 1832; in May served under Capt. G. Kercheval in the Chicago company during the Black Hawk War. [12, 249]

Worthingham, William　listed erroneously as William Worthington in Andreas (volume 1); together with Alanson Sweet, and under contract for John Noble, he built ★★★ **Chicago's 1st** brick house in 1833, standing N of the river on a lot adjacent to the later Lake House hotel; on Sept. 25, 1834 he was appointed firewarden for the first ward; as

per notice in the *Chicago Democrat* of Sept. 29, 1834, he married Jessy [Jennette] Shaw on Sept. 26 at Naper's Settlement; ◆ plasterer, Adams Street near Clark; the death of a son, George, was announced in the *Chicago Democrat* on Feb. 24, 1843. [12, 357]

Wright, Daniel　(1778-1873) born in Rutland, VT; arrived from Ohio in 1833 with wife and several children; soon removed to Dutchman's Point, then in June 1834 built the first house in [Lake County], farther N; in September his wife and youngest son Daniel died, and in 1835 a teen-age son died; in 1836 his daughter Caroline married a William Wigham, his neighbor Hiram Kennicott officiating as justice of the peace. Daniel Wright died on Dec. 30, 1873, and was buried at Half Day, IL.

Wright, Edward　born at Sheffield, MA, in 1821; came in 1833, still a boy, attending Miss Chappel's school in 1834; son of [see] John Wright, brother of John Stephen, Timothy, and Edward; active in real estate speculation and development; ◆ Michigan Avenue, corner of Madison Street; later served as paymaster in the U.S. Army; had died by 1879. [12, 351, 452]

Wright, Freeman G.　born in Shaftsbury, NY, c.1800; arrived in September 1832; by 1879 he lived in Racine, WI. [The name may be identical with {see} Wright, Truman G., the discrepancies resulting from transcription errors; *eds.*] [12]

Wright, John　(1783-1840) often called Deacon Wright, because of his strong religious background and church affiliation; had visited Chicago on horseback in 1815 but found the site unpromising then; on Oct. 28, 1832, he came back by lake schooner with his son John Stephen Wright and merchandise to start a business, intending to settle in Galena, but stayed in Chicago; left his son in

Chicago while fetching more goods from the East, returning in 1833, and in the spring of 1834 brought the remainder of his family from Massachusetts: wife Huldah (née Dewey, married Sept. 26, 1814), Timothy (born 1817), Walter (1819), Edward (1821), Anne Eliza (1824), and Frances Sarah (1827); listed as owner of 180 acres of land consisting of the SW quarter of Section 8, Township 39, prior to 1836, as per Andreas, *History of Chicago*, pp. 112-113; in the original town, he also purchased in November 1832 from Walter Selvey [Searcy] for $100 lot 6 in block 17 [see map on page 44]. In early August 1833 John Wright was one of the "Qualified Electors" who voted to incorporate the town [for a copy of that meeting's report, see entry on incorporation], and was on the voting list for the first town board on Aug. 10, 1833, as John W. Wright; was a charter member of Chicago's first Presbyterian Church under Reverend J. Porter and later served as its deacon, acquiring his nickname. His first store was in a one room log cabin at the SE corner of Lake and Market streets that his son John S. had rented from Mark Beaubien in November 1832. In September 1833, Eliza Chappel took over the log cabin for her school, making it ★★★ **Chicago's 1st** schoolhouse, and Wright moved into a larger store he had built in block 17 on Lake Street; the three younger children—Edward, Anne, and Frances—attended the Chappel school in 1834; legal notices involving John Wright appeared in the Sept. 3, 1834, *Chicago Democrat* as John K. Boyer sought payment for "12 pieces of cotton sheeting and about 30 lbs. of coffee" in a circuit court suit filed July 7. Wright's later residence was at the foot of Madison Street, on Michigan Avenue just S of J.B. Beaubien's house. [12, 432]

Wright, John Stephen　(1815-1874) also James;

born in Sheffield, MA; son of [see] John Wright, brother of Timothy, Walter, and Edward; arrived on Oct. 28, 1832, with his father; initially worked in his father's first two stores, but soon became a successful real estate dealer during the speculative fever that gripped the town in the early 1830s, though he was still underage; tracing from the recorded surveys of the town in the Cook County Clerk's Office, in 1834 he made a ✳ manuscript map [National Archives, Washington, D.C.] that was used in preparing one of two maps published that year in New York by Peter A. Mesier. All four brothers were active in real estate speculation and subdividing. John S. lost his already considerable fortune (c.$200,000) during the crash of 1837, but recovered financially by diversifying into forwarding and commission business as well as manufacture and sale of machinery; ✦ forwarding commission merchant, North Water Street; like his father, he was a charter member of the first Presbyterian church, and financed its construction on the grounds of the Presbyterian church of Chicago's first schoolhouse built for this purpose (1835), allowing the so-called Infant School to move from its makeshift quarters in the First Presbyterian Church building to its own quarters on Clark Street, S of Lake, near the church and still on the church lot. He married Catherine (Kitty) Blackburn Turner in 1846; became the founder and editor of the *Prairie Farmer* newspaper; in 1855 he became a member of the just-formed Old Settlers' Society of Chicago; in 1856 he bought the blockhouse of Fort Dearborn and what remained of the stockade, making the well seasoned oak lumber into furniture; a 300 acre large wooded section of Wright property on the lakeshore two miles N of Lake Street became known as Wrightwood. In 1870, he published *Chicago: Past, Present, Future: Relations to the Great Interior and to the Continent*; died on Sept. 26, 1874; his ▲ grave site is located at Rose-hill Cemetery; ➡ Wrightwood Avenue (2700 N). Also see Wright's Woods. [12, 37, 164, 351, 432, 476, 735]

Wright, Thomas   arrived from New York in 1834; teacher at the English and Classical School for Boys, succeeding Dr. Henry Van der Bogart in 1834, and being succeeded in 1835 by James McClellan; was appointed recording secretary of the Chicago Bible Society on Nov. 25, 1835, elected librarian of the Lyceum on Dec. 12 and president of the Young Men's Temperance Society, organized on Dec. 19; in 1837 he served on the first board of education. [12, 351]

Wright, Timothy   born at Sheffield, MA; arrived in 1833; son of [see] John Wright; brother of [see] John Stephen, Edward and Walter; initially worked in his father's store on Lake Street on block 17; in 1836 worked as a member of a surveying party on the Illinois & Michigan Canal project; ✦ Michigan Avenue, corner of Madison Street; in 1853 he acquired part-ownership of the *Chicago Tribune*; in 1857 served as trustee of the Dearborn Seminary; later moved to Philadelphia. [12, 13, 432]

Wright, Truman G.   arrived from Vermont in 1834 and served as firewarden that year; late in 1835 filed a claim for wharfing privileges; was town trustee in 1836; acquired 160 acres of downtown land in Section 6, Township 39, prior to 1836; plus 80 acres in Section 18, Township 39, as assignee, plus lakeshore property, constituting the SW corner of Section 34 of Township 40, as per Andreas, *History of Chicago*, pp. 112-113; legal notice in the *Chicago American* of Sept. 2, 1837: *Truman G. Wright vs. Sylvester Marsh, attachement*; ✦ speculator, boarded at Tremont House; removed to Racine, prior to 1879, where he still lived in 1885. Also see entry for Wright, Freeman G. [12, 28]

Wright, Walter   born at Sheffield, MA, in 1819; arrived in 1833; son of [see] John Wright, brother of [see] John Stephen, Edward, and Timothy; ✦

Michigan Avenue, corner of Madison Street; active in real estate speculation and development; in 1848 he served as president of the Young Men's Association of Chicago, which had been started in 1841 by Walter L. Newberry, and which later became the Chicago Library Association. Walter had died by 1879. [12, 13, 351, 432]

Wright's Woods   a formerly wooded part of the extensive real estate holdings of members of the John Wright family, on the Near North Side. In *Wau-Bun* Juliette Kinzie describes how she would ride N on the path that preceded Rush Street "to the little prairie W of Wright's Woods"; ➡ Wrightwood Avenue (2700 N).

Wyandotte   schooner from Buffalo under Captain Easterbrook, called at Chicago on Aug. 21, 1834.

Wycoff, Peter   a discharged soldier who worked for A. Clybourne; voted in the elections of July 24 and Nov. 25, 1830.

XY Company   a British fur trading company in the Hudson Bay region; a local but influential contemporary and rival of the Hudson Bay Company and the North West Company.

Y not a letter in this context but an emblem for Chicago that was introduced near the end of the 19th century; for details, see Forks.

You de la Découverte, Pierre   (1658-1718) also Hion, Hyou; trader and soldier, accompanied La Salle in his explorations; signed *proces verbal* of claiming *Louisiane* for France, 1682; from this he took the title sieur de la Découverte by royal permission; married in April 1693 at Chicagou a Miami woman, Elisabeth—★★★ Chicago's 1st marriage. By Elizabeth he had a daughter, Marie-Anne, who married Jean-Baptiste Richard at Montreal in 1718. You leased Ile-aux-Tourtres at the confluence of Ottawa and St. Lawrence rivers, from Governor Vaudreuil and carried on a largely clandestine and unregulated trade in furs and liquor, under the governor's protection; became a wealthy and powerful trader. [205 (1: 573, 2: 672-73), 649]

Young, George   a notice in the *Chicago Democrat* of Dec. 30, 1835, announced the marriage of George Young and Mary Mahaffy.

Young Men's Temperance Society   organized on Dec. 19, 1835; Thomas Wright was chosen as president, H. Markoe and H. Crocker as vice presidents, J.A. Dunn as corresponding secretary, R. Wilkinson as recording secretary, and J.A. Harding, B.H. Clift, and W.G. Austin were chosen as directors.

Young, Richard Montgomery   (1796-1853) born in Kentucky; admitted to the bar in 1817; commissioned judge in the fifth circuit (entire state N of Illinois River) in January 1828; first district judge for the state to hold court in Chicago, at Fort Dearborn in 1831 and in John Kinzie's house the following year; traveled from Galena to Chicago in the spring of 1832 in the company of [see] the attorneys James Strode and Benjamin Mills, and alerted the Chicago community to the hostile intentions of the Indians that he and his party had observed along the way—the Black Hawk War had begun; from 1836 to 1843 he served as U.S. Senator and became a justice of the Illinois Supreme Court in 1843; Judge Caton remembers him as a good fiddle player, in addition to his judicial talents; died in Washington City [now Washington, D.C.]. [13, 37]

Young Tiger   schooner, arrived in 1826 and attempted unsuccessfully to enter the Chicago River.

Young, William   arrived in 1834 and served as a volunteer fireman on the first engine company. [12]

Yoste, Bernard   see Joste, Bernard.

Zarley, J.W.   arrived in 1832 and served under Capt. G. Kercheval in the Chicago company during the Black Hawk War. [12, 714]

Zender, Dr.   from Paris, member of the Botanical Medical Society and of the Phrenological Society of New York; placed an ad in the Nov. 11, 1835, *Chicago Democrat* offering "his professional services in the practice of Medicine to the inhabitants of Chicago"; residing at the Exchange Coffee House, he "will pay particular attention to dyspepsia, consumptions, liver complaints, culaneous diseases, and fevers of every kind" or would provide a class in French or "lessons in the Greek, Latin or Spanish languages, Philosophy, &c. &c."

Zénobe, Père   see Membré, Père Zinobius (Zénobe).

Zeuch, Lucius H., M.D.   Illinois physician and historian; author of *History of Medical Practice in Illinois, Preceding 1850*, which he finished in 1927, the year of his death; together with Robert Knight, he also authored *Mount Joliet: Its Place in Illinois History and Its Location* and *The Location of the Chicago Portage Route of the 17th Century*.

Zimmerman Site   archaeological excavation site near Utica, IL where Father Marquette founded the *Mission de la Conception* at a Kaskaskia village in 1675.

Zinobius, Père   see Membré, Père Zinobius (Zénobe).

This view of Wolf Point has challenged several artists, though none contemporary. The variation shown here is from Andreas' *History of Chicago*, entitled "Wolf Point in 1830", the illustrator unidentified; for others see pages 365 and 366.

CHICAGO:
MEANING OF THE NAME AND LOCATION OF PRE-1800 EUROPEAN SETTLEMENTS

John F. Swenson

The name *Chicago* is derived from the local Indian word *chicagoua* for the native garlic plant (not onion) *Allium tricoccum*. This garlic (in French: *ail sauvage*) grew in abundance on the south end of Lake Michigan on the wooded banks of the extensive river system which bore the same name, *chicagoua*. Father Gravier, a thorough student of the local Miami language, introduced the spelling *chicagoua*, or *chicagou8*, in the 1690s, attempting to express the inflection which the Indians gave to the last syllable of the word.

The French who began arriving here in 1673 were probably confused by the Indian use of this name for several rivers. They usually wrote it as *Chicagou*. Gradually other names were given to the the streams comprising this system: Des Plaines, Saganashkee (Sag), Calumet (Grand and Little), Hickory Creek, Guillory (for the north branch of the present Chicago River), and Chicago or Portage River (for the south branch). Students of early Chicago history likewise tend to get confused, unaware of these name changes, but early French maps and narratives, when carefully interpreted, make it possible to discover who and what was where, and when.

As a name for a place, as distinct from a river, *Chicagou* appears first in *Chicagoumeman*, the native name for the mouth of the present Chicago River, where Fort Dearborn was built in 1803. As a name for a place where people lived, the simple *Chicagou* was first used by the French about 1685 for a Jesuit mission and French army post at the site of Marquette's 1675 camp along the south branch. This interpretation, and the etymology of the name Chicago, derive largely from the memoirs of Henri Joutel, the soldier-naturalist associate of La Salle on his fatal last journey, 1684-1687, to Texas. Joutel spent nearly three weeks in the Chicagou area in 1687-88, and one of his first investigations was into the origin of this name which he had heard from La Salle and many others. His detailed description of the plant, its "ail sauvage" taste, its differences from the native onion and its maple forest habitat, point unambiguously to *Allium tricoccum*.

English accounts tracing the name to a "wild onion" date from after 1800, when different groups of Indians, mainly Potawatomi, had displaced the original Miami. In the Potawatomi language, *chicago* meant both the native garlic and the wild onion.

The downtown Chicago or Fort Dearborn area, exposed to wind, weather and passing enemies, was not where the local Miami and other people lived when Frenchmen, led by Louis Jolliet and Jacques Marquette, S.J., began arriving in 1673. In early 1675 Marquette found a group of Illinois merely camped there before setting out for the Green Bay area. The local population's villages were scattered along rivers and streams in more sheltered environments. Archaeologists have identified dozens of places in the greater Chicago area where they lived, and a few were vaguely recorded by the early French.

Early French forts, camps and settlements, and one or two British army camps are also rather vaguely recorded and can only be approximately located by examination of many obscure pre-1800 maps and documents. The following represents an attempt to piece together all available clues and put these locations and people in a time series. In so doing, it will be necessary to correct some longstanding misconceptions, such as the customary labeling of Jean Baptist Point de Sable as Chicago's first permanent resident. This account, however, will end with the important figure of Point, because with him begins an era for which historical data are available in much greater abundance. Detail may be found in the encyclopedic entries of this volume under the appropriate names, and in the chronology section under the dates given.

• Louis Jolliet, Jacques Marquette and five others; 1673 camp at western end of *portage des chenes*, marked by the Chicago Portage Historical site. Marquette's party also camped here in March 1675.

• Louis Jolliet and associates, 1673-1675; two 1674 maps prepared under Jolliet's direction allude to the explorations made during this period. Jolliet's detailed rendering of the river system in the Chicago area and of the lower St. Joseph River indicate intimate knowledge of the terrain. During this time period, there were probably two building sites on the west bank of the Des Plaines (then Chicagou). One was probably at the mouth of the Tukoquenone (Du Page) River, the other opposite the mouth of Hickory Creek at Mont Jolliet in present Joliet. This distinctive alluvial mound, which the Indians called *Missouratenoui* (place where pirogues were dragged or portaged) was a prominent landmark for native and French travelers, as it was at the crossing of the major east-west Sauk trail. Marquette in early 1675 met two of Jolliet's associates who were living and trading in this area: Pierre Moreau (La Taupine) and Jean Roussel or Rousselière, the unnamed "surgeon" in Marquette's journal.

• Jacques Marquette, S.J.; 1674-75. He and his two companions, the experienced *voyageurs* Jacques Largillier and Pierre Porteret, camped briefly near the mouth of the Chicago River, and in mid-January moved to a site on the south branch, probably selected as a result of 1673-74 explorations in the employ of La Salle, in which Largillier may have taken part.

• Claude Allouez, S.J.; 1677. He visited for several days at a native village somewhere along the Des Plaines, en route to the great Kaskaskia village opposite Starved Rock.

• La Salle's employees; 1677-79. Two trading camps, probably both on Hickory Creek, perhaps near New Lenox. The surgeon Jean Roussel, who worked for La Salle in 1669 and again in 1677-80, may have been in both groups, because he knew the area from his 1673-75 experience. Assuming the same for Michel Accault (Aco) would explain the latter's detailed knowledge of native traders, and of their territories and languages, as early as 1679-80. The 1677 trip produced the buffalo pelts which La Salle showed to Louis XIV in France the following winter. In 1678 the king gave La Salle control over the the Illinois country and the rights to trade in buffalo, which were very abundant southward from Mont Jolliet and Hickory Creek. The 1678-79 trip produced a large quantity of beaver pelts which were taken to present Door County, Wisconsin, and loaded on the *Griffon*, which soon sank with great loss to La Salle's creditors. La Salle seems to have traveled along Hickory Creek twice in 1680, on a route he had not previously seen. On his second trip he found a trace of earlier European presence, a bit of sawed wood.

• La Salle and party, January 1682. Camp along the west bank of the Des Plaines, en route to the mouth of the Mississippi River, probably at Mont Jolliet, opposite the mouth of what the chaplain, Father Zénobe Membré, called the *Chicagou* (Hickory Creek). They were waiting for a party of hunters who had separated from the main group after leaving the St. Joseph River. [Hickory Creek flows west from Skunk Grove in eastern Frankfort Township. *Chicagoua* is the Miami and Illinois word for skunk.]

• La Salle's fort, 1683. Probably at the New Lenox site. In 1994 a team led by archaeologist Rochelle Lurie unearthed, in the midst of an extensive Indian settlement, a rectangular feature of apparently European origin. La Salle, in a letter from here (at the "portage de Chicagou") described it as being 30 leagues, about 72 miles, from his newly completed *Fort St. Louis* at Starved Rock and near a trail (Sauk) from the east. The actual river distance, measured on the plats of the 1822 U.S. Government surveys, is about 32 or 33 leagues. The west end of the *portage des chênes*, the only portage route seriously studied by historians in three centuries, was about ten leagues farther to the north, a route La Salle disliked.

- Jesuit mission and French army post, c.1685-86. Probably on the site of Marquette's 1675 camp, about where Damen Avenue crosses the south branch of the Chicago River. Referred to by Joutel, who described the entire area and the maple forest where he found the native garlic, but not the mission and post which had probably been mostly destroyed by the Iroquois in July 1686. This site is probably the same one farmed 1809-1812 by James Leigh (often erroneously called Charles Lee), a retired sergeant of the Fort Dearborn garrison. In an 1811 letter to his commander-in-chief Col. Jacob Kingsbury, Leigh mentioned the maple-basswood forest here, a typical habitat of the native garlic, *Allium tricoccum*.

- French fort, commanded by Lt. Nicolas d'Ailleboust, sieur de Mantet, 1693-96. Probably at the mouth of the Grand Calumet River, then near present Gary, Indiana. The river is marked *R. de Chicagou* on the "Louvigny" map, which Mantet helped prepare in 1697. Mantet had been ordered to the region to quell Indian unrest in the St. Joseph River area. He and the garrison evacuated this post in May or June of 1696, pursuent to royal orders. This fort, which was erroneously placed in the Fort Dearborn area by the Treaty of Greenville, 1795, may be the same as the *Petit Fort* or "Little Fort" of various British and American accounts of 1779-c.1803, and the mythical progenitor of the later settlement at Waukegan.

- Jesuit Mission of the Guardian Angel, 1696-c.1702. Site of the Merchandise Mart. Headed by Father Bineteau. Two large Miami villages were nearby.

- Trading post of Tonti, Accault and La Forêt, managed by Pierre de Liette, Tonti's cousin, 1697-c.1702. Near site of Tribune Tower. Was probably discontinued with the establishment of Fort Pontchartrain du Détroit by Cadillac.

- Trading post owned by Simon Guillory of Michillimackinac, manager not known; c.1716 -[?]. Opposite Merchandise Mart on the west bank of the north branch of the Chicago River, which was still called Guillory River in 1824 and 1830. Gurdon Hubbard described the site as it appeared in 1818, some time after it had been vacated by French traders forced out of business by the American Fur Company. Guillory's father, also Guillory, was a trader to the Great Lakes as early as 1683.

- British army camp, perhaps two camps, 1779-83. Probably not a fort, but a temporary habitation, somewhere along the south branch of the Chicago River. Alluded to on Linctot's 1779 map, this may have been where Mme Rocheblave, wife of British commandant, took refuge with their children after he was arrested at Fort de Chartres and imprisoned at Williamsburg and New York. Her sister was the widow of Prisque Pagé, prominent Kaskaskia merchant and mill owner, whose family name became attached to the Du Page River and the village, now called Channahon, at its mouth.

- Trading post of Jean Baptiste de Sable, 1788 (or earlier)-1800. Near site of Tribune Tower; later owned by John Kinzie.

TRIBAL MIXTURES IN CHICAGO AREA INDIAN VILLAGES

Helen Hornbeck Tanner

Indian villages are always composed of people from more than one tribe. This mixture of tribal people in Indian communities was characteristic of the region around the base of Lake Michigan, including the Chicago area, as well as other parts of the country.

There are many reasons for people from several tribes to be living in an Indian village as minority populations. Some might be captives brought back from warfare in another region and incorporated in the tribe. Indian people have always been great travelers and traders, and occasionally married young women they met in the villages of trading partners. When Native American peoples visited allied tribes, they might stay a year or two before returning home, sometimes bringing home friends for a return visit. Indian people have always been known for their hospitality, and were proud to be able to entertain travelers as well as official couriers and delegations arriving on inter-tribal business.

Disagreements and sporadic warfare led to the appearance of small groups from other tribes in any major Indian settlement. Since each village or band tried to achieve a consensus in decision-making, the minority faction might voluntarily move to another town to end the dissension. Warfare also brought about the the migration of entire communities, which moved into the territory of another tribe with permission to reside as guests of the host tribe. In major warfare along the American frontier, warriors and their families from eight or ten allied tribes periodically formed a multi-tribal military center that continued in existence for several years. When the tribal groups in the military center dispersed, they often took with them comrades in arms from another tribe.

Epidemic disease was another factor causing new population mixtures in Indian villages. Survivors of an epidemic usually abandoned the site of contamination and went to live with other people. Often their numbers were too small and they were too weak to continue alone. Religious fervor also produced new combinations of tribal people, as converts flocked to the home village of a new prophet or messianic leader.

Non-Indian people also lived in Indian villages of the Chicago district, as they did in other parts of North America. The fur traders who travelled regularly from Montreal or Three Rivers in Canada, and later from St. Louis, Albany, Mackinac Island, Philadelphia, or Pittsburg lived part of the year in Indian towns. Often the traders had Indian families. These traders were of diverse European or African origin, adding to the complexity of populations in Indian communities. In the seventeenth and eighteenth centuries, genetic heritage was not a matter of critical importance. If non-Indians lived according to Indian customs, they were accepted as relatives and kinfolk, though the assignment of clan affiliation presented a problem. White captives who were children were raised as though they were of Indian origin.

All of these factors affected the population composition of the Indian vilages of the Chicago area and surrounding country at one time or another during the past three hundred years. Although historical records for events creating population mixtures exist only for a little over three centuries in the upper Great Lakes, oral traditions provide knowledge of similar occurrences for a much longer period of time.

The group of Indian villages located in the present state of Illinois and on the west bank of the Mississippi river, with large communities on the Illinois river, were known to the first French explorers as the Illinois Indians. These people were involved in the capture and trading of captives from tribes living to the southwest of their own homelands. In French records, these captives were called "panis", apparently an interpretation of "Pawnee", though the term referred to Indian slaves from any tribe west of the Mississippi river. So early Illinois Indian villages could include western Indian slaves. These "panis" were also recorded in census records of the mid-eighteenth century for French and Indian communities on the Straits of Mackinac, Detroit, and Fort Miami (present Fort Wayne, Indiana).

The vicinity of modern Chicago has never been a favorite site for Indian habitation. The sand dunes and swamps, with restricted timber and agricultural land, did not attract large numbers of Indian people. In the late seventeenth century, when there was a fortified post at Chicago for a brief time, Miami Indian people were living south of present Chicago near the bend of the Calumet river and on the Fox river about forty miles west of Chicago. These Miami, whose language is the same as the Illinois, may have been in the process of returning to their customary home base on the Wabash river of Indiana after fleeing temporarily from the rout of Iroquois war parties from New York. The Miami village near the Calumet River nevertheless was attacked in 1687.

In the 1680s, the principal concentration of Indian people in northern Illinois was the vicinity of Fort St. Louis, established by René Robert Cavelier, Sieur de La Salle, in 1682 at Starved Rock, an island in the Illinois river near present Utica, Illinois about ninety miles southwest of Chicago. In addition to the large Kaskaskia village, Shawnee and Miami settled near the fort, which was the objective of an Iroquois expedition in 1683. The long period of Iroquois warfare involving Indians living far north and south of the Great Lakes came to an end with a peace treaty signed in Montreal in 1701. The Kaskaskia representatives from Illinois probably travelled the longest distance to take part in the councils.

Although the Potawatomi became the principal residents of the Chicago area during the eighteenth century, other Great Lakes Indians continued to make their homes for at least part of the year along the branches of the Chicago river and the portage to the Des Plaines river, a well-used route from Lake Michigan to the Illinois river, continuing to the Mississippi river and the Gulf of Mexico. It became a site for prosperous trading posts. Another period of warfare between the French and their Indian allies on one hand and the Mesquakie [Fox] and their allies as opponents, brought a group of Sauk and Mesquakie to the Chicago area in 1742-1743, but they soon moved westward to the Mississippi River Valley, further from French authority.

By the mid-eighteenth century, Potawatomi began expanding around the lower end of Lake Michigan from their headquarter town on the St. Joseph river of southwestern Michigan. The Calumet river system offered particularly attractive sites for villages, but others moved along the western shore of Lake Michigan through northwestern Indiana to present day Chicago, Milwaukee and the Door Peninsula of Wisconsin. Imperial warfare between France and England, ending with the Treaty of Paris in 1763, was a factor in bringing Ottawa and Ojibwa [or Chippewa] Indians into northern Illinois and the Chicago vicinity in the 1760s. In 1760 the French established a fortified trading post at present Ottawa, Illinois a short distance above the site of La Salle's Fort St. Louis, a stretch of the river traditionally occupied by Illinois Indian villages. Apparently, pro-French Ottawa Indians from near Detroit moved to Fort Ottawa when the British took over the French fort at Detroit.

The resistance movement to prevent the British from occupying French forts in the Great Lakes region, a movement headed by Pontiac, the Ottawa leader from Detroit, continued in the Illinois country until 1769. Indian people denied the right of European powers to turn over French forts in Indian country to the British. Although Pontiac was unsuccessful in his attempted siege of Detroit in 1763, his followers relocated on the Maumee river of Ohio, west of present Toledo. Pontiac himself and some of his strongest supporters came to Illinois to prevent the British from occupying Fort Chartres. The Illinois Indians, then concentrated in the southwestern part of the state near Kaskaskia and Cahokia, urged him to continue the ultimately unsuccessful struggle. He had other adherents among the Ojibwa of the present upper peninsula of Michigan near Sault Ste. Marie, Ottawa from the northwestern Lower Peninsula of Michigan near present Petoskey, a few Sauk from northern Illinois, and some Potawatomi. Warriors from these tribal groups congregated at Chicago in the late 1760s, to enter battle if Pontiac decided on further militant action.

Despite the fact that a number of Ottawa and Ojibwa continued to live in the Potawatomi communities around Chicago and present Milwaukee, and even further north on the Lake Michigan shoreline, the local leadership was clearly in the hands of the Potawatomi by the 1770s. Nevertheless, in dealing with Indian people of the southern end of Lake Michigan, the American government usually called them the "United Bands of Chippewa, Ottawa, and Potawatomi." These were the Indian people whom settlers met when they came to Chicago in the 1830s.

By the time of the Treaty of Chicago in 1833, whereby the Potawatomi gave up the last of their lands and reservations, the closest towns to metropolitan Chicago were at the bend of the Calumet river, south of Chicago, and on the Des Plaines river north of the portage from the south branch of the Chicago river. Both the portage site and the mouth of the Chicago river were important trading sites. Important traders at Chicago after the 1770s were of Haitian, French, Scottish, and English origin. By the 1830s, too, the population composition of the Potawatomi towns further from Chicago included other minorities. Potawatomi who moved as far west as the Rock River met the Winnebago, and villages included people from both tribal groups. Other Potawatomi became followers of the Kickapoo prophet, Kennekuk, and lived with his band on Sugar Creek close to the present Indiana state line about one hundred twenty miles south of Chicago. Potawatomi living on the upper Illinois river had Kickapoo living amongst them.

The above discussion indicates Indian tribal distributions and mixtures in Chicago and surrounding territory for the roughly two centuries prior to the removal of the Potawatomi from the town in 1835, and from the remainder of the state soon after 1837. Our knowledge of Indians and their movements prior to the arrival of Europeans is more limited, but they have been in this region ever since the glaciers of the last ice age retreated over 10,000 years ago. It is well to keep in mind that of the total history of human activity in the Chicago region, Native Americans occupied the area for the overwhelming portion of the time period.

Reprinted with minor changes by permission from Dr. Tanner and from Terry Straus, ed., *Indians of the Chicago Area*, 2nd edition (Chicago: NAES College Press, 1990)

"Indians Fishing"

from George Catlin's 1845 book, *Illustrations of the Manners, Customs, and Conditions of the North American Indians: in a Series of Letters and Notes, written during eight Years of Travel and Adventure among the Wildest and most Remarkable Tribes now existing.*

FRENCH CHICAGO DURING THE 18TH CENTURY

ULRICH DANCKERS

Americans tend to attribute their national heritage to the thirteen British colonies established in the 17th and 18th centuries along the Eastern seaboard, and show little awareness of the simultaneous colonization of North America, especially in the Great Lakes region, by the French. As a consequence, remarkably little has been written about the long, turbulent, and fascinating French phase of Chicago as a village prior to Jean Baptist Point de Sable's settlement near the mouth of the Chicago River in the 1780s. One reason for this blind spot in historical knowledge is that the people who made this history left very few written records. Most of them were illiterate, and almost everyone's energies in those early days were absorbed by the never-ending task of assuring survival in the primeval and generally hostile wilderness. Initial and lingering discrimination may also be a factor; after all, in the early 1830s Chicago's French population was quickly overwhelmed by the newly arriving English-speaking settlers, and overwhelmed not only in numbers. Considered by many a "miserable race of men," they were sorely disparaged for the company they kept, and were ushered out of town almost as unceremoniously as were their friends the Indians, with whom many of the French had formed close family ties going back several generations.

The appearance of the French in North America began in 1534 with Jacques Cartier's exploration of the St. Lawrence River, on a commission from his king, Francis I, who was seeking a north-west passage to China. Cartier did not find what we now know never existed, but on May 3, 1536, in a ceremony near what is now Quebec, he claimed the St. Lawrence River and its entire drainage basin for the French crown. When, however, it was learned that he had found neither the passage to China nor a source of precious stones and metals as had been anticipated, French authorities lost interest in further exploration. It was not until the end of the 16th century that efforts to colonialize North America were revived by King Henry IV of France.

From Quebec explorers easily proceeded up the St. Lawrence and then into the Great Lakes. In 1634, exactly 100 years after Cartier's first landing on the Atlantic coast of the continent, the first white man, traveling with seven Huron Indians, entered Lake Michigan by way of the Straits of Mackinac. He was French explorer Jean Nicolet, agent for Governor Champlain of New France, who had been sent westward to explore the unknown territory. On the shore of Green Bay, believing that he had reached China, Nicolet dressed in colorful embroidered silk robes before landing. Encountering Winnebago Indians, he soon realized his mistake.

In the second half of the 17th century the progress of French colonization accelerated. Missions and forts were established in quick succession along the St. Lawrence and at scattered locations around the Great Lakes. The first mission in the Lake Michigan region was built by the Jesuit Father Claude Jean Allouez in 1669 on Green Bay, and in 1671 was moved to the site of the present town of De Pere, Wisconsin, the name referring to Father Allouez. Soon there was a village of traders, and it became the starting point for southern and westward travel via an important water route: the Fox-Wisconsin portage to the Mississippi. Marquette and Jolliet, in 1673, are among the better known French explorers who began their journeys here. (Thirty years later, when traders had established themselves in Chicago as well, overland traffic between the two settlements was maintained by way of the Green Bay Indian Trail. One of the major trails of early Chicago, it can still be traced in the city street pattern as Clark Street, where it follows a former beach ridge of ancient Lake Chicago. At Foster Avenue it angles northwest to Howard Street, where it becomes Chicago Avenue in Evanston, eventually becoming Green Bay Road in the northern suburbs.)

Also in 1671, Father Jacques Marquette founded the St. Ignace Mission on the northern shore of lower Michigan at what is now called Point St. Ignace, where a small village of traders had already formed. For the protection of these missionaries and traders, French soldiers under the command of Louis de Buade, comte de Frontenac, were assigned to the region and built *Fort De Buade* in 1672, later relocated and named Fort Michilimackinac. One year later in September 1673, Father Marquette and Louis Jolliet canoed down the Chicago River on their return trip from exploring the Mississippi. Thus, not only did they discover the Chicago site, but they also recognized the strategic importance of the Chicago portage that linked the Great Lakes with the Mississippi, as documented in Jolliet's report to the French government.

During the next 25 years many other missionaries, traders, and military men followed the pathways opened by Marquette and Jolliet, travelling south from their bases at the north end of Lake Michigan and leaving their footprints at Chicago and in the Illinois River valley. The early French exploration of North America and its penetration of the Great Lakes region were, however, but a prelude to the story of the extensive activity and settlement in the area that is now Chicago. By the year 1700, both a mission and a trading post stood on land that is now almost at the center of the city. And with the year 1701 begins the story as called for in the title.

La Mission de L'Ange Gardien [the Guardian Angel Mission] was founded in 1696 by Father Pierre François Pinet on the Chicago River. Here he served with Father Julian Bineteau, and later with Father Jean Mermet. It probably stood beside the river where Chicago's Merchandise Mart is now located, and flourished until 1702 or 1703. At its peak, the mission was surrounded by a Miami Indian village of 150 cabins. In 1699, it was visited by three priests from the Society of the Foreign Missions of Quebec, conducted to Chicago by Henri de Tonti, the friend and faithful lieutenant of the great explorer René-Robert Cavelier de La Salle, already dead by that time. One of the visitors, Father St. Cosme, supplied a vivid picture of the mission in his report, also indicating that French traders lived nearby. This comes as no surprise; missions and trading posts were usually found in close proximity to one another. Indians were attracted to the posts for the merchandise they offered, thus giving the missionaries opportunities to convert them.

The Chicago traders of that time, referred to by Father St. Cosme only in passing, are well known from other sources. The trading license was held jointly by Sieur Pierre de Liette, in charge of managing the post, and François Daupin de La Forêt. Both were men of noble birth. De Liette was a relative of Tonti, who was also a partner in the trading enterprise, and who visited and helped as often as he could. A fourth partner was Michael Accault, married to an Illinois Indian since 1695, and well known as a former traveling companion of the exploring French priest and author Father Hennepin. In addition to these rather illustrious and educated men there were living nearby, with their Indian wives, various associated traders and helpers, members of the working class, needed to perform the more menial tasks; the names of some are recorded in old notarial records in Quebec. The post was in existence from approximately 1696 to 1702, roughly concurrent with the Guardian Angel Mission. It is not known whether the traders or the missionaries arrived first. After thriving for a few years, the post suffered the same fate as did the nearby mission: it had to be closed because raiding Indian tribes made life in the area too dangerous—at least for a while. Indian attacks became the dominant problem for early French pioneers in Illinois, a problem that remained pathognomonic during most of the century that had just begun.

A war between the French and the Fox Indians started about 1700, and lasted for 40 years. An Algonkian language tribe originally near the western end of Lake Erie, the Fox were driven westward in the middle of the 17th century by the Huron-Iroquois wars. Initially friendly trading partners of the French, who referred to them as *Renards*, they allied with the Iroquois and turned against the French, severely restricting first the Wisconsin-Fox River portage and, around 1700, the Chicago portage. Their actions disrupted community development in the Illinois River valley, along the Mississippi, and in Chicago. For political reasons the seat of French regional government at Michilimackinac, and with it the protective military presence which during the two previous decades had at times extended as far as Chicago and St. Joseph, was transferred to the new *Fort Pontchartrain du Détroit* (the founding of Detroit, Michigan), built in 1701 by Antoine de La Mothe Cadillac. Soon thereafter Indian raids began. Any French traders who held out in isolated Chicago during those most difficult years had to lay low.

In 1711 Joseph Kellog, of English background but a member of a Canadian trading party, traveled with his group by boat from Michillimackinac to the Mississippi River by way of the Chicago portage. In his diary he described the multiple villages he encountered on the trip, but said nothing about Europeans in "Chigaguea," although he reports on the land, vegetation, and game of the locale. Most likely the villagers had temporarily abandoned the place in favor of safer settlements such as Detroit, Cahokia, or Kaskaskia.

On his 1718 map, which he called *Carte de la Louisiane et du Cours du Mississipi*, the French cartographer Guillaume Delisle has printed the name "Chicagou" in its proper place along Lake Michigan, and he shows a settlement on the west bank of the north branch of the Chicago River near the forks, approximately the location where later in the century a trader by the name of Guillory—to whom this story will soon return—had his post. Delisle was a careful, reliable man working for the French crown. He probably used 1717 information to make this map. Nobody knows who owned this post. Perhaps it was an earlier member of the Guillory family [Simon?] of Michilimackinac. If the post was held by the same family for several decades, it would more plausibly explain why the north branch slightly later became known as Guillory's River.

Not all of the French folks calling Chicago their home during the 18th century lived in what we now refer to as the downtown area. All, however, lived along waterways, usually the Chicago portage, also called *Portage des Chenes*. Overland travel with trade goods, because it was difficult and more hazardous, was uncommon, except if one was forced to portage. It is maintained by some historians, that an oak forest at the southwestern end of the Chicago portage harbored a French village from about 1740 on. It was called the "Point of Oaks" and is adjacent to today's Chicago Portage National Historic Site at Harlem Avenue and 48th Street. It is believed that here lived the trader Jean Baptiste Amiot with his Ottawa wife Marianne, and that their son Louis was born here, although it is possible that their cabin stood further downstream on the Des Plaines River. The Amiots were a large French family with members in various parts of Canada. Louis grandfather, Sieur Charles Joseph Amiot, owned a house within the Fort Michilimackinac settlement, as shown on a contemporary map of 1749. We know about Louis and his parents from his baptismal record of June 14, 1746, at Michilimackinac, which reads as follows: "...the said child having been born at the Rivière aux plains near chikago at the beginning of the month of October last." Michilimackinac was the church home for most of the early French Catholic traders in the Chicago region, as it was for the family of Jean Baptiste Amiot. For the greater part of the 18th century no priests lived near Chicago, and contact with the clergy could be maintained only intermittently by traveling long distances. But maintained it was, as historians acknowledge with gratitude, because in an age of general illiteracy only the missionaries could be counted upon to create a measure of written vital statistics.

Of the next known Chicago settlers we have a somewhat mythical report from Governor John Reynolds of Illinois, who during his retirement wrote much about the pioneer history of the state. Reynolds tells of a remarkable woman, born in St. Joseph in 1734 as Marie Joseph Larche. According to Reynolds she lived to the ripe old age of 109, leaving behind four husbands in succession, and it was with her first husband, as Mme Marie Sainte Ange, that she moved from Mackinaw to Chicago in 1765, where they resided for fifteen years. It should be stressed however, that Governor Reynolds' recollections on this subject are in need of independent confirmation. They were, according to his own words, written largely from memory and are in conflict with documents created during Marie's lifetime. For a well researched and more realistic account of "Marie", prepared by

John F. Swenson, we refer the reader to the entry "La Compt, Madam" in the encyclopedic portion of this volume.

In 1763 the French and Indian war ended. It represented the American phase of a worldwide nine year long struggle for supremacy in North America and elsewhere between France and England, and it was won decisively by England. In the same year the Treaty of Paris was signed, and Chicago became officially British. But it was already *de facto* British when, in 1761, the British Lt. Dietrich Brehm visited and mapped the "Chicago" village during his survey of the newly-won territory. He found several settlers there. They were still present in 1763.

In the writings of a later Chicago pioneer, Gurdon Saltonstall Hubbard (1802-1886), there can be found testimony to an early Chicago trader by the name Guillory. As a young man Hubbard hired on with John Jacob Astor's American Fur Company, first came to Chicago in 1818, and in his later years relates that early-on he was shown by several of Astor's veteran traders the outlines of Guillory's former farmstead and trading post, and he was told that it existed prior to 1778. Located strategically on the west bank of the north branch of the Chicago River near the Forks, where Fulton Street now crosses, it allowed for surveillance of all three parts of the waterway. No one knows when it was first established, nor when exactly it was abandoned, but it is likely to have been there for a long time, because, as we indicated above, it gave its name to the north branch, "Guillory's River," a name that was used as late as the 1830s. The name Guillory is often found written in modified versions, such as Guilleroi, Garie, or Guarie. The historian Milo Quaife believes that Guillory's first name was Jean Baptiste. According to Swenson he was of the family of Simon Guillory who died in Mackinac in 1744, and the trading post, while owned by the family, was often run by hired help. We can only speculate as to what doomed the post in the end. Certainly, trade could not thrive in times of warfare, and the American Revolutionary War began in 1775.

In May 1770 Jean Orillat, trader, merchant, land owner, and the wealthiest man in Montreal, financed the travel of two canoes licensed to go to *Chiquagoux* under the direction of Jean Baptiste St.Cyr with eight other *engagés* (a Canadian word from the time of the fur trade, meaning contract laborer). From surviving records we know their names and the merchandise they carried. Interestingly, they took no trade goods, but only their own provision, plus the surprising amount of 200 pounds of chocolate. This is the only license issued in more than a century in which Chicago is the specified destination. Presumably, it was a scouting expedition to size up the current Chicago potential for a new trading post and to gain the local inhabitants' support for such a venture. Perhaps St.Cyr took up residence here, because he does not appear on any subsequent list of *engagés*. But by 1778 Chicago was deserted. Records show that Col. George Morgan, Indian agent appointed by the Continental Congress, and a former prominent trader in Kaskaskia, issued safe-conduct passes in 1776 to "the French people in Chicago" to visit Pittsburgh. The names of these Chicago settlers are not recorded. We know, however, that in 1778 and 1779 Piérre Durand, a Cahokia trader, passed through Chicago en route to Point de Sable's early trading post at *Rivière du Chemin* and encountered only Indians. The historian Clarence W. Alvord found records indicating that in 1782 Jean Baptiste Gaffé of Cahokia sent boatloads of trade goods to Chicago. From this we infer that he had a post there. Over what period of time he maintained this post, we do not know. It could not have been earlier than 1780. Among the preserved papers of the British General Haldimand there is a letter by Philippe François de Rocheblave, deposed last British governor of the Illinois country , who had been taken prisoner by George Rogers Clark at Kaskaskia in 1779, and transported to Virginia, while his wife and children remained behind. He wrote to General Haldimand on Nov. 6, 1783, that he would have to travel from Quebec into the Illinois country and "find Mrs. Rocheblave and the rest of the family at Chikagou." It is not known at whose cabin the Rocheblave family had found refuge at Chicago; it could have been Gaffé's post.

Jean Baptiste Point de Sable is the best known of the early Chicago traders, and a man of many talents. (The "Du" of the misnomer Du Sable is an American corruption of "de" as pronounced in

French, and first appears long after his death.) He earned the respect of his contemporaries, and for those who followed he became a legend, not all of which can be born out by historical research. Legends, however, have their own life, their inherent beauty, and their justification as poetic expressions of the soul's yearning.

Point de Sable first appears in the records of Quebec province in 1768. From recent research by John Swenson, we know that he spent most of his early years traveling as *engagé* for established Montreal traders in the northwestern Great Lakes region. In 1775 he teamed up with the experienced trader Pierre Durand, and both of them left Montreal for Cahokia in the Illinois country. By 1778 Point de Sable operated a trading post at *Rivière du Chemin* [Indiana], where the British Major De Peyster's men arrested him in 1779, assuming he had French or American leanings and connections. Later the major came to know Point de Sable personally and changed his mind about him, attesting to his loyalty toward the British crown by introducing him to Patrick Sinclair, British lieutenant governor of the Province of Quebec and successor to De Peyster as commandant at Michilimackinac. Sinclair's estate near Detroit, the Pinery, was subsequently managed by Point de Sable until 1784, when it had to be sold.

Once Point de Sable became his own man again, he made his home in Chicago, where the Tribune Tower now stands. His Indian wife Catherine came with him. It must have been between 1784 and 1788, and not in 1779, as earlier historians had concluded. Point de Sable may have built from scratch, or moved into an existing abandoned structure and remodeled it. For the first few years there were only the Indians for him to share Chicago with. In Oct. 1788, he and Catherine traveled to her church home in Cahokia and had their marriage of long standing solemnized. They had two children, Jean Baptiste, Jr., and Suzanne, and in Chicago in 1796, they enjoyed the birth of their granddaughter Eulalia Marie Pelletier, child of Suzanne and Jean Baptiste Pelletier. Point de Sable was a skilled farmer, maintained good relationships with his Indian neighbors, spoke French, English, and Indian languages, and he stayed until the year 1800. By then his farm had become a valuable estate that he could sell to his neighbor Jean B. La Lime for 6000 French *livres* [= $1,200], a large amount at the time. While the bill of sale has been preserved and shows La Lime as the purchaser, it turnes out that the trader William Burnett guarantied the payment and was the real new owner. Burnett, of Scottish origin, had his main post at the mouth of the St. Joseph river, but had also maintained a trading post in Chicago since at least 1798.

In 1800, Point de Sable moved to St. Charles in present Missouri, and we will not follow him there in this account. Readers who wish to learn more about this fascinating man may turn to page 388 for a more comprehensive essay about his life and time, prepared by John F. Swenson. Point de Sable left behind a small village of traders, where French and Indian languages were spoken and often mixed. There was Antoine Ouilmette, who says in recorded interviews late in his life, that he became Point de Sable's neighbor in 1790 (the northern Chicago suburb Wilmette is now named after him). In 1792 they were joined by La Lime. Like Point de Sable, both men had Indian wives.

Three years after Point de Sable's departure, the English-speaking element was added when Fort Dearborn was built and the trader, John Kinzie, came with his family in 1804 and bought Point de Sable's old house and farm buildings from La Lime. The village grew slowly for the next three decades, maintaining its French cultural dominance until 1833, when an unprecedented population explosion began, so radically changing the face and fabric of Chicago that it was soon no longer recognizable by its original inhabitants.

JEAN BAPTISTE POINT DE SABLE
THE FOUNDER OF MODERN CHICAGO

John F. Swenson

Jean Baptiste Point de Sable was the founder of modern Chicago and its first black resident. Point de Sable was his chosen legal name; he was never called Du Sable during his lifetime. Point was an inseparable element of his name, which he had assumed by 1778. The prosperous farm he had at the mouth of the Chicagou river (the French spelling) from about 1784 to 1800 helped stabilize a century-old French and Indian fur-trading settlement periodically disrupted by the wars and raids of Indians and Europeans, and abandoned by the French during the Revolution from 1778 to 1782.

The earliest known documents which refer specifically to him establish that in 1778 and 1779, perhaps as early as 1775, Point managed a trading post at the mouth of the *Rivière du Chemin* (Trail Creek), at present Michigan City, Indiana, not at Chicago, as is usually asserted. Pierre Durand of Detroit was associated with him and Michel Belleau in the ownership of this business. Here is Durand's own 1784 account of Point's post translated from his petition to Gen. Frederick Haldimand, then governor of Canada: "I found the waters low in the Chicagou [River]; I did not get to Lake Michigan until the 2nd of October [1778]. Seeing the season so far advanced that I could not reach Canada I decided to leave my packs at the *Rivière du Chemin* with Baptiste point Sable, free negro, and I returned to the Illinois to finish my business. The 1st of March, 1779, I sent off two canoes to take advantage of the deep water [at Chicagou], and I gave orders to my *commis* [business manager] to take these two canoes to the *Rivière du Chemin* loaded with goods and to go ahead of me with all the men, to help me pass at Chicagou.... I met my *commis* [Michel Belleau] at the start of the bad part [of the portage].... Some days later I arrived at the *Rivière du Chemin*, where I found only my packs [of furs]. The guard told me that M. Benette [Lt. William Bennett of the 8th regiment] had taken all my food, tobacco and *eau de vie* and a canoe to carry them...." Durand also learned that this British force had taken Point prisoner as a suspected rebel back to Michillimackinac, which began an important phase of his career as a minor but valuable member of the British Indian Department.

Up to the time of his capture, Point had been an *engagé* in the fur trade, travelling on the Great Lakes, the Illinois River and elsewhere from perhaps 1768 to 1779. From 1775 to 1779 his associate Durand was known to have been active in the upper country, under an official trade license. Only British subjects were allowed to work in the fur trade, which was supervised by military officers and the governor of Quebec. All *engagés* as well as the license holder had to swear an oath of loyalty to the king before the commander at Montreal and sign a printed oath incorporated in the license. Wealthy individuals posted bonds which would be forfeited for the slightest infraction of the rules of the fur trade or acts of disloyalty. The Durand-Belleau license itself and documents of Point's hiring at Michillimackinac have not been found. Point would have signed by a mark, since he was illiterate as most *engagés* were, but he must have been a skilled man by the time Lt. Governor Sinclair hired him in 1780 for his semi-official operation at the Pinery, adjoining Fort Sinclair north of Detroit.

Once Point de Sable settled in Chicagou, in territory regarded by law as Indian-owned, at the end of the Revolution, he was mainly a farmer. His farm was known, as far away as the nation's capital, as the only source of farm produce in the area until after he moved away in 1800. Like all people living in the barter economy of the frontier, he traded with Indians and Europeans alike for goods and services he needed, but he was not a professional trader. William Burnett, who may already have had a financial stake in the farm during the time Point managed it, became the actual owner (of the buildings, not the land) after Point left in 1800, and also used it as his Chicagou trading post until his associate John Kinzie arrived in 1804. By the 1795 Treaty of Greenville the Indians defeated at Fallen Timbers granted the United States a six-mile square tract at the mouth of the river; Point was thus a tenant or licensee, not an owner, of the land.

The cessation of hostilities created an environment in which Point could prosper. He was a British subject in what was still British-controlled territory. It is generally forgotten that the Northwest Territory, ceded by Great Britain to the United States by the 1783 Treaty of Paris, was still almost completely controlled by British military forces and traders until 1796 with the implementation of Jay's Treaty of 1794 and the surrender of military posts, such as Detroit and Michillimackinac, to the United States. However, British agents remained in place until the Treaty of Ghent ended the War of 1812 in 1815. In Chicago the British agent was [see] John Kinzie, who changed allegiance in 1812 at great personal risk. When Point sold his improvements and household goods for 6,000 *livres* ($1,200) in 1800, a value certified by appraisers Kinzie and Burnett, and moved to St. Charles in present Missouri, then the Spanish colony of Upper Louisiana, his farm was comparable to those of prominent people in Cahokia. There is no record that Point ever became a U.S. citizen.

Point de Sable means "sand point" in French and was probably taken as a surname by Jean Baptiste to identify a place (one of many so named) important to him which has not yet been identified. *Pointe* is the proper French spelling, but the final *e* is almost always dropped in the documents. *Sable* means sand. It can also mean black in the aristocratic Norman French or English heraldry, but only because this color was used to represent sand on coats of arms. Point is unlikely to have known this, for his command of English was rudimentary at best. Moreover, people of African descent were always called *nègre* in French America.

Point de Sable in any form is not a French surname found in any vital records of France, Canada or the United States. The fictitious surname Du Sable imposed on Jean Baptiste appeared only long after his death in 1818. *Du* is a corruption of the proper French pronunciation of *de*, which Anglophones write as *du*. George Rogers Clark, for example, had once planned to attack "Dutroit." In nearly all the many surviving documents, from 1779 to 1818, most of them written in French, in which Point was a party or was mentioned, his surname appears as Point de Sable. The Sieur du Sablé (without the Point) was a title of minor nobility used in the 18th century in the Dandonneau family of Quebec. This family had no known connection to Point de Sable, although the related Chaboillez family were prominent fur traders. A Haitian family named Des Sables, again lacking the Point, were French subjects and cannot be related to Chicagou's founder, whose family probably did not even have a surname, despite the elaborate, undocumented assertions of a member of that family in a fanciful 1950 biography.

Point de Sable was born free, as Durand implied by calling him a "free negro." He was the son of parents still not identified, possibly born at Vaudreuil, near Montreal before 1750. A *Jean Baptiste, nègre*, native of Vaudreuil, is listed as an *engagé* in a 1768 fur trade license. Point's mother was a free woman, not a slave. Children of a slave mother, black or Indian, were slaves under Quebec law, regardless of the status of the father.

Where Point was before 1775 has not been reliably documented, but in that year he seems to have been hired at Montreal by Guillaume Monforton or Montforton of Detroit, a trader and notary at Michillimackinac, to travel there from Montreal. In the surviving British license papers he is simply *Baptiste, nègre*; earlier licenses are similarly vague. There is no truth to the two-century old myth that for several years from 1773, to about 1790, he farmed land at Peoria, under a 1773 deed from the supposed British commander there, Jean Baptiste Maillet, and was a member of the militia in 1790. Aside from the fact that Maillet was a travelling *engagé* in the fur trade, under licenses from 1769 to 1776, and lived near Montreal where he had two daughters born in 1768 and 1771, any such grant was illegal under British law. This myth was exploded in 1809 by the U.S. land commissioners hearing land claims at Peoria, who found that no purported British land grant presented to them, of which this was one, was authorized. The militia rolls for Illinois, published in 1890, have many men named Jean Baptiste, but none with a surname resembling Point de Sable.[1]

In 1775 Point de Sable joined forces with the experienced trader Pierre Durand, a Detroit resident, and left Michillimackinac under the trade license of Michel Belleau. His associates were financed and bonded by Jean Orillat, the wealthiest merchant in Montreal. They had previously been in Illinois. Orillat had been trading between Illinois and Montreal since 1767 or earlier. Belleau and Durand travelled to Illinois. Belleau set up a post where Bureau Creek enters the Illinois River. Bureau is an obvious corruption of his name, most likely by local Indians whose dialect replaced the sound of *l* with *r*. For example, the Illinois Indians called themselves *Irenioua* (plural *Ireniouaki*). Bureau was recorded as early as 1790 as the "River of Bureau," or at Bureau's, which helps locate his post. Near this post was a conspicuous peninsula of sand (French, *pointe de sable*), now called Hickory Ridge, behind which was a harbor providing a place to load canoes, pirogues or *batteaux*. They spent some of their time in Cahokia, Peoria and on the Illinois River from 1775 to 1779. They dealt with each other and with various local merchants such as Charles Marois (interestingly, he was illiterate) and Charles Gratiot of Cahokia, and Pepin & Benito and Charles Sanguinette of St. Louis. Point had an account, managed by Marois, with Michel Palmier *dit* Beaulieu (no relation to Belleau), a wealthy farmer and prominent Cahokia citizen. Pierre Belleau, Michel's brother, was hired to go to Illinois in 1776 by Orillat's former partner Gabriel Cerré. Nothing further is known of him, but Pierre and Michel seem to have been killed by Indians along the Illinois River in the spring of 1780. Michel's estate was administered in Cahokia, where his creditors were, although when he went to Montreal in 1777 without Durand to get his trading license renewed he seems to have stated that he lived at Detroit. Perhaps he and Point were the two young male boarders in Durand's modest household noted in the 1779 Detroit census.

Point de Sable was at his trading post on the *Rivière du Chemin* in October 1778, when Durand, with two boatloads of furs, was forced by the lateness of the season to leave his cargo with "Baptiste point Sable, naigre libre" instead of taking it to Montreal as he had planned. Durand had left Kaskaskia in June just before George Rogers Clark occupied it, but was delayed by the turbulent events of the time. He eventually got underway, passing up the Illinois River and through Chicagou, reaching Lake Michigan on October 2, 1778. After leaving his furs with Jean Baptiste, Durand returned to Cahokia and Kaskaskia for the winter. Perhaps he was able to settle his and Point's debts to the estate of Charles Marois, who had died recently.

Durand sent off Michel Belleau and two canoes of furs to the *Rivière du Chemin* on March 1, 1779. He remained in Cahokia and Kaskaskia to collect on his and Point Sable's accounts with Clark's army. In July 1779, Durand stopped at Peoria, where he met his Cahokia friend Capt. Godefroy de Linctot, the leader of a small army that had left Cahokia at the end of June. Linctot had brought with him Clark's commission of Jean Baptiste Maillet as captain of the Virginia militia at Peoria, a community he was expected to defend from attack, although, as Durand later told Lt. Gov. Patrick Sinclair, there was no fort there. A year later Maillet was in St. Louis and his clerk, Pierre Trogé or Trottier, was on the Maumee River in present Ohio. Linctot, coordinating his movements with those of Clark, was planning to attack Detroit. Major Arent Schuyler De Peyster, the British commander at Michillimackinac, got wind of this plan on July 3 and on the 4th dispatched Bennett overland with 20 soldiers, 60 armed traders serving in the militia, and about 200 Indians, to intercept Linctot's force, which, like Clark's, never reached Detroit.

Durand met Belleau and 14 *engagés* at the start of the Chicagou *portage des chênes*. At Chicagou the local Indian leaders brought him some bad news: Point de Sable had been at his post at the *Rivière du Chemin* when a detachment of Bennett's forces under Corporal Gascon arrested him, about August 1, confiscating 10 barrels of rum, food, clothing and a birchbark canoe with repair supplies, all worth 8,705 *livres* (£580), all the property of Durand. Gascon took Point's many packs of furs under guard to Michillimackinac pending Durand's expected arrival with additional packs. These would be brought by 30 horses provided by the Chicagou Potawatomi. Gascon took Point prisoner to Bennett, who was camped on the nearby St. Joseph River.

Bennett and De Peyster must at the least have known of Point, because Bennett's first report to De Peyster of his arrest, written at his St. Joseph camp on August 9, 1779, simply says "Baptiste Point au Sable I have taken into custody, he hopes to make his conduct appear to you spotless," without explaining who Point was or where he lived.

As commandant De Peyster was responsible for keeping track of all traders in his area. Point cannot have been a stranger to him; he was zealous in his enforcement of fur trade rules.

Point must have known some of the traders and Indians with Bennett, because when he arrived at Fort Michilimackinac about September 1, Bennett reported to De Peyster that "the negro Point au Sable" had "many friends who give him a good character," a clue to his earlier trading voyages. Point was married by now, but there is no mention of his family.

Point de Sable met De Peyster upon his arrival at Michillimackinac about Sept. 1, 1779. De Peyster was waiting for news of a glorious military exploit by troops under his command. Instead, he received Point's demand that he pay for the property Bennett had confiscated from his trading post at the *Rivière du Chemin*. De Peyster refused to pay for these goods, valued at £580, treating them as spoils of war owned by a rebel trader. If they were not spoils of war, De Peyster knew he would have to reimburse Durand out of his own pocket. This was a sizable liability for an officer whose annual salary was £75. Durand was finally reimbursed in 1784, probably to De Peyster's relief.

Shortly before De Peyster left for his new command at Detroit, Durand also arrived at Michillimackinac and learned that De Peyster had ordered his arrest. He managed to avoid being detained and wrote out an itemized bill for his property confiscated from Point's post. Translated from the French, the heading of the bill reads "Memorandum of Property which I, Durand, left in the custody of Baptiste Point Sable, free negro, at the Rivière du Chemin, which Mr. Bennett, commander, gave orders to seize." De Peyster refused to pay this bill because, as he explained to Governor Haldimand when it was presented to him again in 1780, there was a rumor (not true) that Durand "had made lampoons upon the King, which were sung at the Cascaskias." The miscreant was later identified as Jean-Marie Arsenault, *dit* Durand, no relation.

There is a widely accepted myth that Point's trading post of 1779 was not at the *Rivière du Chemin*, as amply documented at the time, but at Chicago. The evidence for this myth is worse than flimsy, and can be briefly dealt with. Andreas in his history of Chicago drew upon an uncritical reading of the much later writings of De Peyster which flatly contradicted his own and other documents of 1779 to 1784. De Peyster published a pseudo-historical narrative of his experiences at Michillimackinac in 1813 under the title of *Speech to the Western Indians* in his self-published *Miscellanies by an Officer*. In a fanciful recasting of the arrest of Point de Sable, De Peyster characterizes him as a handsome Negro, well educated and with French sympathies. In fact, Point was illiterate, and in 1780 De Peyster had urged his successor Sinclair to hire him for a position at a sensitive British location. De Peyster further mangled the historical record by stating that Point was arrested by Capt. Charles de Langlade, not Bennett's Corporal Gascon, and that Point was established at "Eschikagou." Amazingly, Andreas and every subsequent historian have swallowed these fantasies whole, although the essential contemporary documents have been available in published form for more than a century. By the time De Peyster wrote this piece of fanciful doggerel, he had probably heard from old friends, like John Askin of Michillimacknac and Detroit, that Point was then at Chicagou (as De Peyster spelled it in his July 1, 1779 order to Langlade), and mixed up the dates. The obvious conflict between the facts and De Peyster's late recollection of them has regrettably never been examined, to the discredit of students of Chicago history. No credence should be given to the late jottings of a retired offficer whose memory had failed him.

Pierre Durand managed to get passage on a boat manned by black sailors that took him to the *Rivière du Chemin* to get the 120 packs of furs he had left there in Point's absence. On Oct. 15, 1779, De Peyster left for his new command at Detroit, replacing Lt. Gov. Henry Hamilton, now a prisoner of war at Williamsburg. Shortly after De Peyster's successor, Lt. Gov. Patrick Sinclair, assumed command at Michillimackinac, Durand arrived with his treasure of furs. Having barely survived a harrowing stormy lake voyage, the exhausted trader landed his cargo in this small leaky sailboat about October 20. Sinclair arrested him, confiscated his papers, and refused to pay the Point de Sable bill. Durand's papers included a copy of Belleau's declaration of loyalty to Virginia, a bill of exchange endorsed to Point de Sable and Virginia paper money, all worthless payments for goods requisitioned from them by Clark's rebel forces in Illinois. This convinced the erratic and generally paranoid Sinclair that Durand and Point were both rebels, and the confiscated property was mere spoils of war. It soon became evident, however, that both were loyal British subjects who had been victimized, like many others, by Clark's impecunious Virginia forces.

Sinclair bought more trade goods from Durand on credit and promised to reimburse Durand for the cost of shipping his furs to Montreal, promises he never kept. He failed to pay Durand for moving and repairing a house for Matchekiwish, a local Chippewa war chief. He also hired him at a piastre (dollar) a day to guide a war party, headed by Langlade, to Chicagou and down the Illinois River in 1780 to join the attack on St. Louis and Cahokia. Ironically this war party passed the post of Michel and Pierre Belleau, who were killed about this time by Indians on British orders. Sinclair had confiscated from Durand a copy of Michel's oath of loyalty to Virginia, which became his death warrant. Durand was never paid for anything but guiding this party and the property confiscated from Point. Sinclair characteristically declined to pay for about 10,000 *livres* of charges on Durand's second bill.

Point de Sable fared much better than Durand. Surprisingly, within a year this prisoner, arrested under suspicion of siding with the Americans, was employed with De Peyster's knowledge and at the request of Meskiash, village chief of the local Ojibway, as manager of Sinclair's Michigan estate, the Pinery. This property, illegally bought from Indians including Meskiash and others in 1765, was near the mouth of the Pine River at present St. Clair. He held this position from August 1780 until 1784, when the property was sold. His wife and children had probably joined him there, in a house built in November and December 1779, by British workmen. This structure was built of squared pine logs covered by hand-sawed boards. The interior was partitioned into rooms, and the board walls were plastered with clay from the bed of the Pine River.

Shortly after his arrival in the Detroit area Point again pressed De Peyster for payment of the 8,705 *livres*. De Peyster again refused because of Durand's supposed rebel sympathies. He was taking a big risk because if, as it turned out, these goods were requisitioned from a British subject, he would be legally responsible for payment out of his own pocket. This uncertainty hung over him until the wartime expenses of the upper posts were finally approved by the auditors in London in 1787.

The Pinery was supplied from Detroit, and the commandant there was responsible for the regulation of this trade, including approval of any voyages there and beyond, as far as Michillimackinac. As the officer who had jurisdiction over the Pinery, De Peyster must have had regular contact with, and intelligence about Point de Sable, who was there with his permission and no doubt was an employe of the Indian Department. One of De Peyster's sources would have been Meskiash, the Ojibway village chief near the Pinery, who participated in a 1781 Indian council which De Peyster had convened at Detroit.

In the late summer of 1781, Point was apparently running a British trading post at Ouiatenon (Lafayette, Ind.). Lt. Valentine T. Dalton, the Virginia commander at Vincennes, was kidnapped from his home by Indians and taken to Quebec. In a letter to George Rogers Clark he describes his experiences and meeting "J^no Batise." At the forks of the Maumee River (Defiance, Ohio) he met Pierre Trogé ("Truchey") of Vincennes, who was running another trading post. Significantly, he mentions one of Trogé's former employers, LeGras of Vincennes, but not Jean Baptiste Maillet, whom he must have encountered at Peoria or Cahokia.

In 1784 Point de Sable shipped his household goods, obviously the furnishings of the comfortable family home of a very loyal British subject, from the Pinery to Detroit, and moved there with his family. Soon he became associated with William Burnett, a wealthy and wide-ranging trader at the mouth of the St. Joseph River, who also had a post at Michillimackinac, and at Chicagou. By 1788 Point de Sable had settled with his family at the Chicago River and was farming the land with his wife and two children. He had probably disposed of the telltale framed portraits which had adorned his home at the Pinery. The subjects included King George III and Queen Charlotte Sophia; the King's younger brother (the Duke of Gloucester); His Serene Highness, Karl Wilhelm Ferdinand, Duke of Braunschweig-Luneberg, a cousin of George III who had sent his Brunswick troops to Canada's defense against the rebels; and Baron Hawke and Viscount Keppel, both First Lords of the Admiralty who had battled

French fleets. These treasures from their home at the Pinery would have exposed him as a loyal British subject in a place now visited by patriotic citizens and soldiers of the new United States, such as the covert intelligence officer Lt. John Armstrong, travelling under secret war department orders in 1789.

In 1788 he and Catherine went from Chicagou to Cahokia to have their marriage solemnized by Father De St. Pierre (né Heiligenstein) in the newly rebuilt church of the Holy Family. Jean Baptiste had established business and personal relationships in and near Cahokia, dating back to 1778 or earlier.

In 1790 the Detroit-Cahokia trader Hugh Heward stopped at Point's farm and traded cloth for food which Point had grown. Cloth was a major item stocked by traders, and Point would not have needed it, if he were himself in the business.

In 1794 the legendary Shawnee war chief Blue Jacket was making plans to move out of Ohio after Gen. Anthony Wayne's defeat of his British-backed Indian forces at Fallen Timbers, near present Toledo. He thought of going to "Chicagou on the Illinois River" in British-controlled territory, but he didn't because the defeated Indians were forced to cede a six-mile square tract at the mouth of the Chicago River to the United States in the 1795 Treaty of Greenville. A 1794 smallpox epidemic which killed 50 Indians at Chicagou must also have discouraged him.

In 1794 Pierre Grignon, a British trader living at Green Bay, paid a visit to Point de Sable at Chicagou. The brief report of this meeting by his brother Augustin Grignon included a cryptic reference to a government commission Point exhibited to his visitor, who probably then considered himself a fellow British subject in British-controlled territory. It seems unlikely that the United States would employ Point as a secret agent, a man who had for several years been a British subject working at the Pinery, a post controlled by the British Indian Department. The Grignons were themselves employes of the Indian Department as late as 1815. In fact [see] John Kinzie, the Chicagou trader who acquired Point's farm in 1803, was an officer of this department who narrowly escaped hanging or being killed by pro-British Indians for treason committed near Detroit, after he had switched his allegiance to the United States, in 1812. He had been reported by Tecumseh as attempting to win Indians to the Amerian side while bringing them gunpowder furnished by his department.

Suzanne Point de Sable was married at Cahokia in 1790 to Jean Baptiste Pelletier; Fr. Pierre Gibault, long sympathetic to the American cause, officiated. The young couple must have lived with or near her parents in Chicagou. Their daughter Eulalie was born there in 1796.

In 1796 Pelletier got a receipt at Chicagou for some furs, credited to his father-in-law's account, signed by the trader Jean Baptiste Gigon as agent for François Duquette of Michillimackinac and St. Charles. The receipt acknowledges payment of two dozen eggs to have the furs pressed and packed for shipment, a service not necessary if Point had a trading post equipped with the press needed to package furs. Three years earlier Duquette, under a British trading license, had been selling trade goods below cost to the Wabash Indians in an effort to keep them loyal to the crown.

The Pelletiers and another pair of Chicagoans, the Le Mais, went to St. Louis in 1799 to have their children baptized. Little Eulalie Pelletier, whose grandparents were not present, had two interesting godparents. Hyacinthe St. Cyr, now a prominent merchant in St. Louis, was the brother of Baptiste St. Cyr who in 1770 had led a group of Jean Orillat's *engagés* to *Chiquagoux* to evaluate it as a site for a trading post, which Orillat never established. Hyacinthe's wife Hélène Hebert acted as godmother. St. Cyr would have known Point de Sable and may have acted as his representative at the ceremony. Hélène's brother François had been Point's fellow *voyageur* from Detroit to Michillimackinac in 1775.

Suzanne's brother Jean Baptiste Point de Sable *fils* [Jr.], of whom little is known, was living in St. Charles before 1810. He worked for Manuel Lisa, a Spanish trader of St. Louis, as an *engagé* on an 1812-1813 trading expedition up the Missouri River. He died in 1814 and his father was administrator of his meager estate. The surviving probate documents do not mention any heirs. It is not known when Catherine died. Point de Sable sold his Chicago property in 1800 to his neighbor Jean La Lime. William Burnett financed the deal, guaranteeing payment because La Lime put up no earnest money. Catherine did not sign the bill of sale, probably because she was no longer living. Jean Baptiste Pelletier may have been alive in 1815, but nothing is known of Suzanne and Eulalia at that time, nor indeed since 1799.

In the fall of 1800 Point de Sable moved from Chicagou to St. Charles in Spanish Upper Louisiana. There he bought a house and lot from Pierre Rondin, a free black, and also acquired two tracts of farm land. François Duquette was now his neighbor. He became involved in various real estate transactions that did not work out, including perhaps even the land he had bought for his home on the basis of Spanish land titles of doubtful validity. In some of these deals he was joined by his son. By 1809 he was in financial difficulties. Duquette got a judgement against Point for negligence in 1813, but the sheriff could not collect because Point was insolvent.

Somehow Point's name had become involved in the rampant land speculation of the time. Two spurious claims were made by men who had supposedly purchased his rights under acts of Congress to land in Illinois. These claims were filed by land jobbers with the U.S. Land Office at Kaskaskia about 1804, based on the fictitious assertion in perjured documents that he and his family had lived and farmed at Peoria from 1773 to after 1783, and that Point had served in the militia there in 1790. Of course, Point has been well documented as being elsewhere. In 1809 the Land Office rejected these claims as unproven. In 1815 it grudgingly and tentatively recommended that Congress consider approving these claims, but only to Point himself, who was probably unaware of the use of his name by swindlers. The disappointed speculator, Nicolas Jarrot, must not have told Point about Congress's tentative approval in 1816; in fact, he seems to have abandoned these and several other dubious Peoria claims, and he did not mention them in his will, written in 1818, the year Point died. Had deeds been issued with Congressional approval, Point would have received title to 800 acres of valuable real estate in Peoria. But this was not to be, and his financial woes increased. No further land claims were made in his name before another land office in 1820, specifically under a law for consideration of Peoria claims, probably because they had already been exposed as fraudulent, and would have been disputed by the testimony of long-time Peoria residents who recalled events well before 1779, but who did not remember the well-known Point de Sable.

By 1813 Point was destitute, and had even been forced to borrow household utensils from his neighbor Eulalie Barada. This Eulalie, who has been carelessly confused with Point's granddaughter Eulalie Pelletier, was the daughter of Louis Barada (Baradat) of St. Charles, a prominent landowner, and Marie Becquet, a native of Cahokia. Eulalie was born in St. Louis, probably in 1788, and married her first husband in 1802.

In 1813 Point de Sable deeded all his remaining property to his "friend" Eulalie, not for money, but for her promise to take care of him for the rest of his life in sickness and in health, to do his washing, provide firewood, repair his house, supply corn to feed his pigs and chickens, and to arrange for his burial in the parish cemetery. She and her third husband Michel De Roi both made their marks on the 1813 deed. Point affixed his usual "signature," the block capitals IBPS, this time writing the S backwards.

On August 28, 1818, Point de Sable died and on the 29th was buried in the St. Charles Borromeo parish cemetery. The priest's handwritten entry on the burial register describes him as *nègre*. Unlike the usual burial records of this period, there is no mention of his age, origin, parents, relatives or people present at the ceremony. Nor is there any record of probate proceedings.

The contemporary documents, long neglected and never assembled, tell a fascinating story of a successful free-born black entrepreneur, advancing through a series of significant careers to a position of wealth and prominence in Chicagou, and then in his final tragic years to poverty and ignominy. The founder of the modern city of Chicago merits nothing less than recognition of the facts of his life and achievements.

[1] For further discussion, refer to the essay on Peoria on page 395, where the fictitious nature of this "grant," which was never produced by the speculators who claimed under it, is considered in an analysis of the poorly-understood French settlement of Peoria.
[PRINCIPAL SOURCES: 9; 18a; 201; 300a; 470; Michigan Pioneer and Historical Collections, vols. 9, 16, 19]

PEORIA:
ITS EARLY HISTORY RE-EXAMINED

John F. Swenson

Peoria, a city on the Illinois River, is the seat of Peoria County. Its name was originally Pimiteoui, an Illinois word referring to the abundance of fat (pimi) wild game there, particularly at the shallow south end of Peoria Lake. The name Peoria, from the Peouareoua Indians first encountered there by Marquette in 1673, probably means *dreamer*, from the Illinois word peouara, *he dreams*, as recorded at Peoria about 1696 by the Jesuit missionary Jacques Gravier in his manuscript dictionary. The first European settlement was La Salle's *Fort Crevecoeur*, built in January 1680, but destroyed by his deserting employes in August of that year. Father Membré, his chaplain, recorded the meaning of Pimiteoui. *Fort St. Louis de Pimiteoui* was built by Tonti in 1691, when the French abandoned *Fort St. Louis des Illinois* at present Starved Rock. This fort stood among the Indian settlements at the south end of the lake, on a slight elevation on the east bank near the outlet; various French forts occupied this site, described by Patrick Kennedy in 1773, until the last of the occasional French garrisons was withdrawn in 1763 and the fort was burned. Peoria was until after 1790 a trading and farming outpost of Cahokia, some 150 miles to the south, and the French inhabitants were mostly residents of Cahokia, Vincennes and other permanent communities.

Until 1784 southern Illinois was part of Virginia, up to the 41st degree of latitude, under its 1609 royal charter; this line crosses Peoria Lake several miles north of the present city. In 1778 Virginia created Illinois County, following the conquest by George Rogers Clark's Virginia militia. The Illinois country was well known in the populous East, whose traders and land speculators had been there since about 1765 under British rule. French traders, settlers, priests and missionaries had established villages along the Mississippi, principally Cahokia and Kaskaskia, starting shortly before 1700. Some of these French had trading posts and farms at Peoria, but the villages on the Mississippi and Vincennes were where they had their homes

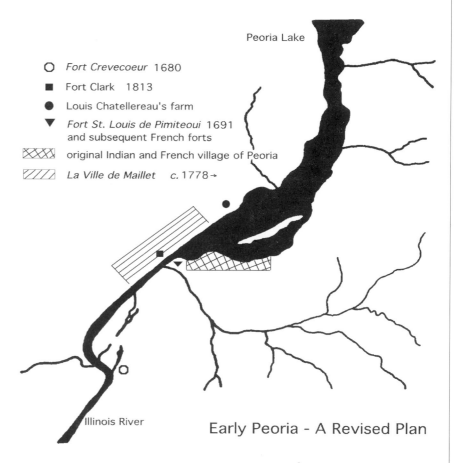

Peoria Lake

○   *Fort Crevecoeur*   1680

■   Fort Clark   1813

●   Louis Chatellereau's farm

▼   *Fort St. Louis de Pimiteoui* 1691
    and subsequent French forts

⊠⊠⊠   original Indian and French village of Peoria

▨▨   *La Ville de Maillet*   c. 1778 →

Illinois River

Early Peoria - A Revised Plan

and churches and did their military duty. The Illinois economy was based on furs and foodstuffs exported to Montreal and New Orleans: Peoria was a source of furs, horses and cattle for the most part. It was in the heart of Indian-controlled territory, and almost constant depredations by the natives made this outpost a hazardous place to live, even for French people with Indian blood and families. While regular censuses were taken in places like Cahokia and Vincennes, and churches provided religious and community centers, none was taken at Peoria; it was never more than an outpost until after 1790, except for a few brave people who lived near the French fort when it was garrisoned. The French of Peoria had their churches, law courts and families elsewhere. When the American Revolution ended in 1783, Virginia had enormous debts accumulated since Clark's conquest. There was little money to pay the accounts owing the Illinois people who had, largely under duress, financed the Virginia occupation. A major part of the resolution of these debts was the plan for Virginia to cede its claims to Illinois lands to the United States, which would then sell them, along with other public lands, to pay the national debts and the state debts which the federal government had assumed. The United States, of course, had to "extinguish" Indian titles to these lands by treaties before it could sell them to its citizens.

Recognizing that the mostly French inhabitants of Illinois and Vincennes had not only helped finance Virginia's conquest but had built valuable communities, the authorities who drafted Virginia's 1784 deed of cession knew that their claims must be dealt with. The deed of cession thus reserved the "possessions and titles" of these ancient inhabitants. Significantly, neither the deed of cession nor the Congressional acts of 1788 and 1791 which authorized land claims for these residents (few of whom could produce a valid deed to their habitations) mentioned Peoria as a place where people had "possessions and titles." The official language of these documents specifically mentions Vincennes and the Illinois settlements along the Mississippi which were well known permanent communities, but deliberately omits Peoria. Peoria as a strategic location was well known; British authorities

had wanted to build a new fort there in 1767 and 1768, and the Treaty of Greenville forced the defeated Indians to grant the United States a six-mile square tract at the southern end of the lake in 1795. The U.S. War Department in 1796 proposed to build a fort there, a plan finally realized in 1813 with the erection of Fort Clark, at the height of the War of 1812.

The 1787 ordinance creating the Northwest Territory, which included Illinois, also recognized the claims of the settlers. Arthur St. Clair became governor, and he visited the area in 1790 under specific instructions from President George Washington. One of St. Clair's duties was to make lists of people who had been residents and declared themselves to be citizens of the United States or Virginia in 1783, when the war ended, and of men who were members of local militias in 1790 which he was expected to organize during his visit. These lists were a means of identifying those settlers who were eligible to claim lands under the laws of 1788 and 1791. None of these 1790 lists, nor additional ones made from 1795 to 1797, mentions Peoria, although some men who were at Peoria occasionally, like Jean Baptiste Maillet (christened Mallet in 1749) of Vincennes, or Louis Chatellereau of Cahokia, who farmed there, were listed in the communities of their residence or militia service. Peoria was abandoned during the Revolution, and people began to return in 1784, well after the 1783 date for eligibility. It should be noted that [see] Jean Baptiste Point de Sable, who lived at Detroit and Chicago during this period, is not mentioned in any of these lists. The 1800 census of Indiana Territory mentions in a footnote that there were "100 souls" at Peoria, but Maillet, an experienced Indian agent who had extensive conferences with St. Clair at Cahokia in May and June of 1790, was one of about ten men encountered at Peoria earlier in May by the respected trader Hugh Heward. Maillet had just come to Peoria from his home in Vincennes where his daughter Veronique was married in April. Heward met no families at Peoria. Clearly Governor St. Clair knew that Peoria was not a permanent, settled community in 1783 or 1790. In fact, he appointed Maillet a captain in the militia, not of St. Clair County, which was based at Cahokia, but of Knox County, which had head-quarters at Vincennes where Maillet and his family lived. Maillet, who had been a judge of the Vincennes court in 1788, was to be stationed at Peoria, which was in Knox County. As captain of the Knox militia, he was basically a peace officer and Indian agent; in case of Indian troubles, he was instructed to send to Cahokia for help. Maillet's Peoria, where he had been a trader and from 1779 to 1780, militia captain under Virginia authority, was what is now called East Peoria, at the south end of the lake but on the east bank of the Illinois River. St. Clair made this portion of the river part of the northern boundary of Knox County, presumably after consultation with Maillet who had just come to Cahokia from there. This is where Heward had just visited several French "settled among the Indians" there. Louis Chatellereau's farm was on the west bank of the river, just outside the newly created Knox County.

Peoria began to grow slowly after 1790. In 1796 two distinguished travellers, Father Levadoux of Detroit and General Collot of France, found some 15 or 20 very poor French families there. In 1792 Chatellereau mortgaged his farm equipment, livestock and personal belongings, including his Indian slave "Pointe Sable," but no real estate, to the trader Gabriel Cerré of St. Louis; the document was drawn up and signed in the presence of Maillet, "commandant" of Peoria and recorded at Vincennes, the seat of Knox County. When Chatellereau died in 1795, his estate, again not including the land, was probated in the Knox County court at Vincennes. Michel Lonval of Cahokia was the administrator and signed the inventory; he acknowledged the assistance of two residents of Peoria.

About this time, real estate speculators began buying up the land claims of the old French settlers along the Mississippi, most of whom had left the chaotic Illinois country for Spanish Louisiana across the river, settling in places like St. Louis and St. Charles. These claims were bought for a few dollars and frequently sold and resold for about ten years, until in 1804 the United States finally set up a land office at Kaskaskia to evaluate the rights created by Congress for citizen-residents of 1783 and militia members of 1790. Chaos reigned, however, because there were few land title records, even of the occasional valid deed. To compound the confusion, Governor St. Clair's lists of eligible claimants had disappeared and could not be found in Illinois. The two land office commissioners, Jones and Backus, moved to Kaskaskia in 1804 and began to receive enormous numbers of written claims. Their rules of evidence were fairly casual, and they began to suspect that many of the claims were fraudulent, filed on behalf of people who did not exist for example, and supported by affidavits of suspicious origin often created by unscrupulous speculators and sworn to before corrupt judges. When these beleaguered commissioners began to make inquiries of the local people with personal knowledge of land occupation and usage, they were unable to speak French, the language of their witnesses. They hired a local bilingual trader to interpret for them, but this man, William Arundel, turned out to be another speculator and fabricator of false documents. They allowed many claims which turned out to be fraudulent, and had to reverse themselves when they were tipped off to the schemes of the land-jobbers. Among the miscreants whom they exposed in their 1809 report to Washington was Judge Robert Reynolds, who had taken many false affidavits from witnesses, some of whom turned out to be imposters. They excoriated him and his son [see] John Reynolds, who was punished ultimately by being elected governor of Illinois in 1830, and then a member of Congress in 1834, the year the Jones and Backus' report was published.

Two of the most ingenious speculators and fabricators of fraudulent claims were the lawyer Isaac Darneille and the trader Nicolas Jarrot. President Thomas Jefferson had enough bad experiences with Darneille, a bold political operator as well, to label him "an unmitigated dissipated swindler" in 1803. These two men presented huge numbers of claims, many of which the commissioners, even under the handicap of inadequate or false information, flatly rejected. Despite their vigilance, the commissioners were not able to expose every fraud or imposition that had been worked on them. To make matters worse, Washington ignored their requests for a copy of St. Clair's missing lists, and the first copy of their report, which detailed the detected frauds of speculators, was stolen from the mail.

Among the many claims Jones and Backus rejected were those originating largely with Darneille and Jarrot for lands supposedly settled at Peoria. The basis for their original rejection, in addition to lack of proof, was that Peoria was not mentioned in the Congressional acts authorizing claims. By about 1806 they had decided not to proceed with these dubious Peoria claims, but the well-connected Jarrot had other ideas. Probably in league with Darneille, bluntly characterized by Jefferson as a "swindler," he concocted a largely fictitious memorial to Congress on behalf of mostly imaginary Peoria residents (few of whose names appear in St. Clair's lists for any place) asking that the laws be amended to include Peoria claims. Jarrot signed most of the names himself for both real people (like the illiterate Point de Sable, a Chicagoan from 1784 to 1800, and since 1800 a resident of St. Charles) and fictitious ones. He even faked a "mark" of Michel Lonval, whose florid signature appears on his inventory of Chatellereau's estate. It is interesting to note that in 1809 Lonval prepared the inventory of Jean Dumoulin of Cahokia, in which he listed a promissory note of Point de Sable as "desperate," meaning uncollectible. The only legitimate signature on this memorial other than Jarrot's was probably William Arundel's, who like Jarrot put his name to a document in which they posed as residents of Peoria, when in fact they lived in Cahokia and Kaskaskia respectively. Congress received this unsupported document in February 1807, and in 1809 amended the law to allow the consideration of the Peoria claims, ignoring the clear evidence gathered on the spot by Governor St. Clair a few years earlier. The role, if any, of Jarrot's contact in Washington is not known.

The Jarrot-Darneille memorial and Congress' gullibility in accepting it opened a floodgate to a host of fraudulent Peoria claims, which has left behind a severely tainted historical record which has seduced practically every historian of Peoria. From 1807 to 1815 and beyond, Jones and Backus and their successors struggled to dismiss the claims of the importunate and well-connected speculators. Finally in 1815, in a report (published in 1834) which has eluded the scrutiny of Peoria historians, they abdicated the decision to Congress, which had allowed the farce to occur with its 1809 amendment. The land office commissioners wisely recommended, however, that if Congress were to allow any of these dubious claims at Peoria, the award should be made only to the original settler or his heirs; the law of April 1816 adopted their suggestion and allowed claims only by the settler or his "legal representative." This discouraged the speculators, who abandoned their spurious Peoria claims. The only Chicago resident who could have benefited from the unlikely granting of such a claim was [see] Jean Baptiste Point de Sable, who has been documented as living elsewhere than Peoria in the period of eligibility, 1783 to 1790, and who was in 1815 living in poverty and hounded by creditors in St. Charles, Missouri Territory. He never received a dime, and died destitute in 1818. This was a proper result, however, because Point had never lived at Peoria, despite Darneille's spurious claim that he had, under a fictitious 1773 British "grant" from Maillet which he never produced and would have been illegal if it had ever existed. In any event, Jones and Backus concluded that no valid British land grant had been presented to them.

Reliable documentation of Peoria history began to reappear in 1813, in the aftermath of Captain Craig's destruction of Peoria and the mass deportation of most of its residents, including the Indian agent Thomas Forsyth, the stepbrother and partner of Chicago's [see] John Kinzie. By 1817 Forsyth and a few former French residents of Peoria, still living in exile in the Missouri Territory, had begun to persuade Congress to reimburse them for their losses of buildings and personal property. They did not claim any lands, probably because they could not assert ownership within the six-mile square tract owned by the United States. Congress responded, not by reimbursing them, but by passing a law in 1820 for the relief of Peoria settlers, basically Craig's victims, providing for a new land claim process. Hearings were held at the land office at Edwardsville, and some 70 claims were presented, most of them supported by the testimony of witnesses appearing before the commissioner, Edward Coles. The published report of these proceedings pointedly observes that the French settled at Peoria without any claims of title (the vernacular would label them squatters), and sold only their improvements, not the land; it sheds considerable light on Peoria history from 1765 to 1812. However, it would be unwise to accept this record at face value.

Central to the testimony of all witnesses was the story, inconsistent with earlier documents, that the original French fort and village had been located on the west bank of the river, more than a mile north of the outlet of the lake, where in fact Heward had found only Chatellereau in 1790. The well-rehearsed story was that about 1778 the villagers, unhappy with the poor quality of the stagnant river water supposedly existing there, moved downstream to the outlet of the lake, where Maillet built a fort as the nucleus of the new *Ville de Maillet*. In fact, the river at both sites was deep and fast-flowing; the water quality could not have been an issue. Further, there is no independent documentation of a fort at Peoria from 1763 to 1813; a British plan to destroy a fort at Peoria in 1779 or 1780 was cancelled because witnesses including Pierre Durand, Point de Sable's associate, had said there was no fort there. The witnesses occasionally contradicted each other as to who had lived where, but they were all in agreement that they and their ancestors and predecessors had always lived along the west bank of the river, either in the "old" or the "new" village.

There is, however, considerable evidence, from 1691 to 1816, that the French fort and the preponderance of settlement were at the south end of Peoria Lake, on the east bank of the river. Perhaps by 1820 this old location was no longer fashionable, because none of the claimants whom Coles heard claimed lands in this area. A study of the topography and hydrography of the area, in a section of the highly detailed U.S. Army Corps of Engineers 1902-1904 map of the Illinois River, helps elucidate the issue of where people lived. There was a gently sloping prairie over a mile deep at the south end of the lake, with very shallow water extending several hundred feet from shore, a condition likely to produce the stagnant water supposedly at the "old" village. From this pleasant site the entire surface of the lake was visible. From the west bank for several miles north of the outlet, however, the view was more limited; the river bank was steep and high, at the edge of a deep and fast-moving river, with a narrow, flat tableland at the foot of steep hills. Liette, describing conditions in the 1690s (which changed little until the river was dredged about 1904) remarked that at times the southern shoreline was so crowded with wading animals browsing on aquatic vegetation that it was difficult for a small boat to reach the shore. There is no place along the entire west bank shallow enough to produce this phenomenon of abundance, reflected in the name Pimiteoui, which Father Membré in 1680 learned meant "plenty of fat beasts here." In 1816 Richard Graham (brother of [see] George Graham), the new Indian agent at Peoria, had complained to his superiors about these shallow, stagnant, grass-choked waters fronting the place in the actual "old" village of Peoria where he was ordered to set up his post. He thought a location on the west bank would be better, much as the French of 1778 had concluded when they began to move across the river, not downstream as the story had been recast by 1820. Patrick Kennedy's description of the south shore site of the fort, the ruins of which he visited in 1773, mentions the "summit" on which the fort had stood. His description does not fit any site on the west bank; his "summit" was probably a low triangular hill, perhaps the remains of a French construction project, within gunshot range of the river outlet, which the fort was built to control. Kennedy also remarked on the view of the entire lake available from this location. There were always a few settlers on the west bank before 1800, of whom Chatellereau is the best documented, but the south shore location was much more defensible, liveable and accessible both by water and by land.

The real growth of Peoria began about 1818, after the War of 1812. Peoria was the effective county seat for Chicago from 1825 to 1832. Both places grew rapidly from that time on, but by 1850 Chicago was far larger and has so remained to the present day.

[PRINCIPAL SOURCES: 9, 10a, 101, 259, 456, 470, 656a]

A TRIP FROM BELLEVILLE TO CHICAGO IN 1836

Memories of Gustave Koerner

Soon after my recovery I was charged with procuring the correction of some deeds for valuable farm-property, the title of which without this correction might become doubtful. As the parties who were to make the title perfect resided near Chicago, it was decided best that I should go there myself. As this was in the line of my business, and the compensation for my services was, for the time, very large, I of course accepted the task. Now-a-days a trip [from Belleville] to Chicago is a pleasant journey of twenty-four hours [Koerner wrote this in 1909], both coming and returning. It was quite a different undertaking in 1836, and so it may not be out of place to give a brief account of my trip.

Going to St. Louis early in May, I took a boat bound for Peru, a place some forty miles north of Peoria on the Illinois River. At Alton, we had a long delay, delivering and receiving goods. When we left late in the evening another boat bound for Galena, near the Mississippi River, left the wharf at the same time. A race immediately sprung up. Though many fatal accidents had happened from such races, the boilers exploding by reason of too great a pressure of steam, yet no passenger remonstrated and all were on deck shouting and cheering. The boats kept close together, and such was the excitement on our boat that we missed the mouth of the Illinois River, about twenty miles above Alton, and actually ran about twelve miles up the Mississippi before the mistake was discovered. This ended the race, and we on board had to turn back to get into the Illinois.

The Illinois was then at high water, quite a fine stream at the mouth, and for about a hundred miles broader than the Main [Frankfurt am Main, Germany, was Koerner's birthplace] while its water, as compared with that of the Missouri or even of the Mississippi, was beautiful. At many places it had overflowed its bank. It was then navigable, even with pretty large boats, some two hundred and fifty miles.

Majestic forests lined both of its shores. Only in a few places did the prairies extend to the river. Peoria, about two hundred miles from St. Louis, has a most beautiful situation. It rises terrace-like on gravel and rocky ground, and is encircled by finely timbered heights. It had even then a number of fine warehouses and residences, and promised the greatness it has since reached. I learned that a good many Germans had already settled there. At Hennepin, about twenty miles above Peoria, I left the boat to catch a stage running from Bloomington to Chicago, at some place east of Hennepin, to which a hack took me and some other passengers. In the night we reached Ottawa, then also a fine and rising place. We had to stop there a few hours, in order to cross the Fox River by ford. The river was high at the time, and the driver would not risk crossing at night, but waited for daylight. The ford was narrow and rather rocky, so that, if the stage had missed the track, it would have been very dangerous. As it was, the water came near running into the stage, which shook terribly, when going over the rough rocks at the bottom of the river. We felt very much relieved when we reached the further bank. From Hennepin on the country had been charming. All rolling prairie, only from time to time dotted with groves of fine timber. Prairies in May and June, covered with a hundred varieties of flowers and studded with numerous patches of strawberries, present a spectacle at which travelers who have seen the most beautiful scenery in the world will feel a great delight.

Not very far from the Fox River we met with a gang of prairie wolves. When first observed they had been standing right in the road; but hearing the rattling of our coach they made off on one side into the prairie. They trotted quite leisurely, turning their heads from time to time in a sort of stealthy way. Their color was that of a fox; in size they were twice as large.

Some ten miles west of Chicago we came into a very wet prairie, with a number of rather deep places filled with water, a sort of Pontine swamps. We were put into a large covered wagon, the wheels of which were very high and stout and the fellies and tires one and a half feet

North American Prairie Wolf [341]

wide to prevent cutting into the mud and getting the wagon stalled. There was no house or field anywhere to be seen until we reached the then little town of Chicago. A few years before only a few shanties and a small wooden fort stood between the lake and the arms of the Chicago River, one of which came from the north and the other from the south. At the time of my visit Chicago had about 5,000 inhabitants. There were only one or two brick houses; all others, even the hotel in which I stopped, were frame buildings. I arrived at noon, having been on my way from Belleville for five days and as many nights, stopping nowhere more than a couple of hours. I immediately went to the recorder's and the circuit clerk's offices, examining the records. In the evening I passed my time at the various places where lands and lots were selling at auction. All over the country, owing to the multitude of banks that had sprung up on the downfall of the great national bank, and to the fact that the national debt had been paid and the surplus of the treasury was about to be divided amongst the States, a spirit of speculation had arisen quite unparalleled at any time or in any country, except when the South Sea Bubble and the Law Mania prevailed in Great Britain and France [Koerner refers to John Law and the Mississippi percolative bubble; for detail see entry "Louisiana Province" in the encyclopedic portion of this volume]. Chicago in the West was at the head of this rage.

Every boat brought hundreds of immigrants, all anxious to make their fortunes by buying up the northern prairies. At places it was supposed the contemplated canal uniting the great lakes and the Mississippi by way of the Illinois River would be located, many towns had been laid out on paper, and here, as well as in towns already existing, as Ottawa, LaSalle, and Peru, lots were sold every night at really fabulous prices, considering the times, as were also all tracts of land within five or ten miles of the canal. Fabulous were the prices, indeed; for, when the crisis came a few years later, all those lots and lands came down to almost nothing, and remained valueless for some ten or twenty years, when a new and more healthy rise took place. These sales were nearly all on long credits; only a very small percentage of the money was paid down. I venture to say that there was not enough cash money in the whole State of Illinois at that time to have paid for the lands and lots that were sold within a month in the city of Chicago alone.

Next morning I started out westward to see the persons I had to deal with. I had to cross the same swamps; but a stout Canadian Indian pony brought me safely through. I had to ford the Des Plaines River, which was pretty deep, before I reached my destination about twelve miles from Chicago. It was in the afternoon when I reached it, and my business took up all the rest of the day. I stayed over night in the place, and the next morning I went with my clients back to Chicago, where our business was completed and the proper deeds made out.

There was an immense deal of life in this new Eldorado. The stores on Water Street were crowded. The river was full of boats. People ran as fast along the muddy unpaved streets as they do now. It had one advantage over the metropolis of today. The river formed by the two arms was nearly as clear as the beautiful lake, the sight of which was then as it is now, a great delight to me. Did I then foresee what Chicago would be in later life? St. Louis, in comparison to Chicago, was in 1836, a stately, magnificent city. Next day I left on the stage, went on it as far as Peoria, took a boat, and after an absence of two weeks, reached St. Louis. [416]

A List of Public Places and Monuments, Inscribed Plaques, Sculptures, Drawings and Paintings Related to Chicago's Earliest History

Editors' comment: A listing of monuments, as presented here, needs continual updating to remain reasonably complete and accurate. For this there are many reasons. Buildings that have featured memorial tablets may be torn down, and someone may determine that new structures need not accommodate an old plaque. Some families eventually forget and neglect grave monuments [✣]. Statues may become "politically incorrect" in what they symbolize and be withdrawn (see Columbus with Indian · 1826). Vandals deface or destroy monuments, thieves abscond with them, and some succumb to weather and acid rain. Some inscriptions contain assertions that were thought to have been historic facts, only to be proven wrong by later research (see Kinzie House · 1837). Historical interpretation is as much subject to change as everything else in this fast-flowing world, and nothing reveals this more than a stroll through the phantasmal realm of historic monuments.

Notes and explanations of symbols: whenever known, the year the monument was erected is listed immediately following the heading.

▼   Symbol indicating monument known to have been present but that has since vanished, or could not be located by the editors as of 1998.

✣   Symbol designating grave monuments.

➡   For street names commemorating early historic events or people, see Encyclopedic Section.

☛   Symbol indicating that the monument's inscription contains some unconfirmed, obsolete, or otherwise mistaken historical data. For clarification, the interested reader may turn to the corresponding entry in the Encyclopedic Section of this volume.

Algonquin Woods · named after a group of related North American Indian tribes sharing a similar language and living between the eastern seaboard and the Great Lakes at the time the first Europeans appeared. Both the Miami and the Potawatomi, the tribes most dominant in the Chicago region—although at different times—belong to the Algonquin group. The woods are located in the southernmost portion of the Des Plaines Division of the Cook County Forest Preserve District, bounded by Oakton Street, Des Plaines River Road, and the Tri-State Tollway.

▼ **Baptist Church** · 1937 · bronze plaque commemorating the first permanent meeting place on the southeast corner of Franklin and South Water streets, inscribed: "Chicago's First Baptist Church – Near this site in the 'Temple Building,' Chicago's first Baptist church held services. The congregation was organized October 19, 1833 by Rev. Allen B. Freeman. – Erected by Chicago's Charter Jubilee – Authenticated by Chicago Historical Society."

✣ **Beaubien, Alexander** · 1907 · son of Jean Baptiste Beaubien; his grave monument is in Graceland Cemetery.

✣ **Beaubien Cemetery** · 1844 · small private cemetery on land set aside for his family by Mark Beaubien in Lisle, IL, immediately west of 2900 W. Ogden Ave., not far from his tavern; while the original ▼ headstones have disappeared over the years, a new granite marker was erected in 1990, inscribed: "The Beaubien Burial Ground – 1844 – Monique Nadeau Beaubien Wife of Mark Beaubien 1800-1847 – Gen. John Baptiste Beaubien 1787-1864 – Millie Beaubien 1844 – Matilda Beaubien 1846-1848 – Monique Beaubien 1847 – Elinore Beaubien Simmons 1835-1870 – Emily Beaubien LeBeau 1825-1919 – Robert Beaubien 1849-1852 – Jessie Beaubien 1860-1862 – William Brian Beaubien 1844-1845 – Mathias Smith (friend) – Ruby Coté Beaubien 1860 – Elizabeth Bennet Beaubien 1854 – DuPage County Historical Marker

INDIAN TRAIL MARKER - see page 408

402

Erected 1990." Mark Beaubien's name does not appear on the marker.

Beaubien House · 1937 · bronze plaque on the east wall of the Cultural Center, southwest corner of Michigan Avenue and Randolph Street, inscribed: "Jean Baptiste Beaubien – On this site, then the lake shore, Jean Baptiste Beaubien, Chicago's second civilian, in 1817, built a 'mansion' to which he brought his bride, Josette LaFramboise. It remained their home until 1845. – Erected by Chicago's Charter Jubilee – Authenticated by Chicago Historical Society – 1937." Beaubien settled permanently in Chicago in 1812, when several houses were already present. The reference to Beaubien as "Chicago's second civilian" has no historical basis chronologically, but does acknowledge his influence in the community, second only to John Kinzie.

Beaubien, Jean Baptiste · also see "Bourbon Spring" and "Forbes Residence."

Beaubien, Mark · Lisle Tavern · 1840 · built in the 1830s by William Sweet in Lisle as his residence. Mark acquired the structure in 1840, turned it into a tavern, and from 1851 to 1857, used it as a tollhouse for the Southwest Plank Road. Now the property of the town of Lisle, it was moved a few blocks in 1989 to the Lisle Station Park, where it can be visited; call (708) 968-2747.

Beaubien Woods · name given in recognition of the Beaubien family to part of the Calumet Division of the Cook County Forest Preserve District. The woods are located on the Little Calumet River and can be reached from east 130th Street, just west of the Calumet Expressway.

▼ **Billy Caldwell's House** · 1937 · bronze plaque on the southeast corner of State Street and Chicago Avenue, inscribed: "Billy Caldwell's House – Here stood home of Billy Caldwell, half-breed Potawatomi Indian known as 'Sauganash' (The Englishman). It was built in 1828 by U.S. Department of Indian Affairs in recognition of his friendly efforts to preserve peace. – Erected by Chicago's Charter Jubilee – Authenticated by Chicago Historical Society – 1937."

Bison · 1893 · two bronze sculptures of the American buffalo at the east entrance of Humbold Park, near the corner of Division Street and Sacramento Boulevard; originally plaster models on the fairgrounds of the 1893 World Columbian Exposition; cast in 1911 by Jules Berchem. Sculptor: Edward Kemeys. Father Marquette still saw large herds of bison on the banks of the Mississippi in 1673, but by 1830 all native wild bison in Illinois had likely been exterminated.

Bourbon Spring · bronze plaque atop a square stone foundation, resembling a well, a few yards east of Barry Point Road, Riverside; inscribed: "July 1832 – General Winfield Scott camped near this spring on way to Blackhawk War. – June 7, 1834 – Election of Jean Baptiste Beaubien as 1st colonel of militia of Cook County, known as 60th Illinois Militia. In celebration of the election, kegs of bourbon were poured into spring, giving it name. – 1837 – Daniel Webster arriving from St. Louis was met at this spring by Chicago delegation. Ceremony took place on this spot."

Caldwell Woods · named in honor of Billy Caldwell, Potawatomi chief, son of an Indian mother and a British Army captain, remembered for his valuable services in assisting treaty negotiations between Indian tribes and the U.S. government. The woods are in the North Branch Division of the Cook County Forest Preserve District, bounded by Caldwell Avenue, Devon Avenue, Milwaukee Avenue, and Harms Road.

Catherine Chevalier Woods · see Robinson Woods.

▼ **Catholic Church** · 1937 · bronze plaque commemorating the first permanent meeting place on the southwest corner of State and Lake streets, inscribed: "Chicago's First Catholic Church – On this site, Old St. Mary's, Chicago's first Catholic Church, was erected in 1833 and dedicated in October of that year. Father John Mary Iranaeus St. Cyr was the first pastor. – Erected by Chicago's Charter Jubilee – Authenticated by Chicago Historical Society – 1937."

Cemeteries · 1937 · bronze plaque at 23rd Street viaduct over Illinois Central Rail Road, inscribed: "First City Cemeteries – This was the site of one of Chicago's first two cemeteries, and comprised sixteen acres. It was laid out in August, 1835, and enclosed in September, after which burials elsewhere on the south side were forbidden. – Erected by Chicago's Charter Jubilee – Authenticated by Chicago Historical Society – 1937." An identical plaque was proposed to designate the northern cemetery of 10 acres on Chicago Avenue, east of Clark Street, but was never placed.

✝ **Chappel, Eliza** · 1888 · one of Chicago's earliest schoolteachers (1833), died in 1888; her grave is in Rosehill Cemetery. Also see entry under Schoolhouse.

Che-che-pin-qua Woods · see Robinson Woods.

Chicago Historical Society Building · Clark Street at North Avenue. Anyone wishing to immerse oneself in a wealth of items relevant to Chicago's early history must visit this, Chicago's oldest cultural institution. Though only a fraction of the society's material is on permanent display, research centers, collections, and special exhibitions provide access to many elusive details.

Chicago Portage National Historic Site · 1952 · Portage Park at 48th Street and Harlem Avenue contains remnants of the portage waterway (Portage Creek) and its associated trails. Near the park entrance is a concrete basin with the text: "Chicago Portage – The Waterway West – Along these waterways and trails history has passed. The Chicago Portage has served as the connecting link between the Great Lakes and the Mississippi River System. – In 1673 led by American Indians explorers Marquette and Jolliet became the first Europeans to cross the portage. This route encouraged the development of the I & M Canal and the growth of Chicago." A monumental iron sculpture of Father Marquette, Louis Jolliet, and an Indian brave was erected within the basin in 1989. Sculptor: Guido Rebechini. ▼ A short walk into the park leads to the edge of Portage Creek and a granite boulder [1930] that once held a bronze plaque commemorating the historic portage in 1673, inscribed: "The Chicago Portage 1673-1836 – This marks the west end of the carrying or connecting place, uniting the waters of the St. Lawrence River and the Great Lakes with those of the Mississippi River, its tributaries and the Gulf of Mexico, the earliest factor in determining Chicago's commercial supremacy. An artery of travel used by the aborigines in their migrations and later by Joliet, Marquette, La Salle, Tonti and the fur traders of New France. An early strategical point in the wars incident to winning the North-West for the settlers. Discovered by Joliet and Marquette in 1673. – Erected by the Chicago Historical Society in pursuance of a plan to give posterity the facts of Chicago's early history. A.D. 1930."

Chicago River · 1953 · bronze plaque on the southwest pylon of the Michigan Avenue bridge, inscribed: "Chicago River – This river, originally flowing eastward from the prairie homelands of the Potawatomi and other Indian tribes, into Lake Michigan, linked the waters of the Atlantic, the St. Lawrence and the Great Lakes with those of the Illinois, the Mississippi and the Gulf of Mexico. From 1673, commerce and civilization followed this natural waterway from the seaboard to the heart of the continent. The strategic importance to early American development of the junction of the Chicago River and Lake Michigan led to the establishment here of Fort Dearborn and to the founding of the city of Chicago. – Erected in 1953 to the memory of those pioneers who plied the water route. – Society of Colonial Wars in the State of Illinois."

Chippewa Woods · honoring the Chippewa [Ojibwa] Indian tribe by attaching its name to the northernmost portion of the Indian Boundary Division of the Cook County Forest Preserve District. The woods are surrounded by Touhy and Devon avenues, Dee and Des Plaines River roads.

Clarke House · 1836 · also called the Henry Brown Clarke House, or the Widow Clarke House, the oldest building in Chicago, built by Henry Brown Clarke at (now) 16th Street and Michigan Avenue, later moved to 45th Street and Wabash Avenue, and again placed near its original site at 1855 S. Indiana Ave., in the Prairie Avenue Historic District bordered by Indiana Avenue, 18th Street, Prairie Avenue and Cullerton Street. Clarke arrived in Chicago in 1835 from Utica, NY, and soon prospered as a merchant and land speculator. His stately Greek revival style house survived the fire of 1871 and is now a historical monument. When built, the residence was at the eastern edge of a seemingly limitless prairie, and the nearest house was about 1 1/2 miles north. At the entrance to the historic district, on 18th Street, is mounted a panel that gives further information about Clarke and his house. The house now belongs to the city of Chicago and can be toured at certain hours; call (312) 744-3200.

✛ **Clybourne, Archibald** · 1872 · this early citizen (1823) and butcher became Chicago's first stockyard owner, died in 1872; his grave is in Rosehill Cemetery.

▼ **Cobweb Castle** · 1937 · bronze plaque at 357 N. State St., inscribed: " 'Cobweb Castle' – Near this site on Wolcott (now State) stood Agency House, known as 'Cobweb Castle'. It was the home of Dr. Alexander Wolcott, Government Indian Agent at Chicago (1820-1830). – Erected by Chicago's Charter Jubilee – Authenticated by Chicago Historical Society – 1937." The house acquired its name during the time Wolcott lived there as a bachelor, before his marriage to Ellen Marion Kinzie in 1823.

Columbus · 1933 · monumental bronze statue of Christopher Columbus, located in Grant Park at Columbus Drive and Roosevelt Road; created for the 1933 Century of Progress Exposition as a gift from the Italian-American community of Chicago. Sculptor: Carl Brioschi.

Columbus · 1891 · monumental bronze statue of Christopher Columbus; exhibited in the Italian pavilion of the 1893 World Columbian Exposition; rededicated in 1966 at the center of a granite fountain, Columbus Plaza within Victor Arrigo Park at 800 S. Polk and 1400 W. Loomis streets. Sculptor: Moses Ezekiel.

▼ **Columbus with Indian** · 1924 · concrete sculpture at 9400 W. Foster Ave., on the northwest corner of River Road in Schiller Park; in elegant garb Christopher Columbus bends to acknowledge a supplicant Indian. No text was inscribed. The Indian's submissive posture offended minority sentiments, and the sculpture has disappeared in recent years. Sculptor: Virgil Rainer.

Cook, Daniel Pope · 1968 · brass plaque on the south side of the lobby of the Cook County Building at 118 N. Clark St., inscribed "Daniel Pope Cook – 1794-1827 – Cook County Illinois, was named in honor of this great American patriot and Illinois citizen – Presented by Independence Hall of Chicago Illinois Sequicentennial – 1818-1968."

✛ **Couch, Ira** · 1858 · a tailor from New York State, came to Chicago in 1835 or 1836 with his brother James. They soon became owners of the Tremont

Hotel, and were said to have become Chicago's first millionaires. Ira died in 1857 while vacationing in Cuba. James placed his brother's remains in a family mausoleum constructed the following year in Lincoln Park (near the Chicago Historical Society north of North Avenue, northwest of the Lincoln monument), the former city cemetery from which all other graves have been transferred.

▼ **Cow Path** · 1937 · bronze plaque over entrance, 100 W. Monroe St., inscribed: "Historic Cow Path – This areaway, 10x177x18 feet, is reserved forever as a cow path by terms of the deed of Willard Jones in 1844, when he sold portions of the surrounding property. – Erected by Chicago's Charter Jubilee – Authenticated by Chicago Historical Society – 1937." Willard Jones came to Chicago in 1833.

Dearborn Street Bridge · bronze bas-relief tablet at the current bridge site with a view of the old bridge, inscribed: "Chicago's first movable bridge was constructed at this site in 1834. The timber span provided only a 60 foot opening for the passage of vessels. So dangerous to ships was this narrow draw, that the bridge was ordered removed by the council in 1839. The present bridge is the fourth at this site."

▼ **Dearborn Street Drawbridge** · 1937 · bronze plaque on the first pylon east of Dearborn Street, north side of Wacker Street; inscribed, "Dearborn Street Drawbridge – First drawbridge over the Chicago River was constructed at Dearborn Street in 1834 by Nelson R. Norton. A primitive wooden affair, 300 feet long with 60 foot opening, the council removed it in 1839. – Erected by Chicago's Charter Jubilee - Authenticated by Chicago Historical Society – 1837." This plaque was likely replaced by the tablet of the preceding entry.

☞ **Defense** · 1928 · concrete sculpture on the southwest pylon of the Michigan Avenue bridge commemorates the Fort Dearborn massacre of 1812, with text tablet: "Defense – Fort Dearborn stood almost on this spot. After an heroic defense in eighteen hundred and twelve, the garrison together with women and children was forced to evacuate the fort. Led forth by Captain Wells, they were brutally massacred by the Indians. They will be cherished as martyrs in our early history. – Erected by the Trustees of the B.F. Ferguson Monument Fund – 1928." Sculptor: Henry Hering.

✛ **Dexter Graves Monument** · 1909 · called "Eternal Silence" and located in Graceland Cemetery, very close to the Kinzie family grave site. In 1831 Dexter Graves owned and ran an unpretentious log cabin hotel called the Mansion House; later he did well in land speculation. After his death, Henry Graves commissioned the monument for his father's grave site: an eight-foot-tall haunting draped and hooded figure, the sunken face blackened by age. Sculptor: Lorado Taft.

Discoverers · 1930 · concrete sculpture on the northeast pylon of the Michigan Avenue bridge honors Louis Jolliet, Jacques Marquette, René-Robert Cavelier, Sieur de La Salle, and Henri de Tonti, shown in the company of Indians and a guardian angel, with text tablet: "The Discoverers – Jolliet, Father Marquette, La Salle, and Tonti will live in American history as fearless explorers who made their way through the Great Lakes and across this watershed to the Mississippi in the late seventeenth century and typify the spirit of brave adventure which has always been firmly planted in the character of the middle west. – Presented to the City by William Wrigley Jr. – 1930." Sculptor: James Earle Frazer.

Eagles · 1931 · at Congress Plaza and Michigan Avenue. Sculptor: Frederick Cleveland Hibbard. American bald eagles appeared regularly along the lakefront before Chicago existed.

Forbes Residence · boulder marker west of the Riverside train station, inscribed: "Site of first home built in Cook County west of Chicago by its first elected sheriff – Stephen Van Rensselaer Forbes – 1831 – Only voting place of Cook County for its first colonel of the state militia – Jean Baptiste Beaubien – June 7, 1834." Forbes first acquired a 160-acre homestead in 1830 and built a large log house the following year; he was elected sheriff of Cook County in 1832.

Forest Park Library · on permanent display in the history room of the library is a collection of authentic Indian silver jewelry from Indian graves in the Chicago area. The artifacts were traded sometime between 1760 and 1820, when silversmiths in Quebec and Montreal crafted laminated ware for the North West Company. They include wristbands, armbands, brooches, gorgets, and earrings. Arrowheads, pottery shards, and early stone axes are also exhibited; located on 7555 Jackson Blvd., Forest Park, IL; call (708) 366-7171.

Fort Crevecoeur · 1939 · mural in the Oak Park post office entitled "The Foundation of Fort Crevecoeur." Artist: J. Theodore Johnson. The fort was built near the lower end of Peoria Lake by La Salle and Tonti in January 1680, but was destroyed by mutinous party members before the end of the same year.

Fort Dearborn · also see Historic Panels.

▼ **Fort Dearborn** · 1880 · marble bas-relief tablet at the southwest corner of Michigan Avenue and River Street [Wacker Drive] on the W.M. Hoyt & Company building (wholesale grocery), previous site of the fort, inscribed: "Blockhouse of Fort Dearborn – This building occupies the site of old Fort Dearborn, which extended a little across Mich. Ave. and somewhat into the river as it now is. The fort was built in 1803 & 4, forming our outmost defense. By order of Gen. Hull it was evacuated Aug. 15, 1812, after its stores and provisions had been distributed among the Indians. Very soon after, the Indians attacked and massacred about fifty of the troops and a number of citizens, including women and children and next day burned the fort. In 1816 it was re-built, but after the Blackhawk war it went into gradual disuse and in May 1837 was abandoned by the army. It was occupied by various government officers till 1857 when it was torn down, excepting a single building, which stood upon this site till the Great Fire of Oct. 9, 1871. – At the suggestion of the Chicago Historical Society this tablet was erected Nov. 1880. – W.M. Hoyt"; the unveiling of the tablet took place on May 21, 1881; pictured was the second fort's blockhouse.

▼ **Fort Dearborn** · 1922 · bronze bas-relief tablet at the southwest corner of Michigan Avenue and Wacker Drive on the London Guarantee and Accident Building erected in 1922, to indicate and illustrate the site of Fort Dearborn, inscribed: "Fort Dearborn Destroyed · 1858 – Office Building Erected · 1922 – This building is erected on the site of Fort Dearborn"; replaced the marble tablet of the previous entry.

Fort Dearborn I · bronze plaque at 360 N. Michigan Ave. showing the first Fort Dearborn with two Indians near the stockade in bas-relief, inscribed: "Here stood Old Fort Dearborn 1803-1812." Near the plaque, bronze markers have been placed in the pavement of and sidewalk along Michigan Avenue tracing the former location of the stockade and blockhouses of the fort.

Fort Dearborn I · 1971 · bronze plaque at northwest corner of Michigan Avenue and Wacker Drive, inscribed: "Chicago Landmark – Site of Fort Dearborn 1803 – Fort Dearborn served as the major western garrison of the United States until destroyed during an Indian uprising in August of 1812. A second fort, erected on the same site in 1816, was demolished in 1856. – Designated a Chicago landmark on September 15, 1971 by the City Council of Chicago, Richard J. Daley, Mayor – Commission on Chicago Historical and Architectural Landmarks."

Fort Dearborn I · 1991· large oil painting in the board room of the Chicago Medical Society building at 515 N. Dearborn St., showing the appearance of the fort in 1810. Artist: Brigitte Kozma.

Fort Dearborn Massacre · 1893 · bronze statue of six figures on a marble base in the Prairie Avenue Historical District Park at 18th Street and Prairie Avenue; also called "Black Partridge Saving Mrs. Helm," referring to the friendly Potawatomi chief who saved Mrs. Margaret Helm's life by ransoming her later; another recognizable figure is that of the fort's physician Dr. Isaac Y. Van Voorhis, who lies mortally wounded on the ground. ▼ On the original base, two bas-relief panels by the sculptor illustrated the march from the fort and Black Partridge's return of the peace medal. Commissioned by the railroad car

manufacturer George Pullman, the sculpture stood at 18th and Calumet streets until 1931, adjoining an old cottonwood tree near Pullman's mansion, believed to have been the site of the massacre; later displayed at the Chicago Historical Society, before its removal to the present location, where it was placed on a new base. Sculptor: Carl Rohl-Smith.

▼ **Fort Dearborn Massacre** · 1937 · bronze plaque on the northeast corner of 18th Street and Calumet Avenue, inscribed: "Near this site, August 15, 1812, took place the fatal encounter between the Indians and the United States troops under Captain Nathan Heald. Erected by Chicago's Charter Jubilee – Authenticated by Chicago Historical Society – 1937."

Fort Dearborn Massacre · bronze plaque on the northeast corner of 18th Street and Prairie Avenue, inscribed: "On August 15, 1812, Indians attacked a small garrison and citizens evacuating Fort Dearborn, killing fifty-three soldiers and women and children. A monument commemorating the tragic event, donated by George M. Pullman, stood on this site from 1894 to 1931. The monument is now in the Chicago Historical Society – Chicago Historical Society." See Fort Dearborn Massacre · 1893.

Fort Dearborn Massacre · see Defense · 1928.

✝ **Foster, John Herbert, M.D.** · 1874 · early Chicago physician (1835) and landowner, part of which land he sold so that Northwestern University could be built; his grave is in Rosehill Cemetery.

✝ **Goodrich, Grant** · 1889 · early Chicago lawyer (1834) who eventually became a respected judge, elected to the Illinois Supreme Court; his grave is in Rosehill Cemetery.

Graue Mill · 1852 · at the corner of York and Spring roads, two blocks north of Ogden Avenue, Hinsdale; the German 1834 immigrant Friedrich Graue built his gristmill in 1852. It was restored in 1950.

✝ **Graves, Dexter** · see Dexter Graves Monument.

Green Bay Road · 1937 · bronze plaque at the northwest end of Michigan Avenue bridge, inscribed: "Green Bay Road – From this point the Green Bay Road ran northwesterly to Clark Street and North Avenue, and followed Clark Street's present route to the vicinity of Peterson Avenue. This road connected Fort Dearborn with Fort Howard, Green Bay, Wisconsin. – Erected by Chicago's Charter Jubilee – Authenticated by Chicago Historical Society – 1937." The road ran mostly on the high ground of one of the ancient ridges created by wave action along the shore of Lake Chicago, a course still evident throughout much of present-day Clark Street.

▼ **Green Tree Tavern** · 1937 · bronze plaque on the Butler Brothers Building, southeast corner of Lake and Canal streets, inscribed: "Green Tree Tavern – Built near this site in 1833 and opened by David Clock. Renamed Stage House in 1835, Chicago Hotel a few years later and afterwards Lake Street House. – Erected by Chicago's Charter Jubilee - Authenticated by Chicago Historical Society – 1937." The tavern was built by Silas B. Cobb for James Kinzie as a two-story frame building and managed initially by David Clock.

☛ ▼ Guardian Angel Mission · 1937 · bronze plaque on the north branch at Foster Avenue bridge, north side, east approach, inscribed: "Guardian Angel Mission – Near this site, from 1696 to 1699, Father Pinet's Mission of the Guardian Angel from which he conducted his evangelical labors among the Miami. – Erected by Chicago's Charter Jubilee – Authenticated by Chicago Historical Society – 1937." From 1696 on, the mission was intermittantly occupied, and it was permanently abandoned in 1702 or 1703. The mission's actual location was most likely the site of the Merchandise Mart; a commemorative ▼ plaque once existed on the Builders Building, southwest corner of LaSalle Street and Wacker Drive.

✝ Hamilton, Richard Jones · 1860 · second lawyer to settle in Chicago (1831); became a judge and held numerous city and county administrative positions before his death in 1860; his grave is in Rosehill Cemetery.

Henry DeTonty Woods · commemorates the French explorer Henri de Tonti, a friend of La Salle, whose first passage through the Chicago Portage was in 1680, followed by many more during his 26 years in North America. The woods are a portion of the Palos Division of the Cook County Forest Preserve District, located between Archer Avenue and the old Illinois & Michigan Canal at the level of 96th Street.

Historic Panels · 1928 · intaglio relief Indiana limestone panels, each seven feet high, on the fifth-floor facade of the 333 N. Michigan Ave. building, depicting seven major subjects: Father Marquette portaging with Indian and *voyageur*, settlers with an oxen team, an Indian brave, a pioneer woman, a trapper, soldiers guarding Ft. Dearborn, and traders exchanging with an Indian. Sculptor: Fred M. Torrey.

✝ Hubbard, Alhira · 1849 · early settler (1830) from Vermont, uncle of Gurdon S. Hubbard and the father of Mary Ann, Gurdon's cousin and third wife; died of cholera in 1849, but was reburied at Graceland Cemetery in 1868.

Hubbard's Folly · 1937 · bronze plaque at the Wacker Drive viaduct between Michigan Avenue and Lake Street, inscribed: " 'Hubbard's Folly' – On this site about 1834, Gurdon S. Hubbard built Chicago's first warehouse, for storing pork and other pioneer produce. Because of its size and substantial construction, early skeptics called the building 'Hubbard's Folly.' – Erected by

Chicago's Charter Jubilee – Authenticated by Chicago Historical Society – 1937."

Illinois & Michigan Canal National Heritage Corridor · though construction of the Illinois & Michigan Canal did not begin until 1836 and was not finished until 1848, the anticipation of this undertaking began to stimulate the growth of Chicago as early as 1832, so much so that by 1837 the modest village had become a city. What remains today of the canal is carefully preserved by Illinois State effort, and is made accessible to the public by publicized canoe routes, hiking and horse trails, and campgrounds. The various portions of the canal extend from Chicago to Peru, IL. For information and brochures, call the Joliet office of the Heritage Corridor at 1-800-926-2262.

Illinois Centennial Monument · 1918 · ornamental Tennessee marble column topped by an eagle at the intersection of Logan Boulevard and Kedzie Avenue; erected by the B.F. Ferguson Monument Fund to celebrate the centennial of Illinois statehood. Architect: Henry Bacon. Sculptor: Evelyn Beatrice Longman Batchelder.

Illinois State Line Marker · 1822 · believed to be the oldest historical monument in Chicagoland—a tall, plain, but harmonious limestone structure with multiple fossils (crinoids?) weathering out on its surface, located where the northwest corner of Indiana touches the eastern border of Illinois. To state that this is the intersection of State Line Road and 103rd Street is correct, except that both streets are interrupted near this point by industrial and railroad developments. The visitor must approach from the north to find the monument in the small Allen J. Benson Park at the entrance to the Commonwealth Edison State Line generating plant. Bronze plaques explain that the "State Line was retraced by Act of Congress 1833" and that the marker is now located 191.09 feet north of its original site, and 159.359 miles due north from the Wabash River.

Indian Alarm · 1884 · bronze sculpture showing an Ottawa Indian family on the move, halting as if alert to some imminent danger; located in Lincoln Park, 3000 N. Four incised granite tablets at the base depict scenes from Ottawa life: "The Peace Pipe – The Corn Dance – Forestry – The Hunt." Sculptor: John J. Boyle. The sculpture was the earliest work in Chicago to realistically portray and feature American Indians.

Indian artifacts and culture · see Mitchell Museum of the American Indian; see Forest Park Library.

Indian Boundary Lines · 1937 · bronze plaque on Rogers Avenue, northeast corner with Clark Street, inscribed: "Indian Boundary Lines – Clark Street honors George Rogers Clark, whose brother William Clark, with Ninian

Edwards and Auguste Chouteau, in 1816 negotiated Indian treaty ceding land including Chicago site from Rogers Avenue to Lake Calumet. – Erected by Chicago's Charter Jubilee – Authenticated by Chicago Historical Society – 1937." The plaque commemorates the successful efforts of Gov. Ninian Edwards and others to negotiate with local Indian tribes, at the 1816 Treaty of St. Louis, the acquisition by the United States of a tract of land, 20 by 70 miles, that extended from Lake Michigan to the Illinois River near Ottawa and included Chicago, the portage, and the area for which construction of a canal between the Great Lakes and the Mississippi River system was contemplated. Rogers Avenue now forms part of the northern boundary of this tract; Indian Boundary Road southwest of Plainfield also follows this northern line.

✛ **Indian Cemetery** · see Robinson grave site.

✛ **Indian Cemetery Marker** · 1941 · a tall triangular granite column on a small hill at Forest Home Cemetery in Forest Park, showing an Indian on horseback in bas-relief and the following inscription: "This is the site of a village and burial ground of the Pottawatomie Indians from ancient times until 1835 when they were exiled to lands beyond the Mississippi. Later this locality was known as Indian Hill. ✧ Here stood the cabin of Leon Bourassa, the trapper. His Indian wife, Margaret, had been reared in this grove and, after the exodus of her tribe, she chose to remain near the graves of her ancestors. ✧ As the years passed, the visits of the Pottawatomies became ever less frequent and this memorial has been erected to perpetuate their memory. ✧ In 1832 federal troops under General Winfield Scott skirted this grove, forded the river a mile north, and marched on to the Black Hawk War in the Rock River country. These soldiers had encamped at a point that is now the Village of Riverside to rest and recover from an epidemic of Asiatic cholera. ✧ Upon the arrival of white settlers these acres became the homestead of Ferdinand Haase and his family. The first person to die in this new home was buried on this hill in 1854. ✧ Thus, many years ago, Ferdinand Haase and his sons re-established and dedicated to sepulcher the ancient forest home of the Pottawatomie to become the present Forest Home of the white man. A.D. 1941." Designer: Paul Strayer. Sculptor: Guido Rebechini.

Indian Council · Within the northwest corner of the U.S. Post Office's Loop Station at 211 S. Clark St. is a five-foot-by-15-foot oil mural entitled, "Great Indian Council, Chicago – 1833." The mural was one of many commissioned by the Treasury Department's Section of Painting and Sculpture, beginning 1934, to decorate the public-works buildings being constructed throughout the country. Painted by the Chicago artist Gustaf Dalstrom for the Chesnut Street Post Office at 840 N. Clark St. in 1938, the work was later moved to its present location; the original ▼ plaque is missing.

Indians · 1928 · two bronze statues of Indians on horseback known as The Bowman and The Spearman, flanking Congress Parkway at Michigan Avenue; erected by the B.F. Ferguson Monument Fund. Sculptor: Ivan Mestrovic.

Indians · also see Historic Panels.

Indian Signal of Peace · 1890 · bronze statue of Sioux chief on horseback, giving the Indian peace sign; exhibited at the 1893 World Columbian Exhibition, then placed on a high granite pedestal in Lincoln Park, north of the entrance to Diversey Harbor. Sculptor: Cyrus Edwin Dallin.

Indian Signal Station and Campground · marked by a granite boulder in the Dan Ryan Woods of the Calumet Division of the Cook County Forest Preserve District, north of 87th at Western Avenue. A bronze plaque on the boulder bears the inscription: "Lookout point used as a signal station on main highway of Indian travel. – Marked by the Dewalt Mechlin Chapter Daughters of the American Revolution. – June 16, 1922." The boulder stands on elevated ground, a moraine of the early Wisconsin glacier, and the rise still affords a distant view to the northeast, where Chicago's skyline is visible above the trees of the preserve.

Indian silver · see Forest Park Library.

▼ **Indian Sun Vow** · 1896 · bronze sculpture of a seated elder Indian observing a young archer releasing an arrow aimed at the sun; exhibited at the Art Institute of Chicago until defaced; now in storage. Sculptor: Hermon Atkins MacNeil.

Indian Trail Marker · 1932 · bronze plaque upon a granite boulder along the Des Plaines River opposite 164 Fairbanks Road, Riverside; inscribed: "This boulder marks the old river-crossing used by the Indians on the trail from north to south by the fur traders, and by the early settlers in the development of the west. – Dedicated July 4, 1932 - Women's Reading Club – Riverside, Illinois – Chicago Historical Society." The crossing is also known as "Riverside Ford," and is believed by some historians to be the location of Laughtons' tavern, separate from the trading post.

Indian Trail Marker · 1942 · the head of an Indian brave carved into a stone boulder at the Forest Home Cemetery in Forest Park, with the following inscription: "An ancient Indian trail once passed this boulder, skirting the forest along the Des Plaines River, through groves of wild plum and hazel thickets. ✧ Eastward the tall grass of the prairie stretched as far as the eye could reach. Later it served as a road for the early settlers in the long months when the flooded prairies were impassable. May those who now follow this trail gain comfort from nature's peace and beauty."

Indian Village and Chipping Station · 1923 · bronze plaque upon a granite boulder on the front lawn of Evanston Hospital on Sheridan Road, inscribed: "This stone marks the site of an ancient Indian village and chipping station, last occupied by the Potawatamie, who were removed from the location in 1835 – Placed by Fort Dearborn Chapter, Daughters of the American Revolution, 1923 – Replaced 1974." Arrowheads and spearheads were fashioned from flint stone at chipping stations.

Iroquois Woods · named after a confederated group of Indian tribes with similar languages who lived mostly in present-day New York State. The triangular woods are located in the southernmost portion of the Des Plaines Division of the Cook County Forest Preserve District, bounded by Touhy Avenue, Algonquin Road, and the Tri-State Tollway.

Isle a la Cache Museum · an island in the Des Plaines River near Romeoville, IL, reached from Chicago via the Chicago Portage in one day's canoe travel on the way toward the Illinois River settlements, was already known to the earliest French traders in the days of Father Marquette's second exploration to Illinois in 1674. They used the island as a campsite and to temporarily hide their valuable trade goods. The Forest Preserve District of Will County now maintains a small museum there that presents the cultural history of the Indian and French fur trade era. It is located at 501 E. Romeo Road in Romeoville; call (815) 886-1467.

Jolliet · also see Chicago Portage National Historic Site; also see Marquette & Jolliet.

Jolliet & Marquette · 1925 · bronze bas-relief plaque located on the east railing of the Michigan Avenue bridge, inscribed: "Chicago Portage – The Waterway West – Along these waterways and trails history has passed. The Chicago portage has served as the connecting link between the Great Lakes and the Mississippi River System. – In 1673 led by American Indians explorers Marquette and Jolliet became the first Europeans to cross the portage. This route encouraged the development of the Illinois & Michigan Canal and the growth of Chicago – This tablet is placed by the Illinois Society of the Colonial Dames of America under the auspices of the Chicago Historical Society – 1925." The tablet pictures an Indian guide, the two explorers, and five *voyageurs* within their canoe.

✛ **Kennison Boulder** · 1903 · aluminum plaque upon a granite boulder in Lincoln Park near Clark and Wisconsin streets, inscribed: "In Memory of – David Kennison, the last survivor of the 'Boston Tea Party,' who died in Chicago, February 24, 1852, aged 115 yrs, 3 mos, 17 da, and is buried near this spot; this stone is erected by the Sons of the Revolution, the Sons of the American Revolution, the Daughters of the American Revolution."

✛ **Kettlestrings, Joseph and Betty** · 1883 · the Kettlestrings arrived at Chicago in 1833; the family grave is in Forest Home Cemetery.

▼ **Kettlestrings' House and Tavern** · 1962 · bronze plaque at 1135 Lake St. in Oak Park, inscribed: "Birthplace of Oak Park – On this site in 1835, Joseph Kettlestrings and his wife, Betty, first settlers of Oak Park, built their cabin amid the oaks on 'the only dry land between Chicago and the Aux Plaines.' It later became an inn, called the Oak Ridge House, and was the area's first public eating place…a stopping point for travelers, and for cattlemen who drove their herds down the trail (now Lake Street) to Chicago. – By proclamation, August 3, 1962 – Oak Park Board of Realtors – John F. Butler, Jr., President."

✛ **Kinzie Family Grave** · 1860 · John Kinzie, patriarch of the Kinzie family, is buried in Graceland Cemetery among many family members. John died in 1828, and his remains were removed from several earlier sites before finding permanent rest.

☛ ▼ **Kinzie House** · 1913 · tablet on the James S. Kirk and Company building (soap factory) at 401 N. Michigan Ave., inscribed: "Site of the First House in Chicago – Erected about 1779 by Jean Baptiste Point De Sable – A Negro from Santo Domingo – Property of the Frenchman Le Mai 1796-1804 – Purchased by John Kinzie and by him occupied from 1804 until the Fort Dearborn Massacre 1812 – Reoccupied by John Kinzie from 1816 until his death in 1828 – Abandoned in 1834 the house soon fell into ruin – With the concurrence of the Chicago Historical Society and the Daughters of the American Revolution – This tablet is dedicated in honor of John Kinzie and of the early inhabitants of Chicago on the centenary of the Fort Dearborn Massacre – This 15th day of August 1812 – By James S. Kirk and Company"; the unveiling of the tablet is believed to have occurred on July 11, 1913.

Kinzie House · 1937 · bronze plaque at 401 N. Michigan Ave., Equitable Building Plaza, inscribed: "Kinzie Mansion – Near this site stood Kinzie Mansion 1784-1832, home of Pointe Du Saible, Le Mai, and John Kinzie, Chicago's 'First Civilian – Here was born, in 1805, the city's first white child, Ellen Marion Kinzie. – Erected by Chicago's Charter Jubilee – Authenticated by Chicago Historical Society – 1937." Subsequent research has shown that some of the statements on the plaque are erroneous: Jean Baptiste Point de Sable built his house about 1784; he sold it to Jean La Lime and William Burnett, not to Le Mai; the structure was occupied by others through 1832; and Ellen Kinzie was born on Dec. 27, 1804.

La Salle · 1889 · bronze statue of the explorer "Robert Cavelier · De La Salle" in Lincoln Park, east side of north Clark Street, north of junction with LaSalle Street; commissioned by Lambert Tree. Sculptor: Count Jacques de La Laing.

La Salle · 1939 · mural in the Oak Park post office entitled "La Salle's Search for Tonti 1680," referring to La Salle's return to Fort Crevecoeur, when he found the fort destroyed and Tonti gone; they were reunited in May 1681 at Mackinac. Artist: J. Theodore Johnson.

▼ **La Salle & Missionaries** · 1937 · bronze plaque in Jackson Park at 67th Street and south Lake Shore Drive, inscribed: "Skirting this lakeshore in October, 1679, La Salle and the Franciscan missionaries, Fathers La Ribourde, Hennepin and Membre, journeyed by canoe to the St. Joseph River, Michigan, and thence to the Illinois country. – Erected by Chicago's Charter Jubilee – Authenticated by Chicago Historical Society – 1937."

La Salle & Tonti · 1925 · bronze bas-relief plaque located on the west railing of the Michigan Avenue bridge, inscribed: "In Honor of Réné-Robert Cavalier [sic] Sieur de La Salle & Henri de Tonti – Who passed through this river on their way to the Mississippi – December 1681 – This tablet is placed by the Illinois Society of the Colonial Dames of America under the auspices of the Chicago Historical Society – 1925." The tablet pictures two Indian guides, an Indian woman with child, the two explorers, and three *voyageurs* portaging their canoe.

Laughton's Tavern · see Indian Trail Marker · 1932.

Laughton's Trading Post · inscribed granite boulder located in the Ottawa Trail Woods Forest Preserve. [When entering the preserve from Harlem Avenue at 46th Street, proceed to the fourth parking area, the one equipped with a water pump; and from there walk westward along a path toward the river.] The boulder is heavily weathered and many of the incised words have become illegible. Old photographs reveal that the inscription once read: "This is the site of the trading post established and operated by Bernardus and David Laughton, fur traders, in 1828 – Laughton's Ford on the Des Plaines lies directly west."

Leif Ericson · 1901 · in Humboldt Park, Humboldt Boulevard, 1400 N; large bronze statue of the Viking standing on a granite bolder, inscribed: "Leif Ericson – Discoverer of America"; commissioned by Chicago's Norwegian community in commemoration of the arrival of Ericson in "Vinland" c. A.D. 1000. Sculptor: Sigvald Asbjornsen.

▼ **Little Fort Road** · 1937 · bronze plaque at 2375 Lincoln Ave., inscribed: "Little Fort Road – Here began the Little Fort Road, now Lincoln Avenue, an Indian trail which became the main road to Little Fort or Waukegan, the first important settlement north of Chicago. – Erected by Chicago's Charter Jubilee – Authenticated by Chicago Historical Society – 1937."

Marquette · also see Historic Panels; also see Jolliet & Marquette.

Marquette · 1930 · bronze plaque with bas-relief sculpture at 6013 S. Damen Ave. showing Father Marquette with an Indian, inscribed: "James Marquette, French priest of the Society of Jesus, on his mission to the Illinois Indians, spent here the winter of 1674-1675. His journal first brought to the world's attention the advantages of soil, climate and transportation facilities in the Mississippi Valley and the Great Lakes basin. – Erected by the City of Chicago – William Hale Thompson, Mayor – Michael J. Faherty, Pres. Board of Local Improvements – Anno Domini MCMXXX." Sculptor: E.P. Seidel, from a sketch by Thomas A. O'Shaughnessy.

Marquette · 1949 · concrete plaque on the northeast pylon of the Lake Shore Drive (Chicago River) bridge, with the seal of the City of Laon, Father Marquette's birthplace, inscribed: "La Ville de Laon - La Ville de Chicago - en memoire de Jacques Marquette - 1949."

☛ **Marquette Boulder Monument** · 1895 · bronze plaque on boulder atop multiboulder base in Summit Park at 5810 S. Archer Road, Summit; in 1920 inscribed: "Father Marquette landed here 1675 – This Monument is constructed of boulders brought by glaciers from Lake Superior region and deposited in this valley, having traversed the route later followed by the earlier French explorers. – La Salle, Joliet and Father Marquette. – Erected by Chicago & Alton Railroad Co. – August 1895." ▼ An earlier tablet included additional text: "On March 31, Fr. Marquette was flooded out from his winter quarters at Robey St., Chicago, and next day camped at this point which is located by a Comparison of his Journal with the original Engineers levels and surveys of the Country."

Marquette Building · 1894 · designed by the architectural firm Holabird & Roche and built by the George A. Fuller Company at 140 S. Dearborn St., this architectural gem's decorative art contains a wealth of references to Chicago's early history: bronze panels over the main doors illustrate incidents in Father Marquette's exploratory travels in Illinois and the Mississippi Valley, with inscriptions taken from the report of his travels, sculpted by Hermon Atkins MacNeil; within the lobby bronze bas-relief portraits of Talon, Frontenac, Marquette, Jolliet, Tonti, La Salle, Moreau, and noted Indian chiefs – among them Chief Chicagou, by Edward Kemeys – over the elevator doors and on the balcony; mosaics of glass and mother-of-pearl illuminating events in Marquette's life, and of armor and weapons used in his time; designed by J.A. Holzer and prepared by the Tiffany Glass and Decorating Company of New York, mounted on the face of the balcony in the rotunda.

Marquette Campsite · 1980 · bronze plaque at 401 N. Michigan Ave., Equitable Building Plaza, inscribed: "On December 4, 1674 Père Jacques Marquette, S.J. and two voyageurs built a shelter near the mouth of the Chicago River.

They were the first Europeans to camp here, the site of Chicago. – Erected by Illinois Society Daughters of Colonial Wars – In our 50th year 1980." Marquette's companions were Pierre Portenet and Jacques Largillier. The group remained for one week, then moved six miles upstream to higher ground near the portage from the south branch of the river, where they camped until the end of March 1675.

Marquette Cross · 1973 · tall cedar cross at 2639 S. Damen Ave., just north of the bridge over the Chicago River's south branch, with an inscribed bronze plaque: "Near this Site Father Jacques Marquette, S.J., Missionary, Explorer and Co-discoverer of the Illinois River, spent the Winter of December 1674 to March 31, 1675." ▼ Old photographs document an earlier wooden cross nearby where Robey Street intersects with the river. A tablet on its base was inscribed: "In memory of Father Marquette, S.J. and Louis Joliet of New France (Canada), first white explorers of the Mississippi & Illinois Rivers & Lake Michigan 1673, navigating 2500 miles, in canoes, in 120 days. In crossing the site of Chicago, Joliet recommended it for its natural advantages as a place of first settlement, & suggested a lakes-to-the-gulf waterway, [see *Jesuit Relations* 58:105] by cutting a canal through the 'portage' west of here where begins, the Chicago Drainage-Ship Canal. Work on this canal was begun Sept. 3, 1892 and received the first waters of Lake Michigan Jan. 2, 1900. This remarkable prophecy made 234 years ago is now being fulfilled. – This end of Robey Street is the historic 'high ground' where Marquette spent the winter 1674-5. – 'To do and suffer everything for so glorious an undertaking' Marquette's journal. – Erected Sat. Sept. 28, 1907 – by – City of Chicago, and Chicago Association of Commerce." ▼ A small iron cross, pictured with the wooden cross in 1909, had been found *in situ* before 1898; the cross still existed in 1950.

Marquette & Joliet · 1926 · monumental bronze figures of Father Jacques Marquette, Louis Jolliet, and an Illinois Indian on an inscribed concrete foundation [text in part badly weathered and covered with graffiti]; located at 24th Street and Marshall Boulevard; erected by the B.F. Ferguson Monument Fund. Sculptor: Hermon Atkins MacNeil.

Marquette & Joliet · also see Chicago Portage National Historic Site · 1952.

Miami Woods · named after the Indian tribe that lived in Chicagoland when the Europeans first arrived. It is located in the North Branch Division of the Cook County Forest Preserve District, and is surrounded by Dempster Street, Lehigh Avenue, Oakton Street, and Caldwell Avenue.

Mitchell Museum of the American Indian · the John M. & Betty Seabury Mitchell Museum of the American Indian was established at Kendall College in 1977. The museum presents prehistoric, historic, and contemporary as-

pects of the lives of the native peoples of the United States and Canada, and exhibits many artifacts of the different cultures. Special programs and lecture series are regularly scheduled. The museum galleries and library are at 2600 Central Park Avenue in Evanston; call (847) 475-1030.

Old Treaty Elm · 1937 · bronze plaque at the intersection of Rogers, Kilbourn, and Caldwell avenues, inscribed: "Old Treaty Elm – This tree which stood here until 1933, marked the northern boundary of the Fort Dearborn Reservation, the trail to Lake Geneva, the center of Billy Caldwell's (Chief Sauganash) reservation, and the site of the Indian Treaty of 1835. – Erected by Chicago's Charter Jubilee – Authenticated by Chicago Historical Society – 1937."

▼ **Old Vincennes Road** · 1937 · bronze plaque placed on the northwest corner of 95th Street and Vincennes Avenue, inscribed: "Old Vincennes Road – This historic trail into Chicago from the South, now Vincennes Avenue, was originally used by the Indians to unite all villages of the Potawatomi nation. It later became the thorough from Ohio and Wabash River settlements. – Erected by Chicago's Charter Jubilee – Authenticated by Chicago Historical Society – 1937."

Ottawa Trail Woods · commemorating the old Indian trail; the woods are part of the Salt Creek Division of the Cook County Forest Preserve District. The trail connected Chicago with the Illinois River valley, bisecting the woods and crossing the Des Plaines River at Laughtons' Ford in [Lyons].

Ouilmette, Antoine · the name of the village of Wilmette, IL, perpetuates the name of this early resident of Chicago and his large family; a short street at 2200 W. Lake Ave. is named Ouilmette Lane.

▼ **Pioneer Court Fountain** · 1965 · 25 names of Chicago pioneers are set in bronze on the circular retaining wall of the fountain on the east side of Michigan Avenue, just north of the Chicago River. They are: Jane Addams · Philip Danforth Armour · Daniel Hudson Burnham · Richard Teller Crane · John Crerar · Steven A. Douglas · Marshall Field · William Rainey Harper · Carter Henry Harrison · Gurdon Saltonstall Hubbard · William Le Baron Jenney · John Kinzie · Cyrus Hall McCormick · Joseph Medill · Walter Loomis Newberry · William Butler Ogden · Potter Palmer · George Mortimer Pullman · Julius Rosenwald · Martin Antoine Ryerson · Jean Baptiste Point Sable · Charles Henry Wacker · Aaron Montgomery Ward · John Wentworth · John Whistler. Among them are seven who arrived in Chicago before 1836, namely Hubbard, Kinzie, Newberry, Ogden, Point de Sable, Wentworth and Whistler. A tablet at the fountain is inscribed: "Pioneer Court – A project developed cooperatively by the Chicago Tribune and the Equitable Life Assurance Society of the United States in commemoration of the pioneers whose names, selected by the Chicago Historical Society for their contribution to Chicago's birth, growth and greatness, are set in bronze in the base of the fountain. – Dedicated June 23, 1965. – By J. Howard Wood, president of the Tribune Company and publisher of the Chicago Tribune, James F. Oates, Jr., Chairman of the Board of Equitable Life Assurance Society of the United States, and by Mayor Richard J. Daley of behalf of the City of Chicago."

Pioneers · 1928 · concrete sculpture on northwest pylon of Michigan Avenue bridge showing early settlers traveling to their new homesteads, with text tablet: "The Pioneers – John Kinzie, fur trader, settled near this spot in the early years of the nineteenth century. One of a band of courageous pioneers – who with their lives at stake – struggled through the wilderness, breaking soil for the seeds of a future civilization. Presented to the City by William Wrigley Jr. – 1928."

☞ **Point du Sable, Catherine and Jean-Baptiste** · 1997 · seven-foot-high, free-standing, three-sided porcelain placard at 401 N. Michigan Ave. honoring the notable couple with the opening statement: "Considered the founders of Chicago, Catherine (1756–1809) and Jean-Baptiste (1745–1818) Point du Sable established a fur trading post on this site in the 1770s or early 1780s, approximately a half-century before Chicago was incorporated." The first of several Tribute Markers of Distinction implemented by the Public Art Program, Chicago Department of Cultural Affairs. [N.B. Of all these dates, only Jean Baptiste's year of death has been documented; *eds.*]

Point Du Sable House · 1977 · bronze plaque at 401 N. Michigan Ave., Equitable Building Plaza, inscribed: "Jean Baptiste Point Du Sable Homesite – Has been dedicated a national historic landmark – This site possesses national significance in commemorating the history of the United States of America – 1977 – National Park Service, United States Department of the Interior"; see Kinzie House · 1913.

Pointe Du Sable · bronze bust of Jean Baptiste Point de Sable by Marion Perkins, 1959; a second bust is by Robert Jones, 1979; six additional sculptures, unveiled and dedicated on September 22, 1978, interpret the "Spirit of Du Sable" in various degrees of abstraction, all located at the Du Sable Museum, 740 E. 56th St. Sculptors: Robert Jones, Ausbra Ford, Geraldine McCullough, Jill N. Parker, Ramon Bertell Price, and Lawrence E. Taylor.

Portage Creek · see Chicago Portage National Historic Site.

✝ **Porter, Rev. Jeremiah** · 1893 · Chicago's first Presbyterian minister (1833); his grave is in Rosehill Cemetery.

Post Office · 1937 · bronze plaque at the northwest corner of Wacker Drive and Lake Street, inscribed: "First Post Office – Near this site in 1833, the log store of John S.C. Hogan, was this section's only post office, serving settlers from miles around. Eastern mail was delivered once a week from Niles, Michigan. – Erected by Chicago's Charter Jubilee – Authenticated by Chicago Historical Society – 1937." Prior to the use of Hogan's store, beginning in 1831, Jonathan Bailey, Chicago's first postmaster, handled postal services from the old Kinzie house, which Bailey had rented.

Potawatomi Indians · 1930 · boulder marker at the entry of Timber Trails Country Club on Plainfield Road near Wolf Road, with bronze plaque inscribed: "Last camp site of the Potawatomie Indians in Cook County – 1835 – Erected by the LaGrange Illinois Chapter – Daughters of the American Revolution – May 15th 1930."

Potawatomi Woods · named for the Chicago area Indian tribe, members of which were part of village life until 1835. The woods are in the northernmost section of the Des Plaines Division of the Cook County Forest Preserve District, surrounded by County Line Road, Portwine Road, Dundee Road, and Milwaukee Avenue.

Prairie Avenue Historic District · bordered by Indiana Avenue, 18th Avenue, Prairie Avenue, and Cullerton Street. See Clarke House; see Fort Dearborn Massacre · 1893.

▼ **Presbyterian Church** · 1937 · bronze plaque commemorating the first permanent meeting place on the southwest corner of Lake and Clark streets, inscribed: "Chicago's First Presbyterian Church – Near this spot was erected in 1833, Chicago's first Presbyterian Church, organized June 26, 1833, by Rev. Jeremiah Porter. The building was dedicated January 4, 1834. – Erected by Chicago's Charter Jubilee – Authenticated by Chicago Historical Society – 1937."

Riverside Ford · see Indian Trail Marker · 1932.

✝ **Robinson, Alexander** · on the west side of the 4800 block of East River Road, within the Schiller Park Forest Preserve, is a granite boulder marking the site where formerly stood two ▼ headstones of the graves of Indian Chief Robinson and his wife Catherine Chevalier. The boulder is inscribed: "Alexander Robinson – (Chee-Chee-Pin-Quay) – Chief of the Potawatomi, Chippewa, and Ottawa Indians who died April 22, 1872 – Catherine (Chevalier) his wife who died August 7, 1860 – And other members of their family are buried on this spot – Part of the reservation granted him by the Treaty of Prairie Du Chien – July 29, 1829, in gratitude for his aid to the family – of John Kinzie and to Capt. and Mrs. Heald at the time of the Fort Dearborn Massacre." ▼ Robinson's last house, built in 1845 on the reservation he had been given for his valuable services, stood nearby until destroyed by fire a few years ago.

Robinson Woods, Che-che-pin-qua Woods, Catherine Chevalier Woods · these three portions of the Indian Boundary Division of the Cook County Forest Preserve District honor Alexander Robinson (whose Indian name was Che-che-pin-qua) and his second wife Catherine Chevalier, reminding us that part of his and his wife's former reservation is now forest preserve land. The woods are located immediately east of Des Plaines River Road between Belmont Avenue and the Kennedy Expressway.

Rush Medical College · bronze plaque on the west wall of the Cook County Medical Society building on the southeast corner of Dearborn and Ohio streets, inscribed: "Site of the first Rush Medical Society – (Est. 1837) – Building Destroyed in the Great Chicago Fire – 1871."

Saganashkee Slough · a large swampy lake, remnant of the prehistoric outlet of early Lake Chicago, has survived as part of the Palos Division of the Cook County Forest Preserve District; located between the Calumet Sag Channel and 107th Street, just west of 104th Avenue.

▼ **Saloon Building** · 1937 · bronze plaque at southeast corner of Lake and [189 N.] Clark streets, inscribed: " 'Saloon Building' – So called because of the upper floor salon where entertainments were held. The Common Council having leased one of the rooms, the building was the City Hall from 1837 to 1842. – Erected by Chicago's Charter Jubilee – Authenticated by Chicago Historical Society – 1937."

Sand Ridge Prairie, Sand Ridge Nature Center · portions of the Thorn Creek Division of the Cook County Forest Preserve District, located in Shabbona Woods, surrounded by 154th and 159th streets and Paxton and Torrence avenues. The names commemorate the long sandy beach ridge created by early Lake Chicago during the Glenwood beach stage 12,000 years ago. Indian trails followed the ridge and early pioneer cabins were built along the crest to avoid the moisture of the surrounding swamps. Where undisturbed, these ridge segments still preserve their unique ecosystems with species of trees, shrubs, and wildflowers requiring modest elevation and sandy soil for drainage. The nature center is at 15891 Paxton Avenue, South Holland; call (708) 868-0606.

▼ **Sauganash Hotel** · bronze plaque with a view of the hotel in bas-relief, at 333 W. Lake St., inscribed: "Sauganash Hotel – Chicago – 1831 – The Sauganash Hotel, also called Sauganash Tavern, was built in 1831 on what is now the southeast corner of Lake Street and Wacker Drive [then Market Street]. It was Chicago's first hotel and soon became the social center of town. In 1833, prominent local citizens met in the Sauganash Hotel to incorporate the town of Chicago. The first election and the first meeting of the town trustees were also held here. The hotel was destroyed by fire in 1851. – Presented by

the Chicago Chapter, Daughters of the American Revolution." The hotel originally began in 1829 as the Eagle Exchange Tavern, owned by Mark Beaubien. The log cabin was enlarged with a two-story blue shuttered clapboard structure that reopened in 1831 under the name Sauganash Tavern. Miller House was actually the first hotel in the village, built in 1827.

Sauk Trail Woods · a portion of the Thorn Creek Division of the Cook County Forest Preserve District, located in South Chicago Heights, between Western and South Chicago avenues, accessible from 26th Street. Sauk Trail Road crosses through the woods, its eastern extension becoming Lincoln Highway, then U.S. Highway 30, still following the old cross-country Indian trail. Nearby, where Sauk Trail Road and South Chicago Avenue intersect, "Browns' Corners" was an important crossroads of the old Northwest, South Chicago Avenue representing part of Hubbard's Trace to Danville.

▼ **Schoolhouse** · a commemorative bronze plaque was formerly present at the site where Eliza Chappel was thought to have taught children in Chicago's first one-room school house in 1833 at the intersection of State and South Water streets. Actually, the schoolhouse was located at the southeast corner of Lake and Market streets, adjacent to Mark Beaubien's Sauganash Tavern. For details, see Chappel, Eliza, in the Encyclopedic Section.

Shabbona Woods · a portion of the Thorn Creek Division of the Cook County Forest Preserve District has been named to commemorate this chief of the Potawatomi Indians. It is located between 154th and 159th streets, and between Paxton and Torrence avenues in Calumet City.

South Water Street · 1926 · bronze bas-relief plaque at the northwest corner of Lake Street and Wacker Drive, showing the appearance of South Water Street in 1834 (on a second panel, in 1924). A third lettered panel indicates that the plaque was installed by the city to commemorate completion of Wacker Drive's construction in 1926.

South Water Street · 1937 · bronze plaque at northwest corner of State State and Wacker Drive, inscribed: "South Water Street – This was Chicago's main business street in 1834, connecting the village with Fort Dearborn. Years before this also was the site of a trading post with the Indians. – Erected by Chicago's Charter Jubilee – Authenticated by Chicago Historical Society – 1937". [It is not clear to which "trading post" the plaque refers; eds.]

✝ **Steele, Ashbel** · 1861 · family grave site in Forest Home Cemetery. Steele and his wife Harriet came to Chicago in 1833; in 1836 they became the first settlers in what is now River Forest.

Stony Ford · one of several ancient fords of the Des Plaines River, existent where the underlying Niagara limestone foundation reaches the surface and resists erosion. Indian trails between Chicago and the Illinois River valley crossed at these fords. This one is located in the Ottawa Trail Woods of the Salt Creek Division of the Cook County Forest Preserve District. It can be seen well, except during high water, as an area of shallow rapids just south of the bridge where Joliet Road [now Lyons] crosses the river.

Talon, Jean Baptiste · first intendant of New France; see Marquette Building.

Thornton Quarry · largest of the regional quarries, where the limestone of the Niagara foundation underlying Chicagoland is still being mined. It was deposited 400 million years ago by shallow tropical seas and contains many fossils. Immediately west of the Thornton-Blue Island Road, Interstate Highway 80 crosses directly over the huge excavation pit.

▼ **U.S. Land Office** · 1937 · bronze plaque on the south side of Lake Street, east of Clark on an iron column, inscribed: "First U.S. Land Office – Near this site, the first United States Land Office was erected in 1835. It stood on the south side of Lake Street between Clark and Dearborn Streets. – Erected by Chicago's Charter Jubilee – Authenticated by Chicago Historical Society – 1937."

Wabansa Stone · 1816 · also Waubansee; a glacial granite boulder, about eight feet in height, with a face carved into one of its upper surfaces, reported to be that of the Potawatomi chief Waubansee. The stone was hollowed out on top and is believed to have been used earlier by the Indians to mill corn; later the stone was hauled within the stockade of the second fort, and a talented soldier chiseled the face; existent in the Chicago Historical Society.

Webber Resource Center · within the Field Museum of Natural History, Roosevelt Road at Lake Shore Drive; established in 1987, the center has become a vital learning source for the history and present concerns of the native cultures of North, Central, and South America. Through a variety of books, maps, videotapes, tribal newspapers, reservation newsletters, and related hands-on items—amid the museum's invaluable collection of artifacts—one can experience or access important materials and information. Members of the center's staff are interactive with those of the D'Arcy McNickle Center, NAES College, and the Mitchell Musem; call (312) 922-9410 ext. 497.

✛ **Wentworth Obelisk** · 1888 · "Long" John Wentworth came to Chicago in 1836 and later served as the city's mayor; later he collected and published a great deal of invaluable historical information. His grave is in Rosehill Cemetery, marked by a 72-foot-tall obelisk, the tallest of any in Chicago private cemeteries, uninscribed and designed by himself, and built reportedly at a cost of $38,000.

Wentworth Woods · to commemorate former Chicago mayor John Wentworth; located in the Thorn Creek Division of the Cook County Forest Preserve District bounded by Wentworth Avenue, State Line Road, Schrum Road, and Michigan City Road.

Wilmette Historical Musem · dedicated to the memory of Antoine [see] Ouilmette and his family and to the history of the northern suburbs of Chicago; located at 609 Ridge Road in Wilmette; call (847) 853-7666.

▼ **Wolf Point** · 1937 · bronze plaque on the southeast corner of Lake and Market [Wacker] streets, inscribed: "In early days this elbow of land, formed by the junction of North and South branches of Chicago River, was the site of three taverns, Wolf Tavern, 'Miller's,' and the Sauganash."

✛ **Wright, John S.** · 1874 · limestone mausoleum at Rosehill Cemetery, probably designed by the architect James Egan. Wright first came to Chicago in 1832, at age 15, with his father John Wright, while other family members followed later. A bold and successful real estate speculator during the land boom, merchant and manufacturer in later years, Wright left his imprint on the town. A wooded section north of the river was owned by him and was formerly called Wright's Grove or Wrightwood.

INDIAN CEMETERY MARKER - see page 408

CHICAGO BIBLIOGRAPHY
An Index of Publications Relating to the History of Chicago prior to 1836

In addition to the material listed numerically as specific references for entries in the Encyclopedic Section of this book, the interested reader may wish to consult sources listed at the end of the Bibliography, comprising both journals and organizations.

1   **Adams, Henry.** *History of the United States of America, 1801-1817.* 2 vols. New York, 1889-1891.

2   **Albach, J.R.** *Annals of the West.* Pittsburgh, 1857.

3   ***Album of Genealogy and Biography, Cook County, Illinois.*** Chicago, 1895.

4   **Allen, John Logan.** *Passage Through the Garden.* Urbana, Ill., 1975.

5   **Alvord, Clarence Walworth.** "Illinois in the Eighteenth Century. A Report on the Documents in the St. Clair County Court House, Belleville, Illinois, Illustrating the early History of the State." *Bulletin of the Illinois State Historical Library* 1, no. 1, 1905.

6   ___. *The Illinois Country, 1673-1818.* Springfield, 1920.

7   **Alvord, Clarence Walworth, ed.** "Laws of the Territory of Illinois, 1809-1811." *Bulletin of the Illinois State Historical Library* 1, no. 2, 1906.

8   ___. "Act Creating the County of Illinois." *Collections of the Illinois State Historical Library* 2, 1907, pp. 9-11.

9   ___. "Cahokia Records, 1778-1790." *Collections of the Illinois State Historical Library* 2, 1907.

9a   ___. See also Illinois Centennial Association.

10   **Alvord, Clarence Walworth, and Clarence Edward Carter, eds.** *The New Regime, British Series.* 2 vols. Springfield, 1916.

10a   ***American State Papers: Public Lands***, Vols. 1, 2, 3. Washington, D.C.: Gales & Seaton, 1834.

11   **Anderson, Thomas G.** "Narrative of Capt. Thomas G. Anderson." *Wisconsin Historical Collections* 9, 1882.

12   **Andreas, Alfred Theodore.** *History of Chicago. From the Earliest Period to the Present Time.* 3 vols. Chicago, 1884-1888. [lists of early settlers, vol. 3, pp. 394-97]

13   ___. *History of Cook County.* Chicago, 1884.

14   **Andreas, Alfred Theodore, ed.** *History of Milwaukee.* Chicago: The Western Historical Company, 1881.

15   **Andrews, Wayne.** See Cochran, Thomas C., and Wayne Andrews, eds.

16   **Angle, Paul McClelland, ed.** *Prairie State, Impressions of Illinois 1673-1967 by Travellers and Other Observers.* Chicago, 1968.

17   ___. "Michael Diversey and Beer in Chicago." *Chicago History* 8, no. 11, spring 1969, pp. 321-26.

18   **Apostol, Lucia.** *Chicago's Riverfront: Its Early History in Maps.* Chicago, 1990.

18a   **Armour, David, and Keith Widder.** *At the Crossroads.* Mackinac Island, Mich., 1978.

19   **Armstrong, P.A.** *The Piaza or the Devil among the Indians.* Morris, Ill., 1887.

20   **Arnold, Hon. Isaac N.** "Address of November 19, 1868, to the Chicago Historical Society, Giving a History of the Society and its Acquisitions up to that Time, with Incidents in the Lives of Abraham Lincoln and Major Anderson; also, of Luther Haven, George Manierre, and other early Settlers of Chicago." *Fergus Historical Series* 10, 1877.

21   ___. "Recollections of Early Chicago and the Illinois Bar. Read Before the Chicago Bar Association on June 10, 1880." *Fergus Historical Series* 22, 1882.

22   ___. "William. B. Ogden; And Early Days in Chicago. A Paper Read Before the Chicago Historical Society, Tuesday, December 29, 1881." *Fergus Historical Series* 17, 1882.

23   **Atkinson, Eleanor.** *The Story of Chicago and National Development, 1534-1910.* Chicago, 1903.

24   **Aubrey, John S.** See Swagerty, William R., with John S. Aubrey.

25   **Bach, Ira J., and Mary Lackritz Gray.** *Chicago's Public Sculptures.* Chicago, 1983.

26   **Bagrow, Leo, and R.A. Skelton.** *History of Cartography.* Chicago, 1984.

27   **Bailey, Robert E.** *Index to the Descriptive Inventory of the Archives of the State of Illinois.* Springfield, 1990.

28   **Bailey, Robert E., and Elaine Shemoney Evans.** *Early Chicago 1833 to 1871, a Selection of City Council Proceedings Files.* Springfield, 1986.

29   **Baird, Elizabeth Thérèse.** "Reminiscences of Early Days on Mackinac Island." *Wisconsin Historical Collections* 14, 1898.

29a   **Bakken, Timothy H.** *Hinsdale.* Hinsdale, Ill., 1976.

30   **Balesi, Charles J.** *The Time of the French in the Heart of North America, 1673-1818.* Chicago, 1992.

31   **Balestier, Joseph N., Esq.** "The Annals of Chicago: A Lecture Delivered Before the Chicago Lyceum, January 21, 1840." *Fergus Historical Series* 1, 1876.

32   **Ball, Rev. T.H., A.M.** *Lake County, Indiana · From 1834-1872.* Chicago, 1873.

33   **Ballance, Charles.** *The History of Peoria, Illinois.* Peoria, 1870.

33a   **Ballantine, Betty, and Ian Ballantine, eds.** *The Native Americans · An Illustrated History.* Atlanta, Ga., 1993.

34   **Bancroft, George.** *History of the United States from the Discovery of the American Continent.* 10 vols. Boston, 1834-1874.

35   **Barce, Elmore.** *The Land of the Potawatomi.* Fowler, Ind., 1919.

36   **Barnhart, John D.** "Documents/A New Letter about the Massacre at Fort Dearborn." *Indiana Magazine of History* 41, no. 2, June 1945.

37   **Bateman, Newton, LL.D.; J. Seymour Currey; and Paul Selby, A.M.; eds.** *Historical Encyclopedia of Illinois, with Commemorative Biographies.* Chicago, 1926.

38   **Bayliss, Clara Kern.** "The Significance of the Piasa." *Transactions of the Illinois State Historical Society* 13, 1908, pp. 114-22.

39   **Beatty, William K.** "ESK – A Medical Original." *Proceedings of the Institute of Medicine, Chicago* 33, 1980.

40   ___. [William Bradshaw Egan] "A Perfect Irish Gentleman." *Proceedings of the Institute of Medicine, Chicago* 36, 1983.

41   **Beaubien, Emily.** Autobiographical typescript. Archives of Sterling Morton Library, Morton Arboretum. Lisle, Ill., n.d.

42 Beaubien, Frank G. "The Beaubiens of Chicago." *Catholic Historical Review* 2, July 1919-January 1920.

43 Beaubien, Madore. "Interview with Madore Beaubien." *Chicago Times*, May 16, 1882.

44 Beck, Lewis Caleb. *Gazetteer of the States of Illinois and Missouri*. Albany, N.Y., 1823.

45 Beckwith, Hiram Williams. *The Illinois and Indiana Indians*. Chicago, 1884.

46 Beckwith, Hiram Williams, ed. *Collections of the Illinois State Historical Society* 1, 1903.

47 Beecher, W.J. *The Chicago Prairie*. The Chicago Academy of Science. Chicago, n.d.

48 Beers, J.S. & Co., publisher. *History of the Great Lakes*. 2 vols. Chicago, 1899.

49 Beeson, Lewis. *Upper Great Lakes · Places of Significance in the Life of Father Jacques Marquette*. St. Ignace, Wis., 1966.

50 Beggs, Rev. Stephen R. *Pages From the Early History of the West and Northwest, &c.* Cincinnati, 1868.

51 Benedetti, Rose Marie and Virginia C. Bulat. *Portage, Pioneers, and Pubs – A History of Lyons, Illinois*. Chicago, 1963.

52 Bennett, R.J. Letter to Rufus Blanchard. Chicago, 1880.

53 Benton, Colbee Chaimberlain. *A Visitor to Chicago in Indian Days – "Journal to the 'Far-Off West.' "* Chicago, 1957.

54 Bernou, Abbé Claude. "Relation of the Discoveries and Voyages of the Sieur de La Salle in 1679-1681." MS, Bibliothèque Nationale, Paris, 1682.

54a Bernstein, Barbara. "Federal Art in Illinois" [a listing of existent public art created during the 1930s, Feb. 15, 1976; Harold Washington Library, Chicago].

55 Berry, Brian J.L. *Chicago: Transformation of an Urban System*. Cambridge, Mass., 1976.

55a Bigelow, Ellen. "Letters Written By A Peoria Woman In 1835." *Journal of the Illinois State Historical Society* 22, July 1929, pp. 335-53.

56 Birkbeck, Morris. *Notes on a Journey in America, from the Coast of Virginia to the Territory of Illinois*. 4th ed. London, 1818.

57 Blair, Emma Helen. *Indian Tribes of the Upper Mississippi Valley and the Region of the Great Lakes*. 2 vols. Cleveland, 1912. Reprint, New York, 1969.

58 Blanchard, Rufus. *Discovery and Conquest of the Northwest, with the History of Chicago*. Wheaton, Ill., 1881; Chicago, 1898.

59 ___. *History of Illinois*. Chicago, 1883.

60 Blodgett, Israel P. "Reminiscences of an Early Settler." Memories collected by his daughter Corac. Downers Grove Historical Society, n.d.

61 Blodgett, Henry W. *Autobiography of Henry W. Blodgett*. Waukegan, 1906.

62 Bodmer, Karl. *Illustrations to Maximilian Prince of Wied's Travels in the Interior of North America*. London, 1844.

63 Boggess, Arthur Clinton. *The Settlement of Illinois 1778-1830*. Chicago, 1908.

64 Bohlen, H. David. *The Birds of Illinois*. Bloomington/Indianapolis, 1989.

65 Bonner, Thomas N. "The Social and Political Attitudes of Midwestern Physicians 1840 to 1940: Chicago as a Case History." *Journal of the History of Medicine and Allied Sciences* 8, no. 2, 1953.

66 ___. *Medicine in Chicago, 1850-1950*. Madison, 1957.

67 Bossu, N. *Nouveaux voyages aux Indes Occidentales*. Paris, 1768.

68 Boyd, Stephen G. *Indian Local Names*. York, Pa., 1885.

69 Brennan, George A. "De Linctot, Guardian of the Frontier." *Journal of the Illinois State Historical Society* 10, 1917.

70 ___. *The Wonder of the Dunes*. Indianapolis, 1923.

71 Brice, Wallace A. *History of Fort Wayne*. Fort Wayne, Ind., 1868.

72 Bross, William. *History of Chicago; Historical and Commercial Statistics, Sketches, Facts and Figures, Republished from the "Daily Democrat Press"; What I remember of Early Chicago. A Lecture, Delivered in McCormick's Hall, January 23, 1876*. Chicago, 1876.

73 ___. *History of Chicago*. 2nd ed. Chicago, 1880.

74 Brown, Franz L. Report of memoirs of Mrs. Callis, daughter of the first Indian agent, Charles Jowett, located at Chicago, 1810-1815. Newberry Library. Chicago, 1914.

75 Brown, George W. See Rousseau, Jacques, and George W. Brown.

76 Brown, G.P. *Drainage Channel and Waterway – A History of the Effort to Secure an Effective and Harmless Method for the Disposal of the Sewage of Chicago, and to Create a Navigable Channel between Lake Michigan and the Mississippi River*. Chicago, 1894.

77 Brown, Henry. "Present and Future Prospect of Chicago: An Address Read Before the Chicago Lyceum, January 20, 1846." *Fergus Historical Series* 9 (1876).

78 ___. *The History of Illinois, from its First Discovery and Settlement to the Present Time*. New York, 1844, 1884.

79 Brown, Lloyd A., and Howard H. Peckham, eds. *Revolutionary War Journals of Henry Dearborn, 1775-1783*. Chicago, 1939.

80 Brown, Samuel R. *The Western Gazetteer; or Emigrant's Directory, Containing a Geographical Description of the Western States and Territories, viz. the States of Kentucky, Indiana, Louisiana, Ohio, Tennessee and Mississippi: and the Territories of Illinois, Missouri, Alabama, Michigan, and North-Western. With an Appendix, Containing some of the Western Counties of New-York, Pennsylvania and Virginia; a Description of the Great Northern Lakes; Indian Annuities, and Directions to Emigrants*. Auburn, N.Y., 1817.

81 Brown, William Hubbard. *The Early History of the State of Illinois. A Lecture Delivered Before the Chicago Lyceum, on the Eighth Day of December 1840*. Chicago, 1840.

82 ___. "Early Movement in Illinois for the Legalization of Slavery: An Historical Sketch Read at the Annual Meeting of the Chicago Historical Society, December 5, 1864." *Fergus Historical Series* 4, 1876.

83 Bryson, Charles Lee. See Gilbert, Paul, and Charles Lee Bryson.

84 Buck, Solon Justus. *Travel and Description 1765 to 1865, together with a List of County Histories, Atlases, and Biographical collections and a List of Territorial and State Laws*. Springfield, 1914.

85 ___. *Illinois in 1818*. Chicago, 1918.

86 Buettinger, Craig. "The Rise and Fall of Hiram Pearson: Mobility on the Urban Frontier." *Chicago History* 9, no. 2, 1980.

87 Buisseret, David. "The Coming of the Grid: Cartographers' Views of the Heartland." Lecture given at the Newberry Library, Chicago, January 16, 1988.

88 ___. *From Sea Charts to Satellite Images*. Chicago, 1990.

89 ___. *Historic Illinois from the Air*. Chicago, 1990.

90 ___. *Mapping of the French Empire in North America*. Chicago: Newberry Library, 1991.

91 ___. See also Karrow, Robert W., and David Buisseret.

92 Bulat, Virginia C. See Benedetti, Rose Marie and Virginia C. Bulat.

93 Buley, R. Carlyle. *The Old Northwest Pioneer Period 1815-1840*. Vol. 1. Bloomington,

Ind., 1957.

93a **Bull, Alfred.** *The Township of Jefferson, Ill. and "Dinner-Pail Avenue" · From Mastodon to Man Whether Red, White, Black or Piebald.* Irving Park, Ill., 1911. [grandfather of Evelyn Marting and Dorothy Marting Sego]

94 **Burden, Philip D.** *The Mapping of North America.* Rickmansworth, Hertfordshire, England, 1996.

95 **Burnet, Jacob.** *Notes on the Early Settlement of the North-Western Territory.* Cincinnati, 1847.

96 **Bushnell, George D.** "Chicago's Rowdy Firefighters." *Chicago History* 2, no. 4, 1973, p. 232.

96a ___. *Wilmette: a history.* Wilmette, Ill., 1976.

97 **Bushnell, William H.** "Biographical Sketches of some of the Early Settlers of Chicago, Part 1: S. Lisle Smith, George Davis, Dr. Phillip Maxwell, John J. Brown, Richard L. Wilson, Col. Lewis C. Kercheval, Uriah P. Harris, Henry B. Clarke, and Sheriff Samuel J. Lowe." [*Fergus Historical Series* 5] "Part 2: William H. Brown, B.W. Raymond, Esq., with Portrait, J. Young Scammon, Charles Walker, Thomas Church." *Fergus Historical Series* 6, 1876.

98 **Butler, Charles.** "William B. Ogden and Early Chicago: An Address delivered in 1881." William B. Ogden Papers. Chicago Historical Society.

99 **Butt, Ernest.** *Chicago Then and Now, a Pictorial History of the City's Development and a Reprint of the First City Directory Published in Chicago in 1844 by J.W. Norris.* Aurora, Ill., 1933.

100 **Butterfield, Consul Willshire.** *History of the Discovery of the Northwest by John Nicolet in 1634, with a Sketch of his Life.* Cincinnati, 1881.

101 **Cadillac, Sieur de Lamothe, and Pierre Liette.** *Memoirs: The Western Country in the 17th Century.* Edited by Milo M. Quaife. Chicago, 1947.

102 **Caldwell, Billy.** Billy Caldwell Papers. Chicago Historical Society.

103 **Caldwell, Norman W.** "The Frontier Army Officer, 1794-1814." *Mid-America* 37, April 1955.

104 ___. "The Enlisted Soldier at the Frontier Post." *Mid-America* 37, October 1955.

105 ___. "Civilian Personnel at the Frontier Military Post (1790-1814)." *Mid-America* 38, April 1956.

106 **Carbutt, John.** *Biographical Sketches of the Leading Men of Chicago.* Chicago, 1868.

106a **Carey, Henry Charles.** See Lea, Isaac, and Henry Charles Carey.

107 **Carriel, Mary Turner.** *Jonathan Baldwin Turner.* Jacksonville, Ill., 1911; Urbana, Ill., 1961.

108 **Carter, Clarence Edwin.** *Great Britain and the Illinois Country, 1763-1774.* New York, 1910.

109 **Carter, Clarence Edwin,** ed. "The Territory of Illinois, 1809-1814," *The Territorial Papers of the United States.* Vol. 16. Washington, D.C.: U.S. Government Printing Office, 1948.

110 ___. See Alvord, Clarence Walworth, and Clarence Edward Carter, eds.

111 **Carver, Jonathan.** *Travels through the Interior Parts of North America in the Years 1766, 1767, and 1768.* London, 1781.

112 **Casas, Don Bartholomew, de las.** *Newe Welt. Warhafftige Anzeigung Der Hispanier grewlichen abschewlichen und unmenschlichen Tyranney von ihnen inn den Indianischen Ländern so gegen Nidergang der Sonnen gelegen und die Newe Welt genennet wird begangen... Jetzt aber erst ins Hochdeutsch durch einen Liebhaber dess Vatterlands....* Frankfurt, 1597. [original Spanish ed.: *Brevissima Relation,* 1552]

113 **Casas, Bartolomé, de las.** *Diario de Colon: Libro de la Primera Navegacion y Descubrimiento de las Indias.* Transcribed by Carlon Sanz. Madrid, 1957-1958.

114 **Cass, Lewis.** *Considerations of the Present State of the Indians, and their Removal to the West of the Mississippi.* Boston, 1828.

115 **Castelnau, Francis, comte de.** *Vues et Souvenirs de L'Amerique du Nord.* Paris, 1842.

116 **Catlin, George.** *Illustrations of the Manners, Customs, and Conditions of the North American Indians: in a Series of Letters and Notes, written during eight Years of Travel and Adventure among the Wildest and most Remarkable Tribes now existing.* 5th ed. London, 1845.

117 ___. *Souvenir of the North American Indians.* London, 1852.

118 **Catlin, George B.** "Oliver Newberry." *Michigan History Magazine* 18, 1934.

119 ___. "Early Settlement in Eastern Michigan." *Michigan History Magazine* 26, 1942.

120 **Caton, John Dean, LL.D.** *Miscellanies.* Contains "The Last of the Illinois, and a Sketch of the Potawatomies"; "Old Chicago – Reply, on behalf of the Old Settlers of Chicago to the Welcome given by the Calumet Club, at its Reception, May 27, 1879"; "American Cervus"; "The Wild Turkey and its Domestication"; "Origin of the Prairies" and others. Boston, 1880.

121 ___. *Early Bench and Bar of Illinois.* Chicago, 1893.

122 **Cauthorn, Henry Sullivan.** *A History of the City of Vincennes, Indiana from 1702 to 1901.* Terre Haute, Ind., 1902.

123 **Cavanagh, Helen M.** *Funk of Funk's Grove.* Bloomington, Ill., 1952.

124 **Celeste, Sister Mary.** "The Miami Indians Prior to 1700." *Mid-America* 16, April 1934.

125 **Chamberlin, Everett.** *Chicago and Its Suburbs, Illustrated.* Chicago, 1874.

126 ___. See Colbert, Elias, and Everett Chamberlin.

127 **Champlain, Samuel de.** *Les Voyages de la Nouvelle France Occidentale, Dicte Canada, Fait Par le Sr. De Champlain....* Paris, 1632.

128 **Charlevoix, Pierre François Xavier de.** *Histoire et description generale de la Nouvelle France, avec le Journal historique d'un Voyage fait par ordre du Roi dans l'Amerique Septentrionnale.* 3 vols. Paris, 1744.

129 ___. *History and General Description of New France by the Rev. P.F.X. de Charlevoix, S.J.* Translated and edited by John G. Shea. New York, 1866-1872.

130 **Chastellux, François Jean, marquis de.** *Voyages dans l'Amerique Septentrionale, dans les années 1780, 1781 & 1782.* Paris, 1788-1791.

131 **Chesnel, Paul.** *Histoire de Cavelier de La Salle; Exploration et Conquete du Bassin du Mississipi....* Paris, 1901.

132 *Chicago City Directory 1844.* Chicago, 1903.

133 **Chicago Department of Development and Planning.** *Historic City/The Settlement of Chicago.* Chicago, 1976.

134 **Chicago Genealogical Society, The.** *List of Letters Remaining in the Post Office · Chicago and Vicinity · January 1834-July 1836.* Chicago, 1970.

135 ___. *Vital Records from the Chicago Newspapers · 1833-1839.* Chicago, 1971.

136 *Chicago in Periodic Literature, A Summary of Articles.* Compiled by the Workers of the

Writers' Program of the Work Projects Administration in the State of Illinois. Vol. 1. Chicago, 1940.

137 **Chicago Medical Society, ed.** *History of Medicine and Surgery and Physicians and Surgeons of Chicago.* Chicago, 1922.

138 "Chicago's Quest for Pure Water." *Chicago Tribune,* January 2, 1900.

139 **Childs, Ebenezer.** "Recollections of Wisconsin since 1820." *Wisconsin Historical Collections* 4, 1859.

140 **Christopher, Louise W.** *Hoofbeats on the Prairie, The Story of a Saddlebag Preacher.* Evanston, Ill., 1987.

141 **Church, Jeremiah.** *Journal of Travels, Adventures, and Remarks of Jerry Church.* Harrisburg, Pa., 1845, 1933.

142 **Clark, George Rogers.** *The Conquest of the Illinois.* Chicago, 1920.

143 **Clark, William.** See Lewis, Meriwether, and William Clark.

144 **Clayton, John.** *The Illinois Fact Book and Historical Almanac, 1673-1968.* Carbondale, Ill., 1970.

145 **Cleaver, Charles, Esq.** "Reminiscences of Early Chicago (1833)." *Fergus Historical Series* 19, 1882.

146 ___. *A History of Chicago from 1833 to 1892.* Chicago, 1892.

147 **Clermont, Alexis.** "Narrative of Alexis Clermont." *Wisconsin Historical Collections* 15, 1900.

148 **Clifton, James A.** *The Prairie People: Continuity and Change in Potawatomi Indian Culture 1665-1965.* Lawrence, Kans., 1977.

149 ___. "Captain Billy Caldwell's Exile in Early Chicago." *Chicago History* 6, no. 4, winter 1977-78, pp. 218-28.

149a ___. "Merchant, Soldier, Broker, Chief; A Corrected Obituary of Captain Billy Caldwell." *Journal of the Illinois State Historical Society* 71, no. 3, August 1978, pp. 185-210.

150 ___. "Chicago, September 14, 1833: The Last Great Indian Treaty in the Old Northwest." *Chicago History* 9, no. 2, summer 1980, pp. 86-97.

151 **Cobb, Charles E., Jr.** "The Great Lakes' Troubled Waters." *National Geographic Magazine* 172, July 1987.

152 **Cochran, Thomas C., and Wayne Andrews, eds.** *Concise Dictionary of American History.* New York, 1962.

153 **Cole, Harry Elsworth.** *Stagecoach and Tavern Tales of the Old Northwest.* Cleveland, 1930.

154 **Colbert, Elias.** *Chicago. Historical and Statistical Sketch of the Garden City: A Chronicle of its Social, Municipal, Commercial and Manufacturing Progress, from the Beginning until Now. Containing Also, Names of the Early Settlers and the Office Holders, with Full Statistical Tables.* Chicago, 1868.

155 **Colbert, Elias, and Everett Chamberlin.** *Chicago and the Great Conflagration.* Cincinnati/New York, 1871.

156 **Colombo, Cristoforo.** *Epistula Cristofori Colom: Cui Etas Nostra Multum Debet; De Insulis Indie Supra Gangem Nuper Inuentis.* Rome, 1493.

157 ___. *Letter of 1493.* Translated by Frank E. Robbins. William L. Clements Library. Ann Arbor, 1952.

158 **Commission on Chicago Historical and Architectural Landmarks, City of Chicago, ed.** *Site of the Wolf Point Settlement.* Chicago, 1975.

159 ___. *Site of the Beaubien Claim.* Chicago, 1975.

160 ___. *Site of the Sauganash Hotel and the Wigwam.* Chicago, 1975.

161 ___. *Site of the Marquette Camp.* Chicago, 1976.

162 ___. *Site of the DuSable/Kinzie House.* Chicago, 1977.

163 **Conger, John Leonard.** *History of the Illinois River Valley.* Chicago, 1932.

164 **Conzen, Michael P., ed.** *Chicago Mapmakers, Essays on the Rise of the City's Map Trade.* Chicago, 1984.

165 **Cook, Frederick Francis.** *Bygone Days in Chicago.* Chicago, 1910.

166 **Cook, Mary Estelle.** *Little Oak Park 1835-1902.* Oak Park, Ill., 1961.

167 **Copley, A.B.** "Early Settlement of Southwestern Michigan." Read at the Annual Meeting of the State Pioneer Society, June 7, 1882.

168 **Corliss, Carlton J.** "Illinois Travel in Olden Days." *Journal of American History* 28, 1934.

169 **Cox, Isaac Joslin.** *The Journeys of René Robert Cavelier Sieur de la Salle.* New York, 1905.

170 **Crafts, James M. and William F.** *The Crafts Family: A Genealogical and Biographical History of the Descendents of Griffin and Allice Crafts, of Roxbury, Massachusetts.* Northampton, Mass., 1893.

171 **Cramton, Willa G.** "Domestic Furnishings of the Northern Illinois Frontier 1833–1850." Master's thesis, Northern Illinois University, Dekalb, 1988.

172 **Crellin, John K.** *Medical Care in Pioneer Illinois.* Springfield, 1982.

173 **Croghan, George.** "Croghan's Journal, February 28, 1765, to October 8, 1765." *Collections of the Illinois State Historical Library* 11, 1916, pp. 1-64.

174 **Cronon, William.** *Nature's Metropolis. Chicago and the Great West.* New York/London, 1991.

175 **Crossley, Fredric B.** *Courts and Lawyers of Illinois.* Chicago, 1912.

176 **Cumming, W.P., R.A. Skelton, and D.B. Quinn.** *The Discovery of North America.* London, 1971.

177 **Currey, J. Seymour.** "Chicago's North Shore." *Transactions of the Illinois State Historical Society* 8, 1904, pp. 101-13.

178 ___. *Chicago: Its History and Its Builders: A Century of Marvelous Growth.* Chicago, 1912.

179 ___. *The Story of Old Fort Dearborn.* Chicago, 1912.

180 **Cutler, Irving.** *Chicago/Metropolis of the Mid-Continent.* Dubuque, Iowa, 1982.

181 **Dale, Edward Everett.** *Medical Practices on the Frontier.* Reprint, *Indiana Magazine of History* 43, December 1947, pp. 307-28.

182 **Dana, Edmund.** *Geographical Sketches on the Western Country; Designed for Emigrants and Settlers: Being the Result of Extensive Researches and Remarks. To Which is Added a Summary of the Most Interesting Matters on the Subjects, Including a Particular Description of the Unsold Public Lands, Collected from a Variety of Authentic Sources. Also a List of the Principal Roads.* Cincinnati, 1819.

183 **Danckers, Ulrich Friedrich.** "Prairie Sky over Fort Dearborn." *Chicago Medicine* 94, no. 15, 1991.

184 ___. "Exploring Chicago's Past." *Chicago Medicine* 96, no. 15, 1993.

185 **Danforth, I.N.** *The Life of Nathan Smith Davis, 1817-1904.* Chicago, 1907.

186 **Darby, William.** *The Emigrant's Guide to the Western and Southwestern States and Territories: Comprising a Geographical and Statistical Description of the States of Louisiana, Mississippi, Tennessee. Kentucky, and Ohio; – the Territories of Alabama, Missouri, Illi-*

nois, and Michigan; and the Western Parts of Virginia, Pennsylvania and New York.... New York, 1818.

187 David, George. "Diary of George David [Extracts] – A Trip From London to Chicago in 1833." *Michigan History Magazine* 18, winter 1934, pp. 53-66.

188 Davis, David J. *History of Medical Practice in Illinois.* Vol. 2. Chicago, 1955.

189 Dedmon, Emmet. *Fabulous Chicago.* enl. ed. New York, 1981.

190 De Gannes. For his copy of Pierre Liette's memoir, see Pease, Theodore Calvin, and Ray Werner, eds. *Collections of the Illinois State Historical Library* 23, 1934, pp. 302-95.

191 Delanglez, Jean, S.J., Ph.D. *The Journal of Jean Cavelier.* Chicago, 1938.

192 ___. *Some of LaSalle's Journeys.* Chicago, 1938.

193 ___. *Frontenac and the Jesuits.* Chicago, 1939.

194 ___. "A Calendar of La Salle's Travels 1643-1683." *Mid-America* 22, 1940.

195 ___. "The 1674 Account of the Discovery of the Mississippi." *Mid-America* 26, 1944.

196 ___. "The Voyages of Tonti in North America, 1678-1704." *Mid-America* 26, 1944.

197 ___. "Marquette's Autograph Map of the Mississippi River." *Mid-America* 27, 1945.

198 ___. "The Joliet Lost Map of the Mississippi." *Mid-America* 28, 1946.

199 ___. *Life and Voyages of Louis Jolliet.* Chicago, 1948.

200 Dennis, Henry C. *The American Indian 1492-1970.* Dobbs Ferry, N.Y., 1971.

201 De Peyster, Col. Arent Schuyler. *Miscellanies, by an Officer.* Dumfries, Scotland, 1813. Reprint, edited by J. Watts De Peyster. New York, 1888.

202 Dickens, Charles. *American Notes for General Circulation.* London, 1842, 1850.

203 ___. *Amerika.* 1st German ed. Leipzig, 1843.

204 Dickinson, Samuel N.. *Hand-Book Specimen of Printing Type, Cuts, Ornaments, Etc.* Boston, 1847.

205 *Dictionary of Canadian Biography.* Vols. 1-6. Toronto: University of Toronto Press, 1966-1987.

206 Dilg, Charles Augustus. "Chicago's Archaic History," MS and typescript written between c.1895-1905 *in* Charles Augustus Dilg Collection. Chicago Historical Society.

207 Dodson, Harriet N. Warren. "The Warrens of Warrenville." *Transactions of the Illinois State Historical Society* 21, 1915, pp. 124-37.

208 Donnelly, Joseph P., S.J. *Jacques Marquette, S.J., 1637-1675.* Chicago, 1968.

209 Dor-Ner, Zvi. *Columbus and the Age of Discovery.* New York, 1991.

210 *Down's Record and Historical View of Peoria.* Peoria, 1850.

211 Drake, Benjamin. *Life and Adventures of Black Hawk: with Sketches of Keokuk, the Sac and Fox Indians, and the Late Black Hawk War.* Cincinnati, 1838, 1841, 1849.

212 ___. *Life of Tecumseh, and his Brother the Prophet; with a Historical Sketch of the Shawanoe Indians.* Cincinnati, 1856.

213 Drake, Daniel, M.D. *A Systematic Treatise, Historical, Etiological and Practical, on the Principal Diseases of the Interior Valley of North America, as they appear in the Caucasian, African, Indian and Esquimaux Varieties of Its Population.* Book 1 Cincinnati, 1850. Book 2 Philadelphia, 1854.

214 Draper, Lyman Copeland. Papers pertaining to the early fur trade at Chicago, and the U.S. Army's history of Fort Dearborn I and II within the Draper Collection: Series S, T, U, YY [detailed *in* Archie Motley's "Manuscript Sources on Frontier Chicago."] Wisconsin State Historical Society, Madison.

215 Drennen, Daniel O. Papers pertaining to Fort Dearborn and Chicago between 1803-1836. Chicago Historical Society.

216 Driggs, Alfred L. "Early Days in Michigan." *St. Joseph County Advertiser,* July 9, 1885.

217 DuCreux, M. *Historia Canadensis.* Paris, 1664.

217a Dugan, Hugh G. *Village on the County Line A History of Hinsdale, Illinois.* Chicago, 1949.

218 Duis, Perry R. *Chicago: Creating New Traditions.* Chicago, 1976.

218a Dunham, Montrew, and Pauline Wandschneider. *Downers Grove 1832-1982.* Downers Grove Historical Society, Downers Grove, Ill., 1982.

219 Dunn, Jacob Piat. *The Mission to the Ouabache.* Indianapolis, 1902.

220 East, Ernest E. "Contributions to Chicago History from Peoria County Records." *Journal of the State of Illinois Historical Society* 31, 1938.

221 Ebert, Albert E. "Early History of the Drug Trade of Chicago, compiled from Records of the Chicago Veteran Druggists Association." *Transactions of the Illinois State Historical Society* 8, 1903, pp. 234-74; 10, 1905, pp. 239-60.

222 Eccles, W.J. *Essays on New France.* Toronto, 1987.

223 Eckert, Allen W. *The Frontiersmen.* Boston, 1967.

224 ___. *Wilderness Empire.* Boston, 1969.

225 ___. *The Conquerors.* Boston, 1970.

226 ___. *Gateway to Empire, A Narrative.* Boston/Toronto, 1983.

227 ___. *The Wilderness War.* Boston, 1987.

228 Edgerton, Michael. See Heise, Kenan, and Michael Edgerton.

229 Edmunds, R. David. *The Potawatomis: Keepers of the Fire.* Norman, Okla., 1978.

230 Edwards, Ninian Wirt. *History of Illinois, from 1778-1833; and Life and Times of Ninian Edwards.* Springfield, 1870.

231 ___. *The Edwards Papers.* Chicago, 1884.

232 Ehrenberg, Ralph E. See Schwartz, Seymour I., and Ralph E. Ehrenberg.

233 Ehresmann, Julia M., ed. *Geneva, Illinois, A History of Its Times and Places.* Geneva, 1977.

234 Elder, Paul Wilson. "Early Taverns and Inns in Illinois." *Journal of the Illinois State Historical Society* 20, 1928.

235 Ellis, Franklin. *History of Berrien and Van Buren Counties, Michigan.* Philadelphia, 1881.

236 Elmes, Philip Robert. "Opening the Great Lakes." *History, Journal of the World Ship Trust,* no. 47. Croton-on-Hudson, N.Y., 1988.

237 Evans, Elaine Shemoney. See Bailey, Robert E., and Elaine Shemoney Evans.

238 Farr, Finis. *Chicago: A Personal History of America's Most American City.* New Rochelle, N.Y., 1973.

239 Farren, Kathy, ed. *A Bicentennial History of Kendall County, Illinois.* Yorkville, Ill., 1976.

240 Faux, William. *Memorable Days in America: Being a Journal of a Tour to the United States, Principally Undertaken to Ascertain, by Positive Evidence, the Condition and Probable Prospects of British Emigrants.* London, 1823.

241 Faye, Stanley, ed. "A Search for Copper on the Illinois River: The Journal of Legardeur DeLisle." *Journal of the Illinois State Historical Society* 38, 1945.

242 Fergus, Robert. "Biographical Sketch of John Dean Caton, Ex-Chief-Justice of Illinois." *Fergus Historical Series* 21, 1882.

243 Fergus, Robert, ed. "Fergus' Directory of the City of Chicago, 1839. With City and County Officers, Churches, Public Buildings, Hotels etc.; also, List of Sheriffs of Cook

County and Mayors of the City since their Organization; together with the Poll-List of the First City Election – Tuesday, May 2nd, 1837; and also a List of Puchasers of Lots in Fort Dearborn Addition, the No. of the Lots and the Prices paid, etc., etc." *Fergus Historical Series* 2, 1876.

244 Fernow, Berthold. *Ohio Valley in Colonial Days.* Albany, N.Y., 1890.

245 Field, Walter. "A Re-examination into the Invention of the Balloon Frame." *Journal of the American Society of Architectural Historians* 2, no. 4, 1942.

246 Fisher, Geo. & Co., publisher. *Biographical Directory of the Voters and Tax Payers of Kendall County, Illinois.* Chicago, 1876.

247 Fisher, Joseph S.J. and Fr. R. von Wieser. *The Oldest Map with the Name America of the Year 1507 and the Carta Marina of the Year 1516 by M. Waldseemüller (Ilacomilus).* Amsterdam, 1968.

248 Fiske, Horace Spencer. *Chicago in Picture and Poetry.* Chicago, 1903.

249 Flinn, John J. *History of the Chicago Police.* Chicago, 1887.

250 Flower, George. *History of the English Settlement in Edwards County, Illinois.* Chicago, 1909.

251 Fonda, John H. "A series of Reminiscences." *Wisconsin Historical Collections* 5, 1868.

252 Ford, Thomas. *A History of Illinois from its Commencement as a State in 1818 to 1847.* Chicago, 1945.

253 Fordam, Elias P. *Personal Narrative of Travels in Virginia, Maryland, Pennsylvania, Ohio, Indiana, Kentucky, and of a Residence in the Illinois Territory: 1817-1818.* Cleveland, 1906.

254 Foreman, Grant. "Illinois and Her Indians." *Transactions of the State Historical Society of Illinois* 46, 1939, pp. 67-111.

255 Forsyth, Thomas. Thomas Forsyth Papers. Wisconsin State Historical Society.

256 ___. Thomas Forsyth Papers. Missouri Historical Society.

257 *Fort Dearborn Papers.* Chicago Historical Society.

258 Foster, J.W. *Chicago's History, Topography, and Architecture.* Chicago, 1872.

259 Franke, Judith A. *French Peoria and the Illinois Country 1673-1846.* Springfield: Illinois State Museum Society, 1995.

260 Frazier, Arthur H. "The Military Frontier: Fort Dearborn." *Chicago History* 9, no. 2, summer 1980.

261 Fryxell, F.M. *The Physiography of the Region of Chicago.* Chicago, 1927.

262 Fuller, Dr. S.S., *et al. Riverside, Then and Now.* Chicago, 1936, 1958.

263 Gagnon, Frederick Ernest. *Louis Jolliet, Decouvreur du Mississippi et du Pays des Illinois.* Montreal, 1902.

264 Gailland, Maurice, S.J. *Diary of the Potawatomi Mission of St. Marie's on the Lake by Father Maurice Gailland.* Edited and translated by James Michael Burke. St. Louis, 1951.

265 Gale, Edward C. "On the Hennepin Trail." *Minnesota History* (St. Paul) 11, no. 1, March 1930, pp. 3-10.

266 Gale, Edwin O. *Reminiscences of Early Chicago and Vicinity.* Chicago, 1902.

267 Garraghan, Gilbert J., S.J. "Early Catholicity in Chicago." *Illinois Catholic Historical Review* 1, no. 1, July 1918.

268 ___. *The Catholic Church in Chicago, 1673-1871. An Historical Sketch.* Chicago, 1921.

269 ___. *Chicago under the French Regime.* Springfield, 1931.

270 Garrett, Wilbur E. "George Washington's Patowmack Canal." *National Geographic Magazine* 172, 1987.

271 Gerhard, Frederick. *Illinois As It Is; Its History, Geography, Statistics, Constitution, Laws, Government..., etc.* Chicago, 1857.

272 Gerwing, Anselm J., O.S.B. "The Chicago Indian Treaty of 1833." *Journal of the Illinois Historical Society* 57, no. 2, summer 1964.

272a Gessner, Conrad. *The History of Four-footed Beasts and Serpents....* London, 1658.

273 Gilbert, Paul, and Charles Lee Bryson. *Chicago and Its Makers. A Narrative of Events from the Day of the first White Man to the Inception of the Second World's Fair.* Chicago, 1929.

274 Gilman, Carolyn. *Where Two Worlds Meet: The Great Lakes Fur Trade.* St. Paul, 1982.

275 Gilpin, Alec R. *The War of 1812 in the Old Northwest.* East Lansing, 1958.

276 Goodspeed, Rev. E.J. *History of the Great Fires in Chicago and the West.* New York, 1871.

277 Goodspeed, Thomas Wakefield. *The University of Chicago Biographical Sketches.* Vol. 1. Chicago, 1922.

278 Goodspeed, Weston Arthur, and Daniel D. Healy, eds. *History of Cook County, Illinois – Being a general Survey of Cook County History, including a condensed History of Chicago and special Account of Districts outside the City Limits, from the earliest Settlement to the present Time.* Chicago, 1909.

279 Gordon, Eleanor Lytle Kinzie. *John Kinzie, the "Father of Chicago," a Sketch.* Chicago, 1912.

280 Gordon, Nelly Kinzie, ed. *The Fort Dearborn Massacre, Written in 1814 by Lieutenant Linai T. Helm, One of the Survivors.* Chicago, 1912.

281 Gravier, Gabriel. *Vie de Samuel Champlain, Fondateur de la Nouvelle-France (1567-1635).* Paris, 1900.

282 ___. *Étude sur Une Carte Inconnue, La premiere dressee par Louis Joliet en 1674 Apres son exploration du Mississipi avec le P. Jacques Marquette en 1673.* Paris, 1880.

283 Gravier, Father Jacques. "Dictionary of the Algonquin Illinois Language, c.1700." MS, Watkinson Library, Trinity College, Hartford, Conn.

284 Gray, James. *The Illinois/Rivers of America Series.* New York, 1940.

285 Gray, Mary Lackritz See Bach, Ira J., and Mary Lackritz Gray.

286 Griffin, Appleton P.G. *The Discovery of the Mississippi: a Bibliographical Account with a Fac-simile of the Map of Louis Joliet, 1674.* New York, 1883.

287 Grignon, Augustin. "Narrative." *Wisconsin Historical Collections* 3, 1857.

288 Griswald, Bert J. "Fort Wayne, Gateway of the West, 1802-1813." *Indiana Historical Collections* 15, 1927.

289 Grossman, Joanne, and Theodore J. Karamanski, eds. *Historic Lighthouses and Navigational Aids of the Illinois Shore of Lake Michigan.* Chicago, 1989.

290 Grover, Frank Reed. *Father Pierre François Pinet, S.J. and his Mission of the Guardian Angel of Chicago (L'Ange Gardien) A.D. 1696-1699.* Chicago, 1907.

291 ___. *Antoine Ouilmette.* Evanston, 1908.

292 ___. "The First Evanstonians." A Paper Read before the Evanston Historical Society, November 2, 1901.

293 Gueroult, Mary Young. "Across the Prairie, a Chapter of Early Chicago." *Journal of the Illinois State Historical Society* 37, July 1935, pp. 250-55.

294 **Guyer, I.D.** *History of Chicago; Its Commercial and Manufacturing Interests and Industry; Together with Sketches of Manufacturers and Men Who Have Most Contributed to Its Prosperity and Advancement, with Glances of Some of the Best Hotels; Also the Principal Railroads which Center in Chicago.* Chicago, 1862.

295 **Habig, Marion Alfonse.** *A Franciscan Père Marquette: A Critical Biography of Fr. Zénobe Membré O.F.M., La Salle's Chaplain and Missionary Companion.* New York, 1934.

296 **Haeger, John Denis.** "The American Fur Company And the Chicago of 1812-1835." *Journal of the Illinois State Historical Society* 61, summer 1968.

297 ___. "Eastern Money and the Urban Frontier, 1833-1842." *Journal of the Illinois State Historical Society* 64, no. 3, autumn 1971.

298 **Hager, Albert D.** "Early Chicago, and the Northwest," *in* Alfred T. Andreas' *History of Chicago. From the Earliest Period to the Present Time,* vol. 1, p. 46.

299 **Haines, Elilah Middlebrook.** *Historical and Statistical Sketches of Lake County, State of Illinois.* Waukegan, 1852.

300 ___. *The American Indian.* Chicago, 1888.

300a **Haldimand, Frederick.** *Haldimand Papers.* British Library, London.

301 **Hall, Albert L.** *History of River Forest, A Suburb of Chicago.* Chicago, 1937.

302 **Hall, James.** *Letters from the West, containing Sketches of Scenery, Manners, and Customs, and Anecdotes connected with the First Settlements of the Western Sections of the United States.* London, 1828.

303 **Hall, Jennie.** *The Story of Chicago.* Chicago/New York/London, 1911.

304 **Halsey, John J., LL.D., ed.** *A History of Lake County, Illinois.* Chicago, 1912.

305 **Hamilton, Henry E.** See Hubbard, Gurdon Saltonstall.

306 **Hamilton, Henry Raymond.** *The Epic of Chicago.* Chicago, 1932.

307 **Hamilton, Raphael N., S.J.** *Marquette's Explorations, The Narratives Re-examined.* Madison/Milwaukee/London, 1970.

308 **Hand, Hon. John Pryor.** "Negro Slavery in Illinois." *Transactions of the Illinois State Historical Society* 15, 1910, pp. 42-49.

309 **Hansel, Ardith K., and David M. Michelson.** *A Reevaluation of the Timing and Causes of the High Lake Phases in the Lake Michigan Basin.* Illinois Department of Energy and Natural Resources, Geology Survey Division. Springfield, 1988.

310 **Hansen, Harry.** *The Chicago/Rivers of America Series.* New York/Toronto, 1942.

311 **Hanson, Philip C.** *Early Chicagoland.* Chicago, 1976.

312 ___. *Geology of Chicago.* Chicago, 1978.

313 ___. *The Presettlement Vegetation of the Plain of Glacial Lake Chicago in Cook County, Illinois.* Chicago, 1981.

314 **Harley, J.B.** *Maps and the Columbian Encounter.* Milwaukee: University of Wisconsin, 1990.

314a **Harmon, Ada Douglas.** *The Story of an Old Town – Glen Ellyn.* Glen Ellyn, 1928.

315 **Harper, Josephine L.** *Guide to the Draper Manuscripts.* Madison, 1983.

316 **Harris, N. Dwight.** *The History of Negro Servitude in Illinois and of the Slavery Agitation in that State · 1719-1864.* Chicago: Lakeside Press, 1904.

317 **Harrisse, Henry.** *John Cabot, The Discoverer of North-America and Sebastian His Son: A Chapter of the Maritime History of England Under the Tudors, 1496-1557.* London, 1896.

318 **Hausman, Harriet.** *Reflections: A History of River Forest.* River Forest, Ill., 1975.

319 **Hayden, James Ryan.** *Chicago's True Founder, Thomas J.V. Owen.* Lombard, Ill., 1934. [list of "500 Chicagoans of 1833," p. 269; list of "Property Owners in Chicago, 1833," p. 288]

320 **Hayner, Don, and Tom McNamee.** *Streetwise Chicago.* Chicago, 1988.

321 **Healy, Daniel D.** See Goodspeed, Weston Arthur, and Daniel D. Healy.

321a **Heard, J. Norman.** *Handbook of the American Frontier: Four Centuries of Indian-White Relationships.* Vol. II. Metuchen, N.J./London, 1990.

322 **Heidenreich, Conrad E.** "Explorations and Mapping of Samuel de Champlain, 1603-1632." *Cartographia* 17, 1976, pp. 1-140.

323 ___. "An Analysis of the 17th Century Map 'Nouvelle France.'" *Cartographia* 25, no. 3, 1988.

324 **Heise, Kenan.** "Is long-lost Chilaga the Camelot of Chicagou?" *Chicago Tribune,* March 4, 1987.

325 **Heise, Kenan, and Michael Edgerton.** *Chicago, Center for Enterprise; An Illustrated History.* Vol. 1. Woodland Hills, Calif., 1982.

326 **Heitman, Francis B.** *Historical Register and Dictionary of the U.S. Army From Its Organization, Sept. 29, 1789, to March 2, 1903.* Washington, D.C., 1903.

327 **Helm, Lieutenant Linai T.** *The Fort Dearborn Massacre.* Edited by Nelly Kinzie Gordon. Chicago/New York, 1912.

328 **Hendrick, Willene, and George Hendrick.** *On the Illinois Frontier: Dr. Hiram Rutherford.* Carbondale/Edwardsville, Ill., 1981.

329 **Henkes, Mark.** *DesPlaines: A History.* DesPlaines, Ill., 1975

330 **Hennepin, Louis.** *Description de la Louisiane, Nouvellement Decouverte au Sud' Oüest de la Nouvelle France, par Ordre du Roy. Avec la Carte du Pays: Les Moeurs et la Maniere de Vivre des Sauvages....* Paris, 1683.

331 ___. *Nouvelle decouverte d'un tres grand pays situé dans l'Amerique, entre le Nouveau Mexique et la Mer Glaciale.* Utrecht, 1697.

332 ___. *Voyage curieux, qui contient une Novelle Decouverte d'un tres-grand pays, situé dans l'Amerique, entre de Nouveau Mexique, & la Mer Glaciale. Qui contient une relation des Caraibes, faite par le Sieur de La Borde.* Leiden, 1704.

333 ___. *A Description of Louisiana.* Translated from the 1683 French ed. by John Gilmary Shea. New York, 1880.

334 ___. *A New Discovery of a Vast Country in America by Father Louis Hennepin.* Translated and edited by Reuben G. Thwaites. Chicago, 1903.

335 **Henry, Alexander.** *Travels and Adventures.* Chicago, 1921.

336 **[Herrington, James]** "A Letter of James Herrington Written from Chicago in 1831." *Bulletin of the Chicago Historical Society* 1, no. 2, February 1935.

337 **Heward, Hugh.** "Journal of a Voyage Made by Hugh Heward to the Illinois Country, 1790." Transcript, Chicago Historical Society.

338 **Hoffmann, Charles Fenno.** *A Winter in the Far West.* London, 1835.

339 ___. *A Winter in the West. By a New Yorker.* New York, 1835.

340 **Hoffmann, John, ed.** *Guide to the History of Illinois.* New York/Westport, Conn./London, 1991.

341 **Hoffmeister, Donald Frederick.** *Mammals of Illinois.* Urbana/Chicago, 1989.

342 Hofmeister, Rudolph A. *The Germans of Chicago*. Champaign, Ill., 1978.

343 Holli, Melvin G., and Peter d'A. Jones, eds. *The Ethnic Frontier: Essays in the History of Group Survival in Chicago and the Midwest*. Grand Rapids, Mich., 1977.

344 ___. *Ethnic Chicago*. Grand Rapids, Mich., 1984.

345 Holt, Glen E., and Dominic A. Pacyga. *Chicago: A Historical Guide to the Neighborhoods. The Loop and South Side*. Chicago, 1979.

346 Hough, Jack L. *Geology of the Great Lakes*. Urbana, Ill., 1958.

347 Howard, Robert P. *Illinois: A History of the Prairie State*. Grand Rapids, Mich., 1972.

348 Howe, Walter A. *Documentary History of the Illinois and Michigan Canal*. Springfield, 1956.

349 Hower, Frances R. *The Story of a French Homestead in the Old Northwest*. Columbus, Ohio, 1907.

349a Hoxie, Frederick E., ed. *Encyclopedia of North American Indians*. Boston/New York, 1996.

350 Hoyt, Homer. *One Hundred Years of Land Value in Chicago. The Relationship of the Growth of Chicago to the Rise of its Land Value, 1830-1933*. Chicago, 1933.

351 Hubbard, Adolphus S. "List of Old Settlers," [Chicagoans who came between January 1831 and December 1836; pp. 424-33] *in* Rufus Blanchard's *Discovery and Conquest of the North-West, with the History of Chicago*.

352 Hubbard, Gurdon Saltonstall. Gurdon Saltonstall Hubbard Papers. Chicago Medical Society.

353 ___. *Incidents and Events in the Life of Gurdon Saltonstall Hubbard*. Collected from personal narrations and other sources and arranged by his nephew, Henry E. Hamilton. Chicago, 1888.

354 ___. *The Autobiography of Gurdon Saltonstall Hubbard: Pa-pa-ma-ta-be, "The Swift Walker."* Chicago, 1911.

355 Hulbert, Archer Butler. *Portage Paths: The Keys to the Continent*. Cleveland, 1903.

356 Hurd, Harvey B., LL.D., and Robert D. Sheppard, D.D., eds. *History of Evanston*. Chicago, 1906.

357 Hurlbut, Henry H. *Chicago Antiquities: Comprising Original Items and Relations, Letters, Extracts, and Notes, pertaining to Early Chicago; embellished with Views, Portraits, Autographs, etc*. Chicago, 1881.

358 Hutton, Paul A. "William Wells, Frontier Scout and Indian Agent." *Indiana Magazine of History* 74, no. 3, September 1978.

359 Hyde, James Nevins, A.M., M.D. "Early Medical Chicago: An Historical Sketch of the First Practitioners of Medicine; with the Present Faculties, and Graduates Since Their Organization of the Medical Colleges of Chicago." *Fergus Historical Series* 11, 1879.

360 Illinois Centennial Association. *The Centennial History of Illinois*. Edited by C.W. Alvord. Springfield, 1919.

361 Imbrie, John, and Katherine Palmer Imbrie. *Ice Ages: Solving the Mystery*. Cambridge, Mass./London, 1979.

362 ***Impartial Enquiry into the Right of the French King to the Territory West of the Great River Mississippi, in North America, Not Ceded by the Preliminaries, Including a Summary Account of That River, and the Country Adjacent; With a Short Detail of the Advantages it Possesses, It's Native Commodities, and How Far They Might Be Improved to the Advantage of the British Commerce. Comprehending a Vindication of*** *the English Claim to That Whole Continent, From Authentic Records, and Indisputable Historical Facts; and Particular Directions to Navigators for Entering the Several Mouths of That Important River*. London, 1762.

363 Ingals, E. Fletcher. *The Life and Works of Daniel Brainard*. Chicago, 1912.

364 Irons, Ernest E., M.D., Ph.D. *The Story of Rush Medical College*. Chicago: Lakeside Press, 1953.

365 Jackson, Donald, ed. *Life of Ma-ka-tai-me-she-kia-kiak or Black Hawk: an autobiography*. Urbana, Ill., 1990.

366 James, Edmund J. *The Territorial Records of Illinois*. Springfield, 1901.

367 Jefferson, Joseph. *The Autobiography of Joseph Jefferson*. New York, 1889.

368 Jefferys, Thomas. *The Natural and Civil History of the French Dominions in North and South America. Giving a Particular Account of the Climate, Soil, Minerals, Animals, Vegetables, Manufactures, Trade, Commerce, Genius, Character, Manners and Customs of the Indians and Other Inhabitants*. London, 1760.

369 Jenison, Marguerite. See Pease, Theodore Calvin, and Marguerite Jenison.

370 Jennings, Jesse D. *Prehistory of North America*. New York, 1974.

371 Jensen, George P. *Historic Chicago Sites*. Chicago, 1953.

372 *Jesuit Relations and Allied Documents*. See Thwaites, Reuben Gold; Kenton, Edna.

373 Jeter, Helen R. *Trends of Population in the Region of Chicago*. Chicago, 1927.

374 Jetté, René. *Dictionaire Généalogique des Familles du Québec des Origins à 1730*. Montreal, 1983.

375 Jewell, Frank. *Annotated Bibliography of Chicago History*. Chicago, 1979.

376 Johnson, Allen. See Malone, Dumas, and Allen Johnson, eds.

377 Johnson, Charles B. *Growth of Cook County*. Vol. 1. Chicago, 1960.

378 Johnson, William. "Notes of a Tour from Fort Wayne to Chicago, 1809." Chicago Historical Society.

379 Jones, Abner D. *Illinois and the West. With a Township Map, Containing the Latest Surveys and Improvements*. Boston, 1838.

380 Jones, Martha Kirker. *Bensenville*. Bensenville, Ill., 1975.

381 Jones, Peter d'A. See Holli, Melvin G., and Peter d'A. Jones, eds.

382 Jordan, Orvis F. *A History of Park Ridge*. Park Ridge, Ill., 1961.

383 Jouan, Henri. "Jean Nicolet, Interpreter and Voyager in Canada 1618-1642." Translated by Grace Clark. *Wisconsin Historical Collections* 11, 1888.

384 Joutel, Henri. *A Journal of the Last Voyage Perform'd by Monsr. de la Sale, to the Gulph of Mexico, to Find Out the Mouth of the Mississippi River, etc*. 1st English ed. London, 1714.

385 ___. "Relation de Henri Joutel." *Découvertes et établissements des Français dans l'ouest et le sud de l'Amerique Septentrionale*. Vol. 3. Edited by M. Pierre Margry. Paris, 1878.

386 Judge, Joseph. "Where Columbus Found the New World." *National Geographic Magazine* 170, November 1986, p. 566.

387 Kappler, Charles, ed. *Indian Treaties 1778-1883*. Vol. 2. Washington, D.C.: U.S. Government Printing Office, 1904. Reprint, New York, 1972.

388 Karamanski, Theodore J. See Grossman, Joanne, and Theodore J. Karamanski, eds.

389 ___. See Mendes, Joel, and Theodore J. Karamanski, eds.

390 Karpinski, Louis C. *Bibliography of Printed Maps of Michigan 1804-1880. With a series of*

over one hundred Reproductions of maps constituting an historical atlas of the Great Lakes and Michigan. Lansing, 1931.

391 **Karrow, Robert W., and David Buisseret.** *Gardens of Delight: Maps and Travel Accounts of Illinois and the Great Lakes from the Collection of Herman Dunlop Smith.* Chicago: Newberry Library, 1984.

392 **Karrow, Robert W., Jr.** *Mapmakers of the Sixteenth Century and Their Maps. Bio-Bibliographies of the Cartographers of Abraham Ortelius, 1570.* Chicago, 1993.

393 **Kaufman, Kevin, ed.** *The Mapping of the Great Lakes in the Seventeenth Century.* Providence, R.I., 1989.

394 **Keating, William Hypolitus.** *Narrative of an Expedition to the Source of the St. Peter's River, Lake Winnepeek, Lake of the Woods, &c., &c. Performed in the Year 1823, by Order of the Hon. J.C. Calhoun, Secretary of War, Under the Command of Stephen H. Long, Major U.S.T.E.* 2 vols. Philadelphia, 1824; London, 1825.

395 **Kelley, John.** "From the Tales of an 1822 Chicagoan." *Journal of the State of Illinois Historical Society* 14, 1921-1922.

396 **Kellogg, Louise Phelps.** *The French Regime in Wisconsin and the Northwest.* Madison, 1925.

397 ___. *The British Regime in Wisconsin and the Northwest.* Madison, 1935.

398 **Kellogg, Louise Phelps, ed.** *Early Narratives of the Northwest (1654-1699).* New York, 1917.

399 **Kenton, Edna, ed.** *The Jesuit Relations and Allied Documents, Selections.* New York, 1954. See also Thwaites, Reuben Gold.

400 **Kingsbury, Jacob.** Col. Jacob Kingsbury Papers. Chicago Historical Society.

401 **Kingston, John T.** *Early Western Days.* Madison, 1876.

402 **Kinietz, W. Vernon.** *The Indians of the Western Great Lakes, 1615-1760.* Ann Arbor, 1940.

403 **Kinney, Janet, M.D.** *Saga of a Surgeon – The Life of Daniel Brainard, M.D.* Springfield, 1987.

404 **Kinzie, John.** "Account Books, Sept. 30, 1803 to Feb. 24, 1822, Chicago." Rev. William Barry's transcript (notation by Gurdon Hubbard), Chicago Historical Society.

405 **Kinzie, Mrs. John H.** (Juliette Augusta [Magill]). "Narrative of the Massacre at Chicago, Saturday, August 15, 1812, and of some Preceding Events." *Fergus Historical Series* 30, 1844.

406 ___. *Wau-Bun. The "Early Days" in the North-West.* Chicago, 1856, 1857, 1901, 1932.

407 ___. *Narrative of the Massacre at Chicago, Saturday, August 15, 1812, and of some Preceding Events.* 2nd ed. Chicago, 1914.

408 **Kirkland, Caroline.** *Chicago Yesterdays, A Sheaf of Reminiscences.* Chicago, 1919.

409 **Kirkland, Caroline Matilda Stansbury.** *A New Home – Who'll Follow? Or, Glimpses of Western Life.* New York, 1841.

410 **Kirkland, Joseph.** *The Story of Chicago.* Chicago, 1892-1894.

411 ___. *The Chicago Massacre of 1812. A Historical and Biographical Narrative of Fort Dearborn (now Chicago). How the fort and city were begun, and who were the beginners. With Illustrations and Historical Documents.* Chicago, 1893.

412 ___. See Moses, John, and Joseph Kirkland.

413 **Knight, Robert, and Lucius H. Zeuch, M.D.** *The Location of the Chicago Portage Route of the Seventeenth Century.* Chicago, 1928.

414 ___. "Mount Joliet: Its Place in Illinois History and Its Location." Lecture given at a special meeting of the Illinois State Historical Society at Joliet, Ill., October 30-31, 1929.

415 **Knoblauch, Marion, ed.** *DuPage County, A Descriptive and Historical Guide, U.S. Federal Writers' Project.* Elmhurst, 1948.

416 **Koerner, Gustave Philip.** *Memoirs of Gustave Koerner 1809-1896.* 2 vols. Edited by Thomas J. McCormack. Cedar Rapids, Iowa, 1909.

417 **Kohl, J.G.** "Eine Deutsche Ansiedlung bei Chicago." *Der Deutsche Pionier* 13, 1881.

418 **Krenkel, John H.** *Illinois Internal Improvements 1818-1848.* Cedar Rapids, Iowa, 1958.

419 **Kurz and Allison, publisher.** *Chicago in Early Days, 1779-1857.* Chicago, 1893.

420 **Lahontan, Louis Armand de Lom d'Arce, baron de.** *Voyages du baron de Lahontan dans l'Amerique Septentrionale … [and] Memoires de l'Amerique Septentrionale.* 2 vols. Amsterdam. 1705.

421 ___. *New Voyages to North America (in the years 1683-1694).* Edited by Reuben G. Thwaites. Chicago, 1905.

422 **Larsen, Curtis E.** *Geological History of Glacial Lake Algonquin and the Upper Great Lakes.* Washington, D.C., 1987.

423 **Larson, John W.** *Those Army Engineers, A History of the Chicago District U.S. Army Corps of Engineers.* Chicago, 1979.

424 **La Salle, Cavelier de.** *Relation of the Discoveries and Voyages of Cavelier de La Salle from 1679 to 1681. The Official Narrative.* Translated by Melville B. Andersen. Chicago, 1901. See also Joutel, Henri; Tonty, Henri de.

425 **Latrobe, Charles J.** *The Rambler in North America, 1832-1833.* London, 1835, 1836.

426 **Laut, Agnes C.** *Cadillac: Knight Errant of the Wilderness; Founder of Detroit; Governor of Louisiana from the Great Lakes to the Gulf.* Indianapolis, 1931.

427 **Law, Judge John.** *The Colonial History of Vincennes, under the French, British and American Governments, from its First Settlement down to the Territorial Administration of Gen. William Henry Harrison, with Additional Notes and Illustrations.* Vincennes, Ind., 1839, 1858.

428 **Lea, Isaac, and Henry Charles Carey.** *The Geography, History, and Statistics, of America, and the West Indies; exhibiting a correct account of the discovery, settlement, and progress of the various kingdoms, states, and provinces of the western hemisphere, to the year 1822.* Philadelphia, 1822.

429 **Lee, George Robert.** *The Beaubiens of Chicago.* Canton, Mo., 1973.

430 **Legler, Henry E.** "Chevalier Henry de Tonty." *Parkman Club Publications* (Milwaukee) no. 3, 1896.

430a **Le Moyne d'Iberville, Pierre.** *Iberville's Gulf Journals.* Tuscaloosa, Ala., 1981.

431 **LePage du Pratz, Antoine Simon.** *Histoire de la Louisiane, Contenant la Découverte de ce Vaste Pays; sa Description Géographiqhe, ….* Paris, 1758.

432 **Lewis, Lloyd, and Henry Justin Smith.** *Chicago: The History of Its Reputation.* Chicago, 1929.

433 **Lewis, Meriwether, and William Clark.** *History of the Expedition under the Command of Captains Lewis and Clark 1804-5-6.* 2 vols. Philadelphia/New York, 1814. Reprint, Dayton, 1840; New York, 1893; New York/London, 1904; Boston, 1953.

434 **Liette, Pierre.** See Cadillac, Sieur de Lamothe and Liette, Pierre.

435 Lindell, Arther G. *Chicago's Corporate Seal*. Chicago, 1962.

436 Long, John. *Voyages and Travels of an Indian Interpreter and Trader, Describing the Manners and Customs of the North American Indians; with an account of the posts situated on the River Saint Laurence, Lake Ontario, &c. To which is added a vocabulary of the Chippeway language....* London, 1791.

436a Long, John H., ed., and Stephen L. Hansen. *Historical Atlas and Chronology of County Boundaries, 1788-1980*. Vol. 2. Boston, Mass., 1984.

436b Long, John H., ed., and Peggy Tuck Sinko. *Atlas of Historical Boundaries · Indiana*. Scholl Center for Family and Community History, Newberry Library. New York, 1996.

436c Long, John H., ed., and Gordon Den Boer. *Atlas of Historical Boundaries · Illinois*. Scholl Center for Family and Community History, Newberry Library. New York, 1997.

437 Long, Maj. L. [Stephen] H. Letter to George Graham, Esq. *The National Register* 3, no. 13, March 29, 1817, pp. 193-98.

438 [Louisiana] *Ausführliche Historische und Geographische Beschreibung des an dem großen Flusse Mississippi in Nord-America gelegenen herrlichen Landes Louisiana; In welches die neu-aufgerichtete Französische große Indianische Compagnie Colonien zu schicken angefangen*. Leipzig, 1720.

439 Luzerne, Frank. *The Lost City! Drama of the Fire Fiend, or, Chicago, as it was, and as it is! And its glorious future!* New York, 1872.

440 Mack, Edwin F. *Old Monroe Street*. Chicago, 1914.

441 MacMillan, Thomas C. *The Scotts and Their Descendants in Illinois*. Springfield, 1922.

442 Malone, Dumas, and Allen Johnson, eds. *Dictionary of American Biography*. Vols. 1-20. New York, 1928-1936.

443 Mannhardt, E. "Die Ersten Beglaubigten Deutschen in Chicago." *Deutsch-Amerikanische Geschichtsblätter* 1, 1901.

444 ___. *Chicago und sein Deutschtum*. Cleveland, 1901-1902.

445 Mansfield, John Brandt, ed. *History of the Great Lakes, Illustrated*. Chicago, 1899.

446 Marcou, Jules. *Nuevas Investigationes Sobre el Origen del Nombre América*. Managua, 1888.

447 Marden, Luis. "The First Landfall of Columbus." *National Geographic Magazine* 170, November 1986, p. 572.

448 Margry, M. Pierre, ed. *Découvertes et établissements des Français dans l'ouest et le sud de l'Amerique Septentrionale (1614-1754)*. 6 vols. Paris, 1879-1886.

449 Marino, Joseph. See Sanders, William T., and Joseph Marino.

450 Marshall, James A. "Rise and Progress of Chicago: An Address Read Before the Centennial Library Association, March 21, 1876." *Fergus Historical Series* 9, 1876.

451 Marshall, James A. "Geometry of the Hopewell Earthworks." *Early Man, an Archaeological Quarterly* spring 1979.

452 ___. "Prehistoric Chicagoland." Lecture before the Central States Anthropological Society Annual Meeting. Covington, Ky., 1996.

453 Martineau, Harriet. *Society in America*. London, 1837.

454 ___. "Chicago in 1836: 'Strange Early Days.' " *Fergus Historical Series* 9, 1876.

455 Mason, Edward G. "Illinois in the Eighteenth Century. Kaskaskia and its Parish Records: Old Fort Chartres: and Col. John Todd's Record Book." *Fergus Historical Series* 12, 1881.

456 Mason, Edward G., ed. *Early Chicago and Illinois*. Chicago, 1890.

457 Matsell, George Washington. *Vocabulum; or The rogue's lexicon*. New York, 1859.

458 Matson, Nehemiah. *Reminiscences of Bureau County*. Princeton, Ill., 1872.

459 ___. *French and Indians of the Illinois River*. Princeton, Ill., 1874.

460 ___. *Memories of Shaubena. With Incidents Relating to the Early Settlement of the West*. Chicago, 1878. Reprint, *Bulletin of the Chicago Historical Society* August 1935.

461 ___. *Pioneers of Illinois*. Chicago, 1882.

462 Mayer, Harold M. "The Launching of Chicago: The Situation and the Site." *Chicago History* 9, no. 2, summer 1980.

463 Mayer, Harold M., and Richard C. Wade. *Chicago: Growth of a Metropolis*. Chicago, 1969.

464 McAfee, Robert B. *History of the Late War in the Western Country*. Lexington, Ky., 1816.

465 McClure, James Baird, publisher. *Stories and Sketches of Chicago*. Chicago, 1884.

466 McConnell, Edward. Letter, 1835, *in* Henry Dummer Papers. Illinois State Historical Library, Springfield, Ill.

467 McCormick, Col. Robert R. "Old Cahokia." *Chicago Tribune* Sec. 1, p. 24, May 15, 1949.

468 McCoy, Isaac. *History of Baptist Indian Missions – embracing remarks on the former and present condition of the aboriginal tribes, their settlement within the Indian Territory, and their future prospects*. Washington, D.C., 1840.

469 McCulloch, David, ed. "History of Peoria County," *in Historical Encyclopedia of Illinois*. Chicago/Peoria, 1902.

470 McDermott, John Francis. *Old Cahokia: A Narrative and Documents illustrating the First Century of its History*. St. Louis, 1949.

471 McEvedy, Colin. *The Penguin Atlas of North American History to 1870*. Hong Kong, 1988.

472 McIlvaine, Mabel. *Chicago, Her History and Her Adornment*. Chicago, 1927.

473 McIlvaine, Mabel, ed. *Reminiscences of Early Chicago, with an Introduction by Mabel McIlvaine*. Chicago, 1912.

474 McIntosh, James T. See Monroe, Haskell M., Jr., and James T. McIntosh, eds.

475 McKenney, Thomas L. *History of the Indian Tribes of North America, with Biographical Sketches and Anecdotes of the Principal Chiefs. Embellished with One Hundred Portraits from the Indian Gallery in the War Department of Washington*. Philadelphia, 1870.

476 McLear, Patrick Edward. "Speculation, Promotion, and the Panic of 1837 in Chicago." *Journal of the Illinois State Historical Society* 62, no. 2, summer 1969, pp. 135-46.

477 ___. "Chicago and the Growth of a Region, 1832 Through 1848" [Ph.D. diss., University of Missouri, 1974]. Ann Arbor, 1990.

478 McLellan, Hugh, ed. See Thomas Nye's *Two Letters*.

479 McMurtrie, Douglas Crawford. *The First Printers of Chicago*. Chicago, 1927.

480 ___. *Chicago Imprints, 1835-1850*. Chicago, 1944.

481 McNamee, Tom. See Hayner, Don, and Tom McNamee.

482 McVicker, J.H. "The Theatre: Its Early Days In Chicago." Paper read before the Chicago Historical Society, February 19, 1884.

483 McWilliams, Richebourg Gaillard. *Iberville's Gulf Journals*. Tuscaloosa, Ala., 1981.

484 Meehan, Thomas. "Jean Baptiste Point du Sable, the First Chicagoan." *Journal of the Illinois State Historical Society* 56, no. 3, autumn 1963.

485 Mendes, Joel, and Theodore J. Karamanski, eds. *The Maritime History of Chicago*. Chicago, 1990.

486 Meyer, Alfred H. "Circulation and Settlement Patterns of the Calumet Region of North-

western Indiana and Northern Illinois (The First Stage of Occupation – the Pottawatomie and the Fur Trader, 1830)." *Annals of the American Association of Geographers* 44, 1954.

487 **Michelson, David M.** See Hansel, Ardith K., and David M. Michelson.

488 **Miller, Andrew.** *New States and Territories, or, The Ohio, Indiana, Illinois, Michigan, Northwestern, Missouri, Louisiana, Mississippi and Alabama in their real characters, in 1818.* Keene, N.H., 1819.

489 **Miller, Donald L.** *City of the Century: The Epic of Chicago and the Making of America.* New York, 1996.

490 **Miller, J.C.** *Riverside, Then and Now.* Riverside, 1936.

491 **Mitchell, Harley Bradford.** *Historical Fragments of Early Chicagoland.* Chicago, 1928.

492 **Mitchell, Samuel Augustus.** *Illinois in 1937; A Sketch Descriptive of the Situation, Boundaries, Face of the Country, Prominent Districts, Prairies, Rivers, Minerals, Animals, Agricultural Productions, Public Lands, Plans of Internal Improvement, Manufacturers, etc. of the State of Illinois: Also Suggestions to Emigrants, Sketches of the Counties, Cities, and Principal Towns of the State: Together with a Letter on the Cultivation of the Prairies by the Hon. H.L. Ellsworth. To Which are Annexed the Letters from a Rambler in the West.* Philadelphia, 1837.

493 **Monette, John W.** *History of the Discovery and Settlement of the Valley of the Mississippi, ….* New York, 1848.

494 **Monroe, Haskell M., Jr., and James T. McIntosh, eds.** *The Papers of Jefferson Davis, 1800-1840.* Vol. 1. Baton Rouge, La., 1971.

495 **Moody, Walter D.** *What of the City?* Chicago, 1919.

496 **Moore, Powell A.** *The Calumet Region, Indiana's Last Frontier.* Indianapolis, 1959.

497 **Morgan, Moses.** Narrative *in* William Richard Head Papers. Chicago Historical Society.

497a **Morison, Samuel Eliot.** *Admiral of the ocean sea, a life of Christopher Columbus.* Boston, 1942.

497b ___, with Mauricio Obregón. *The Caribbean as Columbus Saw It.* Boston, 1964.

498 **Moses, John, and Joseph Kirkland.** *History of Chicago.* Chicago/New York, 1895.

499 **Moskovitz, Denise Pagel, ed.** *Chicago Ancestor File 1974-1984.* Chicago Genealogical Society. Chicago, 1985.

500 **Motley, Archie.** "Manuscript Sources on Frontier Chicago." *Chicago History* 9, no. 2, summer 1980.

501 **Munsell, Joel.** *The Typographical Miscellany.* Albany, N.Y., 1850.

502 **Münster, Sebastian.** *Cosmographey: das ist Beschreibung aller Laender Herrschaften und fuernemsten Stetten des gantzen Erdbodens samt ihren Gelegenheiten Eygenschaften Religion Gebraeuchen Geschichten und Handtierungen &c. Erstlich durch Herrn Sebastian Münster mit grosser Arbeit in sechs Buecher verfasset: Demnach an Welt vnd natuerlichen Historien durch Ihne selbst gebessert: Jetzt aber mit allerley Gedechnuswirdigen Sachen bis ins M.D.XCIII Jar gemehret mit newen Landtaflen vieler Stetten vnd Fuernemmen Maennern Contrafacturen Waapen vnd Geburtslinien so vber die alten Herzukommen gezieret.* Basel, 1598.

503 **Murphy, Edmund R.** *Henry de Tonty: Fur Trader of the Mississippi.* Baltimore, 1941.

504 **Nebenzahl, Kenneth.** *Atlas of Columbus and the Great Discoveries.* Chicago, 1990.

505 **Newcomb, Rexford.** "Beginnings of Architecture in Illinois." *Journal of the Illinois State Historical Society* 39, 1946.

506 **Norris, James Wellington.** *General Directory and Business Advertiser of the City of Chicago, for the Year 1844; together with a Historical Sketch and Statistical Account, to the Present Time.* Chicago, 1844.

507 **Nye, Thomas.** *Two Letters of Thomas Nye Relating to a Journey from Montreal to Chicago in 1837.* Edited by Hugh McLellan. Champlain, N.Y., 1931.

508 ___. *Journal of Thomas Nye Written during a Journey between Montreal and Chicago in 1837.* Champlain, N.Y., 1932.

509 **O'Connor, Mary H.** "Potawatomie Land Cessions in the Old Northwest." Master's thesis, Cornell University, Ithaca, N.Y., 1943.

510 **Ogg, Frederic Austin.** *The Old Northwest.* New Haven, Conn., 1919.

511 **Oliver, William.** *Eight Months in Illinois; with Information to Immigrants.* Newcastle upon Tyne, 1843; Chicago, 1924.

512 **Ordinance for the Government of the Northwest Territory.** New York, July 13, 1787. *Journals of the Continental Congress,* vol. 4, pp. 752-54; see also Francis N. Thorpe, *The Federal and State Constitutions,....* [660a, p. 957 ff.]

513 **Ordinances.** See Statutes for territories, 632a and 632b.

514 **Otis, Philo Adams.** *The First Presbyterian Church 1833-1913, A History of the Oldest Organization in Chicago.* Chicago, 1900.

514a **Pacyga, Dominic A.** See Holt, Glen E., and Dominic A. Pacyga.

515 **Palmer, John M., ed.** *The Bench and Bar of Illinois, Historical and Reminiscent.* Vol. 2. Chicago, 1890.

516 **Parker, Amos Andrew.** *Trip to the West and Texas, Comprising a Journey of 8,000 Miles, Through New York, Michigan, Illinois, Missouri, Louisiana and Texas, in the Autumn of 1834 to 1835.* Concord/Boston, 1836.

517 **Parkman, Francis.** *France and England in North America.* Boston, 1865-1892.

518 ___. *The Jesuits in North America in the Seventeenth Century.* Boston, 1870.

519 ___. *La Salle and the Discovery of the Great West.* Boston, 1897.

520 **Patterson, J.B.** *Life of Ma-Ka-Tai-Me-She Kia-Kiak or Black Hawk, Embracing the Traditions of His Nation – Indian Wars, &c., With an Account of the Cause and General History of the Late War, His Surrender and Confinement at Jefferson Barracks, and Travels through the United States. Dictated by Himself.* 2nd ed. Boston, 1834.

521 **Pattison, William D.** "Beginnings of the American Rectangular Land Survey System, 1784-1800." University of Chicago, Department of Geography research paper N. 50, 1957.

522 **Pease, Theodore Calvin.** *The Frontier State, 1818-1848.* Springfield, 1908; Chicago, 1918, 1922.

523 ___. *The History of Illinois.* Chicago, 1925.

524 **Pease, Theodore Calvin, and Marguerite Jenison.** *George Rogers Clark and the Revolution in Illinois, 1763-1787.* Springfield, 1929.

525 **Pease, Theodore Calvin, and Ray Werner, eds.** "The French Foundations, 1860-1893." *Collections of the Illinois State Historical Library* 23, 1934.

526 ___. "Illinois on the Eve of the Seven Year's War, 1747-1755." *Collections of the Illinois Historical Library* 29, 1940.

527 **Peck, John Mason.** *A Guide for Emigrants, containing Sketches of Illinois, Missouri and the adjacent Parts.* Boston, 1831.

528 ___. Letter to Alexander F. Grant, February 17, 1834. Chicago Historical Society.

529 ___. *A Gazetteer of Illinois*. Boston, 1834.

530 **Peckham, Howard H.** *Old Fort Michilimackinac at Mackinaw City, Michigan*. Ann Arbor, 1938.

531 ___. See Brown, Lloyd A., and Howard H. Peckham, eds.

532 **Petersen, Eugene T.** *France at Mackinac. A pictorial record of French life and culture 1715-1760*. Mackinac Island, Mich., 1968.

533 **Peterson, Jacqueline.** "Ethnogenesis: Metis Development and Influence in the Great Lakes, 1690-1836." Ph.D. diss., University of Illinois at Chicago, 1977.

534 ___. " 'Wild Chicago': The Formation and Destruction of a Multiracial Community on the Midwestern Frontier," *in* Melvin G. Holli's and Peter d'A. Jones's *The Ethnic Frontier: Essays in the History of Group Survival in Chicago and the Midwest*.

535 ___. "Goodbye, Madore Beaubien: The Americanization of Early Chicago Society." *Chicago History* 9, no. 2, summer 1980.

536 ___. "The Founding Fathers: The Approach of French-Indian Chicago 1816-1837," *in* Melvin G. Holli's and Peter d'A. Jones's *Ethnic Chicago*.

537 ___. *New Peoples · Being and Becoming Metis in North America*. Lincoln, Nebr., 1985.

537a **Peto, S. Morton.** *The Resources and Prospects of America*. London/New York, 1866.

538 **Petraitis, Paul W.** "The Road Not Taken – Vanishing Transportation Routes in the Chicago Area." *Conscious Choice*, Wild Onion Alliance. Chicago, c.1992.

539 **Peyster, Arent Schuyler de.** See De Peyster, Col. Arent Schuyler.

540 **Phillips, George S.** *Chicago and Her Churches*. Chicago, 1868.

541 **Phillips, Paul Chrisler.** *The Fur Trade*. Norman, Okla., 1961.

542 **Piehl, Frank J.** "Shall We Gather at the River." *Chicago History* 2, no. 4, 1973, p. 196.

543 **Pierce, Bessie Louise.** *As Others See Chicago: Impressions of Visitors, 1673 to 1933*. Chicago, 1933.

544 ___. *A History of Chicago (1673 to 1893)*. 3 vols. New York, 1937-1957; rev. ed., Chicago, 1975.

545 **Pinkerton, John, ed.** *A general collection of the best and most interesting voyages and travels in all parts of the world....* London, 1812.

546 **Plumb, Ralph Gordon.** *History of Navigation of the Great Lakes*. Washington, D.C., 1911.

547 **Poole, Ernest.** *Giants Gone; Men Who made Chicago*. New York/London, 1943.

548 **Pooley, William Vipond.** *The Settlement of Illinois from 1830 to 1850*. Madison, 1908.

549 **Porter, Rev. Jeremiah.** Letter to Rev. Hovey, August 27, 1833. Chicago Historical Society.

550 ___. "The Earliest Religious History of Chicago: An Address Read before the Chicago Historical Society in 1859." *Fergus Historical Series* 14, 1881.

551 *Potter's American Monthly Magazine* May 1876.

552 **Powell, John Wesley.** *Linguistic Stocks of American Indians North of Mexico*. Washington, D.C., 1891.

553 **Pratt, Harry E., ed.** "John Dean Caton's Reminiscences of Chicago in 1833 and 1834." *Journal of the Illinois State Historical Society* 28, no. 1, 1935.

554 **Prescott, Willian H.** *Ferdinand and Isabella*. Philadelphia, 1837.

555 **Prucha, Francis Paul.** *A Guide to the Military Posts of the United States, 1789-1895*. Madison, 1964.

556 **Prussing, Eugene E.** *Chicago's First Great Lawsuit*. Madison, 1915.

557 **Putnam, James William.** *The Illinois and Michigan Canal*. Chicago, 1918.

558 **Quaife, Milo Milton.** "Some Notes on the Fort Dearborn Massacre." Mississippi Valley Historical Association, *Proceedings for the Year 1910-1911*. Cedar Rapids, Iowa, 1912.

559 ___. *Chicago and the Old Northwest, 1673-1835. A Study of the Evolution of the Northwestern Frontier, together with a History of Fort Dearborn*. Chicago, 1913.

560 ___. *The Development of Chicago 1674 to 1914, Shown in a Series of Contemporary Original Narratives*. Chicago: The Caxton Club, 1916.

561 ___. "The Story of James Corbin, A Soldier of Fort Dearborn." *Mississippi Valley Historical Review* 3, 1916-1917.

562 ___. "The Northwestern Career of Jefferson Davis." *Transactions of the Illinois Historical Society* 30, 1923.

563 ___. *Chicago Highways, Old and New, from Indian Trail to Motor Road*. Chicago, 1923; Ann Arbor, 1968.

564 ___. *Checagou: From Indian Wigwam to Modern City, 1637-1835*. Chicago, 1933.

565 ___. *Lake Michigan/The American Lakes Series*. Indianapolis, 1944.

566 **Quaife, Milo Milton, ed.** *Publications of the State Historical Society of Wisconsin*. Madison, 1916.

567 ___. "Documents: The Chicago Treaty of 1833." *Wisconsin Magazine of History* 1, no. 1, 1917.

568 ___. *Pictures from Illinois One-Hundred Years Ago*. Chicago, 1918.

569 ___. "Documents: Property of Jean Baptiste Point Sable," *Mississippi Valley Historical Review* 15, 1928, pp. 89-96.

570 ___. "Documents: General James Wilkinson's Narrative of the Fallen Timbers Campaign." *Mississippi Valley Historical Review* 16, 1929, pp. 81-90.

571 ___. *History of the Ordinance of 1787 and the Old Northwest Territory*. Marietta, Ohio, 1937.

572 ___. *The Siege of Detroit in 1763 – The Journal of Pontiac's Conspiracy and John Rutherfurd's Narrative of a Captivity*. Chicago, 1958.

573 **Quimby, George I.** *Indian Life in the Upper Great Lakes*. Chicago, 1961.

574 **Quinn, D.B.** See Cumming, W.P., R.A. Skelton, and D.B. Quinn.

575 **Rathbun, Mary Yeater.** *The Illinois and Michigan Canal*. Springfield, 1980.

576 **Rawlings, Eleanor C.** "Wygnancy Polscy w Illinois." Illinois State Historical Society, *Report*, May 12, 1927.

577 **Rawlings, Isaac D., M.S., M.D.** *The Rise and Fall of Disease in Illinois*. Springfield, 1927.

578 *Records of the American Catholic Society of Philadelphia*. (Philadelphia) 20, 1909, pp. 259-64.

578a *Records of the Bureau of Indian Affairs*, Record Groups 11, 75 [detailed *in* Archie Motley's "Manuscript Sources on Frontier Chicago"]. National Archives, Washington, D.C.

579 **Reed, Charles Bert, M.D.** *Masters of the Wilderness*. Chicago, 1814.

580 **Reeling, Viola Crouch.** *Evanston, Its Land and Its People*. Evanston, 1926.

581 **Repplier, Agnes.** *Père Marquette*. New York, 1929.

582 **Reps, John W.** *The Making of Urban America*. Princeton, 1986.

583 **Reynolds, John.** *My Own Times, Embracing also The History of My Life*. Chicago, 1879.

584 ___. *The Pioneer History of Illinois, Containing The Discovery In 1673 And The History Of The Country To The Year 1818, When The State Government Was Organized*. Belleville, Ill., 1852; Chicago, 1887.

585 **Rezek, Antoine Ivan.** *History of the Diocese of Sault Ste. Marie and Marquette Containing*

a Full and Accurate Account of the Development of the Catholic Church in Upper Michigan.... Houghton, Mich., 1906-1907.

586 **Richmond, C.W., and H.F. Valette.** *A History of the County of Du Page, Illinois.* Chicago, 1857.

587 **Roberts, Robert B.** *Encyclopedia of Historic Forts – The Military, Pioneer and Trading Posts of the United States.* New York/London, 1988.

588 **[Robinson, Alexander]** "Article on the life and times of Alexander Robinson, at the occasion of his recent death, based on earlier interviews with the deceased." *Chicago Tribune,* May 14, 1872.

589 **Robson, Charles, ed.** *The Biographical Encyclopædia of Illinois of the Nineteenth Century.* Philadelphia, 1875.

590 **Ross, Harvey Lee.** *The Early Pioneers and Pioneer Events of the State of Illinois.* Chicago, 1899.

591 **Rousseau, Jacques, and George W. Brown.** "The Indians of Northeastern North America." *in Dictionary of Canadian Biography.* Vol. 1. Toronto: University of Toronto Press, 1966.

592 **Rudd, Edward H.** *The Laws and Ordinances of the City of Chicago, Passed in Common Council. Chicago, 1839.* [contains the first business directory of Chicago; reprinted *in* Hurlbut's *Chicago Antiquities....*]

593 **Sabin, Joseph.** *A Dictionary of Books Relating to America, from its Discovery to the Present Time.* 29 vols. New York, 1886-1936.

594 **St. Clair, Arthur.** *The St. Clair Papers; The Life and Public Services of Arthur St. Clair, Soldier of the Revolutionary War; President of the Continental Congress; and Governor of the North-Western Territory. With his Correspondence and other Papers.* Edited by William Henry Smith. Cincinnati, 1882.

595 **[St. Clair County]** *History of St. Clair County, Illinois.* Philadelphia, 1881.

596 **Sanders, William T., and Joseph Marino.** *New World Prehistory/Archeology of the American Indian.* Englewood Cliffs, N.J., 1970.

596a **Saxe, Stephen O., ed.** *Specimen of Printing Types from the Boston Type and Stereotype Foundry, Samuel N. Dickinson, Printer.* Boston, 1832; rev. ed., New York, 1989.

597 **Scammon, Hon. J. Young, and Hon. Isaac N. Arnold,** *et al.* "Addresses Delivered at the Annual Meeting of the Chicago Historical Society, November 19th, 1868." *Fergus Historical Series* 10, 1877.

598 **Schick, L.** *Chicago and Its Environs, a Handbook for the Traveller.* Chicago, 1891.

599 **Schoolcraft, Henry Rowe.** *Narrative Journal of Travels Through the Northwestern Regions of the United States, extending from Detroit through the Great Chain of American Lakes, to the Sources of the Mississippi River, Performed as a Member of the Expedition under Governor Cass in the Year 1820.* Albany, N.Y., 1821; Ann Arbor, 1966.

600 ___. *Travels in the Central Portions of the Mississippi Valley: Comprising Observations on its Mineral, Geography, Internal Resources and Aboriginal Population. Performed under the Sanction of Government, in the Year 1821.* New York, 1825; Milwood, N.Y., 1975.

601 ___. *Notes on the Iroquois; Or Contributions to American History, Antiquities, and General Ethnology.* Albany, N.Y., 1847.

602 ___. *Personal Memoirs of a Residence of Thirty Years with the Indian Tribes on the American Frontier, with Brief Notices of Passing Events, Facts, and Opinions, A.D. 1812 to A.D. 1842.* Philadelphia, 1851.

603 ___. *Historical and Statistical Information Respecting the History, Condition and Prospects of the Indian Tribes of the United States.* 6 vols. Philadelphia, 1851-1857 [vol. 4 contains Schoolcraft's 1820 sketch of Chicago, adapted by Seth Eastman].

604 ___. *Summary Narrative of an Exploratory Expedition to the Source of the Mississippi River, in 1820: resumed and completed, by the Discovery of its Origin in Itaska Lake, in 1832, with Appendices.* Philadelphia, 1855.

605 **Schwartz, Seymour I., and Ralph E. Ehrenberg.** *The Mapping of America.* New York, 1980.

606 **[Scott, Willis]** "An Old Settler/Mr. Willis Scott's Reminiscences of Young Chicago." *Chicago Tribune,* November 12, 1875.

607 **Scott, Winfield.** *Memoirs of Lieutenant-General Scott, LL.D.* New York, 1864.

608 **Seeger, Eugene.** *Chicago, The Wonder City.* Chicago, 1893.

609 **Seelye, Elizabeth E.** *Tecumseh and the Shawnee Prophet.* Chicago, 1878.

610 **Shapiro, Dena.** "Indian Tribes and Trails in the Chicago Region." Master's thesis, University of Chicago, 1929.

611 **Shea, John Gilmary.** *Discovery and Exploration of the Mississippi Valley, with the Original Narratives of Marquette, Allouez, Membré, Hennepin, and Anastase Douay.* New York, 1853; Albany, N.Y., 1903.

612 ___. *History of the Catholic Missions Among the Indian Tribes of the United States, 1529-1854.* New York, 1855, 1973.

613 ___. *Early Voyages Up and Down the Mississippi by Cavelier, St. Cosme, Le Sueur, Gravier and Guignas, with an Introduction and an Index.* Albany, N.Y., 1861, 1902.

614 ___. Also see Charlevoix, P.F.X. de; Hennepin, Louis.

615 **Sheen, Dan R.** *Location of Fort Crevecoeur.* Peoria, 1919.

616 **Sheldon, Electra M.** *Early History of Michigan, From the First Settlement to 1815.* New York, 1846.

617 **Shenstone, William.** *The Poetical Works of Wm. Shenstone, Esqr.* Edinburgh, 1771.

617a **Sheppard, Robert D.** See Hurd, Harvey B., LL.D., and Robert D. Sheppard, D.D., eds.

618 **Shirreff, Patrick.** *A Tour Through North America; Together with a Comprehensive View of the Canadas and the United States, as Adapted for Agricultural Emigration.* Edinburgh, 1835.

619 **Simmons, Noah, M.D.** *Heroes and Heroines of the Fort Dearborn Massacre. Romantic and Tragic History of Corporal John Simmons and His Heroic Wife, Also of the First White Child Born in Chicago. The last Survivor of the Horrid Butchery. A Full and True Recital of Marvellous Fortitude, Matchless Courage and Terrible Suffering During the Battle, the March and the Captivity.* Lawrence, Kans., 1896.

620 **Simond, Charles, directeur.** " Chicago." *Bibliothèque Illustrée des Voyages autour du Monde par terre et par mer* 35, June 1898.

621 **Skelton, R.A.** See Cumming, W.P., R.A. Skelton, and D.B. Quinn.

622 ___. See Bagrow, Leo, and R.A. Skelton.

623 **Smith, Alice E.** *George Smith's Money – A Scottish Investor in America.* Madison, 1966.

624 **Smith, Alice E., ed.** *Guide to the Manuscripts of the Wisconsin Historical Society.* Madison, 1944.

625 **Smith, Dwight L., ed.** *From Greene Ville to Fallen Timbers.* Indianapolis, 1952.

626 **Smith, Herman Dunlop.** *The Des Plaines River, 1673 to 1940. A Brief Consideration of Its Names and History.* Lake Forest, Ill., 1940.

627 Smith, Henry Justin. See Lewis, Lloyd, and Henry Justin Smith.

628 Smith, William, M.D. Letter to James May, dated Fort Dearborn, December 9, 1803. Burton Historical Collection, Detroit Public Library.

629 Sparks, Jared. "Life of Father Marquette." *Library of American Biography*, 1st series. New York, 1848.

630 Sperry, F.M. *A Group of Distinguished Physicians and Surgeons of Chicago*. Chicago, 1904.

631 Sproat, Granville T. "Chicago Life in 1833." *Chicago Tribune*, December 12, 1886.

632 Stackhouse, Perry J. *Chicago and the Baptists, A Century of Progress*. Chicago, 1933.

632a Statute for the Illinois Territory, March 1, 1809. [684a, ch. 13 {1809}, pp. 514-15]

632b Statute for the Indiana Territory, July 4, 1800. [684a, ch. 41 {1800}, pp. 58-59]

633 Steck, Francis Borgia. *The Jolliet-Marquette Expedition*. Quincy, Ill., 1928.

634 ___. *Marquette Legends*. New York, 1960.

634a Stevens, Frank E. "Pierre La Sallier: Lee County's First White Settler." *Journal of the Illinois State Historical Society* 30, April 1937-January 1938, pp. 345-52.

635 Stevens, Frank E. *The Black Hawk War, including a Review of Black Hawk's Life*. Chicago, 1903.

636 Steward, John F. *Lost Maramech and Earliest Chicago*. Chicago, 1903.

637 ___. "Chicago – Origin of the Name of the City and the Old Portages." *Transactions of the Illinois Historical Society* 9, 1904, pp. 460-66.

638 Stoddard, Amos. *Sketches, Historical and Descriptive, of Louisiana*. Philadelphia, 1812.

639 Stoddard, Francis H. *The Life and Letters of Charles Butler*. New York, 1903.

640 Storm, Colton. "Lieutenant John Armstrong's Map of the Illinois River." *Journal of the Illinois State Historical Society* 37, 1944.

641 Storrow, Samuel Appleton. "Tour of the Northwest, 1817," *in* Milo Quaife's *The Development of Chicago 1674 to 1914, Shown in a Series of Contemporary Original Narratives*.

642 Straus, Terry, ed. *Indians of the Chicago Area*. Chicago, 1990.

643 Strong, William Duncan. *Indian Tribes of the Chicago Region*. Chicago, 1938.

643a Sturtevant, William C., ed. *Handbook of North American Indians*. Vols. 4-11, 15, 17. Washington, D.C.: Smithsonian Institution, 1988-1996.

644 Sutton, Robert P., ed. *The Prairie State. Colonial Years to 1860. A Documentary History of Illinois*. Grand Rapids, Mich., 1976.

645 Swagerty, William R., with John S. Aubrey. *America in 1492 · American Civilization on the Eve of the Columbus Voyage*. Chicago: Newberry Library, 1992.

646 Swearingen, James Strode. Journal, typescript; also copy of MS (original *in* Ross County [Ohio] Historical Society). Chicago Historical Society.

647 Swenson. John F. "Chicagoua/Chicago: The Origin, Meaning, and Etymology of a place name." *Illinois Historical Journal* 84, winter 1991, p. 235 ff.

648 ___. "A French Trader named Pagé: The Origin of DuPage." *DuPage History* 3, 1996.

649 ___. Personal communication with author.

650 Taliaferro, Lawrence. "Auto-Biography of Maj. Lawrence Taliaferro," *Collections of the Minnesota Historical Society* 6, 1894, pp. 189-255.

651 Tanner, Helen Hornbeck, ed. *Atlas of Great Lakes Indian History*. London/Norman, 1987.

652 Tanner, John. *A Narrative of the Captivity and Adventures of John Tanner*. New York, 1830.

653 Taylor, James. *Sketches of Some of the Early Settlers of the City of Chicago*. Chicago, 1876.

654 Taylor, Mrs. Charles A. "Diary." *Chicago Tribune*, September 20, 1903.

655 Temple, Wayne C. *Indian Villages of the Illinois Country – Historic Tribes*. Springfield, 1987.

656 ___. See Tucker, Sara Jones, and Wayne C. Temple.

656a *Territorial Papers of the United States*. Vols. 2, 3, 7, 8, 16, 17. Edited by Clarence E. Carter. Washington, D.C.: U.S. Government Printing Office, 1934-1948.

657 Thévenot, Melchisedech. *Recueil de Voyages. Dedié au Roy*. Paris, 1681. [includes *Carte de la decouverte faite l'an 1673 dans l'Amerique Septentrionale*, similar to and apparently drawn from the *Manitoumie* maps]

657a Thompson Bro's. & Burr, publisher. *Combination Atlas Map of DuPage County, Illinois*. Elgin, Ill., 1874. Reprint, DuPage County Historical Society, 1975.

658 Thompson, Joseph J. "The First Catholics in and about Chicago." *Illinois Catholic Historical Review* 3, January 1921.

659 ___. "Chicagou – the Grand Chief of the Illinois, Protonym of the Western Metropolis." *Illinois Catholic Historical Review* 7, 1924-1925.

660 Thompson, Richard A. *DuPage Roots*. DuPage Historical Society, 1985.

660a Thorpe, Francis Newton, ed. *The Federal and State Constitutions, Colonial Charters, and other organic Laws of State, Territories, and Colonies now or heretofore forming the United States of America*. Vol. 2. Washington, D.C.: U.S. Government Printing Office, 1909.

661 Thurston, Henry. *The Sanitary History of Chicago*. Chicago, 1901.

662 Thurston, John Gates. *A Journal of a trip to Illinois in 1836*. Mount Pleasant, Mich., 1971.

663 Thwaites, Reuben Gold. *Father Marquette*. New York, 1902.

664 ___. *France in America, 1497-1763*. New York, 1905.

665 Thwaites, Reuben Gold, ed. *The Jesuit Relations and Allied Documents Travels and Explorations of the Jesuit Missionaries in New France, 1610-1791*. (Cleveland) 73 vols. 1896-1901. Also see Kenton, Edna.

666 ___. *French Regime in Wisconsin*. Madison, 1902-1908.

667 ___. *Early Western Travels, 1748-1846, A Series of Annotated Reprints of Some of the Best and Rarest Contemporary Volumes of Travel, Descriptive of the Aborigines and Social and Economic Conditions in the Middle and Far West, During the Period of Early American Settlement*. 32 vols. Cleveland, 1904-1907.

668 ___. *Frontier Defense on the Upper Ohio, 1777-1778*. Madison, 1912.

669 ___. Also see Hennepin, Louis; Lahontan, baron de.

670 Tipton, John. *John Tipton Papers · Indiana Historical Collections*, Vol. 1, pp. 244-80. Indiana State Library, Indianapolis.

671 Todd, John Howard, A.B. *Illinois, "Thy Wondrous Story" A Collection of 365 Stories of Persons and Events covering the State's History from the Days of the French Explorers down to the Present*. Chicago, 1914.

672 Tonti, Henri, de. *Dernieres découvertes dans L'Amerique Septentrionale de M. de La Sale; mises au jour par M. le chevalier Tonti, gouverneur du Fort Saint Loüis, aux Islinous*. Paris, 1697.

673 ___. *An Account of Monsieur de la Salle's last Expedition and Discoveries in North America.... Made English from the Paris original*. London, 1698.

674 ___. *Relation of Henry Tonti Concerning the Explorations of La Salle from 1678 to 1683*.

Translated by Melville B. Anderson. Chicago: The Caxton Club, 1898.

675 **Tooke, Thomas, and William Newmarch.** *A History of Prices and of the State of the Circulation from 1792 to 1856.* 6 vols. London, 1838-1857; 2nd ed. with introduction by T.E. Gregory, London/New York, 1928.

676 **Tooley, R.V.** *Maps and Mapmakers.* New York, 1987.

677 **Towsley, Genevieve.** *Historic Naperville.* Naperville, 1975.

678 **Travis, Dempsey J.** *An Autobiography of Black Politics.* Chicago, 1987.

679 **[Treaty of Tordesillas, 1494]** *Tratado de limites das conquistas entre os muito altos, e ponderosos senhores D. Joao V. rey de Portugal, e D. Fernando VI. rey de Espanha, pelo qual abolida a demarcaado da linha meridiana, ajustada no Tratado de Tordesillas de 7. de junho de 1494, se determina individualmente a raya dos dominos de huma e outra coroa na America meridional.* Lisbon, 1750.

680 **Trudel, Marcel.** "New France, 1524-1713," *in Dictionary of Canadian Biography.* Vol. 1. Toronto: University of Toronto Press, 1966.

681 **Tucker, Sara J.** *Indian Villages of the Illinois Country. Part I, Atlas.* Springfield, 1942.

682 **Tucker, Sara Jones, and Wayne C. Temple.** *Atlas and Supplement, Indian Villages of the Illinois Country.* Springfield, 1991.

683 **Turner, Frederick Jackson.** "Character and Influence of the Indian Trade in Wisconsin. A Study of the Trading Post as an Institution." *Education, History, and Politics,* 9th ser., no. 11-12. John Hopkins University, Baltimore, Md., 1891. Reprint, Norman: University of Oklahoma Press, 1977.

684 **Tuttle, F.B.** "The Calumet Club," *in Rufus Blanchard's Discovery and Conquest of the Northwest, with the History of Chicago,* p. 735.

684a **United States.** *Statutes at Large of the United States of America, 1789-1873.* Vol. 2. Boston, Mass., 1845.

685 **United States Seventh Circuit Court For The Northern District of Illinois.** *Testimony in the Case George C. Bates vs. Illinois Central Rail Road Company.* Chicago, October term 1858; September term 1859. [Newberry Library, Chicago]

686 **Valette, H.F.** See Richmond, C.W., and H.F. Valette.

687 **Vandiveer, Clarence A.** *The Fur-Trade and Early Western Exploration.* Cleveland, 1929.

688 **VanStone, James W.** "Canadian Trade Silver From Indian Graves in Northern Illinois." *The Wisconsin Archeologist* 51, no. 1, March 1970, pp. 21-30.

689 **Varnum, Jacob Butler.** Journal, pertaining to his life and activity as factor at Fort Dearborn from 1816-1822. Chicago Historical Society.

690 **Vespucci, Amerigo.** See Waldseemüller, Martin.

690a **Vespucci, Amerigo.** *The Solderini Letter.* Strasburg, 1509.

691 **Vieau, Andrew J., Sr.** "Narrative of Andrew J. Vieau, Sr.," *Wisconsin Historical Collections* 11, 1888.

692 **Vierling, Philip E.** *A Self Guided Loop Hiking Trail to the Chicago Portage National Historic Site.* Chicago, 1973, 1974, 1988.

693 **Viger, Jacques.** "Ma Saberdache Rouge." F Archives du Séminaire des Missions Étrangeres. Quebec, 1844.

693a **Villiers du Terrage, Marc, baron de.** *Histoire de la Nouvelle Orléans (1717-1722).* Paris, 1917.

694 ___. *La découverte du Missouri et l'histoire du Fort d'Orléans (1673-1728).* Paris, 1925.

694a ___. *La Louisiane, histoire de son nom et ses frontières successives (1681-1819).* Paris, 1929.

694b ___. "Codex canadiensis," *Les raretés des Indes.* Paris, 1930.

695 **Viola, Herman J.** *Exploring the West.* Washington, D.C., 1987.

696 **Vogel, Virgil J.** "Mystery of Chicago's Name." *Mid-America* 40, July 1958.

697 ___. *Indian Place Names in Illinois.* Springfield, 1963.

698 **Wade, Richard C.** See Mayer, Harold M., and Richard C. Wade.

699 **Wakefield, John Allen.** *History of the War between the United States and the Sac and Fox Nations of Indians, and Parts of Other Disaffected Tribes of Indians, in the Years Eighteen Hundred and Twenty-Seven, Thirty-One, and Thirty-Two.* Jacksonville, Ill., 1834.

700 **Walton, Ivan H.** "Origin of Names of the Great Lakes." *Names Magazine* 3, December 1955.

700a **Wandschneider, Pauline.** See Dunham, Montrew, and Pauline Wandschneider.

701 **Wasson, Isabel B.** "A Village Grows up on a Sandbar." *Forest Leaves* (River Forest, Ill.), June 22, 1977.

702 **Waterman, Arba N.** *Historical Review of Chicago and Cook County.* 3 vols. Chicago/New York, 1908.

703 **Webb, George.** *Chronological List of Engagements Between the Regular Army of the United States and Various Tribes of Hostile Indians which Occured during the Years 1790 to 1898 Inclusive.* New York, 1976.

704 **Weik, Jesse W.** "An Unpublished Chapter in the Early History of Chicago. Reminiscences of James Bucklin, chief engineer of the Illinois and Michigan Canal." *Journal of the Illinois State Historical Society* 7, no. 4, January 1915.

705 **Wendt, Lloyd.** *Swift Walker. An Informal Biography of Gurdon Saltonstall Hubbard.* Chicago/Washington D.C., 1986.

706 **Wentworth, Hon. John, LL.D.** "Early Chicago: A Sunday Lecture Read in McCormick's Hall April 11, 1875; With Supplemental Notes." First lecture, *Fergus Historical Series* 8. Second lecture [May 6, 1876], *Fergus Historical Series* 7, 1876.

707 ___. *Reception to the Settlers of Chicago, prior to 1840, by the Calumet Club, May 27, 1879. Containing Club Members' Names; Origin of Reception; Record of Old Settlers invited; Reception; Speeches of Rev. Stephen R. Beggs, Gen. Henry Strong, Ex-Chief Justice John Dean Caton, Judge Henry W. Blodgett, Judge James Grant, Hon. John Wentworth, Judge Grant Goodrich, Hon. J. Young Scammon, and Hon. William Bross; Tables showing places of birth, year of arrival, and age of those who attended and signed Register; Appendix with letters from John Watkins, Norman K. Towner, Rev. Flavel Bascom, Major-General David Hunter, Judge Ebenezer Peck, Rev. Jeremiah Porter, and the names from whom brief letters of regret were received; Extracts from Chicago Tribune and Evening Journal; and Register of Old Settlers; with names, date of arrival, birthplace, age and present address.* Chicago, 1879.

708 ___. "Early Chicago. Fort Dearborn: An Address Delivered at the Unveiling of the Memorial Tablet to mark the Site of the Block-House, on Saturday Afternoon, May 21st, 1881, under the Auspices of the Chicago Historical Society, to which have been added Notes and an Appendix." *Fergus Historical Series* 16, 1881.

709 **Wentworth, Hon. John,** *et al.* "Chicago River-and-Harbor Convention; An account of Its Origin and Proceedings." *Fergus Historical Series* 18, 1882.

710 **Werner, Ray.** See Pease, Theodore Calvin, and Ray Werner, eds.

711 Western Historical Company, publisher. *History of Milwaukee, Wisconsin.* Chicago, 1881.

711a *Western Springs · A Centennial History of the Village 1886-1986.* The Western Springs Historical Society, Western Springs, Ill., 1985.

712 White, John J. *Arithmetic Simplified: Being a Plain, Practical System, Adapted to the Capacity of Youth, and Designed for the Use of Schools, in the United States.* Hartford, Conn., 1819.

713 White, Marian A. *Book of the Western Suburbs.* Chicago, 1912.

714 Whitney, Ellen M., ed. "The Black Hawk War, 1831-1832." *Illinois State Historical Library* vols. 36-38, spring 1973.

715 *Who Was Who in America · Historical Volume, 1607-1896.* Rev. ed. Chicago, 1967.

715a Widder, Keith. See Armour, David, and Keith Widder.

716 Wieser, R. von, Fr. See Fisher, Joseph S.J. and Fr. R. von Wieser.

717 Wildmann, U. *Bin ka Historica.* Jinotega, 1928.

718 Wilkie, William E. *Dubuque on the Mississippi, 1788-1988.* Dubuque, Iowa, 1987.

719 Will, Drake W. "The Medical and Surgical Practice of the Lewis and Clark Expedition." Reprint, *Journal of the History of Medicine and Allied Sciences* 1959, pp. 273-97.

720 Willman, H.B. *Summary of the Geology of the Chicago Area.* Urbana, Ill., 1971.

721 Wilson, Clyde N., and W. Edwin Hemphill, eds. *The Papers of John C. Calhoun.* 5-12 Columbia, S.C., 1971-1979.

722 Wilson, James Grant. "Chicago from 1803-1812." Chicago Historical Society.

723 ___. "A Sketch of Fort Dearborn." *Historical Magazine* 6, no. 4, April 1862, pp. 108-09.

724 ___. "Sketch of the Life of Lieutenant James Strode Swearingen, Together with the Journal kept by him on the March from Detroit to Chicago in 1803." *New York Herald,* October 4, 1903.

725 Winans, Susan Simmons. Papers and affidavits establishing birth at Fort Dearborn, February 18, 1812. Chicago Historical Society.

726 Winslow, Charles Spaulding. *Historical Events of Chicago.* Chicago, 1937.

727 ___. *Historic Goose Island.* Chicago, 1938.

728 Winslow, Charles Spaulding, ed. *Chicago History: Articles of Historic Interest from Chicago Newspapers and Magazines.* 7 vols. Chicago, 1934. [December 10, 1836 to May 24, 1914]

729 ___. *Indians of the Chicago Region.* Chicago, 1946.

730 Winsor, Justin. *Spanish exploration and settlements in America from the Fifteenth to the Seventeenth Century.* Boston, 1886.

731 ___. *Cartier to Frontenac: Geographical Discovery in the Interior of North America in Its Historical Relations, 1534-1700.* Boston/New York, 1894.

732 ___. *The Cabot Controversies and the Right of England to North America.* Cambridge, Mass., 1896.

732a ___. *The Westward Movement · The Colonies and the republic west of the Alleghenies, 1763-1798.* Boston/New York, 1897.

732b Winsor, Justin, ed. *Narrative and Critical History of America.* 8 vols. Boston/New York, 1884-1889. Reprint, New York, 1967.

733 Wood, David Ward. *Chicago and its Distinguished Citizens, or the Progress of Forty Years.* Chicago, 1881.

734 Woodruff, Hon. George H. *History of Will County.* Chicago: Wm. LeBaron, Jr. & Co., 1878.

735 Wright, John Stephen. *Chicago: Past, Present, Future: Relations to the Great Interior and to the Continent.* Chicago, 1868.

736 Wyant, Elizabeth, ed. "A Merchant of Early Chicago, Four Letters of Eri Baker Hulbert." *Journal of the Illinois State Historical Society* 28, September 1944, pp. 100-09.

737 Young, William T. *Sketch of the Life and Public Services of General Lewis Cass.* 2nd ed. Detroit, 1852.

738 Zeuch, Lucius H., M.D. *History of Medical Practice in Illinois.* Chicago, 1927.

739 Zeuch, Lucius H., M.D. See Knight, Robert, and Lucius H. Zeuch, M.D.

OTHER LITERARY SOURCES RICH IN EARLY CHICAGO HISTORY

American Historical Association
Chicago American, Daily; 1835-1842
Chicago Democrat, 1833-1861
Chicago Genealogical Society, The
Chicago Genealogist
Chicago Historical Society
Chicago Historical Society, Bulletin of the; Chicago History
Chicago Magazine, The West As It Is; March, April, May, June, August 1857
Chicago Tribune, 1847 to present
D'Arcy McNickle Center for American Indian History, Newberry Library
Fergus Historical Series (Fergus Printing Company, Chicago), 1876-1914
Fort St. Joseph Historical Commission
Illinois State Archives, Springfield
Illinois State Historical Library Collections
Illinois State Historical Society, Journal of the (later *Illinois Historical Journal*)
Illinois State Historical Society, Transactions of the
Indiana Historical Society
Indiana Magazine of History
Magazine of History with Notes and Queries, 1905-1919
Magazine of Western History
Michigan History Magazine
Michigan Pioneer and Historical Society Collections
Mid-America (Jesuit Historical Society, Chicago)
Minnesota Historical Society, Collections of the
Minnesota History
Mississippi Valley Historical Association
Mississippi Valley Historical Review
Native American Educational Services (NAES) College Library and Archives, Chicago
Niles' Weekly Register, 1811-1849
Ohio Valley Historical Association
State Historical Society of Wisconsin, Collections of the
Wisconsin Magazine of History